the calorie carb & fat bible

The UK's Most Comprehensive Calorie Counter

the calorie, carb & fat bible 2003

Published by
Weight Loss Resources / Penhaligon Page Ltd
Remus House
Peterborough
PE2 9JX

Note for Journalists
Permission is granted to reproduce up to 100 records for use in articles/features, provided The Calorie Carb & Fat Bible is credited as the source of any such information.

Whilst every effort has been made to ensure accuracy, the publishers cannot be held responsible for any errors or omissions.

ISBN 1 904512 00 3

Contributors
Dr Jeremy Sims MB BS FRIPH FRSH
Tracey Walton, Weight Loss Resources

Compiled by Pat Wilson, Sheila Ashwood
and Rebecca Walton, Weight Loss Resources
Design & Layout by Joanne Readshaw, Forward Press Ltd

Printed and bound in Great Britain by
Antony Rowe Ltd, Chippenham, Wiltshire SN14 6LH

Contents

The Road To A Healthier Weight: Staying Motivated

Anyone will tell you that starting out on a weight loss programme is relatively easy - the DIFFICULT part is staying motivated...

Ask anyone who has successfully lost weight and they will tell you that starting out on a weight loss programme is relatively easy. The difficult part is staying motivated to continue and reach their ultimate goal. They will tell you of the days when they may have been sorely tempted to give up; the times when they felt they would never succeed; the moments when they questioned their reasons for ever trying to lose weight in the first place. Such tests of motivation happen to the best of us and, if you have had similar doubts, you may gain some comfort from the fact that you are far from alone.

But I believe that there are many ways in which we can help ourselves to keep motivated. Below, I have provided some of my top tips. These are not rocket science, but simple ideas and concepts which you *can* put into action. Not all may work for you. Some you may find difficult to implement. But I have tried to give a broad range of ideas from which you can pick and choose, to get you on your way to a new, slimmer, healthier you.

Think Health, Not Diet

I would like to begin by saying that I desperately want to throw out the words "dieting" and "slimming", banishing them for all time, and I urge you to do the same. To me, they both have particular connotations of terrible denial, deprivation, and suffering. This is borne out by the fact that most diets or slimming fads will ultimately fail because for many of us they involve too many negatives. True, they may seem to work initially but in the long-term they all too often leave us right back at square one, as we lose all motivation to carry on with them. They are too rigorous; too

Did you know that it is virtually impossible, to lose more than one pound of FAT weight per week?

unrealistic; paradoxically downright unhealthy; and after a while, just too downright boring. After all there are only so many cabbages or bananas you can consume in a lifetime without feeling physically repulsed by them!

So, I say, let's change our way of thinking a little. Let's think healthy, vitalising, fulfilling. None of which words, I'm afraid, describe the plethora of fad diets we are bombarded with nowadays. However, what they do describe is a change in lifestyle in which, for instance, we look closely at what we eat and when; think carefully about what is in our food; consider the number of calories we consume, monitor the amounts of the different fats and simple carbohydrates. We consider closely our fitness, and improve it within our own safe limits. We tackle the stresses and boredom that drive us to find comfort in food and adopt healthier eating habits. In short, we set out on a new lifestyle which will stay with us for the rest of our lives, and maintain our health into old age.

If you have no other motivation for continuing your weight loss journey, then at least consider its importance to your future long and health-filled life. It will be well worth it, I guarantee.

Don't Rush Things

One of the big traps many people fall into is trying to rush weight loss along. Believe me, the key to success is to take things nice and easy. Think about it for a second or two. It may have taken you years to accumulate that excess weight, so it really shouldn't be a surprise that it is going to take a considerable time to lose it again – if you want to ensure it's healthy weight loss, that is.

Furthermore, taking things steady ensures that the weight you lose is due to fat loss and not essential muscle weight. Did you know that it is virtually impossible, both biochemically and physiologically, to lose more than one pound of fat weight per week?

What I suggest is that you try to lose weight at a steady rate of one or two pounds per week. You will feel comfortable achieving this and, when you have reached your healthier weight, you will find it much easier to maintain for life.

Set Small Goals

Setting unrealistic goals for weight loss is sure-fire way of demotivating yourself. Sadly, many of us expect too much. When we fail to achieve our aims quicly, we lose heart.

Set yourself small steps to your ultimate goal. Steps that you know, with all confidence, you can achieve. Go easy on yourself and make your goals easy. For instance, as mentioned above, aim for one or two pounds weight reduction per week or, if you like, 5% of your weight in three months. Each small step will lead you further along the path to your ultimate goal of a healthier weight. And what's more, you will find that the path is a far less arduous one than you ever expected it to be.

Visualize The End Goal

Never lose sight of your ultimate goal. I think this is true for anything in life.

Before starting out on a weight loss programme, try to sit down and visualize your new life as a slimmer, healthier you. Find somewhere quiet, where you won't be disturbed. Sit in a comfortable chair and close your eyes. In your mind's eye see yourself as the slimmer you. How does it feel? How much more confident are you? What will you be doing in your new life? See yourself not only achieving a new healthier weight, but also achieving all those ambitions you're storing up, but haven't felt confident enough to attempt.

The maxim "Breakfast like a king, lunch like a prince and dine like a pauper" holds more than a element of truth – particularly when it comes to healthy weight loss.

Hold onto this image of the new you, and, as you continue on your path to losing weight, take time to revisit it at regular intervals. The image helps you to stay focused, and boosts your determination when things are not going as well as you hoped.

Have A Good Breakfast

The maxim "Breakfast like a king, lunch like a prince and dine like a pauper" holds more than a element of truth – particularly when it comes to healthy weight loss. Breakfast really does set you up for the day, boosting your metabolism. Maintaining energy levels is very important when you are trying to lose weight.

There is nothing to beat the solidarity of family involvement for helping to maintain your motivation when you are trying to lose weight...

Many people make the mistake of believing that the best way to lose weight is to reduce the number of meals they eat. They miss breakfast, maybe have a very light lunch, if at all, and then return home from work completely ravenous. In this ravenous state they are just about ready to empty all the food cupboards in the kitchen. They have deprived their bodies of vital energy and nutrients for nearly 24 hours, and the body's response is to slow all its metabolic processes because it perceives a state of starvation.

So what happens when you eat a big meal at the end of a day when you have starved yourself? Your body reacts by grabbing as much of the energy in your meal as possible, and storing it as even more fat, just in case it has to endure starvation yet again the next day. You have, in fact, unwittingly entered a very big trap.

The take home message is, therefore, never miss breakfast – to do so is a sure way of blowing all those good weight loss intentions, and leaving you completely demoralised.

Involve Family

It always surprises me how few dieters involve their families in their healthier eating plans. I often think it must be an incredible strain having to prepare separate meals at mealtimes – one meal for yourself and another for the rest of the family. Especially if they are scoffing all those "naughties" that you are trying to cut back on. So, a solution, save yourself the hassle and the guilt and get them all in on your new lifestyle. There is nothing to beat the solidarity of family involvement for helping to maintain your motivation when you are trying to lose weight – it really is a case of "All for one, and one for all!"

Even if your other half, or your little ones, don't need to lose weight, they can still benefit from changing to healthier eating habits – that can't be bad.

Lose Weight With Friends Or Colleagues

Another great way to keep motivation from flagging is to band together with friends or work colleagues. Forming a weight loss group provides much needed support and a strong feeling of shared endeavour. So

Never deny yourself the foods you enjoy, but instead to try to reduce the quantity you eat as much as possible.

much more fun than struggling along on your own, and wonderful for morale. So why not ask around and find out who's ready to join you for a slice of the action (no pun intended) on your path to a healthier more fulfilling life.

Never Punish Yourself......

This is something I see far too much of and it always saddens me. Very often there seems to be the misconception that to lose weight effectively, it is important to deny yourself forever all those "goodies" you enjoyed so much before. Unfortunately, denial only turns into a terrible feeling of deprivation and then a sense of self-loathing when your urges get the better of you and you are tempted by the "forbidden fruit". There is nothing worse for destroying all that motivation for losing weight.

The answer is never to deny yourself the foods you enjoy, but instead to try to reduce the quantity you eat. Ensure your diet is essentially a healthy one, and with this as your basis, allow yourself regular small treats – a little of what you like, as they say. Indeed, as treats you'll enjoy them all the more.

.....Reward Yourself Instead

Last but not least. We have spoken about allowing yourself treats. I think it's also important to reward yourself with something special, *every time* you complete one of those small steps on route to your ultimate weight loss goal. I don't just mean an imaginary congratulatory slap on the back. You deserve far more than that. Reward yourself with something which makes you feel happy, and is a fitting mark of your achievement so far.

Rewards make you realise how wonderful you are. And you really are wonderful!

Dr Jeremy Sims
MB BS FRIPH FRSH DIPN&H

Using this Book to Lose Weight

You only need to eat or drink a sausage roll and a can of cola more than you need each day to create and store a pound of fat in a week

THE CALORIE BALANCE CONCEPT

Calories Consumed	
greater than calories expended	= weight gain
equal to calories expended	= weight maintenance
less than calories expended	= weight loss

Making sure that calories consumed are less than calories expended is the best, if not the only, way to lose weight. After all, we put on weight by doing the exact opposite – eating a little more than we need each day, and becoming less active as each year passes.

You only need to eat or drink 500 calories (a sausage roll and a can of cola) more than you need each day to create and store a pound of fat in a week – 2 stones in just over six months. It's no wonder people say that excess weight tends to 'creep up on you'.

The good news is that the reverse is true. Eat 500 calories less than you need each day and you will lose a pound a week; a stone in 3 months, 2 stones in six months. If you combine this calorie cutting strategy with some exercise or activity that gets you moving, you'll lose weight more quickly.

How Much Weight To Lose

Use the body mass index chart and information on pages 14–15, to determine what is the right weight for you, and set a goal. You may find it helpful to set milestone goals of a stone, or half a stone, to measure your progress by; giving your confidence and motivation a boost as you go along. (Half a stone is the equivalent of 14 (½lb/250g) packs of butter!)

Never give up on a goal because of the time it will take to achieve it – the time will pass anyway...

How Fast to Lose It

A pound a week is probably the best rate of loss for achieving sustained, healthy, permanent weight loss. If you have more than a couple of stones to lose, you could start out at 1½ – 2lb a week and see how you get on. If you begin to find this level too restrictive, slow your rate of loss down a bit – it's better to keep going at a pound a week than to give up because trying to lose 2lb a week is making you miserable! The following words may help you to keep your goal in perspective:

Never give up on a goal because of the time it will take to achieve it – the time will pass anyway.

How Many Calories

Use the calorie tables on pages 15–16318 to find out how many calories you need to consume each day to maintain your current weight. Then subtract the 'calorie deficit' required to lose weight at your chosen rate, from the table below. This will give you a daily calorie allowance.

Rate of Loss	Calorie Deficit
½lb a week	250
1lb a week	500
1½lb a week	750
2lb a week	1000

Keep Track

Write down everything you eat and drink in a day – be as accurate as possible on serving sizes. To start with, eat as you normally would for a few days. This will help you to see opportunities for cutting calories by substituting one food or drink item for another, and/or cutting portion sizes of high calorie foods, or eating them less often. Slowly introduce changes to your diet to bring your consumption within your chosen calorie allowance.

Each time you lose half a stone- celebrate!

Progressing

Each time you lose half a stone – celebrate! Treat yourself to a little luxury – something new to wear, a little pampering or some other (non-food!) treat. Review how well you've done, and set yourself up to lose the next half a stone by calculating a new calorie allowance based on your new weight.

Maintaining the Loss

I lost nearly three stones in just under a year of calorie counting. I reached my goal weight in February 2001, and have had no problem in keeping to that weight. The great thing about calorie counting is that you learn so much about what you eat, and make such important changes to your eating and drinking habits as you go along, that its difficult to go back to your old ways. The couple of times I have put on a pound or two, for example after a holiday, I've spent a few days calorie counting and got right back where I want to be. You can do it too – best of luck!

Tracey Walton

Founder www.weightlossresources.co.uk

Body Mass Index

Body Mass Index is a number calculated from an individual's weight and height, that is used to determine whether a person is within, or outside of, a normal weight range. Use the Body Mass Index Chart to look up your BMI, and use the table below to see what range you fall into.

BMI	
Less than 20	Under Weight
20-25	Normal Weight
25-30	Over Weight
30-40	Obese
Over 40	Severely Obese

The spread from 20-25 shows that what is normal covers quite a big range. This is because 'normal' weight for height covers both men and women, and people of different shapes and body composition. A man would normally be expected to have a higher BMI than a woman of the same height, because men tend to have more muscle than women (women naturally have more fat) and muscle weighs more per square inch than fat. For the same reason a slim, muscular woman will have a higher BMI (i.e. weigh more) than a slim, not very muscular woman of the same height.

What's the Right Weight for You?

As a general rule women, unless they are very strong and muscular, will tend to look at their best at the lower end of the normal range, men around the middle to top of the range. 'Ideal weight' is a very individual thing, probably the best thing to do is set a goal within the normal range as described above and, as you get closer to it, adjust to a level at which you feel at your best.

BODY MASS INDEX CHART

WEIGHT IN STONES / LBS	HEIGHT IN FEET / INCHES														
	4'6	4'8	4'10	5'0	5'2	5'4	5'6	5'8	5'10	6'0	6'2	6'4	6'6	6'8	6'10
6st 7	22.0	20.5	19.1	17.8	16.7	15.7	14.7	13.9	13.1	12.4	11.7	11.1	10.6	10.0	9.5
7st 0	23.7	22.1	20.6	19.2	18.0	16.9	15.9	15.0	14.1	13.3	12.6	12.0	11.4	10.8	10.3
7st 7	25.4	23.6	22.0	20.6	19.3	18.1	17.0	16.0	15.1	14.3	13.5	12.8	12.2	11.6	11.0
8st 0	27.1	25.2	23.5	22.0	20.6	19.3	18.1	17.1	16.1	15.2	14.4	13.7	13.0	12.3	11.8
8st 7	28.8	26.8	25.0	23.3	21.8	20.5	19.3	18.2	17.1	16.2	15.3	14.5	13.8	13.1	12.5
9st 0	30.5	28.4	26.4	24.7	23.1	21.7	20.4	19.2	18.1	17.2	16.2	15.4	14.6	13.9	13.2
9st 7	32.2	29.9	27.9	26.1	24.4	22.9	21.5	20.3	19.2	18.1	17.1	16.2	15.4	14.7	14.0
10st 0	33.9	31.5	29.4	27.4	25.7	24.1	22.7	21.4	20.2	19.1	18.0	17.1	16.2	15.4	14.7
10st 7	35.6	33.1	30.8	28.8	27.0	25.3	23.8	22.4	21.2	20.0	18.9	18.0	17.0	16.2	15.4
11st 0	37.3	34.7	32.3	30.2	28.3	26.5	24.9	23.5	22.2	21.0	19.8	18.8	17.9	17.0	16.2
11st 7	39.0	36.2	33.8	31.6	29.6	27.7	26.1	24.6	23.2	21.9	20.7	19.7	18.7	17.8	16.9
12st 0	40.7	37.8	35.2	32.9	30.8	28.9	27.2	25.6	24.2	22.9	21.6	20.5	19.5	18.5	17.6
12st 7	42.3	39.4	36.7	34.3	32.1	30.1	28.3	26.7	25.2	23.8	22.5	21.4	20.3	19.3	18.4
13st 0	44.0	41.0	38.2	35.7	33.4	31.4	29.5	27.8	26.2	24.8	23.5	22.2	21.1	20.1	19.1
13st 7	45.7	42.5	39.6	37.0	34.7	32.6	30.6	28.8	27.2	25.7	24.4	23.1	21.9	20.8	19.8
14st 0	47.4	44.1	41.1	38.4	36.0	33.8	31.7	29.9	28.2	26.7	25.3	23.9	22.7	21.6	20.6
14st 7	49.1	45.7	42.6	39.8	37.3	35.0	32.9	31.0	29.2	27.6	26.2	24.8	23.5	22.4	21.3
15st 0	50.8	47.3	44.0	41.2	38.5	36.2	34.0	32.0	30.2	28.6	27.1	25.7	24.4	23.2	22.0
15st 7	52.5	48.8	45.5	42.5	39.8	37.4	35.2	33.1	31.2	29.5	28.0	26.5	25.2	23.9	22.8
16st 0	54.2	50.4	47.0	43.9	41.1	38.6	36.3	34.2	32.3	30.5	28.9	27.4	26.0	24.7	23.5
16st 7	55.9	52.0	48.5	45.3	42.4	39.8	37.4	35.2	33.3	31.4	29.8	28.2	26.8	25.5	24.2
17st 0	57.6	53.6	49.9	46.6	43.7	41.0	38.6	36.3	34.3	32.4	30.7	29.1	27.6	26.2	25.0
17st 7	59.3	55.1	51.4	48.0	45.0	42.2	39.7	37.4	35.3	33.3	31.6	29.9	28.4	27.0	25.7
18st 0	61.0	56.7	52.9	49.4	46.3	43.4	40.8	38.5	36.3	34.3	32.5	30.8	29.2	27.8	26.4
18st 7	62.7	58.3	54.3	50.8	47.5	44.6	42.0	39.5	37.3	35.3	33.4	31.6	30.0	28.6	27.2
19st 0	64.4	59.9	55.8	52.1	48.8	45.8	43.1	40.6	38.3	36.2	34.3	32.5	30.8	29.3	27.9
19st 7	66.1	61.4	57.3	53.5	50.1	47.0	44.2	41.7	39.3	37.2	35.2	33.3	31.7	30.1	28.6
20st 0	67.8	63.0	58.7	54.9	51.4	48.2	45.4	42.7	40.3	38.1	36.1	34.2	32.5	30.9	29.4
20st 7	69.4	64.6	60.2	56.3	52.7	49.4	46.5	43.8	41.3	39.1	37.0	35.1	33.3	31.6	30.1
21st 0	71.1	66.2	61.7	57.6	54.0	50.6	47.6	44.9	42.3	40.0	37.9	35.9	34.1	32.4	30.9
21st 7	72.8	67.7	63.1	59.0	55.3	51.9	48.8	45.9	43.3	41.0	38.8	36.8	34.9	33.2	31.6
22st 0	74.5	69.3	64.6	60.4	56.5	53.1	49.9	47.0	44.4	41.9	39.7	37.6	35.7	34.0	32.3
22st 7	76.2	70.9	66.1	61.7	57.8	54.3	51.0	48.1	45.4	42.9	40.6	38.5	36.5	34.7	33.1
23st 0	77.9	72.5	67.5	63.1	59.1	55.5	52.2	49.1	46.4	43.8	41.5	39.3	37.3	35.5	33.8
23st 7	79.6	74.0	69.0	64.5	60.4	56.7	53.3	50.2	47.4	44.8	42.4	40.2	38.2	36.3	34.5
24st 0	81.3	75.6	70.5	65.9	61.7	57.9	54.4	51.3	48.4	45.7	43.3	41.0	39.0	37.0	35.3
24st 7	83.0	77.2	71.9	67.2	63.0	59.1	55.6	52.3	49.4	46.7	44.2	41.9	39.8	37.8	36.0
25st 0	84.7	78.8	73.4	68.6	64.2	60.3	56.7	53.4	50.4	47.6	45.1	42.8	40.6	38.6	36.7
25st 7	86.4	80.3	74.9	70.0	65.5	61.5	57.8	54.5	51.4	48.6	46.0	43.6	41.4	39.4	37.5
26st 0	88.1	81.9	76.3	71.3	66.8	62.7	59.0	55.5	52.4	49.5	46.9	44.5	42.2	40.1	38.2
26st 7	89.8	83.5	77.8	72.7	68.1	63.9	60.1	56.6	53.4	50.5	47.8	45.3	43.0	40.9	38.9
27st 0	91.5	85.1	79.3	74.1	69.4	65.1	61.2	57.7	54.4	51.5	48.7	46.2	43.8	41.7	39.7
27st 7	93.2	86.6	80.8	75.5	70.7	66.3	62.4	58.7	55.4	52.4	49.6	47.0	44.7	42.4	40.4
28st 0	94.9	88.2	82.2	76.8	72.0	67.5	63.5	59.8	56.4	53.4	50.5	47.9	45.5	43.2	41.1
28st 7	96.5	89.8	83.7	78.2	73.2	68.7	64.6	60.9	57.5	54.3	51.4	48.7	46.3	44.0	41.9
29st 0	98.2	91.4	85.2	79.6	74.5	69.9	65.8	62.0	58.5	55.3	52.3	49.6	47.1	44.8	42.6
29st 7	99.9	92.9	86.6	80.9	75.8	71.1	66.9	63.0	59.5	56.2	53.2	50.5	47.9	45.5	43.3

CALORIES REQUIRED TO MAINTAIN WEIGHT
ADULT MALES

AGE / ACTIVITY LEVEL

WEIGHT IN STONES / LBS	VERY SEDENTARY			MODERATELY SEDENTARY			MODERATELY ACTIVE			VERY ACTIVE		
	<30	30-60	60+	<30	30-60	60+	<30	30-60	60+	<30	30-60	60+
9st 0	1856	1827	1502	2010	1979	1627	2320	2284	1878	2784	2741	2254
9st 7	1913	1871	1547	2072	2026	1676	2391	2338	1933	2870	2806	2320
10st 0	1970	1914	1591	2134	2074	1724	2463	2393	1989	2955	2871	2387
10st 7	2027	1958	1636	2196	2121	1772	2534	2447	2045	3041	2937	2454
11st 0	2084	2001	1680	2258	2168	1820	2605	2502	2100	3127	3002	2520
11st 7	2141	2045	1724	2320	2215	1868	2677	2556	2156	3212	3067	2587
12st 0	2199	2088	1769	2382	2262	1916	2748	2611	2211	3298	3133	2654
12st 7	2256	2132	1813	2444	2310	1965	2820	2665	2267	3384	3198	2720
13st 0	2313	2175	1858	2506	2357	2013	2891	2719	2322	3470	3263	2787
13st 7	2370	2219	1902	2568	2404	2061	2963	2774	2378	3555	3329	2854
14st 0	2427	2262	1947	2630	2451	2109	3034	2828	2434	3641	3394	2920
14st 7	2484	2306	1991	2691	2498	2157	3106	2883	2489	3727	3459	2987
15st 0	2542	2350	2036	2753	2545	2205	3177	2937	2545	3813	3525	3054
15st 7	2599	2393	2080	2815	2593	2253	3248	2992	2600	3898	3590	3120
16st 0	2656	2437	2125	2877	2640	2302	3320	3046	2656	3984	3655	3187
16st 7	2713	2480	2169	2939	2687	2350	3391	3100	2711	4070	3721	3254
17st 0	2770	2524	2213	3001	2734	2398	3463	3155	2767	4155	3786	3320
17st 7	2827	2567	2258	3063	2781	2446	3534	3209	2823	4241	3851	3387
18st 0	2884	2611	2302	3125	2828	2494	3606	3264	2878	4327	3917	3454
18st 7	2942	2654	2347	3187	2876	2542	3677	3318	2934	4413	3982	3520
19st 0	2999	2698	2391	3249	2923	2591	3749	3373	2989	4498	4047	3587
19st 7	3056	2741	2436	3311	2970	2639	3820	3427	3045	4584	4112	3654
20st 0	3113	2785	2480	3373	3017	2687	3891	3481	3100	4670	4178	3721
20st 7	3170	2829	2525	3434	3064	2735	3963	3536	3156	4756	4243	3787
21st 0	3227	2872	2569	3496	3112	2783	4034	3590	3211	4841	4308	3854
21st 7	3285	2916	2614	3558	3159	2831	4106	3645	3267	4927	4374	3921
22st 0	3342	2959	2658	3620	3206	2880	4177	3699	3323	5013	4439	3987
22st 7	3399	3003	2702	3682	3253	2928	4249	3754	3378	5098	4504	4054
23st 0	3456	3046	2747	3744	3300	2976	4320	3808	3434	5184	4570	4121
23st 7	3513	3090	2791	3806	3347	3024	4392	3862	3489	5270	4635	4187
24st 0	3570	3133	2836	3868	3395	3072	4463	3917	3545	5356	4700	4254
24st 7	3627	3177	2880	3930	3442	3120	4534	3971	3600	5441	4766	4321
25st 0	3685	3220	2925	3992	3489	3168	4606	4026	3656	5527	4831	4387
25st 7	3742	3264	2969	4054	3536	3217	4677	4080	3712	5613	4896	4454
26st 0	3799	3308	3014	4116	3583	3265	4749	4135	3767	5699	4962	4521
26st 7	3856	3351	3058	4177	3630	3313	4820	4189	3823	5784	5027	4587
27st 0	3913	3395	3103	4239	3678	3361	4892	4243	3878	5870	5092	4654
27st 7	3970	3438	3147	4301	3725	3409	4963	4298	3934	5956	5158	4721
28st 0	4028	3482	3191	4363	3772	3457	5035	4352	3989	6042	5223	4787
28st 7	4085	3525	3236	4425	3819	3506	5106	4407	4045	6127	5288	4854
29st 0	4142	3569	3280	4487	3866	3554	5177	4461	4101	6213	5354	4921
29st 7	4199	3612	3325	4549	3913	3602	5249	4516	4156	6299	5419	4987
30st 0	4256	3656	3369	4611	3961	3650	5320	4570	4212	6384	5484	5054

CALORIES REQUIRED TO MAINTAIN WEIGHT
ADULT FEMALES

	AGE / ACTIVITY LEVEL											
	VERY SEDENTARY			MODERATELY SEDENTARY			MODERATELY ACTIVE			VERY ACTIVE		
WEIGHT IN STONES / LBS	<30	30-60	60+	<30	30-60	60+	<30	30-60	60+	<30	30-60	60+
7st 7	1425	1473	1304	1544	1596	1412	1781	1841	1630	2138	2210	1956
8st 0	1481	1504	1338	1605	1629	1450	1852	1880	1673	2222	2256	2008
8st 7	1537	1535	1373	1666	1663	1487	1922	1919	1716	2306	2302	2059
9st 0	1594	1566	1407	1726	1696	1524	1992	1957	1759	2391	2349	2111
9st 7	1650	1596	1442	1787	1729	1562	2062	1996	1802	2475	2395	2163
10st 0	1706	1627	1476	1848	1763	1599	2133	2034	1845	2559	2441	2214
10st 7	1762	1658	1511	1909	1796	1637	2203	2073	1888	2644	2487	2266
11st 0	1819	1689	1545	1970	1830	1674	2273	2111	1931	2728	2534	2318
11st 7	1875	1720	1580	2031	1863	1711	2344	2150	1975	2813	2580	2370
12st 0	1931	1751	1614	2092	1897	1749	2414	2188	2018	2897	2626	2421
12st 7	1987	1781	1648	2153	1930	1786	2484	2227	2061	2981	2672	2473
13st 0	2044	1812	1683	2214	1963	1823	2555	2266	2104	3066	2719	2525
13st 7	2100	1843	1717	2275	1997	1861	2625	2304	2147	3150	2765	2576
14st 0	2156	1874	1752	2336	2030	1898	2695	2343	2190	3234	2811	2628
14st 7	2212	1905	1786	2397	2064	1935	2766	2381	2233	3319	2858	2680
15st 0	2269	1936	1821	2458	2097	1973	2836	2420	2276	3403	2904	2732
15st 7	2325	1967	1855	2519	2130	2010	2906	2458	2319	3488	2950	2783
16st 0	2381	1997	1890	2580	2164	2047	2976	2497	2362	3572	2996	2835
16st 7	2437	2028	1924	2640	2197	2085	3047	2535	2405	3656	3043	2887
17st 0	2494	2059	1959	2701	2231	2122	3117	2574	2449	3741	3089	2938
17st 7	2550	2090	1993	2762	2264	2159	3187	2613	2492	3825	3135	2990
18st 0	2606	2121	2028	2823	2298	2197	3258	2651	2535	3909	3181	3042
18st 7	2662	2152	2062	2884	2331	2234	3328	2690	2578	3994	3228	3093
19st 0	2719	2182	2097	2945	2364	2271	3398	2728	2621	4078	3274	3145
19st 7	2775	2213	2131	3006	2398	2309	3469	2767	2664	4162	3320	3197
20st 0	2831	2244	2166	3067	2431	2346	3539	2805	2707	4247	3366	3249
20st 7	2887	2275	2200	3128	2465	2383	3609	2844	2750	4331	3413	3300
21st 0	2944	2306	2235	3189	2498	2421	3680	2882	2793	4416	3459	3352
21st 7	3000	2337	2269	3250	2531	2458	3750	2921	2836	4500	3505	3404
22st 0	3056	2368	2303	3311	2565	2495	3820	2960	2879	4584	3552	3455
22st 7	3112	2398	2338	3372	2598	2533	3890	2998	2923	4669	3598	3507
23st 0	3169	2429	2372	3433	2632	2570	3961	3037	2966	4753	3644	3559
23st 7	3225	2460	2407	3494	2665	2608	4031	3075	3009	4837	3690	3611
24st 0	3281	2491	2441	3554	2699	2645	4101	3114	3052	4922	3737	3662
24st 7	3337	2522	2476	3615	2732	2682	4172	3152	3095	5006	3783	3714
25st 0	3394	2553	2510	3676	2765	2720	4242	3191	3138	5091	3829	3766
25st 7	3450	2583	2545	3737	2799	2757	4312	3229	3181	5175	3875	3817
26st 0	3506	2614	2579	3798	2832	2794	4383	3268	3224	5259	3922	3869
26st 7	3562	2645	2614	3859	2866	2832	4453	3307	3267	5344	3968	3921
27st 0	3618	2676	2648	3920	2899	2869	4523	3345	3310	5428	4014	3973
27st 7	3675	2707	2683	3981	2932	2906	4594	3384	3353	5512	4060	4024
28st 0	3731	2738	2717	4042	2966	2944	4664	3422	3397	5597	4107	4076
28st 7	3787	2768	2752	4103	2999	2981	4734	3461	3440	5681	4153	4128

Food Information

Nutritional Information

Calorie values are given per serving, plus calorie and nutrition values per 100g of product. This makes it easy to compare the proportions of fat, protein, carbohydrate and fibre in each food.

The values given are for uncooked, unprepared foods unless otherwise stated.

Finding Foods

The Calorie, Carb & Fat Bible has a new, improved format for this edition. Most foods are grouped together by type, and then put in to alphabetical order. This makes it easy to compare different brands, and will help you to find lower calorie and/or fat alternatives where they are available.

This format also makes it easier to locate foods. Foods are categorised by their main characteristics so, for example, if it is bread, ciabatta or white sliced, you'll find it under "Bread".

There are, however, some foods which are not so easy to categorise, especially combination foods like ready meals. The following pointers will help you to find your way around the book until you get to know it a little better.

Serving sizes vary greatly from person to person...it's very important to be accurate.

FILLED ROLLS AND SANDWICHES - Bagels, baguettes, etc which are filled are listed as "Bagels (filled)" etc. Sandwiches are under "Sandwiches".

CURRIES - Popular types of curry, like Balti or Jalfrezi, are listed under their individual types. Unspecified or lesser known types are listed under "Curry".

BURGERS - All burgers, including chicken-type sandwiches from fast-food outlets, are listed under "Burgers".

CHIPS & FRIES - Are listed seperately, depending on the name of the particular brand. All other types of potato are listed under "Potatoes".

SWEETS & CHOCOLATES - Well-known brands, eg. Aero, Mars Bar, are listed under their brand names. Others are listed under "Chocolate" (for bars) and "Chocolates" (for individual sweets).

READY MEALS - Popular types of dishes are listed under their type, eg. "Chow Mein", "Casserole", "Hot Pot", etc. Others are listed by their main ingredient, eg. "Cicken With", "Chicken In", etc.

Serving Sizes

Many ready-meal type foods are given with calories for the full pack size, so that an individual serving can be worked out by estimating the proportion of the pack that has been consumed. For example, if you have eaten a quarter of a packaged pasta dish, divide the calorie value given for the whole pack by 4 to determine the number of calories you have consumed. Where serving sizes are not appropriate, or unknown, values are given per 1oz/28g. Serving sizes vary greatly from person to person and, if you are trying to lose weight, it's very important to be accurate – especially with foods that are very high in calories such as those that contain a fair amount of fat, sugar, cream, cheese, alcohol etc.

Food Data

Nutrition information for basic (non-branded) foods is from The Composition of Foods 5th Edition (1991) Reproduced under licence from the Controller of Her Majesty's Stationery Office.

Nutrition information for branded goods is from details supplied by retailers and manufacturers, and researched by Weight Loss Resources staff from packaging information. Calorie and nutrition data for all food and drink items are typical values.

The publishers gratefully acknowledge all the manufacturers and retailers who have provided information on their products. All product names, trademarks or registered trademarks belong to their respective owners and are used only for the purpose of identifying products.

Caution

The information in The Calorie, Carb and Fat Bible is intended as an aid to weight loss and weight maintenance, and is not medical advice. If you suffer from, or think you may suffer from a medical condition you should consult your doctor before starting a weight loss and/or exercise regime, If you start exercising after a period of relative inactivity, you should start slowly and consult your doctor if you experience pain, distress or other symptons.

Weights, Measures & Abbreviations

Abbreviations

kcal	kilocalories / calories
prot	protein
carb	carbohydrate
sm	small
med	medium
lge	large
tsp	teaspoon
tbsp	tablespoon
dtsp	desert

METRIC TO IMPERIAL

100g = 3.5oz
1kg = 2.2lb
100ml = 3.4fl oz
1litre = 1.8pints

IMPERIAL TO METRIC

1oz = 28g
1lb = 454g
1fl oz = 30ml
1pint = 0.6litre

Brand Abbreviations

Asda

Good for You .... GFY
SmartPrice .... SP
Healthy Choice .... HC

Marks & Spencer .... M & S

Count on Us .... COU
Steam Cuisine .... SC

Safeway

Eat Smart .... ES
Healthy Choice .... HC

Sainsbury's

Be Good to Yourself .... BGTY
Way to Five .... WTF
Taste the Difference .... TTD
Blue Parrot Cafe .... BPC

Somerfield

Good Intentions .... GI
So Good .... SG
Healthy Selection .... HS

Tesco

Healthy Eating .... HE

	Measure WEIGHT/INFO	per Measure KCAL	Nutrition Values per 100g / 100ml KCAL	PROT	CARB	FAT	FIBRE
ACKEE,							
Canned, Drained	1oz/28g	42	151	2.9	0.8	15.2	0.0
ACTIMEL,							
Yoghurt Drink, Orange, Danone*	1fl oz/30ml	26	88	2.7	16.0	1.5	0.0
Yoghurt Drink, Original, 0% Fat, Danone*	1fl oz/30ml	10	33	2.8	4.9	0.1	1.9
Yoghurt Drink, Original, Danone*	1fl oz/30ml	25	83	2.8	14.3	1.6	0.0
ADVOCAAT	1 Shot/25ml	65	260	4.7	28.4	6.3	0.0
AERO,							
Chocolate, Nestle*	1 Bar/46g	238	518	7.6	57.2	28.8	0.0
Creamy White Centre, Nestle	1 Bar/46g	244	530	7.6	57.4	30.0	0.0
Honeycomb, Nestle*	1 Serving/40g	199	497	5.9	62.2	25.0	0.0
Minis, Nestle*	1 Bar/11g	57	518	7.6	57.2	28.8	0.0
Mint, Nestle*	1 Bar/48g	252	526	6.5	60.2	28.8	0.0
ALCOPOPS, (Calculated Estimate)	1fl oz/30ml	22	73	0.3	5.0	0.0	0.0
ALFALFA Sprouts, Raw	1oz/28g	7	24	4.0	0.4	0.7	1.7
ALLSPICE, Powder	1 Tsp/3g	8	263	6.1	50.5	8.7	0.0
ALMONDS,							
Almonds	6 Whole/10g	61	612	21.1	6.9	55.8	7.4
Flaked, Tesco*	1 Tbsp/7g	43	614	21.1	6.9	55.8	7.4
Nature's Haverst*	5 Nuts/10g	63	630	25.4	5.5	55.8	7.4
Organic Shelled, Waitrose*	1oz/28g	176	630	25.4	6.5	55.8	7.4
Roasted, Sweet Smoke, KP*	1oz/28g	172	616	24.7	8.8	53.6	7.1
Sainsbury's*	1 Nut/1g	6	612	21.1	6.9	55.8	7.4
Whole, Organic, Evernat*	1oz/28g	172	614	21.1	6.9	55.8	7.4
ALPHABITES, Bird's Eye*	9 Bites/56g	75	134	2.0	19.5	5.3	1.4
AMERICAN Hard Gums, Asda*	1 Serving/50g	173	345	0.1	86.0	0.0	0.0
AMICELLI, Galaxy*	1 Serving/13g	66	507	6.2	59.7	27.1	0.0
ANCHOVIES,							
Canned In Oil, Drained	1 Anchovy/3g	8	280	25.2	0.0	19.9	0.0
Fillets, Flat, John West*	1 Can/50g	113	226	25.0	0.1	14.0	0.0
Fillets In Oil, Waitrose*	1 Serving/20g	94	472	16.1	0.0	45.3	0.0
Fillets, Marinated, Waitrose*	1 Serving/5g	9	177	22.0	2.0	9.0	0.0
In Olive Oil, John West*	1oz/28g	63	226	25.0	0.0	14.0	0.0
In Olive Oil, Sainsbury's*	1 Serving/10g	19	185	23.7	0.1	10.0	0.1
Salted, Finest, Tesco*	1 Serving/10g	9	93	18.2	0.0	2.2	0.0
ANGEL DELIGHT,							
Banana Flavour, Kraft*	1 Sachet/59g	289	490	2.5	72.0	21.0	0.0
Banana Toffee Flavour, No Added Sugar, Kraft*	1 Sachet/59g	292	495	4.8	58.5	26.5	0.0
Butterscotch Flavour, Kraft*	1 Sachet/59g	280	475	2.4	73.5	19.0	0.0
Chocolate Flavour, Kraft*	1 Sachet/59g	268	455	3.7	69.5	18.0	0.4
Chocolate Flavour, No Added Sugar, Kraft*	1 Sachet/59g	266	450	6.3	56.5	22.0	0.0
Chocolate Flavour With Topples, Kraft*	1 Sachet/59g	274	465	5.0	67.0	20.0	0.5
Forest Fruit Flavour, Kraft*	1 Sachet/59g	289	490	2.5	71.5	21.5	0.0
Raspberry Flavour, Kraft*	1 Sachet/59g	289	490	2.5	72.0	21.0	0.0
Raspberry Flavour, No Added Sugar, Kraft*	1 Sachet/59g	292	495	4.8	59.5	26.0	0.0
Strawberry Flavour, Kraft*	1 Sachet/59g	286	485	2.5	71.0	21.0	0.0
Strawberry Flavour, No Added Sugar, Kraft*	1 Sachet/59g	289	490	4.8	59.0	26.5	0.0
Strawberry Flavour With Topples, Kraft*	1 Sachet/59g	266	450	2.8	74.5	14.0	0.0
Tangerine Flavour, No Added Sugar, Kraft*	1 Sachet/59g	292	495	4.8	58.0	27.0	0.9
Toffee Flavour, Kraft*	1 Sachet/59g	283	480	2.6	70.0	21.0	0.0
Vanilla Ice Cream Flavour, Kraft*	1 Sachet/59g	289	490	2.5	71.5	21.5	0.0
Vanilla Ice Cream Flavour, No Added Sugar, Kraft*	1 Sachet/59g	295	500	4.8	59.5	27.0	0.0
ANTIPASTO,							
Artichoke, Sainsbury's*	1 Serving/50g	68	135	2.0	3.6	12.5	2.3
Mixed Mushroom, Sainsbury's*	¼ Jar/72g	70	97	2.7	1.4	9.0	3.7

ANTIPASTO,	Measure WEIGHT/INFO	per Measure KCAL	KCAL	PROT	CARB	FAT	FIBRE
			Nutrition Values per 100g / 100ml				
Mixed Pepper, Sainsbury's*	½ Jar/145g	183	126	1.5	11.0	8.4	1.8
Seafood, Drained, Sainsbury's*	½ Jar/84g	150	178	14.3	4.1	11.6	1.4
Sun Dried Tomato, Sainsbury's*	1 Dried Tomato/5g	12	232	4.7	15.5	16.8	6.6
Wild Mushroom, Sainsbury's*	1 Serving/100g	97	97	2.7	1.4	9.0	3.7
APPLE & BLACKCURRANT JUICE DRINK,							
No Added Sugar, Asda*	1 Glass/250ml	13	5	0.0	1.0	0.0	0.0
Robinson's*	1 Glass/250ml	20	8	0.1	1.1	0.0	0.0
Sainsbury's*	1 Carton/250ml	18	7	0.1	1.4	0.1	0.1
With Sweeteners, Sunquen, Aldi*	1 Glass/200ml	5	2	0.0	0.2	0.0	0.0
APPLE & Blueberry Juice, Tesco*	1 Glass/200ml	106	53	0.1	12.6	0.1	0.0
APPLE & Elderflower Juice, Copella*	1 Glass/250ml	108	43	0.4	10.2	0.1	0.0
APPLE & MANGO JUICE,							
M & S*	1 Bottle/250ml	138	55	0.3	13.0	0.0	0.0
Pressed, M & S*	1 Bottle/250ml	138	55	0.3	13.0	0.0	0.3
Sainsbury's*	1 Glass/100ml	54	54	0.3	12.6	0.1	0.1
APPLE JUICE,							
Chilled, Asda*	1 Glass/200ml	98	49	0.1	12.0	0.0	0.0
Copella*	1 Glass/250ml	110	44	0.4	10.3	0.1	0.0
Del Monte*	1 Carton/200ml	94	47	0.3	10.8	0.0	0.0
Apple Juice Drink, HE, Tesco*	1 Glass/100ml	30	30	0.1	7.0	0.1	0.0
Apple Juice Drink, No Added Sugar, Asda*	1 Glass/200ml	10	5	0.0	1.0	0.0	0.0
English Cox, M & S*	1 Glass/200ml	98	49	0.2	11.6	0.0	0.0
English Pressed, Somerfield*	1 Glass/200ml	94	47	0.0	12.0	0.0	0.0
English, Somerfield*	1 Glass/200ml	188	94	0.0	23.0	0.0	0.0
Freshly Pressed, Copella*	1 Glass/200ml	88	44	0.4	10.3	0.1	0.0
M & S*	1 Bottle/250ml	130	52	0.2	12.2	0.0	0.0
Organic, Evernat*	1 Glass/200ml	92	46	0.0	11.0	0.1	0.2
Pressed, M & S*	1 Carton/250ml	113	45	0.3	10.5	0.0	0.1
Pressed, Sainsbury's*	1 Glass/200ml	100	50	0.2	11.8	0.1	0.2
Pure, Sainsbury's*	1 Glass/200ml	90	45	0.1	11.0	0.1	0.1
Pure, SmartPrice, Asda*	1 Glass/200ml	88	44	0.1	10.0	0.1	0.0
Pure, Somerfield*	1 Glass/200ml	94	47	0.0	12.0	0.0	0.0
Pure, Sunpride*	1 Carton/200ml	88	44	0.1	10.2	0.0	0.0
Pure, Tesco*	1 Glass/200ml	94	47	0.1	11.1	0.0	0.0
Pure, Waitrose*	1 Glass/200ml	92	46	0.1	11.0	0.0	0.0
Sparkling, Somerfield*	1 Glass/200ml	112	56	0.0	14.0	0.0	0.0
APPLES,							
Braeburn, Fresh, Sainsbury's*	1 Apple/100g	49	49	0.4	11.6	0.1	1.8
Braeburn, Tesco*	1 Apple/65g	30	46	0.3	10.8	0.2	1.7
Cooking, Baked With Sugar, Flesh Only	1 Serving/140g	109	78	0.5	20.1	0.1	1.7
Cooking, Raw, Peeled	1oz/28g	10	35	0.3	8.9	0.1	1.6
Cooking, Stewed With Sugar	1 Serving/140g	104	74	0.3	19.1	0.1	1.2
Cooking, Stewed Without Sugar	1 Serving/140g	46	33	0.3	8.1	0.1	1.5
Cooking, Weighed With Skin & Core	1oz/28g	7	26	0.2	6.4	0.1	1.1
Eating, Average, Raw	1 Med Apple/112g	53	47	0.4	11.8	0.1	1.8
Eating, Average, Raw, Peeled	1 Med Apple/102g	46	45	0.4	11.2	0.1	1.6
Eating, Dried	1oz/28g	67	238	2.0	60.1	0.5	9.7
English Cox, Sainsbury's*	1 Serving/108g	53	49	0.4	11.6	0.1	1.8
Gala, Organic, Tesco*	1 Apple/152g	70	46	0.3	10.8	0.2	1.7
Gala, Safeway*	1 Apple/100g	49	49	0.4	11.6	0.1	1.8
Gala, Tesco*	1 Med Apple/115g	58	50	11.5	0.3	0.1	1.7
Golden Delicious, Tesco*	1 Serving/100g	46	46	0.3	10.8	0.2	1.7
Granny Smith, Tesco*	1 Sm Apple/75g	36	48	0.3	11.5	0.1	1.7
Pink Lady, Sainsbury's*	1 Apple/125g	61	49	0.4	11.6	0.1	1.8

APPLES,	Measure WEIGHT/INFO	per Measure KCAL	KCAL	PROT	CARB	FAT	FIBRE
			Nutrition Values per 100g / 100ml				
Small & Sweet, Garden Gang, Asda*	1oz/28g	15	55	0.4	12.0	0.1	1.8
APRICOTS,							
Canned, In Juice	1oz/28g	10	34	0.5	8.4	0.1	0.9
Canned, In Syrup	1oz/28g	18	63	0.4	16.1	0.1	0.9
Dried	1oz/28g	53	188	4.8	43.4	0.7	7.7
Dried, Garden Gang, Asda*	1 Pack/50g	74	147	3.4	31.0	0.5	5.0
Dried, Organic, Waitrose*	1oz/28g	50	179	4.3	39.1	0.6	6.9
Dried, Ready To Eat, Tesco*	1 Serving/28g	47	167	4.0	36.5	0.6	6.3
Dried, Ready To Eat, Whitworth's*	1 Pack/87g	144	165	3.9	36.0	0.6	6.3
Dried, Sundora*	1 Serving/50g	83	165	3.9	36.0	0.6	6.3
Dried, Vanilla, Ready to Eat Fruit, Sainsbury's*	1/3 Pack/85g	131	154	2.4	40.3	0.1	4.9
Dried, Waitrose*	½ Pack/125g	209	167	4.0	36.5	0.6	6.3
Halves, Healthy Choice, Asda*	1 Tin/411g	140	34	0.5	8.0	0.0	0.9
Halves, In Fresh Juice, Sainsbury's*	½ Can/120g	49	41	0.5	9.4	0.1	1.2
Halves, In Fruit Juice, Sainsbury's*	½ Can/206g	103	50	0.4	11.5	0.1	1.2
In Fruit Juice, John West*	1oz/28g	11	38	0.5	9.0	0.0	1.0
Raw, Fresh	1 Apricot/65g	20	31	0.9	7.2	0.1	1.7
Raw, Weighed With Stones	1 Apricot/40g	12	29	0.8	6.6	0.1	1.6
Soft, Snack Pack, M & S*	1 Pack/50g	108	215	1.8	51.3	0.2	3.9
ARCHERS*,							
Peach Aqua, Schnapps, Archers (Calculated Estimate)	1 Bottle/275ml	206	75	0.3	5.1	0.0	0.0
Peach Snapps, (Calculated Estimate)	1 Shot/35ml	91	260	0.0	0.0	0.0	0.0
ARTICHOKE,							
Hearts, Drained, Sainsbury's*	½ Can/117g	34	29	2.0	4.9	0.1	2.3
Hearts, Marinated & Grilled, Waitrose*	1 Serving/50g	57	114	3.0	3.0	10.0	3.0
Raw, Fresh	1oz/28g	13	47	3.3	10.5	0.2	5.4
ASPARAGUS,							
Boiled In Salted Water	5 Spears/125g	33	26	3.4	1.4	0.8	1.4
Canned, Re-Heated, Drained	1oz/28g	7	24	3.4	1.5	0.5	2.9
Raw, Fresh	1oz/28g	7	25	2.9	2.0	0.6	1.7
AUBERGINE,							
Baked Topped, M & S*	1 Serving/150g	165	110	2.4	7.4	7.7	0.9
Fried In Blended Oil	1oz/28g	85	302	1.2	2.8	31.9	2.3
Fried In Butter	1oz/28g	85	302	1.2	2.8	31.9	2.3
Parmigiana, M & S*	1 Pack/350g	333	95	4.6	7.6	5.3	1.1
Raw, Fresh	1 Sm/120g	18	15	0.9	2.2	0.4	2.0
AUTHENTIC MIX,							
Bacon & Mushroom Taglietelle, Schwartz*	1 Pack/33g	115	349	8.1	77.5	0.7	0.0
Cajun Chicken, Schwartz*	1 Pack/38g	112	294	6.6	61.5	2.4	0.0
Chicken Balti, Schwartz*	1oz/28g	91	324	13.5	54.4	5.8	0.0
for Spagetti Bolognese, Schwartz*	1 Packet/40g	122	306	10.5	63.0	1.3	0.0
Thai Lemon Chicken, Schwartz*	1 Serving/10g	37	365	3.6	78.3	4.2	0.0
AVOCADO, Average	1 Med/145g	276	190	1.9	1.9	19.5	3.4

	Measure WEIGHT/INFO	per Measure KCAL	Nutrition Values per 100g / 100ml KCAL	PROT	CARB	FAT	FIBRE
BACARDI,							
37.5% Volume	1 Shot/25ml	52	207	0.0	0.0	0.0	0.0
40% Volume	1 Shot/25ml	56	222	0.0	0.0	0.0	0.0
Breezer (Calculated Estimate)	1 Bottle/275ml	198	72	0.3	5.0	0.0	0.0
BACON,							
Back, Dry-Cured, Grilled	1 Rasher/25g	64	257	28.4	0.0	15.9	0.0
Back, Dry-Fried	1 Rasher/25g	74	295	24.2	0.0	22.0	0.0
Back, Drycure, Asda*	1 Rasher/32g	61	192	19.7	0.8	12.2	0.0
Back, Fat Trimmed, Grilled	1 Rasher/23g	49	214	25.7	0.0	12.3	0.0
Back, Fat Trimmed, Raw	1 Rasher/28g	38	136	18.8	0.0	6.7	0.0
Back, Grilled	1 Rasher/25g	72	287	23.2	0.0	21.6	0.0
Back, Grilled Crispy	1 Rasher/25g	78	313	36.0	0.0	18.8	0.0
Back, Lean & Fat, Fried	1 Rasher/25g	116	465	24.9	0.0	40.6	0.0
Back, Microwaved	1 Rasher/25g	77	307	24.2	0.0	23.3	0.0
Back, Rapid Rasher, Danepak*	1 Rasher/19g	51	268	24.0	2.3	18.1	0.0
Back, Raw	1 Rasher/26g	56	215	16.5	0.0	16.5	0.0
Back, Reduced Salt, Grilled	1 Rasher/25g	71	282	24.1	0.0	20.6	0.0
Back, Rindless, No Fat	1oz/28g	68	243	18.4	0.0	17.8	0.0
Back, Smoked, Dry Cure, TTD, Sainsbury's*	1 Rasher/54g	144	267	31.8	0.1	15.5	0.1
Back, Smoked, Grilled	1 Rasher/25g	73	293	23.4	0.0	22.1	0.0
Back, Smoked, Maple Cure, TTD, Sainsbury's*	1 Rasher/31g	70	225	24.0	0.8	14.0	0.7
Back, Smoked, Rindless, Asda*	1 Slice/28g	77	275	23.0	0.7	20.0	0.0
Back, Smoked, Rindless, Somerfield*	1oz/28g	69	246	31.0	0.0	14.0	0.0
Back, Sweetcure, Grilled	1 Rasher/25g	88	351	1.8	78.5	5.3	3.5
Back, Tendersweet, Grilled	1 Rasher/25g	93	372	1.0	77.9	8.2	3.6
Back, Thick Cut Smoked, Sainsbury's*	1 Rasher/25g	68	282	26.3	0.1	19.6	0.1
Back, Unsmoked, Co-Op*	3 Rashers/50g	80	160	17.0	0.0	10.0	0.0
Back, Unsmoked, Danepak*	1 Rasher/25g	61	242	15.5	0.0	20.0	0.0
Back, Unsmoked, Extra Trimmed, Asda*	1 Rasher/27g	67	248	26.0	0.0	16.0	0.0
Back, Unsmoked, Reduced Salt, Rindless, Tesco*	1 Serving/113g	220	195	17.2	0.0	14.0	0.0
Back, Unsmoked, Rindless, Co-Op*	1 Serving/50g	108	215	17.0	0.0	17.0	0.0
Back, Unsmoked, Rindless, Grilled, Asda*	1 Rasher/38g	108	284	26.0	0.0	20.0	0.0
Back, Unsmoked, Rindless, Somerfield*	1oz/28g	69	246	31.0	0.0	14.0	0.0
Back, Unsmoked Rindless, Waitrose*	1 Rasher/25g	62	246	23.6	0.0	17.0	0.0
Back, Unsmoked, Sainsbury's*	1 Rasher/20g	56	282	26.3	0.1	19.6	0.1
Chops, BBQ Sainsbury's*	1 Chop/78g	184	236	21.2	4.6	14.8	0.1
Chops, M & S*	1 Chop/103g	232	225	15.9	0.0	18.0	0.0
Chops, Smoked, Asda*	1oz/28g	56	199	28.7	0.0	9.4	0.0
Collar Joint, Lean & Fat, Boiled	1oz/28g	91	325	20.4	0.0	27.0	0.0
Collar Joint, Lean & Fat, Raw	1oz/28g	89	319	14.6	0.0	28.9	0.0
Collar Joint, Lean Only, Boiled	1oz/28g	53	191	26.0	0.0	9.7	0.0
Crispy Strips,Unsmoked, M & S*	1 Serving/25g	121	485	55.6	0.4	29.2	0.0
Extra Lean, M & S*	1 Rasher/30g	33	110	20.2	0.0	3.4	0.0
Fat Only, Cooked, Average	1oz/28g	194	692	9.3	0.0	72.8	0.0
Fat Only, Raw, Average	1oz/28g	209	747	4.8	0.0	80.9	0.0
Gammon Rasher, Lean Only, Grilled	1oz/28g	48	172	31.4	0.0	5.2	0.0
Lean & Low, Danepak*	1 Serving/26g	44	171	18.3	0.0	10.9	0.0
Lean Only, Fried, Average	1 Rasher/25g	83	332	32.8	0.0	22.3	0.0
Lean Only, Grilled, Average	1 Rasher/25g	73	292	30.5	0.0	18.9	0.0
Lean Only, Raw, Average	1oz/28g	41	147	20.2	0.0	7.4	0.0
Loin Steaks, Grilled	1 Serving/120g	229	191	25.9	0.0	9.7	0.0
Middle, Fried	1 Rasher/40g	140	350	1.0	84.3	3.0	3.6
Middle, Grilled	1 Rasher/40g	123	307	24.8	0.0	23.1	0.0
Middle, Raw	1 Rasher/43g	147	341	1.0	78.3	7.2	3.5
Organic, M & S*	1oz/28g	67	240	18.3	2.1	17.9	0.3

	Measure WEIGHT/INFO	per Measure KCAL	KCAL	PROT	CARB	FAT	FIBRE
			Nutrition Values per 100g / 100ml				
BACON,							
Quorn*	1 Rasher/30g	42	141	13.5	8.1	6.1	3.0
Rashers, Streaky, Fried	1 Rasher/20g	67	335	23.8	0.0	26.6	0.0
Rindless, Smoked, Danish, HE, Tesco*	1 Rasher/20g	21	106	19.8	0.0	3.0	0.0
Smoked, Crispy, Sainsbury's*	1 Serving/10g	44	444	51.7	3.0	25.7	0.1
Smoked, M & S*	1oz/28g	136	485	55.6	0.4	29.2	0.0
Smoked Medallions, BGTY, Sainsbury's*	1 Piece/18g	26	143	29.9	0.8	2.2	0.1
Smoky, Heat 'n' Eat, Thin Sliced, Asda*	1 Slice/50g	81	161	18.7	1.7	8.8	0.5
Streaky, Grilled	1 Rasher/20g	67	337	23.8	0.0	26.9	0.0
Streaky, Raw	1 Rasher/23g	63	276	15.8	0.0	23.6	0.0
Streaky, Smoked, Extra Trimmed, Asda*	1 Rasher/25g	74	297	27.0	0.0	21.0	0.0
Streaky, Unsmoked, Extra Trimmed, Asda*	1 Rasher/25g	74	297	27.0	0.0	21.0	0.0
Unsmoked, Butchers Style, M & S*	1oz/28g	69	246	18.4	0.0	19.1	0.1
Unsmoked, Low Fat, M & S*	1oz/28g	31	112	20.2	0.0	3.4	0.0
Vegetarian, Rashers, Tesco*	1 Rasher/20g	47	237	19.9	14.5	11.0	6.0
BACON BITS,							
Smoked, Sainsbury's*	1 Pack/250g	585	234	18.4	0.1	17.8	0.1
Smoked, Somerfield*	1oz/28g	75	269	24.0	0.0	19.0	0.0
BAGEL, (FILLED)							
Cheese & Jalapeno, Starbucks*	1 Bagel/115g	292	254	10.8	45.8	3.1	1.5
Chicken, Lemon & Watercress, Safeway*	1 Pack/153g	329	215	12.8	28.2	4.1	0.0
Cream Cheese, M & S*	1 Bagel/22.5g	81	352	7.8	31.0	21.8	1.8
Ham, Cream Cheese & Chives, Shapers, Boots*	1 Pack/160g	320	200	12.0	28.0	4.4	1.5
Louisiana Style Chicken, Shapers, Boots*	1 Pack/163g	311	191	11.0	30.0	3.0	1.7
Smoked Salmon & Cream Cheese, M & S*	1 Bagel/23g	64	280	10.9	31.7	12.2	2.9
Smoked Salmon & Soft Cheese, Shapers, Boots*	1 Pack/158g	344	218	12.0	29.0	6.0	0.9
Smoked Salmon, DDs*	1 Serving/140g	284	203	13.7	32.5	2.9	2.1
Tuna & Sweetcorn Relish, Safeway*	1 Bagel/162g	284	175	11.5	26.2	2.7	0.0
Tuna Salad, BGTY, Sainsbury's*	1 Bagel/170g	325	191	10.4	26.0	4.2	1.0
Turkey, Pastrami & American Mustard, Shapers, Boots*	1 Bagel/146g	296	203	11.0	32.0	3.4	1.4
BAGUETTE, (FILLED)							
Cheese & Ham, French, Shell*	1oz/28g	82	292	8.9	37.2	12.0	0.0
Cheese & Onion, Asda*	1oz/28g	102	366	12.0	39.8	17.6	1.3
Cheese, Mixed, & Spring Onion, Asda*	1 Pack/190g	629	331	9.5	32.1	18.3	1.3
Cheese, Tomato & Basil, Asda*	¼ Bread/42g	138	329	10.0	40.8	14.0	1.3
Chicken & Mayonnaise, Asda*	1 Pack/190g	407	214	9.7	30.5	8.7	1.3
Chicken & Stuffing, Hot, Sainsbury's*	1 Baguette/227g	543	239	13.7	29.6	7.2	0.0
Chicken Tikka, Asda*	1 Pack/190g	439	231	10.4	32.8	9.4	1.3
Chicken Tikka, Hot, Sainsburys*	1 Pack/190g	386	203	8.5	28.4	6.1	0.0
Egg and Tomato, Oldfields*	1 Pack/198g	416	210	8.7	27.0	7.6	0.0
Ham & Cheese, French, M & S*	1 Serving/100g	495	495	23.7	56.4	19.5	1.9
Ham & Cheese, Snack 'n' Go, Sainsbury's*	1 Baguette/178g	381	215	12.6	29.6	5.1	1.9
Prawn, French, Shell*	1 Baguette/63g	171	272	9.7	32.4	11.5	0.0
Prawn Mayonnaise, Asda*	1 Pack/190g	399	210	9.1	32.5	4.9	1.3
Steak & Onion, Snack 'n' Go, Sainsbury's*	1 Baguette/177g	396	225	14.3	30.6	5.0	2.2
Tuna Melt, Sainsbury's*	1 Serving/204g	373	183	11.3	25.8	3.9	0.0
Turkey & Ham, Asda*	1 Baguette/360g	774	215	11.6	30.7	5.1	1.3
BAILEYS*, Irish Cream, Original	1 Glass/37g	130	350	3.2	20.0	15.7	0.0
BAKE,							
Bean and Pasta, Asda*	1 Serving/450g	599	133	5.0	17.0	5.0	1.7
Broccoli & Three Cheese, M & S*	1 Serving/225g	315	140	6.3	6.3	9.7	1.8
Cauliflower & Broccoli, Tesco*	½ Pack/250g	178	71	2.8	5.8	4.1	1.0
Chicken & Mushroom, COU, M & S*	1 Serving/360g	324	90	7.3	10.3	2.3	1.1
Chicken and Pasta, Italiano, Tesco*	1 Serving/400g	448	112	9.8	10.3	3.5	1.7
Chicken Arrabbbiata, M & S*	1 Pack/450g	540	120	7.6	16.0	3.0	2.0

B

B

BAKE,	Measure WEIGHT/INFO	per Measure KCAL	KCAL	PROT	CARB	FAT	FIBRE
			Nutrition Values per 100g / 100ml				
Cod & Broccoli, Co-Op*	1 Pack/300g	432	144	8.2	10.8	7.5	1.4
Cod and Prawn, COU, Marks and Spencer*	1 Pack/400g	320	80	6.5	8.8	2.0	1.0
Quorn, Tuscany, Quorn*	1oz/28g	26	94	4.8	11.4	3.2	1.4
Roast Potato, Cheese & Onion, Asda*	½ Pack/200g	288	144	4.2	14.0	8.0	1.1
BAKED BEANS,							
& Jumbo Sausages, Asda*	1 Serving/210g	317	151	7.0	15.0	7.0	2.6
& Meatballs In Tomato Sauce, Sainsbury's*	½ Can/200g	216	108	5.5	13.3	3.6	2.6
& Sausage, GFY, Asda*	1 Serving/217g	178	82	4.7	10.0	2.6	1.8
& Sausage In Tomato Sauce, SmartPrice Asda*	½ Can/203g	256	126	5.0	13.0	6.0	0.0
& Sausages, Asda*	½ Can/205g	252	123	6.0	16.0	3.9	3.0
Barbecue, Heinz*	½ Can/100g	82	82	4.9	14.9	0.3	4.0
Canned In Tomato Sauce	1oz/28g	23	81	4.8	15.1	0.6	3.5
Canned In Tomato Sauce, Reduced Sugar	1oz/28g	21	74	5.4	12.8	0.6	3.8
Cheezy, Heinz*	1oz/28g	53	189	11.6	24.5	4.9	6.2
Corale, Aldi*	½ Can/220g	183	83	4.9	14.3	0.7	3.4
Economy, Sainsbury's*	½ Can/211g	137	65	3.9	12.0	0.2	3.1
Healthy Choice, Asda*	1oz/28g	16	58	2.9	11.0	0.2	2.6
In A Rich Tomato Sauce, Morrisons*	1 Can/420g	294	70	2.9	14.0	0.2	0.0
In Tomato Sauce, Bettabuy, Morrisons*	1 Can/210g	164	78	4.2	14.7	0.3	3.2
In Tomato Sauce, Everyday Saving, Aldi*	1 Can/425g	340	80	4.6	14.2	0.5	0.0
In Tomato Sauce, Healthy Balance, Heinz*	½ Can/207g	139	67	4.6	11.7	0.2	3.7
In Tomato Sauce, Healthy Choice, Safeway*	1 Serving/219g	204	93	4.7	17.3	0.5	3.7
In Tomato Sauce, HE, Tesco*	1 Can/420g	353	84	5.1	15.1	0.3	3.6
In Tomato Sauce, Healthy, HP*	1 Can/420g	266	63	4.4	11.0	0.2	3.7
In Tomato Sauce, Healthy Selection, Somerfield*	1 Can/220g	125	57	3.0	11.0	0.0	0.0
In Tomato Sauce, Heinz*	½ Can/207g	155	75	4.7	13.6	0.2	3.7
In Tomato Sauce, HP*	1 Sm Can/215g	183	85	4.7	15.0	0.7	3.7
In Tomato Sauce, Organic, Sainsbury's*	½ Can/210g	204	97	5.1	18.0	0.5	3.5
In Tomato Sauce, Princes*	½ Can/212g	180	85	4.7	15.5	0.5	4.6
In Tomato Sauce, SmartPrice, Asda*	1 Can/208g	144	69	2.9	14.0	0.2	3.7
In Tomato Sauce, Tesco*	1 Can/210g	179	85	4.6	15.9	0.3	3.5
In Tomato Sauce, Weight Watchers*	½ Can/207g	137	66	4.7	11.3	0.2	3.7
In Tomato Sauce With 8 Pork Sausages, HP*	1 Can/420g	449	107	4.8	12.9	4.0	1.9
Organic, Heinz*	½ Can/207g	157	76	4.9	13.7	0.2	3.9
Reduced Sugar & Salt, Co-Op*	½ Can/210g	126	60	3.0	12.0	0.2	3.0
Reduced Sugar & Salt, Sainsbury's*	½ Can/210g	158	75	4.9	13.0	0.4	5.2
Reduced Sugar & Salt, Tesco*	1 Can/420g	353	84	5.1	15.1	0.3	3.6
Reduced Sugar & Salt, Waitrose*	½ Can/220g	150	68	5.0	11.5	0.2	3.7
Sainsbury's*	½ Can/210g	179	85	4.9	15.5	0.4	5.2
Savers, Morrisons*	1 Can/420g	302	72	3.9	13.5	0.3	0.0
Savers, Safeway*	½ Can/210g	151	72	3.9	13.5	0.3	0.0
SmartPrice, Asda*	1 Serving/100g	69	69	2.9	14.0	0.2	3.7
Value, Tesco*	1 Can/420g	328	78	4.5	16.6	0.3	3.5
Vegetarian, Sausages In Tomato Sauce, Morrisons*	1 Can/420g	496	118	6.4	15.6	3.3	0.0
With Bacon, Heinz*	1oz/28g	25	91	6.6	12.2	1.7	3.1
With Chicken Nuggets, Heinz*	1 Can/200g	210	105	6.7	12.4	3.1	3.2
With Pork Sausages, Heinz*	½ Can/207g	184	89	5.5	11.2	2.5	2.6
With Vegetable Sausages, Heinz*	1 Can/200g	212	106	6.1	12.2	3.6	2.9
BAKES,							
Paprika, Eat Smart, Safeway*	1 Serving/25g	90	360	6.6	76.9	2.5	4.6
Spicy Tomato, BPC, Sainsbury's*	1 Pack/20g	71	353	6.8	76.1	2.4	4.7
Thai Green Curry Flavour, BGTY, Sainsbury's*	½ Pack/50g	178	355	6.0	76.8	2.6	4.5
BAKING POWDER	1 Tsp/2g	3	163	5.2	37.8	0.0	0.0

BALTI,	Measure WEIGHT/INFO	per Measure KCAL	KCAL	PROT	CARB	FAT	FIBRE
Chicken & Naan Bread, Somerfield*	1 Pack/335g	489	146	10.0	16.0	5.0	0.0
Chicken & Rice, COU, M & S*	1 Pack/400g	360	90	7.5	12.5	0.9	1.0
Chicken & Rice, Patak's*	1 Pack/370g	440	119	6.1	16.7	3.5	1.7
Chicken, BPC, Sainsbury's*	1 Can/400g	308	77	8.9	4.6	2.5	0.8
Chicken, COU, M & S*	1 Pack/400g	360	90	6.5	13.6	0.9	1.0
Chicken, Ready Meals, M & S*	1oz/28g	34	120	10.2	4.7	6.5	1.6
Chicken, Sainsbury's*	1 Serving/200g	230	115	12.8	4.2	5.2	3.5
Chicken, Takeaway, Sainsbury's*	1 Pack/400g	404	101	10.4	4.8	4.5	1.4
Chicken Tikka, Tesco*	1 Pack/350g	466	133	11.1	6.4	7.0	0.7
Chicken Tikka, Weight Watchers*	1 Pack/320g	224	70	4.8	10.2	1.1	0.6
Chicken With Naan Bread, Co-Op*	1 Pack/375g	559	149	8.1	11.9	7.6	1.4
Chicken With Naan Bread, Sharwood's*	1 Pack/375g	540	144	6.5	15.4	6.3	2.2
Chicken With Rice, Weight Watchers*	1 Pack/329g	253	77	4.8	10.7	1.7	0.5
Prawn, Budgens*	1 Pack/350g	375	107	5.6	5.2	7.1	1.3
Vegetable, Asda*	½ Can/200g	206	103	2.2	10.0	6.0	2.5
Vegetable, Canned, Flavours of India, Sainsbury's*	½ Can/200g	224	112	2.7	10.0	6.8	2.6
BAMBOO SHOOTS,							
Canned, Drained	1oz/28g	3	11	1.5	0.7	0.2	1.7
BANANA,							
Average, Fresh, Raw, Without Skin	1 Med/150g	143	95	1.2	23.2	0.3	1.1
Chips	1oz/28g	143	511	1.0	59.9	31.4	1.7
Chips, Yoghurt Coated, The Garden of Eden*	1 Serving/25g	133	531	4.5	59.1	32.5	1.7
Junior, Tesco*	1 Serving/100g	100	100	3.5	23.3	0.3	0.0
Organic, Tesco*	1 Banana/110g	110	100	1.2	23.2	0.3	1.1
BARS,							
All Day Breakfast, Weight Watchers*	1 Bar/50g	179	358	6.8	72.2	4.6	3.2
Alpen*	1 Bar/29g	125	431	7.0	68.0	14.5	0.0
Alpen* Apple & Blackberry With Yoghurt	1 Bar/29g	122	421	5.7	73.0	11.8	0.0
Alpen*, Strawberry With Yoghurt	1 Bar/29g	123	425	5.6	73.5	12.1	0.0
Apple & Raisin, Snack, Traidcraft Geobar*	1 Bar/35g	127	362	3.3	76.4	4.8	2.3
Biscuit & Raisin, Reduced Fat, Tesco*	1 Bar/21g	85	406	4.9	68.5	12.5	1.8
Brunch, Hazelnut, Cadbury's*	1 Bar/35g	163	465	7.1	61.0	21.6	0.0
Brunch, Raisin, Cadbury's*	1 Bar/35g	151	430	5.8	66.9	15.8	0.0
Cappuccino Coll, M & S*	1 Bar/35g	185	529	6.0	50.0	35.0	1.0
Caramelised Nut & Raisin Crunch, TTD, Sainsbury's*	1 Serving/50g	206	412	8.3	64.4	13.5	5.3
Cereal & More, M & S*	1 Bar/40g	154	385	20.0	58.2	7.8	2.9
Cereal, Apple & Cinnamonr, Fruit 'n' Grain, Asda*	1 Bar/37g	131	353	4.5	68.0	7.0	2.9
Cereal, Apple & Raisin, Harvest, Quaker*	1 Bar/22g	87	396	5.0	70.0	11.5	4.0
Cereal, Apple & Raspberry, Waitrose*	1 Bar/25g	90	359	5.0	77.1	3.4	4.6
Cereal, Apple & Sultana, Go Ahead, McVitie's*	1 Bar/35g	137	392	4.1	77.6	7.2	1.8
Cereal, Apricot, Organic, Evernat*	1oz/28g	101	360	5.6	64.9	8.7	7.2
Cereal, Apricot Yoghurt, COU, M & S*	1 Bar/25g	90	360	6.1	76.6	2.5	2.9
Cereal, Balance With Fruit, Sainsbury's*	1 Bar/25g	100	401	5.8	75.2	8.6	1.9
Cereal, Banana & Toffee, Boots*	1 Bar/70g	245	350	5.4	75.0	3.1	2.1
Cereal, Blueberry Flavour, Breakfast, Sweet Mornings*	1 Bar/38g	152	399	4.5	66.0	13.0	2.5
Cereal, Coconut Muesli, Kellogg's*	1 Bar/25g	108	430	5.0	65.0	17.0	5.0
Cereal, Cranberry & Apple, Shapers, Boots*	1 Bar/25g	98	391	4.2	76.0	11.0	2.2
Cereal, Cranberry & Orange, BGTY, Sainsbury's*	1 Bar/26g	93	358	2.7	75.8	4.9	2.3
Cereal, Cranberry, New Yorker*	1 Bar/25g	104	417	6.5	73.5	10.3	4.5
Cereal, Fruit & Fibre, Asda*	1 Bar/28g	111	398	6.0	71.0	10.0	3.8
Cereal, Fruit & Fibre, Sainsbury's*	1 Serving/28g	111	397	5.7	70.9	10.1	3.8
Cereal, Fruit & Nut Break, Jordans*	1 Bar/37g	135	374	7.0	63.2	10.4	8.1
Cereal, Ginger & Raisin, BGTY, Sainsbury's*	1 Bar/26g	91	349	2.9	74.5	4.4	2.5
Cereal, Granola, Starbucks*	1 Bar/90g	324	360	8.0	38.6	21.3	4.8

Nutrition Values per 100g / 100ml

B

BARS,	Measure WEIGHT/INFO	per Measure KCAL	Nutrition Values per 100g / 100ml KCAL	PROT	CARB	FAT	FIBRE
Cereal, Lemon, M & S*	1 Bar/25g	90	360	4.1	79.0	2.8	2.8
Cereal, Nuts & Raisins, Organic, Evernat*	1oz/28g	108	385	6.5	62.2	12.3	6.8
Cereal, Organic, Jordans*	1 Bar/33g	150	455	8.0	56.7	21.8	7.8
Cereal, Pure Points,Weight Watchers*	1 Bar/50g	179	358	6.8	72.2	4.6	3.2
Cereal, Raisin & Nut Snack Bar, Benecol*	1 Bar/25g	98	390	3.9	68.5	11.1	2.0
Cereal, Roast Hazelnut, Organic, Jordans*	1 Bar/33g	150	455	8.0	56.7	21.8	7.8
Cereal, Strawberry, COU, M & S*	1 Bar/25g	89	355	4.3	77.8	2.8	3.8
Cereal, Sultana & Honey, Jordans*	1 Bar/36g	130	361	6.0	65.9	8.2	9.2
Cereal, White Chocolate Muesli, Kellogg's*	1 Bar/25g	110	440	5.0	70.0	16.0	2.0
Chewy & Crisp, Apricot & Almond, Tesco*	1 Bar/27g	122	452	6.2	60.0	20.8	2.6
Chewy & Crisp, Apricot & Coconut, Sainsbury's*	1 Bar/27g	123	457	5.2	58.8	22.3	4.0
Chewy & Crisp, Roasted Nut, Sainsbury's*	1 Bar/27g	120	446	10.1	46.6	24.3	3.9
Chewy & Crisp, With Chocolate Chips, Tesco*	1 Bar/27g	125	463	9.2	54.0	23.4	3.8
Chewy, Apple & Cinnamon, GFY, Asda*	1 Bar/27g	95	351	6.0	74.0	3.4	8.0
Chewy, Asda*	1 Bar/27g	133	491	8.0	54.0	27.0	2.8
Chewy, Nuts & Choc Chip, Asda*	1 Bar/27g	127	471	8.0	58.0	23.0	2.8
Chewy Toffee Apple, Eat Smart, Safeway*	1 Bar/25g	89	355	4.0	78.3	2.8	2.9
Chocolate & Orange, Crispy, Freefrom, Sainsbury's**	1 Bar/30g	132	440	4.8	68.2	16.2	1.2
Chocolate & Orange, Shapers Boots*	1 Bar/26g	98	378	4.2	73.0	13.0	1.5
Chocolate & Raspberry, COU, M & S*	1 Bar/25g	90	360	5.4	78.2	2.7	3.2
Chocolate, Crisp, Weight Watchers*	1 Bar/25g	92	369	5.4	75.1	10.2	0.8
Chocolate, Digestive, Farmfoods*	1 Biscuit/21g	104	495	6.7	63.6	23.8	2.3
Coco Pops & Milk Bar, Kellogg's*	1 Bar/20g	90	450	8.0	69.0	16.0	1.0
Cookie, Apple Crumble, COU, M & S*	1 Bar/27g	90	335	5.8	72.6	2.6	2.3
Cookie, Oreo, Nabisco*	1 Bar/35g	180	514	2.0	66.0	29.0	0.0
Cookie, Raisin & Cinnamon, COU, M & S*	1 Bar/26g	88	340	6.7	73.5	1.9	3.4
Corn Flakes & Chocolate Milk, Kellogg's*	1 Bar/40g	176	440	9.0	68.0	15.0	1.5
Crispy Caramel, Shapers, Boots*	1 Bar/24g	96	400	3.9	67.0	17.0	0.4
Crispy Orange, Reduced Fat, Tesco*	1 Biscuit/22g	95	431	3.6	75.5	12.7	0.6
Crunchy, Honey & Almond, Jordans*	1 Bar/33g	153	465	8.8	56.1	22.8	5.8
Crunchy, Honey & Almond, Jordans*	1 Bar/33g	51	155	2.9	18.7	7.6	1.9
Crunchy, Maple & Pecan, Jordans*	1 Bar/33g	153	464	7.7	56.8	22.9	6.5
Double Caramel, Go Ahead, McVitie's*	1 Cake/32g	97	302	4.0	65.3	4.4	0.7
Double Caramel, GFY, Asda*	1 Bar/40g	92	231	5.0	47.0	2.6	0.0
Frosties & Milk, Kellogg's*	1 Bar/27g	122	450	10.0	68.0	16.0	1.0
Fruitsome, Citrus, Rowntree's*	1 Bar/35g	140	400	4.1	65.1	13.7	2.3
Fruitsome, Red Berry, Rowntree's*	1 Bar/35g	148	422	4.1	71.2	13.4	2.9
Fruitsome, Tropical, Rowntree's*	1 Bar/35g	145	415	3.9	70.4	13.5	2.5
Frusli, Absolutely Apricot, Jordans*	1 Bar/33g	120	365	5.0	63.8	10.0	6.3
Frusli, Blueberry Burst, Jordans*	1 Bar/33g	133	402	4.8	68.8	11.9	4.6
Frusli, Raisin & Hazelnut, Jordans*	1 Bar/33g	141	426	6.3	61.3	17.3	3.9
Frusli, Raisin & Hazelnut, Jordans*	1 Bar/33g	140	425	6.3	61.3	17.3	3.9
Frusli, Tangy Citrus, Jordans*	1 Bar/33g	130	393	4.1	70.4	10.5	4.3
Gold Bar, McVitie's*	1 Bar/23g	121	524	6.0	64.6	26.8	0.6
Harvest Chewy, Apple & Raisin, Quaker*	1 Bar/22g	89	405	5.5	68.0	12.0	3.0
Harvest Chewy, Choc Chip, Quaker*	1 Bar/22g	94	426	6.0	64.0	16.0	3.0
Harvest Chewy, White Chocolate Chip, Quaker*	1 Bar/92g	392	426	6.0	66.0	14.0	3.0
Italian Tiramisu, M & S*	1 Bar/35g	184	527	6.3	49.1	34.0	0.8
Mint, Shapers, Boots*	1 Bar/28g	106	378	2.9	75.0	14.0	2.5
Muffin, Cadbury's*	1 Bar/68g	270	403	5.6	38.0	25.4	0.0
Oat Crunchy, Blueberry & Cranberry, Waitrose*	1 Crunchy/60g	262	437	8.0	67.0	15.2	7.4
Perfectly Balanced, Apricot, Waitrose*	1 Bar/25g	89	356	4.9	76.9	3.2	3.8
Perfectly Balanced, Cranberry, Waitrose*	1 Bar/25g	91	363	4.5	78.3	3.5	2.9
Perfectly Balanced, Ginger, Waitrose*	1 Bar/25g	92	367	4.9	79.3	3.3	3.3

BARS,	Measure WEIGHT/INFO	per Measure KCAL	KCAL	PROT	CARB	FAT	FIBRE
Rice Krispies, Kelloggs*	1 Bar/20g	92	460	9.0	66.0	18.0	0.5
Rocky, Caramel, Fox's*	1 Bar/24g	111	461	6.7	61.3	21.0	0.8
Sandwich, Milk Chcoclate, Orange, Somerfield*	1oz/28g	141	504	6.0	66.0	24.0	0.0
Sandwich, Milk Chocolate, SmartPrice, Asda*	1 Bar/25g	132	528	6.0	63.0	28.0	0.0
Sandwich, Milk Chocolate, Somerfield*	1oz/28g	142	507	6.0	66.0	25.0	0.0
Snack, Chocolate & Hazelnut, Benecol*	1 Bar/25g	99	397	4.7	64.5	13.1	2.5
Special K, Kellogg's*	1 Bar/24g	94	390	7.0	75.0	7.0	1.0
Strawberry, Shapers, Boots*	1 Bar/22g	82	374	2.5	79.0	12.0	0.2
Tracker, Breakfast Banana, Mars*	1 bar/37g	176	476	4.7	63.3	22.6	9.4
Tracker, Chocolate Chip, Mars*	1 Bar/27g	137	509	8.6	55.8	27.9	0.0
Tracker, Roasted Nut, Mars*	1 Bar/27g	139	515	9.8	53.5	29.1	0.0
Tracker, Strawberry, Mars*	1 Bar/27g	129	479	4.7	63.6	22.8	0.0
Tracker, Yoghurt, Mars*	1 Bar/27g	133	491	6.3	64.2	23.2	0.0
Wafer, Milk Chocolate, Somerfield*	1oz/28g	148	529	7.0	60.0	29.0	0.0
Wild Berries, Jordans*	1 Bar/33g	130	395	6.0	67.1	11.4	4.9
BASIL,							
Dried, Ground	1 Tsp/1.4g	3	251	14.4	43.2	4.0	0.0
Fresh	1 Tbsp/5.3g	2	40	3.1	5.1	0.8	0.0
BASS,							
Sea, Farmed, Asda*	1oz/28g	29	105	20.5	0.0	2.5	0.0
Sea, Raw	1oz/28g	28	100	19.3	0.0	2.5	0.0
BATON,							
Chicken & Bacon, Tesco*	1 Pack/201g	511	254	9.4	24.7	13.1	1.7
Salmon & Cucumber, HE, Tesco*	1 Serving/100g	248	248	17.5	35.7	3.9	6.2
BATTER MIX,							
SmartPrice, Asda*	1 Pack/128g	421	329	11.0	69.0	1.0	3.3
Tesco*	1 Pack/130g	467	359	12.3	74.4	1.4	7.7
BAY LEAVES, Dried	1oz/28g	88	313	7.6	48.6	8.4	0.0
BEAN & Pea Mix, M & S*	1oz/28g	13	48	4.2	6.5	0.5	6.1
BEAN SPROUTS,							
Amoy*	1oz/28g	6	21	1.9	3.2	0.1	0.0
Asda*	¼ Can/52g	12	23	1.8	3.4	0.2	2.7
Chinese, Sainsbury's*	1 Serving/150g	92	61	1.8	0.7	5.7	1.0
BEANFEAST,							
Bolognese, Batchelors*	1 Serving/65g	196	302	23.9	39.0	5.6	13.5
Mexican Chilli, Batchelors*	1 Serving/65g	203	312	24.3	42.7	4.9	13.6
Savoury Mince, Batchelors*	1 Serving/65g	205	316	24.7	39.5	6.6	12.7
BEANS, ADUKI							
Dried, Boiled In Unsalted Water	1 Tbsp/30g	37	123	9.3	22.5	0.2	5.5
Dried, Raw	1 Tbsp/30g	82	272	19.9	50.1	0.5	11.1
BEANS, BLACK, Sainsbury's*	1oz/28g	20	72	6.0	11.2	0.3	6.4
BEANS, BLACKEYE,							
Canned, Asda*	1 Can/172g	203	118	8.1	19.6	0.8	3.1
Canned, Safeway*	½ Can/117g	142	121	8.8	19.9	0.7	3.5
Dried, Raw	1oz/28g	87	311	23.5	54.1	1.6	8.2
BEANS, BORLOTTI,							
Canned	1oz/28g	29	103	7.4	17.4	0.4	4.7
Canned, Drained, Sainsbury's	1oz/28g	29	103	7.4	17.4	0.4	4.7
Tesco*	1oz/28g	29	103	8.1	16.0	0.7	4.6
BEANS, BROAD,							
Boiled In Unsalted Water	1oz/28g	13	48	5.1	5.6	0.8	5.4
Canned, Re-Heated, Drained	1oz/28g	24	87	8.3	12.7	0.7	5.2
Canned, Young & Tender, Sainsbury's*	½ Can/47g	42	90	8.3	12.7	0.7	5.2
Dried, Raw	1oz/28g	69	245	26.1	32.5	2.1	27.6

Nutrition Values per 100g / 100ml (KCAL, PROT, CARB, FAT, FIBRE)

B

B

BEANS, BROAD,	Measure WEIGHT/INFO	per Measure KCAL	Nutrition Values per 100g / 100ml KCAL	PROT	CARB	FAT	FIBRE
Freshly Frozen, Iceland*	1 Serving/100g	81	81	7.9	11.7	0.6	6.5
Frozen, Great Value, Asda*	1 Serving/100g	81	81	8.0	11.0	0.6	6.0
Prepared, M & S*	1oz/28g	23	81	7.9	11.7	0.6	6.5
Raw	1oz/28g	17	59	5.7	7.2	1.0	6.1
BEANS, BUTTER,							
Canned, Batchelors*	1 Can/130g	108	83	6.0	13.9	0.4	4.8
Canned, Re-Heated, Drained	1oz/28g	22	77	5.9	13.0	0.5	4.6
Canned, Salted Sweetened Water, Safeway*	1 Can/109g	87	80	5.9	13.0	0.5	4.6
Canned, Waitrose*	1 Can/130g	104	80	5.9	13.0	0.5	4.6
Canned, Water, Added Sugar & Salt, Somerfield*	1 Can/220g	176	80	5.9	13.0	0.5	4.6
Dried, Boiled In Unsalted Water	1oz/28g	29	103	7.1	18.4	0.6	5.2
Dried, Raw	1oz/28g	81	290	19.1	52.9	1.7	16.0
Vegetable Oil, Zanae*	1 Pack/140g	158	113	4.8	13.0	4.6	0.0
BEANS, CANNELLINI,							
Asda*	1 Serving/175g	152	87	7.0	14.0	0.3	6.0
Canned, Drained, Sainsbury's*	1oz/28g	24	84	6.8	13.5	0.3	6.0
BEANS, CURRIED, Heinz*	½ Can/100g	103	103	4.9	17.9	1.3	4.0
BEANS, DWARF, Sainsbury's*	1oz/28g	7	25	1.9	3.1	0.5	2.2
BEANS, FLAGEOLET,							
Canned, Sainsbury's*	½ Can/133g	132	99	6.8	16.9	0.5	1.8
Canned, Tesco*	1 Can/175g	180	103	7.5	15.7	1.1	5.9
Canned, Waitrose*	1 Can/265g	193	73	6.7	10.6	0.4	1.9
BEANS, FRENCH,							
Boiled In Unsalted Water	1oz/28g	6	22	1.8	2.9	0.5	2.4
Canned, Re-Heated, Drained	1oz/28g	6	22	1.5	4.1	0.1	2.6
Raw	1oz/28g	7	24	1.9	3.2	0.5	2.2
BEANS, GREEN,							
Cut, Canned, Asda*	1 Can/170g	41	24	1.5	3.8	0.3	2.6
Cut, Iceland*	1 Serving/28g	7	25	1.7	4.7	0.1	4.1
Cut, In Salted Water, Morrisons*	1 Serving/150g	32	21	1.5	3.8	0.0	0.0
Cut, Organic, Waitrose*	1oz/28g	7	24	1.9	3.2	0.5	2.2
Egyptian, Tesco*	1 Serving/50g	13	25	1.9	3.2	0.5	2.2
Fresh, Sliced, Tesco*	1 Serving/100g	25	25	1.7	4.4	0.1	4.1
Sliced, Boiled, Sainsbury's*	1oz/28g	7	25	1.7	4.4	0.1	4.1
Sliced, Frozen, Asda*	1 Serving/50g	13	25	1.7	4.4	0.1	4.1
Sliced, Frozen, Basics, Somerfield*	1oz/28g	6	20	2.0	3.0	0.0	0.0
Whole, Asda*	1oz/28g	7	24	1.5	3.8	0.3	2.6
Whole, Very Fine, Organic, Iceland*	1oz/28g	7	25	1.7	4.7	0.1	4.1
BEANS, HARICOT, Dried, Raw	1oz/28g	80	286	21.4	49.7	1.6	17.0
BEANS, KIDNEY,							
Red, Added Sugar & Salt, Sweet Harvest, Aldi*	1 Can/240g	250	104	6.9	17.8	0.6	6.2
Red, Asda*	1oz/28g	32	113	8.4	18.8	0.5	6.7
Red, Batchelors*	1 Can/130g	118	91	8.1	13.5	0.5	6.4
Red, Canned, Drained	1 Can/240g	240	100	6.9	17.8	0.6	6.2
Red, Dried, Boiled In Unsalted Water	1oz/28g	29	103	8.4	17.4	0.5	6.7
Red, Dried, Raw	1oz/28g	74	266	22.1	44.1	1.4	15.7
Red, Economy, Sainsbury's*	1oz/28g	29	105	8.2	17.0	0.5	8.2
Red, In Chilli Sauce, Sainsbury's*	1 Can/420g	340	81	5.1	14.3	0.4	4.3
Red, In Salted Water, Safeway*	1 Can/130g	135	104	6.9	17.8	0.6	6.2
Red, In Salted Water, Sweet Harvest, Aldi*	1 Can/255g	258	101	8.3	15.5	0.6	0.0
Red, In Water, Organic, Sainsbury's*	½ Can/120g	119	99	8.4	15.9	0.5	6.7
Red, In Water, Sainsbury's*	½ Can/119g	129	108	8.4	17.4	0.5	6.7
Red, In Water, Somerfield*	1 Can/220g	264	120	9.0	20.0	1.0	0.0
Red, In Water, Tesco*	1 Can/420g	391	93	6.9	15.0	0.6	6.2

	Measure	per Measure	Nutrition Values per 100g / 100ml				
	WEIGHT/INFO	KCAL	KCAL	PROT	CARB	FAT	FIBRE
BEANS, KIDNEY,							
Red, Sugar & Salt Added, Sainsbury's*	½ Can/120g	136	113	8.4	18.8	0.5	6.7
Red, Waitrose*	½ Can/90g	82	91	7.1	14.8	0.4	5.7
BEANS, MIXED,							
Hot & Spicy, Tesco*	1 Serving/78g	61	78	5.0	13.3	0.5	3.9
In a Mild Chilli Sauce, Sainsbury's*	½ Can/208g	162	78	5.2	13.5	0.3	5.2
In Spicy Tomato Sauce, Waitrose*	½ Can/211g	154	73	4.3	11.1	1.3	3.6
In Tomato Sauce, Asda*	1 Serving/100g	100	100	5.8	18.0	0.4	4.4
In Tomato Sauce, Safeway*	½ Can/210g	242	115	5.8	22.7	0.1	4.3
BEANS, MUNG,							
Whole, Dried, Boiled In Unsalted Water	1oz/28g	25	91	7.6	15.3	0.4	3.0
Whole, Dried, Raw	1oz/28g	78	279	23.9	46.3	1.1	10.0
BEANS, PINTO,							
Dried, Boiled In Unsalted Water	1oz/28g	38	137	8.9	23.9	0.7	0.0
Dried, Raw	1oz/28g	92	327	21.1	57.1	1.6	0.0
Re-fried Beans	1oz/28g	30	107	6.2	15.3	1.1	0.0
BEANS, RUNNER							
& Carrots, M & S*	1 Serving/240g	60	25	1.0	4.8	0.1	2.1
Boiled In Unsalted Water	1oz/28g	5	18	1.2	2.3	0.5	1.9
Fresh, Sainsbury's*	½ Pack/87g	17	19	1.2	2.3	0.5	1.9
Raw	1oz/28g	6	22	1.6	3.2	0.4	2.0
Runner, Sliced, M & S*	1oz/28g	6	22	1.6	3.1	0.4	2.0
BEANS, SOYA,							
Dried, Boiled In Unsalted Water	1oz/28g	39	141	14.0	5.1	7.3	6.1
Dried, Raw	1oz/28g	104	370	35.9	15.8	18.6	15.7
GMO Free, Organic, Evernat*	1oz/28g	104	370	32.5	15.0	18.0	23.5
BEANS, STRINGLESS, Somerfield*	1 Serving/50g	12	23	1.6	3.2	0.4	2.0
BEANSPROUTS,							
Mung, Raw	1oz/28g	9	31	2.9	4.0	0.5	1.5
Mung, Stir-Fried In Blended Oil	1 Serving/90g	65	72	1.9	2.5	6.1	0.9
Raw	1oz/28g	9	32	2.9	4.0	0.5	1.5
Tesco*	1 Serving/100g	32	32	2.9	4.0	0.5	1.5
BEEF,							
Brisket, Raw, Lean	1oz/28g	39	139	21.1	0.0	6.1	0.0
Brisket, Raw, Lean & Fat	1oz/28g	61	218	18.4	0.0	16.0	0.0
Cooked, Tesco*	1 Slice/13g	14	105	19.6	1.3	2.4	0.0
Diced, Lean, Safeway*	1 Serving/167g	200	120	21.1	0.0	4.0	0.0
Escalope, Healthy Choice, Asda*	1 Escalope/100g	163	163	36.1	0.0	2.1	0.0
Flank, Pot-Roasted, Lean	1oz/28g	71	253	31.8	0.0	14.0	0.0
Flank, Pot-Roasted, Lean & Fat	1oz/28g	87	309	27.1	0.0	22.3	0.0
Flank, Raw, Lean	1oz/28g	49	175	22.7	0.0	9.3	0.0
Flank, Raw, Lean & Fat	1oz/28g	74	266	19.7	0.0	20.8	0.0
Fore-Rib, Raw, Lean	1oz/28g	41	145	21.5	0.0	6.5	0.0
Fore-Rib, Raw, Lean & Fat	1oz/28g	71	253	18.8	0.0	19.8	0.0
Fore-Rib, Roasted, Lean	1oz/28g	66	236	33.3	0.0	11.4	0.0
Fore-Rib, Roasted, Lean & Fat	1oz/28g	84	300	29.1	0.0	20.4	0.0
Joint, Sirloin, Roasted, Lean	1oz/28g	53	188	32.4	0.0	6.5	0.0
Joint, Sirloin, Roasted, Lean & Fat	1oz/28g	65	233	29.8	0.0	12.6	0.0
Mince, British, Tesco*	½ Pack/120g	278	232	18.9	0.0	17.4	0.0
Mince, Extra Lean, Frozen, Morrisons*	1oz/28g	41	145	21.0	0.0	6.9	0.0
Mince, Extra Lean, Raw	1oz/28g	49	174	21.9	0.0	9.6	0.0
Mince, Extra Lean, Sainsbury's*	1oz/28g	49	174	21.9	0.1	9.6	0.1
Mince, Extra Lean, Stewed	1oz/28g	50	177	24.7	0.0	8.7	0.0
Mince, Farmfoods*	1oz/28g	62	221	18.8	0.0	16.2	0.0
Mince, HE, Tesco*	1 Serving/250g	310	124	20.9	0.0	4.5	0.0

B

BEEF,	Measure WEIGHT/INFO	per Measure KCAL	KCAL	PROT	CARB	FAT	FIBRE
Mince, Lean, Tesco*	1oz/28g	50	178	19.7	0.0	11.0	0.0
Mince, M & S*	1oz/28g	37	133	16.0	3.0	7.0	0.1
Mince, Organic, Sainsbury's*	1 Serving/125g	321	257	18.2	0.0	20.5	0.0
Mince, Raw	1oz/28g	63	225	19.7	0.0	16.2	0.0
Mince, Scotch, Extra Lean, Sainsbury's*	1oz/28g	49	174	21.9	0.1	9.6	0.1
Mince, Steak, 95% Fat Free, BGTY, Sainsbury's*	1oz/28g	35	124	21.3	0.1	4.3	0.1
Mince, Steak, Frozen, Asda*	1 Serving/125g	200	160	22.0	0.0	8.0	0.0
Mince, Steak, HE, Tesco*	1 Pack/500g	620	124	20.9	0.0	4.5	0.0
Mince, Steak, Lean, Asda*	1 Serving/150g	246	164	23.0	0.0	8.0	0.0
Mince, Steak, Lean, Co-Op*	1 Serving/125g	231	185	21.0	0.0	11.0	0.0
Mince, Steak, Lean, Less Than 10% Fat, Asda*	1oz/28g	44	158	22.5	0.0	7.5	0.0
Mince, Steak, Lean, Somerfield*	1 Serving/100g	153	153	22.6	0.0	6.5	0.0
Mince, Steak, Lean, Tesco*	1oz/28g	50	178	19.7	0.0	11.0	0.0
Mince, Steak, Somerfield*	1oz/28g	64	229	23.0	0.0	15.0	0.0
Mince, Steak, Super Lean, Less Than 5% Fat, Asda*	1oz/28g	33	119	22.0	0.0	3.6	0.0
Mince, Stewed	1oz/28g	59	209	21.8	0.0	13.5	0.0
Mince, Traditional, Raw, TTD, Sainsbury's*	1oz/28g	63	225	19.7	0.0	16.2	0.0
Minced With Onions, John West*	1oz/28g	27	98	9.2	4.0	5.0	0.0
Patties, Oriental, Perfectly Balanced, Waitrose*	½ Pack/200g	238	119	9.6	13.8	2.8	1.2
Peppered, Carvery, Morrisons*	1 Serving/25g	36	143	23.4	0.1	5.4	1.0
Peppered, Fresh, M & S*	1oz/28g	38	135	11.4	1.7	9.2	0.6
Potted, M & S*	1 Jar/75g	109	145	21.4	1.4	5.9	1.3
Potted, Yorkshire, Sutherland*	1 Serving/10g	20	199	17.2	1.1	14.0	0.0
Rib Eye, Asda*	1oz/28g	49	174	26.1	1.3	7.2	0.4
Salt, Safeway*	1oz/28g	29	105	18.4	1.3	2.9	0.0
Salt, Slices, American Style, Tesco*	1 Slice/7g	8	108	19.9	0.7	2.8	0.3
Salted, Dried, Raw	1oz/28g	70	250	55.4	0.0	1.5	0.0
Salted, Fat Removed, Raw	1oz/28g	33	119	27.1	0.0	0.4	0.0
Shin, Asda*	1oz/28g	50	178	32.7	1.4	4.6	0.4
Silverside, Joint, British, HE, Tesco*	1 Serving/200g	214	107	21.0	0.0	2.6	0.0
Silverside, Pot Roasted, Lean	1oz/28g	54	193	34.0	0.0	6.3	0.0
Silverside, Pot-Roasted, Lean & Fat	1oz/28g	69	247	31.0	0.0	13.7	0.0
Silverside, Raw, Lean	1oz/28g	38	134	23.8	0.0	4.3	0.0
Silverside, Raw, Lean & Fat	1oz/28g	60	215	20.4	0.0	14.8	0.0
Silverside, Salted, Boiled, Lean	1oz/28g	52	184	30.4	0.0	6.9	0.0
Silverside, Salted, Boiled, Lean & Fat	1oz/28g	63	224	27.9	0.0	12.5	0.0
Silverside, Salted, Raw, Lean	1oz/28g	39	140	19.2	0.0	7.0	0.0
Silverside, Salted, Raw, Lean & Fat	1oz/28g	64	227	16.3	0.0	18.0	0.0
Steak, Braising, Braised, Lean	1oz/28g	63	225	34.4	0.0	9.7	0.0
Steak, Braising, Braised, Lean & Fat	1oz/28g	69	246	32.9	0.0	12.7	0.0
Steak, Braising, Raw, Lean	1oz/28g	39	139	21.8	0.0	5.7	0.0
Steak, Braising, Raw, Lean & Fat	1oz/28g	45	160	20.7	0.0	8.6	0.0
Steak, Cubed, HE, Tesco*	1 Serving/142g	142	100	22.7	0.0	1.0	0.0
Steak, Fillet, Fried, Lean	1oz/28g	52	184	28.2	0.0	7.9	0.0
Steak, Fillet, Fried, Lean & Fat	1oz/28g	54	192	28.0	0.0	8.9	0.0
Steak, Fillet, Grilled, Lean	1oz/28g	53	188	29.1	0.0	8.0	0.0
Steak, Fillet, Grilled, Lean & Fat	1oz/28g	56	200	28.7	0.0	9.5	0.0
Steak, Fillet, Raw, Lean	1oz/28g	39	140	21.2	0.0	6.1	0.0
Steak, Fillet, Raw, Lean & Fat	1oz/28g	43	155	20.9	0.0	7.9	0.0
Steak, Fillet, Somerfield*	1oz/28g	51	182	29.0	0.0	7.0	0.0
Steak, Frying, 3.6% Fat, Healthy Choice, Asda*	1oz/28g	33	119	21.6	0.0	3.6	0.0
Steak, Frying, GFY, Asda*	1 Serving/145g	178	123	24.0	0.0	3.0	0.0
Steak, Frying, Prime, Healthy Choice, Safeway*	1 Steak/110g	114	104	21.5	0.0	2.0	0.0
Steak, Frying, Quick Cook, Grilled, Asda*	1 Serving/100g	133	133	22.0	0.0	5.0	0.0

(Nutrition Values per 100g / 100ml apply to the KCAL, PROT, CARB, FAT, FIBRE columns after the per Measure KCAL column.)

BEEF,	Measure WEIGHT/INFO	per Measure KCAL	Nutrition Values per 100g / 100ml KCAL	PROT	CARB	FAT	FIBRE
Steak, Rump, Barbecued, Lean	1oz/28g	49	176	31.2	0.0	5.7	0.0
Steak, Rump, Barbecued, Lean & Fat	1oz/28g	57	203	29.5	0.0	9.4	0.0
Steak, Rump, Fried, Lean	1oz/28g	51	183	30.9	0.0	6.6	0.0
Steak, Rump, Fried, Lean & Fat	1oz/28g	64	228	28.4	0.0	12.7	0.0
Steak, Rump, Grilled, Lean	1oz/28g	50	177	31.0	0.0	5.9	0.0
Steak, Rump, Grilled, Lean & Fat	1oz/28g	61	218	27.3	0.0	12.1	0.0
Steak, Rump, Marinated Strips, Asda*	1oz/28g	66	235	17.6	0.1	18.3	0.1
Steak, Rump, Raw, Lean	1oz/28g	35	125	22.0	0.0	4.1	0.0
Steak, Rump, Raw, Lean & Fat	1oz/28g	49	174	20.7	0.0	10.1	0.0
Steak, Rump, Seared, M & S*	1oz/28g	63	225	19.6	2.9	14.9	0.1
Steak, Sirloin, Fried, Lean	1oz/28g	53	189	28.8	0.0	8.2	0.0
Steak, Sirloin, Fried, Lean & Fat	1oz/28g	65	233	26.8	0.0	14.0	0.0
Steak, Sirloin, Grilled, Medium-Rare, Lean	1oz/28g	49	176	26.6	0.0	7.7	0.0
Steak, Sirloin, Grilled, Medium-Rare, Lean & Fat	1oz/28g	60	213	24.8	0.0	12.6	0.0
Steak, Sirloin, Grilled, Rare, Lean	1oz/28g	46	166	26.4	0.0	6.7	0.0
Steak, Sirloin, Grilled, Rare, Lean & Fat	1oz/28g	60	216	25.1	0.0	12.8	0.0
Steak, Sirloin, Grilled, Well-Done, Lean	1oz/28g	63	225	33.9	0.0	9.9	0.0
Steak, Sirloin, Grilled, Well-Done, Lean & Fat	1oz/28g	72	257	31.8	0.0	14.4	0.0
Steak, Sirloin, Raw, Lean	1oz/28g	38	135	23.5	0.0	4.5	0.0
Steak, Sirloin, Raw, Lean & Fat	1oz/28g	56	201	21.6	0.0	12.7	0.0
Steak, Tender, British, HE, Tesco*	½ Pack/150g	173	115	20.3	0.0	3.7	0.0
Steak, Thin Sliced, M & S*	1 Serving/100g	115	115	23.0	0.0	2.7	0.0
Steak, Top Rump, Asda*	1 Steak/62g	184	302	35.0	0.0	18.0	0.0
Stewing Steak, Raw, Lean	1oz/28g	34	122	22.6	0.0	3.5	0.0
Stewing Steak, Raw, Lean & Fat	1oz/28g	41	146	22.1	0.0	6.4	0.0
Stewing Steak, Stewed, Lean	1oz/28g	52	185	32.0	0.0	6.3	0.0
Stewing Steak, Stewed, Lean & Fat	1oz/28g	57	203	29.2	0.0	9.6	0.0
Thin Sliced, Asda*	1 Slice/13g	13	101	17.6	2.6	2.2	0.8
Topside Joint, Somerfield*	1oz/28g	60	214	27.0	0.0	12.0	0.0
Topside, Raw, Lean	1oz/28g	32	116	23.0	0.0	2.7	0.0
Topside, Raw, Lean & Fat	1oz/28g	55	198	20.4	0.0	12.9	0.0
Topside, Roasted, Medium-Rare, Lean	1oz/28g	49	175	32.2	0.0	5.1	0.0
Topside, Roasted, Medium-Rare, Lean & Fat	1oz/28g	62	222	29.9	0.0	11.4	0.0
Topside, Roasted, Well-Done, Lean	1oz/28g	57	202	36.2	0.0	6.3	0.0
Topside, Roasted, Well-Done, Lean & Fat	1oz/28g	68	244	32.8	0.0	12.5	0.0
Wafer Thin, Roast, Asda*	1 Serving/50g	52	104	20.0	0.3	2.5	0.0
Wafer Thin, Roast, Iceland*	1 Serving/30g	31	102	19.6	0.3	2.5	0.0
Wafer Thin, Tesco*	1 Serving/50g	53	105	19.6	1.3	2.4	0.0
BEEF & GRAVY, Lean Roast, Bird's Eye*	1 Portion/114g	111	97	13.3	3.0	3.5	0.1
BEEF - BOURGUIGNON, Finest, Tesco*	1 Serving/300g	351	117	15.5	3.5	4.5	1.2
BEEF - BRAISED STEAK,							
& Cabbage, COU, M & S*	1 Pack/380g	323	85	8.3	6.7	2.6	1.9
& Carrots, M & S*	1 Pack/200g	140	70	8.0	4.2	2.5	1.3
& Colcannon Mash, Tesco*	1 Pack/450g	477	106	9.5	9.0	3.5	0.9
& Mustard Mash, HE, Tesco*	1 Pack/450g	392	87	7.4	9.5	2.1	0.7
COU, M & S*	½ Pack/225g	180	80	11.9	3.6	2.2	0.7
BEEF - CHASSEUR, & Potato Mash, BGTY, Sainsbury's*	1 Pack/450g	468	104	8.8	11.0	2.8	0.7
BEEF - DAUBE & Peppered Mash, Perfectly Balanced, Waitrose*	1 Pack/402g	346	86	7.2	9.9	2.0	1.2
BEEF - EN CROUTE, Asda*	1 Serving/225g	506	225	11.0	16.0	13.0	1.3
BEEF - GRILL STEAK,							
Aberdeen Angus, Waitrose*	1 Steak/170g	354	208	20.0	1.0	13.8	0.0
Bird's Eye*	1 Steak/66g	205	310	16.2	3.6	25.6	0.1
Black Pepper, Tesco*	1 Serving/87g	261	300	16.2	8.6	22.3	0.0
Iceland*	1 Grillsteak/93g	322	346	24.7	0.8	27.1	0.0

BEEF - GRILL STEAK,	Measure WEIGHT/INFO	per Measure KCAL	Nutrition Values per 100g / 100ml KCAL	PROT	CARB	FAT	FIBRE
Peppered, Asda*	1 Serving/170g	386	227	22.2	5.7	12.8	0.6
Ross*	1 Grillsteak/61g	182	298	15.2	2.0	25.5	0.3
Somerfield*	1 Steak/85g	241	283	17.2	0.5	23.6	0.8
BEEF - HOT & Sour, Tesco*	1 Pack/350g	214	61	7.9	5.5	0.8	0.6
BEEF IN,							
Black Bean Sauce, Chinese Takeaway, Sainsbury's*	1 Pack/386g	432	112	10.9	7.3	4.3	1.1
Gravy, Sliced, Co-Op*	1 Pack/227g	179	79	12.7	2.2	2.2	0.1
Gravy, Sliced, Cooked, Asda*	1 Pack/200g	192	96	16.0	2.6	2.6	0.0
Madras Sauce, BGTY, Sainsbury's*	1 Can/400g	344	86	9.5	4.0	3.6	0.9
Red Wine Sauce, M & S*	1oz/28g	34	120	13.2	3.6	5.9	0.3
Red Wine With Spinach Mash, Waitrose*	1 Pack/400g	304	76	6.7	9.6	1.2	1.3
BEEF - MINCED,							
Vegetables & Gravy, Bird's Eye*	1 Pack/178g	155	87	9.1	5.1	3.4	0.6
With Onions, Co-Op*	½ Can/196g	274	140	12.0	4.0	8.0	0.9
BEEF - ROAST,							
Dinner, Bird's Eye*	1 Pack/283g	297	105	8.2	10.8	3.2	0.0
Dinner, Iceland*	1 Serving/340g	354	104	8.5	9.1	3.7	1.6
BEEF - STEAK, & Chips, HE, Tesco*	1 Pack/450g	473	105	6.3	13.8	2.7	0.5
BEEF - STEWED STEAK,							
& Onions With Gravy, John West*	½ Can/205g	269	131	14.0	3.0	7.0	0.0
SmartPrice, Asda*	1 Serving/205g	230	112	14.0	2.8	5.0	0.0
With Gravy, John West*	1oz/28g	37	131	16.5	5.0	5.0	0.0
BEEF - STIFADO, Tesco*	1 Serving/300g	411	137	11.9	9.3	5.8	0.6
BEEF - WELLINGTON, M & S*	1oz/28g	76	270	10.7	17.5	18.3	1.4
BEEF WITH,							
Honey & Black Pepper, Waitrose*	1 Pack/350g	326	93	9.1	9.4	2.1	1.8
Vegetable Rice, Hot & Sour, COU, M & S*	1 Pack/400g	360	90	5.5	14.4	1.4	0.6
BEER,							
Bitter, Canned	1 Can/440ml	141	32	0.3	2.3	0.0	0.0
Bitter, Draught	1 Pint/568ml	182	32	0.3	2.3	0.0	0.0
Bitter, Keg	1 Pint/568ml	176	31	0.3	2.3	0.0	0.0
Bitter, Low Alcohol	1 Pint/568ml	74	13	0.2	2.1	0.0	0.0
Brown Ale, Bottled	1 Bottle/330ml	99	30	0.3	3.0	0.0	0.0
Guinness, Stout	1 Pint/568ml	170	30	0.4	1.5	0.0	0.0
Mackeson, Stout	1 Pint/568ml	204	36	0.4	4.6	0.0	0.0
Mild, Draught	1 Pint/568ml	136	24	0.2	1.6	0.0	0.0
BEETROOT,							
Baby, Baxters*	1 Jar/340g	102	30	1.5	6.0	0.0	1.2
Baby, In Sweet Vinegar, Sainsbury's*	1 Serving/50g	30	60	1.3	12.9	0.1	1.1
Baby, Pickled, Budgens*	1oz/28g	8	30	1.4	6.0	0.1	0.0
Baby, Whole, Tesco*	1oz/28g	8	28	1.4	4.4	0.1	1.8
Baxters*	1 Slice/10g	5	47	1.5	9.9	0.1	1.2
Boiled In Salted Water	1oz/28g	13	46	2.3	9.5	0.1	1.9
Cooked In Vinegar, Safeway*	1 Serving/79g	36	46	2.3	9.0	0.1	0.0
Cooked, Organic, Waitrose*	1 Serving/65g	31	48	2.3	9.5	0.1	1.9
Crinkle Cut, Baxters*	1 Slice/10g	3	30	1.5	6.0	0.0	1.2
Crinkle Cut, Cooked In Vinegar, Sainsbury's*	1oz/28g	12	43	1.5	8.8	0.2	1.9
Dipped In Malt Vinegar, Traditional Cooked, Tesco*	1 Pack/250g	138	55	0.9	12.0	0.1	1.6
In Natural Juices, Tesco*	1 Serving/50g	24	48	2.3	9.4	0.1	1.9
In Redcurrant Jelly, Baxters*	1 Jar/305g	509	167	0.7	43.9	0.0	0.9
In Sweet Vinegar, Asda*	1 Serving/100g	50	50	1.1	11.0	0.2	1.8
M & S*	1oz/28g	12	44	1.8	9.9	0.0	2.5
Pickled, Drained	1oz/28g	8	28	1.2	5.6	0.2	1.7
Raw	1oz/28g	10	36	1.7	7.6	0.1	1.9

BEETROOT,	Measure WEIGHT/INFO	per Measure KCAL	KCAL	PROT	CARB	FAT	FIBRE
Shredded, In Sweet Vinegar, Sainsbury's*	1 Serving/50g	24	47	1.1	10.3	0.1	1.3
Sliced, Baxters*	1 Slice/10g	3	30	1.5	6.0	0.0	1.2
Sliced,Tesco*	1 Serving/100g	25	25	1.4	4.4	0.1	1.8
BHAJI,							
Aubergine & Potato	1oz/28g	36	130	2.0	12.0	8.8	1.7
Cabbage & Pea With Vegetable Oil	1oz/28g	50	178	3.3	9.2	14.7	3.4
Cauliflower	1oz/28g	60	214	4.0	4.0	20.5	2.0
Mushroom	1oz/28g	46	166	1.7	4.4	16.1	1.3
Okra, Bangladeshi With Butter Ghee	1oz/28g	27	95	2.5	7.6	6.4	3.2
Onion, Asda*	1 Mini Bhaji/49g	96	196	6.0	20.0	10.0	2.0
Onion, Indian Meal For One, Tesco*	1 Bhaji/100g	204	204	5.5	29.2	7.3	1.3
Onion, Mini, Co-Op*	1 Pack/220g	636	289	9.0	33.0	13.4	3.0
Onion, Mini, Farmfoods*	1 Bhaji/30g	65	216	6.4	26.9	9.2	2.4
Onion, Mini, Tesco*	1 Serving/23g	48	210	7.3	26.7	8.2	1.3
Onion, Somerfield*	1 Bhaji/15g	39	262	5.0	15.0	20.0	0.0
Potato & Onion	1oz/28g	45	160	2.1	16.6	10.1	1.6
Potato, Onion & Mushroom	1oz/28g	58	208	2.0	12.0	17.5	1.5
Potato, Spinach & Cauliflower	1oz/28g	47	169	2.2	7.1	15.1	1.4
Spinach	1oz/28g	23	83	3.3	2.6	6.8	2.4
Spinach & Potato	1oz/28g	53	191	3.7	13.4	14.1	2.3
Turnip & Onion	1oz/28g	36	128	1.3	7.1	10.9	2.2
Vegetable With Vegetable Oil	1oz/28g	59	212	2.1	10.1	18.5	2.4
BHAJIA,							
Onion, Indian Starter Selection, M & S*	1 Bhajia/22g	65	295	5.7	15.8	23.3	2.8
Onion, Mini, Sainsbury's*	1 Serving/22g	43	196	5.9	18.7	10.8	3.4
Onion, Sainsbury's*	1 Bhajia/33g	75	226	6.0	31.7	8.3	1.1
Selection, Occasions, Sainsbury's*	1 Serving/15g	32	211	4.8	19.7	12.6	0.0
BIERWURST, Asda*	1 Slice/10g	18	184	15.0	4.0	12.0	0.0
BILBERRIES, Fresh, Raw	1oz/28g	8	30	0.6	6.9	0.2	1.8
BIRYANI,							
Chicken, HE, Tesco*	1 Pack/370g	289	78	8.5	10.0	0.5	0.4
Chicken, Somerfield*	1 Pack/300g	477	159	7.0	19.0	6.0	0.0
Chicken Tikka, BGTY, Sainsbury's*	1 Pack/450gg	491	109	9.7	13.2	1.9	1.3
Chicken Tikka With Basmati Rice, Sharwood's*	1 Pack/373g	481	129	6.3	16.2	4.3	0.9
Vegetable & Rice, Patak's*	1 Pack/370g	481	130	2.5	18.8	5.5	0.7
Vegetable, Sainsburys*	1 Serving/225g	329	146	2.4	16.3	7.9	1.1
BISCUITS, (SEE ALSO COOKIES)							
Abbey Crunch, McVitie's*	1 Biscuit/9g	43	477	6.0	72.8	17.9	2.5
Ace Milk Chocolate, McVitie's*	1 Biscuit/24g	122	510	6.1	66.2	24.5	1.6
After Eight, Nestle*	1 Biscuit/5g	26	525	6.5	62.6	27.7	1.5
All Butter, Asda*	1 Biscuit/9g	44	487	6.0	64.0	23.0	1.9
All Butter, Tesco*	1 Biscuit/9g	44	486	6.3	63.5	23.0	1.9
Almond Fingers, Co-Op*	1oz/28g	109	390	4.0	59.0	15.0	2.0
Almond, M & S*	1oz/28g	140	500	7.3	62.7	24.4	2.2
Almond Thins, Sainsbury's*	1 Biscuit/3g	13	430	7.0	80.3	9.0	1.0
Amaretti, Doria*	1 Biscuit/4g	17	433	6.0	84.8	7.8	0.0
Animals, Milk Chocolate, Cadbury's*	1 Biscuit/19g	94	493	6.6	69.8	20.9	0.0
Animals Mini Packs, Cadburys*	1 Pack/25g	123	491	6.7	70.7	20.2	0.0
Apple & Custard Dessert Creams, Tesco*	1 Biscuit/25g	131	525	4.0	68.3	26.2	1.2
Apple Strudel, Big Softies, Fox's*	1 Biscuit/23g	80	348	5.3	77.0	1.6	2.8
Apricot, Low Fat, M & S*	1 Biscuit/23g	79	343	6.1	69.6	4.4	7.8
Belgian, M & S*	1oz/28g	143	510	5.0	67.0	25.0	2.0
Blue Riband Double Choc, Nestle*	1 Serving/22g	113	513	5.1	63.1	26.7	1.1
BN Chocolate Flavour, McVitie's*	1 Biscuit/18g	83	460	6.6	71.0	16.7	2.6

Nutrition Values per 100g / 100ml

B

B

BISCUITS,	Measure WEIGHT/INFO	per Measure KCAL	Nutrition Values per 100g / 100ml KCAL	PROT	CARB	FAT	FIBRE
BN Strawberry Flavour, McVitie's*	1 Biscuit/18g	71	395	5.6	78.0	6.8	0.0
BN Vanilla Flavour, McVitie's*	1 Biscuit/18g	85	470	5.9	74.0	16.6	1.2
Boasters, Hazelnut & Choc Chip, McVitie's*	1 Biscuit/16g	88	549	7.0	55.5	33.3	2.4
Bourbon Cream, M & S*	1oz/28g	136	485	4.7	70.2	20.4	1.5
Bourbon Cream, Tesco*	1 Biscuit/14g	68	485	5.6	67.8	21.3	2.2
Bourbon Creams, Asda*	1 Biscuit/14g	70	485	6.0	68.0	21.0	2.2
Bourbon Creams, Crawfords*	1 Biscuit/12g	59	495	5.9	71.2	20.7	2.2
Bourbon Creams, Sainsbury's*	1 Biscuit/13g	60	476	5.7	70.4	19.1	1.7
Brandy Snap, All Butter, Fox's*	1 Biscuit/12g	54	452	2.7	79.5	13.9	0.9
Brandy Snaps	1oz/28g	122	437	2.5	64.0	20.3	0.8
Breakaway, Nestle*	1oz/28g	145	519	6.6	57.4	29.2	2.0
Breakaway, Nestle*	1 Biscuit/20g	99	497	6.8	60.2	25.4	2.4
Butter Crinkle Crunch, Fox's*	1 Biscuit/11g	51	464	6.2	69.4	18.0	0.0
Butter Puffs, McVitie's*	1 Biscuit/10g	52	523	10.4	60.7	26.5	2.5
Cantuccini, Sainsbury's*	1 Biscuit/8g	35	440	10.4	63.1	16.2	4.4
Caramel Crisp, Go Ahead, McVitie's*	1 Biscuit/22g	95	431	5.4	72.4	13.3	0.9
Caramel Crisp, Go Ahead, McVitie's*	1 Bar/23g	98	428	4.8	75.1	12.0	0.8
Caramel Crunch, Go Ahead, McVitie's*	1 Bar/24g	106	440	4.7	76.6	13.8	0.8
Caramel Log, Tunnock's*	1 Biscuit/25g	118	472	4.2	64.3	24.0	0.0
Caramel Shortcakes, Co-Op*	1oz/28g	140	500	5.0	53.0	30.0	2.0
Caramelinis, Go Ahead, McVitie's*	1 Biscuit/14g	62	440	5.2	74.2	13.6	1.1
Caramels, Milk Chocolate, McVitie's*	1 Serving/17g	81	478	5.6	65.8	21.4	1.8
Cherry Bakewell, Big Softies, Fox's*	1oz/28g	102	364	5.9	79.8	2.0	2.5
Choc Chip, Mini Cookie, Maryland*	1 Mini Cookie/4g	20	508	6.2	67.0	23.9	0.0
Chocolate Break, Tesco*	1 Serving/21g	110	524	7.9	58.9	28.5	1.7
Chocolate Brownie, Big Softies, Fox's	1 Biscuit/25g	87	348	5.5	74.9	2.9	0.0
Chocolate Caramel Crunch Shortcake, Go Ahead, McVitie's*	1 Biscuit/24g	106	443	4.8	76.8	14.1	0.8
Chocolate Fingers, Caramel, Co-Op*	1 Finger/25g	103	410	5.0	54.0	19.0	0.3
Chocolate Fingers, Milk, Cadbury's*	1oz/28g	147	526	6.9	64.2	26.8	0.0
Chocolate Fingers, Plain, Cadbury's*	1oz/28g	142	508	6.2	60.6	26.8	0.0
Chocolate Fingers, White, Cadbury's*	1oz/28g	148	530	6.7	62.4	28.2	0.0
Chocolate Kimberley, Jacob's*	1 Biscuit/20g	86	428	3.9	64.4	17.2	1.1
Chocolate Snack Sandwich, Cadbury's*	1 Biscuit/26g	137	525	7.2	62.6	27.2	0.0
Chocolate Viennese Sandwich, Fox's*	1 Biscuit/14g	76	542	6.9	57.4	31.6	1.6
Chocolinis, Milk Chocolate, Go Ahead, McVitie's*	1 Biscuit/12g	56	466	7.7	77.2	14.0	2.0
Chocolinis, Plain Chocolate, McVitie's*	1 Biscuit/12g	56	468	6.9	77.0	14.7	2.6
Classic Creams, Fox's*	1 Biscuit/14g	72	516	4.4	65.2	25.8	1.7
Classic, Fox's*	1 Biscuit/9g	43	480	4.6	68.6	20.8	2.2
Classic, Fox's*	1 Bar/24g	120	501	6.3	62.2	27.0	1.2
Classic, Milk Chocolate, Fox's*	1 Biscuit/13g	67	517	6.1	64.9	24.0	1.6
Club, Fruit, Jacob's*	1 Biscuit/25g	124	496	5.6	62.2	25.0	2.3
Club, Milk Chocolate, Jacob's*	1 Biscuit/24g	123	511	5.8	62.6	26.4	2.0
Club, Mint, Jacob's*	1 Biscuit/24g	124	517	5.6	62.5	27.2	1.7
Club, Orange, Jacob's*	1 Biscuit/24g	125	519	5.6	62.2	27.6	1.7
Coconut Crinkle, Sainsbury's*	1 Biscuit/11g	54	500	6.4	59.6	26.2	3.7
Coconut Rings, Tesco*	1 Biscuit/9g	44	485	6.2	66.1	21.7	2.6
Continental Chocolate, Parkwood, Aldi*	1 Biscuit/13g	65	499	7.5	62.5	24.3	2.6
Custard Creams, BGTY, Sainsbury's*	1 Biscuit/12g	57	473	5.8	72.2	17.9	1.2
Custard Creams, Crawfords*	1 Biscuit/11g	57	517	5.9	69.2	24.1	1.5
Custard Creams, Farmfoods*	1 Biscuit/12g	59	492	6.1	67.9	21.8	1.6
Custard Creams, Jacob's*	1 Biscuit/16g	77	481	5.3	68.0	20.9	1.6
Custard Creams, Sainsbury's*	1 Cream/13g	64	496	6.0	67.3	22.6	1.6
Custard Creams, Somerfield*	1 Biscuit/11g	57	514	6.1	69.7	23.4	1.6
Custard Creams, Tesco*	1 Biscuit/12g	61	509	6.1	65.0	25.0	1.5

BISCUITS,	Measure WEIGHT/INFO	per Measure KCAL	Nutrition Values per 100g / 100ml KCAL	PROT	CARB	FAT	FIBRE
Dark Chocolate All Butter, M & S*	1 Biscuit/15g	72	480	6.9	52.4	27.2	11.4
Delicious Digestive, Plain Chocolate, Organic, Doves Farm*	1 Biscuit/13g	56	428	5.8	51.4	22.1	6.4
Digestive, 25% Less Fat, Asda*	1 Biscuit/16g	73	455	7.3	69.8	16.3	2.6
Digestive, 25% Less Fat, Tesco*	1 Biscuit/14g	65	462	7.3	71.0	16.5	3.8
Digestive Bar, Milk Chocolate, M & S*	1 Bar/23g	117	510	6.6	64.6	25.1	1.9
Digestive Bar, Milk Chocolate, McVitie's*	1 Biscuit/23g	118	511	6.6	64.6	25.1	1.9
Digestive, BGTY, Sainsbury's*	1 Biscuit/15g	70	468	7.4	71.0	17.2	3.8
Digestive Caramels, Milk Chocolate, McVitie's*	1 Biscuit/16g	76	477	5.6	65.7	21.4	1.8
Digestive Caramels, Plain Chocolate, McVitie's*	1 Biscuit/17g	82	481	5.7	65.5	22.1	2.1
Digestive, Chocolate	1 Biscuit/ 17g	84	493	6.8	66.5	24.1	2.2
Digestive, Crawfords*	1 Biscuit/12g	58	484	7.1	68.8	20.0	3.4
Digestive Creams, McVitie's*	1 Biscuit/12g	60	502	5.6	68.2	23.0	2.1
Digestive, Economy, Sainsbury's*	1 Biscuit/13g	65	498	6.8	66.3	22.8	3.3
Digestive Finger, Sainsbury's*	1 Finger/8g	39	482	6.8	63.6	22.2	3.2
Digestive, Jacob's*	1 Biscuit/14g	67	479	6.6	65.7	21.1	3.4
Digestive, Light, McVitie's*	1 Biscuit/15g	70	466	7.3	72.9	16.2	3.0
Digestive, M & S*	1oz/28g	143	510	6.5	67.2	23.9	2.8
Digestive, McVitie's*	1 Biscuit/15g	74	495	7.0	67.6	21.9	2.8
Digestive, Milk Chocolate, 25% Less Fat, Tesco*	1 Biscuit/17g	79	466	7.4	69.0	17.8	2.6
Digestive, Milk Chocolate, BGTY, Sainsbury's*	1 Biscuit/17g	77	480	7.4	72.5	17.8	2.6
Digestive, Milk Chocolate, GFY, Asda*	1 Biscuit/17g	79	466	7.0	69.0	18.0	2.6
Digestive, Milk Chocolate Homewheat, Light, McVitie's*	1 Biscuit/16g	76	473	7.4	71.5	17.5	2.6
Digestive, Milk Chocolate Homewheat, McVitie's*	1 Biscuit/17g	86	505	6.8	65.8	23.9	2.3
Digestive, Milk Chocolate, M & S*	1 Biscuit/17g	89	522	6.4	65.3	26.1	2.1
Digestive, Milk Chocolate, Safeway*	1 Biscuit/17g	86	504	7.0	61.5	25.5	2.2
Digestive, Milk Chocolate, Sainsbury's*	1 Biscuit/17g	87	511	6.9	65.9	24.5	2.5
Digestive, Milk Chocolate, Somerfield*	1 Biscuit/17g	87	513	7.0	67.0	24.0	0.0
Digestive, Milk Chocolate, Tesco*	1 Biscuit/17g	85	499	6.9	63.7	24.1	2.4
Digestive, Mini Milk Chocolate, Tesco*	1 Pack/30g	153	510	6.6	59.8	27.1	1.8
Digestive, Plain	1 Biscuit/14g	66	471	6.3	68.6	20.9	2.2
Digestive, Plain Chocolate Homewheat, McVitie's*	1 Biscuit/17g	86	507	6.1	65.6	24.4	2.8
Digestive, Plain Chocolate, Tesco*	1 Biscuit/17g	85	499	6.2	63.5	24.4	2.8
Digestive, Reduced Fat, McVitie's*	1 Biscuit/15g	70	467	7.1	72.8	16.3	3.4
Digestive, SmartPrice, Asda*	1 Biscuit/15g	71	474	7.0	62.0	22.0	5.0
Digestive, Sweetmeal, Sainsbury's*	1 Biscuit/14g	72	498	6.0	66.4	23.1	3.3
Digestive, Sweetmeal, Tesco*	1 Biscuit/18g	80	444	8.4	70.0	14.5	3.1
Digestives, GFY, Asda*	1 Biscuit/14g	65	461	6.0	71.0	17.0	3.6
Digestives, Plain Chocolate, BGTY, Sainsbury's*	1 Biscuit/17g	81	478	6.8	72.6	17.8	3.1
Digestives, Reduced Fat, Safeway*	1 Biscuit/14g	66	469	6.5	73.4	22.9	2.8
Echo, Fox's*	1 Bar/25g	128	510	7.8	59.5	26.7	1.2
Fig Roll, Jacob's*	1 Biscuit/17g	61	357	3.5	67.7	8.0	3.9
Fig Roll, Sainsbury's*	1 Biscuit/18g	70	377	4.8	68.3	9.4	2.6
Fig Rolls, Asda*	1 Biscuit/19g	71	372	4.8	68.0	9.0	0.0
Fig Rolls, Vitalinea, Jacob's*	1 Biscuit/18g	61	339	3.7	68.2	5.8	3.8
Figfuls, Go Ahead, McVitie's*	1 Biscuit/15g	55	365	4.2	76.8	4.6	2.9
Florentines, Sainsbury's*	1 Florentine/8g	40	506	10.0	47.2	30.8	7.0
Fruit Shortcake, Asda*	1 Biscuit/10g	45	445	6.0	67.0	17.0	4.6
Fruit Shortcake, McVitie's*	1 Biscuit/10g	50	495	5.6	67.5	22.5	1.9
Fruit Shortcake, Sainsbury's*	1 Biscuit/8g	39	483	5.9	69.6	20.1	2.1
Fruit Shortcake, Tesco*	1 Biscuit/9g	43	473	5.8	70.1	18.8	1.9
Fruit Shorties, Parkside, Aldi*	1 Biscuit/26g	120	461	6.4	69.1	17.7	2.1
Garibaldi, Crawfords*	1 Biscuit/10g	40	397	5.1	70.8	10.4	2.6
Garibaldi, Sainsbury's*	1 Biscuit/9g	35	389	5.7	67.1	10.9	3.3
Garibaldi, Waitrose*	1oz/28g	109	389	5.7	67.1	10.9	1.3

B

BISCUITS,	Measure WEIGHT/INFO	per Measure KCAL	Nutrition Values per 100g / 100ml KCAL	PROT	CARB	FAT	FIBRE
Ginger Crinkle Crunch, Fox's*	1oz/28g	124	442	4.6	77.0	12.8	1.5
Ginger Crinkle, Sainsbury's*	1 Biscuit/11g	53	486	6.2	63.8	22.9	2.9
Ginger Crunch Creams, Fox's*	1 Biscuit/14g	73	518	4.6	64.8	26.7	0.0
Ginger Nut, Tesco*	1 Biscuit/11g	49	447	5.5	73.3	14.6	1.7
Ginger Nuts, Asda*	1 Biscuit/10g	45	447	5.0	73.0	15.0	0.0
Ginger Nuts, McVitie's*	1 Biscuit/12g	57	473	5.6	75.3	16.6	1.7
Ginger Nuts, Milk Chocolate, McVitie's*	1 Biscuit/14g	68	489	5.8	71.8	19.9	1.5
Ginger Snap, BGTY, Sainsbury's*	1 Biscuit/12g	51	427	6.5	78.2	9.8	1.8
Ginger Snap, Fox's*	1 Biscuit/8g	35	443	4.6	77.1	12.8	1.5
Ginger Snap, M & S*	1 Biscuit/8g	36	445	5.4	76.7	12.9	1.5
Ginger Snap, Starbucks*	1 Cookie/21g	89	426	7.9	73.1	11.3	0.0
Ginger Thins, Asda*	1 Biscuit/5g	23	462	6.0	73.0	16.0	1.9
Gingernut	1 Biscuit/11g	50	456	5.6	79.1	15.2	1.4
Gipsy Creams, McVitie's*	1 Biscuit/12g	62	515	4.8	66.0	25.7	2.7
Golden Crunch Creams, Fox's*	1 Biscuit/13g	66	511	4.3	65.6	25.7	1.2
Golden Crunch, Go Ahead, McVitie's*	1 Biscuit/9g	38	419	7.7	75.2	9.7	2.1
Golden Shortie, Jacob's*	1 Biscuit/11g	54	492	6.0	64.9	23.2	0.0
Happy Faces, Jacob's*	1 Biscuit/16g	78	485	4.8	66.1	22.3	1.6
High Baked Water, Tesco*	3 Biscuits/16g	64	401	10.5	73.1	7.4	3.0
Hob Nobs, Chocolate Creams, McVitie's*	1 Biscuit/12g	60	503	6.7	60.3	26.1	4.0
Hob Nobs, McVitie's*	1 Biscuit/14g	68	485	7.7	63.6	22.1	4.7
Hob Nobs, Milk Chocolate, McVitie's*	1 Biscuit/16g	79	496	7.3	63.0	24.0	3.7
Hob Nobs Munch Bites, McVitie's*	1 Pack/40g	203	508	6.8	63.4	25.2	2.8
Hob Nobs, Plain Chocolate, McVitie's*	1 Biscuit/16.2g	80	498	6.7	63.3	24.3	4.2
Hob Nobs, Vanilla Creams, McVitie's*	1 Biscuit/12g	60	501	6.1	62.3	25.2	3.6
Hovis Digestive, Jacob's*	1 Biscuit/12g	56	469	7.8	66.0	19.3	2.9
Iced Gems, Jacob's*	1 Portion/30g	117	390	5.2	85.2	3.1	1.5
Iced Gems, Yum Tums, Jacob's*	1 Pack/30g	117	390	5.2	85.2	3.1	0.0
Jam Rings, Crawfords*	1 Biscuit/12g	56	470	5.5	73.0	17.2	1.9
Jammie Dodgers, Burton's*	1 Biscuit/19g	85	448	4.8	68.8	16.7	1.7
Jammie Dodgers, Mini, Burton's	1 Biscuit/29g	123	424	6.5	74.3	13.2	0.0
Jestives, Fruit & Nut, Cadbury's*	1 Biscuit/17g	85	500	6.7	60.7	25.6	0.0
Jestives, Milk Chocolate, Cadbury's*	1 Biscuit/17g	86	506	6.4	64.4	24.8	0.0
Lemon Curd Sandwich, Fox's*	1 Biscuit/14g	69	494	4.7	66.2	23.4	1.3
Lemon Puff, Jacob's*	1 Biscuit/13g	69	533	4.3	58.8	31.2	2.8
Lemon Puff, Somerfield*	1oz/28g	149	531	5.0	59.0	30.0	0.0
Lemon Thins, Sainsbury's*	1 Biscuit/10g	47	468	5.6	72.3	17.3	1.7
Lincoln, McVitie's*	1 Biscuit/8g	41	514	6.3	69.0	23.6	2.0
Lincoln, Sainsbury's*	1 Biscuit/8g	40	479	7.2	66.1	20.6	2.1
Malted Milk, Asda*	1 Biscuit/8g	39	490	7.0	66.0	22.0	2.0
Malted Milk, Milk Chocolate, Asda*	1 Biscuit/11g	56	509	7.0	64.0	25.0	1.7
Malted Milk, Sainsbury's*	1 Biscuit/8g	40	488	7.1	65.5	21.9	2.0
Malted Milk, Somerfield*	1oz/28g	137	488	7.0	65.0	22.0	0.0
Malted Milk, Tesco*	1 Biscuit/8g	39	488	7.2	65.6	21.9	2.0
Marie, Crawfords*	1 Biscuit/7g	33	475	7.5	76.3	15.5	2.3
Meringue, Hazlenut, Sainsbury's*	1 Biscuit/6g	24	404	5.0	43.0	23.5	1.1
Milk Chocolate, M & S*	1oz/28g	143	510	6.7	62.0	26.2	1.0
Milk Chocolate Sandwich, Farmfoods*	1 Biscuit/26g	132	506	6.1	65.4	24.4	1.5
Mini Assortment, M & S*	4 Biscuits/10g	48	480	6.1	63.9	22.5	2.8
Morning Coffee, Crawfords*	1 Biscuit/4.8g	19	471	7.6	77.5	14.5	2.4
Morning Coffee, Somerfield*	1oz/28g	132	471	8.0	78.0	15.0	0.0
Nice, Asda*	1 Biscuit/8g	38	480	6.0	68.0	21.0	2.4
Nice, Fox's*	1 Biscuit/8g	38	474	5.9	65.9	20.4	3.8
Nice, Jacob's*	1 Biscuit/7g	33	471	6.1	68.5	19.2	1.8

BISCUITS,	Measure WEIGHT/INFO	per Measure KCAL	Nutrition Values per 100g / 100ml KCAL	PROT	CARB	FAT	FIBRE
Nice, Sainsbury's*	1 Biscuit/8g	34	485	6.5	68.0	20.8	2.4
Nice, Somerfield*	1oz/28g	136	485	7.0	68.0	21.0	0.0
Nice, Tesco*	1 Biscuit/8g	39	485	6.5	68.0	20.8	2.4
Nice, Value, Tesco*	1 Biscuit/5g	24	489	6.9	64.6	22.6	2.4
Oat & Wholemeal, Crawfords*	1 Biscuit/14g	67	482	7.7	64.2	21.6	4.8
Oaten, Organic, Duchy Originals*	1 Biscuit/16g	71	441	9.8	62.3	16.9	5.3
Oatmeal Crunch, Jacob's*	1 Biscuit/8g	37	458	6.8	65.9	18.6	3.6
Orange Creams, Parkwood, Aldi*	1 Biscuit/13g	59	494	4.8	69.8	21.7	1.3
Orange Milk Chocolate Sandwich, Farmfoods*	1 Biscuit/26g	131	503	6.1	65.7	24.1	1.4
Orange Munchy Bites, Blue Riband, Nestle*	1 Box/125g	653	522	5.2	61.4	27.9	2.0
Parmesan Cheese, Sainsbury's*	3 Biscuits/10g	53	553	14.7	56.4	29.9	1.8
Party Rings, Fox's*	1 Biscuit/6g	27	453	4.3	77.8	13.8	1.3
Penguin, McVitie's*	1 Biscuit/25g	133	532	5.4	65.0	27.8	1.5
Penguin, Mint, McVitie's*	1 Biscuit/25g	133	531	5.4	65.0	27.7	1.5
Penguin, Orange, McVitie's*	1 Biscuit/25g	133	531	5.4	65.0	27.7	1.5
Rich Tea, 25% Less Fat, Tesco*	1 Biscuit/10g	44	435	7.1	77.0	11.0	1.3
Rich Tea, Asda*	1 Biscuit/10g	45	447	7.0	71.0	15.0	2.3
Rich Tea, BGTY, Sainsbury's*	1 Biscuit/10g	39	430	7.8	75.9	10.6	2.4
Rich Tea, Economy, Sainsbury's*	1 Biscuit/8g	33	470	7.8	77.5	14.3	2.4
Rich Tea Finger, M & S*	1 Biscuit/5g	24	471	7.4	77.9	14.4	0.4
Rich Tea Finger, Tesco*	1 Biscuit/5g	23	451	7.4	72.9	14.4	2.3
Rich Tea, M & S*	1 Biscuit/10g	46	460	6.9	71.6	15.7	2.4
Rich Tea, McVitie's*	1 Biscuit/8.3g	38	475	7.5	76.3	15.5	2.3
Rich Tea, Milk Chocolate, Somerfield*	1oz/28g	141	504	6.0	69.0	23.0	0.0
Rich Tea, Plain Chocolate, Sainsbury's*	1 Biscuit/13g	65	497	6.6	66.0	23.0	2.6
Rich Tea, Reduced Fat, M & S*	1 Biscuit/10g	43	430	7.8	75.9	10.6	2.4
Rich Tea, Safeway*	1 Biscuit/10g	45	454	7.4	71.5	15.4	2.3
Rich Tea, Sainsbury's*	1 Biscuit/10g	45	454	7.5	71.4	15.4	2.3
Rich Tea, Somerfield*	1oz/28g	134	479	7.0	75.0	17.0	0.0
Rich Tea, Tesco*	1 Biscuit/10g	45	454	7.4	71.5	15.4	2.3
Riva Milk, McVitie's*	1 Biscuit/25.2g	135	540	6.4	57.7	31.5	1.6
Rolo, Nestle*	1 Biscuit/22g	109	494	5.5	62.0	24.9	0.7
Shortcake, Crawfords*	1 Biscuit/10.3g	52	518	6.4	68.1	24.4	2.0
Shortcake, Farmfoods*	1 Biscuit/11g	56	506	6.9	63.1	25.1	1.9
Shortcake, Jacob's*	1 Biscuit/10g	49	485	6.7	65.6	21.8	2.0
Shortcake, Sainsbury's*	1 Biscuit/11g	53	484	7.2	66.6	21.0	2.0
Shortcake, Value, Tesco*	1 Biscuit/10g	48	484	7.3	66.6	21.0	2.1
Shortcake, Waitrose*	1 Biscuit/13g	67	512	6.0	68.1	24.0	1.9
Shorties, Cadbury's*	1 Biscuit/15g	77	511	6.5	67.3	24.0	0.0
Shorties, Sainsbury's*	1 Biscuit/10g	50	500	6.4	69.8	21.8	2.0
St Clements Big Softies, Fox's*	1 Biscuit/14g	50	355	6.0	75.2	2.1	3.3
Strawberry, Cream Tease, McVitie's*	1 Biscuit/19g	97	510	4.8	65.9	25.2	1.2
Strawberry Mallows, Go Ahead, McVitie's*	1 Biscuit/18g	69	385	4.3	70.6	9.5	0.9
Summer Fruits, Big Softies, Fox's	1 Bar/25g	89	356	5.9	77.8	2.6	0.0
Taxi, McVitie's*	1 Biscuit/26.5g	131	504	4.2	63.3	26.0	0.7
Biscuits,Thin Arrowroot, Crawfords*	1 Biscuit/7.4g	33	473	7.4	76.7	15.2	2.2
Toffee Chip Crinkle Crunch, Fox's*	1 Biscuit/11g	51	460	4.6	69.6	18.2	0.0
Toffee Crisp, Nestle*	1 Bar/26g	129	497	4.5	62.1	25.6	0.0
Biscuits,Treacle Crunch Creams, Fox's*	1 Biscuit/13g	65	502	4.5	65.3	24.8	1.4
Viennese Finger, Mr Kipling*	1 Finger/32g	167	523	4.3	54.9	31.8	0.0
Viennese Whirl, Fox's*	1 Biscuit/25g	130	518	6.7	60.1	27.8	0.0
Viscount* Mint	1 Biscuit/16g	83	521	4.8	62.7	27.9	1.3
Water	1oz/28g	123	440	10.8	75.8	12.5	3.1
Water, Carr's*	1 Biscuit/8g	35	436	9.3	76.7	9.2	0.0

B

B

BISCUITS,	Measure WEIGHT/INFO	per Measure KCAL	KCAL	PROT	CARB	FAT	FIBRE
Water, High Bake, Sainsbury's*	1 Biscuit/5g	21	412	9.8	76.3	7.5	3.2
White Chocolate, M & S*	1oz/28g	150	535	6.8	60.8	29.3	0.7
White Chocolate Sundae, Fox's*	1 Biscuit/14g	74	529	7.6	57.8	29.7	0.8
Yoyo, Mint, McVitie's*	1 Biscuit/23g	125	545	3.9	63.1	30.8	1.1
BITES,							
Bacon, Crispy, Shapers, Boots*	1 Bag/23g	99	431	8.0	66.0	15.0	3.0
Bacon Rice, Asda*	1 Pack/30g	136	452	7.0	70.0	16.0	0.4
Balti, COU, M & S*	1 Bag/26g	92	355	6.8	76.8	2.2	4.9
Chicken Tikka, M & S*	1 Serving/50g	95	190	19.9	3.8	10.5	3.2
Chicken Tikka ,Roast, Asda*	1 Pack/250g	485	194	21.0	5.0	10.0	1.0
Chinese Style Chicken, M & S*	1 Serving/100g	170	170	17.0	3.2	10.2	1.9
Mexican Chicken, Somerfield*	1 Pack/227g	508	224	26.0	15.0	7.0	0.0
Pepperoni, COU, M & S*	1oz/28g	99	355	7.1	75.7	2.5	4.7
Southern Fried Chicken, Tesco*	1 Pack/300g	720	240	18.1	16.9	11.1	2.1
Spicy Beastie, Asda*	1 Bag/25g	122	488	6.0	62.0	24.0	1.5
Thai Style Chicken, Organic, Evernat*	1oz/28g	64	230	22.3	11.6	9.4	0.0
BITTER LEMON,							
Diet, Asda*	1 Glass/200ml	4	2	0.0	0.3	0.0	0.0
Organic, Tesco*	1 Sm Can/150ml	68	45	0.0	10.8	0.0	0.0
Sainsbury's*	1 Glass/250ml	45	18	0.1	4.4	0.1	0.1
BLACK GRAM, Urad Gram, Dried, Raw	1oz/28g	77	275	24.9	40.8	1.4	0.0
BLACK PUDDING,							
Asda*	1oz/28g	66	235	8.0	17.0	15.0	1.6
Farmfoods*	1 Slice/44g	136	309	11.7	20.2	20.1	0.7
Scottish, Sliced, Somerfield*	1 Slice/50g	129	257	14.0	14.0	16.0	0.0
BLACKBERRIES,							
Fresh, Raw	1oz/28g	7	25	0.9	5.1	0.2	3.1
In Fruit Juice, John West*	1oz/28g	11	39	0.7	9.0	0.0	0.0
In Fruit Juice, Safeway*	1 Serving/210g	69	33	0.6	7.1	0.2	1.8
In Fruit Juice, Sainsbury's*	1 Serving/115g	46	40	0.6	8.6	0.4	1.5
BLACKCURRANTS,							
Fresh, Raw	1oz/28g	8	28	0.9	6.6	0.0	3.6
In Fruit Juice, Asda*	1oz/28g	10	34	0.6	8.0	0.0	2.2
Stewed With Sugar	1oz/28g	16	58	0.7	15.0	0.0	2.8
Stewed Without Sugar	1oz/28g	7	24	0.8	5.6	0.0	3.1
BLUEBERRIES,							
Fresh, Tesco*	1 Serving/125g	40	32	0.6	6.9	0.2	1.8
BOILED SWEETS,							
Average, Boiled Sweets	1oz/28g	92	327	0.0	87.1	0.0	0.0
Blackcurrant & Liquorice, Co-Op*	1 Sweet/8g	32	405	0.9	91.0	5.0	0.0
Clear Fruits, Sainsbury's*	1 Sweet/7g	26	372	0.1	92.9	0.0	0.0
Cough Sweets, Fundays, Bassett's*	1oz/28g	107	383	0.0	94.9	0.0	0.0
Fruit Drops, Co-Op*	1 Sweet/6g	24	395	0.2	98.0	0.0	0.0
Fruit Drops, Orange & Lemon, Sugar Free, Sula*	1 Sweet/2.5g	9	360	0.0	96.0	0.0	0.0
Fruit Rocks, Assorted, M & S*	1oz/28g	107	381	0.0	95.2	0.0	0.0
Fruit Sherbets, Assorted, M & S*	1 Sweet/8g	34	425	0.0	89.7	7.3	0.0
Lockets, Mars*	1 Pack/43g	165	383	0.0	95.8	0.0	0.0
Pear Drops, M & S*	1oz/28g	109	390	0.0	96.9	0.0	0.0
BOK CHOY, Tesco*	1 Serving/100g	11	11	1.0	1.4	0.2	1.2
BOLOGNESE, Meatless, Granose*	1oz/28g	28	100	8.0	8.0	4.0	0.0
BOMBAY ALOO, M & S*	1oz/28g	20	70	1.8	9.5	2.7	2.0
BOMBAY MIX							
Average Bombay Mix	1oz/28g	141	503	18.8	35.1	32.9	6.2
Tesco*	1 Serving/100g	502	502	13.4	40.3	31.9	5.6

(Nutrition Values per 100g / 100ml: KCAL, PROT, CARB, FAT, FIBRE)

	Measure WEIGHT/INFO	per Measure KCAL	Nutrition Values per 100g / 100ml KCAL	PROT	CARB	FAT	FIBRE
BON BONS,							
Apple, Lemon & Strawberry, Co-Op*	¼ Bag/50g	203	405	1.0	88.0	5.0	0.0
BOOST, Cadbury's*	1 Bar/55g	297	540	5.9	62.3	29.3	0.0
BOUILLON,							
Beef, Made Up, Benedicta*	1floz/30ml	22	73	7.5	9.5	0.5	0.0
Beef, Made Up, Touch of Taste*	1 Serving/15ml	11	73	7.5	9.5	0.5	0.0
Chicken, Made Up, Benedicta*	1fl oz/30ml	23	75	4.0	8.0	3.0	5.6
Swiss Vegetable, Powder, Marigold*	1 teaspoon/4g	8	202	18.4	17.7	6.3	0.7
Vegetable, Made Up, Benedicta*	1fl oz/30ml	30	101	7.5	17.0	0.3	0.0
BOUNTY,							
Calapuno, Mars*	1 Pack/175g	919	525	6.3	54.3	31.4	0.0
Dark, Mars*	1 Funsize/29g	137	471	3.2	54.1	26.8	0.0
Milk, Mars*	1 Funsize/29g	141	485	4.6	56.4	26.8	0.0
BOURNVITA,							
Powder, Made Up With Semi-Skimmed Milk	1 Mug/227ml	132	58	3.5	7.8	1.6	0.0
Powder, Made Up With Whole Milk	1 Mug/227ml	173	76	3.4	7.6	3.8	0.0
BOVRIL,							
Beef Extract, Bovril*	1oz/28g	51	181	39.7	3.9	0.6	0.0
Chicken Savoury Drink, Bovril*	1 Serving/12.5g	15	129	9.7	19.4	1.4	2.1
BOYSENBERRIES, Canned, In Syrup	1oz/28g	25	88	1.0	20.4	0.1	1.6
BRAN, Wheat	1 Tbsp/7g	14	206	14.1	26.8	5.5	36.4
BRANDY,							
37.5% Volume	1 Shot/25ml	52	207	0.0	0.0	0.0	0.0
40% Volume	1 Shot/25ml	56	222	0.0	0.0	0.0	0.0
Cherry	1 Shot/25ml	64	255	0.0	32.6	0.0	0.0
BRANDY SNAP, Baskets, Askeys*	1 Basket/20g	98	490	1.9	72.7	21.3	0.0
BRAZIL NUTS							
Brazil Nuts, Average	6 Whole/20g	136	682	14.1	3.1	68.2	4.3
Kernels, Safeway*	1 Serving/28g	191	682	14.1	3.1	68.2	4.3
Whole, Sainsbury's*	2 Nuts/13g	90	691	16.3	3.1	68.2	4.3
BREAD & BUTTER PUDDING,							
5% Fat, M & S*	1 Pudding/237g	367	155	4.4	24.8	4.2	0.4
Asda*	1 Serving/125g	280	224	4.9	24.0	12.0	0.0
Co-Op*	½ Pudding/170g	425	250	7.0	28.0	13.0	1.0
COU, M & S*	1 Pot/140g	189	135	5.5	24.6	1.7	0.6
Finest, Tesco*	1 Serving/153g	379	248	4.9	24.6	14.4	0.9
Individual, Waitrose*	1 Pudding/116g	247	213	5.4	24.4	10.4	0.3
M & S*	1 Serving/125g	359	287	5.3	24.1	19.4	0.8
Sainsbury's*	1 Pudding/230g	446	194	4.8	21.9	9.7	0.4
BREAD, AMAZING Grain, Nimble*	1 Slice/22g	49	224	10.7	41.3	1.8	7.0
BREAD, BAGEL,							
Cinamon & Raisin, Starbucks*	l Bagel/83g	190	229	44.8	9.4	1.4	1.3
Cinnamon & Raisin, M & S*	1 Bagel/85g	223	262	9.6	52.5	1.8	2.2
Cinnamon & Raisin, New York Bagel Co*	1 Bagel/85g	240	282	10.5	56.0	1.8	2.2
Cinnamon & Raisin, Tesco*	1 Bagel/85g	207	243	9.3	47.5	1.7	2.3
Cinnamon & Raisin, Waitrose*	1 Bagel/86g	229	266	10.5	50.9	2.3	2.1
Multi Grain, Sainsbury's*	1 Bagel/113g	293	259	10.0	49.6	3.1	2.0
Onion & Poppy Seed, M & S*	1 Roll/85g	223	262	9.6	52.5	1.8	2.2
Onion, New York Bagel Co*	1 Bagel/85g	233	274	11.1	53.9	1.6	2.1
Onion, Tesco*	1 Bagel/85g	233	274	10.5	52.4	2.4	1.9
Original, New York Bagel Co*	1 Bagel/85g	230	271	11.2	53.2	1.5	2.2
Plain, M & S*	1 Bagel/85g	230	270	10.4	51.7	2.1	1.3
Plain, Tesco*	1 Bagel/85g	214	252	9.9	48.6	2.0	1.8
Plain, Waitrose*	1 Bagel/85g	226	266	10.4	50.7	2.4	1.5
Sesame, New York Bagel Co*	1 Bagel/84g	228	272	11.4	52.7	1.8	2.2

	Measure	per Measure	Nutrition Values per 100g / 100ml				
BREAD, BAGEL,	**WEIGHT/INFO**	**KCAL**	**KCAL**	**PROT**	**CARB**	**FAT**	**FIBRE**
Simply Plain, M & S*	1 Bagel/85g	230	270	10.4	51.7	2.1	1.3
White, Asda*	1 Bagel/86g	227	264	10.0	49.0	3.1	0.0
BREAD, BAGUETTE,							
Budgens*	1 Baguette/125g	335	268	8.5	55.7	1.2	2.3
Homebake, Half, Tesco*	1 Baguette/150g	353	235	7.8	49.1	0.8	1.2
Mediterranean Herb, Sainsbury's*	1 Serving/85g	288	339	8.5	40.8	15.7	2.3
Ready To Bake, Sainsbury's*	½ Baguette/62g	188	303	9.5	62.9	1.5	3.1
Ready To Bake, St Pierre*	1 Baguette/150g	336	224	7.6	46.2	1.0	1.6
Ready To Bake, Waitrose*	½ Baguette/65g	170	262	8.9	53.8	1.2	2.5
Soft Bake, Somerfield*	1 Serving/100g	284	284	10.3	57.3	1.5	1.9
White, Ready To Bake, Asda*	1 Baguette/115g	322	280	10.0	56.0	1.8	2.6
BREAD, BALTIC Rye, Organic, The Village Bakery*	1oz/28g	68	243	8.0	50.3	1.4	2.9
BREAD, BAPS,							
Brown, Large Sliced, Asda*	1 Bap/58g	140	242	10.0	47.0	1.6	0.0
Cheese Topped, Somerfield*	1 Bap/65g	200	307	12.0	48.0	7.0	0.0
Cheese Topped, White, Tesco*	1oz/28g	86	307	12.2	48.0	7.0	0.7
Floured, M & S*	1 Bap/60g	168	280	11.5	46.8	6.2	2.0
For Burger, Somerfield*	1oz/28g	77	276	10.0	48.0	4.0	0.0
Giant Malted, Sainsbury's*	1 Bap/113g	294	260	0.4	48.5	3.1	5.0
White, Giant, Morrisons*	1 Serving/100g	241	241	8.9	44.0	3.1	0.0
White, Giant, Sainsbury's*	1 Bap/103g	267	259	9.0	49.9	2.6	2.7
White, Giant, Waitrose*	1 Bap/104g	261	251	8.8	45.3	3.8	2.1
White, Large, Tesco*	1 Bap/100g	246	246	9.2	47.5	2.1	2.4
White, Medium, Morrisons*	1 Bap/62g	152	245	8.6	48.5	2.0	2.4
White Sandwich, Kingsmill*	1 Bap/80g	209	261	10.1	46.2	4.0	2.2
White, Sliced, Large, Asda*	1 Bap/58g	148	255	10.0	50.0	1.7	0.0
White, Soft, Floured, M & S*	1 Bap/63g	176	280	11.5	46.8	6.2	2.0
White Soft, Somerfield*	1oz/28g	69	248	11.0	44.0	3.0	0.0
White, Warburton's*	1 Bap/57g	144	252	9.8	43.4	4.3	2.7
Wholemeal, Diet Choice, Waitrose*	1 Bap/68g	171	252	9.6	41.4	5.3	5.6
Wholemeal, Giant, Sainsbury's*	1 Bap/110g	275	250	11.7	43.5	3.2	6.1
Wholemeal, Sainsbury's*	1 Bap/60g	151	252	9.6	41.4	5.3	5.6
Wholemeal, Somerfield*	1oz/28g	66	234	14.0	36.0	3.0	0.0
Wholemeal, Tesco*	1 Bap/46g	104	227	9.6	41.4	5.3	5.6
BREAD, BATCH,							
Seeded, Finest, Tesco*	1 Thick Slice/65g	168	259	9.3	41.8	6.1	6.1
White, Floury, Sainsbury's*	1 Serving/62g	166	267	8.0	48.8	4.5	2.3
White, Warburton's*	1 Slice/42g	98	233	9.8	43.6	2.1	2.7
BREAD, BEST Of Both, Hovis*	1 Slice/40g	88	219	9.0	40.8	2.3	4.5
BREAD, BIG Brown Breadcakes, Morrisons*	1 Breadcake/63g	154	245	9.0	44.6	3.4	4.3
BREAD, BLOOMER,							
Vienna, M & S*	1oz/28g	79	281	9.6	55.8	2.1	2.7
White, Bake Off, Somerfield*	1oz/28g	69	246	9.0	47.0	3.0	0.0
White, Seeded, Bake Off, Somerfield*	1oz/28g	68	243	9.0	46.0	3.0	0.0
Wholemeal, Organic, M & S*	1 Slice/120g	288	240	8.7	35.5	8.0	5.2
BREAD, BRIOCHE,							
Continental Classics*	1 Roll/35g	122	349	8.2	58.3	9.3	0.0
Finest, Tesco*	1 Bun/52g	207	398	10.8	38.3	22.4	2.0
M & S*	1 briochel/50g	182	363	7.8	40.2	20.5	1.5
BREAD, BROWN							
Average Brown	1 Med Slice/34g	74	218	8.5	44.3	2.0	3.5
Crusty Golden, Hovis*	1 Slice/44g	102	231	8.7	43.0	2.7	3.3
Danish, Weight Watchers*	1 Slice/19g	38	200	8.6	37.7	1.6	9.6
Fibre Rich, Allinson*	1 Slice/24g	51	212	13.2	33.6	2.8	8.0

	Measure WEIGHT/INFO	per Measure KCAL	KCAL	PROT	CARB	FAT	FIBRE
BREAD, BROWN,							
Harvest, M & S*	1oz/28g	67	240	8.8	44.5	2.7	3.7
High Fibre, Tukestan*	1 Serving/80g	180	225	12.4	37.2	3.0	7.5
Honey & Oat Bran, Vogel's*	1 Serving/100g	220	220	7.9	39.2	4.5	5.7
Medium Sliced, Tesco*	1 Serving/72g	157	218	8.0	41.6	2.2	4.5
Original Wheatgerm, Medium Sliced, Hovis*	1 Slice/33g	77	233	10.8	40.1	3.3	3.7
Premium Gold Malted, TTD, Sainsbury's*	1 Slice/43g	93	217	8.5	40.3	2.4	2.4
Sainsbury's*	1 Slice/34g	81	239	8.4	46.8	2.1	4.2
Sliced, Medium, Asda*	1 Slice/36g	80	223	8.0	44.0	1.7	4.6
Sliced, Weight Watchers*	1 Slice/12g	25	209	11.9	36.5	1.8	6.3
Soda, M & S*	1 Slice/40g	92	229	9.2	43.6	3.6	4.9
Somerfield*	1 Slice/36g	79	220	7.5	43.8	1.7	4.6
Strong Country, Hovis*	1 Serving/100g	319	319	13.6	62.0	1.8	6.0
Thick, Country Baked, Lidl*	1 Slice/38g	82	217	8.1	42.6	1.6	4.5
Toasted	1 Med Slice/24g	65	272	10.4	56.5	2.1	4.5
Weight Watchers*	1 Slice/12g	25	209	11.9	36.5	1.8	6.3
BREAD, BRUSCHETTINE Ciabatta Slices, M & S*	1 Serving/100g	400	400	14.1	51.4	15.5	10.4
BREAD, BURGER BUNS,							
Farmfoods*	1 Bun/53g	131	248	8.0	47.5	2.9	2.2
Sainsbury's*	1 Bun/56g	162	289	7.8	49.4	6.7	2.4
Sliced, Tesco*	1 Bun/60g	168	280	7.9	47.3	6.6	2.1
Sliced, Waitrose*	1 Bun/61g	158	264	10.0	47.2	3.9	1.8
With Sesame Seeds, Co-Op*	1 Bun/55g	143	260	9.0	44.0	5.0	2.0
BREAD, CHEESE & Onion, Somerfield*	1oz/28g	67	241	8.0	44.0	4.0	0.0
BREAD, CHEESE Onion & Garlic, Sainsbury's*	1 Baguette/190g	688	362	7.8	36.8	20.4	2.0
BREAD, CIABATTA,							
Black Olive, Part Baked, Sainsbury's*	¼ Ciabatta/67g	172	257	8.8	46.8	3.8	2.4
Black Olive, Ready To Bake, Sainsbury's*	¼ Ciabatta/66g	170	257	8.8	46.8	3.8	2.4
Filled With Garlic & Herb Butter, Sainsbury's*	½ Loaf/105g	345	329	8.5	38.8	15.5	0.0
Garlic, Asda*	¼ Loaf/50g	173	345	9.5	41.6	15.6	1.1
Garlic, BGTY, Sainsbury's*	½ Ciabatta/105g	306	291	8.7	36.2	12.4	2.7
Garlic, Finest, Tesco*	1 Serving/65g	200	307	7.7	41.3	12.3	1.8
Garlic, Safeway*	½ Ciabatta/105g	279	266	6.1	38.6	9.7	1.7
Green Olive, Tesco*	¼ Loaf/70g	151	215	7.4	36.3	4.4	1.9
Half, M & S*	1 Loaf/135g	354	262	10.3	48.1	4.1	2.1
Half, TTD, Sainsbury's*	½ Ciabatta/133g	346	260	8.9	47.7	3.7	2.2
Italian Style, Safeway*	¼ Loaf/75g	194	258	8.9	47.7	3.5	2.2
M & S*	1 Ciabatta/130g	341	262	10.3	48.1	4.1	2.1
Organic, M & S*	1oz/28g	59	209	7.8	42.5	0.9	1.9
Organic, Tesco*	1/3 Loaf/100g	240	240	7.6	44.7	3.4	2.1
Ready To Bake, Italia, M & S*	1 Serving/150g	393	262	10.3	48.1	4.1	2.1
Ready To Bake, Sainsbury's*	½ Ciabatta/66g	172	260	8.9	47.7	3.7	2.2
Sundried Tomato & Basil, Tesco*	¼ Loaf/75g	193	257	8.9	42.4	5.7	2.4
Sundried Tomato, Safeway*	1 Serving/127g	375	295	8.8	46.6	8.3	2.8
Tomato & Basil, GFY, Asda*	1 Serving/55g	143	260	9.0	51.0	2.2	0.0
BREAD, COBBLES, Wholemeal, Hovis*	1 Serving/61g	143	235	9.7	31.7	3.4	6.3
BREAD, COUNTRY Grain, COU, M & S*	1 Slice/25g	58	233	11.0	42.8	2.0	5.6
BREAD, FARMHOUSE Loaf, Hovis*	1 Slice/44g	100	228	9.0	44.6	1.5	2.3
BREAD, FOCACCIA,							
Garlic & Herb, Safeway*	1/6 /50g	154	308	9.1	42.9	11.1	2.1
Garlic And Herb, Italian Style, Morrisons*	1oz/28g	95	341	8.5	44.7	14.3	2.5
Garlic and Onion, GFY, Asda*	¼ Focaccia/55g	150	272	12.0	47.0	4.0	0.0
Garlic Butter & Rosemary, Sainsbury's*	¼ Focaccia/75g	219	292	8.0	43.0	9.8	2.8
Mini, Sundried Tomato & Basil, Sainsbury's*	1oz/28g	90	321	8.0	41.8	13.6	0.0
Onion & Herb, Tesco*	½ Pack/190g	547	288	8.7	35.2	12.5	3.7

Nutrition Values per 100g / 100ml (KCAL, PROT, CARB, FAT, FIBRE)

B

BREAD, FOCACCIA,	Measure WEIGHT/INFO	per Measure KCAL	Nutrition Values per 100g / 100ml KCAL	PROT	CARB	FAT	FIBRE
Safeway*	1/6 Slice/47g	131	279	9.5	46.9	5.9	3.4
Sun Dried Tomato & Cheese, M & S*	½ Focaccia/111g	316	285	9.7	40.4	9.6	3.2
BREAD, FOUGASSE, Caramelised Onion & Cheese, Tesco*	1oz/28g	80	284	11.1	43.1	6.3	3.5
BREAD, FRENCH,							
Average Stick	2"" Stick/40g	108	270	9.6	55.4	2.7	1.5
Safeway*	1/5 Slice/41g	110	268	9.8	58.5	0.5	2.4
Stick, Part Baked For Home Baking, Budgens*	1 Stick/200g	526	263	8.4	54.8	1.2	2.3
BREAD, FRUIT							
& Cinnamon Loaf, Tesco Finest*	1 slice/37g	134	363	6.4	54.6	13.2	1.5
Loaf, Asda*	1 Slice/16g	45	280	8.0	54.0	3.5	2.1
Loaf, Co-Op*	1 Slice/36g	97	270	10.0	51.0	3.0	1.0
Loaf, M & S*	1 Slice/33g	79	240	14.7	52.7	1.4	2.2
Loaf, Rich, Soreen*	1/10 Loaf/30g	93	310	7.4	60.7	4.1	0.0
Loaf, Sliced, Tesco*	1 Slice/27g	66	246	8.2	46.7	2.9	2.6
Organic, Evernat*	1oz/28g	81	290	8.5	50.8	5.9	0.0
Soda, M & S*	1 Slice/40g	104	260	5.9	51.3	4.6	2.5
BREAD, GARLIC							
& Herb Feast, Giant, Sainsbury's*	1 Serving/50g	159	317	8.0	42.1	12.9	2.6
& Herb, Low Fat, Bertorelli*	1 Slice/25g	83	333	9.1	49.9	12.6	2.4
& Herb, Perfect Partners, Speedibake*	1 Serving/50g	192	384	7.3	41.2	21.1	2.0
Baguette, 50% Less Fat, Asda*	¼ Baguette/43g	126	294	9.2	45.8	8.2	1.3
Baguette, Asda*	¼ Baguette/42g	158	375	8.9	43.3	18.5	1.2
Baguette, BGTY, Sainsbury's*	1oz/28g	93	333	9.1	49.9	12.6	2.4
Baguette, Extra Strong, Sainsbury's*	½ Baguette/85g	278	327	8.4	40.0	14.8	3.4
Baguette, Frozen, Lidl*	1 Baguette/175g	555	317	7.6	44.7	12.0	0.0
Baguette, GFY, Asda*	½ Baguette/85g	248	292	9.0	46.0	8.0	1.3
Baguette, Good Intentions, Somerfield*	½ Baguette/85g	209	246	7.0	37.8	7.4	1.6
Baguette, HE, Tesco*	1 Serving/42g	111	264	8.0	41.1	7.5	2.6
Baguette, Sainsbury's*	1 Serving/50g	196	391	8.9	48.6	19.2	2.3
Baguette, Slices, Tesco*	1 Serving/35g	109	312	9.8	33.8	15.3	1.7
Baguette, Tesco*	1 Slice/19g	67	355	7.6	39.4	18.6	2.0
Baguette, Value, Asda*	½ Baguette/85g	252	297	9.0	47.0	8.0	1.6
Bread, 25% Less Fat, Sainsbury's*	½ Baguette/85g	268	315	7.8	39.4	14.0	3.1
Bread, 30% Less Fat, Morrisons*	1 Serving/80g	226	283	5.9	41.1	10.8	1.9
Bread, Asda*	½ Baguette/85g	302	355	7.6	39.4	18.6	2.0
Bread, BGTY, Sainsbury's*	1 Serving/40g	126	315	7.8	39.4	14.0	3.1
Bread, Caramelised, TTD, Sainsbury's*	¼ Bread/75g	218	290	9.8	41.5	9.4	3.0
Bread, Finest, Tesco*	¼ Loaf/60g	187	311	7.7	40.3	13.2	1.8
Bread, GFY, Asda*	1 Slice/31g	104	337	11.0	53.0	9.0	1.1
Bread, Half Fat, HE, Tesco*	1 Serving/85g	224	264	8.0	41.1	3.9	2.6
Bread, HE, Iceland*	1 Slice/40g	156	389	7.7	43.9	22.8	0.0
Bread, Homebake, Tesco*	1 Serving/60g	209	348	7.1	33.7	20.5	1.5
Bread, M & S*	1 Slice/20g	76	380	7.5	39.5	21.6	1.0
Bread, Micro, McCain*	½ Bread/54g	202	374	7.8	45.1	18.0	0.0
Bread, Organic, Waitrose*	1 Baguette/170g	536	315	8.7	39.1	13.7	1.8
Bread, Pizza Express*	1 Rest Serving/100g	278	278	7.5	43.0	9.9	0.0
Bread, Pizza Hut*	1 Slice/24g	101	419	8.7	48.1	21.3	2.7
Bread, Reduced Fat, M & S*	1 Slice/85g	289	340	8.0	47.6	13.9	2.3
Bread, Reduced Fat, Waitrose*	1 Pack/170g	551	324	6.9	49.4	11.0	0.9
Bread, Safeway*	¼ Baguette/72g	242	336	8.2	45.9	13.3	2.7
Bread Slices, Farmfoods*	1oz/28g	106	379	8.8	37.9	21.4	3.3
Bread Slices, Sainsburys*	1 Slice/25g	108	433	8.5	39.2	26.9	2.3
Bread, Stonebake, M & S*	1 Loaf/85g	242	285	8.1	41.7	9.4	1.1
Flatbread, BGTY, Sainsbury's*	¼ Bread/56g	177	316	9.6	46.6	10.1	2.7

BREAD, GARLIC,	Measure WEIGHT/INFO	per Measure KCAL	Nutrition Values per 100g / 100ml KCAL	PROT	CARB	FAT	FIBRE
Pitta Breads, Sainsbury's*	1 Pitta/60g	153	255	9.5	52.0	1.0	2.5
Pizza Bread, Co-Op*	1 Pizza/240g	756	315	8.0	41.0	13.0	2.0
Pizza Bread, Domino's Pizza*	1 Slice/40g	115	295	12.0	41.4	9.0	2.3
Slices, GFY, Asda*	1 Slice/31g	104	337	11.0	53.0	9.0	1.1
BREAD, GRANARY							
Average Granary	1 Slice/25g	59	235	9.3	46.3	2.7	4.3
COU, M & S*	1 Slice/25g	62	246	11.7	45.1	2.1	5.7
Hovis*	1 Slice/35g	79	225	9.1	42.7	2.0	3.3
Malted, Medium Brown, Asda*	1 Slice/35g	81	231	9.0	43.0	2.6	3.3
New, Hovis*	1 Slice/44g	101	229	9.0	42.2	2.6	3.3
Waitrose*	1 Slice/40g	88	220	9.4	39.9	2.5	4.3
BREAD, GREEN Olive Country, M & S*	1 Serving/44g	110	250	7.6	40.3	6.3	2.3
BREAD, HIGH BRAN,							
Allinson*	1 Slice/36g	79	219	12.6	35.0	3.2	6.8
M & S*	1 Slice/28g	59	210	12.6	32.5	3.0	6.3
BREAD, IRISH							
Brown, Ormo*	1 Serving/100g	229	229	9.2	43.6	3.6	4.9
Cottage Wheaten, Tesco*	1 Serving/40g	79	198	9.1	35.4	1.9	6.1
BREAD, ITALIAN							
Style, Cheese & Garlic, Morrisons*	½ Pack/135g	431	319	10.8	45.1	10.6	2.1
Style Pesto, TTD Sainsbury's*	¼ Bread/99g	247	249	9.1	39.4	6.1	4.4
Style Red Pepper, Safeway*	1 Serving/80g	184	230	9.1	42.2	2.3	2.1
Style Ring, M & S*	1 Serving/50g	105	210	7.3	42.2	1.3	1.7
Style Stone Baked Garlic, Morrisons*	½ Pack/115g	420	365	7.9	40.4	19.1	1.9
BREAD, MALT LOAF,							
Fruit, Sainsbury's*	1oz/28g	86	308	7.9	63.8	2.4	2.4
Ready Spread Snack, Soreen*	2 Slices/64g	220	344	6.4	57.0	10.0	3.0
Value, Tesco*	1 Slice/25g	72	289	8.9	60.2	1.4	3.3
BREAD, MALTED							
Brown Granary, Medium Sliced, Hovis*	1 Slice/35g	79	225	9.1	42.7	2.0	3.3
Brown, Hovis*	1 Slice/36g	82	229	9.0	42.2	2.6	3.3
Brown, Kingsmill*	1 slice/44g	103	234	9.4	43.4	2.5	2.7
Brown, Morrisons*	1 Slice/38g	96	253	10.3	49.9	1.4	3.1
Brown Slice, BGTY, Sainsbury's*	1 Slice/22g	53	239	12.1	41.4	2.8	5.8
Brown, Thick Sliced, Organic, Tesco*	1 Slice/44g	116	264	7.8	53.8	2.0	3.3
Danish, Nimble*	1 Slice/22g	49	222	8.3	43.7	1.6	5.3
Danish, Sliced, Weight Watchers*	1 Slice/19g	41	218	10.2	41.3	0.3	6.9
Danish, Weight Watchers*	1 Slice/19g	41	218	10.2	41.3	1.4	6.9
Oat, Duchy, Originals*	1 Serving/80g	195	244	8.8	43.6	3.8	3.7
Wheat Country, Kingsmill Gold*	1 Slice/41g	96	234	9.4	43.4	2.5	2.7
Wheat, Eat Smart, Safeway*	1 Slice/26g	60	230	10.0	42.8	1.8	5.3
Wheat Loaf, Thick Sliced, Village Green, Aldi*	1 Slice/38g	96	253	10.3	49.9	1.4	3.1
Wheat, The Best, Safeway*	1 Slice/44g	103	235	9.1	45.6	1.8	4.7
BREAD, MIXED Seed Loaf, Organic, M & S*	1oz/28g	73	261	9.3	37.5	8.7	5.1
BREAD, MULTIGRAIN,							
Bakers Choice, M & S*	1 Slice/25g	61	242	13.4	33.7	6.0	6.4
Tesco*	1 Slice/31g	66	214	11.1	36.8	3.2	8.9
Thick Sliced, Tesco*	1 Slice/50g	113	225	8.4	42.2	2.5	3.9
BREAD, NAAN							
Average Naan	1 Naan/160g	538	336	8.9	50.1	12.5	1.9
Co-Op*	1oz/28g	60	216	7.7	36.9	4.2	1.3
Filled Peshwari, M & S*	1 Serving/127g	394	310	9.2	45.8	10.1	1.9
Fresh, BGTY, Sainsbury's*	1 Serving/150g	368	245	9.4	44.9	3.1	2.2
Fresh, Sharwood's*	1oz/28g	70	251	7.3	48.0	3.3	2.0

B

BREAD, NAAN,	Measure WEIGHT/INFO	per Measure KCAL	KCAL	PROT	CARB	FAT	FIBRE
			Nutrition Values per 100g / 100ml				
Garlic & Coriander, Asda*	½ Naan/74g	260	352	7.0	45.0	16.0	2.3
Garlic & Coriander, Fresh, Sharwood's*	1oz/28g	71	252	7.7	47.8	3.3	2.2
Garlic & Coriander, Mini, Long Life, Sharwood's*	1oz/28g	71	255	7.4	45.3	4.9	2.3
Garlic & Coriander, Mini, Sainsbury's*	1 Naan/50g	148	295	8.6	44.2	9.3	3.7
Garlic & Coriander, Mini, Tesco*	1 Naan/60g	178	296	7.6	47.0	8.6	2.5
Indian Style, Lidl*	1 Naan/140g	332	237	8.7	44.2	2.5	0.0
Long Life, Sharwood's*	1oz/28g	72	258	7.3	45.8	5.1	2.0
Mini, Asda*	1 Serving/100g	304	304	8.0	50.0	8.0	2.8
Mini, Plain, Tesco*	1 Naan/60g	175	292	9.3	47.6	7.2	2.5
Mini, Sainsbury's*	1 Serving/50g	157	314	8.7	41.5	12.4	4.3
Peshwari, Fresh, Sharwood's*	1oz/28g	67	240	6.8	41.9	5.0	2.5
Peshwari, Long Life, Sharwood's*	1oz/28g	71	252	6.2	42.0	6.6	2.6
Peshwari, M & S*	1 Serving/127g	394	310	9.2	45.8	10.1	1.9
Peshwari, Sharwood's*	1 Pack/260g	655	252	6.2	42.0	6.6	2.6
Plain, Farmfoods*	1 Naan/142g	440	310	8.1	50.2	8.5	2.6
Plain, Mini, Fresh, Sharwood's*	1oz/28g	70	251	7.3	48.0	3.3	2.0
Plain, Nisa Heritage*	1 Naan/150g	401	267	9.0	44.2	6.2	1.9
Plain, Sharwood's*	1 Pack/260g	671	258	7.3	45.8	5.1	2.0
Plain, Sharwood's*	1 Pack/235g	606	258	7.3	45.8	5.1	2.0
Plain, Tesco*	1 Naan/150g	429	286	7.8	47.6	7.2	2.5
Safeway*	1 Naan/120g	346	288	8.4	51.4	5.4	2.6
Sainsbury's*	1 Serving/74g	215	291	9.0	44.9	8.4	3.8
Tandoori, Sharwood's*	1 Bread/130g	330	254	7.3	45.0	5.0	2.0
BREAD, OAT, Waitrose*	1oz/28g	71	253	8.5	44.9	4.4	3.6
BREAD, OATMEAL,							
Farmhouse Soft, M & S*	1 Slice/45g	110	245	11.1	39.5	4.4	5.2
Sliced Loaf, Tesco*	1 Slice/50g	111	222	7.4	40.5	3.4	2.8
BREAD, OLIVE, Waitrose*	1 Slice/28g	86	306	9.0	43.6	10.6	2.0
BREAD, PETIT PAIN,							
Homebake, Mini, Tesco*	1 Serving/50g	118	235	7.8	49.1	0.8	0.0
Organic, Tesco*	1 Roll/100g	235	235	7.8	49.1	0.8	1.2
Waitrose*	1 Roll/69g	190	275	9.3	55.9	1.6	3.1
White, Soft Bake, Somerfield*	1 Roll/70g	174	248	9.2	49.9	1.3	1.8
Harvester, Somerfield*	1 Serving/70g	188	269	10.6	52.2	2.0	3.2
Homebake Mini, Tesco*	1 Roll/50g	118	235	7.8	49.1	0.8	1.2
Ready To Bake, Sainsbury's*	1 Petit Pain/44g	132	299	9.4	61.6	1.7	3.2
BREAD, PITTA,							
Brown, Organic, Waitrose*	1 Pitta/61g	138	226	6.4	47.5	1.4	6.6
Cypriana Supreme*	1oz/28g	67	239	8.5	48.6	1.2	0.0
Garlic & Herb, Tesco*	1 Pitta Bread/56g	138	246	8.4	50.3	1.2	2.1
Garlic, Morrisons*	1 Pitta/60g	149	249	9.7	51.1	1.8	0.0
Iceland*	1 Pitta/50g	126	251	8.6	50.0	1.8	2.3
Mini, M & S*	1 Pitta/13g	34	260	9.2	52.1	2.4	1.8
Mini, Sainsbury's*	1 Pitta/30g	75	249	10.3	49.3	1.2	3.5
Organic, Tesco*	1 Pitta/60g	124	206	8.3	40.2	1.4	5.7
Sesame, Sainsbury's*	1 Pitta/59g	156	264	9.8	50.8	2.4	3.1
Sesame Variety, Sainsbury's*	1 Slice/59g	156	264	9.8	50.8	2.4	3.1
Somerfield*	1 Pitta/56g	141	251	8.6	50.0	1.8	2.3
Tesco*	1oz/28g	69	247	8.4	50.7	1.2	2.6
Value, Tesco*	1oz/28g	64	227	6.0	48.8	0.9	2.0
White	1 Pitta/75g	199	265	9.2	57.9	1.2	2.2
White, Asda*	1 Pitta/56g	141	252	9.0	50.0	1.8	2.3
White, Co-Op*	1 Pitta/63g	151	240	10.0	47.0	1.0	3.0
White, Greek Style, Asda*	1 Pitta/50g	127	253	8.0	51.0	1.9	0.0

BREAD, PITTA,	Measure WEIGHT/INFO	per Measure KCAL	Nutrition Values per 100g / 100ml KCAL	PROT	CARB	FAT	FIBRE
White, Iceland*	1 Pitta/50g	126	251	8.6	50.0	1.8	2.3
White, Mini, Safeway*	1 Pitta/54g	119	220	8.0	49.4	1.2	1.9
White, Mini, Sainsbury's*	1 Pitta/31g	88	285	9.8	58.0	1.5	3.5
White, Safeway*	1 Pitta/54g	119	220	8.0	49.4	1.2	1.9
White, Sainsburys*	1 Pittta/59g	151	256	9.5	52.0	1.1	2.3
Wholemeal, Asda*	1 Pitta/56g	128	229	11.0	41.0	2.3	0.0
Wholemeal, Greek Style, Asda*	1 Serving/55g	126	229	11.0	41.0	2.3	0.0
Wholemeal, HE, Co-Op*	1 Pitta/63g	135	215	12.0	37.0	2.0	9.0
Wholemeal, Morrisons*	1 Pitta/60g	135	225	11.9	46.4	2.0	0.0
Wholemeal, Sainsbury's*	1 Pitta/59g	146	247	12.4	46.0	1.5	5.3
Wholemeal, Tesco*	1 Pitta/62g	138	222	9.1	42.5	1.7	5.8
Wholemeal, Waitrose*	1 Pitta/60g	151	251	11.3	53.4	0.6	0.0
BREAD, POTATO & Rosemary, Tesco*	1oz/28g	67	241	8.2	42.0	4.5	2.2
BREAD PUMPERNICKEL Rye, Kelderman*	1 Slice/50g	93	185	6.0	38.0	1.0	0.0
BREAD, RAISIN & Pumpkin Seed, Organic, Tesco*	1 Slice/30g	76	253	9.7	40.6	5.8	3.8
BREAD, RAISIN Loaf With Cinnamon, Warburton's*	1 Slice/33g	91	276	7.5	52.9	3.8	4.2
BREAD, ROASTED Onion, M & S*	1 Slice/50g	125	250	9.0	46.7	3.3	2.1
BREAD, ROLLS,							
Blackpool Milk, Warburton's*	1 Slice/18g	45	251	10.8	45.3	3.0	2.8
Brown, Crusty	1 Roll/50g	128	255	10.3	50.4	2.8	3.5
Brown, Large, Asda*	1 Roll/57g	138	242	10.0	47.0	1.6	0.0
Brown, Malted Grain, Tesco*	1 Roll/58g	142	244	8.7	45.1	3.2	1.9
Brown, Morning, Farmfoods*	1 Roll/50g	135	269	12.0	47.0	3.7	4.2
Brown, Soft	1 Roll/50g	134	268	10.0	51.8	3.8	3.5
Brown, Soft, Somerfield*	1oz/28g	68	243	9.0	42.0	3.0	0.0
Brown, Soft, Tesco*	1 Roll/50g	118	235	9.0	41.6	3.6	4.5
Ciabatta, M & S*	1 Roll/80g	210	262	10.3	48.1	4.1	2.1
Ciabatta, Ready To Bake, Sainsbury's*	1 Roll/75g	198	264	9.1	48.9	3.6	2.3
Ciabatta, Tesco*	1 Serving/75g	200	267	9.0	44.0	6.1	2.1
Crusty, French, M & S*	1 Roll/65g	159	245	8.1	50.5	1.2	3.3
Crusty, Part-Baked, Budgens*	1 Roll/50g	148	296	9.4	61.4	1.4	2.5
Finger, Morrisons*	1 Roll/46g	119	259	10.7	50.0	1.8	2.3
Finger, Sainsbury's*	1 Roll/40g	102	256	10.3	47.9	2.6	2.4
For Hamburgers	1 Roll/50g	132	264	9.1	48.8	5.0	1.5
Granary, Bakers Premium, Tesco*	1 Roll/65g	158	243	9.9	47.8	1.3	2.3
Granary Malted Wheatgrain, Soft, M & S*	1 Roll/80g	208	260	9.3	47.2	3.9	2.3
Hot Dog, Farmfoods*	1 Roll/53g	125	235	8.1	47.0	1.7	2.2
Hot Dog, Sliced, Asda*	1 Roll/84g	197	234	7.0	44.0	3.3	0.0
Hot Dog, Tesco*	1 Roll/85g	200	235	7.3	44.0	3.3	1.9
Kingsmill*	1 Roll/54g	136	252	9.3	44.5	4.1	2.4
Malted Grain, Soft, Weight Watchers*	1 Roll/42g	95	226	9.8	42.2	2.0	4.5
Malted Wheat & Poppy Seed, Safeway*	1 Roll/54g	140	260	10.6	48.7	2.8	3.4
Mixed Mini Selection, M & S*	1 Roll/32g	71	221	9.6	43.4	5.0	1.9
Morning Breakfast, M & S*	1 Roll/55g	160	290	10.3	53.8	4.3	0.6
Morning, Tesco*	1 Roll/48g	117	243	10.4	44.8	2.5	4.7
Oatmeal, Soft, M & S*	1 Roll/80g	224	280	12.3	43.4	6.4	2.7
Pain Raisin, Mini, M & S*	1oz/28g	87	310	5.3	42.3	13.6	1.3
Poppy Seeded Knot, Waitrose*	1 Roll/65g	179	275	9.3	55.9	1.6	3.1
Selection, COU, M & S*	2 Rolls/151g	264	175	11.4	25.6	2.7	0.8
Snack, Mini, Tesco*	1 Roll/35g	95	271	19.0	43.0	6.0	4.0
Sundried Tomato, Homebake, Tesco*	1 Roll/50g	123	246	11.3	44.0	3.0	0.0
White, BGTY, Sainsbury's*	1 Roll/50g	114	227	9.1	45.3	1.0	3.0
White, Boulders, Soft, Hovis*	1 Roll/74g	206	279	11.0	51.5	3.0	2.3
White, Cheese Topped, Asda*	1 Roll/46g	121	264	10.0	46.0	4.4	2.0

B

BREAD, ROLLS,	Measure WEIGHT/INFO	per Measure KCAL	KCAL	PROT	CARB	FAT	FIBRE
White, Cheese Topped, Sainsbury's*	1 Roll/75g	218	291	12.1	41.6	8.5	2.0
White, Crusty	1 Roll/50g	140	280	10.9	57.6	2.3	1.5
White Deli Tesco*	1 Roll/65g	180	277	8.7	52.0	3.8	2.7
White, Finger, Co-Op*	1 Roll/46g	129	280	10.0	52.0	4.0	2.0
White, Finger, SmartPrice, Asda*	1 Roll/50g	121	242	9.0	48.0	1.6	2.1
White Finger, Tesco*	1 Roll/50g	125	251	9.7	55.5	0.4	1.5
White, Finger, Waitrose*	1 Roll/49g	121	247	9.4	45.6	3.0	2.7
White, Floured, Warburton's*	1 Roll/50g	124	247	9.8	43.3	3.8	2.7
White, Hot Dog, Sainsbury's*	1 Roll/85g	235	277	7.3	48.8	5.8	2.4
White, Kingsmill*	1 Roll/60g	151	252	9.3	44.5	4.1	2.4
White, Morning, Co-Op*	1 Roll/47g	134	285	12.0	53.0	3.0	2.0
White, Morning, M & S*	1 Roll/50g	136	272	8.8	53.8	1.5	2.7
White, Old Fashioned, Waitrose*	1 Roll/57g	157	275	8.8	49.8	4.5	2.8
White, Organic, Warburton's*	1 Roll/53g	137	258	10.3	45.3	4.0	2.7
White, Ploughmans, Sainsbury's*	1 Roll/65g	185	285	8.6	54.1	3.8	2.3
White, Scottish, Morning, Safeway*	1 Serving/40g	113	283	10.4	56.4	1.8	1.6
White, Seeded, Sainsbury's*	1 Roll/80g	217	271	10.9	43.4	5.9	4.8
White, Seeded, Soft, M & S*	1 Roll/72g	205	285	11.7	46.2	5.7	1.8
White, Smart Price, Asda*	1 Roll/44g	106	242	9.0	48.0	1.6	2.1
White, Snack, Sainsbury's*	1 Roll/67g	159	237	7.9	49.2	1.0	2.3
White, Soft	1 Roll/45g	121	268	9.2	51.6	4.2	1.5
White, Soft, COU, M & S*	1 Roll/37g	94	255	10.7	47.1	2.7	1.5
White, Soft, Finger, Budgens*	1 Roll/46g	134	291	10.2	54.0	3.8	1.6
White, Soft, Finger, M & S*	1 Roll/64g	189	295	10.1	47.5	7.2	2.2
White, Soft, Premium, Village Green, Aldi*	1 roll/65g	168	259	8.3	47.5	4.0	1.9
White, Soft, Somerfield*	1oz/28g	73	260	10.0	48.0	3.0	0.0
White, Split, Asda*	1 Roll/45g	113	251	10.0	45.0	3.4	2.8
White, Value, Tesco*	1 Roll/35g	81	231	8.0	45.7	1.8	2.3
White, Warburton's*	1 Roll/57g	141	248	9.7	42.8	4.2	0.0
Wholemeal	1 Roll 45g	108	241	9.0	48.3	2.9	5.9
Wholemeal,, Asda*	1 Roll/58g	131	225	11.0	39.0	2.8	6.0
Wholemeal, Deli, With Cracked Wheat, Tesco*	1 Roll/65g	156	240	9.0	40.2	4.8	5.7
Wholemeal, Finger, Soft, M & S*	1 Roll/60g	162	270	13.5	37.9	7.4	4.7
Wholemeal, Floury Batch, Sainsbury's*	1 Roll/67g	157	234	9.0	38.9	4.7	5.7
Wholemeal, HE, Co-Op*	1 Roll/60g	141	235	13.0	37.0	4.0	8.0
Wholemeal, HE, Tesco*	1 Roll/67g	135	202	8.9	37.4	1.9	7.0
Wholemeal, Kingsmill*	1 Roll/68g	167	245	10.7	41.5	4.0	5.1
Wholemeal, Old Fashioned, Waitrose*	1 Roll/57g	135	236	11.1	37.2	4.8	6.6
Wholemeal, Organic, M & S*	1oz/28g	63	224	11.2	42.7	4.2	7.4
Wholemeal, Organic, Sainsbury's*	1 Roll/66g	152	230	10.7	41.0	2.7	6.6
Wholemeal, Ploughmans, Sainsbury's*	1 Roll/65g	171	263	9.0	45.9	4.8	5.7
Wholemeal, Soft, M & S*	1 Roll/55g	128	233	12.4	36.6	4.1	5.8
Wholemeal, Sunflower & Honey, Sainsbury's*	1 Roll/85g	225	265	9.2	45.4	5.1	4.5
Wholemeal With Jumbo Oat Flakes, Eat Smart, Safeway*	1 Roll/53g	125	235	10.6	41.8	2.8	6.2
Wholewhite, Kingsmill*	1 Roll/63g	158	251	9.5	43.7	4.2	3.5
Wholmeal, Deli, Tesco*	1 Serving/65g	156	240	9.0	40.2	4.8	5.7
BREAD, RYE,							
Average Rye	1 Slice/25g	55	219	8.3	45.8	1.7	4.4
German Style, Kelderman*	1 Slice/62g	96	155	5.6	30.2	1.4	7.7
With Sesame Seeds, Ryvita*	1 Serving/9g	31	339	10.5	58.5	7.0	16.0
BREAD, SODA,							
Average Soda	1oz/28g	72	258	7.7	54.6	2.5	2.1
Farl, Tesco*	1 Farl/142g	325	229	7.1	42.2	3.2	2.6
Farls, M & S*	1 Farl/110g	267	243	9.6	50.1	2.7	2.3

(Nutrition Values per 100g / 100ml: KCAL, PROT, CARB, FAT, FIBRE)

	Measure WEIGHT/INFO	per Measure KCAL	Nutrition Values per 100g / 100ml KCAL	PROT	CARB	FAT	FIBRE
BREAD, SOFTGRAIN,							
Farmhouse, M & S*	1 Slice/25g	60	238	8.4	42.8	3.7	3.2
Medium Sliced, GFY, Asda*	1 Slice/35g	79	226	7.0	46.0	1.5	3.7
Mighty White*	1 Slice/36g	81	224	7.2	45.5	1.5	3.7
White, Sliced, Tesco*	1 Med Slice/36g	81	224	7.2	45.5	1.5	3.7
BREAD, STROMBOLI,							
Four Cheese & Sundried Tomato, Finest, Tesco*	1 Serving/67g	206	307	10.8	34.2	14.1	3.4
Sunblush Tom Mozzarella & Basil, TTD, Sainsbury's*	1 Pack/300g	723	241	8.9	35.1	7.5	3.0
BREAD, SUBMARINE,							
Malted Grain, M & S*	1 Roll/109g	300	275	8.9	53.8	4.3	3.0
Mini, M & S*	1 Roll/25g	69	276	11.4	47.7	4.9	1.1
White, Co-Op*	1 Roll/78g	207	265	12.0	45.0	4.0	2.0
BREAD, SUNFLOWER							
& Honey Loaf, M & S*	1 Serving/67g	206	308	12.9	34.0	13.4	5.6
& Pumpin Seed Batched, Organic, Tesco*	1 Slice/30g	73	243	11.0	33.1	7.4	5.2
BREAD, TOASTED,							
Brown	1 Med Slice/30g	72	239	8.4	46.8	2.1	4.2
White	1 Med Slice/33g	79	238	7.5	48.5	1.6	1.8
Wholemeal	1 Med Slice/26g	58	224	8.6	42.3	2.2	5.8
BREAD, TOMATO							
& Garlic, Morrisons*	1 Serving/125g	271	217	5.9	31.4	7.6	2.5
Cheese & Olive, Sharing Bread, BGTY, Sainsbury's*	1 Serving/67g	168	250	9.8	43.4	4.1	2.5
BREAD, WHEATGERM,							
Brown, Original, Medium, Hovis*	1 Slice/33g	77	233	10.8	40.1	3.3	3.7
Thin Sliced, Hovis*	1 Slice/21g	47	222	10.1	38.5	3.0	4.6
BREAD, WHITE							
Average White	1 Slice/25g	59	235	8.4	49.3	1.9	1.5
Bakers Gold, Thick Sliced, Asda*	1 Slice/44g	103	233	8.0	46.0	1.9	2.2
COU, M & S*	1 Slice/26g	60	231	10.6	41.9	2.3	4.6
Crusty, Hovis*	1 Slice/44g	103	233	8.8	44.3	2.2	2.1
Crusty, Sliced Loaf, Tesco*	1 Slice/50g	117	233	7.4	46.0	2.1	2.0
Crusty, Sliced, Premium, Budgens*	1 Slice/50g	121	242	8.8	46.9	2.2	2.2
Danish, Medium Sliced, Morrisons*	1 Slice/17g	42	245	10.2	49.1	1.8	2.2
Danish, Soft & Light, Sainsbury's*	1 Slice/22g	51	232	8.9	45.4	1.6	2.1
Danish, Tesco*	1 Slice/22g	56	254	9.4	49.7	1.9	2.8
Danish, Thick Sliced, Iceland*	1 Slice/22g	51	232	8.9	45.4	1.6	2.1
Danish, Warburton's*	1 Slice/25g	61	243	10.7	46.9	1.4	2.7
Danish, Weight Watchers*	1 Slice/19g	42	222	8.7	43.9	1.3	2.8
Eat Smart, Safeway*	1 Slice/26g	60	230	8.8	45.0	1.8	2.3
Extra Thick Sliced, Kingsmill*	1 Slice/57g	132	232	8.8	43.8	2.4	2.8
Farmhouse Crusty, M & S*	1 Slice/34g	85	250	8.8	48.0	2.6	2.3
Farmhouse Gold Premium, Morrisons*	1 Slice/38g	91	239	9.5	47.3	1.3	2.2
Farmhouse, Hovis	1 Slice/37g	84	228	9.0	44.6	1.5	2.3
Farmhouse Soft, Warburton's*	1 Slice/26g	63	241	10.2	44.3	2.5	2.7
Farmhouse, Waitrose*	1 Slice/40g	94	235	9.5	45.4	1.7	2.6
Fried In Blended Oil	1 Slice/28g	141	503	7.9	48.5	32.2	1.6
Gold Seeded, Kingsmill*	1 Slice/44g	108	245	9.7	38.8	5.7	3.5
Great, Hovis*	1 Slice/40g	90	226	8.8	44.4	1.5	2.2
Healthy, Thick Sliced, Warburtons*	1 Slice/38g	84	222	10.3	41.2	1.8	4.1
Kingsmill*	1 Slice/44g	104	236	8.8	44.2	2.8	2.3
Medium Sliced, Asda*	1 Slice/37g	84	226	7.0	46.0	1.5	2.8
Medium Sliced, Keep Fresh, Safeway*	1 Slice/34g	76	224	7.3	44.3	1.9	2.7
Medium Sliced, Kingsmill*	1 Slice/38g	89	233	8.8	44.1	2.4	2.5
Medium Sliced, Long Life, Asda*	1 Slice/36g	82	228	8.0	45.0	1.8	2.7
Medium Sliced, Longerlife, Sainsbury's*	1 Slice/36g	87	243	8.3	47.6	2.2	1.7

BREAD, WHITE,	Measure WEIGHT/INFO	per Measure KCAL	Nutrition Values per 100g / 100ml KCAL	PROT	CARB	FAT	FIBRE
Medium Sliced, Mother's Pride*	1 Slice/36g	82	229	8.0	45.6	1.6	3.0
Medium Sliced, SmartPrice, Asda*	1 Slice/36g	81	226	7.0	46.0	1.5	2.8
Medium Sliced, Spinaca, Aldi*	1 Slice/25g	59	237	7.2	46.7	1.8	2.3
Medium Sliced, Tesco*	1 Slice/73g	166	228	8.0	45.5	1.6	3.0
Medium Sliced, Warburton's*	1 Slice/24g	57	237	10.2	44.9	1.8	2.7
Organic, M & S*	1oz/28g	73	261	7.6	52.5	2.4	2.2
Premium Gold, TTD, Sainsbury's*	1 Slice/44g	103	233	8.4	45.6	1.9	2.2
Sandwich, Bakery, Sainsbury's*	1 Slice/50g	121	242	10.3	49.0	0.6	2.9
Sliced	1 Med Slice/39g	93	238	7.5	48.5	1.6	1.8
Sliced, BGTY, Sainsbury's*	1 Slice/20g	45	225	10.2	43.9	0.9	4.6
Sliced, Economy, Sainsbury's*	1 Slice/44g	100	228	7.1	46.4	1.5	2.8
Sliced, Longer Life, Co-Op*	1 Slice/44g	99	225	8.0	45.0	2.0	2.0
Sliced, Nimble*	1 Slice/20g	46	232	9.7	44.3	1.8	2.9
Sliced, Organic, Harvestime*	1oz/28g	71	255	8.1	44.6	1.6	2.5
Sliced, Square, Kingsmill*	1 Slice/38g	89	233	8.8	44.1	2.4	2.5
Sliced Toastie, Warburton's*	1 Slice/29g	69	237	10.2	44.9	1.8	2.7
Sliced, Weight Watchers*	1 Slice/12g	27	226	10.3	42.6	1.6	3.6
Soft Crusty, M & S*	1 Slice/25g	64	256	9.3	49.0	2.5	2.4
Soft, Farmhouse, M & S*	1 Slice/25g	60	239	9.8	42.6	3.3	2.5
Square Cut, Hovis*	1 Med Slice/40g	90	226	8.8	44.4	1.5	2.2
Stay Fresh, Tesco*	1 Slice/40g	100	249	8.6	48.3	2.4	1.5
Sunblest*	1 Med Slice/33g	77	232	7.4	46.4	1.9	2.1
Super Toastie, Warburton's*	1 Serving/57g	134	235	10.1	44.6	1.8	2.7
Tasty Crust, Kingsmill*	1 Slice/50g	130	259	9.4	48.8	2.9	2.4
Thick Cut, Lidl*	1 Slice/35g	87	249	8.6	45.4	2.4	2.9
Thick Sliced, Co-Op*	1 Slice/43g	99	230	8.0	46.0	2.0	2.0
Thick Sliced, Family Favourite*	1 Slice/37g	83	225	8.5	44.5	1.4	2.3
Thick Sliced, Kingsmill*	1 Slice/42g	98	233	8.8	44.1	2.4	2.5
Thick Sliced, Long Life, Somerfield*	1 Slice/44g	100	227	7.5	44.9	1.9	2.4
Thick Sliced, M & S*	1 Slice/42g	96	228	7.3	46.7	1.3	2.8
Thick Sliced, Organic, Tesco*	1 Slice/44g	110	249	7.4	51.3	1.6	2.1
Thick Sliced, Sainsbury's*	1 Slice/44g	100	228	7.1	46.4	1.5	2.8
Thick Sliced, SmartPrice Asda*	1 Slice/47g	106	226	7.0	46.0	1.5	2.8
Thick Sliced, Somerfield*	1 Slice/44g	101	229	8.0	45.6	1.6	3.0
Thick Sliced, Tesco*	1 Slice/44g	100	228	7.1	46.4	1.5	2.8
Thick Sliced, Value, Tesco*	1 Slice/44g	109	248	8.4	49.3	1.9	1.5
Thick Sliced, Warbuton's*	1 Slice/28g	65	233	9.8	43.6	2.1	2.7
Thick Sliced, Woolworths*	1 Slice/38g	93	246	7.9	47.6	2.4	3.0
Thin Sliced, Sainsbury's*	1 Slice/29g	66	228	7.1	46.4	1.5	2.8
Toasted	1 Med Slice/33g	87	265	9.3	57.1	1.6	1.8
Toastie Thick Sliced, Warburton's*	1 Slice/44g	103	235	10.1	44.6	1.8	2.7
Weight Watchers*	1 Slice/19g	43	226	10.3	42.6	1.6	3.6
Whole, Kingsmill*	1 Slice/38g	87	230	9.0	42.9	2.5	3.4
BREAD, WHOLEMEAL,							
Average Wholemeal	1 Slice/25g	54	215	9.2	41.6	2.5	5.8
100%, Brennans*	1 Slice/33g	63	190	8.6	36.2	1.9	8.0
Bake Off, Somerfield*	1oz/28g	62	222	11.0	40.0	2.0	0.0
BGTY, Sainsburys*	1 Slice/20g	41	207	12.6	36.8	1.0	7.3
Brown, Nimble*	1 Slice/20g	43	216	11.2	36.9	2.7	6.9
COU, M & S*	1 Slice/21g	45	213	13.6	33.7	2.6	7.0
Country Grain, Hovis*	1 Slice/44g	98	222	11.2	37.4	3.1	5.7
Danish, Better For You, Morrisons*	1 Slice/17g	39	228	11.2	47.9	1.8	6.2
Danish, Warburton's*	1 Slice/25g	57	229	13.3	38.5	2.4	7.2
Economy, Sainsbury's*	1 Slice/28g	61	217	10.3	38.4	2.5	6.5

BREAD, WHOLEMEAL,	Measure WEIGHT/INFO	per Measure KCAL	KCAL	PROT	CARB	FAT	FIBRE
Wholemeal Family Loaf, Safeway*	1 Slice/45g	96	213	9.5	37.4	2.8	6.0
Farmhouse Gold, Morrisons*	1 Slice/38g	78	204	9.2	38.3	1.6	6.0
Farmhouse, Hovis*	1 Slice/44g	91	206	10.2	36.6	2.1	5.3
Farmhouse, Organic, M & S*	1oz/28g	63	224	11.2	42.7	4.2	7.4
Golden, Bakers Choice, M & S*	1 Slice/25g	51	204	10.9	34.3	2.6	7.4
Golden Wheat, Kingsmill*	1 Slice/44g	97	221	10.9	37.8	2.9	6.0
Greggs*	1 Slice/36g	77	215	9.2	41.6	2.5	5.8
Hovis*	1 Slice/35g	75	215	10.1	37.3	2.8	5.9
Keep Fresh, Medium Sliced, Safeway*	1 Slice/37g	75	204	9.1	36.6	2.4	6.2
Kingsmill*	1 Slice/45g	99	221	10.9	37.8	2.9	6.0
Longer Life, Sainsbury's*	1 Med Slice/36g	85	237	10.7	41.0	3.4	6.2
Longerlife, Thick Slice, Sainsbury's*	1 Slice/45g	101	224	10.6	37.4	3.6	5.9
M & S*	1 Slice/38g	80	210	9.6	33.5	4.2	7.2
Medium Cut, Allinson*	1 Slice/36g	78	216	9.5	39.2	2.4	6.5
Medium Cut, Small Sliced, Allinson*	1 Slice/23g	50	219	10.3	38.3	2.7	6.1
Medium Slice, Xtra Life, Waitrose*	1 Slice/36g	85	237	10.7	41.0	3.4	6.2
Medium Sliced, Asda*	1 Slice/37g	80	215	10.0	38.0	2.5	6.0
Medium Sliced, Co-Op*	1 Slice/36g	77	215	11.0	38.0	2.0	6.0
Medium Sliced, Hovis*	1 Slice/36g	79	220	10.5	38.0	2.9	6.3
Medium Sliced, Kingsmill*,	1 Slice/38g	87	228	10.1	39.2	3.4	5.2
Medium Sliced, M & S*	1 Slice/37g	80	215	10.2	32.5	4.5	7.1
Medium Sliced, Morrisons*	1 Slice/32g	68	214	9.9	38.0	2.5	5.8
Medium Sliced, Premium, Waitrose*	1 Med Slice/35g	83	237	10.7	41.0	3.4	6.2
Medium Sliced, Sainsbury's*	1 Slice/36g	80	221	10.8	38.1	2.8	5.9
Medium Sliced, Stay Fresh, Somerfield*	1 Slice/36g	72	200	9.2	36.6	1.8	0.5
Medium Sliced, Stayfresh, Tesco*	1 Slice/36g	84	232	10.5	42.2	2.3	6.3
Medium Sliced, Tesco*	1 Slice/36g	81	226	9.2	41.6	2.5	5.8
Medium Sliced, Warburton's*	1 Slice/36g	84	234	10.3	40.1	3.6	7.2
Multi Grain, Country, Hovis*	1oz/28g	62	222	11.2	37.4	3.1	5.7
Multigrain, Premium Gold, TTD, Sainsbury's*	1 Slice/44g	106	242	10.2	35.9	6.4	5.3
Nimble*	1 Slice/20g	43	216	11.2	36.9	0.8	6.9
Organic, Bake Off, Somerfield*-	1oz/28g	60	216	7.0	44.0	2.0	0.0
Organic, Thick Sliced, Sainsbury's*	1 Slice/44g	92	210	10.0	40.1	1.0	6.7
Premium Gold, TTD, Sainsbury's*	1 Slice/44g	98	223	11.1	37.9	3.0	5.7
Sandwich, Warburton's*	1 Slice/31g	72	232	10.7	40.2	3.1	7.2
Savers, Safeway*	1 Slice/36g	76	211	8.8	38.2	2.5	0.0
Sliced, Organic, Warburton's*	1 Slice/27g	57	212	11.2	34.6	3.2	7.2
Small, Allinson*	1 Slice/23g	49	213	10.1	37.3	2.6	7.5
Small, Kingsmill*	1 Slice/25g	56	224	10.7	38.0	3.2	5.8
Soft Crusty, M & S*	1 Slice/25g	58	230	11.4	39.1	3.1	6.5
Soft, Medium Sliced, Morrisons*	1 Slice/32g	68	214	9.9	38.0	2.5	5.8
Square, Tasty, Kingsmill*	1 Slice/42g	96	228	10.1	39.2	3.4	5.2
Stoneground, Organic, Sainsbury's*	1 Slice/29g	63	217	7.9	39.9	2.9	5.8
Stoneground, Organic, Waitrose*	1 Slice/40g	95	237	10.7	41.0	3.4	6.2
Tasty Crust, Kingsmill*	1 Slice/50g	126	251	11.2	42.2	4.2	5.9
Tesco*	1 Slice/36g	71	198	7.6	37.6	1.9	5.1
Thick Cut, Allinson*	1 Slice/44g	94	213	10.1	37.3	2.6	7.5
Thick Slice, Asda*	1 Slice/45g	97	215	10.0	38.0	2.5	6.0
Thick Sliced, Allied Bakeries*	1 Slice/44g	95	217	10.3	38.4	2.5	6.5
Thick Sliced, Healthy Living, Co-Op*	1 Slice/44g	95	215	11.0	38.0	2.0	7.0
Thick Sliced, Hovis*	1 Slice/44g	97	220	10.5	38.0	2.9	6.3
Thick Sliced Loaf, Tesco*	1 Slice/45g	90	201	8.8	36.4	2.3	5.3
Thick Sliced, Organic, Tesco*	1 Slice/44g	101	229	9.0	42.2	2.7	5.8
Thick Sliced, Sainsbury's*	1 Slice/45g	101	224	8.6	42.3	2.2	5.8

Nutrition Values per 100g / 100ml (KCAL, PROT, CARB, FAT, FIBRE)

BREAD, WHOLEMEAL,	Measure WEIGHT/INFO	per Measure KCAL	Nutrition Values per 100g / 100ml KCAL	PROT	CARB	FAT	FIBRE
Thick Sliced, Stayfresh, Tesco, *	1 Slice/34g	69	204	10.2	34.5	2.9	6.0
Thick Sliced, Waitrose*	1 Slice/44g	111	252	10.9	36.0	7.2	5.8
Toastie, Warburton's*	1 Slice/44g	101	230	10.3	40.2	2.9	7.2
Value, Tesco*	1 Slice/36g	78	217	10.3	38.4	2.5	6.5
With Kibbled Malted Wheat, Kingsmill*	1 Slice/42g	96	228	10.1	39.2	3.4	5.2
BREAD MIX,							
Brown, Gluten-Free, Tritamyl*	1oz/28g	90	323	6.1	78.0	1.2	7.9
Crusty White, Made Up, Tesco*	1 Slice/126g	316	251	9.4	49.3	1.8	2.5
Naan, Sharwood's*	1oz/28g	106	379	11.1	67.4	6.7	3.8
Wholemeal, Crusty, Tesco*	1 Bag/500g	1120	224	9.7	40.7	2.4	7.6
BREADCRUMBS,							
Golden, Sainsbury's*	1oz/28g	93	333	10.5	69.0	1.7	4.6
Homemade	1oz/28g	99	354	11.6	77.5	1.9	2.2
Manufactured	1oz/28g	99	354	10.1	78.5	2.1	0.0
BREADFRUIT,							
Boiled In Unsalted Water	1oz/28g	33	119	1.6	29.0	0.4	0.0
Canned, Drained	1oz/28g	18	66	0.6	16.4	0.2	1.7
Raw	1oz/28g	27	95	1.3	23.1	0.3	0.0
BREADSTICKS,							
Classic, Somerfield*	1 Breadstick/6g	24	396	10.0	82.5	2.9	1.0
Farleys*	1 Serving/12g	50	414	14.0	76.5	5.8	1.1
Grissini Italian, Sainsbury's*	1 Breadstick/5g	20	408	11.6	72.9	7.8	2.9
Italian Cheese, Tesco*	4 Breadsticks/21g	84	399	14.2	67.5	8.0	3.4
Italian Original, Tesco*	1 Pack/125g	510	408	11.6	72.9	7.8	2.9
Original Italian, Mini, Tesco*	1oz/28g	114	408	11.6	72.9	7.8	2.9
Original, Organic, Kallo*	1 Breadstick/6g	24	393	11.8	69.5	7.6	4.7
Pesto Flavour, Safeway*	1 Stick/6g	24	394	13.4	67.5	7.8	5.2
Plain, Asda*	1 Stick/5g	21	412	12.0	73.0	8.0	0.0
Sesame Seed Grissini, Sainsbury's*	1 Breadstick/5g	21	419	12.7	65.5	11.8	3.2
BREAKFAST,							
All Day, Meat Free, HP*	1 Can/415g	452	109	6.4	11.8	4.0	2.1
All Day, With Heinz Baked Beans, Heinz*	1 Pack/403g	463	115	5.8	13.3	4.3	2.4
Big Breakfast, McDonald's*	1 Breakfast/256g	591	231	10.2	15.6	14.2	1.6
Farmhouse, Ready Meals, Waitrose*	½ Pack/250g	385	154	2.9	11.0	10.0	1.2
Fruits, Del Monte*	1 Serving/225g	97	43	0.6	9.6	0.1	0.0
Juice, Del Monte*	1 Glass/200ml	86	43	0.6	9.6	0.0	0.0
Juice, Tesco*	1 Glass/200ml	88	44	0.5	9.7	0.0	0.0
BREAKFAST CEREAL,							
Advantage, Weetabix*	1 Serving/30g	105	350	10.2	72.0	2.4	9.0
All Bran, Apricot Bites, Kellogg's*	1 Serving/45g	126	280	10.0	56.0	3.0	17.0
All Bran, Bite Size, Kellogg's*	1 Serving/50g	145	290	15.0	47.0	4.5	27.0
All Bran Flakes, Kellogg's*	1 Serving/40g	128	320	10.0	66.0	2.5	15.0
All Bran, Kellogg's	1 Serving/40g	108	270	13.0	45.0	4.0	29.0
Alpen, Chocolate Crunch, Weetabix*	1 Serving/40g	155	387	10.6	67.7	8.2	6.7
Alpen, No Added Sugar, Weetabix*	1 Serving/40g	143	357	12.1	61.3	7.1	9.0
Alpen, Nutty Crunch, Weetabix*	1 Serving/40g	154	385	11.0	65.0	9.0	7.5
Alpen, Original, Weetabix*	1 Serving/40g	146	365	10.0	66.0	6.8	7.7
Apricot Wheats, Whole Grain, Sainsbury's*	1 Serving/50g	165	330	7.8	71.4	1.5	8.0
Bananabix, Weetabix*	1 Serving/40g	148	370	8.8	73.0	5.0	8.1
Blackberry & Apple, Alpen*	1 Serving/35g	124	353	9.1	68.9	4.5	8.5
Blueberries & Cranberries, Crisp, Finest, Tesco*	1 Serving/50g	216	431	7.1	64.4	16.1	6.9
Bran Flakes, Asda*	1 Serving/47g	157	333	11.0	65.0	3.2	14.0
Bran Flakes, Co-Op*	1 Serving/30g	99	330	11.0	65.0	3.0	15.0
Bran Flakes, Healthwise, Kellogg's*	1 Serving/40g	128	320	10.0	66.0	2.5	15.0

BREAKFAST CEREAL,	Measure WEIGHT/INFO	per Measure KCAL	Nutrition Values per 100g / 100ml KCAL	PROT	CARB	FAT	FIBRE
Bran Flakes, Honey Nut, Morrisons*	1 Serving/40g	57	143	3.8	28.0	1.8	4.4
Bran Flakes, Honey Nut, Tesco*	1 Serving/40g	143	358	9.6	70.0	4.4	11.0
Bran Flakes, Kellogg's*	1 Serving/30g	99	330	10.0	66.0	2.5	15.0
Bran Flakes, Oat, Kellogg's*	1 Serving/40g	140	350	10.0	66.0	5.0	10.0
Bran Flakes, Oat With Apple & Raisin, Kellogg's*	1 Serving/40g	140	350	10.0	66.0	5.0	10.0
Bran Flakes, Organic, Tesco*	1 Serving/30g	99	330	10.2	67.0	2.4	14.1
Bran Flakes, Tesco*	1 Serving/30g	99	331	10.2	67.1	2.4	14.1
Bran Flakes, Value, Tesco*	1 Bowl/50g	160	320	11.4	63.2	2.4	17.1
Bran Flakes, Waitrose*	1 Serving/30g	100	333	10.1	67.7	2.4	12.7
Bran Flakes, Whole Grain, Sainsbury's*	1 Serving/30g	99	331	10.2	67.1	2.4	14.1
Cheerios, Honey Nut, Nestle*	1 Serving/40g	150	374	7.0	78.9	3.4	5.2
Cheerios, Nestle*	1 Serving/40g	148	369	7.9	75.9	3.8	6.2
Choco Corn Flakes, Kellogg's*	1 Serving/30g	114	380	6.0	83.0	2.5	3.0
Choco Snaps, Tesco*	1 Serving/30g	114	379	5.5	83.9	2.4	2.3
Cinnamon Grahams, Nestle*	1 Serving/40g	166	416	4.6	75.1	10.9	4.2
Clusters, Nestle*	1oz/28g	107	382	10.0	70.2	6.8	8.5
Coco Pops, Kellogg's*	1 Serving/30g	114	380	5.0	85.0	2.5	2.5
Corn Flakes, Chocolate, Co-Op*	1 Serving/40g	146	365	7.0	81.0	2.0	3.0
Corn Flakes, Co-Op*	1 Serving/30g	113	375	8.0	84.0	1.0	1.0
Corn Flakes, Crunchy Nut, Kellogg's*	1 Serving/30g	117	390	7.0	82.0	3.5	3.0
Corn Flakes, Honey Nut, Co-Op*	1 Serving/40g	154	385	7.0	81.0	4.0	1.0
Corn Flakes, Honey Nut, Sainsbury's*	1 Serving/30g	116	387	7.3	80.0	4.2	2.9
Corn Flakes, Honey Nut, Tesco*	1 Sm Bowl/30g	116	387	7.3	80.0	4.2	2.9
Corn Flakes, Kellogg's*	1 Serving/30g	111	370	8.0	82.0	0.8	3.0
Corn Flakes, Milk Chocolate, M & S*	1 Serving/40g	194	485	6.7	60.3	24.1	0.2
Corn Flakes, Organic, Evernat*	1 Serving/30g	111	369	8.0	82.0	1.0	0.0
Corn Flakes, Sainsbury's*	1 Serving/25g	92	367	7.3	82.7	0.8	3.6
Corn Flakes, Tesco*	1 Serving/25g	92	367	7.3	82.7	0.8	3.6
Corn Flakes, Waitrose*	1 Serving/30g	112	374	7.3	84.3	0.8	1.5
Corn Pops, Chocolate, Kellogg's*	1 Serving/30g	117	390	6.0	80.0	5.0	3.5
Corn Pops, Kellogg's*	1 Serving/40g	152	380	6.0	87.0	1.0	2.0
Country Crisp With Strawberries, Jordans*	1 Serving/40g	174	435	7.4	64.5	16.4	8.0
Country Crisp With Whole Raspberries, Jordans*	1 Serving/40g	174	435	7.4	64.5	16.4	8.0
Country Store, Kellogg's*	1 Serving/30g	105	350	9.0	67.0	5.0	8.0
Cranberry & Apple Multigrain, Sainsbury's*	1 Serving/50g	167	333	8.8	66.6	3.5	14.0
Crunchy Bran, Weetabix*	1 Serving/40g	120	299	11.8	52.3	4.7	24.8
Crunchy Nut, Red, Kellogg's*	1 Serving/40g	164	410	7.0	73.0	10.0	3.0
Fibre 1, Nestle*	1 Serving/40g	107	267	10.8	50.2	2.6	30.5
Flakes & Grains, Exotic Fruit, BGTY, Sainsbury's*	1 Serving/30g	113	377	6.8	76.4	4.9	5.9
Flakes, Apple, Blackberry & Raspberry, GFY, Asda*	1 Serving/40g	138	344	9.0	73.0	1.8	11.0
Force, Nestle*	1 Serving/40g	138	344	10.6	70.3	2.3	9.2
Frosted Flakes, Tesco*	1 Serving/30g	112	374	4.9	87.8	0.4	2.4
Frosted Wheats, Kellogg's*	1 Serving/30g	102	340	10.0	72.0	2.0	9.0
Frosties, Chocolate, Kellogg's*	1 Serving/40g	160	400	5.0	84.0	4.5	2.0
Frosties, Kellogg's*	1 Serving/30g	114	380	5.0	88.0	0.6	2.0
Fruit & Fibre, Flakes, Waitrose*	1 Serving/40g	140	350	8.2	65.7	6.0	10.1
Fruit & Fibre, Morrisons*	1 Serving/30g	110	366	8.8	66.5	7.2	8.5
Fruit & Fibre, Organic, Sainsbury's*	1 Serving/40g	147	367	10.0	72.4	4.1	7.8
Fruit & Fibre, Safeway*	1 Serving/40g	143	358	9.0	66.4	6.4	9.0
Fruit & Fibre, Sainsbury's*	1 Serving/30g	108	361	8.1	68.5	6.1	8.9
Fruit & Fibre, Tesco*	1 Serving/30g	113	375	8.5	66.3	8.4	7.8
Fruit & Fibre, Value, Tescp*	1 Serving/40g	144	359	11.4	65.7	5.6	8.0
Fruit & Fibre, Weetabix*	1 Serving/30g	107	358	8.8	66.4	6.4	9.0
Fruit 'n' Fibre, Kellogg's*	1 Serving/50g	175	350	9.0	69.0	4.5	9.0

B

B

BREAKFAST CEREAL,	Measure WEIGHT/INFO	per Measure KCAL	Nutrition Values per 100g / 100ml KCAL	PROT	CARB	FAT	FIBRE
Golden Grahams, Nestle*	1 Serving/40g	152	381	5.6	81.6	3.6	3.2
Golden Nuggets, Nestle*	1 Serving/40g	152	381	6.2	87.4	0.7	1.5
Golden Wheat Pillows, Tesco*	1 Biscuit/25g	85	340	11.5	68.2	2.3	11.9
Grape Nuts, Kraft*	1 Serving/30g	104	345	10.5	72.5	1.9	8.6
Harvest Crunch, Nut, Quaker*	1 Serving/40g	184	459	8.0	62.5	19.5	6.0
Harvest Crunch, Real Red Berries, Quaker*	1 Serving/50g	224	447	7.0	66.0	17.0	4.5
High Fibre Bran, Asda*	1 Serving/50g	137	273	13.0	44.0	5.0	29.0
High Fibre Bran, Co-Op*	1 Serving/40g	108	270	13.0	44.0	5.0	29.0
High Fibre Bran, Sainsbury's*	1oz/28g	80	286	13.4	50.7	3.3	23.6
High Fibre Bran, Tesco*	1 Serving/40g	108	271	13.0	43.6	5.0	29.0
High Fibre Bran, Waitrose*	1oz/28g	79	281	14.4	47.2	3.8	26.0
Honey Loops, Kellogg's*	1 Serving/30g	111	370	8.0	77.0	3.0	7.0
Honey Raisin & Almond, Crunchy, Waitrose*	1 Serving/60g	255	425	10.5	68.8	12.0	5.7
Hot Oat, Instant, Tesco*	1 Serving/30g	107	356	11.5	58.8	8.3	8.9
Hot Oats, Safeway*	1 Serving/20g	71	356	11.6	58.8	8.3	8.9
Hunny B's, Kellogg's*	1 Serving/28g	106	380	6.0	83.0	2.5	3.0
Just Right, Kellogg's*	1 Serving/40g	144	360	7.0	78.0	2.5	4.5
Malt Bites, Safeway*	1 Serving/40g	137	343	10.0	69.2	2.9	10.0
Maple & Pecan, Crisp, Asda*	1 Serving/30g	135	451	8.0	62.0	19.0	6.0
Maple & Pecan, Luxury Crunchy, Jordans*	1 Serving/50g	224	448	9.9	59.9	18.7	6.5
Mini Flakes, Wholewheat, Sainsbury's*	1 Serving/30g	104	348	11.0	71.3	2.1	9.6
Minibix, Banana, Weetabix*	1 Serving/40g	148	370	8.8	73.0	5.0	8.1
Minibix, Chocolate, Weetabix*	1 Serving/39g	149	383	8.4	73.3	6.2	6.7
Minibix, Fruit & Nut, Weetabix*	1 Serving/40g	141	353	8.8	71.2	3.8	8.1
Minibix, Honey, Weetabix*	1 Serving/40g	144	359	8.8	76.1	2.2	0.0
Minibix, Weetabix*	1 Serving/40g	134	335	8.8	71.2	3.8	8.1
Montsters Inc, Nestle*	1 Bowl/40g	149	373	5.1	82.0	2.7	4.2
Muesli, 2% Fat, BGTY, Sainsbury's*	1 Serving/30g	97	324	6.7	70.8	1.6	6.2
Muesli, COU, M & S*	1 Serving/60g	201	335	7.6	70.2	2.5	8.1
Muesli, Cranberry, Luxury, Sainsbury's*	1 Serving/50g	121	241	7.3	62.1	11.9	6.5
Muesli, Crunchy Bran, Nature's Harvest*	1 Serving/50g	176	352	8.8	62.9	9.9	6.4
Muesli, Eat Smart, Safeway*	1 Serving/40g	134	335	8.7	68.6	2.8	7.4
Muesli, Fruit & Bran, Unsweetened, M & S*	1oz/28g	90	320	8.1	68.0	2.7	9.4
Muesli, Fruit & Nut, Iceland*	1 Serving/30g	105	350	9.3	61.0	7.5	8.1
Muesli, Fruit & Nut, Luxury, Co-Op*	1oz/28g	105	375	8.0	64.0	10.0	6.0
Muesli, Fruit & Nut, Luxury, Waitrose*	1oz/28g	102	363	9.0	60.3	9.5	6.5
Muesli, Fruit & Nut, Tesco*	1 Serving/65g	237	365	7.4	57.9	11.5	8.0
Muesli, Fruit, 55%, Asda*	1 Serving/35g	111	318	6.0	67.0	2.9	7.0
Muesli, Fruit, Co-Op*	1oz/28g	98	350	7.0	70.0	5.0	6.0
Muesli, Fruit, GFY, Asda*	1 Serving/50g	152	304	8.0	64.0	1.8	10.0
Muesli, Fruit, HE, Tesco*	1 Serving/40g	129	322	7.0	66.6	4.2	6.9
Muesli, Fruity, Toasted, Hubbard's*	1 Serving/30g	129	429	8.6	69.0	13.0	8.2
Muesli, Luxury Fruit, Safeway*	1 Serving/40g	139	347	7.1	74.3	1.0	2.2
Muesli, Luxury Fruit, Sainsbury's*	1 Serving/50g	162	324	7.1	66.4	3.3	7.0
Muesli, Luxury Fruit, Waitrose*	1 Serving/30g	101	337	7.7	66.3	4.5	6.9
Muesli, Luxury, Jordans*	1 Serving/80g	307	384	9.6	58.4	12.5	8.2
Muesli, Luxury, Sainsbury's*	1oz/28g	101	359	8.5	57.1	10.7	7.7
Muesli, Natural, Jordans*	1 Serving/80g	282	352	10.4	62.4	6.7	8.9
Muesli, No Added Sugar or Salt, Organic, Jordans*	1 Serving/50g	191	381	9.9	62.3	10.2	9.3
Muesli, No Added Sugar, Waitrose*	1oz/28g	102	364	12.0	64.9	6.3	6.7
Muesli, Organic, Jordans*	1oz/28g	105	374	10.9	54.2	12.6	10.5
Muesli, Organic, Waitrose*	1 Serving/50g	179	358	10.8	59.1	8.7	7.8
Muesli, Organic, Whole Earth*	1 Serving/25g	87	347	10.5	61.0	6.4	8.0
Muesli, Original, Holland & Barrett*	1 Serving/30g	105	351	11.1	61.2	8.4	7.1

BREAKFAST CEREAL,	Measure WEIGHT/INFO	per Measure KCAL	KCAL	PROT	CARB	FAT	FIBRE
			Nutrition Values per 100g / 100ml				
Muesli, Original, Sainsbury's*	1 Serving/60g	226	376	9.3	65.7	8.4	7.1
Muesli, Special, Jordans*	1 Serving/40g	143	358	8.4	60.8	9.0	8.1
Muesli, Swiss Style, Co-Op*	1oz/28g	104	370	11.0	67.0	6.0	6.0
Muesli, Swiss Style, No Added Salt Or Sugar, Sainsbury's*	1oz/28g	100	358	10.7	64.3	6.4	7.0
Muesli, Swiss Style, SmartPrice, Asda*	1 Serving/60g	222	370	9.0	70.0	6.0	10.0
Muesli, Swiss Style, Tesco*	1oz/28g	99	353	10.9	65.1	5.4	8.2
Muesli, Swiss Style, Waitrose*	1oz/28g	102	364	10.2	66.1	6.5	7.6
Muesli, Tropical Fruit, Holland & Barrett*	1 Bowl/60g	197	328	7.5	69.8	3.2	5.1
Muesli, Tropical, Tesco*	1 Serving/50g	173	346	7.8	68.2	4.7	9.1
Muesli, Unsweetened, M & S*	1oz/28g	90	322	8.1	68.0	2.7	9.4
Muesli, Value, Tesco*	1 Serving/50g	171	342	7.5	67.6	4.6	8.6
Muesli, Wholewheat, Co-Op*	1oz/28g	98	350	11.0	61.0	7.0	7.0
Muesli, Wholewheat, No Added Sugar & Salt, Tesco*	1oz/28g	106	379	9.6	60.2	11.1	8.1
Muesli, Wholewheat, Sainsbury's*	1oz/28g	95	339	8.5	60.6	6.9	7.6
Multi Flake & Fruit, Perfectly Balanced, Waitrose*	1 Serving/40g	134	335	8.2	68.8	3.0	14.0
Multi Fruit & Flake, COU, M & S	1 Serving/39g	142	365	6.5	81.8	1.1	4.0
Multi Grain, BGTY, Sainsbury's*	1oz/28g	44	157	7.2	24.9	3.1	4.8
Multi Grain, Start, Kellogg's*	1oz/28g	101	360	8.0	79.0	2.0	6.0
Oat Bran, Crispies, Quaker*	1 Serving/40g	153	383	11.0	69.0	6.5	9.0
Oat, Crunchy, Co-Op*	1 Serving/40g	166	415	10.0	65.0	13.0	6.0
Oat, Crunchy, Sainsbury's*	1 Serving/50g	227	453	8.2	59.3	20.3	6.6
Oat, Crunchy, SmartPrice Asda*	1 Serving/40g	171	428	8.0	63.0	16.0	6.0
Oat Krunchies, Quaker*	1 Serving/30g	118	393	9.5	72.0	7.0	5.5
Oat With Tropical Fruits, Crunchy, Tesco*	1 Serving/35g	157	448	8.7	66.0	16.6	3.2
Oatmeal, Instant, Quaker*	1 Serving/35g	126	360	13.6	57.0	8.7	9.7
Oats, Honey, Raisins & Apricot, Geobar*	1 Bar/35g	132	376	5.3	69.0	8.8	3.5
Oats So Simple, Quaker*	1 Serving/27g	100	372	11.0	62.0	8.5	7.0
Oatso Simple, Apple & Cinnamon, Quaker*	1 Satchet/38g	136	358	8.0	68.0	5.5	2.5
Oatso Simple, Baked Apple Flavour, Quaker*	1 Serving/38g	141	370	8.0	70.0	6.0	5.5
Oatso Simple, Berry Burst, Quaker*	1 Serving/38g	141	370	8.0	70.0	6.0	6.5
Oatso Simple, Golden Syrup Flavour, Quaker*	1 Serving/39g	142	364	7.5	70.0	5.5	5.0
Perfect Balance, Weight Watchers*	1 Serving/30g	90	300	7.8	63.3	1.7	15.6
Porage Oats, Scot's, Quaker*	1 Serving/30g	110	368	11.0	62.0	8.0	7.0
Porridge Oats & Bran, Co-Op*	1oz/28g	99	353	12.5	60.0	7.0	12.0
Porridge Oats & Bran, Somerfield*	1oz/28g	108	385	12.0	68.0	7.0	0.0
Porridge Oats, Co-Op*	1oz/28g	102	365	2.0	62.0	8.0	7.0
Porridge Oats, Jordans*	1oz/28g	102	363	12.5	61.5	7.4	8.0
Porridge Oats, Organic, Evernat*	1oz/28g	117	418	13.0	69.0	9.6	7.4
Porridge Oats, Scott, Co-Op*	1oz/28g	102	364	11.8	62.0	7.6	7.2
Porridge Oats, Scottish, Asda*	1oz/28g	107	383	10.0	75.0	4.8	7.0
Porridge Oats, Scottish, Tesco*	1 Serving/50g	182	364	11.8	62.0	7.6	7.2
Porridge Oats, Somerfield*	1oz/28g	108	385	12.0	68.0	7.0	0.0
Porridge Oats, Value, Tesco*	1 Serving/50g	192	384	11.8	68.0	7.2	7.2
Porridge Oats, Whole Rolled, Scottish, Sainsbury's*	1 Serving/50g	191	381	9.7	74.7	4.8	7.0
Porridge, Quick, M & S*	1oz/28g	111	398	15.5	55.1	12.8	5.9
Puffed Wheat, Quaker*	1 Serving/15g	49	328	15.3	62.4	1.3	5.6
Puffed Wheat, Somerfield*	1oz/28g	104	373	14.0	72.0	3.0	0.0
Puffs, Golden Honey, Tesco*	1 Serving/25g	95	378	6.0	84.1	1.9	3.0
Quaker Oats Crunch, Quaker*	1 Serving/40g	178	445	8.0	66.5	16.0	5.0
Quaker Oats, Quaker*	1 Serving/30g	110	368	11.0	62.0	8.0	7.0
Raisin & Almond, Crunchy, Jordans*	1 Serving/56g	230	411	8.4	66.0	12.5	5.0
Raisin & Coconut, Organic, Jordans*	1oz/28g	123	438	10.1	57.2	18.7	7.8
Raisin Wheats, Kellogg's*	1 Serving/30g	96	320	9.0	69.0	2.0	9.0
Raisin Wheats, Sainsbury's*	1 Serving/50g	166	332	8.2	71.5	1.5	8.0

B

BREAKFAST CEREAL,	Measure WEIGHT/INFO	per Measure KCAL	Nutrition Values per 100g / 100ml KCAL	PROT	CARB	FAT	FIBRE
Ready Brek, Banana, Weetabix*	1 Serving/40g	146	365	8.9	68.0	6.4	6.7
Ready Brek, Chocolate, Weetabix*	1 Serving/40g	144	360	9.6	63.7	7.4	8.1
Ready Brek, Strawberry, Weetabix*	1 Serving/40g	146	365	8.7	68.6	6.2	6.8
Ready Brek, Weetabix*	1 Serving/40g	142	356	11.6	58.8	8.3	8.9
Red Berry & Almond Luxury Crunch, Jordans*	1 Serving/75g	331	441	8.2	60.5	18.5	6.6
Rice Krispies, Honey, Kellogg's*	1 Serving/30g	114	380	4.0	89.0	0.7	1.0
Rice Krispies, Kellogg's*	1 Serving/30g	111	370	6.0	85.0	1.0	1.5
Rice Pops, BPC, Sainsbury's*	1 Serving/30g	111	370	7.2	82.3	1.3	2.2
Rice Snaps, Asda*	1 Serving/28g	105	376	7.0	84.0	1.3	1.5
Rice Snaps, HE, Tesco*	1 Pack/25g	93	370	7.2	82.3	1.3	2.2
Rice Snaps, Tesco*	1 Serving/30g	113	378	7.3	84.2	1.3	1.5
Ricicles, Kellogg's*	1 Serving/30g	114	380	4.0	89.0	0.7	1.0
Right Balance, Morrisons*	1 Serving/50g	181	362	6.9	78.6	2.2	5.3
Shredded Wheat, Bitesize, Nestle*	1 Serving/50g	168	335	11.5	67.7	2.2	11.6
Shredded Wheat, Fruitful, Nestle*	1 Serving/50g	177	353	8.4	66.9	5.8	10.3
Shredded Wheat, Honey Nut, Nestle*	1 Serving/40g	151	378	10.9	68.8	6.6	10.4
Shredded Wheat, Nestle*	1 Piece/22g	72	325	11.2	65.2	2.1	12.4
Shreddies, Coco, Nestle*	1 Serving/50g	177	353	8.0	76.1	1.9	9.2
Shreddies, Frosted, Kellogg's*	1 Serving/50g	162	323	0.7	78.5	1.8	4.7
Shreddies, Frosted, Nestle*	1 Serving/50g	178	356	7.3	78.5	1.4	8.3
Shreddies, Frosted, Variety Pack, Nestle*	1 Pack/45g	163	363	6.7	81.1	1.3	6.8
Shreddies, Malt Wheats, Tesco*	1 Serving/45g	151	335	8.3	70.7	2.1	9.7
Shreddies, Nestle*	1 Serving/50g	172	343	9.8	71.7	1.9	11.2
Special K, Kellogg's*	1 Serving/30g	111	370	15.0	75.0	1.0	2.5
Special K, Red Berries, Kellogg's*	1 Serving/30g	111	370	14.0	74.0	1.0	3.0
Strawberry & Almond Crunch, M & S*	1 Serving/40g	186	465	8.0	66.0	18.6	4.9
Strawberry & Maltiflakes, COU, M & S*	1 Serving/40g	146	365	12.7	73.8	2.3	3.5
Sugar Puffs, Quaker*	1 Serving/30g	116	387	6.5	86.5	1.0	3.0
Sultana Bran, Asda*	1 Serving/30g	98	327	9.0	66.0	3.0	11.0
Sultana Bran, Co-Op*	1 Serving/40g	130	325	9.0	66.0	3.0	11.0
Sultana Bran, Healthwise, Kellogg's*	1 Serving/40g	128	320	9.0	66.0	2.0	13.0
Sultana Bran, HE,Tesco*	1 Serving/48g	156	326	8.1	69.0	1.9	9.8
Sultana Bran, Sainsbury's*	1 Serving/30g	97	324	8.2	68.6	1.9	11.6
Tropical, Crunchy, Jordans*	1 Serving/40g	170	425	8.5	65.8	14.2	6.2
Weetabix Crunch, Weetabix*	1 Serving/40g	144	359	8.8	76.1	2.2	7.4
Weetabix*	2 Biscuits/42g	143	340	11.2	67.6	2.7	10.5
Weetos, Weetabix*	1 Serving/30g	115	384	6.2	78.4	5.0	5.6
Wheat Biscuits, HE, Tesco*	2 Biscuits/55g	191	348	11.0	70.0	2.7	8.0
Wheat Biscuits, Morrisons*	1 Biscuit/37g	126	340	11.2	67.6	2.7	10.5
Wheat Biscuits, Nature's Own, Organic, Weetabix*	1 Biscuit/17g	58	339	10.3	69.2	2.4	10.4
Wheat Biscuits, Value, Tesco*	2 Biscuits/30g	103	342	13.7	69.5	1.0	7.5
Wheat Bisks, Asda*	1 Serving/29g	99	340	11.0	68.0	2.7	10.0
Wheat, Corn, Oat & Rice Hoops, Organic, Enjoy, Bird's Eye*	1 Bowl/30g	112	372	8.0	79.0	2.7	5.1
Wholewheat Biscuits, Sainsbury's*	1 Biscuit/36g	122	340	11.2	67.6	2.7	10.5
Yoghurt & Strawberry, Crisp, Somerfield*	1oz/28g	121	432	7.0	67.0	15.0	0.0
BREAM, Sea, Raw	1oz/28g	27	96	17.5	0.0	2.9	0.0
BRESAOLA,							
della Valtellina, Sainsbury's*	1 Slice/14g	23	163	34.7	0.1	2.6	0.1
M & S*	1oz/28g	56	200	34.6	0.0	6.8	0.0
BROCCOLI,							
Baby Courgette & Baby Leeks, Safeway*	1oz/28g	7	24	2.4	2.1	0.8	2.0
Carrot & Mange Tout, M & S*	1oz/28g	10	35	2.9	5.6	0.2	2.1
Cauliflower & Baby Carrots, Safeway*	1 Serving/150g	38	25	2.0	3.0	0.6	2.3
Cauliflower & Carrots, Frozen, Great Value, Asda*	1 Serving/100g	25	25	2.2	2.6	0.6	5.0

	Measure	per Measure	Nutrition Values per 100g / 100ml				
BROCCOLI,	WEIGHT/INFO	KCAL	KCAL	PROT	CARB	FAT	FIBRE
Courgette & Peppers, COU, M & S*	1 Pack/283g	156	55	1.7	2.7	4.1	1.7
Green, Boiled In Salted Water	1 Serving/90g	22	24	3.1	1.1	0.8	2.3
Green, Boiled In Unsalted Water	1 Serving/90g	22	24	3.1	1.1	0.8	2.3
Green, Raw, Fresh	1oz/28g	9	33	4.4	1.8	0.9	2.6
Purple Sprouting, Boiled In Salted Water	1 Serving/90g	17	19	2.1	1.3	0.6	2.3
Purple Sprouting, Boiled In Unsalted Water	1 Serving/90g	17	19	2.1	1.3	0.6	2.3
Purple Sprouting, Raw	1oz/28g	10	35	3.9	2.6	1.1	3.5
With Carrot & Mange Tout, Tender Stem, M & S*	1 Bag/200g	70	35	2.9	5.6	0.2	2.1
BRUSSELS SPROUTS,							
& Sweet Chestnuts, Asda*	1 Serving/100g	73	73	3.1	11.0	1.7	4.2
Boiled In Salted Water	1 Med Serving/90g	32	35	2.9	3.5	1.3	3.1
Boiled In Unsalted Water	1 Med Serving/90g	32	35	2.9	3.5	1.3	3.1
Canned, Drained	1oz/28g	8	28	2.6	2.4	1.0	2.6
Raw	1oz/28g	12	42	3.5	4.1	1.4	4.1
BUBBLE & SQUEAK,							
Aunt Bessie's*	1 Serving/100g	145	145	2.7	17.5	7.1	1.3
Fried In Vegetable Oil	1oz/28g	35	124	1.4	9.8	9.1	1.5
Safeway*	1 Serving/200g	160	80	1.8	10.7	3.3	1.4
Sainsbury's*	1 Pack/55g	84	152	2.2	16.3	8.7	0.7
Tesco*	1 Pack/325g	325	100	1.3	13.5	4.5	1.3
Waitrose*	½ Pack/225g	216	96	1.6	13.4	4.0	1.8
BUBBLE GUM, Seriously Strawberry, Hubba Bubba, Wrigleys*	1 Piece/4g	11	280	0.0	73.0	0.0	0.0
BUCKWHEAT	1oz/28g	102	364	8.1	84.9	1.5	2.1
BUGLES, BBQ Flavour, Golden Wonder*	1 Bag/40g	216	539	4.8	59.9	31.7	0.0
BULGAR WHEAT,							
Bulgur Wheat, Average	1oz/28g	99	353	9.7	76.3	1.7	0.0
Tesco*	1 Serving/50g	180	359	9.7	76.3	1.7	9.1
BUNS,							
Bath, M & S*	1 Bun/71g	217	305	8.3	49.8	8.0	1.9
Belgian, Co-Op*	1 Bun/118g	413	350	5.0	54.0	13.0	2.0
Chelsea	1 Bun/78g	285	366	7.8	56.1	13.8	1.7
Currant	1 Bun/60g	178	296	7.6	52.7	7.5	0.0
Currant, HE, Tesco*	1 Bun/62g	157	253	6.6	50.8	2.6	3.2
Currant, Sainsbury's	1 Bun/72g	197	274	7.0	50.0	5.1	2.8
Dairy Cream, Somerfield*	1 Bun/98g	304	310	6.0	46.9	10.9	0.0
Fruit, Waitrose*	1 Bun/54g	171	316	7.8	55.7	6.9	1.6
Hot Cross	1 Bun/50g	155	310	7.4	58.5	6.8	1.7
Hot Cross, BGTY, Sainsbury's*	1 Bun/60g	145	241	8.3	46.7	2.4	3.5
Hot Cross, Chocolate, Mini, Sainsbury's*	1 Bun/39g	127	325	7.7	48.1	11.3	2.5
Hot Cross, Extra Spicy, M & S*	1 Bun/76g	175	230	8.6	44.1	1.9	4.2
Hot Cross, Finest, Tesco*	1 Bun/75g	203	270	6.9	49.0	5.2	2.6
Hot Cross, Golden Wholemeal, Sainsbury's*	1 Bun/65g	180	277	9.9	45.4	6.2	4.3
Hot Cross, HE, Tesco*	1 Bun/60g	155	258	8.6	50.3	2.5	2.6
Hot Cross, Less Than 3% Fat, M & S*	1 Serving/70g	175	250	8.1	49.8	1.8	2.2
Hot Cross, Luxury, Cafe, M & S*	1 Bun/78g	199	255	8.6	46.2	4.0	2.1
Hot Cross, Luxury, M & S*	1 Bun/79g	201	255	8.6	46.2	4.0	2.1
Hot Cross, Mini, Tesco*	1 Bun/36g	99	274	7.9	48.1	5.5	2.7
Hot Cross, Reduced Fat, Waitrose*	1 Bun/67g	171	255	8.1	54.3	2.1	3.3
Hot Cross, Safeway*	1 Bun/65g	174	268	7.9	46.9	5.4	2.2
Hot Cross, Sainsbury's*	1 Bun/70g	205	293	7.6	53.2	5.5	2.1
Hot Cross, Tesco*	1 Bun/55g	144	262	7.4	46.8	5.0	2.8
Hot Cross, White, Low Fat, Safeway*	1 Bun/65g	161	248	8.7	47.4	2.6	3.0
Hot Cross, White, Mini, Waitrose*	1 Bun/32g	91	284	6.6	51.1	5.9	1.9
Hot Cross, Wholemeal, Organic, Tesco*	1 Bun/55g	140	254	7.6	44.8	4.9	4.5

B

BUNS,	Measure WEIGHT/INFO	per Measure KCAL	Nutrition Values per 100g / 100ml KCAL	PROT	CARB	FAT	FIBRE
Iced & Spiced Soft, M & S*	1 Bun/42g	118	280	7.9	55.0	2.9	1.9
Iced Finger, Tesco*	1 Finger/69g	241	349	6.4	58.3	10.0	1.7
Iced Fruit, M & S*	1 Bun/95g	285	300	8.5	57.9	4.3	1.3
Iced Lemon, Tesco*	1 Bun/48g	156	325	5.2	56.5	8.7	1.9
Iced, M & S*	1 Bun/42g	138	328	8.3	53.7	8.9	2.0
Swiss, Tesco*	1 Bun/100g	334	334	4.0	52.8	11.9	1.4
BURGERS,							
Aberdeen Angus Beef, Mega, Birds Eye*	1 Burger/101g	279	276	16.3	2.4	22.4	0.1
Bean, Quarter Pounder, Mexican Style, Tesco*	1 Burger/101g	215	213	4.3	25.0	10.6	2.8
Beef, 100% Beef, Somerfield*	1 Burger/113.5g	329	289	17.0	1.0	24.0	0.0
Beef, 100% With Seasoning, No Onion, Bird's Eye*	1 Burger/41g	134	326	16.1	0.2	29.0	0.0
Beef, Asda*	1 Burger/114g	259	227	22.2	5.7	12.8	0.6
Beef, Bird's Eye*	1 Burger/41g	134	326	16.1	0.2	29.0	0.0
Beef, Farmfoods*	1 Burger/50g	128	255	14.4	5.4	19.6	0.1
Beef, Flame Grilled, Dalepak*	1 Burger/44g	131	304	15.3	2.1	26.0	0.4
Beef, Giant Chargrilled, Farmfoods*	1 Burger/170g	352	207	17.3	5.6	12.8	1.2
Beef, GFY, Asda*	1 Burger/47g	93	197	20.0	4.4	11.0	0.9
Beef, Herbs, Finest, Tesco*	1 Burger/170g	284	167	16.9	3.6	9.4	0.3
Beef, Quarter Pound, Safeway*	1 Burger/100g	227	227	22.2	5.7	12.8	0.6
Beef, Quarter Pound, Tesco*	1 Burger/113g	292	258	17.8	0.7	20.4	1.3
Beef, Quarter Pounders, 100% Prime, Asda*	1 Burger/86g	254	299	26.0	1.6	21.0	0.0
Beef, Quarter Pounders, Bird's Eye*	1 Burger/139g	386	278	15.3	3.5	22.5	0.2
Beef, Quarter Pounders, Farmfoods*	1 Burger/113g	289	256	14.4	5.4	19.6	0.1
Beef, Quarter Pounders, Flame Grilled, Tesco*	1 Burger/88g	246	280	13.1	4.8	23.2	0.8
Beef, Sainsbury's*	1 Burger/57g	150	267	29.6	1.3	15.9	1.5
Beef With Onion, Bird's Eye*	1 Burger/41g	114	278	15.3	3.5	22.5	0.2
Beef With Onion, Sainsbury's*	1 Burger/42g	102	243	20.7	6.9	14.8	1.0
BGTY, Sainsbury's*	1 Burger/110g	177	161	20.8	7.1	5.5	1.1
Big Mac, McDonald's*	1 Big Mac/215g	492	229	12.4	20.5	10.7	2.5
Cheeseburger, Burger King*	1 Burger/141g	379	269	15.6	30.0	13.4	1.4
Cheeseburger, McDonald's*	1 Burger/122g	300	246	13.0	27.2	9.5	2.1
Chicken, Bird's Eye*	1 Burger/57g	147	258	13.6	16.8	15.2	0.4
Chicken, Crispy Crumb, Farmfoods*	1 Burger/242g	707	292	10.5	20.2	18.8	1.1
Chicken, Crunch Crumb, Tesco*	1 Burger/57g	161	282	12.3	15.6	18.9	0.0
Chicken Fillet, Kentucky Fried Chicken*	1 Burger/213g	469	220	15.0	19.0	9.2	1.6
Chicken Flamer, Burger King*	1 Sandwich/162g	308	190	12.6	18.6	7.3	1.9
Chicken, Sainsbury's*	1 Serving/46g	115	247	15.6	12.2	15.1	1.3
Chicken Sandwich, Burger King*	1 Sandwich/224g	659	294	11.2	23.6	17.4	1.3
Chicken, Spar*	1 Serving/67g	163	244	16.1	20.8	11.2	1.5
Chicken Whopper, Lite, Burger King*	1 Whopper/159g	339	213	15.3	18.4	8.7	0.0
Chicken With Sesame Seed Bun, Breaded, Tesco*	1 Burger/205g	588	287	10.2	26.2	15.7	2.9
Chilli Beef, Quarter Pounder, Farmfoods*	1 Burger/115g	285	248	13.5	2.9	20.3	0.9
Chilli, Quarter Pounder, Iceland*	1 Burger/84g	265	316	18.6	6.5	23.9	0.4
Double Whopper Sandwich, Burger King*	1 Sandwich/353g	918	260	13.5	15.0	16.1	1.1
Double Whopper With Cheese, Burger King*	1 Pack/378g	934	247	14.0	13.0	16.0	1.0
Filet-O-Fish, McDonald's*	1 Pack/161g	388	241	10.0	25.0	11.0	0.7
Fillet Towermeal, Kentucky Fried Chicken*	1 Pack/283g	656	232	13.0	19.8	11.2	1.5
Hamburger, Burger King*	1 Burger/128g	339	265	14.8	23.4	12.5	1.5
Hamburger, McDonald's*	1 Burger/108g	254	235	12.2	30.6	7.1	2.3
Hamburgers In Buns, Farmfoods*	1 Burger/100g	253	253	14.3	29.8	8.5	1.9
In Buns, Farmfoods*	1 Burger/115g	325	283	13.3	21.2	15.0	2.7
Lamb, Quarter Pounders, Bird's Eye*	1 Burger/112g	232	207	13.9	3.8	15.1	0.3
Lamb, Quarter Pounders, Farmfoods*	1oz/28g	76	272	12.3	6.6	21.8	1.0
Low Fat, Iceland*	1 Serving/85g	148	174	27.8	5.0	4.8	1.1

BURGERS,	Measure WEIGHT/INFO	per Measure KCAL	Nutrition Values per 100g / 100ml KCAL	PROT	CARB	FAT	FIBRE
McChicken Grill With BBQ Sauce, McDonald's*	1 Pack/215g	309	144	12.1	18.1	2.6	2.2
McChicken Premiere, McDonald's*	1 Burger/244g	547	224	11.0	15.9	11.5	1.3
McChicken Sandwich, McDonald's*	1 Pack/167g	376	225	9.9	23.1	10.3	2.2
Meat Free, Sainsbury's*	1 Burger/57g	92	161	19.6	3.9	7.4	4.8
Mushroom, Tesco*	1 Serving/87g	144	166	2.8	20.4	8.1	3.1
Pork, Quarter Pounders, Bird's Eye*	1 Burger/122g	292	239	13.9	3.2	19.0	0.2
Prime Beef, Asda*	1 Burger/45g	123	274	22.0	6.0	18.0	0.6
Quarter Pounder, Beef, Steak Country, Lidl*	1 Burger/68g	188	276	16.3	2.4	22.2	0.1
Quarter Pounder, Deluxe, McDonald's*	1 Burger/253g	521	206	11.4	16.1	10.6	1.7
Quarter Pounder, McDonald's*	1 Burger/178g	424	238	14.5	20.9	10.7	2.1
Quarter Pounder, TTD, Sainsbury's*	1 Burger/100g	182	182	22.6	5.5	7.7	1.5
Quarter Pounder With Cheese & Buns, Sainsbury's*	1 Burger/198g	471	238	15.6	19.1	11.5	1.4
Quarter Pounder With Cheese, McDonald's*	1 Burger/206g	515	250	15.1	18.2	13.0	1.8
Quarter Pounders, 95% Fat Free, Good Choice, Iceland*	1 Burger/86g	150	174	27.8	5.0	4.8	1.1
Quarter Pounders, Big Country*	1 Burger/90g	271	301	22.1	1.8	23.1	0.0
Quarter Pounders, Chargrilled, BGTY, Sainsbury's*	1 Burger/114g	184	161	20.8	7.1	5.5	1.1
Quarter Pounders, M & S*	1oz/28g	69	247	18.5	3.2	17.9	0.6
Quorn*	1 Burger/50g	56	112	12.4	5.3	4.6	3.6
Quorn*, Original	1 burger/50g	55	109	12.0	6.9	3.7	4.9
Quorn*, Premium	1 Burger/81g	96	118	11.4	7.1	4.9	3.5
Quorn*, Southern Style	1 Burger/63g	113	180	10.7	12.3	9.8	3.1
Savoury Tofu, Cauldron Foods*	1 Burger/75g	162	216	14.8	13.2	11.5	3.5
Spicy Bean, Burger King*	1 Burger/239g	504	211	7.9	26.2	8.3	3.9
Spicy Bean, Cauldron Foods*	1 Burger/87g	240	276	6.7	26.5	15.9	4.0
Spicy Bean, Dalepak*	1 Burger/118g	242	205	4.6	22.8	10.6	3.0
Spicy Bean, Quarter Pounders, Asda*	1 Serving/108g	257	238	4.5	28.0	12.0	3.0
Spicy Bean, Sainsbury's*	1 Burger/110g	262	240	5.0	27.1	12.4	2.0
Spicy Vegetable, Asda*	1 Burger/56g	108	193	3.4	20.0	11.0	0.0
Spicy Vegetable Bean, BGTY, Sainsbury's*	1 Burger/76g	119	156	5.6	24.3	3.2	3.3
Steak Premiere, McDonald's*	1 Burger/229g	453	198	14.9	19.4	6.2	1.6
Tuna, Morrisons*	1 Burger/117g	209	179	16.9	5.3	10.0	1.9
Tuna, Quarter Pounders, Sainsbury's*	1 Serving/100g	179	179	24.0	10.0	4.8	0.4
Turkey Cheese, Somerfield*	1oz/28g	79	281	14.0	16.0	18.0	0.0
Turkey, Crispy Crumb, Bernard Matthews*	1 Burger/71g	222	313	11.3	19.3	19.8	0.9
Turkey, White Meat, Bernard Matthews*	1oz/28g	57	203	18.7	3.3	13.9	2.4
Value, Farmfoods*	1 Burger/49g	138	282	11.4	9.6	22.1	0.9
Vegeburger Herb & Vegetable, Realeat*	1 Burger/125g	433	346	32.0	32.0	10.0	0.0
Vegeburger, Linda McCartney*	1 Burger/59g	79	134	22.6	2.9	3.6	1.6
Vegetable & Cheese, Tesco*	1 Burger/85g	167	197	7.7	19.5	9.8	1.4
Vegetable, Deluxe, McDonald's*	1 Burger/210g	422	201	4.6	25.8	8.9	2.8
Vegetable, Organic, Tesco*	1 Burger/90g	108	120	2.6	17.6	4.3	2.1
Vegetable, Oven Baked, McCain*	1oz/28g	53	190	3.4	21.6	10.0	0.0
Vegetable, Quarter Pounder, Bird's Eye*	1 Burger/100g	166	166	4.3	19.8	8.0	1.6
Vegetable, Quarter Pounders, Dalepak*	1 Burger/114g	251	220	4.4	20.8	13.2	2.7
Vegetable With Tofu, Organic, Evernat*	1oz/28g	52	186	7.9	16.9	8.3	0.0
Vegetarian, Bean, Mexican Style Quarter Pounder, Tesco*	1 Serving/101g	215	213	4.3	25.0	10.6	2.8
Vegetarian, Flame Grilled, Linda McCartney*	1 Burger/60g	80	134	22.6	2.9	3.6	1.6
Vegetarian, Spicy Bean, Linda McCartney*	1 Burger/85g	190	223	4.3	26.2	11.2	2.9
Vegetarian, Tesco*	1 Burger/56g	92	164	16.0	7.0	8.0	2.5
Veggie, Burger King*	1 Burger/223g	433	194	6.6	24.9	7.6	3.4
Whopper Sandwich With Mayo, Burger King*	1 Whopper/278g	678	244	10.4	19.0	14.0	1.4
Zinger Fillet, Kentucky Fried Chicken*	1 Serving/185g	445	241	13.9	22.4	10.6	1.4
Zinger Tower, Kentucky Fried Chicken*	1 Serving/256g	620	242	12.4	20.2	12.5	1.3
BURRITO, Dinner Kit, Old El Paso*	1 Serving/100g	294	294	8.0	55.0	4.8	0.0

B

BUTTER,	Measure WEIGHT/INFO	per Measure KCAL	Nutrition Values per 100g / 100ml KCAL	PROT	CARB	FAT	FIBRE
Alpine Unsalted, TTD, Sainsbury's*	1 Serving/10g	75	748	0.7	0.6	82.5	0.0
Creamery, Co-Op*	Thin Spread/7g	52	737	0.5	0.0	81.7	0.0
Dairy, M & S*	Thin Spread/7g	29	415	0.9	78.1	11.0	0.0
English, Unsalted, Country Life*	Thin Spread/7g	52	746	0.5	0.0	82.7	0.0
Fresh	Thin Spread/7g	52	737	0.5	0.0	81.7	0.0
Fresh, Kerrygold*	Thin Spread/7g	50	720	0.4	0.0	80.0	0.0
Golden Churn, St Ivel*	Thin Spread/7g	44	628	0.8	1.0	69.0	0.0
Half Fat, Anchor*	Thin Spread/7g	25	363	0.1	0.8	40.0	0.8
Half Fat, Healthy Choice, Asda*	Thin Spread/7g	26	370	2.0	0.5	40.0	0.0
Half Fat, M & S*	Thin Spread/7g	26	370	1.8	2.0	39.5	0.5
Half Fat, Tesco*	Thin Spread/7g	25	361	2.1	0.4	39.0	0.6
Lighter Spreadable, Reduced Fat, Lurpak*	Thin Spread/7g	38	540	0.5	0.5	60.0	0.0
Salted, M & S*	1oz/28g	205	733	0.5	0.5	81.0	0.0
Salted, Organic, M & S*	1oz/28g	202	720	0.1	0.1	81.0	0.0
Spreadable, Anchor*	Thin Spread/7g	52	741	0.4	0.6	81.9	0.0
Spreadable, Country Life*	Thin Spread/7g	51	728	0.3	0.5	80.5	0.0
Spreadable, Fresh	Thin Spread/7g	52	745	0.5	0.0	82.5	0.0
Spreadable, Kerrygold*	Thin Spread/7g	50	720	0.4	0.0	80.0	0.0
Spreadable, Lurpak*	Thin Spread/7g	51	724	0.5	0.5	80.0	0.0
Value, Tesco*	Thin Spread/7g	51	732	0.5	0.7	81.0	0.0
BUTTERMILK							
Buttermilk	1oz/28g	10	37	3.4	5.0	0.5	0.0
Low Fat, Yoplait*	1 Pot/284ml	133	47	5.2	6.0	0.2	0.0
BUTTERSCOTCH, Pieces, Keiller*	1oz/28g	115	412	0.1	89.7	5.8	0.0

CABBAGE,	Measure WEIGHT/INFO	per Measure KCAL	KCAL	PROT	CARB	FAT	FIBRE
& Spring Greens, M & S*	1 Pack/300g	255	85	1.5	4.4	6.8	1.1
Boiled In Salted Water, Average	1 Serving/90g	14	16	1.0	2.2	0.4	1.8
Boiled In Unsalted Water, Average	1 Serving/90g	14	16	1.0	2.2	0.4	1.8
Chinese, Raw	1oz/28g	3	12	1.0	1.4	0.2	1.2
Cut, Fresh, Frozen, Tesco*	1oz/28g	6	22	1.3	3.2	0.5	0.3
Green, Frozen, Asda*	1 Serving/60g	13	22	1.3	3.1	0.5	2.9
Greens, Hand Trimmed, M & S*	1oz/28g	6	22	2.8	2.8	0.0	3.4
Mash, COU, M & S*	1 Pack/225g	169	75	1.9	10.5	2.9	1.8
Mash, Eat Smart, Safeway*	½ Pack/225g	146	65	2.0	9.2	1.8	1.7
Raw, Average	1oz/28g	7	26	1.7	4.1	0.4	2.4
Red & Cranberry Slaw, Tesco*	½ Pack/125g	75	60	0.7	11.3	1.3	0.0
Red, Boiled In Salted Water	1 Serving/90g	14	15	0.8	2.3	0.3	2.0
Red, Raw	1oz/28g	6	21	1.1	3.7	0.3	2.5
Savoy, Boiled In Salted Water	1 Serving/90g	15	17	1.1	2.2	0.5	2.0
Savoy, Raw	1 Serving/90g	24	27	2.1	3.9	0.5	3.1
White, Boiled In Salted Water	1 Serving/90g	13	14	1.0	2.2	0.2	1.5
White, Raw	1oz/28g	8	27	1.4	5.0	0.2	2.1
CAESAR SALAD KIT,							
Asda*	½ Pack/113g	154	136	5.0	11.0	8.0	1.4
Tesco*	½ Pack/150g	237	158	3.2	6.7	13.2	0.7
CAKE,							
Alabama Chocolate Fudge, Farmfoods*	1/6 Cake/61g	201	329	4.7	55.7	9.7	2.7
Almond Flavour Slices, GFY, Asda*	1 Slice/25g	67	268	4.0	56.0	3.1	0.7
Almond Slices, Mr Kipling*	1 Slice/35g	141	403	6.8	58.6	13.4	0.0
Angel, Co-Op*	1/8 Cake/35g	131	375	4.0	52.0	17.0	0.7
Angel, Sainsbury's*	1/8 Cake/41g	171	417	4.1	55.7	19.8	0.8
Angel Slices, Mr Kipling*	1 Slice/38g	138	362	2.6	49.8	16.9	0.4
Apple Bakes, Go Ahead, McVitie's*	1 Cake/35g	129	368	2.8	74.7	8.3	1.2
Apple Crumble, Co-Op*	1/8 Cake/52g	151	290	4.0	41.0	12.0	2.0
Apple, Home Style, M & S*	1 Cake/54g	189	350	5.3	49.4	14.7	1.5
Apple Sponge, M & S*	1 Portion/63g	178	283	3.8	32.0	16.4	0.7
Apricot & Almond, Bakers Delight*	1oz/28g	106	379	5.5	53.2	16.0	1.8
Assorted Cup, Sainsbury's*	1 Cake/38g	130	341	2.2	69.3	6.1	0.4
Bakewell Slices, Mr Kipling*	1 Slice/35g	153	436	3.7	59.5	20.4	0.0
Banana & Date Loaf, Starbucks*	1 Slice/105g	292	278	5.9	57.1	2.9	2.7
Banana, Date & Walnut Slices, BGTY, Sainsbury's*	1 Slice/28g	78	280	5.3	56.1	4.9	2.2
Banana Loaf, Organic, Respect*	1 Serving/40g	151	377	3.5	48.7	19.5	0.9
Battenberg, Somerfield*	1/8 Cake/46g	179	390	5.0	68.0	11.0	0.0
Battenburg, Mini, Mr Kipling*	1 Serving/35g	119	339	3.1	65.6	7.0	0.7
Berry Bakes, Go Ahead, McVitie's*	1 Bar/35g	128	365	2.9	73.9	8.2	1.0
Best Chocolate Orange Explosion, Safeway*	1 Serving/59g	248	421	4.1	48.8	23.3	0.9
Big Party, Morrisons*	1 Serving/85g	338	398	3.8	60.5	15.6	0.8
Birthday, McDonald's*	1 Portion/158g	406	257	1.6	39.6	9.5	0.3
Bounty Bar, McVitie's*	1 Cake/36g	166	461	5.1	55.2	24.5	0.0
Butterfly, Mr Kipling*	1 Cake/29g	114	392	4.4	43.4	22.2	0.6
Cappuccino, Finest, Tesco*	1oz/28g	105	374	2.8	40.4	22.3	0.2
Cappuccino, Indulgent, M & S*	1/6 Cake/74g	311	420	4.5	48.7	23.2	4.2
Caramel Shortcakes, Mr Kipling*	1 Shortcake/36g	178	508	4.2	58.1	28.8	0.0
Caramel Slice, M & S*	1 Slice/64g	304	475	4.9	60.4	25.2	2.6
Carrot & Orange, Finest, Tesco*	1 Serving/50g	171	342	4.1	49.1	14.3	1.0
Carrot & Orange Slices, GFY, Asda*	1 Slice/24g	70	291	3.3	62.0	3.3	1.0
Carrot & Orange Slices, HE, Tesco*	1 Slice/29g	80	277	3.0	56.4	2.7	1.9
Carrot & Orange, Waitrose*	1/6 Cake/47g	165	350	5.3	46.8	15.7	1.8
Carrot, Entenmann's*	1 Serving/40g	156	391	4.1	47.4	20.5	1.5

(Nutrition Values per 100g / 100ml apply to the KCAL, PROT, CARB, FAT, FIBRE columns on the right.)

C

CAKE,	Measure WEIGHT/INFO	per Measure KCAL	KCAL	PROT	CARB	FAT	FIBRE
Carrot, Farmfoods*	1/8 Cake/59g	187	317	3.7	35.4	17.8	1.6
Carrot Loaf, Starbucks*	1 Slice/100g	352	352	4.7	38.4	19.9	2.3
Carrot, M & S*	1oz/28g	98	350	6.1	34.5	21.0	1.5
Carrot Slices, BGTY, Sainsbury's*	1 Slice/27g	62	239	3.0	51.9	3.2	4.9
Carrot Slices, Weight Watchers*	1oz/28g	81	290	3.0	56.7	2.7	1.9
Carrot, Traditional, Farringford Foods*	1oz/28g	115	412	4.4	44.8	25.2	0.0
Carrot Wedge, Tesco*	1 Pack/175g	576	329	4.6	41.7	16.0	1.5
Cherry Bakewell, M & S*	1 Cake/44g	185	420	4.5	61.7	17.7	1.0
Cherry Bakewells, Mini, Morrisons*	1 Tart/27g	107	396	3.7	67.7	12.9	1.5
Cherry Bakewells, Mr Kipling*	1 Cake/45g	186	414	3.9	59.3	17.9	1.2
Cherry, Co-Op*	1/8 Cake/47g	195	415	5.0	49.0	22.0	0.5
Cherry Genoa, M & S*	1oz/28g	99	355	4.5	59.3	10.9	1.6
Choc Chip Bar, Go Ahead, McVitie's*	1 Bar/28g	100	356	6.4	56.9	12.1	1.0
Choc Chip Mini Bar, Go Ahead, McVitie's	1 Bar/27g	93	343	5.7	55.3	12.1	0.9
Chocolate	1oz/28g	128	456	7.4	50.4	26.4	0.0
Chocolate & Orange Bar, Go Ahead, McVitie's*	1 Cake Bar/33g	109	330	4.3	64.9	6.0	1.0
Chocolate & Orange Bars, Less Than 5% Fat, Asda	1 Bar/40g	123	307	7.4	63.9	2.4	1.1
Chocolate & Orange Rolls, M & S*	1 Roll/60g	228	380	3.6	27.0	28.4	1.3
Chocolate & Orange Slices, GFY, Asda*	1 Slice/30g	84	281	3.0	61.0	2.8	0.7
Chocolate Birthday, M & S*	1 Serving/68g	279	410	4.5	43.7	24.1	1.3
Chocolate Birthday, Tesco*	1 Serving/58g	276	475	6.3	50.3	27.6	0.9
Chocolate Box, Asda*	1 Serving/60g	263	439	5.0	53.0	23.0	0.7
Chocolate Brownie, Fudge, Entenmann's*	1/8 Cake/55g	168	306	4.0	62.7	4.4	1.5
Chocolate Brownie, Fudgy, M & S*	1 Brownie/87g	400	460	4.8	56.9	25.2	3.0
Chocolate Brownie, Slices, M & S*	1 Brownie/36g	158	440	5.3	51.1	24.1	1.3
Chocolate Chip Bar, Mr Kipling*	1 Bar/33g	148	448	6.1	45.2	27.0	0.0
Chocolate Chip Bar, Sainsbury's*	1 Cake Bar/25g	108	430	6.1	51.2	22.3	0.6
Chocolate Chip, Co-Op*	1/6 Cake/62.5g	273	440	5.0	44.0	27.0	0.5
Chocolate Chunk, Bakers Delight*	1oz/28g	115	409	5.5	54.7	18.7	0.9
Chocolate Cup, BGTY, Sainsbury's*	1 Cake/38g	121	318	2.5	66.5	4.6	0.8
Chocolate Cup, Lyons*	1 Cake/39g	125	321	2.4	67.5	4.6	0.8
Chocolate Dream Bar, Go Ahead, McVitie's*	1 Bar/36g	141	391	4.6	63.2	13.4	0.9
Chocolate Eclair, Dairy Cream, Co-Op*	1 Eclair/29g	122	420	6.0	23.0	34.0	0.6
Choc Eclair, Fresh Cream, Jumbo, Co-Op*	1 Eclair/94g	357	380	4.0	27.0	28.0	2.0
Chocolate Eclair, Fresh Cream, Safeway*	1 Eclair/59g	210	356	4.1	24.8	26.7	0.4
Chocolate Eclairs, Fresh Cream, M & S*	1 Eclair/62g	234	378	4.1	18.8	32.3	0.2
Chocolate Eclairs, Fresh Cream, Sainsbury's*	1 Eclair/29g	104	360	4.2	32.7	23.6	0.1
Chocolate Eclairs, Fresh Cream, Tesco*	1 Eclair/66g	244	370	4.0	31.2	25.5	0.4
Chocolate Flavour Slice, Eat Smart, Safeway*	1 Slice/28g	95	340	5.3	73.6	2.4	4.0
Chocolate Flavour Slices, GFY, Asda*	2 Slices/55g	141	257	4.3	54.0	2.6	1.4
Chocolate Flavour Slices, HE, Tesco*	1 Slice/25g	79	314	4.7	65.5	2.4	3.7
Chocolate Fudge & Vanilla Cream, M & S*	1/6 Cake/69g	306	450	5.2	49.8	26.0	1.3
Chocolate Fudge, Entenmann's*	1 Serving/48g	173	361	4.4	51.8	15.1	0.9
Chocolate Fudge, M & S*	1oz/28g	109	390	3.7	50.8	20.6	1.4
Chocolate Fudge, Pizza Express*	1 Cake/100g	395	395	4.0	57.2	17.0	0.0
Chocolate Fudge Slice, Waitrose*	1 Slice/60g	230	383	4.7	54.6	16.2	1.5
Chocolate Fudge, Somerfield*	1oz/28g	114	406	5.0	48.0	22.0	0.0
Chocolate, Home Bake, McVitie's*	1oz/28g	99	355	5.7	54.4	14.1	1.4
Chocolate Indulgence, Finest, Tesco*	1 Slice/52g	203	390	3.8	47.8	20.4	0.4
Chocolate Loaf, Somerfield*	1oz/28g	111	396	6.0	44.0	22.0	0.0
Chocolate Nests, Mini, M & S*	1 Cake/16g	74	465	4.4	63.9	21.1	1.5
Chocolate Orange Slices, BGTY, Sainsbury's*	1 Slice/30g	90	301	3.9	62.8	4.8	1.3
Chocolate Slice, Go Ahead, McVitie's*	1 Slice/32g	94	293	4.5	49.4	8.2	1.9
Chocolate Slices, Mr Kipling*	1oz/28g	108	386	4.8	50.4	18.3	0.0

Nutrition Values per 100g / 100ml (KCAL, PROT, CARB, FAT, FIBRE)

C

CAKE,	Measure WEIGHT/INFO	per Measure KCAL	Nutrition Values per 100g / 100ml KCAL	PROT	CARB	FAT	FIBRE
Chocolate Sponge, Less Than 5% Fat, Asda*	1 Sponge/110g	198	180	4.4	32.0	3.8	1.1
Chocolate Sponge Roll, M & S*	¼ Cake/66g	251	380	3.9	50.5	18.4	1.8
Chocolate Swiss Roll, Mini, Tesco*	1 Roll/22g	87	396	4.6	61.0	14.8	0.0
Chocolate, Thorntons*	1 Serving/87g	408	469	5.2	47.1	28.8	0.6
Chocolate Truffle, Somerfield*	1oz/28g	136	485	6.0	51.0	28.0	0.0
Chocolate Victoria Sponge, Co-Op*	1 Slice/61g	201	330	5.0	42.0	16.0	1.0
Chocolate, Viennese, M & S*	1oz/28g	105	375	4.4	54.1	13.6	1.6
Chocolate With Butter Icing	1oz/28g	135	481	5.7	50.9	29.7	0.0
Choux Buns, Fresh Cream, Tesco*	1 Bun/95g	340	358	4.9	28.5	24.9	0.9
Choux Buns, M & S*	1oz/28g	89	317	5.4	25.6	22.2	0.3
Christmas, Conoisseur, M & S*	1 Slice/60g	216	360	4.1	64.7	9.2	3.3
Christmas, Rich Fruit All Iced, Sainsbury's*	1/16th Cake/85g	307	361	4.0	66.4	8.9	1.5
Christmas, TTD, Sainsbury's*	1/16th Cake/85g	315	371	3.7	67.1	8.9	1.3
Coconut	1 Slice/70g	304	434	6.7	51.2	23.8	2.5
Coconut Sponge, Mini Classics, Mr Kipling*	1 Cake/38g	155	409	3.7	47.0	22.9	0.9
Coffee & Walnut Slices, HE,Tesco*	1 Slice/23g	69	301	4.4	65.7	2.3	2.8
Coffee & Walnut, Somerfield*	1oz/28g	123	440	5.0	46.0	26.0	0.0
Country Slices, Mr Kipling*	1oz/28g	104	371	4.8	53.7	15.2	0.0
Cream Oysters, M & S*	1 Oyster/72g	227	315	3.6	27.5	21.2	3.0
Cream Slices, M & S*	1 Slice/80g	310	387	2.3	45.7	22.9	0.6
Crispy Fruit Slices, Apple & Sultana, Go Ahead, McVitie's*	1 Slice/14g	54	386	6.0	72.7	7.9	3.3
Crispy Fruit Slices, Forest Fruit, Go Ahead, McVitie's*	1 Biscuit/14g	56	400	5.5	73.0	8.8	3.7
Crispy Fruit Slices, Orange & Sultana, Go Ahead, McVitie's*	1 Biscuit/15g	60	400	5.1	75.7	8.1	3.0
Crunchie Cake Bar, Cadbury's*	1 Cake Bar/32g	147	460	5.9	58.3	22.6	0.0
Custard Slices, Tesco*	1 Slice/108g	320	296	2.4	37.5	15.2	0.5
Date & Walnut, Bakers Delight*	1oz/28g	88	315	5.2	55.5	8.0	1.2
Date & Walnut Loaf, Sainsbury's*	1/10 Slice/40g	148	371	6.7	40.1	20.4	1.0
Double Chocolate Brownies, Weight Watchers*	1 Pot/83g	153	184	4.5	33.3	3.6	2.2
Double Chocolate Ganache, M & S*	1/12 Cake/61g	281	460	5.9	46.1	27.6	2.5
Double Chocolate Wedge, Tesco*	1 Piece/100g	416	416	5.0	53.4	20.3	0.9
Dundee, Co-Op*	1/8 Cake/71g	238	335	5.0	53.0	11.0	2.0
Dundee, Somerfield*	1/10 Cake/75g	254	339	5.0	57.0	11.0	0.0
Eccles	1 Cake/45g	214	475	3.9	59.3	26.4	1.6
Eclairs, Dairy Cream, Farmfoods*	1 Eclair/34g	106	311	4.5	34.2	17.4	0.5
Fairy, Co-Op*	1oz/28g	105	375	4.0	43.0	21.0	0.8
Fairy, Value,Tesco*	1 Cake/16g	70	436	6.1	53.7	21.9	1.0
Farmhouse Fruit, Bakers Delight*	1oz/28g	107	381	5.2	55.5	15.3	2.1
Farmhouse Slice, Weight Watchers*	1 Slice/23g	73	317	5.5	64.9	4.0	1.3
Flake, Cadbury's*	1 Cake/26g	114	439	6.0	54.1	22.1	0.7
Flake Cake Bar, Cadbury's*	1 Cake/22g	97	442	6.5	51.8	23.3	0.5
Fondant Fancies, M & S*	1oz/28g	107	382	1.8	69.2	10.9	1.4
Fondant Fancies, Sainsbury's*	1 Cake/27g	95	353	2.4	65.7	9.0	0.4
French Fancies, Mr Kipling*	1 Cake/28g	100	356	2.3	65.1	9.6	0.0
Fresh Cream Bramley Apple Sponge, Tesco*	1/6 Slice/43g	130	303	3.6	35.4	16.3	1.0
Fruit & Nut Crisp Bar, Go Ahead, McVitie's*	1 Bar/22g	95	430	5.3	71.3	13.7	1.7
Fruit, Fully Iced, Luxury Rich, Co-Op*	1oz/28g	99	355	3.0	64.0	9.0	4.0
Fruit, Healthy Selection, Somerfield*	1oz/28g	73	260	5.0	55.0	2.0	0.0
Fruit, Iced All Over, Luxury, Somerfield*	1oz/28g	100	356	4.0	62.0	10.0	0.0
Fruit, Iced Bar, Somerfield*	1oz/28g	98	351	4.0	60.0	11.0	0.0
Fruit, Plain, Retail	1 Slice/90g	319	354	5.1	57.9	12.9	0.0
Fruit, Rich, Connoisseur, Somerfield*	1oz/28g	91	326	4.0	54.0	10.0	0.0
Fruit, Rich, Iced	1 Slice/70g	249	356	4.1	62.7	11.4	1.7
Fruit, Rich, Retail	1 Slice/70g	225	322	4.9	50.7	12.5	1.7
Fruit, Rich, Somerfield*	1oz/28g	97	348	4.0	57.0	12.0	0.0

CAKE,	Measure WEIGHT/INFO	per Measure KCAL	Nutrition Values per 100g / 100ml KCAL	PROT	CARB	FAT	FIBRE
Fudgy Chocolate Slices, COU, M & S*	1 Slice/36g	95	265	4.6	66.4	2.2	2.1
Galaxy Cake Bar, McVitie's*	1oz/28g	138	494	5.1	57.5	27.0	0.3
Genoa, Home Bake, McVitie's*	1oz/28g	107	383	4.7	55.9	15.6	1.4
Ginger Drizzle, Iced, Co-Op*	1/6 Cake/64.5g	226	350	3.0	58.0	12.0	1.0
Ginger, Jamaica Bar, McVitie's*	1 Mini Cake/33g	128	388	3.5	60.2	14.7	1.2
Golden Syrup Bar, McVitie's*	1 Mini Cake/33g	127	385	3.6	60.2	14.4	1.2
Hot Fudge, Cadbury's*	1 Cake/260g	980	377	6.2	56.4	14.0	1.3
Jaffa Cake Bar, McVitie's	1 Bar/31g	126	408	3.9	59.0	17.4	0.0
Jaffa Cake, Value, Tesco*	1 Cake/11g	42	386	4.2	72.7	8.7	0.6
Jaffa Cakes, Asda*	1 Serving/11g	42	378	4.2	70.0	9.0	1.4
Jaffa Cakes, McVitie's*	1 Biscuit/12g	46	384	4.4	73.3	8.1	1.3
Jaffa Cakes, Mini, Asda*	1 Cake/5g	21	412	3.9	63.0	16.0	1.9
Jaffa Cakes, Mini, M & S*	1oz/28g	113	405	3.9	62.8	15.8	1.9
Jaffa Cakes, Morrisons*	1 Cake/13g	50	384	4.4	73.2	8.1	0.0
Jaffa Cakes, Plain Chocolate, Sainsbury's*	1 Cake/13g	46	384	4.4	73.3	8.1	1.3
Jammy Strawberry Rolls, Mini, Cadbury's*	1 Roll/29g	119	411	4.9	59.8	16.5	0.5
Lemon Drizzle, Co-Op*	¼ Cake/97.5g	302	310	4.0	46.0	12.0	1.0
Lemon Drizzle, M & S*	1/6 Cake/63g	230	365	4.2	55.8	13.9	1.4
Lemon Drizzle Slices, GFY, Asda*	1 Slice/25g	69	274	3.6	56.0	4.0	0.7
Lemon, Home Bake, McVitie's*	1oz/28g	108	384	4.6	53.9	18.2	1.0
Lemon Iced Madeira, Co-Op*	1 Cake/290g	1131	390	4.0	53.0	18.0	0.6
Lemon Slices, HE, Tesco*	1 Slice/26g	86	329	3.4	69.1	2.6	3.0
Lemon Slices, Lyons*	1 Slice/21g	74	354	3.7	55.3	13.1	0.6
Lemon Slices, Mr Kipling*	1oz/28g	117	417	4.1	58.2	16.3	0.0
Lemon Smoothie Bake, Go Ahead, McVities*	1 bar/35g	130	372	3.0	75.1	8.1	1.0
Lemon Sponge Slices, Deliciously Zesty, M & S*	1 Slice/27g	107	395	3.7	54.4	18.0	0.7
Madeira	1 Slice/40g	157	393	5.4	58.4	16.9	0.9
Marble, Home Bake, McVitie's*	1oz/28g	115	411	3.7	56.9	18.8	0.9
Meringue Nests, M & S*	1 Nest/12g	47	395	6.1	91.6	0.0	0.0
Meringue Nests, Tesco*	1 Nest/15g	58	388	3.9	92.8	0.1	0.0
Meringues, Cream, Sainsbury's*	1 Meringue/25g	98	392	3.9	59.0	15.7	0.8
Meringues, M & S*	1 Meringue/12g	47	389	5.2	92.0	0.0	0.0
Meringues, Mini, M & S*	1oz/28g	111	395	6.1	91.6	0.0	0.0
Milk Chocolate Bar, Cadbury's*	1 Bar/35g	140	401	6.8	48.8	19.8	0.8
Milky Way Cake Bar, McVitie's*	1 Bar/26g	138	530	5.3	53.8	32.6	0.2
Mini Rolls, Cadbury's*	1 Roll/26g	113	434	5.5	55.6	20.6	0.6
Mini Rolls, Chocolate & Vanilla, Somerfield*	1oz/28g	112	399	5.0	62.0	15.0	0.0
Mini Rolls, Chocolate, Somerfield*	1 Roll/26g	114	438	6.0	55.0	22.0	0.0
Mini Rolls, Chocolate, Tesco*	1 Roll/31g	137	442	6.0	56.3	21.4	0.8
Mini Rolls, Easter Selection, Cadbury's*	1oz/28g	122	434	5.5	55.6	20.6	0.0
Penguin Snack, McVitie's*	1 Cake/24g	121	504	5.2	54.6	29.5	0.0
Raspberry & Vanilla Swiss Roll, Morrisons*	1 Serving/28g	98	350	4.2	61.8	9.5	0.0
Raspberry Jam & Buttercream Sponge Sandwich, Somerfield*	1oz/28g	102	364	4.0	61.0	12.0	0.0
Raspberry Sponge, M & S*	1oz/28g	58	207	1.0	18.6	14.3	0.8
Raspberry Swiss Roll, Lyons*	1 Swiss Roll/175g	485	277	5.2	60.6	1.4	0.0
Raspberry Swiss Roll, Somerfield*	1 Swiss Roll/80g	245	306	5.0	66.0	3.0	0.0
Rice Crispy, Somerfield*	1oz/28g	134	479	5.0	77.0	17.0	0.0
Rice, Dark Chocolate, Organic, Kallo*	1 Cake/12g	57	471	6.8	57.2	24.1	7.4
Rich Choc' Roll, Cadbury's*	1/6th Portion/39g	149	381	4.8	50.2	15.6	1.0
Rock	1 Sm Cake/40g	158	396	5.4	60.5	16.4	1.5
Rum Baba	1oz/28g	62	223	3.5	32.2	8.1	0.8
Seriously Chocolatey Celebration, Sainsbury's*	1/8 Cake/77g	336	437	6.3	45.0	25.7	0.3
Shrek Birthday, Tesco*	1/16 Cake/72g	248	344	3.3	64.0	12.2	0.5
Slab, Jam & Buttercream, Co-Op*	1oz/28g	105	375	4.0	54.0	16.0	1.0

	Measure WEIGHT/INFO	per Measure KCAL	Nutrition Values per 100g / 100ml KCAL	PROT	CARB	FAT	FIBRE
CAKE,							
Snowball, Chocolate, Tunnock's*	1 Snowball/25g	97	388	3.9	47.0	21.8	0.0
Snowballs, Sainsbury's*	1 Snowball/18g	80	445	2.5	55.6	23.0	3.6
Sponge	1 Slice/53g	243	459	6.4	52.4	26.3	0.9
Sponge, Fatless	1 Slice/53g	156	294	10.1	53.0	6.1	0.9
Sponge, Iced, M & S*	1 Serving/100g	400	400	3.4	58.4	17.0	1.3
Sponge, Jam Filled	1 Slice/65g	196	302	4.2	64.2	4.9	1.8
Sponge With Butter Icing	1 Slice/65g	319	490	4.5	52.4	30.6	0.6
Stem Ginger, 96% Fat Free, Trimlyne*	¼ Cake/62.5g	170	273	4.4	58.1	3.6	1.2
Sticky Toffee Slices, Eat Smart, Safeway*	1 Cake/85g	259	305	3.6	65.8	2.7	1.3
Strawberry Dream Bar, McVitie's*	1 Cake/33g	104	314	4.1	64.7	6.0	0.8
Strawberry Swiss Roll, Luxury, Somerfield*	1oz/28g	84	301	4.0	62.0	4.0	0.0
Sultana & Cherry Slice, Co-Op*	1oz/28g	87	310	3.0	48.0	12.0	2.0
Sultana, Apple & Cranberry, 99% Fat Free, Trimlyne*,	1/6 Cake/66.6g	130	195	4.6	45.5	0.9	3.3
Summer Strawberry Bakes, Go Ahead, McVitie's*	1 Bar/35g	128	367	2.7	75.1	8.0	1.0
Swiss Roll	1oz/28g	77	276	7.2	55.5	4.4	0.8
Swiss Roll, Chocolate Flavour, Value, Tesco*	1 Slice/20g	79	394	5.5	49.2	19.5	1.4
Swiss Roll, Chocolate, Jumbo, Safeway*	1/12 Roll/35g	129	369	4.1	47.1	18.2	0.9
Swiss Roll, Chocolate, Somerfield*	¼ Roll/43.5g	167	384	6.0	55.0	16.0	0.0
Swiss Rolls, Chocolate, Individual	1 Roll/26g	88	337	4.3	58.1	11.3	0.0
The Ultimate Carrot Passion, Entenmann's*	1 Slice/52g	206	403	4.6	42.4	24.3	1.0
Toffee & Pecan Loaf, Safeway*	1/6 Cake/62g	225	363	3.6	35.5	22.9	0.5
Toffee & Pecan Slices, M & S*	1 Slice/36g	160	445	4.7	54.0	23.7	1.3
Toffee Temptation, Tesco*	1 Slice/67g	228	340	2.9	39.1	19.1	0.3
Triple Chocolate, TTD, Sainsbury's*	1/8 Cake/52g	210	412	4.7	42.6	24.7	0.5
Turkish Delight, Fry's*	1 Cake/26g	96	371	4.5	62.4	10.8	0.5
Vanilla Slices, M & S*	1 Slice/89g	336	377	2.6	42.6	18.5	0.5
Victoria Sandwich, Co-Op*	1oz/28g	101	360	4.0	48.0	17.0	1.0
Victoria Sponge, Lemon, Co-Op*	1 Slice/42g	151	360	4.0	44.0	19.0	0.7
Victoria Sponge Sandwich, Somerfield*	1oz/28g	112	400	4.0	53.0	19.0	0.0
Viennese Whirl, Mr Kipling*	1 Whirl/28g	139	497	4.1	51.5	30.5	1.2
Viennese Whirl, Somerfield*	1oz/28g	133	475	4.0	56.0	26.0	0.0
Viennese Whirl, Tesco*	1 Cake/39g	181	465	4.0	53.2	26.2	1.2
Walnut & Coffee, Co-Op*	¼ Cake/65g	254	390	5.0	47.0	20.0	0.7
Walnut Layer, Somerfield*	¼ Cake/77.5g	295	381	6.0	45.0	20.0	0.0
Welsh	1oz/28g	121	431	5.6	61.8	19.6	1.5
Wild Blueberry & Apple, Bakers Delight*	1oz/28g	99	354	4.6	48.8	15.6	1.5
Winnie The Pooh Birthday, Nestle*	1 Serving/100g	361	361	2.4	63.3	10.9	0.5
Yoghurt & Berry Loaf, Low Fat, Starbucks*	1 Cake/94g	254	270	5.3	50.8	5.1	1.7
Yorkshire Parkin, Bakers Delight*	1oz/28g	111	395	5.1	60.3	14.8	1.5
CALAMARI,							
Battered, Young's*	1 Serving/150g	266	177	7.8	13.0	10.4	1.5
M & S*	1oz/28g	65	231	13.9	11.5	14.4	0.5
Rings In Batter, Waitrose*	½ Pack/85g	227	267	13.9	14.2	17.2	0.6
CAMPINO,							
Oranges & Cream, Bendicks*	1oz/28g	116	416	0.1	85.8	8.1	0.0
Strawberries & Cream, Bendicks*	1oz/28g	117	418	0.1	86.2	8.1	0.0
CAPERS, In Spirit Vinegar, Opies*	1oz/28g	8	27	1.6	2.6	0.4	0.0
CAPPUCCINO,							
Cafe Mocha,Dry, Maxwell House*	1 Serving/23g	100	434	4.3	78.2	10.8	0.0
Cafe Specials, Dry, M & S*	1 Serving/14g	55	395	14.0	59.0	11.5	0.7
Dry, Maxwell House*	1 Mug/15g	53	350	12.0	64.0	9.6	0.4
Dry, Nescafe*	1 Serving/12g	51	427	14.7	53.9	17.0	0.8
Dry, Tesco*	1 Serving/13g	53	411	14.9	52.9	15.5	0.4
Instant, Kenco*	1 Sachet/20g	80	401	13.5	55.7	13.8	0.0

	Measure WEIGHT/INFO	per Measure KCAL	KCAL	PROT	CARB	FAT	FIBRE
			Nutrition Values per 100g / 100ml				
CAPPUCCINO,							
Instant, Made Up, Maxwell House*	1 Serving/280g	123	44	0.6	5.8	1.9	0.0
Pret A Manger*	1 Serving/304ml	70	23	1.7	2.3	0.7	0.0
Unsweetened, Dry, Nescafe*	1 Serving/12g	51	427	14.9	54.7	16.6	0.0
With Chocolate, Pret A Manger*	1 Drink/355ml	67	19	1.4	1.9	0.6	0.0
CARAMAC, Nestle*	1 Bar/30g	163	563	5.8	54.4	35.8	0.0
CARAMEL,							
Cadbury's*	1 Bar/50g	240	480	4.3	61.3	24.3	0.0
Cadbury's*	1 Serving/100g	495	495	5.7	61.1	25.3	0.0
Egg, Cadbury's*	1 Egg/39g	191	490	4.3	58.9	26.1	0.0
CARAMEL MACCHIATO, Starbucks*	1 Grande/100ml	250	250	9.0	36.0	9.0	0.0
CAROB Powder	1 Tsp/2g	3	159	4.9	37.0	0.1	0.0
CARROTS,							
& Peas, Sainsbury's*	1 Serving/200g	100	50	3.3	8.3	0.5	3.8
Baby, Extra Sweet, Organic, Iceland*	1oz/28g	6	22	0.4	4.7	0.3	2.3
Baby, Frozen, Somerfield*	1 Pack/750g	210	28	1.0	6.0	0.0	0.0
Baby, Tesco*	1 Serving/75g	17	22	0.4	4.5	0.3	2.3
Baby, With Fine Beans, Tesco*	1 Pack/200g	58	29	1.3	4.7	0.5	2.3
Batons, Fresh 'N' Ready, Sainsbury's*	1 Serving/100g	26	26	0.6	4.9	0.4	2.5
Batons, M & S*	1oz/28g	9	33	0.7	8.3	0.0	2.9
Broccoli & Cauliflower Florets, M & S*	1oz/28g	8	30	1.8	6.1	0.0	2.8
Canned, Re-Heated, Drained	1oz/28g	6	20	0.5	4.2	0.3	1.9
Cauliflower & Broccoli Florets, Safeway*	1 Serving/125g	44	35	2.6	4.6	0.7	2.3
Cauliflower & Broccoli, Tesco*	1oz/28g	10	35	2.5	4.9	0.6	2.3
Frozen, Co-Op*	1oz/28g	7	25	0.6	5.0	0.4	2.0
Frozen, Iceland*	1 Serving/100g	22	22	0.4	4.7	0.3	2.3
Grated, Asda*	1oz/28g	9	31	0.7	6.0	0.5	2.4
Julienne, Farmfoods*	1oz/28g	10	37	0.6	7.9	0.3	2.4
Raw, Asda*	1 Serving/50g	12	23	0.6	4.9	0.4	2.3
Raw, Organic, Tesco*	1 Serving/100g	37	37	0.6	7.9	0.3	2.4
Sliced, Asda*	1oz/28g	6	20	0.7	4.4	0.0	1.9
Sliced, Basics, Frozen, Somerfield*	1oz/28g	10	37	1.0	8.0	0.0	0.0
Sliced, Frozen, Tesco*	1oz/28g	8	30	0.7	5.7	0.5	2.4
Sliced, In Brine, Asda*	1oz/28g	6	20	0.7	4.4	0.0	1.9
Sliced, In Water, Somerfield*	1oz/28g	6	20	1.0	4.0	0.0	0.0
Sliced, In Water, Tinned, Tesco*	1 Serving/180g	36	20	0.5	3.9	0.3	1.9
Sliced, Tesco*	1 Serving/175g	72	41	1.0	8.4	0.4	2.9
Sliced, Value, Tesco*	½ Can/90g	18	20	0.5	3.9	0.3	1.9
Whole, Tesco*	1oz/28g	6	20	0.5	3.9	0.3	1.9
Young, Boiled In Salted Water	1oz/28g	6	22	0.6	4.4	0.4	2.3
Young, Boiled In Unsalted Water	1oz/28g	6	22	0.6	4.4	0.4	2.3
Young, Raw, Fresh	1oz/28g	8	30	0.7	6.0	0.5	2.4
CARROT & APPLE Juice, With Hint Of Ginger, Pressed, M & S*	1 Glass/250ml	88	35	0.5	8.0	0.1	0.4
CARROT & SWEDE,							
Crush, M & S*	1 Serving/150g	83	55	0.7	2.8	4.5	3.1
Julienne, Frozen, Great Value, Asda*	1 Serving/100g	20	20	0.5	3.7	0.3	1.8
Mash, BGTY, Sainsbury's*	1 Serving/225g	200	89	1.3	16.0	2.2	1.2
Mash. Eat Smart, Safeway*	1 Serving/225g	146	65	1.6	11.8	1.2	1.3
Mash, Fresh, Tesco*	1oz/28g	22	80	1.2	11.1	3.4	1.4
Mix, Freshly Prepared, Asda*	½ Pack/250g	48	19	0.5	3.6	0.3	1.6
CARROT JUICE,							
Organic, Evernat*	1 Glass/200ml	44	22	0.6	4.8	0.0	0.3
P & J*	1 Glass/250ml	60	24	0.5	5.7	0.0	0.0
Pret A Manger*	1 Glass/250ml	60	24	0.5	5.7	0.1	0.0

	Measure WEIGHT/INFO	per Measure KCAL	Nutrition Values per 100g / 100ml KCAL	PROT	CARB	FAT	FIBRE
CASHEW NUTS,							
Organic, Crazy Jack*	1 Pack/100g	573	573	7.7	18.2	48.2	3.2
Plain	10 Whole/10g	57	573	17.7	18.1	48.2	3.2
Roasted & Salted	10 Whole/10g	61	611	20.5	18.8	50.9	3.2
Roasted & Salted, Co-Op*	1 Serving/20g	124	620	20.0	21.0	51.0	4.0
Roasted Salted, Whole, Tesco*	1 Serving/25g	133	531	20.1	36.9	33.7	3.8
Salted, Roasted, KP*	1 Pack/50g	310	619	19.8	20.5	50.9	4.0
Whole, Holland & Barrett*	1 Pack/100g	573	573	17.7	18.2	48.2	3.2
Whole, Tesco*	1oz/28g	173	619	19.8	20.5	50.9	4.0
& Peanuts, Honey Roasted, Tesco*	1 Bag/25g	145	579	21.6	26.6	42.9	4.2
CASSAVA,							
Baked	1oz/28g	43	155	0.7	40.1	0.2	1.7
Boiled In Unsalted Water	1oz/28g	36	130	0.5	33.5	0.2	1.4
Chips	1oz/28g	99	353	1.8	91.4	0.4	4.0
Gari	1oz/28g	100	358	1.3	92.9	0.5	0.0
Raw	1oz/28g	40	142	0.6	36.8	0.2	1.6
Steamed	1oz/28g	40	142	0.6	36.8	0.2	1.6
CASSEROLE,							
Bean & Lentil, Morrisons*	1 Can/410g	287	70	4.1	12.5	0.4	0.0
Beef & Ale, Finest, Tesco*	½ Pack/300g	222	74	12.2	3.9	1.1	0.4
Beef & Dumplings, M & S*	1 Pack/454g	522	115	10.5	7.7	4.7	1.0
Beef & Vegetable, Ready Meals, Waitrose*	1oz/28g	32	114	4.1	12.8	5.2	0.9
Beef, M & S*	1 Serving/200g	240	120	8.1	9.2	5.7	1.0
Beef, Ready Meals, M & S*	1 Meal/454g	622	137	11.1	9.9	6.4	0.7
Caribbean Style Turtle Bean, M & S*	1 Pack/380g	323	85	3.3	11.2	3.3	1.2
Chicken & Asparagus In White Wine, Tesco*	½ Pack/300g	444	148	11.5	7.7	7.9	0.8
Chicken & Dumplings, Asda*	1 Pack/300g	333	111	3.9	14.0	4.4	0.8
Chicken & Herb Dumplings, BGTY, Sainsbury's*	1 Pack/450g	446	99	6.1	9.5	4.1	0.6
Chicken & Tomato, Asda*	¼ Pack/273g	569	208	16.0	2.2	15.0	0.5
Chicken, GFY, Asda*	1 Pack/375g	375	100	5.0	12.0	3.5	0.8
Chicken, M & S*	1 Pack/200g	230	115	7.4	10.9	4.4	0.9
Chicken Mediterranean, Tesco*	1 Pack/400g	260	65	6.7	4.5	2.3	0.9
Chicken, Mega Value, Tesco*	1 Serving/250g	113	45	8.4	1.1	0.8	0.6
Chicken With Dumplings, COU, M & S*	1 Pack/454g	454	100	9.7	9.9	1.9	0.9
Chunky Veg & Butter Bean & Dumplings, Eat Smart, Safeway*	1 Pack/400g	260	65	1.9	9.0	1.9	1.3
Chunky Vegetables, M & S*	1 Bag/450g	90	20	0.7	3.4	0.3	1.4
Country Vegetable, Sainsbury's*	1 Can/400g	300	75	2.2	11.0	2.5	1.1
Diced Beef, Less Than 10% Fat, Asda*	1 Pack/227g	275	121	24.0	0.0	2.8	0.0
Lamb & Rosemary, M & S*	1 Pack/454g	409	90	9.7	5.5	3.3	1.0
Lamb, BGTY, Sainsbury's*	1 Serving/200g	242	121	20.7	0.1	4.3	0.1
Lamb, M & S*	1 Pack/200g	260	130	6.2	10.6	6.8	1.2
Lentil & Vegetable, Granose*	1 Pack/400g	220	55	2.8	7.9	1.4	0.0
Minced Lamb With Mint Dumplings, Sainsbury's*	1 Pack/450g	558	124	5.4	10.4	6.8	1.1
Mix Vegetables, Safeway*	1 Serving/100g	17	17	0.7	3.0	0.3	2.1
Mixed Vegetables, Farmfoods*	1oz/28g	8	29	0.8	5.8	0.3	2.1
Pork With Apple Dumplings, Tesco*	1 Pack/300g	492	164	10.8	12.6	8.0	1.7
Prime Steak, Sainsbury's*	1oz/28g	34	122	22.6	0.1	3.5	0.1
Quorn*, Dumplings	1oz/28g	36	127	4.5	14.2	5.8	1.7
Rabbit	1oz/28g	29	102	11.6	2.6	5.1	0.4
Sausage	1oz/28g	104	373	0.1	85.2	3.5	0.9
Sausage & Potato, M & S*	1 Serving/200g	190	95	3.3	7.5	5.9	0.9
Sausage, SmartPrice, Asda*	1 Can/392g	459	117	3.6	10.0	7.0	0.0
Steak & Ale With Dumplings, M & S*	1 Serving/325g	471	145	10.0	10.1	7.2	1.0
Steak & Mushroom With Mustard Mash, Finest, Tesco*	1 Pack/550g	523	95	5.9	9.0	3.9	1.1
Vegetable & Chicken, Long Life, Sainsbury's*	1 Pack/300g	186	62	4.6	7.4	1.5	0.8

C

CASSEROLE,	Measure WEIGHT/INFO	per Measure KCAL	Nutrition Values per 100g / 100ml KCAL	PROT	CARB	FAT	FIBRE
Vegetable & Dumplings, COU, M & S*	1 Pack/454g	477	105	9.4	10.6	2.6	0.5
Vegetable With Dumplings, Asda*	1 portion/350g	343	98	2.7	12.0	4.3	2.1
Vegetable With Herb Dumplings, COU, M & S*	½ Pack/227g	170	75	2.1	11.1	1.3	1.7
CASSEROLE MIX,							
Beef, Colman's*	1 Pack/40g	119	297	5.2	67.0	0.6	0.0
Beef, Schwartz*	½ Packet/21g	58	276	9.9	53.9	2.3	0.0
Chicken, Colman's*	1 Pack/40g	109	272	5.3	60.0	0.7	0.0
Chicken, Schwartz*	½ Pack/18g	55	304	10.6	62.8	1.2	0.0
Liver & Bacon, Colman's*	1 Pack/40g	116	289	9.3	59.0	1.2	0.0
Sausage, Asda*	¼ Pack/25g	80	321	6.0	65.0	4.1	5.0
Sausage, Colman's*	1 Serving/40g	122	304	8.1	65.7	1.0	5.4
CAULIFLOWER,							
& Broccoli Florets, Asda*	1 Serving/100g	26	26	2.7	2.1	0.7	2.4
& Broccoli Florets, Morrisons*	1 Serving/60g	16	26	2.7	2.3	0.7	0.0
& Broccoli Florets, Sainsbury's*	1 Serving/180g	47	26	3.0	1.6	0.8	2.0
& Broccoli Florets, Tesco*	1oz/28g	9	33	4.0	2.3	0.9	2.2
Boiled In Salted Water	1oz/28g	8	28	2.9	2.1	0.9	1.6
Boiled In Unsalted Water	1oz/28g	8	28	2.9	2.1	0.9	1.6
Florets, In Cheese Sauce, Tesco*	1 Pack/500g	345	69	5.9	4.8	2.9	1.9
Peas & Carrots, Bird's Eye*	1oz/28g	9	32	2.2	4.8	0.4	2.6
Peas & Carrots, Organic, Iceland*	1oz/28g	10	37	2.8	5.5	0.6	2.9
Raw, Asda*	1 Serving/50g	14	28	2.9	2.1	0.9	1.6
Raw, Fresh	1oz/28g	10	34	3.6	3.0	0.9	1.8
CAULIFLOWER CHEESE,							
Asda*	1 Pack/396g	352	89	3.9	4.9	6.0	0.8
Better For You, Morrisons*	1 Pack/300g	231	77	4.5	5.4	4.1	1.2
BGTY, Sainsbury's*	1 Pack/452g	208	46	4.9	3.5	1.4	1.3
Bird's Eye*	1 Pack/329g	354	108	4.8	7.7	6.4	0.8
COU, M & S*	1 Pack/300g	195	65	5.3	5.7	2.2	1.3
Eat Smart, Safeway*	1 Pack/300g	165	55	4.5	4.0	2.1	1.0
Half Fat Cheese, HE, Tesco*	1 Pack/400g	164	41	3.8	3.0	1.5	1.9
HE, Tesco*	1 Pack/500g	345	69	5.9	4.8	2.9	1.9
Made With Semi-Skimmed Milk	1oz/28g	28	100	6.0	5.2	6.4	1.3
Made With Skimmed Milk	1oz/28g	27	97	6.0	5.2	6.0	1.3
Made With Whole Milk	1oz/28g	29	105	6.0	5.2	6.9	1.3
M & S*	1 Pack/200g	290	145	5.4	9.6	9.6	1.2
Ready Meal, Tesco*	1 Pack/300g	264	88	4.2	5.2	5.6	1.2
Ross*	1 Pack/300g	300	100	4.9	5.5	6.6	0.1
Vegetarian, Safeway*	1 Serving/150g	138	92	4.7	5.2	5.8	1.4
CAVIARE, Bottled In Brine, Drained	1oz/28g	26	92	10.9	0.0	5.4	0.0
CELERIAC,							
Boiled In Salted Water	1oz/28g	4	15	0.9	1.9	0.5	3.2
Raw	1oz/28g	5	18	1.2	2.3	0.4	3.7
CELERY,							
Boiled In Salted Water	1 Med Serving/50g	4	8	0.5	0.8	0.3	1.2
Hearts, Tesco*	½ Can/133g	12	9	0.9	1.1	0.1	2.3
Raw	1 Med Stalk/40g	3	7	0.5	0.9	0.2	1.1
CHAMPAGNE	1 Glass/120ml	89	76	0.3	1.4	0.0	0.0
CHAPATTIS,							
Made With Fat	1 Chapati/60g	197	328	8.1	48.3	12.8	0.0
Made Without Fat	1 Chapati/55g	111	202	7.3	43.7	1.0	0.0
Morrisons*	1 Chappatti/40g	105	269	8.6	49.8	6.9	0.0
Patak's*	1 Chapatti/42g	121	287	7.5	53.1	6.4	3.2

C

CHARD,	Measure WEIGHT/INFO	per Measure KCAL	KCAL	PROT	CARB	FAT	FIBRE
Swiss, Boiled In Unsalted Water	1oz/28g	6	20	1.9	3.2	0.1	0.0
Swiss, Raw	1oz/28g	5	19	1.8	2.9	0.2	0.0
CHEDDARIE Light, Kraft*	1 Serving/25g	61	245	17.0	10.0	15.0	0.0
CHEDDARS,							
Cheese & Ham, Mini, McVitie's*	1 Bag/30g	160	534	11.0	55.5	29.8	2.0
Mini, McVitie's*	1 Bag/30g	155	535	11.0	54.4	30.3	2.0
Tangy Salsa, Mini, McVitie's*	1 Bag/50g	266	532	11.0	54.7	29.9	2.1
CHEESE, (SEE ALSO COTTAGE CHEESE)							
15% Fat, Sainsbury's*	1 Serving/100g	261	261	31.5	0.1	15.0	0.0
Applewood, Somerfield*	1oz/28g	119	426	28.0	0.0	35.0	0.0
Asiago, M & S*	1oz/28g	105	375	33.0	0.1	27.0	0.0
Babybel, Fromageries Bel*	1 Cheese/20g	62	308	23.0	0.0	24.0	0.0
Babybel, Light, Mini, Fromageries Bel*	1 Mini Cheese/20g	43	214	26.5	0.0	12.0	0.0
Bavarian Smoked, Processed, Somefield*	1oz/28g	85	302	29.0	0.0	21.0	0.0
Blue Shropshire, Somerfield*	1oz/28g	115	409	22.0	0.0	36.0	0.0
Blue Stilton, Budgens*	1oz/28g	115	410	22.7	0.0	35.5	0.0
Blue Vinney, BGTY, Sainsbury's*	1oz/28g	90	320	30.4	0.1	22.0	0.0
Boursin, Light, Boursin*	1oz/28g	43	153	12.5	4.5	9.5	0.0
Bresse Bleu, M & S*	1oz/28g	99	355	19.0	0.3	31.0	0.0
Brie	1oz/28g	89	319	19.3	0.0	26.9	0.0
Brie, Continental, HE, Tesco*	1 Serving/50g	85	170	20.0	0.0	10.0	0.0
Brie, Cornish, Organic, Waitrose*	1oz/28g	74	265	16.8	0.1	22.0	0.0
Brie, French Creamy, Budgens*	1oz/28g	102	364	19.0	0.1	32.0	0.0
Brie, Half Fat, M & S*	1 Serving/100g	207	207	23.5	1.3	12.0	0.0
Brie, Organic, M & S*	1oz/28g	87	310	19.0	0.1	26.0	0.0
Brie, Somerset, Tesco*	1 Serving/40g	122	306	22.0	0.5	24.0	0.0
Caerphilly	1oz/28g	105	375	23.2	0.1	31.3	0.0
Cambozola Blue Brie, Somerfield*	1oz/28g	122	434	14.0	1.0	42.0	0.0
Camembert	1oz/28g	83	297	20.9	0.0	23.7	0.0
Camembert In Crispy Crumb, Kitchen Range Foods*	1oz/28g	98	349	13.3	14.5	26.5	0.0
Chaumes, M & S*	1oz/28g	85	305	20.2	1.0	26.0	0.0
Cheddar, 3% Fat, M & S*	1oz/28g	48	172	36.2	0.1	2.8	0.0
Cheddar, Average	1oz/28g	115	412	25.5	0.1	34.4	0.0
Cheddar, Canadian, Somerfield*	1oz/28g	114	406	25.0	0.0	34.0	0.0
Cheddar, Canadian, Waitrose*	1 Serving/25g	103	410	25.0	0.1	34.4	0.0
Cheddar, Cathedral City, Dairy Crest Ltd*	1oz/28g	115	410	25.0	0.1	34.4	0.0
Cheddar, Davidstow Extra Mature, Sainsbury's*	1 Serving/100g	410	410	25.0	0.1	34.4	0.0
Cheddar, Davidstow Mature, M & S*	1 Slice/10g	41	410	25.0	0.1	34.4	0.0
Cheddar, English, Extra Mature, Asda*	1oz/28g	114	406	25.0	0.1	34.0	0.0
Cheddar, English Mature, Co-Op*	1 Serving/30g	123	410	25.0	0.1	34.4	0.0
Cheddar, English Mature, Somerfield*	1 Serving/30g	123	410	25.0	0.1	34.4	0.0
Cheddar, English Mature, Tesco*	1oz/28g	115	410	25.0	0.1	34.4	0.0
Cheddar, Extra Mature, Horlicks Farms*	1oz/28g	115	412	25.5	0.1	34.4	0.0
Cheddar, Extra Mature Vintage, M & S*	1oz/28g	115	410	25.0	0.1	34.4	0.0
Cheddar, Full Flavour, Value, Tesco*	1 Serving/30g	123	410	25.0	0.1	34.4	0.0
Cheddar, Grated Mild, Safeway*	1 Serving/50g	205	410	25.0	0.1	34.4	0.0
Cheddar, Half Fat, Tesco*	1oz/28g	73	259	30.9	0.1	15.0	0.0
Cheddar, Irish Mature, Tesco*	1 Serving/100g	410	410	25.0	0.1	34.4	0.0
Cheddar, Mature, 16% Fat, BGTY, Sainsbury's*	1 Serving/100g	260	260	29.3	0.1	15.8	0.0
Cheddar, Mature English, Sainsbury's*	1 Slice/20g	82	410	25.0	0.1	34.4	0.0
Cheddar, Mature, GFY, Asda*	1 Serving/28g	73	259	31.0	0.0	15.0	0.0
Cheddar, Mature Grated, Tesco*	1 Serving/50g	207	413	24.4	1.4	34.4	0.0
Cheddar, Mature, Half Fat, Iceland*	1oz/28g	73	260	29.3	0.1	15.8	0.0
Cheddar, Mature, Half Fat, Waitrose*	1 Serving/40g	105	262	29.1	0.1	16.0	0.0

Nutrition Values per 100g / 100ml (KCAL, PROT, CARB, FAT, FIBRE)

C

CHEESE,	Measure WEIGHT/INFO	per Measure KCAL	Nutrition Values per 100g / 100ml KCAL	PROT	CARB	FAT	FIBRE
Cheddar, Mature Reduced Fat, M & S*	1oz/28g	91	325	29.4	0.1	23.0	0.0
Cheddar, Mature, Sainsbury's*	1 Serving/50g	205	410	25.0	0.1	34.4	0.0
Cheddar, Mature Style, Half Fat, M & S*	1oz/28g	78	277	31.0	0.1	17.0	0.0
Cheddar, Mature, Tesco*	1 Serving/25g	103	410	25.0	0.1	34.4	0.0
Cheddar, Mature White, Morrisons*	1 Serving/28g	115	410	25.0	0.1	34.4	0.0
Cheddar, Mature White, Westacre, Aldi*	1oz/28g	115	410	25.0	0.1	34.4	0.0
Cheddar, Medium, Half Fat, M & S*	1oz/28g	92	327	30.0	0.1	23.0	0.0
Cheddar, Mediumr, Organic, Somerfield*	1oz/28g	114	406	25.0	0.0	34.0	0.0
Cheddar, Mild, Netto*	1 Serving/90g	369	410	25.0	0.1	34.4	0.0
Cheddar, Mild, Organic, Somerfield*	1oz/28g	114	406	25.0	0.0	34.0	0.0
Cheddar, Mild, Sainsbury's*	1 Serving/50g	205	410	25.0	0.1	34.4	0.0
Cheddar, Oak Smoked, M & S*	1oz/28g	115	410	25.0	0.1	34.4	0.0
Cheddar, Scottish Extra Mature, Sainsbury's*	1 Serving/100g	410	410	25.0	0.1	34.4	0.0
Cheddar, Scottish Medium, M & S*	1oz/28g	115	410	25.0	0.1	34.4	0.0
Cheddar, Slow Matured, Anchor*	1oz/28g	120	429	24.0	0.0	37.0	0.0
Cheddar, Smoked, M & S*	1oz/28g	115	412	25.5	0.1	34.4	0.0
Cheddar, Tesco*	1oz/28g	115	410	25.0	0.1	34.4	0.0
Cheddar Type, Reduced Fat	1 Sm Serving/20g	52	261	31.5	0.0	15.0	0.0
Cheddar, Vegetarian	1oz/28g	119	425	25.8	0.0	35.7	0.0
Cheddar, Vintage Davidstow, Safeway*	1oz/28g	115	410	25.0	0.1	34.4	0.0
Cheddar, Vintage Truckle, M & S*	1oz/28g	115	410	25.0	0.1	34.4	0.0
Cheddar, Welsh Extra Mature, Tesco*	1 Serving/25g	103	410	25.0	0.1	34.4	0.0
Cheddar, West Country, TTD, Sainsbury's*	1 Serving/28g	115	410	25.0	0.1	34.4	0.0
Cheddar, Wickedly Extra Mature, M & S*	1oz/28g	115	410	25.0	0.1	34.4	0.0
Cheshire	1oz/28g	106	379	24.0	0.1	31.4	0.0
Chevre Du Berry, M & S*	1oz/28g	55	195	11.8	3.1	15.0	0.0
Coloured, Low Fat, Weight Watchers*	1oz/28g	51	182	34.2	0.1	5.0	0.0
Cotswold, Full Fat With Herbs, Somerfield*	1oz/28g	113	405	25.0	0.0	34.0	0.0
Cream, Average	1 Portion/30g	132	439	3.1	0.0	47.4	0.0
Cream, 95% Fat Free, M & S*	1oz/28g	31	111	13.0	4.2	4.5	0.0
Cream, Extra Light, Tesco*	1oz/28g	36	128	15.0	3.5	6.0	0.0
Cream, Light, Benecol*	1 Serving/34g	58	170	7.8	3.3	14.0	0.7
Cream, Low Fat, BGTY, Sainsbury's*	1oz/28g	31	111	11.0	4.3	5.5	0.4
Cream With Onion & Chives, Morrisons*	1 Serving/20g	38	190	11.0	3.0	15.0	0.0
Creamery Soft With Onion & Chives, BGTY, Sainsbury's*	1 Serving/20g	23	115	13.5	4.0	5.0	1.0
Creamy Chaumes, M & S*	1oz/28g	80	287	17.6	1.0	23.6	0.0
Danish Blue	1oz/28g	97	347	20.1	0.0	29.6	0.0
Dolcelatte, M & S*	1oz/28g	89	317	19.2	0.1	26.0	0.0
Dolcelatte, Tesco*	1oz/28g	108	385	17.3	0.2	35.0	1.1
Double Glouceste, Soft & Chives, M & S*	1oz/28g	100	358	20.0	9.2	26.8	0.0
Double Gloucester	1oz/28g	113	405	24.6	0.1	34.0	0.0
Double Gloucester, Organic, M & S*	1oz/28g	113	404	24.4	0.1	34.0	0.0
Dubliner, Kerrygold*	1oz/28g	110	392	26.0	0.1	32.0	0.0
Edam	1oz/28g	93	333	26.0	0.0	25.4	0.0
Edam Hard, Medium Fat, HE, Tesco*	1 Serving/100g	229	229	32.6	0.1	10.9	0.0
Edam Type, Reduced Fat	1oz/28g	64	229	32.6	0.0	10.9	0.0
Emmental	1oz/28g	107	382	28.7	0.0	29.7	0.0
Extra Light, Low Fat, Morrisons*	¼ Pack/25g	33	130	15.0	3.5	6.0	0.0
Extra Light Soft & Creamy With Garlic & Herbs, Asda*	1oz/28g	36	130	13.0	6.0	6.0	0.0
Extra Light Soft With Garlic & Herb, HE, Tesco*	1 Serving/50g	63	126	13.5	5.6	5.5	0.0
Extra Mature, Reduced Fat, Tesco*	1 Serving/70g	207	295	26.4	0.1	21.0	0.0
Farmhouse, 16% Fat, Sainsbury's*	1oz/28g	73	260	29.3	0.1	15.8	0.0
Farmhouse Mature, HE, Tesco*	1 Serving/50g	131	261	31.5	0.0	15.0	0.0
Feta	1oz/28g	70	250	15.6	1.5	20.2	0.0

CHEESE,	Measure WEIGHT/INFO	per Measure KCAL	KCAL	PROT	CARB	FAT	FIBRE
			Nutrition Values per 100g / 100ml				
French Camembert, Sainsbury's*	1 Serving/30g	84	279	20.0	0.2	22.0	0.0
French Goat, Fresh, Finest, Tesco*	1 Serving/40g	66	166	11.5	2.8	12.1	0.0
Full Flavour, Economy, Sainsbury's*	1oz/28g	115	410	25.0	0.1	34.4	0.0
Garlic & Herb, Soft & Creamy, Extra Light, Asda*	¼ Pack/50g	65	130	13.0	6.0	6.0	0.0
Garlic & Herb, Soft, M & S*	1oz/28g	58	206	8.5	2.7	18.0	0.0
Garlic Roule With Herbs, Somerfield*	1oz/28g	92	329	10.0	3.0	31.0	0.0
Goat Camembert, M & S*	1oz/28g	85	304	20.0	2.0	24.0	0.0
Goats, Disc, M & S*	1 Pack/100g	296	296	15.4	2.9	24.3	0.0
Goats Milk, Soft	1oz/28g	55	198	13.1	1.0	15.8	0.0
Goats, Organic, M & S*	1oz/28g	77	275	14.9	2.5	22.8	0.1
Goats, Sainsbury's*	1oz/28g	79	283	15.0	4.0	23.0	0.0
Goats With Roasted Vegetables, Somerfield*	1oz/28g	55	196	8.0	26.0	7.0	0.0
Gorgonzola, Creamy, M & S*	1oz/28g	92	330	19.0	0.1	26.0	0.0
Gorgonzola, Somerfield*	1oz/28g	95	338	21.0	0.0	28.0	0.0
Gouda	1oz/28g	105	375	24.0	0.0	31.0	0.0
Grated, BGTY, Sainsbury's*	1 Serving/50g	132	264	31.0	0.6	15.0	0.0
Grated, GFY, Asda*	1 Serving/10g	22	220	31.0	1.5	10.0	0.0
Grated Italian, Sainsbury's*	1 Serving/30g	146	485	44.1	0.3	34.2	0.0
Grated Pizza, Safeway*	1 Serving/50g	163	325	25.0	0.6	24.8	0.0
Gruyere	1oz/28g	115	409	27.2	0.0	33.3	0.0
Half Fat, BGTY, Sainsbury's*	1 Serving/30g	80	268	34.5	1.4	14.0	0.0
Hard Coloured, Medium Fat, Tesco*	1 Serving/100g	259	259	30.9	0.1	15.0	0.0
Herbs & Garlic, Creamery Light Soft, Sainsbury's*	1 Serving/30g	54	180	7.2	3.4	15.5	0.3
Italian Ricotta, M & S*	1oz/28g	42	149	10.5	2.0	11.0	0.0
Jarlsberg, M & S*	1oz/28g	98	351	27.0	0.1	27.0	0.0
Lancashire	1oz/28g	104	373	23.3	0.1	31.0	0.0
Leerdammer* Wedge	1 Wedge/250g	933	373	28.3	0.0	28.6	0.0
Leicester	1oz/28g	112	401	24.3	0.1	33.7	0.0
Mascarpone, M & S*	1oz/28g	133	474	5.2	4.1	46.6	0.0
Mature, 95% Fat Free, Weight Watchers*	1 Serving/50g	91	182	34.2	0.1	5.0	0.0
Mature, BGTY, Sainsbury's*	1oz/28g	73	260	29.3	0.1	15.8	0.0
Mature, HE, Tesco*	1oz/28g	73	259	30.9	0.1	15.0	0.0
Mature, Living, Shape*	1oz/28g	87	309	30.0	0.1	21.0	0.0
Mature, Low Fat, Weight Watchers*	1 Serving/40g	75	188	36.1	5.8	2.3	0.0
Mature Stilton, M & S*	1oz/28g	115	411	22.7	0.1	35.5	0.0
Medium Fat Soft, Smooth & Cream Light, Morrisons*	1/8 Pack/25g	50	200	12.0	3.0	15.0	0.0
Mild Coloured, HE, Tesco*	1 Serving/30g	78	259	30.9	0.1	15.0	0.0
Mild, Low Fat, Weight Watchers*	1/5 Pack/40g	73	182	34.2	0.1	5.0	0.0
Mozzarella	1oz/28g	81	289	25.1	0.0	21.0	0.0
Mozzarella For Pizza, Tesco*	¼ Pack/50g	151	301	25.5	1.4	21.5	0.0
Mozzarella, Grated Italian, Sainsbury's*	1 Serving/25g	74	294	24.5	0.6	21.5	0.1
Mozzarella, Italian, Asda*	1 Serving/45g	132	293	20.0	1.5	23.0	0.0
Mozzarella, Italian, Tesco*	1 Serving/50g	134	268	18.0	2.0	20.0	0.0
Mozzarella, Light, BGTY, Sainsbury's*	1oz/28g	48	172	19.0	1.5	10.0	0.0
Mozzarella, Light, Galbani*	1 Serving/50g	95	190	21.2	1.2	11.0	0.0
Mozzarella, Santa Lucia, Galbani*	1 Pack/125g	323	258	18.0	1.5	20.0	0.0
Onion & Chive, Low Fat, Soft, BGTY, Sainsbury's*	1 Serving/30g	35	115	13.5	4.0	5.0	1.0
Parmesan	1oz/28g	127	452	39.4	0.0	32.7	0.0
Parmesan, Continental Fresh, Grated, Tesco*	1 Tbsp/6g	25	415	34.0	0.1	31.0	0.0
Parmesan, Freshly Grated, Parmigiano Reggiano*	1 Serving/10g	39	388	33.0	0.1	28.4	0.1
Parmesan, Grated, Sainsbury's*	1 Serving/30g	146	485	44.1	0.3	34.2	0.0
Parmesan, Organic, M & S*	1oz/28g	110	392	33.0	0.1	28.4	0.0
Parmesan Shavings, Asda*	1 Serving/25g	97	388	33.0	0.0	28.4	0.0
Pastrami Flavour, Sandwich, Swiss Processed, Gerber*	2 Slices/25g	87	348	24.0	0.0	28.0	0.0

C

CHEESE,	Measure WEIGHT/INFO	per Measure KCAL	Nutrition Values per 100g / 100ml KCAL	PROT	CARB	FAT	FIBRE
Patros Feta, Somerfield*	1oz/28g	75	267	19.0	1.0	21.0	0.0
Poivre, Boursin*	1oz/28g	116	414	7.0	2.0	42.0	0.0
Port Salut, M & S*	1oz/28g	90	322	21.0	1.0	26.0	0.0
Processed, Plain	1oz/28g	92	330	20.8	0.9	27.0	0.0
Processed, Smoked	1oz/28g	85	303	20.5	0.2	24.5	0.0
Red Leicester, BGTY, Sainsbury's*	1 Serving/50g	130	259	31.0	0.1	15.0	0.0
Red Leicester, Economy, Sainsbury's*	1oz/28g	112	399	23.8	0.1	33.7	0.0
Red Leicester, Half Fat, Morrisons*	1oz/28g	74	264	31.0	0.0	15.0	0.0
Red Leicester, HE, Tesco*	1oz/28g	73	262	29.1	0.1	16.1	0.0
Red Leicester, M & S*	1oz/28g	112	399	23.0	0.1	33.7	0.0
Red Leicester, Organic, M & S*	1oz/28g	112	399	23.8	0.1	33.7	0.0
Red Leicester, Tesco*	1oz/28g	112	399	23.8	0.1	33.7	0.0
Ricotta	1oz/28g	40	144	9.4	2.0	11.0	0.0
Roquefort	1oz/28g	105	375	19.7	0.0	32.9	0.0
Roule, French, Sainsbury's*	1 Serving/30g	96	321	8.5	3.0	30.5	0.0
Sage Derby	1oz/28g	113	402	24.2	0.1	33.9	0.0
Shaved Pamesan, Fresh, M & S*	1 Serving/10g	39	392	33.0	0.1	28.4	0.0
Shredded Monterey Jack, Kraft*	¼ Cup/28g	101	360	22.0	3.6	28.8	0.0
Shropshire Blue, Sainsbury's*	1 Serving/100g	373	373	20.1	0.1	32.5	0.0
Soft & Creamy, Light, Asda*	1 Serving/65g	127	195	12.0	3.0	15.0	0.0
Soft Cream, Lite, Somerfield*	1 Serving/20g	39	195	12.0	3.0	15.0	0.0
Soft, Extra Light, Co-Op*	1oz/28g	36	128	15.0	3.5	6.0	0.0
Soft, Extra Light, Healthy Choice, Safeway*	1/8 Pack/25g	32	126	15.0	3.0	6.0	0.0
Soft, Extra Light, Low Fat, BGTY, Sainsbury's*	1oz/28g	31	111	11.0	4.3	5.5	0.4
Soft, Extra Light, Morrisons*	1 Serving/20g	26	130	15.0	3.5	6.0	0.0
Soft, Extra Light, Tesco*	1oz/28g	36	128	15.0	3.5	6.0	0.0
Soft, Full Fat	1oz/28g	88	313	8.6	0.0	31.0	0.0
Soft, Less Than 5% Fat, M & S*	1oz/28g	31	111	13.0	4.2	4.5	0.3
Soft, Light, Co-Op*	1 Serving/50g	98	195	12.0	3.0	15.0	0.0
Soft, Light, Tesco*	1oz/28g	55	195	12.0	3.0	15.0	0.0
Soft, Light, Waitrose*	1 Serving/30g	37	122	14.1	3.0	6.0	0.0
Soft, Low Fat, Asda*	1oz/28g	27	96	6.8	5.7	5.1	0.1
Soft, Low Fat, Waitrose*	1oz/28g	36	128	15.0	3.5	6.0	0.0
Soft, Medium Fat	1oz/28g	50	179	9.2	3.1	14.5	0.0
Soft, Reduced Fat, M & S*	1oz/28g	53	190	8.0	3.0	16.0	0.0
Soft With Onion & Chives, Extra Light, Tesco*	1 Serving/30g	36	121	12.9	5.0	5.5	0.0
Somerset Goats, Waitrose*	1oz/28g	95	340	20.6	0.0	28.6	0.0
Soya	1oz/28g	89	319	18.3	0.0	27.3	0.0
Stilton, Blue	1oz/28g	115	411	22.7	0.1	35.5	0.0
Stilton, White	1oz/28g	101	362	19.9	0.1	31.3	0.0
Swiss Fondue, Sainsbury's*	1oz/28g	66	235	14.0	2.5	16.0	0.0
Welsh Goats, Sainsbury's*	1 Serving/30g	85	283	15.0	4.0	23.0	0.0
Wensleydale	1oz/28g	106	377	23.3	0.1	31.5	0.0
Wensleydale With Cranberries, Co-Op*	1 Serving/25g	91	365	18.0	12.0	27.0	3.0
White, Grated, 14% Fat, Somerfield*	1oz/28g	71	253	30.0	1.0	14.0	0.0
White, Mild, Arla*	1 Serving/20g	42	209	22.0	1.0	13.0	0.0
White Stilton & Apricot, M & S*	1oz/28g	94	337	13.8	18.5	23.1	0.0
White Stilton & Cranberry, M & S*	1oz/28g	101	362	18.2	15.5	25.3	0.0
White Stilton With Apricot, Somerfield*	1oz/28g	103	369	16.0	8.0	30.0	0.0
CHEESE ON TOAST	1oz/28g	106	380	13.8	23.8	26.3	0.7
CHEESE PUFFS,							
Farmfoods*	1 Bag/18g	96	532	7.0	54.3	31.9	1.0
Sainsbury's*	1 Pack/100g	530	530	9.1	51.4	32.0	1.9
Shapers, Boots*	1 Bag/16g	84	523	6.4	59.0	29.0	1.6

CHEESE PUFFS,	Measure WEIGHT/INFO	per Measure KCAL	KCAL	PROT	CARB	FAT	FIBRE
SmartPrice, Asda*	1 Bag/18g	92	512	7.0	58.0	28.0	1.3
Value, Tesco*	1 Bag/18g	90	498	7.7	54.1	27.9	1.7
CHEESE SINGLES,							
50% Less Fat, Asda*	1 Slice/20g	38	190	19.0	6.0	10.0	0.0
American, 2% Milk, Kraft*	1 Slice/19g	45	237	21.0	5.3	15.8	0.0
Light, Kraft*	1 Serving/20g	41	205	20.0	6.0	11.0	0.0
Light, Safeway*	1 Slice/20g	38	192	21.2	4.2	10.0	0.0
CHEESE SLICES,							
97% Fat Free, Kraft*	1 Slice/20g	31	155	23.3	9.9	2.3	0.0
Bavarian Smoked, Asda*	1 Slice/18g	50	277	17.0	0.4	23.0	0.0
Better For You, Morrisons*	1 Slice/20g	39	196	21.0	5.4	10.0	0.0
Cheddar, Mature, M & S*	1 Slice/30g	124	412	25.5	0.1	34.4	0.0
Cheddar, Mild, M & S*	1 Slice/30g	124	412	25.5	0.1	34.4	0.0
Cheddar, Reduced Fat, Weight Watchers*	1 Slice/21g	50	239	21.9	5.0	14.7	0.0
Cheese Food, Asda*	1 Slice/20g	58	289	18.0	7.0	21.0	0.0
Cheese Food, Sainsbury's*	1 Slice/20g	52	260	14.5	5.4	20.0	0.0
Dairylea*	1 Slice/25g	76	305	13.0	8.0	24.5	0.0
Farmfoods*	1 Slice/17g	49	286	18.0	4.0	22.0	0.0
Half Fat, Asda*	1 Slice/20g	39	194	20.6	5.4	10.0	0.0
Half Fat, M & S*	1 Slice/30g	83	277	31.0	0.1	17.0	0.0
Jarlsberg*	1slice/15g	54	360	27.0	0.0	27.0	0.0
Kraft*	1 Slice/20g	56	280	13.5	6.6	21.5	0.0
Leerdammer*	1 Slice/28g	101	360	27.1	0.0	27.7	0.0
Light, Dairylea*	1 Slice/25g	55	220	18.5	7.0	12.5	0.0
Light, Kraft*	1 Slice/20g	41	205	20.0	6.0	11.0	0.0
Light, Laughing Cow*	1 Slice/20g	41	203	21.0	6.0	10.5	0.0
Light, Thick, Dairylea*	1 Slice/25g	51	205	17.3	8.6	10.5	0.0
Mature, Asda*	1 Slice/20g	52	259	31.0	0.1	15.0	0.0
Mature, BGTY, Sainsbury's*	1 Slice/24g	63	261	31.5	0.1	15.0	0.0
Mature Cheddar, Tesco*	1 Slice/30g	123	410	25.0	0.1	34.4	0.0
Single, Lite, Somerfield*	1 Slice/20g	42	212	20.0	6.0	12.0	0.0
Singles, Half Fat Tesco*	1 Serving/20g	39	194	21.7	4.2	10.0	0.0
Somerfield*	1 oz/28g	84	300	19.0	2.0	24.0	0.0
Swiss, Leerdammer*	1 slice/25g	90	360	27.1	0.0	27.7	0.0
Thick, Dairylea*	1 Slice/50g	140	280	13.0	7.5	22.0	0.0
CHEESE SPREAD,							
60% Less Fat, Asda*	1 Serving/30g	52	174	16.0	7.3	9.0	0.0
BGTY, Sainsbury's*	1 Serving/25g	28	111	11.0	4.3	5.5	0.4
BPC, Sainsbury's*	1 Serving/30g	84	280	15.5	5.0	22.0	0.0
Chilli, Primula*	1oz/28g	60	216	16.2	5.3	14.4	0.0
Chunky Triangles, BGTY, Sainsbury's*	1 Triangle/25g	43	171	14.8	10.0	8.0	0.0
Cream, Light, Sainsbury's*	1 Serving/50g	94	187	7.8	4.1	15.5	0.3
Creamery, Light, Sainsbury's*	1 Serving/25g	46	185	9.0	3.5	15.0	0.0
Dairylea*	1oz/28g	71	255	7.6	8.0	21.5	0.0
Flavoured	1oz/28g	72	258	14.2	4.4	20.5	0.0
Garlic & Herbs, Light, Benecol*	1 Serving/20g	35	174	7.8	4.2	14.0	0.7
Kerrygold*	1oz/28g	60	213	11.0	8.5	15.0	0.0
Light, Laughing Cow*	1 Triangle/18g	25	141	13.5	6.5	7.0	0.0
Light, Primula*	1oz/28g	48	171	16.0	6.6	9.0	0.0
Light, Triangles, Dairylea*	1oz/28g	52	185	14.5	7.6	11.0	0.0
Light, Tub, Dairylea*	1oz/28g	52	186	14.0	7.3	11.0	0.0
Low Fat, Weight Watchers*	1 Serving/50g	56	112	18.1	3.4	2.9	1.2
Mediterranean Soft & Creamy, Extra Light, Asda*	1 Serving/32g	42	130	13.0	6.0	6.0	0.0
Original, Primula*	1oz/28g	72	257	16.0	1.0	21.0	0.0

Nutrition Values per 100g / 100ml

	Measure WEIGHT/INFO	per Measure KCAL	Nutrition Values per 100g / 100ml KCAL	PROT	CARB	FAT	FIBRE
CHEESE SPREAD,							
Soft, Low Fat, M & S*	1 Pack/100g	111	111	13.0	4.2	4.5	0.3
Triangles, Chunky, Dairylea*	1 Triangle/14g	32	225	9.9	7.3	17.5	0.0
With Chives, Primula*	1oz/28g	71	253	15.0	1.0	21.0	0.0
With Ham, Primula*	1oz/28g	71	253	15.0	1.0	21.0	0.0
With Shrimp, Primula*	1 Tbsp/15g	38	253	15.0	1.0	21.0	0.0
CHEESE STRAWS,							
Cheddar, M & S*	1 Straw/11g	59	535	14.9	40.1	34.9	2.4
Selection, Sainsbury's*	1 Straw/7g	41	558	16.6	34.5	39.3	2.8
CHEESE STRIPS, Dairylea*	1 Pack/21g	72	345	23.5	0.4	27.0	0.0
CHEESE TRIANGLES,							
Big Portions, Laughing Cow*	1 Triangle/18g	48	269	10.0	6.5	22.5	0.0
Chunky, Light, Dairylea*	1 Triangle/23g	37	161	13.5	6.9	8.7	0.0
Half Fat, Safeway*	1oz/28g	52	184	16.0	8.5	9.5	0.0
HE, Tesco*	1oz/28g	52	187	16.8	6.4	10.5	0.0
Light, Dairylea*	1 Triangle/23g	43	185	14.5	7.6	11.0	0.0
Light, Laughing Cow*	1oz/28g	40	143	13.0	7.0	7.0	0.0
CHEESECAKE,							
Cheesecake, Average	1oz/28g	119	426	3.7	24.6	35.5	0.4
Blackcurrant Devonshire, McVitie's*	1/6 Cake/67g	190	288	3.8	29.7	17.1	1.7
Blackcurrant, M & S*	1oz/28g	82	293	3.3	29.4	17.9	0.9
Blackcurrant, Sainsbury's*	1oz/28g	75	267	3.2	29.5	15.1	1.1
Blackcurrant Swirl, Heinz*	1/5 Portion/87g	241	277	4.1	30.3	15.4	3.6
Blackcurrant, Value, Tesco*	1 Serving/70g	174	248	2.8	31.4	12.3	1.0
Blueberry & Lemon Flavour Wedges, Sainsbury's*	1 Serving/80g	262	327	5.1	29.2	21.1	1.2
Caramel Swirl, Cadbury's*	1 Slice/91g	373	410	6.0	40.1	25.8	0.0
Cherry, BGTY, Sainsbury's*	1 Serving/91g	181	199	4.6	35.5	4.3	0.5
Cherry, Low Fat, Tesco*	1 Serving/91g	185	203	3.4	38.0	4.1	0.9
Chocolate, Baked, Ultimate, Entenmann's*	1 Cake/100g	331	331	5.7	34.2	19.0	2.8
Chocolate Chip, M & S*	1oz/28g	109	391	5.1	39.7	23.6	0.2
Chocolate, Farmfoods*	1 Cake/68g	230	338	7.2	35.7	18.5	1.2
Chocolate, M & S*	1oz/28g	106	380	6.5	40.3	21.5	0.4
Chocolate, Weight Watchers*	1 Cake/95g	143	151	7.5	20.7	4.0	0.7
Double Chocolate Wedge, Sainsbury's*	1 Portion/75g	327	436	5.7	29.0	33.0	1.7
Homestyle Chocolate, M & S*	1oz/28g	105	376	6.0	38.0	22.2	0.7
Irish Cream, McVitie's*	¼ Slice/190g	616	324	4.4	33.0	19.4	0.4
Lemon, BGTY, Sainsbury's*	1/6 Cake/71g	142	200	4.4	37.0	3.8	0.5
Lemon, M & S*	1oz/28g	92	330	5.7	38.7	17.1	0.2
Mandarin, Co-Op*	1 Slice/99g	297	300	4.0	32.0	17.0	0.3
Mandarin, GFY, Asda*	1 Serving/97g	194	200	4.0	36.0	4.4	0.8
Mandarin, Healthy Choice, Safeway*	1 Serving/92g	189	205	3.8	37.1	4.6	0.4
Praline, Asda*	1/8 Cake/62g	226	364	7.0	30.0	24.0	3.2
Raspberry Ripple, M & S*	1oz/28g	84	300	5.9	32.8	15.6	0.3
Raspberry Swirl, Heinz*	1 Serving/100g	266	266	3.9	30.1	14.5	2.8
Rhubarb Crumble, Sainsbury's*	1 Serving/114g	268	235	3.1	34.8	9.3	2.4
Sticky Toffee, Tesco*	1 Slice/66g	248	375	4.0	35.3	24.2	0.5
Strawberry, 95% Fat Free, M & S*	1 Slice/98g	187	191	5.1	33.8	4.0	0.3
Strawberry, Individual, Weight Watchers*	1 Cake/103g	199	193	5.5	33.9	3.2	1.8
Strawberry, Sainsbury's*	1 Serving/90g	221	246	3.5	24.4	14.9	4.6
Strawberry, Tesco*	1 Serving/100g	254	254	3.9	32.5	12.0	0.0
Toffee & Banana, M & S*	1oz/28g	88	315	5.0	35.7	16.7	0.2
Toffee, Asda*	1 Cake/87g	295	339	4.3	31.0	22.0	3.5
Toffee, Co-Op*	1oz/28g	74	265	5.0	35.0	11.0	1.0
Toffee, M & S*	1 Serving/105g	357	340	5.2	37.2	21.5	0.9
Triple Chocolate, Waitrose*	1/6 Cake/76g	262	349	5.4	38.3	19.3	1.2

	Measure WEIGHT/INFO	per Measure KCAL	Nutrition Values per 100g / 100ml KCAL	PROT	CARB	FAT	FIBRE
CHEESECAKE,							
Ultimate Vanilla New York Baked, Entenmann's*	1 Cake/100g	327	327	4.1	34.2	19.3	1.7
Vanilla, Tesco*	1 Serving/115g	417	363	5.7	29.4	24.7	0.6
CHEETOS, Cheese, Walkers*	1 Bag/24g	120	500	6.5	61.0	26.0	1.3
CHERRIES,							
Fresh, Raw, Weighed With Stones	1oz/28g	11	39	0.7	9.5	0.1	0.7
Fresh, Raw, Weighed Without Stones	1oz/28g	13	48	0.9	11.5	0.1	0.9
Glace	1oz/28g	70	251	0.4	66.4	0.0	0.9
In Kirsch, M & S*	1oz/28g	35	125	0.4	28.3	0.3	0.4
Stewed With Sugar	1oz/28g	23	82	0.7	21.0	0.1	0.7
Stewed Without Sugar	1oz/28g	12	42	0.8	10.1	0.1	0.8
CHERRYADE, Sugar Free, Tesco*	1 Glass/250ml	3	1	0.0	0.0	0.0	0.0
CHESTNUTS	1 Nut/10g	17	170	2.0	36.6	2.7	4.1
CHEW SWEETS, Average	1oz/28g	107	381	1.0	87.0	5.6	1.0
CHEWING GUM,							
Airwaves, Wrigleys*	1 Piece/1g	2	150	0.0	62.0	0.0	0.0
Doublemint, Wrigleys*	1 Piece/3g	9	306	0.0	73.0	0.0	0.0
Extra Peppermint Maltitol, Wrigleys*	1 Piece/1g	2	165	0.0	63.0	0.0	0.0
Juicy Fruit, Improved, Wrigleys*	1 Piece/3g	9	295	0.0	71.0	0.0	0.0
Orbit, Spearmint, Wrigleys*	1 Piece/3g	6	190	0.0	62.0	0.0	0.0
Spearmint, Wrigleys*	1 Piece/3g	9	295	0.0	73.0	0.0	0.0
CHICK PEAS,							
Canned, Asda*	1 Can/179g	197	110	7.0	14.0	2.9	4.1
Canned, Re-Heated, Drained, Average	1oz/28g	32	115	7.2	16.1	2.9	4.1
In Salted Water, Safeway*	1 Serving/100g	119	119	7.2	16.1	2.9	4.1
In Salted Water, Sainsbury's*	1 Can/130g	144	111	7.2	14.1	2.9	4.1
In Salted Water, Tesco*	1 Can/240g	266	111	7.2	14.1	2.9	4.1
In Water, Salt Added, Drained, Sainsbury's*	1oz/28g	33	119	7.2	16.1	2.9	4.3
Morrisons*	1 Can/130g	155	119	7.2	16.1	2.9	0.0
Organic, Dried, Evernat*	1oz/28g	88	315	21.4	45.2	5.4	10.7
Organic, Waitrose*	1oz/28g	33	119	7.5	20.0	1.0	3.5
Sainsbury's*	1oz/28g	33	119	7.2	16.1	2.9	4.1
Split, Dried, Boiled In Unsalted Water	1 Tbsp/28g	32	114	7.7	17.4	2.0	0.0
Split, Dried, Raw, Average	1 Tbsp/28g	91	325	22.7	49.6	5.4	0.0
Tesco*	1oz/28g	31	111	7.2	14.1	2.9	4.1
Whole, Dried, Boiled In Unsalted Water	1 Heaped Tbsp/28g	34	121	8.4	18.2	2.1	4.3
Whole, Dried, Raw	1oz/28g	90	320	21.3	49.6	5.4	10.7
CHICKEN, BASIC							
Breast, Cured, M & S*	1 Serving/50g	41	82	18.4	0.0	1.0	0.0
Breast, Fillets, Skinless, Fresh, Value, Tesco*	1 Breast/170g	197	116	21.8	0.0	3.2	0.0
Breast, Fillets, Skinless, HE, Tesco*	1 Serving/140g	146	104	23.6	0.0	1.1	0.0
Breast, Fillets, Skinless, Waitrose*	1 Pack/190g	236	124	27.6	0.6	1.6	0.6
Breast, Golden Roasted, Bernard Matthews*	1oz/28g	31	110	23.4	0.6	1.5	0.0
Breast, Meat Only, Minced	1oz/28g	31	110	23.1	0.0	1.2	0.0
Breast, Premium, Bernard Matthews*	1 Slice/20g	24	122	19.3	3.0	3.6	0.0
Breast, Skinless, Boneless, Ready To Eat, Asda*	1oz/28g	31	111	24.3	0.7	1.3	0.0
Breast, Smoked, Premium, Bernard Matthews*	1 Slice/20g	21	107	17.2	1.6	3.5	0.0
Breast, Smoked, Premium, Sainsbury's*	1 Slice/20g	23	114	24.8	0.5	1.7	0.4
Breast, Tandoori, Pieces, Sainsbury's*	1 Serving/100g	140	140	28.6	0.9	2.8	0.9
Breast, Tandoori, Simple Solutions, Tesco*	1 Serving/180g	221	123	16.0	3.7	4.7	1.1
Breasts, Garlic & Herb Flavour, Co-Op*	1 Serving/170g	281	165	19.0	2.0	9.0	0.3
Breasts, Garlic & Pepper, COU, M & S*	1 Breast/120g	162	135	18.2	11.0	1.9	1.3
Crispy, Bird's Eye*	1 Piece/98g	228	233	15.1	12.9	13.4	0.2
Diced, Ready Cooked, Iceland*	1 Serving/100g	117	117	27.0	0.0	4.9	0.0
Fillets - Sweet Chilli & Lime, Mini, M & S*	1 Serving/210g	284	135	24.5	5.6	1.8	1.1

C

CHICKEN, BASIC,	Measure WEIGHT/INFO	per Measure KCAL	KCAL	PROT	CARB	FAT	FIBRE
Meat & Skin, Portions, Deep Fried	1oz/28g	57	204	4.5	26.4	9.3	0.0
Meat & Skin, Raw	1oz/28g	64	230	17.6	0.0	17.7	0.0
Meat & Skin, Roasted	1oz/28g	60	216	22.6	0.0	14.0	0.0
Meat, Average, Raw	1oz/28g	30	108	22.3	0.0	2.1	5.4
Meat, Average, Roasted	1oz/28g	50	177	27.3	0.0	7.5	0.0
Mince, Sainsbury's*	1 Serving/125g	201	161	18.1	0.1	9.8	0.5
O's, Bird's Eye*	10 O's/48g	125	260	13.1	14.6	16.6	0.7
Portions, Hot & Spicy, Asda*	1 Portion/92g	187	203	14.0	12.0	11.0	0.0
Portions, Hot & Spicy, Morrisons*	1 Portion/100g	215	215	14.0	12.1	13.0	1.3
Stuffed With Mushrooms, Finest, Tesco*	1 Serving/150g	177	118	15.9	2.0	5.1	0.6
Tenders, Tex-Mex, Jumbo, M & S*	1 Serving/100g	125	125	22.8	0.7	3.4	0.6
Thigh, Fillets, Fresh, Asda*	1 Serving/100g	195	195	24.0	0.0	11.0	0.0
Thigh, Fillets, Large, Sainsbury's*	1 Thigh/125g	270	216	28.0	0.1	11.6	0.1
Thigh, Fillets, Skinless, Tesco*	2 Thighs/180g	227	126	19.1	0.0	5.5	0.0
Thigh, Roasted, M & S*	1oz/28g	76	270	24.8	0.8	18.7	0.0
Thighs, Chinese, Forest Farms*	1oz/28g	68	242	20.2	1.4	17.3	9.0
Wing Quarter, Meat & Skin, Casseroled	1oz/28g	80	285	3.8	39.1	12.9	0.0
Wing Quarter, Meat & Skin, Raw	1oz/28g	95	340	10.9	71.3	2.7	8.5
Wing Quarter, Meat & Skin, Roasted	1oz/28g	104	371	10.4	71.0	4.3	0.0
Wing Quarter, Meat Only, Casseroled	1oz/28g	75	268	1.5	47.2	8.7	1.2
CHICKEN &,							
Apricot Rice, COU, M & S*	1 Pack/400g	360	90	9.4	10.6	0.9	0.7
Asparagus, BGTY, Sainsbury's*	1 Pack/450g	504	112	8.5	17.4	1.0	0.8
Asparagus, Finest, Tesco*	1 Serving/200g	184	92	12.8	4.3	2.6	0.7
Asparagus, Long Grain & Wild Rice, BGTY, Sainsbury's*	1 Pack/451g	555	123	9.2	17.1	2.0	0.8
Asparagus With Tomato & Balsamic Dressing, Tesco*	1 Serving/200g	184	92	12.8	4.3	2.6	0.7
Bacon Bundles, Sainsbury's*	1 Bundle/123g	231	188	19.9	3.0	10.7	0.2
Bacon Cranberry, Breast, Somerfield*	1oz/28g	41	146	22.0	3.0	5.0	0.0
Black Bean, Chinese Takeaway, Tesco*	1 Serving/200g	190	95	8.3	8.0	3.3	0.5
Black Bean Sauce & Egg Fried Rice, BGTY, Sainsbury's*	1 Pack/450g	527	117	7.2	14.7	3.3	0.5
Black Bean Sauce & Egg Rice, HE, Tesco*	1 Pack/400g	372	93	5.6	12.4	2.3	2.1
Black Bean With Chinese Rice, COU, M & S*	1 Pack/400g	320	80	7.4	7.6	2.4	1.1
Broccoli, White Wine Sauce & Potato, HE, Tesco*	1 Pack/400g	312	78	6.0	10.2	1.5	1.0
Broccoli With Rigatoni Pasta, BGTY, Sainsbury's*	1 Pack/450g	590	131	10.5	15.2	3.1	0.7
Cashew Nut With Egg Fried Rice, Somerfield*	1 Pack/340g	435	128	7.0	13.0	5.0	0.0
Cashew Nuts & Veg Rice, COU, M & S*	1 Pack/400g	320	80	6.9	8.6	2.0	1.0
Cashew Nuts, Asda*	1oz/28g	37	132	8.2	4.2	9.1	0.8
Cashew Nuts, Cantonese, Sainsbury's*	1 Pack/350g	350	100	9.4	3.8	5.2	1.8
Cashew Nuts, Co-Op*	1 Pack/350g	438	125	10.0	8.0	6.0	0.9
Cashew Nuts, M & S*	1 Pack/300g	300	100	10.3	5.0	4.0	1.2
Cashew Nuts, Ready Meals, Waitrose*	1oz/28g	29	104	11.3	8.2	2.9	1.0
Cashew Nuts, Somerfield*	½ Pack/175g	166	95	9.2	6.5	3.6	6.6
Cashew Nuts With Vegetable Rice, COU M & S*	1 Pack/400g	360	90	7.2	9.9	2.5	0.6
Coconut, Lime & Ginger Rice, Perfectly Balanced, Waitrose*	1 Pack/400g	432	108	7.2	15.1	2.7	0.9
Cous Cous, HE, Tesco*	1 Serving/351g	263	75	10.3	7.3	0.5	1.4
Fries For One, M & S*	1 Pack/250g	500	200	7.8	26.3	7.2	2.2
Gravy, COU, M & S*	1 Pack/300g	216	72	7.2	7.8	1.3	1.6
Honey Roasted Root Vegetables, BGTY, Sainsbury's*	1 Pack/450g	500	111	8.3	16.6	1.3	2.7
Leek Cumberland, BGTY, Sainsbury's*	1 Pack/450g	527	117	7.6	12.3	4.2	0.8
Mexican Rice, Spicy, HE, Tesco*	1 Pack/450g	387	86	7.2	12.9	0.7	0.6
Mushroom, Chinese, Iceland*	1 Pack/400g	276	69	8.2	3.8	2.3	0.4
Mushroom, Chinese, Tesco*	1 Pack/460g	474	103	5.7	13.8	2.8	1.0
Mushroom In Oyster Sauce, Tesco*	1 Pack/350g	252	72	8.0	6.3	1.6	0.7
Mushroom With Egg Fried Rice, Farmfoods*	1 Pack/325g	374	115	5.4	15.2	3.6	0.2

Nutrition Values per 100g / 100ml

CHICKEN &,	Measure WEIGHT/INFO	per Measure KCAL	KCAL	PROT	CARB	FAT	FIBRE
Mushrooms, Tesco*	1 Serving/350g	252	72	8.0	6.3	1.6	0.7
Pasta, Dijon, HE, Tesco*	1 Pack/50g	54	108	7.3	13.9	2.6	0.6
Pasta, Mediterranean Style, Eat Smart, Safeway*	1 Pack/400g	340	85	6.6	10.4	1.5	1.9
Pineapple With Egg Fried Rice, Tesco*	1 Pack/450g	450	100	7.6	12.1	2.4	1.2
Prawn Yaki Udan Noodles, M & S*	1 Pack/395g	435	110	8.1	11.9	3.6	0.8
Red Wine Penne, Italiana, Weight Watchers*	1 Pack/395g	249	63	3.7	10.1	0.7	0.6
Red Wine Sauce With Potato Gratin, HE, Tesco*	1 Pack/450g	410	91	7.7	8.9	2.7	2.2
White Wine With Rice, HE, Tesco*	1 Pack/450g	450	100	7.1	14.8	1.4	1.0
Wild Rice Steamer With Lemon Sauce, M & S*	1 Pack/400g	420	105	9.8	11.8	2.2	2.0
CHICKEN - A L' ORANGE, Lean Cuisine*	1 Pack/334g	384	115	5.6	18.0	2.1	0.4
CHICKEN - AL FORNO,							
Arrabbiata, Sainsbury's*	1 Pack/900g	1026	114	6.5	16.4	2.5	1.4
BGTY, Sainsbury's*	1oz/28g	30	107	8.9	12.8	2.2	1.3
CHICKEN - ARRABBIATA,							
Bistro, Waitrose*	½ Pack/175g	156	89	12.9	2.5	3.0	0.5
GFY, Asda*	1 Serving/340g	228	67	4.7	9.0	1.3	0.0
CHICKEN - BALLS,							
Chinese, M & S*	1 Ball/16g	45	280	10.8	29.2	13.6	2.1
Crispy, M & S*	1 Ball/16g	35	220	13.3	23.7	8.1	0.5
Lemon, Asda*	1 Ball/15g	42	279	14.0	19.0	17.0	1.6
CHICKEN - BARBECUE,							
Breast, Steaks, Spicy, M & S*	1 Serving/100g	135	135	17.7	2.0	6.3	0.9
Fillets, Mini, M & S*	1oz/28g	36	130	25.3	5.9	0.6	0.8
Southern Style, GFY, Asda*	1 Serving/165g	213	129	19.0	5.0	3.7	1.0
CHICKEN - BATTERED,							
Breast, Steaks, Iceland*	1 Breasteak/95g	224	236	15.4	14.2	13.1	0.9
Crispy, Asda*	1 Piece/95g	225	237	14.0	16.0	13.0	0.0
CHICKEN - BBQ,							
Chunky, Ready To Eat, Tesco*	½ Pack/85g	118	139	29.0	3.2	1.1	0.3
Thigh, Asda*	1oz/28g	60	216	22.6	0.0	14.0	0.0
Wings, Flavoured, Farmfoods*	1oz/28g	69	247	21.1	8.0	14.5	1.0
Wings, McCain*	1 Serving/135g	298	221	22.3	6.6	11.7	0.0
CHICKEN - BREADED,							
Breast, Fillets, Farmfoods*	1oz/28g	57	204	0.0	16.0	13.8	9.4
Breast, Steaks, Iceland*	1 Breasteak/84g	206	245	18.9	12.9	13.1	1.4
Coronation, Fresh, Bernard Matthews*	1 Piece/143g	352	246	8.7	17.6	15.7	1.7
Fillet, Lemon & Pepper, BGTY, Sainsbury's*	1 Serving/112g	202	180	18.2	18.9	3.5	1.3
Fillets, BGTY, Sainsbury's*	1 Fillet/113g	200	177	18.9	17.3	3.6	1.3
Portions, Crunchy, Asda*	1 Piece/92g	199	216	14.0	13.0	12.0	0.0
Steaks, Tesco*	1 Steak/95g	213	224	13.0	16.9	11.6	0.4
CHICKEN - BUTTER, Sainsbury's*	1 Pack/400g	592	148	12.1	4.4	9.1	1.2
CHICKEN - CAJUN,							
& Potato Hash, HE, Tesco*	1 Pack/450g	428	95	6.6	11.7	2.4	0.9
& Southern Fried Wedges, Colman's*	1 Pack/65g	188	289	8.5	51.0	5.7	11.9
& Wedges, BGTY, Sainsbury's*	1 Pack/450g	482	107	6.9	12.1	3.4	1.0
American Style, Asda*	1 Pack/340g	330	97	7.0	11.0	2.8	0.0
Asda*	1 Serving/150g	327	218	22.0	7.0	11.0	0.4
Breast, Fillets, Marinated, Sainsbury's*	1 Fillet/93g	113	122	24.7	2.6	1.4	0.5
Breast, Pieces, Sainsbury's*	1 Serving/100g	142	142	22.0	6.3	3.2	0.9
HE, Tesco*	1 Pack/350g	298	85	8.8	9.1	1.5	1.4
M & S*	1 Fillet/126g	246	195	16.4	11.0	9.6	0.6
Somerfield*	1 Pack/149g	282	189	6.2	24.4	7.5	1.1
CHICKEN - CALYPSO, With Turmeric Rice, BGTY, Sainsbury's*	1 Pack/450g	495	110	6.7	16.3	2.1	1.0
CHICKEN - CARBONARE, Steam Cuisine, M & S*	1 Pack/400g	560	140	10.4	9.8	6.9	1.2

Nutrition Values per 100g / 100ml

C

	Measure WEIGHT/INFO	per Measure KCAL	KCAL	PROT	CARB	FAT	FIBRE
			Nutrition Values per 100g / 100ml				
CHICKEN - CARIBBEAN,							
Fruity, Rice & Peas, BGTY, Sainsbury's*	1 Pack/450g	509	113	6.7	14.0	3.3	1.9
CHICKEN - CEASAR, COU, M & S*	1 Pack/181g	244	135	12.2	19.9	2.4	4.3
CHICKEN - CHARGRILLED,							
& Lime & Coriander, Asda*	1 Serving/190g	352	185	24.0	2.0	9.0	1.1
& Vegetable Medley, HE, Tesco*	1 Pack/450g	270	60	6.5	5.8	1.2	0.9
Asda*	1 Slice/25g	27	109	23.9	0.5	1.3	0.0
Breast, Cured, M & S*	1 Slice/19g	19	100	20.9	0.3	1.7	0.0
Breast, In Mango Ginger Marinade, GFY, Asda*	½ Pack/190g	234	123	17.0	11.0	1.2	0.5
Breast, Thai Style Marinade, GFY, Asda*	½ Pack/178g	178	100	17.0	1.3	3.0	0.5
Chunky, Tesco*	1oz/28g	32	116	25.5	0.9	1.1	0.0
Fillets, GFY, Asda*	1 Fillet/64g	90	140	30.0	0.4	2.0	1.1
Fillets, Sainsbury's*	1 Serving/119g	214	180	22.1	1.4	9.5	0.7
Fillets, Sliced, M & S*	1 Serving/140g	182	130	29.8	0.6	1.0	0.5
Herb & Red Pepper Sauce, COU, M & S*	1oz/28g	25	90	15.9	1.2	2.1	0.4
In BBQ Sauce, GFY, Breast, Asda*	1 Serving/166g	214	129	19.0	5.0	3.7	1.0
In Tomato & Basil Sauce, M & S*	1 Serving/235g	223	95	12.9	2.1	3.8	1.3
Lemon, COU, M & S*	½ Pack/175g	158	90	16.1	5.5	0.6	0.9
Lime & Coriander, Asda*	1 Serving/190g	352	185	24.0	2.0	9.0	1.1
Mayo, Red Pepper, Somerfield*	1oz/28g	66	234	10.0	21.0	12.0	0.0
Mushroom & Wine, HE, Tesco*	1 Pack/450g	392	87	9.0	10.0	1.2	1.0
Pasta Salsa, HE, Tesco*	1 Pack/450g	396	88	7.3	11.7	1.3	1.0
Spicy, Breast, With Rice, Asda*	1 Pack/400g	372	93	6.0	16.0	0.6	1.0
With Caramelised Peppers, M & S*	½ Pack/237g	225	95	12.9	2.1	3.8	1.3
With Olive Oil, Coriander & Lemon, Sainsbury's*	1 Serving/122g	310	254	22.7	2.2	17.1	0.7
CHICKEN - CHARGRILLS,							
Garlic, Bird's Eye*	1 Piece/76g	169	222	19.2	1.2	15.6	0.0
Original, Birds Eye*	1 Serving/79g	179	227	18.5	1.1	16.5	0.0
CHICKEN - CHASSEUR, Finest, Tesco*	1 Serving/200g	266	133	12.6	1.6	8.4	0.4
CHICKEN - CHILLI,							
& Lemongrass, With Egg Noodles, BGTY, Sainsbury's*	1 Pack/450g	500	111	10.0	10.2	3.4	1.2
Chunks, Breast, Safeway*	1 Serving/100g	142	142	22.2	6.3	3.2	0.0
Sticky, M & S*	2 Pieces/112g	258	230	8.0	26.1	10.0	0.7
Sweet, & Toasted Sweetcorn, M & S*	1oz/28g	27	95	13.8	4.7	2.1	0.5
Sweet, Findus*	1 Pack/350g	420	120	6.0	15.0	3.5	1.5
Sweet, With Rice, HE, Tesco*	1 Pack/400g	392	98	5.0	18.9	0.3	0.5
With Lime, Breast, Simple Solutions, Tesco*	1 Pack/400g	564	141	22.5	0.8	5.3	1.4
CHICKEN - CHINESE,							
M & S*	1 Serving/140g	182	130	22.8	8.5	0.3	0.8
Oriental Express*	1 Pack/350g	326	93	5.7	15.9	0.7	2.2
Sliced, Breast, Fillets, M & S*	1 Pack/140g	182	130	22.8	8.5	0.3	0.8
Style, & Noodles, HE, Tesco*	1 Pack/370g	278	75	6.9	9.4	1.1	0.7
Style, Breast, Fillets, Asda*	1oz/28g	41	148	31.2	1.1	2.1	0.7
Style, Mini, Breast, Fillets, Tesco*	½ Pack/100g	121	121	24.9	2.9	1.1	0.2
Style, Mini, Fillets, M & S*	1 Pack/190g	228	120	22.0	7.5	0.7	1.2
CHICKEN - CIDER, COU, M & S*	1 Pack/400g	300	75	7.2	6.7	2.3	0.8
CHICKEN - CORONATION, COU, M & S*	1oz/28g	34	120	16.3	8.6	2.2	0.7
CHICKEN - DRUMSTICKS,							
American Style, Frozen, Sainsbury's*	1 Drumstick/84g	195	232	21.9	7.3	12.8	0.8
BBQ, Asda*	1oz/28g	53	189	25.0	2.0	9.0	0.3
BBQ, Safeway*	1 Serving/48g	84	176	23.8	3.4	7.9	0.0
BBQ, Sainsbury's*	1 Drumstick/100g	195	195	22.4	6.5	8.7	0.1
Chinese, Sainsbury's*	1 Drumstick/100g	171	171	20.9	5.2	7.4	0.8
Chinese Style, Asda*	1oz/28g	52	184	24.2	1.9	8.8	0.6
Extra Crispy, Kentucky Fried Chicken*	1 Drumstick/67g	195	291	22.3	10.4	17.9	1.4

CHICKEN - DRUMSTICKS,	Measure WEIGHT/INFO	per Measure KCAL	KCAL	PROT	CARB	FAT	FIBRE
Hot & Spicy, Asda*	1oz/28g	49	176	25.0	1.0	8.0	0.4
Jumbo Size, M & S*	1oz/28g	53	190	26.0	0.6	9.5	0.0
Roast, Asda*	1oz/28g	50	180	24.9	1.0	8.5	0.0
Sainsbury's*	1 Drumstick/100g	183	183	25.3	0.1	9.1	0.1
Tesco*	1 Serving/100g	230	230	17.6	0.0	17.7	0.0
With Skin, Asda*	1 Drumstick/125g	231	185	26.0	0.0	9.0	0.0
Without Skin, Tesco*	1 Drumstick/121g	152	126	19.0	0.0	5.5	0.0
CHICKEN - DUNKERS, Domino's Pizza*	1oz/28g	62	220	23.5	1.5	13.3	0.5
CHICKEN - EN CROUTE, Breast, Tesco*	1 Serving/215g	555	258	9.4	20.4	15.4	0.6
CHICKEN - ESCALOPE,							
Bernard Matthews*	1 Escalope/143g	390	273	9.5	18.3	18.0	0.0
Breast, M & S*	1 Pack/310g	372	120	20.2	1.5	4.3	0.6
Tomato & Basil, Safeway*	1 Escalope/150g	242	161	21.2	2.2	7.5	1.2
& Bacon, Sun Valley*	1 Escalope/140g	438	313	15.8	16.0	20.6	0.0
GFY, Asda*	1 Escalope/128g	330	258	15.0	18.0	14.0	0.4
CHICKEN - FILLETS,							
Caesar, Mini, BGTY, Sainsbury's*	½ Pack/100g	142	142	27.5	1.7	2.8	0.5
Coronation, BGTY, Sainsbury's*	1 Fillet/100g	136	136	27.1	2.4	2.6	1.0
Crumbed, Breast, Sainsbury's*	1 Breast Fillet/107g	230	215	16.4	15.6	9.7	1.1
Hickory Barbecue & Chilli, BGTY, Sainsbury's*	1 Fillet/100g	133	133	26.9	3.6	1.2	0.9
Honey & Mustard, Mini, M & S*	1 Serving/105g	142	135	24.9	3.9	2.0	1.3
Hot & Spicy, Breast, Sainsbury's*	1 Fillet/108g	211	195	18.5	14.6	7.0	1.2
Hot & Spicy, Iceland*	1 Serving/92g	171	186	18.2	10.9	7.8	0.9
Lime & Coriander, Mini, Breast, Tesco*	½ Pack/100g	122	122	25.0	2.5	1.3	0.2
Lime & Coriander, Mini, M & S*	1 Fillet/42g	44	105	22.4	2.1	1.2	0.3
Red Japanese, Sainsbury's*	1 Serving/100g	151	151	29.2	2.8	2.5	0.4
Red Pepper, Mini, BGTY, Sainsbury's*	1 Serving/100g	126	126	26.5	3.7	0.6	0.7
Roast, Boneless, Breast, Sainsbury's*	1 Breast/120g	221	184	25.1	0.2	9.2	0.1
Roast, Breast, Morrisons*	1 Fillet/120g	221	184	25.1	0.2	9.2	0.1
Roast Mushroom & Garlic, GFY, Asda*	2 Fillets/360g	425	118	20.0	2.9	2.9	0.5
Roast, Sliced, Skinless, Breast, M & Ss*	1 Serving/240g	312	130	29.8	0.6	1.0	0.5
Skinless, Cooked, Breast, M & S*	1 Serving/100g	130	130	29.8	0.6	1.0	0.5
Skinless, Cooked, Breast, Waitrose*	1 Breast/85g	201	236	52.4	1.2	3.0	1.2
Sundried Tomato & Parmesan, BGTY, Sainsbury's*	½ Pack/100g	138	138	22.1	6.0	2.9	0.5
Tandoori, Mini, Eat Smart, Safeway*	1 Serving/50g	65	130	26.2	1.4	2.0	0.5
Tandoori, Mini, M & S*	1 Serving/100g	125	125	23.2	3.7	2.1	0.2
Tex-Mex, Breast, Eat Smart, Safeway*	1 Breast/123g	160	130	29.5	0.8	1.0	0.9
Tomato & Basil, Mini, Breast, Tesco*	1 Pack/200g	262	131	25.2	2.1	2.4	0.2
Tomato & Basil, Mini, M & S*	1oz/28g	32	115	21.7	2.9	1.8	0.5
Tomato, Basil & Garlic, Mini, BGTY, Sainsbury's*	1 Pack/328g	407	124	19.7	1.7	4.4	0.2
CHICKEN - FINGERS,							
Safeway*	1 Finger/23g	60	259	14.0	20.8	13.1	1.7
Tesco*	1 Serving/75g	181	241	13.4	16.7	13.4	0.6
CHICKEN - FLAME GRILL,							
COU, M & S*	1oz/28g	25	90	7.9	12.1	0.8	1.2
With Rice & Lentils, COU, M & S*	1 Pack/208g	250	120	8.7	16.7	1.8	1.6
CHICKEN - FORRESTIERE, GFY, Asda*	1 Pack/442g	402	91	15.0	2.5	2.3	0.3
CHICKEN - FRENCH Style, BGTY, Sainsbury's*	1 Serving/168g	203	121	15.3	7.7	3.3	0.1
CHICKEN - FRIED, Spicy, Sainsbury's*	1 Serving/150g	414	276	28.8	2.9	16.6	2.1
CHICKEN - FU YUNG, Chinese Takeaway, Tesco*	1 Pack/350g	315	90	5.6	14.5	1.0	0.8
CHICKEN - GARLIC,							
Crunchy, Bird's Eye*	1 Piece/99g	259	262	14.4	16.9	15.2	0.9
Egg Pasta & Roasted Veg, BGTY, Sainsbury's*	1 Pack/450g	396	88	8.9	10.2	1.3	1.3

Nutrition Values per 100g / 100ml

C

CHICKEN - GOUJONS,	Measure WEIGHT/INFO	per Measure KCAL	Nutrition Values per 100g / 100ml KCAL	PROT	CARB	FAT	FIBRE
Breast, Fresh, Asda*	1oz/28g	30	106	24.0	0.0	1.1	0.0
Somerfield*	1 Pack/240g	533	222	15.0	27.0	6.0	0.0
CHICKEN - HONEY,							
& Mustard, BGTY, Sainsbury's*	1 Pack/451g	528	117	8.6	15.5	2.3	0.6
& Mustard, Bird's Eye*	1 Piece/87g	185	213	18.2	3.0	14.2	0.0
& Mustard, GFY, Asda*	1 Pack/402g	478	119	7.0	17.0	2.5	0.1
& Mustard, Oven Baked, Breast, Bird's Eye*	1 Portion/86g	183	213	18.2	3.0	14.2	0.0
& Mustard, Somerfield*	1 Pack/380g	555	146	18.0	8.0	5.0	0.0
Cantonese, Sesame, Sainsbury's*	1/3 Pack/135g	116	86	9.8	5.5	2.7	0.8
Roast, Asda*	2 Slices/50g	59	118	24.0	1.1	1.9	0.1
Roast, Thin Sliced, Asda*	1 Slice/13g	15	116	19.1	3.2	3.0	0.1
CHICKEN IN,							
A Paprika Flavoured Crispy Batter, Bernard Matthews*	1 Portion/110g	249	226	14.5	20.6	9.5	0.0
Asparagus Sauce & New Potatoes, Sainsbury's*	1 Serving/495g	545	110	7.4	9.5	4.7	0.9
Balsamic Vinegar Dressing, Simple Solutions, Tesco*	½ Pack/155g	256	165	16.4	0.1	11.0	0.7
Barbecue Sauce, COU, M & S*	1 Pack/352g	370	105	8.6	13.8	1.6	1.2
Barbeque Sauce, HE, Tesco*	1 Breast/170g	177	104	18.3	4.5	1.4	0.9
Basil & Chilli Sauce With Sticky Rice, BGTY, Sainsbury's*	1 Pack/450g	563	125	6.8	16.9	3.4	0.3
BBQ Sauce, GFY, Asda*	1 Serving/380g	414	109	13.0	13.0	0.5	1.3
BBQ Sauce, Weight Watchers*	1 Pack/339g	332	98	5.8	10.8	3.5	0.9
Black Bean & Rice, HE, Tesco*	1 Pack/450g	387	86	7.4	12.4	0.7	1.6
Black Bean Sauce, Budgens*	1 Pack/350g	333	95	9.9	4.9	4.0	0.9
Black Bean Sauce, Chinese Takeaway, Iceland*	1 Pack/400g	348	87	9.3	5.3	3.2	0.7
Black Bean Sauce, Safeway*	1 Pack/350g	284	81	9.4	7.9	1.3	1.0
Black Bean Sauce, Somerfield*	½ Pack/175g	133	76	10.7	6.1	1.0	1.9
Black Bean Sauce, Waitrose*	1 Pack/300g	243	81	10.9	6.6	1.2	0.8
Black Bean Sauce With Egg Fried Rice, Somerfield*	1 Pack/340g	384	113	7.0	13.0	4.0	0.0
Black Bean Sauce With Rice, Asda*	1 Pack/400g	500	125	7.0	20.0	1.9	0.6
Black Bean Sauce With Rice, Iceland*	1 Pack/400g	388	97	5.1	15.8	1.5	0.8
Broccoli & Mushroom, Good Choice, Iceland*	1 Pack/400g	436	109	7.5	17.1	1.2	0.7
Broccoli & Mushroom With Rice, HE, Tesco*	1 Pack/400g	440	110	7.5	17.1	1.2	0.7
Chilli & Lemon Grass With Rice, Sainsbury's*	1 Pack/450g	527	117	6.2	17.4	2.5	0.7
Citrus Sauce, Eat Smart, Safeway*	1 Serving/185g	185	100	18.3	4.0	1.1	1.0
Citrus Tikka Sauce, Breast, Sainsbury's*	1 Breast/200g	304	152	28.6	3.2	2.7	0.1
Creamy Garlic Sauce, Breast, Tesco*	½ Pack/200g	246	123	15.9	2.5	5.5	0.8
Creamy Mushroom Sauce, Weight Watchers*	1 Pack/330g	264	80	6.8	7.5	2.5	0.5
Creamy Thai Sauce, Somerfield*	1 Pack/440g	748	170	22.0	2.0	8.0	0.0
Garlic & Herbs, Breast, Sainsbury's*	1 Serving/200g	316	158	28.3	5.4	2.6	0.1
Ginger & Chilli With Veg Noodles, COU, M & S*	1 Pack/400g	300	75	6.4	10.7	0.6	1.1
Gravy, Breast, Bird's Eye*	1 Pack/162.5g	130	80	14.9	2.8	1.0	0.1
Gravy, Chunky, M & S*	1 Can/489g	465	95	13.6	1.4	3.9	0.8
Hot Ginger Sauce With Thai Sticky Rice, Sainsbury's*	1 Pack/450g	603	134	6.8	16.3	4.6	0.5
Leek & Bacon Sauce, Chilled, Co-Op*	1 Pack/400g	460	115	15.0	2.0	5.0	0.2
Lemon Flavour Sauce, Breast Fillets, Safeway*	1 Fillet/92g	200	217	17.0	16.0	9.4	1.4
Lemon Sauce, Breast, HE, Tesco*	1 Pack/385g	385	100	15.9	4.7	1.9	0.5
Lemon Sauce With Rice, Sainsbury's*	1 Pack/450g	513	114	8.1	17.0	1.5	0.7
Mexican Salsa, Tesco*	1 Pack/320g	368	115	19.5	3.1	2.7	0.6
Mild & Fruity Curry, Breasts, HE, Tesco*	2 Breasts/345g	321	93	15.8	4.1	1.5	0.5
Mushroom & Ham Sauce With Rice, BGTY, Sainsbury's*	1 Pack/450g	581	129	9.7	18.9	1.6	0.3
Parma Ham, M & S*	½ Pack/282g	367	130	11.6	6.3	6.2	2.0
Pepercorn Sauce, Good Choice, Iceland*	1 Pack/400g	404	101	5.5	15.8	1.7	0.5
Peppercorn Sauce, BGTY, Sainsbury's*	1 Pack/350g	340	97	9.4	9.5	2.4	1.5
Peppercorn Sauce, Weight Watchers*	1 Pack/300g	252	84	4.8	11.9	1.8	0.7
Red Pepper Sauce, Eat Smart, Safeway*	1 Serving/175g	166	95	18.4	2.3	1.3	1.4

C

	Measure WEIGHT/INFO	per Measure KCAL	Nutrition Values per 100g / 100ml KCAL	PROT	CARB	FAT	FIBRE
CHICKEN IN,							
Red Wine & Bacon Sauce, Breast, Somerfield*	1 Breast/150g	131	87	14.0	3.0	2.0	0.0
Red Wine & Mushrooms, Asda*	½ Pack/190g	174	92	17.0	1.8	1.9	0.5
Red Wine & Potato Grattin, HE, Tesco*	1 Pack/450g	410	91	7.7	8.9	2.7	2.2
Red Wine, Mushrooms, Bacon & Onions, M & S*	½ Pack/215g	247	115	15.7	2.4	4.6	0.4
Spicy Tomato Sauce & Basil Mash, PB, Waitrose*	1 Pack/400g	376	94	6.3	10.0	3.2	0.8
Tomato & Basil, BGTY, Sainsbury's*	1 Pack/450g	369	82	9.0	7.9	1.6	1.2
Tomato & Basil Sauce, Breast Fillets, Healthy Choice, Asda*	1 Pack/400g	484	121	22.0	1.2	3.2	2.0
Tomato & Basil Sauce, Breast, GFY, Asda*	1 Pack/392g	447	114	12.0	9.0	3.4	1.5
Tomato & Basil Sauce, Good Choice, Iceland*	½ Pack/170g	153	90	13.3	3.3	2.6	0.6
Tomato & Basil Sauce With Rice, Eat Smart, Safeway*	1 Pack/400g	360	90	8.9	10.2	1.1	1.0
White Sauce, BGTY, Sainsbury's*	1 Can/200g	250	125	14.5	2.5	6.3	1.0
White Sauce, HE, Tesco*	1 Serving/100g	94	94	12.0	4.8	3.0	0.0
White Sauce, Sainsbury's*	1 Can/206g	348	169	9.9	4.7	12.3	0.5
White Wine & Asparagus Panzerotti, Asda*	½ Pack/150g	239	159	8.0	28.0	1.7	0.0
White Wine & Mushroom Sauce, M & S*	1 Serving/200g	260	130	15.6	1.6	6.8	1.0
White Wine Sauce & Wild Rice, GFY, Asda*	1 Pack/400g	500	125	8.0	21.0	1.0	0.4
White Wine Sauce, Budgens*	1 Pack/225g	664	295	9.7	19.5	19.8	0.8
White Wine Sauce, Simple Solutions, Tesco*	½ Pack/200g	198	99	19.3	0.9	2.0	0.5
Wine & Mushroom Sauce, Breast, Good Choice, Iceland*	1 Breast/155g	163	105	17.6	3.1	2.2	0.7
Wine & Mushroom Sauce, Breasts, GFY, Asda*	½ Pack/190g	203	107	17.0	3.0	3.0	1.6
CHICKEN - INDIAN,							
Royal Taj, Sainsbury's*	1 Breast/100g	124	124	27.3	0.1	1.6	0.7
Style, Fillets, Sainsbury's*	1 Pack/200g	233	112	13.7	4.4	4.4	1.2
CHICKEN - ITALIAN,							
Al Forno, Sainsbury's*	½ Pack/452g	565	125	7.8	13.4	4.5	1.2
Good Choice, Iceland*	1 Pack/400g	400	100	5.0	19.0	0.4	0.5
Iceland*	1 Pack/250g	208	83	13.6	4.8	1.0	0.5
Style, BGTY, Sainsbury's*	1 Serving/167g	209	125	16.9	7.6	3.0	0.1
Style, Dinner, Asda*	1 Serving/400g	244	61	6.0	7.0	1.0	1.1
Style, Eat Smart, Safeway*	1 Pack/184g	278	151	11.9	17.3	3.8	4.0
Style, Fillets, GFY, Asda*	1 Serving/158g	190	120	20.0	0.9	4.0	0.5
Style, Meal, Asda*	1 Pack/408g	241	59	6.0	7.0	0.8	0.8
Style, Sainsbury's*	½ Pack/190g	222	117	16.3	3.9	4.0	0.1
CHICKEN - KUNG PO,							
Diet Choice, Waitrose*	1 Pack/300g	342	114	13.4	12.4	1.2	0.7
Sainsbury's*	½ Pack/175g	131	75	9.2	4.0	2.5	1.0
CHICKEN - LEMON,							
& Herb, Bernard Matthews*	1oz/28g	43	154	23.7	4.7	4.5	0.0
& Pepper, M & S*	1 Serving/100g	125	125	24.1	5.2	0.7	0.0
& Pepper, Waitrose*	1 Fillet/150g	296	197	17.1	15.4	7.4	0.8
& Rice, HE, Tesco*	1 Pack/450g	473	105	7.0	19.0	0.1	0.5
& Rice, Lean Cuisine, Findus*	1 Pack/340g	340	100	6.5	16.2	1.0	0.5
Cantonese, Sainsbury's*	½ Pack/140g	217	156	11.0	13.9	6.3	0.6
Cantonese Style, With Egg Fried Rice, Farmfoods*	1 Pack/324g	486	150	4.9	21.8	4.8	0.1
COU, M & S*	1 Pack/150g	150	100	17.9	5.6	0.9	0.8
Cream, With Rice, Perfectly Balanced, Waitrose*	1 Pack/400g	592	148	7.6	21.7	3.4	0.3
Crispy, Take It Away, M & S*	1 Carton/227g	329	145	9.4	19.2	3.4	0.7
Pepper, Bird's Eye*	1 Piece/113g	273	242	15.4	17.5	12.3	0.6
Tesco*	½ Pack/175g	214	122	11.0	10.1	4.2	0.6
Veg, Spicy Cous Cous & Chilli, M & S*	1 Pack/400g	540	135	10.7	14.9	4.8	2.0
CHICKEN - MANGO, With Rice, BGTY, Sainsbury's*	1 Pack/450g	572	127	6.9	21.4	1.5	0.8
CHICKEN - MEXICAN,							
COU, M & S*	1 Pack/255g	395	155	10.3	25.0	2.0	2.0
Spicy, Bird's Eye*	1 Piece/103g	254	247	14.6	16.5	13.6	0.6

C

CHICKEN - MEXICAN,	Measure WEIGHT/INFO	per Measure KCAL	Nutrition Values per 100g / 100ml KCAL	PROT	CARB	FAT	FIBRE
Style, BGTY, Sainsbury's*	1 Serving/260g	255	98	6.9	12.1	2.5	2.2
Style, GFY, Asda*	½ Pack/200g	256	128	17.0	3.7	5.0	0.3
Style, With Potato Wedges, GFY, Asda*	1 Pack/400g	504	126	7.0	14.0	4.7	1.4
With Chilli Cheese Filling, Somerfield*	1 Serving/56g	90	160	17.0	3.0	9.0	0.0
CHICKEN - MUSTARD, Potatoes, Leeks, Spinach, SC, M& S*	1 Pack/400g	400	100	10.2	8.2	3.4	1.3
CHICKEN - NUGGETS,							
Battered, Somerfield*	1oz/28g	69	248	14.0	16.0	14.0	0.0
Breaded, Crunchy, Asda*	1 Nugget/14g	35	253	16.0	18.0	13.0	1.9
Breaded, Iceland*	1 Nugget/13g	35	270	19.4	15.8	14.3	1.1
Breaded, SmartPrice, Asda*	1 Nugget/16g	51	320	15.0	29.0	16.0	1.2
Iceland*	1 Nugget/15g	44	290	14.5	18.9	17.4	2.3
In Crispy Breadcrumbs, Sainsbury's*	4 Nuggets/54g	137	253	12.9	18.1	14.3	1.2
McNuggets, McDonald's*	6 Pieces/109g	254	233	17.1	10.6	13.6	1.9
Somerfield*	1oz/28g	71	252	14.0	15.0	15.0	0.0
Tesco*	1oz/28g	68	243	13.3	16.2	13.9	0.7
CHICKEN - PAPRIKA, Vegetables & Rice, BGTY, Sainsbury's*	1 Pack/451g	555	123	7.2	17.8	2.6	0.8
CHICKEN - PEPPER, Fry, Sainsburys*	1 Pack/400g	508	127	15.0	2.9	6.2	1.6
CHICKEN - PICCATA, HE, Tesco*	1 Pack/405g	518	128	15.7	7.7	3.8	0.5
CHICKEN - PIRI PIRI,							
M & S*	1 Serving/300g	420	140	10.0	7.3	7.7	1.3
Tesco*	1 Serving/290g	307	106	15.8	1.4	4.1	0.5
CHICKEN - POLENTA Paupiettes, Perfectly Balanced, Waitrose*	½ Pack/225g	254	113	19.1	5.0	1.8	0.8
CHICKEN - RENDANG, Sainsbury's*	1 Pack/350g	690	197	9.6	5.1	15.3	1.7
CHICKEN - ROAST,							
Dinner, Bird's Eye*	1 Pack/368g	364	99	8.9	8.9	3.1	1.3
Meal, M & S*	1 Pack/250g	375	150	14.6	5.3	7.7	0.1
CHICKEN - ROLL,							
Asda*	1 Slice/10g	17	174	15.0	3.8	11.0	0.0
Breast, Sainsbury's	1 Slice/10g	15	153	18.4	1.9	8.0	0.7
Breast, Somerfield*	1 Slice/11.3g	15	134	20.0	4.0	4.0	0.0
Broccoli & Mushroom, Sainsbury's*	½ Roll/175g	441	252	8.7	24.3	13.3	1.0
SmartPrice, Asda*	1 Slice/14g	24	174	15.0	3.8	11.0	0.0
Somerfield*	1oz/28g	56	200	17.0	8.0	11.0	0.0
With Pork, Sage & Onion Stuffing, Value, Tesco*	1 Roll/125g	166	133	9.4	7.8	7.1	0.5
CHICKEN - SALSA,							
Mango, Breast, Sainsbury's*	1 Breast/178g	271	152	26.2	6.4	2.4	0.1
Melt, Sainsbury's*	1 Pack/372g	480	129	7.2	10.7	6.4	1.6
CHICKEN - SLICES,							
Roast, Chunks, Breast, Waitrose*	1oz/28g	36	127	25.9	3.6	1.0	1.1
Breast, Bernard Matthews*	1 Slice/20g	24	122	19.3	3.0	3.6	0.0
Cooked, Sainsbury's*	1 Slice/19g	20	106	21.4	2.1	1.3	0.3
Roast, Mattessons*	1 Slice/25g	33	131	24.8	2.2	3.4	0.5
Roast, Premium, Somerfield*	1 Slice/20g	23	114	25.0	1.0	1.0	0.0
CHICKEN - SOUTHERN FRIED,							
Bird's Eye*	1 Steak/98g	272	278	14.6	13.4	18.4	0.9
Drumsticks, Tesco*	1oz/28g	57	202	17.6	8.8	10.7	0.5
Fillets, Asda*	1 Fillet/86g	175	203	21.0	14.0	7.0	0.5
Fillets, Fresh, Sainsbury's*	1 Fillet/104g	220	212	18.2	12.4	9.9	1.0
Fillets, Frozen, Morrisons*	1 Piece/100g	181	181	15.1	9.7	9.1	2.3
Fillets, Mini, Breast, Tesco*	1 Piece/43.7g	87	199	16.5	13.0	9.0	2.3
Nuggets, Bird's Eye*	1 Nugget/17g	42	248	12.9	17.8	14.0	1.2
Portions, Asda*	1 Portion/95g	210	221	14.0	12.0	13.0	0.0
Steaks, Tesco*	1 Steak/137g	293	214	15.4	11.1	12.0	0.9
Strips, Tesco*	1 Pack/300g	699	233	18.7	18.3	9.4	1.4

CHICKEN - SOUTHERN FRIED,	Measure WEIGHT/INFO	per Measure KCAL	Nutrition Values per 100g / 100ml KCAL	PROT	CARB	FAT	FIBRE
Thigh, Tesco*	1oz/28g	68	242	14.7	10.1	15.9	0.5
Wing, Tesco*	1 Serving/100g	238	238	15.0	11.7	14.6	0.5
CHICKEN - STEAKS, Hot & Spicy, Tesco*	1 Steak/95g	200	211	13.5	11.4	12.4	0.8
CHICKEN - STRIPPERS, Domino's Pizza*	1oz/28g	61	219	23.3	13.4	8.0	1.0
CHICKEN - STRIPS, Crispy, Kentucky Fried Chicken*	1 Av Serving/100g	268	268	18.6	14.5	15.1	1.5
CHICKEN - STUFFED, Breast, With Mushrooms, HE, Tesco*	1 Serving/175g	152	87	16.3	1.5	1.8	0.2
CHICKEN - SUPREME,							
John West*	1oz/28g	52	185	14.0	3.0	13.0	0.0
With Rice, HE, Tesco*	1 Pack/400g	384	96	4.9	15.6	1.6	1.5
With Rice, Weight Watchers*	1 Pack/300g	255	85	5.6	11.9	1.6	0.5
CHICKEN - SZECHUAN,							
Chilli & Peppercorn, Sainsbury's*	1 Pack/400g	352	88	9.9	3.2	4.0	0.5
Perfectly Balanced, Waitrose*	1 Pack/465g	479	103	13.4	5.6	3.0	1.5
With Garlic Rice, BGTY, Sainsbury's*	1 Pack/449g	489	109	6.8	15.6	2.1	1.3
With Noodles, Sainsbury's*	1 Pack/450g	423	94	6.0	10.4	3.1	0.9
CHICKEN - TANDOORI, With Spicy Potatoes & Dip, HE, Tesco*	1 Pack/370g	322	87	9.7	10.3	0.8	1.3
CHICKEN - THAI,							
Bird's Eye*	1 Portion/86g	189	220	18.1	3.1	15.0	0.1
Chiang Mai, & Noodles, BGTY, Sainsbury's*	1 Pack/448g	484	108	6.9	11.0	4.0	1.7
Coconut, & Noodles, M & S*	1 Pack/400g	320	80	7.2	8.1	1.8	0.7
Green, Fillets, Mini, Sainsbury's*	½ Pack/100g	130	130	27.9	0.9	1.6	0.8
Red, & Noodles, Deli Meal, Marks and Spencer*	1 Pack/380g	380	100	6.3	10.0	4.1	0.8
Red, Fillets, Mini, BGTY, Sainsbury's*,	1 Serving/100g	125	125	20.9	6.8	1.6	0.8
Red, Fillets, Mini, M & S*	1 Serving/210g	273	130	22.5	4.1	2.5	0.4
Style, BGTY, Sainsbury's*	1 Serving/190g	247	130	15.6	6.8	4.5	0.1
Style, Red, Fillets, Mini, Breast, Tesco*	½ Pack/100g	135	135	26.8	2.8	1.8	0.5
Style, Steam Cuisine, M & S*	1 Pack/400g	440	110	8.8	10.4	3.8	1.7
Style, With Noodles, Tesco*	1 Pack/400g	332	83	7.5	9.5	1.7	1.0
CHICKEN - TIKKA,							
& Cous Cous, Boots*	1 Pack/160g	307	192	6.2	17.0	11.0	1.3
& Lemon Rice, Deli Meal, M & S*	1 Pack/360g	342	95	9.8	10.2	2.0	0.7
BGTY, Sainsbury's	1 Serving/188g	265	141	10.5	21.2	1.6	0.0
Breast Chunks, Safeway*	1 Pack/200g	356	178	32.2	4.1	3.7	0.0
Breast, Citrus, Sainsbury's*	1 Breast/180g	292	162	27.2	6.0	3.3	0.1
Breast Fillets, Mini, Asda*	1oz/28g	34	123	26.0	1.5	1.7	1.0
Breast Fillets, Sliced, M & S*	1 Pack/140g	154	110	21.9	3.2	1.7	0.8
Breast Pieces, Sainsbury's*	1 Serving/150g	233	155	26.1	3.2	4.1	0.5
Chunky, Tesco*	1 Pack/170g	221	130	27.4	0.5	2.1	0.3
COU, M & S*	1 Pack/300g	270	90	9.4	10.6	0.9	0.7
Fillets, Mini, Eat Smart, Safeway*	1 Serving/100g	120	120	27.9	1.2	0.3	0.8
Fillets, Mini, M & S*	1 Serving/100g	125	125	24.2	1.1	2.6	1.3
Fillets, Roast, Asda*	1oz/28g	36	127	26.0	2.3	1.5	0.3
Pieces, Ready Cooked, Iceland*	1 Serving/100g	135	135	26.8	1.6	2.5	0.0
Portions, Asda*	1oz/28g	47	169	17.2	0.5	11.0	1.0
With Basmati Rice, GFY, Asda*	1 Pack/400g	592	148	9.0	24.0	1.8	1.6
With Rice, Vesta*	1 Pack/228g	857	376	14.9	65.1	6.2	2.9
CHICKEN - VINDALOO, Waitrose*	1 Pack/340g	398	117	10.6	6.4	5.4	1.6
CHICKEN - WAFER THIN,							
American Fried, Bernard Matthews*	1oz/28g	31	111	18.0	3.1	3.0	0.0
M & S*	1oz/28g	28	100	18.8	1.5	2.1	0.0
Roast, Asda*	1oz/28g	31	110	21.0	3.6	1.3	0.0
Roast, Safeway*	1 Serving/25g	28	112	20.6	2.4	2.2	0.0
Roast, Sainsbury's*	1oz/28g	34	121	18.3	3.7	3.6	1.6
Roast, Tesco*	1oz/28g	36	129	19.3	3.6	4.1	0.0

C

CHICKEN - WAFER THIN	Measure WEIGHT/INFO	per Measure KCAL	Nutrition Values per 100g / 100ml KCAL	PROT	CARB	FAT	FIBRE
Sage & Onion, Breast, Bernard Matthews*	1 Serving/25g	30	120	19.8	3.5	3.0	0.0
CHICKEN - WINGS,							
Chinese Style, Asda*	1oz/28g	70	250	28.0	3.0	14.0	0.5
Chinese Style, M & S*	1 Serving/100g	260	260	20.5	7.3	17.0	0.6
Hot & Spicy, Asda*	1 Pack/450g	1076	239	21.0	4.9	15.0	1.3
Hot & Spicy, Tesco*	½ Pack/325g	725	223	22.7	5.4	12.3	0.4
In Cantonese Sauce, Asda*	1 Pack/360g	994	276	13.2	19.9	16.0	0.4
Microwave, Tesco*	1oz/28g	72	256	22.7	7.8	14.9	0.4
Take Away, Pizza Hut*	1 Pack/178g	466	262	22.5	1.7	18.4	1.3
With Sour Cream & Chive Dip, Pizza Hut*	1 Pack/178g	680	382	22.8	1.9	31.5	1.3
CHICKEN WITH,							
Apricots & Almonds, HE, Tesco*	1 Pack/500g	465	93	11.8	7.3	1.9	0.5
Baby Potatoes, Basil & Mint, BGTY, Sainsbury's*	1 Pack/450g	306	68	9.1	5.4	1.1	1.6
Bacon & Leeks, BGTY, Sainsbury's*	1 Pack/450g	405	90	8.4	10.1	1.8	0.6
Citrus Wild Rice, BGTY, Sainsbury's*	1 Pack/450g	513	114	8.1	17.0	1.5	0.7
Citrus Wild Rice, GFY, Asda*	1 Pack/393g	511	130	7.0	25.0	0.2	0.0
Coriander & Lime, Asda*	1 Serving/105g	122	116	24.0	2.9	0.9	0.2
Coriander & Lime, Somerfield*	1 Serving/170g	281	165	20.0	0.7	9.1	0.9
Cranberry & Orange, Roast Potatoes, Asda*	1 Pack/400g	664	166	10.0	18.0	6.0	1.3
Cranberry & Orange Stuffing, Sainsbury's*	1 Serving/100g	201	201	23.0	4.1	10.3	0.8
Cranberry Stuffing, Breast, Tesco Finest*	Half Pack/200g	252	126	16.2	9.9	2.4	0.9
Cranberry Stuffing, Finest, Tesco*	1 Serving/200g	252	126	16.2	9.9	2.4	0.9
Cream & Mushroom Sauce, Somerfield	1 Pack/300g	357	119	15.0	3.0	6.0	0.0
Garlic & Herb Butter, Somerfield*	1 Pack/397g	961	242	17.0	1.0	19.0	0.0
Garlic & Herbs, Asda*	1 Slice/25g	29	114	23.9	1.1	1.5	0.0
Garlic Dough Balls, Sainsbury's*	1 Serving/180g	344	191	20.2	11.8	8.2	2.7
Green Peppers, Black Bean Sauce & Rice, Farmfoods*	1 Meal/324g	408	126	5.5	17.1	3.9	0.4
Ham & Rice, COU, M & S*	1oz/28g	28	100	8.9	12.5	1.5	0.7
Leek, Cheese & Smoked Bacon, Breast, M & S*	1 Breast/200g	290	145	18.4	0.6	7.8	0.3
Leeks & Bacon, GFY, Asda*	1 Serving/213g	243	114	17.0	2.2	4.1	0.2
Lime & Coriander, HE, Tesco*	1 Pack/320g	413	129	20.0	8.4	1.7	1.9
Mild & Creamy Goat's Cheese, Breast, M & S*	½ Pack/200g	260	130	16.6	3.1	5.5	0.7
Mushroom & Ham, BGTY, Sainsbury's*	1 Pack/450g	567	126	9.8	19.2	1.1	0.3
Mushroom In Madeira Sauce, HE, Tesco*	½ Pack/200g	182	91	15.0	5.4	1.0	0.4
Mushrooms In Oyster Sauce, Tesco*	1 Packet/350g	189	54	8.0	3.5	0.9	0.8
Pancakes & Plum Sauce, COU M & S*	1 Pack/245g	257	105	7.9	12.7	2.3	0.3
Pancetta & Mozzarella, Finest, Tesco*	1 Serving/150g	297	198	11.6	11.5	11.8	0.9
Pappardelle, Citrus Saffron, Waitrose*	1 Serving/250g	340	136	9.1	8.8	7.1	1.5
Potato Wedges, Healthy Living, Co-Op*	1 Pack/295g	266	90	7.0	11.0	2.0	0.8
Potatoes, Italian Style, Finest, Tesco*	1 Pack/400g	516	129	8.4	7.3	7.4	0.5
Prosciutio, Dolcelatte & 3 Cheese Sauce, Asda*	½ Pack/195g	355	182	30.0	1.9	6.0	1.2
Red Peppers, COU, M & S*	1oz/28g	17	60	9.7	3.4	0.5	0.8
Rice 'n' Peas, Sainsbury's*	1 Pack/300g	489	163	12.5	14.4	6.1	2.1
Rice, Fiesta, Weight Watchers*	1 Pack/330g	277	84	6.0	10.5	2.0	0.4
Rice, Mexicana, Weight Watchers*	1 Pack/320g	275	86	5.0	13.2	1.5	0.5
Roast Red Pepper, Finest, Tesco*	1 Pack/400g	596	149	11.6	5.3	9.1	0.6
Roast Vegetables & Cous Cous, BGTY, Sainsbury's*	1 Pack/450g	621	138	9.7	16.2	3.8	2.1
Roasted Vegetables & Wild Rice, Co-Op*	1 Pack/350g	1523	435	33.0	67.0	4.0	2.0
Rosemary Potatoes & Chorizo, Finest, Tesco*	1 Pack/350g	371	106	11.4	5.8	4.1	0.7
Salsa & Potato Wedges, GFY, Asda*	1 Pack/400g	364	91	6.0	9.0	3.4	2.6
Spicy Tomato, Fresh, Asda*	1 Pack/200g	470	235	34.0	4.4	9.0	1.2
Spinach & Pasta, M & S*	1oz/28g	64	228	9.4	14.0	15.0	1.3
Spinach In A Four Cheese Sauce, Finest, Tesco*	1 Serving/200g	230	115	16.1	2.0	4.7	0.5
Spring Vegetables & Creamy Sauce, Finest, Tesco*	1 Serving/200g	186	93	12.3	3.0	3.5	0.6

C

	Measure WEIGHT/INFO	per Measure KCAL	Nutrition Values per 100g / 100ml KCAL	PROT	CARB	FAT	FIBRE
CHICKEN WITH,							
Stuffing, Breast, TTD, Sainsbury's*	1oz/28g	50	180	21.5	5.2	8.1	0.9
Sun Dried Tomato & Olive Oil, Breast, Waitrose*	1 Serving/95g	132	139	24.1	2.5	3.7	1.2
Sundried Tomato & Basil Butter, Sainsbury's*	1 Breast/185g	363	196	25.0	2.5	9.5	0.2
Tagine, Cous Cous, BGTY, Sainsbury's*	1 Pack/450g	626	139	10.1	15.9	3.9	1.5
Tomato & Basil, Roasted Baby Potatoes, BGTY, Sainsbury's*	1 Pack/450g	369	82	9.0	7.9	1.6	1.2
Tomato & Basil, HE, Tesco*	1 Serving/225g	189	84	11.2	6.1	1.7	1.2
Veg, Red Wine & Potato Gratin, COU, M & S*	1 Pack/400g	380	95	8.8	10.5	2.0	1.2
White Rice, Oriental Express*	1 Pack/340g	347	102	4.5	20.9	0.6	0.6
CHILLI,							
& Potato Wedges, Good Choice, Iceland*	1 Pack/400g	368	92	5.5	9.8	3.4	1.2
& Potato Wedges, Sainsbury's*	1 Pack/370g	393	106	7.2	10.1	4.1	2.2
Beef & Chilli Sauce, Chinese Takeaway, Farmfoods*	1oz/28g	66	234	6.7	20.0	13.0	0.3
Beef, Asda*	½ Pack/200g	190	95	7.0	8.0	3.9	1.2
Beef, Crispy, Sainsbury's*	1 Pack/400g	628	157	12.8	4.9	9.6	1.2
Beef Jacket, M & S*	1 Pack/360g	288	80	5.9	9.6	2.0	0.9
Beef, With Rice, Sainsbury's*	1 Serving/300g	360	120	5.6	20.6	1.7	1.1
Con Carne & Rice, Somerfield*	1 Pack/500g	490	98	5.0	18.0	1.0	0.0
Con Carne, 99% Fat Free, Stagg*	1oz/28g	28	99	7.2	14.2	0.4	2.2
Con Carne, Baked Bean, Heinz*	1 Can/390g	324	83	7.0	10.3	1.5	2.8
Con Carne, Bird's Eye*	1 Pack/300g	324	108	3.9	17.8	2.3	1.6
Con Carne, Frozen, Co-Op*	1 Pack/340g	306	90	6.0	15.0	1.0	1.0
Con Carne, Good Choice, Iceland*	1 Pack/400g	464	116	4.6	22.6	0.8	0.3
Con Carne, Homepride*	1 tin/390g	234	60	2.5	11.2	0.6	0.0
Con Carne, Iceland*	1 Pack/400g	412	103	5.3	19.6	0.4	1.0
Con Carne, Lidl*	1 Serving/250g	278	111	8.0	12.0	3.0	0.0
Con Carne, M & S*	1 Pack/285g	285	100	8.7	7.4	3.7	2.0
Con Carne, Ready Meals, Waitrose*	1oz/28g	39	138	6.0	21.8	3.0	1.5
Con Carne, Sainsbury's*	1 Pack/400g	412	103	4.5	18.4	1.3	1.1
Con Carne, SmartPrice, Asda*	1 Can/392g	372	95	6.0	12.0	2.6	2.4
Con Carne, Tesco*	1 Can/392g	463	118	8.0	10.5	4.9	2.4
Con Carne With Rice, BGTY, Sainsbury's*	1 Pack/449g	503	112	6.5	17.4	1.8	0.8
Con Carne With Rice, COU, M & S*	1oz/28g	25	90	6.3	14.0	1.1	1.4
Con Carne With Rice, Healthy Choice, Asda*	1 Pack/400g	412	103	6.0	15.0	2.1	0.9
Crispy Beef, Ready Meals, M & S*	1oz/28g	74	265	8.9	33.1	10.5	0.7
Crispy Beef, Tesco*	1 Pack/250g	455	182	11.4	19.8	6.3	1.2
Extra Hot, M & S*	1oz/28g	28	100	8.7	9.1	3.1	1.8
Meat Free, Sainsbury's*	1 Pack/400g	308	77	4.0	4.1	5.0	5.2
Medium, Uncle Ben's*	1 Jar/500g	305	61	1.8	11.1	0.8	0.0
Mexican Chilli With Potato Wedges, Weight Watchers*	1 Pack/300g	252	84	5.1	10.3	2.5	1.7
Mexican Style, Aldi*	½ Can/196g	231	118	8.7	9.2	5.2	2.1
Mixed Vegetable, Tesco*	1 Pack/400g	352	88	3.9	11.0	2.9	3.2
Non Carne, Linda McCartney*	1 Pack/340g	252	74	5.8	9.2	2.3	1.7
Quorn*	1oz/28g	23	81	4.7	6.9	4.2	2.5
Quorn*, With Rice	1 Pack/300g	246	82	4.9	11.7	1.7	2.2
Spicy Bean & Vegetable, Safeway*	1 Pack/311g	196	63	3.3	9.6	1.3	2.5
Uncle Ben's*	1oz/28g	17	59	1.8	11.1	0.8	0.0
Vegetable	1oz/28g	16	57	3.0	10.8	0.6	2.6
Vegetable, & Rice, BGTY, Sainsbury's*	1 Pack/450g	405	90	3.5	17.6	0.6	2.1
Vegetable, & Rice, HE,Tesco*	1 Pack/450g	392	87	2.8	16.1	1.2	1.5
Vegetable, & Rice, Safeway*	1 Pack/500g	530	106	3.4	21.2	0.8	1.7
Vegetable, 99% Fat Free, Stagg*	1oz/28g	16	58	3.1	9.3	0.5	3.1
Vegetable, GFY, Asda*	1 Pack/310g	270	87	2.8	17.0	0.9	1.0
Vegetable, Organic, Sainsbury's*	1 Pack/355g	309	87	2.6	16.5	1.2	1.6
Vegetable, Retail	1oz/28g	20	70	4.0	9.4	2.1	0.0

CHILLI,	Measure WEIGHT/INFO	per Measure KCAL	KCAL	PROT	CARB	FAT	FIBRE
Vegetable, Waitrose*	1 Can/392g	227	58	2.9	6.6	2.2	0.0
Wedge Bowl, COU, M & S*	1 Pack/400g	380	95	7.2	11.3	2.3	1.8
Weight Watchers*	1 Pack/320g	269	84	5.1	10.4	2.5	1.7
CHILLIES,							
Green, Tesco*	1oz/28g	4	16	0.8	2.6	0.3	1.6
Mixed, Tesco*	1oz/28g	8	27	1.8	4.2	0.3	1.6
Very Lazy, EPC*	1 Serving/10g	11	114	4.2	15.3	4.0	0.5
CHINESE LEAVES, Tesco*	1 Serving/100g	18	18	3.5	0.3	0.3	2.6
CHINESE MEAL,							
For One, GFY, Asda*	1 Pack/570g	946	166	7.0	28.0	2.9	0.0
For Two, Tesco*	1 Pack/500g	480	96	4.4	16.0	1.6	1.1
CHIPLETS, Salt & Vinegar, M & S*	1 Bag/35g	170	485	6.4	59.5	25.5	2.4
CHIPS,							
11mm Fresh, Deep Fried, McCain*	1oz/28g	66	235	3.2	31.8	10.6	0.0
14mm Fresh, Deep Fried, McCain*	1oz/28g	59	209	2.7	34.2	6.8	0.0
14mm Friers Choice, Deep Fried, McCain*	1oz/28g	56	199	3.5	29.3	8.0	0.0
3 Way Cook, Somerfield*	1 Serving/96g	145	151	2.5	24.0	5.0	1.6
9/16"" Straight Cut Caterpack, Deep Fried, McCain*	1oz/28g	63	225	3.1	32.1	9.4	0.0
American Style Oven, Co-Op*	1 Serving/150g	255	170	2.0	26.0	6.0	3.0
American Style Oven, Safeway*	1 Serving/125g	288	230	4.1	38.2	6.8	3.0
American Style Oven, Sainsbury's*	1 Serving/165g	314	190	5.4	23.6	8.3	1.3
American Style Southern Fried, Iceland*	1 Serving/100g	251	251	4.0	34.0	11.0	3.0
American Style Thin Oven, Tesco*	1 Serving/125g	210	168	2.7	24.6	6.5	2.1
Beefeater, Deep Fried, McCain*	1oz/28g	71	253	3.3	37.7	9.9	0.0
Beefeater, Oven Baked, McCain*	1oz/28g	55	195	4.0	32.2	5.6	0.0
Chippy, Deep Fried, McCain*	1oz/28g	51	182	3.0	27.8	6.5	0.0
Chunky, COU, M & S*	1 Serving/150g	135	90	1.6	17.6	1.7	1.5
Chunky, Eat Smart, Safeway*	1 Serving/158g	150	95	1.6	18.3	1.6	1.4
Chunky Oven, Harry Ramsden's*	1 Serving/150g	185	123	2.8	19.9	3.6	1.6
COU, M & S*	1 Serving/300g	270	90	1.6	17.6	1.7	1.5
Crinkle Cut, Frozen, Fried In Corn Oil	1oz/28g	81	290	3.6	33.4	16.7	2.2
Crinkle Cut Oven, Asda*	1 Serving/100g	244	244	3.8	37.0	9.0	3.0
Crinkle Cut, Oven Baked, McCain*	1oz/28g	51	182	3.3	29.7	5.6	0.0
Crinkle Cut Oven, Safeway*	1 Serving/130g	234	180	3.3	29.5	5.4	2.4
Crinkle Cut Oven, Ultimate Seasoned, McCain*	1 Serving/85g	190	223	3.5	34.0	8.2	3.5
Family Fries Oven, Tesco*	1 Serving/125g	164	131	2.0	22.4	3.7	1.8
Fine Cut, Frozen, Fried In Blended Oil	1oz/28g	102	364	4.5	41.2	21.3	2.4
Fine Cut, Frozen, Fried In Corn Oil	1oz/28g	102	364	4.5	41.2	21.3	2.7
French Fries, Retail	1oz/28g	78	280	3.3	34.0	15.5	2.1
Homemade, Fried In Blended Oil	1oz/28g	53	189	3.9	30.1	6.7	2.2
Homemade, Fried In Corn Oil	1oz/28g	53	189	3.9	30.1	6.7	2.2
Homemade, Fried In Dripping	1oz/28g	53	189	3.9	30.1	6.7	2.2
Homestyle Oven, Sainsbury's*	1 Serving/125g	206	165	2.4	29.2	4.3	2.1
Just Bake, Low Fat, M & S*	1oz/28g	37	133	2.0	24.7	3.7	1.7
Low Fat, Good Choice, Iceland*	1oz/28g	41	147	2.0	25.3	2.6	1.8
Micro, McCain*	1oz/28g	54	194	3.3	27.3	7.9	0.0
Microwave, Cooked	1oz/28g	62	221	3.6	32.1	9.6	2.9
New Crinkle Cut, Oven Baked, McCain*	1oz/28g	55	198	3.5	33.4	5.6	0.0
New Straight Cut, Oven Baked, McCain*	1oz/28g	51	182	3.6	31.4	4.7	0.0
Oven Baked, McCain*	1oz/28g	48	173	2.8	29.3	4.9	0.0
Oven, BGTY, Sainsbury's*	1oz/28g	42	151	2.7	27.1	3.5	2.1
Oven, Champion, Aldi*	1oz/28g	44	158	2.5	27.0	4.5	0.0
Oven, Cooked, Value, Tesco*	1 Serving/125g	308	246	4.5	39.5	7.8	2.9
Oven, Crinkle Cut, Co-Op*	1oz/28g	38	135	2.0	22.0	4.0	3.0

Nutrition Values per 100g / 100ml

C

	Measure WEIGHT/INFO	per Measure KCAL	KCAL	PROT	CARB	FAT	FIBRE
			Nutrition Values per 100g / 100ml				
CHIPS,							
Oven, Crinkle Cut, Tesco*	1oz/28g	40	142	2.1	23.3	4.5	2.0
Oven, Frozen, Baked	1oz/28g	45	162	3.2	29.8	4.2	2.0
Oven, Frozen, McCain*	1oz/28g	39	138	2.5	26.2	4.0	1.9
Oven, Healthy Choice, Safeway*	1 Serving/150g	227	151	2.8	27.1	3.5	2.1
Oven, Morrisons*	1 Serving/100g	134	134	2.4	22.2	3.9	0.0
Oven, Reduced Fat, Waitrose*	1oz/28g	37	133	2.3	24.3	3.0	1.6
Oven, Safeway*	1oz/28g	42	151	2.8	27.1	3.5	2.1
Oven Steak Cut, Asda*	1 Serving/100g	153	153	2.0	27.0	4.1	2.5
Oven, Steak Cut, Sainsbury's*	1 Serving/165g	266	161	2.6	27.1	4.7	2.8
Oven, Straight Cut, 4% Fat, HE, Tesco*,	1oz/28g	35	124	2.3	21.8	3.1	1.9
Oven, Straight Cut, Better For You, Morrisons*	1 Serving/165g	249	151	2.8	27.1	3.5	2.1
Oven, Straight Cut, Great Value Asda*	1 Serving/100g	199	199	3.5	35.0	5.0	3.0
Oven, Straight Cut, Sainsbury's*	1 Serving/200g	340	170	3.4	28.0	4.9	2.5
Oven, Thick Cut, Frozen, Baked	1oz/28g	44	157	3.2	27.9	4.4	1.8
Retail, Fried In Blended Oil	1oz/28g	67	239	3.2	30.5	12.4	2.2
Steakhouse Oven, Tesco*	1 Serving/125g	165	132	2.7	22.7	3.4	1.7
Straight Cut, Frozen, Fried In Blended Oil	1oz/28g	76	273	4.1	36.0	13.5	2.4
Straight Cut, Frozen, Fried In Corn Oil	1oz/28g	76	273	4.1	36.0	13.5	2.4
Straight Cut, Microwave Baked, McCain*	1oz/28g	70	251	3.5	35.0	10.7	0.0
Straight Cut, Oven Baked, McCain*	1oz/28g	48	173	2.8	29.3	4.9	0.0
Straight Cut Oven, Reduced Fat, Tesco*	1 Serving/100g	127	127	2.3	22.7	3.0	2.1
Straight Cut Oven Cooked, HE, Tesco*	1oz/28g	35	124	2.3	21.8	3.1	1.9
Straight Cut Oven Cooked, Tesco*	1oz/28g	46	166	2.6	27.8	4.9	1.7
Straight Cut Oven, GFY, Asda*	1oz/28g	42	150	2.6	27.0	3.5	2.4
Straight Cut Oven, Iceland*	1 Serving/100g	197	197	3.6	31.6	6.2	2.3
Stringfellows, Oven Baked, McCain*	1oz/28g	72	256	4.1	37.0	10.2	0.0
Thick Cut Caterpack, Deep Fried, McCain*	1oz/28g	60	215	3.1	28.8	9.7	0.0
Thick Cut, Frozen, Fried In Corn Oil	1oz/28g	66	234	3.6	34.0	10.2	2.4
Vending 3/8"" Straight Cut, Deep Fried, McCain*	1oz/28g	62	220	3.3	29.6	9.8	0.0
CHIPSTICKS,							
Ready Salted, Smiths, Walkers*	1 Bag/22g	105	476	6.8	59.5	23.5	0.0
Salt & Vinegar, Smiths, Walkers*	1 Bag/22g	105	476	6.8	59.5	23.5	0.0
CHIVES, Fresh	1oz/28g	6	23	2.8	1.7	0.6	1.9
CHOC ICES,							
Choc Ices	1 Bar/50g	139	277	3.5	28.1	17.5	0.0
Chunky, Walls*	1 bar/81g	162	200	2.6	18.9	13.1	0.0
Dark, Somerfield*	1 Choc Ice/62ml	186	300	3.0	25.0	21.0	0.0
Economy Sainsbury's*	1 Choc Ice/31g	92	292	2.6	17.6	23.5	0.9
Fruit & Nut, Safeway*	1 Choc Ice/45g	154	343	3.9	30.6	22.8	1.7
Light, Sainsburys*	1 bar/43g	135	313	3.2	27.0	21.4	0.3
Light, Tesco*	1 Serving/43g	138	322	3.4	27.1	22.1	0.5
Milk Chocolate, M & S*	1oz/28g	86	306	4.1	28.7	19.4	0.5
Neapolitan Chocolate, Co-Op*	1 Ice/62g	120	194	2.0	16.9	13.2	0.4
Neapolitan Chocolate, Farmfoods*	1 Bar/62ml	76	230	2.6	24.9	13.3	0.0
Real Milk, Sainsbury's*	1 Ice/71ml	133	187	2.0	20.0	11.0	0.1
Real White, Tesco*	1 Ice/54g	185	343	4.2	27.4	24.1	0.1
Rum & Rasin, Safeway*	1 Ice/45g	136	303	3.3	28.9	19.3	1.1
SmartPrice, Asda*	1 Choc Ice/31g	81	262	2.8	20.0	19.0	0.0
CHOCOLATE, (SEE ALSO CHOCOLATES)							
All Gold Plain, Terry's*	1oz/28g	134	477	3.8	60.9	24.0	1.1
Animal Bar, Nestle*	1 Bar/19g	97	513	5.8	63.6	26.1	0.0
Assortment, Occasions, Tesco*	1 Serving/150g	705	470	4.6	65.8	20.9	0.5
Barbie, Milk, M & S*	1 Bar/13g	70	540	8.1	54.1	32.4	1.3
Belgian Assortment, Waitrose*	1oz/28g	127	453	6.3	45.5	27.3	3.8

C

CHOCOLATE,	Measure WEIGHT/INFO	per Measure KCAL	Nutrition Values per 100g / 100ml KCAL	PROT	CARB	FAT	FIBRE
Belgian Dark, Extra Special, Asda*	2 Squares/20g	102	508	11.0	26.0	40.0	16.0
Belgian, Finest, Tesco*	1 Chocolate/12g	62	520	5.9	55.6	28.4	5.2
Belgian Plain With Ginger, TTD, Sainsbury's*	2 Squares/20g	114	571	7.2	31.2	46.4	10.9
Belgian Seashells, Woolworths*	1 Box/63g	347	550	5.5	52.9	31.1	0.0
Belgian White With Coffee, TTD, Sainsbury's*	2 Squares/20g	110	548	6.5	56.9	32.7	0.0
Belgian White With Lemon, TTD, Sainsbury's*	2 Squares/20g	109	546	5.7	61.2	30.9	0.1
Black Magic, Nestle*	1oz/28g	128	456	4.4	62.6	20.8	1.6
Bournville, Cadbury's*	1 Bar/50g	248	495	4.6	59.6	26.7	0.0
Brazil Nut Assortment, M & S*	1oz/28g	163	581	9.6	37.5	45.3	1.5
Bubble Bar, M & S*	1 Bar/25g	136	542	9.5	51.8	33.1	2.2
Chocolate Buttons, White, Co-Op*	1 Pack/70g	382	545	7.0	61.0	31.0	0.0
Cafe au Lait, Thorntons*	1 Chocolate/16g	77	481	5.3	58.1	25.0	0.6
Cappuccino Bar, Thorntons*	1 Bar/38g	201	529	5.2	49.7	34.7	0.5
Cappuccino Mountain Bar, M & S*	1oz/28g	149	533	8.4	52.0	32.5	2.6
Chocolat Noir, Lindt*	1/6 Bar/17g	87	510	6.0	50.0	32.0	0.0
Chocolate Orange Bar, Milk, Terry's*	1 Bar/85g	459	540	7.5	55.6	32.0	0.3
Chocolate Orange Bar, Terry's*	1 Bar/40g	212	531	7.7	57.4	30.0	2.1
Chomp, Cadbury's*	1 Treatsize/12g	56	465	3.5	67.9	19.8	0.0
Chunky Hazelnut Bar, M & S*	1 Bar/52g	293	563	8.8	48.1	37.3	1.7
Classic Chocolate Bar, Cadbury's*	1 Bar/26g	134	514	6.5	62.3	26.5	0.8
Dairy Milk, Cadbury's*	1 Treatsize/15g	80	530	7.8	57.1	29.9	0.0
Dairy Milk, Snack Size, Cadbury's*	1 Bar/30g	159	530	7.8	57.1	29.9	0.0
Dark, Bar, Thorntons*	1 Sm Bar/48g	245	511	9.3	31.6	38.8	15.9
Dark, Co-Op*	1 Bar/50g	253	505	4.0	57.0	29.0	6.0
Dark, Organic, Green & Black's*	1 Bar/20g	114	571	10.0	51.0	37.0	0.0
Divine, Milk, Co-Op*	1 Bar/45g	243	540	7.0	57.0	32.0	2.0
Freddo, Cadbury's*	1 Bar/17g	89	525	7.8	56.8	29.4	0.0
Fruit & Nut Assortment, M & S*	1oz/28g	148	527	7.6	49.8	34.3	1.3
Fruit & Nut, Cadbury's*	1 Bar/49g	240	490	8.0	55.7	26.3	0.0
Ginger, Dark, Thorntons*	1 Bar/100g	509	509	5.8	44.3	35.1	8.8
Ginger, Terry's*	1oz/28g	111	395	2.6	68.0	12.4	3.4
Irish Cream Liqueur, Thorntons*	1 Chocolate/14g	67	479	6.1	51.4	25.7	0.0
Jazz Orange Bar, Thorntons*	1 Bar/56g	304	543	6.8	55.7	32.3	1.2
Kinder Bueno, Ferrero*	1 Twin Bar/43g	245	570	8.5	47.6	38.5	0.0
Lemon Mousse, Bar, Thorntons*	1oz/28g	141	503	4.1	55.3	29.3	0.0
Luxury Belgian Milk, Bar,For Baking, Sainsbury's*	1 Serving/175g	973	556	7.6	56.5	33.3	1.5
Luxury Dark Continental, Tesco*	1 Bar/100g	571	571	11.3	46.5	37.8	0.1
Maya Gold, Green & Black's*	1 Bar/20g	110	552	6.0	56.5	33.5	0.0
Milk	1oz/28g	146	520	7.7	56.9	30.7	0.8
Milk Chocolate Excellence, Lindt*	1 Bar/100g	570	570	6.6	48.9	39.6	0.0
Milk, Co-Op*	1 Sm Bar/50g	265	530	9.0	55.0	31.0	2.0
Milk, Extra au Lait, Milch Extra, Lindt*	½ Bar/50g	268	535	6.5	57.0	31.0	0.0
Milk, Extra Fine Swiss, M & S*	1oz/28g	155	553	8.9	50.4	35.3	2.4
Milk, Organic, Green & Black's*	1oz/28g	147	524	9.5	54.0	32.0	0.0
Milk, SmartPrice, Asda*	1 Square/6g	32	536	8.0	54.0	32.0	2.4
Milk, Tesco*	1 Serving/25g	133	533	9.5	54.7	30.7	2.2
Milk, Thorntons*	1 Sm Bar/50g	269	538	7.5	54.8	32.0	1.0
Mint Crisp, Cadbury's*	1oz/28g	141	505	6.4	70.3	22.2	0.0
Mountain Bars, Mini, M & S*	1oz/28g	152	542	8.5	52.3	33.3	2.4
Muffin Chocolate Bar, Asda*	1 Bar/37g	142	385	5.0	53.0	17.0	3.3
Neapolitans, Terry's*	1oz/28g	146	522	6.0	57.3	29.7	4.1
Nuts About Caramel, Cadbury's*	1 Bar/55g	272	495	5.8	56.6	27.4	0.0
Old Jamaica, Cadbury's*	1oz/28g	129	460	5.8	56.9	23.3	0.0
Orange, Plain, Terry's*	1 Orange/175g	889	508	3.8	56.8	29.4	6.2

C

CHOCOLATE,	Measure WEIGHT/INFO	per Measure KCAL	KCAL	PROT	CARB	FAT	FIBRE
			Nutrition Values per 100g / 100ml				
Orange Toffi Chocs, Thorntons*	1oz/28g	125	448	4.4	48.5	26.4	0.3
Original Toffi Chocs, Thorntons*	1oz/28g	125	448	4.4	48.5	26.4	0.3
Pain Au Chocolat, Asda*	1 Serving/23g	106	462	8.0	49.0	26.0	0.0
Pain Au Chocolat, Waitrose*	1 Serving/90g	380	422	8.1	34.9	27.8	1.1
Panettone, M & S*	1 Serving/90g	333	370	5.7	48.4	17.7	2.2
Peanuts, Assorted, Thorntons*	1 Bag/140g	785	561	13.8	34.8	40.8	3.6
Plain	1oz/28g	143	510	5.0	63.5	28.0	2.5
Plain, Cocoa Solids, Finest, Tesco*	1 Square/10g	58	581	7.7	38.5	44.0	5.8
Plain, Organic, Tesco*	1 oz/28g	145	519	6.4	44.7	34.9	9.6
Rich Dark Fruit & Nut Plain, Sainsbury's*	4 Sqs/25g	117	489	5.2	53.9	27.9	5.7
Rich Dark Plain, Co-Op*	1 Bar/200g	1010	505	4.0	57.0	29.0	6.0
Rich Dark Plain, Sainsbury's*	1oz/28g	144	514	3.7	65.0	29.5	0.9
Rich Dark Plain, Somerfield*	1 Bar/200g	1014	507	5.0	52.0	31.0	0.0
Rocher, Thorntons*	1 Chocolate/15g	76	507	6.8	45.3	33.3	2.0
Swiss Dark Extra Fine, M & S*	1 Bar/150g	773	515	6.4	46.7	34.5	9.7
Swiss Milk Chocolate & Hazelnut Bar, M & S*	1oz/28g	156	556	6.4	51.9	36.0	3.3
Swiss Milk, M & S*	1oz/28g	150	535	5.1	60.9	30.1	1.9
Swiss Mountain Bar, M & S*	1 Bar/100g	555	555	6.5	55.2	35.3	0.2
Swiss White, Bar, M & S*	1oz/28g	152	543	8.0	58.3	30.9	0.0
Taz Chocolate Bar, Cadbury's*	1 Bar/25g	121	485	4.8	62.0	24.0	0.0
Teddy, Milk, Thorntons*	1 Teddy/250g	1358	543	7.6	52.6	33.5	1.0
White	1oz/28g	148	529	8.0	58.3	30.9	0.0
White, Organic, Green & Black's*	1 Bag/30g	173	577	7.5	52.5	37.5	0.0
White, Thorntons*	1 Bar/50g	273	546	6.7	59.4	31.4	0.0
Whole Nut, Cadbury's*	1 Bar/49g	270	550	9.3	48.8	35.2	0.0
Wholenut, Cadbury's*	1 Snacksize Bar/30g	165	550	9.3	48.8	35.2	0.0
Wildlife Bar, Cadbury's*	1 Bar/21g	109	520	7.8	56.8	29.3	0.0
CHOCOLATE DROPS,							
Plain, Sainsbury's*	1 Serving/125g	638	510	5.3	60.1	27.6	4.0
White, For Cooking & Decorating, Sainsbury's*	1oz/28g	152	544	6.5	60.3	30.8	0.0
CHOCOLATE ECLAIRS,							
Cadbury's*	1 Sweet/8g	39	485	4.6	75.0	18.8	0.0
Fresh Cream, Co-Op*	1 Eclair/8g	38	470	3.0	71.0	19.0	0.1
M & S*	1 Sweet/7g	34	482	1.9	73.9	20.1	0.0
Sainsbury's*	1 Sweet/7g	32	452	3.0	61.1	19.1	0.6
CHOCOLATE ORANGE,							
Milk, Terry's*	1 Orange/175g	928	530	7.5	57.3	30.0	2.1
Mini Segments, Milk, Terry's*	1 Segment/8g	42	527	7.7	57.9	29.4	2.1
Toffee Eclairs, Terry's*	1oz/28g	132	473	1.7	68.3	21.4	0.1
CHOCOLATE PEANUTS,							
Co-Op*	1oz/28g	153	545	15.0	34.0	39.0	4.0
M & S*	1oz/28g	149	531	12.8	43.1	34.1	4.2
Milk, Somerfield*	1oz/28g	155	553	16.0	34.0	39.0	0.0
Milk, Tesco*	1 Bag/227g	1221	538	17.5	31.8	37.9	4.4
CHOCOLATE RAISINS,							
Assorted, Thorntons*	1 Bag/140g	601	429	4.2	58.8	19.7	2.9
Co-Op*	¼ Pack/50g	205	410	4.0	64.0	15.0	1.0
M & S*	1oz/28g	116	414	4.5	66.5	14.6	1.2
Milk, Sainsbury's*	1oz/28g	117	418	4.7	62.7	16.5	1.4
CHOCOLATE SPREAD							
Chocolate Spread	1 Tsp/12g	68	569	4.1	57.1	37.6	0.0
Cadbury's*	1 Tsp/12g	69	575	4.5	55.0	38.0	0.0
Hazelnut, Nutella, Ferrero*	1oz/28g	149	533	6.5	57.0	31.0	0.0
Milk, Belgian, Sainsbury's*	1 Serving/10g	56	559	11.9	47.2	35.8	1.4

C

	Measure WEIGHT/INFO	per Measure KCAL	Nutrition Values per 100g / 100ml KCAL	PROT	CARB	FAT	FIBRE
CHOCOLATE SPREAD,							
Nutella, Ferrero*	1 Tsp/12g	62	516	6.4	61.2	29.0	0.0
Snickers, Mars*	1 Serving/7g	38	548	8.7	43.3	37.8	0.0
With Nuts	1 Tsp/12g	66	549	6.2	60.5	33.0	0.8
CHOCOLATE WITH Almonds, Dark, Organic, Evernat*	1oz/28g	169	604	16.3	37.4	43.2	0.0
CHOCOLATES,							
All Gold Milk, Terry's*	1oz/28g	137	490	5.6	61.5	24.5	0.6
Almond Mocca Mousse, Thorntons*	1 Chocolate/14g	76	543	8.5	40.7	37.9	2.9
Alpini, Thorntons*	1 Chocolate/13g	70	538	7.0	54.6	32.3	2.3
Apricot Parfait, Thorntons*	1 Chocolate/14g	63	450	4.9	51.2	25.0	2.9
Bittermint, Bendicks*	1 Mint/18.2g	74	411	4.4	63.0	17.6	0.0
Buttons, Cadbury's*	1 Treat Size/14g	74	525	7.8	56.8	29.4	0.0
Buttons, Milk, M & S*	1 Pack/75g	375	500	8.6	59.8	25.3	1.9
Buttons, Milk, Somerfield*	1 Pack/75g	390	520	8.0	58.0	28.0	0.0
Cappuccino, Thorntons*	1 Chocolate/13g	70	538	5.9	48.5	36.2	0.8
Champagne, Thorntons*	1 Chocolate/16g	76	475	6.9	43.1	29.4	2.5
Chocolate Mousse, Thorntons*	1 Chocolate/13g	67	515	7.5	40.0	36.2	3.1
Coffee Creme, Dark, Thorntons*	1 Chocolate/13g	52	400	3.0	71.5	10.8	0.8
Coffee Creme, Milk, Thorntons*	1 Chocolate/13g	52	400	2.8	74.6	10.0	0.8
Country Caramel, Milk, Thorntons*	1 Chocolate/9g	45	500	4.6	62.2	26.7	0.0
Dairy Box, Milk, Nestle*	1 Sm Box/227g	1085	478	5.7	60.8	23.5	0.8
Lemon Parfait, Milk, Thorntons*	1 Chocolate/14g	66	471	3.6	65.0	22.9	0.7
Liquers, Cognac Truffle, Thorntons*	1 Chocolate/14g	65	464	7.3	40.0	27.1	2.9
Liqueurs, Milk Chocolate Luxury Selection, Famous Names*	1 Chocolate/8g	36	456	3.2	60.8	19.6	0.0
Milk Tray, Cadbury's*	1oz/28g	139	495	5.2	60.5	26.0	0.0
Mint Batons, Bendicks*	1 Mint/6g	31	517	6.7	47.0	35.0	0.0
Mint Crisp, Bendicks*	1 Mint/7.7g	40	494	5.2	55.0	29.9	0.0
Mint Crisp, Dark, Elizabeth Shaw*	1 Chocolate/6g	27	458	1.9	68.0	20.7	0.0
Mint Crisp, Milk, Bendicks*	1 Mint/7g	37	529	7.1	57.0	31.4	0.0
Mint Crisp, Milk, Elizabeth Shaw*	1 Chocolate/6g	30	493	4.0	70.9	21.4	0.0
Mint Crisp, Thorntons*	1 Chocolate/7g	34	486	7.7	40.0	31.4	4.3
Mint Crisp, White, Bendicks*	1 Mint/9.5g	56	558	6.3	56.0	36.9	0.0
Mint Crisp, Woolworths*	1 Sweet/6g	29	481	5.1	68.8	24.1	0.0
Praline, Coffee, Thorntons*	1 Chocolate/7g	37	529	7.0	47.1	34.3	2.9
Praline, Double Nut, Thorntons*	1 Chocolate/6g	34	567	8.5	51.7	35.0	3.3
Praline, Hazelnut, Thorntons*	1 Chocolate/5g	27	540	7.0	48.0	36.0	4.0
Praline, Marzipan, Thorntons*	1 Chocolate/14g	63	450	5.9	58.6	21.4	2.1
Praline, Pirouett, Thorntons*	1 Chocolate/11g	60	545	6.8	46.4	36.4	4.5
Praline, Roast Hazelnut, Thorntons*	1 Chocolate/13g	70	538	6.0	51.5	33.8	3.1
Praline, Swiss, Bites, Sainsbury's*	1 Biscuit/7g	37	527	7.3	51.7	32.3	6.0
Strawberry Parfait, Milk, Thorntons*	1 Chocolate/14g	67	479	3.6	65.7	22.9	0.7
Swiss Milk Discs, M & S*	1 Disc/5g	28	553	8.9	50.4	35.3	2.4
Truffle, Amaretto, Thorntons*	1 Chocolate/14g	66	471	5.5	55.0	25.7	2.9
Truffle, Brandy, Thorntons*	1 Chocolate/14g	68	486	6.1	52.1	27.1	0.7
Truffle, Caramel, Thorntons*	1 Chocolate/14g	67	479	4.2	57.9	25.7	2.1
Truffle, Champagne, Petit, Thorntons*	1 Chocolate/6g	31	517	7.5	48.3	31.7	3.3
Truffle, Champagne, Premier, Thorntons*	1 Chocolate/17g	88	518	6.9	45.3	32.9	2.4
Truffle, Cherry, Thorntons*	1 Chocolate/14g	58	414	4.2	50.7	21.4	1.4
Truffle, Continental Champagne, Thorntons*	1 Chocolate/16g	78	488	6.1	51.3	28.0	0.6
Truffle, Grand Marnier, Thorntons*	1 Chocolate/15g	77	513	7.2	40.7	34.0	4.0
Truffle, Honey Nougat, Thorntons*	1 Chocolate/14g	74	529	6.2	52.1	32.9	0.7
Truffle, Irish Milk Chocolate Cream, Elizabeth Shaw*	1 Chocolate/12g	57	477	3.9	63.4	22.8	0.0
Truffle, Lemon, White, Thorntons*	1 Chocolate/14g	63	450	4.6	64.3	25.0	0.7
Truffle, Mocha	1oz/28g	137	488	6.2	63.8	24.9	2.0
Truffle, Rum, Thorntons*	1 Chocolate/13g	63	485	4.8	58.5	24.6	4.8

	Measure WEIGHT/INFO	per Measure KCAL	KCAL	PROT	CARB	FAT	FIBRE
CHOCOLATES,							
Chocolates,Truffle, Seville, Thorntons*	1 Chocolate/14g	76	543	7.1	53.6	33.6	1.4
Truffle, Swiss, Somerfield*	1 Pack/125g	640	512	4.0	52.0	32.0	0.0
Truffle, Thorntons*	1 Chocolate/7g	33	471	6.0	48.6	27.1	1.4
Truffle, Vanilla Almond, Thorntons*	1 Chocolate/15g	84	560	8.8	46.7	38.0	1.3
Truffle, Vanilla, Thorntons*	1 Chocolate/13g	64	492	4.8	57.7	26.9	1.5
Truffle, Viennese, Dark, Thorntons*	1 Chocolate/10g	53	530	5.9	47.0	36.0	3.0
Truffle, Viennese, Milk, Thorntons*	1 Chocolate/10g	56	560	4.9	54.0	36.0	0.0
Truffles, Rum	1oz/28g	146	521	6.1	49.7	33.7	1.9
Wild Raspberry Mousse, Thorntons*	1 Chocolate/12g	61	508	4.7	52.5	30.8	1.7
CHOW MEIN,							
Cantonese Chicken, Sainsbury's*	1 Pack/450g	455	101	6.5	11.5	3.2	1.7
Cantonese Vegetable, Sainsbury's*	½ Pack/100g	85	85	2.2	10.6	3.8	0.0
Chicken, Asda*	1 Serving/460g	488	106	5.0	13.0	3.8	2.1
Chicken, BGTY, Sainsbury's*	1 Meal/450g	410	91	6.9	11.5	1.9	1.2
Chicken, Co-Op*	1 Pack/300g	270	90	8.0	9.0	3.0	0.9
Chicken, COU, M & S*	1 Pack/200g	180	90	9.3	8.1	2.3	1.1
Chicken, Great Value, Asda*	1 Pack/400g	408	102	5.0	14.0	2.9	0.8
Chicken, HE, Tesco*	1 Pack/450g	392	87	8.2	10.8	1.2	0.4
Chicken, Iceland*	1 Pack/340g	343	101	7.8	15.0	1.1	1.4
Chicken, Microwavable, Oriental Express*	1 Pack/300g	246	82	4.6	16.0	0.6	1.2
Chicken, Somerfield*	1 Pack/280g	437	156	4.0	26.0	4.0	0.0
Chicken Stir Fry, Oriental Express*	1 Pack/350g	347	99	5.8	14.9	1.8	2.9
Chicken, Tesco*	1 Pack/350g	322	92	5.1	14.5	1.5	0.8
Chicken With Vegetable Spring Roll, Oriental Express*	1 Pack/300g	213	71	5.5	12.4	0.6	1.9
Chinese Style, Safeway*	1 Serving/150g	167	111	4.0	13.0	4.4	1.1
For 1, Vesta*	1 Pack/107g	340	318	14.8	54.0	4.7	7.7
Pork Perfectly Balanced, Waitrose*	½ Pack/310g	332	107	7.6	17.2	0.9	1.6
Special Chinese, Farmfoods*	1 Pack/400g	276	69	4.3	6.7	2.8	0.8
Special, COU, M & S*	1 Pack/400g	360	90	6.6	12.3	1.4	0.7
Special, Ready Meals, M & S*	1oz/28g	38	135	7.4	18.2	3.7	1.1
Stir Fry, Asda*	1 Pack/350g	270	77	2.1	6.0	5.0	0.0
Stir Fry, Somerfield*	1 Pack/300g	474	158	6.0	32.0	1.0	0.0
Vegetable, Asda*	1oz/28g	25	90	2.9	15.5	1.8	1.2
Vegetable, HE, Tesco*	1 Pack/350g	221	63	6.8	7.9	0.5	1.3
Vegetables & Noodles In Sauce, Safeway*	1 Serving/200g	110	55	3.7	9.5	0.2	1.3
With Vegetable Spring Roll, Oriental Express*	1 Roll/120g	196	163	5.3	28.5	3.2	3.0
CHRISTMAS PUDDING,							
Christmas Pudding	1oz/28g	81	291	4.6	49.5	9.7	1.3
Less Than 5% Fat, GFY, Asda*	½ Pudding/100g	279	279	2.6	58.0	4.1	1.6
Luxury, Budgens*	1 Portion/50g	160	320	3.4	50.7	9.3	1.4
Luxury, Safeway*	1/8 Pudding/114g	316	277	3.1	47.9	8.1	1.3
Luxury, Sainsbury's*	1 Pudding/100g	310	310	3.7	45.2	10.5	1.5
Luxury, Somerfield*	1/6 Pudding/75g	215	287	3.0	47.0	10.0	0.0
Retail	1oz/28g	92	329	3.0	56.3	11.8	1.7
Rich Fruit, Tesco*	1 Serving/114g	331	290	2.4	55.0	5.9	0.0
Sticky Toffee, Tesco*	¼ Pudding/114g	372	326	2.5	64.5	6.4	0.8
Tescos*	1 Serving/113g	305	270	2.4	55.0	5.9	1.5
Traditional, Budgens*	1 Portion/50g	124	247	2.6	55.6	6.0	1.6
Traditional Style, Asda*	1 Pudding/100g	296	296	2.6	58.0	6.0	1.6
Vintage, M & S*	1/8 Pudding/113g	335	295	2.6	59.8	5.6	1.4
CHUTNEY,							
Apricot & Ginger, Safeway*	1 Tsp/15g	24	162	1.4	38.0	0.2	2.0
Apricot, Sharwood's*	1 Tsp/16g	21	131	0.6	32.0	0.1	2.3
Bengal Hot, Sharwood's*	1oz/28g	56	200	0.5	48.7	0.3	1.1

Nutrition Values per 100g / 100ml

C

C

CHUTNEY,	Measure WEIGHT/INFO	per Measure KCAL	Nutrition Values per 100g / 100ml KCAL	PROT	CARB	FAT	FIBRE
Bengal Spice Mango, Sharwood's*	1 Tsp/5g	12	236	0.5	58.0	0.2	1.2
Caramalised Onion, Sainsbury's*	1 Serving/25g	28	111	1.1	23.5	1.4	1.1
Fruit, Spiced, Baxters*	1 Tsp/16g	23	143	6.0	34.8	0.1	0.0
Fruit, Traditional, M & S*	1oz/28g	43	155	0.9	37.2	0.3	1.7
Major Grey Mango, Patak's*	1oz/28g	71	255	0.4	66.0	0.2	0.7
Mango & Apple, Sharwood's*	1oz/28g	65	233	0.4	57.6	0.1	1.1
Mango & Lime, Sharwood's*	1oz/28g	58	206	0.4	50.5	0.3	0.8
Mango, Budgens*	1oz/28g	66	235	0.3	58.2	0.1	0.0
Mango, Green Label, Sharwood's*	1 Serving/10g	23	234	0.3	57.8	0.2	0.9
Mango, Hot, Patak's*	1oz/28g	72	258	0.4	67.1	0.2	0.7
Mango, Somerfield*	1oz/28g	40	143	1.0	35.0	0.0	0.0
Mango, Sweet	1 Heaped Tsp/16g	30	189	0.7	48.3	0.1	0.0
Mango With Ginger, Baxters*	1 Jar/320g	598	187	5.0	45.7	0.2	0.9
Mixed Fruit	1 Heaped Tsp/16g	25	155	0.6	39.7	0.0	0.0
Peach Fruit, Sharwoods*	1oz/28g	48	172	0.4	42.3	0.1	0.9
Ploughmans Plum, EPC*	1 Tsp/10g	16	160	1.3	38.1	0.2	1.6
Spicy Fruit, Safeway*	1 Tsp/16g	16	109	0.5	25.5	0.1	0.1
Spicy Mango, M & S*	1oz/28g	52	185	0.1	46.1	0.3	1.8
Strawberry & Black Pepper, TTD, Sainsbury's*	1 Dtsp/10g	17	169	1.1	39.5	0.4	1.3
Sweet Mango, M & S*	1oz/28g	67	240	0.3	58.8	0.2	1.5
Sweet Mango, Patak's*	1oz/28g	73	259	0.3	67.4	0.1	0.7
Tomato	1 Heaped Tsp/16g	20	128	1.2	31.0	0.2	1.3
Tomato & Red Pepper, Baxters*	1 Jar/312g	512	164	2.0	38.0	0.4	1.5
CIDER,							
Dry	1 Pint/568ml	204	36	0.0	2.6	0.0	0.0
Low Alcohol	1 Pint/568ml	97	17	0.0	3.6	0.0	0.0
Medium Sweet, Somerfield*	1 Pint/568ml	233	41	0.0	5.0	0.0	0.0
Sweet	1 Pint/568ml	239	42	0.0	4.3	0.0	0.0
Value, Tesco*	1 Pint/568ml	153	27	0.0	0.8	0.0	0.0
Vintage	1 Pint/568ml	574	101	0.0	7.3	0.0	0.0
CINNAMON, Powder	1 Tsp/3g	8	261	3.9	55.5	3.2	0.0
CLAMS,							
Baby, In Brine, John West*	1/3 Can/47g	38	81	16.0	3.0	0.6	0.0
Canned In Brine, Drained	1oz/28g	22	77	16.0	1.9	0.6	0.0
CLEMENTINES,							
Weighed With Peel & Pips	1oz/28g	8	28	0.7	6.5	0.1	0.9
Weighed Without Peel	1 Med/60g	22	37	0.9	8.7	0.1	1.2
COBBLER,							
Courgette & Pepper, M & S*	1 Pack/375g	300	80	2.8	11.3	2.8	1.5
Rhubarb & Gooseberry, M & S*	1oz/28g	48	170	2.3	28.2	5.2	2.3
COCKLES,							
Boiled	1 Cockle/4g	2	53	12.0	0.0	0.6	0.0
Bottled In Vinegar, Drained	1oz/28g	17	60	13.3	0.0	0.7	0.0
Cooked & Pickled, Van Smirren*	1oz/28g	23	81	12.0	9.0	1.0	0.0
COCOA BUTTER	1oz/28g	251	896	0.0	0.0	99.5	0.0
COCOA POWDER,							
Cadbury's*	1 Tbsp/16g	52	322	23.1	10.5	20.8	0.0
Made Up With Semi-Skimmed Milk	1 Mug/227ml	129	57	3.5	7.0	1.9	0.2
Made Up With Skimmed Milk	1 Mug/227ml	100	44	3.5	7.0	0.5	0.0
Made Up With Whole Milk	1 Mug/227ml	173	76	3.4	6.8	4.2	0.2
COCONUT,							
Cream	1oz/28g	98	350	4.0	5.9	34.7	0.0
Block	1oz/28g	187	669	6.0	7.0	68.8	0.0
Sharwood's*	1oz/28g	185	662	6.0	6.4	68.0	14.0

	Measure WEIGHT/INFO	per Measure KCAL	KCAL	PROT	CARB	FAT	FIBRE
			Nutrition Values per 100g / 100ml				
COCONUT,							
Desiccated	1oz/28g	169	604	5.6	6.4	62.0	13.7
Fresh	1oz/28g	98	351	3.2	3.7	36.0	7.3
Ice	1oz/28g	104	371	1.7	66.7	12.7	2.6
Milk, Amoy*	1oz/28g	39	140	1.9	1.1	17.0	0.0
Milk, BGTY, Sainsbury's*	¼ Can/100ml	96	96	1.0	3.6	8.6	0.0
Milk, Blue Dragon*	1 Can/400ml	640	160	2.2	2.2	15.7	0.0
Milk, Low Fat, Blue Dragon*	1 Can/400ml	272	68	0.7	1.0	6.7	0.0
Milk, Reduced Fat, Blue Dragon*	1 Can/400ml	408	102	0.9	2.4	9.8	0.0
COD,							
& Chips, Oven Baked, Safeway*	1 Pack/250g	523	209	8.4	25.0	8.4	3.5
Baked	1oz/28g	27	96	21.4	0.0	1.2	0.0
Cakes, Big Time, Bird's Eye*	1 Cake/114g	185	162	7.6	16.7	7.2	1.0
Captains Coins, Bird's Eye*	1 Coin/20g	34	168	10.1	13.3	8.3	0.9
Cheese & Chive Crunchies, Asda*	½ Pack/179g	399	223	8.0	23.0	11.0	1.5
Dried, Salted, Boiled	1oz/28g	39	138	32.5	0.0	0.9	0.0
Fillets, & Chips, M & S*	1 Pack/340g	612	180	7.0	22.1	7.0	1.8
Fillets, Battered, Iceland*	1 Fillet/115g	292	254	13.9	20.9	12.8	1.7
Fillets, Breaded, GFY, Asda*	1 Fillet/123g	185	150	14.0	17.0	2.9	1.5
Fillets, Breaded, Tesco*	1 Fillet/110g	220	200	12.2	17.6	9.0	1.1
Fillets, Breaded, Waitrose*	1 Fillet/150g	282	188	13.4	17.0	7.4	1.5
Fillets, Chargrilled, Sainsbury's*	1 Fillet/112g	184	164	15.4	0.8	11.0	0.0
Fillets, Chunky, Skinless & Boneless Breadcrumbs, Sainsbury's*	1 Fillet/125g	264	211	14.9	16.3	9.6	1.2
Fillets, Crispy Crumb, Farmfoods*	1oz/28g	59	209	13.3	17.0	9.8	0.5
Fillets, Fresh, Asda*	1 Serving/100g	95	95	21.0	0.0	1.2	0.0
Fillets, Frozen, Sainsbury's*	1 Fillet/110g	99	90	20.8	0.1	0.8	0.1
Fillets, In A Crunchy Ovencrisp Crumb, Tesco*	1 Fillet/127g	202	159	12.8	12.9	6.2	1.0
Fillets, In Breadcrumbs, Bird's Eye*	1 Serving/112g	190	170	12.8	14.2	6.9	0.5
Fillets, In Breadcrumbs, Safeway*	1 Fillet/135g	234	173	17.5	11.8	6.3	1.2
Fillets, In Crisp Crumb, Prime Cut Skinless, Waitrose*	1 Fillet/160g	269	168	14.2	11.7	7.1	0.5
Fillets, In Crispy Breadcrumbs, HE, Tesco*	1 Portion/120g	166	138	15.1	13.4	2.7	1.9
Fillets, In Crispy Crumb, Good Choice, Iceland*	1 Serving/127g	267	210	16.2	17.5	8.4	0.9
Fillets, In Crunchy Breadcrumbs, Sainsbury's*	1 Fillet/125g	273	218	13.6	17.1	10.6	1.3
Fillets, In Ovencrisp Batter, Tesco*	1 Portion/142g	240	169	12.1	16.3	6.1	0.3
Fillets, In Parsley Sauce, BGTY, Sainsbury's*	1 Pack/351g	316	90	11.6	1.3	4.3	0.7
Fillets, Smoked, Sainsbury's*	1 Serving/150g	152	101	21.6	0.0	1.6	0.0
Fillets, With A Mediterranean Pepper Sauce, Waitrose*	1 Pack/370g	241	65	12.2	1.1	1.3	0.9
Fish & Chips, Waitrose*	1 Serving/283g	849	300	14.4	33.7	12.0	4.8
In Batter, Chunky, M & S*	1oz/28g	48	172	13.8	10.6	8.6	0.8
In Batter, Fried In Blended Oil	1oz/28g	69	247	16.1	11.7	15.4	0.5
In Breadcrumbs, Chunky, M & S*	1oz/28g	46	166	13.6	9.9	8.0	1.3
In Breadcrumbs, COU, M & S*	1 Serving/136g	170	125	13.2	13.7	1.6	1.3
In Butter Sauce, Ross*	1 Serving/150g	126	84	9.1	3.2	3.9	0.1
In Butter Sauce, Sainsbury's*	1 Serving/170g	184	108	10.5	3.1	5.9	0.3
In Cheese Sauce, BGTY, Sainsbury's*	1 Serving/170g	145	85	12.8	3.1	2.4	0.0
In Mushroom Sauce, BGTY, Sainsbury's*	1 Serving/170g	112	66	9.9	2.8	1.7	0.1
In Oceancrisp Breadcrumbs, Tesco*	1 Fillet/125g	214	171	12.1	11.5	8.5	3.9
In Parsley Sauce, BGTY, Sainsbury's*	1 Pack/170g	143	84	11.4	2.4	3.2	0.3
In Parsley Sauce, COU, M & S*	1 Pack/185g	130	70	10.6	1.4	2.5	0.6
In Parsley Sauce, Eat Smart, Safeway*	1 Serving/200g	150	75	11.5	2.4	1.9	0.9
In Parsley Sauce, M & S*	1oz/28g	30	107	11.5	3.9	5.1	0.5
Loins, Tesco*	1 Loin/150g	120	80	18.3	0.0	0.7	0.0
Mornay, Sainsbury's*	1 Serving/180g	277	154	15.2	2.2	9.4	0.9
Poached	1oz/28g	26	94	20.9	0.0	1.1	0.0
Portions, Asda*	1 Cod Steak/92g	78	85	21.0	0.0	0.1	0.0

	Measure WEIGHT/INFO	per Measure KCAL	KCAL	PROT	CARB	FAT	FIBRE
COD,							
Portions, Breaded, Somerfield*	1 Portion/100g	206	206	13.0	13.0	12.0	0.0
Portions In Breadcrumbs, M & S*	1oz/28g	57	203	10.7	15.4	11.0	0.8
Portions In Parsley Sauce, Asda*	1 Serving/150g	116	77	11.0	3.8	2.0	0.1
Portions In Parsley Sauce, Sainsbury's*	1 Pack/170g	143	84	11.4	2.4	3.2	0.3
Raw	1oz/28g	22	80	18.3	0.0	0.7	0.0
Smoked, Poached	1oz/28g	28	101	21.6	0.0	1.6	0.0
Smoked, Raw	1oz/28g	22	79	18.3	0.0	0.6	0.0
Steaks, In Butter Sauce, Bird's Eye*	1 Pack/170g	165	97	10.0	3.9	4.6	0.1
Steaks, In Cheese Sauce, Bird's Eye*	1 Pack/182g	175	96	10.9	5.2	3.5	0.1
Steaks, In Crispy Batter, Bird's Eye*	1 Steak/124g	241	194	10.4	11.0	12.0	1.1
Steaks, In Parsley Sauce, Bird's Eye*	1 Pack/176g	150	85	10.4	5.0	2.6	0.1
Steaks, Skinless & Boneless, Sainsbury's*	1 Steak/72g	62	86	21.4	0.0	0.1	0.1
Steamed	1oz/28g	23	83	18.6	0.0	0.9	0.0
Sweet Chilli, COU, M & S*	1 Pack/400g	360	90	7.7	13.1	0.5	1.6
With a Thai Crust, Perfectly Balanced, Waitrose*	1 Pack/280g	249	89	15.1	1.6	2.5	0.6
With Roasted Vegetables, M & S*	1 Serving/280g	238	85	8.0	4.9	3.8	1.7
With Salsa & Rosemary Potatoes, BGTY, Sainsbury's*	1 Pack/450g	356	79	4.7	13.1	0.9	1.6
COFFEE,							
Black	1 Mug/270ml	5	2	0.2	0.3	0.0	0.0
Frappuccino, Starbucks*	1 Drink/281ml	190	68	2.1	13.9	1.1	0.0
Ice Mocha Drink, Nescafe, Nestle*	1 Bottle/280ml	160	57	1.1	10.5	1.2	0.0
Infusion, Average With Semi-Skimmed Milk	1 Cup/220ml	14	7	0.6	0.7	0.2	0.0
Infusion, Average With Single Cream	1 Cup/220ml	31	14	0.4	0.3	1.2	0.0
Infusion, Average With Whole Milk	1 Cup/220ml	15	7	0.5	0.5	0.4	0.0
COFFEE MATE,							
Lite, Carnation*	1 Serving	20	398	2.5	83.9	6.9	0.0
Lite, Nestle*	2 Tsps/5g	20	398	2.5	83.9	6.9	0.0
Nestle*	2 Tsp/7g	36	520	1.2	60.5	30.3	0.0
COFFEE WHITENER,							
Half Fat, Co-Op*	1 Tsp/5g	22	430	0.9	78.0	13.0	0.0
Light, HE, Tesco*	1 Tsp/6g	27	449	3.5	71.0	16.8	0.0
Tesco*	1 Tsp/3g	16	533	1.2	61.3	31.4	0.0
UHT Creamer, McDonald's*	1 Cup/14ml	17	123	4.2	4.2	10.0	0.0
COGNAC,							
37.5% Volume	1 Shot/25ml	52	207	0.0	0.0	0.0	0.0
40% Volume	1 Shot/25ml	56	222	0.0	0.0	0.0	0.0
COINTREAU, Liqueur Specialite De France	1 Serving/37g	80	215	0.0	0.0	0.0	0.0
COLA,							
Cola	1 Can/330ml	135	41	0.0	10.9	0.0	0.0
Coca Cola, McDonald's*	1 Med/400ml	172	43	0.0	10.5	0.0	0.0
Coke, Diet, The Coca Cola Co*	1 Can/330ml	1	0	0.0	0.0	0.0	0.0
Coke, The Coca Cola Co*	1 Can/330ml	139	42	0.0	10.9	0.0	0.0
Coke With Lemon, Diet, Coca Cola*	1 Can/330ml	5	1	0.0	0.0	0.0	0.0
Diet, Classic, Sainsbury's*	1 Can/330ml	1	0	0.0	0.0	0.0	0.0
Diet, Just, Asda*	1 Bottle/250ml	1	0	0.0	0.0	0.0	0.0
Diet, M & S*	1 Can/330ml	3	1	0.0	0.3	0.0	0.0
Diet, Morrisons*	1 Glass/250ml	1	0	0.0	0.1	0.0	0.0
Diet, Pepsi*	1 Can/330ml	1	0	0.0	0.0	0.0	0.0
Diet, Virgin*	1 Glass/250ml	1	0	0.1	0.1	0.1	0.0
Pepsi Max*	1fl oz/30ml	0	1	0.1	0.1	0.0	0.0
COLA BOTTLES, Fizzy, M & S*	1 Pack/200g	650	325	6.4	75.0	0.0	0.0
COLCANNON,							
Co-Op*	1 Pack/500g	325	65	2.0	10.0	2.0	2.0
HE, Tesco*	1 Pack/330g	244	74	2.1	12.2	1.9	1.0

Nutrition Values per 100g / 100ml (KCAL, PROT, CARB, FAT, FIBRE)

C

	Measure WEIGHT/INFO	per Measure KCAL	Nutrition Values per 100g / 100ml KCAL	PROT	CARB	FAT	FIBRE
COLCANNON,							
Tesco*	1 Serving/250g	245	98	2.3	11.7	4.7	1.7
COLESLAW,							
3% Fat, M & S*	1oz/28g	47	167	1.3	9.0	14.0	1.4
50% Less Fat, Asda*	1oz/28g	17	61	2.1	6.8	2.8	0.9
Apple, M & S*	1oz/28g	53	190	1.4	9.2	16.6	1.4
Better For You, Morrisons*	1oz/28g	17	62	1.5	6.7	3.5	0.0
BGTY, Sainsbury's*	1oz/28g	19	69	0.9	6.6	4.3	1.9
Cheese, M & S*	1 Serving/30g	98	325	4.2	2.0	33.5	1.7
Cheese, Somerfield*	1oz/28g	48	171	3.0	7.0	14.0	0.0
Chunky, Asda*	1oz/28g	54	194	1.0	7.1	18.0	1.6
Classic, M & S*	1 Pot/190g	124	65	1.9	8.8	2.3	1.3
Co-Op*	1 Serving/50g	65	130	1.0	7.0	11.0	2.0
Creamy, Asda*	1oz/28g	55	195	1.0	7.8	17.7	1.0
Creamy, HE, Tesco*	1 Serving/30g	29	95	2.4	6.8	6.4	1.4
Creamy, Sainsbury's*	1oz/28g	69	245	1.3	4.6	24.6	1.6
Creamy, Tesco*	1oz/28g	52	186	1.1	7.6	16.8	1.5
Crunchy, Budgens*	1 Serving/75g	198	264	1.3	4.6	26.7	1.2
Eat Smart, Safeway*	¼ Pack/50g	30	60	1.8	7.2	2.6	1.9
Finest, Tesco*	1 Serving/50g	107	214	1.2	6.1	20.5	1.6
Garlic & Herb, Asda*	1oz/28g	60	216	1.1	7.2	20.3	1.5
GFY, Asda*	1 Serving/50g	48	96	1.4	9.0	6.0	1.6
Healthy Choice, Safeway*	1 Pot/250g	215	86	1.5	7.4	5.7	1.6
HE, Tesco*	1 Serving/100g	85	85	1.3	7.0	5.8	1.6
Heinz*	1oz/28g	38	135	1.6	9.4	10.2	1.2
Iceland*	1 Serving/110g	112	102	0.7	7.8	7.5	1.6
Kentucky Fried Chicken*	1 Portion/142g	231	163	1.4	18.3	9.5	2.1
Less Than 3% Fat, M & S*	1oz/28g	18	65	1.9	8.8	2.3	1.3
Light, Morrisons*	1oz/28g	59	210	1.2	9.9	18.4	0.0
Low Fat Mayonnaise, Tesco*	1oz/28g	18	64	1.4	4.7	4.4	1.4
Luxury, Asda*	1 Serving/50g	109	217	0.9	6.0	21.0	0.0
Luxury, M & S*	1oz/28g	43	152	1.0	6.0	13.8	1.0
M & S*	1oz/28g	50	180	1.7	6.1	16.5	1.1
Organic, M & S*	1oz/28g	41	145	1.1	7.3	12.4	1.0
Perfectly Balanced, Waitrose*	1 Serving/84g	46	55	1.8	6.8	2.3	1.5
Prawn, Asda*	1oz/28g	54	192	2.4	6.6	17.3	1.4
Premium, Safeway*	1oz/28g	61	219	2.2	5.3	21.0	0.0
Premium, Safeway*	1 Serving/125g	334	267	1.9	3.8	27.2	2.3
Reduced Fat, Asda*	1 Pot/250g	218	87	1.5	6.0	6.3	1.6
Reduced Fat, Co-Op*	1 Serving/50g	45	90	0.9	6.0	7.0	2.0
Reduced Fat, Sainsbury's*	1oz/28g	29	102	1.2	7.3	8.0	1.7
Reduced Fat, Traditional, M & S*	1oz/28g	57	205	1.1	5.4	20.0	2.8
Safeway*	1 Serving/75g	128	170	0.7	6.7	15.6	0.0
Salad, Reduced Fat, Sainsbury's*	1/3 Pot/87g	89	102	1.2	7.3	8.0	1.7
Salad, Sainsbury's*	1 Serving/75g	109	145	1.3	6.8	12.5	1.5
SmartPrice, Asda*	1oz/28g	30	107	0.8	8.0	8.0	2.0
Supreme, Waitrose*	1oz/28g	53	190	1.8	4.9	18.1	1.7
Tesco*	1 Serving/50g	79	158	2.2	5.2	14.3	1.6
Three Cheese, Asda*	1oz/28g	54	192	5.0	7.4	16.4	1.2
Traditional, M & S*	1oz/28g	84	301	1.2	3.9	31.2	1.7
TTD, Sainsbury's*	1oz/28g	74	263	1.6	6.1	25.8	1.5
Value, Tesco*	1oz/28g	32	115	1.2	6.8	9.2	1.6
With Mayonnaise, Retail	1oz/28g	72	258	1.2	4.2	26.4	1.4
With Reduced Calorie Dressing, Retail	1oz/28g	19	67	0.9	6.1	4.5	1.4

C

	Measure WEIGHT/INFO	per Measure KCAL	Nutrition Values per 100g / 100ml KCAL	PROT	CARB	FAT	FIBRE
COLESLAW MIX,							
Shredded, Waitrose*	1 Serving/100g	29	29	1.1	5.6	0.2	2.2
Tesco*	1 Pack/400g	124	31	1.1	6.2	0.2	2.1
COLEY,							
Portions, Tesco*	1 Serving/92g	68	74	16.4	0.0	0.9	0.0
Raw	1oz/28g	23	82	18.3	0.0	1.0	0.0
Steak, Skinless & Boneless, Sainsbury's*	1 Portion/72g	66	92	21.8	0.0	0.5	0.0
Steamed	1oz/28g	29	105	23.3	0.0	1.3	0.0
CONSERVE,							
Apricot, Finest, Tesco*	1 Tbsp/15g	38	255	0.6	63.0	0.1	0.8
Apricot, Sainsbury's*	1 Tbsp/15g	36	241	0.5	58.4	0.1	2.8
Blackcurrant, Sainsbury's*	1 Tsp/15g	37	248	0.7	60.0	0.1	1.7
Raspberry, Finest, Tesco*	1 Tsp/15g	42	277	0.6	67.7	0.1	1.0
Red Cherry, Finest, Tesco*	1 Tsp/15g	42	277	0.6	67.6	0.1	0.8
Strawberry, Continental, Asda*	1 Tsp/15g	36	242	0.4	60.0	0.0	0.0
Strawberry, M & S*	1 Tsp/15g	35	236	0.4	57.6	0.2	0.8
Strawberry, Set, Traditional, Sainsbury's*	1 Tsp/15g	37	245	0.5	59.6	0.1	1.6
Strawberry, Soft, Set, Continental, Sainsbury's*	1 Tsp/15g	38	251	0.5	61.1	0.5	0.4
CONSOMME	1oz/28g	3	12	2.9	0.1	0.0	0.0
COOKEEN*	1oz/28g	252	900	0.0	0.0	100.0	0.0
COOKIES,							
All Butter Sultana, M & S*	1 Cookie/16g	73	455	5.2	66.0	19.0	2.7
Big Milk Chocolate Chunk, Cookie Coach Co*	1 Cookie/35g	174	497	6.2	61.4	25.1	0.0
Choc Chip & Coconut, Maryland*	1oz/28g	143	512	5.1	62.9	23.7	0.0
Choc Chip & Hazelnut, Maryland*	1oz/28g	140	500	5.4	65.2	24.2	0.0
Choc Chip, Asda*	1 Biscuit/11g	56	506	5.0	63.0	26.0	1.8
Choc Chip, Cadbury's*	1oz/28g	138	493	6.5	66.1	22.6	0.0
Choc Chip, Lyons*	1oz/28g	142	506	5.3	68.3	23.5	0.0
Choc Chip, Maryland*	1 Cookie/11g	56	511	6.2	68.0	23.9	0.0
Choc Chip, McVitie's*	1 Biscuit/10g	45	453	5.2	75.5	14.5	1.7
Choc Chunk & Hazelnut, Luxury, Cadbury's*	1oz/28g	146	521	6.3	60.0	28.7	0.0
Chocolate & Nut, Organic, Evernat*	1 Cookie/69g	337	489	7.2	64.1	22.6	0.0
Chocolate & Roasted Hazelnut, TTD, Sainsbury's*	1 Cookie/17g	89	521	6.4	56.3	30.3	2.2
Chocolate Chip & Hazelnut, Asda*	1 Cookie/12g	62	516	6.0	60.0	28.0	0.0
Chocolate Chip, Chips Ahoy*	1 Cookie/11g	55	500	6.0	65.0	25.0	3.0
Chocolate Chip, Co-Op*	1 Cookie/11g	55	500	5.0	65.0	24.0	1.0
Chocolate Chip Tesco*	1oz/28g	139	496	5.4	63.6	24.4	2.0
Chocolate Chip, M & S*	1 Cookie/12g	61	506	6.0	62.1	25.9	1.2
Chocolate Chip, Mini, McVitie's*	1 Pack/50g	260	520	5.7	66.7	25.6	1.9
Chocolate Chip, Mini, Tesco*	1 Bag/30g	148	493	5.4	64.6	23.7	1.7
Chocolate Chip, Sainsbury's*	1 Cookie/11g	56	508	6.2	67.0	23.9	1.3
Chocolate Chip, SmartPrice, Asda*	1 Biscuit/10g	52	508	5.0	68.0	24.0	0.0
Chocolate Orange, Half Coated, Finest, Tesco*	1 Biscuit/22g	107	488	4.9	59.6	25.5	1.2
Coconut & Raspberry, Gluten Free, Sainsbury's*	1 Cookie/20g	102	511	5.9	56.0	29.3	6.7
Coconut, Gluten-Free, Sainsbury's*	1 Serving/20g	103	516	5.6	54.4	30.7	4.1
Cranberry & Orange, Go Ahead, McVitie's*	1 Biscuit/17g	77	452	5.3	78.0	13.2	2.4
Danish Butter, Tesco*	1oz/28g	144	516	4.7	66.7	25.6	1.3
Dark Treacle, Weight Watchers*	2 Cookies/23g	97	423	5.2	66.7	15.1	1.7
Double Choc Chip, Mini, M & S*	1 Biscuit/22g	108	490	5.3	63.6	23.7	1.8
Double Choc Chunk, Luxury, Cadbury's*	1oz/28g	146	521	5.7	59.0	29.0	0.0
Double Choc, Maryland*	1 Cookie/10g	46	510	5.2	64.4	25.7	0.0
Fudge Brownie American Cream, Sainsbury's*	1 Cookie/12g	60	499	4.8	67.9	23.2	2.2
Ginger, Low Fat, M & S*	1 Biscuit/23g	82	358	5.1	74.9	4.3	2.4
Ginger, Safeway*	1 Biscuit/22g	106	480	4.7	66.5	22.7	2.4
Milk Chocolate Chip, Speedibake*	1oz/28g	134	477	4.8	63.3	22.7	1.2

	Measure WEIGHT/INFO	per Measure KCAL	Nutrition Values per 100g / 100ml KCAL	PROT	CARB	FAT	FIBRE
COOKIES,							
Oat & Raisin, Safeway*	1 Cookie/12g	50	414	7.5	77.5	8.8	0.0
Oat and Cranberry, BGTY, Sainsbury's*	1 biscuit/28g	126	449	6.8	65.0	18.0	5.1
Oatflake & Honey, Organic, Sainsbury's*	1 Cookie/17g	82	480	6.3	66.0	21.2	2.6
Oatflake, Jacob's*	1 Biscuit/13g	62	477	6.9	63.1	21.9	3.0
Oreo, Nabisco*	3 Cookies/34g	160	470	6.0	71.0	21.0	3.0
Peanut, Hellema*	1 Biscuit/16g	81	509	11.8	47.3	30.3	0.7
Raisin & Cinnamon, Low Fat, M & S*	1 Biscuit/22g	78	355	6.2	73.0	4.1	3.2
Real Chocolate Chip, Weight Watchers*	2 Cookies/23g	98	427	5.3	66.1	15.7	1.6
Shortbread, Organic, Evernat*	1oz/28g	149	532	5.9	56.7	31.3	0.0
Smarties, Asda*	1 Cookie/100g	175	175	2.3	28.0	6.0	0.6
Stem Ginger, Tesco*	1 Cookie/20g	98	489	4.2	64.0	24.0	2.0
Stem Ginger, TTD, Sainsbury's*	1 Cookie/17g	84	496	4.5	63.4	24.9	1.7
Stem Ginger, Weight Watchers*	1 Cookie/11.5g	46	399	5.0	64.5	13.4	1.4
Sultana & Cinnamon, Weight Watchers*	2 Cookies/23g	92	398	5.0	67.1	12.1	1.8
COQ AU VIN,							
Finest, Tesco*	1 Serving/273g	251	92	14.3	0.7	3.6	1.8
HE, Tesco*	1 Pack/400g	344	86	15.2	2.1	1.9	0.4
Perfectly Balanced, Waitrose*	1 Pack/500g	445	89	12.6	2.7	3.1	0.6
Sainsbury's*	1 Pack/400g	484	121	16.8	3.5	4.4	0.2
CORIANDER,							
Leaves, Dried	1oz/28g	78	279	21.8	41.7	4.8	0.0
Leaves, Fresh	1oz/28g	6	20	2.4	1.8	0.6	0.0
CORN, (SEE ALSO SWEETCORN)							
Baby, & Sugar Snap Peas, Safeway*	½ Pack/100g	27	27	2.9	3.3	0.2	0.0
Baby, Fine Beans & Baby Carrots, Tesco*	1 Pack/250g	68	27	1.7	4.0	0.5	2.2
Baby, Safeway*	1oz/28g	6	23	2.9	1.9	0.4	0.0
Baby, Sweet	1 Serving/100g	24	24	2.5	2.7	0.4	2.0
Cobs, Baby, Asda*	¼ Can/51g	9	17	0.8	3.4	0.0	0.4
Cobs, Organic, Mini, Iceland*	1oz/28g	26	93	3.1	22.3	0.7	2.8
Creamed, Green Giant*	1 Can/418g	238	57	1.2	11.9	0.5	3.0
On The Cob, Kentucky Fried Chicken*	1 Cob/162g	150	93	3.0	21.6	0.9	1.2
On The Cob, Prepared, M & S*	1 Cob/175g	95	54	2.0	9.9	1.0	0.9
On The Cob, Supersweet, Tesco*	1 Cob/250g	143	57	2.0	9.9	1.0	0.9
On The Cob, Supersweet, Tesco*	1 Serving/162g	92	57	2.0	9.9	1.0	0.9
On The Cob, Whole, Boiled In Salted Water	1oz/28g	18	66	2.5	11.6	1.4	1.3
On The Cob, Whole, Boiled In Unsalted Water	1oz/28g	18	66	2.5	11.6	1.4	1.3
On The Cob, Whole, Raw	1oz/28g	15	54	2.0	9.9	1.0	0.9
Whole Kernel, Del Monte*	½ Can/125g	60	48	1.6	8.8	0.8	2.4
CORNED BEEF,							
Asda*	1 Slice/31g	68	218	26.4	0.2	12.4	0.0
BGTY, Saisnbury's*	1 Serving/100g	184	184	26.8	1.2	8.0	0.1
Hydale, Aldi*	1 Serving/100g	225	225	24.8	1.0	13.5	0.0
John West*	1oz/28g	62	221	25.0	1.0	13.0	0.0
Lean, M & S*	1oz/28g	59	210	26.0	1.5	11.0	0.0
Lean, Princes*	½ Can/100g	194	194	25.0	1.0	10.0	0.0
Premium, Sainsbury's*	1oz/28g	58	208	26.8	1.2	10.7	0.1
Premium, Sliced, Sainsbury's*	1 Slice/42g	90	214	27.3	0.5	11.4	0.1
Princes*	1 Can/200g	446	223	24.8	0.5	13.5	0.0
Slices, Economy, Sainsbury's*	1 Slice/37g	87	236	26.5	1.0	14.0	0.1
SmartPrice, Asda*	1oz/28g	64	228	25.0	0.4	14.0	0.0
Tesco*	1 Serving/175g	352	201	26.0	0.5	10.6	0.0
Thin Sliced, Asda*	1oz/28g	60	213	26.0	0.2	12.0	0.0
Value, Tesco*	1oz/28g	63	225	24.8	1.0	13.5	0.0

CORNFLOUR	Measure WEIGHT/INFO	per Measure KCAL	Nutrition Values per 100g / 100ml KCAL	PROT	CARB	FAT	FIBRE
Cornflour, Average	1oz/28g	99	354	0.6	92.0	0.7	0.1
Bestfoods*	1oz/28g	96	343	0.6	83.6	0.7	0.1
COTTAGE CHEESE,							
& Chive, M & S*	1oz/28g	28	100	11.9	3.5	3.9	0.0
& Coronation Chicken, BGTY, Sainsbury's*	1oz/28g	25	91	11.3	8.7	1.2	0.1
& Pineapple, Shape*	1oz/28g	20	73	9.8	8.0	0.2	0.1
Better For You, Morrisons*	1 Pot/125g	110	88	13.0	6.9	0.9	0.0
BGTY, Sainsbury's*	1oz/28g	25	91	12.1	8.4	0.9	0.2
Bio Natural, HE, Tesco*	1 Serving/50g	39	78	11.9	3.6	1.8	0.0
Chargrilled Vegetables, BGTY, Sainsbury's*	1oz/28g	25	88	12.1	7.8	0.9	0.6
Healthy Choice, Asda*	1oz/28g	25	88	13.0	4.0	2.0	0.0
Low Fat, Longley Farm*	1oz/28g	32	114	11.5	3.4	6.0	0.0
Natural	1oz/28g	29	105	12.0	4.0	4.0	0.0
Natural, 95% Fat Free, M & S*	1oz/28g	28	99	11.6	3.5	4.0	0.0
Natural, Asda*	¼ Pot/113g	118	104	12.0	4.0	4.2	0.0
Natural, BGTY, Sainsbury's*	1oz/28g	25	88	13.0	6.9	0.9	0.0
Natural, Deliciously Creamy, M & S	1 Serving/50g	48	95	12.5	4.1	2.9	0.0
Natural, Diet Choice, Waitrose*	1oz/28g	27	98	11.4	3.6	4.2	0.0
Natural, Healthy Choice, Safeway*	1oz/28g	24	87	12.7	4.0	2.0	0.0
Natural, HE, Tesco*	1 Pot/125g	98	78	11.9	3.6	1.8	0.0
Natural, Healthy Living, Co-Op*	1 Pot/250g	188	75	10.0	4.0	2.0	0.0
Natural, Kwik Save*	1 Serving/25g	21	85	13.8	4.4	1.4	0.0
Natural, Tesco*	1 Serving/50g	49	97	11.2	3.5	4.2	0.0
Onion & Chive, BGTY, Sainsbury's*	1 Serving/50g	42	83	12.4	6.4	0.9	0.1
Onion & Chive, GFY, Asda*	1 Serving/50g	43	85	12.0	4.4	1.9	0.1
Onion & Chive, Healthy Choice, Safeway*	1 Pot/125g	105	84	12.0	4.2	1.9	0.1
Pineapple, Healthy Choice, Safeway*	1oz/28g	25	89	10.8	6.9	1.8	0.0
Plain	1oz/28g	27	98	13.8	2.1	3.9	0.0
Plain, Reduced Fat	1oz/28g	22	78	13.3	3.3	1.4	0.0
Poached Salmon & Dill, GFY, Asda*	1/3 Pot/75g	65	86	12.0	2.3	2.7	0.6
Prawn, GFY, Asda*	1oz/28g	25	91	13.0	6.0	1.5	0.0
Smoked Cheese & Onion, GFY, Asda*	½ Pot/114g	100	88	13.0	4.4	1.8	0.1
Tomato & Cracked Black Pepper, Asda*	½ Pot/113g	86	76	10.0	3.1	2.1	1.3
Virtually Fat Free, Eden Vale*	1oz/28g	22	80	12.9	6.5	0.3	0.0
Virtually Fat Free, Sainsbury's*	1oz/28g	22	80	12.9	6.5	0.3	0.0
With Black Pepper, HE, Tesco*	1 Pot/125g	101	81	12.1	4.0	1.8	0.0
With Chives, Good Intentions, Somerfield*	1 Pot/125g	101	81	10.8	3.2	2.8	0.0
With Chives, Somerfield*	1oz/28g	29	105	12.0	5.0	4.0	0.0
With Crunchy Vegetables, HE, Tesco*	1 Pot/125g	91	73	9.9	5.0	1.5	0.2
With Cucumber & Mint, HE, Tesco*	½ Pot/125g	91	73	10.7	3.8	1.7	0.1
With Mango & Peach, HE, Tesco*	1 Pot/250g	188	75	10.4	4.8	1.6	0.1
With Onion & Chive, BGTY, Sainsbury's*	1oz/28g	22	78	12.4	6.4	0.3	0.1
With Onion & Chive, Healthy Choice, Asda*	1oz/28g	23	82	12.0	4.0	2.0	0.1
With Onion & Chive, HE, Tesco*	1oz/28g	22	77	11.0	4.5	1.7	0.2
With Onion & Chive, Perfectly Balanced, Waitrose*	1 Serving/20g	14	70	10.0	3.4	1.8	0.0
With Onion & Chive, Tesco*	1 Serving/250g	235	94	10.9	3.7	4.0	0.0
With Onion & Chives, Low Fat, Sainsbury's*	1oz/28g	28	99	11.6	4.4	4.0	0.1
With Onions & Chives, Better For You, Morrisons*	1oz/28g	22	78	12.4	6.4	0.3	0.1
With Pineapple, Asda*	1oz/28g	31	109	10.0	8.0	3.9	0.0
With Pineapple, BGTY, Sainsbury's*	1oz/28g	24	84	10.5	8.9	0.7	0.1
With Pineapple, GFY, Asda*	1 Serving/200g	184	92	10.0	9.0	1.6	0.2
With Pineapple, HE, Tesco*	1oz/28g	21	75	10.1	5.3	1.5	0.1
With Pineapple, Healthy Living, Co-Op*	½ Pot/125g	119	95	10.0	9.0	2.0	0.2
With Pineapple, Less Than 3% Fat, M & S*	1 Serving/200g	190	95	9.4	9.3	2.2	0.2

C

	Measure WEIGHT/INFO	per Measure KCAL	Nutrition Values per 100g / 100ml KCAL	PROT	CARB	FAT	FIBRE
COTTAGE CHEESE,							
With Pineapple, Sainsbury's*	½ Pot/125g	121	97	9.9	6.8	3.4	2.1
With Pineapple, Somerfield*	1oz/28g	27	97	10.0	7.0	3.0	0.0
With Prawn Cocktail, BGTY, Sainsbury's*	1oz/28g	25	91	12.3	8.3	0.9	0.1
With Salmon & Dill, HE, Tesco*	1oz/28g	25	89	12.0	4.7	2.5	0.5
With Smoked Salmon & Dill, BGTY, Sainsbury's*	1oz/28g	25	89	13.8	6.4	0.9	0.1
With Sweet Chilli Chicken, M & S*	1 Serving/200g	190	95	13.8	4.7	2.1	0.5
With Tuna & Sweetcorn, BGTY, Sainsbury's*	1oz/28g	25	91	12.1	8.4	0.9	0.2
With Tuna & Sweetcorn, Healthy Choice, Asda*	1oz/28g	25	91	12.0	6.0	1.9	0.1
COURGETTE,							
& Sweetcorn, Fresh 'n' Ready, Sainsbury's*	1oz/28g	12	42	2.3	6.7	0.9	1.3
Baby, Tesco*	1 Serving/100g	18	18	1.8	1.8	0.4	0.9
Boiled In Unsalted Water	1oz/28g	5	19	2.0	2.0	0.4	1.2
Fried In Blended Oil	1oz/28g	18	63	2.6	2.6	4.8	1.2
Fried In Butter	1oz/28g	18	63	2.6	2.6	4.8	1.2
Raw	1oz/28g	5	18	1.8	1.8	0.4	0.9
COUS COUS,							
Cous Cous, Average	1oz/28g	64	227	5.7	51.3	1.0	0.0
& Chargrilled Vegetables, M & S*	1 Serving/200g	200	100	3.9	17.3	1.5	1.6
& Spicy Fillet Cod, COU, M & S*	1oz/28g	27	95	6.5	13.1	2.2	1.5
& Vegetable, Organic, M & S*	1oz/28g	47	167	5.6	27.7	3.7	1.2
& Wok Oriental, Findus*	1 Pack/600g	1020	170	4.5	19.0	8.5	0.0
Chargrilled Red & Yellow Pepper, Tesco*	1 Pack/200g	212	106	4.6	17.8	1.8	0.5
Cooked, Sainsbury's*	1 Serving/75g	177	236	8.0	38.8	5.4	2.8
Coriander & Lemon, Sainsbury's*	½ Pack/165g	200	121	4.8	23.5	0.7	0.8
Indian Style, Sainsbury's*	½ Pack/143g	204	143	4.5	25.1	2.7	1.0
Lemon & Coriander, Tesco*	1 Serving/137g	207	151	4.0	28.3	2.4	2.0
Made Up, Asda*	1oz/28g	43	155	4.2	21.4	5.8	2.4
Mediterranean Style, Tesco*	1 Pack/110g	369	335	11.9	65.1	3.0	5.6
Mushrooms, Onion, Garlic & Herbs, Tesco*	½ Pack/50g	167	333	11.3	66.2	2.6	4.9
Oriental, Findus*	1 Serving/100g	170	170	4.5	19.0	8.5	0.0
Plain, Dry Weight, Tesco*	1oz/28g	102	363	15.1	73.1	1.1	0.8
Red Pepper & Coriander, HE, Tesco*	1 Pot/200g	282	141	4.8	26.9	1.6	0.6
Roasted Vegetable, Finest, Tesco*	1 Serving/175g	263	150	4.0	17.4	7.1	1.3
Roasted Vegetables, Waitrose*	1 Serving/200g	324	162	5.2	22.4	5.7	0.0
Salad Bar, BGTY, Sainsbury's*	1 Md Bowl/28g	29	103	3.7	18.5	1.6	0.0
Spicy, Healthy Choice, Safeway*	1 Serving/50g	68	136	4.2	26.0	1.7	0.2
Spicy, HE, Tesco*	1 Pot/250g	325	130	3.6	25.1	1.7	0.6
Sundried Tomato, Somerfield*	1 Jar/110g	176	160	3.0	25.0	5.0	0.0
Vegetable, COU, M & S*	1oz/28g	39	140	2.7	22.5	4.4	1.1
Wild Mushroom & Garlic, Sainsbury's*	½ Pack/100g	239	239	7.0	38.0	6.6	1.0
CRAB,							
Boiled	1oz/28g	36	128	19.5	0.0	5.5	0.0
Cakes, Iceland*	1 Serving/18g	52	288	7.2	25.6	18.0	1.3
Canned In Brine, Drained	1 Sm Can/85g	65	77	18.1	0.0	0.5	0.0
Canned In Brine, Sainsbury's*	½ Can/60g	46	77	18.1	0.1	0.5	0.1
Claws, Asda*	1oz/28g	25	89	11.0	9.0	1.0	0.2
Dressed, In Shell, Asda*	1 Crab/142g	64	45	6.8	0.0	1.9	0.0
Dressed, John West*	1 Can/43g	61	143	18.0	2.0	7.0	0.0
Meat, Orkney, M & S*	1 Pack/100g	100	100	20.8	2.8	0.6	0.0
Meat, White, In Brine, Drained, M & S*	1 Serving/61g	45	74	15.0	2.7	0.4	0.5
Meat, White, In Brine, Glenryck*	1 Can/122g	96	79	16.7	2.0	0.5	0.0
Meat, White, In Brine, John West*	½ Can/60g	43	72	17.0	0.7	0.1	0.0
Sticks, Average	1oz/28g	19	68	10.0	6.6	0.4	0.0
Sticks, Sainsbury's*	1 Stick/16g	18	113	7.0	21.0	0.1	0.1

	Measure	per Measure	Nutrition Values per 100g / 100ml				
CRACKERBREAD,	WEIGHT/INFO	KCAL	KCAL	PROT	CARB	FAT	FIBRE
High Fibre, Ryvita*	1oz/28g	89	318	12.6	60.5	2.8	16.8
Ryvita*	1 Serving/5g	19	383	9.8	79.3	3.0	2.6
Wheat, Original, Ryvita*	1oz/28g	107	383	9.8	79.3	3.0	2.6
CRACKERS,							
99% Fat Free, Rakusen's*	1 Cracker/5g	18	366	10.9	88.9	0.9	0.0
Bath Oliver, Jacob's*	1 Cracker/12g	52	432	9.6	67.6	13.7	2.6
Biscuits For Cheese, TTD, Sainsbury's*	1 Biscuit/8g	39	493	8.6	61.0	23.8	3.1
Bran, Jacob's*	1 Cracker/7g	32	454	9.7	62.8	18.2	3.2
Cheddars, McVitie's*	1 Biscuit/4g	22	543	10.0	55.1	31.3	2.6
Cheese Biscuit Thins, Safeway*	1 Biscuit/4g	22	545	11.9	52.6	31.9	2.5
Cheese Melts, Carr's*	1 Biscuit/4g	19	468	9.4	58.0	22.1	3.0
Cheese Thins, Co-Op*	1 Biscuit/4g	21	530	12.0	49.0	32.0	3.0
Choice Grain, Jacob's*	1 Cracker/7g	30	435	9.2	65.4	15.2	4.7
Corn Thins, 97% Fat Free, Real Foods*	1 Cracker/6g	19	378	10.2	81.7	3.0	8.6
Cornish Wafer, Jacob's*	1 Wafer/9g	48	528	8.0	54.4	31.2	2.4
Cream	1 Cracker/7g	31	440	9.5	68.3	16.3	2.2
Cream, Better For You, Morrisons*	1 Cracker/8g	32	406	10.9	74.4	7.2	2.8
Cream, BGTY, Sainsbury's*	1 Cracker/8g	32	400	10.9	71.7	7.7	3.1
Cream, Biscuits For Cheese, Tesco*	1 Cracker/8g	35	438	10.2	66.7	14.5	2.8
Cream, Half Fat, Safeway*	1 Cracker/8g	32	406	74.4	2.4	7.2	2.9
Cream, Jacob's*	1 Cracker/8g	35	438	10.2	66.9	14.4	2.9
Cream, Roasted Onion, Jacob's*	1 Cracker/8g	35	441	10.2	66.8	14.8	2.9
Cream, Sundried Tomato Flavour, Jacob's*	1 Cracker/8g	35	434	10.2	66.7	14.0	3.0
Cream, Tesco*	1 Biscuit/5g	22	444	8.4	70.0	14.5	3.1
Crispy Cheese, M & S*	1oz/28g	134	478	10.2	57.8	22.6	2.9
Crunchy Vegetable, COU, M & S*	1 Pack/25g	88	350	1.6	82.4	2.0	4.3
Harvest Grain, Sainsbury's*	1 Cracker/6g	27	458	8.5	64.5	18.4	4.1
Herb & Onion, 99% Fat Free, Rakusen's*	1 Cracker/4g	14	361	10.0	78.0	1.0	0.0
Herb & Spice, Jacob's*	1 Biscuit/6g	27	457	9.5	67.5	16.5	2.7
Herbs & Spice Selection, Jacob's*	1 Biscuit/6g	27	451	9.5	68.0	15.7	2.7
Hovis, Jacob's*	1 Cracker/6g	27	447	10.2	60.0	18.5	4.4
Italian, Lightly Salted, Jacob's*	1 Cracker/6g	26	429	10.3	67.6	13.0	2.9
Italian, Olive Oil & Oregano, Jacob's*	1 Cracker/6g	26	437	10.3	66.3	14.5	4.0
Krackawheat, McVitie's*	1 Biscuit/7g	36	515	9.1	62.4	25.4	4.8
Light & Crispy, Sainsbury's*	1 Cracker/11g	42	384	11.3	61.0	10.5	13.0
Matzo, Rakusen's*	1 Cracker/4g	15	370	8.8	80.2	1.5	4.0
Melts, Carr's*	1 Biscuit/4g	18	451	10.2	57.0	20.2	5.0
Multigrain, Tesco*	1 Cracker/6g	27	458	8.5	64.5	18.4	4.1
Oriental Style, Safeway*	1 Serving/25g	88	350	1.5	82.2	1.2	6.2
Poppy & Sesame Thins Savoury, Somerfield*	1oz/28g	147	524	9.0	58.0	28.0	0.0
Ritz, Cheese, Jacob's*	1 Cracker/3g	15	490	10.4	55.5	25.2	2.2
Ritz, Cheese Sandwich, Jacob's*	1 Sandwich/9g	46	510	8.9	52.7	29.3	2.3
Ritz, Original, Jacob's*	1 Cracker/3g	15	509	6.9	55.6	28.8	2.0
Salt & Black Pepper, Jacob's*	1 Cracker/6g	27	457	9.5	67.5	16.5	2.7
Sesame & Poppy, Tesco*	1 Cracker/3g	15	506	9.4	53.7	28.2	3.4
Spicy Vegetable, Tesco*	1 Serving/60g	340	566	2.6	52.4	38.4	1.2
Tuc, Jacob's*	1 Cracker/4.5g	23	512	7.8	57.7	27.8	2.1
Tuc, McVitie's*	1 Biscuit/4g	21	530	7.8	62.2	27.8	2.1
Wheaten, M & S*	1oz/28g	129	460	11.0	54.0	22.0	5.0
CRANBERRIES,							
Dried, Sainsbury's*	1 Pack/75g	253	337	0.1	81.1	1.4	5.1
Fresh, Raw	1oz/28g	4	15	0.4	3.4	0.1	3.0
CRANBERRY & APPLE Juice Drink, Ocean Spray*	1 Glass/200ml	92	46	0.0	11.1	0.0	0.0
CRANBERRY & BLACKCURRANT Juice Drink, Ocean Spray*	1 Bottle/500ml	265	53	0.2	12.7	0.0	0.0

CRANBERRY & RASPBERRY	Measure WEIGHT/INFO	per Measure KCAL	KCAL	PROT	CARB	FAT	FIBRE
Juice Drink, Asda*	1 Serving/250ml	135	54	0.2	13.0	0.0	0.0
Juice Drink, Tesco*	1 Glass/200ml	10	5	0.0	0.8	0.0	0.0
Juice, Low Sugar, Sainsbury's*	1 Glass/250ml	10	4	0.1	0.7	0.1	0.1
Juice, Ocean Spray*	1 Glass/200ml	104	52	0.0	12.7	0.0	0.0
CRANBERRY CLASSIC Light, Ocean Spray*	1 Glass/200ml	48	24	0.0	5.6	0.0	0.0
CRANBERRY GRAPE & Apple Juice, Ocean Spray*	1 Glass/200ml	108	54	0.1	12.9	0.0	0.0
CRANBERRY JUICE DRINK,							
Classic, Ocean Spray*	1 Glass/200ml	98	49	0.0	11.7	0.0	0.0
Del Rivo, Aldi*	1 Glass/100ml	40	40	0.0	9.6	0.0	0.0
Morrisons*	1 Glass/200ml	92	46	0.0	11.6	0.0	0.0
No Added Sugar, Asda*	1 Glass/200ml	12	6	0.1	0.8	0.0	0.0
No Added Sugar, Tesco*	1 Glass/200ml	8	4	0.0	0.7	0.0	0.0
Tesco*	1 Glass/200ml	100	50	0.0	12.0	0.0	0.0
Tropical, Ocean Spray*	1 Glass/200ml	96	48	0.1	11.5	0.0	0.0
CRANBERRY JUICE,							
Low Sugar, Sainsbury's*	1 Glass/200ml	10	5	0.1	0.9	0.1	0.1
M & S*	1 Glass/200ml	120	60	0.0	14.5	0.0	0.0
Sainsbury's*	1 Bottle/250ml	133	53	0.2	12.8	0.1	0.4
CRAYFISH, Raw	1oz/28g	19	67	14.9	0.0	0.8	0.0
CREAM,							
Aerosol, Elmlea*	1oz/28g	71	253	1.5	6.3	24.8	0.0
Aerosol, M & S*	1fl oz/30ml	110	365	2.0	6.1	37.0	0.0
Clotted, Fresh, Waitrose*	1 Serving/28g	157	560	1.5	2.5	60.5	0.0
Dairy, UHT Sweetened, Reduced Fat, Tesco*	1 Tbsp/15g	36	240	2.5	11.2	20.6	0.0
Double, Elmlea*	1 Serving/25ml	87	349	2.4	3.9	36.0	0.3
Double, Fresh, M & S*	1 Tbsp/15ml	67	445	1.7	2.6	47.5	0.0
Double, Fresh, Sainsbury's*	1 Tbsp/15ml	67	445	1.7	2.6	47.5	0.0
Double, Tesco*	1 Tbsp/15ml	68	450	1.7	2.7	48.0	0.0
Extra Thick, Canned, Sterilised, Nestle*	1 Tbsp/50g	117	233	2.6	3.6	23.1	0.0
Extra Thick Double, Tesco*	1 Tbsp/15ml	68	450	1.7	2.7	48.0	0.0
Extra Thick Fresh, BGTY, Sainsbury's*	1 Tbsp/15ml	28	188	2.6	3.9	18.0	0.0
For Coffee, UHT, Kerrygold*	1 Tbsp/15ml	29	190	2.7	3.9	18.3	0.0
Fresh, Clotted	1 Tbsp/15ml	88	586	1.6	2.3	63.5	0.0
Fresh, Double	1 Tbsp/15ml	67	449	1.7	2.7	48.0	0.0
Fresh Double, Waitrose*	1 Tbsp/15ml	67	445	1.7	2.6	47.5	0.0
Fresh Pasteurised Soured, Co-Op*	1 Tbsp/15ml	28	188	2.6	3.9	18.0	0.0
Fresh, Single	1 Tbsp/15ml	30	198	2.6	4.1	19.1	0.0
Fresh Single, Extra Thick, M & S*	1 Tbsp/15ml	34	227	2.8	3.3	22.5	0.0
Fresh, Soured	1 Tbsp/15ml	31	205	2.9	3.8	19.9	0.0
Fresh, Whipping	1 Tbsp/15ml	56	373	2.0	3.1	39.3	0.0
Half Fat, Thick, M & S*	1 Tbsp/15ml	36	241	2.9	3.4	24.0	0.0
Light Double, Elmlea*	1 Tbsp/15ml	37	248	2.8	4.1	24.5	0.3
Light, Real Dairy Aerosol, Anchor*	1 Serving/55ml	25	45	0.6	1.8	3.9	0.0
Light Single, Elmlea*	1 Tbsp/15ml	19	124	3.1	6.4	9.5	0.3
Light Whipping, Elmlea*	1 Tbsp/15ml	30	197	3.1	4.6	18.5	0.2
Pasteurised Double, Morrisons*	1 Serving/50g	225	449	1.7	2.6	48.0	0.0
Cream, Pasteurised Single, Fresh, Tesco*	1 Small Pot/142ml	283	199	2.6	4.1	19.1	0.0
Portion, UHT, Kerrygold*	1 Portion/14g	27	196	2.6	4.0	19.0	0.0
Single, Elmlea*	1 Tbsp/15ml	22	148	3.1	4.6	13.0	0.2
Single, Fresh, Sainsbury's*	1 Tbsp/15ml	28	188	2.6	3.9	18.0	0.0
Soured, Fresh, Sainsbury's*	1 Tbsp/15ml	28	188	2.6	3.9	18.0	0.0
Soured, Tesco*	1fl oz/30ml	56	188	2.6	3.9	18.0	0.0
Sterilised, Nestle*	1 Tbsp/15ml	35	233	2.6	3.6	23.1	0.0
Swirls Light, Half Fat, Anchor*	1 Serving/30ml	14	45	0.6	1.8	3.9	0.0

Nutrition Values per 100g / 100ml

C

CREAM,	Measure WEIGHT/INFO	per Measure KCAL	Nutrition Values per 100g / 100ml KCAL	PROT	CARB	FAT	FIBRE
UHT, Single	1 Tbsp/15g	29	196	2.6	4.0	19.0	0.0
Whipping, Elmlea*	1 Serving/15ml	43	285	2.4	3.5	29.0	0.2
Whipping, Tesco*	1 Tbsp/15ml	56	374	1.9	3.1	39.3	0.0
CREAM LIQUEURS	1 Shot/25ml	81	325	0.0	22.8	16.1	0.0
CREAM SODA, Traditional Style, Tesco*	1 Can/330ml	139	42	0.0	10.4	0.0	0.0
CREME BRULEE,							
M & S*	1 Pot/100g	360	360	3.3	13.0	32.6	0.0
Somerfield*	1 Pot/100g	316	316	4.0	15.0	27.0	0.0
CREME CARAMEL,							
Creme Caramel	1oz/28g	31	109	3.0	20.6	2.2	0.0
La Laitiere*	1 Pot/100g	135	135	5.0	20.0	4.0	0.0
M & S*	1oz/28g	48	172	4.5	18.9	8.7	0.0
Organic, Evernat*	1oz/28g	37	132	4.2	20.1	3.9	0.0
Sainsbury's*	1 Pot/100g	102	102	2.5	21.1	0.9	0.0
SmartPrice, Asda*	1 Pot/100g	102	102	2.5	21.0	0.9	0.0
Somerfield*	1 Pot/100g	114	114	3.0	24.0	1.0	0.0
Tesco*	1 Pot/100g	113	113	2.4	20.0	2.6	0.0
CREME EGG, Cadbury's	1 Egg/39g	174	445	4.0	70.8	15.9	0.0
CREME FRAICHE,							
BGTY, Sainsbury's*	1oz/28g	46	164	3.5	5.0	15.0	0.0
Half Fat, Asda*	1 Serving/50g	87	173	4.9	4.6	15.0	0.0
Half Fat, M & S*	1fl oz/30ml	60	200	4.3	3.5	18.7	0.0
Half Fat, Somerfield*	1fl oz/30ml	51	171	4.0	6.0	15.0	0.0
Half Fat, Waitrose*	1fl oz/30ml	50	165	2.7	5.8	14.6	0.0
Healthy Choice, Safeway*	1fl oz/30ml	50	165	2.7	5.8	14.6	0.0
HE, Tesco*	1fl oz/30ml	51	170	3.5	5.0	15.0	0.0
Low Fat, M & S*	1oz/28g	58	207	4.6	4.3	19.0	0.0
Somerfield*	1oz/28g	106	377	2.0	2.0	40.0	0.0
CREPES,							
Lobster, Finest, Tesco*	1 Serving/160g	250	156	10.7	14.0	6.4	1.2
Mushroom, M & S*	1 Pack/186g	195	105	5.7	17.1	2.4	2.5
CREVETTES, Asda*	1oz/28g	11	41	8.6	0.0	0.7	0.0
CRISPBAKES,							
Bacon & Mushroom, M & S*	1 Crispbake/113g	215	190	4.3	17.7	11.1	2.1
Bubble & Squeak, M & S*	1 Serving/113g	226	200	3.0	22.1	10.8	1.5
Cheese & Chive, Sainsbury's*	1 Serving/108g	273	253	7.1	24.5	14.8	1.7
Cheese & Leek, Iceland*	1 Pack/134g	359	268	5.0	39.9	9.8	4.3
Cheese & Onion, Farmfoods*	1 Crispbake/79g	179	227	4.9	23.2	12.7	1.6
Cheese & Onion, Tesco*	1 Crispbake/109g	275	252	7.9	19.6	15.8	2.1
Chicken & Broccoli, Sainsbury's*	1 Crispbake/99g	224	226	6.1	23.2	12.1	1.3
Corned Beef, Morrisons*	1 Crispbake/105g	154	147	7.8	20.1	4.5	0.6
Corned Beef, Tesco*	1 Crispbake/113g	275	243	9.8	19.9	13.8	0.9
Dutch, Asda*	1 Toast/10g	39	394	14.0	77.0	3.3	3.9
Dutch, Safeway*	1 Bake/10g	39	394	14.0	77.0	3.3	3.9
Dutch, Tesco*	1 Slice/8g	30	371	17.0	72.0	1.7	4.0
Minced Beef, M & S*	1 Crispbake/113g	243	215	9.0	14.8	13.4	1.9
Mushroom & Garlic, Iceland*	1 Crispbake/134g	310	231	4.3	34.2	8.5	3.7
Vegetable, Sainsbury's*	1 Serving/114g	246	216	2.0	26.2	11.4	2.0
CRISPBREAD,							
Currant Crunch, Ryvita*	1oz/28g	94	334	8.7	69.9	2.5	12.8
Dark Rye, Ryvita*	1 Serving/9g	27	303	9.9	62.0	1.7	18.5
Light, M & S*	1 Crispbread/4g	14	360	11.4	71.8	5.0	5.2
Multi-Grain, Ryvita*	1 Slice/11g	37	335	11.5	58.5	6.1	16.2
Organic, Trimlyne*	1 Crispbake/10g	38	380	16.0	73.0	2.3	6.0

C

CRISPBREAD,	Measure WEIGHT/INFO	per Measure KCAL	KCAL	PROT	CARB	FAT	FIBRE
Original, Ryvita*	1 Serving/9g	27	305	9.4	63.3	1.6	17.4
Rye	1 Slice/10g	32	321	9.4	70.6	2.1	11.7
Sesame, Ryvita*	1oz/28g	95	339	10.5	58.5	7.0	16.0
Wholemeal, Organic, Allinson*	1 Crispbread/5g	17	336	14.2	66.0	1.7	12.2
Wholemeal Rye, Kallo*	1 Crispbread/10g	31	314	9.7	65.0	1.7	15.4
With Sesame, Spar*	1 Serving/15g	62	410	12.0	66.0	11.0	5.0
CRISPS,							
Bacon, Shapers, Boots*	1 Bag/23g	99	431	8.0	66.0	15.0	3.0
Baked Potato, COU, M & S*	1 Pack/25g	88	350	8.5	76.4	2.3	5.7
Barbecue, Walkers*	1 Bag/35g	186	530	6.5	50.0	33.0	4.1
Beef & Onion, Walkers*	1 Bag/35g	186	530	6.5	50.0	33.0	4.1
Beefy, Smiths, Walkers*	1 Bag/25g	133	531	4.3	45.2	37.0	0.0
Chargrilled Chicken Crinkles, Shapers, Boots*	1 Bag/20g	96	482	6.6	60.0	24.0	4.0
Chargrilled Steak, Max, Walkers*	1 Bag/55g	289	525	6.5	50.0	33.0	4.0
Cheddar & Onion, Thick & Crunchy, McCoys*	1 Bag/49g	250	511	6.6	52.4	30.6	4.7
Cheese & Branston Pickle Flavour, Walkers*	1 Bag/34.5g	176	510	7.0	49.0	32.0	4.5
Cheese & Chive Flavour, GFY, Asda*	1 Bag/25g	119	476	6.0	59.0	24.0	6.0
Cheese & Chives, Walkers*	1 Bag/35g	186	530	6.5	50.0	33.0	4.1
Cheese & Onion, Asda*	1 Bag/25g	133	530	6.0	50.0	34.0	4.5
Cheese & Onion, BGTY, Sainsbury's*	1 Bag/25g	120	479	7.0	57.0	24.8	5.7
Cheese & Onion, Crinkled, Go Ahead, McVitie's*	1 Bag/26g	116	445	7.0	64.1	17.8	4.2
Cheese & Onion Flavour Crinkles, Shapers, Boots*	1 Bag/20g	96	482	6.6	60.0	24.0	4.0
Cheese & Onion, Golden Wonder*	1 Bag/25g	131	524	6.1	49.2	33.6	2.0
Cheese & Onion, KP*	1 Bag/25g	134	534	6.6	48.7	34.8	4.8
Cheese & Onion, Lites, Walkers*	1 Bag/28g	130	465	7.5	61.0	21.0	4.0
Cheese & Onion, Lower Fat, Asda*	1 Bag/25g	120	481	6.0	58.0	25.0	4.8
Cheese & Onion, M & S*	1 Bag/25g	134	535	5.5	48.8	35.5	5.0
Cheese & Onion, Morrisons*	1 Bag/30g	152	508	7.1	50.5	30.8	4.6
Cheese & Onion, Organic, Tesco*	1 Bag/25g	129	514	5.2	49.9	32.6	7.0
Cheese & Onion, Sainsbury's*	1 Bag/25g	132	527	4.6	48.8	34.8	3.9
Cheese & Onion, Select, Tesco*	1 Bag/25g	134	535	6.6	48.5	34.9	4.8
Cheese & Onion, Smiths, Walkers*	1 Bag/25g	133	531	4.3	45.2	37.0	0.0
Cheese & Onion, Square, Smiths, Walkers*	1 Bag/25g	113	452	6.9	62.5	19.4	0.0
Cheese & Onion, Square, Walkers*	1 Bag/25g	106	425	6.5	59.0	18.0	4.4
Cheese & Onion, Tayto*	1 Bag/25g	137	546	5.8	53.7	34.2	0.0
Cheese & Onion, Value, Tesco*	1 Bag/20g	108	541	6.0	48.3	36.0	4.8
Cheese & Onion, Walkers*	1 Bag/35g	194	553	6.5	50.0	33.0	4.1
Chicken & Thyme Flavour, Oven Roasted, Walkers*	1 Bag/40g	194	485	6.5	54.0	27.0	4.5
Chicken Flavour, HE, Tesco*	1 Bag/12g	43	357	5.1	81.0	1.4	3.4
Chip Shop Curry Max Flavour, Walkers*	1 Pack/55g	289	525	6.5	50.0	33.0	4.0
Cool Sour Cream & Chive Jacket, Half Fat, M & S*	1 Bag/40g	172	430	5.8	61.0	17.0	7.7
Coronation Chicken, Walkers*	1 Bag/25g	131	525	6.5	50.0	33.0	4.0
Crinklins, Original, Go Ahead, McVitie's*	1 Serving/25g	110	441	9.1	68.9	14.3	2.2
Double Cheddar & Chives, Deli Style, Brannigans*	1oz/28g	148	529	7.6	49.5	33.4	3.8
Flame Grilled Steak, Thick & Crunchy, McCoys*	1 Bag/50g	254	508	6.4	52.9	30.1	4.7
Four Cheese & Red Onion Sensations, Walkers*	1 Bag/40g	194	485	6.5	54.0	27.0	4.5
Garlic & Herbs Creme Fraiche, Kettle Chips*	1 Bag/50g	249	497	6.0	54.7	28.3	4.2
Golden Lights, Golden Wonder*	1 Bag/21g	91	435	5.4	64.5	17.2	0.0
Handcooked, M & S*	1 Bag/40g	198	495	5.4	56.9	27.2	4.5
Lightly Salted Crinckle Cut Potato, Lower Fat, Waitrose*	1 Bag/40g	193	483	6.5	58.0	25.0	3.9
Lightly Salted, Golden Lights, Golden Wonder*	1 Bag/21g	92	440	5.1	64.3	18.0	4.3
Lightly Salted, Kettle Chips*	1 Bag/50g	124	247	6.4	51.5	3.0	6.0
Lightly Salted, Traditional Pan Fried, TTD, Sainsbury's*	1 Bag/50g	236	472	6.2	53.6	25.8	5.1
Marmite Flavour, Walkers*	1 Bag/34.5g	176	510	6.5	49.0	32.0	4.0

Nutrition Values per 100g / 100ml (KCAL, PROT, CARB, FAT, FIBRE)

CRISPS,	Measure WEIGHT/INFO	per Measure KCAL	KCAL	PROT	CARB	FAT	FIBRE
			Nutrition Values per 100g / 100ml				
Mediterranean Baked Potato, COU, M & S*	1 Bag/26g	91	350	7.6	73.8	2.6	6.6
New York Cheddar, Kettle Chips*	1 Bag/50g	242	483	6.7	53.9	26.7	4.5
Oven Roasted Chicken & Thyme Sensations, Walkers*	1 Bag/40g	194	485	6.5	54.0	27.0	4.5
Pickled Onion, Golden Wonder*	1 Bag/25g	131	524	5.6	49.0	34.0	2.0
Pickled Onion, Walkers*	1 Bag/35g	186	530	6.5	50.0	33.0	4.1
Potato	1oz/28g	148	530	5.7	53.3	34.2	5.3
Potato, Low Fat	1oz/28g	128	458	6.6	63.5	21.5	5.9
Prawn Cocktail, BGTY, Sainsbury's*	1 Bag/25g	118	473	6.3	58.6	23.7	5.7
Prawn Cocktail, Golden Wonder*	1 Bag/25g	130	521	5.8	49.0	33.5	2.0
Prawn Cocktail, KP*	1 Bag/25g	133	531	5.9	48.4	34.9	4.7
Prawn Cocktail, Sainsbury's*	1 Bag/25g	130	521	4.3	47.5	34.9	3.9
Prawn Cocktail, Smiths, Walkers*	1 Bag/25g	133	531	4.3	45.2	37.0	0.0
Prawn Cocktail, Walkers*	1 Bag/35g	186	530	6.5	50.0	33.0	4.1
Punching Paprika, Max, Walkers*	1 Bag/55g	256	465	7.5	61.0	21.0	4.0
Ready Salted, BGTY, Sainsbury's*	1 Bag/25g	122	486	6.8	55.7	26.2	6.6
Ready Salted Crinkle, Reduced Fat, M & S*	1 Bag/40g	190	475	6.5	58.0	24.0	6.5
Ready Salted, Golden Lights, Golden Wonder*	1 Bag/21g	92	440	5.1	64.3	18.0	0.0
Ready Salted, Golden Wonder*	1 Bag/25g	135	539	5.5	49.9	35.3	2.0
Ready Salted, KP*	1 Bag/24g	131	545	5.6	47.9	36.8	4.9
Ready Salted, Lites, Walkers*	1 Bag/28g	132	470	7.5	60.0	22.0	4.0
Ready Salted, Lower Fat, Asda*	1 Bag/25g	120	481	6.0	58.0	25.0	4.8
Ready Salted, Made With Sunflower Oil, Walkers*	1 Bag/24g	113	470	7.5	60.0	22.0	5.0
Ready Salted, M & S*	1 Bag/25g	136	545	5.6	47.8	36.6	4.9
Ready Salted, Safeway*	1 Bag/25g	143	570	5.8	52.5	37.5	0.0
Ready Salted, Sainsbury's*	1 Bag/25g	135	538	4.3	47.4	36.8	4.1
Ready Salted, Select, Tesco*	1 Bag/25g	136	544	6.2	47.9	36.6	4.5
Ready Salted, SmartPrice, Asda*	1 Bag/20g	111	553	5.0	50.0	37.0	3.0
Ready Salted, Smiths, Walkers*	1 Bag/25g	133	531	4.3	45.2	37.0	0.0
Ready Salted, Square, Smiths, Walkers*	1 Bag/25g	113	452	6.9	62.5	19.4	0.0
Ready Salted, Squares, M & S*	1 Bag/35g	151	430	6.8	63.5	18.1	3.9
Ready Salted, Thick & Crunchy, McCoys*	1 Bag/49g	253	517	6.0	52.3	31.5	4.9
Ready Salted, Value, Tesco*	1 Bag/21g	115	548	6.0	50.0	36.0	0.0
Ready Salted, Walkers*	1 Bag/35g	189	540	6.5	50.0	34.0	4.1
Red Leicester & Spring Onion, M & S*	1 Bag/40g	194	485	6.2	58.7	27.2	4.9
Roast Beef & Mustard, Thick Cut, Brannigans*	1 Bag/40g	203	507	7.6	51.7	30.0	3.7
Roast Beef, KP*	1 Bag/25g	134	534	6.6	47.5	35.3	4.7
Roast Chicken Flavour, Budgens*	1 Bag/25g	129	516	7.3	47.6	33.0	3.6
Roast Chicken, Golden Wonder*	1 Bag/25g	131	522	6.2	48.6	33.6	2.0
Roast Chicken, Select, Tesco*	1 Bag/25g	134	536	6.6	48.6	35.0	4.4
Roast Chicken, Smiths, Walkers*	1 Bag/25g	133	531	4.3	45.2	37.0	0.0
Roast Chicken, Walkers*	1 Bag/35g	186	530	6.5	50.0	33.0	4.1
Salsa With Mesquite, Kettle Chips*	1 Bag/50g	229	458	6.1	54.0	24.3	5.7
Salt & Balsamic Vinegar, M & S*	1 Bag/40g	192	480	6.2	52.5	27.6	5.3
Salt & Black Pepper, Handcooked, M & S*	1 Bag/40g	180	450	5.7	55.0	22.9	5.2
Salt & Malt Vinegar Flavour, Sainsbury's*	1 Bag/25g	135	538	4.9	50.3	35.2	2.3
Salt & Malt Vinegar, Thick & Crunchy, McCoys*	1 Bag/50g	253	506	6.5	52.6	30.0	4.7
Salt & Vinegar, BGTY, Sainsbury's*	1 Bag/25g	121	482	6.5	57.3	25.2	5.2
Salt & Vinegar Flavour, Asda*	1 Bag/25g	133	530	6.0	50.0	34.0	4.5
Salt & Vinegar Flavour Crinkles, Reduced Fat, Boots*	1 Bag/35g	165	471	7.1	59.0	23.0	3.0
Salt & Vinegar Flavour, Half Fat, M & S*	1 Bag/40g	168	420	5.8	61.0	17.0	7.7
Salt & Vinegar, Golden Lights, Golden Wonder*	1 Bag/21g	91	435	4.9	64.1	17.8	4.3
Salt & Vinegar, Golden Wonder*	1 Bag/25g	131	522	5.4	48.5	34.0	2.0
Salt & Vinegar, KP*	1 Bag/25g	133	532	5.5	48.7	35.0	4.7
Salt & Vinegar, Lites, Walkers*	1 Bag/28g	130	465	7.5	61.0	21.0	4.0

CRISPS,	Measure WEIGHT/INFO	per Measure KCAL	KCAL	PROT	CARB	FAT	FIBRE
Salt & Vinegar, Lower Fat, Asda*	1 Bag/25g	120	481	5.0	58.0	25.0	4.8
Salt & Vinegar, Morrisons*	1 Bag/25g	124	497	7.2	48.7	30.4	4.5
Salt & Vinegar, Reduced Fat, Crinkle, M & S*	1 Bag/40g	190	475	7.0	58.0	24.0	6.5
Salt & Vinegar, Sainsbury's*	1 Bag/25g	131	522	4.1	46.9	35.3	3.9
Salt & Vinegar, Smiths, Walkers*	1 Bag/25g	133	531	4.3	45.2	37.0	0.0
Salt & Vinegar, Square, Smiths, Walkers*	1 Bag/25g	113	452	6.9	62.5	19.4	0.0
Salt & Vinegar, Square, Walkers*	1 Bag/25g	105	420	6.0	58.0	18.0	4.5
Salt & Vinegar, Value, Tesco*	1 Bag/20g	109	547	5.7	47.7	37.0	4.8
Salt & Vinegar, Walkers*	1 Bag/35g	186	530	6.5	50.0	33.0	4.1
Salt'n'Shake, Smiths, Walkers*	1 Bag/25g	136	543	4.1	44.2	38.9	0.0
Screaming Salt & Vinegar, Max, Walkers*	1 Bag/55g	256	465	7.5	61.0	21.0	4.0
Sea Salt & Balsamic Vinegar, Kettle Chips*	1 Bag/50g	234	468	5.6	60.9	24.4	4.4
Sea Salt & Cracked Black Pepper, Sensations, Walkers*	1 Bag/40g	194	485	6.5	54.0	27.0	4.5
Sea Salt & Malt Vinegar, Sensations, Walkers*	1 Bag/40g	194	485	6.5	54.0	27.0	4.5
Sea Salt With Crushed Black Peppercorns, Kettle Chips*	1 Bag/50g	225	449	5.7	55.0	22.9	5.2
Smoked Ham & Pickle, Thick Cut, Brannigans*	1 Bag/40g	203	507	7.0	52.8	29.8	3.8
Smokey Bacon, Smiths, Walkers*	1 Bag/25g	133	531	4.3	45.2	37.0	0.0
Smokey Bacon, Walkers*	1 Bag/34g	179	525	6.5	50.0	33.0	4.0
Smoky Bacon, Asda*	1 Bag/25g	133	530	6.0	50.0	34.0	4.5
Smoky Bacon, BGTY, Sainsbury's*	1 Bag/25g	118	472	6.5	58.5	23.6	5.7
Smoky Bacon, Golden Wonder*	1 Bag/25g	131	523	5.9	49.1	33.7	2.0
Smoky Bacon, Walkers*	1 Bag/35g	186	530	6.5	50.0	33.0	4.1
Sour Cream & Chive Crinkles, Shapers, Boots*	1 Bag/20g	96	482	6.6	60.0	24.0	4.0
Sour Cream & Chive, Reduced Fat, M & S*	1 Bag/40g	192	480	6.5	60.0	24.0	6.5
Sour Cream & Chives, Jordans*	1 Bag/30g	125	417	7.3	69.9	12.0	2.7
Sour Cream & Onion, Lights, Golden Wonder*	1 Bag/21g	91	435	5.4	64.5	17.2	5.9
Spring Onion Flavour, Crinklins, Go Ahead, McVitie's*	1 Bag/25g	110	438	9.3	71.2	12.9	2.7
T Bone Steak, Roysters*	1 Bag/31g	160	516	5.7	52.6	31.4	3.6
Thai Sweet Chilli Sensations, Walkers*	1 Bag/35g	170	485	6.5	54.0	27.0	4.5
Tomato Ketchup, Walkers*	1 Bag/35g	186	530	6.5	50.0	33.0	4.1
Tomato, Olive Oil & Basil Traditional Pan Fried, Sainsbury's*	1 Serving/50g	235	469	7.5	51.4	26.0	5.4
Tomato, Olive Oil & Basil, TTD, Sainsbury's*	1 Serving/50g	235	469	7.5	51.4	26.0	5.4
Tomato Sauce, Golden Wonder*	1 Bag/25g	130	521	5.7	49.2	33.5	2.0
Wild Chilli, Thick & Crunchy, McCoys*	1 Bag/50g	255	510	6.0	53.2	30.3	4.8
Worcester Sauce, Walkers*	1 Bag/25g	133	530	6.5	50.0	33.0	4.1
CRISPY PANCAKES,							
Beef Bolognese, Findus*	1 Pancake/65g	104	160	6.6	25.0	4.3	1.2
Chicken & Bacon, Findus*	1 Pancake/62g	90	145	6.1	23.6	2.8	0.9
Chicken, Bacon & Sweetcorn, Findus*	1 Serving/63g	101	160	5.8	24.8	4.1	1.1
Minced Beef & Onion, Green Isle*	1 Pancake/60g	140	234	6.0	31.2	9.5	2.7
Three Cheeses, Findus*	1 Pancake/62g	115	185	7.2	24.4	6.5	0.9
CROISSANT,							
Croissant,	1 Croissant/50g	180	360	8.3	38.3	20.3	1.6
All Butter, BGTY, Sainsbury's*	1 Croissant/44g	176	401	9.8	44.2	20.5	2.2
All Butter, Budgens*	1 Croissant/45g	185	412	7.9	39.7	24.6	3.3
All Butter, Mini, Tesco*	1 Serving/35g	151	430	9.3	45.2	23.5	2.0
All Butter, Reduced Fat, M & S*	1 Croissant/54g	181	335	6.8	38.4	16.9	1.5
All Butter, Sainsbury's*	1 Croissant/44g	196	446	9.3	38.2	28.4	2.0
All Butter, Tesco*	1 Croissant/77g	297	386	6.5	40.4	22.1	1.9
All Butter, TTD, Sainsbury's*	1 Croissant/75g	362	483	8.3	40.2	32.1	2.9
Asda*	1 Croissant/47g	186	405	9.0	45.0	21.0	0.0
Butter, Starbucks*	1 Croissant/82g	289	352	5.9	34.9	21.1	0.0
Chocolate, Pret A Manger*	1 Croissant/70g	322	460	9.3	35.6	31.3	0.0
Flaky Pastry With A Plain Chocolate Filling, Tesco*	1 Pastry/78g	318	408	6.5	41.0	24.3	2.0

Nutrition Values per 100g / 100ml apply to the KCAL, PROT, CARB, FAT and FIBRE columns.

C

	Measure WEIGHT/INFO	per Measure KCAL	Nutrition Values per 100g / 100ml KCAL	PROT	CARB	FAT	FIBRE
CROISSANT,							
Organic, M & S*	1oz/28g	116	415	8.0	45.6	22.3	0.1
Reduced Fat Butter, Tesco*	1 Croissant/52g	165	318	6.6	45.0	12.4	2.1
Smoked Ham & Cheese, M & S*	1 Croissant/105g	341	325	13.4	22.2	21.6	3.9
CROQUETTE,							
Parsnip, Finest, Tesco*	1 Croquette/37g	77	207	5.9	26.2	8.7	1.3
Potato, Asda*	1 Pack/127g	224	176	2.3	26.0	7.0	1.8
Potato, Bird's Eye*	1 Croquette/29g	44	152	2.6	22.6	5.7	1.2
Potato, Farmfoods*	1oz/28g	28	101	2.3	22.6	0.2	2.2
Potato, Fried In Blended Oil	1oz/28g	60	214	3.7	21.6	13.1	1.3
Potato, Sainsbury's*	1 Croquette/28g	50	180	3.9	23.0	8.0	1.0
Potatoes, Tesco*	1 Croquette/30g	43	142	3.0	19.2	5.9	1.5
Spiral, Deep Fried, McCain*	1oz/28g	85	304	3.7	30.4	18.6	0.0
Spiral, Oven Baked, McCain*	1oz/28g	71	253	3.7	28.4	13.8	0.0
Vegetable, Sainsbury's*	1 Serving/175g	392	224	5.8	23.3	11.9	2.2
CROUTONS,							
Cracked Pepper & Sea Salt, Safeway*	1 Serving/10g	45	454	12.8	56.5	19.6	3.9
Fresh, M & S*	1 Serving/10g	53	530	11.4	50.0	32.8	3.2
Italian Salad, Sainsbury's*	1 Pack/40g	204	510	8.5	62.7	25.0	2.5
Roast Onion & Potato, Crosse & Blackwell*	1 Pot/240g	252	105	2.2	13.6	4.7	1.2
CRUDITE PLATTER, Sainsbury*	1 Pack/275g	96	35	1.4	6.6	0.3	1.6
CRUMBLE,							
Apple & Blackberry, M & S*	1 Serving/135g	398	295	3.5	44.9	11.2	1.6
Apple & Blackberry, Tesco*	1 Crumble/335g	667	199	2.6	40.1	3.1	1.9
Apple, Somerfield*	1 Serving/195g	454	233	2.5	36.8	8.4	1.1
Apple, Tesco*	1 Serving/150g	342	228	2.0	33.6	9.5	1.2
Apple, With Sultanas, Weight Watchers*	1 Dessert/110g	196	178	1.4	34.2	3.9	1.3
Fish & Prawn, Youngs*	1 Pie/375g	476	127	5.8	9.7	7.2	1.3
Fruit	1oz/28g	55	198	2.0	34.0	6.9	1.7
Fruit, Wholemeal	1oz/28g	54	193	2.6	31.7	7.1	2.7
Gooseberry, M & S*	1 Serving/133g	379	285	3.5	43.3	10.7	1.7
Ocean, Good Choice, Iceland*	1 Pack/340g	377	111	7.2	14.4	2.7	1.1
Ocean, Low Fat, Ross*	1 Crumble/300g	219	73	5.1	11.4	0.8	0.4
Rhubarb, Co-Op*	¼ Crumble/110g	0	245	2.0	42.0	7.0	1.0
Rhubarb, Farmfoods*	1oz/28g	54	192	2.0	35.0	4.9	2.3
Rhubarb, M & S*	1 Serving/133g	366	275	3.4	42.6	9.9	1.4
Rhubarb, Sainsbury's*	1 Serving/50g	112	224	3.1	40.4	5.6	1.8
Rhubarb, Somerfield*	¼ Crumble/130g	281	216	3.0	38.0	6.0	0.0
Rhubarb, Tesco*	1/6 Crumble/116.7g	228	195	2.8	27.3	8.3	1.7
Salmon, Youngs*	1 Pie/339g	380	112	4.6	13.0	4.6	0.7
Topping, Sainsbury's*	1 Serving/47g	188	401	5.9	50.3	19.6	5.3
CRUMPETS,							
Asda*	1 Crumpet/45g	94	208	6.0	44.0	0.9	0.0
Co-Op*	1 Crumpet/55g	102	185	8.0	36.0	1.0	2.0
Finger, Safeway*	1 Crumpet/30g	55	182	6.9	36.7	0.1	1.8
Less Than 2% Fat, M & S*	1 Crumpet/61g	116	190	8.0	36.9	1.3	2.1
Premium, Sainsbury's*	1 Crumpet/50g	96	191	6.1	38.6	1.4	1.7
Safeway*	1 Crumpet/44g	80	182	7.0	36.6	0.8	1.8
Sainsbury's*	1 Crumpet/44g	91	207	5.6	44.0	0.9	0.5
SmartPrice, Asda*	1 Crumpet/42g	84	199	6.0	42.0	0.8	1.7
Tesco*	1 Crumpet/46g	92	201	6.0	42.6	0.7	1.8
Toasted	1 Crumpet/40g	80	199	6.7	43.4	1.0	2.0
Warburton's*	1 Crumpet/50g	89	178	7.1	35.8	0.7	0.0
CRUNCHIE,							
Cadbury's	1 Standard Bar/41g	193	470	4.4	72.1	18.1	0.0

	Measure WEIGHT/INFO	per Measure KCAL	KCAL	PROT	CARB	FAT	FIBRE
CRUNCHIE,							
Nuggets, Cadbury's*	1 Bag/125g	569	455	3.8	73.1	16.4	0.0
CRUNCHY STICKS,							
Salt & Vinegar, Sainsburys*	1 Bag/25g	119	474	5.9	58.0	24.3	2.4
Salt & Vinegar, Shapers, Boots*	1 Bag/23g	99	430	7.8	66.0	15.0	3.1
Salt & Vinegar, Value, Tesco*	1 Bag/22g	109	497	6.3	58.7	26.3	2.4
CRUSH,							
Morello Cherry, Finest, Tesco*	1 Serving/250ml	115	46	0.0	11.2	0.0	0.0
Orange & Raspberry, Freshly Squeezed, Finest, Tesco*	1fl oz/30ml	17	56	0.5	12.6	0.1	0.2
Orange & Raspberry, Pret A Manger*	1 Bottle/250ml	110	44	0.7	10.0	0.1	0.0
Orange & Raspberry, Safeway*	1 Serving/100ml	57	57	0.5	13.6	0.1	0.2
Orange, Cool, Diet, Sainsbury*	1 Can/330ml	10	3	0.1	0.6	0.1	0.1
CUCUMBER,							
Raw, Fresh	1oz/28g	3	10	0.7	1.5	0.1	0.6
CUMIN, Seeds	1 Tsp/2g	5	235	17.8	0.0	18.2	0.0
CURACAO	1 Shot/25ml	78	311	0.0	28.3	0.0	0.0
CURLY KALE,							
Boiled In Salted Water	1oz/28g	7	24	2.4	1.0	1.1	2.8
Raw	1oz/28g	9	33	3.4	1.4	1.6	3.1
CURLY WURLY,							
Cadbury's*	1 Bar/28g	126	450	4.8	69.9	16.7	0.0
Squirlies, Cadbury's*	1 Squirl/3g	14	450	3.9	69.0	17.8	0.0
CURRANTS	1oz/28g	75	267	2.3	67.8	0.4	1.9
CURRY, (SEE ALSO TYPES, EG. BALTI, MADRAS)							
Aubergine	1oz/28g	33	118	1.4	6.2	10.1	1.5
Beef & Rice, Iceland*	1 Pack/400g	492	123	8.7	16.0	2.6	0.6
Beef, M & S*	1oz/28g	34	120	12.2	3.9	6.1	1.0
Beef, SmartPrice, Asda*	1 Serving/392g	223	57	4.0	9.0	0.5	1.0
Beef With Rice, Asda*	1 Pack/406g	547	135	6.0	19.0	3.9	1.2
Beef With Rice, Bird's Eye*	1 Pack/388g	524	135	6.9	20.8	2.8	0.8
Beef With Rice, Healthy Choice, Asda*	1 Pack/400g	476	119	6.0	18.0	2.6	0.9
Beef With Rice, Tesco*	1 Pack/400g	476	119	5.7	17.3	3.0	0.8
Beef With Rice, Weight Watchers*	1 Pack/328g	249	76	4.2	12.5	1.0	0.3
Blackeye Bean, Gujerati	1oz/28g	36	127	7.2	16.1	4.4	2.8
Bombay Potato	1oz/28g	33	117	2.0	13.7	6.8	1.2
Cabbage	1oz/28g	23	82	1.9	8.1	5.0	2.1
Caribean Style Chicken With Rice & Beans, ES, Safeway*	1 Pack/380g	342	90	6.2	12.5	1.3	1.8
Cauliflower & Potato	1oz/28g	17	59	3.4	6.6	2.4	1.8
Chick Pea, Whole	1oz/28g	50	179	9.6	21.3	7.5	4.5
Chick Pea, Whole & Tomato, Punjabi With Vegetable	1oz/28g	31	112	5.6	12.4	4.9	2.9
Chick Pea, Whole, Basic	1oz/28g	30	108	6.0	14.2	3.6	3.3
Chicken, & Potato Wedges, HE, Tesco*	1 Pack/450g	428	95	7.6	10.3	2.7	1.1
Chicken & Rice, Iceland*	1 Pack/399g	455	114	7.5	13.6	3.3	0.9
Chicken, Asda*	1 Can/200g	210	105	10.0	5.0	5.0	0.0
Chicken Caldina, Sainsbury's*	½ Pack/200g	266	133	12.3	3.2	7.9	1.2
Chicken, Extra Strong, M & S*	1oz/28g	28	100	13.8	2.5	3.9	1.4
Chicken, Good Choice, Iceland*	1 Meal/399g	439	110	5.1	18.3	1.8	7.0
Chicken Malaysian With Rice, Bernard Matthews*	1 Pack/400g	512	128	6.1	17.0	3.9	0.0
Chicken, Mild, BGTY, Sainsbury's*	1 Serving/200g	206	103	10.0	6.7	4.0	1.3
Chicken, Mild, M & S*	1oz/28g	28	100	13.8	2.5	3.9	1.4
Chicken, Mild, Sainsbury's*	1 Can/400g	472	118	10.5	3.5	6.9	1.3
Chicken, Reduced Fat, Asda*	1 Pack/400g	476	119	6.0	18.0	2.6	0.9
Chicken, SmartPrice, Asda*	1 Can/392g	282	72	4.0	11.0	1.3	1.0
Chicken With Naan Bread, Iceland*	1 Portion/260g	484	186	10.1	22.3	6.3	1.4
Chicken With Rice, Asda*	1 Pack/400g	440	110	5.0	17.0	2.4	1.0

(Nutrition Values per 100g / 100ml: KCAL, PROT, CARB, FAT, FIBRE)

C

C

CURRY,	Measure WEIGHT/INFO	per Measure KCAL	KCAL	PROT	CARB	FAT	FIBRE
Chicken With Rice, Bird's Eye*	1 Pack/380g	475	125	5.8	20.5	2.2	0.8
Chicken With Rice For 1, Vesta*	1 Pack/108g	406	376	13.4	64.1	7.4	3.6
Chicken With Rice, Frozen, Co-Op*	1 Pack/350g	385	110	6.0	15.0	3.0	1.0
Chicken With Rice, Healthy Choice, Asda*	1 Pack/400g	492	123	6.0	18.0	3.0	1.0
Chicken With Rice, Morrisons*	1 Pack/300g	345	115	5.5	18.7	2.0	0.4
Chicken With Rice, Sainsbury's*	1 Pack/400g	500	125	5.4	17.5	3.7	0.8
Chicken With Rice, Tesco*	1 Pack/300g	300	100	5.7	14.4	2.2	0.4
Chicken With Rice, Weight Watchers*	1 Pack/300g	273	91	4.7	14.3	1.7	0.5
Chicken With Vegetables, Value, Tesco*	1 Serving/196g	123	63	3.1	7.2	2.4	0.7
Chinese Chicken, Oriental Express*	1 Pack/340g	286	84	4.8	16.2	0.6	0.8
Chinese Chicken, Somerfield*	1 Serving/340g	286	84	4.8	16.2	0.6	0.8
Chinese Chicken With Vegetable Rice, M & S*	1 Pack/400g	320	80	7.1	8.4	2.0	1.3
Courgette & Potato	1oz/28g	24	86	1.9	8.7	5.2	1.2
Dudhi, Kofta	1oz/28g	32	113	2.6	9.4	7.4	2.8
Fish & Vegetable, Bangladeshi	1oz/28g	33	117	9.1	1.4	8.4	0.5
Fish, Bangladeshi	1oz/28g	35	124	12.2	1.5	7.9	0.3
Gobi Aloo Sag, Retail	1oz/28g	27	95	2.2	7.1	6.9	1.4
Green Bean	1oz/28g	37	131	1.7	3.6	12.7	1.6
Green Thai Chicken, Sainsbury's*	1 Serving/200g	306	153	13.6	3.0	9.6	1.6
Green Thai Style Chicken & Sticky Rice, Asda*	1 Pack/450g	585	130	7.0	20.0	2.4	0.1
Hot Chicken With Rice, Asda*	1 Pack/400g	440	110	5.0	18.0	2.0	1.1
Kashmiri Chicken, Heinz*	1 Pack/451g	582	129	7.5	19.9	2.2	0.3
Keralan Shacuti, Sainsbury's*	1 Jar/350g	277	79	1.8	10.5	6.8	2.2
Lamb, Extra Strong, M & S*	1oz/28g	35	125	11.5	4.6	6.9	0.9
Lamb With Rice, Bird's Eye*	1 Pack/382g	520	136	5.6	20.8	3.4	0.9
Curry Leaves, Fresh	1oz/28g	27	97	7.9	13.3	1.3	0.0
Malaysian Chicken & Noodles, COU, M & S*	1oz/28g	24	85	8.6	8.3	1.8	1.1
Mango Chicken, Feeling Great, Findus*	1 Pack/345g	380	110	4.5	16.0	3.5	1.5
Potato & Pea	1oz/28g	26	92	2.9	13.0	3.8	2.4
Prawn & Mushroom	1oz/28g	47	168	7.3	2.5	14.4	1.0
Prawn & Rice, Iceland*	1 Pack/400g	432	108	4.5	15.4	3.2	1.0
Prawn With Rice, Asda*	1 Pack/400g	420	105	3.5	17.0	2.6	1.1
Prawn With Rice, Co-Op*	1 Pack/350g	420	120	3.0	19.0	3.0	0.9
Red Kidney Bean, Punjabi	1oz/28g	30	106	4.7	10.1	5.6	3.8
Red Thai Chicken, New Recipe, Waitrose*	1 Pack/350g	389	111	8.9	5.0	6.2	0.9
Red Thai Fish, Waitrose*	1 Pack/500g	275	55	5.2	3.7	2.2	1.0
Red Thai, Safeway*	1 Pack/324g	369	114	10.0	4.8	6.1	1.6
Red Thai Style Chicken, HE, Tesco*	1 Pack/420g	462	110	6.0	17.7	1.7	0.2
Thai Chicken, Tom Yum, Sainsbury's*	1 Pot/400g	416	104	11.1	3.5	5.1	1.9
Thai Green Chicken, BGTY, Sainsbury's*	1 Pack/400g	268	67	8.1	6.3	1.0	1.5
Thai Red Chicken, 97% Fat Free, Birds Eye*	1 Pack/366g	425	116	5.7	19.0	1.9	0.5
Thai Red Chicken, Asda*	1 Pack/360g	461	128	9.1	5.5	7.7	1.0
Thai Red Chicken, BGTY, Sainsbury's*	1 Pack/450g	545	121	6.2	14.9	4.1	1.1
Thai Red Chicken, Sainsbury's*	1 Serving/200g	300	150	14.3	5.5	7.9	1.0
Thai Red Chicken With Fragrant Rice, Somerfield	1 Pack/340g	503	148	8.0	18.0	5.0	0.0
Thai Red, Sizzle & Stir, Chicken Tonight*	1 Jar/485g	873	180	1.5	4.5	17.3	1.7
Thai Yellow Vegetable, Sainsburys*	½ Pack/200g	256	128	1.7	7.1	10.3	1.5
Vegetable & Rice, Iceland*	1 Pack/400g	528	132	2.3	18.4	5.5	1.2
Vegetable, Budgens*	1 Pack/350g	249	71	1.8	6.9	4.0	2.2
Vegetable, Frozen, Mixed Vegetables	1oz/28g	25	88	2.5	6.9	6.1	0.0
Vegetable, Health Eating, Tesco*	1 Pack/350g	280	80	4.5	13.6	0.8	1.3
Vegetable, Hot, Tesco*	1 Can/425g	340	80	2.2	11.6	2.8	1.5
Vegetable, In Sweet Sauce	1 Serving/330g	162	49	1.4	6.7	2.1	1.3
Vegetable, Indian Meal For One, Tesco*	1 Serving/200g	220	110	1.9	10.5	6.7	1.4

Nutrition Values per 100g / 100ml (KCAL, PROT, CARB, FAT, FIBRE)

CURRY,	Measure WEIGHT/INFO	per Measure KCAL	KCAL	PROT	CARB	FAT	FIBRE
Vegetable, Medium, Tesco*	1 Pack/350g	326	93	2.3	7.1	6.2	1.9
Vegetable, Mild, Tesco*	1 Can/425g	315	74	2.1	10.7	2.5	1.7
Vegetable, Pakistani	1oz/28g	17	60	2.2	8.7	2.6	2.2
Vegetable, Ready Meals, M & S*	1 Pack/300g	495	165	2.4	7.2	14.2	2.1
Vegetable, Retail With Rice	1oz/28g	29	102	3.3	16.4	3.0	0.0
Vegetable, Safeway*	1 Pack/275g	239	87	2.4	7.3	5.4	2.8
Vegetable, SmartPrice, Asda*	½ Can/203g	132	65	2.0	13.0	0.5	1.7
Vegetable, Takeaway	1oz/28g	29	105	2.5	7.6	7.4	0.0
Vegetable, Waitrose*	1 Pack/352g	285	81	3.5	4.9	5.3	2.1
Vegetable With Pilau Rice, BGTY, Sainsbury's*	1 Pack/450g	441	98	2.4	16.9	2.3	0.5
Vegetable With Pilau Rice, Linda McCartney*	1 Pack/339g	224	66	1.6	13.5	0.6	0.5
Vegetable With Rice, Co-Op*	1 Pack/340g	289	85	2.0	17.0	1.0	0.7
Vegetable With Rice, Tesco*	1 Pack/400g	440	110	2.1	18.7	3.0	1.0
Vegetable With Yoghurt	1oz/28g	17	62	2.6	4.6	4.1	1.4
Yellow Vegetable Thai, Sainsbury's*	1 Pack/400g	624	156	2.2	9.4	12.2	1.1
CURRY PASTE,							
Balti, Patak's*	1 Jar/283g	1112	393	5.0	20.3	31.8	3.1
Balti, Patak's*	1oz/28g	107	382	5.8	18.3	31.7	3.1
Balti, Sharwood's*	¼ Pack/72.5g	328	453	5.0	19.2	39.6	3.1
Garam Masala, Cinnamon and Ginger, Hot, Patak's*	1 tbsp/25g	101	403	3.2	17.9	35.4	0.6
Hot, M & S*	1oz/28g	69	245	4.2	13.4	19.2	3.3
Hot, Sharwood's*	1oz/28g	123	439	5.1	18.6	38.3	2.6
Korma, Pataks*	1 tbsp/10g	54	535	4.2	13.0	51.8	2.6
Madras, Pataks*	Half jar/50g	293	586	4.3	21.6	53.6	5.2
Medium, M & S*	1oz/28g	64	230	2.5	10.7	19.5	4.9
Medium, Sharwood's*	1oz/28g	122	434	4.5	16.8	38.8	2.7
Medium, Sharwood's*	1oz/28g	122	434	4.5	16.8	38.8	2.7
Mild, Patak's Original*	1oz/28g	155	552	4.9	14.3	52.8	6.2
Mild, Sharwood's*	1oz/28g	78	279	3.6	17.7	21.5	3.4
Rogan Josh, Patak's*	1 Serving/30g	119	397	4.1	12.7	36.7	5.9
Tandoori, Patak's*	1 Tbsp/25g	28	111	3.1	20.7	1.8	2.6
Tandoori, Sharwood's*	1oz/28g	64	228	5.9	15.5	15.8	1.9
Thai Green, Mild, Sainsbury's*	1 Tbsp/15g	23	156	2.2	14.5	9.9	2.7
Thai Red, Sainsbury's*	1oz/28g	43	154	2.0	8.0	12.0	3.0
Tikka Masala, Patak's*	1oz/28g	101	361	3.4	16.2	31.4	3.2
Tikka Masala, Sharwood's*	1oz/28g	53	191	3.2	9.9	15.4	2.6
CURRY POWDER,							
Curry Powder	1 Tsp/2g	7	325	12.7	41.8	13.8	0.0
Curry Powder	1 Tsp/2g	5	233	9.5	26.1	10.8	23.0
Medium, Sharwood's*	1 Pack/113g	336	297	12.2	52.9	13.4	18.5
Mild, Sharwood's*	1 Tsp/2g	6	300	12.7	54.1	12.3	16.4
Mixed Flavours	1 Tspn/2g	6	316	13.0	34.7	13.9	0.0
CUSTARD,							
Canned, Average	1oz/28g	27	95	2.6	15.4	3.0	0.1
Chocolate, COU, M & S*	1 Pot/140g	147	105	3.1	18.6	2.2	1.0
Chocolate, Tesco*	½ Pot/250g	308	123	2.5	15.0	5.9	0.3
Confectioners'	1oz/28g	48	170	6.4	24.4	5.9	0.2
Devon, Ambrosia*	1oz/28g	29	103	2.7	16.4	3.0	0.1
Devon, Low Fat, Ambrosia*	1oz/28g	20	72	2.9	12.7	1.1	0.1
Economy, Sainsbury's*	½ Can/198g	150	76	3.0	14.4	0.7	0.0
Egg, Average	1oz/28g	33	118	5.7	11.0	6.0	0.0
Fresh, Co-Op*	1 Serving/125g	150	120	5.0	14.0	5.0	0.5
Fresh, HE, Tesco*	1 Serving/100g	103	103	2.3	17.3	2.7	0.2
Fresh, Thick & Creamy, BGTY, Sainsbury's*	1oz/28g	33	119	3.2	14.1	5.5	0.0

Nutrition Values per 100g / 100ml

	Measure WEIGHT/INFO	per Measure KCAL	Nutrition Values per 100g / 100ml KCAL	PROT	CARB	FAT	FIBRE
CUSTARD,							
GFY, Asda*	1 Serving/150g	137	91	2.9	17.0	1.3	0.1
Instant, Dry, Bird's*	1oz/28g	119	425	4.5	76.0	11.5	0.0
Instant, Dry, Low Fat, Bird's*	1oz/28g	113	405	4.3	78.5	8.2	0.0
Instant, Dry, No Added Sugar, Tesco*	1 Serving/Dry/18g	73	406	5.3	77.0	8.5	0.0
Instant, Sainsbury's*	1 Serving/141g	109	77	0.8	14.0	2.0	0.0
Low Fat, Ready To Serve, Bird's*	1oz/28g	24	87	2.8	15.5	1.4	0.0
Low Fat, Ready To Serve, Budgens*	1oz/28g	21	74	2.9	14.0	0.7	0.0
Low Fat, Somerfield*	1 Pot/425g	391	92	3.0	17.0	1.0	0.0
Low Sugar Instant, Co-Op*	1 Pack/74g	56	75	1.1	13.4	1.9	0.1
Made Up With Semi-Skimmed Milk	1oz/28g	26	94	3.8	16.8	1.9	0.0
Made Up With Skimmed Milk	1oz/28g	22	79	3.8	16.8	0.1	0.0
Made Up With Whole Milk	1oz/28g	33	117	3.7	16.6	4.5	0.0
Mix, Chocolate Flavour, Instant, Bird's*	1oz/28g	116	415	5.9	78.5	8.8	0.1
Mix, Instant, 5% Less Sugar, Made Up, Asda*	1 Pack/435g	309	71	0.7	14.0	1.4	0.1
Mix, Instant, Co-Op*	1 Pack/76g	340	448	4.5	68.5	17.3	0.0
Mix, Instant, Made Up, Co-Op*	½ Pack/140ml	118	84	0.7	13.9	2.9	0.0
Original, Ready To Serve, Bird's*	1oz/28g	29	102	2.8	15.5	3.0	0.0
Pot, Forest Fruits Flavour, Hot 'n' Fruity, Bird's*	1 Pot/174g	171	98	0.9	18.5	2.4	0.1
Pot, Ready To Eat, Farmfoods*	1 Pot/150g	146	97	2.9	16.2	2.3	0.0
Pot, Strawberry Flavour, Hot 'n' Fruity, Bird's*	1oz/28g	28	99	1.0	18.5	2.4	0.1
Powder	1oz/28g	99	354	0.6	92.0	0.7	0.1
Powder, Original Flavour, Bird's*	1oz/28g	99	355	0.4	87.0	0.5	0.0
Ready to Eat, GFY, Asda*	1 Serving/150g	137	91	2.9	17.0	1.3	0.1
Ready To Eat, Low Fat, Tesco*	1 Pot/150g	132	88	2.9	16.2	1.3	0.2
Ready To Serve, BGTY, Sainsbury's*	1oz/28g	25	91	2.8	16.9	1.4	0.0
Ready To Serve, Co-Op*	1 Can/425g	425	100	3.0	16.0	3.0	0.0
Ready To Serve, HE, Tesco*	1oz/28g	22	77	2.9	13.0	1.5	0.0
Ready To Serve, Low Fat, Asda*	¼ Pack/142g	109	77	2.9	13.0	1.5	0.0
Ready To Serve Low Fat, Co-Op*	1 Can/425g	319	75	3.0	14.0	0.7	0.0
Ready To Serve, Somerfield*	1oz/28g	29	103	3.0	17.0	3.0	0.0
Sauce, Fresh, Somerfield*	¼ Pack/100g	119	119	3.0	15.0	5.0	0.0
Strawberry Style, Shapers, Boots*	1 Pot/148g	83	56	4.0	8.2	0.8	0.1
Summer, Ambrosia*	1 Pack/500g	490	98	2.7	15.0	3.0	0.0
Thick & Creamy, Fresh, M & S*	¼ Carton/125g	286	229	2.7	16.2	17.0	0.0
Vanilla, COU, M & S*	1 Pot/140g	147	105	4.3	16.6	2.5	0.6
Vanilla With Apple Crunch, Ambrosia*	1 Pack/193g	276	143	3.4	22.4	4.5	0.8
CUTLETS,							
Nut, Goodlife*	1 Serving/88g	248	282	10.2	27.4	14.6	3.0
Nut, Grilled, Cauldron Foods*	1 Cutlet/87g	250	287	10.2	26.8	15.4	4.6
Nut, Retail, Fried In Vegetable Oil	1oz/28g	81	289	4.8	18.7	22.3	1.7
Nut, Retail, Grilled	1oz/28g	59	212	5.1	19.9	13.0	1.8
Vegetable, Nut, Tesco*	1 Serving/88g	271	308	7.7	22.0	21.0	3.5
CUTTLEFISH, Raw	1oz/28g	20	71	16.1	0.0	0.7	0.0

DAB, RAW	Measure WEIGHT/INFO	per Measure KCAL	Nutrition Values per 100g / 100ml KCAL	PROT	CARB	FAT	FIBRE
Dad, Raw, Average	1oz/28g	21	74	15.7	0.0	1.2	0.0
DAIRYLEA DUNKERS,							
Smokey Bacon, Dairylea*	1 Pack/45g	135	300	7.3	24.0	19.5	0.0
Jumbo Munch, Dairylea*	1 Serving/50g	150	300	7.2	26.5	18.5	1.2
DAIRYLEA LUNCHABLES,							
Cheese & Pizza Crackers, Dairylea*	1oz/28g	105	375	10.5	24.5	27.0	1.4
Chicken, Fun Pack, Dairylea*	1 Pack/311g	454	146	5.5	15.0	6.2	0.2
Double Cheese, Dairylea*	1 Pack/110g	413	375	18.0	17.0	26.0	0.3
Ham & Cheese Pizza, Dairylea*	1 Pack/97g	247	255	11.5	26.0	11.0	1.6
Harvest Ham, Dairylea*	1 Pack/110g	314	285	16.5	16.5	17.0	0.3
Tasty Chicken, Dairylea*	1 Pack/110g	314	285	17.0	17.5	16.5	0.3
DAMSONS,							
Raw, Weighed With Stones	1oz/28g	10	34	0.5	8.6	0.0	1.6
Raw, Weighed Without Stones	1oz/28g	11	38	0.5	9.6	0.0	1.8
DANDELION & BURDOCK, Drink, Ben Shaws Original*	1 Lge Can/440ml	128	29	0.0	7.0	0.0	0.0
DANISH PASTRY,							
Danish Pastry	1 Pastry/110g	411	374	5.8	51.3	17.6	1.6
Apple & Sultana, Tesco*	1 Pastry/72g	293	407	5.4	45.0	22.8	1.4
Custard Danish Bar, Sara Lee*	¼ Bar/100g	228	228	6.6	36.1	6.4	0.8
Danish Apple Bar, Sara Lee*	1/6 Bar/70g	160	229	4.3	42.1	5.7	1.7
Danish Twist, Apple & Cinnamon, Entenmann's*	1 Serving/52g	150	288	5.6	62.0	1.9	1.5
Danish Twist, Toasted Pecan, Entenmann's*	1 Slice/48g	171	351	7.0	47.2	15.6	1.4
Pecan, M & S*	1 Serving/67g	287	428	6.2	45.0	26.0	1.3
DATES,							
Dried	1oz/28g	76	270	3.3	68.0	0.2	4.0
Dried, Weighed With Stones	1 Date/20g	45	227	2.8	57.1	0.2	3.4
Fresh, Raw	1oz/28g	35	124	1.5	31.3	0.1	1.8
Medjool	1oz/28g	76	273	2.3	65.5	0.2	2.2
Organic, Waitrose*	1oz/28g	81	290	3.3	67.7	0.7	4.0
Pitted, Asda*	1 Pack/50g	127	254	3.0	60.0	0.2	3.0
Raw, Weighed With Stones	1 Date/30g	32	107	1.3	26.9	0.1	1.5
Tesco*	1 Date/9g	26	287	3.3	68.0	0.2	1.0
DELIGHT,							
Butterscotch Flavour, No Added Sugar, Tesco*	½ Pack/25g	109	434	4.8	66.5	16.5	0.0
Chocolate Flavour, Dry, Tesco*	1 Packet/49g	204	417	6.3	63.0	15.5	0.5
Strawberry Flavour, No Added Sugar, Dry, Tesco*	½ Pack/25g	110	440	4.8	67.0	17.0	0.0
Strawberry, Shapers, Boots*	1 Pot/121g	96	79	4.5	13.0	1.0	0.1
DESSERT,							
Apple Rice, Classic Desserts, M & S*	1 Pot/200g	210	105	2.5	20.0	1.7	0.3
Banana Flavour Custard, Ambrosia*	1 Pack/135g	136	101	2.6	16.2	2.9	0.1
Banoffee, Weight Watchers*	1 Pot/80g	154	192	4.5	35.3	3.7	0.8
Black Cherry & Chocolate, COU, M & S*	1 Pack/115g	132	115	3.6	22.6	1.4	1.2
Black Cherry, COU, M & S*	1 Pot/115g	132	115	3.6	22.6	1.4	1.2
Butterscotch Flavour Whip, Co-Op*	1 Pack/64g	241	377	0.6	93.4	0.1	0.1
Cafe Latte, Iced, BGTY, Sainsbury's*	1 Serving/75g	104	139	2.9	23.7	3.6	3.3
Cappuccino, BGTY, Sainsbury's*	1 Pot/119g	224	188	3.3	25.2	8.1	0.8
Cappuccino, Italian, Co-Op*	1 Pack/90g	257	285	5.0	39.0	12.0	0.1
Caramel, M & S*	1oz/28g	41	147	3.9	22.3	4.1	0.0
Cherry & Chocolate, Eat Smart, Safeway*	1 Serving/100g	150	150	3.2	27.5	2.7	0.1
Chocolate & Cherry, COU, M & S*	1 Pot/130g	156	120	2.6	24.5	1.6	0.9
Chocolate & Honeycomb Iced, Weight Watchers*	1 Pot/58g	92	159	3.1	26.3	4.3	0.8
Chocolate & Marshmallow Swirls, Iced, BGTY, Sainsbury's	¼ Pot/75g	130	173	3.9	33.8	2.5	2.8
Chocolate & Vanilla Caramel, Dairy, Yoplait Petits Filous*	1 Pot/60g	101	169	4.8	23.6	6.2	0.0
Chocolate Creme, Somerfield*	1 Pot/125g	180	144	4.0	22.0	4.0	0.0

D

DESSERT,	Measure WEIGHT/INFO	per Measure KCAL	Nutrition Values per 100g / 100ml KCAL	PROT	CARB	FAT	FIBRE
Chocolate Fudge Brownie, Frozen, Tesco*	1 Pot/100g	171	171	3.5	29.6	4.7	0.9
Chocolate Fudge Brownie, Tesco*	1 Pot/125g	374	299	4.6	40.2	13.3	1.3
Chocolate Muffin, COU, M & S*	1 Serving/110g	149	135	4.6	26.5	1.9	0.9
Chocolate Profiterole, Tesco*	1 Serving/76g	281	370	4.3	27.9	26.7	0.4
Chocolate, Value, Tesco*	1 Pot/115g	112	97	2.8	15.7	2.6	0.0
Chocolate, Weight Watchers*	1 Pot/100ml	92	92	1.8	15.2	2.5	0.5
Corruptible Chocolate, Iced, Weight Watchers*	1 Pot/100ml	92	92	1.8	15.2	2.5	0.5
Dreaming of, Cherry Rice, M & S*	1 pot/200g	220	110	2.4	19.7	2.2	0.1
Dreamy Vanilla, BGTY, Sainsbury's*	1 Serving/58g	146	252	3.5	27.6	14.2	5.3
Galaxy, Mars*	1 Dessert/75g	166	221	4.9	22.7	12.3	0.0
Gulabjam Indian, Waitrose*	1 Pot/180g	476	266	4.8	42.9	8.6	0.6
Lemoncello, Italian, Co-Op*	1 Pack/90g	266	295	3.0	34.0	16.0	0.1
Mandarin, 95% Fat Free, M & S*	1oz/28g	35	125	1.0	19.6	4.5	0.2
Dessert Mix, Chocolate Flavour, Instant, Safeway*	¼ Pack/23g	99	431	8.5	72.4	11.9	1.4
Dessert Mix, Instant Powder, Made Up With Skimmed Milk	1oz/28g	27	97	3.1	14.9	3.2	0.2
Dessert Mix, Instant Powder, Made Up With Whole Milk	1oz/28g	35	125	3.1	14.8	6.3	0.2
Mocha Mallow, Eat Smart, Safeway*	1 Pot/100g	150	150	4.4	26.1	2.7	0.6
Natural Rice, Shape*	1 Pot/175g	149	85	3.5	15.4	1.0	0.1
Peach, Iced, So-Lo, Iceland*	1 Lolly/92ml	98	107	2.3	23.5	0.0	2.2
Pineapple & Passionfruit, M & S*	1 Pot/100g	130	130	0.8	21.7	3.8	0.3
Profiterole, M & S*	1 Dessert/61g	209	342	5.5	29.1	22.1	0.5
Raspberry Flavour Whip, Co-Op*	1 Whip/64g	241	377	1.2	92.5	0.2	0.1
Raspberry Swirl, Iced, Weight Watchers*	1 Scoop/60g	74	124	1.7	23.4	2.5	0.3
Red Devil, Simpsons, St Ivel*	1oz/28g	38	134	2.8	24.3	2.8	0.4
Rolo, Nestle*	1 Pot/78g	191	245	3.1	30.3	12.2	0.3
Strawberries & Cream, Better for You, Morrisons*	1 Serving/200g	244	122	2.2	26.0	1.1	0.1
Strawberry Flavour Custard, Ambrosia*	1 Pack/135g	136	101	2.7	16.1	2.9	0.1
Strawberry Flavour Whip, Co-Op*	1 Pack/64g	246	385	0.9	94.1	0.6	0.1
Strawberry Flavour, With Cream, Somerfield*	1 Dessert/100g	119	119	2.0	16.0	5.0	0.0
Strawberry Rice, Devonshire Style, St Ivel*	1 Pot/150g	182	121	2.8	21.3	2.7	0.1
Strawberry Rice, Shape*	1 Pot/175g	137	78	3.0	14.5	0.9	0.1
Strawberry, SmartPrice, Asda*	1 Pot/100g	120	120	2.3	16.0	5.0	0.0
Summer Fruit, COU, M & S*	1 Serving/105g	110	105	2.1	21.6	1.1	1.2
Supreme, No Added Sugar, Sainsbury's*	¼ Pack/91g	98	108	3.5	13.6	4.4	0.0
Tantalising Toffee, COU, M & S*	¼ Pot/85g	145	170	3.1	32.8	2.9	0.5
Tantalising Toffee Flavour, Iced, Weight Watchers*	1 Serving/57g	93	163	2.7	26.2	4.8	0.2
Toffee Banana Crunch, Farmfoods*	1/6 Dessert/82g	219	267	2.6	38.5	11.4	0.7
Toffee Chocolate, Weight Watchers*	1 Pot/100g	164	164	4.4	31.5	3.2	1.6
Toffee Flavour & Toffee Sauce, Iced, Weight Watchers*	1 Pot/57g	93	163	2.7	26.2	4.8	0.2
Toffee Flavour Custard, Ambrosia*	1 Pack/135g	139	103	2.7	16.4	2.9	0.1
Toffee Flavour Fudge Swirl, Iced, Weight Watchers*	1 Pot/57g	82	143	2.5	22.6	4.4	0.4
Toffee Flavour, Low Fat, So-Lo, Iceland*	1 Serving/100g	65	65	2.1	10.1	1.8	0.3
Toffee Flavoured Dairy, Iced, BGTY, Sainsbury's*	1 Serving/70g	103	147	2.7	24.0	4.5	0.2
Toffee Iced, 3% Fat, M & S*	1oz/28g	51	183	3.1	37.2	2.4	0.5
Toffee With Biscuit Pieces, Iced, Weight Watchers*	1 Pot/100ml	93	93	1.5	14.9	2.7	0.1
Triple Chocolate Truffle, Entenmann's*	1 Serving/100g	304	304	4.5	28.4	19.1	2.2
Vanilla & Raspberry Compote, Iced, Weight Watchers*	1 Scoop/62g	88	142	2.6	23.3	3.9	0.3
Vanilla & Strawberry Compote, Iced, Weight Watchers*	1 Pot/57g	81	142	2.5	23.4	3.9	0.2
Vanilla, COU, M & S*	1 Pot/200g	90	45	4.1	6.1	0.1	0.0
Vanilla Flavour, Iced, HE, Tesco*	1 Serving/50g	67	134	3.9	24.1	2.4	4.6
Vanilla, Frozen, BGTY, Sainsbury's*	1 Serving/75g	89	119	3.0	19.9	3.0	3.7
Vanilla, Frozen, GFY, Asda*	1 Serving/52g	72	139	2.7	22.0	4.5	0.0
Vanilla, Iced, 3% Fat, M & S*	1oz/28g	40	143	3.5	25.9	2.8	0.7
Vanilla Supreme, Sainsbury's*	1 Pot/95g	116	122	3.0	18.0	4.0	0.0

	Measure WEIGHT/INFO	per Measure KCAL	KCAL	PROT	CARB	FAT	FIBRE
			Nutrition Values per 100g / 100ml				
DHAL,							
Blackeye Bean, Patak's*	1oz/28g	29	102	3.6	12.4	4.6	1.8
Black Gram	1oz/28g	21	74	4.2	7.0	3.4	1.7
Chick Pea	1oz/28g	42	149	7.4	17.7	6.1	3.8
Chick Pea, Canned, Asda*	½ Can/194g	198	102	4.3	14.0	3.2	2.9
Lentil, Patak's*	1 Can/283g	156	55	2.8	9.3	1.0	1.0
Lentil, Red Masoor & Tomato With Butter	1oz/28g	26	94	4.0	9.7	4.9	0.9
Lentil, Red Masoor & Vegetable	1oz/28g	31	110	5.8	14.7	3.8	1.8
Lentil, Red Masoor, Punjabi	1oz/28g	39	139	7.2	19.2	4.6	2.0
Lentil, Red Masoor With Vegetable Oil	1oz/28g	48	172	7.6	19.2	7.9	1.8
Lentil, Red Masoorl & Mung Bean	1oz/28g	32	114	4.8	9.9	6.7	1.6
Lentil, Safeway*	1 Serving/200g	182	91	2.4	10.5	4.4	0.9
Lentil, Tesco*	1 Serving/200g	248	124	5.1	10.6	6.6	2.5
Mung Bean, Bengali	1oz/28g	20	73	4.2	7.4	3.3	1.7
Mung Beans, Dried, Boiled In Unsalted Water	1oz/28g	26	92	7.8	15.3	0.4	0.0
Mung Beans, Dried, Raw	1oz/28g	81	291	26.8	46.3	1.1	0.0
Toor, Cooked Dish	1oz/28g	31	109	4.6	13.3	4.6	0.0
DHANSAK,							
Chicken, Ready Meals, M & S*	1oz/28g	50	180	12.4	6.6	11.5	1.6
Chicken With Vegetable Rice, M & S*	1 Pack/400g	360	90	8.9	11.7	0.5	1.4
Vegetable, Sainsbury's*	1 Pack/400g	416	104	2.6	7.2	7.2	1.3
DILL,							
Dried	1 Tsp/1g	3	253	19.9	42.2	4.4	13.6
Fresh	1oz/28g	7	25	3.7	0.9	0.8	2.5
DIME,							
Mini, Terry's*	1 Bag/100g	550	550	4.2	61.0	32.0	0.7
Single, Terry's*	1oz/28g	154	550	3.9	61.6	32.1	0.6
Terry's*	1oz/28g	154	550	4.6	68.5	33.8	0.6
DIP,							
Applewood Cheddar & Onion, Fresh, BGTY, Sainsbury's*	½ Pot/85g	85	100	7.3	7.3	4.6	0.5
Aubergine, Fresh, Waitrose*	1 Serving/85g	159	187	2.5	10.5	15.0	1.7
Blue Cheese, Fresh, Sainsbury's*	1/5 Pot/34g	115	337	3.6	3.1	34.5	0.1
Cheddar & Onion, M & S*	1oz/28g	88	315	5.1	7.5	29.5	0.5
Cheese & Bacon With Breadsticks, Weight Watchers*	1 Pack/50g	98	196	16.0	24.0	4.2	1.4
Cheese & Chive, 50% Less Fat, Asda*	1 Pot/125g	261	209	4.5	9.0	17.2	0.0
Cheese & Chive, Classic, Tesco*	1 Serving/32g	164	511	3.3	3.1	54.0	0.1
Cheese & Chive, Fresh, Sainsbury's*	1oz/28g	109	390	3.9	2.7	40.4	0.0
Cheese & Chive, Healthy Choice, Safeway*	1 Pack/100g	137	137	10.2	6.0	8.0	1.3
Cheese & Chive, HE, Tesco*	1 Tsp/10g	23	228	5.7	6.4	19.9	0.0
Cheese & Chive, Healthy Selection, Somerfield*	1oz/28g	67	239	6.0	5.0	22.0	0.0
Cheese & Chive, M & S*	1oz/28g	120	430	4.5	3.9	44.1	0.5
Cheese, Simply Dippy, Kerrygold*	1 Pack/50g	137	274	9.2	26.4	14.6	0.0
Chilli Cheese, Max, Walkers*	1 Jar/300g	390	130	3.3	9.4	9.1	0.3
Chilli, M & S*	1 Pot/35g	103	295	0.4	73.2	0.2	0.4
Cucumber & Mint, Eat Smart, Safeway*	½ Pot/85g	55	65	7.3	4.9	1.3	0.8
Cucumber & Mint, Fresh, Sainsbury's*	1oz/28g	34	123	4.5	3.7	10.0	0.0
Cucumber & Mint, Somerfield*	1oz/28g	106	380	2.0	4.0	40.0	0.0
Doritos Hot Salsa, Walkers*	1 Jar/326g	130	40	0.9	8.5	0.2	2.2
Doritos Mild Salsa, Walkers*	1oz/28g	11	40	0.9	8.5	0.2	2.2
Feta Cheese, Fresh, Tesco*	1oz/28g	81	288	6.8	7.9	25.5	0.7
Garlic & Herb, M & S*	1oz/28g	88	315	2.4	7.1	30.6	0.5
Garlic & Herb, Morrisons*	1 Pot/100g	699	699	2.0	3.6	75.5	0.5
Garlic & Herb, Primula*	1oz/28g	96	344	4.8	3.6	34.5	0.0
Garlic & Onion, M & S*	1oz/28g	112	400	1.8	3.8	41.8	0.5
Guacamole Avocado, Reduced Fat, The Fresh Dip Company*	1 Serving/113g	128	113	2.5	6.1	8.7	2.3

D

DIP,	Measure WEIGHT/INFO	per Measure KCAL	KCAL	PROT	CARB	FAT	FIBRE
Guacamole, Sainsbury's*	1oz/28g	59	210	1.8	5.3	20.2	2.5
Guacamole, Tesco*	1 Serving/35g	67	190	1.9	4.1	18.4	2.5
Guacomole, Somerfield*	1oz/28g	53	188	2.0	5.0	18.0	0.0
Honey & Mustard, M & S*	1oz/28g	136	485	2.2	10.8	47.9	0.4
Hot Salsa, Fresh, Tesco*	1oz/28g	17	62	1.8	7.9	2.6	0.9
Hot Salsa, Primula*	1oz/28g	10	35	1.8	6.6	0.2	0.0
Hot Salsa, Tesco*	1 Serving/75g	24	32	1.0	6.1	0.4	1.3
Mild Salsa, Amigos, Safeway*	1oz/28g	10	34	1.0	6.1	0.3	0.0
Mustard & Honey, Fresh, Sainsbury's*	1oz/28g	100	356	2.2	5.1	36.3	0.0
Mustard Mash, M & S*	1oz/28g	25	90	2.6	12.7	3.1	1.0
Nacho Cheese, M & S*	1oz/28g	76	270	9.8	3.8	23.7	0.4
Nacho Cheese, Sainsbury's*	1 Serving/50g	244	487	4.8	3.9	50.2	0.0
Onion & Chive, Primula*	1oz/28g	95	341	4.6	2.1	34.9	0.0
Onion & Garlic, 50% Less Fat, Asda*	1oz/28g	59	209	4.5	9.0	17.2	0.0
Onion & Garlic, Fresh, BGTY, Sainsbury's*	1oz/28g	56	201	4.4	4.8	18.2	0.8
Onion & Garlic, Fresh, Sainsbury's*	1oz/28g	104	373	1.8	4.1	38.8	0.0
Onion & Garlic, HE, Tesco*	1oz/28g	70	249	2.9	6.8	23.4	0.0
Onion & Garlic, Healthy Selection, Somerfield*	1oz/28g	62	222	3.0	5.0	21.0	0.0
Pesto, M & S*	1oz/28g	105	375	4.5	4.5	37.4	0.3
Philadelphia & Breadsticks, Light, Kraft*	1 Portion/50g	119	238	8.5	24.5	12.0	1.1
Philadelphia, Chives & Onion With Breadsticks, Kraft*	1 Portion/50g	118	235	8.4	24.5	11.5	1.3
Philadelphia Light With Italian Breadsticks, Kraft*	1 Pack/50g	123	245	8.4	23.0	13.0	1.5
Plum Rib, Sharwood's*	1oz/28g	67	241	0.5	59.4	0.2	0.6
Dip Pot, Barbequesauce, Burger King*	1 Serving/25g	31	125	0.6	28.7	0.3	0.4
Roasted Aubergine, Fresh, BGTY, Sainsbury's*	1oz/28g	79	282	2.3	8.9	26.3	1.9
Roasted Onion & Stilton, Somerfield*	1oz/28g	116	414	6.0	10.0	39.0	0.0
Salsa, Chunky, M & S*	½ Jar/132g	92	70	1.2	12.0	2.4	1.5
Salsa, Extra Hot, Fresh, Somerfield*	1oz/28g	13	47	1.0	8.0	1.0	0.0
Salsa, Fresh, Asda*	1oz/28g	10	35	1.2	6.2	0.6	2.0
Salsa, Fresh, Somerfield*	1oz/28g	12	44	1.0	7.0	1.0	0.0
Salsa, Sainsbury's*	1 Serving/50g	24	48	1.7	7.7	1.1	0.0
Smoked Salmon & Dill, Fresh, Waitrose*	½ Pot/85g	373	439	5.1	4.1	44.7	0.1
Smoked Salmon & Dill, Somerfield*	1oz/28g	134	478	4.0	4.0	49.0	0.0
Sour Cream & Chive, BGTY, Sainsbury's	1oz/28g	46	165	4.9	3.4	14.6	0.7
Sour Cream & Chive, Fresh, Tesco*	½ Pot/75g	305	407	2.1	4.1	42.4	0.0
Sour Cream & Chive, Primula*	1oz/28g	97	346	5.0	1.8	35.3	0.0
Sour Cream & Chive, Reduced Fat, Asda*	1oz/28g	55	197	2.3	7.1	17.9	0.1
Sour Cream & Chive, Sainsbury's*	1 Serving/50g	157	314	2.2	2.5	32.8	0.0
Sour Cream, Co-Op*	1oz/28g	137	490	2.0	3.0	52.0	0.0
Soured Cream & Chive, 95% Fat Free, M & S*	1oz/28g	25	90	6.5	9.6	2.8	0.5
Soured Cream & Chive, BGTY, Sainsbury's*	1 Serving/170g	131	77	6.0	6.6	2.9	0.3
Soured Cream & Chive, M & S*	1oz/28g	83	295	2.5	7.2	28.5	0.6
Spicy Mexican, Primula*	1oz/28g	91	324	4.7	4.8	31.7	0.0
Spicy Salsa, M & S*	1oz/28g	17	60	1.3	7.2	2.7	1.2
Subndried Tomato, Somerfield*	1oz/28g	155	552	1.0	5.0	59.0	0.0
Sweet Mustard, Classic, Fresh, Healthy Choice, Safeway*	1oz/28g	35	124	9.2	7.0	6.6	1.7
Tangy Barbecue, M & S*	1oz/28g	28	100	1.1	22.2	0.6	0.6
Texan Bean, Sainsbury's*	1 Serving/50g	45	90	3.3	13.9	2.3	0.0
Thousand Island, M & S*	1oz/28g	69	245	2.1	9.4	22.2	0.7
Tikka, Classic, Fresh, Healthy Choice, Safeway*	1oz/28g	38	137	10.2	6.0	8.0	1.3
Tomato Ketchip, Asda*	1 Pack/25g	18	71	1.6	16.0	0.1	1.0
Tzatzaki, Somerfield*	1oz/28g	37	131	6.0	3.0	11.0	0.0
Yoghurt & Cucumber Mint, Tesco*	1oz/28g	34	121	7.0	7.2	7.1	0.6
Yoghurt & Cucumber Soured Cream, St Ivel*	1oz/28g	75	267	3.2	4.4	26.3	0.3

Nutrition Values per 100g / 100ml apply to KCAL, PROT, CARB, FAT, FIBRE columns.

	Measure WEIGHT/INFO	per Measure KCAL	Nutrition Values per 100g / 100ml KCAL	PROT	CARB	FAT	FIBRE
DIPPERS,							
Celery, Marks and Spencer*	1 pot/130g	163	125	1.8	4.4	11.0	1.2
Cheese & Spring Onion, Weight Watchers*	1 Serving/50g	98	196	16.0	24.0	4.2	1.4
Cheese, Weight Watchers*	1 Serving/50g	98	196	16.0	24.0	4.2	1.4
Chicken, Battered, Safeway*	5 pieces/90g	219	243	13.4	16.4	13.8	1.2
Chicken, Chinese, Tesco*	½ Pack/150g	255	170	17.3	8.4	7.5	0.9
Chicken, Crispy, Bird's Eye*	1 Dipper/17g	48	280	12.5	12.9	19.8	0.2
Chicken, Crispy, Farmfoods*	1 Dipper/17g	42	247	14.2	16.4	13.9	0.4
Chicken, Tikka, Tesco*	1oz/28g	54	193	21.5	5.0	9.7	1.0
Onion & Garlic Big Dipper, Budgens*	1 Serving/50g	210	419	2.0	3.7	43.9	0.1
DISCOS,							
Pickled Onion, Discos*	1 Bag/31g	155	500	3.7	58.6	27.8	2.9
Salt & Vinegar, KP*	1 Bag/31g	153	493	3.8	57.2	27.6	2.8
DOLLY MIXTURES, M & S*	1 Pack/125g	479	383	1.5	90.7	1.5	0.0
DOPIAZA,							
Chicken, Safeway*	1 Pack/326g	450	138	10.4	5.3	8.4	1.4
Chicken, With Pilau Rice, Tesco*	1 Pack/400g	424	106	5.7	12.3	3.8	1.5
Mushroom, Retail	1oz/28g	19	69	1.3	3.7	5.7	1.1
DORITOS,							
Cheesy 3D's, Walkers*	1 Pack/20g	89	445	7.0	68.0	16.0	3.0
Cool Original, Walkers*	1 Bag/40g	204	510	7.5	62.0	26.0	3.5
Cool Spice 3Ds, Walkers*	1 Bag/24g	108	450	8.0	64.0	18.0	4.4
Dippas Dipping Chips, Doritos*	1 Bag/35g	172	490	7.5	63.0	23.0	3.5
Hint Of Chilli Dippas, Walkers*	1 Bag/35g	173	495	7.0	61.0	25.0	3.5
Hint of Lime, Walkers*	1 Bag/35g	170	485	7.5	58.0	25.0	7.5
Mexican Hot, Walkers*	1 Bag/40g	202	505	8.0	57.0	27.0	3.5
Tangy Cheese, Walkers*	1 Bag/40g	210	525	7.0	63.0	27.0	3.5
Texas Paprika 3Ds, Walkers*	1 Bag/24g	106	440	7.5	66.0	16.0	4.5
DOUBLE DECKER, Cadbury's*	1 Bar/51g	237	465	5.2	64.9	20.7	0.0
DOUGH BALLS,							
Cheese & Garlic, Occasions, Sainsbury's*	1 Dough Ball/12g	41	341	10.3	33.4	18.5	2.1
Garlic & Herb, Occasions, Sainsbury's*	1 Dough Ball/12g	41	343	8.4	38.7	17.2	2.2
Pizza Express*	8 Balls/50g	200	400	14.3	85.0	3.2	0.0
Sainsbury's*	1 Ball/12g	41	343	8.4	38.7	17.2	2.2
DOUGHNUTS,							
Chocolate Donut, McDonald's*	1 Donut/79g	329	417	4.9	45.9	23.8	2.4
Chocolate, Somerfield*	1 Doughnut/57g	203	356	7.8	43.8	16.6	1.7
Cinnamon Donut, McDonald's*	1 Donut/72g	302	419	5.1	43.1	25.1	3.8
Cream & Jam, Tesco*	1 Doughnut/90g	324	360	4.1	39.7	20.5	1.3
Custard, Tesco*	1 Doughnut/91g	266	292	4.1	33.4	15.8	1.0
Custard-Filled	1 Doughnut/75g	269	358	6.2	43.3	19.0	0.0
Dairy Cream, M & S*	1oz/28g	87	310	4.9	40.8	14.1	1.3
Finger, Co-Op*	1 Doughnut/82g	299	365	4.0	45.0	18.0	2.0
Jam	1 Doughnut/75g	252	336	5.7	48.8	14.5	0.0
Jam, M & S*	1 Doughnut/49g	141	287	5.0	57.6	4.0	1.3
Ring	1 Doughnut/60g	238	397	6.1	47.2	21.7	0.0
Ring, Co-Op*	1 Doughnut/106g	392	370	4.0	44.0	20.0	1.0
Ring, Iced	1 Doughnut/70g	268	383	4.8	55.1	17.5	0.0
Sugared Donut, McDonald's*	1 Donut/72g	303	421	5.0	42.6	25.6	3.7
Toffee, Tesco*	1 Doughnut/75g	235	313	8.0	44.2	11.6	1.6
DOVER SOLE, Raw	1oz/28g	25	89	18.1	0.0	1.8	0.0
DR PEPPER*, Soda, Diet	1fl oz/30ml	0	1	0.0	0.1	0.0	0.0
DREAM,							
Cadbury's*	1 Bar/45g	250	555	4.5	59.7	33.3	0.0
Double Fudge, Cadbury's*	1oz/28g	139	495	6.3	61.4	25.2	0.0

	Measure WEIGHT/INFO	per Measure KCAL	Nutrition Values per 100g / 100ml KCAL	PROT	CARB	FAT	FIBRE
DREAM,							
Egg, Cadbury's*	1oz/28g	160	570	6.0	56.0	35.8	0.0
White Chocolate, Cadbury's*	1 Piece/8g	44	555	4.5	59.7	33.3	0.0
DREAM TOPPING,							
Dry, Bird's*	1oz/28g	193	690	6.7	32.5	58.5	0.5
Made Up, Skimmed Milk, Birds*	1oz/28g	21	75	2.0	4.8	5.3	0.0
Sugar Free, Dry, Bird's*	1oz/28g	195	695	7.3	30.5	60.5	0.5
DRESSING,							
& Marinade, Fire Roasted Red Pepper, Tesco*	1 Serving/100ml	171	171	0.9	9.0	14.6	0.5
Balsamic, Extra Virgin Olive Oil, TTD, Sainsbury's*	1 Tsp/5ml	19	376	0.5	12.8	36.0	0.4
Balsamic, Fresh, Somerfield*	1 Tsp/5ml	24	473	1.0	11.0	48.0	0.0
Balsamic Vinegar & Red Pepper, Perfectly Balanced, Waitrose*	1 Tbsp/15ml	22	148	0.6	28.5	3.5	1.1
Balsamic Vinegar & Smoked Garlic, Safeway*	1 Serving/15ml	19	125	0.1	28.3	0.9	0.5
Balsamic Vinegar, Asda*	1 Pack/44ml	121	275	0.9	7.0	27.0	0.0
Balsamic With Garlic & Herbs, Finest, Tesco*	1 Serving/10ml	13	133	0.3	3.4	13.1	0.1
Balsamic With Olive Oil, Pizza Express*	1 Serving/10g	42	421	0.3	10.3	41.2	0.0
Blue Cheese Flavoured, Hellmann's*	1 Jar/235g	1079	459	0.7	6.3	47.2	1.1
Blue Cheese, Fresh, Sainsbury's*	1 Dtsp/10ml	42	423	2.3	0.5	45.7	0.1
Blue Cheese, HE, Tesco*	1 Tsp/5g	4	82	4.4	9.0	3.1	0.1
Blue Cheese, Low Fat, Weight Watchers*	1oz/28g	17	59	1.5	5.8	3.4	0.0
Blue Cheese Salsa, Morrisons*	1fl oz/30ml	78	260	1.5	6.5	26.0	0.0
Caesar, 95% Fat Free, Tesco*	1 Tsp/6g	5	88	4.1	8.9	3.7	0.3
Caesar, Finest, Tesco*	1 Tbsp/15ml	72	477	1.9	2.8	50.9	0.2
Caesar, Fresh, M & S*	1 Tsp/6g	32	525	2.0	1.8	56.4	0.2
Caesar, Fresh, Sainsbury's*	1 Tsp/6g	29	479	3.0	1.1	51.4	0.2
Caesar, Gourmet, Fresh, Waitrose*	1 Tbsp/15ml	72	479	4.5	0.9	50.8	0.5
Caesar, HE, Tesco*	1 Tbsp/15ml	11	74	3.0	8.4	2.8	0.2
Caesar, Hellmann's*	1 Tsp/6g	30	499	2.5	4.5	51.7	0.3
Caesar, Low Fat, Cardini's*	1 Tsp/6g	7	120	1.0	27.0	1.0	1.0
Caesar, M & S*	1 Tsp/6g	31	523	2.0	1.8	56.4	0.2
Caesar Salad, Safeway*	1 Serving/25g	122	488	3.7	13.7	48.5	0.1
Caesar Style, GFY, Asda*	1 Sachet/44ml	34	77	5.0	9.0	2.3	0.0
Caesar Style, Kraft*	1 Tbsp/15ml	15	102	2.1	15.0	3.5	0.1
Caesar Style, Low Fat, Weight Watchers*	1 Tsp/6g	4	60	1.6	5.8	3.4	0.0
Californian Tomato, Virtually Fat Free, EPC*	1oz/28g	21	76	0.9	17.2	0.4	0.0
Classic French, Fresh, M & S*	1 Serving/10ml	52	515	0.6	8.2	53.1	0.2
Classic Italian, Fat Free, Kraft*	1fl oz/30ml	10	32	0.1	6.8	0.0	0.6
Cream Cheese & Chive, Creamy Ranch, Kraft*	1 Serving/15ml	31	205	1.2	11.0	17.0	0.0
Creamy Caesar, Waistline, Crosse & Blackwell*	1 Dtsp/11g	15	135	1.5	11.1	9.2	0.3
Creamy Cocktail, Waistline, Crosse & Blackwell*	1 Dtsp Spoon/10g	14	143	1.0	14.7	8.6	0.5
Creamy Italian, Hellmann's*	1 Tsp/6g	28	460	1.7	6.1	47.1	0.4
Creamy Ranch, 95% Fat Free, Kraft*	1 Tsp/6ml	7	111	1.4	14.5	5.0	0.3
Creamy Roasted Garlic, GFY, Asda*	1 Tbsp/15g	11	70	0.8	8.0	3.9	0.6
Creamy, Waistline, 93% Fat Free, Crosse & Blackwell*	1 Tsp/6g	7	120	1.0	14.4	6.4	0.2
Fine Herb, Better For You, Morrisons*	1 Tbsp/15ml	7	45	0.0	11.0	0.0	0.0
Fire Roasted Tomato Chilli, M & S*	1oz/28g	21	75	0.5	13.5	1.6	0.2
For Tuna, Coronation Style, Weight Watchers*	1 Can/80g	122	152	10.2	6.5	9.5	0.6
French, BGTY, Sainsbury's*	1 Tbsp/15ml	12	79	1.1	8.8	4.4	0.5
French Classic, M & S*	1 Tbsp/15ml	77	516	0.6	8.2	53.1	0.2
French, COU, M & S*	1/3 Bottle/105g	74	70	0.7	11.5	2.6	0.7
French, Fat Free, Worldwide Dressings, Aldi*	1 Serving/20g	6	32	0.1	7.9	0.0	0.9
French, Fresh, HE, Tesco*	1 Tbsp/15ml	8	56	1.1	6.7	2.8	0.0
French, Fresh, M & S*	1 Tbsp/15ml	16	105	0.7	19.3	2.5	0.3
French, Fresh, Morrisons*	1 Tbsp/15ml	75	499	1.5	13.6	48.7	0.0
French, Fresh, Organic, Sainsbury's*	1 Tbsp/15ml	45	301	0.4	5.5	31.0	0.4

D

DRESSING,	Measure WEIGHT/INFO	per Measure KCAL	Nutrition Values per 100g / 100ml KCAL	PROT	CARB	FAT	FIBRE
French, Fresh, Somerfield*	1 Tbsp/15ml	74	490	1.0	7.0	51.0	0.0
French, GFY, Asda*	1 Tbsp/15g	8	50	0.7	7.0	2.1	0.1
French, HE, Tesco*	1 Tbsp/15ml	3	23	0.8	3.1	0.8	0.0
French, Less Than 3% Fat, M & S*	1 Tbsp/15ml	10	68	0.7	11.5	2.6	0.7
French, Low Fat, Hellmann's*	1 Tbsp/15g	9	62	0.1	10.8	1.6	0.5
French, Organic, M & S*	1 Tbsp/15g	98	655	0.2	7.5	69.4	0.3
French, Reduced Fat, M & S*	1 Tbsp/15g	11	70	0.7	11.5	2.8	0.7
French, Sainsbury's*	1 Tbsp/15ml	33	219	0.6	9.8	19.1	0.5
French Style, Eat Smart, Safeway*	1 Serving/15ml	22	145	0.7	28.9	2.5	0.7
Fresh, Oil Free, Safeway*	1 Serving/30ml	23	75	1.6	14.0	1.4	0.0
Fresh, Yoghurt & Mint, Perfectly Balanced, Waitrose*	1 Serving/100ml	130	130	4.6	22.1	2.6	0.7
Garlic & Herb, Reduced Calorie, Hellmann's*	1 Bottle/235ml	545	232	0.6	12.8	19.3	0.4
Get Dressed, Honey Mustard, 5% Fat, Kraft*	1 Serving/15ml	20	131	1.3	19.0	5.0	1.2
Green Olive, M & S*	1oz/28g	40	144	1.5	2.2	14.4	1.3
Green Thai, Coconut & Lemon Grass, Loyd Grossman*	1oz/28g	49	174	0.2	19.3	10.6	0.5
Herb, Eat Smart, Safeway*	1 Tbsp/15ml	9	60	0.5	9.5	2.0	0.5
Herby Ranch, Less Than 5% Fat, Asda*	1oz/28g	26	92	1.0	12.2	4.3	0.2
Honey & Mustard, Finest, Tesco*	1 Serving/25ml	72	288	1.7	19.6	22.5	0.7
Honey & Mustard, Fresh, M & S*	1 Serving/10ml	43	430	1.7	9.7	42.4	0.5
Honey & Mustard, GFY, Asda*	1 Tbsp/15g	13	89	1.5	13.0	3.4	0.8
Honey & Mustard, Low Fat, M & S*	1 Serving/28g	31	110	1.5	20.0	2.5	0.8
Honey & Mustard, M & S*	1oz/28g	95	339	7.9	2.3	29.6	0.0
Honey & Mustard, M & S*	1 Tbsp/15ml	64	427	1.7	9.7	42.4	0.6
Honey & Mustard, More Than A Dressing, EPC*	1 Tsp/7g	6	91	0.5	21.6	0.3	0.0
Honey & Mustard, Sainsbury's*	1 Serving/10ml	37	366	1.0	15.4	33.0	0.1
Hot Lime & Coconut, BGTY, Sainsbury's*	1 Tbsp/15ml	8	51	0.7	5.7	2.9	1.2
Italian, Frank Cooper*	1oz/28g	81	290	1.3	9.1	27.5	0.4
Italian, Reduced Calorie, Hellmann's*	1 Serving/25ml	65	269	0.5	19.5	20.8	0.3
Italian Style, GFY, Asda*	1 Tbsp/15g	10	67	3.1	6.0	3.4	0.0
Italian, Waistline, 99% Fat Free, Crosse & Blackwell*	1 Tsp/6g	2	39	0.7	7.0	0.9	0.3
Lemon & Cracked Black Pepper, GFY, Asda*	1 Tbsp/15g	9	57	0.2	14.0	0.0	0.3
Lemon, Feta & Oregano, M & S*	1 Tbsp/15ml	24	160	1.3	8.2	13.4	0.6
Lime & Coriander, EPC*	1 Serving/50g	29	57	0.3	13.3	0.3	0.0
Mascarpone, Basil & Walnut, Sainsbury's*	1 Tbsp/15ml	39	259	1.8	26.0	16.1	0.2
Mayonnaise Style, 90% Fat Free, Weight Watchers*	1 Tsp/11g	14	125	1.7	8.9	9.2	0.0
Mild Mustard, Low Fat, Weight Watchers*	1 Tbsp/10g	6	63	2.0	5.7	3.6	0.0
Miracle Whip, Kraft*	1floz/30ml	120	400	0.3	11.0	39.0	0.1
Mustard & Dill, Perfectly Balanced, Waitrose*	1 Serving/100ml	159	159	1.1	31.5	3.2	1.1
Oil & Lemon	1 Tbsp/15g	97	647	0.3	2.8	70.6	0.0
Oil Free, French, Waitrose*	1 Tsp/5ml	4	76	1.5	13.1	2.0	0.6
Oil Free, Fresh, Somerfield*	1 Tsp/5ml	2	35	1.0	7.0	0.0	0.0
Oil Free Lime & Coriander, Waitrose*	1 Tsp/5ml	3	65	1.5	11.9	1.3	0.4
Olive Oil & Balsamic Vinegar, Sainsbury's*	1 Serving/25ml	104	415	0.9	9.4	41.8	0.2
Olive Oil, Pizza Express*	2 Tsp/5g	29	573	1.4	3.4	63.0	0.0
Orange & Honey, Hellmann's*	1 Serving/40ml	44	110	0.8	17.5	3.5	0.8
Parmesan & Peppercorn, Loyd Grossman*	1oz/28g	98	349	2.1	5.9	35.2	0.5
Passion Fruit & Mango, HE, Tesco*	1 Tbsp/15ml	25	169	0.6	36.7	2.2	0.4
Pizza Express*	1 Serving/25g	143	573	1.4	3.4	63.0	0.0
Ranch, Kraft*	1oz/28g	118	420	1.7	7.6	42.0	0.1
Ranch Style, Asda*	1 Serving/44ml	37	85	3.5	9.0	3.9	0.0
Raspberry Balsamic Vinegar, EPC*	1 Serving/50g	34	67	0.4	15.7	0.1	0.6
Red Pepper, M & S*	1 Tbsp/15ml	58	385	0.6	7.6	39.2	0.5
Red Pesto, BGTY, Sainsbury's*	1 Serving/30ml	26	85	2.9	13.3	2.3	1.4
Roasted Garlic, More Than A Dressing, EPC*	1 Serving/100ml	55	55	0.6	12.4	0.3	0.0

DRESSING,	Measure WEIGHT/INFO	per Measure KCAL	KCAL	PROT	CARB	FAT	FIBRE
			Nutrition Values per 100g / 100ml				
Salad, BGTY, Sainsbury's*	1 Tbsp/15g	21	140	0.8	10.8	9.9	0.3
Salad Cream Style, Weight Watchers*	1 Tbsp/10g	12	115	1.5	16.2	4.4	0.0
Salad, HE, Tesco*	1 Tbsp/15g	22	144	0.8	12.9	9.9	0.3
Salad, Low Fat, Weight Watchers*	1 Tbsp/10g	11	106	1.5	15.4	4.3	0.0
Salad, Sundried Tomato & Chilli, Loyd Grossman*	1 Tsp/5g	18	361	0.9	5.3	37.3	0.9
Salad, Thousand Island, 95% Fat Free, Asda	1 Tsp/6g	6	99	1.6	12.6	4.7	0.5
Salad, Thousand Island, Hellmann's*	1oz/28g	97	347	0.9	15.2	31.0	1.0
Salad, Thousand Island, Reduced Calorie, Hellmann's*	1oz/28g	73	259	1.0	19.0	19.4	0.9
Salad, Vinaigrette Style, 95% Fat Free, Asda*	1 Tbsp/15ml	6	42	0.1	10.6	0.0	0.3
Smoked Garlic & Parmesan, Sainsbury's*	1 Serving/20ml	83	415	3.0	4.0	41.1	0.3
Smooth Mayonnaise, Frank Cooper*	1 Pot/28g	213	761	1.4	3.6	82.4	0.0
Sundried Tomato, Safeway*	1 Serving/40ml	126	314	1.1	13.8	28.3	0.0
Sundried Tomato, Sainsbury's	1 Serving/15ml	27	179	1.5	10.9	14.4	0.6
Sweetfire Pepper, HE, Tesco*	1 Serving/10ml	7	67	0.6	15.7	0.3	0.1
Texas Ranch, Frank Cooper*	1 Pot/28g	128	457	1.9	9.4	45.8	0.2
Thousand Island	1 Tsp/6g	19	323	1.1	12.5	30.2	0.4
Thousand Island, BGTY, Sainsbury's*	1 Serving/50g	53	105	1.2	21.6	1.1	2.9
Thousand Island, COU, M & S*	1 Serving/30g	26	85	1.4	14.2	2.6	1.1
Thousand Island, Fat Free, Kraft*	1floz/30ml	27	90	0.5	20.5	0.2	2.8
Thousand Island, Frank Cooper*	1 Pot/28g	122	437	1.2	7.2	44.8	0.3
Thousand Island, HE, Tesco*	1 Serving/25ml	47	189	2.9	10.0	15.1	0.0
Thousand Island, Original, Kraft*	1oz/28g	102	365	0.9	19.0	31.5	0.4
Thousand Island, Reduced Calorie	1 Tsp/6g	12	195	0.7	14.7	15.2	0.0
Thousand Island, Somerfield*	1 Serving/30ml	101	335	2.0	23.0	26.0	0.0
Thousand Island, Tesco*	1 Serving/30ml	130	433	1.0	12.3	42.2	0.0
Tomato & Basil, Fresh, Somerfield*	1 Tbsp/15ml	52	348	2.0	7.0	35.0	0.0
Tomato & Basil, HE, Tesco*	1 Serving/10ml	7	73	0.5	12.9	2.0	0.5
Tomato & Red Pepper, BGTY, Sainsbury's*	1 Serving/50ml	42	83	1.1	10.0	4.3	0.6
Tuna Mayonnaise & Sweetcorn Style, Weight Watchers*	1 Can/80g	114	142	11.5	6.2	8.0	0.1
Vinaigrette, BGTY, Sainsbury's*	1fl oz/30ml	23	78	0.6	8.4	4.7	0.7
Vinaigrette, Frank Cooper*	1 Pot/28g	46	163	1.0	14.1	11.4	0.3
Vinaigrette, Perfectly Balanced, Waitrose*	1 Tsp/5ml	4	89	0.4	20.9	0.4	0.5
Waistline, Reduced Fat, Crosse & Blackwell*	1oz/28g	29	105	0.8	11.6	6.0	0.3
Wholegrain Dijon Mustard & Honey, Loyd Grossman*	1oz/28g	93	331	1.2	9.9	31.8	1.3
With Blue Cheese, Ranch, Kraft*	1oz/28g	136	485	1.6	8.9	49.5	0.1
Yoghurt & Mint, GFY, Asda*	1 Tbsp/15ml	9	60	3.9	8.0	1.4	0.0
Yoghurt Mint Cucumber, M & S*	1 Tsp/5ml	6	115	1.0	8.7	8.0	0.0
Zesty Lemon, HE, Tesco*	1 Tsp/5ml	4	70	0.4	8.8	3.1	0.4
DRIED FRUITS, Exotic, Ready To Eat, Sainsbury's*	1/3 Pack/85g	241	284	0.2	70.6	0.1	2.4
DRIED MIXED FRUIT,							
Dried Mixed Fruit, Average	1 Tbsp/25g	67	268	2.3	68.1	0.4	2.2
Tesco*	1 Tbsp/25g	71	284	2.3	67.9	0.4	2.2
DRIFTER, NESTLE*	1 Finger/31g	144	479	4.1	66.7	21.7	0.9
DRINKING CHOCOLATE,							
Asda*	1 Serving/30g	111	370	6.0	73.0	6.0	0.0
Cadbury's*	1 Serving/18g	66	367	6.4	72.4	5.8	0.0
Granules, Impress*	1oz/28g	102	365	5.6	77.0	3.7	6.0
Powder, Made Up With Skimmed Milk	1 Mug/227ml	134	59	3.5	10.8	0.6	0.0
Powder, Made Up With Whole Milk	1 Mug/227ml	204	90	3.4	10.6	4.1	0.0
Waitrose*	3 Tsp/12g	48	403	7.2	79.9	6.1	2.9
DRIPPING, Beef	1oz/28g	249	891	0.0	0.0	99.0	0.0
DUCK,							
A L' Orange, Roast, M & S*	½ Pack/270g	554	205	12.5	4.1	15.6	0.6
A l' Orange With Rice, COU, M & S*	1 Pack/348g	365	105	7.3	17.5	0.5	0.6

	Measure	per Measure	Nutrition Values per 100g / 100ml				
DUCK,	WEIGHT/INFO	KCAL	KCAL	PROT	CARB	FAT	FIBRE
Aromatic, Japanese Noodle Box, Food To Go, M & S*	1 Pack/295g	295	100	6.7	13.4	2.1	0.7
Aromatic Shredded, M & S*	1 Serving/35g	49	140	25.9	0.8	3.8	0.0
Aromatic With Plum Sauce, Tesco*	½ Pack/250g	350	140	9.3	15.2	4.6	0.3
Breast Fillets, Sliced, M & S*	1 Pack/100g	150	150	25.3	3.6	3.7	0.0
Crispy Aromatic, Ready Meals, M & S*	1 Pack/275g	591	215	12.6	10.3	13.6	1.2
Crispy Aromatic, Tesco*	1 Serving/61g	131	214	14.6	12.3	11.8	0.9
Crispy In a Plum Sauce, M & S*	1 Pack/325g	569	175	10.7	11.2	9.6	0.9
Gressingham Fillets & Orange Sauce, TTD Sainsbury's*	½ Pack/250g	633	253	24.9	0.1	17.0	1.0
Gressingham, Skinless Breast Fillet, TTD, Sainsbury's	1 Serving/160g	192	120	25.4	0.1	2.0	0.4
Oriental Stonebake Foldover, COU, M & S*	1 Pack/162g	235	145	11.5	20.5	1.7	2.6
Pancakes With Hoisin Sauce, M & S*	1 Pack/80g	136	170	13.0	19.9	4.0	0.9
Raw, Meat, Fat & Skin	1oz/28g	109	388	13.1	0.0	37.3	0.0
Raw, Meat Only	1oz/28g	38	137	19.7	0.0	6.5	0.0
Roasted, & Plum Sauce, Sainsbury's*	½ Pack/150g	272	181	12.0	13.5	8.8	0.7
Roasted, Meat, Fat & Skin	1oz/28g	118	423	20.0	0.0	38.1	0.0
Roasted, Meat Only	1oz/28g	55	195	25.3	0.0	10.4	0.0
Shanghai Roast With Noodles, Sainsbury's*	1 Pack/450g	581	129	5.6	18.0	3.8	1.2
Traditional Norfolk Breast Fillets, Sainsbury's*	1 Fillet/170g	442	260	22.3	0.0	19.0	0.1
DUMPLINGS,							
Dumplings, Average	1oz/28g	58	208	2.8	24.5	11.7	0.9
Homestyle, Aunt Bessie's*	1 Dumpling/49g	187	382	8.5	39.5	21.1	2.1
Prawn, Cantonese, Crispy, Sainsbury's*	1 Dumpling/11g	27	241	9.3	20.9	13.4	1.1
Prawn Sui Mai With Soy Sauce, M & S*	1 Pack/130g	143	110	13.7	6.7	3.4	0.6

D

E

	Measure WEIGHT/INFO	per Measure KCAL	Nutrition Values per 100g / 100ml KCAL	PROT	CARB	FAT	FIBRE
EEL,							
Jellied	1oz/28g	27	98	8.4	0.0	7.1	0.0
Raw	1oz/28g	47	168	16.6	0.0	11.3	0.0
EGG,							
Medium, Free Range, Tesco*	1 Egg/60g	88	147	12.5	0.0	10.8	0.0
White, Dried	1oz/28g	83	295	73.8	0.0	0.0	0.0
EGGS,							
Boiled	1 Size 1/67g	98	147	12.5	0.0	10.8	0.0
Dried	1oz/28g	159	568	48.4	0.0	41.6	0.0
Duck, Boiled & Salted	1 Egg/75g	149	198	14.6	0.0	15.5	0.0
Duck, Whole, Raw	1 Egg/75g	122	163	14.3	0.0	11.8	0.0
Fried	1 Med/60g	107	179	13.6	0.0	13.9	0.0
Medium, Free Range, Organic, Asda*	1 Egg/56g	83	148	12.0	0.2	11.0	0.0
Poached	1 Med/50g	74	147	12.5	0.0	10.8	0.0
Quail, Whole, Raw	1oz/28g	42	151	12.9	0.0	11.1	0.0
Scrambled With Milk	2 Med Eggs/120g	296	247	10.7	0.6	22.6	0.0
Turkey, Whole, Raw	1oz/28g	46	165	13.7	0.0	12.2	0.0
Whites, Raw	1oz/28g	10	36	9.0	0.0	0.0	0.0
Whole, Raw	1 Size 3/57g	84	147	12.5	0.0	10.8	0.0
Yolks, Raw	1oz/28g	95	339	16.1	0.0	30.5	0.0
ELDERBERRIES	1oz/28g	10	35	0.7	7.4	0.5	0.0
ELDERFLOWER Cordial, Bottle Green*	1 Glass/200ml	46	23	0.0	5.6	0.0	0.0
ENCHILADA,							
Chicken, COU, M & S*	1 Pack/252g	315	125	8.5	16.1	2.9	1.4
Chicken, Iceland*	1 Pack/400g	536	134	9.7	13.3	4.7	0.9
Chicken, M & S*	1 Serving/225g	405	180	9.2	11.5	10.6	2.2
Chicken, Safeway*	1 Serving/230g	384	167	7.9	22.9	4.9	1.0
Quorn, Marlow Foods*	1 Pack/401g	405	101	5.3	11.7	3.7	1.9
Quorn*	1 Pack/400g	384	96	5.3	11.7	3.1	1.9
Vegetable, Asda*	1 Pack/398g	529	133	4.4	19.0	4.4	1.3
Vegetable, Eat Smart, Safeway*	1 Pack/290g	305	105	5.2	15.5	2.3	1.7
Vegetable, GFY, Asda*	1 Pack/350g	399	114	4.4	14.0	4.5	1.3
ENDIVE, Raw	1oz/28g	4	13	1.8	1.0	0.2	2.0
ENERGY DRINK,							
Red Rooster, Hi Energy Mixer, Cott Beverages Ltd*	1 Can/250ml	113	45	0.6	10.3	0.0	0.0
Red Thunder, Aldi*	1 Can/250ml	113	45	0.6	10.3	0.0	0.0
Sitting Bull, Lidl*	1 Can/250ml	128	51	0.1	13.0	0.0	0.0
EVE'S PUDDING,							
Eve's Pudding	1oz/28g	67	241	3.5	28.9	13.1	1.4
5% Fat, M & S*	1 Pudding/223g	323	145	3.0	23.5	4.4	0.6
BGTY, Sainsbury's*	1 Pudding/170g	286	168	2.8	29.4	4.4	1.7
Eat Smart, Safeway*	1 Pudding/87g	131	150	2.3	30.6	1.8	0.9
M & S*	1 Serving/118g	254	215	2.7	32.3	8.3	0.4
With Custard, Less Than 5% Fat, M & S*	1 Pudding/205g	318	155	3.4	24.7	4.6	0.7
With Custard, Snack, M & S*	1 Serving/230g	437	190	3.2	22.6	9.2	0.7
EXOTIC Fruit Juice, Pure, Del Monte*	1 Glass/200ml	96	48	0.3	11.3	0.0	0.0

	Measure WEIGHT/INFO	per Measure KCAL	KCAL	PROT	CARB	FAT	FIBRE
			Nutrition Values per 100g / 100ml				
FAGGOTS,							
In Rich Gravy, Iceland*	1 Faggot/81g	116	143	6.5	15.9	6.4	1.1
FAJITA,							
Chicken, Co-Op*	1 Serving/230g	391	170	11.0	15.0	7.0	3.0
Chicken, COU, M & S*	1 Pack/230g	288	125	10.0	16.5	2.3	1.5
Chicken, Eat Smart, Safeway*	1 Serving/248g	290	117	10.6	14.8	1.7	1.6
Chicken, GFY, Asda*	1 Serving/225g	297	132	10.0	17.0	2.7	1.1
Chicken, HE, Tesco*	½ Pack/225g	248	110	9.2	15.3	1.3	0.5
Chicken, M & S*	1 Pack/230g	345	150	8.6	17.7	5.3	1.0
Chicken, Sainsburys*	½ Pack/250g	360	144	11.5	13.8	4.8	1.2
Chicken, Tesco*	1 Serving/275g	388	141	9.5	14.2	5.1	1.0
Chicken With Sour Cream, Asda*	1 Pack/440g	713	162	10.3	17.1	8.3	1.3
Gammon Steaks, Tesco*	1 Serving/250g	368	147	17.5	5.3	6.2	0.0
Quorn* Ready Meals	1oz/28g	41	148	6.9	22.1	3.5	2.7
Steak, M & S*	1oz/28g	53	190	8.9	17.2	9.1	0.6
Tuna, Eat Smart, Safeway*	1 Pack/263g	302	115	9.7	15.0	1.8	1.4
Vegetable, Somerfield*	1 Pack/500g	640	128	3.0	17.0	5.0	0.0
Vegetable, Tesco*	1 Wrap/112g	133	119	4.2	14.3	5.0	1.1
FALAFEL,							
Cauldron Foods*	1 Falafel/25g	37	149	7.6	15.3	6.4	7.1
Fried In Vegetable Oil	1oz/28g	50	179	6.4	15.6	11.2	3.4
Organic, Cauldron Foods*	1 Falafel/25g	55	220	8.0	23.3	10.5	7.6
FANTA,							
Lemon, The Coca Cola Co*	1 Can/330ml	165	50	0.0	12.0	0.0	0.0
Orange, McDonald's*	1 Reguar/251g	108	43	0.0	10.4	0.0	0.0
FENNEL,							
Florence, Boiled In Salted Water	1oz/28g	3	11	0.9	1.5	0.2	2.3
Florence, Raw	1oz/28g	3	12	0.9	1.8	0.2	2.4
FENUGREEK LEAVES, Raw	1oz/28g	10	35	4.6	4.8	0.2	0.0
FIGS,							
Dried	1 Fig/20g	45	227	3.6	52.9	1.6	7.5
Dried, M & S*	1oz/28g	71	253	3.4	63.6	0.0	4.6
Dried, Organic, Waitrose*	1oz/28g	67	240	3.6	52.9	1.6	7.5
Dried, Whitworth*	1oz/28g	62	220	3.3	48.4	1.5	6.9
Raw	1 Fig/35g	15	43	1.3	9.5	0.3	1.5
FISH & CHIPS,							
Budgens*	1 Pack/284g	625	220	8.0	24.5	10.0	2.3
Safeway*	1 Pack/249g	518	208	8.0	25.0	8.4	3.5
Somerfield*	1 Serving/283g	495	175	8.0	22.0	6.0	0.0
FISH BAKE,							
Cheese Pastry, Bird's Eye*	1 Piece/171g	390	228	9.3	17.2	13.6	1.9
Haddock & Prawn, COU, M & S*	1 Bake/340g	289	85	7.3	7.3	2.8	0.4
Italiano, Bird's Eye*	½ Pack/205g	180	88	11.5	3.6	3.1	0.3
Vegetable Tuscany, Bird's Eye*	½ Pack/201g	195	97	11.8	2.2	4.6	0.6
FISH BALLS, Steamed	1oz/28g	21	74	11.8	5.5	0.5	0.0
FISH BOUILLON, Benedicta*	1fl oz/30ml	21	69	7.5	9.0	0.3	0.0
FISH,							
Breaded, Asda*	1 Serving/150g	351	234	15.0	12.0	14.0	0.5
Fillets, In Oven Crispy Batter, Farmfoods*	1oz/28g	49	176	9.6	16.9	7.8	0.9
Fillets, In Oven Crispy Crumb, Farmfoods*	1oz/28g	76	270	9.6	21.5	16.2	1.1
Fillets, White, Breaded, Tesco*	1 Piece/95g	205	216	10.0	20.9	10.3	1.1
In Batter, Youngs*	1 Serving/100g	315	315	14.9	20.4	19.7	0.8
In Crispy Batter, Bird's Eye*	1 Steak/120g	230	192	13.6	11.6	10.1	0.7
In Light Batter, Iceland*	1 Fillet/120g	230	192	13.6	11.6	10.1	0.7
Nuggets, Battered, Farmfoods*	1oz/28g	60	214	10.9	16.0	11.8	0.7

F

FISH,	Measure WEIGHT/INFO	per Measure KCAL	Nutrition Values per 100g / 100ml KCAL	PROT	CARB	FAT	FIBRE
Salted, Chinese, Steamed	1oz/28g	43	155	33.9	0.0	2.2	0.0
Steak, In Parsley Sauce, Ross*	1 Serving/150g	123	82	9.1	3.1	3.7	0.1
Steaks, In Butter Sauce, Ross*	1 Serving/150g	126	84	9.1	3.2	3.9	0.1
White, Tesco*	1 Med Fillet/100g	78	78	16.6	0.0	0.6	0.0
FISH CAKES,							
Basics, Somerfield*	1 Fish Cake/42g	75	178	9.0	19.0	8.0	0.0
Captain's Coins, Mini, Bird's Eye*	1 Fish Cake/20g	34	168	10.1	13.3	8.3	0.9
Cod & Pancetta, Cafe Culture, M & S*	1 Fish Cake/85g	166	195	9.2	7.2	15.5	2.0
Cod & Parsley, Waitrose*	1 Serving/85g	157	185	10.7	13.1	10.0	2.0
Cod, Homemade	1 Fish Cake/50g	121	241	9.3	14.4	16.6	0.7
Cod, In Crunch Crumb, Bird's Eye*	1 Fish Cake/52g	85	163	8.8	16.2	7.0	0.7
Cod, M & S*	1 Fish Cake/85g	162	190	8.4	15.7	10.1	1.6
Cod, Sainsbury's*	1 Fish Cake/46g	88	192	10.8	17.5	8.8	0.8
Cod, Tesco*	1 Fish Cake/49g	94	192	8.6	18.8	9.1	0.8
Crab, M & S*	1oz/28g	63	225	8.0	18.0	13.2	1.4
Fried In Blended Oil	1 Fish Cake/50g	109	218	8.6	16.8	13.4	0.0
Frozen	1oz/28g	37	132	8.6	16.7	3.9	0.0
Grilled	1 Fish Cake/50g	77	154	9.9	19.7	4.5	0.0
Haddock, Asda*	1 Fish Cake/88g	181	206	8.0	21.0	10.0	1.5
Haddock, M & S*	1 Pack/170g	289	170	8.6	13.7	9.2	1.3
Haddock, Sainsbury's*	1 Fish Cake/90g	173	192	11.7	18.1	8.1	0.7
Haddock, Smoked, Frozen, Waitrose*	1 Cake/85g	157	185	11.0	12.4	10.1	2.1
Haddock, Smoked, Tesco*	1 Fish Cake/90g	171	190	8.6	22.5	7.3	1.1
M & S*	1 Fish Cake/80g	180	225	8.0	18.0	13.3	0.0
Salmon & Broccoli, Morrisons*	1 Fish Cake/60g	126	210	9.8	17.2	11.9	1.3
Salmon & Broccoli, With Bubble & Squeak, Safeway*	1 Pack/389g	513	132	3.9	15.0	6.3	1.0
Salmon & Tarragon, Waitrose*	1 Fish Cake/85g	179	211	11.9	14.3	11.8	2.2
Salmon, Asda*	1 Fish Cake/86g	215	250	8.0	23.0	14.0	1.4
Salmon, Bird's Eye*	1 Cake/50g	84	168	9.5	12.2	9.0	1.4
Salmon, Homemade	1 Fish Cake/50g	137	273	10.4	14.4	19.7	0.7
Salmon, M & S*	1oz/28g	66	235	7.9	20.0	13.8	1.7
Salmon, Morrisons*	1 Cake/90g	241	268	10.1	27.6	13.1	1.5
Salmon, Sainsbury's*	1 Fish Cake/90g	167	186	13.2	17.4	7.1	1.2
Salmon, Tesco*	1 Cake/50g	110	219	10.1	13.7	13.7	0.9
Salmon, With Parsley Sauce, Finest, Tesco*	½ Pack/170g	350	206	8.6	11.7	13.9	1.0
Thai Style, Sainsbury's*	1 Fish Cake/49g	69	141	12.0	13.8	4.2	1.7
Tuna, Asda*	1 Fish Cake/87g	171	196	9.0	22.0	8.0	1.3
Tuna, Marks and Spencer*	1 Serving/85g	170	200	10.0	14.9	11.0	1.6
FISH FINGERS,							
Bird's Eye*	1 Fish Finger/28g	50	177	12.7	14.1	7.7	1.0
Cod Fillet, Bird's Eye*	1 Finger/30g	53	177	12.7	14.1	7.7	1.0
Cod, Fried In Blended Oil	1 Fish Finger/28g	67	238	13.2	15.5	14.1	0.6
Cod, Frozen	1 Fish Finger/28g	48	170	11.6	14.2	7.8	0.6
Cod, Grilled	1 Fish Finger/28g	56	200	14.3	16.6	8.9	0.7
Economy, Sainsbury's*	1 Fish Finger/26g	51	198	12.6	17.7	8.5	1.3
Farmfoods*	1 Fish Finger/27g	49	183	12.2	15.6	8.0	1.2
Haddock, Asda*	1 Finger/30g	62	205	14.0	17.0	9.0	0.0
Haddock Fillet, Bird's Eye*	1 Finger/29g	48	167	12.4	13.2	7.2	0.9
Iceland*	1 Fish Finger/23g	44	192	11.5	17.3	8.5	1.3
In Crispy Batter, Bird's Eye*	1 Fish Finger/29g	63	218	10.4	15.8	12.6	0.4
In Crispy Batter, Jumbo, Morrisons*	1 Fish Finger/71g	146	205	11.3	12.2	12.5	0.6
Ross*	1 Fish Finger/26g	48	186	12.1	17.6	7.5	0.8
Sainsbury's*	1 Fish Finger/27g	52	194	13.4	16.0	8.5	0.7
SmartPrice, Asda*	1 Fish Finger/25g	46	184	12.0	16.0	8.0	1.1

FISH FINGERS,	Measure WEIGHT/INFO	per Measure KCAL	Nutrition Values per 100g / 100ml KCAL	PROT	CARB	FAT	FIBRE
Value, Tesco*	1 Finger/25g	46	182	11.0	16.8	7.9	1.6
FIVE FRUITS Juice Drink, Fruit Burst, Del Monte*	1 Carton/250ml	133	53	0.2	12.4	0.0	0.0
FIVE SPICE Powder, Sharwood's*	1oz/28g	48	172	12.2	11.6	8.6	23.4
FLAKE, Cadbury's*	1 Standard Bar/34g	180	530	8.1	55.7	30.7	0.0
FLAN CASE,							
Golden Bake, Sainsbury's*	1 Case/113g	373	330	5.5	65.6	5.1	1.2
Pastry	1oz/28g	152	544	7.1	56.7	33.6	1.8
Sponge	1oz/28g	83	295	9.8	53.6	6.1	0.8
FLAN,							
Cheese & Onion, M & S*	1oz/28g	81	290	6.1	25.1	18.7	1.4
Chicken & Broccoli, Iceland*	1 Serving/250g	628	251	6.0	24.6	14.3	1.8
Mushroom & Leek, M & S*	1oz/28g	69	245	4.3	19.1	16.9	1.5
Pastry, With Fruit	1oz/28g	33	118	1.4	19.3	4.4	0.7
Spinach & Ricotta, Waitrose*	1 Serving/260g	666	256	6.5	17.1	17.9	3.4
Sponge With Fruit	1oz/28g	31	112	2.8	23.3	1.5	0.6
Three Cheese & Fried Onion, M & S*	1 Serving/260g	699	269	7.0	17.5	19.0	2.8
FLAPJACK,							
Flapjack	1oz/28g	136	484	4.5	60.4	26.6	2.7
All Butter, Sainsbury's*	1 Flapjack/35g	156	446	5.7	54.5	22.8	2.7
Apple & Sultana, Mr Kipling*	1 Flapjack/27g	124	460	4.6	59.6	22.5	0.0
Apricot & Raisin, Waitrose*	1 Flapjack/38g	143	376	4.7	64.3	11.1	5.8
Apricot, COU, M & S*	1oz/28g	96	342	5.4	77.1	2.1	2.0
Cappuccino, Blackfriars*	1 Flapjack/110g	481	437	5.0	61.0	25.0	0.0
Cherry & Sultana, M & S*	1oz/28g	111	395	5.4	63.7	13.0	5.1
Chewy Nutty, Coffee Republic	1 Flapjack/33g	145	440	7.1	50.9	23.2	2.0
Chocolate & Hazelnut, M & S*	1 Flapjack/71g	330	465	7.3	55.6	25.5	3.8
Chocolate Chip, Happy Shopper*	1 Flapjack/35g	163	467	5.7	58.7	23.3	0.0
Chocolate Chunk, Boots*	1 Slice/75g	351	468	5.7	55.0	25.0	3.0
Chocolate Dipped, M & S*	1 Flapjack/96g	442	460	6.1	61.3	22.4	3.0
Fruit & Nut, Organic, Evernat*	1oz/28g	136	484	4.5	60.4	26.6	0.0
Fruit, Mr Kipling*	1 Flapjack/24g	103	430	4.8	51.4	22.9	0.0
Fruit With Raisins, Boots*	1 Pack/75g	329	439	5.4	57.0	21.0	3.5
M & S*	1 Flapjack/53g	228	430	6.0	59.1	19.0	3.5
Mixed Fruit, Organic, Evernat*	1oz/28g	136	484	4.5	60.4	26.6	0.0
Sultana, Tesco*	1 Serving/50g	173	346	5.0	36.2	20.1	3.7
FLATBREAD, (FILLED)							
Cajun Prawn, BGTY, Sainsbury's*	1 Pack/160g	243	152	8.5	27.7	0.8	0.0
Cheese & Onion Swedish Style, Shapers, Boots*	1 Flatbread/127g	265	209	10.0	24.0	8.1	1.3
Chicken & Black Bean Sauce, Shapers, Boots*	1 Pack/204g	249	122	8.7	20.0	0.8	1.7
Chicken Fajita, Shapers, Boots*	1 Serving/200g	276	138	9.0	20.0	2.4	2.6
Chicken Tikka, Shapers, Boots*	1 Flatbread/176g	294	167	9.7	18.0	6.2	3.0
Chinese Chicken, COU, M & S*	1 Flatbread/156g	234	150	13.5	22.8	1.4	2.6
Feta Cheese, Shapers, Boots*	1 Pack/167g	287	172	7.0	21.0	6.7	2.1
Italian Chicken, Shapers, Boots*	1 Pack/168g	319	191	11.0	21.0	7.0	2.8
Italian Salad, Shapers, Boots*	1 Flatbread/204g	294	144	5.5	20.0	4.7	1.7
Mexican Style Cheese & Bean, Sainsbury's*	1 Serving/178g	310	174	9.7	24.8	4.0	0.0
Mexican Style Chicken, Safeway*	1 Pack/150g	248	165	11.6	24.7	2.1	1.9
Oriental Chicken & Mango, Shapers, Boots*	1 Flatbread/179g	288	161	11.0	23.0	2.8	2.2
Rancher's Chicken, COU, M & S*	1 Pack/174g	270	155	10.9	23.0	2.0	1.5
Spicy Mexican, Shapers, Boots*	1 Pack/190g	296	156	7.0	23.0	4.0	3.7
Thai Chicken, Shapers, Boots*	1 Pack/155g	288	186	11.0	21.0	6.4	2.2
Tuscan Style Tuna, Shapers, Boots*	1 Pack/194g	239	123	8.8	19.0	1.3	1.3
FLOUR,							
Brown, Chapati,	1 Tbsp/20g	67	333	11.5	73.7	1.2	0.0

F

FLOUR,	Measure WEIGHT/INFO	per Measure KCAL	KCAL	PROT	CARB	FAT	FIBRE
Brown, Wheat	1oz/28g	90	323	12.6	68.5	1.8	6.4
Chick Pea	1oz/28g	88	313	19.7	49.6	5.4	10.7
Millet	1oz/28g	99	354	5.8	75.4	1.7	0.0
Plain, Organic, M & S*	1oz/28g	95	340	10.9	70.4	1.9	3.7
Potato	1oz/28g	92	328	9.1	75.6	0.9	5.7
Rice	1oz/28g	102	366	6.4	80.1	0.8	2.0
Rye, Whole	1oz/28g	94	335	8.2	75.9	2.0	11.7
Self Raising, Bettabuy, Morrisons*	1 Serving/100g	337	337	9.8	71.4	1.3	3.0
Self-Raising, Organic, M & S*	1oz/28g	92	330	10.3	68.1	1.6	5.3
Soya, Full Fat	1oz/28g	125	447	36.8	23.5	23.5	11.2
Soya, Full Fat, Nature's Harvest, Holland & Barrett*	1oz/28g	111	396	39.0	16.0	20.0	12.0
Soya, Low Fat	1oz/28g	99	352	45.3	28.2	7.2	13.5
Speciality Gluten Free, Doves Farm*	1 Serving/100g	353	353	4.7	85.2	1.8	2.7
Strong, Brown Bread, Sainsbury's*	1 Serving/100g	320	320	14.0	61.0	1.8	6.4
Strong, Canadian, Waitrose*	1oz/28g	94	337	12.6	68.6	1.4	3.1
Strong, White Bread, Allinson*	1 Serving/100g	330	330	11.5	67.9	1.4	3.7
Strong, White Bread, Tesco*	1 Serving/100g	346	346	11.7	71.6	1.4	3.7
Strong, White, Organic, Waitrose*	1oz/28g	89	319	11.5	64.5	1.7	2.7
Strong, Wholemeal Plain, Waitrose*	1 Serving/100g	311	311	14.5	58.3	2.2	9.0
White, Bread, Organic, Waitrose*	1oz/28g	69	246	8.8	48.8	0.5	1.8
White, Chapati,	1 Tbsp/20g	67	335	9.8	77.6	0.5	0.0
White, Organic, Waitrose*	1oz/28g	99	355	8.0	77.7	1.3	3.1
White, Plain, Value, Tesco*	1oz/28g	95	341	9.5	70.7	2.2	3.1
White, Wheat, Plain	1oz/28g	95	341	9.4	77.7	1.3	3.1
White, Wheat, Self-Raising	1oz/28g	92	330	8.9	75.6	1.2	3.1
White, Wheat, White, Breadmaking	1oz/28g	95	341	11.5	75.3	1.4	3.1
Wholemeal, Organic, Waitrose*	1oz/28g	89	319	11.0	63.9	2.2	9.0
Wholemeal, Self Raising, Tesco*	1oz/28g	89	317	11.5	62.9	2.2	9.0
Wholemeal, Wheat	1oz/28g	87	310	12.7	63.9	2.2	9.0
FLYING SAUCERS, Co-Op*	1 Sweet/1g	4	370	0.5	90.0	1.0	0.6
FLYTE,							
Mars*	1 Bar/45g	196	435	3.6	72.3	14.7	0.0
Snacksize, Mars*	1 Bar/22g	96	436	3.8	72.5	14.5	0.0
FOOL,							
Apricot, BGTY, Sainsbury's*	1 Pot/113g	87	77	3.5	8.0	3.4	0.3
Apricot, Fruit, Tesco*	1 Pot/113g	200	177	2.6	16.4	11.2	0.3
Fruit	1oz/28g	46	163	1.0	20.2	9.3	1.2
Gooseberry, Fruit, BGTY, Sainsbury's*	1 Serving/121g	93	77	2.9	10.0	2.8	0.8
Gooseberry, Fruit, Co-Op*	1 Pot/114g	211	185	3.0	22.0	10.0	1.0
Gooseberry, Fruit, Somerfield*	1 Pot/114g	215	189	3.0	19.0	11.0	0.0
Lemon, Fruit, BGTY, Sainsbury's*	1 Pot/113g	94	83	3.4	9.7	3.4	0.3
Lemon, Fruit, Shapers, Boots*	1 Pot/113g	105	93	3.8	11.0	3.8	0.0
Raspberry, Fruit, Tesco*	1 Pot/113g	234	207	2.6	23.6	11.3	0.3
Rhubarb, Fruit, BGTY, Sainsbury's*	1 Pot/120g	90	75	2.9	9.5	2.8	0.3
Rhubarb, Fruit, Somerfield*	1 Pot/114g	201	176	3.0	16.0	11.0	0.0
Strawberry, Fruit, BGTY, Sainsbury's*	1 Pot/120g	100	83	3.0	11.5	2.8	1.0
Strawberry, Fruit, Co-Op*	1 Pot/114g	188	165	2.0	18.0	9.0	0.8
Strawberry, Fruit, Shapers, Boots*	1 Pot/112g	90	81	3.5	9.2	3.4	0.3
Strawberry, Fruit, Somerfield*	1 Pot/114g	201	176	3.0	16.0	11.0	0.0
FRANKFURTERS,							
Herta*	1 Frankfurter/35g	117	335	12.0	2.0	31.0	0.0
Jumbo, Herta*	1 Frankfurter/80g	236	295	11.7	0.4	27.5	0.0
Jumbo, M & S*	1 Frankfurter/94g	277	295	11.7	0.4	27.5	0.0
Vegetarian, Tivall*	3 sausages/90g	220	244	18.0	7.0	16.0	3.0

Nutrition Values per 100g / 100ml (KCAL, PROT, CARB, FAT, FIBRE)

FRAZZLES,	Measure WEIGHT/INFO	per Measure KCAL	Nutrition Values per 100g / 100ml KCAL	PROT	CARB	FAT	FIBRE
Bacon, Smiths, Walkers*	1 Bag/23g	108	470	8.0	59.0	22.4	0.0
FREEZEPOPS,							
Cola, The Simpsons, Calypso*	1 Freezepop/50ml	15	30	0.0	7.1	0.0	0.0
Orange, The Simpsons, Calypso*	1 Freezepop/50ml	15	30	0.0	7.1	0.0	0.0
Raspberry, The Simpsons, Calypso*	1 Freezepop/50ml	15	30	0.0	7.1	0.0	0.0
FRENCH FRIES, (CRISPS)							
Cheese & Onion, Walkers*	1 Bag/22g	94	425	5.4	64.0	16.0	4.2
Ready Salted, Walkers*	1 Bag/22g	95	430	5.1	64.0	17.0	4.3
Salt & Vinegar, COU, M & S*	1 Pack/25g	88	350	5.1	80.9	1.6	2.3
Salt & Vinegar, Walkers*	1 Bag/22g	92	420	5.0	63.0	16.0	4.2
Worcester Sauce, Walkers*	1 Bag/22g	92	420	5.1	64.0	16.0	4.2
FRENCH TOAST,							
Asda*	1 Slice/8g	30	381	10.0	74.0	5.0	4.0
Tesco*	1 Serving/100g	393	393	11.0	72.5	6.6	3.0
FRIES,							
9/16"" Straight Cut Home, Deep Fried, McCain*	1oz/28g	65	233	3.2	32.7	9.9	0.0
9/16"" Straight Cut Home, Oven Baked, McCain*	1oz/28g	53	188	3.2	31.5	5.5	0.0
American, 3 Way Cook, Somerfield*	1oz/28g	43	155	3.0	25.0	5.0	0.0
American, Oven, Asda*	1 Serving/180g	432	240	3.4	34.0	10.0	3.0
American Style, Frozen, Thin, Tesco*	1 Serving/125g	208	166	2.2	21.1	8.1	1.9
American Style Slim, Iceland*	1 Serving/100g	373	373	6.1	55.8	13.9	7.0
Bacon, Smiths, Walkers*	1 Bag/25g	126	504	11.7	44.4	31.2	0.0
Cafe Frites, M & S*	1 Pack/200g	440	220	3.0	32.7	8.7	2.4
Crispy French, McCain*	1 Serving/100g	165	165	2.1	24.3	6.6	0.0
Crispy Savoury Seasoning Southern, McCain*	1 Serving/100g	179	179	2.8	26.4	6.9	0.0
Home Oven Chips, McCain*	1oz/28g	53	188	3.2	31.5	5.5	0.0
King Size, Salted, Burger King*	1 Bag/170g	539	317	3.5	42.3	14.7	2.9
McDonald's *	1 Reg Portion/78g	207	265	3.8	36.3	11.5	3.6
Medium, Kentucky Fried Chicken*	1 Serving/100g	294	294	3.8	36.4	14.8	3.1
Medium, Salted, Burger King*	1 Bag/116g	369	318	3.4	42.2	14.6	3.4
Oven, Straight Cut, Morrisons*	1 Serving/100g	149	149	2.8	24.6	4.3	2.6
Salt & Vinegar, BGTY, Sainsbury's*	1 Bag/15g	50	335	5.5	75.3	1.4	2.7
Scampi, Smiths, Walkers*	1 Bag/27g	134	496	13.0	52.5	26.0	0.0
Small, Salted, Burger King*	1 Bag/74g	229	310	2.7	41.8	14.8	2.7
Southern, Oven Cook, McCain*	1 Serving/80g	146	182	2.7	26.1	8.4	0.0
Southern Spicy Spiral, Deep Fried, McCain*	1oz/28g	58	208	2.7	26.4	10.2	0.0
Southern Spicy Spiral, Oven Baked, McCain*	1oz/28g	46	165	1.7	24.6	6.6	0.0
Southern, Straight Cut, Oven Baked, McCain*	1oz/28g	74	263	4.1	37.1	10.9	0.0
Spicy Curly, Asda*	1 Serving/75g	134	179	2.3	29.0	6.0	2.5
FRISPS,							
Tangy Salt & Vinegar, Frisps*	1 Bag/30g	155	517	5.8	52.2	31.7	4.0
Tasty Cheese & Onion, Frisps*	1 Bag/31g	162	521	6.3	52.4	31.8	4.3
FROMAGE FRAIS,							
Apple Strudel, Safeway*	1 Pot/100g	116	116	6.6	14.8	3.4	0.7
Apricot, Tesco*	1 Pot/100g	77	77	6.5	6.0	3.0	1.3
Bakewell Tart Flavour, BGTY, Sainsbury's*	1 Pot/100g	54	54	7.6	5.5	0.2	1.1
Banoffee Pie Flavour, Low Fat, Safeway*	1 Pot/100g	135	135	6.8	17.6	4.1	0.2
Banoffee Toffee, Weight Watchers*	1 Pot/100g	64	64	5.7	10.0	0.1	1.1
BGTY, Sainsbury's*	½ Pot/100g	47	47	7.5	3.9	0.2	0.0
Blackcurrant, HE, Tesco*	1 Pot/100g	59	59	7.7	6.5	0.2	0.6
BPC, Sainsbury's*	1 Serving/50g	49	98	6.6	11.0	3.1	0.2
Cherry Pie Flavour, BGTY, Sainsbury's*	1 Pot/100g	54	54	7.6	5.5	0.2	1.1
Chocolate & Orange, Weight Watchers*	1 Pot/100g	64	64	5.7	10.0	0.1	1.1
Chocolate Fudge Smooth & Creamy, Tesco*	1 Serving/100g	136	136	6.7	13.3	6.2	0.2

F

	Measure	per Measure	Nutrition Values per 100g / 100ml				
FROMAGE FRAIS,	WEIGHT/INFO	KCAL	KCAL	PROT	CARB	FAT	FIBRE
COU, M & S*	1 Pot/100g	48	48	7.8	4.5	0.1	0.5
Eat Smart, Safeway*	1 Pot/100g	55	55	7.7	5.1	0.2	1.6
Exotic Fruits, Eat Smart, Safeway*	1 Pot/100g	60	60	7.9	6.6	0.2	0.4
Fruit, Weight Watchers*	1 Pot/100g	48	48	5.4	6.3	0.1	0.3
Lemon, Balanced Lifestyle, Aldi*	1 Serving/100g	52	52	5.6	6.6	0.3	0.6
Lemon Pie, Low Fat, Sainsbury's*	1 Pot/90g	108	120	6.7	17.3	2.7	0.2
Lemon Sponge Flavour, BGTY, Sainsbury's*	1 Pot/100g	52	52	7.6	5.0	0.2	1.1
Morello Cherries, Perfectly Balanced, Waitrose*	½ Pot/250ml	260	104	2.5	19.1	1.9	1.8
Natural Creamy Dessert, Co-Op*	1 Pot/200g	204	102	6.1	2.9	7.3	0.0
Natural, GFY, Asda*	1oz/28g	13	45	8.0	3.3	0.0	0.0
Natural Normandy, Sainsbury's*	1 Tbsp/28g	13	47	7.5	3.9	0.2	0.0
Natural, Tesco*	1 Serving/100g	46	46	7.8	3.3	0.2	0.0
Orange & Mandarin, Tesco*	1 Pot/100g	75	75	6.5	5.6	3.0	2.3
Peach, BGTY, Sainsburys*	1 Pot/100g	53	53	7.2	5.5	0.2	0.5
Peach, HE, Safeway*	1 Serving/100g	58	58	7.9	6.3	0.1	0.3
Peach, Weight Watchers*	1 Pot/100g	48	48	5.4	6.4	0.1	0.2
Petit Dessert, Co-Op*	1 Pot/60g	74	123	6.3	14.5	4.4	0.0
Petits Filous, Yoplait*	1 Pot/60g	76	127	6.5	14.5	4.7	0.0
Plain	1oz/28g	32	113	6.8	5.7	7.1	0.0
Raspberry & Redcurrant, BGTY, Sainsbury's*	1 Pot/100g	49	49	7.2	4.5	0.2	1.9
Raspberry & Strawberry, Weight Watchers*	1 Pot/100g	48	48	5.4	6.2	0.1	0.3
Raspberry, COU, M & S*	1 Pot/100g	49	49	7.8	4.9	0.1	0.4
Raspberry, Eat Smart, Safeway*	1 Pot/100g	50	50	7.6	4.5	0.2	1.8
Raspberry, Healthy Choice, Asda*	1 Pot/100g	41	41	6.0	3.8	0.2	0.0
Raspberry, HE, Tesco*	1 Pot/100g	55	55	7.7	5.7	0.2	0.2
Raspberry, Muller*	1 Pot/50g	68	135	6.1	13.5	6.3	0.0
Real Fruit, Tesco*	1 Pot/100g	54	54	5.6	7.6	0.1	0.1
Red Cherry, Tesco*	1 Pot/100g	75	75	6.5	5.5	3.0	2.3
Rhubarb & Crumble, Low Fat, Sainsbury's*	1 Pot/90g	96	107	6.7	14.1	2.6	0.4
Shape*	1 Pot/100g	69	69	6.8	6.8	1.2	0.0
Strawberry, 99.9% Fat Free, Onken*	1 Serving/50g	46	91	6.9	15.3	0.1	0.0
Strawberry, BGTY, Sainsbury's*	1 Pot/100g	48	48	7.2	4.3	0.2	1.4
Strawberry, Healthy Choice, Asda*	1 Pot/100g	41	41	6.0	3.7	0.2	0.0
Strawberry, Low Fat, St Ivel*	1 Pot/100g	69	69	6.9	6.8	1.2	0.0
Strawberry, Puree, Somerfield*	1 Pot/50g	60	120	7.0	14.0	4.0	0.0
Strawberry, Somerfield*	1 Pot/100g	110	110	7.0	14.0	3.0	0.0
Strawberry, Tesco*	1 Pot/100g	75	75	6.5	5.5	3.0	2.5
Strawberry, Weight Watchers*	1 Pot/100g	47	47	5.4	6.2	0.1	0.2
Summer Fruits, Weight Watchers*	1 Pot/100g	48	48	5.4	6.3	0.1	0.4
Toffee & Pecan Pie, Smooth & Creamy, Tesco*	1 Serving/100g	148	148	6.9	14.8	6.8	0.2
Toffee, BGTY, Sainsbury's*	1 Pot/100g	60	60	7.2	7.0	0.3	0.2
Toffee, Weight Watchers*	1 Serving/100g	64	64	5.7	10.0	0.1	1.1
Tropical Fruits, BGTY, Sainsbury's*	1 Pot/100g	54	54	7.3	5.8	0.2	0.3
Very Low Fat	1oz/28g	16	58	7.7	6.8	0.2	0.0
Virtually Fat Free, Healthy Choice, Asda	1oz/28g	13	45	8.0	3.3	0.0	0.0
Virtually Fat Free, Safeway*	1 Serving/100g	41	41	6.7	3.2	0.2	0.0
Virtually Fat Free, Tesco*	1 Pot/100g	56	56	5.6	8.2	0.1	0.0
FRUIT COCKTAIL,							
Fresh & Ready, Sainsbury's*	1 Pack/300g	117	39	0.6	9.0	0.1	1.2
In Apple Juice, Asda*	1/3 Can/80g	40	50	0.3	12.0	0.1	1.6
In Fruit Juice, Sainsbury's*	1 Serving/198g	97	49	0.3	11.9	0.1	1.3
In Grape Juice, Tesco*	1oz/28g	12	43	0.4	10.0	0.0	1.0
In Juice, Del Monte*	1 Can/415g	203	49	0.4	11.2	0.1	0.0
In Light Syrup, Sainsbury's*	½ Can/125g	73	58	0.4	14.0	0.1	1.3

	Measure WEIGHT/INFO	per Measure KCAL	KCAL	PROT	CARB	FAT	FIBRE
			Nutrition Values per 100g / 100ml				
FRUIT COCKTAIL,							
In Syrup, Del Monte*	1 Can/420g	315	75	0.4	18.0	0.1	0.0
In Very Light Syrup, Value,Tesco*	1 Can/410g	123	30	0.4	7.3	0.0	1.0
Fruit Cocktail Juice Drink, Sainsbury's*	1 Glass/200ml	94	47	0.2	11.2	0.1	0.1
Safeway*	1 Serving/205g	117	57	0.4	14.0	0.0	1.0
Tropical, In Syrup, Sainsbury's*	½ Can/130g	95	73	0.5	17.6	0.1	1.4
Tropical, Morrisons*	½ Can/212g	144	68	0.0	17.0	0.0	0.0
Tropical, Safeway*	½ Can/214g	154	72	0.5	17.6	0.0	1.4
FRUIT COMPOTE,							
Apricot & Prune, Yeo Valley*	1 Pot/225g	207	92	0.6	22.3	0.1	1.6
HE, Tesco*	1 Pot/140g	113	81	0.9	19.1	0.2	1.6
Organic, Yeo Valley*	1oz/28g	13	47	0.5	11.2	0.0	0.0
FRUIT DRINK,							
Alive Tropical Torrent, The Coca Cola Co*	1 Glass/200ml	88	44	0.0	11.0	0.0	0.0
Apple & Blackcurrant, No Added Sugar, Safeway*	1fl oz/30ml	2	8	0.1	1.0	0.0	0.0
Blackcurrant & Apple, Shapers, Boots*	1 Bottle/500ml	10	2	0.0	0.2	0.0	0.0
Five Fruits, Five Alive*	1 Carton/250ml	125	50	0.0	12.0	0.0	0.0
FRUIT GUMS,							
& Jellies	1 Tube/33g	107	324	6.5	79.5	0.0	0.0
Dinosaur Family, Asda*	1 Pack/100g	362	362	7.0	79.0	2.0	0.3
Red & Black, M & S*	1 Bag/113g	362	320	5.2	75.8	0.1	0.1
Rowntree's*	1oz/28g	94	337	4.6	79.9	0.0	0.0
Strawberry & Cream, M & S*	1 Pack/100g	341	341	5.7	76.0	0.5	0.0
FRUIT MEDLEY,							
Exotic, Waitrose*	1 Medley/300g	126	42	0.6	9.5	0.2	1.1
Fresh, Waitrose*	1 Pack/300g	114	38	0.6	8.7	0.1	1.4
M & S*	1oz/28g	7	25	0.6	7.1	0.2	1.1
FRUIT PASTILLES,							
Fruit Pastilles, Average	1 Tube/33g	108	327	2.8	84.2	0.0	0.0
Co-Op*	1 Sweet/6g	20	337	2.8	81.5	0.0	0.0
Honey & Lemon, M & S*	1 Pastille 2.5g	11	365	7.3	84.1	0.0	0.0
Rowntree's*	1 Tube/53g	184	348	4.3	82.9	0.0	0.0
FRUIT SALAD,							
Chunky, In Grape Juice, Tesco*	1 Serving/135g	63	47	0.4	11.0	0.2	0.8
Exotic, Sainsbury's*	1oz/28g	11	40	0.6	9.1	0.3	1.0
Exotic, Somerfield*	1 Pot/350g	140	40	0.6	9.0	0.2	1.3
Exotic, Tesco*	1 Serving/225g	86	38	0.7	8.4	0.2	1.5
Fresh, Asda*	1oz/28g	13	45	0.6	11.1	0.1	1.3
Fresh, M & S*	1oz/28g	10	36	0.6	9.5	0.2	0.9
Fresh, Safeway*	1 Pack/300g	135	45	0.7	10.0	0.2	1.5
Fresh, Sainsbury's*	1oz/28g	14	49	0.6	11.3	0.1	1.4
Fresh, Sainsbury's*	1 Serving/120g	55	46	0.6	10.5	0.2	1.4
Fresh, Somerfield	1oz/28g	12	43	1.0	10.0	0.0	0.0
Fresh, Somerfield*	1 Bowl/200g	94	47	0.6	11.0	0.1	1.5
Fresh, Tesco*	1oz/28g	13	45	0.6	10.5	0.1	1.4
Green, M & S*	1 Bowl/400g	200	50	0.6	10.9	0.2	1.2
Homemade	1oz/28g	15	55	0.7	13.8	0.1	1.5
Luxury, M & S*	1oz/28g	11	40	0.6	9.2	0.1	1.1
Mixed, Food To Go, M & S*	1 Pack/400g	400	100	0.9	23.3	0.3	2.8
Mixed, New Improved, Tesco*	1 Pot/225g	79	35	0.8	7.6	0.2	1.2
Mixed, Prepared, Sainsbury's*	½ Pack/230g	97	42	0.7	8.9	0.2	1.2
Mixed, Sainsbury's*	1 Bowl/480g	211	44	0.6	10.2	0.1	1.1
Mixed, Tesco*	1 Salad/225g	86	38	0.7	8.3	0.2	1.3
Pineapple, Mandarin & Grapefruit, Asda*	1 Serving/200g	86	43	0.6	10.0	0.1	0.0
Tropical, Asda*	1oz/28g	10	36	0.6	8.8	0.2	1.2

	Measure WEIGHT/INFO	per Measure KCAL	Nutrition Values per 100g / 100ml KCAL	PROT	CARB	FAT	FIBRE
FRUIT SALAD,							
Tropical, In Light Syrup, Passion Fruit Juice, Tesco*	½ Can/216g	130	60	0.3	14.1	0.1	1.1
Tropical, M & S*	1oz/28g	12	44	0.8	9.6	0.3	1.8
FRUIT SHOOT, Orange & Peach, Robinson*	1 Bottle/200ml	10	5	0.1	0.8	0.0	0.0
FRUIT SPREAD,							
Apricot, Weight Watchers*	1 Tsp/15g	17	110	0.3	27.2	0.0	0.5
Blackcurrant, Weight Watchers*	1 Tsp/15g	16	106	0.2	26.3	0.0	0.9
High, Blueberry, St Dalfour*	1 Tsp/15g	34	228	0.5	56.0	0.2	2.2
Raspberry, Weight Watchers*	1 Tsp/15g	17	111	0.4	27.1	0.1	0.9
Seville Orange, Weight Watchers*	1 Tsp/15g	17	111	0.2	27.5	0.0	0.3
Strawberry, Weight Watchers*	1 Tsp/15g	17	115	0.2	28.4	0.0	0.4
FRUITIES, Weight Watchers*	1 Serving/2g	3	135	0.0	54.0	0.0	34.0
FRUITIME Mixed Fruit Pieces, Tesco*	1 Can/140g	84	60	0.4	14.0	0.0	1.0
FU YUNG, Egg	1oz/28g	67	239	9.9	2.2	20.6	1.3
FUDGE,							
Fudge, Average	1oz/28g	123	441	3.3	81.1	13.7	0.0
All Butter, TTD, Sainsbury's*	1 Pack/125g	536	429	1.3	73.4	14.5	0.0
Butter, Dark, Thorntons*	1 Chocolate/13g	59	454	4.1	63.8	20.8	1.5
Butter, Milk, Thorntons*	1 Chocolate/13g	60	462	3.7	68.5	19.2	0.0
Butter Tablet, Thorntons*	1oz/28g	116	414	0.9	77.6	11.1	0.0
Cadbury's*	1 Standard Bar/26g	116	445	2.8	72.3	16.3	0.0
Cherry & Almond, Thorntons*	1 Bag/100g	464	464	3.2	70.5	19.1	0.4
Chocolate, Thorntons*	1 Bag/100g	459	459	3.1	69.0	19.1	0.6
Clotted Cream, M & S*	1oz/28g	133	474	1.7	67.6	22.1	0.0
Dairy, Co-Op*	1 Sweet/9g	39	430	2.0	76.0	13.0	0.0
Devon, Somerfield*	1 Pack/250g	1060	424	2.0	78.9	11.1	0.0
Double Chocolate Bar, M & S*	1 Bar/43g	202	470	4.2	66.9	21.0	0.7
Vanilla, Bar, M & S*	1 Bar/43g	205	476	3.7	63.0	23.3	0.4
Vanilla, Thorntons*	1 Bag/100g	465	465	1.8	65.9	21.9	0.0
FUSE, Cadbury's*	1 Standard Bar/49g	238	485	7.6	58.2	24.8	0.0

	Measure WEIGHT/INFO	per Measure KCAL	KCAL	PROT	CARB	FAT	FIBRE
GALAXY,							
Caramel, Mars*	1 Bar/49g	239	488	5.3	60.1	25.1	0.0
Chocolate, Mars*	1 Bar/47g	250	532	9.0	56.6	30.0	0.0
Fruit & Hazelnut, Milk, Galaxy*	1 Bar/47g	235	501	7.1	55.2	28.0	0.0
Liaison, Mars*	1 Chocolate Bar/48g	233	485	5.4	60.3	24.7	0.0
Ripple, Mars*	1 Bar/33g	169	528	6.9	59.3	29.3	0.0
Swirls, Mars*	1 Bag/150g	747	498	4.9	60.2	26.5	0.0
GAMMON,							
Breaded, Wiltshire, M & S*	1oz/28g	39	140	23.6	1.6	4.7	0.0
Crumbed, Budgens*	1 Portion/50g	72	143	21.0	0.4	6.4	0.4
Honey Roast, Dry Cured, TTD, Sainsbury's*	1 Slice/35g	50	142	24.0	3.3	3.6	0.1
Mustard Glazed, M & S*	1 Slice/30g	55	184	23.9	0.8	9.6	0.0
GAMMON JOINT,							
Cured, Less Than 5% Fat, Asda*	1/3 Joint/151g	210	139	26.0	7.0	0.8	0.0
Irish, With Honey & Mustard Glaze, Tesco*	1 Serving/100g	161	161	18.1	3.2	8.5	0.2
Lean Only, Boiled	1oz/28g	47	167	29.4	0.0	5.5	0.0
Smoked, Boneless, Sainsbury's*	1 Serving/100g	208	208	25.0	0.0	12.0	0.0
Unsmoked Danish, M & S*	1oz/28g	34	122	16.6	0.0	6.2	0.0
With Honey & Mustard Glaze, Tesco*	1 Pack/450g	725	161	18.1	3.2	8.5	0.2
With Honey & Pineapple, Tesco*	1 Serving/200g	300	150	14.3	11.4	5.2	0.2
With Sticky Mango Salsa, Tesco*	1 Serving/125g	133	106	14.4	9.8	1.0	3.0
With Sweetcure Honey Glaze, M & S*	1 Joint/510g	1071	210	16.1	6.9	12.6	0.8
GAMMON STEAKS,							
Below 5% Fat, Asda*	1 Pack/250g	253	101	19.0	1.0	2.3	0.9
Honey Cured, M & S*	1oz/28g	27	96	19.1	1.5	1.5	0.0
Lean & Low, Danepak	1oz/28g	35	125	20.0	0.0	5.0	0.0
Plate, Smoked, Sainsbury's*	1 Steak/125g	173	138	22.7	0.1	5.2	0.1
Plate, Unsmoked, Sainsbury's*	1 Steak/150g	207	138	22.7	0.1	5.2	0.1
Round, Unsmoked, Asda*	1 Steak/125g	126	101	17.0	0.0	3.7	0.0
Smoked, Prime, Asda*	1 Steak/250g	280	112	18.0	0.2	4.4	0.0
Tendersweet, Lightly Smoked, Sainsbury's*	1 Steak/54g	86	160	27.4	0.1	5.5	0.1
Traditional, M & S*	1oz/28g	31	110	18.2	0.0	4.3	0.0
Unsmoked, HE, Tesco*	1 Serving/110g	100	91	18.6	1.0	1.4	0.0
Unsmoked, Prime, Healthy Choice, Asda*	1 Steak/250g	298	119	18.4	0.2	4.9	0.0
GAMMON TOPPER, Sainsbury's*	1 Serving/154g	342	222	11.9	14.8	12.8	1.7
GARAM MASALA	1oz/28g	106	379	15.6	45.2	15.1	0.0
GARLIC,							
Butter, Somerfield*	1oz/28g	192	686	1.0	2.0	75.0	0.0
Powder	1 Tsp/3g	7	246	18.7	42.7	1.2	9.9
Puree	1 Tbsp/18g	61	380	3.5	16.9	33.6	0.0
Raw	1 Clove/3g	3	98	7.9	16.3	0.6	4.1
GATEAU,							
Black Forest, Tesco*	1 Serving/55g	141	257	3.2	29.9	13.8	0.1
Chocolate, Asda*	1 Serving/100g	176	176	2.4	19.0	10.0	0.4
Chocolate Layer, M & S	1 Serving/86g	278	323	4.2	35.9	18.3	0.9
Chocolate Meringue, M & S*	1oz/28g	112	400	4.0	39.0	25.3	0.2
Chocolate Orange, Co-Op*	1 Slice/97g	320	330	5.0	37.0	18.0	1.0
Coffee, Tesco*	1 Serving/100g	300	300	4.2	32.5	17.0	0.6
Double Chocolate, Sara Lee*	1oz/28g	93	331	5.6	41.3	16.5	0.9
Double Chocolate, Tesco*	1 Serving/45g	124	276	4.4	32.1	14.4	2.2
Ice Cream, Chocolate & Vanilla, Iceland*	1 Serving/130g	252	194	3.3	24.1	9.4	0.6
Lemon & Lime, M & S*	1 Serving/100g	295	295	3.2	35.0	15.6	0.3
Profiterole, TTD, Sainsbury's*	1/6 Gateau/112g	410	365	3.9	26.2	27.2	1.1
Strawberry, Co-Op*	1 Slice/77g	222	288	5.1	29.2	16.7	1.0
Swiss, Cadbury's*	1/6/60g	228	380	5.2	52.0	16.8	0.9

Nutrition Values per 100g / 100ml

G

GATEAU,	Measure WEIGHT/INFO	per Measure KCAL	Nutrition Values per 100g / 100ml KCAL	PROT	CARB	FAT	FIBRE
Triple Chocolate, Tesco*	1 Serving/64g	187	292	3.9	31.1	16.9	0.4
GELATINE	1oz/28g	95	338	84.4	0.0	0.0	0.0
GHEE,							
Butter	1oz/28g	251	898	0.0	0.0	99.8	0.0
Palm	1oz/28g	251	897	0.0	0.0	99.7	0.0
Vegetable	1oz/28g	251	895	0.0	0.0	99.4	0.0
Vegetable, Sharwood's*	1oz/28g	251	897	0.0	0.0	99.7	0.0
GIN,							
37.5% Volume	1 Shot/25ml	52	207	0.0	0.0	0.0	0.0
40% Volume	1 Shot/25ml	56	222	0.0	0.0	0.0	0.0
GINGER ALE,							
American, Low Calorie, Somerfield*	1fl oz/30ml	0	1	0.0	0.0	0.0	0.0
Dry, Average	1 Glass/250ml	38	15	0.0	3.9	0.0	0.0
Dry, Sainsbury's*	1 Glass/250ml	95	38	0.1	9.1	0.1	0.1
GINGER BEER, Traditional Style, Tesco*	1 Can/330ml	218	66	0.0	16.1	0.0	0.0
GINGER,							
Fresh, Average	1oz/28g	14	49	1.7	9.5	0.7	0.0
Ground	1 Tsp/2g	5	258	7.4	60.0	3.3	0.0
Root, Raw	1oz/28g	11	38	1.4	7.2	0.6	0.0
Stem, In Sugar Syrup, Sainsbury's*	1oz/28g	76	271	0.2	67.3	0.1	1.4
GINGERBREAD, Average	1oz/28g	106	379	5.7	64.7	12.6	1.2
GNOCCHI, Fresh, Sainsbury's*	1 Serving/100g	152	152	3.8	33.6	0.3	1.4
GOLDEN DRUMMERS,							
Chicken, Bernard Matthews*	1 Drummer/54g	138	256	12.2	10.1	18.6	0.0
Turkey, Bernard Matthews*	1 Drummer/57g	146	256	12.2	10.1	18.6	0.9
GOOSE,							
Raw, Meat, Fat & Skin	1oz/28g	83	295	38.3	38.2	4.6	21.0
Roast, Meat Only	1oz/28g	89	319	29.3	0.0	22.4	0.0
Roasted, Meat, Fat & Skin	1oz/28g	103	367	14.2	70.4	2.6	4.2
GOOSEBERRIES, Dessert, Raw	1oz/28g	11	40	0.7	9.2	0.3	2.4
GRAPE & RASPBERRY Juice, Pressed, M & S*	1 Sm Bottle/250ml	138	55	0.4	12.9	0.0	0.1
GRAPEFRUIT,							
Canned, In Juice	1oz/28g	8	30	0.6	7.3	0.0	0.4
Canned, In Syrup	1oz/28g	17	60	0.5	15.5	0.0	0.6
Fresh, Raw	1oz/28g	8	30	0.8	6.8	0.1	1.3
In Syrup, Sainsbury's*	½ Can/250g	188	75	0.5	17.5	0.1	0.4
Raw, Weighed With Peel & Pips	1 Med/340g	68	20	0.5	4.6	0.1	0.9
Ruby Red, In Natural Juice, Tesco*	1 Serving/135g	57	42	0.6	10.0	0.0	0.4
Segments, In Grapefruit Juice, John West*	1oz/28g	9	33	0.5	7.0	0.0	0.6
Segments, In Grapefruit Juice, Safeway*	1 Serving/165g	76	46	0.4	11.0	0.0	0.4
Segments, In Juice, Del Monte*	1oz/28g	14	49	0.6	10.9	0.0	0.0
Segments, In Natural Juice, Sainsbury's*	1oz/28g	11	38	0.5	8.7	0.1	0.4
Segments, In Syrup, Sainsbury's*	1oz/28g	20	73	0.5	17.5	0.1	0.4
GRAPEFRUIT & Lime, Quest, M & S*	1 Bottle/330ml	53	16	0.0	4.0	0.0	0.0
GRAPEFRUIT JUICE,							
Asda*	1 Glass/200ml	80	40	0.4	9.0	0.1	0.0
Del Monte*	1 Glass/200ml	82	41	0.5	8.8	0.0	0.0
Florida, M & S*	1 Glass/200ml	60	30	0.4	7.5	0.0	0.0
Florida Pink, Somerfield*	1 Glass/200ml	88	44	1.0	10.0	0.0	0.0
Florida Pink, Squeezed, Sainsbury's*	1 Glass/200ml	82	41	0.5	9.2	0.1	0.3
Freshly Squeezed, Johnsons*	1 Glass/200ml	64	32	0.7	7.4	0.1	0.0
Golden, Tropicana*	1 Glass/200ml	80	40	0.6	8.0	0.0	0.5
Pure, Sainsbury's*	1 Glass/200ml	82	41	0.4	8.6	0.1	0.1
Pure, Somerfield*	1 Glass/200ml	76	38	1.0	9.0	0.0	0.0

G

	Measure WEIGHT/INFO	per Measure KCAL	KCAL	PROT	CARB	FAT	FIBRE
GRAPEFRUIT JUICE,							
Pure, Tesco*	1 Glass/200ml	82	41	0.4	9.0	0.0	0.0
GRAPES,							
Fresh, Average, Raw	1oz/28g	17	60	0.4	15.4	0.1	0.7
Seedless, Selection Pack, Tesco*	¼ Pack/100g	64	64	0.4	15.4	0.1	0.7
GRATIN,							
Cauliflower, Findus*	1 Pack/400g	340	85	3.5	7.0	5.0	0.0
Creamy Potato, M & S*	½ Pack/225g	360	160	2.2	11.9	11.1	0.9
Potato, Somerfield*	½ Pack/225g	356	158	2.0	11.0	12.0	0.0
Spinach, M & S*	½ Pack/200g	340	170	6.9	10.6	11.2	1.8
Vegetable, Somerfield*	1 Pack/300g	417	139	1.0	5.0	13.0	0.0
GRAVADLAX, Sainsbury's*	1 Serving/50g	88	176	19.9	6.5	7.8	0.6
GRAVY,							
Beef, Fresh, Sainsbury's*	1 Serving/83ml	45	54	3.1	3.2	3.3	0.5
Chicken, Fresh, M & S*	1oz/28g	10	35	2.5	5.0	0.1	0.3
For Poultry, M & S*	1 Jar/400g	136	34	2.5	5.0	0.4	0.3
Fresh, Somerfield*	1 Pack/300g	69	23	0.0	4.0	1.0	0.0
Granuals, Dry, Bisto*	1 Serving/10g	38	384	3.1	56.4	16.2	1.5
Granules, Beef, Dry, Tesco*	1 Serving/6g	29	480	5.5	36.4	34.7	1.5
Granules, Beef, Made Up, Oxo*	1 Serving/140ml	27	19	0.6	3.4	0.3	0.0
Granules, Chicken & Hint of Sage & Onion, Oxo*	3/4 Pint Made/30g	95	316	11.1	54.2	6.1	0.7
Granules, Chicken, Dry, Oxo*	1oz/28g	83	296	11.1	54.2	4.9	0.7
Granules, Chicken, Made Up, Oxo*	1fl oz/30ml	5	18	0.7	3.3	0.3	0.0
Granules, Dry, Bisto*	1oz/28g	109	391	3.1	55.2	17.6	1.5
Granules For Chicken, Dry, Bisto*	1 Serving/4g	15	385	3.2	57.9	15.6	1.4
Granules For Chicken, Made Up, SmartPrice, Asda*	1 Serving/100ml	34	34	0.2	3.0	2.3	0.1
Granules For Meat, Made Up, Asda*	1 Serving/100ml	38	38	0.6	4.0	2.4	0.1
Granules for Turkey, Dry, Bisto*	1 Serving/4g	15	367	3.3	53.9	15.3	1.2
Granules, Instant, Dry	1oz/28g	129	462	4.4	40.6	32.5	0.0
Granules, Instant, Made Up	1oz/28g	10	34	0.3	3.0	2.4	0.0
Granules, Made Up, Bisto*	1floz/30ml	9	30	0.2	4.2	1.4	0.2
Granules, Made Up, Oxo*	1 Serving/150ml	29	19	0.6	3.4	0.3	0.0
Granules, Onion, Dry, Oxo*	1oz/28g	92	328	8.2	62.3	4.8	0.8
Granules, Onion, Made Up, Oxo*	1fl oz/30ml	6	20	0.5	3.7	0.3	0.0
Granules, Vegetable, Dry, Oxo*	1oz/28g	88	316	8.4	59.5	4.9	0.9
Granules, Vegetable, Dry, Tesco*	½ Pint/20g	94	470	3.8	38.5	33.4	3.7
Granules, Vegetarian, Dry, Bisto*	1 Serving/28g	110	394	2.6	54.9	18.2	1.3
Granules With Onion, Dry, Bisto*	1 Serving/4g	15	365	2.9	56.1	14.3	1.8
Mix, Instant, Made Up, BGTY, Sainsbury's*	1fl oz/30ml	10	32	0.3	7.4	0.1	0.1
Onion, Fresh, Asda*	1/6 Pot/77g	30	39	1.7	3.3	2.1	0.4
Onion, Fresh, Somerfield*	1 Pack/300g	195	65	1.0	7.0	4.0	0.0
Onion, Rich, M & S*	½ Pack/150g	60	40	2.0	5.9	1.2	0.3
GREENGAGES,							
Raw	1oz/28g	11	41	0.8	9.7	0.1	2.1
GRILLS,							
Cauliflower Cheese, Dalepak*	1 Grill/94g	231	246	4.6	20.0	14.8	2.6
Cheese & Bacon, Danepak*	1 Grill/84g	239	284	15.0	13.4	18.9	1.2
Leek & Potato, Dalepak*	1 Grill/96g	275	286	4.9	28.7	16.8	2.5
Mushroom & Oregano, Organic, Waitrose*	1 Grill/100g	160	160	8.8	12.8	8.2	2.4
Salmon, Tesco*	1 Serving/100g	165	165	20.3	1.1	8.8	1.3
Tikka, Organic, Waitrose*	1 Grill/100g	185	185	6.9	18.5	9.3	3.4
Vegetable, Dalepak*	1 Grill/85g	170	200	5.2	17.2	12.3	3.2
Vegetable, Ross*	1 Grill/114g	252	221	4.3	25.5	11.3	0.9
GROUND ALMONDS,							
Nature's Harvest, Holland & Barrett*	1oz/28g	176	630	25.4	6.5	55.8	7.4

(Nutrition Values per 100g / 100ml: KCAL, PROT, CARB, FAT, FIBRE)

G

	Measure WEIGHT/INFO	per Measure KCAL	Nutrition Values per 100g / 100ml KCAL	PROT	CARB	FAT	FIBRE
GROUND ALMONDS,							
Sainsbury's*	1 Tbsp/20g	123	614	25.4	2.6	55.8	7.4
GROUSE, Roasted, Meat Only	1oz/28g	125	447	6.8	66.4	17.9	0.0
GUACAMOLE,							
Guacamole, Average	1oz/28g	36	128	1.4	2.2	12.7	2.5
Fresh, Sainsbury's*	1oz/28g	59	210	1.8	5.3	20.2	2.5
GUAVA,							
Canned, In Syrup	1oz/28g	17	60	0.4	15.7	0.0	3.0
Fresh, Raw	1oz/28g	7	26	0.8	5.0	0.5	3.7
GUMBO,							
Cajun Vegetable, Sainsbury's*	1 Serving/450g	266	59	1.4	7.7	2.5	1.5
Louisiana Chicken, Perfectly Balanced, Waitrose*	1 Serving/235g	207	88	12.2	3.5	2.8	1.3
GUMMY Milk Bottles, Bassett's*	1 Pack/25g	88	353	6.2	78.3	1.6	0.0

HADDOCK,	Measure WEIGHT/INFO	per Measure KCAL	KCAL	PROT	CARB	FAT	FIBRE
& Chips, M & S*	1oz/28g	52	187	7.0	22.6	7.6	2.1
Fillets, Battered, M & S*	1 Fillet/125g	306	245	12.6	16.0	14.6	0.7
Fillets, In Breadcrumbs, Scottish, Sainsbury's*	1 Fillet/170g	345	203	13.4	16.4	9.3	0.9
Fillets, Butter, Smoked, Tesco*	1 Pack/204g	208	102	19.9	0.6	2.1	0.7
Fillets, Cheese & Chive Sauce, Smoked, Seafresh	1 Serving/170g	201	118	14.7	1.2	6.1	0.1
Fillets, Cheese & Parsley Sauce, Smoked, M & S*	1 Pack/190g	200	105	13.7	1.4	5.0	0.4
Fillets, Crisp Breadcrumbs, Ocean Trader*	1 Fish/120g	229	191	12.4	14.3	9.4	1.0
Fillets, Crispy Battered, Farmfoods*	1oz/28g	38	137	12.3	14.4	3.4	0.5
Fillets, Fresh, M & S*	1 Fillet/113g	90	80	19.0	0.0	0.6	0.0
Fillets, In A Watercress Sauce, BGTY, Sainsbury's*	½ Pack/170g	133	78	13.2	0.9	2.4	0.7
Fillets, In Tomato Herb Sauce, BGTY, Sainsbury's*	½ Pack/165g	150	91	12.9	3.6	2.8	0.1
Fillets, Smoked, Farmfoods*	1oz/28g	23	81	19.0	0.0	0.6	0.0
Fillets, Smoked, M & S*	1 Pack/227g	170	75	17.8	0.0	0.1	0.0
Fillets, Smoked, Steamed, Tesco*	1 Pack/300g	303	101	23.3	0.0	0.9	0.0
Fillets, Smoked, Tesco*	1 Serving/100g	87	87	20.4	0.0	0.6	0.0
Fillets, Somerfield*	1oz/28g	23	81	19.0	0.0	1.0	0.0
Fillets, Tesco*	1 Serving/150g	122	81	19.0	0.0	0.6	0.0
Fillets, Undyed, Smoked, Sainsbury's*	1 Fillet/175g	154	88	22.0	0.5	0.4	0.5
Florentine, HE, Tesco*	1 Pack/370g	303	82	8.2	10.0	1.0	0.5
Goujons, Crispy Batter, M & S*	1 Serving/100g	250	250	11.7	18.5	14.1	0.8
Grilled	1oz/28g	29	104	24.3	0.0	0.8	0.0
In Batter, Fried In Blended Oil	1oz/28g	65	232	17.1	10.0	14.0	0.4
In Breadcrumbs, Chunky, M & S*	1oz/28g	64	230	5.3	12.6	17.1	3.7
In Breadcrumbs, M & S*	1oz/28g	50	178	13.7	10.8	8.9	1.4
In Cheese & Chive Sauce, HE, Tesco*	1 Pack/360g	284	79	12.7	2.6	2.0	0.1
In Crispy Batter, Iceland*	1 Serving/179g	392	219	15.0	16.0	10.5	1.3
In Crumbs, Fried In Blended Oil	1oz/28g	49	174	21.4	3.6	8.3	0.2
In Flour, Fried In Blended Oil	1oz/28g	39	138	21.1	4.5	4.1	0.2
In Tomato & Herb Sauce, BGTY, Sainsbury's*	1 Serving/180g	164	91	12.9	3.6	2.8	0.1
In Watercress Sauce, GFY, Asda*	1 Pack/400g	268	67	6.0	7.0	1.7	1.4
Mornay, COU, M & S*	1 Pack/190g	152	80	12.3	2.1	2.7	0.2
Mornay, Waitrose*	1 Serving/180g	140	78	14.2	1.9	1.6	0.7
Mustard Sauce, Smoked, Tesco*	1 Pack/450g	342	76	6.9	5.9	2.7	1.0
Poached	1oz/28g	32	113	17.7	1.1	4.3	0.0
Portions, Breaded, Somerfield*	1 Portion/100g	212	212	12.0	13.0	12.0	0.0
Potato Topped, Cumberland, M & S*	1 Pack/300g	390	130	8.2	10.6	6.0	0.4
Rarebit, Smoked, Finest, Tesco*	1 Rarebit/180g	326	181	5.6	19.1	9.2	0.4
Raw	1oz/28g	23	81	19.0	0.0	0.6	0.0
Skinless Fillets, Farmfoods*	1oz/28g	20	73	16.8	0.0	0.6	0.0
Smoked, Poached	1oz/28g	38	134	18.7	1.1	6.1	0.0
Smoked, Raw	1oz/28g	23	81	19.0	0.0	0.6	0.0
Smoked, Steamed	1oz/28g	28	101	23.3	0.0	0.9	0.0
Smoked, Tesco*	1 Serving/150g	152	101	23.3	0.0	0.9	0.0
Steaks, Crispy Batter, Bird's Eye*	1 Steak/145g	307	212	11.0	13.7	12.6	0.5
Steamed	1oz/28g	25	89	20.9	0.0	0.6	0.0
HAGGIS,							
Neeps & Tatties, M & S*	1 Pack/300g	330	110	3.8	12.3	4.8	0.8
Vegetarian, McSween*	1 Serving/100g	216	216	6.6	26.8	10.2	2.4
HAKE,							
Fillets, Sainsbury's*	1 Fillet/85g	86	101	21.1	0.1	1.8	0.1
Goujons, M & S*	1oz/28g	69	245	12.0	21.4	12.6	1.5
Grilled	1oz/28g	32	113	22.2	0.0	2.7	0.0
In Breadcrumbs, M & S*	1oz/28g	60	215	13.1	11.1	13.5	0.4
Raw	1oz/28g	26	92	18.0	0.0	2.2	0.0

Nutrition Values per 100g / 100ml apply to the KCAL, PROT, CARB, FAT and FIBRE columns.

H

HALIBUT,	Measure WEIGHT/INFO	per Measure KCAL	KCAL	PROT	CARB	FAT	FIBRE
Grilled	1oz/28g	34	121	25.3	0.0	2.2	0.0
Poached	1oz/28g	43	154	24.7	1.1	5.7	0.0
Raw	1oz/28g	29	103	21.5	0.0	1.9	0.0
Steamed	1oz/28g	37	131	23.8	0.0	4.0	0.0
HALLOUMI, Total*	1oz/28g	90	320	20.0	0.8	25.0	0.0
HALWA	1oz/28g	107	381	1.8	68.0	13.2	0.0
HAM,							
Applewood Smoked, Safeway*	1 Slice/28g	29	104	19.8	0.2	2.7	0.0
Baked, Danepak*	1 Slice/17g	26	152	18.9	1.4	7.9	0.0
Baked, Organic, Waitrose*	1 Slice/22g	33	149	27.0	0.3	4.4	0.0
Baked, Somerfield*	1oz/28g	43	153	16.0	3.0	9.0	0.0
Bavarian, Asda*	1 Slice/15g	18	121	21.4	0.5	3.7	0.0
Beechwood Smoked, Dry Cure, Somerfield*	1oz/28g	38	135	25.0	2.0	3.0	0.0
Breaded, Asda*	1 Slice/37g	56	150	24.0	0.9	5.6	3.2
Breaded Wiltshire, M & S*	1oz/28g	38	135	23.6	1.0	3.7	0.0
British Cooked, Somerfield*	1oz/28g	26	94	18.0	1.0	2.0	0.0
British, Extra Lean, M & S*	1 Slice/11g	10	90	18.0	1.4	1.4	0.0
British Honey Roast, Somerfield*	1oz/28g	27	97	18.0	2.0	2.0	0.0
Brunswick, Sliced, Sainsbury's*	1 Slice/20g	32	160	19.5	0.6	8.8	0.1
Brunswick, Smoked, German, Waitrose*	1 Slice/20g	32	160	19.5	0.6	8.8	0.0
Chargrilled, Wafer Thin, M & S*	1 Serving/100g	120	120	21.3	0.5	3.9	0.0
Cooked, HE, Tesco*	1 Slice/25g	29	117	24.4	0.0	2.2	0.0
Cooked, Sainsbury's*	2 Slices/25g	29	116	18.2	0.1	4.7	0.1
Cooked, Sliced, Tesco*	1 Slice/30g	35	118	21.2	0.8	3.3	0.1
Cooked, Tesco*	1 Slice/13g	13	97	17.6	0.4	2.8	0.0
Cooked, Wafer Thin, Budgens*	2 Slices/20g	20	102	16.8	0.8	3.5	0.5
Cooked, Waifos, Denny*	1 Packet/85g	79	93	17.3	1.3	2.0	0.0
Crumbed, Safeway*	1 Slice/28g	32	113	19.5	1.2	3.4	0.0
Danish, Honey Roast, Lean, M & S*	1 Serving/25g	28	110	19.5	3.1	2.2	0.0
Danish, M & S*	1 Slice/11g	10	95	17.7	2.0	1.6	0.0
Danish Prime Quality, Lean, M & S*	1oz/28g	25	90	18.0	0.0	2.0	0.0
Dry Cure Honey Roast, Tesco*	1 Slice/25g	33	133	23.5	1.6	3.6	0.0
Dry Cure, Ovenbaked, Asda*	1 Slice/32g	47	147	22.0	3.5	5.0	1.0
Dry Cure Smoked, Finely Sliced, Sainsbury's*	1 Slice/18g	24	135	21.2	1.0	5.1	0.1
Dry Cured Breaded, TTD, Sainsbury's*	1 Slice/27g	35	130	21.1	2.5	3.9	0.1
Dry Cured Cooked, Organic, Sainsbury's*	1 Slice/22g	31	141	26.4	1.4	3.3	1.1
Dry Cured Honey Roast, Finely Sliced, Sainsbury's*	1 Slice/18g	24	136	21.4	1.0	5.1	0.1
Dry Cured Honey Roast, TTD, Sainsbury's*	1 Slice/27g	35	135	21.7	2.6	4.2	0.1
Dry Cured Oak Smoked, TTD, Sainsbury's*	1 Slice/27g	32	119	22.5	1.7	2.5	0.1
Dry Cured Premium Cooked, Plumrose*	1 Slice/20g	28	142	19.9	0.0	7.0	0.0
Dry Cured Smoked, Finely Sliced, Sainsbury's*	1 Slice/18g	24	135	21.2	1.0	5.1	0.1
Economy, Sainsbury's*	1 Slice/13g	13	102	16.8	0.8	3.6	0.6
English Smoked, Waitrose*	1oz/28g	39	140	21.4	0.0	6.0	0.0
Extra Lean, M & S*	1 Pack/113g	102	90	18.0	1.4	1.4	0.0
Gammon, Cooked, Somerfield*	1oz/28g	45	159	20.0	1.0	8.0	0.0
Gammon Joint, Boiled	1oz/28g	57	204	23.3	0.0	12.3	0.0
Gammon Joint, Raw	1oz/28g	39	138	17.5	0.0	7.5	0.0
Gammon Smoked, Dry Cured, Waitrose*	1 Serving/100g	132	132	22.0	0.9	4.4	0.0
Genuilne Parma, M & S*	1 Serving/10g	20	200	30.0	0.0	9.0	0.0
German Black Forest, Safeway*	½ Pack/35g	93	267	27.2	1.3	17.0	0.5
German Black Forest, Sainsbury's*	1 Slice/8g	21	267	27.2	1.3	17.0	0.5
Great Value, Harris*	1 Slice/10g	10	96	16.3	0.8	3.1	0.0
Honey & Mustard, Wafer Thin, M & S*	1 Pack/100g	140	140	20.8	4.6	4.3	0.0
Honey Cured Wafer Thin, TTD, Sainsbury's*	1 Serving/75g	95	126	20.8	1.8	4.0	0.0

Nutrition Values per 100g / 100ml

H

HAM,	Measure WEIGHT/INFO	per Measure KCAL	Nutrition Values per 100g / 100ml KCAL	PROT	CARB	FAT	FIBRE
Honey Roast, Asda*	1 Slice/12g	12	101	17.0	3.4	0.1	1.6
Honey Roast, Bernard Matthews*	1 Slice/21g	24	112	20.4	2.0	2.5	0.0
Honey Roast, Co-Op*	1 Slice/23g	28	120	19.0	0.6	5.0	0.0
Honey Roast Dry Cure, Asda*	1 Slice/31g	42	137	22.0	2.0	4.5	0.5
Honey Roast Gammon, Waitrose*	1 Slice/43g	60	139	22.8	0.1	5.3	0.0
Honey Roast, HE, Tesco*	1 Slice/25g	27	107	22.2	1.7	1.2	0.0
Honey Roast, M & S*	1 Slice/11g	12	110	19.5	3.1	2.2	0.0
Honey Roast, Organic, Waitrose*	1 Slice/45g	63	140	20.6	1.4	5.8	0.0
Honey Roast, Oven Baked, Asda*	1 Slice/31g	42	137	22.0	2.0	4.5	0.5
Honey Roast, Premium, Safeway*	1 Slice/28g	34	121	19.3	1.8	4.1	0.0
Honey Roast, Safeway*	1 Slice/12g	12	102	17.4	1.7	2.8	0.0
Honey Roast, Sainsbury's*	1 Slice/13g	15	119	18.6	1.7	4.2	0.1
Honey Roast, Tesco*	1 Slice/31g	37	120	21.4	1.1	3.3	0.0
Honey Roast, Thin, Dry Dured, Somerfield*	1 Slice/32g	40	126	21.9	0.4	4.1	0.0
Honey Roast, Thin Sliced, Asda*	1 Slice/13g	15	116	19.0	2.9	3.1	1.6
Honey Roast, TTD, Sainsbury's*	1 Slice/38g	51	135	21.7	2.6	4.2	0.0
Honey Roast, Wafer Thin, Asda*	1oz/28g	31	112	16.8	3.9	3.2	0.0
Honey Roast, Wafer Thin, Premium, Cut, Safeway*	1 Slice/12g	23	194	23.4	2.6	10.0	0.0
Honey Roast, Wafer Thin, Safeway*	¼ Pack/25g	28	112	16.8	3.9	3.2	0.0
Honey Roast, Wafer Thin, Sainsbury's*	1 Slice/10g	11	113	16.8	5.8	2.5	0.1
Honey Roast, Wafer Thin, Tesco*	1 Serving/25g	27	107	17.1	1.6	3.6	0.0
Honey Roast, Wafer Thin, Waitrose*	1 Slice/10g	10	104	18.7	1.5	2.6	0.0
Honey Roast, Waitrose*	1 Serving/65g	90	139	22.8	0.1	5.3	0.0
Honey Roasted Mustard, Thin Sliced, Asda*	1 Slice/16g	16	103	17.5	3.8	2.0	1.6
Honey Roasted, Wafer Thin, Somerfield*	1 Serving/50g	62	124	14.2	5.6	5.0	0.0
Italian Dry Cured, Waitrose*	1 Slice/29g	65	223	28.0	0.2	12.0	0.0
Italian Parma, TTD, Sainsbury's*	1 Slice/15g	34	225	28.2	0.1	12.4	0.1
Italian Rostello, Safeway*	1 Serving/60g	78	130	21.0	0.2	5.0	0.0
Joint, Easy Carve, Asda*	1oz/28g	41	146	22.8	1.2	5.9	0.6
Joint, Honey Roast, Asda*	1oz/28g	35	124	23.9	1.7	2.8	0.7
Joint, Oven Baked, Asda*	1oz/28g	33	118	21.7	1.5	1.9	0.6
Lean, BGTY, Sainsbury's*	1 Slice/145g	158	109	23.1	1.5	1.2	0.5
Mild Cure, Courtway, Aldi*	1 Slice/11g	13	120	16.8	1.6	5.2	0.0
Mustard, Thin Sliced, Asda*	1 Slice/13g	13	101	17.0	3.8	2.0	0.0
Norfolk Smoked, Bernard Matthews*	1 Piece/38g	41	108	23.8	0.6	1.0	0.0
Oak Smoked, Asda*	1 Slice/38g	51	134	20.6	1.2	5.2	0.8
Oak Smoked Gammon, Waitrose*	1 Slice/43g	62	145	24.2	0.0	5.3	0.0
On The Bone, Breaded, Somerfield*	1oz/28g	45	161	21.0	0.0	9.0	0.0
Oven Baked, Sliced, Asda*	1 Slice/32g	47	147	22.0	3.5	5.0	1.0
Ovenbaked, Safeway*	1 Slice/20g	23	116	19.5	0.2	4.1	0.0
Parma, M & S*	1oz/28g	56	200	30.0	0.0	9.0	0.0
Parma, Somerfield*	1oz/28g	63	226	29.0	0.0	12.0	0.0
Peppered, Thin Sliced, Asda*	1 Slice/12g	12	99	17.0	3.7	1.8	0.0
Princes*	1 Serving/225g	349	155	12.0	1.5	11.0	0.0
Prosciutto, Asda*	1 Serving/50g	117	233	29.0	0.0	13.0	0.6
Prosciutto di Speck, TTD, Sainsbury's*	1 Slice/12g	26	220	28.4	0.1	11.7	0.1
Safeway*	1 Slice/12g	11	95	17.8	0.7	2.3	0.0
Scrumpy Cured, Tesco*	1 Slice/34g	60	176	27.2	0.9	7.1	0.0
Sliced, Thin, SmartPrice, Asda*	1 Slice/12g	11	92	16.0	0.8	2.7	0.0
Slices, Cooked, Sainsbury's*	1 Slice/28g	32	116	18.2	0.1	4.7	0.1
Smoked, Iceland*	1 Slice/24g	30	127	20.6	0.7	4.6	0.0
Smoked, M & S*	1 Slice/6g	6	105	19.7	0.2	3.0	0.0
Smoked, Safeway*	2 Slices/25g	26	103	17.3	1.8	2.9	0.0
Smoked, Sainsbury's*	1 Slice/12.5g	14	115	18.5	0.1	4.5	0.1

H

HAM,	Measure WEIGHT/INFO	per Measure KCAL	Nutrition Values per 100g / 100ml KCAL	PROT	CARB	FAT	FIBRE
Smoked, Slices, Sainsbury's*	1 Serving/27g	32	119	22.5	1.7	2.5	0.1
Smoked, Somerfield*	1oz/28g	29	102	17.0	1.0	3.0	0.0
Smoked, Tesco*	1 Slice/31g	36	117	21.7	0.5	3.1	0.0
Smoked, Thin Sliced, Asda*	1 Slice/52	50	96	18.0	2.4	1.6	0.9
Smoked, Wafer Thin, Asda*	1oz/28g	27	96	16.1	0.8	3.1	0.0
Smoked, Wafer Thin, Sainsbury's*	1 Serving/40g	36	90	16.2	2.0	1.9	0.0
Smoked, Wafer Thin, Tesco*	1 Serving/50g	53	105	16.6	0.8	3.9	0.0
Smoked, Wafer Thin, TTD, Sainsbury's*	1 Slice/5g	6	124	21.3	0.6	4.0	0.1
Tesco*	1 Serving/40g	47	118	21.2	0.8	3.3	0.1
Thick Cut, Tesco*	1 Serving/85g	119	140	20.6	1.4	5.8	0.0
Thin Sliced, Cooked, Asda*	1 Slice/13g	15	114	20.0	3.8	2.1	0.8
Thinly Sliced, Somerfield*	1oz/28g	36	130	15.0	3.0	7.0	0.0
Tinned, Ye Olde Oak*	100g/100g	108	108	12.5	2.0	5.5	0.0
Traditional Cured Danish Breaded, M & S*	1oz/28g	41	145	21.8	0.7	5.9	0.0
Traditional Cured Danish Roasted, M & S*	1 Slice/28g	42	150	22.6	1.9	5.8	0.0
Traditional Dry Cure, Finest, Tesco*	1 Slice/25g	42	169	25.4	0.0	7.5	0.0
Traditional Wiltshire Cured, Wafer Thin, Finest, Tesco*	1 Serving/100g	140	140	24.1	0.0	4.8	0.0
Turkey, Smoked, Wafer Thin, Bernard Matthews*	1 Serving/10g	11	112	14.4	3.8	4.4	0.0
Turkey, Wafer Thin, Bernard Matthews*	1oz/28g	27	98	13.6	3.5	3.3	0.0
Wafer Danish, M & S*	1oz/28g	28	100	17.6	1.7	2.9	0.0
Wafer Thin, Asda*	1oz/28g	27	95	16.0	0.8	3.1	0.0
Wafer Thin, Bernard Matthews*	1 Slice/45g	42	93	15.7	0.9	2.9	0.0
Wafer Thin Dry Cure, Tesco*	1 Thin/30g	39	130	23.5	0.9	3.6	0.0
Wafer Thin, Iceland*	1 Slice/9g	8	94	16.4	0.8	2.8	0.0
Wafer Thin Roast, HE, Tesco*	½ Pack/50g	48	95	22.0	0.0	0.8	0.0
Wafer Thin, Sainsbury's*	1 Serving/10g	9	93	16.5	2.0	2.1	0.1
Wafer Thin, Tesco*	1 Pack/200g	210	105	16.6	0.8	3.9	0.0
Wiltshire Crumbed, Traditional, Finest, Tesco*	1 Slice/44g	62	140	24.1	0.0	4.8	0.1
HARIBO*,							
American Hard Gums	1 Pack/175g	630	360	0.3	85.5	1.9	0.2
Cola Bottles	1 Sm Pack/16g	57	358	7.7	78.9	1.3	0.3
Cola Bottles, Fizzy	1 Med Pack/175g	628	359	6.3	78.3	2.3	0.5
Dolly Mixtures	1 Pack/175g	719	411	1.8	90.2	4.8	0.2
Fantasy Mix	1 Sm Pack/100g	360	360	6.6	79.0	2.0	0.3
Fried Eggs	1 Pack/175g	630	360	6.6	79.0	2.0	0.3
Gold Bears	1 Pack/100g	358	358	7.7	78.9	1.3	0.3
Horror Mix	1 Sm Pack/100g	360	360	6.6	79.0	2.0	0.3
Jelly Beans	1 Pack/100g	360	360	3.8	89.2	1.2	0.0
Kiddies Super Mix	1 Pack/100g	401	401	1.1	95.3	1.7	0.8
Liquorice Favourites	1 Pack/175g	625	357	2.8	78.8	3.0	2.3
Milky Mix	1 Pack/175g	644	368	7.1	79.6	2.3	0.4
Mint Imperials	1 Pack/175g	695	397	0.4	98.8	0.5	0.1
Pasta Frutta	1 Pack/200g	718	359	1.3	87.0	0.7	0.5
Pontefract Cakes	1 Pack/100g	306	306	5.3	68.2	1.3	5.6
Starmix	1 Pack/100g	360	360	6.6	79.0	2.0	0.3
Tangfastics	1 Pack/100g	359	359	6.3	78.3	2.3	0.5
Wine Gums	1 Pack/175g	655	374	6.2	85.9	0.6	0.1
HASH BROWNS,							
Birds Eye*	1 Serving/63g	126	200	2.0	21.9	11.6	1.6
Burger King*	1 Hash Brown/102g	318	312	7.2	32.3	19.4	3.8
Deep Fried, McCain*	1oz/28g	69	246	2.0	24.3	15.3	0.0
Farmfoods*	1oz/28g	35	124	2.1	18.2	4.7	2.1
Frozen, McCain*	1 Hash Brown/40g	70	174	3.0	24.0	7.3	0.0
McDonald's*	1 Portion/56g	127	227	2.2	25.3	13.0	3.8

H

	Measure WEIGHT/INFO	per Measure KCAL	Nutrition Values per 100g / 100ml KCAL	PROT	CARB	FAT	FIBRE
HASH BROWNS,							
Oven Baked, McCain*	1oz/28g	55	196	1.7	25.5	8.6	0.0
Potato, Iceland*	1 Hash/33g	75	227	2.2	27.1	12.2	2.6
Tesco*	1oz/28g	43	154	2.4	20.0	7.2	1.7
HASH,							
Chicken Salsa, HE, Tesco*	1 Pack/350g	242	69	5.6	9.5	1.0	1.1
Corned Beef, Asda*	1 Pack/400g	416	104	6.0	12.0	3.6	1.1
Corned Beef, Chilled, Co-Op*	1 Pack/300g	345	115	9.0	5.0	6.0	1.0
Farmhouse, HE, Tesco*	1 Serving/300g	264	88	2.2	13.6	2.7	1.1
Vegetable & Lentil, Asda*	1 Pack/289g	254	88	3.2	14.0	2.1	0.0
HASLET, Somerfield*	1oz/28g	57	205	15.0	10.0	12.0	0.0
HAZELNUTS	10 Whole/10g	65	650	14.1	6.0	63.5	6.5
HERB CUBES,							
Basil, Knorr*	1 Cube/10g	47	472	6.1	35.9	33.8	0.6
Parsley & Garlic, Knorr*	1 Cube/10g	42	422	8.6	35.2	27.4	1.8
HEROES,							
Miniature, Cadbury's*	3 Sweets/30g	147	490	5.6	59.2	25.6	0.0
HERRING,							
Canned In Tomato Sauce	1oz/28g	54	193	12.8	3.2	14.4	0.0
Dried, Salted	1oz/28g	47	168	25.3	0.0	7.4	0.0
Fillets, In Tomato Sauce, John West*	1 Can/190g	416	219	11.5	4.6	17.2	0.4
Grilled	1oz/28g	51	181	20.1	0.0	11.2	0.0
In Horseradish Sauce, John West*	1oz/28g	64	230	13.0	4.0	18.0	0.0
Oatmeal, Fried In Vegetable Oil	1oz/28g	66	234	23.1	1.5	15.1	0.1
Pickled	1oz/28g	59	209	16.7	10.0	11.1	0.0
Raw	1oz/28g	53	190	17.8	0.0	13.2	0.0
Rollmop, With Onion, Asda*	1 Rollmop/65g	89	137	13.2	10.3	4.8	0.8
HIGH LIGHTS,							
Cadbury's*	1 Cup/200ml	40	20	1.0	2.5	0.7	0.3
Choc Malt Hot Chocolate, Cadbury's*	1 Serving/200ml	44	22	1.0	2.9	0.7	0.3
Choc Mint, Cadbury's*	1 Serving/200ml	40	20	1.0	2.5	0.7	0.3
Chocolate Orange, Cadbury's*	1 Serving/200ml	40	20	1.0	2.3	0.7	0.3
Dairy Fudge, Cadbury's*	1 Serving/200ml	40	20	1.0	2.8	0.5	0.2
HOKI,							
Fillets, In White Wine Sauce, BGTY, Sainsbury's*	1 Pack/360g	281	78	13.4	1.7	1.9	0.0
Grilled	1oz/28g	34	121	24.1	0.0	2.7	0.0
Raw	1oz/28g	24	85	16.9	0.0	1.9	0.0
HONEY,							
Honey	1 Tsp/6g	49	288	0.4	76.4	0.0	0.0
Australian Eucalyptus, Finest, Tesco*	1 Tsp/4g	12	307	0.4	76.4	0.0	0.0
Clear, Frank Cooper*	1 Tsp/6g	18	292	0.4	72.6	0.0	0.0
Greek, Waitrose*	1 Tsp/6g	18	307	0.4	76.4	0.0	0.0
Organic, M & S*	1 Tsp/6g	21	355	0.2	88.4	0.1	0.1
Pure, Clear, Asda*	1 Tbsp/15g	46	306	0.4	79.0	0.0	0.0
Pure, Clear, Blended, Sainsbury's*	1 Serving/6g	20	331	0.4	82.3	0.1	0.0
Pure, Clear, Chivers*	1 Tsp/6g	19	311	0.6	77.2	0.0	0.0
Pure, Frank Cooper*	1 Tsp/6g	18	292	0.4	72.6	0.0	0.0
Pure, Set, Tesco*	1 Tsp/5g	15	307	0.4	76.4	0.0	0.0
Pure, Set, Waitrose*	1 Tsp/9g	28	307	0.4	76.4	0.0	0.0
Set, Safeway*	1 Tsps/15g	48	322	0.4	80.0	0.0	0.0
Spanish Orange Blossom, Sainsbury's*	1 Tbsp/15g	51	339	0.1	84.7	0.0	0.3
Tasmanian Leatherwood, TTD, Sainsbury's*	1 Serving/6g	20	339	0.1	84.7	0.1	0.3
HOOCH,* Vodka, (Calculated Estimate)	1 Bottle/330ml	244	74	0.3	5.1	0.0	0.0
HORLICKS,							
Hot Chocolate, Light, SmithKline Beecham*	1 Serving/32g	128	399	8.8	72.6	8.1	3.7

	Measure WEIGHT/INFO	per Measure KCAL	KCAL	PROT	CARB	FAT	FIBRE
			Nutrition Values per 100g / 100ml				
HORLICKS,							
Low Fat Instant Powder, Made Up With Water	1 Mug/227ml	116	51	2.4	10.1	0.5	0.0
Powder, Made Up With Semi-Skimmed Milk	1 Mug/227ml	184	81	4.3	12.9	1.9	0.0
Powder, Made Up With Skimmed Milk	1 Mug/227ml	159	70	4.3	12.9	0.5	0.0
Powder, Made Up With Whole Milk	1 Mug/227ml	225	99	4.2	12.7	3.9	0.0
HORSERADISH,							
Mustard, Sainsbury's*	1 Tsp/5g	4	82	5.3	2.3	5.8	0.0
Raw	1oz/28g	17	62	4.5	11.0	0.3	6.2
HOT CHOCOLATE,							
Caramel Flavoured, Instant, Aldi*	1 Serving/11g	40	363	18.5	40.6	14.1	8.5
Chocolate Time, Safeway*	1 Serving/30g	123	411	9.4	67.8	11.4	1.8
Galaxy*	1 Mug/28g	115	411	7.0	68.7	12.1	0.0
Instant, Cadbury's*	1 Serving/14g	60	426	10.9	64.2	14.0	2.3
Instant, Tesco*	1 Serving/32g	132	414	8.0	68.3	12.1	0.7
Low Calorie, Somerfield*	1 Sachet/12g	40	330	18.0	48.0	8.0	0.0
McDonald's*	1 Floz/30ml	101	336	3.4	60.9	8.7	2.0
Mint Flavour, BGTY, Sainsbury's*	1 Serving/180ml	101	56	2.1	10.5	0.6	0.4
Orange Flavour, BGTY, Sainsbury's*	1 Serving/180ml	101	56	2.2	10.2	0.7	0.4
SmartPrice, Asda*	4 Tsp/23g	89	388	13.0	66.0	8.0	3.9
Velvet, Cadbury's*	1 Serving/28g	136	487	8.6	57.8	24.6	2.0
HOT DOG,							
& Ketchup, McDonald's*	1 Serving/116g	296	255	9.6	25.8	12.6	1.3
American Style, Sainsbury's*	1 Sausage/50g	144	288	13.0	0.5	26.0	0.0
American Style, Tesco*	1 Hot Dog/75g	164	218	12.7	3.4	17.1	0.0
Canned, Ye Olde Oak*	1 Hot Dog/33g	54	165	11.5	5.0	12.0	0.0
Farmfoods*	1 Sausage/50g	84	168	10.0	5.0	12.0	1.0
Lancaster*	4 Sausages/92g	138	150	10.0	4.0	10.5	0.0
Lite, Princes*	1oz/28g	42	150	10.5	5.5	9.5	0.6
Meatfree, Sainsbury's*	1 Sausage/30g	70	235	17.8	4.2	16.4	1.9
Mini, Tesco*	1 Hot Dog/10g	22	218	12.7	3.4	17.1	0.0
Princes*	1 Sausage/23g	42	183	8.0	5.0	14.5	0.0
SmartPrice Asda*	1 Sausage/23g	31	135	10.0	3.5	9.0	0.0
Value, Tesco*	1 Sausage/27g	59	218	12.7	3.4	17.1	0.0
HOT POT,							
Beef, Weight Watchers*	1 Hotpot/320g	288	90	5.8	10.0	3.0	1.4
Chicken & Cider, Ready Meals, Waitrose*	1 Pack/400g	500	125	6.8	12.9	5.1	1.1
Chicken, Co-Op*	1 Serving/340g	289	85	6.0	9.0	3.0	0.7
Chicken, Good Choice, Iceland*	1 Pack/400g	276	69	5.0	9.3	1.3	1.0
Chicken, Weight Watchers*	1 Pack/340g	306	90	5.3	11.3	2.6	0.9
Lamb & Vegetable, Asda*	1 Pot/500g	240	48	4.0	7.0	0.4	0.0
Lancashire, Asda*	1 Hotpot/401g	269	67	3.8	10.0	1.3	0.9
Lancashire, Safeway*	1 Pack/400g	336	84	8.4	6.6	2.7	1.3
Lancashire, Sainsbury's*	½ Pack/225g	203	90	6.7	9.5	2.8	0.5
Lancashire, Tesco*	½ Pack/360g	400	111	5.5	8.3	6.2	0.9
Minced Beef & Vegetable, Tesco*	1 Pack/300g	282	94	3.5	11.9	3.6	1.9
Minced Beef, Asda*	1 Pack/375g	409	109	7.0	10.0	4.6	1.7
Minced Beef Classic, Sainsbury's*	1 Pack/450g	491	109	6.1	13.4	3.4	1.0
Minced Beef, Long Life, Sainsbury's*	1 Pack/300g	207	69	3.9	10.0	1.5	0.9
Minced Beef, SmartPrice, Asda*	1 Pack/296g	237	80	3.2	10.0	3.0	1.0
Minced Beef, Tesco*	1 Pack/750g	765	102	3.6	11.7	4.5	0.9
Sausage, SmartPrice, Asda*	1 Pack/302g	251	83	3.6	9.0	3.6	0.8
Sausage With Heinz Baked Beans, Heinz*	1 Pack/340g	367	108	5.4	13.1	3.8	2.5
Vegetable, Somerfield*	1 Pack/300g	348	116	4.0	11.0	6.0	0.0
Vegetable, Tesco*	1 Pack/340g	326	96	2.9	10.5	4.7	1.3
Vegetable, Weight Watchers*	1 Pack/335g	228	68	2.6	9.9	1.9	1.5

H

	Measure WEIGHT/INFO	per Measure KCAL	Nutrition Values per 100g / 100ml KCAL	PROT	CARB	FAT	FIBRE
HOUMOUS,							
30% Less Fat, Asda*	1oz/28g	77	275	8.8	16.4	19.4	2.1
BGTY, Sainsbury's*	1oz/28g	54	192	5.9	15.6	11.8	1.3
Fresh, Healthy Choice, Safeway*	1oz/28g	74	264	9.1	13.6	19.2	0.0
Fresh, Tesco*	1oz/28g	83	296	7.8	7.9	25.9	3.3
GFY, Asda*	½ Pot/85g	209	246	9.0	12.0	18.0	4.3
Lemon & Chilli, Fresh, Tesco*	1oz/28g	84	299	8.4	7.3	26.2	3.2
Light, Morrisons*	½ Pack/85g	200	235	7.4	10.9	18.0	0.0
M & S*	1oz/28g	87	310	7.1	9.5	27.3	3.3
Organic, Tesco*	1 Pot/170g	544	320	6.5	12.3	27.2	2.4
Reduced Fat, Fresh, Tesco*	1oz/28g	66	236	7.5	12.9	17.2	3.3
Reduced Fat, M & S*	1oz/28g	67	240	7.5	12.9	17.2	3.3
Reduced Fat, Waitrose*	1oz/28g	67	239	7.7	11.3	18.1	2.6
Roasted Red Pepper, Tesco*	1 Pot/170g	510	300	6.6	11.9	25.1	3.1
Sainsbury's*	1oz/28g	87	312	7.3	8.9	27.5	2.2
Somerfield*	1oz/28g	87	309	8.0	11.0	26.0	0.0
Spicy Red Pepper, M & S*	¼ Pot/75g	158	210	7.3	14.8	13.7	2.5
HULA HOOPS,							
Barbecue Beef Flavour, Hula Hoops*	1 Bag/34g	170	500	3.9	58.7	27.5	2.4
Beef & Mustard, KP*	1 Bag/50g	260	519	3.9	55.0	31.5	1.8
Cheese & Onion, KP*	1 Bag/34g	179	525	3.9	56.8	31.4	2.2
Nacho Cheese Flavour Tortilla Rings, KP*	1 Bag/50g	258	516	4.7	59.2	28.9	2.7
Original, KP*	1 Bag/33g	166	504	3.3	58.9	28.1	2.5
Prawn Cocktail, KP*	1 Bag/34g	168	493	3.3	58.9	27.1	2.4
Salt & Vinegar, KP*	1 Bag/34g	169	497	3.7	58.4	27.4	2.5
Sizzling Bacon, KP*	1 Bag/34g	175	514	3.2	54.7	31.4	2.1
Totally Cheese Flavour Shoks, KP*	1 Bag/55g	285	519	3.8	54.5	31.8	2.1

H

ICE CREAM, (SEE ALSO CHOC ICE)	Measure WEIGHT/INFO	per Measure KCAL	Nutrition Values per 100g / 100ml KCAL	PROT	CARB	FAT	FIBRE
Apricot, Finest, Tesco*	1 Serving/100g	225	225	3.3	29.2	10.6	0.3
Baileys, Haagen-Dazs*	1oz/28g	73	260	4.5	22.2	17.1	0.0
Banana, Thorntons*	1oz/28g	63	225	4.0	23.8	12.6	0.0
Banoffee, Criminally Creamy, Co-Op*	1oz/28g	66	235	3.0	26.0	13.0	0.1
Banoffee Fudge, Sainsbury's*	1/8 Pot/67g	119	178	2.8	28.7	5.9	0.2
Ice Cream Bar, Baileys, Haagen-Dazs*	1oz/28g	86	307	4.1	24.8	21.2	0.0
Ice Cream Bar, Caramel, Cadbury's*	1 Bar/64g	188	294	3.7	32.4	16.6	0.0
Ice Cream Bar, Choc Chip, Haagen-Dazs*	1oz/28g	90	320	4.3	27.4	21.5	0.0
Ice Cream Bar, Chocolate Covered	1oz/28g	90	320	5.0	24.0	23.3	0.0
Ice Cream Bar, Chuncky Chocolate, Co-Op*	1 Bar/60g	204	340	5.0	35.0	20.0	1.0
Ice Cream Bar, Chunky Toffee, Co-Op*	1 Bar/60g	204	340	4.0	34.0	21.0	1.0
Ice Cream Bar, Deam, Cadbury's*	1 Serving/118g	260	220	3.6	26.0	11.9	0.0
Ice Cream Bar, Peanut, Farmfoods*	1 Bar/60ml	187	360	5.3	36.6	21.4	1.2
Ice Cream Bar, Racer, Aldi*	1 Bar/59g	194	328	6.0	34.2	18.6	0.0
Ice Cream Bar, Toffee Cream, Haagen-Dazs*	1oz/28g	97	346	4.1	32.2	22.3	0.0
Belgian Chocolate, Haagen-Dazs*	1oz/28g	89	318	4.6	28.4	20.7	0.0
Bounty, Mars*	1oz/28g	77	274	3.3	23.8	18.3	0.0
Bournville, Cadbury's*	1 Bar/120g	258	215	3.5	26.0	11.6	0.0
Cappuccino, Thorntons*	1oz/28g	61	218	4.4	20.7	12.9	0.0
Choc Chip Cookie Dough, Ben & Jerrys*	1 Serving/100g	230	230	3.0	23.0	14.0	0.0
Choc Chip, Cookie Dough, Haagen-Dazs*	1oz/28g	83	296	4.2	27.7	18.8	0.0
Choc Chip, Haagen-Dazs*	1oz/28g	80	286	4.7	24.8	18.7	0.0
Chocolate, 98% Fat Free, Too Good, Wall's*	1 Spoonful/20ml	15	75	2.2	14.1	1.0	0.2
Chocolate, COU, M & S*	1 Serving/140g	231	165	3.9	35.0	2.9	0.8
Chocolate, Easy Serve, Co-Op*	1oz/28g	46	165	3.0	22.0	7.0	0.3
Chocolate Flavour, Soft Scoop, Sainsbury's*	1 Serving/70g	122	174	3.1	23.6	7.5	0.3
Chocolate Fudge Swirl, Haagen-Dazs*	1oz/28g	77	276	4.6	25.6	17.2	0.0
Chocolate Honeycomb, COU, M & S*	1 Serving/100ml	150	150	3.5	31.5	2.6	0.7
Chocolate Midnight Cookies, Haagen-Dazs*	1oz/28g	81	289	4.9	28.7	17.2	0.0
Chocolate Orange, Deliciously Dairy, Co-Op*	1oz/28g	55	195	4.0	29.0	7.0	0.8
Chocolate, Organic, Iceland*	1oz/28g	58	208	4.9	28.6	8.2	0.0
Chocolate, Organic, M & S*	1oz/28g	71	255	5.0	24.0	16.0	1.5
Chocolate Soft Scoop, Asda*	1 Scoop/47g	84	179	3.7	23.0	8.0	0.0
Chocolate, Thorntons*	1oz/28g	67	238	4.6	25.1	12.9	0.0
Chocolate, Weight Watchers*	1 Serving/100ml	92	92	1.8	15.2	2.5	0.5
Cookies & Cream, Haagen-Dazs*	1oz/28g	73	262	4.6	22.6	17.0	0.0
Cornish Clotted, M & S*	1 Pot/90g	207	230	2.8	21.8	14.5	0.1
Cornish Style, Co-Op*	1oz/28g	53	190	4.0	23.0	9.0	0.1
Cornish Vanilla, Organic, Iceland*	1oz/28g	60	214	4.1	21.4	12.4	0.0
Cornish Vanilla, Soft Scoop, M & S*	1oz/28g	56	199	3.9	21.8	10.7	0.2
Creamy Chocolate & Nut, Co-Op*	1oz/28g	66	235	4.0	25.0	13.0	0.5
Crunchie, Cadbury's*	1 Pot/500ml	710	142	2.3	19.4	12.5	0.0
Dairy Cornish, Tesco*	1 Serving/49g	112	228	3.2	24.7	12.3	0.1
Dairy, Flavoured	1oz/28g	50	179	3.5	24.7	8.0	0.0
Dairy Milk, Cadbury's*	1 Stick/120ml	286	238	3.5	25.9	14.0	0.0
Dairy, Pizza Hut*	1 Portion/141.7g	273	192	4.6	23.3	8.9	0.2
Dairy, Vanilla	1oz/28g	54	194	3.6	24.4	9.8	0.0
Demon Chocolate, M & S*	1 Serving/79g	208	263	3.7	37.1	11.1	0.6
Dulce de Leche, Bar, Haagan-Daaz*	1 Bar/105g	370	352	3.8	32.3	22.9	0.0
Flake, Cadbury's*	1 Serving/125ml	204	163	2.4	19.6	8.8	0.0
Heavenly Vanilla, Cadbury's*	1 Serving/250ml	355	142	2.5	12.8	9.3	0.0
Knickerbocker Glory	1oz/28g	31	112	1.5	16.4	5.0	0.2
Lemon Pie, Haagen-Dazs*	1oz/28g	73	262	3.9	24.5	16.3	0.0
Light Chocolate Ices, Co-Op*	1 Ice/62g	121	195	2.0	18.0	13.0	0.5

ICE CREAM,	Measure WEIGHT/INFO	per Measure KCAL	Nutrition Values per 100g / 100ml KCAL	PROT	CARB	FAT	FIBRE
Magic Maple, M & S*	1 Ice Cream/93g	259	278	2.9	39.0	12.3	0.6
Magnum Moments, Wall's*	1 Serving/18ml	58	323	4.0	30.0	20.8	0.0
Maple & Walnut American, Sainsbury's*	1/8 Pot/68g	121	179	3.1	25.6	7.2	0.2
Maple Brazil, Thorntons*	1oz/28g	66	236	4.1	24.4	13.6	0.0
Mars, Mars*	1 Bar/75g	260	346	5.1	37.2	19.7	0.0
Mint Choc Chip, Organic, Iceland*	1oz/28g	55	197	4.7	25.8	8.3	0.0
Mint Choc Chip Soft Scoop, Asda*	1 Serving/46g	86	187	2.9	24.0	9.0	0.3
Mint Ripple, Good Choice, Iceland*	1 Scoop/50g	59	117	3.0	21.7	2.1	0.1
Mint, Thorntons*	1oz/28g	66	237	4.0	25.0	13.4	0.0
Mocha Coffee Indulgence, Sainsbury's*	¼ Pot/82g	178	217	3.2	22.1	12.9	0.1
Monster Mint, Sainsbury's*	1/8 Pot/67g	121	180	3.0	26.3	6.9	0.3
Neapolitan Brick, Co-Op*	1oz/28g	43	155	3.0	20.0	7.0	0.2
Neapolitan Easy Serve, Co-Op*	1oz/28g	42	150	3.0	20.0	7.0	0.2
Neapolitan, Iceland*	1oz/28g	46	164	3.0	21.3	7.4	0.0
Neapolitan, Organic, Iceland*	1oz/28g	55	196	4.2	26.4	8.2	0.0
Neapolitan, Soft Scoop, M & S*	1 Scoop/65g	120	185	3.8	23.9	8.2	0.1
Non-Dairy, Mixes	1oz/28g	51	182	4.1	25.1	7.9	0.0
Non-Dairy, Reduced Calorie	1oz/28g	33	119	3.4	13.7	6.0	0.0
Non-Dairy, Vanilla	1oz/28g	50	178	3.2	23.1	8.7	0.0
Peach Melba, Soft Scoop, M & S*	1oz/28g	46	165	2.8	21.4	7.6	0.3
Picnic, Cadbury's*	1 Cone/125ml	258	207	3.4	28.9	9.4	0.3
Praline & Chocolate, Thorntons*	1oz/28g	87	309	4.6	21.3	22.9	0.6
Pralines & Cream, Haagen-Dazs*	1oz/28g	77	276	4.2	26.2	17.2	0.0
Rage Chocolate With Caramel Sauce, Treats*	1 Ice Cream/60g	177	295	3.3	30.9	17.5	0.0
Raspberry & Shortcake, Co-Op*	1oz/28g	64	230	3.0	23.0	14.0	0.3
Raspberry, Easy Serve, Co-Op*	1oz/28g	43	152	2.5	22.3	5.9	0.0
Raspberry Ripple Brick, Tesco*	1 Serving/48g	71	148	2.6	20.8	6.0	0.2
Raspberry Ripple, Co-Op*	1oz/28g	45	160	3.0	23.0	7.0	0.2
Raspberry Ripple, Organic, Iceland*	1oz/28g	50	180	4.8	22.6	7.8	0.0
Raspberry Ripple, Soft Scoop, Asda*	1 Scoop/46g	75	164	2.5	25.0	6.0	0.0
Raspberry Ripple, Soft Scoop, Tesco*	2 Scoops/50g	79	157	2.5	23.0	6.1	0.2
Really Creamy Chocolate, Asda*	1 Serving/100g	227	227	4.1	28.0	11.0	0.4
Rocky Road, Sainsbury's*	1/8 Pot/67g	137	205	3.8	30.9	7.3	1.0
Rum & Raisin, Organic, Iceland*	1oz/28g	55	195	4.5	28.1	7.2	0.0
Screwball, Co-Op*	1 Lolly/95g	190	200	2.0	31.0	7.0	0.0
Screwball, Farmfoods*	1 Lolly/72ml	101	177	3.3	27.1	6.1	0.0
Screwball, Safeway*	1 Serving/65g	129	198	3.1	24.5	9.7	0.6
Screwball, Tesco*	1 Screwball/61g	116	190	2.9	25.2	8.6	0.3
Smarties, Nestle*	1 Serving/50g	125	250	3.6	32.3	11.9	0.2
Strawberries & Cream, Deliciously Dairy, Co-Op*	1oz/28g	46	165	3.0	24.0	6.0	0.3
Strawberry & Cream, Organic, Sainsbury's*	1 Serving/100g	193	193	3.6	22.6	9.8	0.4
Strawberry Cheesecake, Haagen-Dazs*	1oz/28g	74	266	3.9	26.5	16.1	0.0
Strawberry, Fromage Frais, Asda*	1 Pot/46g	87	190	3.7	28.0	7.0	0.3
Strawberry, Haagen-Dazs*	1oz/28g	67	241	4.0	21.5	15.5	0.0
Strawberry, Thorntons*	1oz/28g	52	185	3.2	22.5	9.3	0.1
Strawberry, Weight Watchers*	1 Pot/57g	81	142	2.5	23.4	3.9	0.2
Toffee Creme, Haagen-Dazs*	1oz/28g	74	265	4.5	26.7	15.6	0.0
Toffee, Deliciously Dairy, Co-Op*	1oz/28g	45	160	3.0	21.0	7.0	0.2
Toffee Fudge, Soft Scoop, Asda*	1 Serving/50g	93	185	2.6	28.0	7.0	0.0
Toffee, Somerfield*	1 Serving/75g	172	229	3.4	33.2	9.2	0.9
Toffee, Thorntons*	1oz/28g	61	218	4.1	24.5	11.6	0.0
Toffee, Too Good To Be True, Wall's*	1fl oz/30ml	23	75	2.2	14.9	0.4	0.1
Toffee, Weight Watchers*	1 Serving/100ml	93	93	1.5	14.9	2.7	0.1
Traditional Cornish Blackberry, M & S*	1oz/28g	61	218	2.3	28.0	10.8	0.3

ICE CREAM,	Measure WEIGHT/INFO	per Measure KCAL	Nutrition Values per 100g / 100ml KCAL	PROT	CARB	FAT	FIBRE
Traditional Cornish Strawberry, M & S*	1oz/28g	64	229	2.3	29.7	11.2	0.2
Vanilla Brick, Co-Op*	1oz/28g	45	160	3.0	21.0	7.0	0.2
Vanilla Choc Fudge, Haagen-Dazs*	1oz/28g	75	267	4.3	23.5	17.2	0.0
Vanilla, COU, M & S*	¼ Pot/79g	111	140	1.7	25.9	2.8	0.8
Vanilla, Criminally Creamy, Co-Op*	1oz/28g	60	215	3.0	18.0	15.0	0.1
Vanilla Dairy, Finest, Tesco*	1 Serving/92g	227	247	4.5	18.0	17.4	0.3
Vanilla, Deliciously Dairy, Co-Op*	1oz/28g	49	175	3.0	23.0	8.0	0.2
Vanilla, Easy Serve, Co-Op*	1oz/28g	39	140	3.0	18.0	7.0	0.2
Vanilla, Everyday, Co-Op*	1oz/28g	41	145	3.0	18.0	7.0	0.2
Vanilla Flavour, Budgens*	1oz/28g	45	159	3.0	21.7	6.7	0.1
Vanilla Flavour, Soft Scoop, Sainsbury's*	1 Serving/70g	111	159	3.0	21.7	6.7	0.1
Vanilla, Haagen-Dazs*	1oz/28g	70	250	4.5	19.7	17.1	0.0
Vanilla, Light Soft Scoop, 25% Less Fat, Morrisons*	1 Scoop/50g	75	150	2.9	23.2	5.0	0.2
Vanilla, Organic, Iceland*	1oz/28g	61	217	4.5	22.2	12.2	0.0
Vanilla, Organic, Sainsbury's*	1 Serving/85g	176	207	4.3	20.5	12.0	0.1
Vanilla, SmartPrice, Asda*	1 Scoop/40g	55	137	2.8	19.0	6.0	0.2
Vanilla, Soft Scoop, 25% Less Fat, Asda*	1oz/28g	42	149	2.9	23.0	5.0	0.0
Vanilla, Soft Scoop, Light, 94% Fat Free, Wall's*	1 Serving/100ml	80	80	1.4	12.4	2.9	0.1
Vanilla, Soft Scoop, Tesco*	1oz/28g	39	138	2.7	21.6	4.5	0.2
Vanilla, Thorntons*	1oz/28g	63	225	4.9	20.5	13.6	0.0
Vanilla, Value, Tesco*	1 Serving/56g	75	134	2.7	18.3	5.5	0.2
Viennetta, Biscuit Caramel, Walls*	1/6th/58g	183	315	3.3	27.8	20.9	0.0
Viennetta, Cappuccino, Wall's*	1 Serving/75g	191	255	3.5	22.0	17.0	0.0
Viennetta, Mint, Wall's*	1 Serving/80g	204	255	3.4	23.0	16.6	0.0
Viennetta, Strawberry Cheesecake Biscuit, Wall's*	1 Serving/100g	305	305	3.5	28.1	20.7	0.0
Viennetta, Strawberry, Walls*	1 Serving/80g	204	255	3.4	22.1	16.8	0.0
Viennetta, Vanilla, Wall's*	¼ Bar/80gg	204	255	3.3	23.0	16.7	0.0
Virtuous Vanilla & Strawberry, Weight Watchers*	1 Serving/100ml	81	81	1.4	13.3	2.2	0.1
Voluptuous Vanilla, COU, M & S*	¼ Pot/125ml	175	140	1.7	25.9	2.8	0.8
Ice Cream Wafers, Cornet, Askeys*	1 Cornet/4g	15	370	11.0	77.0	2.5	0.0
White Vanilla Flavour, Soft Scoop, Sainsbury's*	1oz/28g	38	136	2.9	18.8	5.5	0.2
White Vanilla, Soft Scoop, Tesco*	1oz/28g	46	164	3.1	21.8	7.1	0.1
Zesty Lemon Meringue, COU, M & S*	¼ Pot/73g	120	165	2.6	33.0	2.5	0.5
ICE CREAM CONE,							
Average, Ice Cream Cone	1 Cone/75g	140	186	3.5	25.5	8.5	0.0
Carousel Wafer Company*	1 Cone/2g	7	342	12.6	65.0	3.7	0.0
Choc 'n' Nut, Farmfoods*	1 Cone/120ml	183	278	5.0	33.0	14.0	1.0
Chocolate & Nut, Co-Op*	1 Cone/110g	307	279	3.9	31.0	15.5	0.6
Chocolate & Vanilla, Good Choice, Iceland*	1 Cone/110ml	161	146	2.7	22.9	6.5	0.8
Chocolate & Vanilla, M & S*	1oz/28g	83	295	4.2	31.8	17.0	0.7
Chocolate Flavour, Somerfield*	1 Cone/110ml	329	299	4.0	38.0	15.0	0.0
Chocolate, M & S*	1oz/28g	94	335	4.0	28.0	23.0	2.3
Chocolate, Vanilla & Hazelnut, Sainsbury's*	1 Cone/62g	190	306	4.5	33.9	16.9	0.6
Cone, Haagen-Dazs*	1oz/28g	85	303	4.7	25.5	20.3	0.0
Cornetto, Wall's*	1 Cone/75g	195	260	3.7	34.5	12.9	0.0
Creme Egg, Cadbury's*	1 Cone/115ml	270	235	2.9	29.3	11.6	0.0
Extreme Raspberry, Cornetto, Nestle*	1 Cornetto/88g	220	250	2.5	36.0	10.0	0.2
Flake 99, Cadbury's*	1 Cone/125ml	204	163	2.4	19.6	8.8	0.0
Flake, Cadbury's*	1 Cone/130g	298	229	3.5	28.0	12.2	0.5
McDonald's*	1 Cone/98g	157	160	4.5	24.4	5.0	0.0
Mini, Tesco*	1 Cone/48g	152	316	4.1	31.5	19.3	0.8
Mint Choc Chip, Iceland*	1 cone/72g	210	292	3.3	40.4	13.0	1.0
Sticky Toffee, Farmfoods*	1 Cone/120ml	177	272	3.2	36.0	12.8	2.0
Strawberry & Vanilla, Farmfoods*	1 Cone/120ml	170	257	3.0	32.0	13.0	2.0

I

ICE CREAM CONE,	Measure WEIGHT/INFO	per Measure KCAL	KCAL	PROT	CARB	FAT	FIBRE
Strawberry & Vanilla, Iceland*	1 Serving/70g	182	260	3.3	37.5	10.8	0.7
Strawberry & Vanilla, M & S*	1oz/28g	81	290	4.2	30.9	16.5	0.7
Strawberry & Vanilla, Sainsbury's*	1 Cone/62g	153	247	2.8	36.5	10.0	0.3
Strawberry, BGTY, Sainsbury's*	1 Cone/69g	151	219	2.6	37.5	6.5	1.3
Strawberry, Co-Op*	1 Cone/110g	283	257	3.5	33.6	12.1	0.5
Strawberry, M & S*	1oz/28g	74	263	3.5	31.1	14.0	0.4
Strawberry, Somerfield*	1 Cone/110g	299	272	3.0	40.0	11.0	0.0
Sweets, Tesco*	1 Bag/60g	197	328	6.0	75.8	0.1	0.0
Toffee Flavoured, Somerfield*	1 Cone/110ml	320	291	4.0	39.0	14.0	0.0
Tropical, GFY, Asda*	1 Cone/100g	135	135	2.6	20.0	5.0	0.3
With Flake, McDonald's*	1 Cone/107g	204	191	4.8	27.0	7.2	0.0
ICE CREAM ROLL,							
Artic	1 Portion/70g	140	200	4.1	33.3	6.6	0.0
Basics, Somerfield*	1/6 Roll/110ml	233	212	4.0	35.0	6.0	0.0
M & S*	1oz/28g	60	215	3.6	35.2	6.7	0.0
Mini, Cadbury's*	1 Roll/45ml	99	220	3.4	24.3	13.1	0.0
Tesco*	¼ Roll/57g	131	230	3.7	34.5	8.6	0.4
ICE LOLLY,							
Assorted, Farmfoods*	1 Lolly/56ml	35	62	0.0	15.6	0.0	0.0
Assorted, Safeway*	1 Lolly/31ml	26	85	0.0	20.9	0.0	0.1
Blackcurrant, Ribena*	1 Lolly/52ml	41	79	0.0	19.2	0.0	0.0
Blackcurrant Split, Iceland*	1 Lolly/75g	61	81	1.1	12.0	3.2	0.1
Choc & Almond, Mini, Tesco*	1 Lolly/31g	103	331	4.4	24.8	23.8	0.9
Chocolate, Plain, Mini, Tesco*	1 Lolly/31g	94	304	3.1	24.8	21.4	1.2
Chocolate, Pooh Stick, Nestle*	1 Lolly/40g	36	89	2.1	12.9	3.6	0.0
Cola Lickers, Farmfoods*	1 Lolly/56ml	37	68	0.0	17.0	0.0	0.0
Elderflower,Tubes, Frozen, M & S*	1oz/28g	23	82	0.1	20.5	0.1	0.2
Exotic Fruit, Tesco*	1 Lolly/31.5g	41	131	1.8	26.4	2.0	0.6
Exotic Split, Bars, M & S*	1oz/28g	36	127	2.5	25.0	1.9	0.4
Fab, Nestle*	1 Lolly/57g	82	144	0.8	23.7	4.9	0.0
Frenzy, Farmfoods*	1 Lolly/92ml	235	255	3.1	23.1	16.8	0.6
Fruit Assorted, Basics, Somerfield*	1 Lolly/56ml	32	58	0.0	15.0	0.0	0.0
Fruit, Assorted, Waitrose*	1 Lolly/73g	59	81	0.0	20.0	0.0	0.1
Fruit Fusion, Mini, Farmfoods*	1 Lolly/45ml	36	79	0.2	19.2	0.1	0.2
Fruit Luxury, Mini, Co-Op*	1 Lolly/45g	59	130	2.0	18.0	6.0	0.2
Fruit Pastille, Rowntree's*	1 Lolly/65ml	59	90	0.0	21.0	0.0	0.0
Fruit, Red, Tesco*	1 Lolly/31.5g	40	128	1.8	25.6	2.0	0.6
Fruit Split, Assorted, Co-Op*	1 Lolly/73g	80	110	1.0	20.0	3.0	0.1
Fruit Splits, Assorted, Somerfield*	1 Split/73ml	74	102	0.0	18.0	3.0	0.0
Lemon & Lime, Mini Bar, M & S*	1 Bar/50g	48	95	0.1	23.6	0.1	0.2
Lemon & Lime, Tubes, Frozen, M & S*	1oz/28g	27	95	0.1	23.6	0.1	0.2
Milk Chocolate & Crisped Wheat, Co-Op*	1 Lolly/110g	259	235	3.0	28.0	12.0	0.7
Milk Flavour, Farmfoods*	1 Lolly/50ml	91	182	2.8	20.1	10.1	0.1
Orange & Lemon Splits, Farmfoods*	1 Lolly/56ml	56	124	1.6	19.8	4.3	0.2
Orange Juice, Bar, M & S*	1 Bar/75g	65	86	0.5	21.0	0.0	0.1
Orange Juice, Co-Op*	1 Lolly/73g	51	70	0.4	17.0	0.1	0.1
Orange Juice, Freshly Squeezed, Finest,Tesco*	1 Lolly/80ml	89	111	0.7	27.0	0.0	0.0
Orange Juice, Safeway*	1 Lolly/73ml	62	85	0.7	20.4	0.1	0.0
Orange Juice, Tropicana*	1 Lolly/50g	43	85	0.5	20.7	0.0	0.0
Orange Maid, Nestle*	1 Lolly/73ml	66	91	0.5	21.6	0.0	0.0
Orange, Real Juice, Sainsbury's*	1 Lolly/72ml	63	88	0.7	21.0	0.1	0.1
Orange Real Juice, Tesco*	1 Lolly/32g	25	78	0.6	18.7	0.0	0.3
Pineapple Split, Iceland*	1 Ice Lolly/75g	89	118	1.4	18.5	4.6	0.1
Polar Snappers, Double, Farmfoods*	1 Lolly/60ml	40	66	0.0	16.5	0.0	0.0

Nutrition Values per 100g / 100ml

I

	Measure WEIGHT/INFO	per Measure KCAL	Nutrition Values per 100g / 100ml KCAL	PROT	CARB	FAT	FIBRE
ICE LOLLY,							
Raspberry, Real Fruit Juice, Sainsbury's*	1 Lolly/72g	62	86	0.3	21.0	0.1	0.1
Real Fruit, Dairy Split, Sainsbury's*	1 Serving/73ml	100	137	2.1	22.8	4.2	0.1
Real Fruit Juice, Rocket, BPC, Sainsbury's*	1 Lolly/58ml	45	77	0.2	19.1	0.0	0.1
Refresher, Bassett's*	1 Lolly/40g	47	117	2.7	22.2	2.7	0.3
Rocket, Co-Op*	1 Lolly/60g	42	70	0.0	17.0	0.0	0.0
Strawberry & Banana, Smoothies, Sainsbury's*	1 Lolly/60g	100	166	1.5	28.0	5.3	0.2
Strawberry & Vanilla, 99% Fat Free, So-Lo, Iceland*	1 Lolly/92g	98	107	2.3	23.5	0.4	2.2
Strawberry Split, Co-Op*	1 Lolly/71ml	75	105	1.0	17.0	3.0	0.1
Traffic Light, Co-Op*	1 Lolly/52g	55	105	0.4	25.0	0.8	0.0
Tropical Fruit, Starburst, Mars*	1 Lolly/93ml	94	101	0.3	24.8	0.1	0.0
Vanilla, Pooh Stick, Nestle*	1 Lolly/40g	34	86	1.9	12.9	3.5	0.0
Wonka Super Sour Tastic, Nestle*	1 Serving/60ml	84	140	0.0	26.1	3.6	0.0
INDIAN							
Channa Masala, Sainsbury's*	1 Serving/149g	165	111	4.2	12.4	4.9	3.3
Daal, Sainsbury's*	1 Pack/300g	264	88	3.7	8.4	4.4	0.7
Meal For One, 5% Fat, Morrisons*	1 Pack/500g	560	112	5.5	15.3	3.2	0.8
Meal For One, GFY, Asda*	1 Serving/495g	644	130	8.0	14.0	4.7	1.0
Meal For One, HE, Tesco*	1 Pack/420g	437	104	7.4	14.0	2.1	1.4
Menu, COU, M & S*	1 Meal/550g	413	75	8.4	7.5	1.2	2.1
Menu Meal For Two, Tesco*	1 Serving/537g	811	151	6.3	17.0	6.4	0.8
Snack Selection, Safeway*	1 Serving/170g	347	204	4.0	25.8	9.4	1.9
Sweets, Waitrose*	1 Serving/125g	511	409	6.7	54.7	18.8	1.4
Takeaway, Ready Meals, M & S*	1oz/28g	42	150	6.7	15.3	7.1	1.5
INDONESIAN Nasi Goreng, Asda*	1 Pack/360g	778	216	7.4	32.3	6.3	1.3
IRON BRU, Diet, Barr's*	1 Can/330ml	2	1	0.0	0.0	0.0	0.0

I

JALFREZI,	Measure WEIGHT/INFO	per Measure KCAL	Nutrition Values per 100g / 100ml KCAL	PROT	CARB	FAT	FIBRE
Chicken, Safeway*	1 Pack/333g	360	108	12.1	4.5	4.6	1.3
Chicken, Sainsbury's*	1 Pack/400g	436	109	12.1	3.4	5.2	1.7
Chicken With Basmati Rice, Eat Smart, Safeway*	1 Pack/390g	351	90	5.7	11.2	2.0	1.1
Chicken With Pilau Rice, BGTY, Sainsbury's*	1 Pack/450g	432	96	7.0	14.3	1.2	0.8
Chicken With Pilau Rice, Tesco*	1 Pack/400g	408	102	5.3	13.3	3.0	0.9
Pilau Rice, Ready Meals, Patak's*	1oz/28g	37	131	7.8	13.5	5.3	0.9
Vegetable, Eastern Indian, Sainsbury's*	1 Pack/400g	208	52	3.4	2.0	3.4	1.7
Vegetable, Take Away Menu For 1, BGTY, Sainsbury's*	1 Pack/148g	43	29	1.8	5.4	0.0	2.3
JAM,							
Apricot & Peach, 25% Less Sugar, Asda*	1 Tsp/15g	28	184	0.5	45.4	0.1	1.1
Apricot, Baxters*	1 Tsp/15g	32	210	0.0	53.0	0.0	0.8
Apricot, Frank Cooper*	1 Tsp/15g	44	242	0.4	60.1	0.0	0.7
Apricot, Fruit, Asda*	1 Serving/20g	37	183	0.5	45.0	0.5	0.0
Apricot, Grandessa, Aldi*	1 Serving/25g	64	255	0.4	63.0	0.0	0.7
Apricot, Luxury, Baxters*	1 Tsp/15g	38	252	0.0	63.0	0.0	8.0
Apricot, Reduced Sugar, Sainsbury's*	1 Tsp/15g	29	190	0.4	47.0	0.1	0.8
Apricot, Sainsbury's*	1 Tsp/15g	40	264	0.3	65.7	0.0	0.8
Apricot, Tesco*	Thin Spead/7g	19	265	0.3	65.0	0.0	0.7
Apricot, Thick, Rhapsodie de Fruit, St Dalfour*	1 Serving/20g	45	227	0.4	56.0	0.3	1.7
Black Cherry, Rhapsodie de Fruit, St Dalfour*	2 Tsp/30g	69	230	0.7	56.0	0.3	1.2
Blackcurrant, 25% Less Sugar, Asda*	1 Tsp/15g	27	180	0.5	45.5	0.0	1.8
Blackcurrant, Baxters*	1 Tsp/15g	32	210	0.0	53.0	0.0	1.3
Blackcurrant, Better For You, Morrisons*	1 Serving/10g	20	196	0.6	46.4	0.4	0.0
Blackcurrant, Co-Op*	1 Heaped Tsp/18g	45	250	0.2	63.0	0.0	0.9
Blackcurrant, Extra, Morrisons*	1 Serving/20g	51	253	0.3	63.0	0.0	2.7
Blackcurrant, Frank Cooper*	1 Tsp/15g	36	243	0.3	60.6	0.0	1.1
Blackcurrant, Luxury, Baxters*	1 Tsp/15g	38	252	0.0	63.0	0.0	1.4
Blackcurrant, Reduced Sugar, Sainsbury's*	1 Tsp/15g	29	190	0.4	47.0	0.1	1.4
Blackcurrant, Robertson's*	1 Tsp/7g	17	246	0.3	60.5	0.0	0.0
Blackcurrant, Tesco*	1 Tsp/15g	39	261	0.2	65.0	0.0	1.0
Blueberry & Blackberry, Baxters*	1 Tsp/15g	38	252	0.0	63.0	0.0	1.2
Country Berries, Luxury, Baxters*	1 Tsp/15g	38	252	0.0	63.0	0.0	1.1
Damson, Extra Fruit, Best, Hartley's*	1 Tsp/5g	12	244	0.2	60.8	0.0	0.0
Damson, Sainsbury's*	1 Serving/25g	40	160	0.4	39.6	0.0	0.4
Fruit With Edible Seeds	1 Tsp/15g	39	261	0.6	69.0	0.0	0.0
Golden Peach, Rhapsodie de Fruit, St Dalfour*	2 Tsp/20g	45	227	0.5	56.0	0.1	1.3
Kiwi & Goosberry, 66% Fruit, Asda*	1 Serving/30g	56	187	0.5	45.0	0.5	0.0
Mixed Fruit, Budgens*	1 Tbsp/15g	39	261	0.2	65.0	0.0	0.8
Mixed Fruit, SmartPrice, Asda*	1 Tbsp/15g	36	241	0.2	60.0	0.0	1.0
Mixed Fruit, Value, Tesco*	1 Tsp/5g	13	253	0.2	63.0	0.0	0.8
Original, Hartley's*	1 Tsp/15g	38	252	0.2	62.8	0.0	0.6
Raspberry, Baxters*	1 Tsp/15g	38	252	0.0	63.0	0.0	1.2
Raspberry, Classic, Robertson's*	1 Tsp/10g	25	247	0.3	60.8	0.0	0.0
Raspberry, Frank Cooper*	1 Tsp/15g	37	247	0.6	60.9	0.1	1.2
Raspberry, Reduced Sugar, Asda*	1 Tsp/15g	28	185	0.7	45.0	0.2	0.0
Raspberry, Reduced Sugar, Sainsbury's*	1 Tsp/15g	29	190	0.6	47.0	0.1	1.1
Raspberry, Seedless, Budgens*	1 Tbsp/15g	39	262	0.5	65.0	0.0	0.0
Raspberry, Seedless, Robertson's*	1 Tsp/10g	25	247	0.3	60.8	0.0	0.0
Raspberry, Seedless, Sainsbury's*	1 Tsp/15g	40	264	0.5	65.5	0.0	1.1
Raspberry, Seedless, Tesco*	1 Tsp/15g	38	254	0.5	63.0	0.0	0.0
Raspberry, Somerfield*	1 Tsp/15g	39	261	1.0	64.0	0.0	0.0
Reduced Sugar	1 Tsp/15g	18	123	0.5	31.9	0.1	0.8
Rhubarb & Ginger, Baxters*	1 Tsp/15g	32	210	0.0	53.0	0.0	0.6
Strawberry & Redcurrant, Reduced Sugar, Streamline*	1 Tsp/15g	29	192	0.4	46.8	0.3	0.0

JAM,	Measure WEIGHT/INFO	per Measure KCAL	Nutrition Values per 100g / 100ml KCAL	PROT	CARB	FAT	FIBRE
Strawberry, 25% Less Sugar, Asda*	1 Tsp/15g	28	184	0.4	45.5	0.1	0.9
Strawberry, 66% Fruit, Asda*	1 Serving/10g	19	187	0.5	45.0	0.5	0.0
Strawberry, Asda*	1 Tsp/15g	39	257	0.3	64.0	0.0	1.0
Strawberry, Baxters*	1 Tsp/15g	32	210	0.0	53.0	0.0	5.0
Strawberry, Best, Hartley's*	1 Serving/10g	24	244	0.4	60.6	0.0	0.0
Strawberry, Co-Op*	1 Tsp/15g	39	260	0.3	64.6	0.1	0.6
Strawberry, Frank Cooper*	1 Tsp/15g	37	248	0.4	61.5	0.0	0.5
Strawberry, Iceland*	1 Serving/15g	39	258	0.1	64.0	0.1	0.1
Strawberry, Light, Robertson's*	1 Tsp/15g	32	210	0.2	52.2	0.0	0.0
Strawberry, Luxury, Baxters*	1 Tsp/15g	38	252	0.0	63.0	0.0	0.5
Strawberry, Reduced Sugar, Bonne Maman*	1 Tsp/15g	28	184	0.5	45.0	0.2	0.0
Strawberry, Reduced Sugar, Sainsbury's*	1 Tbsp/15g	29	190	0.4	47.0	0.1	0.5
Strawberry, Rhapsodie de Fruit, St Dalfour*	1 Tsp/10g	23	227	0.4	56.0	0.1	0.0
Strawberry, Robertson's*	1 Tsp/10g	25	249	0.2	61.2	0.0	0.0
Strawberry, Safeway*	1 Tbsp/15g	39	261	0.3	64.6	0.1	0.6
Strawberry, Sainsbury's*	1 Serving/13g	33	252	0.3	62.7	0.0	0.6
Strawberry, Somerfield*	1 Tsp/15g	39	260	0.0	65.0	0.0	0.0
Strawberry, Tesco*	1 Heaped Tsp/20g	53	265	0.3	65.0	0.0	0.6
Strawberry, With Extra Fruit, Reduced Sugar, Streamline*	1 Tsp/5g	10	192	0.3	47.1	0.3	0.0
Wild Blackberry Jelly, Baxters*	1 Tsp/15g	32	210	0.0	53.0	0.0	1.2
JAMBALAYA,							
Cajun Chicken, BGTY, Sainsburys*	1 Serving/450g	536	119	6.4	14.6	3.9	1.0
COU, M & S*	1 Pack/400g	340	85	6.5	10.8	2.0	0.9
JELLIES, Blackcurrant, Thorntons*	1 Jelly/10g	30	300	0.1	75.0	0.0	0.0
JELLY BABIES,							
Bassett's*	1 Baby/6g	20	335	4.0	79.5	0.0	0.0
Co-Op*	1 Mini Jelly/4g	13	335	4.0	80.0	0.0	0.0
M & S*	1 Pack/125g	418	334	5.2	78.0	0.0	0.0
Mini, Waitrose*	1 Bag/125g	370	296	4.3	68.7	0.4	0.0
Somerfield*	1 Sweet/6g	21	343	4.7	80.7	0.0	0.0
Tesco*	1 Baby/6g	20	332	5.3	77.4	0.1	0.1
Tropical Fruit Flavours, Mini, Bassett's*	1 Baby/4.6g	13	336	4.0	79.9	0.0	0.0
JELLY BEANS, Rowntree's*	1 Pack/35g	128	367	0.0	91.8	0.0	0.0
JELLY BEARS, Co-Op*	1 Sweet/3g	10	325	6.0	76.0	0.1	0.0
JELLY,							
Blackcurrant, Made Up, Sainsbury's*	¼ Jelly/150g	98	65	1.2	15.1	0.0	0.0
Blackcurrant, Sugar Free, Rowntree's*	1 Pack/24g	73	305	66.5	0.3	0.0	0.4
Crystals, Black Cherry, Sugar Free, Bird's*	1oz/28g	92	330	61.0	9.1	0.1	0.0
Crystals, Lemon & Lime, Sugar Free, Bird's*	1oz/28g	92	330	62.5	7.3	0.2	0.0
Crystals, Peach & Pear, Sugar Free, Bird's*	1oz/28g	91	325	64.5	3.3	0.2	0.0
Double Cherry, Safeway*	1 Serving/100g	84	84	0.3	20.6	0.0	1.4
Fresh Fruit, M & S*	1 Pot/175g	131	75	0.2	18.4	0.1	0.3
Fruit Cocktail, M & S*	1oz/28g	31	110	0.4	16.4	4.7	0.3
Lemon, Co-Op*	1 Pack/135g	412	305	5.0	71.0	0.0	0.0
Lemon, Somerfield*	1 Pack/135g	393	291	6.0	66.0	0.0	0.0
Lime, Co-Op*	1 Pack/135g	397	294	5.5	68.1	0.1	1.0
Lime Flavour, Waitrose*	1 Square/11g	33	296	4.5	69.5	0.0	0.0
Lime, Somerfield*	1 Pack/135g	392	290	6.0	66.0	0.0	0.0
Made With Water	1oz/28g	17	61	1.2	15.1	0.0	0.0
Mandarin, Aroma, M & S*	1oz/28g	17	60	0.2	14.6	0.0	0.4
Orange, Co-Op*	1 Pack/135g	402	298	5.5	68.9	0.1	0.0
Orange Flavour, Somerfield*	1 Pack/128g	379	296	5.0	69.0	0.0	0.0
Orange, Somerfield*	1 Pack/135g	393	291	6.0	66.0	0.0	0.0
Peach, Co-Op*	1 Pack/135g	401	297	5.5	68.7	0.1	0.0

J

JELLY,	Measure WEIGHT/INFO	per Measure KCAL	Nutrition Values per 100g / 100ml KCAL	PROT	CARB	FAT	FIBRE
Pineapple, Co-Op*	1 Pack/135g	398	295	5.6	68.1	0.1	0.0
Raspberry & Rose, Aroma, M & S*	1oz/28g	14	50	0.2	11.9	0.2	0.4
Raspberry, Co-Op*	1 Pack/135g	402	298	5.5	68.9	0.1	0.0
Raspberry, M & S*	1 Serving/175g	109	62	0.3	14.6	0.3	0.0
Strawberry & Raspberry, Sainsbury's*	½ Pot/280g	230	82	0.2	20.2	0.0	1.2
Strawberry, Basics, Somerfield*	¼ Jelly/32g	95	296	5.0	69.0	0.0	0.0
Strawberry, Co-Op*	1 Pack/135g	402	298	5.5	69.1	0.1	0.0
Strawberry, Somerfield*	¼ Jelly/33.75g	99	291	6.0	66.0	0.0	0.0
Summer Fruit, Co-Op*	1 Pack/135g	401	297	5.5	68.7	0.1	0.0
Tropical Fresh Fruit, Eat Smart, Safeway*	1 Serving/185g	120	65	0.6	14.5	0.3	1.1
Wild Rowan, Baxters*	1oz/28g	75	268	0.0	67.0	0.0	0.0
JELLY TOTS, Rowntree's*	1 Pack/42g	145	346	0.1	86.5	0.0	0.0

J

KEBAB,	Measure WEIGHT/INFO	per Measure KCAL	Nutrition Values per 100g / 100ml KCAL	PROT	CARB	FAT	FIBRE
Barbecue Chicken Tikka, Mini, Somerfield*	1oz/28g	38	134	21.0	4.0	4.0	0.0
Cajun Salmon, Tesco*	1 Kebab/75g	100	133	19.8	3.9	4.2	1.3
Chicken, Honey & Mustard, M & S*	1oz/28g	41	145	16.7	8.2	4.8	1.0
Chicken Mango Flavour, Cooked, Waitrose*	1 Kebab/73g	86	118	24.1	4.5	0.4	0.1
Chicken, Thin Sliced, Heat 'n' Eat, Asda*	½ Pack/50g	92	184	15.0	3.9	12.0	1.1
Chicken With Jasmine Rice & Pineapple, ES, Safeway*	1 Pack/380g	380	100	5.8	16.5	1.2	1.2
Chicken With Sweet Chilli Sauce, Finest, Tesco*	½ Pack/175g	242	138	17.9	14.7	0.8	1.2
Chicken With Sweet Chilli Sauce, M & S*	1 Serving/165g	228	138	17.9	14.7	0.8	1.2
Chilli & Coriander Chicken Breast, COU, M & S*	½ Pack/200g	200	100	20.6	1.0	1.4	0.0
Chinese Chicken, Mini, M & S*	1 Kebab/11g	24	215	19.5	5.1	12.9	0.6
Chinese Salmon, Iceland*	1 Kebab/75g	115	153	23.8	4.1	4.6	1.6
Citrus Tikka Chicken Breast, Sainsbury's*	1 Kebab/61g	79	129	25.6	5.4	0.5	0.9
Citrus Tikka Lamb Kofta, Sainsbury's*	1 Kebab/84g	199	235	18.1	9.8	13.7	2.6
Doner, Heat 'n' Eat Thin Sliced, Asda*	1 Pack/100g	196	196	16.7	8.4	10.6	1.7
Greek Style Lamb, Sainsbury's*	1 Kebab/168g	428	255	17.4	7.7	17.0	2.3
Green Pesto Chicken Breast, COU, M & S*	1 Serving/200g	160	80	15.1	1.5	1.4	1.0
Green Thai Chicken Waitrose*	1 Serving/180g	223	124	20.5	1.4	4.0	1.4
Lamb Kofta With A Mint & Coriander Raita, Safeway*	1 Pack/290g	632	218	16.9	8.4	13.0	1.2
Mango Salsa Chicken Breast, Sainsbury's*	1 Kebab/60g	85	142	26.3	5.5	1.6	0.6
Pork & Pepper, Asda*	½ Pack/170g	250	147	25.0	5.0	3.0	1.4
Shish In Pitta Bread With Salad	1oz/28g	137	491	13.8	61.4	21.1	2.9
Shish, M & S*	1 Serving/100g	185	185	13.8	1.6	13.5	0.6
Shish With Onions & Peppers	1oz/28g	54	192	3.2	27.6	8.4	0.3
Spicy Tomato Creole King Prawn, M & S*	1 Pack/240g	240	100	14.3	2.9	3.3	0.7
Sticky Barbecue Chicken Thigh, M & S*	1 Kebab/100g	160	160	15.6	7.4	7.5	0.8
Sweet Oriental Chicken Breast, COU, M & S*	½ Pack/200g	220	110	20.8	4.3	1.0	0.1
Sweetcorn, Tesco*	1 Kebab/130g	74	57	2.0	9.9	1.0	0.9
Tandoori, M & S*	1oz/28g	34	120	23.3	1.0	2.5	0.0
Thai Style Chicken, Eat Smart, Safeway*	1 Kebab/85g	85	100	15.3	6.4	1.3	1.4
Tiger Prawn, Asda*	1oz/28g	17	59	14.6	0.0	0.1	0.0
Tikka Chicken, Mini, Somerfield*	1oz/28g	38	134	21.0	4.0	4.0	0.0
Tikka, Mini, M & S*	1 Kebab/11g	23	205	18.4	4.0	12.7	0.6
Tomato & Basil Chicken, Eat Smart, Safeway*	1 Kebab/71.5g	82	115	18.0	5.0	2.1	1.5
Vegetable, Asda*	1 Kebab/40g	25	63	1.8	4.5	4.3	2.4
Vegetable, Sainsbury's*	1 Kebab/100g	36	36	1.5	6.4	0.5	1.2
Vegetable, Tesco*	1 Kebab/120g	47	39	1.7	6.8	0.6	1.1
Zesty Lime & Coriander Chicken Breast, M & S*	1 Kebab/100g	125	125	20.8	0.5	4.4	0.4
KEDGEREE,							
Kedgeree, Average	1oz/28g	48	171	15.9	7.8	8.7	0.1
COU, M & S*	1 Pack/370g	426	115	7.9	14.4	2.6	0.8
Perfectly Balanced, Waitrose*	1 Pack/400g	368	92	7.0	10.8	2.3	0.6
Smoked Haddock, Big Dish, M & S*	1 Pack/450g	585	130	8.5	13.0	5.0	1.9
KETCHUP,							
BBQ, Heinz*	1 Serving/10g	14	137	1.3	31.3	0.3	0.3
Dip Pot, Burger King*	1 Pot/25g	27	107	1.0	24.7	0.1	0.6
Sachet, Burger King*	1 Sachet/15g	16	107	1.0	24.7	0.1	0.6
Tomato	1oz/28g	32	115	1.6	28.6	0.1	0.9
Tomato, 25% Less Sugar, Asda*	1 Tbsp/10g	7	71	1.6	16.0	0.1	0.0
Tomato, Budgens*	1oz/28g	36	127	2.3	29.2	0.1	0.6
Tomato, Daddies, HP*	1oz/28g	31	110	0.9	26.5	0.3	0.0
Tomato, Frank Cooper*	1 Sachet/12g	14	119	1.0	27.9	0.3	0.6
Tomato, Heinz*	1 Tbsp/15g	16	107	1.0	24.7	0.1	0.6
Tomato, McDonald's*	1 Portion/20g	26	131	1.4	31.2	0.1	0.0
Tomato, Organic, Evernat*	1oz/28g	26	92	1.0	22.0	0.0	0.0

	Measure WEIGHT/INFO	per Measure KCAL	Nutrition Values per 100g / 100ml KCAL	PROT	CARB	FAT	FIBRE
KETCHUP,							
Tomato, Sainsbury's*	1 Tbsp/15g	19	128	0.9	28.7	0.5	1.0
Tomato, SmartPrice, Asda*	1 Tbsp/10g	12	122	0.7	29.0	0.2	0.7
Tomato, Value, Tesco*	1 Tbsp/15ml	21	139	2.3	32.2	0.1	1.4
Wicked Orange, Heinz*	1 Serving/11g	12	108	1.0	24.7	0.1	0.6
KIDNEY,							
Lamb, Fresh, Sainsbury's*	1 Kidney/50g	94	188	23.7	0.1	10.3	0.0
Lamb, Fried	1oz/28g	74	264	6.2	40.7	8.2	2.3
Ox, Raw	1oz/28g	25	88	17.2	0.0	2.1	0.0
Pig, Fried	1oz/28g	77	275	10.5	53.4	1.6	2.3
Pig, Raw	1oz/28g	24	86	15.5	0.0	2.7	0.0
KIEV,							
Breaded, Fresh, Value, Bernard Matthews*	1 Kiev/125g	374	299	10.6	13.9	22.3	2.7
Cheese & Ham Chicken, Asda*	1 Kiev/150g	348	232	17.4	12.0	12.6	0.7
Cheese & Mushroom Chicken, Somerfield*	½ Pack/142g	294	207	14.0	15.0	11.0	0.0
Cheese & Smoked Ham Chicken, Sainsbury's*	1 Serving/136g	299	220	15.9	12.0	12.8	0.3
Cheesy Garlic, Meat Free, Sainsbury's*	1 Kiev/123g	263	214	17.3	10.6	11.4	3.0
Chicken, 25% Less Fat, Asda*	1 Kiev/132g	294	223	12.0	10.0	15.0	108.0
Chicken, Bernard Matthews*	1 Kiev/125g	374	299	10.6	13.9	22.3	2.7
Chicken, BGTY, Sainsbury's*	1 Kiev/125g	253	202	14.3	11.3	11.1	1.0
Chicken, Breaded, Mini, Family, Bernard Matthews*	1 Kiev/23g	46	199	15.7	12.1	9.8	0.0
Chicken Breast, Garlic Butter, Sun Valley*	1 Kiev/141g	436	309	13.2	11.8	23.2	0.9
Chicken, Cheese & Ham, Tesco*	1 Kiev/142g	338	238	16.3	11.3	14.2	0.6
Chicken, COU, M & S*	1 Pack/142g	163	115	18.4	8.2	1.2	0.8
Chicken, Creamy Pepper, Safeway*	1 Serving/133g	306	230	11.9	11.1	15.4	1.1
Chicken, Creamy Peppercorn, Tesco*	1 Serving/141g	303	215	12.8	8.1	14.6	1.5
Chicken, Garlic, Safeway*	1 Kiev/147g	413	281	12.9	11.2	20.5	0.9
Chicken, Grampian*	1 Serving/138g	313	227	11.9	15.5	13.0	0.9
Chicken, Mini, M & S*	1 Mini Kiev/39g	94	242	11.6	21.0	12.4	0.8
Chicken, Premium, M & S*	1 Kiev/150g	353	235	16.3	10.4	14.0	0.6
Chicken, Somerfield*	½ Pack/142g	398	280	12.0	13.0	20.0	0.0
Chicken, Tesco*	1oz/28g	70	251	16.7	8.8	16.5	1.1
Chicken Tikka Masala, Tesco*	1oz/28g	61	219	12.4	9.7	14.5	1.2
Chicken, Whole Breast, COU, M & S*	1 Serving/150g	188	125	15.8	10.8	1.8	0.5
Chicken With Cheese & Broccoli, Sainsbury's*	1 Serving/124g	260	210	15.6	8.6	12.5	1.5
Chicken With Garlic Butter, Tesco*	1 Kiev/125g	343	274	13.7	8.8	20.4	0.7
Creamy Garlic Chicken, Tesco*	1 Serving/142g	334	235	12.2	9.7	16.4	0.6
Garlic & Parsley Chicken, BGTY, Sainsbury's*	1 Kiev/133g	318	239	15.0	11.7	14.7	1.3
Garlic Butter Chicken, Lower Fat, Asda*	1 Kiev/136g	282	207	13.0	14.0	11.0	0.7
Garlic Butter Chicken, Safeway*	1 Kiev/115g	316	275	13.3	12.5	19.1	1.1
Garlic Butter, Sainsbury's*	1 Kiev/121g	289	239	13.0	11.8	15.5	0.5
Garlic Butter, Tesco*	1 Kiev/142g	462	325	14.4	22.1	19.9	0.8
Garlic Chicken, GFY, Asda*	1 Pack/138g	302	219	15.0	15.0	11.0	1.0
Ham & Cheese Chicken, Somerfield*	½ Pack/142g	294	207	14.0	14.0	11.0	0.0
Lemon Butter Chicken, Somerfield*	½ Pack/142g	409	288	12.0	12.0	21.0	0.0
Smokey Ham & Cheese, Asda*	1 Kiev/129g	262	203	13.0	13.0	11.0	3.0
Thai Chicken, Sainsbury's*	1 Kiev/133g	290	218	12.8	15.3	11.7	1.2
Tikka Chicken, Asda*	1 Kiev/150g	326	217	15.6	15.6	10.2	0.8
Vegetarian, Garlic Butter, Tesco*	1 Kiev/142g	462	325	14.4	22.1	19.9	0.8
Vegetarian, Garlic, Safeway*	1 Serving/142g	423	298	13.2	20.3	18.2	0.7
KING PRAWN,							
& Mushroom Provencale, M & S*	½ Pack/185g	120	65	7.2	3.9	2.5	0.9
Creole, With Vegetable Rice, COU, M & S*	1 Pack/400g	300	75	4.5	13.3	0.6	0.7
Ginger & Spring Onion, Budgens*	1 Pack/350g	151	43	5.9	2.1	1.2	0.7
Japanese Noodle Box, M & S*	1 Pack/300g	330	110	5.8	16.0	2.7	1.6

K

	Measure WEIGHT/INFO	per Measure KCAL	Nutrition Values per 100g / 100ml KCAL	PROT	CARB	FAT	FIBRE
KING PRAWN,							
Salad, Thai Style, M & S*	1 Serving/295g	266	90	4.4	12.6	2.5	1.3
KIPPER,							
Baked	1oz/28g	57	205	25.5	0.0	11.4	0.0
Boil In Bag, Boiled	1oz/28g	66	237	20.0	0.0	17.4	0.0
Fillets, BGTY, Sainsbury's*	1 Pack/220g	691	314	18.0	0.1	26.9	0.1
Fillets, In Brine, John West*	1 Can/140g	269	192	21.0	0.0	12.0	0.0
Fillets, In Sunflower Oil, John West*	1 Can/140g	321	229	19.0	0.0	17.0	0.0
Fillets, Sainsbury's*	½ Pack/150g	383	255	20.1	0.1	19.4	0.0
Fillets, Smoked Scottish, Macrae*	1 Pack/171g	375	219	20.4	0.0	15.1	0.0
Fillets, With Butter, Farmfoods*	1oz/28g	64	229	17.5	0.0	17.7	0.0
Grilled	1oz/28g	71	255	20.1	0.0	19.4	0.0
Raw	1oz/28g	64	229	17.5	0.0	17.7	0.0
KISSES, Hershey*	1 Kiss/5g	28	561	7.0	59.0	32.0	0.0
KIT KAT,							
2 Finger, Nestle*	2 Finger Bar/21g	106	506	6.7	60.6	26.3	0.0
4 Fingers, Nestle*	4 Fingers/48g	243	507	6.8	60.2	26.5	1.2
Chunky, Nestle*	1 Bar/55g	283	514	6.5	59.8	27.6	0.0
Individual Bars, Nestle*	1 Bar/28g	144	513	6.6	60.4	27.2	0.0
Mini, Nestle*	1 Bar/15g	75	502	7.5	59.4	26.0	0.0
Mint, Nestle*	4 Finger Bar/48g	243	506	6.0	61.4	26.3	1.1
Orange, 2 Finger, Nestle*	2 Finger Bar/20g	101	506	6.7	60.6	26.3	0.0
White, Nestle*	1 Chunky Bar/53g	278	525	8.0	58.3	28.9	0.0
KIWI FRUIT,							
Fresh, Raw	1oz/28g	14	49	1.1	10.6	0.5	1.9
Weighed With Skin	1 Kiwi/60g	25	42	1.0	9.1	0.4	1.6
KOHL RABI,							
Boiled In Salted Water	1oz/28g	5	18	1.2	3.1	0.2	1.9
Raw	1oz/28g	6	23	1.6	3.7	0.2	2.2
KORMA,							
Chicken & Basmati Rice, Tesco*	1 Pot/350g	588	168	4.3	16.9	9.3	2.3
Chicken & Pilau Rice, BGTY, Sainsbury's*	1 Pack/450g	513	114	9.0	14.6	2.2	1.2
Chicken & Pilau Rice, GFY, Asda*	1 Pack/400g	600	150	8.0	16.0	6.0	1.3
Chicken & Pilau Rice, Somerfield*	1 Pack/340g	687	202	9.0	16.0	11.0	0.0
Chicken & Rice, 95% Fat Free, Bird's Eye*	1 Pack/370g	444	120	6.2	19.6	1.9	1.1
Chicken & Rice, COU, M & S*	1 Pack/400g	420	105	8.1	13.7	1.7	0.5
Chicken & Rice, HE, Tesco*	1 Pack/420g	487	116	7.2	17.9	1.8	0.3
Chicken & Rice, Organic, Tesco*	1 Pack/450g	923	205	6.0	21.5	10.6	0.4
Chicken & Rice, Patak's*	1 Pack/370g	466	126	5.9	15.8	4.8	0.4
Chicken Coconut, Sainsbury's*	1 Pack/400g	664	166	13.0	5.3	10.3	1.6
Chicken, Creamy, Weight Watchers*	1 Pack/330g	343	104	6.6	12.0	3.3	0.5
Chicken, Indian Takeaway, Iceland*	1 Pack/400g	656	164	11.8	4.5	11.0	1.4
Chicken Meal, BGTY, Restaurant, Sainsbury's*	1 Serving/201g	223	111	15.0	4.0	4.1	1.2
Chicken, Safeway*	1 Pack/350g	648	185	14.1	8.4	10.6	2.0
Chicken, Sainsbury's*	1 Pack/400g	580	145	14.1	3.3	8.4	0.7
Chicken, Tesco*	1 Pack/350g	620	177	10.8	6.8	11.8	0.6
Chicken With Pilau Rice, Perfectly Balanced, Waitrose*	1 Pack/400g	528	132	8.9	18.3	2.6	1.1
Chicken With Pilau Rice, Sharwood's*	1 Pack/375g	566	151	6.7	15.4	7.0	0.9
Quorn	1oz/28g	39	140	3.7	16.7	7.0	0.0
Vegetable & Rice, Tesco*	1 Pack/450g	621	138	2.9	18.3	5.9	1.6
Vegetable, Sainsbury's*	1 Serving/200g	302	151	2.7	6.6	12.6	2.2
KRISPROLLS							
Golden Wheat, Pogen*	1 Serving/10g	41	410	11.0	72.0	8.5	4.0
Original Cracked Wheat, Pogen*	1 Piece/10g	38	380	12.0	67.0	7.0	9.0
KULFI	1oz/28g	119	424	5.4	11.8	39.9	0.6

K

KUMQUATS,	Measure WEIGHT/INFO	per Measure KCAL	Nutrition Values per 100g / 100ml KCAL	PROT	CARB	FAT	FIBRE
Canned, In Syrup	1oz/28g	39	138	0.4	35.4	0.5	1.7
Raw	1oz/28g	12	43	0.9	9.3	0.5	3.8

K

	Measure WEIGHT/INFO	per Measure KCAL	Nutrition Values per 100g / 100ml KCAL	PROT	CARB	FAT	FIBRE
LAGER,							
Lager	1 Pint/568ml	165	29	0.3	2.4	0.0	0.0
Amstel, Heinekin N V*	1 pint/568ml	227	40	0.5	3.0	0.0	0.0
Lager, Budweiser, Anheuser-Busch*	1 Bottle/330ml	133	40	0.3	2.9	0.0	0.0
Export, Fosters*	1 Pint/568ml	210	37	0.0	2.2	0.0	0.0
French Premier, Somerfield*	1 Bottle/250ml	108	43	0.0	4.0	0.0	0.0
Heineken, Heineken N V*	1 Pint/568ml	256	45	0.5	3.0	0.0	0.0
Low Alcohol	1 Can/440ml	44	10	0.2	1.5	0.0	0.0
Miller Pilsner*	1 Bottle/500ml	150	30	0.3	2.4	0.0	0.0
Pilsner, German, Somerfield*	1 Bottle/250ml	73	29	1.0	0.0	0.0	0.0
Premium	1 Can/440ml	260	59	0.3	2.4	0.0	0.0
LAMB,							
Average, Trimmed Lean, Raw	1oz/28g	44	156	20.2	0.0	8.3	0.0
Chop, Leg, Bernard Matthews*	1oz/28g	55	196	18.4	0.0	13.6	0.0
Chop, Loin, Bernard Matthews*	1 Pack/600g	1476	246	18.4	0.0	13.6	0.0
Chop, M & S*	1oz/28g	56	200	16.9	2.4	13.5	0.0
Chop, Somerfield*	1oz/28g	78	277	18.0	0.0	23.0	0.0
Diced, HE, Tesco*	½ Pack/165g	215	130	20.1	0.0	5.5	0.0
Leg, Joint, M & Ss*	1 Joint/510g	612	120	18.4	1.0	5.2	0.0
Leg, Somerfield*	1oz/28g	60	215	26.0	0.0	12.0	0.0
Mince, New Zealand, Sainsbury's*	1 Serving/100g	257	257	21.4	0.0	19.0	0.4
Mince, Premium, Bernard Matthews*	1oz/28g	55	198	17.0	0.9	14.0	0.0
Mince, Raw	1oz/28g	55	196	19.1	0.0	13.3	0.0
Mince, Scottish, Tesco*	1oz/28g	71	254	17.2	0.0	20.4	0.0
Mince, Tesco*	1 Serving/150g	381	254	17.2	0.0	20.0	0.0
Minced, Frozen, Morrisons*	1oz/28g	68	242	18.0	0.0	19.0	0.0
Minced, M & S*	1oz/28g	43	155	15.6	2.0	9.4	0.3
Rack, Raw, Lean & Fat	1oz/28g	79	283	17.3	0.0	23.8	0.0
Shank, Sainsburys*	1 Serving/200g	188	94	13.2	3.1	3.8	0.3
Shoulder,	1oz/28g	88	316	20.0	0.0	26.0	0.0
Shoulder, Half, Bernard Matthews*	1oz/28g	73	262	15.9	0.0	22.1	0.0
Shoulder, Raw, Lean & Fat	1oz/28g	66	235	17.6	0.0	18.3	0.0
Steak, Asda*	1 Serving/100g	197	197	29.0	0.0	9.0	0.0
Steak, Bernard Matthews*	1 Steak/140g	151	108	18.2	0.7	3.6	0.0
Steak, BGTY, Sainsbury's*	1 Serving/125g	185	148	24.1	0.1	5.8	0.1
Steak, Leg, HE, Tesco*	1 Steak/150g	165	110	20.1	0.0	3.3	0.0
Stewing, Raw, Lean & Fat	1oz/28g	57	203	22.5	0.0	12.6	0.0
LAMB &,							
Pepper Koftas, Waitrose*	1 Kofta/138g	264	191	14.9	0.9	14.3	1.2
LAMB - CASSOULET, M & S*	1oz/28g	25	90	7.4	7.2	3.4	2.0
LAMB - DONER Sandwich, Steak, Farmfoods*	1oz/28g	84	300	15.0	2.3	25.6	0.0
LAMB - ESCALOPE, British, Tesco*	1 Piece/95g	105	110	20.1	0.0	3.3	0.0
LAMB - GRILL STEAK,							
Bird's Eye*	1 Grillsteak/71g	170	239	16.5	1.9	18.4	0.7
Prime, Asda*	1 Steak/63g	192	304	22.0	2.2	23.0	0.0
LAMB - GRILLED, Shoulder, Diced, Lean & Fat	1oz/28g	81	288	28.5	0.0	19.3	0.0
LAMB IN,							
Mint Gravy, Sliced, Sainsbury's*	1 Pack/125g	134	107	15.3	2.9	3.8	0.8
Minted Gravy, Shanks, Iceland*	1 Pack/400g	824	206	20.1	1.6	13.2	0.7
LAMB - INDIAN, Fillet, Somerfield*	1 Pack/300g	570	190	17.0	4.0	12.0	0.0
LAMB - MEDITERRANEAN,							
Shanks, Finest, Tesco*	1 Serving/404g	671	166	15.0	6.6	8.8	2.0
Style Sardinian, Tesco*	1 Serving/263g	295	112	9.3	2.8	7.1	0.7
LAMB - MINTED,							
Chop, Asda*	1 Serving/113g	312	276	26.0	2.6	18.0	0.0

	Measure WEIGHT/INFO	per Measure KCAL	Nutrition Values per 100g / 100ml KCAL	PROT	CARB	FAT	FIBRE
LAMB, MINTED,							
Grill Sticks, Asda*	1 Stick/57g	133	234	22.0	5.0	14.0	0.3
Steak, Leg, With Onion Gravy, Tesco*	1 Pack/400g	408	102	13.0	5.4	3.2	0.3
LAMB - MOUSSAKA,							
Finest, Tesco*	1 Pack/330g	521	158	7.7	9.1	10.1	2.0
Somerfield*	1 Pack/300g	480	160	7.4	8.7	10.6	2.1
LAMB - POT ROASTED, Leg, M & S*	1 Pack/625g	750	120	10.0	6.6	6.1	1.2
LAMB - ROAST,							
Bernard Matthews*	1 Pack/567g	777	137	16.0	0.1	13.5	0.9
In Gravy, Bird's Eye*	1 Pack/239g	160	67	8.1	3.8	2.2	0.1
Meal, Ready Meals, M & S*	1 Pack/340g	459	135	7.5	14.1	5.7	1.5
Minted, In Gravy, M & S*	1 Pack/200g	140	70	6.8	6.6	1.5	0.9
LAMB - ROASTED,							
Leg, Whole, Medium, Lean	1oz/28g	57	203	29.7	0.0	9.4	0.0
Leg, Whole, Medium, Lean & Fat	1oz/28g	67	240	28.1	0.0	14.2	0.0
Leg, Whole, New Zealand, Chilled, Lean	1oz/28g	58	207	28.8	0.0	10.2	0.0
Leg, Whole, New Zealand, Chilled, Lean & Fat	1oz/28g	64	230	28.0	0.0	13.1	0.0
Leg, Whole, Well Done, Lean	1oz/28g	58	208	31.3	0.0	9.2	0.0
Leg, Whole, Well Done, Lean & Fat	1oz/28g	68	242	29.8	0.0	13.6	0.0
Rack, Lean	1oz/28g	63	225	27.1	0.0	13.0	0.0
Rack, Lean & Fat	1oz/28g	102	363	23.0	0.0	30.1	0.0
Shoulder, Whole, Lean	1oz/28g	61	218	27.2	0.0	12.1	0.0
Shoulder, Whole, Lean & Fat	1oz/28g	83	298	24.7	0.0	22.1	0.0
LAMB - STEWED,							
Stewing, Lean	1oz/28g	67	240	26.6	0.0	14.8	0.0
Stewing, Lean & Fat	1oz/28g	78	279	24.4	0.0	20.1	0.0
LAMB WITH,							
Carrot & Swede Mash, Braised, Eat Smart, Safeway*	1 Pack/388g	330	85	7.6	7.4	2.4	1.4
Cherry Tomatoes & Mediterranean Style Veg, Leg, Finest, Tesco*	½ Pack/267g	240	90	7.4	7.9	3.2	0.5
Chunky Vegetables, Braised Shank, M & S*	½ Pack/425g	808	190	24.7	2.0	9.0	0.7
Redcurrant & Rosemary Sauce, Leg Joint, Sainsbury's*	1 Serving/100g	164	164	18.0	7.2	7.2	0.3
Sweet Mint Dressing, Joint, Tesco*	1 Serving/50g	97	193	19.9	1.8	11.8	0.6
LANGGOUSTINES, Shelled*	1oz/28g	27	97	19.4	0.0	0.1	0.0
LARD	1oz/28g	249	891	0.0	0.0	99.0	0.0
LATTE,							
'A' Mocha, Cafe Met*	1 Bottle/290ml	174	60	3.2	9.0	1.4	0.0
Cafe, M & S*	1 Serving/190g	143	75	4.3	8.3	2.8	0.0
Nescafe*	1 Sachet/21g	98	469	14.5	52.4	22.5	0.0
Single, Pret A Manger*	1 Serving/200ml	84	42	3.5	4.0	1.4	0.0
Skimmed Milk, Starbucks*	1 Serving/260ml	88	34	3.4	5.0	0.1	0.0
LAVERBREAD	1oz/28g	15	52	3.2	1.6	3.7	0.0
LEEKS,							
Baby, Tesco*	1 Pack/175g	40	23	1.6	2.9	0.5	2.2
Boiled In Salted Water	1oz/28g	6	21	1.2	2.6	0.7	1.7
Boiled In Unsalted Water	1oz/28g	6	21	1.2	2.6	0.7	1.7
Creamed, Frozen, Waitrose*	1 Serving/225g	115	51	1.8	5.5	2.4	0.0
Cut, Farmfoods*	1oz/28g	6	23	1.6	2.9	0.5	2.2
Prepared, M & S*	1oz/28g	9	31	1.9	6.0	0.0	3.1
Raw	1oz/28g	6	22	1.6	2.9	0.5	2.2
LEMON CURD,							
Lemon Curd	1 Tsp/15g	42	283	0.6	62.7	5.0	0.2
Luxury, Waitrose*	1 Tsp/15g	52	344	3.2	60.1	10.1	0.0
Tesco*	1 Serving/10g	30	298	0.6	62.5	4.8	0.0
Waitrose*	1 Tsp/15g	45	301	0.6	65.3	4.1	0.1
LEMON DRINK, No Added Sugar, Somerfield*	1 Glass/200ml	12	6	0.0	1.0	0.0	0.0

	Measure WEIGHT/INFO	per Measure KCAL	Nutrition Values per 100g / 100ml KCAL	PROT	CARB	FAT	FIBRE
LEMON,							
Fresh, Raw	1 Slice/5g	0	7	0.3	1.6	0.0	1.7
Juice, Fresh	1 Tsp/5ml	0	7	0.3	1.6	0.0	0.1
LEMON SOLE,							
& Butter, M & S*	1oz/28g	49	174	15.1	0.1	12.6	0.0
Breadcrumbs, M & S*	1oz/28g	63	225	11.2	17.1	12.7	0.7
Fillets, Chunky, Boneless, Sainsbury's*	1 Fillet/160g	329	207	12.8	13.5	11.3	1.9
Fillets, COU, M & S*	1 Serving/220g	88	40	8.2	1.2	0.4	2.0
Fillets, In A Light Crispy Crumb, Iceland*	1 Fillet/150g	422	281	15.5	21.8	14.6	0.0
Fillets, M & S*	½ Pack/110g	193	175	15.1	0.1	12.6	0.0
Goujons, Fried In Blended Oil	1oz/28g	105	374	15.5	14.3	28.7	0.0
Goujons, With Citrus Mayonnaise, Tesco*	1 Serving/250g	610	244	11.7	19.6	13.2	0.8
Grilled	1oz/28g	27	97	20.2	0.0	1.7	0.0
In Crumbs, Fried	1oz/28g	60	216	16.1	9.3	13.0	0.4
Raw	1oz/28g	23	83	17.4	0.0	1.5	0.0
Steamed	1oz/28g	25	91	20.6	0.0	0.9	0.0
Whole, Filleted, Waitrose*	1 Fillet/87g	158	182	14.8	11.9	8.3	0.5
LEMONADE,							
Lemonade	1 Glass/250ml	53	21	0.1	5.0	0.1	0.1
7-Up, Light, Britvic*	1 Can/330ml	4	1	0.1	0.2	0.0	0.0
Lemonade, Asda*	1 Glass/250ml	83	33	0.0	8.0	0.0	0.0
Cloudy, Sainsbury's*	1 Glass/250ml	118	47	0.1	12.0	0.1	0.1
Diet, Lilt Light, The Coca Cola Co*	1fl oz/30ml	1	3	0.0	0.4	0.0	0.0
Diet, Schweppes*	1 Bottle/500ml	8	2	0.0	0.0	0.0	0.0
Diet, Traditional Style, Sainsbury's*	1 Glass/250ml	8	3	0.1	0.2	0.1	0.1
Fresh Squeezed, M & S*	1 Bottle/250ml	113	45	0.1	11.8	0.0	0.0
Lime, Safeway*	1 Can/144ml	63	44	0.0	10.6	0.0	0.0
Shapers, Boots*	1 Bottle/500ml	13	3	0.0	0.0	0.0	0.0
Somerfield*	½ Pint/296ml	80	27	0.0	7.0	0.0	0.0
Sprite, Light, Sprite*	1fl oz/30ml	0	2	0.0	0.0	0.0	0.0
Sprite, McDonald's*	1 Regular/251ml	108	43	0.0	10.5	0.0	0.0
Still, M & S*	1 Glass/250ml	5	49	0.1	12.9	0.0	0.0
Still, Tesco*	1 Glass/200ml	100	50	0.0	12.0	0.0	0.0
Tesco*	1 Serving/100ml	16	16	0.1	3.8	0.0	0.0
Traditional Style, Tesco*	1 Glass/200ml	100	50	0.0	12.3	0.0	0.0
LENTILS,							
Continental, Dried, Tesco*	1 Serving/50g	146	292	24.4	44.4	1.9	8.9
Green & Brown, Whole, Dried, Boiled In Salted Water	1oz/28g	29	105	8.8	16.9	0.7	3.8
Green & Brown, Whole, Dried, Raw	1oz/28g	83	297	24.3	48.8	1.9	8.9
Green, Dried, Tesco*	1 Serving/227g	708	312	20.4	55.6	0.9	10.6
Green In Water, Sainsbury's*	1 Serving/133g	145	109	8.8	16.9	0.7	3.8
Green, Organic, Evernat*	1oz/28g	87	312	20.4	55.6	0.9	10.6
Green, Canned, Tesco*	1 Can/195g	125	64	5.0	10.2	0.4	2.3
Red, Dried, Organic, Evernat*	1oz/28g	87	312	23.8	51.3	1.3	4.9
Red, Split, Dried, Boiled In Unsalted Water	1oz/28g	28	100	7.6	17.5	0.4	1.9
Red, Split, Dried, Raw	1oz/28g	89	318	23.8	56.3	1.3	4.9
LETTUCE,							
Average, Raw	1oz/28g	4	14	0.8	1.7	0.5	0.9
Chinese Leaf, Tesco*	1 Serving/200g	36	18	3.5	0.3	0.3	2.6
Hearts Of Tomaine, Sainsbury's*	1oz/28g	4	16	1.0	1.7	0.6	1.2
Iceberg, Herbs, M & S*	1oz/28g	4	14	0.8	1.8	0.4	0.8
Iceberg, Morrisons*	1 Serving/100g	13	13	0.7	1.9	0.3	0.0
Iceberg, Prepared, M & S*	1oz/28g	4	13	0.7	1.9	0.3	0.6
Iceberg, Shredded, Asda*	1 Serving/100g	13	13	0.7	1.8	0.3	0.6
Iceberg, Shredded, Sainsbury's*	1oz/28g	4	13	0.7	1.8	0.3	0.6

	Measure WEIGHT/INFO	per Measure KCAL	Nutrition Values per 100g / 100ml KCAL	PROT	CARB	FAT	FIBRE
LETTUCE,							
Iceberg, Somerfield*	1oz/28g	4	13	1.0	2.0	0.0	0.0
Romaine, Organic, Tesco*	½ Lettuce/100g	15	15	0.8	1.7	0.5	0.9
Round, Tesco*	1 Serving/100g	15	15	1.0	1.7	0.5	0.0
LIME JUICE,							
Cordial, Co-Op*	1fl oz/30ml	8	25	0.0	4.0	0.0	0.0
Cordial, Concentrated	1floz/30ml	34	112	0.1	29.8	0.0	0.0
Cordial, Diluted	1 Glass/250ml	55	22	0.0	6.0	0.0	0.0
Cordial, Princes*	1fl oz/30ml	8	27	0.0	4.3	0.0	0.0
Cordial, Sainsbury's*	1 Glass/250ml	24	9	0.1	1.9	0.1	0.1
Cordial, Tesco*	1 Serving/75ml	35	46	0.0	9.3	0.0	0.0
Fresh	1 Tsp/5ml	0	9	0.4	1.6	0.1	0.1
LINSEEDS,							
Golden, Organic, Evernat*	1oz/28g	127	452	22.0	6.0	38.0	25.0
Chopped, Risetti*	1 Serving/5g	22	448	23.0	38.0	22.0	31.0
LION BAR,							
Mini, Nestle*	1 Bar/16g	80	486	4.6	67.7	21.7	0.0
Nestle*	1 Bar/55g	260	472	4.7	64.5	21.7	0.0
LIQUEURS, High Strength	1 Shot/25ml	79	314	0.0	24.4	0.0	0.0
LIQUORICE,							
Allsorts, Average	1 Sm Bag/56g	195	349	3.7	76.7	5.2	2.0
Allsorts, Smart Price, Asda*	1oz/28g	87	312	2.5	69.0	2.9	1.4
Catherine Wheels, Sainsbury's*	1 Wheel/17g	49	286	3.8	67.2	0.3	0.7
Comfits, M & S*	1oz/28g	100	357	2.4	86.2	0.3	0.7
Shapes, Average	1oz/28g	78	278	5.5	65.0	1.4	1.9
LIVER,							
Calves, Fried	1oz/28g	49	176	22.3	0.0	9.6	0.0
Calves, Raw	1oz/28g	29	104	18.3	0.0	3.4	0.0
Calves, With Garlic Butter, M & S*	1oz/28g	56	200	13.3	7.3	13.5	0.4
Chicken, Raw	1oz/28g	26	92	17.7	0.0	2.3	0.0
Lamb's, Fried	1oz/28g	77	274	7.9	52.3	4.4	4.3
Lamb's, Raw, Tesco*	1 Serving/125g	171	137	20.3	0.0	6.2	0.0
Lamb's With Onions, M & S*	1oz/28g	52	185	14.1	6.8	11.3	0.1
Ox, Raw	1oz/28g	43	155	21.1	0.0	7.8	0.0
Pig's, Raw	1oz/28g	117	418	6.8	46.7	23.3	2.0
LIVER &,							
Bacon, British Classics, Tesco*	1 Pack/400g	496	124	10.7	7.1	5.9	0.7
Bacon, In Onion Gravy, With Mash, Sainsbury's*	1 Pack/450g	509	113	6.4	10.9	4.9	0.7
Bacon, Morrisons*	1 Pack/400g	452	113	11.5	5.7	5.1	0.5
Bacon, Ready Meals, M & S*	1 Pack/400g	520	130	12.4	3.6	7.6	1.2
Bacon, With Mash, GFY, Asda*	1 Pack/450g	437	97	6.0	11.0	3.2	0.8
Bacon, With Mash, Tesco*	1 Pack/500g	470	94	4.8	9.4	4.1	0.9
Bacon, With Mashed Potato, Safeway*	1 Pack/450g	491	109	7.9	8.8	4.7	1.3
Bacon, With Potato, Somerfield*	1 Pack/320g	445	139	8.0	13.0	6.0	0.0
Onion & Dumplings, M & S*	1 Pack/204g	255	125	7.6	10.5	6.0	0.9
Onions With Mash, Tesco*	1 Pack/500g	470	94	4.8	9.4	4.1	0.9
LIVER SAUSAGE,							
Asda*	1oz/28g	57	204	17.0	2.0	14.2	0.4
Sainsbury's*	1 Slice/13g	27	212	14.4	4.7	15.1	0.5
Sliced, Somerfield*	1 Slice/11g	27	247	14.0	5.0	19.0	0.0
Value, Tesco*	1 Slice/10g	20	200	15.8	6.1	12.5	0.0
LOADED SKINS,							
HE, Tesco*	1 Serving/340g	425	125	7.7	17.9	2.5	0.6
With Cheese & Bacon, Asda*	1 Serving/65g	185	284	10.6	21.4	17.4	2.0
With Cheese & Jalapeno, Asda*	1 Serving/65g	164	252	8.9	21.0	14.7	2.2

	Measure	per Measure	Nutrition Values per 100g / 100ml				
LOBSTER,	WEIGHT/INFO	KCAL	KCAL	PROT	CARB	FAT	FIBRE
Boiled	1oz/28g	29	103	22.1	0.0	1.6	0.0
Cooked, Asda*	1oz/28g	32	115	22.1	0.0	3.4	0.0
Dressed, John West*	1 Can/43g	45	105	13.0	2.0	5.0	0.0
Dressed, M & S*	1oz/28g	76	273	14.3	0.8	23.6	0.1
Half, M & S*	1oz/28g	66	235	12.1	2.4	19.6	0.2
LOGANBERRIES, Raw	1oz/28g	5	17	1.1	3.4	0.0	2.5
LOLLIPOPS,							
Assorted, Co-Op*	1 Lollipop/10g	40	400	0.0	97.0	0.0	0.0
M & S*	1oz/28g	107	383	0.0	95.4	0.0	0.0
LONGANS, Canned, In Syrup, Drained	1oz/28g	19	67	0.4	17.1	0.3	0.0
LOQUATS, Raw	1oz/28g	8	28	0.7	6.3	0.2	0.0
LUCOZADE,							
Orange Energy Drink, Smithkline Beecham*	1 Bottle/500ml	350	70	0.0	17.2	0.0	0.0
Original, Smithkline Beecham*	1 Sm Bottle/345ml	252	73	0.0	17.9	0.0	0.0
Sport Isotonic Lemon Body Fuel, Smithkline Beecham*	1 Bottle/500ml	140	28	0.0	6.4	0.0	0.0
Sport, Orange, SmithKline Beecham*	1 Bottle/500ml	140	28	0.0	6.4	0.0	0.1
LUNCHEON MEAT,							
Pork, John West*	1oz/28g	83	297	13.0	5.0	25.0	0.0
Pork, Slices, Asda*	1oz/28g	78	280	12.9	3.0	24.0	0.0
Pork, Tesco*	1 Slice/14g	40	287	14.0	4.0	23.9	0.0
LYCHEES,							
Canned, In Syrup	1oz/28g	19	68	0.4	17.7	0.0	0.5
Fresh, Raw	1oz/28g	16	58	0.9	14.3	0.1	0.7
In Juice, Amoy*	1oz/28g	13	46	0.4	10.9	0.0	0.0
Lotus, In Syrup, Amoy	1oz/28g	19	68	0.4	17.7	0.0	0.0
Raw, Weighed With Skin & Stone	1oz/28g	10	36	0.5	8.9	0.1	0.4

M&M'S,	Measure WEIGHT/INFO	per Measure KCAL	Nutrition Values per 100g / 100ml KCAL	PROT	CARB	FAT	FIBRE
Funsize, Mars*	1 Funsize/20g	97	487	4.7	69.6	21.1	0.0
Mini, Mars*	1 Sm Pack/36g	176	489	6.3	63.6	23.2	0.0
Peanut, Mars*	1 Pack/45g	231	514	10.2	57.3	27.1	0.0
Plain, Mars*	1 Pack/48g	240	499	4.1	70.7	20.8	2.1
MACADAMIA NUTS, Salted	6 Nuts/10g	75	748	7.9	4.8	77.6	5.3
MACKEREL,							
Crushed Peppercorns, Smoked, Tesco*	1 Serving/90g	267	297	20.7	0.0	23.8	1.6
Fillets, In Brine, Asda*	1 Can/88g	193	219	18.6	0.0	16.1	0.0
Fillets, In Brine, John West*	1 Can/94g	219	233	20.0	0.0	17.0	0.0
Fillets, In Brine, Sainsbury's*	1 Can/90g	215	239	20.0	0.1	17.7	0.1
Fillets, In Curry Sauce, John West*	1oz/28g	65	233	16.0	4.0	17.0	0.3
Fillets, In Mustard Sauce, John West*	1oz/28g	60	215	15.0	5.0	15.0	0.2
Fillets, In Mustard Sauce, Tesco*	1 Can/120g	274	228	13.9	4.7	17.1	0.0
Fillets, In Spicy Tomato Sauce, John West*	1oz/28g	55	198	15.0	3.0	14.0	0.0
Fillets, In Spicy Tomato Sauce, Princes*	1 Can/125g	250	200	13.6	4.7	14.1	0.0
Fillets, In Sunflower Oil, John West*	1 Can/94g	244	260	20.0	0.0	20.0	0.0
Fillets, In Tomato Sauce, John West*	1oz/28g	60	213	17.0	2.5	15.0	0.1
Fillets, In Tomato Sauce, Princes*	1 Can/125g	254	203	13.6	3.3	15.0	0.0
Fillets, In Tomato Sauce, Sainsbury's*	1 Can/125g	204	163	14.0	2.0	11.0	0.1
Fillets, Peppered, Asda*	½ Pack/130g	430	331	22.0	0.0	27.0	0.0
Fillets, Peppered, John West*	½ Pack/62g	184	297	15.7	0.0	26.0	0.0
Fillets, Peppered, M & S*	1 Serving/100g	350	350	22.4	0.0	28.7	0.6
Fillets, Peppered, Smoked, Sainsbury's*	1 Serving/106g	388	366	20.8	0.6	31.1	0.1
Fillets, Smoked, Farmfoods*	1oz/28g	99	354	18.9	0.0	30.9	0.0
Fillets, Smoked, M & S*	1oz/28g	80	284	18.1	2.6	22.4	0.1
Fillets, Smoked, Sainsbury's*	1 Serving/100g	386	386	20.1	0.0	34.0	0.1
Fillets, Smoked, Tesco*	1 Serving/100g	297	297	19.7	0.0	24.2	0.0
Fillets, Smoked, Waitrose*	1 Fillet/100g	339	339	20.4	0.3	28.5	0.0
Fillets, Smoked, With Crushed Peppercorns, Waitrose*	1 Can/120g	385	321	18.7	1.6	26.6	0.0
Fried In Blended Oil	1oz/28g	76	272	24.0	0.0	19.5	0.0
Grilled	1oz/28g	67	239	20.8	0.0	17.3	0.0
Headless Gutted, Somerfield*	1oz/28g	62	220	19.0	0.0	16.0	0.0
In Sunflower Oil, Peppered, Smoked, John West*	1oz/28g	87	311	21.0	0.5	25.0	0.5
In Tomato Sauce	1oz/28g	58	206	16.4	1.4	15.0	0.0
Raw	1oz/28g	62	220	18.7	0.0	16.1	0.0
Smoked	1oz/28g	99	354	18.9	0.0	30.9	0.0
Smoked, Asda*	1 Serving/100g	331	331	22.0	0.0	27.0	0.0
Steak, In Brine, John West*	1oz/28g	68	243	18.0	0.0	19.0	0.0
Steak, In Tomato Sauce, John West*	1oz/28g	62	221	15.0	2.0	17.0	0.0
MADRAS,							
Chicken, & Pilau Rice, Somerfield*	1 Pack/340g	496	146	7.0	14.0	7.0	0.0
Chicken, Budgens*	1 Pack/350g	553	158	10.7	3.9	11.1	1.8
Chicken, Indian, Sainsbury's*	1 Pack/400g	636	159	13.3	1.8	10.9	2.6
Chicken, Indian Takeaway, Frozen, Iceland*	1oz/28g	29	104	8.1	6.2	5.2	1.7
Chicken, Meals To Go, Somerfield*	1 Pack/299g	416	139	8.7	3.5	10.0	0.4
Chicken, Tesco*	1 Pack/350g	326	93	10.6	3.6	4.1	0.6
Chicken, Waitrose*	1oz/28g	47	168	14.6	3.7	10.5	1.8
MAKHANI,							
Chicken, & Rice, Sainsbury's*	1 Pack/501g	752	150	8.6	14.1	6.6	0.8
Chicken Tikka, Waitrose*	1 Pack/400g	644	161	13.2	4.2	10.1	1.8
Chicken Tikka, With Pilau Rice, BGTY, Sainsbuy's*	1 Pack/450g	428	95	7.8	12.7	1.4	0.9
MALTESERS, Mars*	1 Sm Pack/37g	183	494	10.0	61.4	23.1	0.0
MANDARIN ORANGES,							
Canned, In Juice	1oz/28g	9	32	0.7	7.7	0.0	0.3

M

MANDARIN ORANGES,	Measure WEIGHT/INFO	per Measure KCAL	KCAL	PROT	CARB	FAT	FIBRE
Canned, In Syrup	1oz/28g	15	52	0.5	13.4	0.0	0.2
In Fruit Juice, Waitrose*	1 Can/295g	112	38	0.6	9.0	0.0	0.0
In Light Syrup, Del Monte*	1 Can/298g	182	61	0.6	13.9	0.1	0.0
Segments, In Fruit Juice, Sainsbury's*	1 Pack/175g	77	44	0.7	10.0	0.1	0.4
Segments, In Mandarin Juice, Co-Op*	½ Can/149g	49	33	0.7	7.6	0.0	0.3
Segments, In Natural Juice, John West*	¼ Can/102g	43	42	0.6	10.0	0.0	0.8
Segments, In Natural Juice, Morrisons*	1 Can/298g	125	42	0.6	10.0	0.0	1.5
Segments, In Natural Juice, Tesco*	½ Can/149g	51	34	0.7	7.7	0.0	0.3
Segments, Spanish, Sainsbury's*	1oz/28g	12	44	0.7	10.0	0.1	0.4
Tesco*	1 Serving/150g	59	39	0.9	8.7	0.1	1.2
Without Peel	1 Sm/50g	17	34	0.9	8.0	0.1	1.3
MANGE TOUT,							
& Sugar Snap Peas, Tesco*	1 Pack/150g	102	68	7.0	9.2	0.4	3.8
Boiled In Salted Water	1oz/28g	7	26	3.2	3.3	0.1	2.2
Raw	1oz/28g	9	32	3.6	4.2	0.2	2.3
Safeway*	1 Serving/25g	8	33	3.6	4.2	0.2	0.0
Stir-Fried In Blended Oil	1oz/28g	20	71	3.8	3.5	4.8	2.4
MANGO & APPLE Juice, Copella*	1 Serving/200ml	86	43	0.4	10.1	0.1	0.0
MANGO,							
Fresh, M & S*	1 Pack/200g	120	60	0.7	14.1	0.2	2.6
Pieces, Freshly Prepared, Waitrose*	1 Serving/100g	59	59	0.7	14.1	0.2	2.6
Pineapple & Passionfruit, M & S*	1 Pack/400g	200	50	0.6	10.9	0.2	1.7
Ripe, Canned, In Syrup	1oz/28g	22	77	0.3	20.3	0.0	0.7
Ripe, Raw	1oz/28g	16	57	0.7	14.1	0.2	2.6
Ripe, Raw, Weighed With Skin & Stone	1oz/28g	11	39	0.5	9.6	0.1	1.8
Slices, Amoy*	1 Can/425g	327	77	0.3	20.3	0.0	0.9
Slices, In Syrup, Sainsbury's*	1 Serving/255g	217	85	0.2	20.8	0.1	1.1
Unripe, Raw	1 Slice/40g	18	46	0.5	11.2	0.2	2.9
MANGO JUICE, Canned	1 Glass/200ml	78	39	0.1	9.8	0.2	0.0
MARBLE, Cadbury's*	1 Bar/46g	246	535	8.4	54.8	31.2	0.0
MARGARINE,							
Margarine	Thin Spread/7g	52	739	0.2	1.0	81.6	0.0
Best For Baking, Asda*	1 Tsp/10g	66	659	0.1	0.5	73.0	0.0
Clover*	Thin Spread/7g	46	654	0.6	0.2	72.0	0.0
Low Fat, Asda*	1 Serving/10g	35	346	1.0	0.0	38.0	0.0
Stork*, Packet	1oz/28g	202	720	0.0	0.1	80.0	0.0
Stork*, Tub	1 Level Tbsp/14g	92	658	0.1	0.1	73.0	0.0
Soya, Granose*	1oz/28g	209	745	0.1	0.1	82.0	0.0
Sunflower, Granose*	Thin Spread/7g	50	720	0.0	0.0	84.0	0.0
MARINADE,							
Barbecue, COU, M & S*	1 Serving/35g	53	150	1.2	35.5	0.2	1.0
Barbecue, In Minutes, Knorr*	1 Pack/110g	337	306	6.2	66.4	1.3	3.4
Chinese, Classic, Sharwood's*	1oz/28g	32	113	1.8	16.1	4.8	1.0
Citrus & Black Pepper, Asda*	1/16 Jar/17g	51	300	2.1	28.0	20.0	0.3
Coconut & Lime, Sainsbury's*	1 Jar/125g	198	158	1.1	3.2	15.3	1.4
Hot & Spicy Barbecue, M & S*	1 Serving/18g	23	130	1.0	31.1	0.3	0.8
Sundried Tomato & Basil With Peri-Peri, Nando's*	1 Bottle/270g	319	118	0.1	15.3	9.5	0.8
Thai Coconut, Coriander & Lime, Lea & Perrins*	1oz/28g	45	159	1.3	25.7	6.1	0.0
Tomato & Herb, Lea & Perrins*	1oz/28g	28	100	1.2	24.1	0.5	0.0
White Wine, Garlic & Pepper, Lea & Perrins*	1oz/28g	28	99	0.1	23.7	0.7	0.0
MARJORAM, Dried	1 Tsp/0.6g	3	271	12.7	42.5	7.0	0.0
MARLIN,							
Steaks, Chargrilled, Sainsbury's*	1 Serving/240g	367	153	23.6	0.8	6.1	0.6
Steaks, Raw, Sainsbury's*	1 Steak/110g	109	99	24.3	0.0	0.2	0.0

(Nutrition Values per 100g / 100ml)

MARMALADE,	Measure WEIGHT/INFO	per Measure KCAL	Nutrition Values per 100g / 100ml KCAL	PROT	CARB	FAT	FIBRE
25% Less Sugar, Asda*	1 Tsp/15g	28	185	0.4	45.6	0.0	0.9
Breakfast, Chivers*	1 Tsp/15g	39	260	0.3	64.7	0.0	0.6
Breakfast, Fine Cut, Frank Cooper*	1 Tsp/15g	37	249	0.2	61.9	0.0	0.3
Christmas Orange & Whisky, M & S*	1oz/28g	67	240	0.3	59.5	0.2	1.9
Golden Shred, Robertson's*	1 Tsp/15g	38	253	0.2	62.3	0.0	0.0
Grapefruit & Cranberry, M & S*	1 Tsp/15g	36	240	0.3	60.3	0.0	1.5
Grapefruit, Fine Cut, Duerr's	1 Tsp/15g	39	261	0.2	65.0	0.0	0.0
Lemon & Lime, M & S*	1 Tsp/15g	41	274	0.1	67.9	0.2	0.8
Lemon Jelly, No Peel, Tesco*	1 Tsp/15g	39	263	0.1	65.0	0.0	0.4
Lemon Shred, Somerfield*	1 Tsp/15g	39	260	0.0	65.0	0.0	0.0
Lime Shred, Asda*	1 Tbsp/15g	38	253	0.1	63.0	0.1	0.3
Lime Shred, Sainsbury's*	1 Tsp/15g	40	269	0.2	67.0	0.1	0.4
Olde English, Chivers*	1 Tsp/15g	41	276	0.3	68.7	0.0	0.6
Orange & Lemon, Reduced Sugar, Zest*	1 Tsp/6g	12	195	0.3	47.1	0.2	0.0
Orange, Asda*	1 Serving/28g	52	187	0.5	45.0	0.5	0.0
Orange, Fine Cut, Crystal, Tiptree, Wilkin & Sons*	1 Tsp/15g	40	268	0.1	67.0	0.0	0.0
Orange Jelly, Shredless, Sainsbury's*	1 Tsp/15g	39	261	0.2	65.0	0.1	0.4
Orange, Lemon & Grapefruit, Baxters*	1 Tsp/15g	38	252	0.0	63.0	0.0	0.1
Orange, Medium Cut, Somerfield*	1 Tsp/15g	39	257	0.0	64.0	0.0	0.0
Orange, Reduced Sugar, Diced Cut, Streamline*	1 Tsp/15g	29	192	0.4	47.0	0.3	0.0
Orange, Reduced Sugar, Sainsbury's*	1 Tsp/15g	29	190	0.4	47.0	0.1	0.7
Orange, Scothch, Baxters*	1 Tsp/15g	32	210	0.0	53.0	0.0	0.1
Orange, Seville, Fine Cut, Duerr's*	1 Tsp/14g	37	261	0.2	65.0	0.0	0.0
Orange, Seville, Organic, Waitrose*	1 Serving/12g	31	261	0.3	65.0	0.0	0.7
Orange, Seville, Thick Cut, Organic, Sainsbury's*	1 Tsp/15g	39	261	0.3	65.0	0.1	0.4
Orange, Seville, Thin Cut, Baxters*	1 Tsp/15g	38	252	0.0	63.0	0.0	0.1
Orange Shred, Fine Cut, Jelly, Sainsbury's*	1 Tsp/15g	38	253	0.2	63.0	0.1	0.4
Orange Shred, Fine Cut, Tesco*	1 Tsp/15g	39	263	0.1	65.0	0.0	0.4
Orange, Shredless, Duerr's*	1 Tsp/10g	26	261	0.2	65.0	0.0	0.0
Orange, Thick Cut, Co-Op*	1 Tsp/15g	43	285	0.3	70.0	0.2	0.4
Orange, Thin Cut, Saver, Safeway*	1 Serving/28g	69	245	0.7	60.0	0.1	0.0
Orange, Value, Tesco*	1 Serving/28g	71	255	0.2	63.1	0.0	0.5
Thick Cut, Somerfield*	1 Tsp/15g	39	260	0.0	65.0	0.0	0.0
Three Fruits, Fresh Fruit, Sainsbury's*	1 Tsp/15g	38	250	0.0	61.3	0.0	0.0
MARMITE, Yeast Extract, Marmite*	1 Tsp/9g	21	234	43.0	14.8	0.4	2.6
MARROW,							
Boiled In Salted Water	1oz/28g	3	9	0.4	1.6	0.2	0.6
Boiled In Unsalted Water	1oz/28g	3	9	0.4	1.6	0.2	0.6
Raw	1oz/28g	3	12	0.5	2.2	0.2	0.5
MARS BAR,							
5 Little Ones, Mars*	1 Piece/8g	38	477	4.5	73.6	18.3	0.0
Standard Bar, Mars*	1 Bar/42g	190	452	4.0	69.6	17.5	0.0
MARSHMALLOW, Squares, Rice Krispies, Chewy, Kellogg's*	1 Med Bar/18g	74	410	3.0	78.0	10.0	1.0
MARSHMALLOWS,							
Marshmallows, Average	1oz/28g	92	327	3.9	83.1	0.0	0.0
Pink & White, Co-Op*	1 Sweet/7g	24	340	3.0	82.0	0.0	0.0
Princess*	1oz/28g	88	314	3.4	80.0	0.0	0.0
MARZIPAN,							
Almond, Dark, Thorntons*	1 Chocolate/13g	62	477	7.2	58.5	24.6	3.8
Bar, Chocolate, Plain, Thorntons*	1 Bar/46g	206	448	5.2	69.1	17.4	2.0
Golden, Waitrose*	1oz/28g	118	420	6.4	67.4	13.9	1.5
Retail	1oz/28g	113	404	5.3	67.6	14.4	1.9
MAYONNAISE,							
Mayonnaise, Average	1 Tsp/11g	80	724	1.9	0.2	79.3	0.0

M

MAYONNAISE,	Measure WEIGHT/INFO	per Measure KCAL	Nutrition Values per 100g / 100ml KCAL	PROT	CARB	FAT	FIBRE
50% Less Fat, GFY, Asda*	1 Tbsp/10g	32	322	0.8	10.0	31.0	0.0
Dijonnaise, Hellmann's*	1 Tsp/6g	13	210	2.9	5.1	19.7	0.0
French, Sainsbury's*	1 Tsp/6ml	41	678	1.2	2.4	73.6	1.4
French Style, BGTY, Sainsbury's*	1 Tbsp/15ml	55	366	0.6	7.5	36.9	0.0
Garlic & Herb, M & S*	1 Tsp/6g	43	712	3.4	2.4	76.9	0.9
Garlic Flavoured, Frank Cooper*	1 Tsp/6g	28	460	2.2	8.8	46.2	0.1
Garlic, Waitrose*	1 Tsp/6g	21	346	0.6	8.6	34.3	0.0
Half Fat, Healthy Choice, Safeway*	1 Tsp/11g	35	319	0.8	10.8	30.3	0.0
Hellmann's*	1 Tsp/11g	79	722	1.1	1.3	79.1	0.0
Light, Auchan*	1 Tsp/11g	39	351	0.5	8.5	35.0	0.0
Light, BGTY, Sainsbury's*	1 Tsp/11g	33	296	0.5	7.2	29.3	0.0
Light, Morrisons*	1 Tsp/11g	32	287	1.4	8.5	27.5	0.0
Light, Reduced Calorie, Hellmann's*	1 Tsp/11g	33	300	0.7	6.7	29.8	0.0
Mediterranean, Hellmann's*	1 Tsp/11g	79	722	1.1	1.3	79.1	0.0
Mild Dijon Mustard, Frank Cooper*	1 Pot/28g	114	406	3.3	9.3	39.5	0.1
Onion & Chive, BGTY, Sainsbury's*	1 Tbsp/15ml	19	127	2.0	11.8	8.0	0.7
Organic, Evernat*	1 Tsp/11g	83	752	1.3	2.8	81.0	0.0
Real, Hellmann's*	1 Tbsp/15ml	101	676	1.0	1.2	74.0	0.0
Reduced Calorie	1 Tsp/11g	32	288	1.0	8.2	28.1	0.0
Reduced Calorie, Healthy Selection, Somerfield*	1 Tbsp/15ml	49	326	0.8	9.8	31.5	0.0
Reduced Calorie, Waitrose*	1 Tsp/11g	32	287	1.4	8.5	27.5	0.0
Reduced Fat, Tesco*	1 Tbsp/15ml	44	292	0.8	7.9	28.6	0.0
Sainsbury's*	1 Tsp/11g	75	686	0.4	1.2	75.4	0.0
Vegetarian, Tesco*	1 Tsp/12g	89	738	1.5	0.8	81.0	0.0
MCFLURRY,							
Crunchie, McDonald's*	1 Portion/183g	321	175	4.2	26.1	6.2	0.0
Dairy Milk, McDonalds's*	1 Portion/181g	280	154	4.5	24.3	7.2	0.0
Jammie Dodger, McDonald's*	1 Serving/128g	256	200	3.9	33.6	6.4	0.3
Smarties, McDonald's*	1 Serving/185g	327	177	4.2	26.2	6.2	0.2
MCMUFFIN,							
Bacon & Egg, Double, McDonald's*	1 Pack/226g	573	253	14.7	11.4	16.4	0.8
Bacon & Egg, McDonald's*	1 McMuffin/141g	345	245	14.2	18.5	12.8	1.3
Egg, McDonald's*	1 McMuffin/127g	281	221	12.2	20.4	10.1	1.5
Sausage & Egg, McDonald's*	1 McMuffin/176g	426	242	13.8	14.7	14.1	1.0
Scrambled Egg, McDonald's*	1 McMuffin/147g	294	200	10.9	17.5	9.6	1.3
MEAT CAPELLETTI, Fresh, Asda*	1oz/28g	48	172	8.0	26.0	4.0	1.7
MEAT LOAF,							
Somerfield*	1 Pack/454g	867	191	10.0	8.0	13.0	0.0
Turkey & Bacon, Sainsbury's*	1 Serving/185g	318	172	15.2	5.1	10.1	0.5
Turkey & Bacon, Tesco*	1 Serving/225g	401	178	14.7	7.4	9.9	1.1
MEATBALLS,							
Aberdeen Angus, Waitrose*	3 Meatballs/107g	223	208	20.0	1.0	13.8	0.0
Al Forno, Safeway*	1 Pack/450g	684	152	6.0	16.8	6.8	0.4
Beef, Asda*	1 Serving/287g	362	126	11.0	7.0	6.0	0.6
Galician, M & S*	½ Pack/240g	300	125	9.3	6.6	7.0	0.9
Herby With Pasta Tomato Sauce, COU, M & S*	1 Pack/300g	360	120	10.4	15.2	1.7	0.9
In Bolognese Sauce, Somerfield*	1 Pack/454g	704	155	7.0	7.0	11.0	0.0
In Gravy, Campbells*	½ tin/205g	164	80	5.6	8.6	2.6	0.0
Italian Pork, Al Forno, Sainsbury's*	1 Pack/450g	644	143	6.1	17.6	5.3	1.4
M & S*	1oz/28g	58	208	10.9	10.7	13.5	2.4
Spaghetti With Chicken In Tomato Sauce, Heinz*	1 Can/400g	352	88	4.1	11.0	3.0	0.5
Spicy Tom Sauce & Spaghetti, COU, M & S*	1 Pack/360g	342	95	6.3	13.5	1.9	1.2
Swedish, Findus*	½ Pack/100g	230	230	13.0	7.0	17.0	0.0
Swedish, Sainsbury's*	1 Serving/200g	430	215	14.0	6.0	15.0	2.6

	Measure WEIGHT/INFO	per Measure KCAL	Nutrition Values per 100g / 100ml KCAL	PROT	CARB	FAT	FIBRE
MEATBALLS,							
Swedish, Scan*	¼ Pack/88g	189	215	14.0	6.0	15.0	2.6
Tomato Sauce, SmartPrice, Asda*	1 Can/201g	320	159	3.7	9.0	12.0	0.0
Turkey, GFY, Asda*	½ Pack/330g	333	101	10.0	7.0	3.7	0.0
MEDAGLIONE, Cheese & Red Bell Pepper, ES, Safeway*	1 Serving/125g	175	140	6.3	21.1	2.9	1.0
MELBA TOAST,							
Asda*	1 Toast/5g	20	396	12.0	79.0	3.6	2.8
Buitoni*	1 Serving/33g	130	395	12.1	75.5	4.9	4.6
Dutch, Tesco*	1 Serving/20g	75	377	16.0	73.0	2.3	5.0
Organic, Trimlyne*	1 Slice/3g	12	390	13.0	78.0	2.9	5.5
Original, Van Der Meulen*	1 Slice/3g	12	399	12.8	80.5	2.9	3.9
Safeway*	1 Serving/3g	11	362	12.0	72.0	2.9	3.9
With Sesame, Tesco*	1 Slice/3g	11	370	12.8	61.7	8.0	3.8
MELON,							
Average, Weighed With Skin	1oz/28g	4	16	0.4	3.6	0.1	0.5
Fresh, Average, Raw	1oz/28g	7	24	0.6	5.5	0.1	0.7
Galia, Portions, Somerfield*	1oz/28g	7	25	1.0	6.0	0.0	0.0
Honeydew, Portion, Somerfield*	1oz/28g	8	30	1.0	7.0	0.0	0.0
Just Melon, Shapers, Boots*	1 Pot/139g	39	28	0.6	6.2	0.1	0.6
Kiwi & Strawberry Mixed Fruits, Sainsbury's*	1oz/28g	9	33	0.8	6.3	0.2	1.3
M & S*	1 Serving/50g	13	25	0.5	5.6	0.2	0.5
Mixed, M & S*	1 Pot/225g	56	25	0.5	5.6	0.2	0.5
Pineapple & Strawberry, Food To Go, M & S*	1 Serving/200g	70	35	0.6	7.1	0.2	1.1
Pineapple & Strawberry, Fully Prepared, Sainsbury's*	1 Serving/245g	86	35	0.6	7.8	0.1	0.9
Seeds	1oz/28g	163	583	28.5	9.9	47.7	0.0
Slice Selection, Waitrose*	1 Serving/225g	45	20	0.4	4.3	0.1	0.4
MELON MEDLEY,							
M & S*	1 Pot/450g	135	30	0.5	5.6	0.2	0.5
Sainsbury's*	1 Serving/145g	41	28	0.6	6.2	0.1	0.6
Salad Bar, Asda*	1oz/28g	7	26	0.6	6.6	0.0	0.7
Tesco*	1 Serving/250g	68	27	0.6	6.0	0.1	0.5
MELT,							
Cheesy Fish, Young's*	1 Serving/340g	418	123	7.6	8.3	6.6	0.9
Mushroom & Broccoli Potato Wedge, Weight Watchers*	1 Pack/310g	285	92	3.3	12.6	3.1	1.0
Tuna & Wedges, Tesco*	1 Pack/400g	360	90	6.1	9.2	3.2	1.8
MERINGUE,							
Meringue	1oz/28g	106	379	5.3	95.4	0.0	0.0
Layered, Tesco*	1/5 Meringue/52g	146	280	3.5	63.2	1.5	1.4
Lemon, Iced, 3% Fat, M & S*	1oz/28g	47	167	2.4	33.9	2.4	1.5
Lemon, Weight Watchers*	1 Serving/85g	161	189	2.4	43.1	0.5	0.6
Nests, Asda*	1 Nest/15g	59	390	3.7	93.0	0.3	0.0
Nests, Sainsbury's*	1 Nest/15g	58	387	3.9	92.8	0.0	0.0
Nests, Tropical Fruit, Sainsbury's*	1 Nest/95g	234	246	2.0	42.0	7.8	2.4
Raspberry, Farmfoods*	¼ Meringue/46g	148	322	2.9	38.8	17.2	0.7
Raspberry, M & S*	1 Serving/105g	215	205	1.8	20.6	13.1	3.1
Shells, Mini, Asda*	1 Shell/4g	16	388	4.8	92.0	0.1	0.0
Summer Fruits, 90% Fat Free, Sara Lee*	1 Meringue/135g	308	228	2.5	35.7	8.5	2.2
Toffee, M & S*	1 Meringue/30g	125	415	4.1	52.2	20.9	0.8
Tropical, M & S*	1 Serving/53g	212	400	3.1	37.0	26.9	0.0
MILK,							
Condensed, Skimmed, Sweetened	1oz/28g	75	267	10.0	60.0	0.2	0.0
Condensed, Whole, Sweetened	1oz/28g	93	333	8.5	55.5	10.1	0.0
Dried Skimmed	1oz/28g	97	348	36.1	52.9	0.6	0.0
Dried Skimmed, Instant, Tesco*	1oz/28g	100	358	35.0	52.0	1.1	0.0
Dried Skimmed, Powder, Tesco*	1 Tbsp/6g	21	358	35.0	52.0	1.1	0.0

M

MILK,	Measure WEIGHT/INFO	per Measure KCAL	KCAL	PROT	CARB	FAT	FIBRE
			Nutrition Values per 100g / 100ml				
Dried Whole	1oz/28g	137	490	26.3	39.4	26.3	0.0
Milk Drink, Banana, Sterilised Skimmed, Happy Shopper*	1 Bottle/500ml	245	49	3.2	8.8	0.1	0.0
Milk Drink, Chocolate Sterilised Skimmed, Happy Shopper*	1 Bottle/500ml	295	59	3.6	10.4	0.3	0.0
Milk Drink, Mars Extra Milk Chocolate Caramel, Mars*	1 Bottle/330g	224	68	3.5	12.1	0.3	0.0
Evaporated, Full Cream, Waitrose*	1 Tbsp/15ml	24	160	8.2	11.5	9.0	0.0
Evaporated, Light, Carnation*	1 Serving/25g	28	110	7.5	10.5	4.0	0.0
Evaporated, Low Fat, Somerfield*	1oz/28g	31	109	8.0	11.0	4.0	0.0
Evaporated, Safeway*	1 Serving/69g	110	160	8.2	11.5	9.0	0.0
Evaporated, Tesco*	1 Serving/95g	153	161	8.4	11.6	9.0	0.0
Evaporated, Whole	1oz/28g	42	151	8.4	8.5	9.4	0.0
Full Fat, Pasteurised Standardised, Sainsbury's*	1fl oz/30ml	20	68	3.2	4.7	4.0	0.0
Goats, Pasteurised	1fl oz/30ml	18	60	3.1	4.4	3.5	0.0
Half Fat, M & S*	1fl oz/30ml	15	49	3.4	5.0	1.7	0.0
Low Fat, Calcia Extra Calcium, Unigate*	1fl oz/30ml	14	45	4.3	6.3	0.5	0.0
Semi Skimmed, Arla*	½ Pint/296ml	145	49	3.4	5.0	1.7	0.0
Semi Skimmed, Asda*	¼ Pint/125ml	61	49	3.4	5.0	1.7	0.0
Semi Skimmed, British Long Life UHT, Sainsbury's*	1 Serving/100ml	49	49	3.4	5.0	1.7	0.0
Semi Skimmed, Budgens*	1 Glass/250ml	123	49	3.3	5.2	1.7	0.0
Semi Skimmed, Cravendale*	1 Serving/200ml	98	49	3.4	5.0	1.7	0.0
Semi Skimmed, Long Life, Tesco*	1 Serving/20ml	10	49	3.4	5.0	1.7	0.0
Semi Skimmed, Organic, M & S*	1 Bottle/568ml	278	49	3.4	5.0	1.7	0.0
Semi Skimmed, Sainsbury's*	1fl oz/30ml	15	49	3.4	5.0	1.7	0.0
Semi-Skimmed	1fl oz/28ml	13	46	3.3	5.0	1.6	0.0
Semi-Skimmed, Co-Op*	1 Serving/100ml	50	50	3.0	5.0	1.7	0.0
Semi-Skimmed, Tesco*	1 Glass/200ml	96	48	3.3	5.0	1.6	0.0
Skimmed	1fl oz/28ml	9	33	3.3	5.0	0.1	0.0
Skimmed, Budgens*	1 Glass/250ml	88	35	3.4	5.2	0.1	0.0
Skimmed, Co-Op*	1 Serving/100ml	35	35	3.0	5.0	0.1	0.0
Skimmed, Long Life British UHT, Sainsbury's*	1 Glass/200ml	70	35	3.4	5.0	0.1	0.0
Skimmed, Long Life UHT, SmartPrice, Asda*	1fl oz/30ml	10	35	3.2	5.2	0.1	0.0
Skimmed, M & S*	1 Serving/100ml	34	34	3.4	5.0	0.1	0.0
Skimmed, Organic, Tesco*	1 Serving/250ml	85	34	3.3	5.0	0.1	0.0
Skimmed, Powdered, Organic, Evernat*	1oz/28g	96	344	34.0	52.0	0.0	0.0
Skimmed, Tesco*	1 Pint/50ml	17	34	3.3	5.0	0.1	0.0
Skimmed, UHT, Asda*	1floz/30ml	10	34	3.4	5.0	0.1	0.0
Skimmed, UHT, Tesco*	1 Serving/100ml	34	34	3.3	5.0	0.1	0.0
Skimmed, Unsweetened Condensed, HE, Tesco*	1 Sm Can/205g	221	108	7.5	10.5	4.0	0.0
Soya, Flavoured	1floz/30mls	12	40	2.8	3.6	1.7	0.0
Soya, No Added Sugar, Calcium Enriched, Granose*	1floz/30ml	11	36	3.3	1.9	1.9	0.0
Soya, No Added Sugar, Organic, Granose*	1floz/30ml	10	33	3.3	1.8	1.7	0.0
Soya, Plain	1floz/30ml	10	32	2.9	0.8	1.9	0.0
Soya, So Good*	1fl oz/30ml	15	50	3.4	5.3	1.7	0.0
Soya, Sweetened, Asda*	1fl oz/30ml	14	47	3.3	4.2	1.9	0.0
Soya, Sweetened, Calcium Enriched, Granose*	1floz/30ml	14	45	3.3	4.2	1.9	0.0
Soya, Sweetened, Calcium Enriched, White Wave*	1floz/30ml	14	47	3.3	4.1	1.9	0.0
Soya, Sweetened, Safeway*	1fl oz/30ml	12	41	3.3	3.3	1.6	0.2
Soya, Sweetened, Sainsbury's*	1fl oz/30ml	14	45	3.6	2.9	2.1	0.1
Soya, Tesco*	1 Serving/100ml	45	45	3.6	2.9	2.1	1.0
Soya, Unsweetened, Asda*	1fl oz/30ml	11	38	3.3	1.9	1.9	0.0
Soya, Unsweetened, Sainsbury's*	1 Serving/125ml	45	36	3.6	0.6	2.1	0.1
Soya, Unsweetened, Value, Tesco*	1 Serving/250ml	65	26	2.8	0.2	1.6	0.9
UHT Portions, Kerrygold*	1 Portion/14g	9	66	3.2	4.8	3.9	0.0
Whole, Fresh	1fl oz/28ml	18	66	3.2	4.8	3.9	0.0
Whole, Organic, M & S*	1 Bottle/568ml	386	68	3.2	4.7	4.0	0.0

MILK SHAKE,	Measure WEIGHT/INFO	per Measure KCAL	KCAL	PROT	CARB	FAT	FIBRE
Banana, Frijj*	1 Serving/500ml	310	62	3.4	10.1	0.8	0.0
Banana, McDonald's*	1 Regular/336g	396	118	3.2	19.8	3.0	0.0
Chocolate Flavour, BGTY, Sainsbury's*	1 Bottle/500ml	290	58	5.3	8.0	0.5	0.9
Chocolate Flavoured, Fresh, Thick, Frijj*	1 Bottle/500ml	345	69	3.5	11.6	1.0	0.0
Chocolate, McDonald's*	1 Regular/336g	403	120	3.4	19.9	3.0	0.0
Chocolate, Thick, Somerfield*	1 Shake/250ml	285	114	4.0	15.0	4.0	0.0
Flying Custard Flavour, Low Fat, Frijj*	1 Bottle/500ml	325	65	3.4	11.0	0.8	0.0
Powder, Made Up With Semi-Skimmed Milk	1 Serving/250ml	173	69	3.2	11.3	1.6	0.0
Powder, Made Up With Whole Milk	1 Serving/250ml	218	87	3.1	11.1	3.7	0.0
Strawberry Flavour, Thick, Low Fat, Frijj*	1 Bottle/250ml	155	62	3.4	10.1	0.8	0.0
Strawberry, McDonald's*	1 Regular/336g	400	119	3.2	20.0	3.0	0.0
Strawberry, Thick, Somerfield*	1 Milkshake/250ml	275	110	4.0	15.0	4.0	0.0
Vanilla Flavour, BGTY, Sainsbury's*	1 Bottle/500ml	230	46	5.3	5.9	0.1	0.4
Vanilla, McDonald's*	1 Regular/336g	383	114	3.2	18.8	3.0	0.0
MILKY BAR,							
Buttons, Nestle*	1 Mini Bag/16g	87	542	7.6	57.5	31.3	0.0
Choo, Nestle*	1oz/28g	131	468	4.7	73.2	17.6	0.0
Crunchies, Nestle*	1 Pack/30g	168	560	7.0	54.9	34.7	0.0
Nestle*	1 Bar/12g	65	542	7.6	57.5	31.3	0.0
MILKY WAY,							
Fun Size, Mars*	1oz/28g	125	447	3.7	71.6	16.2	0.0
Magic Stars, Mars*	1 Bag/33g	184	557	8.8	51.8	35.0	0.0
Mars*	1 Single Bar/26g	118	454	4.2	72.0	16.6	0.0
MILO, Nestle*	1 Serving/20g	76	380	8.2	72.9	6.0	4.7
MINCEMEAT,							
Mincemeat	1oz/28g	77	274	0.6	62.1	4.3	1.3
Organic, Waitrose*	1oz/28g	81	290	0.9	65.8	2.6	2.0
Traditional, Sainsbury's*	1 Tbsp/23g	65	282	0.9	62.4	3.2	1.4
MINI EGGS, Milk Chocolate, Cadbury's*	1 Egg/3g	15	495	5.6	67.7	22.2	0.0
MINSTRELS, Galaxy, Mars*	1 Pack/42g	206	491	6.0	69.5	21.0	0.0
MINT,							
Dried	1oz/28g	78	279	24.8	34.6	4.6	0.0
Fresh	1oz/28g	12	43	3.8	5.3	0.7	0.0
Jelly, Baxters*	1oz/28g	74	264	0.0	66.0	0.0	0.0
Jelly, Safeway*	1 Serving/10g	17	174	0.3	41.6	0.0	0.0
Jelly, Sainsbury's*	1 Serving/10g	27	269	0.1	66.6	0.2	0.3
Matchmakers, Nestle*	1oz/28g	134	477	5.1	68.7	20.2	0.0
Twix, Mars*	1 Pack/58g	289	498	4.7	63.8	24.9	0.0
MINTS,							
After Dinner, Dark, Elizabeth Shaw*	1 Chocolate/9g	42	469	2.8	62.5	23.1	0.0
After Dinner, Sainsbury's*	1 Mint/7g	32	456	4.1	62.1	21.2	4.1
After Eight, Nestle*	1 Mint/8g	34	419	2.5	72.4	13.3	0.0
Butter Mintoes, M & S*	1 Sweet/9g	35	391	0.0	84.0	6.8	0.0
Buttermints, M & S*	1oz/28g	120	428	0.6	85.8	9.1	0.0
Clear, Co-Op*	1 Sweet/6g	24	395	0.0	98.0	0.0	0.0
Cream, Luxury, Thorntons*	1 Chocolate/13g	62	477	4.2	62.3	23.8	2.3
Everton, Co-Op*	1 Sweet/6g	25	410	0.6	92.0	4.0	0.0
Extra Strong, Trebor*	3 Mints/10g	40	396	0.3	98.8	0.0	0.0
Glacier, Fox's*	1 Mint/5g	19	386	0.0	96.4	0.0	0.0
Humbug, Thorntons*	1 Sweet/9g	31	340	1.0	87.8	4.4	0.0
Humbugs, Co-Op*	1 Sweet/8g	34	425	0.6	89.9	7.0	0.0
Humbugs, M & S*	1 Sweet/9g	37	407	0.6	91.1	4.4	0.0
Humbugs, Somerfield*	1oz/28g	105	374	1.0	84.0	4.0	0.0
Humbugs, TTD, Sainsbury's*	1oz/28g	113	405	0.7	86.3	6.3	0.0

Nutrition Values per 100g / 100ml

M

M

MINTS,	Measure WEIGHT/INFO	per Measure KCAL	KCAL	PROT	CARB	FAT	FIBRE
			Nutrition Values per 100g / 100ml				
Imperials, Co-Op*	1 Sweet/3g	12	395	0.3	98.0	0.2	0.0
Imperials, M & S*	1oz/28g	109	391	0.0	97.8	0.0	0.0
Mint Assortment, M & S*	1 Sweet/7g	29	414	0.7	85.4	7.7	0.0
Mint Favourites, Bassett's*	1 assorted sweet/6g	22	367	0.9	77.4	5.9	0.0
Polo, Sugar Free, Nestle*	1oz/28g	67	238	0.0	99.1	0.0	0.0
Rocks, M & S*	1oz/28g	108	385	0.0	96.2	0.0	0.0
Toffi, Thorntons*	1oz/28g	125	448	4.4	48.5	26.4	0.3
MISO	1oz/28g	57	203	13.3	23.5	6.2	0.0
MIXED FRUIT,							
Pieces In Custard Banana Sauce, Fruitini*	1 Can/140g	101	72	1.2	15.7	0.9	0.0
Pieces In Orange Jelly, Fruitini*	1 Can/140g	94	67	0.3	15.8	0.1	0.0
Somerfield*	1oz/28g	80	285	2.0	68.0	1.0	0.0
Sultanas, Currants, Raisins & Citrus Peel, Asda*	1 Serving/100g	283	283	2.6	67.0	0.5	1.7
MIXED GRILL, Farmfoods*	1 Pack/300g	471	157	8.1	12.7	8.2	0.6
MIXED PEEL	1 Heaped Tbsp/25g	58	231	0.3	59.1	0.9	4.8
MIXED VEGETABLES,							
Canned, Drained, Sainsbury's*	1 Can/200g	114	57	3.0	10.6	0.3	2.3
Canned, Re-Heated, Drained	1oz/28g	11	38	1.9	6.1	0.8	1.7
Farmhouse, Tesco*	1 Serving/80g	32	40	3.6	4.6	0.8	3.0
Fresh, Asda*	1oz/28g	7	26	1.9	3.0	0.7	1.0
Freshly Frozen, Iceland*	1 Serving/100g	52	52	3.4	8.3	0.9	3.4
Frozen, Asda*	1 Serving/100g	53	53	3.1	8.0	0.9	4.0
Frozen, Boiled In Salted Water	1oz/28g	12	42	3.3	6.6	0.5	0.0
Frozen, Safeway*	1 Serving/120g	70	58	3.0	9.4	0.9	3.4
Frozen, Sainsbury's*	1 Serving/90g	49	54	2.8	8.4	1.0	3.1
Frozen, Tesco*	1 Serving/100g	49	49	2.9	7.8	0.7	3.2
Frozen, Waitrose*	1 Serving/100g	54	54	3.1	8.7	0.8	3.5
In Salted Water, Asda*	1oz/28g	13	48	2.6	9.0	0.2	1.7
In Water, Straight to Wok, Amoy*	½ Pack/110g	27	25	1.8	3.7	0.3	0.0
Organic, Waitrose*	1oz/28g	19	69	4.4	10.0	1.3	2.7
Red Peppers & Courgette, Tesco*	1 Pack/250g	68	27	1.7	3.8	0.5	2.0
MOLASSES	1 Tbsp/20g	53	266	0.0	68.8	0.1	0.0
MONKEY NUTS, Roasted, Somerfield*	1oz/28g	111	396	20.0	7.0	32.0	0.0
MONKFISH,							
Grilled	1oz/28g	27	96	22.7	0.0	0.6	0.0
Raw	1oz/28g	18	66	15.7	0.0	0.4	0.0
Tails, Asda*	1oz/28g	27	96	22.7	0.0	0.6	0.0
MONSTER MUNCH,							
Flamin' Hot, Walkers*	1 Bag/25g	118	470	7.0	55.0	25.0	1.8
Pickled Onion, Walkers*	1 Bag/25g	120	480	6.0	57.0	25.0	1.7
Spicy, Walkers*	1 Bag/25g	125	500	5.0	55.0	29.0	1.3
MOROCCAN VEGETABLES,							
COU, M & S*	½ Pack/150g	83	55	2.4	8.2	1.5	1.7
With Cous Cous, WTF, Sainsburys*	1 Serving/450g	495	110	3.2	16.8	3.3	2.5
MOUSSAKA,							
Beef, HE, Tesco*	1 Pack/300g	294	98	6.1	10.1	3.7	0.0
COU, M & S*	1 Pack/300g	285	95	6.6	12.1	2.4	0.6
Perfectly Balanced, Waitrose*	1 Pack/300g	255	85	6.6	7.6	3.1	1.0
Ready Meals, Waitrose*	1 Pack/300g	492	164	8.2	10.9	9.7	1.7
Vegetable, M & S*	1 Pack/300g	330	110	4.4	11.8	5.2	1.1
Vegetable, Ready Meals, Waitrose*	1oz/28g	38	134	3.7	12.3	7.8	2.3
MOUSSE,							
Aero Chocolate, Nestle*	1 Pot/59g	109	185	5.1	21.0	8.9	0.5
Aero Twist Cappuccino & Chocolate, Nestle*	1 Pot/75g	135	180	4.2	16.8	10.8	0.2

MOUSSE,	Measure WEIGHT/INFO	per Measure KCAL	Nutrition Values per 100g / 100ml KCAL	PROT	CARB	FAT	FIBRE
Apricot, Lite, Onken*	1 Pot/150g	156	104	4.6	18.0	1.5	0.3
Banoffee, COU, M & S*	1 Pot/70g	102	145	2.9	28.8	2.1	1.5
Black Cherry, Lite, Onken*	1 Pot/150g	156	104	4.6	17.9	1.5	0.3
Blackcurrant, Onken*	1 Pot/150g	210	140	5.2	14.6	6.8	0.0
Blackcurrant, Shape*	1oz/28g	12	43	3.0	3.9	1.8	0.2
Cadbury's Buttons, Twinpot, St Ivel*	1 Pot/100g	262	262	5.6	27.2	14.6	0.0
Cadbury's Flake, Twinpot, St Ivel*	1 Pot/100g	257	257	5.6	27.4	13.9	0.0
Cadbury's Light Chocolate, St Ivel*	1 Pot/64g	79	123	6.2	17.3	3.2	0.0
Cadbury's Mint Flavour Chocolate, St Ivel*	1 Pot/64g	115	180	5.4	22.6	7.5	0.0
Caramelised Orange, COU, M & S*	1 Pot/70g	91	130	2.8	26.3	1.7	3.4
Chocolate	1 Carton/60g	83	139	4.0	19.9	5.4	0.0
Chocolate & Hazelnut, Onken*	1 Pot/125g	173	138	3.3	17.8	6.0	0.0
Chocolate & Hazelnut Puree, Onken*	½ Pot/185g	222	120	3.4	19.5	3.1	0.0
Chocolate & Mint, COU, M & S*	1 Serving/90g	108	120	5.4	17.8	2.6	0.5
Chocolate & Orange, COU, M & S*	1 Pot/70g	77	110	5.9	16.0	2.6	0.9
Chocolate, BGTY, Sainsbury's*	1 Pot/62.5g	74	120	4.8	18.4	3.0	0.4
Chocolate Co-Op*	1 Mousse/63g	129	205	4.0	25.3	9.8	1.1
Chocolate, COU, M & S*	1 Pot/70g	81	115	5.8	16.6	2.7	1.0
Chocolate, Eat Smart, Safeway*	1 Pot/62g	81	130	4.1	21.5	2.7	1.1
Chocolate, HE, Tesco*	1 Mousse/60g	64	107	3.1	17.9	2.6	2.1
Chocolate, Healthy Selection, Low Fat, Somerfield*	1 Pot/60g	81	135	5.3	18.2	4.6	0.0
Chocolate, Iceland*	1 Pot/62g	113	183	4.0	26.3	6.9	0.0
Chocolate, Italian Style, Tesco*	1 Pot/90g	243	270	5.0	32.8	13.2	2.4
Chocolate, Organic, Evernat*	1oz/28g	83	296	10.1	21.1	19.1	0.0
Chocolate, Safeway*	1 Pot/62g	127	205	4.0	25.3	9.8	1.1
Chocolate, Sainsbury's*	1 Pot/62g	122	197	4.0	25.4	8.8	1.1
Chocolate With Vanilla Layer, Cadbury's*	1 Pot/100g	162	162	4.8	21.9	6.1	0.0
Fruit Juice, Shape*	1 Pot/100g	115	115	3.5	18.5	2.8	0.0
Layered Lemon, Co-Op*	1 Mousse/100g	140	140	3.0	24.0	3.0	0.2
Layered Strawberry, Co-Op*	1 Mousse/100g	120	120	3.0	19.0	3.0	0.2
Lemon, COU, M & S*	1 Pot/70g	81	115	2.9	19.4	2.4	3.5
Lemon, Dessert, Sainsbury's*	1oz/28g	51	182	3.6	20.7	9.4	0.6
Lemon, Eat Smart, Safeway*	1 Pot/70g	95	135	3.4	23.5	2.7	0.4
Lemon, Less Than 3% Fat, BGTY, Sainsbury's*	1 Pot/62g	59	95	3.4	14.3	2.7	0.7
Lemon, Less Than 3% Fat, HE, Tesco*	1 Serving/60g	57	95	3.4	14.3	2.7	0.0
Lemon, Lite, Onken*	1 Pot/150g	156	104	4.6	18.0	1.6	0.0
Lemon, Low Fat, Morrisons*	1 Pot/110g	175	159	3.1	30.5	2.7	0.1
Lemon, Onken*	1 Pot/150g	219	146	5.1	15.8	6.9	0.1
Lemon, Perfectly Balanced, Waitrose*	1 Pot/95g	150	158	3.1	30.2	2.7	0.1
Milk Chocolate, Cadbury's, St Ivel*	1 Pot/55g	106	192	6.0	25.8	7.2	0.0
Milky Way, Mars*	1 Pot/50g	115	229	4.5	20.0	14.5	0.0
Orange & Nectarine, Shape*	1oz/28g	13	47	3.0	4.9	1.9	0.0
Peach & Passion Fruit, Perfectly Balanced, Waitrose*	1 Serving/95g	118	124	3.5	21.2	2.8	0.5
Peach, Onken*	1 Pot/150g	200	133	4.8	13.5	6.6	0.0
Peach, Shape*	1oz/28g	12	43	3.0	3.9	1.8	0.1
Pineapple, COU, M & S*	1 Pot/70g	84	120	3.3	20.7	2.4	3.5
Pineapple, Shape*	1oz/28g	12	43	2.9	3.8	1.8	0.1
Raspberry & Blackcurrant, Shape*	1 Pot/125g	58	46	3.0	4.5	1.8	0.1
Raspberry, COU, M & S*	1 Pot/70g	81	115	3.0	19.6	2.4	3.9
Raspberry, Lite, Onken*	1 Pot/150g	152	101	4.6	17.3	1.5	1.0
Raspberry Ripple, Tesco*	1 Mousse/100ml	149	149	2.9	20.5	6.1	0.1
Rhubarb, Lite, Onken*	1 Pot/150g	155	103	4.6	17.8	1.5	0.3
Starburst Juicy Eden Vale*	1 pot/90g	139	154	4.2	21.9	5.5	0.1
Strawberry, Asda*	1 Pot/64g	107	167	3.5	18.0	9.0	0.2

M

	Measure WEIGHT/INFO	per Measure KCAL	Nutrition Values per 100g / 100ml KCAL	PROT	CARB	FAT	FIBRE
MOUSSE,							
Strawberry Fruity, Organic, Sainsbury's*	1 Pot/125g	129	103	6.2	15.7	3.0	3.6
Strawberry, Lite, Onken*	1 Pot/150g	153	102	4.6	17.3	1.6	1.1
Strawberry, Low Fat, Waitrose*	1 Serving/95g	112	118	3.2	20.0	2.8	0.6
Strawberry, Onken*	1 Pot/150g	200	133	4.8	13.5	6.6	0.0
Strawberry, Safeway*	1 Mousse/63g	106	168	3.5	17.3	9.4	0.1
Strawberry, Sainsbury's*	1 Pot/63g	106	168	3.4	17.5	9.4	0.1
Strawberry, Shape*	1oz/28g	12	44	3.0	4.0	1.8	0.0
Summer Fruits, Light, Muller*	1 Pot/149g	143	96	4.3	18.7	0.4	0.0
Tropical, Eat Smart, Safeway*	1 Pot/90g	122	135	3.3	24.5	2.3	3.2
Tropical Fruits, Light, Muller*	1 Pot/150g	150	101	4.3	20.0	0.4	0.0
Tropical Pineapple, Shape*	1 Pot/125ml	51	41	2.6	3.6	1.8	0.0
MUFFIN,							
Average Muffin	1 Muffin/57g	161	283	10.1	49.6	6.3	2.0
Blueberry Buster, McVitie's*	1 Muffin/95g	408	429	4.3	49.9	23.6	1.1
Blueberry, Made Up, Jane Asher*	1 Muffin/79g	217	275	4.8	40.6	10.4	1.3
Blueberry, M & S*	1oz/28g	105	376	4.8	52.4	16.4	1.2
Blueberry, Sainsbury's*	1 Muffin/75g	242	322	5.4	46.7	12.6	2.2
Blueberry, Tesco*	1 Muffin/70g	279	398	4.8	39.7	24.4	1.3
Blueberry, Waitrose*	1 Muffin/65g	239	367	4.7	55.2	14.2	1.7
Blueberry, Weight Watchers*	1 Serving/65g	172	265	6.4	46.9	5.7	2.6
Bran	1 Muffin/57g	155	272	7.8	45.6	7.7	7.7
Bran & Sultana, Weight Watchers*	1 Muffin/60g	144	240	4.5	50.7	2.1	2.3
Buttered, McDonald's*	1 Muffin/63g	158	250	8.6	40.7	5.9	2.9
Buttered With Preserve, McDonald's*	1 Muffin/93g	234	252	5.9	48.1	4.0	2.0
Carrot Cake, Entenmanns*	1 Muffin/105g	344	328	5.1	45.8	15.1	3.0
Cheese & Black Pepper, Sainsbury's*	1 Muffin/65g	142	218	12.9	34.6	2.0	1.2
Cheese, Tesco*	1 Muffin/75g	183	244	12.5	38.1	4.6	2.0
Choc Chip, BGTY, Sainsbury's*	1 Muffin/75g	282	376	5.2	51.8	16.4	1.6
Choc Chip, Mini, Weight Watchers*	1 Muffin/15g	47	312	6.6	52.1	8.6	3.1
Chocolate, BGTY, Sainsbury's*	1 Muffin/75g	282	376	5.2	51.8	16.4	1.6
Chocolate Chip, American Style, Sainsbury's*	1 Muffin/75g	328	437	5.9	52.4	22.7	0.6
Chocolate Indulgence, McVitie's*	1 Muffin/75g	254	338	5.8	57.9	9.2	1.3
Chunky Chocolate Chip, McVitie's*	1 Muffin/94g	393	418	5.3	50.6	21.6	0.8
Dairy Cream Lemon, Safeway*	1 Cake/110g	409	372	4.4	44.5	19.6	0.0
Double Berry Burst, Entenmann's*	1 Muffin/59g	140	238	4.6	50.1	2.1	1.6
Double Choc Chip, Mini, Asda*	1 Mini Muffin/19g	74	390	6.0	51.0	18.0	0.0
Double Choc Chip, Weight Watchers*	1 Muffin/65g	189	291	6.8	47.2	8.3	3.6
Double Chocolate, 95% Fat Free, Entemann's*	1 Muffin/58g	152	262	2.6	52.3	4.7	1.8
Double Chocolate Chip, Co-Op*	1oz/28g	115	410	6.0	49.0	21.0	3.0
Double Chocolate Chip, Tesco*	1 Muffin/72g	302	419	6.1	48.0	22.5	1.4
Double Chocolate, M & S*	1 Muffin/75g	313	417	5.2	48.7	22.4	1.9
Double Chocolate, Mini, M & S*	1 Muffin/30g	131	438	5.7	52.8	22.7	1.2
Double Chocolate, Mini, Weight Watchers*	1 Muffin/15g	45	300	7.0	48.5	8.7	3.5
Double Chocolate, Somerfield*	1 Muffin/70g	298	425	6.8	46.5	23.5	0.0
Lemon & Blueberry, Tesco*	1 Muffin/110g	411	374	4.0	42.4	20.9	1.1
Lemon & Poppy Seed, Entenmann's*	1 Muffin/105g	417	397	5.6	52.8	19.3	2.5
Lemon & Poppy Seed, M & S*	1 Muffin/72g	281	390	6.3	46.1	19.8	1.5
Lemon & Sultana, BGTY, Sainsbury's*	1 Muffin/75g	211	281	4.5	55.6	4.5	1.4
Lemon, Boots*	1 Muffin/110g	424	385	3.6	50.0	19.0	1.3
M & S*	1 Muffin/56g	126	225	11.2	43.7	1.9	2.9
Mixed Fruit, Low Fat, Abbey Bakery*	1 Muffin/35g	93	267	4.5	55.6	4.5	1.4
Oven Bottom, Asda*	1 Muffin/68g	173	255	10.0	50.4	1.5	2.2
Oven Bottom, Mini, Morrisons*	1 Serving/42g	107	255	10.0	50.4	1.5	2.2
Oven Bottom, Tesco*	1 Muffin/68g	173	255	10.0	50.4	1.5	2.2

MUFFIN,	Measure WEIGHT/INFO	per Measure KCAL	Nutrition Values per 100g / 100ml KCAL	PROT	CARB	FAT	FIBRE
Oven Bottom, Warburton's*	1 Muffin/69g	175	253	10.9	45.8	2.9	0.0
Plain Chocolate Chip, Sainsbury's*	1 Muffin/75g	313	423	6.4	51.3	21.4	0.6
Premium White, Sainsbury's*	1 Muffin/65g	135	208	8.0	41.4	1.1	2.0
Rolo, Nestle*	1 Serving/80g	289	361	5.4	44.3	18.0	0.8
Skinny Sunrise, Starbucks*	1 Muffin/130g	255	194	4.6	36.7	3.0	1.3
Somerfield*	1 Muffin/60g	130	216	12.2	39.3	1.6	1.9
Spiced Fruit, Co-Op*	1 Muffin/60g	159	265	11.0	52.0	2.0	3.0
Spicy Fruit, Sainsbury's*	1 Muffin/63g	140	222	9.6	43.3	1.2	2.7
Toffee Choo Choo, Tesco*	1 Muffin/95g	402	423	6.4	49.1	22.4	1.0
Toffee Temptation, McVitie's*	1 Muffin/85.5g	295	347	4.7	60.8	9.5	0.8
White, Asda*	1 Muffin/72g	174	242	9.0	48.0	1.6	2.0
White, Sainsbury's*	1 Muffin/65g	147	226	10.3	43.2	1.3	2.8
White, Tesco*	1 Muffin/60g	143	238	10.2	42.0	3.2	2.1
White, Waitrose*	1 Muffin/60g	128	213	10.7	39.4	1.4	4.2
Wholemeal, Organic, Waitrose*	1 Muffin/65g	129	198	12.4	32.9	1.9	7.6
Wholemeal, Perfectly Balanced, Waitrose*	1 Muffin/65g	137	211	11.8	36.1	2.2	5.8
Wholemeal, Tesco*	1 Muffin/65g	134	206	11.1	35.9	2.0	5.2
MULBERRIES, Raw	1oz/28g	10	36	1.3	8.1	0.0	0.0
MULLET,							
Grey, Grilled	1oz/28g	42	150	25.7	0.0	5.2	0.0
Grey, Raw	1oz/28g	32	115	19.8	0.0	4.0	0.0
Red, Grilled	1oz/28g	34	121	20.4	0.0	4.4	0.0
Red, Raw	1oz/28g	31	109	18.7	0.0	3.8	0.0
MULTIVITAMINS Drink, Tropicana*	1fl oz/30ml	16	52	0.5	10.5	0.0	0.1
MUNCHIES, Mint, Rowntree, Nestle*	1 Pack/61g	268	433	3.8	67.4	16.5	0.0
MUSHROOMS,							
Breaded, Home-Style, Kitchen Range Foods*	1oz/28g	32	113	4.3	23.2	0.4	0.0
Button, Baby, Tesco*	1 Serving/75g	10	13	1.8	0.4	0.5	1.1
Button, Sliced, Sainsbury's*	1 Can/156g	22	14	2.1	0.5	0.5	1.2
Button, Whole, In Salted Water, Tesco*	1 Serving/50g	6	11	1.7	0.6	0.2	1.4
Chestnut, Tesco*	1 Pack/250g	33	13	1.8	0.4	0.5	1.1
Chinese, Dried, Raw	1oz/28g	80	284	10.0	59.9	1.8	0.0
Closed Cup, Tesco*	1oz/28g	4	13	1.8	0.4	0.5	1.1
Common, Boiled In Salted Water	1oz/28g	3	11	1.8	0.4	0.3	1.1
Common, Canned, Re-Heated, Drained	1oz/28g	3	12	2.1	0.0	0.4	1.3
Common, Fried In Blended Oil	1oz/28g	44	157	2.4	0.3	16.2	1.5
Common, Fried In Butter	1oz/28g	44	157	2.4	0.3	16.2	1.5
Common, Raw	1oz/28g	4	13	1.8	0.4	0.5	1.1
Creamed, Asda*	½ Can/145g	132	91	1.2	8.0	6.0	0.3
Creamed, Chesswood*	1oz/28g	24	86	1.3	9.0	5.0	0.8
Creamed, Tesco*	1oz/28g	19	68	1.3	3.4	5.5	0.3
Creamy, COU, M & S*	½ Pack/150g	75	50	3.2	4.5	2.3	1.6
Crispy, M & S*	1oz/28g	84	300	4.2	12.5	25.7	1.8
Dried	1oz/28g	45	159	21.8	4.8	6.0	13.3
Frozen, Tesco*	1oz/28g	4	13	1.8	0.4	0.5	1.1
Garlic	1oz/28g	39	139	2.1	0.6	14.4	1.2
Garlic, Breaded, Asda*	1 Serving/100g	173	173	5.7	17.9	8.8	0.9
Garlic, Breaded, Farmfoods*	1oz/28g	57	203	5.3	24.8	9.3	0.8
Garlic, Breaded, Iceland*	1 Pack/340g	816	240	5.6	18.6	15.9	1.6
Garlic, Italian Style, Organic, Asda*	1 Serving/42g	107	254	11.0	30.0	10.0	2.5
Garlic, Pizza Hut*	1 Pack/112.2g	217	192	5.9	19.7	9.9	3.4
Garlic, Tex-Mex Style, Morrisons*	1 Box/310g	527	170	5.5	19.4	7.8	1.7
Garlic, With BBQ Dip, Pizza Hut*	1 Pack/112.2g	264	234	6.2	30.5	10.0	3.4
Garlic, With Sour Cream & Chive Dip, Pizza Hut*	1 Pack/112.2g	429	380	6.4	20.0	30.8	3.4

MUSHROOMS,	Measure WEIGHT/INFO	per Measure KCAL	KCAL	PROT	CARB	FAT	FIBRE
			Nutrition Values per 100g / 100ml				
Oyster, Raw, Unprepared	1oz/28g	2	8	1.6	0.0	0.2	0.0
Porcini, Dried, Merchant Gourmet*	1 oz/28g	36	128	12.3	5.0	6.5	0.0
Provencale, COU, M & S*	1 Pack/300g	150	50	2.4	4.2	2.3	1.5
Shiitake, Cooked	1oz/28g	15	55	1.6	12.3	0.2	0.0
Shiitake, Dried, Raw	1oz/28g	83	296	9.6	63.9	1.0	0.0
Sliced, Frozen, Asda*	1 Serving/28g	3	12	1.8	0.4	0.3	1.1
Sliced, In Salted Water, Tesco*	1 Serving/100g	11	11	1.7	0.6	0.2	1.4
Straw, Canned, Drained	1oz/28g	4	15	2.1	1.2	0.2	0.0
Stuffed, Finest, Tesco*	1 Serving/130g	224	172	4.0	7.4	14.0	1.9
Stuffed, With Cheese & Herb Breadcrumbs, Waitrose*	1 Serving/165g	215	130	4.6	16.2	5.2	2.1
Stuffed With Cheese, Mustard & Herbs, Sainsbury's*	1 Serving/115g	150	130	7.4	6.3	8.3	1.2
MUSSELS,							
Boiled	1 Mussel/7g	7	104	16.7	3.5	2.7	0.0
Canned & Bottled, Drained	1oz/28g	27	98	16.9	3.1	2.1	0.0
Garlic Butter Sauce, Cooked, Scottish, Morrisons*	½ Pack/250g	218	87	4.6	3.6	6.0	0.3
Greenshell, New Zealand, Sainsbury's*	1 Serving/60g	74	123	19.2	4.3	2.3	0.1
Raw	1oz/28g	21	74	12.1	2.5	1.8	0.0
Thai Fragrant, M & S*	½ Pack/325g	358	110	10.6	4.5	5.7	0.1
Vegetable Oil, Smoked, John West*	1oz/28g	58	207	20.0	7.0	11.0	0.0
White Wine Cream Sauce, Cooked, Scottish, Morrisons*	½ Pack/250g	263	105	9.0	5.4	5.3	0.5
MUSTARD & Cress, Raw	1oz/28g	4	13	1.6	0.4	0.6	1.1
MUSTARD,							
American, French's*	tablespoon/15g	27	180	6.0	16.0	12.0	0.0
Cajun, Colman's*	1 Tsp/6g	11	187	7.0	23.0	6.5	2.7
Coarse Grain, Frank Cooper*	1 Tsp/6g	12	206	8.9	17.0	11.4	0.0
Colman's*	1 Tsp/5ml	9	188	7.0	19.0	9.3	1.6
Dijon, Frank Cooper*	1 Tsp/6g	11	179	7.2	10.0	12.3	0.0
Dijon, M & S*	1 Tsp/6g	9	153	10.0	7.2	9.5	1.0
English, Frank Cooper*	1 Tsp/6g	11	188	5.7	22.0	8.6	0.2
English, M & S*	1 Tsp/6g	14	226	12.6	8.7	15.9	1.0
English, Powder, Colman's*	1 Tsp/5g	26	518	29.0	24.0	34.0	6.2
English, Safeway*	1 Tsp/6g	10	163	6.1	18.3	6.7	0.0
English, With Chillies, Sainsbury's*	1 Tsp/5g	10	204	8.3	18.1	10.9	6.4
French Classic Yellow, Colman's*	1 Tsp/6g	4	73	4.3	2.6	4.2	0.0
French, Frank Cooper*	1 Tsp/6g	7	113	4.6	7.0	7.4	0.0
French Mild, Colman's*	1 Tsp/6g	6	104	6.3	4.0	7.0	3.8
Garlic, Colman's*	1 Tsp/6g	12	203	9.2	19.0	9.0	3.2
Herb & Tomato, Colman's*	1 Tsp/6g	14	228	9.5	26.0	8.5	3.6
Honey, Colman's*	1 Tsp/6g	12	208	7.4	24.0	8.2	0.0
Mayonnaise, BGTY, Sainsbury's*	1 Tsp/6g	9	146	2.9	13.4	8.8	0.5
Peppercorn, Colman's*	1 Tsp/6g	11	182	8.8	12.0	10.0	4.9
Powder	1 Tsp/3.3g	14	452	28.9	20.7	28.7	0.0
Powder, Colman's*	1oz/28g	145	518	29.0	24.0	34.0	0.0
Powder, Made Up	1oz/28g	63	226	14.5	10.4	14.4	0.0
Smooth	1 Level Tsp/8g	11	139	7.1	9.7	8.2	0.0
Sweet Peppers, Colman's*	1 Tsp/6g	13	218	7.9	20.0	11.0	4.9
Tarragon, Tesco*	1 Tbsp/15ml	59	396	0.9	8.6	39.8	0.2
Wholegrain	1 Level Tsp/8g	11	140	8.2	4.2	10.2	4.9
Wholegrain, Colman's*	1 Tsp/6g	10	173	8.5	8.5	11.0	5.9
Wholegrain, Safeway*	1 Tbsp/15g	27	183	8.0	15.2	9.1	0.0
Wholegrain, Tesco*	1 Tsp/6g	0	153	8.2	8.7	9.5	5.8

	Measure WEIGHT/INFO	per Measure KCAL	Nutrition Values per 100g / 100ml KCAL	PROT	CARB	FAT	FIBRE
NACHOS,							
Chicken, Safeway*	½ Pack/170g	352	207	10.3	15.7	11.4	1.8
Chilli, Sainbury's*	½ Pack/250g	695	278	10.9	29.5	12.9	1.3
Kit, Old El Paso*	½ Pack/260g	598	230	4.0	31.0	10.0	0.0
NECTARINES,							
Fresh, Raw	1oz/28g	11	40	1.4	9.0	0.1	1.2
Weighed With Pips	1 Med/140g	50	36	1.2	8.0	0.1	1.1
NESQUIK,							
Banana Flavour, Made With Semi Skimmed Milk, Nestle*	1 Serving/200ml	790	395	0.0	97.3	0.5	0.0
Chocolate Flavour, Nestle*	3 Tsp/15g	57	380	2.5	86.5	2.8	2.2
Strawberry, Dry, Nestle*	1 Serving/10g	39	390	0.0	96.7	0.5	0.0
NIBBLES, Cheese & Ham, Sainsbury's*	½ Pack/50g	257	514	13.1	54.8	27.1	2.6
NIK NAKS,							
Cream 'n' Cheesy, Golden Wonder*	1 Bag/34g	185	545	5.1	56.1	33.4	0.0
Nice 'n' Spicy, Golden Wonder*	1 Bag/34g	185	545	4.7	55.5	33.4	1.0
Rib 'n' Saucy, Golden Wonder*	1 Bag/34g	185	545	5.1	55.7	33.4	1.1
NOBBLE, Cadbury's*	1 Bar/30g	138	460	4.8	68.6	18.4	0.0
NOODLE BOWL,							
Chicken, Cantonese Style, Tesco*	1 Bowl/400g	356	89	5.8	12.6	1.7	1.6
Szechuan Style Prawn, Tesco*	1 Bowl/400g	376	94	5.5	17.3	0.3	0.9
NOODLES,							
99% Fat Free, Dry, Heinz*	1 Serving/85g	257	302	9.5	65.3	0.4	2.7
Cantonese, Sainsburys*	1 Serving/200g	248	124	4.3	17.2	4.2	1.9
Char Sui, BGTY, Sainsbury's*	1 Pack/450g	423	94	7.1	10.8	2.5	0.8
Char Sui, Cantonese, Sainsbury's*	1 Pack/450g	378	84	6.8	10.5	1.6	1.5
Chicken, Chinese, Asda*	1 Pot/302g	305	101	6.0	16.0	1.4	0.8
Chicken, Chinese Style, GFY, Asda*	1 Pack/393g	295	75	6.0	9.0	1.7	0.6
Chicken, Coconut & Coriander, M & S*	1 Pack/400g	440	110	8.8	10.4	3.8	1.7
Chicken Flavour, 3 Minute, Dry, Blue Dragon*	1 Pack/85g	403	475	9.3	61.2	21.4	0.0
Chicken Flavour, Instant, Dry, Bettabuy, Morrisons*	1 Pack/65g	295	454	10.5	63.6	17.5	0.9
Chilli Chicken, GFY, Asda*	1 Pack/415g	461	111	6.0	20.0	0.8	1.0
Chow Mein, Sainsbury's*	1 Pack/125g	136	109	3.9	19.2	1.8	0.8
Chow Mein, Stir Fry, Tesco*	1 Serving/200g	116	58	2.1	9.7	1.2	1.0
Egg, Asda*	1 Pack/184g	280	152	4.8	31.0	0.8	1.3
Egg, Boiled	1oz/28g	17	62	2.2	13.0	0.5	0.6
Egg, Fine, Dry, Sharwood's*	1oz/28g	95	340	10.8	70.1	1.8	2.9
Egg, Fine Thread, Dry, M & S*	1 Serving/63g	221	350	14.3	71.6	0.9	5.1
Egg Fried, Cantonese, Safeway*	1oz/28g	29	104	3.4	10.7	5.3	1.1
Egg, Medium, Asda*	1 Layer/190g	289	152	4.8	31.0	0.8	1.3
Egg, Medium, Dry, Sharwood's*	1oz/28g	95	340	10.8	70.1	1.8	2.9
Egg, Dry, Raw	1oz/28g	109	391	12.1	71.7	8.2	2.9
Egg, Straight To Wok, Amoy*	½ Pack/75g	113	151	4.2	29.0	2.1	1.3
Egg, Thread, Amoy*	1 Serving/150g	227	151	4.2	29.0	2.1	1.3
Egg, Thread, Sharwood's*	1oz/28g	30	107	3.6	21.8	0.6	1.1
Egg, Tossed In Sesame Oil, Asda*	½ Pack/150g	174	116	2.3	11.0	7.0	0.0
Fresh, Tesco*	1 Serving/150g	102	68	2.8	11.4	1.3	0.6
Fried	1oz/28g	43	153	1.9	11.3	11.5	0.5
Instant, Made Up, Blue Dragon*	1 Serving/75g	124	165	2.8	25.7	5.7	0.0
Instant, Dry, Sainsburys*	1 packet/100g	392	392	9.4	57.0	14.0	0.2
Japanese Udon, Sainsbury*	1 Serving/150g	210	140	3.9	27.1	1.8	1.2
Medium, Dry, Sharwood's*	1oz/28g	95	340	10.8	70.1	1.8	2.9
Medium, Straight To Wok*	1oz/28g	47	169	6.0	24.5	5.2	0.0
Oriental Beef & Sweet Red Pepper, Dry Colman's*	1 Serving/80g	254	317	4.2	73.4	0.7	5.1
Plain, Boiled	1oz/28g	17	62	2.4	13.0	0.4	0.7
Plain, Dry, Raw	1oz/28g	109	388	11.7	76.1	6.2	2.9

N

NOODLES,	Measure WEIGHT/INFO	per Measure KCAL	Nutrition Values per 100g / 100ml KCAL	PROT	CARB	FAT	FIBRE
Prawn, Eat Smart, Safeway*	1 Pack/200g	190	95	5.6	13.5	1.6	0.7
Ramen, With Chilli Beef, M & S*	1 Pack/484g	532	110	8.1	11.9	3.6	0.8
Rice, Dry, Amoy*	1oz/28g	101	361	6.5	86.6	1.0	0.0
Rice, Ho Fun, Dry, Amoy*	1 Serving/50g	172	343	12.1	71.1	1.1	0.0
Rice, Thai, Dry, Sharwood's*	1 Pack/250g	903	361	6.5	86.8	1.0	2.4
Savoury, COU, M & S*	1oz/28g	17	60	2.9	11.5	0.6	1.2
Savoury Vegetable, COU, M & S*	1 Pack/450g	270	60	2.9	11.5	0.6	1.2
Singapore, M & S*	1oz/28g	38	135	5.9	18.7	4.3	0.5
Singapore, Sainsbury's*	1 Pack/350g	441	126	3.2	11.9	7.3	2.4
Singapore, Somerfield*	1 Pot/300g	261	87	5.0	15.0	1.0	0.0
Singapore, Tesco*	1 Pack/350g	389	111	6.3	16.8	2.1	0.7
Singapore, Waitrose*	1 Pack/400g	476	119	7.3	12.6	4.4	2.1
Straight to Wok, Amoy*	1 Pack/180g	272	151	4.2	29.0	2.1	1.3
Thai Style, Sainsbury's*	1 Pack/340g	381	112	3.3	19.4	2.3	0.7
Thai, Waitrose*	1 Pack/300g	357	119	6.8	18.4	2.1	1.7
Thick, Dry, Sharwood's*	1 Pack/250g	850	340	10.8	70.1	1.8	2.9
Thread, Dry, Sharwood's*	1oz/28g	95	340	10.8	70.1	1.8	2.9
Thread, Straight To Wok, Amoy*	1oz/28g	47	169	6.0	24.5	5.2	0.0
NOUGAT,							
Nougat	1oz/28g	108	384	4.4	77.3	8.5	0.9
Raspberry & Orange Hazelnut, Thorntons*	1 Chocolate/9g	39	433	4.8	60.0	20.0	2.2
NUGGETS, Meat Free, BPC, Sainsbury's*	1 Nugget/18g	41	228	17.3	12.5	12.1	3.0
NUT ROAST,							
Nut Roast	1oz/28g	99	352	13.3	18.3	25.7	4.2
Cashew Roast, Granose*	1 Pack/150g	720	480	22.0	26.0	32.0	0.0
Leek, Cheese & Mushroom, Organic, Cauldron Foods*	Half Pack/143g	343	240	13.2	13.2	14.9	4.1
Lentil	1oz/28g	62	222	10.6	18.8	12.1	3.8
Tomato & Courgette, Organic, Waitrose*	½ Pack/142g	295	208	11.7	12.5	12.3	4.9
Vegetarian, Tesco*	1 Serving/160g	218	136	5.4	11.4	7.6	2.0
NUTMEG, Powder	1 Tsp/3g	16	525	5.8	45.3	36.3	0.0
NUTRI-GRAIN,							
Apple, Kellogg's*	1 Bar/37g	130	350	4.0	68.0	8.0	3.0
Blueberry, Kellogg's*	1 Bar/37g	130	350	4.0	68.0	8.0	3.0
Cappuccino, Kellogg's*	1 Bar/37g	137	370	5.0	66.0	10.0	2.5
Cherry, Kellogg's*	1 Bar/37g	133	360	4.0	68.0	8.0	3.0
Chocolate, Kellogg's*	1 Bar/37g	137	370	4.5	67.0	10.0	3.0
Elevenses, Kellogg's*	1 Bar/45g	162	360	5.0	67.0	8.0	3.5
Forest Fruits & Yoghurt Twists, Kellogg's*	1 Bar/37g	133	360	3.5	69.0	8.0	2.0
Mixed Fruits Twists, Kellogg's*	1 Bar/37g	133	360	3.5	69.0	8.0	2.0
Strawberry, Kellogg's*	1 Bar/37g	133	360	4.0	69.0	8.0	3.0
Strawberry Twists, Kellogg's*	1 Bar/37g	130	350	3.5	69.0	8.0	2.0
Tangy Orange, Kellogg's*	1 Bar/38g	141	370	5.0	68.0	9.0	4.0
NUTS & RAISINS,							
Mixed	1 Pack/40g	192	481	14.1	31.5	34.1	4.5
Mixed, Safeway*	1 Serving/50g	264	527	18.6	30.7	36.7	4.8
Mixed, Somerfield*	1oz/28g	159	568	18.0	24.0	45.0	0.0
Mixed, Unsalted, Sainsbury's*	1oz/28g	143	510	16.2	28.0	37.0	4.8
NUTS - MIXED,							
Mixed	1 Pack/40g	243	607	22.9	7.9	54.1	6.0
Mixed, Chopped, Sainsbury's*	1 Serving/100g	605	605	27.1	9.6	50.9	6.0
Mixed, Luxury, Unsalted, Somerfield*	1oz/28g	186	663	18.0	10.0	61.0	0.0
Mixed, Natural, Luxury, Tesco*	1oz/28g	179	639	22.6	6.9	57.9	5.6
Mixed, Roast Salted, Somerfield*	1oz/28g	175	625	24.0	11.0	54.0	0.0
Mixed, Sainsbury's*	1 Bag/200g	1346	673	18.8	4.6	64.5	5.3

NUTS - MIXED,	Measure WEIGHT/INFO	per Measure KCAL	Nutrition Values per 100g / 100ml KCAL	PROT	CARB	FAT	FIBRE
Organic Luxury , M & S*	1oz/28g	179	640	21.1	11.6	56.6	6.1
Roast Salted, Luxury, KP*	1oz/28g	181	646	21.9	10.1	57.6	5.9
Selection, Honey Roast, M & S*	1oz/28g	175	625	18.1	20.5	52.2	5.1
NUTSERS, Cheese & Onion, KP*	1 Bag/175g	900	514	14.3	47.3	29.8	5.4

N

	Measure WEIGHT/INFO	per Measure KCAL	KCAL	PROT	CARB	FAT	FIBRE
OATCAKES,							
Fine, Nairn's*	1 Oatcake/7g	32	463	10.9	61.3	19.3	6.0
Nairn's*	1 Serving/10g	45	446	11.0	59.3	18.3	6.6
Organic, Safeway*	1 Oatcake/13g	56	445	11.2	56.7	19.3	6.6
Retail	1oz/28g	123	441	10.0	63.0	18.3	0.0
Rough, Nairn's*	1 Oatcake/11g	48	436	10.6	64.7	18.2	7.2
Rough Scottish, Sainsbury's*	1 Oatcake/11g	51	462	12.3	59.9	19.3	6.5
Scottish, Organic, Waitrose*	1 Biscuit/13g	58	447	11.2	57.0	19.4	6.6
OATMEAL, Raw	1oz/28g	112	401	12.4	72.8	8.7	6.8
OATS,							
Jumbo, Organic, Evernat*	1oz/28g	117	418	13.0	69.0	9.6	7.4
Jumbo, Organic, Waitrose*	1oz/28g	101	361	11.0	61.1	8.1	7.8
Porridge Scottish, Organic, Sainsbury's*	1 Serving/45g	172	383	10.0	74.4	5.0	7.9
TTD, Sainsbury's*	1 Serving/40g	152	381	9.7	74.7	4.8	0.0
OCEAN,							
Pinks, Asda*	1oz/28g	24	86	10.0	10.0	0.7	0.2
Prawnies, Mini, Asda*	1 Prawnie/11g	9	84	11.0	8.0	0.9	0.5
Snacks, Sainsbury's*	1 Serving/16g	18	113	7.0	21.0	0.1	0.1
Stix, Farmfoods*	1 Stick/14g	15	110	7.0	20.0	0.2	0.0
OCTOPUS, Raw	1oz/28g	23	83	17.9	0.0	1.3	0.0
OIL,							
Chilli, Sainsbury's*	1 Tsp/5ml	41	823	0.0	0.0	91.4	0.0
Chilli, Waitrose*	1 Tsp/5ml	41	824	0.0	0.0	91.6	0.0
Chinese Stir Fry, Asda*	1 Tbsp/15ml	123	823	0.0	0.0	91.4	0.0
Coconut	1 Tsp/5ml	45	899	0.0	0.0	99.9	0.0
Corn	1 Tsp/5ml	45	899	0.0	0.0	99.9	0.0
Corn, Mazola*	1 Tsp/5ml	42	830	0.0	0.0	92.0	0.0
Flora*	1oz/28g	252	900	0.0	0.0	100.0	0.0
Grapeseed	1 Tsp/5ml	45	899	0.0	0.0	99.9	0.0
Groundnut, Co-Op*	1 Tsp/5ml	41	824	0.0	0.0	91.6	0.0
Groundnut, Somerfield*	1 Tsp/5ml	41	824	0.0	0.0	92.0	0.0
Hazelnut	1 Tsp/5ml	45	899	0.0	0.0	99.9	0.0
Olive	1 Tbsp/15ml	135	899	0.0	0.0	99.9	0.0
Olive, Central Italian, Sainsbury's*	1 Serving/10ml	82	823	0.1	0.0	91.0	0.0
Olive, Extra Virgin, Asda*	1 Tbsp/15ml	123	819	0.0	0.0	91.0	0.0
Olive, Extra Virgin, Bertolli*	1 Tbsp/15ml	123	820	0.0	0.0	91.0	0.0
Olive, Extra Virgin, Co-Op*	1 Tbsp/15ml	135	900	0.0	0.0	100.0	0.0
Olive, Extra Virgin, Fruity & Peppery Flavour, Sainsbury's*	1 Tbsp/15ml	123	823	0.1	0.0	91.4	0.0
Olive, Extra Virgin, Mist Spray, Belolive*	1fl oz/30ml	150	500	0.0	0.0	55.0	0.0
Olive, Extra Virgin, Sainsbury's*	1 Tbsp/15ml	123	823	0.1	0.0	91.4	0.0
Olive, Extra Virgin, Somerfield*	1fl oz/30ml	270	900	0.0	0.0	100.0	0.0
Olive, Extra Virgin, Tesco*	1 Tbsp/10g	90	900	0.0	0.0	100.0	0.0
Olive, Extra Virgin, Waitrose*	1 Tbsp/10ml	82	823	0.0	0.0	91.4	0.0
Olive, Lemon Flavoured, Sainsbury's*	1 Tbsp/15ml	123	823	0.1	0.0	91.4	0.1
Olive, Organic, M & S*	1floz/30ml	270	900	0.0	0.0	100.0	0.0
Olive, Pure, Napolina*	1 fl oz/30ml	248	828	0.0	0.0	92.0	0.0
Olive, Spray, Fry Light*	5 Sprays/1ml	5	498	0.0	0.0	55.2	0.0
Olivio*	1oz/28g	252	900	0.0	0.0	100.0	0.0
Palm	1 Tsp/5ml	45	899	0.0	0.0	99.9	0.0
Peanut	1 Tsp/5ml	45	899	0.0	0.0	99.9	0.0
Rapeseed	1 Tsp/5ml	45	899	0.0	0.0	99.9	0.0
Safflower	1 Tsp/5ml	45	899	0.0	0.0	99.9	0.0
Sesame	1 Tsp/5ml	45	898	0.2	0.0	99.7	0.0
Sesame, Blended, Amoy*	1 Tsp/5ml	44	880	0.0	0.0	100.0	0.0
Sesame, Finest, Tesco*	1 Tsp/3g	27	900	0.0	0.0	100.0	0.0

Nutrition Values per 100g / 100ml apply to the KCAL, PROT, CARB, FAT and FIBRE columns.

	Measure WEIGHT/INFO	per Measure KCAL	KCAL	PROT	CARB	FAT	FIBRE
			Nutrition Values per 100g / 100ml				
OIL,							
Sesame, Organic, Evernat*	1 Tsp/5ml	45	900	0.0	0.0	100.0	0.0
Sesame, Pure, Sharwood's*	1 Tsp/5ml	44	881	0.2	0.0	99.7	0.0
Soya	1 Tsp/5ml	45	899	0.0	0.0	99.9	0.0
Stir Fry, Sharwood's*	1fl oz/30ml	269	897	0.0	0.0	99.7	0.0
Sunflower	1 Tsp/5ml	45	899	0.0	0.0	99.9	0.0
Sunflower, Flora*	1 Tbsp/15ml	124	826	0.0	0.0	92.0	0.0
Sunflower, Fry Light Spray	1 Spray/0.2ml	1	522	0.0	0.0	55.2	0.0
Sunflower, Mazola*	1 Tsp/5ml	42	830	0.0	0.0	92.0	0.0
Sunflower, Organic, Evernat*	1 Tsp/5ml	45	900	0.0	0.0	100.0	0.0
Sunflower, Pure, Sainsbury's*	I Tsp/5ml	41	829	0.1	0.0	92.0	0.0
Sunflower, Pure, Tesco*	1oz/28g	252	900	0.0	0.0	100.0	0.0
Sunflower With Vitamin E, Flora*	1 Serving/5g	45	900	0.0	0.0	100.0	0.0
Vegetable, Blended, Average	1 Tsp/5ml	45	899	0.0	0.0	99.9	0.0
Vegetable, Iceland*	1 Serving/5g	45	900	0.0	0.0	100.0	0.0
Vegetable, Pure, Sainsbury's*	1 Tbsp/15ml	124	825	0.1	0.0	91.7	0.0
Vegetable, Pure, Tesco*	1fl oz/30ml	270	900	0.0	0.0	100.0	0.0
Vegetable, Safeway*	1 Serving/15ml	124	825	0.0	0.0	91.7	0.0
Vinaigrette, Balsamic Vinegar & Pistachio, Finest, Tesco*	1 Tbsp/15ml	56	370	0.2	2.8	39.2	0.0
Walnut	1 Tsp/5ml	45	899	0.0	0.0	99.9	0.0
Wheatgerm	1 Tsp/5ml	45	899	0.0	0.0	99.9	0.0
OKRA,							
Boiled In Unsalted Water	1oz/28g	8	28	2.5	2.7	0.9	3.6
Canned, Drained	1oz/28g	6	21	1.4	2.5	0.7	2.6
Raw	1oz/28g	9	31	2.8	3.0	1.0	4.0
Stir-Fried In Corn Oil	1oz/28g	75	269	4.3	4.4	26.1	6.3
OLIVES,							
Black, Pitted, Sainsbury's*	1 Sm Tin/85g	132	155	0.6	0.1	16.9	4.6
Black, Pitted, Somerfield*	1 Olive/3g	4	126	1.0	6.0	11.0	0.0
Green, Pimiento Stuffed, Somerfield*	1 Olive/3g	4	126	1.0	4.0	12.0	0.0
Green, Pitted, Somerfield*	1 Olive/3g	4	147	1.0	1.0	14.0	0.0
Green, Queen, M & S*	1oz/28g	34	120	1.4	0.2	12.8	2.4
In Brine	1 Olive/3g	3	103	0.9	0.0	11.0	2.9
In Brine, Weighed With Stones	1 Olive/3g	2	82	0.7	0.0	8.8	2.3
Kalamata, M & S*	1oz/28g	67	240	1.6	1.4	25.1	1.6
Pimento Stuffed, In Brine, Tesco*	1 Serving/25g	38	153	0.8	0.1	16.4	2.1
Sliced, In Brine, Tesco*	1oz/28g	39	141	1.1	0.1	15.1	0.0
OMELETTE,							
Average , Cheese,	2 Egg /180g	479	266	15.9	0.0	22.6	0.0
Average, Plain	2 Egg /120g	229	191	10.9	0.0	16.4	0.0
Average, Spanish	1oz/28g	34	120	5.7	6.2	8.3	1.4
Ham & Mushroom, Farmfoods*	1 Omelette/120g	200	167	8.7	1.8	13.9	0.1
Mushroom & Cheese, Tesco*	1 Omelette/120g	248	207	9.8	1.6	17.9	0.2
ONION RINGS,							
Asda*	¼ Pack/25g	122	489	6.0	60.0	25.0	2.4
Battered, Asda*	1 Serving/100g	343	343	3.8	31.0	22.7	1.7
Battered, Natural, Kitchen Range Foods*	1oz/28g	52	187	2.3	21.6	10.2	0.0
Battered, Sainsbury's*	1 Ring/12g	32	268	3.6	28.9	15.3	2.2
Breadcrumbs, Tesco*	1 Serving/100g	294	294	4.3	34.1	15.6	2.3
Breaded, Farmfoods*	1oz/28g	66	235	4.4	29.6	11.0	1.4
Breaded, Iceland*	4 Rings/45g	132	293	4.4	34.2	15.4	2.7
COU, M & S*	1oz/28g	95	340	4.7	80.7	1.5	3.7
Large, Burger King*	1 Serving/120g	348	290	4.8	36.4	13.9	3.8
Maize Snacks, Sainsbury's*	½ Pack/50g	240	479	8.5	57.8	23.8	3.9
Oven Crisp Batter, Tesco*	1 Onion Ring/17g	40	236	4.2	24.8	13.3	2.5

O

O

	Measure WEIGHT/INFO	per Measure KCAL	Nutrition Values per 100g / 100ml KCAL	PROT	CARB	FAT	FIBRE
ONION RINGS,							
Pickled, BGTY, Sainsbury's*	1 Bag/10g	34	340	4.7	77.0	1.5	3.7
Pickled, COU, M & S*	1 Bag/20g	68	340	4.7	80.7	1.5	3.7
Pickled, HE, Tesco*	1 Pack/15g	51	340	6.2	74.7	1.8	6.5
Red Mill*	1 Bag/50g	249	498	7.5	58.8	25.9	2.2
Regular, Burger King*	1 Serving/90g	261	290	4.8	36.4	13.9	3.8
Value, Tesco*	1 Bag/16g	77	482	7.6	58.3	24.3	2.5
ONIONS,							
Baked	1oz/28g	29	103	3.5	22.3	0.6	3.9
Boiled In Unsalted Water	1oz/28g	5	17	0.6	3.7	0.1	0.7
Borettane, In Balsamic Vinegar, Waitrose*	1/3 Pack/60g	20	34	0.8	4.9	1.2	1.0
Diced, Organic, Iceland*	1 Lge Bag/907g	154	17	0.6	3.7	0.1	0.7
Fried In Blended Oil	1oz/28g	46	164	2.3	14.1	11.2	3.1
Fried In Butter	1oz/28g	46	164	2.3	14.1	11.2	3.1
Pickled, Cocktail Silverskin, Drained	1oz/28g	4	15	0.6	3.1	0.1	0.0
Pickled, Drained	1 Med Onion/10g	2	24	0.9	4.9	0.2	1.2
Raw	1oz/28g	10	36	1.2	7.9	0.2	1.4
Red, Organic, Tesco*	1 Onion/100g	38	38	1.2	7.9	0.2	1.4
Salad, M & S*	1 Serving/10g	3	25	2.3	2.9	0.2	1.7
OPTIONS*,							
Choca Mocha Drink	1 Sachet/10g	36	359	14.1	50.1	11.4	7.0
Chocolate Au Lait Drink	1 Sachet/10g	36	355	11.8	54.5	10.0	7.3
Hot Chocolate, Belgian Chocolate, Instant	1 Serving/11g	40	363	12.4	54.9	10.4	7.5
Hot Chocolate, Diet Friendly	1 Sachet/11ml	40	364	14.3	50.6	11.6	7.1
Hot Chocolate, Mint, Made Up	1 Serving/200ml	40	20	0.8	2.8	0.7	0.4
Hot Chocolate, Orange Flavour	1 Serving/11ml	40	364	14.2	50.8	11.6	7.1
Hot Chocolate, Pleasure	1 Serving/18g	68	377	16.7	48.4	13.0	7.8
Irish Cream Drink	1 Sachet/10g	36	357	13.9	50.0	11.3	8.1
Marshmallow Melts Drink	1 Sachet/14g	48	344	11.3	56.3	8.2	5.9
Mint Drink	1 Sachet/10g	36	364	14.3	50.6	11.6	7.1
Outrageous Orange Drink	1 Sachet/10g	36	364	14.2	50.8	11.6	7.1
Toffee Drink	1 Sachet/13g	52	400	10.5	68.9	9.2	0.0
Turkish Delight Drink	1 Sachet/10g	37	365	14.4	50.4	11.7	7.2
ORANGE & BANANA Juice, Asda*	1 Glass/200ml	108	54	0.7	12.0	0.1	0.2
ORANGE & CRANBERRY Juice Drink, Ocean Spray*	1fl oz/30ml	14	48	0.0	11.5	0.0	0.0
ORANGE & GRAPEFRUIT JUICE,							
Pure, Asda*	1 Glass/200ml	82	41	0.7	9.0	0.0	0.2
Pure, Sainsbury's*	1 Glass/250ml	105	42	0.7	9.0	0.1	0.1
ORANGE & GRAPEFRUIT Segments In Juice, Del Monte*	1 Can/411g	197	48	0.6	10.6	0.0	0.0
ORANGE & KIWI Fruit Juice, Tropicana*	1 Serving/175ml	90	51	0.5	12.0	0.0	0.0
ORANGE & PEACH Juice Drink, Somerfield*	1fl oz/30ml	22	72	0.0	11.0	0.0	0.0
ORANGE & PINEAPPLE JUICE,							
Del Monte*	1 Glass/200ml	96	48	0.5	11.0	0.0	0.0
Pure, Asda*	1 Glass/120ml	54	45	0.4	10.0	1.0	1.0
ORANGE & RASPBERRY, Fresh Squeezed, M & S*	1 Glass/200ml	96	48	0.7	11.9	0.0	0.0
ORANGE, APPLE & Passionfruit Juice, Del Monte*	1 Glass/200ml	90	45	0.5	10.1	0.0	0.0
ORANGE CREAM, Cadbury's*	1 Bar/51g	217	425	2.6	68.6	15.4	0.0
ORANGE DRINK, No Added Sugar, Asda*	1 Glass/250ml	13	5	0.1	0.9	0.0	0.0
ORANGE JUICE,							
Del Monte*	1 Glass/200ml	88	44	0.6	9.9	0.0	0.0
Florida, M & S*	1 Bottle/250ml	85	34	0.5	8.5	0.0	0.0
Florida, Pure, Somerfield*	1 Glass/200ml	86	43	1.0	10.0	0.0	0.0
Florida, Pure Squeezed, Somerfield*	1 Glass/200ml	92	46	1.0	11.0	0.0	0.0
Florida, Smooth, Safeway*	1 Glass/200ml	96	48	0.7	10.7	0.0	0.3
Freshly Squeezed, Asda*	1 Glass/200ml	88	44	0.6	10.0	0.0	0.1

	Measure WEIGHT/INFO	per Measure KCAL	Nutrition Values per 100g / 100ml KCAL	PROT	CARB	FAT	FIBRE
ORANGE JUICE,							
Freshly Squeezed, Boots*	1 Glass/200ml	84	42	0.6	9.0	0.1	0.1
Freshly Squeezed, Finest, Tesco*	1 Glass/200ml	92	46	0.8	10.4	0.1	0.1
Freshly Squeezed, M & S*	1 Glass/200ml	90	45	0.7	9.8	0.1	0.0
Freshly Squeezed, Safeway*	1 Glass/200ml	80	40	0.5	9.1	0.1	0.1
Freshly Squeezed, TTD, Sainsbury's	1 Glass/200ml	98	49	0.6	10.5	0.0	0.4
Lidl*	1 Glass/200ml	78	39	0.6	9.0	0.4	0.4
Organic, Evernat*	1 Glass/200ml	86	43	0.7	9.0	0.2	0.2
Pure, Co-Op*	1 Glass/200ml	80	40	0.5	9.0	0.1	0.1
Pure, McDonald's*	1 Regular/200ml	94	47	0.7	10.3	0.0	0.1
Pure, Morrisons*	1 Glass/200ml	72	36	0.6	9.0	0.0	0.0
Pure, Organic, BPC, Sainsbury's*	1 Carton/250ml	115	46	0.5	10.4	0.1	0.1
Pure, Organic, Waitrose*	1 Serving/328g	154	47	1.0	11.0	0.0	0.0
Pure, Premium, Somerfield*	1 Glass/200ml	88	44	1.0	10.0	0.0	0.0
Pure, Rio D'oro, Aldi*	1 Glass/200ml	80	40	0.2	10.0	0.0	0.0
Pure, Sainsbury's*	1 Glass/200ml	94	47	0.5	10.5	0.1	0.1
Pure, SmartPrice, Asda*	1 Bottle/200ml	90	45	0.5	10.0	0.1	0.1
Pure, Smooth, Tesco*	1 Glass/125ml	58	46	1.0	10.5	0.0	0.0
Pure, Somerfield*	1 Glass/200ml	90	45	1.0	10.0	0.0	0.0
Pure, Tesco*	1 Glass/200ml	92	46	0.5	10.5	0.0	0.0
Pure, Value Tesco*	1 Glass/200ml	86	43	0.6	9.4	0.0	0.0
Pure, Waitrose*	1 Glass/200ml	90	45	0.7	10.0	0.0	0.0
Smooth, M & S*	1 Glass/200ml	82	41	0.7	9.1	0.0	0.0
Smooth Style, Tropicana*	1 Carton/250ml	108	43	0.7	9.0	0.0	0.5
Unsweetened	1 Glass/200ml	72	36	0.5	8.8	0.1	0.1
Unsweetened, Long Life, Economy, Sainsbury's*	1 Glass/200ml	84	42	0.5	9.1	0.2	0.2
With Juicy Bits, 100% Squeezed, Sainsbury's*	1 Serving/150ml	72	48	0.7	10.7	0.1	0.3
With Juicy Bits, Pure Squeezed, Tropicana*	1 Glass/200ml	86	43	0.7	9.0	0.0	0.5
ORANGE JUICE DRINK,							
HE, Tesco*	1 Glass/200ml	56	28	0.3	6.1	0.1	0.0
Value, Tesco*	1 Glass/250ml	33	13	0.0	3.3	0.0	0.0
Pouch, M & S*	1 Bottle/200ml	98	49	0.2	11.7	0.0	0.0
ORANGE SPARKLE, M & S*	1 Bottle/330ml	162	49	0.0	11.7	0.0	0.0
ORANGE WITH CRANBERRY Juice, M & S*	1 Sm Bottle/250ml	138	55	0.5	14.0	0.5	1.0
ORANGES,							
Fresh, Raw	1 Med/160g	59	37	1.1	8.5	0.1	1.7
Weighed With Peel & Pips	1oz/28g	7	26	0.8	5.9	0.1	1.2
OREGANO,							
Dried, Ground	1 Tsp/1g	3	306	11.0	49.5	10.3	0.0
Fresh	1oz/28g	18	66	2.2	9.7	2.0	0.0
OVALTINE,							
Hi Malt, Light, Instant Drink	1 Sachet/20g	72	358	9.1	67.1	5.9	2.8
Powder, Made Up With Semi-Skimmed Milk	1 Mug/227ml	179	79	3.9	13.0	1.7	0.0
Powder, Made Up With Whole Milk	1 Mug/227ml	220	97	3.8	12.9	3.8	0.0
OXTAIL,							
Raw	1oz/28g	118	423	3.9	81.0	9.5	0.7
Stewed	1oz/28g	121	432	4.4	78.1	11.6	1.1
OYSTERS,							
In Vegetable Oil, Smoked, John West*	1oz/28g	64	230	16.0	10.0	14.0	0.0
Raw	1oz/28g	18	65	10.8	2.7	1.3	0.0

O

	Measure WEIGHT/INFO	per Measure KCAL	KCAL	PROT	CARB	FAT	FIBRE
			Nutrition Values per 100g / 100ml				
PAELLA,							
Big Dish Chicken & Chorizo, M & S*	1 Pack/450g	630	140	7.9	18.4	3.9	1.6
Chicken, HE, Tesco*	1 Pack/400g	416	104	8.9	15.4	0.8	2.2
Chicken, New, HE, Tesco*	1 Pack/370g	329	89	7.2	10.4	2.0	1.2
Chicken, Steam Pack, HE, Tesco*	1 Pack/350g	291	83	8.1	11.8	0.4	7.0
Enjoy, Bird's Eye*	1 Pack/500g	620	124	7.7	16.2	3.2	0.6
Prawn, Chorizo, Chicken, Boots*	1 Pack/170g	231	136	7.0	18.0	4.0	0.5
Seafood, M & S*	1 Pack/450g	518	115	6.4	13.7	3.8	3.2
Seafood, Sainsbury's*	1 Pack/400g	504	126	8.3	20.3	1.3	0.6
Vesta	1 Paella/160g	558	349	10.9	69.6	2.9	3.0
PAIN AU Chocolate, Tesco*	1 Pain/56g	235	420	7.0	46.5	22.9	1.4
PAK CHOI, Tesco*	1 Serving/100g	11	11	1.0	1.4	0.2	1.2
PAKORA,							
Bhajia, Onion, Fried In Vegetable Oil	1oz/28g	76	271	9.8	26.2	14.7	5.5
Bhajia, Potato Carrot & Pea, Fried In Vegetable Oil	1oz/28g	100	357	10.9	28.8	22.6	6.1
Bhajia, Vegetable, Retail	1oz/28g	66	235	6.4	21.4	14.7	3.6
Vegetable, Indian Starter Selection, M & S*	1 Pakora/23g	61	265	6.3	19.6	18.1	2.9
Vegetable, Somerfield*	1 Pakora/15g	46	305	7.0	19.0	23.0	0.0
PANCAKE,							
Apple & Sultana, M & S*	1 Serving/80g	160	200	2.2	30.2	7.9	1.2
Chinese Roll, Farmfoods*	1 Roll/88g	125	142	4.3	21.6	4.3	1.0
HE, Tesco*	1 Pancake/30g	74	246	7.3	49.9	1.9	1.5
Irish, M & S*	1 Pancake/35g	85	243	7.1	53.8	1.4	1.3
Mini, Tesco*	1 Pancake/14g	39	277	6.7	50.0	5.6	1.4
Mix, Traditional, Asda*	1 Pack/256g	545	213	6.0	27.0	9.0	1.8
Morrisons*	1 Pancake/60g	133	221	8.4	37.3	5.0	1.5
Plain, Sainsbury's*	1 Pancake/63g	144	228	8.4	37.3	5.0	1.5
Raisin & Lemon, Co-Op*	1 Pancake/34g	122	360	8.0	60.0	10.0	2.0
Raisin & Lemon, Tesco*	1 Pancake/36g	99	275	5.8	49.3	6.1	2.7
Savoury, Made With Skimmed Milk	1oz/28g	70	249	6.4	24.1	14.7	0.8
Savoury, Made With Whole Milk	1oz/28g	76	273	6.3	24.0	17.5	0.8
Scotch	1 Pancake/50g	146	292	5.8	43.6	11.7	1.4
Scotch, BGTY, Sainsbury's*	1 Pancake/30g	76	252	5.3	48.5	4.1	1.3
Scotch, Low Fat, Asda*	1 Pancake/32g	87	272	6.0	57.0	2.2	0.0
Scotch, Mini, Sainsbury's*	1 Pancake/23g	69	302	7.9	49.5	8.0	1.3
Scotch, Sainsbury's	1 Pancake/30g	98	337	7.5	54.4	9.9	1.6
Sultana & Syrup Scotch, Sainsbury's*	1 Pancake/35g	113	322	6.7	55.2	8.3	1.7
Sweet, Made With Skimmed Milk	1oz/28g	78	280	6.0	35.1	13.8	0.8
Sweet, Made With Whole Milk	1oz/28g	84	301	5.9	35.0	16.2	0.8
Traditional, Tesco*	1 Pancake/62g	137	221	8.4	35.6	5.0	1.5
Vegetable Roll	1 Roll/85g	185	218	6.6	21.0	12.5	0.0
PANCAKES, & Sausage, McDonald's*	1 Portion/262g	671	256	6.1	34.3	10.3	1.1
PANCETTA, Cubetti, Italian, Sainsbury's*	½ Pack/65g	207	318	20.0	0.1	26.4	0.1
PANINI,							
Chicken & Baby Spinach, Costa*	1 Serving/440g	832	189	9.8	32.5	2.5	0.0
Ham & Swiss Cheese, Coffee Republic*	1 Panini/223g	558	250	15.7	20.5	11.7	0.0
Mozarella, Tomato & Pesto, Costa*	1 Panini/209g	487	233	9.6	35.1	7.2	5.0
Mozzarella & Tomato, Coffee Republic*	1 Panini/255g	566	222	11.1	23.6	10.0	0.0
Roasted Vegetables & Cheese, Starbucks*	1 Pack/215g	542	252	8.7	20.6	15.1	0.0
PAPAYA,							
Dried, Sweetened, Tesco*	4 Pieces/25g	59	235	0.4	56.3	0.9	2.9
Unripe, Raw	1oz/28g	8	27	0.9	5.5	0.1	1.5
PAPPADS, Green Chilli & Garlic, Sharwood's*	1oz/28g	75	267	19.9	43.3	1.6	9.7
PAPPADUMS, Patak's*	1 Serving/10g	28	275	21.5	43.2	1.9	0.0
PAPRIKA	1 Tsp/2g	6	289	14.8	34.9	13.0	0.0

	Measure WEIGHT/INFO	per Measure KCAL	KCAL	PROT	CARB	FAT	FIBRE
			Nutrition Values per 100g / 100ml				
PARATHA,							
Average Paratha	1oz/28g	90	322	8.0	43.2	14.3	4.0
PARCELS,							
Cheese & Ham, Sainsbury's*	1 Pack/250g	445	178	7.4	19.9	7.6	1.5
Filo, Mushroom, Bistro, Waitrose*	1 Parcel/92g	270	294	4.7	28.0	18.1	1.4
Filo, Mushroom, Savoury, Creamy, Somerfield*	1oz/28g	86	308	5.0	24.0	21.0	0.0
Smoked Salmon, M & S*	1 Parcel/55g	151	275	15.4	0.7	23.6	0.0
Smoked Salmon, Tesco*	1 Serving/50g	147	293	16.4	0.0	25.3	0.2
Spinach & Feta, Tesco*	1 Parcel/108g	306	283	7.1	23.5	17.8	0.9
PARSLEY,							
Dried	1 Tsp/1.3g	2	181	15.8	14.5	7.0	26.9
Fresh	1oz/28g	10	34	3.0	2.7	1.3	5.0
Thyme & Lemon Stuffing, Paxo*	1 Serving/45g	68	150	4.3	28.4	2.1	2.4
PARSNIP,							
Boiled In Salted Water	1oz/28g	18	66	1.6	12.9	1.2	4.7
Boiled In Unsalted Water	1oz/28g	18	66	1.6	12.9	1.2	4.7
Honey Roasted, Tesco*	½ Pack/125g	238	190	2.1	28.4	7.5	3.6
Organic, Tesco*	1 Serving/100g	67	67	1.8	12.5	1.1	4.6
Raw	1oz/28g	18	64	1.8	12.5	1.1	4.6
Roasted, M & S*	1 Serving/112g	134	120	1.8	14.3	6.4	0.8
Roasting, Tesco*	1 Parsnip/75g	77	103	1.7	14.5	4.2	4.4
PARTRIDGE, ROASTED, Meat Only	1oz/28g	59	212	36.7	0.0	7.2	0.0
PASANDA,							
Chicken, M & S*	½ Pack/150g	240	160	11.3	3.8	10.9	1.3
Chicken, Waitrose*	1oz/28g	52	185	14.8	3.8	12.3	1.1
Chicken, With Pilau Rice, Sharwoods*	1 Serving/376g	538	143	5.8	15.2	6.6	0.8
PASSATA,							
Basil, Del Monte*	1 Jar/500g	160	32	1.4	5.9	0.2	0.0
Classic Italian With Onion & Garlic, Sainsbury's*	1oz/28g	10	37	1.4	7.7	0.1	1.3
Heinz*	1 Serving/100g	17	17	0.7	2.9	0.3	1.0
Onion Garlic & Herbs, Safeway*	1 Serving/138g	47	34	1.4	5.7	0.6	1.2
SmartPrice, Asda*	1 Serving/15g	4	25	1.4	4.5	0.1	0.2
Traditional, Del Monte*	1 Jar/500g	155	31	1.4	5.5	0.1	0.0
With Garlic & Italian Herbs, Tesco*	1 Serving/165g	53	32	1.2	6.4	0.2	1.1
PASSION FRUIT,							
Juice	1 Glass/200ml	94	47	0.8	10.7	0.1	0.0
Raw, Fresh	1 Fruit/15g	5	36	2.6	5.8	0.4	3.3
Weighed With Skin	1oz/28g	6	22	1.7	3.5	0.2	2.0
PASTA BAKE,							
Bacon & Leek, Tesco*	1 Pack/450g	774	172	8.1	16.1	8.3	2.0
Cheese & Broccoli, Fish Bakes, Bird's Eye*	½ Pack/200g	264	132	12.5	6.1	6.4	0.3
Cheese & Tomato, Tesco*	1 Pack/400g	388	97	3.4	17.8	1.4	1.2
Chicken & Bacon, Tesco*	1oz/28g	46	166	6.9	19.3	6.8	0.5
Chicken & Broccoli, Morrisons*	1 Pack/400g	452	113	6.1	13.3	4.0	0.6
Chicken & Broccoli, Weight Watchers*	1 Bake/305g	290	95	6.0	14.2	1.5	0.9
Chicken & Spinach, GFY, Asda*	1 Pack/335g	281	84	4.9	10.0	2.7	0.6
Chicken & Spinach, Sainsbury's*	1 Pack/340g	286	84	4.9	10.0	2.7	0.6
Chicken & Vegetable, HE, Tesco*	1 Pack/400g	344	86	6.0	11.8	1.7	0.5
Chicken, GFY, Asda*	1 Serving/340g	299	88	5.0	9.0	3.5	0.5
Chicken, Somerfield*	1 Pack/300g	351	117	8.0	8.0	6.0	0.0
Chicken, Tesco*	1 Serving/400g	344	86	6.0	11.8	1.7	0.5
Chicken, Tesco*	1 Pack/400g	448	112	9.8	10.3	3.5	1.7
Creamy Mushroom, Dolmio*	½ Jar/245g	267	109	1.1	5.5	9.2	0.0
Creamy Tomato, Dolmio*	1 Serving/125g	141	113	2.3	8.4	7.2	0.0
Ham & Broccoli, Asda*	1 Pack/340g	309	91	3.4	10.0	4.1	0.5

P

PASTA BAKE,	Measure WEIGHT/INFO	per Measure KCAL	Nutrition Values per 100g / 100ml KCAL	PROT	CARB	FAT	FIBRE
Ham & Mushroom, Dolmio*	1oz/28g	33	118	1.9	3.3	10.8	0.0
Italiano Cheese & Tomato, Tesco*	1 Bake/300g	354	118	3.9	16.1	4.2	1.0
Italiano Chicken, Tesco*	1 Serving/190g	238	125	7.3	13.3	4.7	0.5
Lasagne, Creamy, Napolina*	1 Jar/525g	452	86	2.9	9.4	4.0	0.0
Meatball, Tesco*	1 Pack/400g	576	144	5.9	19.3	4.8	0.5
Penne Mozzarella, Tesco*	1 Pack/340g	408	120	4.7	19.7	2.5	0.6
Roast Vegetable, Eat Smart, Safeway*	1 Pack/330g	380	115	3.8	19.6	1.9	1.3
Spicy Tomato & Pepperoni, Asda*	1 Pack/440g	431	98	1.1	10.0	6.0	1.2
Spicy Tomato & Pepperoni, Homepride*	1 Jar/450g	324	72	1.5	8.1	3.7	0.0
Sun-Dried Tomato, Dolmio*	1 Serving/100ml	83	83	2.2	10.5	3.0	0.0
Tomato & Herb, Asda*	1 Jar/436g	715	164	1.8	10.0	13.0	1.2
Tuna & Tomat & Fish Sauce, Schwartz*	1 Jar/315g	246	78	2.6	12.1	2.2	0.0
Tuna & Tomato, BGTY, Sainsbury's*	1 Pack/450g	554	123	8.7	12.6	4.2	0.4
Tuna, Co-Op*	1 Serving/340g	306	90	7.0	12.0	2.0	1.0
Tuna, COU, M & S*	1 Pack/360g	378	105	8.0	13.4	2.0	1.1
Tuna, Eat Smart, Safeway*	1 Pack/345g	345	100	5.7	17.7	0.4	1.3
Tuna, HE, Tesco*	1 Pack/340g	258	76	5.4	11.9	0.8	0.5
Tuna, Safeway*	1 Pack/400g	620	155	8.9	12.0	7.9	1.1
Tuna, Somerfield*	1 Bake/300g	411	137	9.0	10.0	7.0	0.0
Tuna, Tesco*	1oz/28g	36	129	6.9	11.7	6.1	0.9
Vegetable, Asda*	1 Serving/300g	231	77	2.4	9.0	3.5	0.8
Vegetable, Ready Meals, Waitrose*	1oz/28g	44	157	5.9	14.4	8.6	1.0
Vegetable, Tesco*	1 Pack/380g	467	123	5.6	12.6	5.6	1.6
PASTA BREAK,							
Cheese & Ham, Asda*	1 Pot/66g	75	113	3.3	17.0	3.5	0.0
Chicken & Herb, Knorr*	1 Pot/347g	382	110	3.7	16.5	3.3	0.9
Chicken & Mushroom Flavour, Asda*	1 Pot/231g	254	110	2.7	19.0	2.6	0.0
Korma, Asda*	1 Pot/68g	74	109	2.3	19.0	2.6	0.0
PASTA, CANNELLONI,							
Beef, Geat Value, Asda*	1 Pack/400g	384	96	6.0	12.0	2.7	1.6
Beef, Italiano, Tesco*	1 Serving/340g	442	130	5.3	12.4	6.6	0.7
Findus*	1 Pack/342g	445	130	5.6	11.1	6.7	1.0
HE, Tesco*	1 Pack/400g	360	90	6.7	12.4	1.5	1.3
Italia Ready Meal, M & S*	1 Pack/360g	540	150	7.4	8.6	9.2	1.0
Italian Chicken & Pesto, Sainsbury's*	1 Pack/450g	675	150	6.1	14.4	7.5	1.1
Mushroom, Tesco*	1 Pack/450g	639	142	5.4	17.7	5.5	1.2
Parmesan & Basil, M & S*	1 Pack/360g	504	140	5.9	11.4	7.9	0.8
Ricotta & Spinach, COU, M & S*	1 Pack/360g	288	80	5.8	9.7	1.9	1.5
Roasted Vegetable, Morrisons*	1 Pack/350g	312	89	3.9	12.5	2.5	2.3
Spinach & Ricotta, GFY, Asda*	1 Pack/303g	418	138	6.0	21.0	3.3	0.5
Spinach & Ricotta, HE, Tesco*	1 Pack/340g	326	96	4.5	13.7	2.6	1.3
Spinach & Ricotta, Ross*	1 Pack/300g	300	100	4.3	13.7	3.1	0.5
Spinach & Ricotta, Safeway*	1 Pack/401g	565	141	6.5	14.4	6.4	0.4
Spinach & Ricotta, Sainsbury's*	1 Pack/288g	372	129	5.1	10.5	7.4	1.2
Spinach & Ricotta, Somerfield*	1 Pack/300g	393	131	5.0	13.0	7.0	0.0
Spinach & Ricotta, Tesco*	1 Pack/340g	490	144	4.5	6.4	11.2	0.5
Spinach & Wild Mushroom, Linda McCartney*	1 Pack/340g	381	112	4.9	14.1	4.0	1.7
Wild Mushroom, Tesco*	1 Serving/225g	320	142	5.4	17.7	5.5	1.2
PASTA, CONCHIGLIE,							
Asda*	1 Serving/50g	173	346	12.0	71.0	1.5	3.0
Chicken & Mushroom, Heinz*	1 Pack/300g	276	92	3.1	11.2	3.8	0.3
Dried, Napolina*	1oz/28g	99	352	11.5	73.0	1.5	2.2
Dried, Sainsbury's*	1 Serving/90g	321	357	12.3	73.1	1.7	2.5
Safeway*	1 Serving/50g	174	348	13.2	70.1	1.7	2.9

	Measure WEIGHT/INFO	per Measure KCAL	Nutrition Values per 100g / 100ml KCAL	PROT	CARB	FAT	FIBRE
PASTA, CONCHIGLIE,							
Shells, Asda*	1 Serving/50g	173	346	12.0	71.0	1.5	3.0
Shells, Tesco*	1 Serving/100g	345	345	13.2	68.5	2.0	2.9
Whole Wheat, Asda*	1oz/28g	90	323	14.0	60.0	3.0	10.0
Wholewheat, Organic, Sainsbury's*	1 Serving/100g	316	316	12.7	61.9	2.0	10.0
PASTA, FARFALLE,							
Asda*	1 Serving/100g	366	366	12.0	75.0	2.0	3.0
Bows, Morrisons*	1 Serving/75g	266	354	12.0	72.0	2.0	3.0
Bows, Tesco*	1 Serving/100g	354	354	11.0	73.1	1.9	2.7
Dried, Napolina*	1oz/28g	99	352	11.5	73.0	1.5	2.2
Sainsbury's*	1 Serving/100g	357	357	12.3	73.1	1.7	2.5
PASTA, FETTUCCINE,							
Buitoni*	1oz/28g	101	362	12.2	74.4	1.7	0.0
Bolognese, Enjoy, Bird's Eye*	1 Serving/290g	500	173	9.5	19.3	6.4	0.6
Tricolour, Asda*	1 Serving/100g	162	162	7.0	28.0	2.4	3.9
PASTA, FUSILLI,							
Bolognese, Ready Meals, M & S*	1oz/28g	38	135	7.0	13.1	6.2	1.0
Dried, Napolina*	1oz/28g	99	352	11.5	73.0	1.5	2.2
Dried, Waitrose*	1 Serving/120g	452	377	10.8	82.8	0.3	0.0
Egg, Fresh, Waitrose*	1 Serving/125g	361	289	11.4	53.1	3.4	2.1
Fresh, Asda*	1oz/28g	48	170	7.0	31.0	2.0	1.4
Fresh, Cooked, Safeway*	1 Serving/200g	318	159	5.8	30.3	1.6	2.1
M & S*	1oz/28g	100	358	13.1	70.2	2.7	2.7
Organic, Seeds Of Change*	1 Serving/75g	263	350	11.5	75.0	0.3	0.0
Quorn, Basil, Quorn*	1 Pack/400g	412	103	4.9	12.8	3.6	1.6
Safeway*	1oz/28g	29	102	3.9	20.1	0.7	1.2
Sainsbury's*	1oz/28g	100	357	12.3	73.1	1.7	2.5
Somerfield*	1 Serving/250g	865	346	13.0	69.0	2.0	4.0
Spirals, Fresh, Tesco*	1 Serving/125g	360	288	11.9	51.8	3.7	1.5
Tricolore, Dried, Safeway*	1 Serving/75g	261	348	13.2	70.1	1.7	2.9
Tricolore, Dry, Napolina*	1oz/28g	99	352	11.5	73.0	1.5	2.2
Tricolore, Sainsbury's*	1 Serving/90g	321	357	12.3	73.1	1.7	2.5
Twists, Asda*	1 Serving/50g	173	346	12.0	71.0	1.5	3.0
Twists, Tesco*	1 Serving/100g	345	345	13.2	68.5	2.0	2.9
Wholewheat, Italian, Sainsbury's*	1 Serving/90g	284	316	12.7	61.9	2.0	10.0
Wholewheat, Safeway*	1oz/28g	90	321	14.4	60.2	2.5	8.4
With Chicken & Courgettes, Sainsbury's*	1 Pack/450g	675	150	8.6	14.6	6.4	0.5
PASTA, LASAGNE,							
Lasagne, Boiled	1oz/28g	28	100	3.0	22.0	0.6	0.9
Lasagne, Raw	1oz/28g	97	346	11.9	74.8	2.0	3.1
Al Forno, M & S*	1 Pack/330g	528	160	9.6	12.3	8.3	1.4
Asda*	1 Pack/378g	427	113	6.0	11.0	5.0	1.1
Asparagus, M & S*	1 Pack/360g	414	115	4.7	12.1	5.2	1.2
Beef, Asda*	1 Pack/400g	1972	493	29.0	56.0	17.0	4.0
Beef, Bird's Eye*	1 Pack/384g	515	134	7.0	12.5	6.2	0.7
Beef, Eat Smart, Safeway*	1 Pack/380g	380	100	7.6	10.9	2.7	1.3
Beef, Frozen, Co-Op*	1 Pack/340g	388	114	7.5	10.7	4.6	1.4
Beef, GFY, Asda*	1 Pack/350g	385	110	9.0	14.0	2.0	1.0
Beef, Ready Meals, Waitrose*	1oz/28g	41	145	6.7	13.1	7.3	1.4
Beef, Reduced Fat, Waitrose*	1 Pack/325g	345	106	5.5	12.1	4.0	0.8
Beef, Weight Watchers*	1 Pack/300g	297	99	7.4	11.0	2.8	0.7
BGTY, Sainsbury's*	1 Pack/450g	504	112	7.2	12.3	3.8	0.3
Bird's Eye*	1 Pack/375g	420	112	6.1	11.6	4.6	0.7
Cheese, Onion & Tomato, Bird's Eye*	1 Pack/375g	390	104	3.9	15.0	3.1	0.6
Chicken, Italian, Sainsbury's*	1 Pack/450g	549	122	8.4	12.6	4.2	0.5

P

PASTA, LASAGNE,	Measure WEIGHT/INFO	per Measure KCAL	KCAL	PROT	CARB	FAT	FIBRE
Chicken, Ready Meals, Waitrose*	1 Pack/300g	411	137	6.3	13.0	6.6	0.9
Chilli, Tesco*	1 Pack/440g	730	166	7.9	11.9	9.6	1.4
COU, M & S*	1 Pack/360g	324	90	6.9	11.7	1.7	1.0
Deep Filled Classic, M & S*	1oz/28g	53	190	10.0	11.2	11.9	0.6
Family, M & S*	¼ Pack/225g	281	125	10.3	6.9	6.2	1.1
Findus*	1 Pack/350g	385	110	6.1	11.5	4.2	0.7
Finest, Tesco*	½ Pack/300g	432	144	7.4	13.1	6.9	0.5
Fresh, Findus*	1 Pack/350g	403	115	6.2	11.7	4.5	0.0
GFY, Asda*	1 Pack/340g	330	97	4.6	12.0	3.4	0.2
Good Intentions, Somerfield*	1 Pack/300g	303	101	5.3	13.9	2.7	0.4
Healthy Choice, Asda*	1 Pack/348g	383	110	9.0	14.0	2.0	1.5
HE, Tesco*	1 Pack/340g	343	101	5.1	13.4	3.0	0.9
Italian, Sainsbury's*	¼ Pack/225g	401	178	8.6	15.6	9.0	0.4
Italiano, Tesco*	1 Pack/425g	595	140	8.0	12.0	6.7	0.5
Layered, Asda*	1 Pack/300g	444	148	5.0	14.0	8.0	0.3
Lidl*	1 Serving/200g	336	168	8.0	13.7	9.0	0.0
Low Fat, Co-Op*	1 Pack/300g	255	85	6.0	10.0	3.0	1.0
Meat, Somerfield*	1 Pack/600g	768	128	6.0	12.0	6.0	0.0
No Pre Cooking, Sainsbury's*	1 Serving/150g	536	357	12.3	73.1	1.7	2.5
Pasta Reale*	1 Pack/300g	843	281	11.2	55.1	1.9	2.9
Perfectly Balanced, Waitrose*	1 Pack/340g	330	97	5.1	11.1	3.6	1.0
Quorn*	1 Pack/300g	252	84	4.7	7.7	3.8	1.4
Ready Meal, M & S*	1 Pack/360g	594	165	11.3	11.7	8.2	1.3
Roasted Mushroom & Spinach, COU, M & S*	1 Pack/360g	288	80	5.0	12.1	1.2	1.1
Safeway*	1 Pack/300g	354	118	5.7	11.5	5.5	0.5
Salmon & Spinach, Tesco*	1 Pack/400g	292	73	4.9	10.0	1.5	0.8
Seafood, COU, M & S*	1 Pack/300g	285	95	9.6	9.4	2.2	1.5
Seafood, Findus*	1 Pack/330g	396	120	4.5	13.0	5.0	0.0
Sheets, Egg, Italian, Fresh, Sainsbury's*	2 Sheets/85g	150	176	6.7	32.1	2.3	1.5
Sheets, Fresh, Somerfield*	1oz/28g	76	270	11.0	56.0	1.0	0.0
Sheets, Fresh, Tesco*	1 Serving/150g	410	273	11.0	50.6	2.9	2.9
Sheets, SmartPrice. Asda*	1 Sheet/13g	46	353	11.0	75.0	1.0	3.0
Sheets, Tesco*	1oz/28g	97	346	12.0	72.3	1.0	2.8
Sheets, Value, Tesco*	1oz/28g	95	341	11.0	72.0	1.0	3.0
Triangles With Chicken, COU, M & S*	1 Pack/360g	324	90	7.8	11.9	1.8	1.0
Triple Cheese Spicy Vegetable, The Little Big Food Company*	1 Pack/360g	472	131	5.8	15.0	5.8	0.8
Vegetable	1oz/28g	29	102	4.1	12.4	4.4	1.0
Vegetable, Italiano, Tesco*	1 Pack/340g	286	84	2.8	11.9	2.8	1.0
Vegetable, Low Fat, Co-Op*	1 Pack/300g	195	65	4.0	10.0	2.0	1.0
Vegetable, Luxury Roasted, Safeway*	1 Pack/400g	492	123	3.4	15.8	5.1	1.1
Vegetable, Mediterranean, Linda McCartney*	1 Pack/320g	333	104	3.2	15.8	3.1	1.5
Vegetable, Mediterranean Style, Eat Smart, Safeway*	1 Pack/380g	228	60	3.0	10.1	0.8	1.5
Vegetable, Mediterranean, Waitrose*	1 Pack/351g	397	113	3.7	12.7	5.3	1.0
Vegetable, Ready Meals, Waitrose*	1oz/28g	36	127	3.2	13.8	6.5	1.4
Vegetable, Retail	1oz/28g	33	117	4.8	13.4	5.3	0.0
Vegetable, Weight Watchers*	1 Pack/330g	251	76	3.6	11.8	1.7	0.7
Vegetarian, Linda McCartney*	1 Pack/320g	374	117	7.0	14.2	3.5	1.9
Verdi, No Pre-Cook, Sainsbury's*	1oz/28g	100	357	12.3	73.1	1.7	2.5
PASTA, LINGUINE,							
Chicken & Pesto, Sainsbury's*	1 Pack/450g	653	145	8.2	13.8	6.3	1.0
Pomodoro, M & S*	1 Serving/300g	360	120	4.1	17.6	3.5	1.2
Sainsbury's*	1 Serving/50g	179	357	12.3	73.1	1.7	2.5
Sun-Dried Tomato & Egg, Asda*	1 Serving/200g	324	162	7.0	28.0	2.4	3.9
Tesco*	1 Serving/100g	273	273	13.2	54.0	2.0	2.9

Nutrition Values per 100g / 100ml

P

	Measure WEIGHT/INFO	per Measure KCAL	Nutrition Values per 100g / 100ml KCAL	PROT	CARB	FAT	FIBRE
PASTA, LINGUINE,							
Vegetable & Ham, BGTY, Sainsbury's*	1 Pack/450g	410	91	4.4	11.7	3.0	0.9
PASTA, MACARONI,							
& Cheese, Kraft*	1 Serving/50g	205	410	11.0	47.0	17.5	1.0
Boiled	1oz/28g	24	86	3.0	18.5	0.5	0.9
Cheese	1oz/28g	50	178	7.3	13.6	10.8	0.5
Cheese, BGTY, Sainsbury's*	1 Pack/450g	549	122	5.4	19.8	2.3	2.4
Cheese, Bird's Eye*	1 Pack/302g	374	124	4.2	15.6	5.0	0.4
Cheese, Canned	1oz/28g	39	138	4.5	16.4	6.5	0.4
Cheese, Co-Op*	1 Pack/350g	455	130	6.0	19.0	4.0	1.0
Cheese, Eat Smart, Safeway*	1 Pack/315g	394	125	6.5	19.2	2.1	0.8
Cheese, Findus*	1 Pack/360g	576	160	6.3	14.3	8.5	0.0
Cheese, Frozen, Co-Op*	1 Pack/300g	420	140	6.8	12.1	7.2	1.4
Cheese, Heinz*	1 Can/400g	380	95	3.4	9.8	4.7	0.3
Cheese, Italian, Sainsbury's*	½ Pack/225g	360	160	7.3	15.3	7.7	1.6
Cheese, Ready Meals, M & S*	1 Pack/360g	540	150	6.9	12.1	8.4	0.7
Cheese, Sainsbury's*	1 Pack/300g	426	142	5.3	15.5	6.5	1.1
Cheese, Somerfield	1oz/28g	71	255	6.0	29.0	13.0	0.0
Cheese, Tesco*	1 Can/410g	513	125	4.5	10.1	6.3	0.3
Dried, Napolina*	1oz/28g	99	352	11.5	73.0	1.5	2.2
Italian, Sainsbury's*	1 Serving/100g	357	357	12.3	73.1	1.7	2.5
Quick Cook, Sainsbury's*	1oz/28g	100	357	12.3	73.1	1.7	2.5
Raw	1oz/28g	97	348	12.0	75.8	1.8	3.1
Tesco*	1 Serving/135g	269	199	4.8	30.2	6.5	1.3
PASTA 'N' SAUCE,							
Cheese, Leek & Ham, Batchelors*	1 Pack/126g	478	379	14.1	68.3	5.5	2.3
Chicken & Mushroom, Batchelors*	1 Pack/126g	455	361	12.4	73.5	2.0	2.7
Creamy Tomato & Mushroom, Batchelors*	1 Pack/125g	458	366	13.0	71.0	3.3	3.2
Macaroni Cheese, Batchelors*	1 Pack/115g	435	378	17.2	63.6	6.1	2.8
Mild Cheese & Brocolli, Batchelors*	1 Pack/129g	479	371	13.5	69.0	4.5	2.8
Mushroom & Wine, Batchelors*	1 Pack/132g	498	377	12.0	71.3	4.9	2.5
Tomato & Bacon Flavour, Batchelors*	1 Pack/134g	476	355	13.0	70.0	2.6	3.0
Tomato Onion & Herb Flavour, Batchelors*	1 Pack/135g	470	348	13.2	64.5	4.1	5.8
PASTA, PAPPARDELLE,							
Basil, Fresh, Sainsbury's*	1 Serving/240g	281	117	5.0	21.2	1.4	2.0
Chilli, Fresh, Sainsbury's*	1 Serving/250g	303	121	5.7	20.7	1.7	2.0
Cracked Black Pepper, Safeway*	1 Bowl/120g	173	144	5.7	26.5	1.8	1.9
Egg, Italia, M & S*	1 Serving/100g	355	355	13.9	68.5	2.8	3.0
PASTA, PENNE ,							
Al Forno, Leek & Bacon, Asda*	½ Pack/300g	531	177	5.0	10.0	13.0	0.5
Arrabbiata, BGTY, Sainsbury's*	1 Pack/450g	414	92	2.9	16.5	1.6	1.9
Asda*	1 Serving/50g	173	346	12.0	71.0	1.5	3.0
Bolognese, Heinz*	1 Pack/300g	213	71	3.8	11.8	0.9	0.6
Chicken & Red Wine, Weight Watchers*	1 Pack/394g	248	63	3.7	10.1	0.7	0.6
Chicken & Tomato , Italian, Sainsbury's*	½ Pack/350g	473	135	7.6	19.0	3.2	1.6
Chilli & Garlic, Asda*	1 Serving/75g	260	346	12.0	71.0	1.5	3.0
Creamy Sundried Tomato & Mascarpone, Somerfield*	1 Pack/500g	775	155	5.0	21.0	6.0	0.0
Dried, Napolina*	1oz/28g	99	352	11.5	73.0	1.5	2.2
Dry, Buitoni*	1oz/28g	101	362	12.2	74.4	1.7	2.0
Egg, Asda*	1 Serving/100g	170	170	7.0	31.0	2.0	1.4
Egg, Fresh, Safeway*	¼ Pack/125g	429	343	12.6	65.3	3.5	4.5
Fresh, Asda*	1oz/28g	50	178	7.0	31.0	2.0	1.4
Fresh, Egg, Safeway*	1 Bowl/100g	159	159	5.8	30.3	1.6	2.1
Fresh, Tesco*	1 Serving/125g	360	288	11.9	51.8	3.7	1.5
Hickory Steak, M & S*	1 Pack/500g	675	135	6.9	19.3	3.1	1.3

P

	Measure WEIGHT/INFO	per Measure KCAL	KCAL	PROT	CARB	FAT	FIBRE
PASTA, PENNE ,							
Italian, Fresh, Sainsbury's*	1 Serving/215g	361	168	7.8	29.4	2.1	1.8
M & S*	1oz/28g	99	355	13.6	68.7	2.9	3.1
Microwaveable, Dolmio*	1 Sachet/220g	299	136	5.3	26.3	1.0	0.0
Nicoise, Sainsbury's*	1 Pack/450g	401	89	2.9	12.4	3.1	1.1
Organic, Sainsbury's*	1 Serving/50g	179	357	12.3	73.1	1.7	2.5
Plain, Dried, Tesco*	1oz/28g	97	345	13.2	68.5	2.0	2.9
Quick Cook, Italian, Sainsbury's*	1 Serving/250g	893	357	12.3	73.1	5.0	2.5
Quick Cook, Sainsbury's*	1 Serving/50g	179	357	12.3	73.1	1.7	2.5
Rigate, Sainsbury's*	1oz/28g	100	357	12.3	73.1	1.7	2.5
Tesco*	1 Serving/100g	133	133	5.0	26.4	0.8	1.1
Tomato & Basil Sauce, Asda*	½ Pack/314g	185	59	0.8	6.0	3.5	2.0
Tubes, Egg, Fresh, Waitrose*	1 Serving/150g	434	289	11.4	53.1	3.4	1.6
Tuna, Tomato & Olive, Asda*	1 Pack/340g	173	51	4.2	4.2	1.9	0.6
Waitrose*	1 Serving/100g	354	354	11.3	73.1	1.8	2.9
With Chilli & Red Peppers, Asda*	1 Can/400g	224	56	1.3	10.0	1.2	0.6
With Tomato, Mozarella & Basil, Enjoy, Bird's Eye*	1 Serving/250g	333	133	4.6	19.9	3.9	0.5
PASTA QUILLS,							
Cooked, Co-Op*	1 Serving/200g	302	151	5.7	30.2	0.9	1.8
Morrisons*	1 Serving/50g	173	346	12.0	72.3	1.0	0.0
Value, Tesco*	1 Serving/75g	248	330	12.0	71.7	1.5	3.0
PASTA, RAVIOLI,							
Amatriciana, TTD, Sainsbury's*	1 Serving/125g	390	312	16.6	33.3	12.5	3.5
Asparagus & Ham, HE, Tesco*	½ Pack/125g	203	162	8.2	26.5	2.6	0.6
Basil & Parmesan, Organic, Sainsbury's*	½ Pack/192g	290	151	7.4	21.1	5.2	2.1
Beef Bolognese, Asda*	1 Serving/125g	206	165	7.0	28.0	2.8	1.2
Beef, Fresh, Safeway*	1 Serving/137g	352	257	10.0	39.4	6.6	3.0
Beef, Tesco*	1 Serving/194g	175	90	4.3	12.3	2.6	1.5
Cheese & Sun Dried Tomato, Co-Op*	½ Pack/125g	356	285	12.0	38.0	9.0	2.0
Cheese & Tomato, Fresh, Organic, Tesco*	1 Serving/125g	343	274	12.5	30.8	11.2	1.1
Cheese & Tomato, Heinz*	1 Can/410g	332	81	2.7	14.1	1.5	0.6
Cheese, Tomato & Basil, Italiano, Tesco*	½ Pack/125g	304	243	13.6	24.1	10.2	0.5
Chicken & Mushroom, Finest, Tesco*	½ Pack/125g	268	214	11.6	25.8	7.1	1.1
Chicken & Rosemary, Perfectly Balanced, Waitrose*	½ Pack/125g	266	213	14.9	30.4	3.5	2.1
Chicken & Tomato, Perfectly Balanced, Waitrose*	1 Serving/125g	265	212	13.5	33.4	2.7	2.8
Four Cheese, Italia, M & S*	1 Pack/360g	432	120	6.7	13.1	4.6	1.0
Fresh, Pasta Reale*	1 Serving/150g	459	306	13.1	53.3	5.9	0.0
In Tomato Sauce, Carlini, Aldi*	1 Can/400g	324	81	3.1	15.0	1.0	0.5
In Tomato Sauce, Farmfoods*	1 Can/400g	340	85	2.7	14.0	2.0	1.3
In Tomato Sauce, Heinz*	1 Can/410g	299	73	2.6	13.0	1.1	0.6
In Tomato Sauce, Meat Free, Heinz*	1 Can/410g	308	75	2.4	14.4	0.8	0.5
In Tomato Sauce, Sainsbury's*	1oz/28g	23	83	3.1	15.5	1.0	0.5
In Tomato Sauce, Tesco*	1 Can/400g	276	69	2.7	14.2	0.1	1.3
Meat, Italian, Fresh, Asda*	½ Pack/150g	261	174	8.0	26.0	4.2	0.0
Mediterranean Vegetable, HE, Tesco*	1 Serving/125g	199	159	6.7	27.2	2.6	0.9
Mozzarella Tomato & Basil, Tesco*	1 Serving/125g	304	243	13.6	24.1	10.2	0.5
Mushroom & Mascarpone, The Best, Safeway*	1 Pack/175g	466	266	9.9	31.8	11.0	1.0
Mushroom, Italian, Fresh, Somerfield*	½ Pack/125g	336	269	10.8	34.4	9.8	1.8
Mushroom, Ready Meals, M & S*	1oz/28g	38	135	8.1	22.0	1.9	2.2
Prosciuttoi, Ready Meal, M & S*	1 Pack/100g	195	195	13.3	17.0	8.1	1.0
Red Onion & Brunello Wine, TTD, Sainsbury's*	1 Serving/125g	235	188	7.5	23.0	7.3	2.5
Salmon, Open, Finest, Tesco*	1oz/28g	37	131	6.8	15.5	4.6	0.5
Smoked Salmon, Ready Meals, M & S*	1 Pack/125g	256	205	13.8	19.6	8.0	1.1
Spinach & Ricotta, Waitrose*	1 Serving/125g	309	247	10.5	35.0	7.2	1.9
Tomato Cheese & Meat, Sainsbury's*	1 Serving/125g	314	251	12.4	21.4	12.9	2.2

P

	Measure WEIGHT/INFO	per Measure KCAL	Nutrition Values per 100g / 100ml KCAL	PROT	CARB	FAT	FIBRE
PASTA, RAVIOLI,							
Vegetable In Tomato Sauce, Italiana, Weight Watchers*	1 Can/385g	266	69	1.7	11.0	2.1	0.5
Vegetable, Morrisons*	1 Can/400g	276	69	2.4	13.9	0.4	0.0
Vegetable, Tesco*	½ Can/200g	164	82	2.6	16.3	0.7	0.7
Wild Mushroom, Al Forno, TTD, Sainsbury's*	1 Pack/300g	459	153	7.0	14.0	7.7	1.2
PASTA, RIGATONI,							
Asda*	1 Serving/25g	87	346	12.0	71.0	1.5	3.0
Carbonara, Heinz*	1 Pot/300g	270	90	3.0	10.7	3.9	0.3
Carbonara, Tesco*	1 Serving/205g	236	115	5.2	10.6	5.8	1.2
Spicy Vegetable, HP*	1 Can/400g	230	58	1.8	9.2	1.5	0.9
Tomato & Cheese, Perfectly Balanced, Waitrose*	1 Pack/400g	664	166	7.6	28.6	2.3	2.3
With Broccoli, Linda McCartney*	1 Pack/340g	340	100	4.3	15.9	2.2	1.7
PASTA SALAD,							
Pasta Salad	1oz/28g	36	127	2.6	13.3	7.4	1.6
Basil & Parmesan, Tesco*	1 Serving/50g	65	130	4.3	20.2	3.6	0.6
Carbonara, Waitrose*	1oz/28g	72	257	5.4	8.1	22.6	0.5
Chargrilled Chicken, M & S*	1 Serving/190g	285	150	9.6	23.6	2.9	1.6
Chargrilled Chicken, Shape*	1 Pack/250g	248	99	6.1	12.9	2.6	0.8
Chargrilled Vegetables & Tomato, Boots, Shapers*	1 Serving/175g	187	107	2.8	17.0	3.1	1.5
Chicken & Smoked Bacon, M & S*	1 Salad/380g	817	215	7.5	19.0	12.3	1.9
Chicken, Sundried Tomato & Basil, HE, Tesco*	1 Serving/190g	215	113	7.6	15.0	2.5	0.9
Crayfish, Rocket & Lemon, Finest, Tesco*	1 Serving/250g	728	291	8.9	28.0	15.9	4.2
Farfalle, Prawns Tomatoes & Cucumber, Sainsbury's*	1 Serving/260g	270	104	4.5	10.9	4.7	0.7
Feta Cheese, Sun Blush Tomatoes, M & S*	1 Serving/190g	361	190	5.5	17.2	11.1	2.1
Garlic Mushroom, Salad Bar, Asda*	1oz/28g	59	212	2.5	12.5	16.9	0.8
Ham & Pineapple, Salad Bar, Asda*	1oz/28g	62	221	3.3	15.6	16.2	1.4
Honey & Mustard Chicken, M & S*	1 Serving/190g	304	160	8.7	26.7	2.5	1.5
Honey & Mustard Chicken, Sainsbury's*	1 Pack/260g	447	172	7.3	16.9	8.3	1.4
Italian Style, Asda*	1oz/28g	42	149	3.2	19.1	6.6	1.2
Italian Style Chargrilled Chicken, Fresh, Asda*	1 Pack/200g	318	159	7.0	17.0	7.0	0.4
Italian Style, Safeway*	1 Serving/225g	234	104	2.9	17.2	2.6	0.6
Italian Style, Sainsbury's*	1/3 Pot/84g	129	153	3.5	20.5	6.3	1.4
King Prawns, COU, M & S*	1 Serving/100g	95	95	5.1	16.4	1.5	0.9
Kraft*	½ Cup/68g	183	269	4.0	26.5	16.2	0.0
Lime & Coriander Chicken, M & S*	1 Serving/190g	371	195	7.6	14.4	12.2	0.6
Mediterranean Chicken, Waitrose*	1 Serving/200g	314	157	7.0	16.9	6.8	2.1
Mediterranean Style, Layered, Waitrose*	1 Pot/275g	190	69	2.6	11.8	1.3	1.0
Mediterranean, Tesco*	1oz/28g	24	87	2.1	9.6	4.5	1.4
Mediterranean Tuna, Shapers, Boots*	1 Serving/239g	232	97	6.2	15.0	1.3	0.9
Mediterranean Vegetable & Bean, BGTY, Sainsbury's*	1 Serving/66g	53	80	3.2	12.5	1.9	2.8
Mozzarella & Plum Tomatoes, COU, M & S*	1 Bowl/255g	204	80	4.6	11.5	1.6	1.7
Pepper, HE, Tesco*	1 Salad/210g	139	66	2.4	13.3	0.4	1.0
Prawn Cocktail, Shapers, Boots*	1 Pack/304g	250	82	5.7	11.0	1.7	0.9
Prawn, COU, M & S*	1 Pack/274g	260	95	5.1	16.4	1.5	0.9
Prawn, Shapers, Boots*	1 Pot/250g	250	100	4.1	14.0	3.1	0.4
Ready To Eat, Somerfield*	½ Pack/123g	175	142	2.8	17.1	6.9	1.6
Roasted Mushroom, Spinach & Tarragon, Tesco*	1 Pot/200g	216	108	4.3	17.2	2.4	0.8
Sainsbury's*	½ Pack/160g	235	147	3.2	20.0	6.0	1.5
Salmon, M & S*	1 Serving/380g	817	215	6.8	12.7	15.2	0.7
Spinach & Nuts, M & S*	1oz/28g	64	229	6.9	18.2	15.0	1.6
Sweetcorn & Pepper, GFY, Asda*	1 Serving/175g	68	39	1.9	7.0	0.4	0.0
Sweetcorn, M & S*	1oz/28g	30	107	2.8	14.9	4.0	1.8
Sweetcorn, Waitrose*	1oz/28g	31	112	6.4	18.9	1.2	1.1
Tiger Prawn, Waitrose*	1 Serving/225g	545	242	5.4	16.7	17.1	0.4
Tomato & Basil Chicken, M & S*	1 Serving/279g	446	160	7.0	14.8	7.9	1.8

P

	Measure WEIGHT/INFO	per Measure KCAL	Nutrition Values per 100g / 100ml KCAL	PROT	CARB	FAT	FIBRE
PASTA SALAD,							
Tomato & Basil, Sainsbury's*	1 Serving/250g	383	153	3.5	20.5	6.3	1.4
Tomato & Chargrilled Vegetable, Tesco*	1 Serving/200g	248	124	3.7	18.6	3.9	1.4
Tomato & Mozzarella, Leaf, Shapers, Boots*	1 Pack/185g	356	192	5.1	16.0	12.0	2.5
Tomato & Mozzarella, Waitrose*	1 Pack/225g	380	169	4.3	10.0	12.4	0.6
Tuna & Spinach, COU, M & S*	1 Pack/270g	257	95	6.8	14.3	1.8	3.8
Tuna & Sweetcorn, COU, M & S*	1 Pack/200g	210	105	7.1	18.3	0.9	1.2
Tuna & Sweetcorn, HE, Tesco*	1 Pot/200g	230	115	5.7	17.0	2.7	1.3
Tuna & Sweetcorn, Sainsbury's*	1 Serving/100g	111	111	7.1	18.3	1.2	1.2
Tuna, Tesco*	1 Pot/300g	399	133	6.2	10.5	7.3	0.0
Vegetable, Healthy Selection, Somerfield*	1 Pot/200g	180	90	2.8	19.6	0.0	0.7
Vegetable, Somerfield*	1 Salad/200g	288	144	3.0	20.0	6.0	0.0
Waitrose*	1oz/28g	24	87	3.0	18.3	0.2	0.7
Wholemeal	1oz/28g	37	131	3.1	13.8	7.5	2.7
Wild Mushroom, TTD, Sainsbury's*	1 Serving/259g	464	179	4.6	16.6	10.5	1.5
PASTA SAUCE,							
Amatriciana, Fresh, Safeway*	½ Pot/175g	89	51	2.5	5.6	2.1	1.2
Amatriciana, Fresh, Sainsbury's*	½ Pot/153g	69	45	3.5	3.5	1.9	1.3
Amatriciana, GFY, Asda*	½ Pot/175g	88	50	2.3	6.0	1.9	0.0
Amatriciana, Tesco*	1 Serving/175g	109	62	2.3	4.0	4.1	0.7
Arrabbiata, Barilla*	1 Jar/400g	232	58	1.5	6.2	3.0	0.0
Arrabbiata, BGTY, Sainsbury's*	1 Jar/150g	107	71	1.3	7.6	3.9	0.7
Arrabbiata, Fresh, Co-Op*	½ Pot/150g	83	55	1.0	5.0	3.0	1.0
Arrabbiata, Fresh, Safeway*	½ Pot/176g	58	33	1.2	5.1	0.9	1.0
Arrabbiata, Fresh, Tesco*	1 Serving/110ml	29	26	0.7	3.7	0.9	0.9
Arrabbiata, GFY, Asda*	1 Serving/350g	133	38	1.1	6.0	1.1	0.0
Arrabbiata, Italiano, Tesco*	½ Pot/175g	65	37	1.7	6.1	0.6	1.0
Arrabbiata, M & S*	1 Jar/320g	240	75	1.2	6.2	5.3	0.8
Arrabbiata, Sainsbury's*	1oz/28g	13	45	1.4	3.3	2.9	1.6
Aubergine & Pepper, Sacla*	½ Pot/95g	238	250	1.8	5.6	24.5	0.0
Aubergine, M & S*	1oz/28g	41	148	1.6	8.4	13.4	3.0
Basil & Oregano For Bolognese, Ragu*	1 Serving/200g	76	38	2.0	7.6	0.0	0.8
Basil Pesto Stir In, Waitrose*	½ Bottle/85g	394	463	12.8	8.2	42.1	1.4
Beef Bolognese, Fresh, Asda*	¼ Pot/82g	78	95	4.3	3.4	7.3	0.4
Black Olive Pesto, Sacla*	1oz/28g	115	409	2.9	4.3	42.2	0.0
Bolognese, Dolmio*	¼ Jar/175g	91	52	1.8	10.3	0.0	0.0
Bolognese, Finest, Tesco*	1 Serving/175g	170	97	7.0	3.8	6.1	0.5
Bolognese, Fresh, Sainsbury's*	½ Pot/150g	120	80	6.0	4.7	4.1	1.2
Bolognese, Fresh, Waitrose*	1 Pot/350g	277	79	5.1	5.3	4.2	0.7
Bolognese, M & S*	1 Jar/100g	115	115	7.0	10.8	4.9	1.2
Bolognese, Organic, Seeds Of Change*	1 Jar/530g	313	59	1.5	10.5	1.2	1.2
Bolognese, Original Light, Dolmio*	1 Serving/125g	44	35	1.6	6.9	0.1	0.0
Bolognese, Original, Sainsbury's*	¼ Jar/136g	90	66	1.9	9.9	2.1	1.3
Bolognese, SmartPrice, Asda*	½ Jar/226g	88	39	0.9	7.0	0.8	0.6
Bolognese, Somerfield*	1 Pack/300g	243	81	3.0	8.0	4.0	0.0
Bolognese, Tesco*	1 Serving/175g	100	57	4.2	4.0	2.6	0.8
Bolognese With Beef, Tesco*	½ Can/213g	179	84	4.9	5.5	4.7	0.0
Cacciatore, Fresh, Sainsbury's*	½ Pot/150g	152	101	5.4	8.1	5.9	1.5
Chargrilled Vegetable With Extra Virgin Olive Oil, Bertolli*	½ Jar/250g	150	60	2.1	8.7	1.9	2.4
Cheese & Bacon, Asda*	1 Pack/116g	476	410	13.0	67.0	10.0	2.3
Cheese & Bacon Bake, Homepride*	1oz/28g	27	95	2.0	2.5	8.6	0.0
Cheese, Fresh, Perfectly Balanced, Waitrose*	½ Pot/175g	144	82	6.1	7.9	2.9	0.5
Cherry Tomato & Basil, Sacla*	1 Serving/96g	90	94	1.2	5.3	7.4	0.0
Chunky Vegetable, Asda*	1 Serving/250g	123	49	1.4	7.0	1.7	1.2
Chunky Vegetables, Somerfield*	1 Jar/525g	226	43	2.0	7.0	1.0	0.0

P

PASTA SAUCE,	Measure WEIGHT/INFO	per Measure KCAL	Nutrition Values per 100g / 100ml KCAL	PROT	CARB	FAT	FIBRE
Cream & Mushroom, M & S*	1oz/28g	45	160	1.5	6.6	14.3	0.6
Creamy Mushroom, Baxters*	1 Jar/320g	294	92	1.3	6.3	6.8	0.2
Creamy Mushroom, Chicken Tonight*	¼ Jar/125g	110	88	0.7	2.8	8.2	0.4
Creamy Mushroom, Dolmio*	1 Pack/150g	167	111	1.3	3.7	10.0	0.0
Creamy Mustard, Colman's*	1 Pack/29g	108	374	11.0	46.0	16.0	0.0
Creamy Pepper & Mushroom, Colman's*	1 Pack/25g	82	327	8.1	56.0	9.1	0.0
Creamy Pesto, Pasta Reale*	1 Pack/200g	302	151	2.1	4.5	13.8	0.2
Creamy Tomato & Bacon Bake, Homepride*	1 Serving/110g	99	90	1.9	6.5	6.3	0.0
Creamy Tomato & Basil, BGTY, Sainsbury's*	½ Jar/250g	173	69	1.7	7.6	3.6	1.0
Creamy Tomato & Herb Bake, Homepride*	1 Jar/455g	464	102	2.0	7.5	7.1	0.0
Dolmio*	1 Serving/100g	133	133	4.3	22.5	2.5	0.0
Extra Mushrooms Bolognese, Dolmio*	1 Jar/500g	235	47	1.6	9.3	0.1	0.0
Extra Spicy Bolognese, Dolmio*	1 Serving/250g	133	53	1.7	9.2	1.1	0.0
Fiorentina, Fresh, Sainsbury's*	½ Pot/157g	165	105	3.2	4.3	8.4	0.9
Florentina, Fresh, Tesco*	1 Pot/175g	233	133	2.6	4.1	11.8	0.4
Four Cheese, BGTY, Sainsbury's*	1 Serving/150g	104	69	2.9	5.5	4.0	0.1
Four Cheese, Fresh, Asda*	½ Pot/162g	309	191	5.4	2.2	17.8	0.5
Four Cheese, Loyd Grossman*	1 Jar/350g	476	136	2.6	4.6	11.9	0.0
Four Cheese, Sainsbury's*	1 Serving/150g	296	197	6.6	4.5	17.0	0.8
Garlic, Perfectly Balanced, Waitrose*	1 Jar/440g	330	75	2.3	12.7	1.7	2.3
Green Pesto, Bertolli*	1 Serving/47g	202	429	5.4	4.2	43.0	1.3
Green Pesto, Fresh, Tesco*	1oz/28g	141	505	6.5	12.2	48.0	0.1
Green Pesto, Sainsbury's*	1oz/28g	120	430	5.4	8.3	41.7	0.0
Ham & Mushroom, Creamy, Stir & Serve, Homepride*	1 Serving/92g	124	135	1.8	5.5	11.7	0.0
Hot & Spicy, Morrisons*	1 Serving/130g	82	63	1.3	9.3	2.4	1.0
Hot Mixed Peppers Bolognese, Sainsbury's*	1oz/28g	18	66	2.0	9.7	2.1	1.5
Italian Cheese, Finest, Tesco*	½ Pot/175g	172	98	4.8	8.4	5.1	0.0
Italian Mushroom, Sainsbury's*	1 Serving/85g	56	66	2.0	9.8	2.1	1.7
Layered Tomato & Mozarella, Finest, Tesco*	1 Jar/160g	232	145	6.6	6.9	10.1	0.7
Mascarpone, BGTY, Sainsbury's*	1 Serving/120g	379	316	8.6	2.8	30.0	0.0
Mediterrainean Vegetable Pasta, Tesco*	1 Serving/166g	95	57	1.4	9.0	1.7	1.2
Mediterranean, Fresh, Waitrose*	1 Pot/350g	214	61	1.4	5.0	3.9	2.4
Mediterranean Sizzling, Homepride*	1 Serving/96g	83	86	0.9	6.3	6.4	0.0
Mediterranean Tomato, Asda*	1 Jar/500g	285	57	1.5	10.0	1.2	0.0
Mediterranean Vegetable, Organic, Pasta Reale*	1 Pack/300g	183	61	1.0	3.9	4.6	0.3
Mushroom & Garlic, 98% Fat Free, Homepride*	1 Jar/450g	230	51	1.1	8.9	1.4	0.5
Mushroom & Garlic, Deliciously Good, Homepride*	1/3 Jar/147g	109	74	0.9	6.9	4.8	0.3
Mushroom & Garlic, Somerfield*	1 Pack/110g	158	144	4.0	18.0	6.0	0.0
Mushroom & Marsala Wine, Sacla*	½ Pot/85g	165	194	2.2	3.9	18.8	0.0
Mushroom & Mascarpone, HE, Tesco*	½ Jar/175g	86	49	2.1	5.3	2.2	0.3
Mushroom & White Wine, Knorr*	1oz/28g	27	98	1.0	4.0	8.0	0.0
Mushroom Alfredo, Five Brothers*	1 Jar/445g	543	122	3.3	2.5	10.8	1.4
Mushroom, Colman's*	1 Pack/27g	97	358	14.0	53.0	9.7	0.0
Mushroom, Fresh, Waitrose*	1 Serving/175g	142	81	1.6	5.7	5.7	0.5
Mushroom, GFY, Asda*	1 Serving/175g	112	64	2.7	7.0	2.8	0.0
Mushroom, M & S*	1oz/28g	61	218	4.9	5.0	21.3	3.4
Mushroom Pasta, Romano, Aldi*	1 Jar/470g	310	66	1.8	10.3	1.9	1.6
Mushroom, Perfectly Balanced, Waitrose*	1 Jar/440g	330	75	2.6	11.8	1.9	2.2
Mushroom, Sainsbury's*	1 Serving/100g	66	66	2.0	9.8	2.1	1.7
Mushroom, Somerfield*	1 Jar/525g	252	48	2.0	8.0	1.0	0.0
Napoletana, BGTY, Sainsbury's*	½ Pot/151g	71	47	1.2	5.0	2.5	1.3
Napoletana, Fresh, Asda*	1 Pot/330g	135	41	2.2	6.0	1.3	1.4
Napoletana, Fresh, Safeway*	½ Pot/175g	67	38	1.5	6.1	0.8	1.2
Napoletana, Fresh, Sainsbury's*	1oz/28g	25	91	1.9	7.9	5.8	1.1

PASTA SAUCE,	Measure WEIGHT/INFO	per Measure KCAL	Nutrition Values per 100g / 100ml KCAL	PROT	CARB	FAT	FIBRE
Napoletana, Fresh, Waitrose*	1 Serving/175g	82	47	1.3	6.6	1.7	1.0
Napoletana, GFY, Asda*	1 Serving/175g	58	33	1.0	5.0	1.0	0.0
Napoletana, Sainsbury's*	½ Pot/150g	126	84	1.9	6.6	5.6	0.9
Olive & Tomato, Sacla*	1 Serving/95g	87	92	1.3	3.6	8.0	0.0
Olive, Barilla*	1 Serving/100g	92	92	1.5	10.3	5.0	0.0
Olive, M & S*	1oz/28g	94	335	2.1	5.7	33.7	2.6
Onion & Garlic Bolognese, Extra, Dolmio*	1 Serving/125g	66	53	1.7	9.0	1.0	0.0
Onion & Garlic, Co-Op*	1 Serving/125g	106	85	2.0	12.0	3.0	0.7
Onion & Garlic For Bolognese, Ragu*	1 Serving/125g	80	64	2.2	11.4	1.1	1.2
Onion & Garlic, Somerfield*	1 Jar/525g	257	49	2.0	8.0	1.0	0.0
Onion & Garlic, Tesco*	1 Serving/225g	83	37	1.2	7.6	0.3	0.8
Original For Bolognese, Ragu*	1 Jar/525g	268	51	1.7	10.7	0.1	1.0
Original, Tesco*	1 Jar/455g	155	34	1.2	6.5	0.1	0.8
Pepper & Tomato, M & S*	1 Jar/320g	224	70	1.6	6.1	4.2	0.9
Pesto, Fresh, Waitrose*	1 Tbsp/26g	120	463	12.8	8.2	42.1	1.4
Porcini Mushroom & Pepperoni, Asda*	½ Jar/140g	158	113	3.8	11.0	6.0	0.0
Porcini Mushroom Stir In, BGTY, Sainsbury's*	½ Jar/75g	57	76	3.8	5.7	4.2	1.9
Primavera, Fresh, Morrisons*	½ Pot/175g	152	87	2.4	6.1	5.9	0.0
Puttanesca, Loyd Grossman*	1oz/28g	25	90	1.7	6.8	6.2	0.9
Puttanesca, M & S*	1 Jar/320g	256	80	1.5	6.2	5.5	1.9
Puttanesca, Sainsbury's*	1 Serving/110g	132	120	2.0	8.1	8.8	0.0
Puttanesca, The Best, Safeway*	1 Serving/170g	139	82	1.0	5.6	6.2	0.0
Red Pesto, M & S*	1oz/28g	93	331	3.6	6.9	33.2	3.5
Roasted Vegetable, Microwaveable, Dolmio*	½ Pack/190g	103	54	1.4	7.6	2.0	0.0
Roasted Vegetable, Tesco*	1 Pack/175g	114	65	1.5	8.0	3.0	0.8
Roasted Vegetables & Tuna, BGTY, Sainsbury's*	½ Pot/150g	74	49	3.5	4.5	1.9	3.1
Romano, Aldi*	1 Serving/235g	141	60	1.7	8.8	2.0	1.1
Salsina With Onions & Garlic, Valfrutta*	1 Serving/150g	36	24	1.6	4.5	0.0	1.4
Sliced Mushroom, Tesco*	1 Jar/460g	161	35	1.3	7.0	0.2	0.8
Smoky Bacon, Loyd Grossman*	1oz/28g	27	98	3.1	5.4	7.2	0.7
Spicy Italian Chilli, Microwaveable, Dolmio*	1 Sachet/170g	92	54	1.4	7.6	2.0	0.0
Spicy Pepper & Tomato, Sacla*	½ Jar/95g	132	139	1.4	6.8	11.8	0.0
Spicy With Peppers, Tesco*	1 Jar/455g	177	39	1.2	7.9	0.3	1.1
Stir & Serve, Homepride*	1 Bottle/480g	187	39	1.2	6.0	1.2	0.0
Sun Dried Tomato & Garlic, Sacla*	1 Serving/95g	177	186	3.0	10.3	14.7	0.0
Sun Dried Tomato & Garlic, The Best, Safeway*	1 Jar/340g	496	146	2.2	6.2	12.5	0.0
Sun Dried Tomato & Olive Oil, Loyd Grossman*	1oz/28g	52	187	0.8	10.3	15.8	0.3
Sun Dried Tomato, M & S*	1oz/28g	102	363	3.6	12.4	34.9	5.7
Sun Ripened Tomato & Basil, Dolmio*	1 Serving/150g	117	78	1.3	7.9	4.6	0.0
Sun Ripened Tomato & Basil, Microwaveable, Dolmio*	½ Pack/190g	106	56	1.4	7.9	2.1	0.0
Sweet Pepper, Dolmio*	1 Serving/150g	239	159	1.6	8.8	13.4	0.0
Sweet Red Pepper, Loyd Grossman*	1oz/28g	24	87	1.7	7.3	5.6	1.2
Three Cheeses, Co-Op*	1 Pack/300g	405	135	6.0	6.0	9.0	0.1
Tomato & Basil, Loyd Grossman*	1oz/28g	24	87	1.7	7.3	5.6	1.2
Tomato & Basil, Organic, Pasta Reale*	1 Pack/300g	216	72	1.0	5.1	5.3	0.4
Tomato & Basil, Organic, Seeds Of Change*	1 Jar/390g	234	60	1.4	8.5	2.2	1.1
Tomato & Chilli, Loyd Grossman*	1oz/28g	25	88	1.7	7.3	5.7	0.9
Tomato & Chunky Mushroom, Dolmio*	1 Pack/475g	323	68	1.2	7.6	3.7	0.0
Tomato & Herb, Iceland*	1 Serving/100g	59	59	1.4	8.9	2.0	0.7
Tomato & Herb, M & S*	1 Jar/500g	400	80	2.6	10.1	3.1	1.7
Tomato & Herb, Organic, M & S*	1 Jar/320g	176	55	1.1	6.8	2.6	1.8
Tomato & Herb, Organic, Sainsbury's*	1 Serving/75g	38	51	1.2	6.6	2.0	0.5
Tomato & Mascarpone, M & S*	½ Pack/175g	175	100	3.3	6.6	6.2	0.8
Tomato & Mascarpone, Pasta Reale*	1 Pack/300g	318	106	2.9	5.9	7.9	0.5

	Measure WEIGHT/INFO	per Measure KCAL	Nutrition Values per 100g / 100ml KCAL	PROT	CARB	FAT	FIBRE
PASTA SAUCE,							
Tomato & Mushroom, Asda*	1 Serving/127g	71	56	1.8	8.0	1.9	1.2
Tomato & Parmesan, Seeds Of Change*	1 Serving/150g	101	67	2.5	7.8	2.9	1.1
Tomato & Smokey Bacon, Dolmio*	1 Pot/150g	240	160	5.5	5.8	13.1	0.0
Tomato & Spicy Sausages, M & S*	1 Jar/330g	215	65	4.0	5.5	3.0	0.8
Tomato & Tuna, Loyd Grossman*	1oz/28g	25	88	4.4	7.5	4.4	0.8
Tomato & Wild Mushroom, Waitrose*	1 Serving/175g	65	37	1.7	6.0	0.7	0.9
Tomato, Basil & Parmesan Stir In, BGTY, Sainsbury's*	1 Serving/75g	69	92	2.9	7.8	5.5	1.0
Tomato, Organic, Evernat*	1oz/28g	18	64	2.8	10.2	1.3	0.0
Tomato, Pepers & Herb, Somerfield*	1 Pack/110g	138	125	3.0	17.0	5.0	0.0
Tomato, Roasted Garlic & Mushroom, Bertoli*	1 Jar/500g	255	51	1.9	6.4	2.0	1.5
Tomato Romano & Garlic, Five Brothers*	1 Serving/145g	107	74	2.9	8.6	3.0	2.2
Tomato With Herbs & Garlic, Italian, Safeway*	1 Serving/120g	73	61	1.9	8.7	2.1	1.3
Tomato With Italian, Safeway*	½ Jar/235g	146	62	2.0	8.8	2.1	1.9
Tomato With Onions & Garlic, Italian, Safeway*	1 Serving/50g	35	69	2.3	10.2	2.1	1.8
Tomato With Peppers, Italian, Safeway*	1 Serving/100g	63	63	2.0	8.5	2.1	1.4
Traditional, Healthy Choice, Safeway*	1 Jar/475g	257	54	1.8	8.2	1.6	1.3
Traditional, Ragu	1 Jar/515g	345	67	2.0	9.9	2.1	1.2
Traditional, Somerfield*	1 Jar/525g	263	50	2.0	8.0	1.0	0.0
Whole Cherry Tomato & Red Chilli, Sacla*	1 Serving/96g	85	89	1.5	6.2	6.5	0.1
PASTA SHAPES,							
Cooked, Tesco*	1 Serving/260g	356	137	5.1	26.3	0.8	1.1
Economy, Sainsbury's*	1oz/28g	97	346	12.0	72.2	1.0	2.3
In A Cheese & Broccoli Sauce, Tesco*	1 Serving/84g	317	377	13.1	66.2	6.6	4.1
In Rich Chicken, Garilc & Wine Sauce, Tesco*	1 Pack/110g	393	357	14.0	66.1	4.1	4.2
Postman Pat, HP*	1 Can/410g	279	68	1.8	14.3	0.4	0.7
Quick Cook Somerfield*	1oz/28g	97	346	13.0	69.0	2.0	0.0
Scooby Doo, HP*	1 Can/410g	279	68	1.8	14.3	0.4	0.7
Teletubbies, Heinz*	1 Can/400g	244	61	2.0	12.3	0.4	0.6
PASTA, SHELLS							
Egg, Tesco*	1 Serving/125g	343	274	11.4	49.5	3.4	3.0
In Bolognese Sauce, Weight Watchers*	1 Pack/395g	280	71	5.2	9.6	1.3	0.7
Tesco*	1oz/28g	99	354	13.2	68.5	2.0	2.9
PASTA SNACK,							
Ham and Mushroom, Tesco*	1 Serving/300g	618	206	4.2	15.0	14.3	1.1
Tomato & Herb, Morrisons*	1 Pot/247g	247	100	3.1	19.5	1.1	0.0
Tuna Sweetcorn, Tesco*	1 Serving/100g	210	210	5.9	16.9	13.2	1.1
PASTA, SPAGHETTI							
Amatriciana, BGTY, Sainsbury's*	1 Pack/450g	383	85	5.5	14.7	0.5	1.4
Bolgnese, Meat Sauce, Tomatoes, Sainsbury's*	½ Can/205g	150	73	3.9	10.3	1.8	1.0
Bolognaise, Meat Free, Sainsbury's*	1 Can/400g	280	70	3.4	12.0	0.9	1.2
Bolognaise, Sainsbury's*	1 Pack/300g	237	79	4.9	10.5	1.9	0.9
Bolognaise, Tesco*	1 Pack/257g	339	132	6.5	14.1	5.5	1.2
Bolognese, Asda*	1 Pack/400g	388	97	5.0	17.0	1.0	0.9
Bolognese, BGTY, Sainsbury's*	1 Pack/450g	392	87	4.7	14.8	1.0	1.1
Bolognese, Bird's Eye*	1 Pack/362g	404	112	4.8	13.4	4.4	0.9
Bolognese, Canned, Asda*	½ Can/205g	174	85	4.2	10.7	2.8	0.6
Bolognese, COU, M & S*	1 Pack/360g	360	100	6.1	14.9	1.4	0.9
Bolognese, Eat Smart, Safeway*	1 Pack/393g	350	89	5.9	13.1	1.4	1.3
Bolognese, Healthy Choice, Asda*	1 Pack/400g	388	97	5.0	17.0	1.0	0.9
Bolognese, Healthy Choice, Iceland*	1 Pack/400g	428	107	6.8	17.8	1.0	1.1
Bolognese, HE, Tesco*	1 Pack/340g	326	96	5.3	13.7	2.2	1.5
Bolognese, Heinz*	1 Can/400g	344	86	3.4	12.8	2.3	0.7
Bolognese, HP*	1 Pack/410g	312	76	3.8	11.3	1.9	0.7
Bolognese In Tomato & Beef Sauce, Carlini, Aldi*	1 Can/410g	324	79	3.7	10.2	2.6	1.2

P

P

PASTA, SPAGHETTI,	Measure WEIGHT/INFO	per Measure KCAL	Nutrition Values per 100g / 100ml KCAL	PROT	CARB	FAT	FIBRE
Bolognese, Lean Cuisine, Findus*	1 Pack/320g	275	86	4.5	11.5	2.3	1.1
Bolognese, Meat Free, Heinz*	1 Serving/200g	162	81	3.3	13.1	1.7	0.6
Bolognese, Quorn, Sainsbury's*	1 Pack/450g	347	77	4.9	11.9	1.1	1.8
Bolognese, Quorn*	1oz/28g	20	73	5.7	9.4	1.4	2.4
Bolognese, Quorn*	1 Pack/400g	292	73	5.7	9.4	1.4	2.4
Bolognese, Ready Meals, M & S*	1 Pack/360g	576	160	8.8	12.7	8.1	1.2
Bolognese, Safeway*	1 Pack/301g	322	107	6.7	15.5	2.0	0.5
Bolognese, Sainsbury's*	1 Pack/400g	408	102	4.9	16.9	1.6	0.6
Bolognese, Tesco*	1 Pack/400g	356	89	4.9	13.4	1.8	0.7
Bolognese, Weight Watchers*	1 Pack/320g	301	94	5.8	14.6	1.3	1.0
Bolognese With Mushrooms, Colman's*	1 Pack/45g	67	149	4.0	29.9	1.4	2.8
Canned In Tomato Sauce	1oz/28g	18	64	1.9	14.1	0.4	0.7
Carbonara, GFY, Asda*	1 Pack/120g	151	126	4.4	20.0	3.2	0.7
Carbonara, M & S*	1 Pack/360g	630	175	7.6	14.3	9.5	0.1
Carbonara, Tesco*	1 Pack/450g	612	136	5.9	15.2	5.7	1.3
Cooked, Sainsbury's	1 Serving/240g	322	134	4.6	27.4	0.6	1.0
Dried, Spar*	1 Serving/100g	346	346	12.0	71.0	1.6	0.0
Dry, Buitoni*	1 Serving/150g	543	362	12.2	74.4	1.7	0.0
Dry, Happy Shopper*	1 Serving/75g	259	345	12.0	72.0	1.0	3.0
Dry, Italian, Sainsbury's*	1 Serving/100g	357	357	12.3	73.1	1.7	2.5
Dry, Safeway*	1oz/28g	95	338	13.2	67.3	1.8	2.9
Dry, Sainsbury's*	1 Serving/92g	318	346	12.0	72.2	1.0	2.3
Durum Wheat, Seeds Of Change*	1 Serving/75g	263	350	11.5	75.0	0.3	0.0
Durum Wheat, Tesco*	1 Serving/85g	293	345	13.2	68.5	2.0	2.9
Egg, Fresh, Asda*	¼ Pack/124g	167	135	6.0	23.0	2.1	1.6
Egg, Fresh, Italiano, Tesco*	½ Pack/125g	360	288	11.9	51.8	3.7	1.5
Egg, Tesco*	1 Pack/150g	533	355	14.5	66.4	3.5	2.6
Faster, Asda*	1 Serving/50g	173	346	12.0	71.0	1.5	3.0
Fresh, Asda*	1oz/28g	38	135	6.0	23.0	2.1	1.6
Fresh, Sainsbury's*	1 Serving/240g	358	149	6.4	27.5	1.5	1.6
Fresh, Spar*	1 Serving/100g	257	257	9.0	54.2	1.8	3.0
Hoops 'n' Hot Dogs, Heinz*	1 Can/400g	304	76	2.8	11.0	2.4	0.4
Hoops In Tomato Sauce, Heinz*	1 Can/400g	224	56	1.9	11.7	0.2	0.6
Hoops, Tesco*	½ Can/205g	123	60	1.6	12.9	0.2	0.5
Hoops With Pork Sausages & Tomato, Happy Shopper*	1 Can/410g	443	108	3.2	14.0	4.4	0.3
In Tomato Sauce, Heinz*	1 Can/400g	244	61	1.7	13.0	0.2	0.5
In Tomato Sauce, HP*	1 Can/410g	247	60	1.5	13.1	0.2	0.4
In Tomato Sauce, Sainsbury's*	1 Can/410g	262	64	1.9	13.3	0.4	0.5
In Tomato Sauce, Somerfield*	1 Can/4255g	268	63	2.0	14.0	0.0	0.0
In Tomato Sauce, Value, Tesco*	½ Can/205g	131	64	1.9	13.3	0.4	0.5
In Tomato Sauce With Parsley, Weight Watchers*	1 Can/400g	196	49	1.8	10.0	0.2	0.6
In Tomatoe Sauce, Asda*	1 Serving/200g	122	61	1.7	13.0	0.2	0.5
Loops, SmartPrice Asda*	1 Serving/205g	127	62	1.7	13.0	0.3	0.4
Quick Cook, Sainsbury's*	1 Serving/50g	179	357	12.3	73.1	1.7	2.5
Quick Cook, Somerfield*	1oz/28g	97	346	13.0	69.0	2.0	0.0
Short, Dry, Napolina*	1oz/28g	99	352	11.5	73.0	1.5	2.2
Strands, Tesco*	1oz/28g	97	345	13.2	68.5	2.0	2.9
White, Boiled	1oz/28g	29	104	3.6	22.2	0.7	1.2
White, Dry, Raw	1oz/28g	96	342	12.0	74.1	1.8	2.9
Whole Wheat, Asda*	1 Serving/90g	291	323	14.0	60.0	3.0	10.0
Wholemeal, Boiled	1oz/28g	32	113	4.7	23.2	0.9	3.5
Wholemeal, Raw	1oz/28g	91	324	13.4	66.2	2.5	8.4
Wholewheat, Co-Op*	1 Pack/500g	1600	320	14.0	60.0	3.0	8.0
Wholewheat, Tesco*	1oz/28g	90	321	14.4	60.2	2.5	8.4

	Measure WEIGHT/INFO	per Measure KCAL	KCAL	PROT	CARB	FAT	FIBRE
PASTA, SPAGHETTI,							
Wholewheati, Sainsbury's*	1oz/28g	92	330	13.3	61.9	3.2	9.3
With Sausages, Heinz*	1 Can/400g	328	82	3.7	11.0	2.6	0.5
With Tomato & Cheese, Tesco*	½ Pack/250g	280	112	4.0	18.1	2.6	1.1
PASTA, TAGLIATELLE							
Carbonara, Low Fat, Bertorelli*	1 Pack/350g	301	86	5.3	12.0	2.2	0.9
Carbonara, Naturally Less 5% Fat, Asda*	1 Pack/400g	440	110	4.2	18.0	2.4	0.8
Carbonara, Perfectly Balanced, Waitrose*	1 Pack/350g	357	102	5.3	12.1	3.6	0.7
Carbonara, Reduced Fat, Waitrose*	1 Pack/350g	399	114	5.0	12.1	5.1	0.6
Carbonara, Safeway*	1 Serving/298g	277	93	3.7	13.2	2.8	0.6
Chicken & Tomato, Eat Smart, Safeway*	1 Pack/400g	360	90	7.5	10.8	1.4	1.1
Chicken, Garlic & Lemon, BGTY, Sainsbury's*	1 Pack/450g	509	113	8.9	10.8	3.8	0.3
Chicken, Italia, M & S*	1 Pack/360g	342	95	8.1	12.1	1.8	1.2
Dry, Morrisons*	1 Serving/50g	173	345	12.0	72.3	1.0	0.0
Dry, Sainsbury's*	1oz/28g	100	357	12.3	73.1	1.7	2.5
Dry, Tesco*	1 Serving/100g	345	345	13.2	68.5	2.0	2.9
Egg & Spinach, Finest, Tesco*	1oz/28g	75	268	11.7	47.5	3.5	2.7
Egg & Spinach, Dry, Safeway*	1 Serving/125g	435	348	13.2	67.3	2.9	2.9
Egg, Fresh, Tesco*	¼ Pack/125g	360	288	11.9	51.8	3.7	1.5
Fresh, Co-Op*	1oz/28g	78	280	11.0	56.0	2.0	3.0
Fresh, Morrisons*	½ Pack/125g	364	291	11.3	54.0	3.3	2.5
Garlic & Herb, Cooked, Sainsbury's*	1oz/28g	41	147	6.5	26.3	1.8	1.9
Garlic & Herb, Fresh, Co-Op*	1oz/28g	78	280	12.0	43.0	7.0	4.0
Garlic & Herb, Fresh, Tesco*	1 Serving/125g	361	289	12.0	51.8	3.7	1.5
Garlic & Herbs, Cooked, Pasta Reale*	1 Pack/250g	390	156	6.2	30.4	1.1	1.0
Garlic Mushroom, BGTY, Sainsbury's*	1 Pack/450g	369	82	3.6	12.3	2.0	1.0
Ham & Mushroom, Asda*	1 Pack/340g	469	138	6.0	20.0	3.8	0.2
Ham & Mushroom, Better For You, Morrisons*	1 Pack/350g	326	93	5.3	9.4	3.8	0.8
Ham & Mushroom, BGTY, Sainsbury's*	1 Pack/450g	486	108	5.3	14.5	3.2	0.8
Ham & Mushroom, Co-Op*	1 Pack/300g	270	90	6.0	10.0	3.0	2.0
Ham & Mushroom, COU, M & S*	1oz/28g	25	90	5.3	12.0	2.2	0.9
Ham & Mushroom, GFY, Asda*	1 Pack/340g	408	120	6.0	14.0	4.4	0.4
Ham & Mushroom, Good Intentions, Somerfield*	1 Serving/300g	333	111	5.6	15.6	2.9	0.3
Ham & Mushroom, Healthy Choice, Safeway*	1 Pack/400g	400	100	5.5	12.1	3.3	0.3
Ham & Mushroom, HE, Tesco*	1 Meal/340g	306	90	4.3	13.6	2.0	0.9
Ham & Mushroom, Italiano, Tesco*	1 Pack/340g	445	131	5.4	18.0	4.2	1.0
Ham & Mushroom, Morrisons*	1 Pack/350g	462	132	5.1	9.6	8.4	0.1
Ham & Mushroom, Organic, Tesco*	1 Pack/350g	665	190	5.4	25.8	7.2	1.3
Ham & Mushroom, Somerfield*	1 Serving/285g	325	114	4.0	13.0	5.0	0.0
Ham & Mushrooms, COU, M & S*	1 Serving/360g	360	100	5.9	13.5	2.7	0.9
Ham, Ready Meals, M & S*	1 Pack/360g	414	115	5.8	10.5	5.7	1.0
Italian, Organic, Dry, Waitrose*	1 Serving/75g	263	350	11.5	75.0	0.3	0.0
Mushroom & Tomato, Asda*	1 Pack/340g	211	62	2.5	10.0	1.3	1.2
Nests, Dry, Napolina*	1oz/28g	93	332	11.5	68.0	1.5	3.7
Red Pepper, Organic, Sainsbury's*	½ Bag/125g	183	146	5.4	27.8	1.5	1.4
Smoked Salmon, Ready Meals, M & S*	1 Pack/360g	612	170	6.2	10.6	11.2	0.9
Tomato & Basil Chicken, Weight Watchers*	1 Pack/330g	254	77	5.9	11.8	0.6	0.8
Tricolore, Waitrose*	½ Pack/125g	351	281	12.0	51.6	2.9	1.6
Vegetable, Tesco*	1 Pack/300g	261	87	2.5	12.4	3.0	0.4
Vegetables, Retail	1oz/28g	21	74	1.6	11.0	3.0	0.7
Verdi, Fresh, Asda*	1oz/28g	38	134	5.0	25.0	1.6	1.5
Verdi, Fresh, Sainsbury's*	1 Serving/240g	353	147	6.4	26.4	1.8	1.8
Verdi, Fresh, Tesco*	1 Serving/125g	163	130	5.2	25.1	1.0	2.0
Verdi, Pasta Reale*	1oz/28g	72	257	8.7	52.4	1.5	4.1
PASTA, TORTELLINI,							

Nutrition Values per 100g / 100ml apply to the last five columns.

P

	Measure WEIGHT/INFO	per Measure KCAL	Nutrition Values per 100g / 100ml KCAL	PROT	CARB	FAT	FIBRE
PASTA, TORTELLINI,							
3 Cheese, Sainsbury's*	1 Serving/50g	196	391	14.4	63.8	8.7	3.0
Cheese & Tomato, M & S*	1 Meal/125g	238	190	10.0	29.1	3.6	1.8
Chicken & Mushroom, Asda*	1 Serving/125g	206	165	7.0	21.0	3.9	1.6
Chicken & Mushroom, Less Than 5% Fat, Asda*	½ Pack/150g	209	139	7.0	22.0	2.5	0.0
Four Cheese, Asda*	1 Serving/150g	201	134	6.0	20.0	3.3	0.0
Four Cheese, Fresh, Asda*	1 Serving/100g	134	134	6.0	20.0	3.3	0.0
Four Cheese With Tomato & Basil Sauce, Tesco*	1 Pack/400g	500	125	6.1	16.9	3.7	0.6
Garlic & Herb, Morrisons*	½ Pack/150g	428	285	11.4	43.2	7.5	2.3
Garlic, Basil & Ricotta Tortellini, Asda*	1 Serving/150g	227	151	6.0	24.0	3.4	0.0
Ham & Cheese, Asda*	1 Serving/125g	191	153	7.0	20.0	5.0	1.8
Ham & Cheese, Fresh, Asda*	½ Pack/150g	198	132	6.0	20.0	3.1	0.0
Ham & Cheese, Tesco*	1 Serving/225g	578	257	13.5	38.1	5.6	1.8
Italiana, Weight Watchers*	1 Can/395g	237	60	2.1	8.5	1.9	0.5
Mozzarella & Tomato Tortellini, Fresh, Asda*	1oz/28g	46	166	8.0	25.0	3.8	0.0
Mushroom, Asda*	1 Serving/125g	218	174	6.0	28.0	4.2	2.3
Mushroom, BGTY, Sainsbury's*	1 Pack/400g	308	77	2.5	10.0	3.0	2.5
Mushroom, Perfectly Balanced, Waitrose*	1 Pack/250g	573	229	9.4	39.8	3.6	2.4
Pork & Beef, BGTY, Sainsbury's*	½ Can/200g	142	71	2.3	11.9	1.6	1.2
Ricotta & Spinach, Sainsbury's*	1oz/28g	109	388	15.0	62.5	8.7	2.2
Ricotta & Spinach, Somerfield*	1 Can/250g	283	113	12.0	4.0	6.0	0.0
Smoked Bacon & Tomato, Asda*	1 Pack/300g	591	197	9.0	29.0	5.0	0.0
Smoked Ham & Cheese, Ready Meals, Waitrose*	1oz/28g	73	261	12.9	38.7	6.1	1.3
Spicy Pepperoni, Asda*	½ Pack/150g	252	168	7.0	26.0	4.0	0.0
Spinach & Ricotta, Tesco*	1 Serving/125g	323	258	11.9	36.2	7.3	1.9
Spinach & Ricotta, Verdi, Asda*	1 Serving/125g	186	149	6.0	21.0	4.5	2.4
Spinach and Ricotta, Fresh, Sainsbury's*	½ Pack/125g	269	215	10.0	31.3	5.5	3.7
Tomato & Mozzarella, Fresh, Asda*	½ Pack/150g	236	157	8.0	25.0	2.8	0.0
Trio, Fresh, Tesco*	½ Pack/125g	323	258	12.8	35.8	7.1	2.0
PASTA, TORTELLONI,							
Carbonara, Sainsbury's*	1 Serving/154g	416	270	13.1	27.7	12.6	2.5
Cheese & Pesto, Somerfield*	1 Pack/250g	788	315	12.0	40.0	12.0	0.0
Garlic & Herb, Cooked, Pasta Reale*	1 Pack/300g	546	182	6.7	30.1	3.9	0.9
Goats Cheese & Pesto, Sainsbury's*	1 Pack/250g	518	207	8.9	24.6	8.1	2.6
Spinach & Ricotta, Fresh, Safeway*	½ Pack/202g	341	169	7.4	24.0	4.8	2.4
Spinach & Ricotta, Fresh, Sainsbury's*	½ Pack/150g	323	215	10.0	31.3	5.5	3.7
Tubes, Dried, Safeway*	1oz/28g	95	338	13.2	67.3	1.8	2.9
PASTA, TWISTS,							
Asda*	1 Serving/50g	173	346	12.0	71.0	1.5	3.0
Co-Op*	1oz/28g	97	345	13.0	69.0	2.0	3.0
Morrisons*	¼ Pack/125g	455	364	12.0	72.3	1.0	0.0
Romano, Aldi*	1oz/28g	101	362	12.0	75.0	1.5	2.9
PASTA,							
& Chicken & Mushroom Sauce, SmartPrice, Asda*	½ Pack/180g	299	166	5.0	23.0	6.0	2.2
& Chicken With Spicy Arrabbiata Sauce, COU, M & S*	1 Pack/360g	252	70	5.2	8.7	1.4	1.3
& Roasted Vegetables, Waitrose*	1oz/28g	43	154	2.4	14.2	9.7	1.0
& Sauce, Tomato, Onion & Herb, Morrisons*	1 Serving/110g	141	128	3.2	18.7	4.5	2.3
& Sun Dried Tomatoes, GFY, Asda*	½ Pack/125g	146	117	3.1	19.0	3.2	0.0
& Vegetables, M & S*	1oz/28g	21	76	3.6	13.5	0.8	1.9
Agnolotti Mushroom, Cooked, Pasta Reale*	1 Pack/300g	474	158	5.6	25.0	3.9	0.6
Angel Hair, Sainsbury's*	1 Serving/100g	357	357	12.3	73.1	1.7	2.5
Arrabbiata, Tesco*	1 Serving/205g	144	70	2.6	12.1	1.2	1.1
Bolognese Shells, BGTY, Sainsbury's*	1 Can/400g	340	85	5.0	11.8	2.0	0.7
Bolognese Shells, Italiana, Weight Watchers*	1 Can/395g	284	72	5.3	9.8	1.3	0.8
Bolognese Shells, Ready Meals, M & S*	1 Pack/390g	585	150	7.8	11.4	8.3	0.9

P

PASTA,	Measure WEIGHT/INFO	per Measure KCAL	Nutrition Values per 100g / 100ml KCAL	PROT	CARB	FAT	FIBRE
Cajun Chicken, HE, Tesco*	1 Pack/365g	412	113	7.9	17.3	1.3	0.7
Cappelletti, Chicken & Ham, Fresh, Safeway*	½ Pack/177g	320	181	9.7	27.7	3.5	1.8
Cappelletti, Fresh, Sainsbury's*	1 Serving/125g	294	235	12.9	33.5	5.5	2.7
Carbonara, Ready Meals, M & S*	1 Pack/360g	630	175	7.6	14.3	9.5	0.8
Cavatelli, Egg, Asda*	1 Serving/100g	203	203	9.0	34.0	3.4	3.0
Cellantani, Buitoni*	1 Serving/195g	706	362	12.2	74.4	1.7	0.0
Chargrill Chicken, Shapers*	1 Serving/100g	324	324	16.0	46.0	8.4	2.0
Chargrilled Vegetables & Tomato, Shapers, Boots*	1 Bowl/175g	187	107	2.8	17.0	3.1	1.5
Cheesey, Kraft*	1 Serving/169g	389	230	5.9	27.0	10.5	1.3
Cherry Tomato & Mozzarella, Shapers, Boots*	1 Pot/163g	186	114	3.3	19.0	2.7	1.6
Chicken & Spinach, Waitrose*	1 Pack/350g	483	138	7.0	14.0	6.0	0.8
Chicken Napolitana, Good Intentions, Somerfield*	1 Pack/300g	279	93	6.1	14.0	1.4	0.5
Cooked, Standard, Buitoni*	1 Serving/100g	129	129	4.8	25.9	0.7	1.2
Creamy Mushroom, Asda*	1 Pack/250g	588	235	2.5	14.0	18.8	1.0
Duetto, Green & White, Pasta Reale*	1oz/28g	79	281	10.9	49.4	6.0	3.6
Duetto, Red & White, Pasta Reale*	1oz/28g	85	304	12.9	47.5	8.0	2.5
Egg, Fresh, Somerfield*	1 Serving/125g	148	118	4.4	22.1	1.4	1.4
Eliche, Buitoni*	1 Serving/75g	272	362	12.2	74.4	1.7	0.0
Farfalline, Bows, Mini, Tesco*	1oz/28g	93	333	13.2	65.6	2.0	2.9
Fiorelli, Egg, M & S*	1 Serving/100g	355	355	13.9	68.5	2.8	3.0
Fireroast Tomato & Peppert, Finest, Tesco*	1 Serving/200g	384	192	3.9	19.4	11.0	1.4
Gemelli, Durum Wheat, Tesco*	1 Serving/100g	354	354	13.2	68.5	2.0	2.9
Honey & Mustard Chicken, Shapers, Boots*	1 Pack/241g	304	126	7.0	19.0	2.4	1.7
In Herb Sauce, Sainsbury's*	1 Pack/420g	441	105	3.5	22.4	0.2	0.8
In Mushroom & Tomato Sauce, Sainsbury's*	½ Pack/200g	370	185	5.1	24.8	7.3	1.1
Lasagnetta, Dried, Napolina*	1oz/28g	99	352	11.5	73.0	1.5	2.2
Lasagnette, Vegetable, HP*	1 Can/400g	240	60	1.8	9.5	1.6	0.9
Messicani, Egg, M & S*	1 Serving/100g	355	355	13.9	68.5	2.8	3.0
Orecchiette Shells, TTD, Sainsbury's*	1 Serving/50g	184	367	11.5	79.1	0.5	2.0
Parcels, Italian Tomato & Mozzarella, Sainsbury's*	½ Pack/175g	340	194	7.5	23.0	8.0	3.4
Parcels, Cheese & Sweet Pepper Sauce, Somerfield*	½ Pack/125g	349	279	12.4	30.7	11.8	2.2
Spaghetti In Tomato Sauce, Tesco*	1 Can/410g	246	60	1.6	12.9	0.2	0.5
Pennette, Tricolore, Sainsbury's*	1 Serving/100g	357	357	12.3	73.1	1.7	2.5
Pot, Spinach, M & S*	1oz/28g	71	254	6.7	22.9	15.1	1.7
Pronto, Mushroom & Garlic, Safeway*	1 Serving/203g	315	155	5.0	21.7	5.3	0.9
Puglian & Meatballs, M & S*	1 Serving/500g	650	130	6.3	15.2	4.7	1.5
Radiatore, Sainsbury's*	1 Serving/75g	268	357	12.3	73.1	1.7	2.5
Radiatore, Somerfield*	1oz/28g	97	346	13.0	69.0	2.0	0.0
Roast Vegetable & Tomato, Bird's Eye*	1 Pack/350g	284	81	2.8	15.2	1.0	0.9
Sacchetini, Italian Meat & Cheese, Tesco*	½ Pack/125g	323	258	13.8	34.4	7.2	2.1
Seafood, Retail	1oz/28g	31	110	8.9	7.6	4.8	0.4
Snails, Lumache, Tesco*	1 Serving/100g	354	354	11.5	72.6	1.9	2.7
Spaghettini Express, Buitoni*	1 Serving/200g	724	362	12.2	74.4	1.7	0.0
Spicy Meatball, M & S*	1 Pack/400g	540	135	8.8	12.0	6.0	1.4
Spicy Tomato, Good Intentions, Somerfield*	1 Pack/299g	257	86	2.8	15.7	1.3	0.8
Spirali, Cooked, Asda*	1 Serving/50g	173	346	12.0	72.0	1.6	3.0
Spirals, Glutenfree, Glutano*	1oz/28g	100	357	4.0	83.0	1.0	0.0
Spirals, Spicy, Tesco*	1oz/28g	20	72	4.5	11.6	0.8	0.8
Stortelli, Microwaveable, Dolmio*	1 Serving/220g	299	136	5.3	26.3	1.0	0.0
Tomato & Mushroom, Waitrose*	1oz/28g	39	141	2.3	11.1	9.7	0.9
Tomato, Bacon & Mushroom, HE, Tesco*	1 Pack/450g	486	108	4.7	17.0	2.3	1.9
Tomato, HE, Tesco*	½ Pot/100g	88	88	2.8	17.0	1.0	0.0
Tomato, Parmesan & Spinach, Shapers, Boots*	1 Pot/280g	288	103	3.8	15.0	3.1	1.6
Tuna & Sweetcorn, Sainsbury's*	1 Pasta/300g	327	109	6.7	14.7	2.6	1.4

P

	Measure	per Measure	Nutrition Values per 100g / 100ml				
PASTA,	**WEIGHT/INFO**	**KCAL**	**KCAL**	**PROT**	**CARB**	**FAT**	**FIBRE**
Tuna & Vegetable, Waitrose*	1 Pack/350g	329	94	5.9	9.0	3.8	0.6
Tuna, Eat Smart, Safeway*	1 Serving/210g	210	100	8.0	12.2	1.6	0.5
Tuscany, Better For You, Morrisons*	1 Pack/350g	305	87	3.0	17.7	0.5	1.1
Vegetable, Asda*	1 Serving/50g	105	209	2.4	16.0	15.0	0.9
Vegetarian, Spaghetti & Meatballs Style, Safeway*	1 Pack/350g	382	109	5.0	13.7	3.8	0.5
Vermicelli, Dry	1oz/28g	99	355	8.7	78.3	0.4	0.0
Wholemeal, Tesco*	1 Serving/125g	419	335	13.0	65.0	2.1	6.8
Wholewheat, Barilla*	1oz/28g	95	340	13.0	67.5	2.0	6.0
Wholewheat Spaghetti In Tomato Sauce, Sainsbury's*	1 Serving/205g	125	61	2.0	11.9	0.6	1.1
With Broad Beans, Fine Beans, Peas & Spinach, Sainsbury's	1 Pack/450g	441	98	4.5	16.7	1.5	2.0
With Meatballs, Sainsbury's*	1 Can/300g	339	113	6.6	10.6	4.9	1.6
With Tomato & Basil Chicken, M & S*	1 Serving/190g	171	90	6.8	10.6	2.1	1.4
With Tomato & Chargrilled Chicken, Tesco*	1 Pot/300g	381	127	6.0	14.6	4.9	1.0
With Vegetables, Superdrug*	1 Serving/180g	259	144	3.0	21.8	5.0	0.7
PASTE,							
Bacon & Tomato, Tesco*	1 Serving/38g	89	233	14.0	3.4	18.1	0.1
Beef, Princes*	1 Serving/18g	40	220	14.4	5.2	15.8	0.0
Chicken & Ham, Asda*	½ Jar/38g	82	217	14.0	2.1	17.0	0.0
Chicken & Ham, Sainsbury's*	Thin Spread/9g	14	158	16.0	1.1	10.0	1.1
Chicken & Stuffing, Asda*	½ Jar/35g	71	203	16.0	3.3	14.0	0.0
Chicken, Asda*	Thin Spread/7g	13	184	16.0	0.8	13.0	0.0
Chicken, Princes*	Thin Spread/9g	22	240	12.6	5.6	18.5	0.0
Chicken, Tesco*	1 Serving/12g	30	248	14.8	2.3	20.0	0.1
Chicken, Value, Tesco*	Thin Spread/9g	18	196	15.1	1.8	14.3	0.1
Crab, (Classic), Shippams*	1 small jar/35g	48	138	14.1	6.0	6.4	0.0
Crab, Princes*	1 Pot/35g	36	104	13.4	4.8	3.5	0.0
Salmon & Shrimp, Somerfield*	Thin Spread/9g	10	112	17.0	4.0	3.0	0.0
Salmon, Asda*	1 Serving/53g	76	143	15.0	5.0	7.0	0.0
Salmon, Princes*	1 Serving/30g	59	195	13.5	6.5	12.8	0.0
Salmon, Sainsbury's*	1 Serving/20g	42	208	13.4	4.4	15.2	0.7
Salmon, Smart Price, Asda*	1 Serving/75g	78	104	15.0	4.6	2.8	0.0
Salmon, Value, Tesco*	Thin Spread/9g	12	131	14.0	4.8	6.2	0.1
Sardine & Tomato, Asda*	Thin Spread/9g	11	123	14.0	3.3	6.0	0.0
Sardine & Tomato, Princes*	1 Jar/75g	110	146	15.4	5.0	7.2	0.0
Sardine & Tomato, Somerfield*	Thin Spread/9g	13	144	15.0	5.0	7.0	0.0
Sausage & Baked Bean, Tesco*	1 Jar/75g	137	182	13.7	4.8	12.0	0.8
Tuna & Mayonnaise, Princes*	1 Pot/75g	158	210	16.6	1.3	15.4	0.0
Tuna & Mayonnaise, Somerfield*	Thin Spread/9g	19	209	15.0	2.0	16.0	0.0
Vegetable, Sainsbury's*	1 Serving/17g	26	154	7.4	5.9	11.2	3.4
PASTRAMI,							
American Style, Safeway*	1 Slice/15g	21	140	23.8	2.0	4.1	0.0
Asda*	1 Slice/25g	35	141	24.0	2.0	4.1	0.0
Slices, TTD, Sainsbury's*	1 Slice/10g	14	140	23.8	2.0	4.1	0.1
Slices, Waitrose*	1 Slice/10g	12	124	24.3	0.0	3.0	0.0
Turkey, Wafer Thin, M & S*	1 Serving/100g	113	113	23.6	1.4	1.6	0.0
Wafer Thin, M & S*	1 Pack/75g	101	135	23.5	0.9	4.7	0.1
PASTRY,							
Cheese & Onion, Proper Cornish Real Pastries*	1 Pasty/255g	709	278	8.1	31.7	13.2	1.8
Chinese Flaky	1oz/28g	110	392	5.4	59.3	16.4	0.0
Choux, Cooked	1oz/28g	91	325	8.5	29.8	19.8	1.2
Choux, Raw	1oz/28g	59	211	5.5	19.4	12.9	0.8
Filo, Jus-Rol*	1 Sheet/45g	128	285	8.9	60.0	1.0	0.0
Filo, Sainsbury's*	1 Sheet/33g	104	315	9.2	62.1	4.1	0.8
Flaky, Cooked	1oz/28g	157	560	5.6	45.9	40.6	1.8

P

	Measure WEIGHT/INFO	per Measure KCAL	Nutrition Values per 100g / 100ml KCAL	PROT	CARB	FAT	FIBRE
PASTRY,							
Flaky, Raw	1oz/28g	119	424	4.2	34.8	30.7	1.4
Greek	1oz/28g	90	322	4.7	40.0	17.0	0.0
Pastry Mix, Short Crust, Somerfield*	1oz/28g	134	479	7.0	49.0	28.0	0.0
Puff, Frozen, Jus-Rol*	1 Sheet/213g	846	397	6.1	37.0	25.0	0.0
Puff, Frozen, Raw	1 Shell/47g	175	373	5.7	37.0	23.5	0.0
Puff, Ready Rolled, Jus-Rol*	1 Sheet/240g	998	416	4.2	39.0	27.0	0.0
Shortcrust, Cooked	1oz/28g	146	521	6.6	54.2	32.3	2.2
Shortcrust, Frozen, Jus-Rol*	1 Sheet/225g	1055	469	6.6	41.0	31.0	0.0
Shortcrust, Frozen, Raw	1oz/28g	123	440	4.5	44.3	28.4	1.9
Shortcrust, Raw	1oz/28g	126	449	5.7	46.8	27.9	1.9
Wholemeal, Cooked	1oz/28g	140	499	8.9	44.6	32.9	6.3
Wholemeal, Raw	1oz/28g	121	431	7.7	38.5	28.4	5.4
PASTY,							
Bite Size Pasties, Food To Go, Sainsburys*	1 Serving/60g	226	377	8.2	31.2	24.4	1.5
Cheese & Onion, Co-Op*	1 Pasty/75g	235	313	9.2	24.5	19.8	1.7
Cheese & Onion, Farmfoods*	1 Pasty/191g	485	254	6.6	25.5	14.0	2.0
Cheese & Onion, Geo Adams*	1 Pasty/150g	420	280	6.9	27.9	15.6	1.1
Cheese & Onion, Somerfield*	1 Pasty/145g	419	289	7.0	24.0	18.0	0.0
Corned Beef, Mega, M & S*	1oz/28g	87	310	9.5	22.3	20.2	0.9
Cornish, Asda*	1 Pasty/100g	287	287	7.0	22.0	19.0	1.2
Cornish, BGTY, Sainsbury's*	1 Pasty/135g	308	228	7.7	28.2	9.4	1.6
Cornish, Cheese & Onion, Ginsters*	1 Pasty/130g	511	393	10.4	30.7	25.4	2.3
Cornish, Chicken & Bacon, Ginsters*	1 Pasty/227g	579	255	5.4	25.7	14.5	0.9
Cornish, Chunky Steak, Ginsters*	¼ Pasty/56g	316	565	15.1	52.7	32.7	3.6
Cornish, Co-Op*	1 Pasty/75g	200	267	6.4	23.4	16.4	1.6
Cornish, M & S*	1 Pasty/150g	480	320	6.5	27.3	20.3	1.5
Cornish, Mega, M & S*	1oz/28g	84	300	6.0	18.7	22.1	1.2
Cornish, Mini, M & S*	1 Pastie/72g	227	315	6.7	21.0	22.6	1.0
Cornish, Mini, Tesco*	1 Pasty/24g	66	274	5.6	23.2	17.7	0.5
Cornish, Morrisons*	1 Pasty/200g	626	313	7.5	29.1	18.5	0.0
Cornish, Original, Ginsters*	1 Pasty/227g	568	250	6.0	19.0	15.8	1.1
Cornish, Safeway*	1 Pasty/170g	490	288	7.5	22.6	18.6	1.5
Cornish, SmartPrice, Asda*	1 Pasty/94g	286	304	8.0	32.0	16.0	1.7
Cornish, Somerfield*	1oz/28g	85	303	6.0	28.0	18.0	0.0
Steak & Onion, M & S*	1 Pasty/164g	459	280	8.7	19.2	18.8	1.4
Tandoori & Vegetable, Holland & Barrett*	1 Pack/110g	232	211	4.3	29.4	8.5	1.8
Vegetable	1oz/28g	77	274	4.1	33.3	14.9	1.9
Vegetarian, Cornish, Linda McCartney*	1 Pasty/170g	420	247	5.2	25.5	13.8	1.5
PATE,							
Ardennes, Asda*	1 Serving/50g	143	286	13.9	3.6	24.0	1.3
Ardennes, BGTY, Sainsbury's*	1 Serving/50g	95	189	18.1	2.4	11.9	0.1
Ardennes, HE, Tesco*	1 Serving/50g	119	238	16.5	2.6	17.9	1.6
Ardennes, Reduced Fat, Safeway*	1 Serving/50g	97	194	18.5	3.1	11.9	0.1
Ardennes, Safeway*	1 Serving/50g	166	331	12.8	6.0	28.4	0.8
Ardennes, Sainsbury's*	1 Serving/20g	60	299	16.5	2.1	24.9	0.1
Ardennes, Tesco*	1 Tbsp/15g	53	354	13.3	0.5	33.2	1.2
Asparagus, Sainsbury's*	½ Pot/57g	88	153	3.4	5.4	13.1	1.0
Brussels, Asda*	1 Serving/50g	175	350	10.7	4.4	32.2	1.7
Brussels, BGTY, Sainsbury's*	1 Serving/50g	137	273	12.6	6.2	22.0	0.1
Brussels, Fat Reduced, Somerfield*	1 Serving/50g	96	192	14.0	2.0	14.0	0.0
Brussels, HE, Tesco*	1 Serving/28g	66	235	16.4	2.3	17.8	1.9
Brussels, Reduced Fat, Asda*	1 Serving/44g	88	199	15.0	2.1	15.0	1.9
Brussels, Reduced Fat, Somerfield*	1 Serving/50g	139	277	14.0	8.0	21.0	0.0
Brussels, Sainsbury's*	1 Pack/170g	663	390	10.6	1.1	38.2	0.1

P

PATE,	Measure WEIGHT/INFO	per Measure KCAL	Nutrition Values per 100g / 100ml KCAL	PROT	CARB	FAT	FIBRE
Brussels, Tesco*	1 Serving/28g	92	330	11.0	3.0	30.5	1.1
Brussels With Garlic, Asda*	1 Serving/50g	170	340	10.7	4.0	31.3	2.5
Carrot, Ginger & Spring Onion, M & S*	1 Serving/50g	73	145	1.5	9.6	11.0	0.9
Chicken Liver & Brandy, Asda*	1 Serving/50g	177	353	9.0	5.5	32.8	3.2
Chicken Liver, M & S*	1oz/28g	79	281	14.0	1.9	24.1	0.1
Chicken Liver Parfait, TTD, Sainsbury's*	1 Serving/20g	72	359	8.0	2.0	35.0	0.5
Chicken Liver With Brandy, Tesco*	1oz/28g	82	293	11.8	3.5	25.8	1.4
Coarse Farmhouse, Organic, Sainsbury's*	1 Serving/56g	138	246	13.3	3.7	19.7	0.8
Coarse Pork Liver With Olives & Tomatoes, Sainsbury's*	1 Serving/85g	236	278	16.0	1.5	23.1	0.0
Crab, M & S*	1oz/28g	63	225	12.1	5.9	17.3	0.0
Crab, Waitrose*	1oz/28g	59	209	14.5	0.5	16.6	0.0
Duck & Champagne, Luxury, M & S*	1oz/28g	106	380	8.3	8.3	35.2	7.8
Duck & Orange, M & S*	1oz/28g	88	315	10.6	2.8	29.0	0.5
Duck With Port Wine, Somerfield*	1oz/28g	102	365	12.0	3.0	34.0	0.0
Farmhouse With Christmas Ale, Sainsbury's*	1oz/28g	67	239	15.4	1.6	19.1	0.0
Farmhouse With Mushrooms & Garlic, Tesco*	1 Serving/90g	257	285	13.8	0.6	25.3	1.3
Garlic & Herb Yeast, Tartex*	1 Serving/10g	23	230	7.0	10.0	18.0	0.0
Isle of Skye Smoked Salmon, TTD, Sainsbury's*	½ Pot/58g	161	277	16.5	0.8	23.1	0.1
Liver Spreading, Somerfield*	1oz/28g	77	275	14.0	3.0	23.0	0.0
Mackerel, Smoked	1oz/28g	103	368	13.4	1.3	34.4	0.0
Mediterranean Roast Vegetable, Tesco*	1 Serving/28g	31	112	2.4	4.3	9.4	1.2
Mushroom & Herb, Somerfield*	1oz/28g	81	289	4.0	8.0	27.0	0.0
Mushroom & Tarragon, Cauldron Foods*	1oz/28g	43	155	2.8	5.5	13.5	1.4
Mushroom, COU, M & S*	1oz/28g	17	60	2.9	7.4	1.9	0.9
Mushroom, New, Tesco*	1 Serving/85g	117	138	3.3	9.8	9.5	1.0
Mushroom, Organic, Cauldron Foods*	1oz/28g	33	119	2.8	4.3	10.1	1.0
Mushroom, Sainsbury's*	1oz/28g	47	168	3.1	5.9	15.2	1.3
Mushroom, Tesco*	1oz/28g	42	151	3.2	9.1	11.3	0.9
Poached Salmon & Watercress, Tesco*	1 Serving/25g	60	238	19.2	0.4	17.7	0.2
Pork & Garlic, Somerfield*	1oz/28g	83	295	14.0	3.0	25.0	0.0
Pork & Mushroom, Somerfield*	1oz/28g	95	339	11.0	3.0	31.0	0.0
Pork With Port & Cranberry, Tesco*	1 Serving/28g	83	296	12.1	4.3	25.6	0.6
Quorn, Brussels Style, Quorn*	1 Pack/130g	150	115	10.8	5.7	5.4	3.4
Quorn, Country Style Coarse, Quorn*	½ Pot/65g	68	104	9.2	7.3	4.2	2.7
Quorn Deli, Quorn*	1oz/28g	32	115	10.8	5.7	5.4	3.4
Red Pepper, M & S*	1oz/28g	52	185	3.0	6.6	16.2	0.9
Roasted Carrot, Ginger & Spring Onion, M & S*	1 Serving/50g	73	145	1.5	9.6	11.0	0.9
Roasted Red Pepper & Humous, Princes*	¼ Jar/27g	32	120	4.6	12.4	5.8	0.0
Roasted Red Pepper, Oven Roasted, Castle MacLellan*	1oz/28g	46	163	3.3	8.2	13.5	0.8
Salmon, Organic, M & S*	1oz/28g	76	270	16.9	0.0	22.5	0.0
Salmon, Smoked, M & S*	1oz/28g	74	265	16.9	0.0	22.0	0.0
Salsa, Princes*	1 Serving/25g	21	84	3.6	16.7	0.3	0.0
Smoked Mackerel, M & S*	1oz/28g	104	370	13.4	0.7	34.7	0.3
Smoked Salmon, HE, Tesco*	1 Serving/50g	65	130	17.5	2.6	5.5	0.0
Smoked Salmon, Organic, Waitrose*	1oz/28g	83	296	13.9	2.4	25.6	0.0
Spiced Parsnip & Carrot, Organic, Asda*	½ Pot/58g	63	109	3.7	10.0	6.0	2.6
Spicy Bean, Princes*	½ Pot/55g	46	84	3.6	16.7	0.3	0.0
Spinach, Parmesan & Almond, Cauldron Foods*	1/3 Pack/38g	66	173	7.2	6.3	13.2	2.3
Tomato, Lentil & Basil, Cauldron Foods*	1oz/28g	43	154	7.5	15.6	6.8	1.5
Tuna, M & S*	1oz/28g	99	355	18.0	0.0	31.3	0.0
Tuna With Butter & Lemon Juice, Sainsbury's*	½ Pot/58g	209	360	19.0	0.1	31.6	0.3
Vegetable	1oz/28g	48	173	7.5	5.9	13.4	0.0
Vegetarian, Spicy Mexican, Organic, Waitrose*	1 Serving/50g	58	115	6.2	8.6	6.2	3.5
Vegetarian, Spinach, Soft Cheese & Onion, Co-Op*	1oz/28g	48	170	5.0	3.0	15.0	4.0

P

PATE,	Measure WEIGHT/INFO	per Measure KCAL	KCAL	PROT	CARB	FAT	FIBRE
			Nutrition Values per 100g / 100ml				
Vegetarian, Yeast, Wild Mushroom, Grano Vita*	1oz/28g	60	213	10.0	5.0	17.0	0.0
Yeast With Mushrooms, Organic, Tartex*	1oz/28g	56	200	7.0	7.0	16.0	0.0
PAVLOVA,							
Bucks Fizz Mini Champagne, Co-Op*	1 Pavlova/19g	62	325	3.0	38.0	18.0	0.5
Raspberry, Co-Op*	1/6 Pavlova/49g	147	300	3.2	44.8	12.0	1.1
Raspberry, Individual, M & S*	1 Pavlova/65g	133	205	4.0	41.8	2.4	0.2
Raspberry, M & S*	1 Serving/84g	193	230	2.3	33.3	9.6	0.3
Raspberry, Mini, Co-Op*	1 Pavlova/19g	61	320	3.0	56.0	9.0	0.6
Raspberry, Tesco*	1 Serving/65g	191	294	2.7	41.8	12.9	1.1
Sticky Toffee, Farmfoods*	1/6 Pack/49g	186	380	3.4	47.8	19.5	0.3
Sticky Toffee, Sainsbury's*	1/6 Pack/61g	249	415	3.7	63.1	16.4	0.9
Strawberry & Champagne, Mini, Co-Op*	1 Pavlova/19g	65	340	3.0	40.0	19.0	0.8
Strawberry, Co-Op*	1 Serving/52g	177	340	3.0	50.0	14.0	0.4
Strawberry, COU, M & S*	1 Pot/95g	147	155	2.4	30.5	2.4	0.8
Strawberry, Farmfoods*	1/6 Cake/52g	152	292	2.3	36.9	15.0	2.2
Toffee, Co-Op*	1/6 Pavlova/53g	193	365	3.0	52.0	16.0	0.6
Toffee, Mini, Co-Op*	1 Pavlova/18g	69	385	4.0	64.0	13.0	0.0
Toffee Pecan, M & S*	1oz/28g	118	420	3.9	41.5	26.6	0.4
PAW-PAW,							
Raw, Fresh	1oz/28g	10	36	0.5	8.8	0.1	2.2
Raw, Weighed With Skin & Pips	1oz/28g	8	27	0.4	6.6	0.1	1.7
PEACH & PEAR Fruit Express, Del Monte*	1 Serving/185g	87	47	0.4	10.8	0.1	0.9
PEACH & PEAR Pieces, Fruit Express, Del Monte*	1 Serving/185g	87	47	0.4	10.8	0.1	0.9
PEACHES,							
& Pears, Pieces In Juice, Fruiti, Sainsbury's*	1 Can/139g	78	56	0.3	13.9	0.1	0.5
Canned, In Juice	1oz/28g	11	39	0.6	9.7	0.0	0.8
Canned, In Syrup	1oz/28g	15	55	0.5	14.0	0.0	0.9
Dried	1oz/28g	61	219	3.4	53.0	0.8	7.3
Fruit Express, Del Monte*	1 Serving/185g	91	49	0.5	11.2	0.1	0.9
Halves In Apple Juice, Asda*	1 Can/234g	117	50	0.5	12.0	0.0	1.0
Halves In Grape Juice, Safeway*	1 Serving/145g	70	48	0.4	11.7	0.0	1.0
Halves In Grape Juice, Tesco*	1 Can/410g	180	44	0.5	10.0	0.1	1.0
Halves In Syrup, Del Monte*	1 Can/235g	181	77	0.4	18.5	0.1	0.0
In Fruit Juice, John West*	1 Serving/100g	38	38	0.5	9.0	0.0	0.9
In Juice, Del Monte*	1 Can/415g	203	49	0.5	11.2	0.1	0.0
In Juice, Fruitini*	1 Can/140g	77	55	0.4	13.0	0.1	0.0
In Syrup, Del Monte*	1 Can/420g	323	77	0.4	18.5	0.1	0.0
Pieces In Strawberry Jelly, Fruitini*	1 Can/140g	91	65	0.3	15.3	0.1	0.0
Raw, Fresh	1 Med Peach/110g	36	33	1.0	7.6	0.1	1.5
Raw, Weighed With Stone	1oz/28g	8	30	0.9	6.8	0.1	1.3
Slices In Apple Juice, Asda*	1 Can/213g	89	42	0.6	10.0	0.0	0.9
Slices In Fruit Juice, Sainsbury's*	½ Can/206g	99	48	0.4	11.7	0.1	1.0
Slices In Fruit Juice, Waitrose*	1 Can/409g	176	43	0.5	10.2	0.0	1.0
Slices In Grape Juice, Tesco*	1 Can/250g	110	44	0.5	11.0	0.0	1.0
Slices, In Light Syrup, Tesco*	1 Serving/135g	90	67	0.4	16.0	0.1	0.8
Slices In Light Syrup, Sainsbury's*	½ Can/203g	118	58	0.4	14.0	0.1	0.8
Slices In Syrup, Del Monte*	1 Can/227g	175	77	0.4	18.5	0.1	0.0
PEANUT BRITTLE	1oz/28g	135	483	8.6	73.8	19.0	2.0
PEANUT BUTTER,							
Creamy, Smooth, Sun Pat*	1 Tsp/15g	93	620	24.0	17.5	50.2	6.1
Crunchy, Asda*	1 Tsp/10g	61	611	28.0	12.0	51.0	6.0
Crunchy, Budgens*	1oz/28g	166	592	23.6	12.5	49.7	6.9
Crunchy, No Added Sugar, Whole Earth*	1 Tsp/10g	59	592	24.9	10.1	50.2	7.3
Crunchy, Organic, Evernat*	1 Tsp/10g	64	641	29.0	13.0	53.0	7.0

P

	Measure WEIGHT/INFO	per Measure KCAL	Nutrition Values per 100g / 100ml KCAL	PROT	CARB	FAT	FIBRE
PEANUT BUTTER,							
Crunchy, Organic, No Added Sugar, Waitrose*	1 Tbsp/12g	71	592	24.9	10.1	50.2	7.3
Crunchy, Route 66*	1 Tsp/10g	65	648	20.0	13.0	58.0	5.4
Crunchy, Sainsbury's*	1 Tsp/10g	59	594	23.2	12.4	50.2	6.7
Crunchy, Somerfield*	1 Tsp/10g	59	586	24.0	12.0	49.0	0.0
Crunchy, Tesco*	1 Tsp/10g	61	614	27.8	12.0	50.5	6.5
Original Crunchy, Sun Pat*	1 Tsp/10g	63	630	26.6	12.6	52.8	6.5
SmartPrice, Asda*	1 Tbsp/15g	87	582	23.0	10.0	50.0	6.0
Smooth	1 Tsp/10g	62	623	22.6	13.1	53.7	5.4
Smooth, 25% Less Fat, Tesco*	1 Serving/30g	159	529	22.6	30.7	35.1	6.7
Smooth, BGTY, Sainsbury's*	1 Tsp/10g	53	533	22.6	31.7	35.1	6.7
Smooth, Budgens*	1 Tsp/10g	0	596	23.3	12.4	50.3	6.8
Smooth Light, Kraft*	1 Tsp/20g	114	571	16.3	40.1	38.6	0.0
Smooth, Somerfield*	1 Tsp/10g	59	592	24.0	11.0	50.0	0.0
Smooth, Tesco*	1 Tsp/10g	61	614	27.8	12.0	50.5	6.5
Stripy, Sun Pat*	1 Tsp/10g	62	617	13.0	35.0	47.0	3.0
Wholegrain	1 Tsp/10g	61	606	24.9	7.7	53.1	6.0
PEANUTS & RAISINS,							
Peanuts & Raisins	1 Pack/40g	174	435	15.3	37.5	26.0	4.4
Somerfield*	1oz/28g	133	474	19.0	37.0	28.0	0.0
PEANUTS,							
Chilli, Sainsbury's*	1 Serving/50g	306	612	28.4	7.2	52.2	6.2
Dry Roasted	1oz/28g	165	589	25.5	10.3	49.8	6.4
Dry Roasted, Budgens*	1oz/28g	166	594	23.9	13.7	49.3	6.5
Dry Roasted, KP*	1 Pack/50g	298	596	27.4	8.9	50.1	5.9
Dry Roasted, Sainsbury's*	1 Serving/20g	113	567	26.2	14.3	45.0	6.1
Honey Roasted, KP*	1 Pack/49g	297	607	34.2	15.3	49.9	5.3
Honey Roasted, Waitrose*	1 Bag/200g	1206	603	19.5	31.8	44.2	5.7
Organic, Waitrose*	1 Serving/25g	153	610	22.8	11.9	52.4	5.9
Plain	10 Whole/10g	56	564	25.6	12.5	46.1	6.2
Redskin, Organic, Evernat*	1oz/28g	161	574	17.5	18.3	48.0	3.8
Roast Salted, Jumbo, M & S*	1oz/28g	174	622	28.5	7.8	53.0	6.2
Roast Salted, Somerfield*	1oz/28g	168	600	29.0	9.0	50.0	0.0
Roasted & Salted	10 Whole/10g	60	602	24.5	7.1	53.0	6.0
Salted, Budgens*	1oz/28g	166	593	28.1	10.5	48.7	8.6
Salted, Golden Wonder*	1 Bag/50g	303	605	24.4	10.6	51.6	5.8
Salted, Large, Asda*	1 Serving/50g	309	617	28.3	6.6	53.0	6.0
Salted, Roast, Somerfield*	1oz/28g	168	600	29.0	9.0	50.0	0.0
Salted Roasted, KP*	1 Sm Pack/50g	311	622	28.5	7.8	53.0	6.2
Salted, SmartPrice, Asda*	1 Serving/25g	154	617	28.0	7.0	53.0	6.0
Sea Salt, Organic, KP*	1oz/28g	174	622	28.5	7.8	53.0	6.2
Spicy Chilli, Shots, KP*	1 Pack/45g	274	608	28.1	7.7	51.7	6.2
PEAR JUICE, With A Hint Of Ginger, Pressed, M & S*	1 Glass/250ml	125	50	0.3	11.7	0.1	0.0
PEARL BARLEY,							
Boiled	1oz/28g	34	120	2.7	27.6	0.6	0.0
Raw	1oz/28g	101	360	7.9	83.6	1.7	0.0
PEARS,							
Average, Raw	1 Med Core/170g	68	40	0.3	10.0	0.1	2.2
Canned, In Juice	1oz/28g	9	33	0.3	8.5	0.0	1.4
Canned, In Syrup	1oz/28g	14	50	0.2	13.2	0.0	1.1
Comice, Raw	1 Med/170g	56	33	0.3	8.5	0.0	2.0
Dried, M & S*	1oz/28g	63	225	2.7	53.0	0.5	14.5
Halves, In Fruit Juice, Safeway*	1 Serving/170g	78	46	0.4	11.2	0.0	1.8
Halves, In Grape Juice, Waitrose*	½ Can/205g	100	49	0.3	11.6	0.1	2.0
Halves, In Juice, Somerfield*	1oz/28g	14	49	0.0	12.0	0.0	0.0

	Measure WEIGHT/INFO	per Measure KCAL	Nutrition Values per 100g / 100ml KCAL	PROT	CARB	FAT	FIBRE
PEARS,							
Halves, In Light Syrup, Sainsbury's*	1oz/28g	16	56	0.4	13.9	0.1	1.6
Halves, In Light Syrup, Tesco*	1oz/28g	18	65	0.2	15.9	0.0	1.1
Halves, In Natural Juice, Sainsbury's*	1oz/28g	13	45	0.5	10.4	0.1	1.6
Halves, In Syrup, John West*	1oz/28g	18	63	0.4	15.0	0.1	1.6
Halves, Tesco*	1 Serving/100g	35	35	0.3	8.5	0.0	1.4
In Juice, Del Monte*	1oz/28g	13	45	0.3	10.5	0.1	0.0
Organic, Tesco*	1 Pear/170g	71	42	0.3	10.0	0.1	2.2
Peeled, Raw, Average, Weighed With Skin & Core	1oz/28g	8	29	0.2	7.3	0.1	1.1
Prickly, Raw, Fresh	1oz/28g	14	49	0.7	11.5	0.3	0.0
Quarters, In Fruit Juice, Sainsbury's*	1oz/28g	11	41	0.4	9.7	0.1	1.6
Quarters, In Natural Juice, Tesco*	¼ Can/112g	52	46	0.3	11.0	0.0	1.4
Tinned, Asda*	1 Can/241g	89	37	0.3	9.0	0.0	1.4
William, Raw	1 Med/170g	58	34	0.4	8.3	0.1	2.2
PEAS,							
& Sweetcorn, Fresh, M & S*	1oz/28g	21	75	4.8	11.4	1.5	3.0
Boiled In Unsalted Water	1oz/28g	22	79	6.7	10.0	1.6	4.5
Canned, Re-Heated, Drained	1oz/28g	22	80	5.3	13.5	0.9	5.1
Dried, Bigga, Batchelors*	1oz/28g	73	262	23.1	37.6	2.1	20.2
Dried, Boiled In Unsalted Water	1oz/28g	31	109	6.9	19.9	0.8	5.5
Dried, Raw	1oz/28g	85	303	21.6	52.0	2.4	13.0
Frozen, Bird's Eye*	1 Serving/85g	53	62	4.9	9.0	0.7	4.5
Frozen, Boiled In Salted Water	1oz/28g	19	69	6.0	9.7	0.9	5.1
Frozen, Boiled In Unsalted Water	1oz/28g	19	69	6.0	9.7	0.9	5.1
Frozen, Raw	1oz/28g	18	66	5.7	9.3	0.9	5.1
Garden, Bird's Eye*	1 Serving/85g	53	62	4.9	9.0	0.7	4.5
Garden, Canned, Drained, Sainsbury's*	1oz/28g	23	83	5.3	13.5	0.9	5.1
Garden, Canned, No Salt Or Sugar, Sainsbury's*	1 Can/80g	34	43	4.2	5.5	0.5	3.0
Garden, Freshly Frozen, Morrisons*	1 Serving/100g	83	83	6.9	11.3	1.5	0.0
Garden, In Sugared Salted Water, Drained, Tesco*	1 Serving/68g	46	67	5.3	9.4	0.9	5.1
Garden, In Sweetened Salted Water, Safeway*	1 Can/44g	22	50	4.6	7.0	0.3	5.1
Garden, In Water, Asda*	1 Serving/90g	44	49	4.6	7.0	0.3	5.0
Garden, In Water, No Added Sugar or Salt, Morrisons*	1 Can/185g	87	47	4.6	6.5	0.3	0.0
Garden, M & S*	1oz/28g	19	67	5.8	10.6	0.4	5.2
Garden, Mint Flavoured, Sainsbury's*	¼ Bag/227g	161	71	6.0	9.7	0.9	5.1
Garden, Tesco*	1oz/28g	19	67	5.3	9.4	0.9	5.1
Garden, Tinned, Asda*	1oz/28g	15	53	4.6	8.0	0.3	5.0
Garden, Young, M & S*	1 Serving/100g	70	70	5.8	10.6	0.4	5.2
Giant Marrowfat, Farrows, Batchelors*	1 Can/173g	133	77	5.9	12.3	0.5	4.9
Hand Shelled, M & S*	1oz/28g	19	67	5.8	10.6	0.4	5.2
Marrowfat, Asda*	1 Serving/90g	75	83	6.2	13.7	0.4	4.8
Marrowfat, Canned, Drained, Re-Heated,	1oz/28g	28	100	6.9	17.5	0.8	4.1
Marrowfat, Processed, Bigga, Batchelors*	1 Sm Can/160g	106	66	5.6	10.1	0.3	4.0
Marrowfat, Processed, Bigga, Batchelors*	1oz/28g	26	94	6.5	15.7	0.6	3.5
Marrowfat, Processed, Canned, Co-Op*	1oz/28g	28	99	6.9	16.0	0.8	4.1
Marrowfat, Processed, In Sugared Salt Water, Tesco*	1 Can/180g	167	93	6.9	14.5	0.8	4.1
Marrowfat, Sainsbury's*	1 Serving/90g	95	105	6.9	17.5	0.8	4.1
Marrowfat, Tesco*	1 Serving/60g	50	83	6.2	13.7	0.4	0.0
Minted, Farmfoods*	1oz/28g	24	86	6.9	11.3	1.5	5.0
Mushy, Batchelors*	1 Can/415g	320	77	5.2	13.5	0.2	2.7
Mushy, Canned, Re-Heated	1oz/28g	23	81	5.8	13.8	0.7	1.8
Mushy, Chip Shop, Batchelors*	1oz/28g	22	78	4.9	13.8	0.3	3.3
Mushy, Farmfoods*	1oz/28g	41	146	10.5	25.4	0.3	5.9
Mushy, Lockwoods*	¼ Pack/113.5g	112	99	8.0	15.9	0.3	0.0
Mushy Peas With Vinegar, Chip Shop, Budgens*	1 Can/300g	240	80	5.8	12.5	0.7	1.8

	Measure WEIGHT/INFO	per Measure KCAL	Nutrition Values per 100g / 100ml KCAL	PROT	CARB	FAT	FIBRE
PEAS,							
Mushy, Processed, Safeway*	1 Can/300g	255	85	5.8	13.8	0.7	1.8
Mushy, SmartPrice, Asda*	1 Serving/151g	130	86	6.0	14.0	0.7	2.7
Mushy, Somerfield*	1 Serving/100g	80	80	5.9	13.1	0.4	0.0
Mushy, Value, Tesco*	1oz/28g	20	71	5.8	11.3	0.7	1.8
Organic, Waitrose*	1oz/28g	18	66	5.7	9.3	0.9	5.1
Petit Pois, Farmfoods*	1oz/28g	14	49	4.8	5.3	0.9	4.5
Processed, Canned, Re-Heated, Drained	1oz/28g	28	99	6.9	17.5	0.7	4.8
Processed, Economy, Sainsbury's*	1oz/28g	29	104	6.9	17.5	0.7	4.8
Processed, SmartPrice, Asda*	1oz/28g	24	84	6.0	14.0	0.4	4.8
Processed, Somerfield*	1oz/28g	23	83	6.0	14.0	0.0	0.0
Processed, Sweet Harvest, Aldi*	1oz/28g	23	83	6.2	13.7	0.4	0.0
Processed, Value, Tesco*	½ Can/95g	93	98	6.9	16.0	0.7	0.0
Raw	1oz/28g	23	83	6.9	11.3	1.5	4.7
Small Processed, Batchelors*	1oz/28g	24	87	5.4	15.5	0.4	4.8
Sugar Snap, COU, M & S*	1oz/28g	22	80	3.8	5.8	4.6	2.8
Sugar Snap, Tesco*	1oz/28g	10	35	3.4	5.0	0.2	1.5
Sugar-Snap, Boiled In Salted Water	1oz/28g	9	33	3.1	4.7	0.3	1.3
Sugar-Snap, Raw	1oz/28g	10	34	3.4	5.0	0.2	1.5
Summer Sweet, Green Giant*	3/4 Cup/175ml	107	61	3.4	11.0	0.4	0.0
Value, Farmfoods*	1oz/28g	19	68	5.7	9.3	0.9	5.1
PEASE PUDDING, Canned, Re-Heated, Drained	1oz/28g	26	93	6.8	16.1	0.6	1.8
PECAN NUTS	3 Nuts/18g	124	689	9.2	5.8	70.1	4.7
PEPERAMI,							
Hot, Peperami*	1oz/28g	155	554	19.0	2.5	52.0	1.2
Mini, Pepperami*	1 Peperami/10g	54	536	22.0	1.7	49.0	0.1
Salami Sausage, Peperami*	1oz/28g	150	536	22.0	1.7	49.0	0.1
PEPPER,							
Cayenne, Ground	1 Tsp/1.8g	6	318	12.0	31.7	17.3	0.0
Frank Cooper*	1 Serving/1g	1	68	12.2	0.0	2.1	0.0
PEPPERMINT Cream, Fry's*	1 Bar/51g	217	425	2.6	68.8	15.4	0.0
PEPPERONI,							
American Style, Tesco*	1 Piece/5g	19	387	20.0	3.2	32.7	0.0
Asda*	1 Slice/6g	24	405	22.0	6.6	32.3	0.0
Ready to Eat, Sainsbury's*	1 Serving/25g	94	376	24.9	0.1	30.7	0.1
Spicy Italian, M & S*	1 Pack/50g	158	316	20.9	1.1	25.3	0.0
Tomato Spicy, Stir In, Dolmio*	1oz/28g	41	147	3.4	7.9	11.5	0.0
PEPPERS,							
Capsicum, Chilli, Green, Raw	1oz/28g	6	20	2.9	0.7	0.6	0.0
Capsicum, Chilli, Red, Raw	1oz/28g	7	26	1.8	4.2	0.3	0.0
Capsicum, Green, Boiled In Salted Water	1oz/28g	5	18	1.0	2.6	0.5	1.8
Capsicum, Green, Raw	1oz/28g	4	15	0.8	2.6	0.3	1.6
Capsicum, Red, Boiled In Salted Water	1oz/28g	10	34	1.1	7.0	0.4	1.7
Capsicum, Red, Raw	1oz/28g	9	32	1.0	6.4	0.4	1.6
Capsicum, Yellow, Raw	1oz/28g	7	26	1.2	5.3	0.2	1.7
Green, Filled, Tesco*	1 Pepper/150g	117	78	2.6	9.0	3.5	0.7
Jalapeno, Co-Op*	1oz/28g	74	265	5.0	31.0	13.0	0.9
Jalapeno, Flamin' Hot, Kitchen Range Foods*	1oz/28g	62	223	4.6	22.9	12.7	0.0
Marinated, Sainsbury's*	1 Serving/100g	81	81	1.0	4.8	6.4	0.0
Mixed, M & S*	1oz/28g	29	103	1.5	11.3	7.0	2.7
Mixed, Organic, Iceland*	1oz/28g	8	28	1.1	5.1	0.4	1.8
Mixed, Sliced, Farmfoods*	1oz/28g	7	24	0.9	4.3	0.4	1.6
Mixed, Sliced, Ready, Frozen, Tesco*	1 Serving/28g	7	25	1.0	4.6	0.3	1.6
Red, Filled, M & S*	1 Serving/115g	86	75	2.9	11.1	2.4	1.5
Stuffed, Fresh, Asda*	1 Pepper/150g	144	96	3.8	9.0	5.0	1.2

P

	Measure WEIGHT/INFO	per Measure KCAL	KCAL	PROT	CARB	FAT	FIBRE
			Nutrition Values per 100g / 100ml				
PEPPERS,							
Stuffed, Perfectly Balanced, Waitrose*	1 Pack/300g	243	81	3.0	11.8	2.4	1.3
Stuffed, Sainsbury's*	1 Serving/137g	169	123	3.3	11.8	6.9	1.0
Stuffed With Rice	1oz/28g	24	85	1.5	15.4	2.4	1.3
Stuffed With Vegetables, Cheese Topping	1oz/28g	31	111	3.4	9.8	6.7	1.5
Yellow, Stuffed, Italian, Ready to Roast, Sainsbury's*	1 Pack/136g	144	106	5.3	9.9	5.0	1.3
PETIT POIS,							
& Baby Carrots, Safeway*	1 Can/138g	57	41	2.5	7.4	0.0	1.0
& Baby Carrots, Safeway*	½ Can Drained/132g	41	31	2.9	3.7	0.5	3.1
Canned, Drained	1 Serving/65g	29	45	5.2	4.9	0.6	4.3
Fresh Frozen, Tesco,*	1 Serving/100g	48	48	5.0	5.5	0.9	4.5
Frozen, Asda*	1 Serving/100g	48	48	5.0	5.0	0.9	4.5
Frozen, Boiled In Salted Water	1 Serving/65g	32	49	5.0	5.5	0.9	4.5
Frozen, Boiled In Unsalted Water	1 Serving/65g	32	49	5.0	5.5	0.9	4.5
M & S*	1oz/28g	16	56	4.9	7.6	0.7	4.5
Organic, Evernat*	1oz/28g	17	61	5.4	8.7	0.5	0.0
Organic, Waitrose*	1oz/28g	18	64	5.0	9.0	0.9	0.0
Somerfield*	1oz/28g	16	58	4.0	9.0	1.0	0.0
Waitrose*	½ Can/100g	64	64	5.9	9.4	0.3	2.6
With Baby Carrots, Waitrose*	½ Can/200g	100	50	3.9	8.2	0.2	1.9
PHEASANT, Roasted, Meat Only	1oz/28g	76	270	13.2	48.1	2.4	3.3
PHILADELPHIA,							
Cheese Spread, Cream, Extra Light, Kraft*	1oz/28g	28	101	11.0	3.0	5.0	0.6
Cheese Spread, Garlic & Herbs, Light, Kraft*	1oz/28g	50	180	7.2	3.4	15.5	0.2
Cheese Spread, Kraft*	1oz/28g	78	280	6.0	2.5	27.5	0.1
Cheese Spread, Light, Kraft*	1oz/28g	53	190	7.6	3.4	16.0	0.3
Cheese Spread, Soft Cream, Full Fat, Kraft*	1 Serving/25g	63	250	5.9	3.2	24.0	0.2
Cheese Spread, With Chives, Light, Kraft*	1oz/28g	52	185	7.5	3.4	15.5	0.3
Cheese Spread, With Ham, Light, Kraft*	1oz/28g	52	184	7.9	4.3	15.0	0.2
Herb Ciabatta, Snack, Light, Kraft*	1 Serving/50g	118	235	7.9	16.5	15.0	2.0
Spread, Cheese, Tomato & Basil, Light, Kraft*	1 Tbsp/20g	38	190	7.6	4.3	16.0	0.5
PICCALILLI,							
Haywards*	1 Serving/28g	18	66	1.4	13.9	0.5	0.0
Morrisons*	1 Tsp/10g	7	72	1.7	14.7	0.7	0.0
PICKLE,							
Branston	1 Tsp/10g	14	140	0.7	34.2	0.3	1.3
Brinjal, Patak's*	1 Tsp/16g	57	355	2.1	36.5	24.4	0.9
Chilli, Branston*	1 Tsp/16g	21	130	0.7	30.0	0.7	1.5
Chilli, Patak's*	1 Tsp/16g	49	305	4.1	1.4	33.7	0.0
Chilli Tomato, Patak's*	1oz/28g	27	95	2.5	16.0	3.2	1.5
Garlic, Patak's*	1 Tsp/16g	43	267	3.6	21.3	18.5	1.6
Lime, Hot, Asda*	1 Dtsp/10g	12	123	2.2	6.0	10.0	1.0
Lime, Hot, Patak's*	1 Tsp/16g	30	186	2.6	4.2	18.7	0.3
Lime, M & S*	1 Tsp/16g	34	215	0.8	42.5	4.8	2.4
Lime, Oily	1oz/28g	50	178	1.9	8.3	15.5	0.0
Lime, Sharwood's*	1 Tsp/16g	24	152	2.2	15.0	9.3	2.9
Mango, Hot, Patak's*	1 Tsp/16g	42	265	2.3	8.0	25.7	1.9
Mild Mustard, Heinz*	1 Tbsp/10g	13	129	2.2	25.7	1.3	0.9
Mixed, Sainsbury's*	1oz/28g	14	49	2.3	7.7	0.5	1.3
Original, Tesco*	1 Tsp/25g	33	132	0.8	30.4	0.2	1.1
Ploughmans, Heinz*	1 Tbsp/10g	12	117	0.8	26.7	0.2	0.9
Sandwich, Branston*	1 Tsp/10g	14	140	0.7	34.2	0.3	1.3
Sandwich, Somerfield*	1 Tsp/10g	15	150	1.0	36.0	0.0	0.0
Smooth, Branston*	1 Serving/13g	18	139	0.6	34.0	0.1	1.4
Spicy, Branston*	1 Heaped Tsp/15g	21	140	0.7	34.7	0.3	1.3

P

	Measure WEIGHT/INFO	per Measure KCAL	Nutrition Values per 100g / 100ml KCAL	PROT	CARB	FAT	FIBRE
PICKLE,							
Sweet	1 Tsp/10g	14	141	0.6	36.0	0.1	1.2
Sweet, Budgens*	1 Tsp/10g	14	141	0.8	34.0	0.2	0.0
Sweet, Frank Cooper*	1 Pot/20g	21	104	0.5	25.3	0.1	0.8
Sweet, Hartley's*	1 Tsp/16g	7	140	0.5	36.2	0.0	0.0
Sweet Harvest, Asda*	1 Serving/25g	39	154	0.8	37.0	0.3	0.8
Sweet, SmartPrice, Asda*	1 Tbsp/15g	16	106	0.9	25.0	0.3	1.0
Sweet, Somerfield*	1 Tsp/10g	14	137	1.0	33.0	0.0	0.0
Tangy, Sandwich, Heinz*	1 Tsp/10g	13	134	0.7	31.4	0.2	0.9
Tomato, Tangy, Heinz*	1 Tsp/10g	10	102	2.0	22.0	0.3	1.5
PICKLES,							
Dill, Cucumbers, Safeway*	1oz/28g	5	19	0.9	3.5	0.2	0.0
Gherkins, Drained	1oz/28g	4	14	0.9	2.6	0.1	1.2
Gherkins, Sainsbury's*	1 Gherkin/40g	12	30	0.9	6.3	0.1	1.2
Mixed, Salad Bar, Asda*	1oz/28g	11	40	0.5	9.2	0.1	0.0
Red Cabbage, Asda*	1 Serving/50g	16	32	1.6	6.0	0.1	0.0
Red Cabbage In Vinegar, Healthy Selection, Somerfield*	1oz/28g	4	13	1.0	2.0	0.0	0.0
PICNIC, Cadbury's*	1 Bar/48g	228	475	7.5	58.3	23.6	0.0
PIE,							
Admiral's, Ross*	1 Pie/340g	357	105	4.8	10.9	4.6	0.7
Apple & Blackberry, Shortcrust, M & S*	1 Serving/142g	469	330	4.3	50.2	12.5	1.1
Apple & Blackberry, Somerfield*	¼ Pie/106g	280	264	4.0	36.0	12.0	0.0
Apple, American, Iceland*	1 Portion/92g	258	280	4.8	39.2	11.6	2.2
Apple, Cooked, Speedibake*	1 Serving/120g	340	283	3.4	38.5	12.8	1.5
Apple, Deep Filled, Farmfoods*	1oz/28g	74	266	3.6	34.3	12.7	2.2
Apple, Deep Filled, Iceland*	1 Portion/116g	332	286	2.5	39.2	13.2	1.1
Apple, Deep Filled, Sainsbury's*	¼ Pie/137g	374	273	3.8	35.6	12.8	1.6
Apple, Deep Filled, Somerfield*	1/6 Pie/90g	239	265	3.0	36.0	12.0	0.0
Apple, McDonald's*	1 Pie/78g	225	289	2.8	33.2	16.1	1.4
Apple, McVitie's*	1 Slice/117g	316	270	3.0	39.0	11.0	2.0
Apple, Pastry Top & Bottom	1oz/28g	74	266	2.9	35.8	13.3	1.7
Apple, Puff Pastry, M & S*	1 Pie/135g	338	250	2.4	31.3	12.7	1.0
Apple, Safeway*	1 Serving/80g	241	301	3.3	45.5	11.8	0.0
Apple Slice, Colonels Pies, Kentucky Fried Chicken*	1 Slice/113g	310	274	1.7	38.9	12.3	0.0
Apple, SmartPrice, Asda*	1 Serving/47g	178	379	3.5	53.0	17.0	1.3
Apple, Tesco*	1 Pie/47g	191	406	3.3	59.4	17.2	1.5
Apricot Fruit, GFY, Asda*	1 Serving/52g	162	311	3.3	52.0	10.0	0.0
Banoffee Cream, American Dream, McVitie's*	1 Portion/70g	277	396	4.3	36.7	25.5	0.8
Banoffee, Tesco*	1 Pie/112g	381	340	3.7	45.4	15.9	1.2
Beef & Kidney, Farmfoods*	1oz/28g	68	242	5.6	23.9	13.8	1.1
Blackcurrant, Deep Filled, Sainsbury's*	1 Slice/137g	440	321	5.8	42.6	14.1	2.2
Blackcurrant, Shortcrust, M & S*	1 Pie/142g	412	290	3.9	45.6	10.1	1.3
Bramley Apple & Blackberry, M & S*	¼ Pie/146g	380	260	3.4	39.8	9.9	1.3
Bramley Apple & Custard, Lattice Topped, Mr Kipling*	1 Pie/64g	217	339	3.6	48.3	14.6	1.1
Bramley Apple, Deep Filled, Mr Kipling*	1 Pie/66g	220	333	3.4	50.7	13.0	1.3
Bramley Apple, Deep Filled, Sainsbury's*	1/6 Pie/120g	329	274	3.7	38.0	11.9	1.9
Bramley Apple, M & S*	1 Pie/55g	184	335	2.9	57.6	11.7	1.6
Bramley Apple, Reduced Fat, Asda*	1 Pie/56g	176	314	3.3	55.1	9.4	1.3
British Chicken & Vegetable, Somerfield*	1 Pie/350g	270	77	3.7	8.8	3.0	2.0
Buffet Pork, Farmfoods*	1 Pie/65g	252	388	8.8	28.2	26.7	1.0
Cheese & Pickle Pork, Mini, Tesco*	1 Pie/49g	191	389	9.2	29.3	26.1	1.2
Cheese & Potato	1oz/28g	39	139	4.8	12.6	8.1	0.7
Cherry, Deep Filled, Somerfield*	1/6 Pie/90g	259	288	3.0	41.0	12.0	0.0
Cherry, Shortcrust, M & S*	1 Pie/142g	412	290	3.6	43.4	10.9	0.8
Chicken & Asparagus, McDougalls*	1 Serving/170g	490	288	8.0	19.0	20.0	0.9

P

PIE,	Measure WEIGHT/INFO	per Measure KCAL	Nutrition Values per 100g / 100ml KCAL	PROT	CARB	FAT	FIBRE
Chicken & Bacon, Filo Pastry, Finest, Tesco*	1 Serving/160g	362	226	11.3	18.9	11.7	1.7
Chicken & Basil, M & S*	1oz/28g	59	210	8.9	17.0	11.9	1.1
Chicken & Broccoli, COU, M & S*	1 Pack/300g	240	80	6.8	8.9	2.0	1.5
Chicken & Broccoli, Good Intentions, Somerfield*	1 Pack/350g	315	90	8.0	10.6	1.7	1.5
Chicken & Broccoli, HE, Tesco*	1 Pie/450g	374	83	6.7	9.4	2.1	1.0
Chicken & Broccoli Lattice, Sainsbury's*	½ Pie/192g	520	271	9.3	22.4	16.0	0.9
Chicken & Broccoli, Lattice, Tesco*	½ Pie/200g	496	248	8.5	18.9	15.4	2.1
Chicken & Gravy, HE, Tesco*	1 Pie/200g	368	184	10.6	24.3	5.0	1.9
Chicken & Ham, Deep Filled, Somerfield*	¼ Pie/138g	348	252	11.0	21.0	14.0	0.0
Chicken & Ham, Family, Farmfoods*	1oz/28g	67	241	9.9	19.4	13.8	1.2
Chicken & Leek, Deep Filled, Somerfield*	1 Pie/200g	550	275	12.0	21.0	16.0	0.0
Chicken & Leek, M & S*	1oz/28g	70	250	10.1	18.8	15.1	1.1
Chicken & Mushroom, Asda*	1 Pie/ 150g	444	296	7.7	25.4	18.2	1.0
Chicken & Mushroom Cumberland, Somerfield*	1 Pie/300g	441	147	7.0	14.0	7.0	0.0
Chicken & Mushroom, Farmfoods*	1 Pie/110g	271	246	5.6	22.4	14.9	0.9
Chicken & Mushroom, Individual, Co-Op*	1 Pie/149g	465	312	8.6	24.5	19.9	1.2
Chicken & Mushroom, Shortcrust, Somerfield*	¼ Pie/125g	410	328	6.2	24.7	22.7	1.2
Chicken & Sweetcorn, Co-Op*	¼ Pie/113g	333	295	6.0	24.0	20.0	1.0
Chicken & Vegetable, Asda*	1 Pack/400g	360	90	7.0	13.0	1.1	0.8
Chicken & Vegetable, BGTY, Sainsbury's*	1 Serving/102g	205	201	9.7	20.7	8.8	1.4
Chicken & Vegetable, Farmfoods*	1 Pie/128g	384	300	7.2	25.4	18.8	1.4
Chicken & Vegetable, Fray Bentos*	¼ Pie/100g	173	173	7.4	12.3	10.5	0.0
Chicken & Vegetable, Freshbake*	¼ Pie/114g	298	261	6.2	23.2	15.9	1.1
Chicken & Vegetable, Perfectly Balanced, Waitrose*	1 Serving/375g	285	76	5.1	10.8	1.4	1.3
Chicken & Vegetable, Somerfield*	1 Pie/95g	226	238	15.0	4.0	18.0	0.0
Chicken & Vegetable, Value, Tesco*	1 Pie/150g	378	252	5.5	19.7	16.8	1.0
Chicken, Bacon & Cheese, Lattice, Bird's Eye*	1 Lattice/157g	403	257	10.4	17.0	16.4	1.1
Chicken, Bird's Eye*	1 Pie/143g	435	304	9.6	25.1	18.3	1.3
Chicken, Bird's Eye*	1 Pie/158g	414	262	7.2	23.1	15.6	1.3
Chicken, Cheese & Brocolli Lattice, Bird's Eye*	1 Lattice/150g	380	253	10.3	18.4	14.8	1.0
Chicken Cottage, Tesco*	1 Pack/400g	324	81	5.9	11.5	1.3	0.8
Chicken, Eat Smart, Safeway*	1 Pack/400g	340	85	8.2	9.0	1.7	1.2
Chicken, Individual Shortcrust, Asda*	1 Pie/175g	534	305	10.0	28.0	17.0	1.0
Chicken, Mushroom & Broccoli, BGTY Sainsbury's*	1 Pack/450g	423	94	8.2	10.5	2.2	0.7
Chicken, Mushroom & White Wine, Morrisons*	1 Serving/117g	310	265	7.5	24.4	15.2	0.9
Chicken, Short Crust, M & S*	1 Pie/170g	510	300	9.7	26.2	17.4	1.7
Chicken, Tesco*	1 Serving/150g	425	283	11.2	21.9	16.7	1.1
Classic British Steak, Shortcrust Pastry, Sainsbury's*	¼ Pie/130g	519	299	9.9	27.1	16.8	0.9
Cod & Haddock, COU, M & S*	1 Pack/300g	225	75	6.5	8.8	1.2	0.9
Cod & Prawn, M & S*	1oz/28g	43	155	10.6	8.7	8.9	0.7
Cod & Smoked Haddock, M & S*	1 Pack/300g	225	75	6.5	8.8	1.2	0.9
Cottage, Aberdeen Angus, Waitrose*	1 Pie/350g	340	97	5.3	11.0	3.5	0.9
Cottage, Asda*	1 Pie/300g	258	86	4.3	11.0	2.8	0.9
Cottage, Classic British, Sainsburys*	1 Pack/450g	500	111	6.3	11.1	4.6	0.6
Cottage, COU, M & S*	1oz/28g	27	95	8.0	11.0	1.9	0.6
Cottage, Good Intentions, Somerfield*	1 Serving/300g	261	87	6.2	11.0	2.0	1.2
Cottage, Good Intentions, Somerfield*	1 Pack/299g	239	80	5.3	10.6	1.8	1.2
Cottage, HE, Tesco*	1 Pie/450g	347	77	4.7	9.9	2.0	0.7
Cottage, HE, Tesco*	1 Pack/400g	348	87	6.0	10.6	2.3	1.0
Cottage, Iceland*	1 Pack/400g	468	117	5.1	13.6	4.7	0.7
Cottage, Large, Tesco*	1 Pack/475g	575	121	5.5	10.8	6.2	0.5
Cottage, M & S*	1 Pie/400g	480	120	7.1	9.0	6.3	1.3
Cottage, Quorn, Sainsburys*	1 Pack/450g	329	73	3.0	10.2	2.2	1.8
Cottage, Quorn*	1 Pie/300g	213	71	2.7	10.7	1.9	1.3

P

PIE,	Measure WEIGHT/INFO	per Measure KCAL	KCAL	PROT	CARB	FAT	FIBRE
			Nutrition Values per 100g / 100ml				
Cottage, Ready Meals, Waitrose*	1oz/28g	32	116	6.3	9.3	6.0	0.7
Cottage, Safeway*	1 Pack/450g	486	108	6.0	9.4	5.2	1.1
Cottage, Sainsbury's*	1 Pack/300g	207	69	3.8	10.4	1.4	1.2
Cottage, SmartPrice, Asda*	1 Pie/159g	149	94	3.1	12.0	3.7	0.7
Cottage, Spar*	1 Pack/500g	585	117	4.6	16.1	3.8	1.4
Cottage, Tesco*	1 Pie/300g	300	100	3.3	12.5	4.1	0.5
Cottage, Weight Watchers*	1 Pack/320g	230	72	3.8	11.3	1.2	0.5
Cumberland Chicken, British Classics, Tesco*	1 Pack/450g	441	98	6.5	8.0	4.5	2.1
Cumberland Fish, HE, Tesco*	1 Pack/450g	378	84	6.0	10.0	2.2	0.8
Cumberland, Individual, Tesco*	1 Pie/350g	389	111	6.9	11.6	4.1	0.8
Cumberland, M & S*	1 Pie/195g	312	160	6.9	10.1	10.4	1.1
Cumberland, Tesco*	1 Pie/500g	575	115	6.3	10.9	5.1	1.3
Deep Apple, Somerfield*	1oz/28g	110	392	4.0	59.0	16.0	0.0
Dutch Apple, Burger King*	1 Pie/113g	339	300	1.7	46.0	12.3	0.8
Fish	1 Serving/250g	263	105	8.0	12.3	3.0	0.7
Fish, Asda*	1 Serving/338g	372	110	6.0	11.0	4.7	1.3
Fisherman's Chilled, Co-Op*	1 Pie/300g	345	115	4.0	11.0	6.0	0.7
Fisherman's, HE, Tesco*	1 Pie/400g	308	77	5.1	9.2	2.2	1.3
Fisherman's, Healthy Options, Asda*	1 Pie/406g	337	83	5.0	10.0	2.5	0.9
Fisherman's, Sainsbury's*	1 Serving/299g	287	96	4.3	12.0	3.4	0.9
Fisherman's, Tesco*	1 Pie/300g	390	130	7.0	12.3	5.9	1.2
Fruit, Pastry Top & Bottom	1oz/28g	73	260	3.0	34.0	13.3	1.8
Fruit Selection, Deep Filled, Mr Kipling*	1 Pie/66g	220	333	3.5	50.5	12.9	1.4
Haddock Cumberland, M & S*	1 Pie/300g	390	130	8.2	10.6	6.0	0.4
Haddock, Eat Smart, Safeway*	1 Pack/400g	300	75	5.2	10.0	1.4	1.0
Key Lime, Sainsbury's*	¼ Pie/80g	280	350	4.2	51.8	14.0	0.7
Lamb Shepherd's, Waitrose*	1 Pie/350g	448	128	7.1	10.5	6.4	1.0
Lemon Meringue	1oz/28g	89	319	4.5	45.9	14.4	0.7
Lemon Meringue, I Need A, M & S*	1 Pot/105g	221	210	2.1	23.3	12.0	2.6
Lemon Meringue, M & S*	1/6 Pie/78g	215	275	3.9	40.4	11.0	0.8
Lemon Meringue, Mr Kipling*	1 Cake/51g	184	360	2.9	59.9	12.1	3.0
Lemon Meringue, Sara Lee*	1oz/28g	77	276	2.6	46.6	9.2	0.9
Lemon Meringue, Tesco*	1 Pie/385g	989	257	4.0	43.7	7.3	0.5
Luxury Cottage, M & S*	½ Pack/310g	403	130	7.7	9.5	6.9	1.6
Luxury Fish, M & S*	1 Pack/300g	330	110	7.3	7.6	5.6	1.5
Luxury Mince, M & S*	1 Pie/59g	227	385	4.6	58.4	14.4	1.5
Luxury Roast Chicken & Mushroom, M & S*	½ Pie/275g	880	320	9.9	20.0	22.5	1.0
Mariner's, Ross*	1 Pie/340g	435	128	5.0	13.9	5.9	1.0
Meat & Potato, Shortcrust, Co-Op*	¼ Pie/137g	403	294	7.3	23.3	19.1	1.4
Meat & Potato, Value, Tesco*	1 Pie/95g	274	288	6.9	23.8	18.4	3.5
Melton Mowbray Cured Pork, M & S*	1 Pie/290g	1044	360	10.1	25.9	24.5	1.0
Melton Mowbray Pork, Tesco*	1 Sm Pie/148g	679	459	10.0	29.0	33.7	1.3
Melton Pork, Mini, M & S*	1oz/28g	112	400	10.8	28.4	27.3	1.2
Mince, Deep, Sainsbury's*	1 Pie/67g	240	358	3.5	55.0	13.8	1.4
Mince, Individual	1 Pie/48g	203	423	4.3	59.0	20.4	2.1
Mince, Lattice, Tesco*	1 Pie/52g	208	400	3.3	64.4	14.4	2.5
Mince, Luxury, M & S*	1 Pie/60g	215	360	3.2	59.2	12.4	2.3
Mince, Mr Kipling*	1 Pie/62g	231	372	3.8	56.8	14.4	1.5
Mince, Somerfield*	1oz/28g	111	398	4.0	56.0	17.0	0.0
Minced Beef & Onion, Bird's Eye*	1 Pie/145g	419	289	7.1	26.3	17.3	0.7
Minced Beef & Onion, Farmfoods*	1 Pie/128g	378	295	7.3	24.4	18.7	1.0
Minced Beef & Onion, Iceland*	1 Portion/190g	551	290	7.1	23.1	18.8	1.2
Minced Beef & Onion, Sainsbury's*	1 Pie/150g	410	273	6.8	27.8	15.0	0.9
Minced Beef & Onion, Somerfield*	1 Pie/150g	440	293	8.0	27.0	17.0	0.0

PIE,	Measure WEIGHT/INFO	per Measure KCAL	KCAL	PROT	CARB	FAT	FIBRE
			Nutrition Values per 100g / 100ml				
Minced Beef & Onion, Tesco*	1 Pie/150g	455	303	5.7	27.4	19.0	1.7
Minced Beef, Plate, M & S*	1oz/28g	71	253	7.6	20.7	16.0	2.0
Minced Steak & Onion, Aberdeen Angus, Tesco*	1 Serving/232g	490	211	9.9	17.9	11.1	0.5
Moroccan Filo, M & S*	1 Serving/130g	215	165	5.5	22.8	5.9	1.6
Ocean, BGTY, Sainsbury's*	1 Pack/350g	270	77	5.4	10.5	1.5	1.1
Ocean, M & S*	1 Pie/650g	532	95	8.2	7.6	3.5	0.9
Ocean With Cod, Weight Watchers*	1 Pack/295g	251	85	5.4	10.0	2.6	0.8
Pork & Cider Potato, BGTY, Sainsbury's*	1 Pack/450g	504	112	8.4	14.5	2.3	0.5
Pork & Egg, M & S*	1 Pie/435g	1527	351	9.7	19.8	25.9	0.8
Pork & Kentish Cider With Mustard Mash, COU, M & S*	1 Pack/300g	240	80	6.7	9.0	1.8	1.4
Pork & Pickle, Bowyers*	1 Pie/150g	576	384	10.0	26.3	27.3	0.0
Pork and Pickle, Pork Farms*	1 pie/50g	185	370	8.5	30.1	24.0	0.0
Pork, Crusty Bake, Sainsbury's*	1 Pie/75g	293	390	10.5	27.0	26.7	1.0
Pork, Melton Mowbray, Medium, Somerfield*	¼ Pie/70g	275	393	11.0	27.0	27.0	0.0
Pork, Mini, Tesco*	1 Pie/45g	162	359	10.2	25.9	23.8	1.0
Pork, Small Melton Mowbray, Somerfield*	½ Pie/64g	237	371	12.0	30.0	23.0	0.0
Pork, Somerfield*	1 Pie/110g	442	402	11.0	24.0	29.0	0.0
Pork With Egg, Morrisons*	1 Serving/100g	356	356	8.6	21.3	26.3	0.0
Potato & Meat, Farmfoods*	1 Pie/158g	416	263	5.4	22.0	17.0	1.0
Potato Topped Chicken Cumberland, M & S*	1 Serving/227g	329	145	6.8	9.7	8.6	1.0
Potato Topped Cottage, M & S*	1 Pack/190g	238	125	5.8	10.0	6.8	0.7
Potato Topped Salmon, M & S*	1 Pie/300g	285	95	6.2	10.3	3.3	1.1
Quorn & Mushroom, Tesco*	1 Pie/141g	378	268	5.3	23.8	16.8	1.3
Quorn & Vegetable	1oz/28g	52	186	6.9	14.7	11.5	2.0
Quorn, Creamy Mushroom, Quorn*	1 Pie/134g	355	265	5.1	24.7	16.2	1.9
Roast Chicken & Ham, Deep Filled, Sainsbury's*	1 Pie/210g	594	283	8.0	23.0	17.7	1.0
Roast Chicken, COU, M & S*	1 Pack/300g	240	80	7.3	9.1	1.3	1.2
Roast Chicken, Sainsbury's*	1/3 Pie/173g	535	311	10.5	27.2	17.8	0.9
Roast Chicken, Shortcrust Pastry, Classic, Sainsbury's*	1/3 Pie/173g	522	302	10.2	26.6	17.2	0.9
Salmon & Broccoli, Bird's Eye*	1 Pie/351g	449	128	6.6	11.4	6.2	0.7
Salmon & Broccoli, Filo Pastry, Finest, Tesco*	1 Pie/170g	386	227	7.9	18.9	13.3	2.1
Salmon & Broccoli Lattice Bar, Asda*	1/3 Bar/133g	360	271	6.0	28.0	15.0	0.8
Salmon & Broccoli, Premium, Tesco*	1 Serving/170g	425	250	6.1	17.7	17.2	0.7
Salmon & Broccoli, Safeway*	1 Serving/135g	427	316	6.8	19.6	23.4	1.4
Salmon Cottage, Sainsbury's*	1 Pack/218g	159	73	4.6	10.4	1.4	1.3
Sausage & Onion, Tesco*	1 Pack/300g	333	111	2.3	11.7	6.1	0.5
Scotch, Co-Op*	1 Pie/132g	408	309	7.3	27.3	18.9	1.5
Scotch, Farmfoods*	1 Pie/151g	430	285	7.8	26.8	16.3	1.2
Scotch, Somerfield*	1oz/28g	65	232	6.0	29.0	10.0	0.0
Shepherd's	1oz/28g	60	216	3.8	28.2	11.0	1.2
Shepherd's, Asda*	1 Pie/153g	193	126	5.0	13.0	6.0	0.8
Shepherd's, Baked Bean Cuisine, Heinz*	1 Pie/340g	299	88	4.1	11.6	2.8	1.5
Shepherd's, BGTY, Sainsbury's*	1 Pack/300g	225	75	3.6	10.2	2.2	1.7
Shepherd's, British Classics, Tesco*	1 Pack/500g	715	143	4.8	10.5	9.1	1.4
Shepherd's, COU, M & S*	1 Pack/300g	210	70	5.2	8.6	1.3	1.6
Shepherd's, Great Value, Asda*	1 Pack/400g	376	94	4.7	12.0	3.0	0.6
Shepherd's, Healthy Choice, Safeway*	1 Pack/333g	333	100	6.3	10.7	3.5	0.9
Shepherd's, M & S*	1 Pack/400g	380	95	5.3	9.7	3.9	1.4
Shepherd's, Reduced Fat, Waitrose*	1 Pack/350g	301	86	5.7	10.6	2.3	0.8
Shepherd's, Safeway*	1 Serving/200g	200	100	7.5	7.5	4.4	1.4
Shepherd's, Sainsbury's*	1 Pack/300g	315	105	4.4	10.3	5.1	0.8
Shepherd's, Tesco*	1 Pie/400g	380	95	6.0	10.5	3.2	0.7
Shepherd's, Vegetable	1oz/28g	32	113	4.6	15.8	4.0	2.4
Shepherd's With Lamb, Weight Watchers*	1 Pack/320g	234	73	3.8	11.6	1.2	0.5

	Measure	per Measure	Nutrition Values per 100g / 100ml				
	WEIGHT/INFO	KCAL	KCAL	PROT	CARB	FAT	FIBRE
PIE,							
Steak & Ale, Budgens*	1 Pack/225g	583	259	7.2	19.5	16.9	0.9
Steak & Ale, Deep Filled, Somerfield*	1 Pie/200g	550	275	12.0	22.0	16.0	0.0
Steak & Ale, Fray Bentos*	1 Pie/425g	697	164	7.6	13.0	9.1	0.0
Steak & Ale, Pub Style, Co-Op*	1 Pie/250g	538	215	9.0	17.0	12.0	2.0
Steak & Gravy, Somerfield*	1oz/28g	67	239	13.0	23.0	11.0	0.0
Steak & Kidney, Bird's Eye*	1 Pie/146g	419	287	7.5	24.4	17.7	1.7
Steak & Kidney, Deep Filled, Somerfield*	¼ Pie/140g	332	237	10.0	21.0	13.0	0.0
Steak & Kidney, Double Crust, Homemade	1oz/28g	151	540	8.2	56.3	31.4	3.8
Steak & Kidney, Individual	1 Pie/200g	646	323	9.1	25.6	21.2	0.9
Steak & Kidney, Morrisons*	1 Serving/142g	351	247	8.1	21.8	14.1	0.0
Steak & Kidney, Puff Pastry, Sainsbury's*	1 Pie/150g	423	282	8.2	26.9	15.7	0.9
Steak & Kidney, Shortcrust Pastry, Classic, Sainsbury's*	1/3 Pie/174g	515	296	10.2	26.5	16.6	0.8
Steak & Kidney, Single Crust, Homemade	1oz/28g	76	273	16.4	15.8	16.4	0.6
Steak & Kidney, Tinned, Fray Bentos*	½ Pie/212g	346	163	8.2	12.9	8.8	0.0
Steak & Mushroom, Asda*	1 Serving/300g	270	90	5.0	10.0	3.3	0.7
Steak & Mushroom, Bird's Eye*	1 Pie/142g	389	274	7.5	22.7	17.0	2.0
Steak & Mushroom, Co-Op*	1 Pie/454g	1158	255	9.0	20.0	15.0	1.0
Steak & Mushroom, HE, Tesco*	1 Serving/200g	380	190	10.5	24.2	5.7	1.9
Steak & Mushroom, Sainsbury's*	¼ Pie/130g	372	286	8.6	26.0	16.4	1.0
Steak & Mushroom, Tesco*	1 Pie/142g	410	289	7.1	22.5	18.9	1.2
Steak & Onion, Farmfoods*	1 Pie/127g	382	301	6.0	26.4	19.1	1.0
Steak & Red Wine, Puff Pastry, Pub, Sainsbury's*	1 Pie/240g	497	207	7.2	16.8	12.3	2.1
Steak, Asda*	1 Pie/150g	453	302	9.2	25.1	18.3	1.0
Steak, M & S*	1oz/28g	64	230	10.0	19.0	12.7	1.2
Steak, Safeway*	¼ Pie/130g	381	293	9.4	27.4	16.2	1.1
Steak, Short Crust, Sainsbury's*	¼ Pie/131g	392	299	9.9	27.1	16.8	0.9
Steak, Tesco*	1 Serving/205g	556	271	7.2	23.3	16.5	1.4
Strawberry Creme, Slice, Kentucky Fried Chicken*	1 Slice/78g	279	358	5.4	41.0	19.2	2.5
Summer Fruit, Orchard Tree, Aldi*	1/8 Pie/75g	242	323	3.0	46.6	13.8	1.2
Tuna & Sweetcorn, COU, M & S*	1 Pie/300g	255	85	6.4	11.6	1.5	1.5
Turkey & Ham, Farmfoods*	1 Pie/147g	404	275	8.6	26.5	14.9	1.4
Turkey & Ham, Shortcrust, M & S*	1/3 Pie/183g	494	270	11.9	19.5	15.9	1.0
Vegetable	1oz/28g	42	151	3.0	18.9	7.6	1.5
Vegetable & Cheddar Cheese, Waitrose*	1 Pie/210g	475	226	4.9	17.8	15.0	1.2
Vegetable & Cheese, Safeway*	1 Pie/132g	372	282	5.5	27.3	16.8	1.6
Vegetable Cumberland, M & S*	1 Serving/200g	210	105	4.2	12.9	4.3	4.4
Vegetable, HE, Tesco*	1 Pack/450g	360	80	2.7	11.1	2.7	0.8
Vegetable, Tesco*	1 Serving/142g	386	272	4.9	23.6	17.5	1.2
Vegetarian, Chunky Vegetable, Linda McCartney*	1 pie/179g	516	288	5.7	17.5	21.7	1.5
Vegetarian, Cottage, Sainsbury's*	1 Pack/380g	344	91	4.4	11.7	3.0	0.7
Vegetarian, Cottage, Tesco*	1 Pack/400g	432	108	4.4	12.9	4.3	0.9
Vegetarian, Deep Country, Linda McCartney*	1 Pie/176g	444	252	6.8	27.6	13.3	1.4
Vegetarian, Porkless, Holland & Barrett*	1 Pie/120g	380	317	11.0	31.6	16.8	2.5
Vegetarian, Shepherd's, Linda McCartney*	1 Pack/340g	317	93	4.6	13.9	2.1	1.6
Welsh Lamb, Sainsbury's*	¼ Pie/120g	290	242	9.1	19.2	14.3	0.8
West Country Chicken, Sainsbury's*	1 Serving/240g	614	256	11.9	17.1	15.6	2.1
PIE FILLING,							
Black Cherry, Fruit, Sainsbury's*	1 Serving/100g	73	73	0.3	17.7	0.1	0.3
Blackcurrant, Fruit, Sainsbury's*	1 Serving/100g	82	82	0.4	20.0	0.1	1.6
Cherry	1oz/28g	23	82	0.4	21.5	0.0	0.4
Fruit	1oz/28g	22	77	0.4	20.1	0.0	1.0
Summer Fruits, Fruit, Tesco*	1 Can/385g	377	98	0.4	24.1	0.0	0.9
PIGEON, Roasted, Meat Only	1oz/28g	82	293	10.7	54.3	3.3	2.3
PIKELETS,							

	Measure WEIGHT/INFO	per Measure KCAL	KCAL	PROT	CARB	FAT	FIBRE
PIKELETS,							
Less Than 2% Fat, M & S*	1 Pikelet/35g	70	200	7.3	39.1	1.3	1.6
Tesco*	1 Pikelet/35g	68	193	5.8	40.9	0.7	1.7
PILAF,							
Forest Mushroom & Pine Nut, Bistro, Waitrose*	1 Serving/225g	338	150	7.0	15.8	6.5	1.5
With Tomato	1oz/28g	40	144	2.5	28.0	3.3	0.4
PILAU, Plain	1oz/28g	39	141	2.3	24.8	4.6	0.3
PILCHARDS,							
Canned In Tomato Sauce	1oz/28g	40	144	16.7	1.1	8.1	0.0
Fillets, In Tomato Sauce, Skinless, Glenryck*	1 Can/120g	109	91	16.1	3.5	1.5	1.0
In Brine, Pacific, Glenryck*	½ Can/77g	110	143	22.3	0.0	6.0	0.0
In Brine, Princes*	1 Serving/155g	229	148	19.0	0.0	8.0	0.0
In Tomato Sauce, Glenryck*	1oz/28g	32	114	16.7	2.3	4.3	0.0
In Tomato Sauce, John West*	1oz/28g	40	144	16.7	1.0	8.1	0.0
In Tomato Sauce, Princes*	1 Serving/78g	105	135	16.0	2.5	6.8	0.0
PINE NUTS	1oz/28g	193	688	14.0	4.0	68.6	1.9
PINEAPPLE & Coconut Juice, Sainsbury's*	1 Glass/250ml	128	51	0.4	11.9	0.1	0.1
PINEAPPLE & Grapefruit Drink, Shapers, Boots*	1 Bottle/500ml	10	2	0.1	0.2	0.1	0.0
PINEAPPLE,							
& Papaya, Dried, Garden Gang, Asda*	1 Pack/50g	142	283	2.8	64.0	1.7	8.0
Canned, In Juice	1oz/28g	13	47	0.3	12.2	0.0	0.5
Canned, In Syrup	1oz/28g	18	64	0.5	16.5	0.0	0.7
Chunks, Fruit Express, Del Monte*	1 Pot/130g	85	65	0.4	15.0	0.1	0.0
Chunks, In Juice, Somerfield*	1oz/28g	17	61	0.0	15.0	0.0	0.0
Chunks, In Light Syrup, Somerfield*	1oz/28g	21	75	0.0	18.0	0.0	0.0
Chunks, In Pineapple Juice, Asda*	1 Can/272g	133	49	0.3	12.0	0.1	0.0
Chunks, In Pineapple Juice, St Michael*	1 Serving/115g	63	55	0.5	12.2	0.2	0.5
Chunks, Sainsbury's*	¼ Pack/84g	37	44	0.0	10.1	0.2	1.2
Crushed, Del Monte*	1 Serving/28g	14	50	0.4	12.2	0.1	0.4
Dried, Tesco*	1 Serving/15g	35	230	0.4	52.9	1.9	1.7
Fresh Ideas, Tesco*	1 Pack/200g	88	44	0.4	10.1	0.2	1.3
Fresh, M & S*	1 Pack/260g	117	45	0.4	10.1	0.2	1.2
Fresh, Raw	1oz/28g	11	41	0.4	10.1	0.2	1.2
Fresh, Waitrose*	1 Serving/250g	110	44	0.4	10.1	0.2	1.2
In Own Juice, Del Monte*	1 Can/432g	281	65	0.4	15.0	0.1	0.0
Organic, Waitrose*	1oz/28g	12	44	0.4	10.1	0.2	1.2
Pieces, In Juice, Princes*	1 Can/227g	114	50	0.3	12.2	0.0	0.5
Pieces, In Natural Juice, Sainsbury's*	1 Can/140g	85	61	0.4	14.7	0.1	0.7
Pieces, In Natural Juice, Tesco*	1oz/28g	15	52	0.3	12.0	0.0	0.5
Pieces, In Own Fruit Juice, Safeway*	1 Serving/170g	83	49	0.3	12.0	0.0	1.4
Pieces, In Pineapple Juice, Fruitime, Tesco*	1 Can/140g	84	60	0.3	14.0	0.0	0.5
Rings, In Pineapple Juice, John West*	1 Can/106g	43	41	0.3	10.0	0.0	0.7
Rings, Safeway*	1 Serving/25g	17	68	0.5	16.5	0.0	0.7
Rings, Sainsbury's*	1 Serving/50g	22	44	0.4	10.1	0.2	1.2
Slices, In Fruit Juice, Waitrose*	½ Can/67g	34	50	0.5	12.2	0.0	0.5
Slices, In Natural Juice, Sainsbury's*	½ Can/216g	132	61	0.4	14.7	0.1	0.7
Slices, In Natural Juice, Tesco*	1 Slice/56g	28	50	0.3	12.2	0.0	0.5
PINEAPPLE JUICE,							
Asda*	1 Glass/250ml	125	50	0.3	11.6	0.1	0.3
Del Monte*	1 Glass/200ml	104	52	0.4	12.0	0.0	0.0
Fresh Squeezed, M & S*	1 Glass/250ml	75	30	0.2	8.8	0.0	0.6
Pure, Asda*	1 Glass/200ml	100	50	0.3	11.6	0.1	0.0
Pure, Sainsbury's*	1 Glass/200ml	106	53	0.4	12.3	0.1	0.1
Pure, Waitrose*	1 Glass/200ml	106	53	0.3	12.4	0.0	0.0
Unsweetened	1 Glass/200ml	82	41	0.3	10.5	0.1	0.0Pink

Nutrition Values per 100g / 100ml apply to columns KCAL, PROT, CARB, FAT, FIBRE.

	Measure WEIGHT/INFO	per Measure KCAL	Nutrition Values per 100g / 100ml KCAL	PROT	CARB	FAT	FIBRE
PINEAPPLE JUICE,,							
Grapefruit Fruit & Barley Drink, Tesco*	1 Glass/200ml	24	12	0.2	1.2	0.0	0.0
PINK GRAPEFRUIT In Natural Juice, Waitrose*	1 Serving/100g	32	32	0.6	7.3	0.0	0.4
PINK GRAPEFRUIT Juice Drink, Ocean Spray*	1 Glass/200ml	84	42	0.3	9.7	0.0	0.0
PINK GRAPEFRUIT JUICE,							
Freshly Squeezed, M & S*	1 Glass/200ml	70	35	0.5	7.8	0.1	0.0
Sainsbury's*	1 Glass/200ml	82	41	0.5	9.2	0.1	0.3
PISTACHIO NUTS,							
Golden Wonder*	1 Bag/40g	246	615	21.1	7.8	55.5	5.5
Roast Salted, KP*	1oz/28g	176	630	20.8	11.9	55.5	6.0
Roasted & Salted	10 Nuts/8g	48	601	17.9	8.2	55.4	6.1
Roasted & Salted, Waitrose*	1 Serving/25g	144	576	18.5	8.2	52.1	6.1
Roasted & Salted, Sainsbury's*	1 Serving/50g	312	625	21.2	11.2	55.1	6.2
Unsalted, Roasted, KP*	1oz/28g	179	640	20.8	14.2	55.5	6.0
Whole Shelled, Sainsbury's*	1 Serving/25g	151	602	20.7	7.5	54.3	6.0
PIZZA BASE,							
Deep Pan, Napolina*	1 Base/260g	757	291	7.9	58.0	3.0	0.2
Deep, Standard Recipe, Pizza Two Four*	1oz/28g	63	225	7.0	48.7	0.2	0.0
Italian, Sainsbury's*	1 Base/150g	452	301	7.6	57.0	4.8	1.5
Medium, Standard Recipe, Pizza Two Four*	1oz/28g	63	225	7.0	48.7	0.2	0.0
Mini, Napolina*	1 Base/75g	218	291	7.9	58.0	3.0	0.2
PIZZA BASE							
Thin & Crispy, Napolina*	1 Base/150g	437	291	7.9	58.0	3.0	0.2
Thin & Crispy, Safeway*	1 Base/140g	393	281	9.0	54.0	3.2	2.4
Thin & Crispy, Sainsbury's*	1 Base/140g	421	301	9.9	62.8	1.1	1.1
Thin & Crispy, Tesco*	1 Serving/110g	348	316	9.2	52.9	7.5	1.5
PIZZA BASE MIX, Morrisons*	1 Serving/77g	313	407	12.7	77.9	5.0	3.6
PIZZA,							
American Hot, Pizza Express*	½ Pizza/264g	517	196	10.6	26.8	5.1	1.1
Bacon & Cheese Stonebake, Hot & Crispy, M & S*	1 Pack/160g	472	295	14.6	25.8	14.9	1.6
Bacon & Mushroom Pizzeria, Sainsbury's*	1 Pizza/355g	880	248	11.7	34.5	7.0	3.7
Bacon & Mushroom, Stone Bake, M & S*	1 Pizza/375g	750	200	9.9	27.2	6.4	1.6
Bacon & Mushroom, Thin & Crispy, Sainsbury's*	½ Pizza/150g	396	264	12.9	29.2	10.6	1.7
Bacon & Mushroom, Thin & Crispy, Somerfield*	¼ Pizza/81g	189	233	11.0	24.0	10.0	0.0
Bacon, Mushroom & Tomato, Stonebaked, Tesco*	1 Serving/173g	351	203	9.9	24.1	7.4	2.0
Baked Beans & Cheese, Heinz*	½ Pizza/222g	460	207	9.7	30.1	5.3	2.0
Baked Beans & Sausage, Heinz*	½ Pizza/221g	420	190	9.1	26.2	5.4	2.1
Baked Beans, Microwave, Heinz*	1 Pizza/150g	335	223	8.7	29.8	7.7	1.9
BBQ Chicken, Deep Dish, Schwan's*	1 Pizza/170g	393	231	8.8	26.3	10.1	0.0
BBQ Chicken Stuffed Crust, Asda*	½ Pizza/245g	613	250	13.0	27.0	10.0	2.7
BBQ Chicken, Thin & Crispy, Sainsbury's*	½ Pizza/147g	384	261	13.8	33.1	8.2	1.6
Big Fill Meat Feast, Somerfield*	1 Pizza/455g	1019	224	11.0	26.0	8.0	0.0
Bistro Cheese & Tomato, Waitrose*	½ Pizza/205g	488	238	10.0	27.6	9.7	1.2
Bistro Mushroom & Roasted Onion, Waitrose*	½ Pizza/187g	402	215	9.8	28.9	6.7	1.3
Bistro Salami & Pepperoni, Waitrose*	½ Pizza/190g	492	259	12.9	28.8	10.2	1.5
Cajun Chicken, BGTY, Sainsbury's*	½ Pizza/165g	363	220	11.0	36.0	3.6	1.7
Cajun Style Chicken, Stonebaked, Tesco*	1 Pizza/561g	1318	235	11.9	24.8	9.8	1.4
Caprina, Pizza Express*	1 Pizza/300g	635	212	8.0	31.0	7.3	0.0
Chargrilled Chicken & Bacon Pizzeria, Sainsbury's*	½ Pizza/181g	554	306	12.8	35.4	12.6	1.2
Chargrilled Chicken & Vegetable, GFY, Asda*	½ Pizza/166g	355	214	13.0	36.0	2.0	2.0
Chargrilled Chicken & Vegetable, Low Fat, Bertorelli*	1 Pizza/180g	439	244	14.2	39.3	4.4	2.3
Chargrilled Chicken, Iceland*	1 Pizza/381g	804	211	12.3	25.4	6.7	2.0
Chargrilled Chicken, Thin & Crispy, Asda*	1 Serving/185g	387	209	9.0	32.0	5.0	1.6
Chargrilled, Safeway*	1 Serving/172g	301	175	10.2	27.6	2.1	2.6
Chargrilled Turkey Tikka Indian Sauce, Bernard Matthews*	½ Pizza/165g	335	203	10.1	31.0	4.3	0.0

PIZZA,	Measure WEIGHT/INFO	per Measure KCAL	Nutrition Values per 100g / 100ml KCAL	PROT	CARB	FAT	FIBRE
Chargrilled Vegetable, COU, M & S*	½ Pizza/294g	397	135	6.0	23.4	2.4	1.9
Chargrilled Vegetable, Eat Smart, Safeway*	1 Pizza/206g	361	175	10.2	27.6	2.1	2.6
Chargrilled Vegetable, HE, Tesco*	½ Pizza/143g	320	224	10.4	39.6	2.7	1.1
Cheese & Tomato	1oz/28g	66	237	9.1	25.2	11.8	1.4
Cheese & Tomato, 9.5"", Domino's Pizza*	1 Slice/52g	125	241	12.8	34.9	5.6	3.2
Cheese & Tomato, Basics, Somerfield*	1 Serving/80g	194	242	9.7	35.1	7.0	1.9
Cheese & Tomato, Deep & Crispy, Tesco*	1oz/28g	65	231	10.8	31.7	6.8	1.2
Cheese & Tomato, Deep Pan, Sainsbury's*	1 Pizza/182g	470	258	11.7	33.1	8.7	1.9
Cheese & Tomato, Economy, Sainsbury's*	1 Pizza/60g	142	237	11.2	34.1	6.2	1.8
Cheese & Tomato French Bread, Co-Op*	1 Pizza/135g	270	200	9.0	27.0	6.0	2.0
Cheese & Tomato French Bread, Findus*	1 Piece/143g	336	235	9.1	32.2	7.7	1.5
Cheese & Tomato, HE, Tesco*	1 Serving/100g	211	211	11.9	35.5	2.4	1.6
Cheese & Tomato, Italiano Range, Tesco*	1 Pizza/380g	969	255	11.4	31.7	9.2	3.3
Cheese & Tomato, M & S*	1oz/28g	63	225	11.5	29.3	6.9	1.3
Cheese & Tomato, Mini, M & S*	1 Pizza/95g	233	245	10.0	38.7	5.8	1.6
Cheese & Tomato, Morrisons*	1 Serving/143g	204	143	7.0	19.0	4.3	0.7
Cheese & Tomato, Retail, Frozen	1oz/28g	70	250	7.5	32.9	10.7	1.4
Cheese & Tomato, Sainsbury's*	1 Pizza/247g	706	286	13.7	35.4	9.9	2.4
Cheese & Tomato Slice, Ross*	1 Slice/77g	148	192	6.5	22.2	8.6	2.0
Cheese & Tomato, SmartPrice, Asda*	1 Pizza/125g	356	285	13.0	38.0	9.0	0.0
Cheese & Tomato, Stonebaked, Safeway*	½ Pizza/190g	437	230	12.0	32.3	5.9	1.5
Cheese & Tomato, Stonebaked, Thin & Crispy, Tesco*	½ Pizza/161g	388	241	11.6	29.4	8.6	2.1
Cheese & Tomato, Thin & Crispy, Morrisons*	1 Pizza/335g	787	235	11.6	27.4	8.7	0.0
Cheese & Tomato, Thin & Crispy, Organic, Tesco*	½ Pizza/147g	369	251	10.6	30.1	9.8	1.3
Cheese & Tomato, Thin & Crispy, Safeway*	1oz/28g	69	245	12.2	31.0	8.0	1.4
Cheese & Tomato, Thin & Crispy, Sainsbury's*	1 Serving/135g	329	244	11.4	26.0	11.1	1.5
Cheese & Tomato, Thin & Crispy, Waitrose*	½ Pizza/118g	245	208	9.2	25.0	7.9	1.3
Cheese & Tomato, Value, Tesco*	1 Serving/140g	319	228	10.0	28.7	8.1	2.4
Cheese Feast, Big Fill, Somerfield*	1 Pizza/430g	1135	264	13.0	28.0	11.0	0.0
Cheese Supreme, New Recipe, Goodfella's*	¼ Pizza/102g	269	264	12.3	31.2	10.0	2.2
Cheese, Thin & Crispy, Goodfella's*	1 Serving/275g	729	265	15.7	27.6	10.1	1.8
Cheese Triple, Chicago Town*	1 Serving/170g	418	246	9.9	27.6	10.7	0.0
Chicken & Maple Bacon Carbonara, Asda*	½ Pizza/195g	484	248	11.0	33.0	8.0	2.2
Chicken & Red Pepper, HE, Tesco*	1 Pizza/260g	608	234	12.7	40.1	2.5	0.7
Chicken & Spinach, Eat Smart, Safeway*	1 Pizza/165g	322	195	19.0	24.0	2.1	2.5
Chicken & Sweetcorn, Stonebaked, Tesco*	1 Serving/177g	354	200	11.9	26.0	5.4	2.0
Chicken Salsa, Healthy Choice, Safeway*	½ Pizza/177g	437	246	13.3	40.9	3.2	1.6
Chicken Salsa, HE, Tesco*	½ Pizza/169g	313	185	13.0	30.3	1.3	1.5
Chicken Supreme, Medium Pan, Pizza Hut*	½ Pizza/300g	810	270	13.0	29.0	12.0	2.0
Chilli Beef, Stone bake, M & S*	1 Pizza/395g	790	200	9.6	26.7	5.8	1.9
Delicata Four Season Ultra Thin, TTD, Sainsbury's*	½ Pizza/168g	445	265	13.3	24.3	12.9	2.3
Delicata Mushroom & Red Onion, TTD, Sainsbury's*	½ Pizza/165g	507	307	12.0	28.7	16.0	2.6
Deluxe, 9.5", Domino's Pizza*	1 Slice/66g	171	259	12.8	29.1	10.1	2.4
Double Cheese, Chicago Town*	1 Pizza/405g	932	230	11.7	30.6	6.7	0.0
Fire Roasted Pepper, Sainsbury's*	1 Pizza/344g	605	176	5.3	35.3	1.5	1.6
Flamed Chicken & Vegetables, BGTY, Sainsbury's*	1 Pizza/260g	660	254	14.2	39.3	4.4	2.3
Focaccia Goats Cheese & Caramel Onion, Sainsbury's*	1 Pizza/186g	543	292	8.6	34.1	13.5	1.9
Focaccia Tomato & Black Olive, TTD, Sainsbury's*	½ Pizza/222g	515	232	9.3	28.7	8.9	2.9
Four Cheese, Freschetta, Schwan*	¼ Slice/75g	205	273	11.3	34.8	9.8	1.4
Four Cheese, M & S*	1oz/28g	67	240	13.2	30.3	7.5	1.2
French Bread, BPC, Sainsbury's*	1 Pizza/132g	271	205	10.7	30.8	4.3	1.3
Full House, 9.5"", Domino's Pizza*	1 Slice/74g	183	247	12.5	25.5	10.5	1.8
Garlic & Mushroom, Asda*	½ Pizza/241g	696	289	10.0	24.0	17.0	1.6
Garlic & Mushroom, Thin & Crispy, Sainsbury's*	1 Pizza/260g	829	319	11.1	31.2	16.6	1.7

P

PIZZA,	Measure WEIGHT/INFO	per Measure KCAL	KCAL	PROT	CARB	FAT	FIBRE
			Nutrition Values per 100g / 100ml				
Garlic Chicken & Spinach, Perfectly Balanced, Waitrose*	½ Pizza/172g	351	204	13.3	30.8	3.1	2.3
Garlic Mushroom, Classico, Tesco*	½ Pizza/203g	471	232	8.9	29.1	8.9	2.2
Garlic Mushroom, Italian Style, Somerfield*	½ Pizza/175g	460	263	9.0	33.0	10.0	0.0
Garlic Mushroom, Safeway*	½ Pizza/155g	482	311	9.4	39.2	12.9	1.7
Grilled Pepper, Weight Watchers*	1 Pizza/220g	392	178	10.0	29.3	2.3	1.8
Ham & Cheese, Mini, Tesco*	1 Serving/92g	228	248	13.6	31.3	7.6	3.2
Ham & Mushroom, BGTY, Sainsbury's*	½ Pizza/158g	291	184	10.2	26.4	4.2	2.9
Ham & Mushroom Calzone, Waitrose*	½ Pizza/145g	363	250	10.0	31.6	9.3	1.6
Ham & Mushroom, COU, M & S*	1 Pack/245g	392	160	9.2	25.7	2.4	1.3
Ham & Mushroom, Deep & Crispy, Tesco*	1 Serving/210g	420	200	9.7	29.2	4.9	1.1
Ham & Mushroom, Eat Smart, Safeway*	1 Serving/208g	385	185	13.6	27.2	2.4	2.5
Ham & Mushroom, Go Ahead, McVitie's*	1 Pizza/120g	272	227	11.1	34.7	4.9	1.3
Ham & Mushroom, GFY, Asda*	1 Serving/165g	342	207	11.0	34.0	3.0	2.0
Ham & Mushroom, HE, Tesco*	1 Pizza/252g	491	195	10.4	35.6	1.2	2.0
Ham & Mushroom Slices, Farmfoods*	1 Slice/89g	170	191	8.0	34.0	2.6	0.9
Ham & Mushroom, Stone Baked, Goodfella's*	½ Pizza/175g	439	251	9.6	27.6	11.4	1.2
Ham & Mushroom, The Italian, Medium 12"", Pizza Hut*	1 Slice/96g	270	281	13.6	35.4	10.6	2.6
Ham & Mushroom, Thin & Crispy, Somerfield*	½ Pizza/170g	357	210	10.8	24.0	7.9	1.0
Ham & Mushroom, Thin & Crispy, Tesco*	1 Serving/166g	349	210	13.0	23.9	6.9	2.4
Ham & Pineapple, American Deep Pan, Sainsbury's*	1 Pizza/412g	1001	243	10.5	32.6	7.8	1.7
Ham & Pineapple, Chicago Town*	1 Pizza/435g	866	199	10.0	29.7	4.5	0.0
Ham & Pineapple, Deep Dish, Chicago Town*	1 Serving/170g	403	237	8.0	26.1	11.2	0.0
Ham & Pineapple, Deep Pan, American Style, Goodfella's*	1 Pizza/445g	1095	246	14.7	26.7	9.6	1.6
Ham & Pineapple, Eat Smart, Safeway*	1 Serving/151g	279	185	13.6	27.2	2.4	2.5
Ham & Pineapple, HE, Tesco*	1 Serving/169g	343	203	11.9	35.4	1.5	1.3
Ham & Pineapple, Loaded, Tesco*	½ Pizza/265g	557	210	11.3	28.7	5.5	1.4
Ham & Pineapple, Stone Bake, M & S*	1 Pizza/345g	690	200	10.1	28.3	5.7	1.6
Ham & Pineapple, Stonebaked, Tesco*	1 Serving/171g	363	212	11.5	27.1	6.4	1.9
Ham & Pineapple, Thin & Crispy, Good Choice, Iceland*	1 Pizza/600g	1338	223	11.7	33.1	4.9	1.7
Ham & Pineapple, Thin & Crispy, Goodfella's*	1 Serving/163g	333	204	10.6	22.8	7.8	2.4
Ham & Pineapple, Thin & Crispy Italian Morrisons*	1 Pizza/375g	746	199	10.2	24.9	6.1	0.0
Ham & Pineapple, Thin & Crispy, Sainsbury's*	1 Pizza/305g	824	270	13.5	29.8	10.7	1.7
Ham & Pineapple, Thin & Crispy, Somerfield*	½ Pizza/192g	405	211	10.7	21.5	9.1	2.4
Ham, Mushroom & Tomato, BGTY, Sainsbury's*	½ Pizza/150g	307	206	11.8	30.4	4.1	1.2
Hawaiian, Medium Pan, Pizza Hut*	1 Slice/96g	241	251	12.6	29.2	9.3	1.4
Honey Roast Salmon & Broccoli, BGTY, Sainsbury's*	1 Serving/280g	613	219	10.2	34.4	4.5	3.5
Hot & Spicy Chicken, M & S*	1oz/28g	59	210	15.5	20.9	7.3	1.9
Hot & Spicy, Deep Dish, Schwan's*	1 Pizza/170g	423	249	9.1	27.6	11.4	0.0
Hot & Spicy, Thin & Crispy, Somerfield*	1 Pizza/305g	918	301	12.0	25.0	17.0	0.0
Hot Chicken, Stone Bake, M & S*	1 Pizza/380g	798	210	11.5	25.1	6.8	1.3
Italian Meats, Finest, Tesco*	½ Pizza/217g	449	207	13.6	29.4	3.9	1.3
La Reine, Takeaway, Pizza Express*	¼ Pizza/138g	324	235	12.4	30.0	7.3	1.9
Margharita, Stone Baked, BGTY, Sainsbury's**	1 Serving/145g	315	217	11.0	39.0	1.9	1.8
Margheria, Stone Baked, GFY, Asda*	¼ Pizza/73g	158	217	11.0	39.0	1.9	1.8
Margherita, Classico, Tesco*	1 Serving/150g	383	255	11.4	31.7	9.2	3.3
Margherita, Finest, Tesco*	1 Serving/207g	441	213	11.0	30.5	5.2	1.2
Margherita, Italian Stone Baked, Somerfield*	1 Pizza/290g	554	191	10.0	22.0	7.0	0.0
Margherita, Italian Style, Somerfield*	½ Pizza/190g	424	223	10.0	32.0	6.0	0.0
Margherita, Medium Pan, Pizza Hut*	1 Slice/85g	239	281	12.7	31.1	11.8	2.1
Margherita, Pizza Express*	½ Pizza/135g	263	195	10.2	30.5	3.6	1.4
Margherita, Stone Baked, Goodfella's*	1 Slice/36g	95	263	10.9	31.9	11.4	7.6
Margherita, Stuffed Crust Original, Pizza Hut*	1 Slice/125.3g	330	262	14.9	28.5	9.8	1.0
Margherita, The Italian, Medium, Pizza Hut*	1 Slice/95g	292	307	15.2	39.5	10.8	2.3
Meat Feast, Asda*	¼ Pizza/100g	316	316	14.0	38.0	12.0	2.0

P

PIZZA,	Measure WEIGHT/INFO	per Measure KCAL	Nutrition Values per 100g / 100ml KCAL	PROT	CARB	FAT	FIBRE
Meat Feast, Medium Pan, Pizza Hut*	1 Slice/114g	324	284	14.6	24.4	14.2	0.9
Meat Feast, The Italian, 12"", Pizza Hut*	1 Slice/113g	341	302	15.4	30.3	14.3	2.3
Meat Feast, Thin & Crispy, Somerfield*	½ Pizza/150g	369	246	11.1	26.9	10.4	1.5
Meaty, The Edge, Pizza Hut*	1 Slice/64g	207	323	16.6	23.3	18.2	0.0
Mexican Chicken, COU, M & S*	1 Pizza/248g	384	155	10.3	25.0	2.0	2.0
Mexican, Deep Pan, Farmfoods*	1oz/28g	53	188	8.4	31.7	3.1	0.9
Micro, McCain*	½ Serving/133g	388	292	12.4	26.9	15.0	0.0
Mighty Meaty, 9.5"", Domino's Pizza*	1/6 Pizza/71g	177	249	13.9	25.5	10.2	2.8
Mixed Grill, 9.5"", Domino's Pizza*	1 Slice/75g	178	237	12.0	26.2	9.3	2.3
Mozzarella, Lidl*	1 Serving/175g	436	249	10.1	22.7	13.1	0.0
Mushroom & Bacon, Thin & Crispy, Waitrose*	1 Pizza/336g	726	216	11.4	23.9	8.3	1.7
Mushroom & Red Onion, TTD, Sainsbury's*	1 Pizza/258g	789	306	11.8	33.0	14.1	2.5
Mushroom, Pizza Express*	1 Pizza/400g	627	157	7.5	21.9	5.2	0.0
Neptune, Pizza Express*	1 Pizza/300g	604	201	10.9	29.9	5.3	0.0
Pepperonata Delicata, Sainsbury's*	1 Pizza/330g	917	278	12.9	24.3	14.4	2.6
Pepperoni & Onion, 9"", Sainsbury's*	½ Pizza/207g	615	297	13.4	31.7	13.0	1.9
Pepperoni, American Style Deep Pan, Co-Op*	1 Pizza/395g	988	250	12.0	28.0	10.0	1.0
Pepperoni, Chicago Town*	1 Sm Pizza/170g	471	277	11.5	28.8	12.9	0.0
Pepperoni, Chilli & Vegetable, Fresh, Tesco*	1 Pizza/260g	660	254	9.5	35.1	8.4	1.7
Pepperoni, Classico, Tesco*	½ Pizza/205g	586	286	11.6	27.3	14.5	1.9
Pepperoni, Deep & Crispy, Somerfield*	¼ Slice/101g	236	234	10.7	31.6	7.2	1.6
Pepperoni, Deep & Crispy, Tesco*	1 Pizza/375g	881	235	10.1	31.8	7.5	1.2
Pepperoni, Deep Pan, Goodfella's*	¼ Slice/109g	294	270	12.7	28.9	11.6	1.6
Pepperoni, Deep Pan, Safeway*	½ Pizza/198g	558	283	13.9	28.9	12.4	2.5
Pepperoni Deluxe, American Deep Pan, Sainsbury's*	1 Pizza/424g	1077	254	13.3	28.7	9.5	2.7
Pepperoni Extra, Chicago Town*	1 Pizza/460g	994	216	9.6	27.7	7.4	0.0
Pepperoni Feast, Deep Dish, Schwan's*	1 Pizza/435g	1188	273	9.9	26.3	14.2	0.0
Pepperoni, Freschetta, Schwan's*	1 Pizza/310g	846	273	10.8	31.6	11.5	0.0
Pepperoni, Goodfella's*	1 Pizza/337g	900	267	13.2	26.3	12.9	1.7
Pepperoni, Italian Style, Somerfield*	1 Pizza/380g	920	242	11.0	32.0	8.0	0.0
Pepperoni, Italian, Thin & Crispy, Morrisons*	1 Pizza/365g	843	231	11.1	25.0	9.6	0.0
Pepperoni, Micro, McCain*	1 Serving/135g	405	300	12.1	26.5	16.2	0.0
Pepperoni Passion, 9.5"", Domino's Pizza*	1 Slice/65g	186	286	13.6	31.5	11.6	1.4
Pepperoni, Pizza Outler*	1 Slice/100g	410	410	19.0	45.0	17.0	3.0
Pepperoni, Pizzeria, Sainsbury's*	½ Pizza/197g	528	268	12.5	34.7	8.8	1.3
Pepperoni, Stateside Foods*	½ Pizza/370g	988	267	12.2	32.3	9.8	1.4
Pepperoni, Stone Baked, Farmfoods*	1oz/28g	76	270	11.1	29.1	12.1	1.4
Pepperoni, Stonebaked, Goodfella's*	½ Pizza/181g	503	278	11.9	27.4	14.4	2.4
Pepperoni, The Insider, Pizza Hut*	1 Slice/137g	360	263	12.4	25.5	12.4	1.5
Pepperoni, Thin & Crispy, Co-Op*	1 Pizza/270g	689	255	11.0	26.0	11.0	1.0
Pepperoni, Thin & Crispy, Sainsbury's*	½ Pizza/132g	395	299	13.7	27.0	15.1	5.1
Pepperoni, Thin & Crispy, Tesco*	¼ Pizza/132g	379	287	11.5	30.3	13.3	2.3
Pleasure With Fire Roasted Vegetables, Heinz*	½ Pizza/200g	418	209	9.5	24.8	8.0	2.4
Prosciutto & Mascarpone, Safeway*	½ Pizza/200g	522	261	12.3	29.8	10.3	2.2
Prosciutto Con Funghi, Lidl*	½ Pizza/200g	454	227	9.5	31.5	7.0	0.0
Quattro Formaggi Pizzeria, Sainsbury's*	½ Pizza/175g	490	280	12.8	30.8	12.1	2.5
Real Big Triple Cheese, Family, Chicago Town*	½ Pizza/365g	931	255	11.5	29.4	10.2	0.0
Roast Vegetable, COU, M & S*	1 Pizza/294g	397	135	6.0	23.4	2.3	1.9
Roast Vegetable, Freschetta, Schwan's*	1 Pizza/380g	802	211	9.3	28.4	6.7	0.0
Roasted Pepper & Feta Cheese, BGTY, Sainsbury's*	1 Serving/280g	532	190	6.5	35.7	2.4	2.6
Roasted Pepper & Ham, Perfectly Balanced, Waitrose*	½ Pizza/215g	376	175	10.2	25.0	3.8	2.4
Roasted Peppers, Weight Watchers*	1 Pizza/220g	392	178	10.0	29.3	2.3	1.8
Salami & Ham, Pizzeria, Waitrose*	½ Pizza/205g	443	216	10.1	28.7	6.7	1.8
Salami Con Mozarella, Lidl*	½ Pizza/200g	534	267	9.9	31.5	11.2	0.0

P

PIZZA,	Measure WEIGHT/INFO	per Measure KCAL	Nutrition Values per 100g / 100ml KCAL	PROT	CARB	FAT	FIBRE
Sicilian, Premium, Co-Op*	1 Pizza/600g	1320	220	9.0	27.0	8.0	2.0
Slice Selection, M & S*	1 Serving/52g	120	230	9.4	30.3	7.8	1.9
Sloopy Giuseppe, Pizza Express*	½ Pizza/181g	310	171	8.4	27.7	3.0	1.9
Smoked Ham & Mushroom, Thin & Crispy, Co-Op*	1 Pizza/400g	792	198	9.0	30.3	4.5	1.7
Smoked Ham & Pineapple, Deep Pan, Co-Op*	1 Pizza/395g	1142	289	11.6	36.7	10.6	1.7
Smoked Ham & Pineapple, Weight Watchers*	1 Pizza/241g	429	178	10.3	27.6	2.9	1.5
Speciality Cheese, Deep Pan, TTD, Sainsbury's*	½ Pizza/160g	432	270	12.1	34.5	9.3	1.6
Spicy Chicken Fajita, Sainsbury's*	½ Pizza/232g	509	219	13.3	32.9	3.9	1.9
Spicy Chicken, Healthy Living, Co-Op*	1 Serving/174g	296	170	9.0	28.0	2.0	3.0
Spicy Chicken, Micro, McCain*	1 Pizza/133g	388	292	12.4	26.9	15.0	0.0
Spicy Vegetable, Low Fat, Bertorelli*	1 Pizza/180g	243	135	6.0	23.4	2.4	1.9
Spinach & Bacon, Thin & Crispy, M & S*	1 Pizza/290g	740	255	10.6	26.8	12.1	1.0
Spinach & Goats Cheese, BGTY, Sainsbury's*	½ Pizza/160g	304	190	6.8	31.8	3.9	2.4
Spinach & Ricotta, Classico, Tesco*	1 Pizza/208g	437	210	8.6	27.3	7.3	2.0
Spinach & Ricotta, Extra Special, Asda*	1 Pizza/400g	940	235	9.0	34.0	7.0	1.9
Spinach & Ricotta, Pizzaroma, Safeway*	1 Pizza/420g	1042	248	10.9	31.4	8.8	3.6
Spinach & Ricotta Pizzeria, Sainsbury's*	1 Pizza/390g	1002	257	11.4	30.8	10.7	2.1
Steak, Stone Bake, M & S*	1 Pizza/400g	820	205	9.9	25.7	6.7	1.4
Sunblushed Tomato & Mascarpone, Pizzadella, Tesco*	1 Serving/275g	894	325	8.5	36.7	16.0	1.5
Super Supreme, Family, Chicago Town*	¼ Pizza/225g	527	234	9.6	24.5	10.8	0.0
Suprema, Freschetta, Schwan's*	1 Pizza/355g	905	255	10.3	28.5	11.1	0.0
Supreme, Deep Pan, Safeway*	1 Serving/189g	450	238	10.8	27.0	9.6	4.7
Supreme, Medium Pan, Pizza Hut*	1 Slice/105.7g	292	275	12.6	25.1	13.8	1.2
Supreme, Square To Share, Farmfoods*	1 Serving/93g	196	211	10.7	22.9	8.6	1.1
Supreme, The Italian, Medium, Pizza Hut*	1 Slice/106g	297	280	13.0	33.4	11.4	2.1
Tandoori Hot, 9.5"", Domino's Pizza*	1 Slice/67g	137	205	12.2	27.8	5.2	2.8
The Big Cheese, Deep Pan, Goodfella's*	1/6 Pizza/118g	295	250	12.2	25.9	10.8	1.1
The Works, The Edge, Pizza Hut*	1 Slice/64g	161	252	12.9	22.0	12.5	0.0
Three Cheeses & Tomato, Stonebaked, Co-Op*	1 Pizza/415g	888	214	10.0	25.2	8.1	1.5
Three Meat, Thin & Crispy, Sainsbury's*	½ Pizza/147g	344	234	12.5	23.4	10.7	1.3
Tomato	1oz/28g	54	193	3.3	22.6	10.6	1.4
Tomato & Cheese French Bread, Farmfoods*	1 Pizza/89g	164	184	5.6	9.9	13.5	1.2
Tomato & Cheese, Ross*	1 Pizza/81g	181	224	7.4	31.5	7.6	2.5
Tomato & Cheese, Snack Size, Farmfoods*	1 Pizza/89g	164	184	5.6	9.9	13.5	1.2
Tomato & Cheese, Stone Bake, M & S*	1 Pizza/340g	782	230	10.8	30.1	8.4	1.6
Tomato & Cheese, Thin & Crispy, M & S*	1 Pizza/300g	705	235	11.0	27.7	9.4	1.2
Tomato & Red Pepper, Perfectly Balanced, Waitrose*	½ Pizza/163g	313	192	6.6	38.1	1.5	1.9
Tomato, Mushroom & Bacon, Deep Pan, Co-Op*	1 Pizza/420g	882	210	9.0	25.0	8.0	2.0
Triple Cheese, Deep Dish, Chicago Town*	1 Serving/170g	418	246	9.9	27.6	10.7	0.0
Tuscan Vegetable & Mozzarella, WTF, Sainsbury's*	1 Pizza/317g	552	174	5.7	26.6	5.0	2.3
Vegetable, COU, M & S*	1 Pizza/294g	397	135	6.4	23.2	2.4	1.9
Vegetable, Deep Pan, Co-Op*	1 Pizza/425g	829	195	8.0	25.0	7.0	2.0
Vegetable Feast, Thin & Crispy 9"", Farmfoods*	1oz/28g	47	167	8.5	23.7	4.2	0.9
Vegetable, Stone Bake, M & S*	1 Serving/465g	837	180	7.8	25.0	5.6	1.5
Vegetable, Thin & Crispy, Iceland*	½ Pizza/200g	442	221	8.3	23.2	10.6	1.7
Vegetarian, Organic, Evernat*	1oz/28g	59	212	7.5	36.4	4.0	0.0
Vegetarian, Original Medium, Pizza Hut*	1 Slice/93.5g	227	241	11.2	28.0	9.4	1.9
Vegetarian, Supreme, 9.5"", Domino's Pizza*	1 Slice/71g	137	193	10.8	27.0	4.6	2.4
Veggie, The Edge, Pizza Hut*	1 Slice/60g	137	228	11.4	24.6	9.3	0.0
PIZZA POCKET,							
Chargrilled Chicken & Veg, HE Tesco*	1 Pocket/190g	304	160	11.4	23.1	2.4	2.8
Hot, HE, Tesco*	1 Serving/190g	304	160	11.4	23.1	2.4	2.8
PLAICE,							
Breaded, Asda*	1 Serving/150g	351	234	15.0	12.0	14.0	0.5

P

	Measure	per Measure	Nutrition Values per 100g / 100ml				
PLAICE,	WEIGHT/INFO	KCAL	KCAL	PROT	CARB	FAT	FIBRE
Breaded, Chunky, Somerfield*	1oz/28g	59	209	12.0	17.0	10.0	0.0
Filled With Prawns & Garlic, Somerfield*	1 Plaice/171g	366	214	12.0	14.8	11.9	0.7
Fillet, Boneless, Chunky, Sainsbury's*	1 Fillet/153g	314	205	12.6	16.6	9.8	0.5
Fillets, Baked, Sainsbury's*	1 Serving/100g	234	234	13.0	19.2	11.7	1.1
Fillets, Breaded, Waitrose*	1 Fillet/150g	291	194	13.2	9.9	11.3	0.3
Fillets, Crunchy Breadcrumbs, Boned, Asda*	1oz/28g	66	237	11.0	19.0	13.0	0.9
Fillets, In Crispy Breadcrumbs, Somerfield*	1 Serving/150g	290	193	12.0	17.0	8.6	1.4
Fillets, Somerfield*	1oz/28g	22	79	17.0	0.0	1.0	0.0
Fillets, Tesco*	1 Serving/100g	79	79	16.7	0.0	1.4	0.0
Goujons, Baked	1oz/28g	85	304	8.8	27.7	18.3	0.0
Goujons, Fried In Blended Oil	1oz/28g	119	426	8.5	27.0	32.3	0.0
Grilled	1oz/28g	27	96	20.1	0.0	1.7	0.0
In Batter, Fried In Blended Oil	1oz/28g	72	257	15.2	12.0	16.8	0.5
In Crumbs, Fried In Blended Oil	1oz/28g	64	228	18.0	8.6	13.7	0.2
Lightly Dusted, M & S*	1 Fillet/113g	183	162	12.3	11.0	7.4	0.5
Raw	1oz/28g	22	79	16.7	0.0	1.4	0.0
Steamed	1oz/28g	26	93	18.9	0.0	1.9	0.0
PLANTAIN,							
Boiled In Unsalted Water	1oz/28g	31	112	0.8	28.5	0.2	1.2
Raw	1oz/28g	33	117	1.1	29.4	0.3	1.3
Ripe, Fried In Vegetable Oil	1oz/28g	75	267	1.5	47.5	9.2	2.3
PLOUGHMANS,							
Cheddar Cheese, Waitrose*	1 Pack/172g	416	242	8.6	19.8	14.3	1.4
Cheese, BGTY, Sainsbury's*	1 Pack/161g	264	164	8.4	24.0	3.8	0.0
Cheese, Eat Smart, Safeway*	1 Roll/166g	266	160	12.4	21.7	2.1	1.6
PLUMS,							
Average, Raw, Weighed With Stones	1oz/28g	10	34	0.5	8.3	0.1	1.5
Average, Stewed Without Sugar	1oz/28g	8	30	0.5	7.3	0.1	1.3
Fresh, Raw	1oz/28g	10	36	0.6	8.8	0.1	1.6
Safeway*	1 Serving/68g	26	38	0.6	8.7	0.1	1.6
POLO,							
Citrus Sharp, Nestle*	1 Tube/34g	134	393	0.0	96.6	1.0	0.0
Smoothies, Nestle*	1 Polo/4g	16	408	0.1	86.9	6.8	0.0
POMEGRANATE,							
Raw, Fresh	1oz/28g	14	51	1.3	11.8	0.2	3.4
Weighed With Skin	1oz/28g	9	33	0.9	7.7	0.1	2.2
POP TARTS,							
Chocolate, Kellogg's*	1 Pop Tart/50g	200	400	6.0	67.0	11.0	2.5
Cream Cheese & Cherry Swirl, Kelloggs*	1 Serving/62g	250	403	3.2	59.7	17.7	1.0
Frosted Brown Sugar Cinnamon, Kelloggs*	1 pastry/50g	210	420	6.0	68.0	14.0	2.0
Strawberry Sensation, Kellogg's*	1 Pop Tart/50g	195	390	4.0	69.0	11.0	2.0
POPCORN,							
Butter Toffee, Tesco*	1 Pack/350g	1418	405	2.2	81.7	7.7	4.3
Plain	1oz/28g	166	593	6.2	48.7	42.8	0.0
Popping Corn, Organic, Evernat*	1oz/28g	165	588	6.2	44.4	42.8	6.6
Salted, Blockbuster*	1 Bowl/25g	121	482	8.2	57.8	24.3	5.5
Toffee, 90% Fat Free, Butterkist*	1 Pack/35g	142	406	2.8	77.7	9.3	0.0
Toffee, Blockbuster*	¼ Pack/50g	221	441	2.2	77.4	13.7	2.9
Toffee, Sainsbury's*	1 Pack/100g	423	423	2.6	80.8	9.9	1.5
POPPADUMS,							
Extra Large, Sharwood's*	1oz/28g	78	279	21.3	44.7	1.7	10.3
Fried In Vegetable Oil	1oz/28g	103	369	17.5	39.1	16.9	0.0
Garlic & Coriander, Sharwood's*	1oz/28g	130	464	17.7	37.9	26.8	7.7
Madras Spiced, Sharwood's*	1oz/28g	79	281	20.4	45.6	1.9	10.3

P

	Measure WEIGHT/INFO	per Measure KCAL	Nutrition Values per 100g / 100ml KCAL	PROT	CARB	FAT	FIBRE
POPPADUMS,							
M & S*	1 Poppadum/9g	42	467	17.4	39.3	26.6	8.4
Mercifully Mild, Phileas Fogg*	1 Serving/30g	150	499	14.8	36.8	32.6	6.0
Plain, Asda*	1 Poppadum/9g	44	484	18.0	40.0	28.0	0.0
Spicy, COU, M & S*	1 Pack/26g	85	325	23.5	51.9	2.4	8.1
POPPETS*,							
Chocolate Raisins	1 Box/100g	409	409	4.8	66.0	14.0	0.0
Mint Cream	1oz/28g	119	424	2.0	75.0	13.0	0.0
Peanut	1 Box/100g	544	544	16.4	37.0	37.0	0.0
Toffee, Milk Chocolate	1 Box/100g	484	484	4.6	67.0	22.0	0.0
POPPY SEEDS, Asda*	1 Serving/2g	11	556	21.0	19.0	44.0	0.0
PORK,							
Cantonese Red Lion Balls With Pak Choi, Sainsbury's*	1 Pack/400g	452	113	5.0	10.6	5.6	0.8
Char Sui In Cantonese Sauce, Asda*	1 Pack/360g	623	173	9.8	28.4	2.2	0.5
Char Sui, Takeaway, Iceland*	1 Pack/400g	412	103	7.9	12.5	2.4	1.2
Chops, In Mustard & Cream	1oz/28g	65	231	0.7	57.0	0.0	0.3
Leg, Diced, Waitrose*	1oz/28g	30	108	22.8	0.0	0.8	0.0
Leg, Joint, M & S*	¼ Pack/125g	138	110	19.9	0.4	3.1	0.0
Lemon & Thyme, TTD, Sainsbury's*	1 Serving/67g	159	238	19.8	5.6	15.2	0.3
Loin, Joint, Raw, Lean & Fat	1oz/28g	66	235	7.7	46.0	1.8	2.7
Loin, Steak, Fried, Lean	1oz/28g	68	243	9.4	48.7	2.1	5.0
Loin, Steak, Fried, Lean & Fat	1oz/28g	57	203	8.8	40.4	2.1	6.7
Loin, Steak, M & S*	1 Serving/125g	281	225	19.9	0.0	16.1	0.0
Loin, Steak, Raw, Lean & Fat	1oz/28g	62	223	8.7	44.8	2.0	4.6
Loin, Steak, Sainsbury's*	1 Serving/74g	167	225	26.1	0.3	13.3	0.8
Mince, HE, Tesco*	1 Pack/400g	444	111	20.2	0.7	3.0	0.0
Mince, Raw	1oz/28g	62	221	9.6	44.1	2.3	7.3
Steak, Raw, Lean	1oz/28g	76	270	7.0	48.3	7.4	4.6
Steak, Raw, Lean & Fat	1oz/28g	111	396	7.1	73.0	12.0	0.0
Tongue, Lunch, Asda*	1 Slice/21g	37	175	21.4	1.5	9.3	0.0
Trimmed, Lean, Raw	1oz/28g	150	535	10.0	50.8	34.0	0.0
PORK &,							
Chestnut Stuffing, M & S*	1oz/28g	64	230	5.3	12.6	17.1	3.7
PORK - CHINESE,							
Steak, Asda*	1 Serving/250g	508	203	22.0	4.0	11.0	1.3
PORK - ESCALOPES,							
BGTY, Sainsbury's*	½ Pack/200g	274	137	31.1	0.0	1.4	0.0
British, HE, Tesco*	1 Escalope/125g	138	110	21.3	0.0	2.7	0.0
PORK - GRILLED,							
Steak, Lean	1oz/28g	47	169	33.9	0.0	3.7	0.0
Steak, Lean & Fat	1oz/28g	83	295	5.2	52.2	8.8	7.7
PORK - HONEY Roast, Loin, Sainsbury's*	1 Slice/12g	20	165	23.6	2.7	6.6	0.1
PORK - HOT & Spicy, Steak, Shoulder, Waitrose*	1 Steak/100g	207	207	19.5	1.3	13.7	0.0
PORK IN,							
Light Mustard Sauce, COU, M & S*	1 Serving/390g	312	80	12.2	3.2	2.1	0.4
Mustard Sauce With Colcannon Mash, BGTY, Sainsbury's*	1 Pack/450g	369	82	6.2	10.0	1.9	0.6
PORK - MEDALLIONS, Loin, BGTY, Sainsbury's*	1 Pack/220g	142	129	27.2	0.0	2.2	0.8
PORK - ROAST,							
Dinner, Bird's Eye*	1 Pack/362g	340	94	7.5	10.9	2.3	1.4
Joint, GFY, Asda*	½ Joint/283g	314	111	23.0	3.4	0.6	0.7
Loin, Asda*	1oz/28g	38	134	21.5	0.9	4.9	0.0
Tesco*	1oz/28g	32	116	24.2	0.0	2.1	0.0
PORK - ROASTED,							
Cured, British, Loin, M & S*	1 Slice/10g	14	140	25.2	0.7	4.4	0.0
Loin, Joint, Lean	1oz/28g	68	243	7.5	48.7	2.7	2.9

P

	Measure WEIGHT/INFO	per Measure KCAL	KCAL	PROT	CARB	FAT	FIBRE
			Nutrition Values per 100g / 100ml				
PORK - ROASTED,							
Loin, Joint, Lean & Fat	1oz/28g	74	264	8.2	53.0	2.9	3.1
PORK - ROLL, With Stuffing, John West*	1oz/28g	86	306	13.0	5.0	26.0	0.0
PORK - ROULADE, Tenderloin, Waitrose*	1 Pack/171g	282	165	18.4	5.9	7.5	1.8
PORK - SLICES,							
Roast, Co-Op*	1 Slice/30g	38	125	22.0	0.0	4.0	0.0
Roast, Safeway*	1 Slice/28g	40	142	23.4	0.9	5.0	0.0
Shoulder, Cured	1oz/28g	29	103	16.9	0.9	3.6	0.0
PORK - SMOKED, Cured, Loin, M & S*	1oz/28g	43	155	18.1	0.0	9.1	0.0
PORK - STEWED,							
Mince	1oz/28g	60	213	7.4	32.1	6.1	1.1
Steak, Lean	1oz/28g	49	176	33.6	0.0	4.6	0.0
Steak, Lean & Fat	1oz/28g	64	229	5.2	43.6	3.3	1.8
PORK WITH,							
Sage & Onion Stuffing, Joint, BGTY, Sainsbury's*	1 Serving/150g	246	164	29.5	3.3	3.6	1.3
Sage, Onion & Lemon Stuffing, Joint, Sainsbury's*	1 Serving/260g	699	269	27.4	2.2	16.7	1.4
PORK SCRATCHINGS,							
KP*	1 Pack/20g	125	624	47.3	0.5	48.1	0.5
Tavern Snacks*	1 Pack/30g	187	624	47.3	0.5	48.1	0.5
PORT	1 Serving/50ml	79	157	0.1	12.0	0.0	0.0
POT NOODLE*,							
Beef & Tomato	1 Pot/90g	382	424	10.7	60.3	15.5	3.7
Burger Fun	1 Pot/59g	248	420	12.3	59.4	14.9	3.3
Chicken & Mushroom	1 Pot/89g	389	437	12.1	60.9	16.1	3.1
Chicken Curry, Hot	1 Pot/87g	383	440	10.1	63.6	16.1	2.7
Chow Mein	1 Pot/89g	385	433	11.6	60.5	16.0	2.7
Nice'n'Spicy	1 Pot/87g	380	437	9.7	61.5	16.9	2.7
Pizza Flavour	1 Pot/87g	388	446	10.7	63.1	16.8	2.5
Sausage & Tomato	1 Pot/89g	389	437	10.0	63.1	16.0	2.7
Spicy Curry	1 Pot/89g	379	426	9.8	61.5	15.6	3.0
Sweet & Sour	1 Pot/86g	376	437	9.4	63.2	16.2	2.7
POT RICE,							
Chicken & Sweetcorn, Pot Rice*	1 Pot/68g	243	357	13.1	65.8	4.6	4.0
Chicken Curry, Pot Rice*	1 Pot/74g	253	342	11.0	67.2	2.3	3.3
POTATOES,							
Baked, Flesh & Skin	1 Med/180g	245	136	3.9	31.7	0.2	2.7
Baked, Flesh Only	1 Med/160g	123	77	2.2	18.0	0.1	1.4
New, Average, Raw	1oz/28g	20	70	1.7	16.1	0.3	1.0
New, Boiled In Salted Water	1oz/28g	21	75	1.5	17.8	0.3	1.1
New, Boiled In Unsalted Water	1oz/28g	21	75	1.5	17.8	0.3	1.1
New, Canned, Re-Heated, Drained	1oz/28g	18	63	1.5	15.1	0.1	0.8
New, Chipped, Fried In Corn Oil	1oz/28g	64	228	4.4	33.3	9.5	1.7
New, In Skins, Boiled In Salted Water	1oz/28g	18	66	1.4	15.4	0.3	1.5
New, In Skins, Boiled In Unsalted Water	1oz/28g	18	66	1.4	15.4	0.3	1.5
Old, Average, Raw	1oz/28g	21	75	2.1	17.2	0.2	1.3
Old, Boiled In Salted Water	1oz/28g	20	72	1.8	17.0	0.1	1.2
Old, Boiled In Unsalted Water	1oz/28g	20	72	1.8	17.0	0.1	1.2
Old, Roast In Blended Oil	1oz/28g	42	149	2.9	25.9	4.5	1.8
Old, Roast In Lard	1oz/28g	42	149	2.9	25.9	4.5	1.8
POTATO - BAKE,							
Cheese & Onion, Tesco*	1 Pack/400g	376	94	2.4	10.0	4.9	1.0
Chicken & Mushroom, Homepride*	1 Serving/105g	128	122	2.3	1.9	11.7	0.0
Garlic & Herb, Homepride*	1 Serving/100g	148	148	0.7	4.2	14.2	0.0
POTATO - BAKE MIX,							
Creamy Cheddar Cheese, Colman's*	1 Pack/45g	189	420	11.5	34.8	26.0	9.6

	Measure WEIGHT/INFO	per Measure KCAL	KCAL	PROT	CARB	FAT	FIBRE
POTATO - BAKE MIX,							
Garlic & Herb, Colman's*	1 Pack/45g	149	330	8.9	52.7	11.1	3.8
Ham & Leek, Colman's*	1 Pack/44g	181	412	9.9	40.4	24.0	2.1
POTATO - BAKED,							
Leek & Cheese, M & S*	1 Serving/206g	206	100	3.8	13.4	3.1	3.2
With Cheddar Cheese, COU, M & S*	1 Potato/164g	164	100	2.9	17.3	1.9	2.0
With Cheddar Cheese, Farmfoods*	1 Potato/143g	196	137	4.7	21.0	3.8	1.9
With Cheese, Tesco*	1 Pack/400g	448	112	2.7	18.7	2.9	1.0
With Chilli Con Carne, Eat Smart, Safeway*	1 Serving/300g	225	75	6.1	8.9	1.3	1.9
With Chilli, COU, M & S*	1 Pack/300g	270	90	6.0	11.0	2.1	1.2
With Tuna & Sweetcorn, COU, M & S*	1 Pack/300g	270	90	5.1	12.8	1.8	1.4
POTATO - BOMBAY,							
Asda*	½ Can/204g	202	99	1.5	12.0	5.0	1.6
Canned, Tesco*	1 Can/400g	296	74	1.6	11.9	2.2	0.7
M & S*	1 Pack/300g	300	100	1.5	12.1	4.8	1.6
Medium, Chilled, Tesco*	1oz/28g	29	103	1.7	8.4	7.0	0.8
Mild, Flavour Of India, Sainsbury's*	½ Can/200g	166	83	2.0	13.0	2.5	1.4
Sainsbury's*	1 Pack/300g	303	101	1.8	11.8	5.2	1.7
Tesco*	1 Pack/350g	413	118	1.8	13.5	6.4	1.1
POTATO - CAKES,							
Fried In Vegetable Oil	1oz/28g	59	210	3.9	31.4	8.5	1.6
Rosti, M & S*	1 Serving/100g	140	140	1.5	16.8	7.5	1.8
Sainsbury's*	1 Cake/65g	114	176	4.3	36.2	1.6	3.2
Toasted, Tesco*	1 Cake/58g	116	200	4.4	40.5	2.3	2.2
Warburton's*	1 Cake/45g	119	264	5.9	38.6	9.6	0.0
POTATO - CREAMED, With Cabbage, Asda*	1 Pack/350g	256	73	1.3	11.0	2.6	0.0
POTATO - FARLS, M & S*	1 Farl/55g	79	144	4.2	33.8	0.4	4.7
POTATO - FRIED, Crispy, M & S*	1 Pack/400g	660	165	2.0	22.6	7.1	1.4
POTATO - FRITTERS,							
Crispy, Bird's Eye*	1 Fritter/20g	29	145	2.0	16.3	8.0	1.2
With Sweetcorn, M & S*	1 Pack/135g	304	225	4.4	24.1	12.6	2.3
POTATO - INSTANT,							
Mashed, Made Up, Sainsbury's*	1 Serving/220g	114	52	1.8	10.9	0.1	1.0
Mashed, Made Up With Water, Smash*	1 Serving/160g	96	60	1.4	13.2	0.2	0.6
Mashed, Mr Mash*	1oz/28g	18	64	1.1	14.4	0.2	0.8
Powder, Made Up With Water	1 Med Serving/180g	103	57	1.5	13.5	0.1	1.0
POTATO - JACKET,							
Beef Chilli, Asda*	1 Pack/300g	372	124	5.0	22.0	1.8	2.1
Cheese & Butter, Tesco*	1 potato/200g	214	107	4.2	14.6	3.5	1.0
Cheese Filled, Farmfoods*	2 Halves/255g	349	137	4.7	21.0	3.8	1.9
Creamy Mushroom, Asda*	1 Serving/100g	124	124	3.5	22.0	2.4	1.7
Oven Baked, McCain*	1oz/28g	29	105	2.3	23.8	0.1	0.0
Scallops, Slices, Waitrose*	1 Serving/150g	171	114	2.2	19.8	2.9	1.7
Tuna & Sweetcorn, Deep Filled, M & S*	1 Pack/300g	270	90	4.9	13.1	2.2	1.2
Tuna, COU, M & S*	1oz/28g	24	85	4.8	10.8	2.4	1.4
With Baked Beans & Mozzarella , Eat Smart, Safeway*	1 Pack/283g	255	90	5.8	12.8	1.4	2.3
With Cheese Mash, GFY, Asda*	1 Potato/200g	194	97	2.9	17.0	1.9	0.0
With Chicken Tikka, COU, M & S*	1 Serving/300g	240	80	5.4	10.9	1.6	1.3
With Chilli Con Carne, COU, M & S*	1 Potato/300g	270	90	6.0	11.0	2.1	1.2
With Chilli Con Carne, Eat Smart, Safeway*	1 Pack/300g	225	75	6.1	8.9	1.3	1.9
With Chilli Con Carne, Pro Cuisine*	1 Pack/340g	347	102	4.6	18.7	1.0	0.0
With Garlic Butter Filling, Morrisons*	1 Serving/210g	239	114	1.7	13.6	5.9	0.9
With Garlic, Mini, Asda*	1 Serving/65g	59	91	2.2	13.0	3.3	0.0
With Garlic Mushrooms, Eat Smart, Safeway*	1 Pack/300g	210	70	2.7	8.1	2.7	1.6
With Herb & Rock Salt Seasoning, M & S*	1 Pack/500g	375	75	2.0	14.2	1.1	1.7

Nutrition Values per 100g / 100ml

P

POTATO - JACKET,	Measure WEIGHT/INFO	per Measure KCAL	Nutrition Values per 100g / 100ml KCAL	PROT	CARB	FAT	FIBRE
With Tuna & Sweetcorn, COU, M & S*	1 Pack/300g	270	90	5.1	12.8	1.8	1.4
With Tuna & Sweetcorn, Eat Smart, Safeway*	1 Pack/300g	240	80	5.3	10.3	1.9	1.4
POTATO - MASH,							
Bacon & Spring Onion, Finest, Tesco*	½ Pack/200g	214	107	4.3	10.8	5.2	1.6
Cabbage & Spring Onion, COU, M & S*	1 Serving/225g	180	80	1.7	11.8	2.5	1.9
Cabbage & Spring Onion, Sainsbury's*	½ Pack/225g	279	124	2.0	14.8	6.3	1.1
Carrot & Swede, Sainsbury's*	½ Pack/225g	230	102	1.9	11.7	5.3	1.5
Cheddar, Tesco*	1 Pack/500g	555	111	2.7	13.0	5.4	1.0
Creamy, Finest, Tesco*	½ Pack/250g	373	149	2.0	12.4	10.1	1.2
Fresh, Tesco*	1 Pack/400g	368	92	2.1	11.1	4.4	1.9
Fresh, With Butter, Sainsbury's*	½ Pack/225g	290	129	1.5	15.4	6.8	1.1
Instant, SmartPrice, Asda*	½ Pack/60g	209	349	8.0	78.0	0.5	7.0
Leek & Cheese, COU, M & S*	1 Pack/225g	180	80	3.0	12.0	2.1	1.3
Maris Piper, Sainsbury's*	1 Serving/225g	290	129	1.5	15.4	6.8	1.1
Mustard, With Caramelised Onions, Finest, Tesco*	1 Serving/200g	232	116	2.6	16.0	4.6	1.8
Olive Oil, HE, Tesco*	1 Serving/100g	90	90	2.1	15.5	2.2	0.9
Sundried Tomato & Basil, COU, M & S*	1 Serving/170g	128	75	1.0	14.4	1.5	1.2
With Carrot & Swede, COU, M & S*	1oz/28g	17	60	1.0	12.2	1.2	1.9
With Leeks, Creamy, Bird's Eye*	1 Pack/300g	300	100	2.0	7.3	7.0	0.8
POTATO - MASHED,							
Asda*	1 Serving/175g	159	91	1.8	16.0	2.2	1.1
Fresh, Sainsbury's*	½ Pot/200g	192	96	2.0	14.6	2.8	1.0
Frozen, Sainsbury's*	1/3 Pack/228g	249	109	1.7	13.4	5.4	2.3
GFY, Asda*	½ Pack/200g	176	88	1.9	17.0	1.4	0.0
Iceland*	1 Serving/230g	196	85	2.0	17.0	1.0	2.0
Instant, Tesco*	1 Serving/60g	206	343	7.3	76.2	1.0	5.8
Spring Onion, Iceland*	1 Serving/230g	209	91	2.0	14.0	3.0	3.0
With Butter, Old	1oz/28g	29	104	1.8	15.5	4.3	1.1
With Margarine, Old	1oz/28g	29	104	1.8	15.5	4.3	1.1
POTATO - ROAST,							
Baby, Finest, Tesco*	½ Pack/150g	149	99	3.6	15.1	2.7	1.4
COU, M & S*	½ Pack/150g	158	105	2.2	18.1	2.6	3.3
Crispy, Aunt Bessie's*	1 Serving/83g	154	185	2.3	22.9	9.3	1.8
Deep Fried, McCain*	1oz/28g	47	167	3.0	22.5	7.2	0.0
Garlic, Somerfield*	1 Pack/320g	422	132	2.0	20.0	5.0	0.0
Home Roasts, Crispy, McCain*	1 Serving/75g	95	126	2.2	23.6	3.6	0.0
Oven Baked, McCain*	1oz/28g	31	109	2.6	21.6	1.4	0.0
Oven Ready, Budgens*	1 Serving/180g	184	102	2.0	21.7	0.8	2.1
¼ Cut, Deep Fried, McCain*	1oz/28g	45	161	3.1	22.5	6.5	0.0
¼ Cut, Oven Baked, McCain*	1oz/28g	42	149	3.5	25.9	3.5	0.0
POTATO - SKINS,							
¼ Cut, Deep Fried, McCain*	1oz/28g	52	186	3.0	30.1	6.0	0.0
¼ Cut, Oven Baked, McCain*	1oz/28g	53	190	3.7	33.1	4.8	0.0
Cheese & Bacon, Tesco*	1 Serving/95g	241	254	9.2	19.5	15.5	3.0
Loaded, New York Style, Tesco*	1 Burger/35g	89	254	9.2	19.5	15.5	3.0
Loaded, With Soured Cream, M & S*	½ Pack/150g	308	205	9.1	15.8	11.9	0.9
POTATO - SLICES,							
Crispy, M & S*	1oz/28g	55	195	3.2	20.2	11.3	2.8
Garlic & Herb, Heinz*	1oz/28g	23	82	1.7	10.2	3.9	0.7
Tomato & Red Pepper, Heinz*	1 Serving/250g	168	67	1.8	11.3	1.6	1.0
POTATO - SMILES,							
Deep Fried, McCain*	1oz/28g	64	227	3.7	31.3	9.7	0.0
Oven Baked, McCain*	1oz/28g	62	220	3.9	31.9	8.6	0.0
POTATO - WAFFLES,							

P

	Measure WEIGHT/INFO	per Measure KCAL	Nutrition Values per 100g / 100ml KCAL	PROT	CARB	FAT	FIBRE
POTAT - WAFFLES,							
Bird's Eye*	1 Waffle/56g	94	167	2.0	20.7	8.5	1.5
Deep Fried, Mini, McCain*	1oz/28g	64	227	3.8	31.2	9.7	0.0
Farmfoods*	1 Waffle/56g	146	260	2.3	25.9	16.3	2.0
Findus*	1 Waffle/55g	94	170	2.9	25.7	6.2	0.0
Frozen, Cooked	1oz/28g	56	200	3.2	30.3	8.2	2.3
Frozen, Grilled, Asda*	1 Waffle/57g	104	183	2.0	21.0	10.1	1.7
Kitchen Range Foods*	1oz/28g	35	125	1.1	22.9	3.8	0.0
Mini, Farmfoods*	1oz/28g	41	145	1.9	21.6	5.7	1.7
Mini, Tesco*	1 Waffle/15g	23	151	1.9	21.6	6.3	1.6
Oven Baked, Mini, McCain*	1oz/28g	62	221	3.9	32.0	8.6	0.0
Safeway*	1 Waffle/52g	120	230	2.5	23.8	13.6	2.0
Tesco*	1 Waffle/56g	97	174	2.4	23.8	7.7	0.8
POTATO - WEDGES,							
& Dip, M & S*	1 Pack/450g	698	155	2.5	20.4	7.4	1.8
& Italian Style Tomato Sauce, COU, M & S*	½ Pack/200g	180	90	3.1	15.4	1.7	1.8
Asda*	1 Wedge/40g	57	142	3.4	21.0	4.9	1.7
Chunky, McCain*	10 Wedges/175g	242	138	2.4	23.3	4.7	0.0
Co-Op*	1oz/28g	38	135	2.0	20.0	6.0	2.0
Garlic & Herb, COU, M & S*	1 Pack/300g	300	100	2.3	16.4	2.6	3.2
Garlic & Herb, Kitchen Range Foods*	1oz/28g	42	151	1.6	18.5	7.8	0.0
In BBQ Sauce, Micro, McCain*	1 Box/200g	234	117	2.2	23.5	2.4	0.0
Kentucky Fried Chicken*	1 Portion/135g	279	207	3.7	20.7	9.6	3.7
New York Style, HE, Tesco*	½ Pack/125g	124	99	2.3	16.4	2.7	1.3
Savoury, McCain*	1 Serving/200g	300	150	2.9	22.7	6.2	0.0
Savoury, Waitrose*	1/3 Bag/250g	350	140	2.3	22.9	4.3	1.9
Southern Fried, Asda*	1 Serving/188g	263	140	2.9	23.0	4.0	1.8
Southern Fried, Farmfoods*	1oz/28g	49	174	2.7	23.2	7.8	2.2
Southern Fried Style, Tesco*	1 Serving/155g	233	150	3.0	14.1	9.1	2.0
Spicy, Asda*	1 Serving/100g	145	145	1.8	21.8	5.7	2.1
Spicy, Deep Fried, McCain*	1oz/28g	52	187	3.6	27.3	8.1	0.0
Spicy, M & S*	½ Pack/225g	349	155	2.4	21.8	6.5	1.3
Spicy, Occasions, Sainsbury's*	1 Serving/100g	144	144	2.5	23.7	4.3	0.4
Spicy, Oven Baked, McCain*	1oz/28g	61	219	4.2	34.8	8.4	0.0
Spicy, Simple Solutions, Tesco*	1 Serving/150g	141	94	4.6	12.2	3.0	1.4
Tesco*	1 Serving/110g	135	123	3.0	18.4	4.2	1.5
With Broccoli & Mozzerella Cheese, Weight Watchers*	1 Pack/320g	294	92	3.1	13.3	3.0	1.0
With Soured Cream & Chive Dip, Safeway*	1 Pack/450g	639	142	3.1	22.1	4.6	2.1
POTATOES IN,							
Herb Marinade, New, Tesco*	1 Serving/90g	73	81	2.4	13.0	2.1	0.3
POTATOES WITH,							
Butter & Herbs, Baby, Sainsbury's*	¼ Pack/141g	135	96	1.4	14.7	3.5	1.5
Butter, Parsley, Chives & Mint, New, M & S*	1 Serving/100g	80	80	1.6	9.7	3.7	1.5
Herb Butter, Baby, Safeway*	1 Serving/200g	158	79	1.4	15.6	1.2	1.4
Parsley Butter, New, TTD, Sainsbury's*	1 Serving/150g	126	84	2.2	13.3	2.4	1.0
Sunblush Tomato, New, M & S*	1 Pack/385g	347	90	1.6	17.2	1.8	1.3
POUSSIN, Raw, Meat & Skin	1oz/28g	65	232	1.8	34.9	10.0	1.0
PRAWN COCKTAIL,							
Asda*	1oz/28g	124	443	8.6	3.3	43.6	0.0
Better For You, Morrisons*	1 Serving/100g	149	149	4.7	9.7	10.3	0.1
BGTY, Sainsbury's*	1oz/28g	45	160	7.5	2.3	13.4	0.5
COU, M & S*	1oz/28g	24	85	11.6	4.9	2.2	0.5
Light, Asda*	1oz/28g	45	160	9.9	4.8	11.2	0.0
M & S*	1oz/28g	97	345	8.7	3.0	33.1	1.2
Reduced Fat, M & S*	1oz/28g	43	152	9.1	2.9	11.6	1.1

P

	Measure WEIGHT/INFO	per Measure KCAL	KCAL	PROT	CARB	FAT	FIBRE
			Nutrition Values per 100g / 100ml				
PRAWN COCKTAIL,							
Reduced Fat, Tesco*	1 Serving/200g	304	152	7.6	6.5	10.6	0.4
Reduced Fat, Waitrose*	1oz/28g	63	225	5.7	6.6	22.9	1.3
Safeway*	½ Pot/100g	373	373	7.6	3.4	36.5	0.2
Tesco*	1 Tub/200g	834	417	7.3	3.5	41.5	0.1
PRAWN CRACKERS,							
Asda*	1 Serving/25g	134	535	2.0	53.0	35.0	0.0
M & S*	1 Pack/15g	83	550	3.0	62.3	32.0	0.0
Sainsbury's*	1 Cracker/3g	16	537	2.4	60.4	31.7	0.8
Tesco*	1/3 Pack/20g	114	568	3.7	44.0	41.9	0.5
Uncooked, Sharwood's*	1oz/28g	136	487	0.7	52.7	29.7	1.7
PRAWN Layered Salad, M & S*	1 Pack/450g	338	75	4.1	10.0	2.3	0.7
PRAWN SHELLS, Shapers, Boots*	1 Bag/21g	98	469	6.6	68.0	19.0	1.6
PRAWN TOAST,							
Dim Sum Selection, Sainsbury's*	1 Toast/8g	23	283	9.9	19.2	18.5	2.0
M & S Party Food*	1 Toast/13g	36	280	11.5	18.4	18.1	2.2
M & S*	1oz/28g	78	280	11.5	18.4	18.1	2.2
PRAWNS,							
& Mushroom Provencale With Pasta, COU, M & S*	1 Pack/400g	360	90	5.9	15.7	0.5	0.0
& Noodles In Sweet Chilli Sauce, COU, M & S*	1 Pack/400g	340	85	4.8	14.7	1.1	1.2
Batter Crisp, Lyons*	1 Pack/160g	350	219	8.0	18.2	12.7	1.1
Bhuna Indian Tandoori, Sainsbury's*	½ Pack/200g	152	76	5.5	4.5	4.0	1.7
Black Tiger, Raw, Asda*	1oz/28g	20	71	17.4	0.0	0.1	0.0
Boiled	1 Prawn/3g	3	99	22.6	0.0	0.9	0.0
Brine, John West*	½ Can/60g	58	97	21.0	1.0	1.0	0.0
Chilli & Coriander, M & S*	1 Serving/70g	67	95	17.9	0.6	2.2	0.6
Chilli, Battered, M & S*	1oz/28g	63	225	7.2	23.8	11.5	0.5
Chilli, M & S*	1oz/28g	22	79	17.9	0.6	0.5	0.6
Chinese, Oriental Express*	1 Serving/320g	218	68	3.2	13.8	0.6	1.9
Cocktail, M & S*	1oz/28g	27	95	20.2	0.0	1.2	0.0
Cold Water, Finest, Tesco*	1oz/28g	18	66	14.3	0.1	0.2	0.1
Cooked & Peeled, Frozen, Tesco*	1 Serving/100g	99	99	22.6	0.0	0.9	0.0
Cooked & Peeled, Somerfield*	1oz/28g	18	66	14.0	0.0	1.0	0.0
Cooked & Peeled, Tesco*	1 Serving/75g	54	72	15.6	1.0	0.6	0.1
Dried	1oz/28g	79	281	62.4	0.0	3.5	0.0
Extra Large, Frozen, North Atlantic, TTD, Sainsbury's*	1 Serving/106g	82	77	17.0	0.1	1.0	0.1
Extra Large, M & S*	1oz/28g	27	97	21.0	0.2	1.4	0.0
Hot & Spicy, Lyons*	1oz/28g	89	318	11.0	26.1	18.9	2.8
Iceland*	1 Serving/100g	104	104	22.8	0.0	1.3	0.0
In Creamy Garlic Sauce, Youngs*	1 Serving/158g	261	165	8.5	0.3	14.5	0.0
King, Jumbo, M & S*	1 Serving/80g	56	70	13.9	0.0	1.8	0.0
King, Large, Honduran, M & S*	1 Pack/140g	98	70	15.1	0.2	0.9	0.0
King, M & S*	1oz/28g	19	68	15.2	0.0	0.8	0.0
King, Peeled, M & S*	1oz/28g	19	69	15.1	0.2	0.9	0.0
King, Sainsbury's*	1 Serving/70g	47	67	14.9	0.1	0.8	0.0
King, Tiger, Cooked & Peeled, Tesco*	½ Pack/125g	96	77	17.5	0.3	0.6	0.0
Morrisons*	1 Serving/100g	77	77	17.0	0.0	1.0	0.0
North Atlantic, Farmfoods*	1oz/28g	17	60	14.0	0.0	0.4	0.0
North Atlantic, M & S*	½ Pack/100g	95	95	20.0	0.0	1.6	0.0
Peeled, Sainsbury's*	1 Serving/125g	85	68	16.0	0.1	0.4	0.1
Peeled, Youngs*	1oz/28g	28	99	22.6	0.0	0.9	0.0
Raw, Weighed Whole With Shell	1oz/28g	21	76	17.6	0.0	0.6	0.0
Small, Sainsbury's*	1oz/28g	22	77	17.0	0.1	1.0	0.1
Spicy Thai, Tesco*	1 Serving/100g	77	77	13.0	1.7	2.0	0.3
Sweet Chilli Sauce, Asda*	1 Pack/360g	500	139	4.1	15.0	6.9	0.3

PRAWNS,	Measure WEIGHT/INFO	per Measure KCAL	Nutrition Values per 100g / 100ml KCAL	PROT	CARB	FAT	FIBRE
Sweet Chilli, Tesco*	1 Pack/300g	633	211	6.7	21.9	10.8	1.2
Sweet Chilli, With Rice, Tesco*	1 Pack/460g	488	106	2.4	19.2	2.2	0.5
Thai, M & S*	1oz/28g	29	103	5.2	13.6	3.1	1.3
Tiger, Cooked & Peeled, Somerfield*	1 Pack/180g	122	68	15.0	0.0	1.0	0.0
Tiger, Cooked, Asda*	1oz/28g	30	107	22.6	0.0	1.8	0.0
Tiger, Japanese Noodle Box, M & S*	1 Box/300g	330	110	5.8	16.0	2.7	1.6
Tiger, Jumbo, M & S*	1oz/28g	27	95	22.8	0.6	0.1	0.0
Tiger, Jumbo, Sainsbury's*	1 Serving/250g	168	67	14.9	0.1	0.8	0.0
Tiger, M & S*	1oz/28g	19	69	15.1	0.2	0.9	0.0
Tiger, Raw, Safeway*	1 Serving/100g	67	67	14.9	0.0	0.8	0.0
Tiger, Sainsbury's*	1 Pack/250g	168	67	14.9	0.1	0.8	0.1
Tiger, Tesco*	1oz/28g	19	67	14.5	0.0	1.0	0.0
Tiger, Whole Raw, Asda*	1oz/28g	11	41	8.6	0.0	0.7	0.0
Tiger, Wrapped, M & S*	1 Pack/190g	477	251	11.3	20.7	13.6	1.3
PREMIUM Crumpets, Safeway*	1 Serving/60g	111	185	7.5	36.3	1.1	2.4
PREMIUM Frozen Seafood Collection, Tesco*	1 Serving/100g	70	70	12.2	2.4	1.3	0.0
PRETZELS,							
American Style, Salted, Sainsbury's*	1 Serving/50g	191	381	9.6	81.8	4.0	5.2
Ham & Cheese, COU, M & S*	1 Pack/136g	245	180	15.3	24.5	2.4	1.4
Lightly Salted, Tesco*	1 Serving/25g	99	395	9.3	73.4	7.1	5.5
Mini, Eat Smart, Safeway*	1 Bag/25g	90	360	9.6	79.7	2.5	5.5
New York Style, Shapers, Boots*	1 Bag/24g	94	391	11.0	81.0	2.5	3.8
Salt & Cracked Black Pepper, COU, M & S*	1 Pack/25g	95	380	9.7	83.3	2.4	2.7
Selection Tray, M & S*	1oz/28g	112	401	9.7	75.5	6.7	3.4
Sour Cream & Onion, Tesco*	1 Serving/25g	114	457	8.4	67.7	17.0	2.3
PRINGLES,							
Barbecue, Pringles*	1 Serving/50g	267	533	4.9	48.0	36.0	5.1
Cheese & Onion, Pringles*	1 Serving/50g	266	532	4.5	47.0	36.0	4.9
Curry, Pringles*	1 Serving/50g	266	531	5.2	46.0	36.0	3.4
Original, Pringles*	1 Serving/50g	274	547	4.7	47.0	38.0	5.1
Paprika, Pringles*	1 Serving/50g	268	535	5.7	46.0	36.0	5.0
Pizza, Pringles*	1 Serving/50g	268	536	5.1	43.0	37.0	4.8
Salt & Vinegar, Pringles*	1 Serving/50g	265	530	4.5	47.0	36.0	4.8
Sour Cream & Onion, Pringles*	1 Serving/50g	270	539	5.3	46.0	37.0	4.9
Sour Cream & Onion, Right, Pringles*	1 Serving/50g	233	466	5.4	56.0	25.0	4.6
PROBIOTIC Drink, Orange, Health, Tesco*	1 Serving/100g	67	67	1.5	13.4	0.9	1.3
PROFITEROLES,							
Classic French, Sainsbury's*	1 Serving/90g	264	293	6.0	32.2	15.5	0.1
Dairy Cream, Co-Op*	¼ Pack/70g	242	345	6.0	24.0	25.0	0.5
Large, Dairy Cream, Farmfoods*	1oz/28g	95	340	5.2	27.5	23.2	0.6
Somerfield*	1 Serving/100g	273	273	5.0	31.0	14.0	0.0
PROMITE, Master Foods Asia Pacific*	1 Serving/5g	9	170	15.9	25.2	1.7	0.0
PROVAMEL*,							
Banana Flavour Soya Alternative To Milk	½ Pint/284	213	75	3.6	10.5	2.1	1.2
Black Cherry Yofu	1 Pot/125g	106	85	3.7	12.9	2.1	1.2
Chocolate Dessert,	1 Dessert/100g	105	105	1.2	10.2	6.6	0.0
Chocolate Soya Dessert	1 Pot/125g	116	93	3.0	14.9	2.3	1.3
Fruits Of The Forest Soya Dessert	1 Serving/125g	98	78	3.0	11.9	1.8	0.3
Hazelnut Soya Dessert	1 Pot/125g	126	101	3.0	16.0	2.8	1.2
Peach & Mango Yofu, Organic	1 Pot/125g	116	93	3.7	14.7	2.1	1.2
Peach & Pear Flavour Yofu, Junior	1 Pot/125g	105	84	3.8	12.4	2.2	0.0
Peach Yofu	1 Pot/125g	109	87	3.8	13.3	2.1	1.2
Red Cherry Yofu, Organic	1 Pot/125g	116	93	3.7	14.8	2.1	1.2
Soya Alternative To Milk	½ Pint/284ml	102	36	3.6	0.6	2.1	1.2

PROVAMEL*,	Measure WEIGHT/INFO	per Measure KCAL	Nutrition Values per 100g / 100ml KCAL	PROT	CARB	FAT	FIBRE
Soya Alternative To Milk, No Added Sugar Or Salt	1 Carton/500ml	180	36	3.6	0.6	2.1	1.0
Soya Alternative To Milk, Organic	1 Carton/500ml	255	51	3.6	4.3	2.1	1.0
Soya Dream	1 Carton/250ml	445	178	3.0	1.7	17.7	1.1
Strawberry & Banana Flavour Yofu, Junior	1 Pot/125g	106	85	3.8	12.7	2.2	0.0
Strawberry Flavour Soya Alternative To Milk	1 Carton/250ml	160	64	3.6	7.7	2.1	1.2
Strawberry Ice Dessert,	1 Dessert/100g	103	103	1.2	10.7	6.2	0.0
Strawberry Yofu	1 Pot/125g	106	85	3.8	12.6	2.1	1.3
Vanilla Flavour Organic Soya Dessert	1oz/28g	29	105	3.0	19.1	1.8	1.0
Vanilla Flavour Yofu	1 Pot/125g	96	77	4.1	10.0	2.3	1.3
Vanilla Soya Dessert	1 Pot/125g	108	86	3.0	14.4	1.8	1.0
Yofu, Organic	1oz/28g	15	53	4.5	2.8	2.6	1.5
PROVENCAL Chicken, Steam Cuisine, M & S*	1oz/28g	34	120	9.6	12.7	3.8	1.4
PRUNE JUICE, Pure, Tesco*	1 Glass/250ml	180	72	0.7	16.8	0.1	1.2
PRUNES,							
Agen, Snack Pack, M & S*	1 Pack/50g	98	195	1.4	46.7	0.3	4.1
Breakfast, In Fruit Juice, Sainsbury's*	1 Serving/130g	113	87	1.1	20.7	0.1	1.1
Californian, In Syrup, Safeway*	1 Serving/104g	98	94	0.8	22.4	0.1	1.9
Californian, Tesco*	1 Serving/30g	45	149	2.5	33.9	0.4	5.7
Canned In Juice	1oz/28g	22	79	0.7	19.7	0.2	2.4
Canned In Syrup	1oz/28g	25	90	0.6	23.0	0.2	2.8
Dried, M & S*	1oz/28g	68	244	2.3	62.3	0.1	4.2
French, Waitrose*	1 Serving/40g	60	149	2.5	33.9	0.4	5.7
In Apple Juice, Tesco*	1 Can/213g	198	93	0.7	22.0	0.2	2.4
Large, Waitrose*	1oz/28g	47	169	2.8	38.4	0.5	6.5
Pitted, Organic, Waitrose*	1oz/28g	47	169	2.8	38.4	0.5	6.5
Raw, Fresh	1oz/28g	45	160	2.8	38.4	0.5	6.5
Stewed With Sugar	1oz/28g	29	103	1.3	25.5	0.2	3.1
Stewed Without Sugar	1oz/28g	23	81	1.4	19.5	0.3	3.3
Sweet, Pitted, Stoneless, Asda*	1 Pack/50g	75	149	2.5	34.0	0.3	6.0
With Stones, Ready to Eat, Tesco*	1 Serving/50g	64	128	2.1	29.2	0.3	4.9
PUDDING, (SEE ALSO PUDDING TYPES - EG. SPONGE)							
Apple & Blackberry Crumble, Custard Style, Somerfield*	1oz/28g	34	123	3.0	17.0	5.0	0.0
Apple Pie Custard Style, Somerfield*	1oz/28g	34	123	3.0	17.0	5.0	0.0
Banana Fudge Crunch, Bird's*	1oz/28g	125	445	5.4	75.0	14.0	0.8
Blackberry & Bramley Apple, M & S*	¼ Pudding/152g	365	240	3.3	38.2	8.2	2.0
Bread	1oz/28g	83	297	5.9	49.7	9.6	1.2
Chocolate, BGTY, Sainsbury's*	1 Pudding/110g	293	266	4.7	51.5	4.7	0.6
Chocolate, GFY, Asda*	1 Pudding/124g	274	221	4.4	42.0	3.9	2.7
Chocolate, Perfectly Balanced, Waitrose*	1 Serving/105g	196	187	3.8	36.0	3.1	0.8
Chocolate With Chocolate Sauce, Heinz*	¼ Can/77g	213	277	2.1	47.2	8.8	0.8
Christmas, Traditional, M & S*	1/8 Pudding/113g	345	305	3.4	62.8	5.4	1.9
Lemon Crunch , Bird's*	1oz/28g	125	445	5.5	74.0	14.0	0.7
Lemon, M & S*	1 Pudding/105g	328	312	4.3	39.4	15.2	2.3
Lemon, Perfectly Balanced, Waitrose*	1 Serving/105g	212	202	3.4	41.7	2.4	0.6
Lemon, Sainsbury's*	1 Pudding/110g	304	276	3.4	41.4	10.8	0.6
Macaroni, Creamed, Ambrosia*	1 Can/425g	374	88	3.6	14.6	1.7	0.3
Pudding Mix, Chocolate Crunch, Bird's*	1oz/28g	125	445	6.3	72.5	14.0	1.0
Queen of Puddings	1oz/28g	60	213	4.8	33.1	7.8	0.2
Rhubarb Crumble Custard Style, Somerfield*	1oz/28g	33	119	3.0	16.0	5.0	0.0
Rich Chocolate, Tryton Foods*	1oz/28g	76	273	4.7	41.7	9.5	1.8
Sticky Toffee & Sticky Toffee Sauce, BGTY, Sainsbury's*	1 Serving/130g	319	245	5.0	49.3	4.1	2.2
Sticky Toffee, Bread, M & S*	1oz/28g	83	295	4.1	46.3	10.6	2.2
Sticky Toffee, Co-Op*	¼ Pudding/100g	355	355	3.0	40.0	20.0	0.7
Sticky Toffee, Farmfoods*	¼ Pudding/186g	627	337	4.1	65.7	6.4	0.3

P

	Measure WEIGHT/INFO	per Measure KCAL	Nutrition Values per 100g / 100ml KCAL	PROT	CARB	FAT	FIBRE
PUDDING,							
Sticky Toffee, M & S*	1 Pudding/105g	337	321	3.5	51.9	11.0	1.1
Sticky Toffee, Tryton Foods*	1oz/28g	88	314	3.7	62.7	5.4	1.0
Sticky Toffee, With Custard, Somerfield*	1 Pack/245g	576	235	3.0	38.0	8.0	0.0
Strawberry Jam With Custard, Farmfoods*	1 Serving/145g	525	362	3.2	35.5	23.9	0.9
Summer Fruit, Co-Op*	1 Pack/260g	273	105	1.0	25.0	0.2	1.0
Summer Fruit, M & S*	1oz/28g	25	90	2.0	20.9	0.2	4.1
Summer Fruit, Tesco*	1 Serving/100g	72	72	1.3	16.3	0.2	2.9
Summer Pudding, BGTY, Sainsbury's*	1 Pot/110g	223	203	3.2	40.9	4.6	2.4
Summer Pudding, HE, Tesco*	1 Serving/100g	89	89	1.9	19.1	0.6	2.2
Summer Pudding, Safeway*	1 Pudding/135g	196	145	2.5	32.9	0.4	3.1
Summer Pudding, Waitrose*	1 Pot/120g	125	104	2.0	23.1	0.4	1.4
Summerfruit, HE, Tesco*	1 Pudding/100g	72	72	1.3	16.3	0.2	2.9
Summerfruit, Somerfield*	1 Pudding/110g	306	278	3.0	42.0	11.0	0.0
Syrup, Individual, Co-Op*	1 Pudding/170g	604	355	3.0	38.0	21.0	1.0
Syrup, M & S*	1 Serving/105g	370	352	3.9	61.7	10.0	0.8
PULSES, Mixed In Water, Sainsbury's*	½ Can/120g	131	109	8.7	13.6	2.2	4.6
PUMPKIN,							
Boiled In Salted Water	1oz/28g	4	13	0.6	2.1	0.3	1.1
Raw	1oz/28g	4	13	0.7	2.2	0.2	1.0
Seeds	1oz/28g	159	569	24.4	15.2	45.6	5.3
Seeds, Organic, Evernat*	1oz/28g	158	565	24.4	15.2	45.6	5.3

	Measure WEIGHT/INFO	per Measure KCAL	Nutrition Values per 100g / 100ml KCAL	PROT	CARB	FAT	FIBRE
QUALITY STREET,							
Nestle*	1 Serving/25g	117	466	4.0	66.0	20.7	0.8
QUAVERS,							
Cheese, Walkers*	1 Bag/20g	103	515	3.0	61.0	29.0	1.2
Prawn Cocktail, Walkers*	1 Bag/20g	102	510	2.6	61.0	28.0	1.2
Salt & Vinegar, Walkers*	1 Bag/20g	100	500	2.3	58.0	29.0	1.1
QUICHE,							
Baby Spinach & Gruyere, Sainsbury's*	¼ Quiche/93g	228	245	7.4	15.1	17.2	1.0
Bacon & Cheese, Pork Farms*	1 Pack/120g	378	315	11.1	20.8	20.0	0.0
Bacon & Leek, Asda*	¼ Quiche/109g	311	285	9.0	15.0	21.0	0.8
Bacon & Tomato, Good Intentions, Somerfield*	1 Serving/145g	255	176	5.7	5.1	14.8	0.1
Bacon & Tomato, Safeway*	¼ Quiche/100g	287	287	8.6	20.3	19.0	1.4
Bacon, Leek & Mushroom, M & S*	¼ Quiche/100g	250	250	8.7	14.2	17.9	2.1
Broccoli & Cheese, Healthy Choice, Safeway*	1oz/28g	49	176	7.8	18.3	10.0	1.8
Broccoli & Tomato, M & S*	1oz/28g	59	210	6.7	14.7	13.8	1.6
Broccoli, Extra Value, Tesco*	1 Serving/125g	341	273	10.0	15.1	19.2	0.8
Broccoli, HE, Tesco*	1 Quiche/175g	308	176	6.7	21.5	7.0	1.4
Broccoli, Tesco*	1 Quiche/175g	340	194	7.0	20.9	9.2	1.4
Broccoli, Tomato & Cheese, BGTY, Sainsbury's*	1 Quiche/390g	632	162	6.4	15.7	8.2	1.3
Broccoli, Tomato & Cheese, Sainsbury's*	1 Serving/125g	274	219	6.1	15.5	14.7	1.3
Cheese & Bacon, HE, Tesco*	1 Serving/155g	307	198	9.1	19.9	9.1	1.4
Cheese & Bacon, SmartPrice, Asda*	¼ Quiche/82g	208	257	6.0	20.0	17.0	0.7
Cheese & Bacon, Tesco*	¼ Quiche/100g	324	324	10.5	16.4	24.0	1.7
Cheese & Broccoli, Good Intentions, Somerfield*	1 Quiche/145g	229	158	2.4	17.8	8.6	0.8
Cheese & Chive, HE, Tesco*	1 Serving/86g	169	197	10.4	22.1	7.4	1.2
Cheese & Egg	1oz/28g	88	314	12.5	17.3	22.2	0.6
Cheese & Ham, Basics, Somerfield*	¼ Quiche/81g	187	231	7.0	20.1	13.6	0.7
Cheese & Ham, Sainsbury's*	1 Serving/100g	266	266	9.3	14.4	19.0	1.2
Cheese & Ham, Somerfield*	1 Quiche/325g	835	257	7.0	18.0	18.0	0.0
Cheese & Mushroom, Budgens*	½ Quiche/170g	474	279	7.8	18.4	19.3	1.4
Cheese & Onion, M & S*	1oz/28g	76	270	7.9	16.4	19.0	1.2
Cheese & Onion, Mini, Somerfield*	1oz/28g	110	394	9.0	27.0	28.0	0.0
Cheese & Onion, Safeway*	1 Serving/310g	797	257	7.2	25.2	14.2	0.0
Cheese & Onion, Sainsbury's*	1 Quiche/390g	956	245	8.0	15.0	17.0	0.9
Cheese & Onion, Somerfield*	1 Quiche/300g	696	232	8.0	14.0	16.0	0.0
Cheese & Onion, Value, Tesco*	½ Quiche/200g	526	263	8.6	16.1	18.2	0.7
Cheese & Onion, Waitrose*	1 Serving/85g	182	214	6.4	13.9	14.8	3.6
Cheese & Tomato, Asda*	¼ Quiche/105g	274	261	8.0	19.0	17.0	0.9
Cheese & Tomato, M & S*	1 Serving/100g	230	230	7.7	15.1	15.6	1.6
Cheese & Tomato, Morrisons*	½ Quiche/64g	195	304	7.3	22.8	20.5	1.0
Cheese & Tomato, Somerfield*	1 Quiche/135g	416	308	10.0	23.0	19.0	0.0
Cheese, Broccoli & Tomato, Nisa Heritage*	1 Serving/85g	234	275	7.3	17.5	19.5	1.4
Cheese, Onion & Chive, HE, Tesco*	1 Slice/100g	202	202	10.9	21.2	8.2	1.3
Cheese, Onion & Chive, SmartPrice, Asda*	¼ Quiche/83g	213	257	6.0	20.0	17.0	0.7
Cheese, Onion & Chive, Somerfield*	1oz/28g	87	310	9.0	16.0	23.0	0.0
Cheese, Onion & Chive, Tesco*	1oz/28g	90	320	10.6	15.5	24.0	0.6
Cheese Potato & Onion, Safeway*	1/3 Quiche/115g	361	314	8.8	24.1	20.3	1.5
Chicken & Basil, Finest, Tesco*	1 Serving/134g	381	284	9.3	19.8	18.6	1.3
Chicken & Mushroom, Somerfield*	1oz/28g	90	320	12.0	22.0	21.0	0.0
Cumberland Sausage & Onion, Sainsbury's*	1 Serving/180g	486	270	7.0	18.8	18.5	1.3
Egg, Bacon & Cheese, Iceland*	1 Serving/90g	299	332	7.7	23.5	23.0	1.9
Gammon, Leek & Cheddar Cheese, Somerfield*	¼ Quiche/95g	251	264	7.6	19.9	17.1	0.9
Goats Cheese & Red Pepper, Tesco*	1 Serving/87g	271	312	5.8	19.2	23.6	0.9
Ham & Mustard, GFY, Asda*	1 Quiche/155g	327	211	9.0	19.0	11.0	3.9
Ham & Tomato, M & S*	½ Pack/200g	440	220	8.1	12.4	15.5	2.9

Q

QUICHE,,	Measure WEIGHT/INFO	per Measure KCAL	KCAL	PROT	CARB	FAT	FIBRE
Leek & Sweet Potato, Waitrose*	½ Quiche/200g	440	220	5.3	17.0	14.5	2.3
Leek, Cheese & Chive, Sainsbury's*	1/3 Quiche/125g	293	234	7.1	14.9	16.2	1.3
Lorraine	1oz/28g	109	391	16.1	19.8	28.1	0.7
Lorraine, Asda*	1 Serving/106g	318	300	9.0	21.0	20.0	2.3
Lorraine, BGTY, Sainsbury's*	1 Serving/128g	273	213	10.9	17.7	10.9	0.7
Lorraine, Budgens*	1 Pack/180g	520	289	8.2	25.6	17.1	0.8
Lorraine, Co-Op*	1/3 Quiche/108g	313	290	11.0	20.0	21.0	3.0
Lorraine, Finest, Tesco*	1 Serving/100g	330	330	8.4	17.5	25.1	1.5
Lorraine, HE, New Improved Recipe, Tesco*	¼ Quiche/100g	202	202	13.0	20.9	7.4	1.3
Lorraine, Improved Recipe, M & S*	1oz/28g	78	280	12.5	14.9	18.9	0.9
Lorraine, Individual, M & S*	1 Serving/170g	544	320	13.1	14.4	23.2	1.9
Lorraine, Individual, Sainsbury'*	1 Quiche/180g	540	300	10.9	18.7	20.2	1.2
Lorraine, Large, Somerfield*	¼ Quiche/81g	223	275	11.0	19.0	17.0	0.0
Lorraine, M & S*	1oz/28g	85	305	13.7	12.0	22.5	0.9
Lorraine, Mini, M & S*	1oz/28g	95	340	11.6	21.0	23.6	1.6
Lorraine, Sainsbury's*	1/3 Quiche/128g	341	265	9.3	14.4	19.0	0.9
Lorraine, Tesco*	1 Serving/81g	262	324	9.8	18.4	23.5	0.8
Lorraine, Waitrose*	¼ Flan/90g	306	340	10.0	15.5	26.4	0.7
Mature Cheddar & Slow Roasted Onion, M & S*	½ Pack/200g	560	280	8.2	16.7	20.0	1.2
Mediterranean, M & S*	1oz/28g	64	230	6.6	16.6	15.3	0.9
Mediterranean Vegetable, BGTY, Sainsbury's*	1/3 Quiche/133g	321	241	6.3	14.6	17.5	2.2
Mediterranean Vegetable, Mini, M & S*	1oz/28g	78	280	6.8	23.9	17.5	1.6
Mushroom	1oz/28g	80	284	10.0	18.3	19.5	0.9
Mushroom, M & S*	¼ Quiche/100g	235	235	6.1	14.6	16.7	2.8
Mushroom Medley, Waitrose*	¼ Quiche/100g	222	222	6.4	15.0	15.2	2.9
Mushroom, Safeway*	¼ Quiche/82g	192	234	6.7	18.2	15.0	2.0
Mushroom, Somerfield*	¼ Quiche/82g	212	258	9.0	20.0	16.0	0.0
Roasted Mediterranean Vegetable, M & S*	1oz/28g	62	220	5.6	14.5	15.3	1.3
Salmon & Asparagus, HE, Tesco*	1 Quiche/345g	621	180	7.5	20.2	7.7	1.2
Salmon & Broccoli, Asda*	¼ Quiche/106g	289	273	10.0	20.0	17.0	2.6
Salmon & Broccoli, Budgens*	½ Quiche/187g	539	288	11.2	17.7	19.1	0.6
Salmon & Broccoli, Tesco*	1 Serving/133g	355	267	8.8	17.0	18.0	1.8
Smoked Ham, Cream Cheese & Chive, Sainsbury's*	1 Quiche/180g	421	234	7.7	18.7	14.3	1.2
Smoked Salmon & Spinach, Asda*	1 Serving/83g	212	256	10.0	18.0	16.0	1.0
Spicy Meat Feast, Sainsbury's*	1 Serving/188g	425	226	6.7	14.6	15.6	1.3
Spinach & Gruyere, Mini, Somerfield*	1oz/28g	108	384	11.0	25.0	27.0	0.0
Spinach & Ricotta, M & S*	1oz/28g	73	260	8.0	14.9	18.8	1.7
Spinach & Ricotta, Safeway*	¼ Quiche/85g	193	227	7.9	22.6	11.7	1.7
Spinach, Ricotta & Gruyere Slice, Somerfield*	1 Slice/130g	348	268	7.0	15.0	20.0	0.0
Spinach Ricotta Cheese & Red Pepper, Safeway*	1 Serving/120g	304	253	6.2	20.2	16.4	1.2
Summer Vegetable, M & S*	¼ Quiche/100g	225	225	4.9	14.5	16.5	1.7
Sweet Cherry Pepper & Fontal Cheese, Finest, Tesco*	¼ Slice/100g	293	293	6.7	16.9	22.1	0.9
Tomato & Cheese, Sainsbury's*	1/3 Quiche/133g	374	281	7.9	20.9	18.4	1.5
Tomato, Broccoli & Cheese, Sainsbury's*	1 Serving/180g	437	243	6.7	19.6	15.3	1.5
Tomato, Cheese & Courgette, Asda*	1 Quiche/100g	333	333	11.0	34.0	17.0	5.0
Tomato Cheese & Courgette, GFY, Asda*	1 Serving/155g	333	215	7.0	22.0	11.0	3.3
Tuna, Tomato & Basil, Asda*	1 Serving/125g	305	244	9.0	16.0	16.0	1.5
Vegetable, Tesco*	1 Serving/100g	257	257	6.9	17.5	17.7	1.5
QUICK SNACK,							
Chicken & Mushroom Flavour, Value Tesco*	1 Pot/80g	274	342	14.9	60.6	4.5	7.0
Mash, Roasted Onion, Sainsburys*	1 pot/58g	75	130	1.8	14.8	7.1	0.0
Rice, Chilli, Sainsbury's*	1 Pack/280g	241	86	2.5	18.6	0.2	0.0
QUINCES	1oz/28g	7	26	0.3	6.3	0.1	0.0
QUINOA	1oz/28g	87	309	13.8	55.7	5.0	0.0

Nutrition Values per 100g / 100ml (KCAL, PROT, CARB, FAT, FIBRE)

Q

	Measure WEIGHT/INFO	per Measure KCAL	Nutrition Values per 100g / 100ml KCAL	PROT	CARB	FAT	FIBRE
QUORN DELI,							
Chicken Style, Slices, Quorn*	3 Slices/33g	36	108	16.9	4.0	2.7	3.2
Ham Flavour, Quorn*	1 Slice/20g	26	130	19.3	6.1	3.1	3.1
Ham, Wafer Thin, Quorn*	1 Serving/18g	23	130	19.3	6.1	3.1	3.1
Turkey Flavour With Stuffing, Quorn*	1 Slice/13g	13	102	13.7	8.3	1.5	4.5
QUORN Escalopes, Garlic & Herb, Quorn*	1 Escalope/140g	293	209	8.9	16.9	11.8	3.8
QUORN FILLETS,							
& Mushroom & White Wine Sauce, Quorn*	1oz/28g	18	65	6.3	6.0	1.8	2.1
Cajun Spice, Quorn*	1 Serving/100g	176	176	10.9	14.7	8.2	3.4
Chinese Style Char Grilled, Mini, Quorn*	1 Serving/85g	115	135	12.1	15.6	2.7	4.7
Hot and Spicy, Quorn*	1 fillet/100g	176	176	10.9	14.7	8.2	6.4
In Breadcrumbs, Quorn	1 Fillet/94g	184	196	11.0	14.2	10.6	3.8
Lemon & Black Pepper, Quorn*	1oz/28g	53	189	8.8	18.4	8.9	3.0
Lemon & Pepper, Sainsbury's*	1 Fillet/100g	198	198	11.6	16.9	9.3	3.8
Oriental, Sainsbury's*	1 Serving/294g	353	120	4.0	24.6	0.6	1.8
Provencale, Morrisons*	1 Serving/165g	94	57	5.4	5.8	1.4	1.1
Quorn*	2 Fillets/102g	88	86	13.1	4.9	1.5	4.9
With A Crispy Seasonal Coating, Quorn*	1 Fillet/100g	197	197	8.8	18.4	9.8	3.0
QUORN Goujons, With Chunky Salsa Dip, Quorn*	1oz/28g	57	204	10.4	17.0	10.5	3.0
QUORN Grills, Lamb Flavour, Quorn*	1 Grill/90g	104	116	11.4	10.4	3.2	4.2
QUORN Mince, Quorn*	1 Pack/300g	273	91	15.0	1.4	2.8	4.9
QUORN, Myco-Protein	1oz/28g	24	86	11.8	2.0	3.5	4.8
QUORN NUGGETS,							
Quorn*	1 nugget/20g	38	191	10.6	15.7	9.5	3.5
Southern Style, Quorn*	1 Nugget/20g	39	197	12.1	15.7	9.5	3.5
Quorn Pieces	1 Serving	44	86	13.1	4.9	1.5	4.9
Quorn Pieces, Quorn*	1 Pack/300g	276	92	14.0	1.8	3.2	4.8
QUORN STEAKS,							
Peppered, Quorn*	1 Steak/100g	126	126	11.6	10.5	4.2	3.7
Peppered, Sainsbury's*	1 Steak/95g	124	130	11.9	11.9	4.2	4.5
Quorn* Chicken Style Roast, Quorn*	1oz/28g	30	108	16.9	4.0	2.7	3.2
Quorn* Chunky Pieces	1 Serving/87g	90	103	14.0	5.8	2.6	6.0

	Measure WEIGHT/INFO	per Measure KCAL	KCAL	PROT	CARB	FAT	FIBRE
RABBIT,							
Raw, Meat Only	1oz/28g	38	137	21.9	0.0	5.5	0.0
Stewed, Meat Only	1oz/28g	88	313	5.5	55.5	9.4	8.2
RADDICCIO, Raw	1oz/28g	4	14	1.4	1.7	0.2	1.8
RADISH,							
Red, Raw	1oz/28g	3	12	0.7	1.9	0.2	0.9
Sainsbury's*	1 Pack/150g	18	12	0.7	1.9	0.2	0.9
White/Mooli, Raw	1oz/28g	4	15	0.8	2.9	0.1	0.0
RAISIN TOAST, Jacob's*	1 Biscuit/14g	52	368	13.1	70.1	3.9	4.4
RAISINS,							
Raisins	1 Tbsp/30g	82	272	2.1	69.3	0.4	2.0
Raisins & Sultanas, Jumbo, M & S*	1 Pack/50g	133	265	2.4	62.4	0.5	2.6
Califorian, Seedless, Safeway*	1 Pack/14g	44	316	3.3	77.5	0.4	0.0
California, Sun Dried, Sun-Maid*	1 Pack/42g	128	304	3.0	71.4	0.7	5.8
Californian, Organic, Evernat*	1 Serving/65g	188	289	2.1	69.3	0.4	2.0
Seedless, Somerfield*	1oz/28g	92	330	3.0	77.0	1.0	0.0
Seedless, Tesco*	1 Serving/10g	27	265	1.1	64.1	0.5	6.8
RAITA,							
Raita	1oz/28g	16	58	4.3	5.7	2.1	0.2
RASPBERRIES,							
Canned, In Syrup	1oz/28g	25	88	0.6	22.5	0.1	1.5
Fresh, Raw	1oz/28g	7	25	1.4	4.6	0.3	2.5
Fresh, Tesco*	1 Pack/125g	34	27	1.4	4.6	0.3	2.5
Frozen, Asda*	1 Serving/100g	26	26	1.4	4.5	0.3	2.5
In Apple Juice, Asda*	½ Can/145g	48	33	0.9	7.0	0.2	1.5
In Fruit Juice, John West*	1 Serving/100g	27	27	0.7	6.0	0.0	2.4
M & S*	1oz/28g	7	25	0.9	5.6	0.0	7.4
RATATOUILLE,							
Provencale, Asda*	½ Can/195g	98	50	1.0	7.0	2.0	1.0
Provencale, Sainsbury's*	½ Can/190g	80	42	0.8	5.7	1.8	1.0
Provencale, Tesco*	½ Can/195g	72	37	1.1	4.2	1.8	0.9
Provencale, Waitrose*	½ Can/195g	107	55	1.5	7.8	2.1	0.8
Safeway*	1 Serving/200g	78	39	1.0	3.0	2.5	1.6
Sainsbury's*	1 Pack/300g	99	33	1.5	5.5	0.6	1.6
Vegetable, M & S*	1 Pack/300g	135	45	2.3	2.5	3.0	2.1
RED BULL	1 Can/250ml	113	45	0.0	11.3	0.0	0.0
RED CABBAGE, Braised With Red Wine, M & S*	½ Pack/150g	180	120	1.4	17.1	4.8	1.0
RED GRAPE JUICE,							
Safeway*	1 Serving/120ml	77	64	0.1	15.5	0.0	0.0
Sainsbury's*	1 Glass/200ml	138	69	0.1	16.6	0.0	0.0
REDCURRANT JELLY,							
Redcurrant Jelly	1oz/28g	67	240	0.3	63.8	0.0	0.0
Baxters*	1oz/28g	73	260	0.0	65.0	0.0	0.0
REDCURRANTS, Raw	1oz/28g	6	21	1.1	4.4	0.0	3.4
REFRESHERS, Bassett's*	1oz/28g	106	377	4.3	78.1	0.0	0.0
RELISH,							
Hamburger, Bick's*	1oz/28g	27	96	1.3	22.3	0.2	0.0
Onion, M & S*	1oz/28g	46	165	1.0	32.1	3.0	1.1
Salsa, Waitrose*	1oz/28g	21	74	2.1	14.7	0.2	2.0
Sweetcorn, Bicks*	1 Tbsp/22g	23	103	1.3	24.3	0.2	0.0
Sweetcorn, Safeway*	1 Serving/50g	69	137	1.0	32.4	0.4	0.5
Tomato & Chilli Texan Style, Tesco*	1 Tbsp/14g	20	140	1.7	32.0	0.1	1.1
Tomato & Onion, Somerfield*	1 Tsp/10g	5	53	1.0	8.0	2.0	0.0
Tomato, M & S*	1oz/28g	36	130	1.8	30.2	0.3	1.5
REVELS, Mars*	1 Sm Bag/35g	173	495	6.2	65.6	23.1	0.0

Nutrition Values per 100g / 100ml

	Measure WEIGHT/INFO	per Measure KCAL	Nutrition Values per 100g / 100ml KCAL	PROT	CARB	FAT	FIBRE
RHUBARB,							
Fresh, Raw	1oz/28g	2	7	0.9	0.8	0.1	1.4
In Light Syrup, Sainsbury's*	1oz/28g	9	31	0.5	6.9	0.1	0.8
No Added Sugar, Asda*	¼ Can/133g	8	6	0.8	0.7	0.0	1.3
Stewed With Sugar	1oz/28g	13	48	0.9	11.5	0.1	1.2
Stewed Without Sugar	1oz/28g	2	7	0.9	0.7	0.1	1.3
RIBENA*,							
Apple Juice Drink	1 Carton/287ml	132	46	0.0	11.1	0.0	0.0
Blackcurrant, Diluted With Water	1 Serving/180ml	81	45	0.0	11.0	0.0	0.0
Blackcurrant Juice Drink	1 Carton/288ml	164	57	0.0	14.0	0.0	0.0
Blackcurrant Juice Drink, Toothkind	1 Carton/288ml	12	4	0.0	0.7	0.0	0.0
Light	1 Bottle/288ml	63	22	0.0	5.2	0.0	0.0
Orange Tropical Juice Drink, Toothkind	1 Carton/288ml	9	3	0.0	0.6	0.0	0.0
Strawberry Juice Drink, Toothkind	1 Carton/288ml	12	4	0.0	0.7	0.0	0.0
RIBS,							
Chinese King, Farmfoods*	1 Rib/79g	185	234	11.9	4.0	19.0	1.5
In Spicy BBQ Sauce, Asda*	1 Pack/360g	842	234	19.8	7.6	13.8	0.0
Pork, BBQ Flavoured, Farmfoods*	1oz/28g	84	301	20.6	12.5	18.7	0.8
Pork, BBQ, Sainsbury's*	1 Rib/60g	188	314	28.5	3.8	20.5	0.1
Pork, Chinese Style, Farmfoods*	1oz/28g	63	224	14.9	5.4	15.9	1.7
Pork, Chinese Style, Jumbo, Sainsbury's*	1oz/28g	82	293	27.3	4.2	18.6	0.1
Pork, Rib Rack, Smokey Barbecue, Farmfoods*	1oz/28g	83	296	15.3	5.7	23.5	0.6
Pork, Single, BBQ, Asda*	1oz/28g	58	206	23.7	3.5	10.7	0.0
Pork, Spare, Chops, Braised, Lean	1oz/28g	117	417	8.1	79.0	6.9	3.0
Pork, Spare, Chops, Braised, Lean & Fat	1oz/28g	113	402	7.9	84.1	3.8	1.7
Pork, Spare, Chops, Raw, Lean & Fat	1oz/28g	64	229	7.7	25.0	10.8	0.0
Pork, Spare, Steaks, Raw, Lean & Fat	1oz/28g	88	316	7.1	44.2	12.3	0.0
RIBSTEAKS,							
Chinese Style, Dalepak*	1 Ribsteak/63g	186	295	17.7	10.4	20.3	0.9
Smokey Barbecue Style, Dalepak*	1 Ribsteak/58g	164	282	16.2	8.8	20.3	0.9
RICE,							
American Easy Cook, Dry Weight, Sainsbury's*	1 Serving/50g	179	358	6.8	76.6	2.6	0.8
American Easy Cook, Cooked, Sainsbury's*	1 Serving/50g	71	142	2.7	30.6	1.0	0.3
Arborio Risotto, Dry, Asda*	1 Serving/125g	438	350	7.0	78.0	1.1	0.0
Arborio Risotto, Dry, Sainsburys*	1 Serving/120g	419	349	7.0	78.5	0.8	1.4
Arborio, Dry, Tesco*	1 Serving/80g	277	346	7.4	78.3	0.4	1.1
Basmati, & Wild, Easy Cook, Dry, Tilda*	1oz/28g	98	349	9.4	77.0	0.4	0.9
Basmati, & Wild, M & S*	1 Pack/180g	189	105	2.8	22.5	0.4	1.2
Basmati, Brown, Dry, Asda*	1 Serving/50g	181	362	10.0	71.0	4.0	2.3
Basmati, Brown, Dry, Tesco*	1 Serving/50g	176	351	9.4	73.0	2.4	2.3
Basmati, Brown, Dry, Tilda*	1oz/28g	97	347	9.2	71.4	2.7	1.9
Basmati, Easy Cook, Dry, Tesco*	1 Serving/50g	178	356	8.1	79.8	0.5	0.4
Basmati, Easy Cook, Dry, Tilda*	1oz/28g	98	349	8.5	78.4	0.1	0.4
Basmati, Easy Cook, Dry, Uncle Ben's*	1 Serving/63g	216	343	9.0	76.0	0.6	1.9
Basmati, Express, Uncle Ben's*	½ Pack/125g	173	138	2.8	29.9	1.3	0.0
Basmati, Indian, Dry, Tesco*	1 Serving/56g	194	347	8.4	76.1	0.9	0.1
Basmati, Pure, Rizazz, Tilda*	1 Bag/250g	383	153	2.6	30.2	2.4	0.0
Basmati, Safeway*	1oz/28g	44	157	6.7	16.7	7.0	1.6
Basmati, Dry, Sainsbury's*	1 Serving/50g	176	352	7.4	80.0	0.3	0.2
Basmati, Sainsbury's*	1 Serving/150g	191	127	2.6	28.6	0.2	0.1
Basmati, Dry, Somerfield*	1 Serving/100g	343	343	9.3	75.4	0.5	1.6
Basmati, Steamed, Sainsbury's*	1 Serving/250g	298	119	3.6	25.9	0.1	1.5
Basmati, Dry, Tilda*	1oz/28g	97	348	8.6	77.6	0.4	0.4
BBQ & Spicy, M & S*	1 Pack/250g	463	185	6.1	23.7	7.2	1.2
Brown, American Easy Cook, Dry, Tilda*	1oz/28g	99	352	8.1	75.1	2.1	1.9

R

RICE,	Measure WEIGHT/INFO	per Measure KCAL	KCAL	PROT	CARB	FAT	FIBRE
Brown, Boiled	1oz/28g	39	141	2.6	32.1	1.1	0.8
Brown, Italian Easy Cook, Sainsbury's*	1 Serving/50g	87	173	3.5	36.4	1.5	1.6
Brown, Raw	1oz/28g	100	357	6.7	81.3	2.8	1.9
Brown, Wholegrain, American, Sainsbury's*	1 Serving/50g	68	135	2.7	28.6	1.1	1.3
Brown, Wholegrain, Dry, Sainsbury's*	1 Serving/40g	135	338	6.8	71.5	2.8	2.5
Carnaroli Risotto, Dry, Tesco*	1 oz/28g	99	352	7.6	77.2	1.4	1.2
Chinese Five Spice, Special Recipe, Sainsbury's*	1oz/28g	37	133	2.9	29.9	0.3	0.9
Chinese Savoury, Dry, Batchelors*	1 Serving/50g	177	354	9.9	73.1	2.4	2.8
Coriander & Herbs, Dry, Batchelors*	1/3 Pack/76g	280	369	7.9	79.6	3.5	5.0
Curry Style Savoury, Safeway*	1 Serving/100g	112	112	2.2	23.4	1.1	1.6
Egg Fried	1oz/28g	58	208	4.2	25.7	10.6	0.4
Egg Fried, Asda*	1oz/28g	43	152	4.2	23.4	4.4	1.8
Egg Fried, Chinese, Sainsbury's*	1 Pack/200g	350	175	4.5	27.8	5.1	1.2
Egg Fried, Chinese Style, Tesco*	1 Portion/250g	418	167	4.4	27.9	4.2	0.7
Egg Fried, M & S*	1 Pack/200g	420	210	4.1	32.4	7.0	0.3
Egg Fried, Oriental Express*	1 Packet/425g	531	125	4.0	22.2	2.3	1.3
Egg Fried, Tesco*	½ Pack/250g	313	125	4.7	23.3	1.5	1.8
Egg Fried, Waitrose*	1 Pack/300g	426	142	3.0	20.6	5.2	1.0
Fried, Chicken, Chinese Takeaway, Iceland*	1 Pack/340g	510	150	6.5	20.7	4.6	0.6
Fried, Duck, Chicken & Pork Celebration, Sainsbury's*	1 Pack/450g	545	121	7.9	14.2	3.6	1.5
Golden Savoury, Batchelors*	½ Pack/62g	226	364	10.1	74.7	2.8	2.4
Golden Savoury, Cooked, Tesco*	1 Serving/178g	219	123	3.0	25.0	1.0	1.0
Golden Savoury, Nirvana, Aldi*	1 Pack/120g	161	134	3.4	28.1	0.9	0.8
Golden Vegetable, Tesco*	1 Serving/125g	135	108	2.6	21.9	1.1	0.6
Imperial Red, Dry, Merchant Gourmet*	1oz/28g	85	305	8.6	61.2	2.5	8.6
Italian, Easy Cook, Dry, Tesco*	1 Serving/75g	260	347	7.0	77.6	0.9	0.4
Italian, Risotto, Dry, M & S*	1oz/28g	94	336	6.8	76.0	0.5	2.6
Lemon Pepper Speciality, Asda*	1 Serving/52g	67	129	2.0	27.0	1.4	0.1
Lentil & Roast Aubergine, M & S*	1oz/28g	1	125	3.8	15.4	5.3	2.3
Long Grai, Dry	1oz/28g	90	320	8.0	74.4	0.9	3.9
Long Grain, & Wild, American, Dry, Sainsbury's*	1 Serving/75g	231	308	6.2	69.0	0.8	2.0
Long Grain, & Wild, Dry, Asda*	1 Serving/75g	272	363	9.0	77.0	2.1	0.0
Long Grain, & Wild, Cooked, Tesco*	1 Serving/200g	300	150	3.0	31.8	1.3	0.2
Long Grain, American, Dry, Asda*	1 Serving/70g	252	360	7.0	81.0	0.9	0.4
Long Grain, American, Dry, Co-Op*	1 Serving/50g	175	350	8.0	77.0	1.0	1.0
Long Grain, American, Cooked, Sainsbury's*	½ Pack/138g	214	155	3.4	27.9	3.3	0.3
Long Grain, American Easy Cook, Dry, Tesco*	1 Serving/75g	260	347	7.0	77.6	0.9	0.4
Long Grain, American Easy Cook, Dry, Tilda*	1oz/28g	99	355	7.6	79.9	0.6	0.4
Long Grain, Canned, M & S*	1oz/28g	44	158	3.6	33.6	1.0	0.4
Long Grain, White, Frozen, Microwavable, Sainsbury's*	1 Sachet/200g	210	105	2.7	22.4	0.5	1.1
Mexican, Ready Meals, Waitrose*	1 Pack/300g	432	144	2.6	27.8	2.5	0.5
Mushroom & Coconut, Organic, Waitrose*	1 Pack/300g	474	158	3.7	24.5	5.0	1.4
Original Vegetable, Bird's Eye*	1oz/28g	29	105	4.0	20.8	0.6	1.1
Pilau	1oz/28g	61	217	2.7	25.7	11.5	0.6
Pilau, 3 Colour Indian, Sainsbury's*	1 Pot/520g	1175	226	3.9	33.7	8.4	0.6
Pilau, Basmati, Rizazz, Tilda*	1 Serving/125g	183	146	2.5	28.7	2.4	0.0
Pilau, Dry, Batchelors*	1/3 Pack/76g	280	369	7.9	79.6	3.5	5.0
Pilau, Bengali, Sainsbury's*	1 Pack/200g	330	165	4.2	26.5	4.7	2.2
Pilau, Express, Uncle Ben's*	½ Pack/125g	211	169	3.1	31.0	3.6	0.0
Pilau, Indian Mushroom, Sainsbury's*	1 Serving/100g	119	119	3.0	21.3	2.4	1.9
Pilau, Mild, Sainsbury's*	1 Pack/200g	332	166	4.1	32.1	2.4	0.5
Pilau, Safeway*	1 Serving/250g	493	197	3.5	31.8	6.2	1.1
Pilau, Dry, Sharwood's*	1oz/28g	99	354	9.0	76.8	1.2	1.8
Pilau, Takeaway Menu For 1, BGTY, Sainsbury's*	1 Pack/151g	227	150	4.8	32.8	0.0	1.7

Nutrition Values per 100g / 100ml

R

RICE,	Measure WEIGHT/INFO	per Measure KCAL	Nutrition Values per 100g / 100ml KCAL	PROT	CARB	FAT	FIBRE
Pilau, Tesco*	1oz/28g	45	162	3.4	31.1	2.7	0.3
Saffron, M & S*	1 Pack/200g	310	155	2.9	23.7	5.6	1.0
Savory Mushroom Basmati, Tilda*	1 Pack/250g	353	141	2.6	27.5	2.3	0.0
Savoury, Beef, Dry, Batchelors*	½ Pack/62g	222	358	9.4	74.9	2.3	3.2
Savoury, Chicken, Dry, Batchelors*	1 Pack/124g	443	357	9.9	74.5	2.2	2.9
Savoury, Chicken, SmartPrice, Asda*	½ Pack/168g	210	125	3.2	26.0	0.9	2.4
Savoury, Chicken, Tesco*	1 Serving/87g	177	204	6.4	39.4	2.2	6.7
Savoury, Golden Vegetable, Asda*	½ Pack/176g	208	118	2.6	25.0	0.8	2.5
Savoury, Golden Vegetable, Morrisons*	1 Serving/50g	71	141	3.4	30.1	0.8	1.1
Savoury, Golden Vegetable, Sainsbury's*	¼ Pack/100g	122	122	2.9	25.4	1.0	0.3
Savoury, Mild Curry, Dry, Batchelors*	½ Pack/61g	217	355	8.4	76.0	1.9	1.8
Savoury, Mixed Vegetable, Dry, Tesco*	1 Serving/63g	219	347	8.8	71.1	3.0	6.4
Savoury, Mushroom & Pepper, Cooked, Morrisons*	1 Serving/200g	204	102	2.3	21.5	0.8	0.0
Savoury, Mushroom, Asda*	½ Pack/168g	207	123	3.2	26.0	0.7	2.9
Savoury, Mushroom, Dry, Batchelors*	1 Sachet/122g	439	360	10.9	74.3	2.1	2.5
Savoury, Sweet & Sour, Dry, Batchelors*	1 Serving/135g	419	310	9.4	75.6	2.1	3.1
Savoury, Sweet & Sour, Somerfield*	1 Pack/120g	127	106	2.0	23.0	1.0	0.0
Savoury, Vegetable, Dry, Co-Op*	½ Pack/60g	210	350	9.0	76.0	1.0	3.0
Spanish, Of The World, Dry, Batchelors*	1oz/28g	101	360	9.5	75.5	2.2	2.5
Spanish Paella, Dry, Sainsbury's*	1 Serving/100g	349	349	7.0	78.5	0.8	1.4
Spanish Style Savoury, Safeway*	1 Pack/394g	449	114	2.7	23.7	0.9	1.4
Special Fried, Asda*	1oz/28g	42	149	5.4	21.0	4.9	1.5
Special Fried, Chilled, Co-Op*	1 Pack/300g	348	116	6.2	13.9	3.9	1.1
Special Fried, M & S*	1 Pack/450g	923	205	6.2	27.2	7.8	0.5
Special Fried, Somerfield*	1 Pack/200g	316	158	5.0	25.0	4.0	0.0
Sticky Chicken, Chinese Takeaway, Tesco*	1 Box/350g	434	124	5.8	12.6	5.6	1.0
Thai, Chicken, Enjoy, Bird's Eye**	1 Pack/500g	535	107	6.9	13.2	3.0	0.7
Thai, Fragrant, Dry, Asda*	1 Serving/75g	264	352	7.0	79.0	0.9	0.0
Thai, Fragrant, Dry, Tesco*	1 Serving/75g	262	349	7.3	79.1	0.4	0.8
Thai, Fragrant, Waitrose*	1 Serving/175g	243	139	2.7	28.7	1.5	0.3
Thai, Jasmine, Dry, Tilda*	1oz/28g	97	348	7.1	79.5	0.2	0.4
Thai, Sticky, Sainsbury's*	1 Serving/100g	132	132	2.3	26.1	2.0	0.3
Valencia For Paella, Dry, Asda*	1 Serving/125g	435	348	6.0	79.0	0.8	0.0
Vegetable, Frozen, Tesco*	1 Serving/100g	105	105	4.0	20.8	0.6	1.1
White, Farmfoods*	1oz/28g	37	131	2.7	27.1	1.3	0.1
White, Flaked, Raw	1oz/28g	97	346	6.6	77.5	1.2	0.0
White, Fried	1oz/28g	37	131	2.2	25.0	3.2	0.6
White, Glutinous, Boiled	1oz/28g	18	65	1.7	14.7	0.3	0.0
White, Glutinous, Raw	1oz/28g	101	359	8.4	74.9	1.6	0.0
White, Microwaveable, Safeway*	1 Sachet/200g	210	105	2.7	22.4	0.5	1.1
White, Polished, Boiled	1oz/28g	34	123	2.2	29.6	0.3	0.2
White, Polished, Raw	1oz/28g	101	361	6.5	86.8	1.0	0.5
Wild With Sunblush Tomatoes, TTD, Sainsbury's*	1 Serving/50g	78	155	2.7	21.4	6.5	1.8
Yellow, Farmfoods*	1oz/28g	37	131	2.7	27.1	1.3	0.1
Yellow, Ready Cooked, Tesco*	1oz/28g	32	113	2.7	27.1	1.3	0.1
RICE BOWL,							
Chicken & Mushroom, Sharwood's*	1 Pack/350g	392	112	4.8	17.1	2.7	0.7
Chicken Tikka Masala, Uncle Bens*	1 Serving/350g	382	109	5.9	15.9	2.4	0.0
Honey BBQ Chicken, Uncle Bens*	1 Serving/350g	420	120	5.4	23.1	0.6	0.0
Balti, Asda*	1 Pot/60g	60	100	3.8	20.0	0.5	0.0
RICE CAKES,							
Ryvita*	1 Cake/7g	28	395	8.8	82.1	3.4	1.3
Savoury, Kallo*	1 Cake/8g	28	355	14.2	67.5	3.2	4.4
Savoury With Yeast Extract, Kallo*	1 Slice/11g	40	364	12.7	72.0	2.8	4.7

R

RICE CAKES,	Measure WEIGHT/INFO	per Measure KCAL	Nutrition Values per 100g / 100ml KCAL	PROT	CARB	FAT	FIBRE
Slightly Salted, Thick Slice, Organic, Kallo*	1 Cake/8g	30	372	8.0	78.7	2.8	5.1
Snack Size, Kallo*	1 Cake/2g	7	372	8.0	78.7	2.8	5.1
Thin Slice, Organic, Waitrose*	1 Cake/6g	23	391	9.0	81.3	3.3	3.8
Wholegrain, Organic, Kallo*	1 Cake/7.5g	26	368	8.5	74.5	4.0	4.8
With Sesame, Organic, Evernat*	1 Cake/4g	15	368	8.5	74.5	4.0	0.0
With Sesame, Thick Sliced, Kallo*	1 Cake/10g	37	373	8.0	78.0	3.2	5.4
RICE CRACKERS,							
Japanese, Holland & Barrett*	1oz/28g	111	397	9.0	79.7	4.7	0.3
Thin, Blue Dragon*	3 Crackers/5g	20	395	6.1	84.4	3.7	0.0
RICE POT, Caramelised Pineapple, Waitrose*	1 Pot/229g	499	218	3.2	27.6	10.5	0.1
RICE PUDDING,							
& Conserve, M & S*	1oz/28g	53	190	2.3	17.4	12.5	0.3
50% Less Fat, Asda*	½ Can/212g	170	85	3.3	16.2	0.8	0.2
BGTY, Sainsbury's*	½ Can/212g	180	85	3.3	16.2	0.8	0.2
Canned	1oz/28g	25	89	3.4	14.0	2.5	0.2
Caramel, Muller Rice, Muller*	1 Pot/200g	210	105	3.5	17.4	2.4	0.0
Clotted Cream, M & S*	1 Pudding/185g	431	233	3.0	19.2	16.6	0.2
Co-Op*	1oz/28g	49	175	5.0	20.0	9.0	2.0
Creamed, Canned, Ambrosia*	1 Can/425g	383	90	3.1	15.2	1.9	0.0
Creamed, Co-Op*	1 Can/170g	153	90	3.0	16.0	1.5	0.0
Creamed, HE, Tesco*	1oz/28g	19	68	3.6	11.4	0.6	0.0
Creamed, Low Fat, Ambrosia*	1 Serving/150g	129	86	3.3	16.1	0.9	0.0
Creamed, Morrisons*	1 Can/212g	189	89	3.1	15.7	1.6	0.0
Creamed, Pot, Ambrosia*	1 Pot/150g	152	101	3.2	16.5	2.5	0.0
Creamy Rice, Shape*	1 Serving/175g	149	85	3.5	15.4	1.0	0.4
Creamy Rice With Tropical Crunch, Ambrosia*	1 Pack/210g	307	146	3.6	23.4	4.2	0.6
Creamy With Strawberry Crunch, Ambrosia*	1 Pack/205g	297	145	3.9	23.0	4.2	0.7
Everyday, Co-Op*	1 Can/396	333	84	3.4	15.5	0.9	0.1
Low Fat, Budgens*	1 Can/425g	370	87	3.4	16.3	0.9	0.0
Low Fat, Canned, Ambrosia*	½ Can/200g	162	81	3.2	15.2	0.8	0.0
Low Fat, Co-Op*	1 Sm Can/170g	145	85	3.0	16.0	0.8	0.0
Low Fat, Healthy Selection, Somerfield*	1 Pot/213g	173	81	4.0	15.0	1.0	0.0
Low Fat, No Added Sugar, Weight Watchers*	½ Can/212g	155	73	3.7	11.4	1.5	0.0
Low Fat, Pot, Ambrosia*	1 Pot/150g	129	86	3.3	16.1	0.9	0.0
Luxury, Co-Op*	1 Can/425g	536	126	3.3	15.9	5.5	0.1
Milk, Economy, Sainsbury's*	½ Can/198g	139	70	3.2	12.6	0.8	0.2
Organic, Ambrosia*	1 Can/425g	455	107	3.4	15.1	3.7	0.0
Organic, Co-Op*	1 Can/425g	446	105	3.0	16.0	3.0	0.2
Organic, Evernat*	1oz/28g	39	141	5.5	22.9	3.0	0.0
Safeway*	1 Serving/19g	66	349	7.3	77.3	1.2	0.2
Thick & Creamy, Co-Op*	1 Can/425g	531	125	3.0	16.0	6.0	0.0
Thick & Creamy, Nestle*	1 Can/425g	527	124	3.1	15.4	5.6	0.2
Value, Tesco*	½ Can/212g	178	84	3.3	15.5	0.9	0.2
With Sultanas & Nutmeg, Ambrosia*	1 Pack/425g	446	105	3.2	16.6	2.9	0.1
With Sultanas & Nutmeg, Co-Op*	1 Can/425g	446	105	3.0	18.0	3.0	0.1
RIESEN Chocolate Chew, Bendicks*	1oz/28g	126	450	5.0	73.0	17.0	0.0
RISOTTO,							
Beef, For 1, Vesta*	1 Risotto/95g	329	346	15.3	57.8	5.9	5.6
Caramelised Onion & Gruyere Cheese, M & S*	1 Pack/200g	350	175	3.0	17.8	10.3	1.7
Chicken & Lemon, Weight Watchers*	1 Pack/330g	317	96	5.9	12.3	2.6	0.5
Chicken & Mushroom, Finest, Tesco*	1 Pack/400g	496	124	7.4	17.2	2.8	0.5
Chicken & Mushroom, Good Intentions, Somerfield*	1 Pack/300g	345	115	5.7	19.0	1.8	0.3
Chicken, Co-Op*	1 Pack/340g	442	130	6.0	16.0	5.0	2.0
Chicken, Ready Meal, M & S*	1 Pack/360g	450	125	6.7	14.4	4.4	0.9

	Measure WEIGHT/INFO	per Measure KCAL	Nutrition Values per 100g / 100ml KCAL	PROT	CARB	FAT	FIBRE
RISOTTO,							
Haddock & Mushroom, COU, M & S*	1 Pack/400g	320	80	6.4	12.1	0.8	2.0
Hot Smoked Salmon & Spinach, M & S*	½ Pack/300g	420	140	6.4	11.0	8.0	0.6
King Prawn, Pea & Mint, M & S*	½ Pack/300g	405	135	3.8	15.9	6.2	0.9
Lemon & Mint, Healthy Balalnce,Waitrose*	1 Serving/350g	462	132	3.9	20.7	3.7	1.0
Mushroom, Asda*	1 Pack/340g	340	100	2.3	15.0	3.4	0.6
Mushroom, Finest, Tesco*	1 Pack/350g	550	157	3.1	16.4	8.8	1.2
Mushroom, Italiano, Tesco*	1 Pack/340g	367	108	2.4	20.0	2.0	4.6
Mushroom, Ready Meals, M & S*	1 Pack/360g	450	125	2.8	16.9	4.9	1.0
Mushroom, Somerfield*	1 Pack/300g	333	111	2.0	16.0	4.0	0.0
Mushroom, Waitrose*	1 Pack/350g	277	79	1.9	6.9	4.9	0.5
Roasted Vegetables, Stir-in, Uncle Ben's*	½ Pack/75g	86	115	1.7	5.0	9.7	0.0
Spring Vegetable, M & S*	1 Serving/330g	330	100	2.0	14.2	4.0	0.9
Vegetable	1oz/28g	41	147	4.2	19.2	6.5	2.2
Vegetable, Brown Rice	1oz/28g	40	143	4.1	18.6	6.4	2.4
RISPINOS,							
Apple & Cinnamon, Uncle Ben's*	1 Bag/60g	230	383	4.7	90.0	0.5	0.0
Barbecue, Uncle Ben's*	1 Pack/50g	182	363	8.4	82.0	0.2	0.0
Caramel, Uncle Ben's*	1 Pack/60g	229	382	5.1	89.0	0.7	0.0
Cheese & Onion, Uncle Ben's*	1 Pack/50g	181	361	8.4	81.0	0.4	0.0
Chocolate, Uncle Ben's*	1oz/28g	108	385	5.3	89.0	1.1	0.0
Coconut, Uncle Ben's*	1oz/28g	111	396	6.7	86.0	2.8	0.0
Pizza, Uncle Ben's*	1 Pack/50g	182	363	8.4	82.0	0.2	0.0
Vanilla, Uncle Ben's	1oz/28g	107	383	7.7	87.0	0.5	0.0
RISSOLES, Lentil, Fried In Vegetable Oil	1oz/28g	59	211	8.9	22.0	10.5	3.6
ROASTED VEGETABLES,							
Italian, M & S*	1 Serving/95g	219	230	1.8	7.1	21.0	1.7
Italiano Marinated, Tesco*	½ Tub/100g	121	121	1.7	9.2	8.6	0.8
With Sundried Tomato, Finest, Tesco*	½ Pack/150g	153	102	1.9	7.3	7.2	1.2
ROCKET,							
Wild, Sainsbury's*	1oz/28g	8	28	3.9	2.6	0.2	0.6
Wild, Tesco*	1 Bag/50g	9	18	3.3	0.6	0.3	1.7
ROCKY, Fox's*	1 Bar/25g	129	516	8.2	58.8	27.5	1.4
ROE,							
Cod, Hard, Coated In Batter, Fried	1oz/28g	53	189	12.4	8.9	11.8	0.2
Cod, Hard, Fried In Blended Oil	1oz/28g	57	202	20.9	3.0	11.9	0.1
Cod, Hard, Raw	1oz/28g	29	104	21.7	0.0	1.9	0.0
Cod, Pressed, John West*	1 Can/200g	198	99	17.6	1.4	2.6	0.1
Herring, Soft, Fried In Blended Oil	1oz/28g	74	265	26.3	4.7	15.8	0.2
Herring, Soft, Raw	1oz/28g	25	91	16.8	0.0	2.6	0.0
ROGAN JOSH,							
Chicken, Patak's*	1oz/28g	34	123	8.1	17.2	2.4	0.7
Chicken, With Pilau Rice, Farmfoods*	1 Pack/325g	354	109	5.3	17.1	2.1	0.4
Lamb, M & S*	1 Pack/300g	360	120	14.4	3.9	5.1	1.2
Lamb, Tesco*	1 Pack/350g	504	144	12.2	6.7	7.6	2.4
Lamb, With Pilau Rice, Eastern Classics*	1 Pack/400g	604	151	5.6	19.9	5.4	1.0
Prawn, COU, M & S*	1 Pack/400g	360	90	4.9	16.2	0.6	0.8
ROLLS, (FILLED)							
Bacon With Brown Sauce, McDonald's*	1 Roll/118g	289	245	12.8	31.2	8.4	1.4
Brie & Grapes, M & S*	1 Roll/57g	174	306	11.1	24.5	18.2	1.4
Brown, Roast Chicken & Mayonnaise, Big, Sainsbury's*	1 Pack/185g	479	259	9.6	21.8	14.8	0.0
Cheese & Chutney, M & S*	1 Roll/165g	256	155	13.9	23.1	0.7	1.2
Cheese & Onion, Co-Op*	1 Roll/66g	195	295	7.0	26.0	18.0	2.0
Cheese & Onion, M & S*	1oz/28g	91	325	10.1	27.5	19.4	1.0
Cheese & Onion, Sainsbury's*	1 Roll/67g	205	306	8.0	22.9	20.3	1.9

R

ROLLS,	Measure WEIGHT/INFO	per Measure KCAL	Nutrition Values per 100g / 100ml KCAL	PROT	CARB	FAT	FIBRE
Cheese & Onion, Somerfield*	1 Roll/70g	242	345	8.0	28.0	22.0	0.0
Cheese & Pickle, Sainsbury's*	1 Roll/136g	359	264	10.6	35.1	10.0	0.0
Chicken & Sundried Tomato, Weight Watchers*	1 Pack/170g	272	160	12.9	22.7	1.9	1.2
Chicken Salad, HE, Tesco*	1 Serving/224g	289	129	10.3	16.0	2.6	1.1
Ham & Pineapple, Eat Smart, Safeway*	1 Serving/180g	225	125	11.2	17.2	1.1	2.6
Ham Salad, BGTY, Sainsbury's*	1 Roll/178g	292	164	10.0	23.3	3.4	0.0
Mushroom & Bacon Crusty, M & S*	1 Roll/160g	424	265	8.7	29.0	12.6	2.3
Oak Smoked Salmon, M & S*	1 Roll/55g	139	252	14.6	23.1	11.3	1.2
Smoked Ham & Honey Roasted Pineapple, M & S*	1 Roll/179g	260	145	9.9	22.7	1.4	3.0
Soft White, Bacon & Cheese, Shell*	1 Pack/123g	331	269	11.4	33.0	10.2	0.0
Spicy Chicken, Crusty, M & S*	1 Roll/150g	383	255	12.8	25.8	11.1	2.0
White, Cheese & Onion, Shell*	1 Roll/178g	554	311	14.5	30.2	14.8	0.0
ROLO,							
Giant, Nestle*	1 Rolo/9g	42	468	3.2	70.0	19.5	0.0
Minis, Nestle*	1 Pack/26g	124	473	3.5	69.1	20.3	0.0
Standard, Nestle*	1 Rolo/9g	43	473	3.5	69.1	20.3	0.0
ROLY POLY,							
Jam, & Custard, Co-Op*	¼ Pack/100g	235	235	4.0	36.0	8.0	0.7
Jam & Custard, Safeway*	1 Serving/112g	299	267	3.8	43.0	8.9	0.8
Jam & Custard, Sainsbury's*	1 Pack/205g	521	254	3.3	34.1	11.6	0.5
Jam, Farmfoods*	1oz/28g	101	359	5.0	55.0	13.2	1.9
Jam, M & S*	1 Serving/75g	260	346	3.6	61.7	11.1	1.4
Jam, Tesco*	1 Serving/82g	308	375	4.7	51.5	16.7	1.2
Strawberry Jam, Tryton Foods*	1oz/28g	108	384	5.4	53.9	16.3	1.7
Syrup, With Fresh Custard, Sainsbury's*	1 Pack/225g	524	233	3.4	29.9	11.1	0.4
ROOT BEER	1 Can/330ml	135	41	0.0	10.6	0.0	0.0
ROSEMARY,							
Dried	1 Tsp/1g	3	331	4.9	46.4	15.2	0.0
Fresh	1oz/28g	28	99	1.4	13.5	4.4	0.0
ROSES, Cadbury's*	1oz/28g	136	485	4.8	60.9	24.8	0.0
ROSTI,							
Coriander & Chilli Potato, M & S*	1 Cake/110g	187	170	6.1	10.0	12.0	2.4
Lamb, Tesco*	1 Pack/350g	350	100	5.3	13.6	2.7	0.8
Leek & Mushroomi, Morrisons*	1 Serving/100g	149	149	2.8	19.7	6.6	2.1
Oven Baked, McCain*	1 Rosti/95g	234	246	3.7	29.7	12.8	0.0
Potato, Fresh, Safeway*	1 Rost/100g	138	138	2.8	19.2	5.5	2.8
Potato, McCain*	1 Rosti/95g	161	169	2.2	19.6	9.1	0.0
Potato, Onion & Gruyere, Finest, Tesco*	1 Pack/350g	403	115	3.5	11.9	5.9	1.4
Vegetable, Waitrose*	1 Pack/400g	248	62	1.4	8.8	2.3	1.3
Waitrose*	½ Pack/200g	190	95	1.1	15.1	3.3	1.4
ROULADE,							
Chocolate, Finest, Tesco*	1 Serving/80g	222	277	3.4	53.2	5.6	2.3
Lemon, Asda*	1 Serving/100g	343	343	2.7	56.0	12.0	0.0
Lemon Meringue, M & S	1 Serving/74g	230	311	3.2	46.6	12.5	0.3
Orange & Lemon Meringue, Co-Op*	1 Serving/82g	287	350	3.0	57.0	12.0	0.3
Passion Fruit, M & S*	1oz/28g	83	295	2.8	50.0	9.2	0.2
Raspberry & Vanilla, Somerfield*	1oz/28g	118	420	3.0	56.0	20.0	0.0
Raspberry, M & S*	1oz/28g	88	315	3.3	50.3	11.0	0.1
Salmon & Spinach, Tesco*	1 Serving/60g	155	258	9.5	1.7	23.7	0.2
Toffee & Walnut, Somerfield*	1oz/28g	130	465	4.0	50.0	28.0	0.0
Toffee, M & S*	1oz/28g	104	371	4.1	56.0	14.5	0.3
RUBY Breakfast Juice, Tropicana*	1 Glass/200ml	86	43	0.7	9.0	0.0	0.5
RUBY Orange Juice, M & S*	1 Bottle/250ml	125	50	0.7	11.5	0.0	0.2
RUFFLE, Jameson's*	1 Bar/28g	120	444	2.1	67.9	18.2	0.0

RUM,	Measure WEIGHT/INFO	per Measure KCAL	Nutrition Values per 100g / 100ml KCAL	PROT	CARB	FAT	FIBRE
37.5% Volume	1 Shot/25ml	52	207	0.0	0.0	0.0	0.0
40% Volume	1 Shot/25ml	56	222	0.0	0.0	0.0	0.0
White	1 Shot/25ml	52	207	0.0	0.0	0.0	0.0

R

	Measure WEIGHT/INFO	per Measure KCAL	Nutrition Values per 100g / 100ml KCAL	PROT	CARB	FAT	FIBRE
SAAG,							
Aloo, Sainsbury's*	½ Pack/150g	177	118	2.4	9.0	8.0	1.6
Aloo, Tesco*	1 Serving/200g	144	72	2.1	8.0	3.5	2.0
Chicken, M & S*	1 Pack/300g	435	145	11.1	4.0	9.4	1.9
Chicken, Masala, Sainsbury's*	1oz/28g	80	284	30.2	10.8	13.3	1.0
Chicken, Safeway*	1 Serving/350g	504	144	11.6	5.4	8.4	1.4
Gobi Aloo, Indian Takeaway, Sainsbury's*	1 Pack/334g	164	49	1.7	8.0	1.1	1.5
Gobi Aloo, Morrisons*	1 Pack/350g	305	87	2.0	9.1	4.7	0.4
Gobi Aloo, Tesco*	1 Serving/175g	182	104	2.3	7.3	7.3	1.4
Paneer, Sainsbury's*	1 Pack/400g	1520	380	17.0	9.0	30.6	2.4
SAFFRON	1 Tsp/0.7g	3	310	11.4	61.5	5.9	0.0
SAGE,							
Dried, Ground	1 Tsp/1g	3	315	10.6	42.7	12.7	0.0
Fresh	1oz/28g	33	119	3.9	15.6	4.6	0.0
SAGO, Raw	1oz/28g	99	355	0.2	94.0	0.2	0.5
SALAD,							
Alfresco Style, Tesco*	1 Serving/200g	40	20	0.9	3.3	0.3	1.4
All Seasons, Sainsbury's*	1oz/28g	3	12	1.0	1.5	0.2	1.2
American Ranch, Asda*	1 Serving/220g	253	115	2.5	6.0	9.0	2.0
American Style, Morrisons*	1 Serving/25g	5	22	1.1	3.9	0.3	2.3
Baby Leaf & Herb, Asda*	1 Serving/50g	7	14	2.3	0.7	0.2	2.4
Baby Leaf, Fully Prepared, Sainsbury's*	½ Bag/63g	10	16	1.3	1.9	0.4	1.5
Baby Leaf, M & S*	1 Pack/100g	15	15	2.1	1.4	0.3	1.4
Baby Leaf, Organic, Sainsbury's*	1 Serving/20g	3	14	1.5	1.4	0.3	1.1
Baby Leaf, Sainsbury's*	1 Serving/60g	13	21	1.3	1.7	1.0	3.3
Baby Leaf, Somerfield*	1 Pack/80g	14	18	2.0	1.0	1.0	0.0
Baby Leaf With Watercress, Tesco*	¼ Bag/25g	5	19	2.0	1.3	0.7	1.4
Baby Tomato, Tesco*	1 Pack/205g	35	17	0.8	2.8	0.3	0.9
Bacon Caesar, M & S*	1oz/28g	48	170	5.5	5.7	14.0	1.2
Bacon Caesar, Sainsburys*	1 Pack/256g	415	162	4.7	7.3	12.7	1.4
Salad Bag, Tesco*	1 Serving/200g	38	19	0.9	3.0	0.4	1.4
Bean & Sweetcorn, Side, M & S*	1 Serving/125g	131	105	2.5	7.0	7.2	1.3
Bean, M & S*	1 Serving/80g	72	90	6.4	14.3	0.9	3.9
Bean, Retail	1oz/28g	41	147	4.2	12.8	9.3	3.0
Beetroot	1oz/28g	28	100	2.0	8.4	6.8	1.7
Beetroot, 1% Fat, M & S*	1 Serving/225g	131	58	1.1	7.7	2.7	1.7
Beetroot, GFY, Asda*	1 Serving/84g	46	55	1.0	12.0	0.3	1.8
Beetroot, Organic, M & S*	1oz/28g	20	73	1.5	9.1	3.4	1.9
Bistro, Asda*	1 Serving/180g	29	16	1.4	2.7	0.0	2.5
Bistro, Sainsbury's*	1 Pack/150g	33	22	1.1	3.6	0.4	1.3
Bistro, Washed Ready To Eat, Tesco*	1 Pack/140g	22	16	1.1	1.7	0.5	1.0
Caesar, BGTY, Sainsbury's*	½ Bag/127g	168	132	3.6	8.6	9.9	1.7
Caesar, Half Fat, Safeway*	½ Pack/133g	117	88	3.8	3.2	6.7	1.3
Caesar, HE, Tesco*	1 Serving/100g	101	101	3.2	8.0	6.2	0.7
Caesar, M & S*	1 Serving/100g	151	151	2.6	8.0	12.1	0.7
Caesar, Sainsbury's*	½ Bag/128g	227	177	3.6	6.7	15.1	1.0
Caesar, Waitrose*	1 Serving/115g	175	152	6.4	6.3	11.2	0.8
Caesar, Washed & Ready to Eat, Somerfield*	½ Bag/125g	155	124	5.0	6.5	8.7	0.8
Carrot & Nut With French Dressing, Retail	1oz/28g	61	218	2.1	13.7	17.6	2.4
Carrot, Eat Smart, Safeway*	1 Serving/75g	71	95	0.9	15.6	3.0	3.9
Ceasar, So Good, Somerfield*	½ Bag/125g	155	124	5.0	6.5	8.7	0.8
Celery, Nut & Sultana, Asda*	1oz/28g	76	272	2.9	11.2	23.9	1.9
Celery, Nut & Sultana, Waitrose*	1oz/28g	54	192	2.8	8.4	16.4	1.0
Chargrilled Chicken Wholefood, M & S*	1 Pot/219g	230	105	10.1	11.6	1.9	4.8
Cheese & Apple, Somerfield*	1 Serving/175g	319	182	12.3	27.5	2.5	1.9

S

SALAD,	Measure WEIGHT/INFO	per Measure KCAL	Nutrition Values per 100g / 100ml KCAL	PROT	CARB	FAT	FIBRE
Cheese Coleslaw, Sainsbury's*	1oz/28g	61	218	5.1	6.0	19.3	0.1
Cheese Layered, M & S*	1 Pack/450g	923	205	4.3	9.0	17.0	0.7
Cheese Layered, Tesco*	1 Serving/165g	264	160	4.4	9.9	11.4	1.0
Chicken Caesar Bistro, M & S*	½ Pack/135g	189	140	5.0	6.5	10.6	0.6
Chicken Caesar, Boots*	1 Salad/155g	192	124	7.7	6.0	7.7	0.6
Chicken Caesar, Shapers, Boots*	1 Pack/180g	331	184	9.9	24.0	5.4	2.1
Chicken Caesar, Tesco*	1 Pack/300g	330	110	6.8	10.6	4.5	0.8
Chicken, HE, Tesco*	1 Salad/216g	296	137	8.4	22.6	1.4	1.2
Chicken, Tesco*	1 Serving/300g	348	116	5.3	7.0	7.4	1.0
Chickpea & Spinach, M & S*	1 Serving/260g	299	115	7.3	12.5	4.1	2.7
Chilli Chicken & Spicy Cous Cous, HE, Tesco*	1 Serving/190g	251	132	6.5	21.1	2.4	1.5
Chilli, Tomato, Chickpea & Butterbean, Tesco*	1 Pack/130g	146	112	3.4	14.3	4.6	0.5
Chunky, Somerfield*	1 Serving/250g	40	16	1.0	3.0	0.0	0.9
Classic Caesar, M & S*	½ Pack/112g	174	155	2.9	6.8	12.7	0.5
Club, Safeway*	1 Serving/215g	226	105	1.3	6.0	8.4	1.3
Coleslaw & Potato, 3% Fat, M & S*	1oz/28g	20	72	2.7	7.7	3.4	1.5
Continental Four Leaf, Sainsbury's*	1oz/28g	5	18	1.6	2.1	0.3	0.8
Continental Leaf, Asda*	1oz/28g	4	16	1.4	1.4	0.5	1.4
Coronation Chicken & Rice, Asda*	1oz/28g	67	241	6.7	15.2	17.0	0.4
Coronation Chicken, Salad Bar, Asda*	1oz/28g	82	293	5.7	16.4	22.7	0.7
Cous Cous & Vegetable, 2% Fat, M & S*	1oz/28g	39	139	3.9	17.5	4.9	2.0
Cous Cous, Better For You, Morrisons*	½ Pot/113g	164	145	4.6	23.8	3.5	0.5
Cous Cous, Tesco*	1 Serving/25g	35	141	4.8	26.9	1.6	0.6
Creamy Ranch Style, Kraft*	1 Tsp/5ml	4	85	0.9	14.5	2.3	2.4
Crisp & Sweet, Asda*	1 Serving/100g	19	19	0.9	3.1	0.3	1.7
Crisp Mixed, Tesco*	1 Pack/200g	38	19	1.1	2.8	0.3	1.5
Crispy Green, Safeway*	1 Bag/165g	21	13	1.0	1.6	0.3	1.1
Crispy Leaf, Asda*	1oz/28g	4	14	0.8	1.6	0.5	0.9
Crispy Mix, M & S*	1oz/28g	10	36	1.3	6.6	0.5	1.2
Crispy, Somerfield*	1 Pack/140g	17	12	1.0	2.0	0.0	0.0
Crispy, Tesco*	1oz/28g	6	20	1.2	3.0	0.3	1.6
Crunchy Layered, Tesco*	1 Serving/54g	15	27	1.1	4.9	0.3	1.7
Crunchy, M & S*	1oz/28g	6	21	1.1	3.5	0.3	1.4
Crunchy Mix, Co-Op*	1oz/28g	7	25	1.0	4.0	0.3	2.0
Crunchy Shredded, Safeway*	1 Serving/50g	10	19	1.2	2.9	0.3	1.5
Crunchy Spring, M & S*	1oz/28g	6	21	1.1	3.5	0.3	1.4
Crunchy Spring, Side, M & S*	1 Serving/160g	32	20	0.9	4.1	0.2	1.3
Egg & Potato Fresh, M & S*	1 Serving/250g	150	60	3.0	4.6	2.9	0.9
Egg & Potato, GFY, Asda*	1 Serving/290g	206	71	2.6	5.0	4.5	0.0
Endive & Radicchio, Somerfield*	1 Pack/150g	20	13	2.0	1.0	0.0	0.0
English Garden, Tesco*	1 Serving/180g	22	12	0.7	1.8	0.2	0.7
Family, Somerfield*	1 Serving/67g	12	18	0.8	2.9	0.4	1.3
Fine Cut, Asda*	1oz/28g	7	24	1.2	4.1	0.3	2.1
Florida, Retail	1oz/28g	63	224	0.9	9.7	20.5	1.0
Four Leaf, Tesco*	1oz/28g	4	15	0.8	1.8	0.5	0.9
Fresh & Crispy, Tesco*	1 Salad/230g	30	13	0.7	1.9	0.3	0.7
Fresh Green With Sweetcorn & Radish, Safeway*	1 Pack/210g	55	26	1.1	4.8	0.3	1.1
Fresh Sugar Plum Tomato, Safeway*	1 Serving/160g	46	29	1.1	3.2	1.3	1.2
Garden, Ready to Eat, Tesco*	1 Pack/225g	34	15	1.0	2.0	0.3	0.9
Garden, Safeway*	1oz/28g	6	23	1.1	4.0	0.3	2.0
Garden With Watercress, M & S*	1 Salad/80g	10	12	1.5	1.4	0.1	1.4
Garden With Yoghurt & Mint Dressing, GFY, Asda*	1 Serving/195g	51	26	1.1	3.2	1.0	0.0
Gourment Nicoise, M & S*	1 Serving/500g	575	115	4.8	3.9	8.9	0.0
Gourmet Caesar, M & S*	1 Serving/100g	155	155	4.1	7.1	12.1	0.8

S

SALAD,	Measure WEIGHT/INFO	per Measure KCAL	Nutrition Values per 100g / 100ml KCAL	PROT	CARB	FAT	FIBRE
Gourmet Continental, Waitrose*	1 Serving/150g	23	15	0.8	1.6	0.5	0.9
Greek	1oz/28g	36	130	2.7	1.9	12.5	0.8
Greek Layered, Perfectly Balanced, Waitrose*	½ Pack/140g	67	48	2.4	3.2	2.8	0.7
Greek, M & S*	1 Serving/125g	119	95	2.5	2.4	8.2	0.7
Greek Style Layered, Perfectly Balanced, Waitrose*	1 Serving/280g	134	48	2.4	3.2	2.8	0.7
Green	1oz/28g	3	12	0.7	1.8	0.3	1.0
Green, Fresh, Safeway*	½ Pack/98g	14	14	0.9	1.9	0.3	0.8
Green, M & S*	1oz/28g	4	13	0.8	1.7	0.3	0.9
Green Pesto, Waitrose*	1 Serving/100g	193	193	6.7	2.3	17.4	0.7
Green, Side, Sainsbury's*	1 Pack/200g	28	14	0.8	2.1	0.3	0.8
Green With Honey & Mustard Dressing, M & S*	1 Pack/200g	120	60	0.9	2.7	4.8	0.8
Ham, Healthier Choice, Ginsters*	1 Pack/176g	231	131	9.3	16.2	4.3	0.0
Herb, M & S*	1 Pack/100g	20	20	2.9	1.4	0.4	1.9
Herb, Sainsbury's*	1 Serving/40g	10	26	1.9	2.0	1.1	1.7
Herb, Tesco*	1oz/28g	4	16	1.1	1.8	0.5	0.9
Hot Smoked Salmon & Rice, Deli Meal, M & S*	1 Pack/380g	570	150	6.5	15.1	6.9	0.2
Iceberg & Cabbage, Asda*	½ Pack/125g	24	19	1.0	3.1	0.3	1.5
Italian, Organic, M & S*	1oz/28g	5	17	1.3	1.8	0.5	0.1
Italian Style, Asda*	1 Serving/20g	2	12	1.5	1.3	0.1	1.2
Italian Style, Sainsbury's*	1/3 Pack/60g	80	134	2.1	8.0	10.9	1.1
Italian Style, Tesco*	1oz/28g	4	14	1.1	1.4	0.4	1.3
Italian Wild Rocket & Parmesan, Sainsbury's*	1 Serving/50g	89	177	7.5	3.4	14.8	0.5
Layered Tuna, Tesco*	1 Serving/370g	466	126	4.4	9.4	7.9	1.0
Layered With Egg, Somerfield*	1 Pot/300g	543	181	3.0	3.0	18.0	0.0
Layered With Tuna, Somerfield*	1 Pot/255g	599	235	5.0	5.0	22.0	0.0
Leafy Mixed, Safeway*	1oz/28g	4	14	0.9	1.5	0.5	1.0
Leafy, Tesco*	1oz/28g	4	14	1.2	1.5	0.4	1.2
Luxury Potato, Asda*	1 Serving/50g	119	237	1.0	11.0	21.0	0.0
Mediterranean Style, Asda*	½ Pack/135g	22	16	1.0	3.0	0.0	0.0
Mediterranean Style, Morrisons*	1 Serving/90g	13	14	1.5	1.9	0.2	0.0
Mediterranean Style, Side, Sainsbury's*	1 Pack/245g	0	25	0.9	3.0	1.0	1.2
Mediterranean Tuna, John West*	1oz/28g	30	106	8.0	5.0	6.0	2.0
Mixed Bean, Asda*	½ Can/145g	129	89	5.8	13.7	1.2	6.3
Mixed Bean, Tesco*	1 Serving/70g	49	70	3.2	13.1	0.5	1.9
Mixed Bean, Waitrose*	1 Serving/210g	229	109	8.7	13.6	2.2	4.6
Mixed Bean, WTF, Sainsbury's*	1 Can/270g	227	84	5.4	13.5	0.9	3.8
Mixed Leaf, Asda*	1 Serving/100g	21	21	1.5	3.2	0.2	2.1
Mixed Leaf With Olive Oil Dressing, Pizza Express*	1 Pack/240g	326	136	0.9	2.1	14.1	0.7
Mixed Leaves, Somerfield*	1 Pack/140g	17	12	1.0	2.0	0.0	0.0
Mixed Leaves, Tesco*	1 Serving/20g	3	14	0.9	1.6	0.4	0.9
Mixed, Sainsbury's*	1 Serving/100g	21	21	1.4	3.4	0.2	2.1
Mixed With Peppers & Iceberg Lettuce, Somerfield*	1 Pack/200g	50	25	1.0	5.0	0.0	0.0
Moroccan Style Cous Cous, M & S*	½ Pack/100g	160	160	5.0	32.8	1.2	4.8
New Potato & Egg, WTF, Sainsbury's*	1 Serving/315g	192	61	2.5	5.0	3.4	0.6
New Potato & Egg With Salad Cream, Side, M & S*	1 Pack/305g	183	60	3.0	4.6	2.9	0.9
New Potato & Sweet Chilli Prawn, M & S*	1 Pack/210g	147	70	2.8	14.0	0.5	0.7
New Potato, Less Than 3% Fat, M & S*	1 Pot/190g	143	75	1.7	14.4	1.3	1.2
New Potato, M & S*	1oz/28g	55	195	1.9	10.4	16.2	0.7
Nicoise, Lunch Pot, M & S*	1 Pot/330g	330	100	5.6	4.9	6.7	1.0
Nicoise, Pizza Express*	1 Salad/400g	729	182	10.0	16.3	9.3	0.0
Nicoise Style, Layered, Waitrose*	1 Bowl/275g	129	47	2.7	5.8	1.4	1.0
Noodle With Thai Style Chicken, M & S*	½ Pot/145g	160	110	5.2	11.6	4.9	1.4
Pollo, Pizza Express*	1 Serving/100g	572	572	41.2	32.5	31.8	0.0
Potato, 50% Less Fat, Asda*	½ Pot/62g	47	76	1.6	11.2	2.7	1.5

S

SALAD,	Measure WEIGHT/INFO	per Measure KCAL	Nutrition Values per 100g / 100ml KCAL	PROT	CARB	FAT	FIBRE
Potato, Asda*	¼ Pot/57g	67	117	0.9	12.5	7.0	1.1
Potato Baby, With Mint, TTD, Sainsbury's*	1 Serving/100g	204	204	2.0	10.8	17.0	0.7
Potato, Chunky, Somerfield*	1oz/28g	59	212	1.0	3.0	22.0	0.0
Potato, Creamy, Asda*	1oz/28g	61	219	1.0	11.9	18.6	0.7
Potato, Eat Smart, Safeway*	½ Pack/121g	85	70	1.7	10.2	2.0	1.9
Potato, GFY, Asda*	½ Pack/125g	145	116	1.3	12.0	7.0	0.0
Potato, HE, Tesco*	1 Pot/250g	218	87	2.2	12.0	3.4	0.9
Potato, Kentucky Fried Chicken*	1 Portion/160g	229	143	2.5	14.3	8.7	1.8
Potato, Less Than 4% Fat, Safeway*	1 Serving/250g	213	85	2.1	13.1	2.7	0.9
Potato, Less Than 5% Fat, Somerfield*	1oz/28g	24	86	2.0	11.0	4.0	0.0
Potato, M & S*	1oz/28g	55	195	1.2	8.5	17.3	1.3
Potato, Reduced Calorie, Waitrose*	1oz/28g	22	77	2.2	10.4	2.9	0.9
Potato, Reduced Fat, Sainsbury's*	1oz/28g	34	121	1.0	11.8	7.3	1.6
Potato, Salad Bar, Asda*	1oz/28g	52	187	0.6	11.6	15.4	1.1
Potato, Tesco*	1 Pot/125g	219	175	1.5	12.2	13.3	0.9
Potato With Mayonnaise	1oz/28g	67	239	1.6	12.2	20.8	0.9
Potato With Mayonnaise, Retail	1oz/28g	80	287	1.5	11.4	26.5	0.8
Potato With Reduced Calorie Dressing, Retail	1oz/28g	27	97	1.3	14.8	4.1	0.8
Prawn & Egg, Leaf, Shapers, Boots*	1 Pack/182g	193	106	6.7	2.1	7.9	1.0
Prawn Cocktail, Tesco*	1 Pack/300g	360	120	5.7	10.9	6.0	0.8
Primavera, Finest, Tesco*	1 Pack/100g	25	25	2.4	2.4	0.6	1.3
Ranch Style, TTD, Sainsbury's*	½ Pack/80g	122	153	3.1	9.8	11.3	1.1
Ratatouille & Roast Vegetables, Waitrose*	1oz/28g	31	110	2.2	16.0	4.1	1.0
Red Cheddar & Edam, Sainsbury's*	1 Bowl/450g	482	107	4.4	12.8	4.2	1.1
Red Leaf & Rocket, Sainsbury's*	1 Serving/50g	11	21	3.5	1.6	0.1	1.7
Red Thai Chicken With Noodles, Tesco*	1 Pack/300g	342	114	7.2	20.2	0.5	1.4
Ribbon, M & S*	1oz/28g	5	17	0.8	3.2	0.2	1.7
Roast Chicken, Tesco*	1 Salad/300g	348	116	5.3	7.0	7.4	1.0
Roasted Vegetables & Cous Cous, Sainsbury's*	1 Pot/225g	349	155	5.5	26.3	3.1	0.0
Rocket, Tesco*	1oz/28g	4	16	1.3	1.7	0.5	1.2
Salmon & Roquette, M & S*	1 Serving/255g	306	120	3.9	8.5	8.0	1.0
Santa Tomato, Side, M & S*	1 Pack/225g	146	65	0.8	3.3	5.5	0.9
Selection, Fresh, M & S*	1 Pack/230g	32	14	0.7	2.1	0.3	0.9
Selection, Side, M & S*	1 Serving/255g	153	60	1.1	2.5	5.0	1.3
Skipjack Tuna, John West*	1 Can/192g	190	99	7.3	3.7	6.1	0.0
Smoked Ham, Weight Watchers*	1 Pack/181g	233	129	11.0	16.6	2.0	3.0
Spicy Bean, Tesco*	1 Serving/125g	111	89	4.9	12.1	2.3	2.5
Spicy Chickpea Feta & Chilli, M & S*	1oz/28g	56	200	7.2	13.1	13.4	2.9
Summer Bean, M & S*	1 Pack/225g	225	100	5.8	16.7	1.3	3.9
Summer, M & S*	1oz/28g	6	20	0.8	3.6	0.4	1.2
Sweet & Crispy, Fresh, Safeway*	1 Serving/90g	19	21	0.9	3.7	0.3	1.5
Sweet & Crispy, Side, Sainsbury's*	1 Serving/74g	32	43	1.3	8.2	0.5	1.3
Sweet & Crispy, Somerfield*	1 Pack/100g	25	25	1.0	5.0	0.0	0.0
Sweet & Crunchy, Morrisons*	1 Serving/100g	20	20	0.8	4.0	0.3	1.3
Sweet & Crunchy, Tesco*	1 Pack/285g	51	18	0.8	3.0	0.3	1.7
Sweet & Sour Prawn Noodle, HE, Tesco*	1 Pack/190g	122	64	5.0	9.4	0.7	0.4
Sweet Carrot, 3% Fat, M & S*	1oz/28g	21	75	1.3	16.7	1.2	1.4
Sweet Crispy, Eat Smart, Safeway*	1 Serving/220g	59	27	1.0	4.9	0.4	1.3
Sweet Crispy, Safeway*	1 Serving/220g	132	60	2.2	10.8	0.9	2.9
Sweet Crunchy, Sainsbury's*	1oz/28g	6	20	1.1	3.5	0.3	1.4
Sweet, Layered, Tesco*	1 Serving/285g	117	41	1.9	7.4	0.5	2.1
Sweet Leaf & Carrot, Asda*	½ Pack/164g	34	21	0.9	3.6	0.3	1.4
Sweet Leaf, Sainsbury's*	1 Serving/100g	21	21	0.8	3.2	0.5	1.5
Sweet Mix With Endive, Safeway*	1 Serving/30g	4	13	1.7	0.9	0.3	1.7

S

	Measure WEIGHT/INFO	per Measure KCAL	Nutrition Values per 100g / 100ml KCAL	PROT	CARB	FAT	FIBRE
SALAD,							
Sweet Pepper With Corn, Tesco*	1 Pack/270g	103	38	1.3	7.2	0.5	1.5
Tabbouleh Feta, Finest Tesco*	1 Serving/100g	118	118	4.2	13.7	5.2	0.6
Thai Style Chicken, M & S*	1 Serving/195g	205	105	6.7	15.1	1.9	1.9
Three Bean, Tesco*	1 Can/300g	330	110	7.7	17.6	1.0	5.3
Tomato & Mozarella, M & S*	1oz/28g	49	175	10.6	2.6	13.3	0.5
Tomato & Onion	1oz/28g	20	72	0.8	4.0	6.1	1.0
Tuna, HE, Tesco*	1 Serving/300g	399	133	6.2	10.5	7.3	0.9
Tuna Nicoise, Sainsbury's*	1 Pack/183g	234	128	11.3	1.8	8.4	0.0
Vegetable, Canned	1oz/28g	40	143	1.6	13.0	9.8	1.2
Vegetable, Heinz*	1 Can/195g	259	133	1.5	12.6	8.5	1.3
Waldorf	1oz/28g	54	193	1.4	7.5	17.7	1.3
Watercress & Spinach, Asda*	1 Serving/50g	8	16	2.1	1.7	0.1	1.7
Watercress, Morrisons*	1 Bag/100g	17	17	1.7	1.2	0.7	0.0
Watercress, Spinach & Rocket, Sainsbury's*	1oz/28g	7	25	3.0	1.2	0.9	1.7
Wheat With Roasted Vegetables, Sainsbury's*	1 Pack/220g	339	154	3.3	17.0	8.3	4.5
Wild Rocket, Safeway*	1 Serving/75g	14	18	1.3	2.1	0.5	1.1
With Sweetcorn, Side, Tesco*	1 Serving/135g	51	38	1.3	7.2	0.5	1.5
SALAD BOWL,							
Avocado & Tomato, Sainsbury's*	1 Pack/180g	97	54	1.0	6.7	2.6	1.3
Cheese & Coleslaw, COU, M & S*	1 Serving/260g	130	50	4.6	4.7	1.6	1.3
Coleslaw, Tesco*	1 Bowl/300g	327	109	1.0	3.4	10.1	1.3
Cottage Cheese, Asda*	1 Serving/149g	97	65	8.0	3.2	2.2	0.0
Crispy, M & S*	1 Serving/250g	88	35	1.3	6.6	0.5	1.2
French Style, Sainsbury's*	1oz/28g	15	55	1.0	4.8	3.5	1.5
Greek, M & S*	1 Serving/bowl/255g	242	95	2.5	2.4	8.2	0.7
Greek Style, Somerfield*	1 Bowl/225g	178	79	2.2	3.5	6.2	1.1
Tomato & Basil, M & S*	1 Serving/245g	233	95	0.8	4.4	8.4	0.7
Tomato, Sainsbury's*	½ Bowl/150g	93	62	0.9	4.4	4.5	1.6
Tuna, Fresh, Asda*	1 Serving/160g	184	115	8.0	5.0	7.0	0.0
SALAD CREAM,							
Salad Cream	1 Serving/30g	104	348	1.5	16.7	31.0	0.0
60% Less Fat, Asda*	1 Serving/10g	14	138	0.8	11.0	10.0	0.0
BGTY, Sainsbury's*	1 Tbsp/15g	21	140	0.8	10.8	9.9	0.3
Heinz*	1 Tbsp/10g	33	331	1.4	20.3	26.7	0.0
Light, Heinz*	1 Tbsp/10g	24	244	1.8	13.5	19.9	0.0
Morrisons*	1 Tsp/5g	16	312	1.4	19.0	25.0	0.0
Reduced Calorie	1 Serving/30g	58	194	1.0	9.4	17.2	0.0
Sainsbury's*	1 Tbsp/15g	50	333	2.7	17.0	27.7	0.0
Somerfield*	1 Serving/30g	104	348	1.0	20.0	29.0	0.0
Tesco*	1 Tbsp/25g	85	338	2.4	18.5	27.7	0.4
Value, Tesco*	1 Serving/50g	68	135	1.1	12.1	8.5	0.4
SALAMI,							
Danish, Asda*	1 Slice/8g	43	540	13.0	0.5	54.0	0.0
German, Asda*	1 Slice/8g	29	367	19.0	2.9	31.0	0.0
German, Somerfield*	1 Pack/100g	322	322	22.0	1.0	26.0	0.0
Milanoi, Asda*	1 Slice/5g	21	425	24.0	3.4	35.0	0.0
Napoli, M & S*	1oz/28g	104	371	27.3	0.7	28.2	0.0
Napolii, Sainsbury's*	1 Slice/8g	27	343	24.2	1.5	27.0	0.1
Pepper, German, Sainsbury's*	1 Slice/10g	33	326	22.0	1.0	26.0	0.3
Peppered, German, Asda*	1 Slice/20g	79	394	21.5	4.3	32.3	0.0
Peppered, German, Somerfield*	1 Pack/100g	341	341	24.0	4.0	25.0	0.0
SALMON,							
Appetisers, Smoked, Tesco*	1 Pack/100g	224	224	15.1	0.7	17.9	1.7
Blinis, Smoked, M & S*	1oz/28g	67	240	11.9	18.9	13.0	1.8

S

SALMON,	Measure WEIGHT/INFO	per Measure KCAL	Nutrition Values per 100g / 100ml KCAL	PROT	CARB	FAT	FIBRE
Dill & Sauce, Youngs*	1 Pack/435g	265	61	6.1	4.2	2.3	0.1
En Croute, Luxury, M & S*	1oz/28g	59	210	11.9	9.4	13.7	2.2
En Croute, Retail	1oz/28g	81	288	11.8	18.0	19.1	0.0
En Croute, Sainsbury's*	1 Serving/179g	533	298	9.7	18.4	20.0	1.2
Fillets, & Butter, M & S*	1oz/28g	64	230	16.7	0.0	18.0	0.0
Fillets, Boneless, Sainsbury's*	1 Serving/100g	215	215	24.2	0.0	13.1	0.0
Fillets, Boneless, Tesco*	1 Serving/150g	270	180	20.2	0.0	11.0	0.0
Fillets, Cajun, Waitrose*	1 Serving/150g	215	143	20.6	0.4	6.5	0.0
Fillets, Chargrilled, Sainsbury's*	1 Serving/270 g	270	243	20.9	0.2	17.6	0.0
Fillets, Creamy Watercress Sauce, Scottish, Seafresh*	1 Pack 300g	528	176	13.7	1.2	12.9	0.1
Fillets, Iceland*	1 Fillet/150g	293	195	22.3	0.0	11.7	0.0
Fillets, In Creme Fraiche & Red Pepper Sauce, Sainsbury's*	1 Serving/168g	227	135	13.8	2.0	8.0	0.0
Fillets, In Brine, John West*	1oz/28g	52	187	22.0	0.0	11.0	0.0
Fillets, Lime & Coriander Marinade, Pacific, Sainsbury's*	1 Serving/100g	139	139	24.4	1.3	4.1	0.9
Fillets, M & S*	1 Serving/150g	203	135	20.2	0.2	5.8	0.0
Fillets, Organic, M & S*	1oz/28g	56	200	20.3	0.1	13.4	0.0
Fillets, Poached, M & S*	1oz/28g	56	200	21.7	0.1	12.7	0.0
Fillets, Sainsbury's*	1 Serving/180g	387	215	24.2	0.0	13.1	0.0
Fillets, Scottish Caledonian, M & S*	1 Fillet/130g	260	200	20.3	0.1	13.4	0.0
Fillets, Skinless & Boneless, Asda*	1 Fillet/130g	280	215	24.2	0.0	13.1	0.0
Fillets, Somerfield*	1oz/28g	50	180	20.0	0.0	11.0	0.0
Fillets, With a Cream Sauce, Scottish, M & S*	1 Serving/200g	360	180	13.8	1.0	13.0	0.1
Flakes, Honey Roast, M & S*	1oz/28g	56	200	27.6	3.2	8.8	0.0
Flakes, Honey Roast, Sainsbury's*	1 Serving/100g	169	169	23.8	0.5	8.0	0.1
Flakes, Honey Roasted, Tesco*	1 Serving/100g	211	211	21.5	2.3	12.9	0.0
Flakes, Poached, M & S*	1oz/28g	53	190	24.0	0.0	10.5	0.0
Fresh, Waitrose*	1 Fillet/163g	290	178	20.7	0.0	10.5	3.3
Frozen, Iceland*	1 Steak/150g	293	195	22.3	0.0	11.7	0.0
Goujons, Tesco*	1 Pack/150g	305	203	19.2	5.9	11.4	0.6
Grilled	1oz/28g	60	215	24.2	0.0	13.1	0.0
Lightly Smoked, Scottish, M & S*	1 Portion/141g	228	162	19.5	0.1	8.8	0.2
Lunchbox, COU, M & S*	1 Pack/235g	200	85	5.1	13.1	1.4	0.9
Mornay, With Broccoli, Weight Watchers*	1 Pack/290g	261	90	9.6	9.0	1.7	0.7
Oak, Smoked, M & S*	1oz/28g	52	185	22.4	0.0	10.8	0.0
Organic, Scottish, Waitrose*	1oz/28g	50	180	20.2	0.0	11.0	0.0
Pink, Canned In Brine, Flesh & Bones, Drained	1oz/28g	43	153	23.5	0.0	6.6	0.0
Pink, Canned In Brine, Flesh Only, Drained	1oz/28g	43	153	23.5	0.0	6.6	0.0
Pink, John West*	½ Can/87g	135	155	23.0	0.0	7.0	0.0
Pink, Skinless & Boneless, John West*	1oz/28g	35	124	22.0	0.0	4.0	0.0
Pink, Skinless & Boneless, Sainsbury's*	1 Can/125g	173	138	21.5	0.1	6.0	0.1
Pink, SmartPrice, Asda*	½ Can/78g	121	155	23.0	0.0	7.0	0.0
Pink, Wild, Princes*	1 Serving/50g	62	124	18.3	0.0	5.6	0.0
Platter, GFY, Asda*	1 Pack/400g	376	94	7.0	8.0	3.8	1.4
Potatoes & Vegetables, Scottish, M & S*	1 Pack/400g	460	115	7.9	5.8	6.9	0.9
Raw	1oz/28g	50	180	20.2	0.0	11.0	0.0
Red, Asda*	1 Serving/105g	166	158	16.8	0.0	10.1	0.0
Red, Canned In Brine, Flesh & Bones, Drained	1oz/28g	43	153	23.5	0.0	6.6	0.0
Red, Canned In Brine, Flesh Only, Drained	1oz/28g	47	167	21.6	0.0	9.0	0.0
Red, John West*	1 Can/105g	176	168	24.0	0.0	8.0	0.0
Red, Medium, John West*	½ Can/89g	142	160	22.0	0.0	8.0	0.0
Red, Pacific, Tesco*	1 Can/212g	335	158	16.8	0.0	10.1	0.0
Red, Sainsbury's*	1 Serving/106g	169	159	16.8	0.1	10.1	0.1
Red, Skinless & Boneless, Canadian, M & S*	1 Serving/100g	160	160	19.0	0.0	9.1	0.0
Red, Skinless & Boneless, Glenryck*	1 Serving/73g	91	124	21.7	0.3	4.1	0.3

	Measure WEIGHT/INFO	per Measure KCAL	Nutrition Values per 100g / 100ml KCAL	PROT	CARB	FAT	FIBRE
SALMON,							
Red, Skinless & Boneless, John West*	1oz/28g	40	142	22.0	0.0	6.0	0.0
Red, Skinless & Boneless, Tesco*	1 Serving/180g	302	168	22.5	0.0	8.7	0.0
Red, Wild Pacific, Safeway*	1 Can/213g	328	154	23.5	0.0	6.6	0.0
Slices, Smoked, M & S*	1oz/28g	52	185	22.4	0.0	10.8	0.0
Slices, Smoked, Tesco*	1oz/28g	50	179	22.9	0.0	9.7	0.0
Smoked	1oz/28g	40	142	25.4	0.0	4.5	0.0
Smoked, Hot, Sainsbury's*	1 Serving/62g	100	161	22.0	1.1	7.2	0.1
Smoked, Irish, M & S*	1oz/28g	38	136	23.3	0.0	4.8	0.0
Smoked, Organic, Scottish, Sainsbury's*	1 Serving/100g	186	186	22.7	1.6	9.9	0.1
Smoked, Pink, John West*	1oz/28g	43	155	23.0	0.0	7.0	0.0
Smoked, Scottish, Asda*	1 Slice/26g	46	182	23.0	0.0	10.0	0.0
Smoked, Scottish, Morrisons*	1 Serving/100g	243	243	21.6	0.3	17.3	0.0
Smoked, Scottish, Sainsbury's*	1oz/28g	48	172	23.3	0.1	8.8	0.1
Smoked, Scottish, Somerfield*	1oz/28g	45	161	22.0	1.0	8.0	0.0
Smoked, Waitrose*	1 Serving/100g	176	176	22.9	0.0	9.4	0.6
Steaks, Asda*	1oz/28g	60	215	24.2	0.0	13.1	0.0
Steaks, M & S*	1 Serving/150g	308	205	19.1	0.5	14.2	0.0
Steaks, Somerfield*	1oz/28g	50	180	20.0	0.0	11.0	0.0
Steaks, Tesco*	1 Steak/175g	315	180	20.2	0.0	11.0	0.0
Steamed	1oz/28g	55	197	20.1	0.0	13.0	0.0
Strips, Smoked, Scottish, Tesco*	½ Pack/100g	179	179	22.9	0.0	9.7	0.0
Tail Joint, Lemon & Herb Butter, M & S*	1 Pack/480g	864	180	18.8	0.8	11.4	0.2
Thai Noodles, HE, Tesco*	1 Pack/350g	231	66	6.7	7.1	1.2	1.5
Thinly Sliced, Smoked, Sainsbury's*	1 Slice/20g	31	157	23.6	0.1	7.0	0.1
Wafer Thin, Scottish, M & S*	1oz/28g	52	187	22.4	0.0	10.8	0.0
With Herb Vegetables, HE, Tesco*	1 Pack/350g	228	65	6.6	3.8	2.6	0.9
With Spinach & Cheese, Atlantic, Bird's Eye*	1 Serving/241g	415	172	9.8	4.2	12.9	0.1
SALSA,							
Fresh, Sainsbury's*	1oz/28g	15	54	1.7	7.0	2.1	0.9
Fresh, Waitrose*	1oz/28g	16	57	1.2	6.9	2.7	1.0
M & S*	½ Jar/136g	95	70	1.2	12.0	2.4	1.5
Medium Hot, Discovery*	1oz/28g	16	58	1.1	8.1	2.4	2.1
Mild, Organic, Evernat*	1oz/28g	136	484	4.5	60.4	26.6	0.0
Spicy Bean, Princes*	1 Serving/110g	92	84	3.6	16.7	0.3	0.0
Spicy, Less Than 3% Fat, M & S*	½ Pot/85g	30	35	1.3	5.6	0.8	0.8
Taco, Old El Paso*	¼ Pack/29g	13	46	1.5	10.0	0.0	0.0
Taco, Tex 'n' Mex, Sainsbury's*	1 Serving/100g	37	37	1.3	7.3	0.1	0.4
Tomato, Chunky, Tex Mex, Tesco*	1 Serving/50g	26	52	1.0	6.4	2.5	1.0
Tuna, Good Intentions, Somerfield*	1 Pack/51g	142	278	17.4	47.4	2.1	2.7
SALT, Sea, Organic, M & S*	1oz/28g	132	472	5.3	54.2	24.0	7.0
SAMBAL Oelek Wok, Findus*	½ Bag/300g	255	85	3.0	17.0	0.4	0.0
SAMOSAS,							
Chicken Tikka, Sainsbury's*	2 Samosas/100g	239	239	8.3	22.5	12.9	3.1
Co-Op*	1oz/28g	70	250	6.0	34.0	10.0	2.0
Dim Sum Selection, Sainsbury's*	1 Samosas/12g	24	196	3.4	28.6	7.6	2.8
Lamb, Waitrose*	1oz/28g	87	310	8.5	18.1	22.6	0.8
Mini, Sainsbury's*	1 Serving/28g	82	294	6.9	33.2	14.8	2.7
Vegetable	1oz/28g	132	472	3.1	22.3	41.8	1.8
Vegetable, M & S*	1 Samosa/45g	115	255	5.1	24.8	15.3	2.8
Vegetable, Retail	1oz/28g	61	217	5.1	30.0	9.3	2.5
Vegetable, Tesco*	1 Samosa/50g	126	252	5.0	28.4	13.2	2.7
Vegetable, Waitrose*	1 Samosas/50g	107	214	3.3	26.3	10.6	0.8
SANDWICH,							
All Day Breakfast, Finest, Tesco*	1 Pack/275g	660	240	9.7	16.4	15.1	1.6

SANDWICH,	Measure WEIGHT/INFO	per Measure KCAL	Nutrition Values per 100g / 100ml KCAL	PROT	CARB	FAT	FIBRE
Bacon, Chicken & Avocado Ultimate, M & S*	1 Pack/241g	552	229	10.7	17.9	12.7	2.8
Bacon, Chicken, Cheese, Big, Sainsbury's*	1 Pack/254g	734	289	11.7	18.0	17.9	0.0
Bacon, Chicken, Cheese Triple, BGTY, Sainsbury's*	1 Pack/263g	534	203	11.7	19.4	7.6	4.4
Bacon, Lettuce & Tomato & Chicken Salad, Co-Op*	1 Pack/230g	472	205	10.0	21.0	9.0	2.0
Bacon, Lettuce & Tomato, Asda*	1 Pack/262g	618	236	12.2	20.3	12.0	3.0
Bacon, Lettuce & Tomato, Boots*	1oz/28g	75	268	10.0	21.0	16.0	2.2
Bacon, Lettuce & Tomato, COU, M & S*	1 Pack/174g	270	155	11.0	22.4	2.3	2.4
Bacon, Lettuce & Tomato Deep Filled, Asda*	1 Pack/206g	606	294	13.3	21.8	17.0	3.0
Bacon, Lettuce & Tomato, HE, Tesco*	1 Pack/165g	221	134	10.3	19.8	1.5	2.0
Bacon, Lettuce & Tomato, Healthy Selection, Budgens*	1 Pack/183g	388	212	10.1	21.3	9.6	2.8
Bacon, Lettuce & Tomato, Shapers, Boots*	1 Pack/171g	328	192	10.0	22.0	7.1	2.3
Bacon, Lettuce & Tomato, Starbucks*	1 Serving/190g	437	230	7.7	28.3	9.6	0.0
Bacon, Lettuce & Tomato, Tesco*	1 Serving/203g	629	310	8.0	18.4	22.7	1.4
Bap, Cheese & Coleslaw, Eat Smart, Safeway*	1 Bap/200g	624	312	9.9	24.4	19.8	2.6
Bap, Malted, Chargrilled Chicken, Co-Op*	1 Bap/201g	492	245	9.0	23.0	13.0	2.0
Bap, Malted, Chicken Salad, Co-Op*	1 Bap/252g	491	195	8.0	19.0	10.0	2.0
Bap, Malted, Three Cheese & Spring Onion, Co-Op*	1 Bap/226g	768	340	9.0	21.0	25.0	1.0
Bap, Malted, Tuna & Sweetcorn, Co-Op*	1 Bap/212g	530	250	9.0	24.0	13.0	2.0
Barm, White, Corned Beef & Onion, Open Choice Foods*	1 Roll/144g	331	230	12.7	30.7	6.1	0.0
BBQ Chicken With Mayonnaise, Somerfield*	1oz/28g	77	276	13.0	23.0	15.0	0.0
Beef & Horseradish, Deep Filled, BGTY, Sainsbury's*	1 Pack/202g	313	155	11.4	22.0	2.4	2.4
Beef & Onion, American Style, The Big One, Sainsbury's*	1 Pack/386g	737	191	11.7	21.2	6.6	0.0
Beef Salad, COU, M & S*	1 Pack/183g	225	123	12.1	14.6	1.8	2.7
Beef Salad, GFY, Asda*	1 Pack/160g	250	156	12.0	20.0	3.1	3.1
Big Chicken Salad, M & S*	1 Serving/283g	509	180	9.8	19.4	7.3	1.5
Big Prawn & Mayonnaise on Oatmeal Bread, Sainsbury's*	1 Pack/259g	686	265	10.1	21.1	15.6	0.0
Bloomer, Honey & Mustard Chicken, BGTY, Sainsbury's*	1 Pack/162g	288	178	12.0	25.0	3.3	0.0
BLT, GFY, Asda*	1 Pack/171g	294	172	9.0	26.0	3.5	1.6
BLT, Waitrose*	1 Pack/210g	578	275	9.3	25.6	15.0	2.3
Breakfast, Co-Op*	1 Pack/242g	653	270	11.0	21.0	16.0	2.0
Breast of Chicken, Millers*	1 Pack/162g	343	212	13.8	19.3	8.9	0.0
Brie & Bacon, Asda*	1 Pack/181g	603	333	13.3	22.9	21.1	1.3
Brie & Grape, Finest, Tesco*	1 Pack/209g	527	252	8.5	20.6	15.1	1.5
Brie With Apple & Grapes, Sainsbury's*	1 Pack/220g	515	234	8.4	21.7	13.6	0.0
Brunch, St Ivel*	1 Serving/225g	581	258	10.2	26.0	12.6	0.0
Chargrill Chicken With Honey Mustard Mayo, Spar*	1 Pack/168g	428	255	13.1	25.0	11.4	0.0
Chargrilled Chicken & Tomato Relish, Shapers, Boots*	1 Pack/190g	295	155	12.0	20.0	3.0	3.1
Chargrilled Chicken & Watercress, BGTY, Sainsbury's*	1 Pack/172g	318	185	14.5	24.1	3.4	0.0
Chargrilled Chicken & Watercress, M & S*	1 Packet/173g	285	165	12.8	23.9	1.7	2.1
Chargrilled Chicken Caesar, Big, Sainsbury's*	1 Pack/216g	657	304	12.2	25.3	17.1	0.0
Chargrilled Chicken Salad, Weight Watchers*	1 Pack/186g	296	159	9.9	20.4	4.2	1.9
Chargrilled Chicken Salsa, BGTY, Sainsbury's*	1 Pack/225g	306	136	10.6	19.9	1.6	2.9
Chargrilled Chicken With Mango, TTD, Sainsbury's*	1 Pack/217g	352	162	11.0	22.2	3.2	0.0
Chargrilled Vegetable, Eat Smart, Safeway*	1 Pack/183g	265	145	7.4	23.4	2.3	2.8
Cheddar Cheese & Celery, Somerfield*	1oz/28g	78	280	10.0	16.0	20.0	0.0
Cheese & Carrot, Somerfield*	1oz/28g	50	180	11.0	24.0	4.0	0.0
Cheese & Celery, M & S*	1 Pack/180g	466	259	10.8	14.7	17.4	2.9
Cheese & Coleslaw, Asda*	1 Pack/262g	799	305	10.1	22.1	19.6	3.3
Cheese & Coleslaw, Safeway*	1 Pack/187g	501	268	8.4	22.9	17.1	0.5
Cheese & Coleslaw, Sutherland*	1 Serving/185g	376	203	10.7	29.9	4.5	0.0
Cheese & Onion, Tesco*	1 Pack/178g	621	349	11.5	17.1	26.1	2.2
Cheese & Onion, Weight Watchers*	1 Serving/100g	275	275	21.9	38.8	3.6	2.1
Cheese & Onion With Mayo, Somerfield*	1oz/28g	111	395	12.0	17.0	31.0	0.0
Cheese & Pickle, Shapers, Boots*	1 Pack/165g	342	207	9.8	31.0	4.9	2.3

S

SANDWICH,	Measure WEIGHT/INFO	per Measure KCAL	Nutrition Values per 100g / 100ml KCAL	PROT	CARB	FAT	FIBRE
Cheese & Spring Onion, Asda*	1 Pack/172g	635	369	11.6	22.6	25.8	3.1
Cheese & Spring Onion, Co-Op*	1 Pack/164g	607	370	12.0	21.0	26.0	3.0
Cheese & Spring Onion, Sutherland*	1oz/28g	104	371	12.0	21.4	26.4	0.0
Cheese & Tomato, Asda*	1 Pack/154g	388	252	11.0	23.2	12.8	3.7
Cheese & Tomato, Co-Op*	1 Pack/161g	394	245	10.0	23.0	12.0	2.0
Cheese & Tomato, Organic, M & S*	1 Pack/165g	559	339	11.8	24.8	21.4	1.9
Cheese & Tomato, Tesco*	1 Pack/182g	582	320	9.2	22.6	21.4	1.1
Cheese, Asda*	1 Pack/262g	618	236	12.2	20.3	12.0	3.0
Cheese Coleslaw, M & S*	1 Pack/186g	498	268	10.2	17.6	17.4	3.2
Cheese, Ham BLT Triple Pack, Asda*	1 Pack/260g	614	236	12.2	20.3	12.0	3.0
Cheese Salad, GFY, Asda*	1 Pack/100g	270	270	20.0	34.0	6.0	4.9
Cheese Salad, Shapers, Boots*	1 Pack/205g	308	150	9.7	22.0	2.5	2.2
Cheese, Tomato & Apple Chutney, Half Fat, Starbucks*	1 Pack/200g	318	159	8.8	21.3	4.2	0.0
Cheese, Tomato & Spring Onion, Shapers, Boots*	1 Pack/178g	306	172	12.0	24.0	3.1	2.0
Cheese Tomato Spring Onion, Shapers, Boots*	1 Pack/179g	344	192	11.0	22.0	6.7	3.3
Chicken & Bacon Club, Starbucks	1 Pack/252g	590	234	11.5	12.8	15.3	0.0
Chicken & Bacon, COU, M & S*	1 Pack/181g	244	135	12.2	17.1	2.2	3.8
Chicken & Bacon, Deep Filled, Co-Op*	1 Pack/166g	556	335	16.0	23.0	20.0	3.0
Chicken & Bacon, HE, Tesco*	1 Pack/155g	240	155	10.4	24.6	1.7	1.7
Chicken & Bacon, Shapers, Boots*	1 Pack/179g	317	177	14.0	19.0	5.0	3.1
Chicken & Bacon, Tesco*	1 Pack/195g	538	276	11.2	18.7	17.4	1.3
Chicken & Basil, Safeway*	1 Pack/179g	303	169	12.3	20.7	4.9	1.7
Chicken & Cress, COU, M & S*	1 Pack/161g	261	162	12.8	23.9	1.7	2.1
Chicken & Guacamole Bistro, Waitrose*	1 Pack/212g	363	171	10.5	20.5	5.2	3.5
Chicken & Maple Bacon, Somerfield*	1oz/28g	78	280	14.0	20.0	16.0	0.0
Chicken & Roast Tomatoes, COU, M & S*	1 Pack/195g	273	140	12.0	21.7	2.1	4.2
Chicken & Salad, COU, Cafe, M & S*	1 Pack/193g	261	135	9.8	19.0	1.9	1.6
Chicken & Salad, Low Fat, Waitrose*	1 Pack/188g	291	155	10.4	18.6	4.3	2.1
Chicken & Salad, M & S*	1 Pack/200g	408	204	9.2	17.6	10.8	1.5
Chicken & Stuffing, M & S*	1 Pack/166g	412	248	12.2	20.1	13.2	2.9
Chicken & Sweetcorn, Asda*	1 Pack/217g	536	247	10.8	20.7	13.5	2.9
Chicken & Sweetcorn, M & S*	1 Pack/186g	394	212	10.9	19.8	10.0	2.0
Chicken & Sweetcorn, Somerfield*	1oz/28g	71	252	10.0	28.0	11.0	0.0
Chicken & Sweetcorn, Tesco*	1 Pack/194g	433	223	9.4	22.1	10.8	1.7
Chicken & Watercress, HE, Tesco*	1 Pack/160g	253	158	13.8	21.7	1.8	1.7
Chicken, Burger King*	1 Sandwich/224g	659	294	11.2	23.6	17.4	1.3
Chicken Caesar, COU, M & S*	1 Serving/181g	244	135	12.2	19.9	2.4	4.3
Chicken Caesar, Finest, Tesco*	1 Pack/199g	454	228	15.4	19.2	10.0	1.4
Chicken Caesar Pocket, Shapers, Boots*	1 Pack/185g	332	179	11.0	21.0	5.7	2.9
Chicken Caesar Salad, Sainsbury's*	1 Pack/186g	299	161	11.2	20.4	3.8	0.0
Chicken Caesar Salad, Somerfield*	1oz/28g	71	255	15.0	20.0	13.0	0.0
Chicken Caesar Style Salad, GFY, Asda*	1 Pack/163g	289	177	11.0	27.0	2.8	2.1
Chicken Club, Burger King*	1 Sandwich/242g	620	256	12.3	22.3	13.2	1.6
Chicken Club, Wendy's*	1 Pack/213g	409	192	13.1	20.2	7.0	0.9
Chicken Cordon Bleu, Somerfield*	1oz/28g	78	279	14.0	19.0	17.0	0.0
Chicken, Eat Smart, Safeway*	1 Pack/141g	240	170	14.9	22.2	2.0	0.6
Chicken Fajita, Shapers, Boots*	1 Pack/192g	307	160	9.3	24.0	3.0	1.7
Chicken Jalfrezi Naan, Ready To Go, M & S*	1 Pack/288g	576	200	9.8	26.3	6.3	2.9
Chicken, Lightly Spiced, Starbucks*	1 Pack/200g	286	143	11.2	18.2	2.4	0.0
Chicken, No Mayo, Cafe Revive, M & S*	1 Pack/153g	230	150	14.1	17.9	2.4	3.1
Chicken No Mayo, M & S*	1 Pack/142g	220	155	15.0	17.5	3.0	3.1
Chicken, Prawn, Ham Salad Triple, HE, Tesco*	1 Pack/248g	350	141	10.4	20.8	1.8	2.1
Chicken Salad, Baxter & Platts*	1 Pack/165g	254	154	11.4	17.8	4.2	2.8
Chicken Salad, Best For You, BHS*	1 Pack/315g	992	315	23.2	43.1	5.3	3.3

S

SANDWICH,	Measure WEIGHT/INFO	per Measure KCAL	Nutrition Values per 100g / 100ml KCAL	PROT	CARB	FAT	FIBRE
Chicken Salad, BGTY, Sainsbury's*	1 Pack/197g	278	141	10.3	18.6	3.0	0.0
Chicken Salad, Co-Op*	1 Pack/195g	429	220	10.0	20.0	11.0	3.0
Chicken Salad, COU, M & S*	1 Pack/194g	256	132	9.8	19.0	1.9	1.6
Chicken Salad, Deep Filled, Asda*	1 Pack/247g	551	223	18.1	22.2	7.4	1.3
Chicken Salad, Deep Filled, Co-Op*	1 Pack/213g	437	205	10.0	20.0	9.0	1.0
Chicken Salad, Eat Smart, Safeway*	1 Pack/183g	265	145	13.7	17.1	2.3	0.8
Chicken Salad, GFY, Asda*	1 Pack/194g	310	160	10.0	22.0	3.5	1.4
Chicken Salad, Healthy Choice, Safeway*	1 Pack/185g	287	155	10.7	20.5	3.4	1.9
Chicken Salad, HE, Tesco*	1 Pack/193g	266	138	9.6	19.0	2.6	1.6
Chicken Salad, Homestyle, Somerfield*	1oz/28g	56	201	13.0	20.0	7.0	0.0
Chicken Salad, Millers*	1 Pack/200g	310	155	11.3	16.3	4.9	0.0
Chicken Salad, Montagu's*	1 Pack/162g	275	170	10.5	20.9	5.3	0.0
Chicken Salad On Malted Bread With Mayo, Safeway*	1 Pack/195g	392	201	10.9	18.7	9.2	2.1
Chicken Salad, Prawn Mayo, Egg & Bacon, Waitrose*	1 Pack/246g	608	247	9.8	17.8	15.2	2.4
Chicken Salad, Somerfield*	1oz/28g	48	171	10.0	24.0	4.0	0.0
Chicken Salad, Superdrug*	1 Pack/181g	257	142	10.1	18.7	2.6	68.6
Chicken Salad, Sutherland*	1 Pack/181g	302	167	10.3	23.1	3.7	0.0
Chicken Salad Wedge, Tesco*	1 Wedge/220g	458	208	9.4	18.2	10.8	1.2
Chicken Salsa, BGTY, Sainsbury's*	1 Pack/224g	332	148	10.8	20.8	2.3	2.3
Chicken Tandoori, Waitrose*	1 Serving/181g	302	167	11.6	23.0	3.1	4.1
Chicken Tikka & Salad Pack, COU, M & S*	1 Pack/253g	215	85	9.7	9.6	1.0	3.2
Chicken Tikka, Asda*	1 Pack/186g	316	170	11.0	21.0	4.7	1.5
Chicken Tikka, COU, M & S*	1 Pack/158g	174	110	12.9	12.6	1.2	4.0
Chicken Tikka, Eat Smart, Safeway*	1 Pack/159g	240	151	11.8	21.6	1.9	2.5
Chicken Tikka, Garlic & Herb Bread Pocket, Somerfield*	1 Pack/168g	341	203	11.0	30.0	4.3	2.0
Chicken Tikka, HE, Tesco*	1 Pack/159g	270	170	14.5	21.9	2.7	1.8
Chicken Tikka, M & S*	1 Pack/180g	391	217	10.4	19.5	10.9	2.0
Chicken Tikka Naan, Ready To Go, M & S*	1 Pack/298g	641	215	9.9	26.5	7.8	4.0
Chicken Tikka, Weight Watchers*	1 Pack/158g	289	183	12.8	23.4	4.3	1.6
Chinese Chicken, Low Calorie, Tesco*	1 Pack/169g	270	160	11.8	22.6	2.5	2.0
Chinese Chicken, Malted Brown Bread, Waitrose*	1 Pack/164g	333	203	13.5	21.9	6.8	3.3
Ciabatta, Ham & Cheese, Asda*	¼ Bread/74g	231	312	11.6	38.9	12.2	1.2
Ciabatta, Italian Ham With Plum Tomato & Rocket, Costa*	1 Serving/50g	115	231	23.1	24.9	4.4	0.0
Coronation Chicken & Mild Curry Mayo, Somerfield*	1oz/28g	82	294	10.0	24.0	18.0	0.0
Coronation Chicken, M & S*	1 Pack/210g	420	200	11.2	20.2	9.7	3.1
Cottage Cheese & Tomato, Shapers, Boots*	1 Serving/150g	219	146	7.8	18.0	4.8	2.4
Cream Cheese Salad, The Sandwich Box*	1 Pack/138g	250	181	5.6	26.3	5.8	0.0
Danish Ham Salad, COU, M & S*	1 Pack/138g	181	131	9.3	17.4	2.7	1.9
Double Whopper, Burger King*	1 Sandwich/353g	918	260	13.5	15.0	16.1	1.1
Egg & Bacon, Bacon & Tomato, Sausage & Egg, Tesco*	1 Pack/256g	778	304	9.7	19.4	20.8	1.2
Egg & Bacon, Burger King*	1 Pack/139g	296	213	11.1	21.7	9.1	1.9
Egg & Bacon, Co-Op*	1 Pack/188g	536	285	13.0	20.0	17.0	2.0
Egg & Bacon, Deep Fill, Ginsters*	1 Round/210g	590	281	11.5	18.8	18.2	0.0
Egg & Bacon, M & S*	1 Pack/215g	525	244	13.4	15.8	14.2	2.1
Egg & Bacon, Scottish Slimmers, Tesco*	1 Pack/139g	279	201	13.6	26.3	4.6	1.2
Egg & Bacon, Shell*	1 Pack/191g	579	303	12.2	18.7	19.9	0.0
Egg & Bacon, Tesco*	1 Pack/179g	530	298	10.6	20.2	19.4	1.3
Egg & Cress, BGTY, Sainsbury's*	1 Pack/166g	317	191	9.6	26.0	5.4	0.0
Egg & Cress, Co-Op*	1 Pack/159g	398	250	9.0	21.0	15.0	2.0
Egg & Cress, M & S*	1 Pack/182g	331	182	10.1	13.6	9.7	3.2
Egg & Cress, Reduced Fat, M & S*	1 Pack/113g	170	150	10.8	20.8	5.8	1.1
Egg & Cress, Sainsbury's*	1 Pack/170g	357	210	9.2	22.1	9.5	0.0
Egg & Cress, Tesco*	1 Pack/174g	445	256	10.0	20.3	15.0	1.7
Egg & Salad Cream, Heinz*	1 Pack/228g	456	200	8.1	21.4	9.1	1.6

S

SANDWICH,	Measure WEIGHT/INFO	per Measure KCAL	Nutrition Values per 100g / 100ml KCAL	PROT	CARB	FAT	FIBRE
Egg & Tomato, Organic, Waitrose*	1 Pack/192g	359	187	9.7	15.3	9.7	4.0
Egg & Tomato With Salad Cream, Shell*	1 Pack/183g	311	170	7.7	21.4	6.0	0.0
Egg and Tomato, With Salad Cream, Big, Sainsbury's*	1 Pack/266g	463	174	9.1	21.3	5.8	0.0
Egg Mayo & Cress, Starbucks*	1 Pack/202g	450	223	9.5	18.5	12.3	0.0
Egg Mayonnaise & Cress, Millers*	1 Pack/166g	369	222	9.4	18.8	12.2	0.0
Egg Mayonnaise & Cress, Shapers, Boots*	1 Pack/161g	304	189	9.4	24.0	6.1	0.0
Egg Mayonnaise & Cress, Somerfield*	1oz/28g	71	252	10.0	18.0	16.0	0.0
Egg Mayonnaise & Cress, Wheatgerm Bread, Asda*	1 Pack/158g	371	235	9.7	21.3	12.4	1.9
Egg Mayonnaise & Cress, Wheatgerm, Tesco*	1 Pack/146g	368	252	9.8	18.4	15.5	1.3
Egg Mayonnaise & Salad, Superdrug*	1 Pack/169g	286	169	7.6	18.3	7.3	2.4
Egg Mayonnaise & Tomato, Shapers Boots*	1 Pack/197g	339	172	7.6	22.0	5.9	2.6
Egg Mayonnaise On Hi Bran Bread, Ginsters*	1 Pack/143g	343	240	10.7	17.6	15.2	0.0
Egg Mayonnaise, Shell*	1 Pack/189g	522	276	9.8	24.7	15.4	0.0
Egg Mayonnaise, Waitrose*	1 Pack/180g	396	220	10.1	19.1	11.4	3.4
Egg Mayonnaise With Cress, Reduced Fat, Waitrose*	1 Serving/162g	300	185	10.4	18.1	7.9	3.4
Egg Salad, Deep Filled, Asda*	1 Pack/231g	404	175	7.3	18.5	7.9	1.3
Egg Salad, GFY, Asda*	1 Pack/163g	262	161	7.0	23.0	4.5	1.3
Egg Salad, HE, Tesco*	1 Pack/169g	279	165	7.6	22.5	4.9	2.0
Egg Salad, Malted Brown Bread, HE, Tesco*	1 Pack/182g	264	145	7.2	19.6	4.2	1.8
Egg Salad, Shapers, Boots*	1 Pack/184g	304	165	6.9	24.0	4.6	1.1
Egg Salad With Mayonnaise Wholemeal, Waitrose*	1 Pack/180g	257	143	8.3	16.5	4.9	3.6
Filet-O-Fish, McDonald's*	1 Pack/161g	388	241	10.0	25.0	11.0	0.7
Grilled Chicken & Watercress, COU, M & S*	1 Pack/164g	266	162	12.8	23.9	1.7	2.1
Grilled Vegetable, Safeway*	1 Pack/150g	236	157	5.6	24.9	3.9	2.4
Ham & Cheese, Baxter & Platts*	1 Pack/168g	408	243	11.3	20.5	13.0	1.7
Ham & Cheese Toasted, Coffee Republic*	1 Pack/160g	429	268	15.7	24.4	12.7	0.0
Ham & Cream Cheese, Tesco*	1 Sandwich/212g	655	309	11.0	27.2	17.3	1.2
Ham & Egg, Asda*	1 Pack/262g	590	225	10.4	16.8	12.8	2.1
Ham & Mustard, Eat Smart, Safeway*	1 Pack/139g	250	180	13.7	26.3	2.2	2.0
Ham & Mustard, Tesco*	1 Pack/147g	437	297	10.6	20.8	19.0	1.2
Ham & Swiss Cheese, M & S*	1 Pack/159g	393	247	14.7	18.9	12.6	3.3
Ham & Turkey, Asda*	1 Pack/190g	393	207	12.9	15.8	10.2	2.3
Ham & Turkey Salad, Co-Op*	1 Pack/188g	263	140	9.0	21.0	3.0	2.0
Ham, Cheese & Pickle, M & S*	1 Pack/197g	459	233	13.0	15.9	13.1	2.4
Ham Cheese & Pickle, Sutherland*	1 Pack/230g	727	316	11.3	20.6	20.9	0.0
Ham, M & S*	1 Pack/200g	220	110	17.2	3.2	2.6	0.0
Ham Salad, Co-Op*	1 Pack/193g	299	155	9.0	19.0	5.0	1.0
Ham Salad, HE, Tesco*	1 Serving/163g	215	132	10.6	17.5	2.2	2.0
Ham Salad, Prawn Mayo & Chicken, HE, Tesco*	1 Serving/248g	350	141	10.4	20.8	1.8	2.1
Ham Salad, Safeway*	1 Pack/272g	403	148	8.3	24.5	1.8	1.9
Ham Salad Wedge, HE, Tesco*	1 Serving/198g	269	136	7.1	23.0	1.7	1.0
Houmous & Crunchy Salad, Oldfields*	1 Pack/180g	256	142	6.3	20.0	4.2	0.0
Houmous, Costa*	1 Pack/165g	263	160	6.4	25.9	2.8	0.0
Lean Danish Ham & Salad, COU, M & S*	1 Pack/182g	255	140	10.6	18.7	2.4	1.9
Lemon Chicken & Relish, Perfectly Balanced, Waitrose*	1 Pack/151g	243	161	12.3	21.4	2.9	3.5
Lime & Coriander Chicken, BGTY, Sainsbury's*	1 Pack/168g	282	168	10.6	23.5	3.5	0.0
Luxury Smoked Salmon, M & S*	1 Pack/137g	333	243	15.0	19.0	11.9	1.8
Mature Cheddar, Apple, & Chutney, TTD, Sainsbury's*	1 Pack/200g	472	236	10.2	26.4	10.0	0.0
McChicken, McDonald's*	1 Sandwich/167g	376	225	9.9	23.1	10.3	2.2
Mozzarella & Tomato Calzone, Waitrose*	1 Pack/175g	410	234	10.8	22.7	11.1	2.2
Mushroom & Herb Pocket, Boots*	1 Serving/200g	376	188	7.8	27.0	5.4	2.8
Naan, Chicken Tikka, Tesco*	1 Roll/185g	326	176	8.3	28.9	3.0	1.6
Oriental Chicken Triple, Shapers, Boots*	1 Pack/215g	398	185	12.0	22.0	5.4	2.6
Parmesan & Rocket, Egg, Cheese & Tomato, Boots*	1 Pack/241g	422	175	8.7	23.0	5.4	2.1

S

SANDWICH,	Measure WEIGHT/INFO	per Measure KCAL	Nutrition Values per 100g / 100ml KCAL	PROT	CARB	FAT	FIBRE
Pastrami & Gherkin, BGTY, Sainsbury's*	1 Pack/230g	357	155	9.8	23.1	2.6	3.0
Pitta Pocket, Chargrilled Chicken, M & S*	1 Pack/208g	279	134	11.2	14.5	3.5	1.6
Ploughman's & Onion Mayonnaise, Somerfield*	1oz/28g	77	275	10.0	30.0	13.0	0.0
Ploughman's, HE, Tesco*	1 Pack/180g	261	145	11.6	21.0	1.6	2.0
Ploughmans, Cheese, M & S*	1 Pack/185g	451	244	9.3	21.5	13.4	1.5
Ploughmans, Deep Filled, Asda*	1 Pack/254g	650	256	10.3	21.3	14.5	2.9
Poached Salmon, Coffee Republic*	1 Pack/191g	350	183	10.3	18.4	7.6	0.0
Poached Salmon, M & S*	1 Pack/171g	397	232	12.9	16.2	12.8	2.6
Poached Salmon With Salad On Oatmeal, Costa*	1 Pack/151g	224	148	7.7	22.9	2.8	0.0
Prawn & Egg, Deep Filled, Asda*	1 Pack/250g	570	228	12.0	17.0	12.0	2.3
Prawn & Mayonnaise, BGTY, Sainsbury's*	1 Pack/165g	312	189	10.4	20.3	7.3	3.1
Prawn & Mayonnaise, COU, M & S*	1 Pack/141g	254	180	11.9	20.3	2.7	1.7
Prawn & Mayonnaise, Healthy Selection, Budgens*	1 Pack/143g	296	207	11.0	22.0	8.3	1.8
Prawn & Mayonnaise, Reduced Fat, Waitrose*	1 Pack/146g	276	189	9.2	24.1	6.2	2.5
Prawn & Mayonnaise, Safeway*	1 Pack/168g	402	239	9.0	21.1	13.2	3.1
Prawn Cocktail, HE, Tesco*	1 Pack/154g	245	159	11.0	22.0	2.7	1.8
Prawn Cocktail Salad, Shapers, Boots*	1 Pack/167g	296	177	10.0	18.0	7.2	2.9
Prawn Cocktail, Weight Watchers*	1 Pack/168g	252	150	8.9	18.1	4.6	2.8
Prawn, Lemon & Chilli Mayonnaise, Shapers, Boots*	1 Pack/159g	266	167	8.6	22.0	4.9	3.0
Prawn Marie Rose, Waitrose*	1 Pack/164g	303	185	9.4	17.3	8.7	2.7
Prawn Mayo, Ham Salad Triple Pack, Sutherland*	1 Pack/253g	620	245	9.8	24.8	11.9	0.3
Prawn Mayonnaise, Ginsters*	1 Pack/152g	415	273	12.4	17.8	17.8	0.0
Prawn Mayonnaise, GFY, Asda*	1 Pack/160g	270	169	10.0	22.0	4.6	2.1
Prawn Mayonnaise, Healthy Choice, Asda*	1 Pack/156g	343	220	12.8	19.3	10.2	1.9
Prawn Mayonnaise, HE, Tesco*	1 Pack/154g	270	175	11.9	22.7	4.1	1.9
Prawn Mayonnaise, M & S*	1 Pack/156g	382	245	10.5	20.2	13.5	2.7
Prawn Mayonnaise On Oatmeal Bread, Weight Watchers*	1 Pack/158g	254	161	10.4	23.7	2.7	2.3
Red Salmon & Cucumber, Healthy Choice, Asda*	1 Pack/149g	285	191	10.6	19.9	7.7	2.1
Red Salmon & Cucumber, Tesco*	1 Pack/144g	251	174	11.3	24.2	3.5	1.9
Roast Beef & Horseradish, Starbucks*	1 Pack/200g	546	273	18.7	23.1	11.1	1.0
Roast Beef & Onion, Deep Filled, Asda*	1 Pack/258g	550	213	11.3	22.6	10.8	1.1
Roast Beef, Deep Fill, Woolworths*	1 Pack/191g	283	148	10.5	17.9	3.9	0.0
Roast Chicken & Bacon, Sainsbury's*	1 Pack/167g	433	259	14.1	18.6	14.2	0.0
Roast Chicken & Coleslaw, Sainsbury's*	1 Pack/186g	348	187	11.4	21.0	7.9	0.0
Roast Chicken & Ham, Ginsters*	1 Pack/180g	425	236	11.2	18.5	13.6	0.0
Roast Chicken & Stuffing, Tesco*	1 Pack/164g	370	227	13.5	24.3	8.4	1.7
Roast Chicken, No Mayo, COU, M & S*	1 Serving/147g	250	170	14.5	21.1	2.6	1.4
Roast Chicken, Prawn Mayo, BLT, Shapers, Boots*	1 Pack/221g	402	182	12.0	22.0	5.1	2.9
Roast Chicken, Prawn, Triple Pack, BLT, Waitrose*	1 Pack/241g	653	271	9.2	18.8	17.7	1.6
Roast Chicken Salad, Ginsters*	1 Pack/210g	506	241	9.8	18.8	14.6	0.0
Roast Chicken Salad, Luxury, Boots*	1 Pack/288g	697	242	10.0	19.0	14.0	2.3
Roast Chicken Salad, Shapers Boots*	1 Pack/193g	284	147	11.0	19.0	3.0	2.3
Roast Chicken Salad, Weight Watchers*	1 Pack/186g	266	143	10.3	15.8	4.3	2.8
Roast Chicken Triple, Perfectly Balance, Waitrose*	1 Pack/254g	356	140	8.7	19.2	3.2	2.8
Roast Peppers & Goats Cheese Focaccia, Finest, Tesco*	1 Focaccia/150g	419	279	7.0	21.5	18.3	1.7
Salmon & Cucumber, BGTY, Sainsbury's*	1 Pack/161g	266	165	9.7	21.0	3.0	3.5
Salmon & Cucumber Brown Bread, Waitrose*	1 Pack/150g	296	197	10.5	22.7	7.1	1.4
Salmon & Cucumber, Healthy Living, Co-Op*	1 Pack/159g	286	180	10.0	24.0	5.0	2.0
Salmon & Cucumber, M & S*	1 Pack/168g	329	196	11.0	19.5	8.3	2.6
Sausage & Egg Wedge, Tesco*	1 Pack/269g	699	260	9.1	23.6	14.4	1.1
Sausage, Bacon & Egg, Burger King*	1 Pack/182g	430	236	13.2	17.5	12.7	1.7
Seafood Cocktail, Asda*	1 Pack/190g	486	256	6.7	21.3	15.8	1.6
Seafood Medley, M & S*	1 Pack/227g	468	206	7.2	16.3	12.4	3.5
Simply Egg Mayonnaise, Boots*	1 Pack/181g	449	248	9.2	19.0	15.0	2.9

S

SANDWICH,	Measure WEIGHT/INFO	per Measure KCAL	Nutrition Values per 100g / 100ml KCAL	PROT	CARB	FAT	FIBRE
Simply Prawn Mayonnaise, Boots*	1 Pack/261g	736	282	11.0	19.0	18.0	2.2
Simply Salad, Shapers, Boots*	1 Pack/216g	300	139	5.2	23.0	2.9	1.8
Simply Tuna Mayonnaise & Cucumber, Boots*	1 Pack/200g	498	249	12.0	21.0	13.0	2.4
Smoked Cheese Folded Focaccia, TTD, Sainsbury's*	¼ Focaccia/220g	607	276	13.1	34.6	9.4	2.9
Smoked Ham & Cheese, Co-Op*	1 Serving/167g	334	200	15.0	24.0	5.0	2.0
Smoked Ham & Cream Cheese, HS, Budgens*	1 Pack/136g	269	197	11.4	25.7	5.5	3.4
Smoked Ham & Edam, Shapers, Boots*	1 Pack/183g	315	172	9.3	19.0	6.5	2.7
Smoked Ham & Mustard, M & S*	1 Pack/149g	347	233	10.1	18.8	13.0	2.0
Smoked Ham & Mustard, Sainsbury's*	1 Pack/175g	406	232	10.6	21.9	11.3	0.0
Smoked Ham, Cheese & Pickle, COU, M & S*	1 Pack/174g	270	155	14.4	20.0	1.8	3.7
Smoked Ham, Cheese & Pickle, Shapers, Boots*	1 Pack/172g	296	172	13.0	19.0	4.9	2.9
Smoked Ham, Pineapple Soft Cheese, BGTY, Sainsbury's*	1 Pack/193g	344	178	10.5	26.5	3.3	0.0
Smoked Ham Salad, Weight Watchers*	1 Pack/181g	244	135	10.9	16.5	2.8	2.8
Smoked Salmon Cream Cheese, M & S*	1 Pack/162g	437	270	11.7	19.3	16.2	2.5
Smoked Tomato Ham, Starbucks*	1 Pack/206g	297	144	5.2	22.0	3.9	0.0
Smoked Turkey Summer Salad, Starbucks*	1 Pack/198g	303	153	10.8	22.3	2.4	1.5
Soft Cheese & Roasted Pepper, Weight Watchers*	1 Pack/158g	289	183	9.4	27.7	3.8	1.5
Southern Spiced Chicken, M & S*	1 Pack/179g	421	235	11.2	21.7	13.0	3.1
Sub, Chicken & Stuffing, Safeway*	1 Roll/275g	605	220	10.3	21.3	10.4	4.2
Sub, Chicken Salad, Asda*	1 Sub/200g	460	230	9.4	17.4	13.6	0.9
Tandoori Chicken, Finest, Tesco*	1 Pack/224g	421	188	10.8	19.2	7.5	1.4
Thai Chicken, Tesco*	1 Pack/244g	634	260	8.5	21.1	15.7	1.5
Three Cheese & Onion, New Style, Weight Watchers*	1 Pack/148g	275	186	14.8	26.2	2.4	1.4
Three Cheese & Spring Onion, Shell*	1 Pack/168g	672	400	11.1	20.8	30.3	0.0
Tomato, Parmesan, Rocket, Tomato Bread, Shapers, Boots*	1 Pack/164g	303	185	7.5	24.0	6.6	1.7
Triple Chicken, Shapers, Boots*	1 Serving/228g	440	193	13.0	23.0	5.4	2.3
Tuna & Celery, Perfectly Balanced, Waitrose*	1 Pack/172g	272	158	11.7	20.5	3.2	3.9
Tuna & Chargrilled Vegetables, BGTY, Sainsbury's*	1 Pack/196g	329	168	10.7	21.5	4.4	0.0
Tuna & Cucumber, BGTY, Sainsbury's*	1 Pack/164g	275	169	12.0	21.6	3.9	3.0
Tuna & Cucumber, Ginsters*	1 Pack/171g	238	139	9.9	19.4	3.2	0.0
Tuna & Cucumber, Healthy Choice, Asda*	1 Pack/164g	315	192	10.9	22.3	6.6	1.1
Tuna & Cucumber, Healthy Choice, Sutherlands*	1 Pack/179g	344	192	12.2	22.0	6.2	0.0
Tuna & Cucumber, M & S*	1 Pack/170g	430	253	12.0	18.0	14.8	2.4
Tuna & Cucumber, Red Cal Mayo, BGTY, Sainsbury's*	1 Pack/182g	288	158	12.2	22.5	2.3	0.0
Tuna & Cucumber, Shapers, Boots*	1 Pack/179g	322	180	11.0	24.0	4.4	1.7
Tuna & Cucumber, Shell*	1 Pack/188g	431	229	12.3	21.9	10.2	0.0
Tuna & Lemon Mayo, Shapers, Boots*	1 Pack/206g	318	154	10.0	18.0	4.7	1.7
Tuna & Sweetcorn, Asda*	1 Pack/205g	592	289	11.5	21.8	17.2	2.7
Tuna & Sweetcorn, COU, M & S*	1 Pack/180g	270	150	12.6	19.0	2.4	3.8
Tuna & Sweetcorn, Eat Smart, Safeway*	1 Pack/152g	251	165	13.4	21.9	2.5	2.8
Tuna & Sweetcorn, HE, Tesco*	1 Pack/154g	263	171	11.4	25.6	2.5	2.1
Tuna & Sweetcorn, M & S*	1 Pack/185g	453	245	11.0	20.9	13.0	2.1
Tuna & Sweetcorn, Tesco*	1 Pack/174g	432	248	11.3	24.4	11.7	1.8
Tuna Mayonnaise, White Bread, Open Choice Foods*	1 Pack/120g	298	248	12.0	29.6	8.4	0.0
Tuna Mayonnaise With Spring Onions, Starbucks*	1 Pack/209g	318	152	9.0	19.9	4.0	1.5
Tuna Melt, Swedish Bread, Shapers, Boots*	1 Pack/163g	258	158	13.0	20.0	2.9	1.6
Tuna Pepper & Sweetcorn Salad, Shapers, Boots*	1 Pack/204g	345	169	9.2	24.0	4.0	1.9
Tuna Salad, M & S*	1 Pack/250g	575	230	12.5	16.8	12.6	2.1
Tuna Salad, Weight Watchers*	1 Pack/191g	248	130	10.6	15.8	2.7	2.6
Tuna, Tomato & Onion, COU, M & S*	1 Pack/177g	250	141	11.1	18.8	2.4	2.2
Turkey & Ham Salad, Sutherland*	1 Pack/185g	303	164	9.8	25.2	2.6	0.0
Turkey Breast & Ham, Subway*	1 Pack/235g	294	125	8.5	19.6	2.1	1.7
Vegetarian, Salad, Waitrose*	1oz/28g	74	266	9.8	19.6	16.5	1.9
Wensleydale & Carrot, M & S*	1 Pack/183g	430	235	9.9	21.4	12.3	2.8

S

	Measure WEIGHT/INFO	per Measure KCAL	KCAL	PROT	CARB	FAT	FIBRE
			Nutrition Values per 100g / 100ml				
SANDWICH FILLER,							
Cheese & Spring Onion, HE, Tesco*	1 Serving/85g	185	218	13.2	6.8	15.4	0.6
Cheese & Spring Onion, M & S*	1 Serving/56g	199	355	8.5	5.0	33.6	0.2
Chicken & Bacon With Sweetcorn, Sainsbury's*	1 Serving/60g	155	258	12.0	3.8	21.6	1.0
Chicken & Sweetcorn, Deli, M & S*	1 Pot/170g	306	180	11.6	4.2	12.9	1.5
Chicken, Sweetcorn & Sage, HE, Tesco*	1 Serving/125g	105	84	9.4	8.8	1.3	1.3
Chicken Tikka, BGTY, Sainsbury*	Half Pot/85g	99	117	16.5	6.0	3.0	1.0
Chicken With Salad Vegetables, Heinz*	1 Filling/56g	114	203	5.1	11.7	15.1	0.5
Egg & Bacon, Fresh, Tesco*	1 Serving/45g	112	248	12.7	4.2	20.1	0.6
Egg Mayonnaise, Deli, Somerfield*	1 Serving/40g	120	301	9.7	0.2	29.2	0.0
Egg Mayonnaise, M & S*	1oz/28g	62	220	10.1	0.8	19.7	1.1
Egg Mayonnaise, Tesco*	1 Serving/50g	122	243	10.5	2.5	21.2	0.8
Ham & Salad Vegetables, Heinz*	1oz/28g	57	204	5.3	10.0	15.9	0.4
Prawn Mayonnaise, M & S*	1oz/28g	91	325	8.7	0.7	31.7	0.8
Seafood, BGTY, Sainsbury's*	1oz/28g	36	128	8.7	7.6	7.0	0.5
Seafood Cocktail, M & S*	1oz/28g	76	272	6.4	8.2	23.8	0.2
Tex-Mex Chicken, Tesco*	1 Pack/250g	255	102	12.3	11.2	0.9	1.2
Tuna & Sweetcorn, M & S*	1oz/28g	70	250	14.2	2.3	20.7	1.3
Tuna & Sweetcorn With Salad Vegetables, Heinz*	1oz/28g	53	191	5.8	12.1	13.2	0.7
SANDWICH FILLING,							
Cheese & Onion, Asda*	1 Serving/56g	288	515	9.8	4.4	50.9	0.3
Cheese & Onion, Co-Op*	1 Serving/56g	269	480	10.0	4.0	47.0	0.5
Cheese & Spring Onion, Better For You, Morrisons*	½ Pot/85g	216	254	10.4	7.0	20.0	2.2
Chicken & Sweetcorn, Asda*	1 Serving/60g	187	312	11.0	4.0	28.0	2.0
Chicken & Sweetcorn, Low Fat, Morrisons*	1 Serving/56g	101	180	8.8	8.5	12.3	1.6
Chicken Tikka, Less Than 5% Fat, Asda*	1 Serving/56g	65	116	11.0	7.3	4.7	1.2
Crab, BGTY, Sainsbury's*	1oz/28g	36	128	8.7	7.6	7.0	0.5
Egg Mayonnaise, Asda*	1oz/28g	72	258	10.3	1.9	23.3	0.7
Egg Mayonnaise, Co-Op*	1oz/28g	69	245	11.0	3.0	21.0	0.8
Egg Mayonnaise With Chives, Asda*	1oz/28g	92	327	9.1	1.1	31.8	0.0
Houmous & Vegetable, Asda*	1/3 tub/57g	133	233	8.0	12.0	17.0	3.5
Prawns With Seafood Sauce, Asda*	1oz/28g	107	382	11.7	1.4	36.8	0.0
Tuna & Sweetcorn, Asda*	1oz/28g	83	295	8.2	6.0	26.5	0.6
Tuna & Sweetcorn, GFY, Asda*	1/3 Pot/57g	87	152	13.0	7.0	8.0	3.3
Tuna & Sweetcorn, Reduced Fat, Co-Op*	1 Serving/50g	103	205	13.0	7.0	14.0	0.9
Tuna & Sweetcorn, Reduced Fat, Morrisons*	1oz/28g	50	178	13.0	7.8	10.5	1.2
Tuna & Sweetcorn, Tesco*	1 Serving/60g	172	287	9.4	10.0	23.3	0.9
Tuna & Sweetcorn With Mayonnaise, Morrisons*	1 Serving/25g	72	289	13.1	5.9	23.7	0.6
SANDWICH SPREAD,							
Cucumber, Heinz*	1oz/28g	46	164	1.7	12.7	11.6	0.6
Original, Heinz*	1oz/28g	66	237	1.7	15.2	18.6	0.7
Somerfield*	1oz/28g	59	212	1.0	26.0	11.0	0.0
SARDINES,							
Canned In Brine, Drained	1oz/28g	48	172	21.5	0.0	9.6	0.0
Canned In Oil, Drained	1oz/28g	62	220	23.3	0.0	14.1	0.0
Canned In Tomato Sauce	1oz/28g	45	162	17.0	1.4	9.9	0.0
Grilled	1oz/28g	55	195	25.3	0.0	10.4	0.0
Headless, Somerfield*	1oz/28g	46	165	21.0	0.0	9.0	0.0
In Brine, John West*	1 Can/90g	156	173	23.0	0.0	9.0	0.0
In Brine, Portuguese, Sainsbury's*	1 Can/90g	165	183	22.4	0.1	10.3	0.1
In Brine, Tesco*	½ Can/42g	79	189	22.8	0.0	10.9	0.0
In Extra Virgin Olive Oil, Princes*	1 Can Drained/90g	203	226	24.2	0.0	13.9	0.0
In Olive Oil, John West*	1 Can/96g	243	253	25.0	0.0	17.0	0.0
In Olive Oil, Portuguese, M & S*	1 Can/90g	176	195	23.0	0.0	11.3	0.0
In Olive Oil, Portuguese, Sainsbury's*	1 Can/90g	194	216	25.5	0.1	12.6	0.3

S

SARDINES,	Measure WEIGHT/INFO	per Measure KCAL	KCAL	PROT	CARB	FAT	FIBRE
			Nutrition Values per 100g / 100ml				
In Sunflower Oil, John West*	1 Can/96g	209	218	23.0	0.0	14.0	0.0
In Tomato Sauce, Asda*	1 Can/120g	218	182	18.0	0.5	12.0	0.0
In Tomato Sauce, John West*	1oz/28g	46	164	17.0	1.5	10.0	0.0
In Tomato Sauce, Portuguese, M & S*	1 Can/120g	160	133	19.4	1.2	5.6	0.2
In Tomato Sauce, Portuguese, Sainsbury's*	1 Can/120g	212	177	17.4	2.2	11.0	0.4
In Tomato Sauce, Princes*	1 Can/120g	228	190	19.0	1.6	11.9	0.0
In Tomato Sauce, Skinless & Boneless, Sainsbury's*	1 Can/120g	143	119	22.1	1.0	3.0	0.1
In Tomato Sauce, Tesco*	1 Can/120g	214	178	17.8	0.5	11.6	0.0
Raw	1oz/28g	46	165	20.6	0.0	9.2	0.0
SATAY,							
Chicken & Turkey, Co-Op*	1 Pack/120g	264	220	20.0	4.0	14.0	0.1
Chicken & Turkey, Sainsbury's*	1 Stick/20g	44	222	20.0	4.0	14.0	1.9
Chicken, A Taste of Indonesia*	1 Serving/160g	232	145	22.0	3.0	5.0	0.0
Chicken, M & S*	1 Satay/43g	90	210	19.1	4.4	12.7	0.7
Chicken, Morrisons*	1 Satay/10g	17	171	23.5	3.5	7.0	0.7
Chicken, Thai Cocktail Sel & Peanut Sauce, Somerfield*	1oz/28g	43	152	23.0	2.0	6.0	0.0
Chicken Tikka Cocktail Selection, Somerfield*	1oz/28g	48	171	24.0	4.0	7.0	0.0
SATSUMAS,							
Fresh, Raw	1oz/28g	10	36	0.9	8.5	0.1	1.3
Weighed With Peel	1 Med/80g	21	26	0.6	6.0	0.1	0.9
SAUCE, (SEE ALSO KETCHUP & PASTA SAUCE)							
Apple, Baxters*	1 Tsp/15g	7	49	0.1	11.1	0.4	0.7
Apple, Bramley, Asda*	1 Tsp/15g	14	94	0.2	23.0	0.1	0.9
Apple, Bramley, Colman's*	1 Tsp/15ml	16	108	0.2	26.0	0.0	0.0
Apple, Bramley, Morrisons*	1 Tsp/15g	21	139	0.2	34.5	0.0	1.2
Apple, Bramley, Sainsbury's*	1 Tsp/15g	17	111	0.2	27.2	0.1	1.8
Apple, Heinz*	1 Tsp/15g	8	56	0.3	13.4	0.2	1.5
Arrabbiata, Fusilli, Heinz*	1 Serving/388g	198	51	1.9	10.1	0.4	0.8
Balti, Cooking, BGTY, Sainsbury's*	¼ Jar/129g	98	76	1.1	10.9	3.1	0.6
Balti, Cooking, Eat Smart, Safeway*	1 Serving/88g	66	75	1.1	10.0	2.9	0.8
Balti, Cooking, Organic, Sainsbury's*	1 Serving/225g	158	70	2.2	10.0	2.3	0.5
Balti, Cooking, Sharwood's*	1 Jar/420g	370	88	1.1	9.1	5.2	0.5
Balti, Cooking, Tesco*	1 Serving/500g	575	115	2.3	8.6	7.8	1.6
Balti, Deliciously Good, Homepride*	1/3 Jar/153g	89	58	1.1	9.1	1.9	0.6
Balti Indian, M & S*	1oz/28g	25	90	1.4	9.2	5.5	1.1
Balti, Indian Style, Iceland*	1 Serving/220g	154	70	1.6	10.1	2.6	0.5
Balti, Sizzle & Stir, Chicken Tonight*	1/3 Jar/168g	195	116	1.3	6.3	9.5	2.9
Barbecue, Asda*	1 Serving/135g	128	95	1.2	22.0	0.2	0.6
Barbecue, Chicken Tonight*	¼ Jar/125g	76	61	2.0	12.4	0.4	0.9
Barbecue, Cooking, BGTY, Sainsbury's*	¼ Jar/124g	46	37	0.4	8.4	0.2	0.7
Barbeque, Cook In, Homepride*	1 Serving/130g	96	74	0.8	14.0	1.6	0.0
Barbeque, McDonald's*	1 Portion/32g	55	173	2.2	38.3	1.2	0.0
Barbeque, Simply Sausages Ranch, Colman's*	1 Serving/130g	96	74	1.8	16.6	0.1	1.1
BBQ, HP*	1 Serving/20ml	29	143	0.8	33.1	0.2	0.0
BBQ, Smokey Tomato, HP*	1oz/28g	40	143	0.8	33.1	0.2	0.0
Beef In Ale, Cooking, Asda*	1 Jar/500g	160	32	1.6	6.0	0.2	0.0
Black Bean & Green Pepper, Stir Fry, Sharwood's*	1 Serving/150g	83	55	2.0	11.0	0.3	0.5
Black Bean, Amoy*	1oz/28g	42	150	10.0	23.0	2.0	0.0
Black Bean, Canton, Stir Fry, Blue Dragon*	1 Pack/100g	88	88	2.8	14.8	2.0	1.5
Black Bean, Fresh, Sainsbury's*	1 Sachet/50ml	78	156	6.7	27.5	2.6	1.7
Black Bean, Stir Fry, Amoy*	1oz/28g	29	104	1.8	12.0	5.6	0.0
Black Bean, Stir Fry, Asda*	1 Serving/50ml	54	108	2.9	21.0	1.4	0.0
Black Bean, Stir Fry, Fresh Ideas, Tesco*	½ Sachet/25g	33	132	4.2	22.6	2.8	0.8
Black Bean, Stir Fry, M & S*	1 Serving/60g	108	180	6.3	20.0	8.0	2.0

S

SAUCE,	Measure WEIGHT/INFO	per Measure KCAL	KCAL	PROT	CARB	FAT	FIBRE
Black Bean, Stir Fry, Morrisons*	½ Jar/237g	135	57	1.7	11.2	0.6	0.0
Black Bean, Stir Fry, Safeway*	1/3 Pack/33g	43	129	3.7	20.2	3.7	0.9
Black Bean, Stir Fry, Sainsbury's*	1 Serving/70ml	107	153	6.7	25.8	2.6	1.7
Black Bean, Stir Fry, Sharwood's*	1 Jar/160g	149	93	0.3	19.9	1.3	1.2
Black Bean, Stir Fry, Straight To Wok, Amoy*	1 Pack/220g	411	187	2.7	42.7	0.6	0.0
Black Bean, Stir Fry, Tesco*	½ Jar/220g	216	98	2.3	17.9	1.6	0.7
Black Pepper, Hong Kong, Straight To Wok*	1oz/28g	40	142	2.2	20.5	5.7	0.0
Bolognese, Original, Deliciously Good, Homepride*	¼ Jar/112g	39	35	1.3	7.1	0.2	0.8
Brandy Flavour, Kraft*	1oz/28g	25	91	2.5	15.5	1.4	0.0
Bread, Made With Semi-Skimmed Milk	1 Serving/45g	42	93	4.3	12.8	3.1	0.3
Brown, Bottled	1 Tsp/6g	6	99	1.1	25.2	0.0	0.7
Brown, Daddies Favourite, HP*	1 Tsp/6g	6	102	0.9	24.3	0.1	0.0
Brown, Tesco*	1 Tsp/10g	10	104	0.7	25.1	0.1	0.6
Butter & Tarragon, Chicken Tonight*	1oz/28g	30	106	1.0	2.1	10.4	0.7
Cajun, Sizzle & Stir, Chicken Tonight*	1/3 Jar/150g	189	126	0.8	12.0	8.3	0.0
Carbonara, BGTY, Sainsbury's*	1 Serving/150g	110	73	3.5	4.5	4.5	0.5
Carbonara, Co-Op*	1 Pack/300g	555	185	8.0	7.0	14.0	0.1
Carbonara, Creamy, Loyd Grossman*	1oz/28g	52	186	3.8	8.9	15.0	0.3
Carbonara, Creamy, Microwaveable, Dolmio*	1 Serving/75g	116	155	3.3	4.0	13.5	0.0
Carbonara, Fresh, Safeway*	1 Serving/175g	285	163	7.1	5.2	12.6	0.5
Carbonara, Fresh, Sainsbury's*	½ Pot/150g	333	222	5.9	2.2	21.1	0.8
Carbonara, GFY, Asda,*	1 Serving/170g	167	98	5.0	6.0	6.0	0.0
Carbonara, HE, Tesco*	1 Serving/175g	121	69	5.2	6.2	2.6	0.0
Carbonara, Perfectly Balanced, Waitrose*	½ Pot/175g	154	88	7.8	6.0	3.6	1.2
Carbonara, Stir In, Dolmio*	1 Serving/75g	140	186	6.5	3.7	15.8	0.0
Carmelised Onion & Red Wine, M & S*	1 Serving/52g	31	60	1.9	6.7	3.1	0.6
Casserole, Sausage, Cook In , Homepride*	1 Jar/720g	504	70	0.8	16.0	0.2	0.0
Chasseur, Cook In, Homepride*	1 Can/390g	156	40	0.7	9.2	0.1	0.0
Chausseur, Classic, Chicken Tonight*	1 Serving/100g	45	45	0.7	3.9	2.9	1.3
Cheese, Cheddar, Colman's*	1 Pack/40g	156	389	19.0	46.0	14.0	0.0
Cheese, Fresh, Waitrose*	1 Pot/350g	459	131	5.1	5.7	9.8	0.0
Cheese, Granules, Made Up, Bisto*	1floz/30ml	30	100	1.2	6.4	7.6	0.0
Cheese, Italiano, Tesco*	1 Pot/350g	368	105	5.3	8.0	5.7	0.0
Cheese, Made With Semi-Skimmed Milk	1 Serving/60g	107	179	8.1	9.1	12.6	0.2
Cheese, Made With Whole Milk	1 Serving/60g	118	197	8.0	9.0	14.6	0.2
Cheese, Perfectly Balanced, Waitrose*	1 Serving/50g	41	82	6.1	7.9	2.9	0.5
Chicken, Sizzling, Dolmio*	1 Serving/100g	102	102	1.2	7.5	7.5	0.0
Chicken, Spanish, Chicken Tonight*	1oz/28g	12	44	1.7	5.8	1.5	1.3
Chili & Garlic, Amoy*	1oz/28g	31	112	12.0	27.0	0.0	0.0
Chilli & Garlic, Lea & Perrins*	1 Tsp/6g	4	60	1.0	14.9	0.0	0.0
Chilli & Garlic, Stir Fry, M & S*	½ Jar/125g	188	150	1.5	35.2	0.4	1.2
Chilli, Amoy*	1 Tsp/6g	2	25	1.0	5.2	0.0	1.0
Chilli Con Carne, Cooking, BGTY, Sainsbury's*	1 Jar/500g	190	38	0.8	8.2	0.2	0.6
Chilli, Cooking, SmartPrice, Asda*	1 Serving/140g	80	57	2.5	11.0	0.3	1.1
Chilli, HP*	1 Tsp/6g	8	134	1.2	32.3	0.1	0.0
Chilli, Medium, Deliciously Good, Homepride*	1 Jar/460g	258	56	2.3	10.4	0.5	1.2
Chilli, Mild, Asda*	1 Pack/128g	88	69	2.1	10.0	2.3	1.7
Chilli, Mild, Colman's*	1 Pack/35g	113	322	9.2	60.0	3.9	0.0
Chilli, Mild, HE, Asda*	½ Jar/250g	173	69	2.1	10.0	2.3	1.7
Chilli, Seeds Of Change*	1 Jar/400g	408	102	4.0	18.2	1.5	2.2
Chilli With Kidney Beans, Old El Paso*	1 Serving/115g	92	80	4.3	14.8	0.4	0.0
Chinese 5 Spice, Stir It Up, Chicken Tonight*	1 Jar/80g	478	597	2.4	34.1	50.1	6.6
Chop Suey, Stir Fry, Sharwood's*	1 Jar/160g	120	75	0.7	14.6	1.5	0.2
Chow Mein, Sainsbury's*	1 Serving/50g	36	71	1.8	10.5	2.4	0.0

Nutrition Values per 100g / 100ml

SAUCE,	Measure WEIGHT/INFO	per Measure KCAL	Nutrition Values per 100g / 100ml KCAL	PROT	CARB	FAT	FIBRE
Chow Mein, Stir Fry, Blue Dragon*	1 Sachet/120g	110	92	1.1	15.4	2.9	0.4
Chunky Onions & Garlic, Ragu*	¼ Jar/129g	66	51	1.9	7.6	1.4	2.0
Coronation, Heinz*	1 Tbsp/10g	33	334	0.8	13.1	31.0	0.9
Country French, Chicken Tonight*	¼ Jar/125g	123	98	0.7	3.3	9.1	0.7
Country Mushroom, Ragu*	¼ Jar/129g	88	68	2.0	9.5	2.1	1.2
Cracked Black Pepper, M & S*	1 Jar/300g	345	115	2.7	6.7	8.9	0.4
Cranberry & Orange With Port, Colman's*	1 Serving/14ml	38	274	0.2	67.0	0.2	0.0
Cranberry & Red Onion, Sizzling, Homepride*	1 Serving/100g	83	83	0.5	17.7	1.0	0.0
Cranberry Jelly, Baxters*	1 Tsp/15g	40	268	0.0	67.0	0.0	0.0
Cranberry, M & S*	1 Tsp/15g	31	205	0.2	51.1	0.1	1.5
Cranberry, Safeway*	1 Tsp/15g	25	168	0.2	41.0	0.3	1.3
Cranberry, Sainsbury's*	1 Tsp/15g	23	154	0.8	37.1	0.3	1.3
Cranberry, Tesco*	1 Tsp/15g	23	156	0.1	38.8	0.0	0.9
Creamy Leek & Wholegrain Mustard, Colman's*	1 Serving/160g	187	117	1.3	4.8	10.6	1.4
Creamy Tomato & Basil, Cooking, BGTY, Sainsbury's*	¼ Jar/125g	88	70	1.7	7.6	3.6	1.0
Cumberland Sausage, Colman's*	¼ Jar/126g	43	34	0.7	7.4	0.2	0.8
Curry, 98% Fat Free, Homepride*	1oz/28g	15	54	1.4	9.2	1.5	0.6
Curry, Chinese, Farmfoods*	1 Sachet/200g	220	110	0.6	7.1	8.8	0.7
Curry, Creamy, BGTY, Sainsbury's*	¼ Jar/125g	84	67	1.4	6.8	3.8	0.5
Curry, Creamy, Chicken Tonight*	¼ Jar/125g	106	85	1.5	4.6	6.7	0.8
Curry, Deliciously Good, Homepride*	1/3 Jar/149g	91	61	1.1	10.0	1.8	0.5
Curry, Green Thai, Asda*	1 Jar/340g	309	91	0.5	4.3	8.0	0.2
Curry, Green Thai, Loyd Grossman*	½ Jar/175g	228	130	2.3	10.1	9.0	1.2
Curry, Mild, Tesco*	1 Jar/500g	420	84	1.1	13.4	2.8	0.8
Curry, Red Pepper Ras, Sainsbury's*	½ Jar/175g	86	49	2.2	9.0	0.5	1.1
Curry, Singapore, Blue Dragon*	1 Sachet/120g	89	74	1.8	9.0	3.4	3.7
Curry, Spicy Durban, New World, Knorr*	1 Pack/500g	305	61	0.6	8.7	2.7	0.4
Curry, Sweet	1oz/28g	25	91	1.2	9.6	5.6	1.4
Curry, Sweet, McDonald's*	1 Portion/32g	61	192	1.2	41.1	2.5	0.0
Curry, Tenghai, Sharwood's*	1 Jar/420g	487	116	1.2	9.6	7.8	1.8
Curry, Thai Green, Barts*	½ Pack/150ml	210	140	2.0	6.0	12.0	0.0
Curry, Thai Green, Sainsbury's*	¼ Pack/125g	170	136	1.8	10.8	9.5	2.1
Curry, Thai Green, Sharwood's*	1oz/28g	30	107	1.1	8.4	7.6	0.1
Curry, Thai Panang, Sainsbury's*	1/3 Pack/166g	229	138	1.4	6.6	11.8	1.4
Curry, Thai Red, Sainsbury's*	½ Pouch/250g	390	156	1.7	5.0	14.3	1.5
Curry, Thai Red, Sharwood's*	1oz/28g	22	80	0.9	8.8	4.6	0.2
Curry, Tuna In Thai, Princes*	1 Can/185g	250	135	16.4	2.3	6.7	0.0
Dhansak, Medium, Sharwood's*	1 Jar/420g	370	88	3.6	11.1	3.2	1.0
Dhansak, Sharwood's*	1 Jar/445g	668	150	4.7	15.2	7.8	1.4
Diane, Safeway*	½ Pot/85g	40	47	0.8	3.3	3.5	0.3
Dill, Sainsbury's*	1 Tsp/5g	23	466	1.9	19.7	42.2	0.9
Dipping For Dim Sum, Amoy*	1 Tbsp/15ml	29	190	0.0	48.0	0.0	0.0
Dopiaza, Patak's*	1 Serving/212g	235	111	1.7	9.1	7.6	1.3
Enchilada, Medium, Old El Paso*	1 Can/270g	92	34	0.0	5.0	1.7	0.0
Fajita, Asda*	¼ Jar/125g	79	63	1.0	5.0	4.3	1.0
Fajita, M & S*	1oz/28g	24	85	1.3	6.4	6.1	2.2
Fajita, Stir It Up, Chicken Tonight*	1 Jar/80g	494	617	4.6	25.1	55.4	2.8
Fish, Nam Plam, Blue Dragon*	1 Tbsp/15ml	12	80	13.4	6.7	0.0	0.0
For Lasagne, Light, Ragu*	1 Serving/100g	72	72	0.5	6.3	5.0	0.2
For Lasagne, Tomato, Ragu*	1 Jar/515g	191	37	1.5	7.4	0.2	1.0
For Lasagne, White, Dolmio*	1 Serving/140g	154	110	2.1	3.7	9.6	0.0
For Lasagne, White, Ragu	¼ Jar/123g	205	167	0.5	4.7	16.3	0.3
Fruity, HP*	1 Tsp/6g	8	141	1.2	35.1	0.1	0.0
Garlic, Lea & Perrins*	1 Tsp/6g	20	337	1.8	17.8	29.0	0.0

SAUCE,	Measure WEIGHT/INFO	per Measure KCAL	Nutrition Values per 100g / 100ml KCAL	PROT	CARB	FAT	FIBRE
Garlic, Onion & Basil For Sizzling Chicken, Dolmio*	1 Jar/520g	530	102	1.2	7.5	7.5	0.0
Ginger & Honey, Stir Fry, Sharwood's*	1 Jar/150g	138	92	1.3	21.4	0.1	0.1
Green Peppercorn, Sainsbury's*	1 Tbsp/15ml	68	455	0.4	3.8	48.5	0.1
Green Tandoori, M & S*	1 Jar/385g	501	130	3.6	6.8	9.9	1.5
Ham & Mushroom For Pasta, Stir & Serve, Homepride*	1 Serving/100g	95	95	1.5	1.3	9.3	0.0
Hoi-Sin & Spring Onion, Stir Fry, Sharwood's*	1 Jar/165g	223	135	2.6	27.8	1.5	0.9
Hoi-sin, Stir Fry, Asda*	1 Serving/100g	165	165	2.6	36.9	0.8	1.0
Hollandaise, Colman's*	1 Pack/27g	102	379	10.0	54.0	13.0	0.0
Hollandaise, Full Fat, M & S*	1 Tbsp/20g	67	336	1.1	4.5	34.9	0.1
Hollandaise, Homemade	1oz/28g	198	707	4.8	0.0	76.2	0.0
Hollandaise, M & S*	1oz/28g	56	200	1.6	2.4	20.5	0.1
Hollandaise, Pour Over, Knorr*	1oz/28g	44	158	0.0	7.0	14.0	0.0
Hollandaise, Sainsbury's*	1 Tbsp/15ml	77	515	0.5	4.2	55.0	0.0
Hollandaise, Schwartz*	1 Pack/25g	98	392	11.3	61.5	11.2	0.0
Honey & Coriander, Stir Fry, Blue Dragon*	1 Pack/120g	115	96	0.5	22.1	0.6	0.3
Honey & Mustard, Chicken Tonight*	¼ Jar/130g	139	107	1.6	13.5	5.2	1.3
Honey & Mustard, COU, M & S*	½ Jar/160g	112	70	2.3	9.2	2.9	0.7
Horseradish, Creamed, Colman's*	1 Tsp/16g	37	229	4.3	21.4	13.3	0.0
Horseradish, Creamed, Waitrose*	1 Tbsp/16g	30	185	2.4	19.6	9.9	2.3
Horseradish, Hot, Colman's*	1 Tbsp/15ml	16	105	1.8	9.7	5.7	0.0
Horseradish, Sainsbury's*	1 Dtsp/10g	15	145	1.5	17.8	6.6	2.4
Hot Chilli, Sharwood's*	1fl oz/30ml	36	120	0.5	29.4	0.6	1.3
Hot Chilli, Uncle Ben's*	1 Jar/500g	250	50	2.0	9.6	0.4	0.0
Hot Pepper	1oz/28g	7	26	1.6	1.7	1.5	0.0
HP*	1oz/28g	33	119	0.9	27.5	0.2	0.0
Italian Tomato & Herb, For Pasta, BGTY, Sainsbury's*	½ Jar/250g	138	55	2.1	10.9	0.3	0.0
Italian Tomato Feast, Chicken Tonight*	1 Serving/167g	65	39	1.3	7.0	0.6	1.5
Jalfrezi, Cooking, Asda*	1 Jar/500g	470	94	1.0	9.0	6.0	0.7
Jalfrezi, Cooking, Tesco*	¼ Jar/125g	144	115	2.6	11.4	6.5	1.6
Jalfrezi Hot, Cooking, Sharwood's*	1 Jar/440g	264	60	1.4	7.8	2.6	1.5
Jalfrezi, Hot, Tesco*	1 Serving/220g	125	57	1.1	8.3	2.1	0.8
Jalfrezi, M & S*	1 Jar/385g	308	80	1.7	6.6	5.2	1.9
Jalfrezi, Mild, Sharwood's*	1 Jar/445g	347	78	1.4	10.6	3.3	1.3
Jalfrezi, Stir Fry, Patak's*	1 Jar/250g	260	104	1.4	7.6	7.5	1.4
Jamaican Jerk, Chicken Tonight*	1oz/28g	174	621	3.9	25.7	55.8	5.0
Juicy Pineapple, Onion, Red Peppe, Ginger, Exotic, Heinz*	1 Serving/45ml	63	140	0.3	33.7	0.1	0.4
Kaffir Lime Chilli & Basil, Stir Fry, Sainsbury's*	1 Serving/150g	158	105	1.2	10.6	6.4	1.0
Kashmiri, Butter, Patak's*	1 Jar/420g	533	127	2.1	14.4	7.1	0.7
Korma, Asda*	1 Serving/225g	434	193	2.5	12.0	15.0	2.2
Korma, Cooking, BGTY, Sainsbury's*	¼ Jar/129g	119	92	1.1	10.8	4.9	1.4
Korma, Cooking, Sainsbury's*	¼ Jar/125g	159	127	1.4	8.0	9.9	1.0
Korma, Deliciously Good, Homepride*	1 Jar/450g	396	88	1.4	10.6	4.4	1.4
Korma, HE, Tesco*	1 Jar/435g	439	101	2.2	8.2	6.5	0.9
Korma, Homepride*	1 Serving/160g	110	69	1.3	11.6	2.0	0.0
Korma, Indian, M & S*	1oz/28g	60	215	3.8	11.7	17.3	0.9
Korma, Patak's*	1 Jar/540g	751	139	2.4	11.4	9.4	1.0
Korma, Tin, Patak's*	1 Can/283g	478	169	3.6	8.5	13.4	2.3
Korma, Uncle Ben's*	1 Jar/500g	625	125	1.2	11.4	7.8	0.0
Leek & Fontal, Sainsbury's*	½ Pot/150g	296	197	4.5	3.8	18.2	0.7
Lemon, Amoy*	1 Tsp/5ml	5	104	0.0	26.0	0.0	0.0
Lemon Butter, Schwartz*	1 Serving/9g	35	388	10.2	61.4	11.3	0.0
Lemon Pepper, Stir It Up, Chicken Tonight*	1 Jar/80g	527	659	5.2	26.1	59.3	2.7
Lemon, Stir Fry, Straight to Wok, Amoy*	½ Sachet/50g	81	162	0.3	40.0	0.2	0.0
Lemon, Stir Fry, Tesco*	1 Jar/450g	369	82	0.1	19.3	0.2	0.1

S

SAUCE,	Measure WEIGHT/INFO	per Measure KCAL	Nutrition Values per 100g / 100ml KCAL	PROT	CARB	FAT	FIBRE
Lemongrass & Coriander, Asda*	½ Jar/96g	52	54	1.7	11.0	0.4	0.1
Lemongrass & Ginger, Stir Fry, Sharwood's*	1oz/28g	20	72	1.2	11.1	2.5	0.2
Lime Honey & Ginger, Stir Fry, Sharwood's*	1 Serving/50g	35	69	0.3	16.6	0.1	0.2
Madras, Cooking, Sharwood's*	1 Tsp/2g	2	86	1.5	6.9	5.8	1.3
Madras Cumin & Chilli, Patak's*	¼ Jar/135g	162	120	2.1	11.9	7.1	1.8
Madras, M & S*	1 Jar/385g	289	75	1.5	7.2	4.7	2.1
Madras, Spicy Hot, Sharwood's*	1 Pack/350g	473	135	1.8	7.2	11.0	1.3
Makhani, Sainsbury's*	1 Jar/175g	135	77	2.9	11.6	2.2	0.8
Mediterranean, Rich, Baxters*	1 Jar/320g	173	54	1.2	7.9	1.9	1.4
Mediterranean Vegetable, Roasted, Sainsbury's*	½ Pot/150g	102	68	1.6	6.7	3.9	0.4
Mexican Style, Cooking, Eat Smart, Safeway*	1 Serving/178g	134	75	1.3	15.8	0.6	1.2
Mint, Baxters*	1oz/28g	17	62	1.7	13.2	0.3	0.0
Mint, Classic, Colman's*	1 Serving/5ml	6	122	0.8	26.0	0.1	0.0
Mint Jelly, Sweet, Colman's*	1 Serving/14ml	35	249	0.2	61.0	0.0	0.0
Mint Raita, Patak's*	1 Jar/270g	340	126	3.9	13.6	5.5	0.1
Mint, Sainsbury's*	1 Dtsp/10g	13	126	2.5	28.7	0.1	4.0
Mint, SmartPrice, Asda*	1 Serving/5g	3	52	0.1	13.0	0.0	1.2
Moroccan Seven Vegetable Cous Cous, Sainsbury's*	1 Serving/50g	89	178	2.6	5.9	16.0	0.0
Moroccan Tagine, Pan Fry, Loyd Grossman*	1oz/28g	15	53	0.9	5.4	3.1	0.4
Mustard & Dill, M & S*	1oz/28g	113	405	2.9	17.0	36.6	0.1
Mustard & Sweet Dill, Sainsbury's*	1 Serving/20g	50	248	2.8	25.8	14.9	2.6
Mustard, Mild, McDonald's*	1 Portion/30g	64	212	1.0	24.8	12.1	0.0
Napoletana, Sainsbury's*	1 Serving/100g	42	42	1.0	4.0	2.5	1.0
Olive & Smoked Garlic, Sacla*	1 Serving/150g	131	87	1.2	4.4	7.2	0.0
Onion, Colman's*	1 Sachet/35g	111	316	8.3	68.0	1.0	0.0
Onion, Made With Semi-Skimmed Milk	1 Serving/60g	52	86	2.9	8.4	5.0	0.4
Onion, Made With Skimmed Milk	1 Serving/60g	46	77	2.9	8.4	4.0	0.4
Orange & Green Ginger, Blue Dragon*	1 Pack/120g	118	98	0.5	20.4	1.6	0.5
Oyster & Garlic, Stir Fry, Straight To Wok, Amoy*	½ Pack/50g	98	195	4.9	37.0	3.0	0.0
Oyster & Spring Onion, Blue Dragon*	1 Serving/80g	74	92	1.6	19.9	0.7	1.1
Oyster Flavoured, Amoy*	1 Tsp/5ml	5	108	2.0	25.0	0.0	0.0
Oyster, Stir Fry, Sainsbury's	1 Tbsp/15g	9	61	1.6	13.3	0.1	0.2
Paprika Chicken, Chicken Tonight*	1 Serving/250g	240	96	0.9	3.5	8.7	1.4
Parsley, Colman's*	1 Sachet/20g	64	320	10.4	66.0	1.7	0.0
Parsley, Made Up, Semi Skim Milk, Sainsbury's*	¼ Sachet/51ml	34	67	3.5	8.6	2.1	0.1
Peking Lemon, Stir Fry, Blue Dragon*	1 Serving/35g	58	166	0.3	36.8	1.9	0.1
Peking, Sizzle & Stir, Chicken Tonight*	1 Jar/510g	617	121	0.8	9.4	8.9	1.6
Pepper & Brandy, Pour Over, Knorr*	1oz/28g	29	104	1.0	4.0	9.0	0.0
Pepper, Creamy, Colman's*	1 Pack/25g	88	352	13.0	50.0	11.0	0.0
Peppercorn, Creamy, Chicken Tonight*	¼ Jar/125g	100	80	1.0	3.8	6.7	0.5
Peppercorn, M & S*	1oz/28g	38	135	1.8	7.1	10.8	0.2
Peppercorn, Milk, Creamy, Schwartz*	1 Pack/25g	93	373	12.9	64.7	6.9	0.0
Peri-Peri, Hot, Nando's*	1oz/28g	18	63	0.1	4.5	2.7	1.4
Pesto	1oz/28g	145	517	20.4	2.0	47.5	0.0
Pesto, Bertolli*	1 Serving/20g	78	391	5.6	4.4	39.0	1.4
Pesto, Chargrilled Aubergine, Sacla' *	1 Serving/47.6g	79	164	1.9	3.5	16.0	0.0
Pesto, Classic Green, Sacla' *	1oz/28g	142	507	4.1	8.5	50.7	0.0
Pesto, M & S*	1oz/28g	115	411	3.2	3.5	43.3	3.9
Pesto, Red, Eat Smart, Safeway*	½ Pot/70g	42	60	4.3	6.4	1.9	2.1
Pesto, Red, Sacla*	1 Serving/25g	82	327	4.3	8.9	30.4	0.0
Pesto, Red, Sainsbury's*	1 Serving/60g	242	404	4.8	17.0	35.5	0.8
Pesto, Roasted Pepper, Sacla' *	1 Serving/47.6g	115	239	4.5	6.0	23.0	0.0
Pesto, Spinach & Parmesan, Sainsbury's*	½ Heap Tsp/16g	63	396	5.6	3.4	40.0	0.0
Pineapple & Red Pepper, Kwazulu, New World, Knorr*	1 Pack/500g	260	52	0.2	12.4	0.1	0.5

S

SAUCE,	Measure WEIGHT/INFO	per Measure KCAL	Nutrition Values per 100g / 100ml KCAL	PROT	CARB	FAT	FIBRE
Plum & Sesame, Stir Fry, M & S*	½ Jar/115g	138	120	0.9	29.0	0.1	1.8
Plum, Straight To Wok*	1oz/28g	69	246	0.2	61.0	0.2	0.0
Prawn Cocktail, Frank Cooper*	1 Tbsp/15g	47	316	0.8	18.3	26.7	0.1
Primavera, Loyd Grossman*	¼ Jar/88g	86	98	1.4	6.3	7.4	0.9
Real Oyster, Sharwood's*	1 Jar/150ml	113	75	1.3	17.0	0.2	0.3
Red & Yellow Pepper, Roasted, Sacla*	1 Serving/290g	232	80	1.1	5.5	5.9	0.0
Red Pepper, Fresh, Asda*	¼ Pot/82g	35	43	1.4	6.8	1.2	1.1
Red Pepper, GFY, Asda*	1 Serving/100g	43	43	1.2	7.0	1.1	0.0
Red Thai, Loyd Grossman*	1oz/28g	34	123	2.6	11.7	7.3	1.1
Red Wine & Herb, Safeway*	1 Jar/680g	347	51	1.1	8.3	1.5	0.5
Red Wine & Herbs, Ragu*	¼ Jar/130g	81	62	2.1	8.8	2.0	1.1
Red Wine & Onion, Rich, Simply Sausages, Colman's*	¼ Jar/125g	49	39	0.9	8.5	0.2	1.3
Red Wine, Cook In, Homepride*	¼ Can/98g	47	48	0.5	10.1	0.6	0.0
Red Wine, Cooking, BGTY, Sainsbury's*	1 Serving/125g	53	42	0.5	8.8	0.5	0.8
Redcurrant, Colman's*	1 Tsp/12g	44	368	0.7	90.0	0.0	0.0
Risotto, Mushroom & White Wine, Sacla' *	1 Serving/95g	151	159	3.7	6.9	13.0	0.0
Roasted Vegetable, Stir In, Dolmio*	1oz/28g	36	128	1.4	7.3	10.4	0.0
Rogan Josh, Cooking, Budgens*	1oz/28g	15	53	1.4	10.0	0.9	0.4
Rogan Josh, Cooking, Sharwood's*	1oz/28g	29	102	2.2	9.5	6.1	2.6
Rogan Josh, Culinary, Somerfield*	1 Jar/440g	339	77	2.0	6.0	5.0	0.0
Rogan Josh, Deliciously Good, Homepride*	1 Jar/460g	276	60	1.8	11.6	0.7	1.5
Rogan Josh, Homepride*	1 Jar/460g	285	62	1.9	11.9	0.7	0.0
Rogan Josh, Medium, Sharwood's*	½ Jar/210g	151	72	1.4	8.6	3.6	0.5
Rogan Josh, Patak's*	1 Serving/270g	192	71	1.8	9.4	2.9	0.0
Rogan Josh, Tesco*	½ Can/220g	130	59	1.5	11.5	0.6	0.9
Salami & Tomato Stir In For Pasta, Sainsbury's*	1 Serving/75g	134	178	3.4	6.6	15.3	1.1
Salmon, Oriental, Schwartz*	1 Serving/105g	138	131	2.0	27.5	1.5	0.0
Satay, Amoy*	1 Tsp/5ml	10	198	10.2	11.6	12.3	0.0
Satay, Indonesian, Sharwood's*	1oz/28g	31	112	2.8	11.8	6.0	0.6
Seafood, 25% Less Fat, Tesco*	1 Tsp/5g	17	344	2.7	18.2	28.5	0.3
Seafood, Baxters*	1oz/28g	149	533	1.5	9.9	54.2	0.7
Seafood, BGTY, Sainsbury's*	1 Serving/15ml	23	150	0.8	15.1	9.3	0.1
Seafood, Colman's*	1 Serving/14ml	47	335	0.9	20.0	28.0	0.0
Seafood, GFY, Asda*	1 Dstp/10ml	31	313	0.6	17.0	27.0	0.0
Seafood, Sainsbury's*	1 Tbsp/15ml	50	330	0.7	16.7	26.8	0.1
Seafood, Somerfield*	1oz/28g	97	345	2.0	12.0	32.0	0.0
Sizzle & Stir Smokey Texan, Chicken Tonight*	1 Serving/150g	149	99	1.1	5.8	7.9	1.8
Sizzling Chicken, Mediterranean Vegetables, Dolmio*	1 jar/520g	520	100	1.2	8.0	6.9	0.0
Smoked Ham & Cheese, For Pasta, Eat Smart, Safeway*	1 Serving/125g	94	75	5.8	6.1	2.5	0.9
Smokey Bacon & Tomato, Stir In, Dolmio*	1 Pot/150g	240	160	5.5	5.8	13.1	0.0
Smoky Barbecue, Medium Hot, Uncle Ben's*	1 Jar/400g	316	79	2.6	16.6	0.3	0.0
Soy	1 Tsp/5ml	3	64	8.7	8.3	0.0	0.0
Soy, Dark, Amoy*	1 Tsp/5ml	4	73	1.9	16.3	0.0	0.0
Soy, Light, Amoy*	1 Tsp/5ml	3	55	3.2	11.5	0.0	0.0
Soy, Light, Sharwood's*	1 Tsp/5ml	1	18	4.4	0.2	0.0	0.3
Soy, Reduced Salt, Amoy*	1 Tsp/5ml	3	56	4.0	10.0	0.0	0.0
Soy, Rich, Sharwood's*	1 Tsp/5ml	2	48	4.6	7.5	0.0	0.3
Soy, Superior Dark, Amoy*	1 Tsp/5ml	3	63	1.9	16.3	0.0	0.0
Soya, Japanese, Waitrose*	1 Tbsp/15ml	11	74	7.7	9.4	0.6	0.8
Spaghetti Bolognaise, Colman's*	1 Pack/45g	149	330	8.9	66.5	3.1	6.2
Spicy Bolognese, Cooking, Ragu*	1 Jar/510g	326	64	1.6	9.3	2.3	1.2
Spicy Peanut, Sharwood's*	1oz/28g	29	103	2.5	12.1	5.0	0.6
Spicy Pepper & Tomato, Stir Through, M & S*	½ Jar/95g	166	175	1.6	7.5	15.4	0.0
Spicy Pepper, Eat Smart, Safeway*	1 Serving/84g	42	50	1.4	7.0	1.7	1.3

S

SAUCE,	Measure WEIGHT/INFO	per Measure KCAL	KCAL	PROT	CARB	FAT	FIBRE
Spicy Red Pepper & Roasted Vegetable, For Pasta, Asda*	1 Serving/175g	140	80	1.2	9.0	4.4	1.0
Spicy Red Pepper & Roasted Vegetable, Sainsbury's*	1 Pot/302g	220	73	1.5	8.9	3.4	1.0
Spicy Sweet & Sour, Cooking, Eat Smart, Safeway*	1 Serving/178g	125	70	0.4	14.7	0.9	0.6
Spicy Tikka, Cooking, Sharwood's*	1oz/28g	27	95	1.3	9.4	5.9	0.8
Spicy Tomato, Fresh, Somerfield*	1/3 Pot/100g	41	41	0.8	6.4	1.3	1.1
Spinach & Ricotta, Eat Smart, Safeway*	1 Serving/125g	69	55	2.1	5.6	2.4	0.7
Stroganoff, M & S*	1oz/28g	30	107	3.8	4.9	8.0	0.6
Sun Dried Tomato, Stir In, Light, Dolmio*	1 Serving/75g	62	83	1.7	9.8	4.7	0.0
Sun-Dried Tomato For Pasta, Stir & Serve, Homepride*	1 Serving/100g	62	62	1.0	7.6	3.0	0.0
Sun-Dried Tomato, Stir-In, Dolmio*	1 Serving/75g	124	165	1.5	9.3	14.0	0.0
Sundried Tomato & Basil, Seeds Of Change*	1 Serving/100g	169	169	1.8	9.3	13.2	0.0
Sundried Tomato, Balsamic, Mushroom, ES, Safeway*	1oz/28g	17	60	1.8	10.7	0.7	0.7
Sundried Tomato, Heinz*	1 Serving/10g	8	75	1.6	15.1	0.7	0.9
Sundried Tomato With Vodka & Chilli, TTD, Sainsbury's*	½ Pot/150g	99	66	1.7	6.9	3.5	0.5
Sweet & Sour Chinese, Sainsbury's*	½ Jar/150g	222	148	0.2	36.6	0.1	0.1
Sweet & Sour, Colman's*	1 Pack/40g	134	334	3.4	78.0	0.1	0.0
Sweet & Sour, Cooking, Healthy Choice, Asda*	1 Jar/500g	175	35	0.6	8.0	0.1	0.5
Sweet & Sour, Culinary, Healthy Selection, Somerfield*	1 Jar/440g	176	40	1.0	9.0	0.0	0.0
Sweet & Sour, Extra Pineapple, Uncle Ben's*	1 Serving/165g	144	87	0.3	21.4	0.0	0.0
Sweet & Sour, Fresh Ideas, Tesco*	1 Serving/50ml	77	154	1.1	34.3	1.4	0.5
Sweet & Sour, Fresh, Safeway*	1 Sachet/50g	101	201	0.9	37.8	5.1	0.3
Sweet & Sour, Fresh, Sainsbury's*	1 Sachet/50ml	103	205	0.8	31.2	8.6	0.3
Sweet & Sour, Homepride*	1 Serving/195g	193	99	0.4	24.4	0.1	0.0
Sweet & Sour, Light, Uncle Ben's*	1 Serving/200g	128	64	0.5	15.5	0.0	0.0
Sweet & Sour, McDonald's*	1 Portion/32g	59	183	0.4	43.5	0.8	0.0
Sweet & Sour, Oriental, Chicken Tonight*	¼ Jar/125g	115	92	0.6	20.9	0.7	0.9
Sweet & Sour, Original, Uncle Ben's*	1 Pack/300g	264	88	0.5	21.7	0.0	0.0
Sweet & Sour, Peking Style, Safeway*	1 Jar/340g	214	63	0.6	14.9	0.1	0.9
Sweet & Sour, Sizzle & Stir, Chicken Tonight*	1 Jar/465g	693	149	0.6	19.5	7.7	1.6
Sweet & Sour Spicy, Stir Fry, Sainsbury's*	1 Jar/500g	430	86	0.7	20.0	0.1	0.7
Sweet & Sour, Spicy, Uncle Ben's*	1 Jar/400g	364	91	0.6	22.1	0.1	0.0
Sweet & Sour, Stir Fry, Asda*	½ Pack/50ml	116	232	0.8	46.0	5.0	0.0
Sweet & Sour, Stir Fry, Asda*	1 Serving/63g	146	232	0.8	46.0	5.0	0.0
Sweet & Sour, Stir Fry, Blue Dragon*	1 Serving/120g	150	125	0.7	23.3	3.2	0.9
Sweet & Sour, Stir Fry, HE, Tesco*	1 Jar/440g	167	38	0.6	8.0	0.1	0.8
Sweet & Sour, Stir Fry, Sharwood's*	1 Jar 160g	160	100	0.8	24.1	0.1	1.0
Sweet & Sour, Stir Fry, Straight To Wok, Amoy*	1 Pack/220g	486	221	0.5	54.6	0.2	0.0
Sweet & Sour, Stir Fry, Tesco*	½ Jar/222g	164	74	0.6	17.0	0.2	0.4
Sweet & Sour, Straight To Wok*	1oz/28g	52	186	0.3	45.5	0.3	0.0
Sweet & Sour, Take-Away	1oz/28g	44	157	0.2	32.8	3.4	0.0
Sweet & Sour, Two Stage, Uncle Ben's*	½ Jar/200g	314	157	1.0	18.1	9.1	0.0
Sweet & Sour, Uncle Ben's*	1 Serving/200g	168	84	0.4	21.7	0.0	0.0
Sweet Barbecue, Deliciously Good, Homepride*	1/3 Jar/149g	110	74	1.4	12.0	2.2	1.2
Sweet Chilli & Coriander, Sharwood's*	1 Pack/370g	407	110	0.3	24.4	1.2	0.1
Sweet Chilli & Coriander, Sizzling, Homepride*	1 Serving/100g	51	51	0.7	11.5	0.2	0.0
Sweet Chilli & Garlic Noodle, Sharwood's*	1oz/28g	30	107	0.9	18.9	3.1	0.4
Sweet Chilli & Ginger, Stir Fry, M & S*	1 Serving/60ml	207	345	0.5	44.9	18.1	0.6
Sweet Chilli & Lemon Grass, Sharwood's*	1 Serving/155g	119	77	0.4	18.3	0.2	0.3
Sweet Chilli & Red Pepper, Sharwood*	1 Serving/250g	178	71	0.8	16.4	0.2	1.1
Sweet Chilli, Asda*	1 Tbsp/15ml	18	123	0.4	30.0	0.1	0.8
Sweet Chilli Dipping, Blue Dragon*	1 Tsp/5ml	12	230	0.0	56.0	0.0	0.0
Sweet Chilli Dipping, M & S*	1 Tbsp/15g	37	245	0.2	61.1	0.1	0.5
Sweet Chilli, Sharwood's*	1 Jar/150ml	281	187	0.6	44.4	0.8	1.5
Sweet Pepper, Stir In, Dolmio*	1 Pot/150g	239	159	1.6	8.8	13.4	0.0

Nutrition Values per 100g / 100ml (KCAL, PROT, CARB, FAT, FIBRE)

SAUCE,	Measure WEIGHT/INFO	per Measure KCAL	KCAL	PROT	CARB	FAT	FIBRE
Sweet Soy & Sesame, Uncle Ben's*	1 Serving/100g	110	110	0.7	23.0	1.7	0.0
Szechuan, Hot n Spicy, Safeway*	1 Jar/225g	281	125	1.2	17.9	5.4	0.9
Szechuan Spicy Tomato, Stir Fry, Blue Dragon*	1 Sachet/120g	151	126	1.3	17.6	5.6	2.0
Szechuan, Stir Fry, Sharwood's*	1 Jar/150g	126	84	3.0	15.5	1.1	0.4
Szechuan, Stir Fry, Tesco*	½ Jar/220g	205	93	1.0	14.7	3.2	0.9
Szechuan Style, Stir Fry, Fresh Ideas, Tesco*	1 Sachet/50g	114	228	1.9	33.4	9.7	0.1
Szechuan Sweet & Sour, Sainsbury's*	½ Jar/100g	151	151	0.5	37.0	0.1	0.1
Tartar, Kraft*	2 Tbsp/30ml	162	539	1.3	0.0	58.3	0.0
Tartare	1oz/28g	84	299	1.3	17.9	24.6	0.0
Tartare, Baxters*	1oz/28g	144	515	1.0	8.0	53.3	0.3
Tartare, Colman's*	1 Serving/14ml	37	263	1.1	14.0	21.7	0.0
Tartare, Frank Cooper*	1 Pot/20g	54	271	0.8	16.8	22.3	0.1
Tartare, Sainsbury's*	1 Serving/20ml	94	469	0.4	5.8	49.0	1.0
Tartare, Tesco*	1 Tbsp/15g	43	287	1.5	19.6	21.8	0.3
Teriyaki, Blue Dragon*	½ Pack/60g	104	173	2.0	28.6	0.0	0.0
Teriyaki, Stir Fry, Sharwood's*	1 Jar/150g	137	91	0.9	19.7	1.0	0.3
Thai Chilli, Dipping, Sainsbury's*	1 Tbsp/15g	30	201	0.2	49.8	0.0	5.0
Thai Red Curry, Stir Fry, Blue Dragon*	1 Serving/60g	55	91	1.0	7.3	6.4	1.2
Thai Satay, Sharwood's*	1oz/28g	160	573	17.2	18.0	48.0	6.3
Thai, Stir Fry, Sainsbury's*	1 Serving/53g	66	124	2.5	6.9	9.6	0.2
Thai Style, Stir Fry, M & S*	1 Pack/60g	81	135	3.6	10.3	9.0	2.5
Thai Sweet Chilli, Sizzle & Stir, Chicken Tonight*	1 Jar/510g	694	136	0.6	7.5	11.4	2.9
Tikka Bhuna, Sizzle & Stir, Chicken Tonight*	1 Jar/460g	561	122	1.1	7.2	9.9	2.7
Tikka, Creamy, Chicken Tonight*	1oz/28g	36	129	1.7	12.1	8.2	0.7
Tikka Masala, 25% Fat Reduced, Asda*	1 Jar/500g	380	76	2.9	9.0	3.2	0.5
Tikka Masala, 98% Fat Free, Homepride*	1oz/28g	14	49	1.4	7.9	1.7	0.8
Tikka Masala, Cooking, BGTY, Sainsbury's*	1 Jar/516g	516	100	1.5	12.1	4.9	1.3
Tikka Masala, Cooking, Budgens*	1oz/28g	27	96	1.6	10.1	5.5	0.2
Tikka Masala, Cooking, Eat Smart, Safeway*	½ Jar/180g	117	65	1.9	9.9	1.7	1.1
Tikka Masala, Cooking, HE, Tesco*	1 Serving/250g	220	88	2.1	8.1	5.1	0.8
Tikka Masala, Cooking, Organic, Asda*	1 Jar/450g	504	112	1.2	11.0	7.0	1.1
Tikka Masala, Cooking, Sharwood's*	1 Tsp/2g	2	122	1.2	11.9	7.8	0.9
Tikka Masala, COU, M & S*	½ Pack/100g	80	80	4.5	9.9	2.6	1.7
Tikka Masala, Deliciously Good, Homepride*	¼ Jar/149g	121	81	2.1	10.0	3.6	1.5
Tikka Masala, Fresh, Somerfield*	1 Pack/250g	308	123	3.0	10.0	8.0	0.0
Tikka Masala, Jar, Sharwood's*	1 Jar/435g	492	113	1.4	9.6	7.6	1.4
Tikka Masala Lemon & Coriander, Patak's*	1 Jar/270g	265	98	2.6	10.8	4.9	0.0
Tikka Masala, Organic, Seeds Of Change*	1 Jar/385g	343	89	1.7	9.1	5.5	0.7
Tikka Masala, Organic, Tesco*	½ Jar/220g	229	104	1.9	9.4	6.2	0.8
Tikka Masala, Sizzle & Stir, Chicken Tonight*	1/3 Jar/168g	336	200	2.0	8.4	17.3	2.6
Tomato	1oz/28g	25	89	2.2	8.6	5.5	1.4
Tomato & Basil, Cooking, M & S*	1 Serving/130g	78	60	1.4	5.7	3.4	1.2
Tomato & Basil, Eat Smart, Safeway*	1 Serving/250g	150	60	1.7	7.4	2.5	1.4
Tomato & Basil For Pasta Stir & Serve, Homepride*	1 Jar/480g	278	58	1.2	6.7	2.9	0.0
Tomato & Basil, Fresh, Organic, Waitrose*	¼ Pot/175g	77	44	1.0	6.2	1.7	0.8
Tomato & Basil, Sun-Ripened, Microwaveable, Dolmio*	1 Sachet/170g	95	56	1.4	7.9	2.1	0.0
Tomato & Basil, Tesco*	½ Jar/175g	84	48	0.7	3.8	3.3	0.8
Tomato & Garlic, For Pasta, Asda*	¼ Jar/125g	80	64	2.7	8.0	2.3	1.1
Tomato & Herb, Somerfield*	1oz/28g	11	41	1.0	6.0	1.0	0.0
Tomato & Herbs, Italienne, Stir It Up, Chicken Tonight*	1/3 Pot/26g	164	632	4.8	18.3	60.0	4.4
Tomato & Mascarpone, Fresh, Sainsbury's*	1/3 Pot/100g	118	118	2.2	4.2	10.3	1.1
Tomato & Mascarpone, Fresh, Tesco*	½ Pot/175g	207	118	2.8	7.1	8.7	0.6
Tomato & Mozarella, Finest, Tesco*	1 Serving/175g	89	51	1.6	4.1	3.2	0.6
Tomato & Mozzarrella, Eat Smart, Safeway*	½ Pot/175g	114	65	3.1	6.9	2.7	1.2

Nutrition Values per 100g / 100ml (KCAL, PROT, CARB, FAT, FIBRE)

S

SAUCE,	Measure WEIGHT/INFO	per Measure KCAL	Nutrition Values per 100g / 100ml KCAL	PROT	CARB	FAT	FIBRE
Tomato & Onion, Cook In, Homepride*	1 Can/390g	183	47	0.9	9.8	0.5	0.0
Tomato & Roasted Garlic, Stir In, Dolmio*	½ Pack/75g	94	125	1.2	7.7	10.2	0.0
Tomato & Tuna, Safeway*	½ Pot/175g	159	91	5.5	9.0	3.7	2.2
Tomato & Wild Mushroom, Organic, Fresh, Sainsbury's*	1 Serving/152g	102	67	1.9	3.9	4.9	1.7
Tomato Base For Recipes, Salsina*	1oz/28g	7	24	1.6	4.5	0.0	1.4
Tomato, Fresh, M & S*	1oz/28g	11	40	1.4	6.5	0.6	0.8
Tomato, Indian, Sizzling, Homepride*	1 Serving/240g	82	34	0.9	7.0	0.2	0.0
Tomato, Parmesan & Dill, Tesco*	1 Serving/70g	81	115	3.1	4.8	9.2	0.7
Tomato, Roasted Garlic & Mushroom, Bertolli*	¼ Jar/125g	68	54	1.9	6.4	2.0	1.5
Tomato, Value, Tesco*	1 Serving/10g	14	139	2.3	32.2	0.1	1.4
Vegetable & Garlic, For Pasta, Dolmio*	1 Serving/150g	108	72	1.3	7.4	4.1	0.0
Vegetables, Hoi Sin & Plum, Stir Fry, Sharwood's*	1 Pack/360g	367	102	1.1	21.4	1.3	0.2
Vindaloo, Extra Hot, Sharwood's*	1 Pack/350g	382	109	1.7	7.5	8.0	1.3
Vodka & Chilli, Finest, Tesco*	1 Serving/350g	343	98	2.2	9.4	5.7	2.1
Vodka Chilli Finest, Tesco*	½ Pot/175g	98	56	1.3	5.4	3.3	1.2
Watercress, M & S*	1oz/28g	32	115	3.4	6.5	8.2	0.7
White Granules, Sauce In Seconds Asda*	1 Pack/57g	237	415	3.7	73.0	12.0	0.9
White, Savoury, Colman's*	1 Pack/25g	93	371	11.0	58.0	9.9	0.0
White, Savoury, Made With Semi-Skimmed Milk	1oz/28g	36	128	4.2	11.1	7.8	0.2
White, Savoury, Made With Whole Milk	1oz/28g	42	150	4.1	10.9	10.3	0.2
White Wine & Herb, Creamy, Del Good, Homepride*	1/3 Jar/150g	102	68	0.6	6.3	4.5	0.3
White Wine & Mushroom, BGTY, Sainsbury's*	1 Serving/166g	93	56	1.2	4.9	3.5	0.5
White Wine, Cooking, Iceland*	1 Serving/220g	198	90	1.1	8.3	5.8	0.2
White Wine, Creamy, Cooking, BGTY, Sainsbury's*	¼ Jar/125g	70	56	1.2	4.9	3.5	0.5
White Wine Mushroom & Herb, 98% Fat Free, Homepride*	1 Jar/450g	180	40	0.8	7.0	1.2	0.5
Wild Mushroom, Finest, Tesco*	½ Pack/175g	158	90	1.9	5.2	6.8	0.4
Wine, Chardonnay, M & S*	1oz/28g	42	150	1.6	5.8	13.2	0.3
Worcestershire	1 Tsp/5g	3	65	1.4	15.5	0.1	0.0
Worcestershire, Lea & Perrins*	1 Tsp/5ml	4	88	1.1	22.0	0.0	0.0
Yellow Bean, Sharwood's*	1 Jar/160g	211	132	0.3	28.9	1.7	1.5
Yellow Bean, Stir Fry, Straight To Wok, Amoy*	1oz/28g	44	159	1.6	36.9	0.5	0.0
Yellowbean & Cashew Nut, Asda*	1 Serving/50g	60	119	2.7	21.0	2.7	0.9
SAUCE MIX,							
Beef Stroganoff, Colman's*	1 Pack/40g	160	399	12.4	48.4	17.3	6.4
Bread, Colman's*	1 Pack/40g	130	325	12.0	66.0	1.3	0.0
Bread, Knorr*	½ Pint/40g	177	442	7.9	49.9	23.3	2.1
Cheese, Instant, Safeway*	1 Pack/54g	202	374	4.1	62.0	12.2	8.5
Cheese, Knorr*	1 Pack/58g	132	227	7.8	38.0	4.9	1.8
Cheese, Made Up With Skimmed Milk	1 Serving/60g	47	78	5.4	9.5	2.3	0.0
Chicken Chasseur, Colman's*	1 Pack/45g	123	273	12.0	53.0	1.0	0.0
Chicken Chasseur, Schwartz*	½ Pack/20g	64	322	9.1	64.5	3.1	0.0
Coq Au Vin, Colman's*	1 Pack/50g	141	281	7.5	59.0	1.0	0.0
Creamy Cheese & Bacon, For Pasta, Colman's*	1 Pack/50g	197	394	16.6	44.6	16.6	5.7
Garlic, Mushroom & Cream, Schwartz*	1 Serving/13g	48	373	10.9	59.4	10.2	0.0
Garlic Mushrooms, Creamy, Schwartz*	1 Pack/35g	38	108	2.5	21.0	1.6	0.0
Garlic Mushrooms, Creamy, Schwartz*	1 Pack/35g	109	310	7.1	60.1	4.6	0.0
Mushroom Stroganoff, Schwartz*	1 Pack/35g	41	117	3.3	21.7	1.9	0.0
Parsley, Knorr*	1 Sachet/48g	210	437	4.2	50.6	24.2	0.8
Parsley, Somerfield*	1 Sachet/24g	17	72	4.0	9.0	2.0	0.0
Rum Flavour, Kraft*	1oz/28g	116	415	6.1	76.5	9.5	0.0
Spaghetti Bolognese, Schwartz*	1 Serving/40g	122	306	10.0	63.0	1.0	0.0
Tuna & Mushroom Pasta Melt, Schwartz*	1 Pack/40g	138	344	8.4	54.8	10.1	0.0
Tuna & Pasta Bake, Colman's*	1 Pack/45g	144	319	10.4	57.1	5.4	5.2
Tuna & Pasta, Colman's*	1 Pack/44g	138	314	11.0	54.0	4.9	0.0

S

SAUCE MIX,	Measure WEIGHT/INFO	per Measure KCAL	KCAL	PROT	CARB	FAT	FIBRE
Tuna Napolitana, Schwartz*	1 Sachet/29g	107	368	9.7	53.0	13.0	0.0
White, Instant, Sainsbury's*	1 Serving/90ml	65	72	0.8	10.9	2.8	0.1
White, Made Up With Semi-Skimmed Milk	1oz/28g	20	73	4.0	9.6	2.4	0.0
White, Made Up With Skimmed Milk	1oz/28g	17	59	4.0	9.6	0.9	0.0
White, Savoury, Knorr*	½ Pint Pack/16g	46	290	7.8	52.2	5.6	5.2
SAUERKRAUT	1oz/28g	3	9	1.1	1.1	0.0	2.2
SAUSAGE,							
3% Fat, HE, Tesco*	1 Sausage/56g	66	117	14.2	8.5	2.9	0.9
Aberdeen Angus Beef, Asda*	1 Sausage/77g	203	263	16.0	7.0	19.0	0.5
Aberdeenshire Beef, Safeway*	1 Sausage/48g	126	262	15.9	10.5	17.4	0.9
Aberdeenshire, Butchers Choice, Tesco*	1 Sausage/57g	168	294	9.6	8.5	24.6	2.1
Bangers & Cabbage Mash, Eat Smart, Safeway*	1 Pack/400g	340	85	6.4	9.0	2.5	1.3
Bangers & Mash, Co-Op*	1 Pack/300g	375	125	4.0	13.0	6.0	0.8
Beef, Somerfield*	1 Sausage/51g	122	240	13.0	10.0	17.0	0.0
Beef, With Onion & Red Wine, Finest, Tesco*	1 Sausage/63g	117	185	13.2	8.5	10.9	1.2
BGTY, Sainsbury's*	1 Sausage/50g	95	189	16.9	10.9	8.6	0.5
Bockwurst German, Princes*	1 Sausage/45g	113	251	10.5	0.5	23.0	0.0
Butchers, M & S*	1oz/28g	87	310	11.1	6.7	26.8	0.6
Chicken & Tarragon, Butchers Choice, Sainsbury's*	1 Sausage/47g	106	225	18.1	5.8	14.4	0.2
Chipolata, Basics, Somerfield*	1 Sausage/28g	76	271	10.0	14.0	20.0	0.0
Chipolata, Cumberland, Asda*	1 Sausage/33g	84	255	13.0	17.0	15.0	1.5
Chipolata, Cumberland, Finest, Tesco*	1 Chipolata/28g	66	235	15.6	3.1	17.8	0.7
Chipolata, Lamb & Rosemary, Tesco*	1 Sausage/31.6g	69	218	11.3	8.3	15.5	0.0
Chipolata, Pork & Tomato, Organic, Tesco*	1 Chipolata/28g	79	283	12.2	4.3	24.1	0.9
Chipolata, Pork, Extra Lean, BGTY, Sainsbury's*	1 Chipolata	46	189	16.9	10.9	8.6	0.5
Chipolata, Pork, Finest, Tesco*	1 Sausage/28g	78	280	13.7	3.9	23.3	0.2
Chipolata, Pork, Somerfield*	1 Chipolata/28g	80	286	12.0	10.0	22.0	0.0
Chipolata, Pork, Ultimate, TTD, Sainsbury's*	1 Sausage/45g	112	248	17.6	5.3	17.4	1.2
Choice Pork, Co-Op*	1 Sausage/57g	200	350	10.0	9.0	31.0	2.0
Chorizo, & Jalapeño, Pizzadella, Tesco*	1 Pizza/600g	1272	212	9.9	27.9	6.8	1.7
Chorizo (Tapas Selection), Sainsburys*	1slice/5g	15	304	20.0	2.0	24.0	0.2
Chorizo, Gran Dobion, Somerfield*	1oz/28g	108	387	23.0	4.0	31.0	0.0
Chorizo, M & S*	1 Sausage/57g	140	245	14.4	7.0	18.3	1.7
Chorizo, Spanish, Chorizo, Sainsbury's*	1 Serving/23g	70	304	20.0	2.0	24.0	0.1
Chorizo, Spanish Slices, Tesco*	1 Slice/20g	59	297	26.8	2.6	19.9	0.0
Chorizo, Spanish, Waitrose*	1 Slice/5g	15	304	20.0	2.0	24.0	0.0
Chorizo, Spicy, M & S*	1 Sausage/67g	154	230	13.0	10.3	15.6	0.9
Chorizo, Tesco*	1 Sausage/53g	161	303	11.7	4.4	26.5	0.9
Classic Sicilian Style, TTD, Sainsbury's*	1 Sausage/49g	135	275	16.8	0.5	22.5	0.9
Classic Toulouse, TTD, Sainsbury's*	1 Sausage/44.5g	138	310	23.2	2.1	23.3	0.9
Cocktail, Budgens*	1 Sausage/14g	44	309	10.5	9.0	25.7	0.0
Cocktail, M & S*	1oz/28g	105	375	10.7	10.3	32.8	0.9
Cocktail, Occasions, Sainsbury's*	1 Sausage/9g	31	353	12.1	9.8	29.5	0.3
Cumberland, Butchers Choice, Tesco*	1 Sausage/56g	180	321	11.1	7.6	27.4	1.8
Cumberland, GFY, Asda*	1 Sausage/49g	72	147	17.0	10.0	4.3	0.7
Cumberland, M & S*	1oz/28g	86	306	13.1	5.2	25.9	0.3
Cumberland Pork, Budgens*	1 Serving/100g	319	319	12.1	9.0	26.1	0.0
Cumberland Pork, Butcher's Choice, Sainsbury's*	1 Sausage/57g	148	260	19.8	4.3	18.2	0.1
Cumberland Pork, Safeway*	1 Sausage/57g	156	273	14.2	10.0	19.6	1.0
Cumberland Pork, Waitrose*	1 Sausage/112g	317	283	13.3	5.8	23.0	2.0
Cumberland Ring, TTD, Sainsbury's*	1 Sausage/142g	410	289	17.7	6.2	21.5	0.8
Cumberland, Sainsbury's*	1 Serving/53g	148	279	15.5	10.1	19.6	0.3
Cumberland, Somerfield*	1oz/28g	86	308	11.0	19.0	21.0	0.0
Extra Lean, Grilled, BGTY, Sainsbury's*	1 Sausage/49g	96	196	16.7	13.9	8.2	0.6

(KCAL, PROT, CARB, FAT, FIBRE: Nutrition Values per 100g / 100ml)

S

SAUSAGE,	Measure WEIGHT/INFO	per Measure KCAL	Nutrition Values per 100g / 100ml KCAL	PROT	CARB	FAT	FIBRE
Extra Lean, M & S*	1 Sausage/55g	61	110	15.3	7.2	3.3	2.9
Extra Lean Pork, BGTY, Grilled, Sainsbury's*	1 Sausage/50g	95	189	16.9	10.9	8.6	0.5
French Garlic, Sainsbury's*	1 Slice/13g	30	228	16.6	0.4	17.8	0.0
French Saucisson, Tesco*	1 Slice/5g	19	379	26.7	4.1	28.4	0.0
Frozen, HE, Tesco*	1 Sausage/100g	82	82	7.0	5.9	3.4	0.4
Frozen, SmartPrice, Asda*	1 Sausage/40g	116	291	8.0	13.0	23.0	0.9
Garlic, Mild, Co-Op*	1 Slice/10g	24	235	17.0	0.7	19.0	0.0
Garlic, Strong, Asda*	1 Slice/11g	24	217	15.0	1.0	17.0	0.0
Garlic, Tesco*	1 Slice/12g	22	183	17.7	3.0	11.1	0.0
Great British Banger Lincolnshire, 5% Fat, Asda*	1 Sausage/42g	96	229	15.0	13.0	13.0	1.2
Grilled, HE, Tesco*	1 Sausage/46g	82	178	15.0	13.0	7.0	1.0
Half The Fat, Bowyers*	1oz/28g	55	196	12.6	10.2	11.9	0.0
Hot & Spicy Pork Cocktail, Cooked, Asda*	1 Sausage/10g	31	312	13.0	11.0	24.0	1.3
Hot Mustard Porker, Tesco*	1 Sausage/52g	143	275	16.1	8.1	19.8	3.1
Irish Recipe, Morrisons*	1 Serving/50g	176	351	8.7	28.1	22.6	1.0
Irish Recipe, Sainsbury's*	1 Sausage/40g	111	277	12.2	18.8	17.2	0.6
Jumbo Pork, Asda*	1 Sausage/74g	155	209	17.0	15.0	9.0	1.0
Lamb & Mint, M & S*	1oz/28g	63	225	13.3	6.6	16.3	1.7
Lincolnshire, GFY, Asda*	1 Sausage/50g	74	147	17.0	10.0	4.3	1.0
Lincolnshire Pork, Tesco*	1 Sausage/46g	161	349	9.7	10.6	29.8	0.5
Lincolnshire, Somerfield*	1 Sausage/28.5g	79	281	13.0	8.0	22.0	0.0
Lincolnshire, Tesco*	1 Sausage/60g	177	295	11.4	5.3	25.4	0.0
Lincolnshire, Thick, Premium, Sainsbury's*	1 Sausage/48g	147	306	14.1	12.3	22.3	0.3
Lincolnshire, TTD, Sainsbury's*	1 Sausage/59g	150	258	19.8	6.1	17.1	0.8
Lincolnshire, Waitrose*	1 Sausage/48g	91	189	13.3	6.0	12.4	0.9
Linda McCartney*	1 Sausage/35g	86	245	24.9	8.4	13.1	1.6
Low Fat, BPC, Sainsbury's*	1 Serving/180g	331	184	17.9	13.4	6.5	0.3
Mediterranean Style, 95% Fat Free, Bowyers*	1 Sausage/50g	60	120	13.9	8.9	3.2	0.0
Mediterranean Style Paprika, Waitrose*	1 Sausage/67g	190	283	12.1	4.6	24.0	1.9
Micro, Wall's*	1 Sausage/45g	149	330	12.2	13.4	25.3	2.3
Mini, Skinless, Asda*	1 Sausage/8g	22	279	10.0	17.0	19.0	0.3
Mini, Tesco*	1oz/28g	96	342	12.6	8.9	28.4	0.8
No Meat Bangers, Asda*	1 Sausage/47g	89	189	20.0	7.0	9.0	2.9
Pistachio, Waitrose*	1 Slice/12g	32	267	14.0	1.0	23.0	0.1
Polony Slicing, Asda*	1oz/28g	60	214	11.0	11.0	14.0	0.0
Pork & Apple, Finest, Tesco*	1 Sausage/75g	180	240	12.4	7.3	17.9	1.9
Pork & Apple, M & S*	1 Sausage/57g	125	220	12.1	8.8	15.9	2.2
Pork & Apple, Sainsbury's*	1 Sausage/67g	184	275	18.4	7.8	18.9	1.7
Pork & Beef, Farmfoods*	1 Sausage/45g	125	277	9.3	7.9	23.1	0.9
Pork & Beef, Freshbake*	1 Sausage/45g	114	253	8.7	14.3	17.9	1.9
Pork & Beef, Somerfield*	1 Sausage/57g	164	288	8.0	14.0	22.0	0.0
Pork & Beef, Thick, Iceland*	1 Sausage/53g	165	312	10.4	12.1	24.7	0.6
Pork & Beef, Thin, Tesco*	1 Sausage/20g	60	302	6.7	18.7	22.3	0.5
Pork & Leek, Safeway*	1 Serving/100g	256	256	14.4	5.4	19.7	1.1
Pork & Leek, Tesco*	1 Sausage/75g	226	301	10.0	6.8	26.0	0.4
Pork & Leek, The Best, Safeway*	1 Sausage/52g	133	256	14.4	5.4	19.7	1.1
Pork & Leek, TTD, Sainsbury's*	1 Sausage/44g	125	284	23.0	2.2	20.4	1.2
Pork & Onion, Asda*	1 Sausage/42g	108	257	20.0	6.0	17.0	1.8
Pork & Smoked Bacon, Finest, Tesco*	1oz/28g	76	271	13.9	4.8	21.8	0.2
Pork & Stilton Cheese, Budgens*	1 Sausage/57g	175	308	13.1	7.0	25.3	0.0
Pork & Stilton, Finest, Tesco*	1 Sausage/75g	244	325	13.3	4.7	28.1	0.6
Pork & Tomato, Somerfield*	1 Sausage/57g	157	275	13.0	6.0	22.0	0.0
Pork, 95% Fat Free, Bowyers*	1 Serving/52g	55	105	15.3	7.0	2.4	0.0
Pork, Apricot & Lovage, Waitrose*	1 Sausage/67g	165	246	11.2	12.9	16.6	1.3

SAUSAGE,	Measure WEIGHT/INFO	per Measure KCAL	KCAL	PROT	CARB	FAT	FIBRE
Pork, Bacon & Cheese, Asda*	¼ Pack/114g	329	289	18.0	7.0	21.0	0.4
Pork, BGTY, Sainsbury's*	1 Sausage/50g	95	189	16.9	10.9	8.6	0.5
Pork, Breakfast, Sainsbury's*	1 Sausage/20g	46	230	17.9	14.7	11.1	0.8
Pork, Chilled, Grilled	1 Thin Sausage/35g	103	294	14.5	9.8	22.1	0.7
Pork, Chilli & Coriander, Grilled, Sainsbury's*	1 Sausage/54g	123	228	18.9	3.5	15.4	1.8
Pork Cocktail, Cooked, Asda*	1 Sausage/10g	31	312	13.0	11.0	24.0	1.3
Pork, Cocktail, Cooked, Sainsbury's*	1 Sausage/10g	30	302	13.0	9.5	23.6	1.1
Pork Cocktail, M & S*	1 Sausage/50g	170	340	12.6	10.7	27.5	0.9
Pork Cocktail , Tesco*	1 Sausage/14g	39	279	12.1	9.2	21.5	1.1
Pork, COU, M & S*	1 Sausage/57g	66	115	15.6	9.5	2.1	1.4
Pork, Eat Smart, Grilled, Safeway*	2 Sausages/91g	120	132	22.7	7.3	1.3	1.2
Pork, Extra Lean, Butchers Choice, Sainsbury's*	1 Serving/50g	91	181	20.7	4.1	9.1	0.1
Pork, Extra Lean Premium, Waitrose*	1 Serving/57g	89	156	17.2	2.7	8.5	1.8
Pork, Farmfoods*	1 Sausage/45g	151	336	11.5	8.8	28.3	1.0
Pork, Free Range, Waitrose*	1 Sausage/57g	144	252	16.2	2.4	19.7	0.3
Pork, Fried	1 Thin Sausage/35g	108	308	13.9	9.9	23.9	0.7
Pork, HE, Tesco*	1 Sausage/46g	117	254	11.7	24.1	12.3	0.5
Pork, Jumbo, Budgens*	1 Sausage/113g	351	309	10.5	9.0	25.7	0.0
Pork, Low Fat, 95% Fat Free, Asda*	1 Sausage/50g	73	145	17.3	10.5	4.3	1.0
Pork, M & S*	1oz/28g	98	350	11.4	8.8	30.3	1.0
Pork, Olde English Style, Safeway*	1 Sausage/53g	155	293	13.9	10.4	21.7	1.5
Pork, Organic, Sainsbury's*	1 Sausage/40g	127	312	18.5	0.9	26.0	1.1
Pork, Organic, Tesco*	1 Sausage/50g	116	231	14.8	6.5	16.2	0.7
Pork, Premium, Waitrose*	1oz/28g	68	242	14.6	1.4	19.8	1.5
Pork, Ready Cooked, Iceland*	1 Sausage/24g	68	284	13.4	12.3	20.1	0.3
Pork, Reduced Fat, Chilled, Frozen, Raw	1 Thin Sausage/35g	63	180	13.0	8.7	10.6	1.2
Pork, Roasted Pepper & Chilli, COU, M & S*	1 Sausage/57g	57	100	15.2	7.1	2.0	2.1
Pork, Sainsbury's*	1 Sausage/49g	141	287	12.6	12.4	20.8	0.3
Pork, Somerfield*	1 Sausage/124g	340	274	15.3	8.3	20.0	1.8
Pork, Thick, HE, Tesco*	1 Sausage/52g	61	117	14.2	8.5	2.9	0.9
Pork, Thick, Lean Recipe, Wall's*	1 Sausage/57g	75	132	15.4	8.5	4.1	2.1
Pork, Wall's*	1 Serving/100g	323	323	11.8	8.7	26.5	0.8
Pork With Bramley Apple, Safeway*	1 Serving/100g	287	287	15.1	6.2	22.5	1.7
Premium Beef, Morrisons*	1 Sausage/67g	164	245	15.5	4.6	18.3	1.0
Premium Pork, Asda*	1 Sausage/75g	179	239	18.0	3.5	17.0	1.0
Premium Pork, Somerfield*	1 Sausage/57g	147	258	12.0	8.0	20.0	0.0
Premium Pork, Thick, Sainsbury's	1 Sausage/49g	147	301	15.1	7.7	23.3	0.2
Premium Turkey, Somerfield*	1 Sausage/57g	76	134	18.0	7.0	4.0	0.0
Quorn, Linda McCartney*	1 Serving/35g	88	252	23.2	8.6	13.8	1.2
Quorn*	1 Sausage/42g	47	111	13.4	5.9	3.8	2.6
Rich Venison & Redcurrant, Grilled, TTD, Sainsbury's*	1 Sausage/46g	138	299	21.2	3.0	22.5	1.8
Roasted Garlic & Oregano, Cauldron Foods*	1 Sausage/50g	90	179	13.1	9.0	10.1	2.1
Scottish Lorne, Somerfield*	1 Slice/53g	168	317	10.0	19.0	22.0	0.0
Skinless Pork, Somerfield*	2 Sausages/57g	170	299	10.0	7.0	26.0	0.0
Sliced, Farmfoods*	1 Sausage/71g	175	247	9.7	12.5	17.6	1.0
Smoked Pork, Original, Mattessons*	1 Serving/113g	362	320	13.0	0.5	30.0	0.9
Smoked Pork, Reduced Fat, Mattessons*	1 Serving/75g	191	255	14.0	7.0	19.0	0.9
Smoked, Sainsbury's*	1 Serving/250g	700	280	13.0	5.0	25.0	0.1
Smokey Barbeque Chunky Pork, Waitrose*	1 Sausage/174g	459	264	14.1	2.0	22.2	1.3
Snack Size, Tesco*	1 Sausage/10g	23	234	14.8	11.9	14.1	2.0
Somerfield*	1 Sausage/57g	174	305	8.0	15.0	24.0	0.0
Spanish, Wafer Thin, Asda*	1 Slice/4g	12	298	25.4	4.1	20.0	0.0
Special Value, Budgens*	1 Sausage/57g	176	309	11.8	5.2	26.8	0.0
Spicy Pork, Polenta & Sun-Dried Tomato, Waitrose*	1 Sausage/67g	165	247	11.8	9.8	17.8	0.9

(Nutrition Values per 100g / 100ml: KCAL, PROT, CARB, FAT, FIBRE)

S

SAUSAGE,	Measure WEIGHT/INFO	per Measure KCAL	KCAL	PROT	CARB	FAT	FIBRE
Spicy Pork With Red Peppers & Onions, Tesco*	1oz/28g	51	182	12.5	9.2	10.6	1.2
Spring Onion, Chive, Summer Collection, TTD, Sainsbury's*	1 Sausage/39g	101	258	21.5	1.8	18.3	1.2
Sticky, M & S*	1oz/28g	62	220	7.1	18.2	12.8	1.5
Strong Garlic, Somerfield*	1oz/28g	65	231	15.0	1.0	19.0	0.0
Thick Low Fat, Iceland*	1 Sausage/50g	95	189	12.3	19.4	6.9	0.0
Thick Pork, Half Fat, Butchers Choice, Tesco*	1 Sausage/57g	112	196	13.5	9.1	11.5	1.6
Thin Economy, Sainsbury's*	1 Sausage/33g	95	288	13.5	18.7	17.7	0.6
Toulouse, M & S*	1 Sausage/57g	123	215	12.4	5.8	15.6	1.3
Tuna & Herb, Sainsbury's*	1 Sausage/47g	109	231	19.6	10.0	12.5	1.5
Tuna, Mediterranean Style, Sainsbury's*	1 Serving/50g	102	204	15.1	14.7	9.5	1.2
Turkey & Pork, Bernard Matthews*	1 Sausage/55g	137	249	10.2	13.1	17.3	0.0
Turkey, Asda*	1 Serving/56g	98	175	14.0	5.0	11.0	0.0
Turkey, Somerfield*	1 Sausage/114g	186	163	15.0	7.0	9.0	0.0
Tuscan, M & S*	1 Sausage/66g	145	220	14.9	4.6	16.0	0.6
Ultimate Pork, TTD, Sainsbury's*	1 Sausage/54g	136	252	17.1	5.2	18.1	1.0
Value, Sainsbury's*	1 Sausage/37g	109	294	11.6	17.3	19.8	0.7
Vegetable, Granose*	1oz/28g	63	226	8.5	17.5	13.5	0.0
Vegetarian, Cumberland, Grilled, Cauldron Foods*	1 Sausage/50g	80	160	12.6	12.3	6.7	2.4
Vegetarian, Cumberland, Waitrose*	1 sausage/50g	80	160	12.6	12.3	6.7	2.4
Vegetarian, Leek & Cheese, Organic, Cauldron Foods*	1 Sausage/41g	80	194	14.5	11.2	5.2	1.7
Vegetarian, Lincolnshire, Cauldron Foods*	1 Sausage/50g	106	212	14.7	14.5	10.6	2.2
Vegetarian, Lincolnshire, Tesco*	1 Sausage/50g	106	212	14.7	14.5	10.6	2.2
Vegetarian, Linda McCartney*	1 Sausage/35g	88	252	23.2	8.6	13.8	1.2
Vegetarian, Meat Free, Asda*	1 Sausage/43g	81	189	20.0	7.0	9.0	2.9
Vegetarian, Sundried Tomato & Herb, Linda McCartney*	1 Sausage/35g	93	266	21.8	10.1	15.4	1.7
SAUSAGE & MASH,							
Asda*	1 Pack/400g	324	81	3.5	11.0	2.6	2.9
Onion, M & S*	1 Pack/300g	315	105	4.1	9.0	5.7	1.5
Quorn, Sainsbury's*	1 Pack/394g	339	86	3.8	11.0	3.0	0.7
Quorn, Tesco*	1 Pack/400g	292	73	4.1	8.8	2.4	1.3
Vegetarian, Tesco*	1 Pack/410g	435	106	4.4	10.0	5.4	2.0
With Onion Gravy, Budgens*	1 Pack/450g	765	170	4.9	12.4	11.2	1.5
With Onion Gravy, HE, Tesco*	1 Pack/450g	369	82	4.6	11.3	2.1	1.0
With Onion Gravy, Tesco*	1 Pack/500g	525	105	3.0	11.1	5.4	1.6
SAUSAGE & ONION Puff Pastry Plait, Sainsbury's*	1/3 Plait/120g	451	376	9.9	18.6	29.1	4.3
SAUSAGE MEAT,							
M & S*	1oz/28g	98	350	9.8	11.3	29.9	1.3
Pork, Somerfield*	1oz/28g	95	338	10.0	9.0	29.0	0.0
SAUSAGE ROLL,							
Asda*	1 Roll/64g	248	388	8.0	26.0	28.0	1.0
Basics, Party Size, Somerfield*	1 Roll/13g	45	343	7.0	29.0	22.0	0.0
BGTY, Sainsburys*	1 roll/65g	200	308	9.6	27.9	17.6	1.4
Cocktail, M & S*	1oz/28g	113	405	9.2	25.2	29.7	1.0
Farmfoods*	1 Lge Roll/34g	101	297	6.7	22.9	19.8	0.4
Ginsters*	1 Roll/140g	753	538	13.0	33.7	39.1	2.2
HE, Tesco*	1 Roll/70g	195	278	9.6	31.2	12.8	1.5
Lincolnshire, COU, M & S*	1 Roll/175g	280	160	10.0	23.2	2.7	2.6
Lincolnshire, Somerfield*	1 Roll/96g	373	389	8.0	30.0	26.0	0.0
M & S*	1 Roll/32g	130	405	9.2	21.4	31.2	0.9
Mini, M & S*	1oz/28g	122	435	9.8	29.6	30.9	1.8
Mini, Tesco*	1 Roll/15g	53	356	9.0	23.9	24.9	1.5
Party, Sainsbury's*	1 Roll/12g	54	422	8.7	26.7	31.1	1.2
Party Size, Tesco*	1 Roll/12g	39	327	6.2	26.2	21.9	1.3
Pork Farms*	1 Roll/54g	213	395	9.6	21.6	30.0	0.0

Nutrition Values per 100g / 100ml

S

SAUSAGE ROLL,	Measure WEIGHT/INFO	per Measure KCAL	KCAL	PROT	CARB	FAT	FIBRE
Pork, Large, M & S*	1 Roll/63g	236	375	9.0	22.5	27.9	0.7
Puff Pastry	1oz/28g	107	383	9.9	25.4	27.6	1.0
Puff Pastry, Sainsbury's*	1 Roll/65g	250	384	8.3	25.0	27.9	0.9
Somerfield*	1 Sausage Roll/35g	149	426	9.0	32.0	29.0	0.0
Vegetarian, Linda McCartney*	1 Roll/51g	133	260	10.9	23.1	14.5	1.6
Waitrose*	1 Roll/75g	287	383	10.1	27.0	26.1	1.3
SAUSAGE SCRAMBLES, Chicago Town*	1 Serving/170g	423	249	8.6	31.6	9.8	2.2
SAUSAGES & BEANS, Spar*	1 Can/220g	231	105	4.7	13.8	3.4	5.4
SAUSAGES, ONION, Gravy & Potato Crush, BGTY, Sainsbury's*	1 Pack/450g	401	89	5.7	10.4	2.7	1.4
SAVELOY, Unbattered, Takeaway	1 Saveloy/65g	192	296	13.8	10.8	22.3	0.8
SAVOURY EGG,							
Mini, Asda*	1 Egg/19g	58	303	10.3	17.7	21.2	1.5
Mini, New Improved Recipe, Tesco*	1 Egg/20g	65	323	12.5	18.3	22.2	1.3
Mini,, Tesco*	1 Egg/20g	68	342	11.2	23.0	22.8	0.9
Scallops,							
& Bacon Brochettes, Finest, Tesco*	1 Pack/300g	402	134	14.4	3.2	7.1	0.7
SCAMPI,							
& Chips, Tesco*	1 Serving/450g	689	153	5.1	22.4	4.8	1.6
& Chips, Youngs*	1oz/28g	42	150	5.0	20.3	5.4	1.7
Breaded, Asda*	1 Serving/70g	181	258	14.0	19.0	14.0	1.3
Breaded, Farmfoods*	1oz/28g	35	124	8.5	22.1	0.2	1.2
Breaded, Scottish, Sainsbury's*	1oz/28g	61	219	11.0	17.4	11.7	1.4
Golden In Ovencrisp Breadcrumbs, Tesco*	1oz/28g	49	175	10.0	16.0	7.9	1.0
In Breadcrumbs, Frozen, Fried In Blended Oil	1oz/28g	66	237	9.4	20.5	13.6	0.0
In Breadcrumbs, Whole, M & S*	1oz/28g	56	199	11.4	15.5	10.2	0.7
Whole, M & S*	1oz/28g	64	229	11.1	18.5	12.2	0.8
Whole, Scottish Island, Youngs*	1oz/28g	50	179	9.7	15.8	8.5	0.7
SCONE,							
3% Fat, M & S*	1 Scone/65g	179	275	7.2	55.1	2.5	2.3
All Butter, Tesco*	1 Scone/41g	126	308	7.2	52.3	7.8	1.6
Cheese	1 Scone/40g	145	363	10.1	43.2	17.8	1.6
Cherry, M & S*	1 Scone/60g	202	337	6.9	49.7	12.2	1.9
Cream, Sainsbury's*	1 Scone/50g	173	345	4.6	42.5	17.4	3.1
Derby, Asda*	1 Scone/59g	202	342	7.0	56.0	10.0	0.0
Derby, Somerfield*	1 Scone/60g	208	347	5.3	49.9	14.0	1.9
Devon, Sainsbury's*	1 Scone/54g	201	372	7.1	51.1	15.5	1.6
Fruit	1 Scone/40g	126	316	7.3	52.9	9.8	0.0
Fruit, Economy, Sainsbury's*	1 Scone/34g	111	326	7.9	52.5	9.4	1.7
Fruit, SmartPrice, Asda*	1 Scone/41g	139	338	7.0	55.0	10.0	3.0
Fruit, Somerfield*	1 Scone/35g	134	382	8.0	53.0	10.0	0.0
Plain	1 Scone/40g	145	362	7.2	53.8	14.6	1.9
Potato	1 Scone/40g	118	296	5.1	39.1	14.3	1.6
Strawberry, M & S*	1 Scone/63g	247	392	4.5	45.9	22.5	1.2
Sultana, BGTY, Sainsbury's*	1 Scone/63g	178	283	7.7	56.7	2.8	2.4
Sultana, Finest, Tesco*	1 Scone/70g	225	321	8.9	46.7	10.9	2.1
Sultana, Less Than 5% Fat, Asda*	1 Scone/60g	198	330	7.0	62.0	6.0	1.8
Sultana, Reduced Fat, Waitrose*	1 Scone/65g	187	287	6.6	53.2	5.3	2.6
Sultana, Somerfield*	1 Scone/34g	108	318	5.7	55.4	8.2	0.0
Sultana, Tesco*	1 Scone/70g	215	307	6.8	53.8	7.2	2.0
Wholemeal	1 Scone/40g	130	326	8.7	43.1	14.4	5.2
Wholemeal, Fruit	1 Scone/40g	130	324	8.1	47.2	12.8	4.9
SCOTCH EGGS,							
Asda*	1 Egg/114g	286	251	11.2	13.7	16.8	1.4
Ginsters*	1 Egg/95g	228	240	15.3	9.7	15.9	0.6

Nutrition Values per 100g / 100ml (KCAL, PROT, CARB, FAT, FIBRE)

S

	Measure WEIGHT/INFO	per Measure KCAL	KCAL	PROT	CARB	FAT	FIBRE
			Nutrition Values per 100g / 100ml				
SCOTCH EGG,							
M & S*	1 Egg/125g	344	275	11.7	15.0	18.7	0.5
Retail	1 Egg/120g	301	251	12.0	13.1	17.1	0.0
Sainsbury's*	1 Egg/116g	287	247	11.4	13.2	16.5	0.6
Tesco*	1 Egg/114g	309	271	11.5	17.0	17.4	0.9
SEAFOOD,							
Cocktail, Asda*	1oz/28g	26	92	14.0	5.7	1.5	0.1
Cocktail, Premium Quality, Lyons*	1 Serving/100g	76	76	13.2	3.7	0.9	1.1
Cocktail, Somerfield*	1oz/28g	23	81	14.0	2.0	2.0	0.0
Frozen, Tesco*	1 Pack/400g	280	70	12.2	2.4	1.3	0.0
Medley, Steam Cuisine, M & S*	1 Pack/400g	320	80	8.5	4.5	3.1	1.3
Selection, HE, Tesco*	1 Pack/250g	175	70	12.2	2.4	1.3	0.0
Sticks, Healthy Choice, Asda*	1 Stick/12g	14	113	7.0	21.0	0.1	0.1
Sticks, Morrisons*	1 Stick/15g	16	108	7.0	19.8	0.1	0.0
Sticks, Sainsbury's*	1 Stick/16g	17	107	7.0	21.0	0.1	0.1
Sticks, Tesco*	1 Stick/16g	15	96	5.7	15.9	1.1	0.0
Sticks, With Cocktail Dip, Asda*	1 Pot/95g	126	133	6.0	16.0	5.0	0.1
SEASONING,							
Aromat, Knorr*	1oz/28g	46	164	12.4	20.5	3.6	1.0
SEASONING CUBES,							
For Rice, Pilau, Knorr*	1 Cube/10g	31	305	11.4	13.9	22.6	1.4
For Rice, Saffron, Knorr*	1 Cube/10g	29	291	13.8	17.5	18.4	2.2
For Stir Fry, Oriental Spices, Knorr*	1 Cube/10g	41	414	9.7	25.0	30.6	1.1
Oriental Spice, Knorr*	1 Cube/10g	41	409	9.5	23.7	30.7	0.0
Perfect Pasta, Knorr*	1 Cube/10g	28	278	10.3	5.2	24.0	0.0
Wild Mushroom, Knorr*	1 cube/10g	37	365	10.3	21.3	26.5	0.2
SEASONING MIX,							
Beef Taco, Colman's*	1 Pack/30g	76	252	9.1	26.9	12.0	14.0
Fajita, Chicken, Colmans*	per 40g packet/40g	149	373	10.8	13.3	30.7	13.8
Fajita, Old El Paso*	1oz/28g	88	313	11.0	56.0	5.0	0.0
Mediterranean Roast Vegetable, Schwartz*	1oz/28g	92	330	7.0	65.6	4.4	0.0
Shepherd's Pie, Colman's*	1 Pack/50g	129	257	14.0	47.0	0.9	0.0
Shepherd's Pie, Schwartz*	1 Pack/38g	110	289	9.3	58.5	2.0	0.0
Taco, Old El Paso*	¼ Pack/9g	30	334	5.5	69.0	4.0	0.0
Wholegrain Mustard & Herb Potato Mash, Colman's*	1 Pack/30g	153	510	9.7	19.1	44.1	0.0
SEAWEED,							
Crispy, Blue Dragon*	1 packet/55g	345	628	6.2	19.2	58.0	8.9
Crispy, Budgens*	1 Serving/50g	304	608	7.0	14.2	58.1	6.4
Crispy, M & S*	1oz/28g	168	600	6.5	16.8	56.1	6.3
Irish Moss, Raw	1oz/28g	2	8	1.5	0.0	0.2	12.3
Kombu, Dried, Raw	1oz/28g	12	43	7.1	0.0	1.6	58.7
Nori, Dried, Raw	1oz/28g	38	136	30.7	0.0	1.5	44.4
Wakame, Dried, Raw	1oz/28g	20	71	12.4	0.0	2.4	47.1
SEMOLINA,							
Co-Op*	1oz/28g	97	345	11.7	70.5	1.8	2.1
Flemings*	1oz/28g	98	350	10.7	77.5	1.8	2.1
Instant, Bird's*	1/3 Pack/33g	145	440	5.1	76.5	13.0	1.1
Raw	1oz/28g	98	350	10.7	77.5	1.8	2.1
SEMOLINA PUDDING,							
Creamed, Ambrosia*	1 Can/425g	344	81	3.3	13.1	1.7	0.2
Creamed, Co-Op*	1 Can/425g	383	90	4.0	15.0	2.0	0.0
SESAME SEEDS,							
Sesame Seeds	1oz/28g	167	598	18.2	0.9	58.0	7.9
Organic, Evernat*	1oz/28g	174	623	26.4	6.4	54.8	7.6
SESAME SNAPS, Anglo Dal Ltd*	1 Pack/30g	141	471	9.7	65.0	20.9	0.0

S

SHALLOTS,	Measure WEIGHT/INFO	per Measure KCAL	Nutrition Values per 100g / 100ml KCAL	PROT	CARB	FAT	FIBRE
Shallots, Raw	1oz/28g	6	20	1.5	3.3	0.2	1.4
SHANDY,							
Bitter, Original, Ben Shaws*	1 Can/330ml	89	27	0.0	6.0	0.0	0.0
Homemade	1 Pint/568ml	148	26	0.2	2.9	0.0	0.0
Lemonade, Traditional Style, Tesco*	1 Can/330ml	63	19	0.0	4.7	0.0	0.0
SHARK, Raw	1oz/28g	29	102	23.0	0.0	1.1	0.0
SHARON FRUIT	1oz/28g	20	73	0.8	18.6	0.0	1.6
SHERBERT Cocktails Sweets, Sainsbury's*	1 Sweet/9g	36	400	0.0	83.1	7.5	0.0
SHERBERT Lemons, M & S*	1oz/28g	107	382	0.0	93.9	0.0	0.0
SHERRY,							
Dry	1 Serving/50ml	58	116	0.2	1.4	0.0	0.0
Medium	1 Serving/50ml	58	116	0.1	5.9	0.0	0.0
Sweet	1 Serving 50ml	68	136	0.3	6.9	0.0	0.0
SHORTBREAD,							
Shortbread	1oz/28g	139	498	5.9	63.9	26.1	1.9
All Butter, Assorted, Parkwood, Aldi*	1oz/28g	143	511	6.5	61.0	26.8	2.0
All Butter, Fingers, Tesco*	1 Finger/13g	67	519	5.8	60.3	28.3	1.8
All Butter, McVitie's*	Twin Finger/40g	216	541	6.3	62.6	29.5	1.9
All Butter, Royal Edinburgh, Asda*	1 Finger/18g	93	519	5.8	60.3	28.3	1.8
Chocolate & Caramel, TTD, Sainsbury's*	1 Serving/55g	245	446	4.7	45.0	27.7	1.3
Chocolate Chip, Jacob's*	1 Biscuit/17g	87	513	5.2	61.2	27.5	1.8
Chocolate, Waitrose*	1oz/28g	144	516	5.5	61.2	27.7	1.8
Crawfords*	1 Biscuit/12.5g	64	533	6.6	65.0	27.4	2.0
Farmhouse, TTD, Sainsbury's*	1 Finger/20g	106	528	5.1	61.6	29.0	1.7
Fingers, Asda*	1 Finger/18g	93	519	5.8	60.3	28.3	18.0
Fingers, M & S*	1oz/28g	143	510	5.9	60.8	27.0	1.6
Fingers, Safeway*	1 Finger/21g	109	520	5.8	58.5	29.2	18.9
Fingers, Scottish, M & S*	1oz/28g	143	510	5.9	60.8	27.0	1.6
Highland Demerara Rounds, Sainsbury's*	1 Biscuit/20g	113	565	5.5	70.5	29.0	2.0
Petticoat Tails, Sainsbury's*	1 Segment/13g	68	520	5.4	60.5	28.5	1.8
Pure Butter, Jacob's*	1 Biscuit/20g	105	525	5.7	58.6	29.7	1.8
Rounds, TTD, Sainsbury's*	1 Biscuit/20g	108	538	5.0	59.5	31.1	1.6
Scottish, M & S*	1oz/28g	143	512	4.4	59.7	27.9	2.6
Shrewsbury, M & S*	1oz/28g	128	458	7.5	63.9	23.3	4.5
SHRIMPS,							
Boiled	1oz/28g	33	117	23.8	0.0	2.4	0.0
Canned In Brine, Drained	1oz/28g	26	94	20.8	0.0	1.2	0.0
Dried	1oz/28g	69	245	55.8	0.0	2.4	0.0
Frozen	1oz/28g	20	73	16.5	0.0	0.8	0.0
SKATE,							
Grilled	1oz/28g	22	79	18.9	0.0	0.5	0.0
In Batter, Fried In Blended Oil	1oz/28g	47	168	14.7	4.9	10.1	0.2
Raw	1oz/28g	18	64	15.1	0.0	0.4	0.0
SKIPS,							
Easy Cheesy, KP*	1 Bag/19g	100	525	3.9	59.5	30.1	0.9
Prawn Cocktail, KP*	1 Bag/17g	88	516	3.4	59.9	29.2	1.4
Tangy Tomato, KP*	1 Bag/17g	88	517	3.2	59.6	29.5	1.2
SKITTLES, Mars*	1 Pack/55g	220	400	0.0	90.5	4.2	0.0
SLICES, (PASTY TYPE)							
Beef, Minced Steak & Onion, Tesco*	1 Slice/150g	425	283	8.7	21.3	18.1	1.6
Beef, Minced With Onion, Sainsbury's*	1 Slice/120g	328	273	6.8	24.5	16.4	1.1
Beef, Pepper Steak, Ginsters*	1 Slice/155g	415	268	9.9	21.5	15.8	1.9
Cheese & Garlic, Safeway*	1 Slice/31g	123	398	11.4	44.1	19.5	2.2
Cheese & Ham, Sainsbury's*	1 Slice/112g	313	280	6.6	25.3	16.9	1.5

S

	Measure WEIGHT/INFO	per Measure KCAL	Nutrition Values per 100g / 100ml KCAL	PROT	CARB	FAT	FIBRE
SLICES,							
Cheese & Ham, Savoury, Somerfield*	1 Slice/150g	399	266	7.0	23.0	16.0	0.0
Cheese & Onion, Tesco*	1 Slice/150g	503	335	8.0	20.1	24.7	1.4
Chicken & Mushroom, Asda*	1 Slice/165g	474	287	8.0	21.0	19.0	1.2
Chicken & Mushroom, Ginsters*	1 Slice/155g	420	271	6.6	21.8	17.5	1.7
Chicken & Mushroom, Sainsbury's*	1 Slice/165g	464	281	7.3	20.9	18.7	1.4
Ham & Cheese, Ginsters*	1 Slice/155g	625	403	9.8	31.9	28.2	4.2
Spinach & Ricotta, Safeway*	1 Slice/165g	513	311	6.7	29.1	18.6	1.3
Turkey, Ham & Mushroom, Pork Farms*	1 Slice/165g	431	261	7.2	19.7	17.0	0.0
SLIMFAST,							
Apple Cobbler, Meal On The Go Bar, SlimFast*	1 Bar/56g	220	392	14.2	58.9	8.9	3.5
Banana Deluxe Meal Replacement Drink, SlimFast*	1 Serving/325ml	215	66	4.2	11.3	0.8	1.4
Breakfast & Lunch Bar, Dutch Chocolate, SlimFast*	1 Bar/34g	140	411	14.7	58.8	14.7	5.8
Breakfast & Lunch Bar, Peanut Butter, SlimFast*	1 Bar/34g	150	441	17.6	55.8	17.6	5.8
Chocolate Chip Snack Bar, SlimFast*	1 Bar/26g	99	382	4.9	70.4	11.4	1.8
Chocolate Meal Replacement Bar, SlimFast*	1 Bar/78g	245	314	19.9	46.2	9.4	5.5
Chocolate Muesli Snack Bar, SlimFast*	1 Bar/26g	99	379	4.7	64.5	13.3	6.5
Chocolate Royale, Ready To Drink, Ultra SlimFast*	1 Serving/11floz	220	71	3.2	12.8	0.9	1.6
French Vanilla, Ready To Drink, SlimFast*	1 Can/325ml	215	66	4.2	10.6	0.8	1.5
Soup, Mediterranean Tomato, Dry, SlimFast*	1 Sachet/62g	213	343	22.6	39.8	9.0	10.7
Strawberry Supreme, Ready To Drink, SlimFast*	1 Can/325ml	215	66	4.2	10.6	0.8	1.5
Toffee Delight Meal Replacement Bar, SlimFast*	1 Bar/78g	248	318	20.6	45.3	9.6	5.9
Tropical Treat Shake, SlimFast*	1 Serving/327ml	216	66	4.2	10.6	0.8	1.5
Vanilla Shake, Dry, SlimFast*	1 Serving/35g	123	351	12.7	57.0	7.5	17.1
SMARTIES,							
Mini Cones, Nestle*	1 Serving/44g	145	330	4.5	45.0	13.1	0.0
Nestle*	1oz/28g	129	459	5.4	71.1	17.0	0.0
SMILES, McCain*	1 Piece/14g	27	192	3.2	29.2	6.9	0.0
SMOOTHIE,							
Apple, Raspberries & Banana, P & J*	1 Bottle/330ml	188	57	0.7	12.2	0.3	0.0
Apricot & Peach, COU, M & S*	1 Serving/250ml	100	40	0.9	8.3	0.4	0.4
Banana, M & S*	1 Bottle/500ml	270	54	1.7	12.2	0.1	0.8
Banana, Measure Up, Dry, Asda*	1 Serving/61g	203	333	17.0	55.0	5.0	14.0
Blackberry & Blueberry, Innocent*	1 Bottle/250ml	120	48	0.6	11.5	0.1	0.0
Boysenberry & Raspberry, WTF, Sainsbury's*	1 Bottle/250ml	108	43	0.7	10.0	0.1	1.6
Boysenberry, Blackberry & Blueberry, M & S*	1 Bottle/500ml	200	40	0.5	9.0	0.2	0.9
Cranberries & Rasperries, Pure Fruit, Innocent*	1 Serving/250ml	103	41	0.5	9.5	0.2	0.0
Cranberries & Strawberries, Innocent*	1 Serving/250ml	103	41	0.5	9.5	0.2	0.0
Mango & Passion Fruit, Innocent*	1 Bottle/250ml	138	55	0.4	12.8	0.2	0.0
Mango, Pineapple & Passionfruit, M & S*	1 Bottle/500ml	290	58	0.7	12.1	0.5	0.9
Mixed Berry Tropicana, Muller*	1 Serving/250ml	190	76	1.2	16.0	0.0	0.8
Orange & Mango, Safeway*	1 Bottle/250ml	130	52	0.5	12.1	0.2	0.7
Orange, Strawberry & Guava, Sainsbury's*	1 Serving/300ml	159	53	0.3	12.0	0.2	0.8
Oranges Mangos & Bananas, P & J*	1 Bottle/330ml	195	59	0.9	13.6	0.2	0.7
Peach & Banana, Waitrose*	1 Smoothie/330ml	201	61	0.5	14.4	0.0	0.3
Peaches & Bananas, P & J*	1 Bottle/330ml	188	57	0.7	13.6	0.3	0.0
Pineapple, Banana & Coconut, P & J*	1 Bottle/330ml	234	71	0.8	12.3	1.4	0.0
Pineapple, Banana & Mango Fruit, Finest, Tesco*	1 Glass/200ml	94	47	0.1	11.2	0.2	0.0
Raspberry & Blackcurrant, COU, M & S*	1 Bottle/250ml	93	37	0.9	8.1	0.0	0.4
Raspberry & Cranberry, Shape*	1 Serving/250ml	190	76	2.8	14.9	0.6	0.9
Raspberry, M & S*	1 Bottle/500ml	300	60	1.5	13.4	0.1	0.7
Raspberry, M & S*	1 Serving/250ml	138	55	1.7	12.2	0.6	1.9
Strawberries & Bananas, P & J*	1 Bottle/330ml	172	52	0.9	11.5	0.3	0.0
Strawberry & Banana Fruit, Finest, Tesco*	1 Bottle/250ml	135	54	0.3	12.5	0.3	0.5
Strawberry & White Chocolate, M & S*	1 Serving/250ml	100	40	2.5	5.5	1.0	0.1

S

	Measure WEIGHT/INFO	per Measure KCAL	Nutrition Values per 100g / 100ml KCAL	PROT	CARB	FAT	FIBRE
SNACK BREAKPACK,							
Cadbury's*	1 Biscuit/10g	53	525	7.0	64.2	26.8	0.0
SNACK EGGS, Sainsbury's*	1 Egg/53g	154	290	10.5	15.3	20.7	1.0
SNACK SALAD,							
Chicken Noodle, Sainsburys*	1 Snack/240g	278	116	5.2	12.4	5.1	1.4
Hoi Sin Chicken & Noodle, TTD, Sainsburys*	1 Serving/230g	214	93	4.7	15.2	1.5	1.8
Pasta & Tuna, Healthy Living, Co-Op.*	1 Tub/225g	146	65	5.0	10.0	0.4	1.0
Pasta & Tuna, Healthy Selection, Somerfield*	1 pot/190g	194	102	6.5	13.0	2.7	1.1
Pasta and Tuna, BGTY, Sainsburys*	1 Serving/260g	218	84	6.0	11.5	1.6	2.3
Pasta, Cheese, Somerfield*	1 Salad/200g	422	211	8.0	14.0	14.0	0.0
Pasta, Egg Mayo, Asda*	1 Serving/180g	364	202	4.0	12.8	15.0	0.3
Pasta, Tuna, Asda*	1 Serving/180g	196	109	5.5	13.2	3.8	0.9
Pasta, Tuna, Sainsbury's*	1 Pot/260g	218	84	6.0	11.5	1.6	2.3
SNACK SHORTCAKE, Cadbury's*	1 Biscuit/8g	42	525	7.0	64.2	26.6	0.0
SNACK STOP,							
Creamy Chicken Pasta, Crosse & Blackwell*	1 Pot/247g	210	85	2.7	15.7	1.6	0.0
Macaroni Cheese, Light, Crosse & Blackwell*	1 Pack/248g	260	105	3.2	16.4	3.0	0.9
Melting Cheese & Pepperoni, Crosse & Blackwell*	1 Serving/237g	237	100	2.9	13.3	4.1	0.0
Mushroom Pasta Twirls, Crosse & Blackwell*	1 Pot/248g	248	100	3.1	15.9	2.7	0.9
Roast Onion & Potato, Crosse and Blackwell*	1 Pot/210g	210	100	1.7	14.4	3.7	0.0
Roast Parsnip & Potato, Crosse & Blackwell*	1 Pot/210g	200	95	1.7	13.6	3.6	0.0
Spicy Tomato Pasta, Crosse & Blackwell*	1 Pot/412g	358	87	2.4	15.9	1.5	0.0
Sun Ripened Tomato & Herb, Crosse & Blackwell*	1 pot/ 237g	201	85	2.6	16.1	1.1	0.0
SNACK-A-JACKS,							
Apple Danish Flavour, Quaker*	1 Ricecake/13g	51	390	5.0	87.0	2.5	1.0
Barbecue Flavour, Jumbo, Quaker*	1 Serving/10g	38	376	7.0	80.0	2.5	1.0
Barbecue Flavour, Quaker*	1 Pack/30g	126	421	6.5	77.0	10.0	1.0
Barbecue, Invidual Bag, Quaker*	1 Bag/30g	122	407	7.0	79.0	6.5	1.0
Caramel Flavour, Jumbo, Quaker*	1 Cake/13g	52	397	5.0	87.0	2.5	1.0
Caramel, Quaker*	1 Bag/35g	140	401	5.5	86.0	3.5	0.5
Cheddar Cheese Flavour, Jumbo, Quaker*	1 Cake/10g	40	399	8.5	81.0	4.0	1.0
Cheddar Cheese Flavour, Quaker*	1 Bag/30g	128	427	8.0	73.0	10.0	1.0
Chocolate Flavour, Quaker*	1 Cake/14g	57	406	5.5	85.0	4.5	1.0
Chocolate, Jumbo, Quaker*	1 Cake/12g	49	406	5.5	85.0	4.5	1.0
Chocolate, Quaker*	1 Bag/35g	144	410	5.0	85.0	4.5	1.0
Snack-a-Jacks Crispy Cheese, Quaker*	1 Pack/30g	122	407	8.0	78.0	6.5	1.0
Crispy Chocolate Flavour, Quaker*	1 Pack/30g	122	407	5.5	85.0	4.5	1.0
Salt & Vinegar, Quaker*	1 Bag/30g	123	410	6.5	77.5	8.0	1.0
Savoury Salted, Quaker*	1 Bag/30g	124	414	7.5	77.0	8.0	1.0
Sour Cream & Chive, Quaker*	1 Serving/30g	123	410	7.5	77.0	8.0	1.0
SNAPPER,							
Red, Fried In Blended Oil	1oz/28g	35	126	24.5	0.0	3.1	0.0
Red, Raw	1oz/28g	25	90	19.6	0.0	1.3	0.0
SNAPS,							
Savoury Cheese Flavour, Walkers*	1 Bag/18g	86	508	1.5	65.5	26.8	0.0
Spicy Tomato, Walkers*	1 Bag/18g	91	508	1.5	65.5	26.8	0.0
SNICKERS,							
Cruncher, Mars*	1 Bar/40g	209	523	9.0	57.0	30.0	2.3
Mars*	1 Standard/61g	311	510	10.2	55.3	27.6	0.0
SNOWFLAKE, Cadbury's*	1 Bar/36g	198	550	7.2	60.1	30.9	0.0
SOFTMINTS, Trebor*	1 Tube/40g	156	391	0.0	93.3	2.0	0.0
SORBET,							
Blackcurrant, Del Monte*	1oz/28g	30	106	0.4	27.1	0.1	0.0
Blackcurrant, Iceland*	¼ Pot/100g	100	100	0.0	25.0	0.0	0.0
Lemon	1 Scoop/60g	79	131	0.9	34.2	0.0	0.0

SORBET,	Measure WEIGHT/INFO	per Measure KCAL	Nutrition Values per 100g / 100ml KCAL	PROT	CARB	FAT	FIBRE
Lemon, Del Monte*	1 Sorbet/500g	570	114	0.1	29.2	0.1	0.0
Lemon Harmony, Haagen-Dazs*	1 Serving/90ml	214	238	1.5	32.5	11.3	0.0
Lemon, Organic, Evernat*	1oz/28g	27	96	0.1	22.8	0.5	0.0
Lemon, Sticks, Haagen-Dazs*	1oz/28g	67	238	1.5	32.5	11.3	0.0
Lemon, Tesco*	1 Serving/75g	80	106	0.0	26.2	0.0	0.4
Mango, Del Monte*	1 Sorbet/500g	575	115	0.2	29.6	0.1	0.0
Mango, Tropicale, Haagen-Dazs*	1oz/28g	32	116	0.2	28.6	0.1	0.0
Mango, Waitrose*	1 Pot/100g	90	90	0.1	22.1	0.0	0.6
Orange, Del Monte*	1 Sorbet/500g	625	125	0.2	32.1	0.1	0.0
Passion Fruit, Fat Free, M & S*	1 Sorbet/125g	129	103	0.4	25.0	0.0	0.4
Peach & Strawberry, Haagen-Dazs*	1oz/28g	30	108	0.0	27.0	0.0	0.0
Pear, Organic, Evernat*	1oz/28g	33	119	0.0	28.3	0.6	0.0
Pineapple, Del Monte*	1 Sorbet/500g	600	120	0.3	30.6	0.1	0.0
Raspberry & Blackberry, Fat Free, M & S*	1 Sorbet/125g	140	112	0.4	27.5	0.0	0.6
Raspberry, Haagen-Dazs*	1oz/28g	33	119	0.3	29.2	0.2	0.0
Raspberry, Sticks, Haagen-Dazs*	1oz/28g	28	99	0.2	24.2	0.1	0.0
Raspberry, Tesco*	1 Serving/70ml	97	138	0.5	34.0	0.0	0.0
Strawberry, Fruit Ice, Starburst, Mars*	1 Stick/93ml	99	106	0.1	26.7	0.1	0.0
Strawberry, M & S*	1oz/28g	27	95	0.3	23.4	0.1	0.5
Summer Berry, Swirl, Asda*	¼ Pack/89g	97	109	3.0	26.0	0.4	0.0
Tropical, Really Fruity, Asda*	1 Scoop/75g	90	120	0.1	30.0	0.0	0.3
SORBET CONE,							
Raspberry,Yoghurt & Sorbet, BGTY, Sainsbury's*	1 Cone/69g	151	219	2.6	37.5	6.5	1.3
SOSMIX,							
Direct Foods*	1oz/28g	124	443	18.5	27.0	29.0	0.0
Organic*	1oz/28g	122	435	20.0	37.0	23.0	0.0
SOUFFLE,							
Cheese	1oz/28g	71	253	11.4	9.3	19.2	0.3
Plain	1oz/28g	56	201	7.6	10.4	14.7	0.3
Raspberry & Amaretto, M & S*	1oz/28g	83	298	2.8	33.1	16.7	0.1
SOUP,							
American Potato & Leek Chowder, Knorr*	1 Pack/68g	244	359	8.1	58.3	10.4	5.7
Asparagus & Chicken, New Covent Garden Soup Co*	1 Pack/284g	74	26	1.9	3.7	0.4	0.6
Asparagus & Chicken, Tarragon, Special Recipe, Sainsbury's*	½ Can/206g	97	47	2.1	6.6	1.3	0.4
Asparagus, Batchelors*	1 Serving/223g	143	64	0.5	9.2	2.8	0.4
Asparagus, HE, Dry, Tesco*	1 Serving/19g	67	351	3.6	60.3	10.6	3.2
Asparagus, Less Than 60 Cals, Waitrose*	1 Serving/204ml	51	25	0.4	4.3	0.7	0.7
Asparagus, New Covent Garden Soup Co*	1 Carton/568ml	153	27	1.3	3.0	1.1	0.6
Aubergine & Red Pepper, New Covent Garden Soup Co*	½ Pint/296ml	71	24	0.9	4.8	0.1	0.4
Autumn Vegetable, Baxters*	1 Can/425g	170	40	1.8	8.0	0.2	1.5
Beef & Tomato Cup A Soup, Batchelors*	1 Serving/215g	71	33	0.6	7.3	0.2	0.5
Beef & Vegetable Big, Heinz*	½ Can/200g	90	45	2.4	7.3	0.7	0.9
Beef & Vegetable Mighty, Asda*	½ Can/81g	32	40	2.3	6.0	0.8	0.6
Beef & Vegetable, Tesco*	1 Serving/410g	312	76	2.0	5.3	4.8	0.6
Beef Broth Big, Heinz*	½ Can/200g	82	41	2.0	6.8	0.6	0.7
Beef Chilli Baked Potato Big, Heinz*	1 Can/400g	232	58	3.4	9.1	0.9	1.3
Beef Consomme, Sainsbury's*	1 Can/415g	46	11	2.0	0.7	0.0	0.0
Beef, Heinz*	½ Can/200g	82	41	2.0	4.9	1.5	0.2
Blended Autumn Vegetable, Heinz*	½ Can/200g	114	57	1.2	6.4	3.0	0.7
Blended Carrot & Coriander, Heinz*	½ Can/200g	104	52	0.7	6.2	2.7	0.6
Blended Leek & Bacon, Heinz*	½ Can/200g	108	54	1.9	5.0	2.9	0.5
Blended Red Pepper With Tomato, Heinz*	½ Can/200g	102	51	0.8	5.2	2.9	0.7
Blended Sweetcorn & Yellow Pepper, Heinz*	½ Can/200g	98	49	0.9	6.6	2.1	0.6
Broccoli & Cauliflower Cup, Better For You, Morrisons*	1 Sachet/15g	56	376	4.9	57.2	14.2	4.9

S

SOUP,	Measure WEIGHT/INFO	per Measure KCAL	KCAL	PROT	CARB	FAT	FIBRE
			Nutrition Values per 100g / 100ml				
Broccoli & Cauliflower, Slim A Soup, Made Up, Batchelors*	1 Serving/203g	59	29	0.5	4.9	0.8	0.4
Broccoli & Potato, Organic, Baxters*	1 Can/425g	132	31	1.3	5.8	0.3	0.7
Broccoli & Stilton, Asda*	1 Pack/302g	172	57	2.2	6.0	2.7	0.0
Broccoli & Stilton, Canned, Sainsbury's*	½ Can/207g	126	61	1.7	4.8	3.9	0.4
Broccoli & Stilton, Canned, Tesco*	1 Can/400g	224	56	1.8	4.2	3.5	0.3
Broccoli & Stilton, Fresh, Sainsbury's*	½ Bottle/300ml	156	52	2.1	3.9	3.1	0.9
Broccoli & Stilton, Fresh, Tesco*	½ Pot/300g	219	73	3.3	5.0	4.4	0.7
Broccoli & Stilton, Homestyle, Somerfield*	1 Pack/500g	350	70	2.0	5.0	4.0	0.0
Broccoli & Stilton, Special Recipe, Sainsbury's*	½ Can/208g	127	61	1.7	4.8	3.9	0.4
Broccoli & Stilton, Tesco*	1 Pack/600g	564	94	2.9	2.5	8.1	0.7
Broccoli, Baxters*	1 Can/425g	191	45	1.3	5.9	1.8	0.4
Broccoli, Leek, Horseradish, New Covent Garden Soup Co*	1 Serving/284g	97	34	1.6	3.9	1.3	0.2
Broccoli With Mustard, New Covent Garden Soup Co*	1 Carton/568g	204	36	1.3	3.3	1.9	1.2
Broccoli With Stilton, New Covent Garden Soup Co*	1floz/30ml	14	47	2.0	2.5	3.2	1.0
Brocoli & Stilton, Fresh, Safeway*	1 Serving/500g	290	58	3.5	4.8	2.8	0.7
Butternut Squash & Red Pepper, Baxters*	1 Can/425g	153	36	0.7	6.1	1.0	0.6
Cajun Spicy Vegetable, Slim A Soup, Batchelors*	1 Sachet/211g	57	27	0.8	5.0	0.5	0.6
Cantonese Hot & Sour Noodle, Baxters*	1 Serving/215g	133	62	1.4	11.1	1.3	0.5
Carrot & Butterbean, Baxters*	1 Can/425g	234	55	1.6	7.9	1.9	1.7
Carrot & Coriander, Asda*	1 Pack/297g	92	31	1.0	6.0	0.3	0.0
Carrot & Coriander, Baxters*	1 Can/425g	162	38	0.8	5.5	1.4	0.8
Carrot & Coriander, Carton, Campbell's*	1 Serving/250ml	110	44	0.7	5.4	2.2	0.0
Carrot & Coriander, Classic Homestyle, M & S*	1 Can/425g	170	40	0.6	5.6	2.0	0.7
Carrot & Coriander, Fresh, Sainsbury's*	½ Bottle/300ml	150	50	1.4	4.1	3.1	0.6
Carrot & Coriander, Fresh, Tesco*	1 Pack/600g	270	45	0.6	5.9	2.1	0.9
Carrot & Coriander, Fresh, Waitrose*	½ Pot/300g	117	39	0.5	5.4	1.7	0.9
Carrot & Coriander, GFY, Asda*	½ Pot/251g	88	35	1.2	4.0	1.6	0.4
Carrot & Coriander, Heinz*	1 Can/400g	208	52	0.7	6.2	2.7	0.6
Carrot & Coriander, Less Than 5% Fat, Asda	1 Serving/300g	96	32	1.0	6.0	0.3	0.8
Carrot & Coriander, M & S*	1oz/28g	7	25	0.4	4.3	0.7	0.5
Carrot & Coriander, New Covent Garden Soup Co*	1floz/30ml	13	42	0.8	3.9	2.6	0.6
Carrot & Coriander, Packet, Sainsbury's*	1oz/28g	7	24	0.7	3.9	0.6	0.7
Carrot & Coriander, Perfectly Balanced, Waitrose*	1 Can/413ml	66	16	0.5	3.1	0.2	1.0
Carrot & Coriander, Seeds Of Change*	1 Pack/500g	210	42	0.5	5.7	1.9	0.9
Carrot & Coriander, Somerfield*	1 Pack/450g	212	47	1.0	3.0	4.0	0.0
Carrot & Coriander, Soup-A-Cup, Asda*	1 Serving/26g	102	392	4.6	62.0	14.0	4.5
Carrot & Coriander, Tesco*	½ Can/210g	92	44	0.7	5.4	2.2	0.8
Carrot & Ginger, Perfectly Balanced, Waitrose*	½ Pot/300g	66	22	0.4	3.1	0.9	1.0
Carrot & Lentil, Weight Watchers*	1 Can/295g	91	31	1.4	6.0	0.1	0.7
Carrot & Orange	1oz/28g	6	20	0.4	3.7	0.5	1.0
Carrot & Orange, Pouch, Heinz*	½ Pack/300g	165	55	0.6	8.3	2.2	1.0
Carrot & Parsnip, M & S*	1oz/28g	9	32	0.5	4.9	1.2	0.9
Carrot, Onion & Chick Pea, Baxters*	1 Can/425g	145	34	1.7	7.1	0.1	1.5
Carrot, Orange & Coriander, COU, M & S*	1 Pack/415g	145	35	0.6	6.9	0.6	1.2
Carrot, Parsnip & Nutmeg, Organic, Baxters*	1 Can/425g	115	27	0.7	5.7	0.2	1.0
Carrot Potato & Coriander, Weight Watchers*	1 Can/295g	74	25	0.5	5.5	0.1	0.6
Carrot With Creme Fraiche, Baxters*	1 Can/415g	166	40	0.6	5.8	1.7	0.7
Cauliflower Cheddar, Dijon, New Covent Garden Soup Co*	1 Pack/284ml	287	101	2.3	10.7	5.4	0.5
Cauliflower Cheese, Somerfield*	1 Pack/500g	345	69	3.0	3.0	5.0	0.0
Cheese & Broccoli & Tagliatelle, Cup A Soup, Batchelors*	1 Sachet/291g	160	55	1.8	8.1	1.7	0.7
Cheese, Leek & Bacon, Somerfield*	1 Carton/300g	441	147	5.0	5.0	12.0	0.0
Chicken & Asparagus, Eat Smart, Safeway*	1 Pack/450g	248	55	3.3	3.2	2.7	0.7
Chicken & Broccoli Cup A Soup, Asda*	1 Serving/16g	55	341	7.0	58.0	9.0	6.0
Chicken & Broccoli, Soup-a-Slim, Asda*	1 Sachet/16g	55	341	7.0	58.0	9.0	6.0

S

SOUP,	Measure WEIGHT/INFO	per Measure KCAL	Nutrition Values per 100g / 100ml KCAL	PROT	CARB	FAT	FIBRE
Chicken & Ham Big, Heinz*	½ Can/200g	92	46	2.3	6.9	1.0	0.7
Chicken & Leek Big, Heinz*	½ Can/200g	118	59	2.3	7.8	2.0	0.5
Chicken & Leek Cup A Soup, Batchelors*	1 Serving/213g	77	36	0.6	6.7	0.9	0.3
Chicken & Leek In A Mug, Slim Choice, Safeway*	1 Sachet/12g	53	439	7.2	55.9	20.7	10.0
Chicken & Leek, TTD, Sainsbury's*	½ Bottle/300ml	177	59	4.7	2.1	3.5	0.3
Chicken & Mushroom In A Cup, Sainsbury's*	1 Sachet/223ml	107	48	0.7	7.1	1.9	0.1
Chicken & Mushroom In A Cup, Tesco*	1 Sachet/15g	9	57	1.4	8.5	2.0	0.2
Chicken & Mushroom, Slim A Soup, Batchelors*	1 Sachet/203g	59	29	0.7	4.1	1.1	0.3
Chicken & Mushroom, Soup-a-Slim, Asda*	1 Sachet/14g	51	362	10.0	58.0	10.0	4.2
Chicken & Mushroom, Tesco*	1 Serving/100g	53	53	0.8	5.7	3.0	0.4
Chicken & Mushroom With Baked Potato, Big Soup, Heinz*	1 Can/400g	228	57	2.6	6.7	2.2	0.3
Chicken & Mushroom With Pasta, Cup A Soup, Batchelors*	1 Serving/250g	115	46	1.3	7.1	1.4	0.5
Chicken & Pasta Big, Heinz*	½ Can/200g	68	34	1.8	5.9	0.4	0.8
Chicken & Sweet Corn Cup, Morrisons*	1 Serving/14g	48	341	14.0	57.5	6.1	2.5
Chicken & Sweetcorn, Baxters*	1 Can/425g	166	39	1.6	6.2	0.9	0.6
Chicken & Sweetcorn, BGTY, Sainsbury's*	1 Serving/200g	42	21	1.2	3.5	0.2	0.1
Chicken & Sweetcorn, Fresh, Morrisons*	1 Pot/500g	205	41	2.1	6.7	0.6	0.2
Chicken & Sweetcorn, Fresh, Sainsbury's*	½ Bottle/300ml	135	45	2.1	7.9	0.5	0.5
Chicken & Sweetcorn, GFY, Asda*	1 Can/400g	108	27	1.5	4.2	0.5	0.2
Chicken & Sweetcorn, HE, Tesco*	1 Serving/200ml	64	32	1.5	5.3	0.5	0.2
Chicken & Sweetcorn In A Cup, BGTY, Sainsbury's*	1 Sachet/200ml	50	25	0.7	3.8	0.8	0.6
Chicken & Sweetcorn In A Mug, Tesco*	1 Sachet/28g	122	434	4.8	63.4	17.9	1.1
Chicken & Sweetcorn, Slim A Soup, Batchelors*	1 Sachet/203g	59	29	0.6	4.5	0.9	0.1
Chicken & Sweetcorn, Slim Choice, Safeway*	1 Sachet/13g	47	363	12.2	48.8	13.2	5.1
Chicken & Sweetcorn, Tesco*	1 Can/400ml	128	32	1.5	5.3	0.5	0.2
Chicken & Sweetcorn With Croutons, Sainsbury's*	1oz/28g	17	60	1.4	8.2	2.4	0.4
Chicken & Tarragon, Thick & Creamy, Batchelors*	1 Sachet/281g	118	42	0.8	5.7	2.3	0.3
Chicken & Vegetable Big, Heinz*	1 Can/400g	188	47	2.4	7.3	1.0	0.9
Chicken & Vegetable Cup A Soup, Batchelors*	1 Sachet/30g	131	437	4.8	62.7	18.6	1.1
Chicken & Vegetable Cup A Soup & Croutons, Batchelors*	1 Serving/222g	133	60	0.7	7.8	3.0	1.5
Chicken & Vegetable Cup, Tesco*	1 Sachet/29ml	122	422	5.6	61.3	17.1	0.5
Chicken & Vegetable, Healthy Choice, Baxters*	1 Can/426g	132	31	1.3	5.6	0.5	1.6
Chicken & Vegetable, M & S*	1oz/28g	17	59	5.3	5.7	1.7	1.1
Chicken & Vegetable Mighty, Asda*	1 Can/410g	176	43	2.5	6.8	1.3	0.7
Chicken & Vegetable, Perfectly Balanced, Waitrose*	1 Can/68g	23	34	1.8	5.4	0.6	1.0
Chicken & Vegetable, Thick, Heinz*	1 Can/400g	152	38	1.2	6.2	0.9	0.6
Chicken & Vegetable With Croutons Cup, Co-Op*	1 Sachet/28g	122	435	5.0	60.0	19.0	3.0
Chicken & Vegetable With White Wine, Heinz*	1 Serving/215g	120	56	2.4	6.7	2.2	0.6
Chicken & White Wine, Campbell's*	1 Serving/295g	145	49	1.0	4.0	3.3	0.0
Chicken Broth, Baxters*	1 Can/425g	145	34	1.2	5.3	0.9	0.6
Chicken Broth, Fresh, Baxters*	1 Serving/300g	117	39	4.9	2.1	1.2	0.7
Chicken Broth, Traditional, Baxters*	½ Can/207g	62	30	1.2	5.3	0.4	0.6
Chicken, Campbell's*	1 Can/295g	142	48	1.1	3.5	3.6	0.0
Chicken, Condensed, 99% Fat Free, Campbell's*	1 Can/295g	100	34	1.6	5.0	0.9	0.0
Chicken, Cream of Canned	1oz/28g	16	58	1.7	4.5	3.8	0.0
Chicken Cup A Soup, Batchelors*	1 Serving/213g	98	46	0.7	5.8	2.2	0.3
Chicken Fusion, Fresh, Covent Garden*	½ carton/300g	162	54	2.6	4.8	2.7	0.4
Chicken In a Cup, Sainsbury's*	1 Serving/221ml	86	39	0.7	5.3	1.7	0.1
Chicken In A Cup, Symingtons*	1 Serving/22g	93	424	7.0	57.7	18.4	11.7
Chicken, Leek & White Wine, Finest,Tesco*	1 Pack/300g	216	72	2.8	5.7	4.2	0.3
Chicken, M & S*	1 Pack/213g	196	92	1.6	5.5	7.2	0.2
Chicken Mulligatawny, Asda*	1 Serving/300g	150	50	3.8	7.0	0.8	0.8
Chicken Mulligatawny, Perfectly Balanced, Waitrose*	1 Serving/300g	138	46	1.7	5.3	2.0	0.4
Chicken Mulligatawny, Tesco*	1 Pack/600g	570	95	3.6	5.4	6.6	0.4

SOUP,	Measure WEIGHT/INFO	per Measure KCAL	KCAL	PROT	CARB	FAT	FIBRE
Chicken, Mushroom & Pasta Cup A Soup, Batchelors*	1 Serving/286g	132	46	1.3	7.1	1.4	0.5
Chicken, Mushroom & Rice, Chilled, M & S*	½ Pot/300g	240	80	3.4	8.6	3.8	0.6
Chicken Noodle & Vegetable, Slim A Soup, Batchelors*	1 Serving/203g	59	29	0.8	4.9	0.7	0.3
Chicken Noodle, Asda*	1 Can/410g	107	26	1.6	4.0	0.4	0.1
Chicken Noodle Cup A Soup, Batchelors*	1 Serving/217g	89	41	1.7	7.4	0.6	0.2
Chicken Noodle, Cup, Asda*	1 Sachet/13g	40	305	9.0	63.0	1.9	3.6
Chicken Noodle, HE, Tesco*	1 Pack/500g	215	43	1.6	6.6	1.1	0.4
Chicken Noodle, Heinz*	1oz/28g	8	27	1.1	4.9	0.3	0.2
Chicken Noodle Packet, Batchelors*	1 Pack/284g	71	25	1.6	4.2	0.2	0.3
Chicken Noodle, Safeway*	1 Can/425g	111	26	1.4	3.5	0.7	0.3
Chicken Noodle, Sainsbury's*	1 Sachet/600ml	102	17	0.8	3.0	0.2	0.1
Chicken Noodle, Weight Watchers*	1 Can/295g	50	17	0.7	3.1	0.1	0.2
Chicken, Thick & Creamy, M & S*	1oz/28g	31	110	5.8	3.9	8.0	0.5
Chicken Vegetable Broth, Morrisons*	1 Serving/200g	50	25	1.2	4.5	0.2	0.5
Chicken, Weight Watchers*	1 Can/295g	89	30	1.2	4.1	1.0	0.1
Chilli Bean, M & S*	½ Carton/300g	150	50	2.5	4.7	2.5	2.7
Chinese Chicken Noodle Cup A Soup, Batchelors*	1 Sachet/100g	36	36	1.3	6.8	0.4	0.7
Chinese Chicken Noodle, Dry, Knorr*	1 Pack/45g	138	307	15.1	51.8	4.4	2.9
Chinese Tomato & Noodle, Dry, Knorr*	1 Pack/51g	168	329	9.3	60.1	5.7	4.6
Chunky Chicken & Vegetable, M & S*	1 Can/425g	276	65	5.2	6.6	1.8	0.6
Chunky Chicken & Vegetable Meal, Tesco*	1 Can/410g	176	43	2.3	7.2	0.5	0.7
Chunky Chicken & Vegetable, Soup Sensations*	1 Pack/450g	248	55	3.1	5.8	2.1	0.6
Chunky Chicken, Leek & Potato, Heinz*	1 Can/400g	236	59	2.3	7.8	2.0	0.5
Chunky Minestrone Meal, Tesco*	½ Can/205g	78	38	1.3	6.8	0.6	0.9
Chunky Roasted Vegetable, M & S*	1 Can/400g	140	35	1.3	5.8	0.6	1.1
Chunky Tuscan Style Bean & M & S*	1 Can/415g	249	60	2.4	7.7	2.2	1.0
Chunky Vegetable, Fresh, Baxters*	1 Serving/300ml	117	39	1.6	7.8	0.2	1.1
Chunky Vegetable & Pasta Twists & Herbs, Safeway*	1 Can/400g	160	40	1.5	7.2	0.5	1.2
Chunky With Pasta Minestrone, Co-Op*	1 Pack/400g	140	35	1.0	6.0	0.6	0.7
Cock-a-Leekie Traditional, Baxters*	1 Can/425g	98	23	1.0	4.1	0.3	0.3
Country Garden, Baxters*	1 Can/425g	149	35	0.9	6.5	0.6	0.7
Country Mushroom, Baxters*	1 Pot/600g	360	60	0.9	5.4	3.9	0.3
Country Vegetable, Chilled, M & S*	½ Pot/300g	105	35	0.5	3.2	2.1	1.0
Country Vegetable, Fresh, Asda*	1 Carton/500g	195	39	1.9	7.0	0.4	0.0
Country Vegetable, Fresh, Chilled, M & S*	1 Pot/600g	210	35	0.5	3.2	2.1	1.0
Country Vegetable, Fresh, Morrisons*	½ Pot/250g	108	43	1.0	6.3	1.5	1.2
Country Vegetable, Fresh, Somerfield*	½ Pack/300g	123	41	1.1	4.6	2.0	1.2
Country Vegetable, Fresh, Waitrose*	1 Serving/300g	165	55	2.1	7.1	2.0	1.6
Country Vegetable, Heinz*	1oz/28g	14	51	2.3	9.3	0.5	1.1
Country Vegetable, M & S*	1oz/28g	14	50	1.8	7.0	1.4	1.0
Country Vegetable, Thick, Asda*	1 Pack/410g	164	40	1.6	7.0	0.6	1.2
Country Vegetable, Weight Watchers*	1 Can/295g	89	30	1.1	5.9	0.2	1.0
Courgette & Parmesan, Sainsbury's*	1 Pack/300ml	198	66	1.5	2.5	5.6	0.4
Courgette, Parmesan & Bacon, Somerfield*	1 Pack/500g	255	51	2.0	2.0	4.0	0.0
Cream of Asparagus, Baxters*	1 Can/415g	266	64	1.2	5.3	4.2	0.2
Cream Of Asparagus, Campbell's*	½ Can/150g	68	45	0.5	4.6	2.8	0.0
Cream of Asparagus, Heinz*	1oz/28g	13	46	1.1	4.5	2.6	0.2
Cream of Asparagus In Seconds, Dry, Knorr*	1 Pack/61g	320	524	6.5	42.2	36.6	1.1
Cream of Asparagus, Dry, Morrisons*	1oz/28g	109	390	3.2	70.0	11.0	0.0
Cream of Asparagus Soup In a Cup, Sainsbury's*	1 Serving/230ml	129	56	0.7	8.2	2.3	0.1
Cream Of Celery, Campbell's*	1 Serving/150g	71	47	0.6	3.2	3.4	0.0
Cream of Celery, Heinz*	1oz/28g	12	44	0.8	4.1	2.7	0.2
Cream of Chicken & Mushroom, Campbell's*	1 Can/250g	108	43	0.5	3.5	3.1	0.0
Cream of Chicken & Mushroom, Heinz*	1oz/28g	14	49	1.3	4.6	2.9	0.1

Nutrition Values per 100g / 100ml apply to KCAL, PROT, CARB, FAT, FIBRE.

S

SOUP,	Measure WEIGHT/INFO	per Measure KCAL	Nutrition Values per 100g / 100ml KCAL	PROT	CARB	FAT	FIBRE
Cream of Chicken & Mushroom In Seconds, Dry, Knorr*	1 Pack/58g	302	521	9.5	41.5	35.3	0.7
Cream Of Chicken & Mushroom, Sainsbury's*	1 Can/400g	232	58	1.1	5.1	3.7	0.1
Cream Of Chicken, Asda*	1 Can/410g	209	51	1.2	4.0	3.4	0.1
Cream Of Chicken, Cambell's*	1 Can/590g	295	50	3.7	1.0	3.5	0.0
Cream of Chicken Condensed, Made Up, Heinz*	1oz/28g	12	42	1.1	3.1	2.8	0.0
Cream of Chicken, Fresh, Somerfield*	1 Carton/450g	234	52	2.0	4.0	3.0	0.0
Cream of Chicken, Fresh, Tesco*	1 Serving/300g	294	98	3.3	6.3	6.6	0.2
Cream Of Chicken, Fresh, Waitrose*	1 Serving/300g	180	60	2.6	3.7	3.9	0.2
Cream of Chicken, Heinz*	1oz/28g	14	51	1.3	4.4	3.2	0.1
Cream of Chicken, Homepride*	¼ Bottle/250ml	113	45	1.3	4.0	2.9	0.0
Cream of Chicken In Seconds, Dry, Knorr*	1 Pack/58g	300	518	11.2	36.0	36.6	0.3
Cream of Chicken, Dry, Knorr*	1 Pack/71g	344	484	16.5	33.7	31.5	0.3
Cream of Chicken Microwave, Heinz*	1oz/28g	15	52	1.3	4.6	3.2	0.1
Cream of Chicken Packet, Batchelors*	1 Pack/289g	165	57	1.1	5.6	3.3	0.3
Cream Of Chicken, Sainsbury's*	½ Can/200g	130	65	1.5	6.2	3.8	0.1
Cream of Chicken, Somerfield*	1 Serving/215g	129	60	1.5	4.4	4.1	0.1
Cream of Leek In Seconds, Dry, Knorr*	1 Pack/64g	326	509	5.9	45.2	33.8	1.4
Cream of Leek, Traditional, Baxters*	1 Can/425g	196	46	0.7	5.2	2.5	0.4
Cream of Mushroom, Asda*	1 Can/410g	258	63	1.0	6.0	3.9	0.3
Cream of Mushroom, Co-Op*	1 Pack/400g	240	60	1.0	5.0	4.0	0.0
Cream of Mushroom, Condensed, Campbell's*	1 Can/295ml	204	69	1.7	5.3	4.5	0.0
Cream of Mushroom Condensed, Made Up, Heinz*	1oz/28g	12	42	0.9	3.5	2.7	0.1
Cream Of Mushroom Cup A Soup, Batchelors*	1 Serving/219g	125	57	0.6	7.5	2.8	0.4
Cream Of Mushroom, GFY, Asda*	1 Serving/250g	93	37	2.1	6.0	0.5	0.3
Cream of Mushroom, Heinz*	1oz/28g	14	51	1.4	5.1	2.7	0.1
Cream Of Mushroom In A Bottle, Homepride*	¼ Bottle/250ml	110	44	0.5	3.5	3.1	0.0
Cream of Mushroom, Sainsbury's*	1 Can/400g	220	55	0.6	1.4	5.2	0.1
Cream Of Mushroom, Tesco*	1 Serving/200g	108	54	0.9	4.6	3.5	0.1
Cream of Potato & Leek, Sainsbury's*	½ Can/200g	116	58	0.9	6.8	3.0	0.4
Cream of Scottish Smoked Salmon, Baxters*	1 Can/415g	241	58	1.5	5.7	3.2	0.5
Cream Of Sweetcorn, Condensed, Campbell's*	1 Can/295g	150	51	0.6	6.2	2.7	0.0
Cream of Tomato & Basil, Somerfield*	1 Pack/450g	279	62	1.0	5.0	4.0	0.0
Cream Of Tomato, Asda*	½ Can/205g	150	73	0.8	9.0	3.7	0.5
Cream of Tomato, Campbell's*	1 Can/295g	195	66	0.7	7.6	3.6	0.0
Cream of Tomato Condensed, Made Up, Heinz*	1oz/28g	15	55	0.9	7.1	2.6	0.4
Cream of Tomato, Fresh, Sainsbury's*	½ Bottle/300ml	126	42	0.9	7.0	1.2	0.6
Cream of Tomato, Fresh, Somerfield*	1 Carton/450g	311	69	1.0	6.0	5.0	0.0
Cream Of Tomato, Fresh, Waitrose*	½ Pot/300g	210	70	1.0	4.9	5.1	0.5
Cream of Tomato, Heinz*	1oz/28g	18	64	0.9	7.1	3.6	0.4
Cream Of Tomato, Homepride*	¼ Bottle/250ml	138	55	0.9	7.7	2.6	0.0
Cream Of Tomato, Improves, Tesco*	½ Can/200g	142	71	0.9	8.7	3.6	0.5
Cream of Tomato, Dry, Knorr*	1 Pack/90g	392	435	4.3	51.3	23.6	3.3
Cream of Tomato Microwave, Heinz*	1oz/28g	19	68	0.9	7.5	3.8	0.4
Cream Of Tomato, SmartPrice, Asda*	1 Can/408g	290	71	0.7	9.0	3.6	0.0
Cream of Tomato, Tesco*	1 Pack/600g	474	79	2.2	5.7	5.3	0.5
Cream of Tomato, Traditional, Baxters*	1 Can/425g	302	71	1.5	10.6	2.5	0.7
Cream of Vegetable Cup A Soup, Batchelors*	1 Sachet/33g	134	406	5.8	59.8	16.0	6.2
Creamed Asparagus, Asda*	1 Sachet/30g	131	451	6.0	55.0	23.0	1.1
Creamed Tomato In A Cup, Sainsbury's*	1 Sachet/233ml	112	48	0.7	9.3	0.9	0.1
Creamed Veg Granules & Croutons In A Cup, Sainsbury's*	1 Sachet/230ml	138	60	1.0	8.5	2.4	0.2
Creamed Vegetable In A Mug, Safeway*	1 Sachet/29g	117	405	5.6	57.9	16.8	3.2
Creamy Leek With Croutons In A Cup, Sainsbury's*	1 Serving/228g	130	57	1.1	7.2	2.6	0.1
Creamy Mushroom, Somerfield*	1 Pack/450g	225	50	1.0	4.0	3.0	0.0
Creamy Potato & Leek Cup A Soup, Batchelors*	1 Sachet/280ml	132	47	0.8	7.4	1.5	1.1

S

SOUP,	Measure WEIGHT/INFO	per Measure KCAL	Nutrition Values per 100g / 100ml KCAL	PROT	CARB	FAT	FIBRE
Creamy Potato, Bacon & Onion Cup A Soup, Batchelors*	1 Sachet/280ml	106	38	0.9	7.3	1.0	0.5
Creamy Tomato, Seeds Of Change*	1 Pack/500g	320	64	1.1	10.9	1.8	0.5
Crofter's Thick Vegetable, Dry, Knorr*	1 Pack/66g	240	364	10.8	52.9	12.2	3.3
Cucumber Pea & Mint, New Covent Garden Soup Co*	1 Serving/200ml	90	45	1.8	4.7	2.1	0.6
English Broccoli & Stilton, Dry, Knorr*	1 Pack/65g	331	509	11.7	30.3	37.9	1.6
Farmhouse Chicken Leek, Dry, Knorr*	1 Pack/54g	248	459	10.3	39.3	29.0	1.5
Farmhouse Vegetable, BGTY, Sainsbury's*	1 Serving/200ml	52	26	0.5	4.4	0.8	0.9
Farmhouse Vegetable, Sainsbury's*	1/3 Sachet/223g	58	26	0.9	4.8	0.4	0.3
Farmhouse Vegetable, Thick, Co-Op*	1 Can/400g	140	35	1.0	7.0	0.4	0.3
Fire Flamed Tomato & Red Onion, Sainsbury's*	½ Bottle/300ml	129	43	0.8	5.0	2.2	1.0
Flame Grilled Aubergine, Red Pepper, Covent Garden Co*	½ Pack/284g	68	24	0.9	4.8	0.1	0.4
Florida Spring Vegetable, Dry, Knorr*	1 Pack/36g	104	290	7.8	52.2	5.6	5.2
Forest Mushroom, Heinz*	1oz/28g	12	43	1.0	4.5	2.3	0.1
French Onion	1oz/28g	11	40	0.2	5.7	2.1	1.0
French Onion & Cider, Waitrose*	1 Can/425g	94	22	0.5	4.8	0.1	0.4
French Onion, Asda*	1 Can/297g	101	34	1.6	4.4	1.1	0.0
French Onion, Baxters*	1 Can/425g	94	22	0.7	4.2	0.2	0.4
French Onion, Chilled, M & S*	½ Pot/300g	150	50	2.0	7.2	1.5	1.0
French Onion Condensed, Campbell's*	1 Serving/150ml	57	38	1.7	5.0	1.3	0.8
French Onion, GFY, Asda*	½ Pot/253g	91	36	1.9	6.0	0.5	0.4
French Onion, Heinz*	1 Pack/400g	100	25	0.5	5.7	0.1	0.4
French Onion, Dry, Knorr*	1 Pack/40g	118	296	6.0	62.5	2.5	6.6
French Onion, Made Up, Sainsbury's*	1/3 Serving/205g	39	19	0.4	4.0	0.1	0.1
French Onion, Safeway*	½ Pot/250g	85	34	0.8	3.9	1.7	0.5
Gazpacho, M & S*	½ Pack/390g	117	30	1.3	5.7	0.2	1.5
Giant Minestrone, Big, Heinz*	1oz/28g	12	44	1.7	8.1	0.5	1.0
Golden Vegetable, Asda*	1 Pack/300g	150	50	1.9	6.0	2.0	0.0
Golden Vegetable Calorie Counter, Cup, Co-Op*	1 Sachet/12g	40	335	7.0	54.0	10.0	5.0
Golden Vegetable Cup A Soup, Batchelors*	1 Serving/212g	70	33	0.5	7.3	0.2	0.4
Golden Vegetable Instant, Tesco*	1 Sachet/17g	60	351	8.2	62.0	7.8	3.7
Golden Vegetable, Dry, Knorr*	1 Pack/76g	299	394	10.4	45.4	19.0	3.3
Golden Vegetable, Reduced Calorie Quick, Waitrose*	1 Sachet/16g	4	27	0.6	4.9	0.6	0.3
Golden Vegetable, Slim A Soup, Batchelors*	1 Sachet/207g	58	28	0.5	4.7	0.8	0.7
Golden Vegetable Soup-A-Slim, Asda*	1 Sachet/15g	50	336	6.0	60.0	8.0	1.9
Golden Vegetable With Croutons Cup Soup, Co-Op*	1 Sachet/25g	120	480	4.0	56.0	26.0	2.0
Golden Vegetable With Croutons, Instant, Morrisons*	1 Sachet/27g	118	438	5.3	60.7	19.3	0.0
Green Pea & Mint, Fresh, Waitrose*	1oz/28g	27	97	1.8	5.5	7.7	1.2
Haddock, Chowder, Smoked, Asda*	1 Serving/300g	135	45	2.4	6.0	1.3	0.7
Haggis Broth, Baxters*	1 Can/425g	221	52	1.9	6.8	1.9	0.7
Harvest Carrot & Lima Bean, Heinz*	1oz/28g	11	40	0.8	6.9	1.0	1.3
Highlanders Broth, Baxters*	1 Can/425g	183	43	1.6	6.1	1.4	0.5
Hot & Sour Noodles & Vegetables, Cupa Soup, Batchelors*	1 Serving/270g	89	33	0.9	6.8	0.3	0.4
Italian Bean & Pasta, Baxters*	1 Can/425g	162	38	1.9	7.0	0.2	1.3
Italian Chicken & Pasta, Big, Heinz*	1oz/28g	15	55	2.4	9.7	0.7	0.8
Italian Chicken Broth, Healthy Choice, Baxters*	½ Can/210g	84	40	1.5	6.6	0.8	0.8
Italian Minestrone, Dry, Knorr*	1 Pack/62g	193	311	11.5	57.1	4.1	7.8
Italian Plum Tomato & Basil, Perfectly Balanced, Waitrose*	½ Pot/300g	69	23	0.9	3.8	0.5	0.9
Italian Style Tomato & Basil, Co-Op*	1 Pack/500g	200	40	1.0	4.0	2.0	0.6
Italian Style Tomato & Chicken, BGTY, Sainsbury's*	1 Can/400g	148	37	3.1	5.5	0.3	0.4
Italian Style Tomato, Safeway*	½ Pot/248g	134	54	1.3	5.7	2.9	0.9
Italian Tomato With Basil, Baxters*	1 Can/425g	242	57	2.6	9.3	1.0	1.1
Italian Tomato With Penne Pasta, Baxters*	1 Can/425g	153	36	1.2	7.3	0.2	1.0
Lamb & Vegetable, Big, Heinz*	1oz/28g	16	56	2.4	9.3	1.0	1.1
Lamb & Vegetable Mighty, Asda*	1 Can/410g	246	60	3.2	7.0	2.1	0.9

S

SOUP,	Measure WEIGHT/INFO	per Measure KCAL	KCAL	PROT	CARB	FAT	FIBRE
			Nutrition Values per 100g / 100ml				
Leek & Potato, Chilled, M & S*	1 Serving/300g	240	80	0.9	5.2	6.2	0.6
Leek & Potato, Cup A Soup, Batchelors*	1 Sachet/28g	121	432	5.2	63.2	17.6	1.8
Leek & Potato, Eat Smart, Safeway*	½ Pot/225g	113	50	1.1	6.0	2.4	0.6
Leek & Potato, Fresh, Morrisons*	½ Pot/250g	185	74	2.0	6.4	4.5	0.7
Leek & Potato, Fresh, Sainsbury's*	1 Bowl/300ml	189	63	1.1	3.9	4.8	0.5
Leek & Potato, Fresh, Tesco*	½ Pack/300g	201	67	1.4	6.3	4.0	0.8
Leek & Potato In A Cup, BGTY, Sainsbury's*	1 Sachet/196ml	55	28	0.3	4.9	0.8	0.8
Leek & Potato In A Cup, Tesco*	1 Sachet/15g	51	343	5.3	66.4	6.2	3.5
Leek & Potato, New Covent Garden Soup Co*	½ Carton/284g	105	37	1.2	7.1	1.5	0.8
Leek & Potato, Slim A Soup, Batchelors*	1 Serving/204g	57	28	0.4	5.0	0.7	0.2
Leek & Potato, Tastebreaks, Knorr*	1 Pot/225g	162	72	1.1	9.1	3.4	0.5
Leek Potato, Reduced Calorie Quick, Waitrose*	1 Sachet/190ml	51	27	0.4	5.3	0.5	0.4
Lemon Chicken & Ginger In A Cup, Waitrose*	1 Serving/108ml	50	46	0.5	6.7	1.9	1.7
Lentil	1 Serving/220g	218	99	4.4	12.7	3.8	1.1
Lentil & Bacon, Baxters*	1 Can/425g	255	60	2.7	7.9	1.9	0.8
Lentil & Bacon Cup A Soup, Batchelors*	1 Sachet/26g	87	336	12.6	64.8	2.9	4.6
Lentil & Bacon, M & S*	1oz/28g	18	63	4.1	8.6	1.6	0.7
Lentil & Bacon, Sainsbury's*	½ Can/200g	116	58	3.0	8.9	1.1	1.0
Lentil & Bacon, Tesco*	1 Serving/200g	96	48	3.2	7.2	0.7	0.5
Lentil & Chickpea, Organic, Tesco*	1 Serving/300ml	117	39	1.9	6.1	0.8	0.5
Lentil & Parsley, Organic, Sainsbury's*	1 Pot/500g	285	57	4.8	9.1	0.2	1.7
Lentil & Vegetable, Baxters*	1 Can/423g	144	34	1.9	6.8	0.1	1.5
Lentil & Winter, New Covent Garden Soup Co*	1 Serving/250ml	133	53	3.1	7.7	1.1	0.9
Lentil, Asda*	½ Can/202g	89	44	2.6	8.0	0.2	0.7
Lentil, Bacon & Mixed Bean, Low Fat, Aldi*	1 Meal/400g	260	65	4.7	9.5	0.9	1.6
Lentil, Canned	1 Serving/220g	86	39	3.1	6.5	0.2	1.2
Lentil, Heinz*	1 Can/300g	117	39	2.3	7.1	0.2	1.0
Lobster Bisque, Baxters*	1 Can/415g	220	53	3.4	5.2	2.1	0.1
Luxury Game, Baxters*	1 Can/415g	187	45	3.7	5.9	0.7	0.5
Malaysian Chicken & Sweetcorn, Dry, Knorr*	1 Pack/57g	211	370	10.6	56.3	11.4	1.8
Mediteranean Vegetable, Homepride*	1 Serving/250ml	83	33	0.9	4.3	1.3	0.0
Mediterranean Fish, Waitrose*	½ Pot/300g	108	36	3.4	3.5	0.9	0.7
Mediterranean Style Tomato, HE, Dry, Tesco*	1 Serving/22g	78	353	9.7	64.3	6.3	3.0
Mediterranean Tomato & Chicken Pasta, Weight Watchers*	½ Can/200g	80	40	1.5	7.3	0.5	0.3
Mediterranean Tomato & Vegetable, Weight Watchers*	1 Can/295g	47	16	0.4	3.0	0.3	0.4
Mediterranean Tomato, Baxters*	1 Can/425g	140	33	1.0	6.9	0.2	0.7
Mediterranean Tomato, Campbell's*	1 Can/295g	83	28	0.6	6.4	0.0	0.0
Mediterranean Tomato, Chicken & Pasta, HE, Tesco*	1 Serving/400ml	160	40	1.5	7.3	0.5	0.3
Mediterranean Tomato, COU, M & S*	1 Pack/415g	104	25	0.7	4.8	0.5	0.6
Mediterranean Tomato, Fresh, Baxters*	1 Can/300g	171	57	2.2	8.1	1.8	1.4
Mediterranean Tomato, Fresh, Organic, Sainsbury's*	1 Serving/250ml	78	31	1.3	3.3	1.4	1.0
Mediterranean Tomato In A Cup, Sainsbury's*	1 Serving/214ml	60	28	0.7	5.3	0.4	0.2
Mediterranean Tomato Quick, Reduced Calorie, Waitrose*	1 Serving/200ml	52	26	0.7	4.2	0.7	0.3
Mediterranean Tomato, Slim A Soup, Batchelors*	1 Serving/207g	54	26	0.5	4.7	0.6	0.4
Mediterranean Vegetable, Tesco*	½ Can/200g	76	38	0.6	6.8	0.9	0.5
Mild Curry With Pasta In a Mug, Safeway*	1 Sachet/34g	130	382	6.3	66.6	10.0	0.6
Minestone With Wholemeal Pasta, Batchelors*	1 Serving/415g	133	32	0.9	6.7	0.2	1.0
Minestrone	1oz/28g	18	63	1.8	7.6	3.0	0.9
Minestrone, Baxters*	1 Can/425g	145	34	1.3	6.0	0.6	0.8
Minestrone, Canned	1oz/28g	9	32	1.4	5.1	0.8	0.6
Minestrone, Chilled, M & S*	½ Pot/300g	66	22	1.4	2.5	0.7	1.2
Minestrone, Cup A Soup, Batchelors*	1 Serving/217g	100	46	0.9	8.3	1.1	0.5
Minestrone Cup A Soup, BGTY, Sainsbury's*	1 Serving/200ml	54	27	0.8	6.0	0.1	0.6
Minestrone For One, Heinz*	1 Can/303g	97	32	1.4	5.2	0.7	0.7

S

SOUP,	Measure WEIGHT/INFO	per Measure KCAL	Nutrition Values per 100g / 100ml KCAL	PROT	CARB	FAT	FIBRE
Minestrone, Fresh, Baxters*	1 Box/568ml	233	41	1.8	6.2	1.0	0.6
Minestrone, Fresh, Safeway*	½ Pot/250g	83	33	1.0	6.2	0.5	0.8
Minestrone, Fresh, Sainsbury's*	½ Bottle/300ml	93	31	1.2	4.4	0.9	0.9
Minestrone, Fresh, Tesco*	1 Serving/300g	126	42	1.4	6.9	1.0	0.6
Minestrone, Fresh, Waitrose*	1 Pack/600g	240	40	1.1	5.8	1.4	0.8
Minestrone, HE, Tesco*	1 Pack/500g	140	28	1.0	4.4	0.7	0.6
Minestrone, Heinz*	1 Can/300g	96	32	1.4	5.2	0.7	0.7
Minestrone In a Cup, Sainsbury's*	1 Serving/227ml	84	37	1.4	6.3	0.7	0.2
Minestrone In a Mug, HE, Tesco*	1 Sachet/21g	72	342	3.6	67.7	6.3	3.2
Minestrone, Instant, Under 60 Calories, Tesco*	1 Sachet/19g	58	307	7.3	63.6	2.6	2.3
Minestrone Instant With Croutons, Value, Tesco*	1 Sachet/21g	68	325	6.4	60.2	6.5	1.7
Minestrone, Dry, Knorr*	1 Pack/61g	178	292	9.2	53.9	4.4	6.5
Minestrone, M & S*	1oz/28g	13	46	2.3	7.8	0.6	0.8
Minestrone, New Covent Garden Soup Co*	1 Serving/250ml	83	33	1.7	5.8	0.4	0.7
Minestrone, Organic, M & S*	1 Pack/208g	83	40	1.4	8.9	0.5	1.1
Minestrone Packet, Batchelors*	1 Serving/296g	77	26	0.7	5.1	0.3	0.4
Minestrone Pasta In a Mug, Safeway*	1 Sachet/32g	99	310	9.4	65.9	1.0	0.6
Minestrone, Safeway*	1 Pack/425g	132	31	1.1	6.4	0.1	0.5
Minestrone Simmer, Dry, Asda*	1 Pack/50g	131	262	6.0	57.0	1.1	15.0
Minestrone, Slim A Soup, Batchelors*	1 Serving/203g	53	26	0.7	4.5	0.6	0.6
Minestrone, Slim Choice, Dry, Safeway*	1 Serving/14g	42	298	11.2	54.4	4.0	5.7
Minestrone Soup a Slim, Dry, Asda*	1 Serving/17g	53	311	6.0	69.0	1.2	4.5
Minestrone Special In A Cup, Somerfield*	1 Sachet/22g	80	362	8.0	65.0	8.0	0.0
Minestrone, Tesco*	1 Pack/600g	222	37	0.9	4.0	2.0	0.6
Minestrone, Weight Watchers*	1 Can/295g	59	20	0.8	3.3	0.4	0.5
Minestrone With Croutons, Quick, Waitrose*	1 Serving/236g	85	36	0.8	6.5	0.8	0.3
Minestrone With Wholemeal Pasta, Baxters*	1 Can/415g	133	32	0.9	6.7	0.2	1.0
Minted Lamb Hot Pot Big, Heinz*	1oz/28g	14	51	2.2	8.5	1.0	0.9
Soup Mix, Leek & Potato, Sainsbury's*	½ Pack/204g	39	19	0.6	3.6	0.2	0.5
Soup Mix, Scotch Broth, Sainsbury's*	1 Serving/175g	32	18	0.2	3.8	0.2	0.6
Mixed Bean & Pepper, Organic, M & S*	1 Pack/208g	94	45	2.3	7.7	0.3	1.8
Moroccan Chick Pea, M & S*	1oz/28g	20	70	3.6	8.8	2.1	2.0
Moroccan Lentil, Waitrose*	½ Pot/300g	153	51	3.5	8.2	0.5	3.4
Mulligatawny	1 Serving/220g	213	97	1.4	8.2	6.8	0.9
Mulligatawny, Baxters*	1 Can/425g	230	54	2.3	7.3	1.7	0.7
Mulligatawny Beef Curry, Heinz*	1oz/28g	17	60	1.8	7.2	2.7	0.5
Mulligatawny In A Cup, Symingtons*	1 Serving/232ml	95	41	0.7	8.3	0.6	0.5
Mulligatawny, New Covent Garden Soup Co*	½ Pint/296ml	139	47	2.6	6.2	1.2	0.8
Mulligatawny, Symingtons*	1 Serving/227ml	98	43	0.6	8.6	0.6	0.2
Mulligatawny, Tesco*	1 Can/400g	144	36	1.2	6.8	0.5	0.3
Mushroom & Chicken, Co-Op*	1 Pack/400g	220	55	0.9	5.0	4.0	0.0
Mushroom & Garlic, Slim Choice, Dry, Safeway*	1oz/28g	108	384	8.3	61.4	11.7	6.2
Mushroom & Garlic, Slimming Cup A Soup, Dry, Tesco*	1 Serving/16g	58	360	5.8	61.1	10.3	3.2
Mushroom & Garlic, Tesco*	1 Sachet/16g	58	360	5.8	61.1	10.3	3.2
Mushroom & Madeira Flavour, Soup In A Mug, Safeway*	1 Sachet/28g	114	406	3.2	67.3	13.8	1.0
Mushroom, 98% Fat Free, Baxters*	1 Can/425g	170	40	0.9	5.6	1.6	0.3
Mushroom, 99% Fat Free, Campbell's*	1oz/28g	7	24	0.6	3.5	0.9	0.0
Mushroom, Budgens*	1 Can/400g	284	71	1.2	6.6	4.5	0.1
Mushroom, Chilled, M & S*	1 Pack/300g	135	45	1.9	3.3	2.6	0.5
Mushroom, Cream of, Canned	1 Serving/220g	101	46	1.1	3.9	3.0	0.1
Mushroom, M & S*	1oz/28g	15	52	0.6	4.4	3.5	0.3
Mushroom, Morrisons*	1 Serving/500g	250	50	1.3	3.2	3.6	0.3
Mushroom Potage, Baxters*	1 Can/415g	303	73	1.6	5.6	4.9	0.4
Mushroom, Dry, Symingtons*	1 Serving/23g	80	348	17.8	48.4	9.2	6.7

S

SOUP,	Measure WEIGHT/INFO	per Measure KCAL	KCAL	PROT	CARB	FAT	FIBRE
Mushroom, Weight Watchers*	1 Can/295g	86	29	1.2	5.6	0.2	0.1
Oxtail, Canned	1 Serving/220g	97	44	2.4	5.1	1.7	0.1
Oxtail Cup A Soup, Batchelors*	1 Serving/211g	76	36	0.8	6.5	0.8	0.5
Oxtail Cup Soup, Co-Op*	1 Sachet/19g	67	355	7.0	63.0	9.0	1.0
Oxtail, Heinz*	1oz/28g	11	41	1.9	6.7	0.8	0.3
Oxtail, Sainsbury's*	½ Can/200g	66	33	2.3	5.1	0.4	0.2
Oxtail Soup In A Cup, Sainsbury's*	1 Serving/223ml	69	31	1.0	5.7	0.5	0.2
Oxtail, Tesco*	1 Can/400g	152	38	2.0	5.9	0.7	0.3
Parsnip & Coconut, New Covent Garden Soup Co*	½ Pint/296ml	260	88	1.7	6.7	6.1	1.3
Parsnip & Cranberry, New Covent Garden Soup Co*	½ Pint/296ml	142	48	1.3	7.9	1.2	0.5
Parsnip, Fresh, Morrisons*	½ Pot/250g	100	40	0.9	5.8	1.5	1.4
Parsnip, Honey & Ginger, COU, M & S*	1 Can/415g	125	30	0.7	5.3	0.6	0.7
Pasta, Tomato & Basil, Bertolli*	1 Serving/100g	47	47	1.5	7.9	1.1	1.6
Pea & Ham	1oz/28g	20	70	4.0	9.2	2.1	1.4
Pea & Ham, Asda*	½ Can/205g	107	52	2.6	9.0	0.6	0.6
Pea & Ham, Baxters*	1 Can/425g	247	58	2.9	8.1	1.6	1.2
Pea & Ham, M & S*	1oz/28g	17	62	4.0	9.2	1.0	1.2
Pea & Ham, Morrisons*	1 Serving/250g	93	37	2.0	4.8	1.1	1.2
Pea & Ham, Tesco*	1 Pack/400g	240	60	2.5	9.7	1.2	0.6
Pea & Ham, Thick, Heinz*	1 Can/400g	204	51	3.2	8.7	0.4	1.0
Pea & Mint, Baxters*	1 Serving/300g	186	62	2.3	6.1	3.2	1.5
Pea & Mint, Fresh, M & S*	1 Serving/164g	49	30	1.8	6.3	0.1	1.5
Pea & Mint, Fresh, Tesco*	1 Serving/300g	207	69	2.4	5.1	4.4	0.0
Pea & Mint, Tesco*	½ Pouch/250g	198	79	2.0	5.6	5.4	1.5
Pea Ham, Fresh, Sainsbury's*	½ Bottle/302ml	136	45	2.6	4.9	1.7	1.1
Peking Shiitake Mushroom Noodle, Baxters*	1 Serving/215g	90	42	1.3	7.5	0.8	0.2
Pepper & Chorizo, Sainsbury's*	1 Bowl/400ml	172	43	7.0	2.0	1.0	0.0
Potato & Leek	1oz/28g	15	52	1.5	6.2	2.6	0.8
Potato & Leek, Asda*	½ Pack/292ml	158	54	1.2	6.0	2.8	0.7
Potato & Leek, Baxters*	1 Can/425g	170	40	1.0	6.3	1.2	0.5
Potato & Leek Chunky With Peppers & Chicken, Safeway*	1 Pack/400g	172	43	2.3	6.8	0.7	0.6
Potato & Leek, Fresh, Asda*	½ Pot/250g	98	39	1.2	7.0	0.7	0.0
Potato & Leek, Morrisons*	½ Can/205ml	62	30	0.8	6.6	0.0	0.5
Potato & Leek, Ready To Serve, Campbell's*	1 Pot/500ml	220	44	0.9	5.3	2.1	0.0
Potato & Leek, Tesco*	1 Serving/100g	53	53	0.8	5.7	3.0	0.4
Potato & Leek, Thick, Heinz*	1 Can/400g	136	34	0.7	6.5	0.6	0.5
Potato, Leek & Chicken, BGTY, Sainsbury's*	1 Can/400g	152	38	2.1	5.4	0.9	0.5
Potato, Leek & Ham, M & S*	1oz/28g	18	64	1.2	6.7	3.6	0.5
Pumpkin, New Covent Garden Soup Co*	½ Pint/296ml	95	32	1.1	4.8	0.9	1.0
Red Lentil & Lemon, Baxters*	1 Can/425g	196	46	2.0	7.5	0.9	0.7
Red Pepper & Tomato, Perfectly Balanced, Waitrose*	1 Can/415g	154	37	0.8	4.5	1.8	0.9
Red Pepper, Tomato & Basil, M & S*	1 Can/415g	83	20	1.3	2.7	0.3	0.8
Roast Chicken Broth, New Covent Garden Soup Co*	1 Serving/284g	85	30	1.9	4.3	0.5	0.5
Roasted Mediterranean Vegetable, Fresh, Waitrose*	1 Pot/600g	234	39	0.9	3.7	2.3	0.6
Roasted Mediterranean Vegetable, Heinz*	1 Can/400g	128	32	0.7	4.8	1.2	0.5
Roasted Pepper, Eat Smart, Safeway*	½ Pot/225g	79	35	0.8	3.7	1.8	1.4
Roasted Vegetable, Eat Smart, Safeway*	1 Serving/450g	180	40	0.8	4.1	2.2	2.0
Roasted Vegetable, Fresh, Sainsbury's*	½ Pot/273ml	71	26	0.5	4.8	0.5	1.2
Roasted Winter Vegetable, Sainsbury's*	1 Serving/300ml	129	43	0.5	3.4	3.0	1.0
Royal Game, Baxters*	1 Can/425g	153	36	2.4	5.5	0.5	0.4
Scotch Broth	1 Serving/220g	180	82	8.3	5.0	3.4	1.2
Scotch Broth, Asda*	½ Can/205g	90	44	1.6	6.0	1.5	0.6
Scotch Broth, Baxters*	1 Can/425g	200	47	1.9	7.1	1.2	0.9
Scotch Broth, Co-Op*	1 Pack/400g	180	45	2.0	6.0	2.0	0.6

Nutrition Values per 100g / 100ml apply to the KCAL, PROT, CARB, FAT and FIBRE columns.

S

SOUP,	Measure WEIGHT/INFO	per Measure KCAL	Nutrition Values per 100g / 100ml KCAL	PROT	CARB	FAT	FIBRE
Scotch Broth, Fresh, Morrisons*	1 Pack/500g	155	31	2.5	3.6	0.7	1.9
Scotch Broth, New Covent Garden Soup Co*	½ Pint/296ml	118	40	1.6	2.8	2.5	0.5
Scotch Broth, Sainsbury's*	½ Can/200g	108	54	1.9	8.2	1.5	0.8
Scotch Vegetable, Baxters*	1 Can/425g	183	43	1.9	7.4	0.6	1.3
Sicilian Tomato, New Covent Garden Soup Co*	½ Pint/284ml	114	40	1.6	4.8	1.6	0.8
Smoked Haddock Chowder, Covent Garden Soup Co*	½ Pint/284ml	142	50	2.2	8.1	1.0	0.5
Spiced Spinach & Green Lentil, Asda*	½ Pot/250g	123	49	2.7	5.0	2.0	0.0
Spicy Bean, Co-Op*	1 Pack/500g	200	40	2.0	7.0	0.5	1.0
Spicy Bean, Eat Smart, Safeway*	1 Pack/450g	293	65	3.6	9.1	1.0	3.5
Spicy Lentil & Tomato Soup A Slim, Dry, Asda*	1 Serving/17g	56	327	12.0	63.0	3.0	4.6
Spicy Lentil, COU, M & S*	1 Pack/415g	187	45	2.6	6.7	0.9	1.2
Spicy Lentil, Seeds Of Change*	1 Pack/500g	345	69	2.8	9.4	2.2	0.8
Spicy Mulligatawny, Sainsbury's*	1 Serving/300ml	105	35	2.1	4.5	0.9	0.9
Spicy Parsnip, Baxters*	1 Can/425g	217	51	1.1	6.1	2.5	1.5
Spicy Parsnip, BGTY, Sainsbury's*	1 Pack/400g	180	45	2.2	7.1	0.9	1.0
Spicy Parsnip, Fresh, Tesco*	1 Serving/300g	102	34	0.6	4.5	1.6	1.6
Spicy Parsnip Homestyle, Somerfield*	1 Carton/500g	250	50	2.0	5.0	3.0	0.0
Spicy Parsnip, Perfectly Balanced, Waitrose*	1 Can/415g	125	30	1.0	4.8	0.7	1.1
Spicy Parsnip, Tesco*	1 Pack/600g	330	55	0.8	4.4	3.9	1.7
Spicy Sausage & Bean Meal, Tesco*	1 Can/500g	265	53	2.8	6.4	1.4	1.2
Spicy Thai Chicken, Baxters*	1 Can/415g	278	67	1.8	7.1	3.5	0.3
Spicy Tomato & Lentil, Asda*	1 Can/410g	156	38	1.0	6.0	1.1	0.4
Spicy Tomato & Rice With Sweetcorn, Baxters*	½ Can/207g	93	45	1.3	9.2	0.3	0.6
Spicy Tomato Cup A Soup, Batchelors*	1 Sachet/23g	74	322	7.6	65.8	3.2	3.2
Spinach & Watercress, New Covent Garden Soup Co*	½ Carton/298g	60	20	1.3	2.8	0.4	0.8
Spinach With Nutmeg, New Covent Garden Soup Co*	½ Pint/284ml	102	36	1.7	2.5	2.1	0.8
Split Pea & Ham, Asda*	1 Serving/300g	129	43	3.5	6.9	0.2	0.7
Spring Vegetable, Heinz*	1 Can/400g	124	31	0.8	6.2	0.4	0.7
Super Chicken Noodle In Seconds, Dry, Knorr*	1 Pack/37g	111	299	17.9	46.1	4.7	0.3
Super Chicken Noodle, Dry, Knorr*	1 Pack/56g	182	325	14.3	56.0	4.9	1.8
Sweetcorn & Chicken Chowder, Heinz*	1 Serving/200g	108	54	1.5	5.2	3.0	0.3
Szechuan Chicken Noodle, Fresh, Sainsbury's*	1 Bottle/600ml	204	34	1.4	4.8	1.0	0.4
Tangy Tomato With Pasta, Cup A Soup, Batchelors*	1 Pack/285g	137	48	1.2	9.0	0.8	0.4
Thai Chicken Noodle, Baxters*	1 Serving/430g	202	47	1.7	6.8	1.4	0.3
Thai Chicken, Safeway*	1 Serving/200g	178	89	4.1	2.5	7.0	1.3
Thai Pumpkin Coconut, New Covent Garden Soup Co*	1 Carton/568ml	182	32	1.3	3.5	1.3	1.1
Thai Red Chicken, Fresh, Sainsbury's*	½ Pot/300ml	159	53	1.9	5.0	2.8	0.5
Three Bean, Organic, Seeds of Change*	1 Pack/500g	285	57	1.7	9.9	1.2	1.1
Tomato & Basil, 1% Fat, M & S*	1 Can/400g	152	38	0.6	9.0	0.4	1.4
Tomato & Basil, 99% Fat Free, Baxters*	½ Can/207g	75	36	0.7	6.1	1.0	0.6
Tomato & Basil, Chilled, M & S*	1 Serving/300g	105	35	0.9	6.2	0.7	0.7
Tomato & Basil Cup, Co-Op*	1 Sachet/45g	158	350	2.0	76.0	4.0	4.0
Tomato & Basil, Finest, Tesco*	½ Pot/300g	204	68	1.0	4.1	5.2	0.6
Tomato & Basil, Fresh, Sainsbury's*	1 Pack/300ml	78	26	0.8	4.0	0.7	0.7
Tomato & Basil, Fresh, Tesco*	1 Pack/300g	129	43	1.0	5.7	1.8	0.7
Tomato & Basil, GFY, Asda*	1 Serving/250ml	103	41	1.4	3.9	2.2	0.4
Tomato & Basil, M & S*	1oz/28g	7	24	0.8	4.4	0.4	0.6
Tomato & Basil, New Covent Garden Soup Co*	1 Pack/568g	187	33	1.8	5.7	0.4	0.5
Tomato & Basil Soup-a-Slim, Asda*	1 Sachet/16g	52	326	7.0	70.0	2.0	3.9
Tomato & Basil, Thick & Creamy, Batchelors*	1 Serving/281g	104	37	0.5	6.7	0.9	0.6
Tomato & Brown Lentil, Baxters*	1 Can/425g	166	39	2.4	8.7	0.1	1.5
Tomato & Butterbean, Baxters*	1 Can/425g	234	55	2.0	8.8	1.3	1.8
Tomato & Herb, Campbell's*	1 Carton/500ml	180	36	1.0	5.0	1.3	0.0
Tomato & Herb, M & S*	1oz/28g	20	72	1.3	7.9	4.0	0.4

SOUP,	Measure WEIGHT/INFO	per Measure KCAL	Nutrition Values per 100g / 100ml KCAL	PROT	CARB	FAT	FIBRE
Tomato & Lentil, Heinz*	1 Can/400g	216	54	2.7	10.4	0.2	1.0
Tomato & Orange, Baxters*	1 Can/425g	183	43	1.1	8.4	0.5	0.5
Tomato & Orange, HE, Tesco*	1 Pack/400g	132	33	0.6	7.1	0.2	0.4
Tomato & Red Pepper, Campbell's*	1 Can/590g	366	62	0.5	7.7	3.3	0.0
Tomato & Red Pepper, Soupreme*	1 Serving/250ml	90	36	1.1	5.7	1.0	1.7
Tomato & Red Pepper, Weight Watchers*	1 Serving/205g	25	12	0.4	2.5	0.1	0.4
Tomato & Spinach, Organic, Waitrose*	1 Serving/300g	126	42	1.4	4.9	1.9	0.7
Tomato & Three Bean, BGTY, Sainsbury's*	1 Can/400g	216	54	2.9	8.5	0.9	0.8
Tomato & Vegetable Cup A Soup, Batchelors*	1 Serving/218g	107	49	1.1	8.5	1.2	0.6
Tomato & Vegetable Cup, Soupreme*	1 Sachet/24g	87	361	6.0	64.6	8.7	1.4
Tomato & Vegetable In A Cup, Asda*	1 Sachet/24g	86	360	7.0	65.0	8.0	3.7
Tomato & Vegetable, Organic, Baxters*	1 Can/425g	140	33	0.9	6.6	0.3	0.6
Tomato, 99% Fat Free, Campbell's*	1 Can/200g	88	44	0.7	8.0	1.0	0.0
Tomato, Cream of, Canned	1oz/28g	15	52	0.8	5.9	3.0	0.7
Tomato Cup A Soup, Batchelors*	1 Serving/212g	85	40	0.4	8.1	0.7	0.6
Tomato, Fresh Country, New Covent Garden Soup Co*	½ Pint/284ml	114	40	1.9	6.4	0.8	0.8
Tomato, Fresh, Tesco*	1 Serving/100g	44	44	0.7	5.2	2.3	0.4
Tomato In A Cup, Dry, Tesco*	1 Serving/23g	75	328	6.4	68.5	3.2	0.1
Tomato, Onion & Basil, Asda*	1 Can/400g	116	29	0.8	5.0	0.6	0.3
Tomato Rice, Campbell's*	1oz/28g	13	46	0.9	8.3	1.0	0.0
Tomato, Weight Watchers*	1 Can/295g	74	25	0.7	4.6	0.5	0.3
Vegetable	1oz/28g	15	52	0.9	3.2	4.0	0.9
Vegetable & Beef, Sainsbury's*	1 Can/400g	260	65	2.1	8.5	2.5	1.3
Vegetable & Ham, Big, Heinz*	1 Can/400g	200	50	2.9	8.7	0.4	1.0
Vegetable & Lentil, Fresh, Somerfield*	½ Pack/300g	183	61	2.7	8.4	1.9	1.5
Vegetable Broth, HE, Tesco*	1 Can/400g	148	37	1.2	7.4	0.2	1.0
Vegetable Broth, M & S*	1 Pack/213g	85	40	1.0	6.3	1.4	0.8
Vegetable, Canned	1oz/28g	13	48	1.4	9.9	0.6	1.5
Vegetable Chowder, New Covent garden Soup Co*	Half carton/300g	159	53	2.9	6.6	1.7	1.1
Vegetable Cup, Soupreme*	1 Sachet/26g	111	444	8.1	49.7	23.6	2.3
Vegetable, Extra Thick, Sainsbury's*	1 Can/400g	176	44	1.6	8.0	0.6	1.3
Vegetable, Heinz*	1 Can/400g	188	47	1.4	8.4	0.9	1.1
Vegetable In A Cup, BGTY, Sainsbury's*	1 Sachet/200g	52	26	0.5	4.4	0.8	0.9
Vegetable In A Mug, Dry, HE, Tesco*	1 Mug/18g	66	365	7.0	66.3	8.0	2.6
Vegetable, New Covent Garden Soup Co*	½ Pint/284ml	88	31	1.1	5.9	0.4	1.1
Vegetable, Safeway*	1 Can/295g	109	37	1.5	7.1	0.3	1.2
Vegetable, Sainsbury's*	1 Can/400g	184	46	1.5	8.3	0.7	1.2
Vegetable, Tesco*	½ Can/200g	88	44	1.3	9.3	0.2	1.0
Vegetable, Weight Watchers*	1 Serving/295ml	83	28	0.9	5.6	0.2	0.8
Vegetable With Chicken Broth, Covent Garden Soup Co*	1 fl oz/30ml	9	30	1.9	4.3	0.5	0.5
Vegetable With Chicken Chunky, Safeway*	1 Serving/200g	78	39	2.5	6.2	0.5	0.6
Wild Mushroom & Mascarpone, Tesco*	½ Pot/300g	219	73	1.4	2.9	6.2	1.6
Wild Mushroom, BGTY, Sainsbury's*	1 Serving/189ml	53	28	0.5	4.7	0.8	0.6
Wild Mushroom, Fresh, Tesco*	1 Serving/300g	159	53	1.3	4.7	3.2	0.3
Wild Mushroom, New Covent Garden Soup Co*	1 fl oz/30ml	15	49	1.3	3.7	3.2	0.5
SOYA,							
Chunks, Dried, Sainsbury's*	1oz/28g	27	98	14.0	9.8	0.3	1.1
Mince, Dried, Sainsbury's*	1 Serving/200g	164	82	11.8	8.3	0.2	0.9
Mince, Granules	1oz/28g	74	263	43.2	11.0	5.4	0.0
Mince, Savoury Flavoured, Nature's Harvest*	100g dry/100g	345	345	60.0	30.0	1.0	4.0
Mince, Savoury Flavoured Protein, Natures Way*	1oz/28g	97	345	60.0	35.0	1.0	4.0
Mince, Unflavoured, Nature's Harvest*	1 Serving/100g	345	345	50.0	35.0	1.0	4.0
Mince, With Onion, Sainsbury's*	½ Pack/180g	122	68	5.4	8.0	1.6	1.8
Protein Powder, Holland & Barrett*	1oz/28g	109	390	88.0	0.5	4.0	0.0

S

SOYA,	Measure WEIGHT/INFO	per Measure KCAL	KCAL	PROT	CARB	FAT	FIBRE
Vanilla, Organic, Heinz*	1 Serving/200ml	106	53	2.6	6.9	1.6	0.2
SPACE RAIDERS,							
Cheese, Space Raiders*	1 Bag/16g	76	473	7.1	61.6	22.0	3.1
Pickled Onion, Space Raiders*	1 Bag/16g	74	461	7.0	61.4	20.8	3.4
SPARE RIBS,							
American Style, Somerfield*	½ Pack/125g	303	242	18.8	15.6	11.6	1.8
Barbecue, Chinese Style, Farmfoods*	1 Pack/400g	464	116	9.3	5.6	6.3	0.1
Barbecue Style	1oz/28g	43	152	4.5	18.9	6.5	0.6
Cantonese, Sainsbury's*	1 Serving/300g	633	211	18.1	10.3	10.8	0.4
Chinese, Iceland*	1oz/28g	61	219	14.7	9.6	13.5	0.2
Spare Ribs,Chinese, Somerfield*	1oz/28g	70	251	14.0	13.0	16.0	0.0
Chinese Style, Meal Solutions, Co-Op*	1 Serving/165g	215	130	8.0	4.0	9.0	0.2
Chinese Style, Safeway*	½ Pack/285g	633	222	16.5	16.1	10.2	2.1
M & S*	1oz/28g	57	205	16.6	8.6	11.5	0.2
Mini, Ready Meals, M & S*	1oz/28g	57	205	16.6	8.6	11.5	0.2
Raw, Lean & Fat	1oz/28g	80	285	6.5	40.7	10.8	0.0
Sweet Chinese Style, Co-Op*	1 Pack/250g	553	221	13.9	15.9	11.3	0.8
SPICE BLEND,							
Balti, Sharwood's*	1oz/28g	34	122	1.8	7.1	9.6	1.2
Malay, Sharwood's*	1 Pack/260g	380	146	1.9	14.1	9.1	0.9
Thai, Sharwood's*	1 Pack 260g	424	163	1.8	12.0	11.9	1.0
Tikka, Sharwood's*	1 Pack/260g	263	101	2.7	10.2	5.4	1.7
SPICE MIX,							
Cajun Potato Wedge, Coating, Schwartz*	1 Serving/100g	163	163	3.3	26.3	5.0	0.0
Chicken Tikka Masala & Pilau Rice, Colman's*	1 Pack/85g	309	364	11.5	39.9	18.0	11.2
Chili Mix for Chilli, Schwartz*	1oz/28g	96	344	9.6	63.6	5.7	1.0
Chilli & Garlic Seed, The Food Doctor*	1 Serving/15g	88	584	30.5	3.7	49.7	11.0
Chilli Con Carne, Colman's*	1 Pack/50g	154	308	8.6	62.0	1.7	0.0
Chilli Con Carne, Hot, Schwartz*	1 Pack/41g	141	344	10.8	59.0	7.2	0.0
Green Thai Chicken Curry, Schwartz*	1 Pack/41g	137	334	11.3	67.6	3.2	0.3
Mexican Chili Potato Wedges, Schwartz*	1oz/28g	45	162	3.4	26.1	4.9	0.0
SPICED Puppodums, Sharwood's*	1oz/28g	127	455	19.6	42.1	23.0	9.3
SPINACH,							
& Carrot Pilau, Waitrose*	1oz/28g	44	158	5.8	22.9	5.8	0.0
Baby Leaf, Organic, Sainsbury's*	1 Serving/90g	23	25	2.8	1.6	0.8	2.1
Baby, Waitrose*	1 Serving/110g	28	25	2.8	1.6	0.8	2.1
Boiled In Salted Water	1oz/28g	5	19	2.2	0.8	0.8	2.1
Boiled In Unsalted Water	1oz/28g	5	19	2.2	0.8	0.8	2.1
Canned, Drained	1oz/28g	5	19	2.8	0.8	0.5	1.6
Chopped, Sainsbury's*	1 Serving/100g	22	22	3.1	0.5	0.8	2.1
Frozen, Boiled In Unsalted Water	1oz/28g	6	21	3.1	0.5	0.8	2.1
Leaf, Iceland*	1 Serving/100g	21	21	3.1	0.5	0.8	2.1
Leaf, In Brine, Tesco*	1 Can/265g	66	25	2.2	3.4	0.3	3.0
Raw	1oz/28g	7	25	2.8	1.6	0.8	2.1
Steamed, Tesco*	1oz/28g	7	25	2.8	1.6	0.8	2.1
SPIRA, Cadbury's*	2 Twists/40g	210	525	7.8	56.8	29.4	0.0
SPIRALS, Salt & Vinegar, Bobby's	1 Bag/26g	113	436	3.9	65.8	17.5	0.0
SPIRITS,							
37.5% Volume	1 Shot/25ml	48	207	0.0	0.0	0.0	0.0
40% Volume	1 Shot/25ml	51	222	0.0	0.0	0.0	0.0
SPLIT PEAS,							
Dried, Boiled In Unsalted Water	1oz/28g	35	126	8.3	22.7	0.9	2.7
Dried, Raw	1oz/28g	92	328	22.1	58.2	2.4	6.3
Yellow, Organic, Dried, Evernat*	1oz/28g	87	310	22.1	56.6	1.0	0.0

Nutrition Values per 100g / 100ml

S

SPLIT PEAS,	Measure WEIGHT/INFO	per Measure KCAL	KCAL	PROT	CARB	FAT	FIBRE
Yellow, Sainsbury's*	1 Tbsp/35g	36	104	8.3	16.9	0.3	5.1
SPONGE FINGERS,							
Boudoir, Sainsbury's*	1 Biscuit/5g	20	396	8.1	82.8	3.6	0.4
Tesco*	1 Finger/5g	19	386	7.6	80.6	3.7	1.0
SPONGE PUDDING,							
Sponge Pudding	1oz/28g	95	340	5.8	45.3	16.3	1.1
Banoffee, Heinz*	¼ Can/78g	239	307	2.8	46.6	12.2	0.6
Blackberry & Apple, HE, Tesco*	1 Serving/90g	119	132	2.8	27.5	1.2	1.3
Blackberry & Apple, Tesco*	1 Serving/90g	139	154	2.1	34.4	0.9	1.6
Blackcurrant, BGTY, Sainsbury's*	1 Serving/110g	277	252	2.8	50.0	4.5	1.4
Blackcurrant, Low Fat, Iceland*	1 Pudding/90g	159	177	2.2	39.5	1.1	1.6
Canned	1 Portion/75g	214	285	3.1	45.4	11.4	0.8
Cherry & Almond Flavour, Sainsbury's*	¼ Pudding/110g	334	304	3.5	40.3	14.3	0.7
Cherry & Chocolate, Eat Smart, Safeway*	1 Serving/86g	151	175	2.7	35.6	2.4	0.8
Chocolate & Chocolate Sauce, HE, Tesco*	1 Pudding/90g	186	207	3.9	38.7	4.1	2.1
Chocolate & Sauce, Co-Op*	1 Pack/225g	608	270	5.0	34.0	13.0	0.6
Chocolate, 5% Fat, M & S*	1oz/28g	62	221	5.9	41.1	3.6	1.5
Chocolate, Asda*	1 Pot/105g	307	292	4.9	32.0	16.0	0.0
Chocolate, BGTY, Sainsbury's*	1 Serving/110g	259	236	3.9	45.3	4.3	0.5
Chocolate Custard, Muller*	1 Pot/175g	298	170	3.2	30.2	4.0	0.0
Chocolate, Eat Smart, Safeway*	1 Pudding/88g	150	170	4.5	32.6	2.0	2.0
Chocolate, GFY, Asda*	1 Serving/115g	323	281	2.8	59.0	3.8	2.0
Chocolate, HE, Tesco*	1 Pudding/90g	184	204	4.2	45.4	0.6	1.3
Chocolate Orange, 95% Fat Free, Tesco*	1 Pudding/100g	220	220	3.8	45.2	2.7	1.1
Chocolate, Somerfield*	¼ Pudding/100g	369	369	5.0	35.0	23.0	0.0
Citrus, BGTY, Sainsbury's*	1 Pudding/110g	230	209	3.5	39.7	4.0	0.7
Fruit, Co-Op*	1 Can/300g	1110	370	3.0	53.0	16.0	2.0
Ginger, With Plum Sauce, Waitrose*	1 Pudding/120g	424	353	3.1	51.7	14.9	0.7
Golden Syrup, Co-Op*	1 Can/300g	945	315	2.0	47.0	13.0	0.6
Jam & Custard, Co-Op*	1 Pack/244g	598	245	3.0	37.0	9.0	0.3
Jam & Custard, Somerfield*	¼ Pudding/62g	143	231	3.0	38.0	8.0	0.0
Jam, M & S*	1oz/28g	87	311	3.6	51.5	10.1	1.6
Lemon Curd, Heinz*	¼ Can/78g	236	302	2.6	46.7	11.7	0.6
Lemon, M & S*	1 Pudding/105g	326	310	4.3	39.4	15.2	2.3
Lemon, Waitrose*	1 Serving/105g	212	202	3.4	41.7	2.4	1.4
Raspberry & Custard, Low Fat, Shape*	1 Pot/120g	122	102	4.3	18.2	1.3	0.2
Raspberry, Tesco*	1 Pudding/105g	257	245	3.3	33.3	10.9	1.7
Sticky Toffee, Heinz*	¼ Can/77g	235	305	3.1	45.2	12.5	0.7
Sticky Toffee, Mini, Somerfield*	1 Pudding/110g	349	349	3.0	54.0	13.0	0.0
Sticky Toffee, Somerfield*	1 Pudding/440g	1456	364	3.0	56.0	14.0	0.0
Strawberry, Co-Op*	1 Can/300g	960	320	2.0	48.0	13.0	0.8
Strawberry Jam, Heinz*	¼ Can/82g	230	281	2.6	50.4	7.6	0.6
Summer Fruit, BGTY, Sainsbury's*	1 Serving/110g	243	221	2.7	42.9	4.3	1.0
Syrup, & Custard, M & S*	1oz/28g	76	271	3.3	44.9	8.7	1.1
Syrup & Custard, Morrisons*	1 Serving/125g	290	232	3.4	39.1	6.9	0.8
Syrup, GFY, Asda*	1 Sponge/105g	256	244	3.0	50.0	3.6	0.6
Syrup, M & S*	1oz/28g	104	370	4.1	65.9	10.2	1.1
Syrup, Sainsbury's*	¼ Pudding/110g	404	371	2.7	63.5	11.8	0.4
Syrup, Somerfield*	¼ Pudding/100g	341	341	3.0	57.0	11.0	0.0
Toffee, BGTY, Sainsbury's*	1 Pudding/100g	271	271	4.1	54.3	4.1	0.4
Treacle, Heinz*	¼ Can/80g	222	277	2.3	48.7	8.2	0.5
Treacle, With Custard, Farmfoods*	1 Serving/145g	539	372	3.2	38.4	22.8	0.8
With Dried Fruit	1oz/28g	93	331	5.4	48.1	14.3	1.2
With Jam or Treacle	1oz/28g	93	333	5.1	48.7	14.4	1.0

S

	Measure	per Measure	Nutrition Values per 100g / 100ml				
SPOTTED DICK,	WEIGHT/INFO	KCAL	KCAL	PROT	CARB	FAT	FIBRE
Spotted Dick	1oz/28g	92	327	4.2	42.7	16.7	1.0
& Custard, Co-Op*	1 Serving/245g	527	215	4.0	33.0	8.0	0.7
& Custard, Sainsbury's*	1 Pack/205g	504	246	3.3	32.6	11.4	0.7
Co-Op*	1 Pudding/485g	1310	270	3.0	42.0	10.0	0.8
Heinz*	¼ Can/75g	244	325	3.3	49.8	12.5	0.9
Iceland*	1 Pudding/324g	1186	366	4.6	46.0	18.2	1.4
M & S*	1 Pudding/105g	329	313	4.7	49.7	10.6	1.2
Tryton Foods*	1oz/28g	105	374	5.6	47.5	18.0	2.0
SPRATS,							
Fried	1oz/28g	116	415	24.9	0.0	35.0	0.0
Raw	1oz/28g	48	172	18.3	0.0	11.0	0.0
SPREAD,							
63% Fat, Benecol*	1 Serving/12g	69	573	0.6	1.0	63.0	0.0
Blended, You'd Never Believe It, Co-Op*	1oz/28g	168	600	0.5	2.0	66.0	0.0
Butter, Low Fat, M & S*	Thin Spread/7g	26	374	3.5	0.0	40.0	0.0
Butter Me Up, Tesco*	Thin Spread/7g	44	631	1.0	1.5	69.0	0.0
Butter, Sunflower, Asda*	1 Serving/25g	160	638	0.9	1.2	70.0	0.0
Butterlicious, Sainsbury's*	Thin Spread/7g	44	628	0.6	1.1	69.0	0.1
Buttery Gold, Somerfield*	1 Tbsp/15g	94	627	0.5	1.0	69.0	0.0
Diet, Delight*	1oz/28g	64	228	3.6	1.6	23.0	0.0
Don't Flutter With Butter, Safeway*	Thin Spread/7g	45	636	0.4	1.0	70.0	0.0
Fat, Carapelli, St Ivel*	Thin Spread/7g	38	537	0.6	0.8	59.0	0.0
Flora Buttery, Flora*	Thin Spread/7g	45	637	1.1	0.5	70.0	0.0
Flora Diet Light, Flora*	1 Tbsp/10g	23	227	3.5	1.6	23.0	0.0
Flora Light, Flora*	1oz/28g	100	357	0.1	3.7	38.0	0.6
Flora, Low Salt, Flora*	1oz/28g	176	630	0.1	0.1	70.0	0.0
Flora Original, Flora*	1 Serving/10g	63	630	0.1	0.1	70.0	0.0
Flora Pro-Activ, Flora*	1 Serving/10g	33	328	0.1	3.2	35.0	0.3
Gold, Low Fat, St Ivel*	Thin Spread/7g	26	365	2.1	2.9	38.0	0.0
Gold, Lowest, Low Fat, St Ivel*	Thin Spread/7g	18	259	0.7	3.3	27.0	0.0
Gold, Semi Skimmed, St Ivel*	1 Serving/5g	18	359	0.9	3.3	38.0	0.0
Gold, Unsalted, Low Fat, St Ivel*	Thin Spread/7g	25	360	0.7	3.9	38.0	0.0
Golden, Light, HE, Tesco*	1 Serving/10g	35	354	1.5	1.5	38.0	0.0
Half Fat, Anchor*	1 Tsp/15g	54	363	0.1	0.8	40.0	0.0
I Can't Believe It's Not Butter*	Thin Spread/7g	44	625	0.4	0.7	69.0	0.0
Low Fat 32%, Benecol*	1 Serving/12g	36	300	2.8	0.2	32.0	0.0
Low-Fat	Thin Spread/7g	27	390	5.8	0.5	40.5	0.0
Morning Gold, Low Fat, Morrisons*	1 Tbsp/15g	56	372	7.5	0.0	38.0	0.0
Olive, BGTY, Sainsbury's*	1 Tsp/14g	50	356	2.0	1.5	38.0	0.0
Olive Gold, Reduced Fat, Co-Op*	1oz/28g	150	535	0.2	1.0	59.0	0.0
Olive Gold, With Olive Oil, Low Fat, Asda*	1 Serving/10g	54	537	0.2	1.2	59.0	0.0
Olive Light, Low Fat, BGTY, Sainsbury's*	Thin Spread/ 7g	25	356	2.0	1.5	38.0	0.0
Olive Light, Low Fat, Tesco*	1 Serving/15g	52	348	1.5	0.0	38.0	0.0
Olive, M & S*	Thin Soread/7g	38	536	0.2	1.2	59.0	0.0
Olive Oil, 55% Reduced Fat, Benecol*	Thin Spread/7g	35	498	0.3	0.5	55.0	0.0
Olive Oil, 59% Reduced Fat, Safeway*	Thin Spread/7g	37	532	0.1	0.1	59.0	0.0
Olive Oil, 59% Vegetable Fat, Olivio*	Thin Spread/7g	38	536	0.2	1.0	59.0	0.0
Olive, Organic, Reduced Fat, Sainsbury's*	Thin Spread/7g	37	531	0.0	0.0	59.0	0.0
Olive, Reduced Fat, Asda*	Thin Spread/7g	38	537	0.2	1.2	59.0	0.0
Olive, Reduced Fat, Morrisons*	Thin Spread/7g	38	537	0.9	0.0	59.3	0.3
Olive, Tesco*	1 Serving/28g	150	537	0.2	1.2	59.0	0.0
Olivio Light, Olivio*	Thin Soread/7g	34	486	0.0	0.0	55.0	0.0
Olivio, Van Den Bergh Foods Ltd*	Thin Spread/7g	38	536	0.2	1.0	59.0	0.0
Olivite, Low Fat, Weight Watchers*	Thin Spread/7g	25	351	0.0	0.2	38.9	0.0

S

SPREAD,	Measure WEIGHT/INFO	per Measure KCAL	Nutrition Values per 100g / 100ml KCAL	PROT	CARB	FAT	FIBRE
Pure Gold, GFY, Asda*	1 Serving/10g	35	353	1.7	1.0	38.0	0.0
Pure Gold, Light, 65% Less Fat, Asda*	1 Serving/10g	24	239	2.5	1.0	25.0	0.0
Soft, Economy, Sainsbury's*	1oz/28g	126	450	0.2	1.0	50.0	0.0
Sunflower, Co-Op*	Thin Spread/7g	44	635	0.2	1.0	70.0	0.0
Sunflower, Light, 38% Less Fat, Asda*	Thin Spread/7g	24	342	0.0	0.0	38.0	0.0
Sunflower Light, BGTY, Sainsbury's*	1 Serving/10g	35	352	1.0	1.5	38.0	0.0
Sunflower, Light, GFY, Asda*	1 Serving/10g	35	351	0.0	0.0	39.0	0.0
Sunflower, Light, HE, Tesco*	1 Serving/6g	21	347	0.3	1.0	38.0	0.0
Sunflower, Light, Summerlite, Aldi*	1 Serving/10g	34	344	0.2	0.3	38.0	0.0
Sunflower, Light, Tesco*	Thin Spread/7g	24	348	1.4	0.0	38.0	0.0
Sunflower, Low Fat, Somerfield*	1 Serving/10g	34	342	0.0	0.0	38.0	0.0
Sunflower, M & S*	Thin Spread/7g	44	635	0.2	1.0	70.0	0.0
Sunflower, Reduced Fat, Asda*	Thin Spread/7g	37	531	0.2	1.0	58.5	0.0
Sunflower, Sainsbury's*	Thin Spread/7g	44	631	0.2	0.1	70.0	0.1
Sunflower, Tesco*	1 Serving/15g	95	631	0.0	0.2	70.0	0.0
Sunflower, Value, Tesco*	Thin Spread/7g	31	439	0.1	0.4	48.6	0.0
Tuna & Mayonnaise, Shippam's*	1 Pot/75g	189	252	18.3	3.1	18.5	0.0
Utterly Butterly*	1 Tbsp/10g	63	630	1.0	1.5	69.0	0.0
Utterly Butterly* Scandinavian Style	1 Serving/25g	152	606	0.3	0.5	67.0	0.0
Vegetable, Dairy Free, Sainsbury's*	1 Serving/10g	63	630	0.0	0.0	70.0	3.0
Vitalite Lite, St Ivel*	Thin Spread/7g	24	348	1.5	0.0	38.0	0.0
Vitalite, St Ivel*	Thin Spread/7g	40	578	0.4	1.2	63.0	0.0
You'd Butter Believe It, Low Fat, Dairy, Asda*	1 Serving/10g	63	627	0.5	1.0	69.0	0.0
SPRING GREENS,							
Boiled In Salted Water	1oz/28g	6	20	1.9	1.6	0.7	2.6
Boiled In Unsalted Water	1oz/28g	6	20	1.9	1.6	0.7	2.6
Raw	1oz/28g	9	33	3.0	3.1	1.0	3.4
SPRING ONIONS,							
Bulbs & Tops, Raw	1oz/28g	6	23	2.0	3.0	0.5	1.5
Bulbs Only, Raw	1oz/28g	10	35	0.9	8.5	0.0	1.7
Tesco*	1 Serving/4g	1	25	2.0	3.0	0.5	1.5
SPRING ROLLS,							
Chicken & Chilli, Sainsbury's*	1 Roll/50g	93	185	9.6	15.6	9.3	2.8
Co-Op*	1oz/28g	67	240	6.0	29.0	11.0	0.4
Dim Sum, Sainsbury's*	1 Spring Roll/12g	26	216	4.1	28.2	9.6	2.9
Duck, M & S*	1oz/28g	70	250	8.7	25.2	12.9	2.1
Mini, Sainsbury's	1 Roll/12g	27	221	4.2	28.7	9.9	1.6
Prawn, Chinese, Sainsbury's*	1 Roll/30g	65	217	9.6	21.8	10.2	1.3
Prawn, M & S*	1oz/28g	62	220	9.4	21.4	10.8	1.6
Prawn, Tesco*	1 Spring Roll/33g	61	186	10.8	21.5	6.3	1.4
M & S*	1 Packet/180g	333	185	3.5	24.2	8.4	2.3
Vegetable, Chinese, Sainsbury's*	1 Roll/26g	69	193	4.1	26.9	7.7	1.4
Vegetable, Chinese Takeaway, Sainsbury's*	1Roll/59g	100	170	4.0	24.4	6.3	2.8
Vegetable, Mini, Occasions, Sainsbury's*	per roll/24g	52	216	4.1	28.2	9.6	2.9
Vegetable, Mini, Party Food, M & S*	1 Spring Roll/17g	35	205	3.5	26.3	9.7	2.0
Vegetable, Tempura, M & S*	1 Pack/140g	280	200	2.8	27.9	8.6	1.8
Vegetable, Tesco*	1 Roll/60g	100	166	4.0	21.2	7.2	2.0
Vegetable, Waitrose*	1 spring roll/57g	107	187	3.7	22.1	9.3	3.4
SQUARES,							
Rice Krispies, Chocolate Caramel, Kelloggs*	1 Bar/21g	90	430	4.5	74.0	13.0	0.5
Rice Krispies, Chocolate, Kellogg's*	1 Bar/18g	74	410	4.5	76.0	10.0	1.5
SQUASH,							
Acorn, Baked	1oz/28g	16	56	1.1	12.6	0.1	3.2
Acorn, Raw	1oz/28g	11	40	0.8	9.0	0.1	2.3

S

	Measure WEIGHT/INFO	per Measure KCAL	KCAL	PROT	CARB	FAT	FIBRE
SQUASH,							
Apple & Blackcurrant, No Added Sugar, Somerfield*	1fl oz/30ml	2	8	0.1	0.5	0.0	0.0
Apple & Blackcurrant, Tesco*	1 Glass/250ml	13	5	0.1	1.0	0.0	0.0
Apple & Strawberry High Juice, Sainsbury's*	1 Serving/250ml	83	33	0.1	8.2	0.1	0.1
Apple, Hi Juice, Tesco*	1fl oz/30ml	53	176	0.3	42.7	0.1	0.0
Blackcurrant High Juice, M & S*	1 Glass/250ml	50	20	0.1	5.2	0.0	0.1
Butternut, Baked	1oz/28g	9	32	0.9	7.4	0.1	1.4
Butternut, Raw	1oz/28g	10	36	1.1	8.3	0.1	1.6
Fruit & Barley Orange, Robinson's*	1 Av Serving/50ml	8	16	0.3	2.6	0.0	0.0
Lemon, High Juice, Sainsbury's*	1 Glass/250ml	98	39	0.1	9.1	0.1	0.1
Lemon, Whole, Low Sugar, Sainsbury's*	1 Glass/250ml	5	2	0.1	0.2	0.1	0.1
Mixed Fruit, Low Sugar, Sainsbury's*	1 Glass/250ml	5	2	0.1	0.2	0.1	0.1
Orange & Mango, Low Sugar, Sainsbury's*	1 Serving/250ml	5	2	0.1	0.2	0.1	0.1
Orange & Pineapple, No Added Sugar, Asda*	1 Serving/55ml	5	9	0.2	0.9	0.0	0.1
Orange, Hi Juice, Tesco*	1 Serving/75ml	140	187	0.3	45.0	0.1	0.0
Orange, Lemon & Pineapple, Low Sugar, Sainsbury's*	1fl oz/30ml	0	1	0.1	0.1	0.1	0.1
Orange, No Added Sugar, Asda*	1fl oz/30ml	2	7	0.0	0.6	0.0	0.0
Orange, Original, Robinson's*	1fl oz/30ml	14	45	0.1	10.0	0.0	0.0
Peach, High Juice, Robinson's*	1fl oz/30ml	54	180	0.5	43.1	0.1	0.0
Pineapple, High Juice, Tesco*	1 Serving/75ml	152	203	0.2	49.1	0.1	0.0
Pink Grapefruit, Fruit & Barley, Robinson's*	1fl oz/30ml	5	15	0.3	2.1	0.0	0.0
Pink Grapefruit High Juice, Robinson's*	1 Glass/250ml	455	182	0.2	43.3	0.1	0.0
Spaghetti, Baked	1oz/28g	6	23	0.7	4.3	0.3	2.1
Spaghetti, Raw	1oz/28g	7	26	0.6	4.6	0.6	2.3
Summer Fruits, High Juice, Robinson's*	1fl oz/30ml	61	203	0.1	49.0	0.1	0.0
Tropical Fruits, High Juice Sainsbury's*	1 Serving/250ml	95	38	0.1	9.3	0.1	0.1
Whole Orange, No Added Sugar, Tesco*	1fl oz/30ml	2	7	0.1	0.6	0.0	0.0
Whole Orange, Tesco*	1 Serving/100ml	45	45	0.2	10.1	1.0	1.0
SQUEELINGLY Fizzy Pigs, M & S*	1 Sweet/5g	17	330	4.8	77.0	0.0	0.0
SQUID,							
Dried	1oz/28g	88	313	63.3	4.8	4.6	0.0
in Batter, Fried In Blended Oil	1oz/28g	55	195	11.5	15.7	10.0	0.5
Prepared, Asda*	1oz/28g	23	82	15.4	1.2	1.7	0.0
Raw	1oz/28g	23	81	15.4	1.2	1.7	0.0
Rings, Asda*	1oz/28g	23	81	15.4	1.2	1.7	0.0
STARBAR, Cadbury's*	1 Bar/53g	286	540	9.1	55.0	31.6	0.0
STARBURST							
Joosters, Mars*	1 Pack/45g	160	356	0.0	88.8	0.1	0.0
Juicy Gums, Mars*	1 Pack/45g	139	309	5.9	71.0	4.1	0.0
Mars*	1 Pack/45g	185	411	0.3	85.3	7.6	0.0
Smilers, Mars*	1 Pack/50g	160	319	3.9	75.8	0.0	0.0
Tropical Fruit Chews, Mars*	1 Tube/45g	168	373	0.0	76.9	7.3	0.0
STARS,							
Chicken Flavour, HE, Tesco*	1 Serving/12g	43	357	5.1	81.0	1.4	3.4
Spicy, COU, M & S*	1 Bag/20g	69	345	4.2	82.6	1.6	4.0
STEAK & KIDNEY PUDDING,							
Fray Bentos*	1 Tin/213g	477	224	7.8	19.8	12.6	0.0
M & S*	1 Pudding/100g	215	215	10.5	18.1	11.3	1.0
STEAK &, Vegetable Medley, HE, Tesco*	1 Pack/400g	264	66	7.6	5.3	1.6	0.8
STEAK Chasseur, HE, Tesco*	1 Pack/450g	347	77	10.0	5.3	1.8	0.5
STEAK In Creamy Green Peppercorn Sauce, M & S*	½ Pack/200g	260	130	16.2	2.9	6.0	0.5
STEAMED PUDDING,							
Apple With Wild Berry Sauce, BGTY, Sainsburys*	1 Pudding/110g	308	280	2.6	59.7	3.4	1.4
Chocolate, BGTY, Sainsbury's*	1 Pudding/110g	308	280	3.0	59.0	3.6	1.8
Chocolate Fudge, Aunty's*	1 Pudding/110g	314	285	3.0	59.0	4.2	1.8

Nutrition Values per 100g / 100ml (KCAL, PROT, CARB, FAT, FIBRE)

S

	Measure WEIGHT/INFO	per Measure KCAL	Nutrition Values per 100g / 100ml KCAL	PROT	CARB	FAT	FIBRE
STEAMED PUDDING,							
Golden Syrup, Aunty's*	1 Pudding/110g	366	333	2.6	69.0	5.0	2.3
STEW,							
Beef & Dumplings, Asda*	1 Pack/400g	392	98	6.0	11.0	3.3	0.8
Beef & Dumplings, Eat Smart, Safeway*	1 Pack/394g	335	85	8.1	6.8	2.5	1.1
Beef & Dumplings, HE, Tesco*	1 Pack/450g	495	110	6.0	12.5	4.0	0.9
Beef & Dumplings, Ready Meals, Waitrose*	1oz/28g	38	136	8.0	13.3	5.6	0.8
Beef & Dumplings, Traditional English Meals, Bird's Eye*	1 Pack/338g	355	105	6.7	11.5	3.6	0.0
Beef & Dumplings, Weight Watchers*	1 Pack/327g	262	80	5.2	10.0	2.1	0.8
Beef, Asda*	½ Can/196g	178	91	10.0	7.0	2.5	1.5
Beef With Dumplings, Classic British, Sainsbury's*	1 Pack/450g	531	118	7.7	10.2	5.2	0.5
Beef With Dumplings, COU, M & S*	1 Pack/454g	431	95	8.9	9.1	2.6	0.8
Beef With Dumplings, Tesco*	½ Pack/360g	641	178	5.7	14.0	12.1	0.8
Chicken & Dumplings, Tesco*	1 Serving/300g	402	134	7.4	11.0	6.7	0.6
Chicken, Morrisons*	1 Pack/400g	492	123	17.6	8.9	1.9	0.5
Irish, Asda Smartprice*	1 tin/392g	298	76	3.0	8.0	3.6	0.9
Irish, Plumrose*	1 Tin/392g	318	81	7.5	7.2	2.5	0.0
Mixed Vegetable Topped With Herb Dumplings, Tesco*	1 Pack/420g	508	121	1.9	14.5	6.2	1.3
Vegetable & Dumplings, Linda McCartney*	1 Pack/340g	384	113	2.5	13.7	1.8	0.5
STIR FRY,							
Beansprout & Vegetable, Tesco*	1 Serving/150g	47	31	2.1	4.8	0.4	1.9
Beansprout, Sainsbury's*	1 Pack/300g	144	48	1.9	5.1	2.8	1.5
Beansprouts & Vegetables, Asda*	½ Pack/173g	107	62	2.0	4.5	4.0	1.8
Beansprouts, Asda*	½ Pack/175g	56	32	2.9	4.0	0.5	1.5
Beansprouts, Safeway*	½ Pack/150g	83	55	2.3	4.4	3.1	1.9
Beef, BGTY, Sainsbury's*	½ Pack/125g	156	125	22.0	0.1	4.1	0.0
Beef, Less Than 10% Fat, Asda*	1 Pack/227g	275	121	24.0	0.0	2.8	0.8
Cantonese Style Egg Fried Noodles, Sainsbury's*	¼ Pack/107g	110	104	3.4	10.7	5.3	1.1
Chinese Bean Sprout, Sainsbury's*	½ Pack/313g	150	48	1.9	5.1	2.8	1.5
Chinese Chicken, Iceland*	1 Pack/298g	262	88	6.2	12.7	1.4	2.9
Chinese Chop Suey Veg, Sharwood's*	1 Pack/310g	223	72	1.5	13.9	1.1	0.6
Chinese Exotic Vegetable, Sainsbury's*	1 Pack/350g	133	38	1.7	2.8	2.2	1.8
Chinese Mixed Vegetable, Sainsbury's*	1 Serving/150g	75	50	1.7	4.7	2.7	0.0
Chinese Noodles, Oriental Express*	1oz/28g	20	70	2.7	14.7	0.5	1.4
Chinese Prawn, Asda*	1 Serving/375g	345	92	3.6	18.0	0.6	1.8
Chinese Prawn, Farmfoods*	1oz/28g	31	110	4.1	20.3	1.4	2.7
Chinese Style, Asda*	1oz/28g	19	68	1.7	4.1	5.0	0.0
Chinese Style, Co-Op*	1 Pack/300g	105	35	3.0	6.0	0.4	2.0
Chinese Style, M & S*	1oz/28g	7	25	2.5	3.6	0.4	1.5
Chinese Vegetables, Tesco*	1 Serving/175g	93	53	1.6	10.8	0.4	1.3
Exotic, Tesco*	1 Pack/191g	42	22	1.3	3.8	0.2	1.5
Green Vegetable, M & S*	1 Pack/220g	165	75	3.1	2.5	5.9	2.2
Imperial Noodles, Fresh, Amoy*	1oz/28g	31	112	1.6	17.0	4.4	0.0
Lamb Strips, Tesco*	1 Serving/200g	212	106	13.9	6.8	2.6	0.8
Lime, Honey & Ginger Vegetables, Sharwood's*	1 Pack/345g	235	68	0.7	16.0	0.1	0.1
Mixed Vegetables, Asda*	1oz/28g	7	26	1.1	3.1	1.0	2.6
Mixed Vegetables, Sainsbury's*	½ Pack/140g	70	50	1.7	7.7	2.7	3.0
Mushroom & Vegetables, Asda*	1oz/28g	19	68	2.2	3.8	4.9	0.0
Mushroom, M & S*	1 Pack/500g	150	30	3.0	3.1	0.5	1.4
Mushroom, Safeway*	1 Pack/500g	315	63	2.6	4.2	4.0	1.7
Mushroom, Sainsbury's*	1 Serving/175g	67	38	1.7	4.0	2.4	1.7
Mushroom, Somerfield*	1 Pack/350g	109	31	3.0	5.0	0.0	0.0
Mushroom, Tesco*	1 Pack/350g	102	29	2.4	4.0	0.4	1.7
Noodles, Sainsbury's*	1 Pack/300g	555	185	6.0	31.0	4.8	1.5
Oriental Style Pak Choi, M & S*	1 Pack/220g	165	75	2.2	3.5	5.7	2.4

S

STIR FRY,	Measure WEIGHT/INFO	per Measure KCAL	Nutrition Values per 100g / 100ml KCAL	PROT	CARB	FAT	FIBRE
Oriental Style Vegetables, Sainsbury's*	1oz/28g	17	62	1.5	5.2	3.9	1.5
Oriental Vegetables, Frozen, Asda*	1 Serving/150g	116	77	2.1	7.0	4.5	1.7
Oriental Vegetables, Safeway*	1 Serving/175g	196	112	2.6	15.5	4.4	0.5
Plum Hoisin Noodle, Tesco*	1 Carton/400g	392	98	3.6	17.5	1.5	1.8
Pork, BGTY, Sainsbury's*	¼ Pack/113g	104	92	21.4	0.1	0.7	0.1
Pork, HE, Tesco*	1 Serving/150g	152	101	21.7	0.0	1.6	0.0
Pork Strips, Asda*	1oz/28g	57	203	35.0	0.0	7.0	0.0
Quorn, Spicy Chilli With Vegetables & Rice, Quorn*	½ Pack/170g	162	95	5.9	15.6	1.0	1.8
Singaporean Noodle, Sainsbury's*	½ Pack/160g	202	126	3.2	11.9	7.3	2.4
Spicy Oriental Vegetable, Sainsbury's*	½ Pack/175g	112	64	1.3	4.9	4.4	1.7
Sweet & Sour, M & S*	1oz/28g	19	68	1.1	15.2	0.3	0.5
Sweet & Sour Vegetable, Somerfield*	1 Pack/350g	249	71	2.0	14.0	1.0	0.0
Sweet Pepper, M & S*	1 Pack/400g	160	40	2.3	3.5	1.8	0.6
Szechuan Spicy Oriental Vegetable, Sainsbury's*	1 Pack/350g	224	64	1.3	4.9	4.4	1.7
Stir Fry,Thai Style, M & S*	1 Serving/150g	75	50	2.3	3.0	3.0	1.2
Turkey Breast Strips, HE, Tesco*	1 Serving/175g	180	103	23.2	0.0	1.1	0.0
Vegetable & Noodle, Tesco*	1 Pack/300g	243	81	3.5	13.2	1.6	2.1
Vegetable & Sprouting Beans, Waitrose*	1 Pack/300g	213	71	4.8	10.4	1.1	2.7
Vegetable, Asda*	½ Pack/250g	178	71	1.7	4.9	5.0	1.7
Vegetable Mix, Fried In Vegetable Oil	1oz/28g	18	64	2.0	6.4	3.6	0.0
Vegetable Noodles, BGTY, Sainsbury's*	1 Pack/455g	391	86	3.2	14.0	2.0	1.4
Vegetable, Premium, Sainsbury's*	½ Pack/150g	90	60	2.8	4.2	3.5	2.7
Vegetable, Safeway*	½ Pack/150g	68	45	1.1	3.2	3.1	1.6
Vegetable, Tesco*	1 Pack/300g	90	30	1.7	4.9	0.4	2.1
Vegetables & Beansprout, M & S*	1 Pack/350g	105	30	1.8	4.6	0.4	2.0
Vegetables, Amoy*	1 Can/250g	30	12	1.0	2.1	0.0	2.7
Vegetables, Asda*	1oz/28g	7	26	1.1	3.1	1.0	2.6
Vegetables, Cantonese Style, Tesco*	1 Serving/125g	40	32	2.0	4.1	0.9	1.4
Vegetables, Family Pack, Co-Op*	½ Pack/300g	90	30	2.0	5.0	0.4	5.0
Vegetables, Somerfield*	1 Pack/300g	93	31	2.0	5.0	0.0	0.0
Vegetables, Tesco*	1oz/28g	8	27	1.7	4.4	0.3	1.9
Rice Noodles, Blue Dragon*	1 Serving/100g	372	372	7.0	86.0	0.0	0.0
STOCK,							
Fish, Fresh, Finest, Tesco*	1 Serving/100g	10	10	0.6	1.8	0.0	0.5
Fresh, Finest, Tesco*	1 Pot/300g	33	11	1.9	0.8	0.0	0.2
STOCK CUBES,							
Beef, Bovril*	1 Cube/7g	12	173	9.1	24.8	4.1	0.0
Beef, Knorr*	1 Cube/10g	33	326	11.1	21.0	22.0	0.2
Beef, Oxo*	1 Cube/10g	27	265	17.3	38.4	4.7	1.5
Chicken	1 Cube/6g	14	237	15.4	9.9	15.4	0.0
Chicken, Just Bouillon, Kallo*	1 Cube/12g	30	247	11.8	26.1	10.6	1.0
Chicken, Knorr*	1 Cube/10g	30	301	10.1	23.6	18.5	0.2
Chicken, Oxo*	1 Cube/6g	15	243	15.6	36.6	3.4	1.4
Chinese, Oxo*	1 Cube/6g	16	263	11.0	40.9	6.1	3.6
Fish, Knorr*	1 Cube/10g	32	321	18.9	15.9	20.2	0.7
Garlic, Oxo*	1 Cube/6g	18	298	13.4	48.5	5.5	3.6
Ham, Knorr*	1 Cube/10g	31	313	11.8	24.4	18.7	0.0
Indian, Oxo*	1 Cube/6g	17	291	11.5	43.9	7.7	6.7
Italian, Oxo*	1 Cube/6g	19	309	11.9	48.9	7.3	4.6
Lamb, Knorr*	1 Cube/10g	30	301	14.7	12.9	21.2	0.2
Mexican, Oxo*	1 Cube/6g	15	248	11.8	36.8	6.0	3.7
Original, Oxo*	1 Cube/6g	16	265	17.3	38.4	4.7	1.5
Vegetable	1 Cube/7g	18	253	13.5	11.6	17.3	0.0
Vegetable, Knorr*	1 Pack/80g	246	308	11.9	21.7	19.3	1.3

S

	Measure WEIGHT/INFO	per Measure KCAL	Nutrition Values per 100g / 100ml KCAL	PROT	CARB	FAT	FIBRE
STOCK CUBES,							
Vegetable, Oxo*	1 Cube/6g	15	253	11.2	41.9	4.5	1.7
STRAWBERRIES,							
Fresh, Raw	1oz/28g	8	27	0.8	6.0	0.1	1.1
In Apple Juice, Safeway*	1 Serving/145g	73	50	0.4	12.0	0.0	1.0
In Fruit Juice, Asda*	½ Can/206g	103	50	0.4	12.0	0.0	0.7
In Grape Juice, Tesco*	1 Serving/100g	43	43	0.5	11.0	0.0	0.9
In Light Syrup, Sainsbury's*	1oz/28g	17	62	0.4	15.0	0.1	1.0
Scottish, Safeway*	1oz/28g	8	28	0.8	6.0	0.1	0.0
Tesco*	1 Serving/227g	64	28	0.8	6.0	0.1	1.1
STRAWBERRY LACES,							
Co-Op*	1 Sweet/6g	21	345	7.0	79.0	0.0	1.0
Somerfield*	1 Pack/100g	374	374	3.0	86.0	0.0	0.0
STREAKY STRIPS, Meat Free, Morningstar Farms*	1 Strip/8g	28	348	11.5	13.4	27.6	3.9
STREUSEL, Baked Apple & Plum, HE, Tesco*	1 Serving/120g	161	134	1.9	29.4	1.0	2.0
STROGANOFF,							
Beef, Finest, Tesco*	1 Pack/200g	200	100	13.4	3.9	3.4	0.0
Beef, With Mixed Rice, Tesco*	1 Pack/450g	558	124	7.5	15.2	3.7	1.5
Chicken & Mushroom, COU, M & S*	1 Pack/400g	380	95	8.8	10.3	2.0	2.0
Mushroom, BGTY, Sainsbury's*	1 Pack/450g	545	121	2.7	19.4	3.6	0.4
Mushroom With Rice, Eat Smart, Safeway*	1 Pack/400g	280	70	2.7	11.3	1.3	1.6
Mushroom With Rice, Tesco*	1 Pack/450g	500	111	3.0	12.8	5.3	1.3
Pork With Rice, HE, Tesco*	1 Pack/450g	482	107	7.0	15.8	1.8	0.5
STRUDEL,							
Apple & Mincemeat, Tesco*	1 Serving/100g	322	322	3.3	39.6	16.7	2.0
Apple, Co-Op*	1 Slice/100g	225	225	3.0	28.0	12.0	3.0
Apple, Sainsbury's*	1/6 Portion/90g	269	299	3.6	36.4	15.4	1.9
Summer Fruit, Co-Op*	1/6 Strudel/100g	225	225	3.0	29.0	11.0	3.0
Woodland Fruit, Iceland*	1 Serving/150g	387	258	3.2	33.0	12.6	1.8
Woodland Fruit, Tesco*	1 Serving/100g	257	257	3.2	31.5	13.1	1.8
STUFFING,							
Chestnut & Pork, M & S*	1oz/28g	67	240	6.6	16.3	16.7	2.9
Luxury Apricot, Sultana & Amaretto, Somerfield*	1 Pack/150g	557	371	7.0	61.0	10.0	0.0
Luxury Vine Fruit, Port & Cranberry, Somerfield*	1 Pack/150g	489	326	7.0	68.0	1.0	0.0
Parsley & Thyme, Co-Op*	1 Serving/28g	95	340	10.0	67.0	3.0	6.0
Sage & Onion, Balls, Aunt Bessie's*	1 Stuffing Ball/26g	56	214	7.5	29.6	7.3	2.4
Sage & Onion, Somerfield*	1oz/28g	100	358	6.0	74.0	5.0	0.0
STUFFING MIX,							
Chestnut & Cranberry, Celebration, Paxo*	1 Serving/25g	35	141	4.0	26.7	2.0	2.4
Date, Walnut & Stilton, Special Recipe, Sainsbury's*	1 Serving/25g	49	196	5.2	25.0	8.4	2.0
Dried, Made Up	1oz/28g	27	97	2.8	19.3	1.5	1.3
Parsley, Thyme & Lemon, Sainsbury's*	1 Pack/170g	240	141	4.2	28.2	1.3	1.3
Sage & Onion, Asda*	1 Serving/27g	29	107	3.4	22.0	0.6	1.3
Sage & Onion, Paxo*,	1 Serving/60g	90	150	4.5	27.1	2.6	2.4
Sage & Onion, SmartPrice, Asda*	¼ Pack/75g	262	349	11.0	68.0	3.7	4.7
Sage & Onion, Tesco*	1 Pack/85g	295	347	11.3	71.0	2.0	4.4
SUET,							
Beef, Tesco*	1 Serving/100g	854	854	0.6	6.2	91.9	0.1
Pudding	1oz/28g	94	335	4.4	40.5	18.3	0.9
Shredded Vegetable, Atora Light*	1oz/28g	197	704	3.8	28.5	63.9	1.2
Vegetable	1oz/28g	234	836	1.2	10.1	87.9	0.0
SUGAR,							
Dark Brown Muscovado, Waitrose*	1 Tsp/7g	25	360	0.0	90.0	0.0	0.0
Demerara, Tesco*	1 Tsp/5g	17	339	0.5	99.3	0.0	0.0
For Making Jam, Silver Spoon*	1oz/28g	111	398	0.0	99.5	0.0	0.0

S

	Measure WEIGHT/INFO	per Measure KCAL	KCAL	PROT	CARB	FAT	FIBRE
			Nutrition Values per 100g / 100ml				
SUGAR,							
Granulated, Morrisons*	1 Tsp/5g	20	394	0.0	99.9	0.0	0.0
Granulated, Silver Spoon*	1 Tsp/4g	16	400	0.0	100.0	0.0	0.0
Half Spoon Granuated, With Sweetners, Silver Spoon*	1 Tsp/5g	20	398	0.0	99.5	0.0	0.0
Icing	1 Tsp/4g	16	393	0.0	104.9	0.0	0.0
Light Brown, Soft, Silver Spoon*	1 Serving/2g	8	386	0.1	96.4	0.0	0.0
Light Muscovado, Sainsbury's*	1oz/28g	108	384	0.1	96.0	0.0	0.0
Organic, M & S*	1 Tsp/4g	16	394	0.0	99.9	0.0	0.0
White	1 Tsp/4g	16	394	0.0	105.0	0.0	0.0
SULTANAS,							
Sultanas	1oz/28g	77	275	2.7	69.4	0.4	2.0
Australian, Waitrose*	1oz/28g	82	292	2.7	69.4	0.4	2.0
Dried, M & S*	1oz/28g	87	309	2.4	73.1	0.8	5.7
Homebaker, Safeway*	1oz/28g	82	292	2.7	69.4	0.4	2.0
Organic, Waitrose*	1oz/28g	82	292	2.7	69.4	0.4	2.0
Sainsbury's*	1 Serving/30g	88	292	2.7	69.4	0.4	2.0
Somerfield*	1oz/28g	82	292	3.0	69.0	0.0	0.0
Sun Dried, Organic, Crazy Jack*	1 Serving/100g	292	292	2.7	69.4	0.4	0.0
SUMMER FRUITS,							
Frozen, Asda*	1 Serving/100g	28	28	0.9	6.0	0.0	2.5
Frozen, Sainsbury's*	1 Serving/80g	26	33	0.9	7.4	0.1	2.4
In Syrup, Sainsbury's*	1 Pudding/289g	188	65	0.5	15.6	0.1	1.2
Mix, Sainsbury's*	1 Serving/80g	26	32	0.9	7.4	0.0	2.4
Mix, M & S*	1oz/28g	9	33	1.0	6.7	0.3	2.5
Shearway*	1oz/28g	10	34	0.9	6.9	0.1	0.0
SUNDAE,							
Butter Toffee, Mini, Eat Smart, Safeway*	1 Sundae/63g	101	160	2.9	32.5	1.8	3.7
Chocolate & Orange, Weight Watchers*	1 Pot/102g	137	134	1.2	25.2	2.2	0.2
Chocolate Brownie, Tesco Finest*	1 Serving/215g	808	376	3.1	30.1	27.0	0.4
Chocolate, COU, M & S*	1 Serving/100g	190	190	4.3	35.7	3.1	1.1
Chocolate, COU, M & S*	1 Pot/119g	190	160	3.7	30.7	2.7	0.9
Chocolate, Eat Smart, Safeway*	1 Serving/97g	150	155	3.5	29.0	2.7	4.3
Chocolate, HE, Tesco*	1 Serving/130g	199	153	4.5	24.9	3.9	0.6
Chocolate, Individual, M & S*	1oz/28g	69	247	4.1	28.5	12.9	0.6
Chocolate, M & S*	1oz/28g	80	285	3.1	27.2	18.2	0.0
Chocolate Mint, COU, M & S*	1 Pot/90g	108	120	5.4	17.8	2.6	0.5
Chocolate Nut	1 Portion/70g	195	278	3.0	34.2	15.3	0.1
Chocolate Sensation, Go Ahead, McVitie's*	1 Pot/80g	144	180	5.0	32.4	3.4	1.8
Citrus Sensation, Go Ahead, McVitie's*	1 Serving/80g	138	172	4.4	32.9	2.6	1.0
Hot Caramel, McDonald's*	1 Sundae/189g	357	189	3.8	33.9	4.4	0.0
Hot Fudge, McDonald's*	1 Sundae/187g	352	188	4.5	30.0	5.7	0.0
No Topping, McDonald's*	1 Sundae/149g	219	147	4.2	21.6	5.1	0.0
Peach & Apricot, Perfectly Balanced, Waitrose*	1 Pot/175ml	142	81	1.7	17.7	0.4	0.0
Raspberry, Mini, Eat Smart, Safeway*	1 Sundae/100g	95	95	1.9	19.0	1.2	2.4
Raspberry, Perfectly Balanced, Waitrose*	1 Pot/175ml	151	86	1.7	18.9	0.6	0.0
Strawberry & Vanilla, Weight Watchers*	1 Pot/105g	148	141	1.2	29.1	2.1	0.3
Strawberry Cream, Tesco*	1 Pot/130g	307	236	2.5	16.9	17.6	0.3
Strawberry, M & S*	1 Sundae/45g	173	385	3.4	53.3	17.8	1.0
Strawberry, McDonald's*	1 Sundae/186g	296	159	3.4	27.5	4.1	0.0
Toffee Fudge, HE, Tesco*	1 Serving/100g	172	172	4.0	30.6	3.7	0.2
Tropical, COU, M & S*	1oz/28g	34	120	2.6	21.9	1.9	3.3
SUNFLOWER & Sesame Roast, Granose*	1oz/28g	121	432	20.6	32.4	27.2	0.0
SUNFLOWER SEEDS,							
Sunflower Seeds	1 Tbsp/14g	81	581	19.8	18.6	47.5	6.0
Evernat*	1oz/28g	171	609	26.8	6.3	52.9	6.1

S

	Measure WEIGHT/INFO	per Measure KCAL	KCAL	PROT	CARB	FAT	FIBRE
			Nutrition Values per 100g / 100ml				
SUNNY DELIGHT*							
Sunny Delight*	1 Glass/200ml	88	44	0.1	10.0	0.2	0.0
Apple & Kiwi Kick	1 Glass/200ml	15	7	0.2	1.3	0.2	0.2
Light	1 Glass/200ml	16	8	0.1	1.0	0.2	0.0
Tropical Tornade	1fl oz/30ml	3	10	0.1	1.5	0.2	0.1
SUPERNOODLES,							
Curry, Mild, Batchelors*	1oz/28g	134	480	10.0	63.6	20.7	3.2
Tomato & Herbs, Italian, Batchelors*	1oz/28g	134	479	10.0	63.7	20.7	3.3
Vindaloo Flavour, Batchelors*	1 Pack/105g	465	443	7.0	64.9	17.3	1.9
SUSHI,							
Advent, Medium, Tesco*	1 Serving/210g	307	146	3.8	25.7	3.1	0.9
California Roll Box, M & S*	1 Box/230g	391	170	7.0	22.0	5.2	1.1
Fish Medium Box, M & S*	1 Serving/100g	285	285	13.3	39.8	8.1	1.4
Fish Nigiri, Adventurous, Tesco*	1 Med Pack/200g	270	135	7.1	21.7	2.2	0.5
Fish Selection Box, M & S*	1 Serving/220g	396	180	6.6	27.1	4.5	0.9
Fish, Tesco*	1 Serving/290g	423	146	4.9	25.8	2.6	0.8
GFY, Asda*	1 Pack/220g	352	160	4.9	32.0	1.4	0.0
Hana Set, Waitrose*	1 Serving/175g	324	185	5.4	35.7	2.3	1.4
Komachi Set, Waitrose*	1 Box/235g	425	181	6.1	31.3	3.5	1.4
Large, Boots*	1 Pack/324g	480	148	5.0	28.0	1.8	0.7
Large Box, Food To Go, M & S*	1oz/28g	41	145	5.1	27.4	1.5	0.5
Maki Selection, Shapers, Boots*	1 Pack/158g	225	142	3.5	29.0	1.3	1.1
Medium Box, M & S*	1 Serving/215g	366	170	9.7	24.3	2.8	0.9
Mini, Boots	1 Serving/182g	269	148	4.2	29.0	1.7	1.2
Nigiri, M & S*	1 Serving/190g	285	150	5.2	25.7	2.5	0.9
Oriental Fish Box, M & S*	1 Box/205g	318	155	6.1	23.3	4.1	0.9
Prawn Feast, M & S*	1 Box/219g	350	160	5.7	25.8	3.7	1.1
Selection, Boots*	1 Pack/268g	434	162	5.5	27.0	3.6	1.6
Taiko Vegetable Set, Waitrose*	1 Serving/135g	254	188	4.4	37.1	2.4	1.4
Tesco*	1 Pack/195g	285	146	5.1	25.9	2.3	0.7
Trial Pack, Asda*	1 Pack/115g	186	162	4.1	31.0	2.4	0.0
Vegetarian, M & S*	1 Pack/223g	290	130	4.1	25.5	1.5	1.3
Vegetarian, Tesco*	1 Pack/132g	185	140	3.1	27.2	2.1	0.9
SWEDE & CARROT,							
Cubes, Sainsbury's*	1 Serving/250g	43	17	0.4	3.5	0.2	1.5
For Mashing, Safeway*	½ Pack/250g	43	17	0.4	3.3	0.2	1.4
For Mashing, Tesco*	1 Serving/100g	28	28	0.7	5.5	0.4	2.1
Mash, Asda*	1 Serving/150g	107	71	1.3	10.0	2.9	1.7
Mix, Tesco*	1 Serving/75g	23	30	0.7	6.2	0.3	2.2
SWEDE,							
Boiled In Salted Water	1oz/28g	3	11	0.3	2.3	0.1	0.7
Boiled In Unsalted Water	1oz/28g	3	11	0.3	2.3	0.1	0.7
Mash, COU, M & S*	1oz/28g	15	55	1.1	9.5	1.2	2.1
Raw	1oz/28g	7	24	0.7	5.0	0.3	1.9
SWEET & SOUR,							
Beef, Feeling Great, Findus*	1 Pack/350g	385	110	4.0	19.0	2.0	1.5
Chicken & Egg Fried Rice, BGTY, Sainsbury's*	1 Pack/450g	612	136	7.0	19.2	3.5	0.6
Chicken & Noodles, Chinese Takeaway, Tesco*	1 Pack/350g	350	100	5.7	18.8	0.2	0.2
Chicken & Rice, Mega Value, Tesco*	1 Pack/500g	675	135	4.4	25.0	1.9	1.9
Chicken, Asda*	1oz/28g	28	99	9.2	14.5	0.5	1.4
Chicken, Battered, Tesco*	1 Serving/100g	149	149	7.7	22.1	3.3	0.9
Chicken Cantonese, Sainsbury's*	1 Pack/350g	368	105	10.4	14.6	0.6	0.6
Chicken, Chinese Takeaway, Sainsbury's*	1 Pack/264g	515	195	13.1	21.3	6.4	1.0
Chicken, COU, M & S*	1oz/28g	34	120	6.9	20.5	0.9	0.9
Chicken, Crispy, Iceland*	1 Serving/125g	221	177	18.3	14.2	5.2	1.2

SWEET & SOUR,	Measure WEIGHT/INFO	per Measure KCAL	Nutrition Values per 100g / 100ml KCAL	PROT	CARB	FAT	FIBRE
Chicken, GFY, Asda*	1 Serving/165g	213	129	16.0	15.0	0.5	1.6
Chicken, Healthy Choice, Safeway*	1 Pack/400g	580	145	6.5	25.6	1.8	1.4
Chicken In Crispy Batter, Cantonese, Sainsbury's*	1 Pack/300g	546	182	9.0	21.4	6.7	1.1
Chicken, Low Fat, Iceland*	1 Pack/400g	444	111	8.1	15.7	1.7	1.1
Chicken, Take It Away, M & S*	1 Pack/200g	200	100	9.4	13.2	0.8	1.2
Chicken, Tesco*	1 Can/392g	341	87	6.4	13.3	0.9	0.4
Chicken, Weight Watchers*	1 Pack/320g	304	95	5.2	17.4	0.4	0.3
Chicken With Noodles, HE, Tesco*	1 Pack/350g	277	79	8.3	10.4	0.4	0.8
Chicken With Noodles, Tesco*	1 Pack/350g	441	126	5.7	24.4	0.6	1.4
Chicken With Rice, BGTY, Sainsbury's*	1 Pack/450g	675	150	8.1	21.1	3.7	0.9
Chicken With Rice, Eat Smart, Safeway*	1 Pack/390g	312	80	5.4	12.2	0.9	1.2
Chicken, With Rice, Farmfoods*	1 Pack/300g	324	108	5.9	19.2	0.9	0.7
Chicken With Rice, HE, Tesco*	1 Pack/450g	450	100	8.0	16.3	0.3	0.8
Chicken With Rice, Iceland*	1 Pack/400g	400	100	5.0	19.8	0.1	0.6
Chicken With Rice, Oriental Express*	1 Pack/340g	350	103	4.4	21.3	0.6	0.7
Chicken With Rice, Weight Watchers*	1 Pack/320g	282	88	4.4	16.4	0.5	0.4
Chicken With Vegetable Rice, COU, M & S*	1 Pack/400g	320	80	6.7	10.7	1.2	1.0
Chicken With Vegetable Rice, M & S*	1 Pack/400g	380	95	6.8	13.6	1.5	1.1
Dip, M & S*	1oz/28g	36	130	0.7	31.4	0.1	0.5
Gherkins, Tesco*	1 Serving/100g	34	34	1.0	6.0	0.5	1.2
Pork	1oz/28g	93	331	0.8	77.9	0.9	1.3
Pork, Cantonese, & Egg Fried Rice, Farmfoods*	1 Pack/327g	520	159	4.8	22.0	5.8	0.1
Pork, In Crispy Batter, Sainsbury's*	½ Pack/150g	293	195	10.0	20.0	8.3	1.1
Quick Snack, Rice, Sainsbury's*	1 Serving/237g	230	97	2.5	20.5	0.5	0.0
Roasted Vegetables, Cantonese, Sainsbury's*	1 Pack/348g	327	94	1.1	19.6	1.2	0.9
Vegetables With Rice, Waitrose*	1 Pack/400g	384	96	1.9	19.5	1.1	1.1
SWEET PICCALILLI, Somerfield*	1 Tsp/10g	11	107	1.0	24.0	1.0	0.0
SWEET POTATO,							
Baked	1oz/28g	32	115	1.6	27.9	0.4	3.3
Boiled In Salted Water	1oz/28g	24	84	1.1	20.5	0.3	2.3
Raw	1oz/28g	24	87	1.2	21.3	0.3	2.4
Steamed	1oz/28g	24	84	1.1	20.4	0.3	2.3
SWEETBREAD,							
Lamb, Fried	1oz/28g	135	481	5.4	66.8	22.6	2.5
Lamb, Raw	1oz/28g	131	467	6.1	68.9	18.8	0.8
SWEETCORN,							
& Petit Pois, M & S*	1oz/28g	20	73	4.6	10.8	1.3	3.6
Baby, Canned, Drained	1oz/28g	6	23	2.9	2.0	0.4	1.5
Baby, Fresh & Frozen, Boiled In Salted Water	1oz/28g	7	24	2.5	2.7	0.4	2.0
Golden, Princes*	1oz/28g	17	59	2.9	12.2	0.2	0.0
Green Giant*	1 Can/200g	140	70	2.7	13.3	0.7	2.7
In Water, No Added Sugar or Salt, Sainsbury's*	1oz/28g	17	61	2.8	10.6	0.8	1.4
In Water, Sugar & Salt Added, Sainsbury's*	½ Can/78g	85	109	2.9	21.8	1.1	1.8
In Water, Tesco*	1 Serving/130g	107	82	2.4	15.5	1.1	2.2
Kernels, Boiled In Salted Water	1oz/28g	31	111	4.2	19.6	2.3	2.2
Kernels, Boiled In Unsalted Water	1oz/28g	31	111	4.2	19.6	2.3	2.2
Kernels, Canned, Re-Heated, Drained	1oz/28g	34	122	2.9	26.6	1.2	1.4
Kernels In Water With Salt & Sugar, SmartPrice, Asda*	¼ Can/72g	74	103	2.9	21.0	0.8	2.1
Kernels, Raw	1oz/28g	26	93	3.4	17.0	1.8	1.5
Naturally Sweet In Water, Sainsbury's*	1oz/28g	17	61	2.8	10.6	0.8	1.4
Niblets In Water, Sugar & Salt Added, Green Giant*	1oz/28g	28	100	2.7	20.8	0.7	1.2
Niblets, No Salt, No Sugar, Green Giant*	1 Serving/80g	62	77	2.6	16.7	0.0	2.6
Niblets With Peppers, Green Giant*	1 Serving/165g	135	82	2.6	17.9	0.0	1.3
Whole Kernel, Green Giant*	1 Can/270g	176	65	1.6	14.6	0.4	0.0

S

	Measure WEIGHT/INFO	per Measure KCAL	Nutrition Values per 100g / 100ml KCAL	PROT	CARB	FAT	FIBRE
SWEETCORN,							
With Peppers, Canned, Asda*	1 Serving/50g	38	76	2.7	15.0	0.6	0.0
SWEETENER,							
Canderel, Spoonful, Canderel*	2 Tsp/1g	4	384	2.9	93.0	0.0	0.0
Canderel*	1 Tsp/2g	8	379	24.7	70.0	0.0	5.3
Granulated, Asda*	1 Tsp/1g	4	400	3.0	97.0	0.0	0.0
Granulated, Nothing Comes Closer to Sugar, Silver Spoon*	1 Tsp/1g	4	387	1.0	96.8	0.0	0.0
Granulated, Tesco*	1 Tsp/1g	4	400	3.0	97.0	0.0	0.0
SlendaSweet, Sainsbury's*	1 Tsp/1g	4	395	1.8	97.0	0.0	0.1
Tablets, Tesco*	5 Tablets/5g	1	20	2.0	2.0	0.5	0.0
SWORDFISH,							
Grilled	1oz/28g	39	139	22.9	0.0	5.2	0.0
Loins, Asda*	1oz/28g	41	147	25.5	0.0	5.1	0.0
Raw	1oz/28g	31	109	18.0	0.0	4.1	0.0
SYRUP,							
Corn, Dark	1 Tbsp/20g	56	282	0.0	76.6	0.0	0.0
Golden	1 Tbsp/20g	60	298	0.3	79.0	0.0	0.0
Maple	1 Tbsp/20g	52	262	0.0	67.2	0.2	0.0

TABOULEH,	Measure WEIGHT/INFO	per Measure KCAL	Nutrition Values per 100g / 100ml KCAL	PROT	CARB	FAT	FIBRE
Tabouleh, Average	1oz/28g	33	119	2.6	17.2	4.6	0.0
Meal Kit, Sainsbury's*	1 Serving/100g	153	153	4.1	19.7	6.7	1.1
Share The Taste, M & S*	1oz/28g	31	110	3.4	15.1	4.0	2.0
TACO,							
Mixed Beans, Tesco*	1 Serving/140g	108	77	4.7	13.5	0.5	3.9
Shells, Old El Paso*	1 Taco/12g	57	478	7.4	60.8	22.8	0.0
TAHINI PASTE	1 Heaped Tsp/19g	115	607	18.5	0.9	58.9	8.0
TAMARILLOS	1oz/28g	8	28	2.0	4.7	0.3	0.0
TAMARIND,							
Tamarind	1oz/28g	67	238	2.3	56.5	0.3	0.0
Leaves, Fresh	1oz/28g	32	115	5.8	18.2	2.1	0.0
Pulp	1oz/28g	76	273	3.2	64.5	0.3	0.0
TANDOORI CHICKEN,							
Healthy Choice, McCain*	1 Pack/270g	297	110	7.5	17.5	1.0	0.0
Masala, Asda*	1 Pack/400g	580	145	7.0	18.0	5.0	1.3
Safeway*	1 Pack/350g	595	170	13.7	5.7	10.3	1.3
Tesco*	1 Serving/175g	198	113	10.6	6.7	4.9	1.0
TANDOORI CHICKEN SIZZLER,							
Sainsbury's*	1 Pack/400g	536	134	12.8	4.3	7.3	1.7
Tesco*	1 Serving/175g	243	139	10.0	10.0	6.6	1.0
TANGERINES,							
Fresh, Raw	1oz/28g	10	35	0.9	8.0	0.1	1.3
Weighed With Peel & Pips	1 Med/70g	18	25	0.7	5.8	0.1	0.9
TAPAS, Pequillo Peppers, Sainsbury's*	½ Can/115g	110	96	3.6	8.6	5.2	1.8
TAPIOCA,							
Co-Op*	1oz/28g	97	348	0.4	86.4	0.1	0.4
Raw	1oz/28g	101	359	0.4	95.0	0.1	0.4
TAPIOCA PUDDING,							
Creamed, Ambrosia*	1 Can/425g	340	80	2.5	13.8	1.6	0.0
Creamed, Co-Op*	1 Can/425g	383	90	3.0	17.0	2.0	0.0
TARAMASALATA,							
Taramasalata	1oz/28g	141	504	3.2	4.1	52.9	0.0
Fresh, BGTY, Sainsbury's*	1oz/28g	71	253	4.3	13.5	20.2	0.7
Fresh, HE, Tesco*	1 Pot/170g	430	253	4.3	13.5	20.2	0.7
Fresh, Safeway*	1 Pot/170g	797	469	3.4	8.7	46.7	0.0
TARRAGON,							
Dried, Ground	1 Tsp/1.6g	6	295	22.8	42.8	7.2	0.0
Fresh	1oz/28g	14	49	3.4	6.3	1.1	0.0
TART,							
Apricot Lattice, Sainsbury's*	1 Slice/125g	321	257	3.4	35.3	11.4	2.6
Bakewell	1oz/28g	128	456	6.3	43.5	29.7	1.9
Bakewell, Co-Op*	1oz/28g	123	440	6.0	57.0	21.0	2.0
Bakewell, Somerfield*	¼ Tart/80g	296	370	5.0	45.0	19.0	0.0
Chocolate, Co-Op*	1 Tart/22g	102	465	4.0	42.0	31.0	0.7
Coconut, M & S*	1 Tart/53g	220	415	5.8	57.8	18.1	3.6
Congress, Morrisons*	1 Tart/38g	149	393	6.0	59.7	14.4	2.4
Custard, Individual	1 Tart/94g	260	277	6.3	32.4	14.5	1.2
Custard, Tesco*	1 Tart/82g	214	261	6.2	31.5	12.2	1.1
Egg Custard, M & S*	1 Tart/85g	243	286	6.3	34.7	14.5	0.7
Egg Custard, Safeway*	1 Tart/85g	225	265	5.3	33.3	12.6	0.8
Egg Custard, Sainsbury's	1 Tart/85g	230	270	6.1	30.1	14.1	0.7
Egg Custard, Somerfield*	1 Tart/85g	206	242	5.1	29.9	11.3	0.7
Egg Custard, Tesco*	1 Cake/82g	214	261	6.2	31.5	12.2	1.1
Egg Custard, Waitrose*	1 Serving/150g	356	237	5.7	25.1	12.6	0.5

T

TART,	Measure WEIGHT/INFO	per Measure KCAL	Nutrition Values per 100g / 100ml KCAL	PROT	CARB	FAT	FIBRE
Filo Asparagus Tartlette, M & S*	1 Serving/15g	45	300	4.4	25.2	20.4	2.1
Fruit, Safeway*	1 Tart/180g	425	236	2.7	30.6	11.4	0.0
Goats Cheese & Onion, M & S*	1 Serving/161g	451	280	5.8	22.4	18.7	1.5
Italian Lemon & Almond, Sainsbury's*	1 Slice/49g	182	371	7.4	31.9	23.7	4.1
Jam	1 Slice/90g	342	380	3.3	62.0	14.9	1.6
Jam, Farmfoods*	1 Tart/34g	132	387	3.6	60.5	14.5	2.8
Jam, Real Fruit, Mr Kipling*	1 Tart/35g	136	389	3.5	61.0	14.5	0.0
Jam, Real Fruit, Sainsbury's*	1 Tart/37g	142	383	3.4	60.9	14.0	1.4
Lemon Curd, Lyons*	1 Serving/30g	122	406	3.7	59.3	17.0	0.0
Manchester, M & S*	1oz/28g	104	370	4.1	36.0	23.5	1.1
Mixed Fruit, M & S*	1oz/28g	59	210	2.8	26.9	10.4	0.8
Pear & Chocolate With Brandy, TTD, Sainsbury's*	1/6 Tart/90g	261	290	3.5	32.0	16.4	1.4
Raspberry, Reduced Sugar, Asda*	1 Tart/34g	129	380	4.6	67.5	10.1	1.2
Roasted Vegetable & Goats Cheese Filo, M & S*	1 Tart/120g	276	230	7.4	16.6	14.8	1.3
Roasted Vegetable, Finest, Tesco*	1 Serving/130g	250	192	3.0	19.6	11.3	1.2
Strawberry & Fresh Cream, Finest, Tesco*	1 Tart/129g	350	271	3.3	31.1	14.8	1.2
Strawberry, Reduced Sugar, Asda*	1 Tart/37g	141	380	4.6	67.5	10.1	1.2
Toffee Apple, Co-Op*	1 Tart/20g	69	345	3.0	47.0	16.0	0.7
Toffee Pecan, M & S*	1 Tart/91g	414	455	6.0	48.5	26.5	2.0
Tomato, Mozzarella & Basil Puff, Sainsbury's	1/3 Tart/120g	318	265	9.2	10.2	20.8	0.9
Treacle	1oz/28g	103	368	3.7	60.4	14.1	1.1
Treacle Lattice, Mr Kipling*	1/6 Tart/70g	256	365	4.4	59.8	12.1	1.1
Treacle, Somerfield*	1/6 Tart/59g	232	394	5.0	64.0	14.0	0.0
Treacle, Teatime Selection, Safeway*	1 Tart/45g	171	380	4.2	63.9	12.0	1.1
TARTE,							
au Chocolat, Finest, Tesco*	1/6 Tarte/85g	421	495	5.1	44.0	33.2	1.6
au Citron, TTD, Sainsburys*	1 Serving/105g	360	343	3.7	36.6	20.2	0.6
Aux Abricots, Sainsbury*	1 tarte/120g	404	337	4.9	37.7	18.8	1.3
Aux Fruits, Finest, Tesco*	1 Tart/147g	345	235	3.0	33.4	9.9	1.1
Aux Fruits Rouge des Bois, TTD, Sainsbury*	1/6th tarte/83g	270	325	4.9	31.1	20.1	2.3
Aux Pommes, TTD, Sainsbury's*	1oz/28g	107	381	6.4	46.0	19.0	1.7
Citron, M & S*	1oz/28g	98	350	5.7	36.2	20.9	0.4
TARTLETS,							
Onion, Caramelised, Creamy, Somerfield*	1 Tartlet/105g	310	295	4.0	21.0	22.0	0.0
Roast Pepper & Mascarpone, Sainsbury's*	1 Tart/100g	232	232	3.5	17.7	16.4	1.5
Roast Vegetable, Filo, Mini, Somerfield*	1oz/28g	71	255	8.0	34.0	10.0	0.0
TASTE BREAKS,							
Pasta, Funghi With Croutons, Knorr*	1 Serving/350g	424	121	3.2	16.9	4.6	0.9
Pasta, Tomato Mozzarella With Croutons, Knorr*	1 Pot/348g	393	113	3.8	16.6	3.5	1.3
Rice, Indian Tikka Masala, Knorr*	1 Pot/340g	340	100	2.4	17.3	2.3	1.0
TASTERS,							
Dairy Milk, Cadbury's*	1 Bag/45g	234	520	7.7	57.0	29.2	0.0
Fruit & Nut, Cadbury's*	1 Bag/46g	232	505	9.3	52.1	29.0	0.0
TEA,							
Earl Grey, Iced, Twinings*	1fl oz/30ml	10	34	0.1	8.0	0.0	0.0
Fruit Punch, London Fruit & Herb Company*	1 Mug/200ml	4	2	0.0	0.5	0.0	0.0
Fruit, Whittards*	1fl oz/30ml	12	40	0.0	1.2	0.0	0.0
Green & Lemon, Twinings*	1 Serving/250ml	65	26	0.0	7.3	0.0	0.0
Herbal	1 Mug/227ml	2	1	0.0	0.2	0.0	0.0
Lemon, Instant Drink, Reduced Sweetness, Lift*	1 Serving/15g	53	352	0.0	87.0	0.0	0.0
Lemon, Original, Instant Drink, Lift*	1 Serving/15g	53	352	0.0	87.0	0.0	0.0
Made With Water	1 Mug/227ml	1	0	0.1	0.0	0.0	0.0
Made With Water With Semi-Skimmed Milk	1 Cup/200ml	14	7	0.4	0.5	0.4	0.0
Made With Water With Skimmed Milk	1 Mug/227ml	14	6	0.5	0.7	0.2	0.0

T

	Measure WEIGHT/INFO	per Measure KCAL	Nutrition Values per 100g / 100ml KCAL	PROT	CARB	FAT	FIBRE
TEA,							
Made With Water With Whole Milk	1 Cup/200ml	22	11	1.2	1.5	0.2	0.0
TEACAKES,							
Fresh	1oz/28g	83	296	8.0	52.5	7.5	0.0
Fruited, M & S*	1 Serving/60g	156	260	8.9	53.4	1.0	2.0
Fruited, Warburton's*	1 Teacake/62g	162	261	9.7	48.0	3.4	2.7
Jam, Burton's*	1 Teacake/10g	43	429	3.6	66.0	16.7	1.0
Milk Chocolate, M & S*	1oz/28g	121	431	5.0	65.4	16.7	1.0
Reduced Fat, M & S*	1 Teacake/17g	68	401	5.0	69.1	11.7	0.9
Sainsbury's*	1 Cake/70g	171	244	8.0	45.0	3.6	2.6
Sainsbury's*	1 Serving/76g	170	224	4.5	45.0	3.6	2.6
Tesco*	1 Teacake/61g	163	267	7.8	51.1	3.5	2.4
Toasted	1oz/28g	92	329	8.9	58.3	8.3	0.0
Tunnock's*	1 Biscuit/22g	91	413	5.3	61.0	18.1	0.0
Value, Tesco*	1oz/28g	74	265	7.5	49.1	4.3	2.3
TEMPEH	1oz/28g	46	166	20.7	6.4	6.4	4.3
TERIYAKI Chicken, Asda*	1 Pack/360g	299	83	9.1	8.6	1.4	0.8
TERIYAKI Chicken Japanese Noodle Box, M & S*	1 Box/300g	345	115	8.1	15.5	2.5	1.8
TERRINE,							
Chicken, With Pork, Sage & Onion Stuffing, Somerfield*	1oz/28g	32	114	25.0	1.0	1.0	0.0
Lobster & Prawn, Slices, M & S*	1 Serving/55g	107	195	18.2	0.7	13.4	0.7
Poached Salmon, Tesco*	1 Pack/113g	349	309	15.5	0.8	27.1	0.0
Salmon & Crayfish, Slice, Finest, Tesco*	1 Slice/110g	149	135	21.9	0.1	5.2	0.1
Salmon, Reduced Fat, Tesco*	1 Serving/56g	100	179	15.5	1.1	12.5	3.5
Scottish Smoked Salmon, Tesco*	1 Slice/25g	56	225	13.9	4.9	16.6	0.5
Smooth Pork Liver & Green Peppercorns, TTD, Sainsbury's*	1 Serving/45g	155	345	11.0	2.2	32.5	0.5
Vegetarian, Stack, Tesco*	1 Serving/230g	207	90	1.9	12.0	3.8	2.9
TEVIOT,							
Chicken & Vegetable, HE, Tesco*	½ Pie/275g	325	118	8.6	14.6	2.8	1.1
Chicken & Vegetable, Tesco*	½ Pack/275g	490	178	7.0	17.8	8.7	1.0
Minced Beef & Onion, Safeway*	½ Pie/270g	470	174	10.3	16.5	7.5	1.5
Steak, Tesco*	1 Serving/275g	391	142	14.2	5.9	6.8	0.8
TEX MEX Platter, M & S*	1 Pack/415g	934	225	12.6	10.5	14.6	0.9
THAI BITES,							
Lightly Salted, Jacob's*	1 Pack/25g	94	375	6.9	79.7	3.2	0.1
Oriental Spice, Jacob's*	1 Pack/25g	93	373	7.1	78.0	3.6	0.2
Seaweed Flavour, Jacob's*	1 Pack/25g	94	377	7.1	80.0	3.2	0.5
Sweet Herb, Jacob's*	1 Pack/25g	93	372	7.1	78.8	3.2	0.2
THAI STYLE Lanterns, Shapers, Boots*	1 Pack/18g	81	450	4.2	61.0	21.0	5.2
THYME,							
Dried, Ground	1 Tsp/1.2g	3	276	9.1	45.3	7.4	0.0
Fresh	1 Tsp/0.8g	1	95	3.0	15.1	2.5	0.0
TIA MARIA	1 Shot/25ml	35	140	0.0	0.0	0.0	0.0
TIC TAC,							
Fresh Mint, Ferrero*	2 Tic Tacs/1g	4	390	0.0	97.5	0.0	0.0
Lime & Orange, Ferrero*	2 Tic Tacs/1g	4	386	0.0	95.5	0.0	0.0
Orange, Ferrero*	2 Tic Tacs/1g	4	385	0.0	95.5	0.0	0.0
Spearmint, Ferrero*	1 BOX/16g	62	390	0.0	97.5	0.0	0.0
TIDGY Puds, Tryton Foods*	1oz/28g	97	346	11.3	43.5	14.1	2.1
TIKKA MASALA,							
Chicken & Basmati Rice, Patak's*	1 Pack/400g	580	145	9.9	15.1	5.0	0.2
Chicken & Pilau Rice, GFY, Asda*	1 Pack/400g	596	149	8.0	19.0	4.6	1.1
Chicken Breasts, Good Choice, Iceland*	1 Serving/156g	172	110	14.4	6.2	3.1	1.1
Chicken, COU, M & S*	1 Pack/300g	300	100	12.1	6.0	2.8	1.3
Chicken, Healthy Choice, Iceland*	1 Pack/399g	431	108	6.5	18.0	1.1	0.9

T

	Measure WEIGHT/INFO	per Measure KCAL	KCAL	PROT	CARB	FAT	FIBRE
			Nutrition Values per 100g / 100ml				
TIKKA MASALA,							
Chicken, HE, Tesco*	1 Pack/350g	333	95	12.3	6.6	2.2	0.8
Chicken, Hot, Sainsbury's*	1 Pack/400g	604	151	13.2	3.6	9.3	1.5
Chicken, Indian, Medium, Sainsbury's*	1 Pack/400g	848	212	13.2	5.3	15.3	0.1
Chicken, Indian Takeaway, Iceland*	1 Pack/400g	316	79	7.5	6.9	2.4	1.2
Chicken, Low Fat, Iceland*	1 Pack/400g	360	90	7.8	12.5	1.0	0.5
Chicken, M & S*	1 Pack/300g	585	195	12.2	5.3	13.8	1.5
Chicken, Medium, Tesco*	1 Pack/350g	532	152	11.2	4.9	9.8	0.6
Chicken, Sainsbury's*	1 Pack/400g	736	184	12.8	4.6	12.7	0.2
Chicken, Smart Price, Asda*	1 Serving/300g	405	135	7.0	17.0	4.3	0.3
Chicken, Somerfield*	1 Pack/350g	553	158	11.7	3.6	10.8	1.5
Chicken, Take Away Menu, BGTY, Sainsbury's	1 Pack/251g	226	90	13.4	4.2	2.2	1.3
Chicken, Tinned, Asda*	½ Can/200g	238	119	8.0	6.0	7.0	0.9
Chicken With Basmati Rice, Eat Smart, Safeway*	1 Pack/363g	290	80	6.4	9.6	1.4	0.7
Chicken With Pilau Rice, BGTY, Sainsbury's*	1 Pack/450g	428	95	7.8	12.7	1.4	0.9
Chicken With Pilau Rice, Co-Op*	1 Pack/400g	560	140	7.0	12.0	7.0	1.0
Chicken With Pilau Rice, Waitrose*	1 Pack/400g	520	130	7.7	16.9	3.5	1.1
Chicken With Rice, Bird's Eye*	1 Pack/375g	506	135	5.8	19.5	3.7	0.8
Chicken With Rice, HE, Tesco*	1 Pack/400g	472	118	6.1	17.0	2.8	1.8
Chicken With Tumeric Rice, BGTY, Sainsburys*	1 Pack/369g	446	121	6.7	20.5	1.3	0.4
HE, Tesco*	1 Serving/220g	191	87	1.0	10.2	4.7	0.5
Prawns, Youngs*	1 Serving/150g	149	99	7.6	4.9	5.5	0.1
Quorn, Basmati Rice, Sainsbury's*	1 Pack/450g	567	126	4.8	18.1	3.8	2.0
Quorn, Pilau Rice, Quorn*	1 Pack/400g	540	135	4.9	18.5	5.3	1.6
Vegetable & Rice, Patak's*	1 Pack/370g	503	136	2.5	19.0	6.1	0.9
Vegetable, Asda*	½ Can/204g	190	93	2.0	10.0	5.0	2.0
Vegetable, Waitrose*	1 Can/200g	204	102	2.4	6.4	7.4	0.0
TILAPIA FILLET, M & S*	1 Pack/220g	209	95	19.8	0.0	1.8	0.0
TIME OUT,							
Cadbury's*	2 Fingers/35g	189	540	5.4	61.8	29.9	0.0
Orange, Snack Size, Cadbury's*	1 Finger/11g	61	555	5.0	59.4	32.9	0.0
TIP TOP, Nestle*	1 Serving/40g	45	112	4.8	9.0	6.3	0.0
TIRAMISU,							
COU, M & S*	1 Serving/95g	138	145	3.7	26.9	2.7	0.6
Italian, Co-Op*	1 Pack/90g	230	255	5.0	37.0	10.0	0.4
Morrisons*	1 Pot/90g	248	276	4.0	38.0	11.0	0.0
Raspberry, M & S*	1 Serving/84g	197	235	3.8	22.9	14.4	0.2
Somerfield*	1 Pot/100g	286	286	5.0	39.0	11.0	0.0
TOAD IN THE HOLE,							
Toad In The Hole	1oz/28g	36	128	0.4	32.6	0.0	0.0
Co-Op*	1 Pack/170g	366	215	7.8	12.3	14.9	2.6
Vegetarian, Linda McCartney*	1 Pack/190g	359	189	13.6	13.9	8.8	1.1
Vegetarian, Meat Free, Asda*	1 Toad/173g	407	235	9.0	25.0	11.0	3.1
Vegetarian, Tesco*	1 Pack/190g	471	248	13.1	26.5	10.0	2.8
Vegetarian, Tryton Foods*	1oz/28g	73	262	14.8	18.6	14.2	1.6
With Three Sausages, Asda*	1 Pack/150g	435	290	10.0	22.0	18.0	1.0
TOAST TOPPERS,							
Chicken & Mushroom, Heinz*	1 Serving/56g	31	56	5.1	5.7	1.4	0.2
Ham & Cheese, Heinz*	1oz/28g	27	96	7.4	7.3	4.1	0.1
Mushroom & Bacon, Heinz*	1 Serving/56g	53	94	6.9	6.6	4.4	0.3
TOASTIES,							
Cheese & Ham, Tayto*	1 Serving/50g	260	519	6.8	58.0	29.7	0.0
Cheese & Onion, Warburton's*	1 Toastie/42g	120	286	7.5	33.1	13.7	0.0
TOBLERONE, Milk, Toblerone*	1oz/28g	147	525	5.3	60.7	29.0	2.7
TOFFEE,							

T

	Measure	per Measure	Nutrition Values per 100g / 100ml				
TOFFEE,	WEIGHT/INFO	KCAL	KCAL	PROT	CARB	FAT	FIBRE
Assorted, Sainsbury's*	1 Sweet/8g	37	457	2.2	76.5	15.8	0.2
Burst, Aldi Stores*	1 Bar/45g	217	483	4.5	63.7	23.4	2.4
Chocolate Coated, Thorntons*	1 Bag/100g	521	521	3.5	57.9	30.7	0.3
Devon Butter, Thorntons*	1 Sweet/9g	40	444	1.7	72.2	16.7	0.0
Double Devon, M & S*	1 Sweet/8g	37	460	1.8	73.1	19.9	0.0
English Butter, Co-Op*	1 Toffee/8g	38	470	2.0	71.0	20.0	0.0
Liquorice, Thorntons*	1 Bag/100g	506	506	1.9	58.8	29.4	0.0
Mixed	1oz/28g	119	426	2.2	66.7	18.6	0.0
TOFFEE CRISP,							
Mini, Nestle*	1 Bar/18g	92	507	4.1	60.8	27.5	0.0
Nestle*	1 Bar/48g	237	494	4.1	62.1	25.5	0.0
TOFU,							
Deep Fried, Organic, Evernat*	1oz/28g	44	156	17.3	2.6	8.5	0.0
Marinated Organic Pieces, Cauldron Foods Ltd*	1oz/28g	64	230	19.3	2.4	15.9	0.7
Natural, Organic, Evernat*	1oz/28g	34	120	14.4	1.8	6.2	0.0
Organic, Cauldron Foods*	1oz/28g	33	118	12.9	1.2	6.8	0.2
Smoked, Organic, Evernat*	1oz/28g	36	127	16.3	0.8	6.6	0.0
Soya Bean, Fu Juk	1oz/28g	108	387	45.1	23.3	16.2	0.0
Soya Bean, Steamed	1oz/28g	20	73	8.1	0.7	4.2	0.0
Soya Bean, Steamed, Fried	1oz/28g	73	261	23.5	2.0	17.7	0.0
TOMATO & Cheese Spaghetti, Sainsbury's*	1 Pack/300g	345	115	4.4	16.8	3.4	1.4
TOMATO & Herb Chicken, BGTY, Sainsbury's*	1 Serving/200g	320	160	9.1	23.6	2.2	2.1
TOMATO & Mozarella Pasta, Tesco*	1 Serving/200g	220	110	4.5	15.8	3.2	1.4
TOMATO FLAVOUR Knobbles, Organic, Sainsbury's*	1 Bag/30g	132	440	6.0	77.1	12.0	2.7
TOMATO FRITO, Heinz*	1oz/28g	20	73	1.3	7.7	4.1	0.8
TOMATO JUICE,							
Tomato Juice	1 Glass/200ml	28	14	0.8	3.0	0.0	0.6
Del Monte*	1 Glass/200ml	38	19	0.8	3.5	0.0	0.0
Fresh Pressed, Tesco*	1 Glass/200ml	42	21	0.6	4.6	0.0	0.6
Sainsbury's*	1 Serving/526ml	100	19	0.9	3.7	0.1	0.6
Somerfield*	1fl oz/30ml	7	23	1.0	5.0	0.0	0.0
TOMATO PASTE, Sun Dried, Sainsbury's*	1 Heaped Tsp/10g	37	373	3.4	14.8	33.3	0.0
TOMATO PUREE,							
Tomato Puree	1 Tbsp/16g	12	76	5.0	14.2	0.3	2.8
Double Concentrate, Safeway*	1oz/28g	20	71	4.4	12.9	0.2	2.8
Heinz*	1 Des Sp/11g	6	57	3.7	10.1	0.2	2.3
Napolina*	1oz/28g	28	99	3.9	20.0	0.4	2.0
Sainsbury's*	1 Tbsp/16g	13	82	4.7	14.9	0.4	2.0
Tesco*	1oz/28g	26	92	4.8	18.1	0.0	2.5
Tinned, Sharwood's*	1oz/28g	15	55	4.1	9.5	0.4	2.3
Tube, Sharwood's*	1oz/28g	20	72	5.3	12.3	0.5	3.0
Value, Tesco*	1 Tbsp/16g	11	66	3.6	13.0	0.0	2.6
TOMATOES,							
Canned, Whole Contents	1 Can/410g	66	16	1.0	3.0	0.1	0.7
Cherry, Asda*	1oz/28g	5	19	0.8	3.0	0.4	1.0
Cherry, Canned, Waitrose*	1 Can/395g	83	21	1.1	4.0	0.1	0.9
Cherry, Organic, Tesco*	1 Serving/100g	19	19	0.8	3.2	0.4	2.4
Cherry, Raw, Fresh	1oz/28g	5	18	0.8	3.0	0.4	1.0
Cherry, Safeway*	1 Serving/73g	12	16	0.7	3.0	0.3	0.0
Cherry, Somerfield*	1 Pack/100g	18	18	0.8	3.0	0.4	1.0
Cherry, Tesco*	1 Serving/75g	14	19	0.8	3.0	0.4	1.0
Chopped & Garlic, Asda*	1 Can/400g	92	23	1.0	4.0	0.3	0.0
Chopped, Asda*	1 Can/410g	86	21	1.2	3.8	0.1	0.8
Chopped, Canned, For Bolognese, Napolina*	1 Can/400g	120	30	1.3	5.7	0.2	0.7

	Measure	per Measure	Nutrition Values per 100g / 100ml				
TOMATOES,	WEIGHT/INFO	KCAL	KCAL	PROT	CARB	FAT	FIBRE
Chopped, Chunky, Tesco*	½ Can/200g	62	31	1.5	5.8	0.2	0.9
Chopped, Economy, Sainsbury's*	1 Serving/100g	20	20	1.2	3.5	0.1	0.9
Chopped, In Rich Tomato Sauce, Heinz*	1 Serving/130g	21	16	0.7	2.9	0.2	0.9
Chopped, Italian, Organic, Waitrose*	½ Can/200g	40	20	1.1	4.0	0.0	0.9
Chopped, Italian, Tesco*	1oz/28g	6	23	1.4	4.0	0.2	0.9
Chopped, Italian, Waitrose*	1 Can/227g	45	20	1.1	4.0	0.0	0.9
Chopped, Italian, With Olive Oil & Garlic, Waitrose*	1 Serving/100g	33	33	1.1	3.6	1.6	0.0
Chopped, Italian, With Olives, Waitrose*	1 Can/400g	184	46	1.4	6.0	1.8	0.8
Chopped, Itlalian, With Herbs, Tesco*	1 Can/400g	116	29	1.1	5.7	0.2	0.7
Chopped, M & S*	1oz/28g	6	20	1.2	3.5	0.1	0.9
Chopped, Napolina*	1 Sm Can/227g	50	22	1.1	3.5	0.4	0.3
Chopped, Organic, Biona*	½ Can/200g	37	19	1.1	2.9	0.4	0.0
Chopped, Organic, Tesco*	1 Can/400g	112	28	1.1	5.7	0.1	0.7
Chopped, Princes*	1 Can/400g	68	17	1.1	3.0	0.1	0.7
Chopped, Sainsbury's*	1 Can/400g	80	20	1.2	3.5	0.1	0.9
Chopped, Sugocasa, Premium, Sainsbury's*	¼ Jar/172g	59	34	1.6	6.5	0.2	0.9
Chopped, Thick, Asda*	1oz/28g	8	29	1.2	5.8	0.1	0.9
Chopped, Value, Tesco*	1 Can/400g	68	17	1.0	2.9	0.1	0.7
Chopped, With Chilli & Peppers, Asda*	1 Pack/400g	92	23	1.0	4.0	0.3	0.0
Chopped, With Chilli, Sainsbury's*	½ Can/200g	44	22	1.0	3.5	0.5	0.9
Chopped, With Garlic, Sainsbury's*	½ Can/200g	40	20	1.2	3.5	0.1	0.9
Chopped, With Herbs In Tomato Juice, Co-Op*	1 Serving/110g	19	17	1.0	2.9	0.1	0.7
Chopped, With Herbs, Napolina*	1 Can/400g	100	25	1.0	5.1	0.1	0.4
Chopped, With Herbs, Sainsbury's*	½ Can/200g	40	20	1.2	3.5	0.1	0.9
Chopped, With Onion & Herbs, Napolina*	1 Can/400g	84	21	1.0	4.0	0.1	0.4
Chopped, With Peppers & Onions, Sainsbury's*	½ Can/200g	40	20	1.2	3.5	0.1	0.9
Creamed, Sainsbury's*	1 Carton/500g	150	30	1.1	6.0	0.1	0.8
Fried In Blended Oil	1 Av/85g	77	91	0.7	5.0	7.7	1.3
Grilled	1oz/28g	14	49	2.0	8.9	0.9	2.9
Organic, M & S*	1oz/28g	6	20	1.4	3.5	0.2	1.4
Plum, Asda*	1 Serving/100g	23	23	1.3	4.0	0.2	0.9
Plum, Canned, M & S*	1oz/28g	6	20	1.2	3.5	0.1	0.9
Plum, In Tomato Juice, Value, Tesco*	1 Can/400g	64	16	0.7	3.4	0.0	0.0
Plum, Peeled, Italian, Tesco*	1oz/28g	7	24	1.3	4.0	0.2	0.9
Plum, Peeled, Napolina*	1oz/28g	6	23	1.2	3.5	0.5	0.3
Plum, Peeled, Premium, Sainsbury's*	1 Can/400g	148	37	2.2	7.0	0.1	1.6
Plum, Peeled, SmartPrice, Asda*	½ Can/200g	32	16	1.0	3.0	0.0	0.8
Plum, Peeled, Somerfield*	1oz/28g	4	16	1.0	3.0	0.0	0.0
Plum, Tinned, Sainsbury's*	1 Can/233g	42	18	1.1	3.5	0.1	0.8
Raw, Fresh	1 Med/85g	14	17	0.7	3.1	0.3	1.0
Ripened On The Vine, Safeway*	1 Serving/100g	18	18	0.7	3.0	0.3	0.0
Selected, Merevale, Aldi*	1oz/28g	5	17	0.7	3.1	0.3	1.0
Stuffed With Rice	1oz/28g	59	212	2.1	22.2	13.4	1.1
Sugar Plum, The Best, Safeway*	½ Punnet/100g	18	18	0.7	3.0	0.3	0.0
Sun Blush, Sainsbury's*	1 Serving/65g	79	121	2.9	13.6	7.4	4.3
Sun Dried	1oz/28g	139	495	3.3	5.4	51.3	0.0
Sun Dried, M & S*	1oz/28g	65	232	4.7	15.5	16.8	6.6
Sun Dried, Sacla*	1 Serving/28g	55	195	4.7	10.4	15.0	0.0
Toasted , Cracked Black Pepper, M & S*	1 Pot/200g	190	95	11.7	5.5	2.5	0.0
Whole, Peeled, Heinz*	1 Serving/240g	38	16	0.7	2.9	0.2	0.8
TONGUE,							
Lunch, John West*	1oz/28g	48	173	19.5	3.0	10.4	0.0
Ox, Wafer Thin, Traditional, M & S*	1oz/28g	64	230	22.3	0.0	15.5	0.0
Slices	1oz/28g	56	201	18.7	0.0	14.0	0.0

T

	Measure WEIGHT/INFO	per Measure KCAL	KCAL	PROT	CARB	FAT	FIBRE
TONIC WATER,							
Tonic Water	1 Glass/250ml	83	33	0.0	8.8	0.0	0.0
Diet, Asda*	1 Glass/200ml	2	1	0.0	0.0	0.0	0.0
Indian, Low Calorie, Tesco*	1 Serving/200ml	2	1	0.0	0.0	0.0	0.0
Indian, Slimline, Schweppes*	1 Pub Measure/188ml	3	2	0.4	0.1	0.0	0.0
TOOTY FROOTIES, Rowntree's*	1oz/28g	113	402	0.4	92.1	3.6	0.0
TOPIC, Mars*	1 Bar/47g	232	493	6.0	58.1	26.3	0.0
TOPPING,							
Bruschetta	1serving/115g	30	26	1.2	3.6	0.8	1.1
Bruschetta, Safeway*	1 Serving/100g	26	26	1.2	3.6	0.8	0.0
Cappuccino & Chocolate Flavour, Asda*	1 Satchet/13g	48	372	23.0	43.0	12.0	0.0
Mediterranean, For Cod, Schwartz*	½ Jar/147g	128	87	1.7	9.5	4.7	0.0
Pizza, Italian Tomato & Herb, Sainsbury's*	1/5 Jar/50g	19	38	1.6	7.1	0.4	1.1
Pizza, Tomato With Cheese & Onion, Napolina*	1 Jar/250g	195	78	2.9	7.0	4.0	0.8
Pizza, Traditional Tomato With Basil, Napolina*	1 Jar/250g	153	61	1.2	7.8	2.6	0.7
Pizza, With Herbs, Napolina*	1 Serving/100g	49	49	0.9	6.3	2.2	0.6
TORTE,							
Chocolate, Tesco*	1 Serving/50g	126	251	3.6	32.3	11.9	1.0
Lemon & Mango, Waitrose*	1 Serving/80g	142	177	3.9	33.6	3.0	0.6
Lemon, Farmfoods*	1/6 Cake/70g	137	195	4.3	21.9	10.0	0.5
Raspberry, Safeway*	1/6 Serving/54g	93	172	1.2	25.1	7.4	1.5
TORTELLONI, (SEE ALSO PASTA, TORTELLINI)							
Cheese & Ham, Safeway*	¼ Pack/113g	325	288	13.5	37.1	9.5	2.8
Cheese & Sundried Tomato, Safeway*	1 Serving/125g	229	183	7.7	24.2	6.2	2.7
Five Cheese, Safeway*	1 Serving/150g	275	183	7.8	24.2	6.2	2.7
Five Cheese, Sainsbury's*	1 Pack/250g	435	174	8.5	23.4	5.1	2.2
Five Cheese, Somerfield*	1 Pack/250g	668	267	14.0	35.0	8.0	0.0
Garlic Mushroom & Onion, Eat Smart, Safeway*	1 Serving/125g	231	185	9.3	31.4	2.0	1.4
Mountain Gorgonzola & Chianti, Safeway*	½ Pack/125g	253	202	8.4	27.7	6.3	1.5
Ricotta & Fine Herb, Sainsbury's*	1 Serving/175g	340	194	7.4	22.8	8.1	2.7
Spinach & Ricotta, Eat Smart, Safeway*	1 Serving/125g	225	180	6.8	32.6	2.2	1.6
TORTILLA CHIPS,							
Chilli Flavour, Somerfield*	1 Serving/50g	242	484	6.8	60.1	24.1	5.3
Chilli, Organic, Evernat*	1oz/28g	137	490	8.0	65.0	22.0	0.0
Cool, Salted, Sainsbury's*	1 Serving/50g	253	506	6.5	58.6	27.3	4.3
Cool, Tesco*	1 Serving/50g	246	492	7.4	58.9	25.2	4.6
Easy Cheesy!, Sainsbury's*	1 Serving/50g	249	498	7.1	58.7	26.1	4.5
Lightly Salted, Waitrose*	1 Bag/40g	188	471	6.5	58.6	23.4	4.3
Natural, Evernat*	1oz/28g	137	490	8.0	65.0	22.0	0.0
Phileas Fogg*	1 Serving/50g	243	486	6.1	62.4	10.1	3.3
Salsa Flavour, Somerfield*	1oz/28g	140	499	6.0	62.0	25.0	0.0
Waitrose*	1 Serving/25g	128	510	7.9	65.5	24.0	4.5
TORTILLA WRAP,							
M & S*	1 Wrap/44g	134	305	8.1	51.8	8.4	2.9
Morrisons*	1 Serving/35g	84	240	6.8	45.8	3.8	1.9
Nacho Flavoured, Tesco*	1 Serving/64g	184	288	8.6	48.8	6.5	1.7
Plain Flour, Tesco*	1 Serving/63g	171	272	6.9	48.2	5.7	2.0
Spicy Tomato, Tesco*	1 Wrap/63g	175	278	7.8	49.2	5.6	2.4
Wheat Flour, Waitrose*	1 Wrap/62g	203	327	8.5	51.5	9.8	0.0
TORTILLAS,							
Asda*	1 Tortilla/34g	106	311	8.0	54.0	7.0	2.5
Corn, Old El Paso*	1oz/28g	88	315	10.0	44.0	11.0	0.0
Flour, Tex "n"" Mex 12, Sainsbury's*	1 Tortilla/26g	85	326	8.6	53.9	9.6	2.5
Made With Wheat Flour	1oz/28g	73	262	7.2	59.7	1.0	2.4
Mexican Style, Asda*	1 Tortilla/42g	127	303	9.0	51.0	7.0	0.0

T

TORTILLAS,	Measure WEIGHT/INFO	per Measure KCAL	Nutrition Values per 100g / 100ml KCAL	PROT	CARB	FAT	FIBRE
Old El Paso*	1 Wrap/41g	140	342	10.0	60.0	6.6	0.0
TRAIL MIX	1oz/28g	121	432	9.1	37.2	28.5	4.3
TREACLE, Black	1 Tbsp/20g	51	257	1.2	67.2	0.0	0.0
TRIFLE,							
Trifle, Average	1oz/28g	45	160	3.6	22.3	6.3	0.5
Banana & Mandarin, Co-Op*	¼ Trifle/125g	238	190	2.0	21.0	11.0	0.1
Blackforest, Sainsburys, BGTY*	1 pot/125g	171	137	2.1	21.9	4.5	1.6
Caramel, Galaxy*	1 Pot/100g	255	255	4.5	30.0	13.0	1.0
Cherry & Almond, Somerfield*	1 Trifle/125g	230	184	2.0	23.0	9.0	0.0
COU, M & S*	1oz/28g	34	120	3.0	21.8	2.3	0.3
Cream Mandarin, GFY, Asda*	1 Serving/113g	151	134	1.6	27.0	4.4	0.2
Fruit Cocktail, Co-Op*	1 Trifle/125g	213	170	2.0	23.0	8.0	0.2
Fruit Cocktail, Individual, Shape*	1 Trifle/115g	136	118	3.2	19.6	2.7	1.6
Fruit Cocktail, Individual,Tesco*	1 Pot/113g	175	155	1.7	19.6	7.8	0.6
Fruit Cocktail, Luxury Devonshire, St Ivel*	1 Trifle/125g	211	169	1.9	22.6	7.9	0.2
Fruit Cocktail, Somerfield*	1 Trifle/125g	211	169	2.0	23.0	8.0	0.0
Fruit Cocktail, St Ivel*	1 Trifle/113g	206	182	2.5	23.1	8.8	0.4
Fruit, M & S*	1 Trifle/50g	83	166	1.9	19.0	9.1	0.4
Light Chocolate, Cadbury's, St Ivel*	1 Pot/100g	178	178	5.3	22.7	7.3	0.7
Mandarin & Banana, Luxury Devonshire, St Ivel*	1/5 Trifle/100g	192	192	2.4	21.1	10.9	0.1
Mandarin, Asda*	1 Serving/113g	151	134	1.6	22.0	4.4	0.0
Trifle Mix, Fruit Cocktail Flavour, Bird's*	1oz/28g	119	425	2.7	78.0	11.0	1.2
Trifle Mix, Raspberry Flavour, Bird's*	1oz/28g	119	425	2.7	78.0	10.5	1.2
Trifle Mix, Sherry Flavour, Bird's*	1oz/28g	119	425	2.7	78.0	11.0	1.2
Trifle Mix, Strawberry Flavour, Bird's*	1oz/28g	119	425	2.7	78.0	10.5	1.2
Peach & Zabaglione, COU, M & S*	1 Glass/130g	150	115	2.8	20.6	2.3	0.8
Raspberry, Asda*	1 Serving/100g	175	175	1.8	24.0	8.0	0.1
Raspberry, Co-Op*	1 Trifle/125g	206	165	2.0	22.0	8.0	0.3
Raspberry, Individual, St Ivel*	1 Trifle/113g	195	173	2.5	21.1	8.7	0.4
Raspberry, Luxury Devonshire, St Ivel*	1 Trifle/125g	208	166	2.1	21.6	7.9	0.3
Raspberry, Sainsbury's*	1 Pot/125g	204	163	1.7	21.5	7.8	0.6
Raspberry, Somerfield*	1 Trifle/125g	208	166	2.0	22.0	8.0	0.0
Sherry, Co-Op*	¼ Trifle/188g	320	170	2.0	24.0	7.0	0.5
Sherry, Homestyle, M & S*	1oz/28g	59	212	2.5	19.0	13.3	0.1
Sherry Sainsbury's*	1 Serving/132g	215	162	2.4	20.1	7.5	0.3
Sherry, Traditional English, Waitrose*	1 Pot/125g	258	206	3.0	21.5	11.4	0.9
Trifle Sponges, Safeway*	1 Sponge/23g	73	318	5.3	70.8	1.5	1.1
Trifle Sponges, Somerfield*	1 Sponge/24g	81	339	5.0	76.0	2.0	0.0
Trifle Sponges, Tesco*	1 Sponge/24g	78	325	5.4	72.2	1.6	1.1
Strawberry, Co-Op*	1 Serving/123g	234	190	2.0	21.0	11.0	0.2
Strawberry, COU, M & S*	1 Serving/142g	170	120	3.0	21.8	2.3	0.3
Strawberry, HE, Tesco*	1 Serving/113g	114	101	1.7	18.5	2.2	0.6
Strawberry, Individual, Shape*	1 Pot/115g	137	119	3.3	19.8	2.7	1.6
Strawberry, Individual, Somerfield*	1 Trifle/125g	208	166	2.0	22.0	8.0	0.0
Strawberry, Low Fat, Shape*	1oz/28g	38	137	3.8	22.8	3.1	1.8
Strawberry, Luxury Devonshire, St Ivel*	1 Trifle/125g	208	166	2.0	21.7	7.9	0.2
Strawberry, M & S*	1 Trifle/50g	81	161	2.0	17.7	9.2	0.6
Strawberry, Sainsbury's*	¼ Trifle/125g	232	186	2.2	21.7	10.0	0.2
Strawberry, Somerfield*	¼ Trifle/125g	235	188	2.0	21.0	11.0	0.0
Strawberry, St Ivel*	1 Trifle/113g	194	172	2.4	21.0	8.7	0.2
Strawberry, Tesco*	1 Serving/83g	140	169	1.6	17.7	10.2	0.7
Summerfruit, BGTY, Sainsbury's*	1 Trifle/125g	151	121	1.2	19.2	4.4	0.5
Triple Chocolate, Farmfoods*	¼ Trifle/86.25g	223	259	2.1	21.6	18.2	1.2
With Fresh Cream	1oz/28g	46	166	2.4	19.5	9.2	0.5

TRIPE & ONIONS,	Measure WEIGHT/INFO	per Measure KCAL	KCAL	PROT	CARB	FAT	FIBRE
Stewed	1oz/28g	26	93	8.3	9.5	2.7	0.7
TROPICAL FRUIT DRINK,							
Iceland*	1 Glass/200ml	106	53	0.2	13.0	0.0	0.0
Tesco*	1 Glass/250ml	125	50	0.1	12.1	0.0	0.0
TROPICAL FRUIT JUICE DRINK,							
Safeway*	1 Glass/250ml	118	47	0.2	11.2	0.0	0.0
Somerfield*	1 Glass/250ml	130	52	0.0	12.0	0.0	0.0
With Sweeteners, Somerfield*	1 Carton/250ml	8	3	0.0	0.0	0.0	0.0
TROPICAL FRUIT MIX,							
Four Seasons*	1 Serving/150g	111	74	0.6	17.1	0.3	0.9
M & S*	1oz/28g	14	50	0.6	12.6	0.0	1.0
TROPICAL FRUITS, M & S*	1 Serving/120g	48	40	1.5	8.2	0.2	1.5
TROPICAL JUICE DRINK,							
Juice Burst, Purity*	1 Serving/200ml	96	48	0.2	11.5	0.0	0.0
M & S*	1 Pouch/200ml	94	47	0.2	11.2	0.0	0.0
TROPICAL JUICE,							
No Added Sugar, Safeway*	1 Glass/200ml	10	5	0.1	0.9	0.0	0.0
Pure, Sainsbury's*	1 Glass/200ml	104	52	0.5	12.0	0.1	0.1
TROPICAL MIXED Fruit, Fruit Express, Del Monte*	1 Pot/185g	89	48	0.2	11.2	0.1	1.2
TROPICAL TUNES, Mars*	1 Pack/37g	143	387	0.0	96.6	0.0	0.0
TROUT,							
Brown, Raw	1oz/28g	31	112	19.4	0.0	3.8	0.0
Brown, Steamed	1oz/28g	38	135	23.5	0.0	4.5	0.0
Fillets, Fresh, Loch Etive, Waitrose*	1 Serving/125g	156	125	19.6	0.0	5.2	0.0
Fillets, Scottish Loch, Tesco*	1 Fillet/115g	144	125	19.6	0.0	5.2	0.0
Fillets, Smoked, Organic, Waitrose*	2 Fillets/135g	219	162	26.5	0.0	6.2	0.0
Rainbow, Grilled	1oz/28g	38	135	21.5	0.0	5.4	0.0
Rainbow, Raw	1oz/28g	35	125	19.6	0.0	5.2	0.0
Rainbow, Sainsbury's*	1 Trout/265g	358	135	21.5	0.0	5.4	0.0
Rainbow, Smoked, M & S*	1 Pack/135g	169	125	20.1	0.1	5.0	0.0
Rainbow, Smoked, Somerfield*	1oz/28g	34	120	22.0	0.0	4.0	0.0
Rosemary Crusted, Finest, Tesco*	1 Trout/150g	264	176	16.2	12.2	6.9	1.0
Smoked, M & S*	1oz/28g	34	120	20.2	0.0	4.5	0.0
Smoked, Sainsbury's*	1 Serving/100g	141	141	23.7	0.1	5.1	0.1
Whole, Somerfield*	1oz/28g	35	125	20.0	0.0	5.0	0.0
TUNA,							
All Day Light Meal, Italian, John West*	1 Serving/100g	141	141	11.0	13.0	5.0	0.0
Canned In Brine, Drained	1oz/28g	28	99	23.5	0.0	0.6	0.0
Canned In Oil, Drained	1oz/28g	53	189	27.1	0.0	9.0	0.0
Chunks, In Brine, Asda*	1oz/28g	30	106	26.0	0.0	0.2	0.0
Chunks, In Brine, Canned, Sailor*	½ Can/92g	104	113	27.0	0.0	0.6	0.0
Chunks, In Brine, Heinz*	1oz/28g	28	99	23.5	0.0	0.6	0.0
Chunks, In Brine, John West*	1oz/28g	32	113	27.0	0.0	0.5	0.0
Chunks, In Brine, Princes*	1oz/28g	29	105	25.0	0.0	0.5	0.0
Chunks, In Brine, Safeway*	1oz/28g	28	99	23.5	0.0	0.6	0.0
Chunks, In Brine, Sainsbury's*	¼ Can/71g	80	113	27.0	0.1	0.5	0.0
Chunks, In Brine, Skipjack, Safeway*	1oz/28g	28	99	23.5	0.0	0.6	0.0
Chunks, In Brine, Skipjack, Waitrose*	¼ Can/70g	77	110	26.1	0.0	0.6	0.0
Chunks, In Brine, Somerfield*	1oz/28g	28	99	24.0	0.0	1.0	0.0
Chunks, In Brine, Tesco*	1 Serving/80g	83	104	25.9	0.0	0.6	0.0
Chunks, In Brine, Value, Tesco*	1oz/28g	28	101	23.8	0.0	0.6	0.0
Chunks, In Oil, Somerfield*	1oz/28g	53	189	27.0	0.0	9.0	0.0
Chunks, In Spring Water, Asda*	½ Can/77g	82	106	26.0	0.0	0.2	0.0
Chunks, In Spring Water, Princes*	1 Can/139g	147	106	26.0	0.0	0.2	0.0

Nutrition Values per 100g / 100ml

T

TUNA,	Measure WEIGHT/INFO	per Measure KCAL	Nutrition Values per 100g / 100ml KCAL	PROT	CARB	FAT	FIBRE
Chunks, In Springwater, John West*	1oz/28g	32	113	27.0	0.0	0.5	0.0
Chunks, In Sunflower Oil, John West*	1oz/28g	53	189	27.0	0.0	9.0	0.0
Chunks, In Sunflower Oil, Tescos*	½ Can/92g	174	189	27.1	0.0	9.0	0.0
Chunks, In Water, Sainsbury's*	1oz/28g	35	125	26.2	0.1	2.2	0.0
Chunks, SmartPrice, Asda*	1 Can/130g	138	106	26.0	0.0	0.2	0.0
Flakes, In Brine, Value, Tesco*	1oz/28g	28	101	23.8	0.0	0.6	0.0
Flakes, SmartPrice, Asda*	½ Can/59g	53	90	22.0	0.0	0.2	0.0
In Brine, John West*	1oz/28g	32	113	27.0	0.0	0.5	0.0
In Chilli Sauce, Safeway*	1 Serving/100g	158	158	16.8	4.8	7.9	0.5
In Garlic & Herb Mayonnaise, John West*	½ Can/92g	243	264	12.0	4.0	22.2	0.2
In Spring Water, John West*	½ Can/93g	92	99	23.5	0.0	0.6	0.0
In Spring Water, M & S*	1 Can/180g	189	105	25.0	0.0	0.5	0.0
In Sweet & Sour Sauce, Safeway*	1 Can/185g	148	80	10.9	5.6	1.6	1.0
In Thousand Island Dressing, John West*	1 Can/185g	287	155	18.0	5.1	7.0	0.2
Light Lunch, French Style, John West*	1 Pack/250g	208	83	7.8	7.6	2.4	1.0
Light Lunch, Mediterranean, John West*	1 Pack/250g	180	72	8.0	7.5	1.1	1.1
Light Lunch, Tomato Salsa, John West*	1 Serving/250g	180	72	8.0	7.5	1.1	1.1
Lime & Black Pepper, John West*	1 Serving/85g	133	156	15.6	2.8	9.2	0.0
Loins, Asda*	1oz/28g	37	132	24.0	0.0	4.0	0.0
Mayonnaise With Sweetcorn, John West*	½ Can/92g	231	251	12.0	4.5	20.6	0.2
Raw, Average	1oz/28g	38	136	23.7	0.0	4.6	0.0
Snack Pot, Italian, Weight Watchers*	1 Pot/240g	245	102	9.1	8.5	3.6	0.5
Steak, In Vegetable Oil, Heinz*	1oz/28g	53	189	27.1	0.0	9.0	0.0
Steaks, Chargrilled, Italian, Sainsbury's*	1 Serving/125g	199	159	25.1	0.2	6.4	0.5
Steaks, Finest, Tesco*	1 Serving/120g	138	115	26.0	0.6	0.9	0.0
Steaks, Fresh, Asda*	1 Steak/96g	118	123	29.0	0.0	0.8	0.0
Steaks, Fresh, M & S*	1 Steak/120g	156	130	23.1	0.0	3.9	0.0
Steaks, Fresh, Sainsbury's*	1 Serving/100g	117	117	28.9	0.0	0.4	0.0
Steaks, Frozen, Iceland*	1 Steak/150g	201	134	32.0	0.0	0.6	0.0
Steaks, Frozen, Sainsbury's*	1 Steak/150g	210	140	34.8	0.1	0.1	1.1
Steaks, In Brine, John West*	1 Can/150g	170	113	27.0	0.0	0.5	0.0
Steaks, In Brine, Princes*	1oz/28g	29	105	25.0	0.0	0.5	0.0
Steaks, In Brine, Sainsbury's*	1oz/28g	32	115	26.2	0.1	1.1	0.0
Steaks, In Brine, Skipjack, Morrisons*	½ Can/75g	65	86	20.4	0.0	0.5	0.0
Steaks, In Brine, Skipjack, Waitrose*	½ Tin/75g	82	109	26.0	0.0	0.6	0.0
Steaks, In Brine, Tesco*	1 Can/149g	155	104	25.9	0.0	0.6	0.0
Steaks, In Cajun Marinade, Sainsbury's*	1 Steak/100g	141	141	29.8	0.0	2.4	0.0
Steaks, In Oil, Somerfield*	1oz/28g	53	189	27.0	0.0	9.0	0.0
Steaks, In Olive Oil, Sainsbury's*	1oz/28g	53	189	26.9	0.0	9.0	0.0
Steaks, In Spring Water, Sainsbury's*	1 Sm Can/75g	85	113	27.0	0.0	0.5	0.0
Steaks, In Springwater, Waitrose*	1 Serving/200g	198	99	23.5	0.0	0.6	0.0
Steaks, In Sunflower Oil, John West*	½ Can/75g	142	189	27.0	0.0	9.0	0.0
Steaks, In Sunflower Oil, Sainsbury's*	1 Can/75g	136	181	27.0	0.1	8.1	0.0
Steaks, In Water, Sainsbury's	1oz/28g	35	125	26.2	0.0	2.2	0.0
Steaks, Marinated, Sainsbury's*	1 Serving/100g	153	153	25.1	1.3	5.3	0.5
Steaks, With Sweet Red Pepper Glaze, Sainsbury's*	1 Steak/100g	135	135	28.5	5.0	0.1	0.1
Steaks, Yellowfin, In Spring Water, Sainsbury's*	½ Can/75g	85	113	27.0	0.1	0.5	0.0
Twists, Italian, Weight Watchers*	1 Can/385g	239	62	4.3	8.2	1.4	0.6
With A Twist Touch Of Water, John West*	1 Serving/85g	87	102	23.4	0.8	0.6	0.0
With Light Mayonnaise, Princes*	1 Sachet/100g	112	112	20.5	3.0	2.0	0.0
With Onion, John West*	1oz/28g	33	118	19.0	6.0	2.0	0.0
TURBOT,							
Grilled	1oz/28g	34	122	22.7	0.0	3.5	0.0
Raw	1oz/28g	27	95	17.7	0.0	2.7	0.0

T

TURKEY,	Measure WEIGHT/INFO	per Measure KCAL	Nutrition Values per 100g / 100ml KCAL	PROT	CARB	FAT	FIBRE
Breast, Cooked With Stuffing, Somerfield*	1oz/28g	29	104	17.0	6.0	2.0	0.0
Breast, Diced, Asda*	1 Serving/150g	155	103	24.0	0.0	0.8	0.0
Breast Escalopes, Safeway*	1 Serving/141g	304	217	13.9	18.8	9.6	0.9
Breast Fillet Strips, Fresh, Sainsbury's*	1 Serving/100g	143	143	30.8	0.1	2.1	0.1
Breast Fillet, Y Cut, Non Breaded, Bernard Matthews*	1oz/28g	29	105	23.8	0.1	1.0	0.0
Breast, Golden Roasted, Bernard Matthews*	1 Piece/38g	43	113	24.3	0.4	1.6	0.0
Breast, Hand Carved, Butter Basted, TTD, Sainsbury's*	1oz/28g	40	142	24.7	1.2	4.1	0.3
Breast, Honey Roast, Bernard Matthews*	1 Serving/50g	54	107	23.5	1.1	1.0	0.0
Breast, Honey Roast, Wafer Thin, Bernard Matthews*	1 Serving/50g	48	96	18.6	4.4	0.4	0.0
Breast Joint, Butter Basted, Boneless, Tesco*	1 Serving/100g	136	136	18.6	4.0	5.1	0.4
Breast Joint, Lemon & Pepper Basted, Tesco*	¼ Pack/132g	238	180	19.7	0.0	11.2	0.0
Breast Joint, M & S*	¼ Pack/130g	143	110	19.6	0.2	3.3	0.0
Breast Joint, Sage & Onion, Glazed, GFY, Asda*	1 Serving/100g	101	101	19.0	2.5	1.7	1.0
Breast Joint With Cranberry & Orange Glaze, Sainsbury's*	1 Serving/180g	281	156	29.6	3.0	2.9	1.0
Breast, M & S*	1oz/28g	39	140	24.5	0.0	4.4	0.0
Breast, Norfolk, Premium, Bernard Mathews*	1 Serving/40g	40	100	19.7	2.5	1.2	0.0
Breast, Premium, Smoked, Bernard Matthews*	1 Slice/20g	19	97	20.8	1.4	0.9	0.0
Breast, Roast, Bernard Matthews*	1oz/28g	30	106	18.5	1.3	3.2	0.4
Breast, Roast, Premium, Sainsbury's*	1 Slice/20g	25	127	28.5	0.8	1.2	0.2
Breast, Roast, Somerfield*	1oz/28g	27	98	21.0	2.0	1.0	0.0
Breast, Roasted, Less Than 5% Fat, Asda*	1oz/28g	32	116	25.6	0.2	1.4	0.2
Breast Roll, Cooked, Bernard Matthews*	1 Slice/10g	9	92	17.6	3.5	0.8	0.0
Breast Roll, Norfolk, Cooked, Bernard Matthews*	1 Slice/10g	9	92	17.6	3.5	0.8	0.0
Breast, Sage & Onion Style, Premium, Bernard Matthews*	1 Slice/20g	21	104	19.6	2.2	2.0	0.0
Breast, Sainsbury's*	1 Serving/170g	318	187	25.8	0.1	9.3	0.2
Breast, Smoked, Somerfield*	1oz/28g	36	129	26.0	0.0	3.0	0.0
Breast, Somerfield*	1oz/28g	34	122	20.0	0.0	5.0	0.0
Breast Steaks & Pieces, SmartPrice, Asda*	1 Serving/100g	105	105	24.0	0.0	1.0	0.1
Breast Steaks, Bernard Matthews*	1 Steak/71g	163	229	13.2	15.3	12.8	0.0
Breast Steaks, Farm Assumed, Safeway*	1 Serving/100g	105	105	24.4	0.0	0.8	0.0
Breast Steaks, Fresh, Co-Op*	1 Serving/112g	118	105	23.0	0.0	1.0	0.0
Breast Steaks, Fresh, Waitrose*	1oz/28g	29	105	24.4	0.0	0.8	0.0
Breast Steaks, HE, Tesco*	1 Serving/200g	206	103	23.2	0.0	1.1	0.0
Breast Steaks, Quick Cook, Sainsbury's*	1 Serving/100g	133	133	30.0	0.1	1.4	0.1
Breast Steaks, Sainsbury's*	1oz/28g	37	133	30.0	0.0	1.4	0.0
Breast Strips, Chinese Style, Sainsbury's*	1 Pack/650g	1274	196	26.4	12.5	4.5	0.5
Breast, Wafer Thin, Chinese Style, Bernard Matthews*	1 Pack/100g	110	110	18.0	6.1	1.5	0.0
Cooked Roll, Dinosaur, Bernard Matthews*	1 Slice/10g	17	170	13.6	6.0	10.2	1.1
Cooked, Sainsbury's	1 Slice/20g	20	98	19.8	2.1	1.1	0.7
Cooked, Tesco*	1 Slice/20g	23	114	22.6	1.4	2.0	0.4
Dark Meat, Raw	1oz/28g	74	266	8.7	51.1	4.7	7.5
Dark Meat, Roasted	1oz/28g	101	362	5.4	56.1	13.2	0.0
Diced Breast, British, HE, Tesco*	1 Serving/100g	103	103	23.2	0.0	1.1	0.0
Diced Thigh, British, Tesco*	1 Pack/300g	342	114	20.3	0.0	3.6	0.0
Escalope, Asda*	1 Serving/140g	399	285	13.0	20.0	17.0	0.6
Escalope, Bernard Matthews*	1 Escalope/143g	380	266	10.7	18.4	16.6	0.0
Escalope, Breaded, Tesco*	1 Escalope/138g	298	216	13.7	13.4	11.9	1.6
Escalope, Lemon & Pepper, Bernard Matthews*	1 Escalope/143g	362	253	11.2	17.2	15.5	0.0
Escalope, Southern Fried, Somerfield*	1 Pack/280g	700	250	16.0	13.0	15.0	0.0
Escalope, Spicy Mango, Bernard Matthews*	1 Escalope/136g	354	260	11.6	24.6	12.8	0.0
Escalope With Cheese & Leek Sauce, Bernard Matthews*	1 Portion/134g	340	254	9.2	17.6	16.3	0.0
Fillets, Chinese Marinated, Bernard Matthews*	1 Pack/200g	304	152	23.4	7.2	3.3	0.0
Fillets, Safeway*	1 Serving/160g	248	155	35.0	0.0	1.7	0.0
Fillets, Tikka Marinated, Bernard Matthews*	1 Pack/200g	310	155	21.8	5.2	5.2	1.6

T

TURKEY,	Measure WEIGHT/INFO	per Measure KCAL	Nutrition Values per 100g / 100ml KCAL	PROT	CARB	FAT	FIBRE
Free Range, Fresh Bronze, TTD, Sainsbury's*	1 Serving/100g	166	166	26.4	0.1	6.7	0.1
Honey Roast, Wafer Thin, Asda*	1oz/28g	33	119	19.6	4.7	2.4	0.0
Honey Roast, Wafer Thin, Safeway*	1 Serving/50g	57	114	19.7	3.9	2.2	0.0
Honey Roast, Wafer Thin, Sainsbury's*	1 Serving/100g	107	107	18.8	3.7	1.9	0.7
Leg Roast, Bernard Matthews*	1 Leg/567g	777	137	15.4	0.5	5.4	1.2
Leg Roast, Uncooked, Bernard Matthews*	1 Serving/283g	317	112	15.4	0.5	5.4	0.0
Light Meat, Raw	1oz/28g	78	277	8.6	50.2	4.3	3.2
Light Meat, Roasted	1oz/28g	43	153	33.7	0.0	2.0	0.0
Meat For Casseroles, Bernard Matthews*	1oz/28g	33	118	19.3	0.0	4.5	0.0
Mince, Frozen, Asda*	1 Serving/100g	147	147	21.0	0.0	7.0	0.0
Mince, HE, Tesco*	1 Serving/175g	217	124	18.0	0.0	5.8	0.0
Mince, Sainsbury's*	½ Pack/250g	495	198	28.6	0.0	9.6	0.0
On The Bone, Honey Roast, Somerfield*	1oz/28g	42	149	26.0	0.0	5.0	0.0
Rashers, Bernard Matthews*	1 Slice/25g	26	105	18.0	3.7	2.0	0.0
Rashers, Healthy Choice, Safeway*	1 Rasher/27g	27	99	20.0	2.4	1.0	0.0
Rashers Lightly Smoked, HE, Tesco*	1 Serving/75g	76	101	19.8	1.5	1.8	0.0
Rashers, Lightly Smoked, Tesco*	1 Serving/75g	76	101	19.8	1.5	1.8	0.0
Rashers, Original, Unsmoked, Mattesons*	1 Rasher/26g	26	99	19.3	1.8	1.6	0.0
Roast Dinner, Bird's Eye*	1 Pack/359g	330	92	6.7	9.5	3.0	1.4
Roast, Frozen, Cooked	1oz/28g	48	170	26.7	0.0	7.0	0.0
Roast, Meat & Skin	1oz/28g	48	171	28.0	0.0	6.5	0.0
Roast, Thin Sliced, Asda*	1 Slice/13g	15	112	20.0	3.6	2.0	0.0
Schnitzel, Lidl*	1 Schnitzel/115g	210	183	19.0	11.0	7.0	0.0
Slices	1oz/28g	32	114	23.0	1.2	1.9	0.0
Slices, 97% Fat Free, Bernard Matthews*	1 Slice/37g	42	113	24.3	0.4	1.6	0.0
Slices, Honey Roast, Tesco*	1 Slice/20g	24	122	24.5	2.1	1.7	0.5
Smoked, Wafer Thin, Tesco*	1 Serving/50g	58	116	19.1	3.6	2.8	0.0
Steak, Tesco*	1 Serving/114g	117	103	23.2	0.0	1.1	0.0
Steaks In Crumbs, Frozen, Grilled	1oz/28g	83	295	17.6	18.9	17.1	0.6
Steaks, Quick Cook, HE, Tesco*	1 Serving/80g	82	103	23.2	0.0	0.3	0.0
Strips, Stir-Fried	1oz/28g	93	333	5.0	51.6	12.2	0.0
Stuffed Roll, GFY, Asda*	½ Pack/225g	320	142	14.0	12.0	4.2	0.8
Thigh, Diced, Co-Op*	1 Serving/85g	102	120	19.0	0.0	5.0	0.0
Thigh, Lean Diced, Sainsbury's*	1oz/28g	58	207	34.3	0.5	7.5	0.1
Thin Sliced Honey Roast, Asda*	1 Slice/13g	15	116	19.1	3.2	3.0	0.1
Wafer Thin, 92% Fat Free, Bernard Matthews*	¼ Pack/38g	55	144	14.8	5.5	7.0	0.0
Wafer Thin, Cooked, Bernard Matthews*	5 Slices/38g	55	144	14.8	5.5	7.0	0.0
Wafer Thin, Smoked, Bernard Matthews*	1oz/28g	26	93	18.6	2.1	1.5	0.0
TURKEY. Breast, Grilled, Asda*	1 Serving/200g	206	103	24.0	0.0	0.8	0.0
TURKISH DELIGHT,							
Bar, M & S*	1 Bar/55g	219	399	1.6	79.0	8.5	0.0
Bar, Shapers, Boots*	1 Bar/32g	99	310	2.0	76.0	8.0	0.8
Dark, Thorntons*	1 Chocolate/10g	39	390	2.7	69.0	11.0	2.0
Fry's*	1 Bar/51g	186	365	2.0	73.3	7.2	0.0
Without Nuts	1oz/28g	83	295	0.6	77.9	0.0	0.0
TURMERIC, Powder	1 Tsp/3g	11	354	7.8	58.2	9.9	0.0
TURNIP,							
Boiled In Salted Water	1oz/28g	3	12	0.6	2.0	0.2	1.9
Boiled In Unsalted Water	1oz/28g	3	12	0.6	2.0	0.2	1.9
Raw	1oz/28g	6	23	0.9	4.7	0.3	2.4
TURNOVER,							
Apple, Co-Op*	1 Turnover/77g	308	400	4.0	35.0	27.0	1.0
Apple, Tesco*	1 Turnover/88g	294	334	3.2	29.8	22.4	0.9
TWIGLETS,							

T

	Measure	per Measure	Nutrition Values per 100g / 100ml				
TWIGLETS,	WEIGHT/INFO	KCAL	KCAL	PROT	CARB	FAT	FIBRE
Curry, Jacob's*	1 Bag/30g	134	448	8.0	55.7	21.5	6.0
Original, Jacob's*	1 Bag/30g	117	390	12.0	61.3	10.8	6.8
Tangy, Jacob's*	1 Bag/30g	136	454	8.1	55.9	22.0	5.4
TWILIGHT, Terry's*	1oz/28g	145	519	2.9	61.4	28.9	3.9
TWIRL, Cadbury's*	1 Finger/22g	116	525	8.1	55.9	30.1	0.0
TWIRLS, Salt & Vinegar, Tesco*	1 Bag/80g	349	436	3.9	65.8	17.5	2.4
TWISTER, Kentucky Fried Chicken*	1 Twister/240g	600	250	9.1	21.6	14.1	1.6
TWISTS, Tomato & Herb, Shapers, Boots*	1 Pack/20g	94	468	3.7	66.0	21.0	3.9
TWIX,							
Fingers, Mars*	1 Serving/29g	143	494	4.6	64.8	24.1	0.0
Mars*	1 Single Bar/29g	144	495	5.8	63.5	24.2	0.0
Top, Mars*	1 Bar/28g	143	511	5.2	60.2	27.7	0.0
Twixels, Mars*	1 Finger/6g	31	513	5.0	64.0	26.1	0.0
TZATZIKI,							
Tzatziki	1oz/28g	18	66	3.7	2.0	4.9	0.2
Fresh, Sainsbury's*	1oz/28g	35	126	4.0	3.7	10.6	0.3
M & S*	1oz/28g	41	145	5.6	5.9	10.9	0.4
Tesco*	1 Serving/85g	121	142	5.1	4.1	11.7	1.0
Total*	1oz/28g	27	98	4.9	4.1	7.0	0.0

T

	Measure	per Measure	Nutrition Values per 100g / 100ml				
	WEIGHT/INFO	KCAL	KCAL	PROT	CARB	FAT	FIBRE
VEAL,							
Escalope, Fried	1oz/28g	55	196	33.7	0.0	6.8	0.0
Mince, Raw	1oz/28g	40	144	20.3	0.0	7.0	0.0
Mince, Organic*	1oz/28g	53	189	17.0	7.8	10.0	0.0
Mince, RealEat*	1 Serving/125g	220	176	15.5	6.0	10.0	2.0
VEGE ROAST, Chicken Style, Realeat*	1 Pack/454g	844	186	23.0	3.2	9.0	0.0
VEGEBANGER Herb, Realeat*	1 Vegebanger/110g	319	290	42.0	21.0	4.2	0.0
VEGEBANGER Spicy, Realeat*	1 Vegebanger/110g	294	267	25.3	12.1	13.2	0.0
VEGEBITES, Realeat*	1oz/28g	68	243	12.1	11.2	16.6	0.0
VEGEBURGER, Retail, Grilled	1oz/28g	55	196	16.6	8.0	11.1	4.2
VEGEMINCE, Realeat*	1oz/28g	100	356	34.0	15.5	18.5	0.0
VEGEMITE, Kraft*	Thin Spread/1g	2	180	30.0	14.0	0.0	0.0
VEGESTEAK, Realeat*	1 Pack/400g	1056	264	28.4	15.0	10.0	0.0
VEGETABLE - ROAST,							
Arrabbiata, HE, Tesco*	1 Pack/450g	437	97	3.3	18.4	1.1	1.1
Lavash, Ready Meals, Waitrose*	1oz/28g	67	239	4.7	28.9	11.6	1.8
VEGETABLE BAKE,							
Potato & Vegetable, Co-Op*	1 Bake/340g	425	125	4.0	11.0	8.0	1.0
Root Vegetable, M & S*	1 Bake/270g	621	230	6.6	35.0	6.5	3.9
Salsa, WTF, Sainsbury's*	1 Pack/400g	460	115	4.1	11.7	5.7	1.6
Vegetable & Lentil, Somerfield*	1 Pack/350g	319	91	4.9	13.8	1.8	2.5
Vegetarian, Iceland*	1 Pack/332g	408	123	4.5	14.5	5.2	2.6
Vegetarian, Tesco*	1 Pack/400g	440	110	4.1	9.9	6.0	0.9
VEGETABLE BIRIYANI With Vegetable Curry, Budgens*	1 Serving/250g	378	151	3.4	22.9	5.1	1.5
VEGETABLE ENCHILLIADAS, Chilled, Co-Op*	1 Pack/270g	378	140	6.0	21.0	4.0	3.0
VEGETABLE FINGERS,							
Crispy, Birds Eye*	1 Finger/29g	50	171	3.8	21.0	8.0	1.2
Crispy Crunchy, Dalepak*	1 Finger/28g	78	277	4.1	25.8	17.5	8.7
VEGETABLE JUICE, Organic, Evernat*	1 Glass/200ml	36	18	0.9	3.5	0.1	0.2
VEGETABLE MEDLEY,							
Asparagus Tips, Perfectly Balanced, Waitrose*	1 Serving/225g	122	54	1.3	4.6	3.4	1.4
Basil & Oregano Butter, Waitrose*	1 Serving/113g	59	52	1.7	3.7	3.4	1.9
M & S*	½ Pack/250g	88	35	2.9	3.9	0.7	3.5
Tesco*	1 Serving/200g	52	26	1.8	3.6	0.5	2.4
VEGETABLE PRIMAVERA, HE, Tesco*	1 Pack/350g	235	67	3.4	10.0	1.5	1.0
VEGETABLE PULAO, Perfectly Balanced, Waitrose*	1 Pack/400g	380	95	2.9	14.1	3.0	1.8
VEGETABLES, Chinese Water, Amoy*	1 Pack/200g	46	23	1.8	3.7	0.3	1.5
VEGETARIAN MINCE,							
& Onions, Organic*	1 Pack/120g	418	348	19.0	59.0	4.0	0.0
Mince, Meat Free, Asda*	1oz/28g	49	176	27.0	7.0	4.4	4.1
VEGETARIAN STEAK, Lamb & Mint Style, Safeway*	1 Steak/100g	210	210	26.6	9.9	7.4	2.0
VEGETARIAN STEAKS, Gammon Style, Safeway*	1 Serving/100g	250	250	25.0	9.6	12.4	2.0
VEGETERIAN MINCE, Easy Cook, Linda McCartney*	1oz/28g	35	126	21.4	9.3	0.4	1.7
VENISON,							
Grill Steak, Finest, Tesco*	1 Steak/170g	202	119	19.0	5.0	2.5	1.9
In Red Wine & Port	1oz/28g	105	375	0.1	93.5	0.8	0.1
Raw	1oz/28g	64	227	6.8	28.7	9.3	0.0
Roasted	1oz/28g	46	165	35.6	0.0	2.5	0.0
Steaks, Prime, Tesco*	1 Steak/140g	154	110	23.0	0.0	2.0	0.0
VERMOUTH,							
Dry	1 Shot/25ml	27	109	0.1	3.0	0.0	0.0
Sweet	1 Shot/25ml	38	151	0.0	15.9	0.0	0.0
VIENESSE BOMBES, Gold Selection, Somerfield*	1 Bombe/115g	398	346	4.0	29.0	24.0	0.0
VIMTO*,							
Vimto*	1 Can/330ml	147	45	0.0	11.0	0.0	0.0

	Measure WEIGHT/INFO	per Measure KCAL	Nutrition Values per 100g / 100ml KCAL	PROT	CARB	FAT	FIBRE
VIMTO,							
Cordial	1 Serving/10ml	3	30	0.0	7.4	0.0	0.0
Grape Blackcurrant & Raspberry Juice Drink	1 Bottle/500ml	223	45	0.0	11.0	0.0	0.0
Light	1 Can/330ml	17	5	0.0	1.2	0.0	0.0
VINAIGRETTE,							
Bean, 2% Fat, M & S*	1 Pack/225g	203	90	6.4	14.3	0.9	3.9
French, Full Flavoured, Fat Free, Kraft*	1 Tbsp/15ml	7	47	0.1	10.5	0.0	0.3
French Style, Finest, Tesco*	1 Tbsp/15ml	69	461	0.8	5.9	47.4	0.2
Italian & Garlic, Kraft*	1 Tsp/5ml	6	128	0.4	7.2	10.5	0.2
Luxury French, Hellmann's*	1 Tsp/5ml	15	305	0.8	16.0	26.1	0.4
Portuguese, Nando's*	1 Tbsp/15g	61	409	1.0	2.1	44.0	0.3
Waistline, 99% Fat Free, Crosse & Blackwell*	1 Tbsp/15ml	1	9	1.0	0.7	0.2	0.2
VINE LEAVES,							
Preserved In Brine	1oz/28g	4	15	3.6	0.2	0.0	0.0
Stuffed, M & S*	1oz/28g	31	110	3.8	13.1	4.4	2.2
Stuffed With Rice	1oz/28g	73	262	2.8	23.8	18.0	0.0
VINEGAR,							
Balsamic	5ml	0	3	0.3	0.6	0.0	0.0
Malt, Frank Cooper*	1 Sachet/8g	0	4	0.4	0.6	0.0	0.0
Malt, Heinz*	1 Tsp/5ml	1	18	0.2	0.6	0.0	0.0
Rice, White, Amoy*	1 Tsp/5ml	0	4	0.0	1.0	0.0	0.0
Wine, White, Heinz*	1 Tsp/5ml	1	21	0.1	0.6	0.0	0.0
VODKA,							
Vodka	1 Shot/25ml	52	207	0.0	0.0	0.0	0.0
37.5% Volume	1 Shot/25ml	52	207	0.0	0.0	0.0	0.0
40% Volume	1 Shot/25ml	56	222	0.0	0.0	0.0	0.0
VOL AU VENTS,							
Broccoli, M & S*	1oz/28g	105	375	6.8	28.5	26.4	1.0
Chicken & Mushroom, M & S*	1oz/28g	98	350	7.7	25.2	24.3	2.1
Ham & Cheese, M & S*	1oz/28g	106	380	8.8	25.7	26.7	1.8
Mushroom, M & S*	1oz/28g	94	335	6.3	24.2	23.6	1.5
Mushroom, Sainsbury's*	1 Vol Au Vent/14g	49	350	6.9	30.8	22.1	1.4
Party Seafood, Youngs*	1 Vol Au Vent/17g	60	354	8.3	26.0	24.8	1.0
Prawn, M & S*	1oz/28g	101	360	8.0	26.2	24.7	1.9
Tomato, M & S*	1oz/28g	87	310	4.5	26.7	20.4	1.7

V

	Measure	per Measure	Nutrition Values per 100g / 100ml				
WAFERS,	WEIGHT/INFO	KCAL	KCAL	PROT	CARB	FAT	FIBRE
Cafe Curls, Rolled, Askeys*	1 Curl/5g	21	422	5.8	80.3	8.6	0.0
Caramel, Dark Chocolate, Tunnock's*	1 Wafer/26g	128	492	5.2	60.7	25.4	0.0
Caramel, M & S*	1oz/28g	136	486	5.4	63.1	23.5	0.5
Caramel, Tunnock's*	1 Biscuit/26g	118	454	4.6	68.0	20.1	0.0
Chocolate, Cadbury's*	1oz/28g	147	526	7.0	61.2	29.8	0.0
Chocolate Curl, Mini, M & S*	1 Biscuit/5g	28	550	5.8	56.0	33.6	1.5
Chocolate Mint, Plain, Somerfield*	1oz/28g	151	538	9.0	56.0	31.0	0.0
Filled	1oz/28g	150	535	4.7	66.0	29.9	0.0
Ice Cream	1oz/28g	96	342	10.1	78.8	0.7	0.0
Ice Cream, Askeys*	2 Wafers/3g	11	380	11.0	79.0	2.5	0.0
Milk Chocolate Caramel, Farmfoods*	1 Biscuit/22g	105	475	5.9	61.9	22.8	3.1
Milk Chocolate Caramel, M & S*	1oz/28g	133	475	5.9	61.9	22.8	3.1
Milk Chocolate, Sainsbury's*	1 Biscuit/10g	51	506	6.2	60.5	26.7	1.4
Orange Break, Somerfield*	1oz/28g	149	531	8.0	57.0	30.0	0.0
Pink, Crawfords*	1 Biscuit/7g	36	521	2.5	68.6	26.5	1.1
WAFFLES,							
Barbecue Flavour, American Style, Shapers, Boots*	1 Pack/20g	95	476	4.5	65.0	22.0	3.7
Caramel, The Big Cereal Company*	1 Serving/23g	84	367	7.5	80.1	1.9	2.8
Ready Salted, M & S*	1 Bag/40g	194	485	2.1	65.6	23.6	1.6
Smokey Bacon, BGTY, Sainsbury's*	1 Bag/12g	41	344	5.6	76.3	1.8	1.5
Toasting, McVitie's*	1 Waffle/23g	108	469	5.9	53.9	25.6	0.9
WAGON WHEEL, Burton's*	1 Wheel/36g	159	441	4.9	67.3	16.9	1.3
WALNUT HALVES,							
Organic, Evernat*	1oz/28g	193	689	14.7	3.3	68.5	3.5
Somerfield*	1oz/28g	193	688	15.0	3.0	69.0	0.0
WALNUT PIECES, Asda*	1 Serving/10g	69	694	15.0	3.3	69.0	3.5
WALNUT WHIP,							
Vanilla, Nestle*	1 Whip/34g	160	486	5.7	60.5	24.6	0.0
WALNUTS,							
Walnuts	6 Halves/20g	138	688	14.7	3.3	68.5	3.5
Organic Shelled, Waitrose*	1oz/28g	195	698	17.3	3.1	68.5	3.5
Sainsbury's*	1 Nut/3g	21	688	14.7	3.3	68.5	3.5
WATER CHESTNUTS,							
Amoy*	1oz/28g	12	42	0.9	10.1	0.0	0.0
Canned, Drained	1oz/28g	9	31	0.9	7.4	0.0	0.0
Raw	1oz/28g	13	46	1.4	10.4	0.2	0.0
Whole, Asda*	1oz/28g	5	17	0.8	3.4	0.0	0.4
Whole, Sainsbury's*	1 Can/141g	24	17	0.8	3.4	0.1	0.4
WATER ICE,							
Fruit, Iceland*	1 Lolly/75ml	74	98	0.2	24.4	0.0	0.2
Orange, Iceland*	1 Ice/75ml	73	98	0.2	24.4	0.0	0.2
Pineapple, Iceland*	1 Ice/75ml	65	86	0.0	21.5	0.0	0.2
Raspberry, Iceland*	1 Ice/75ml	67	89	0.0	22.2	0.0	0.2
WATER,							
Lemon & Elderflower, Slightly Sparkling, Tesco*	1 Glass/200ml	2	1	0.0	0.1	0.0	0.0
Lemon & Lime Flavoured, M & S*	1 Glass/250ml	13	5	0.0	1.0	0.0	0.0
Mandarin & Cranberry, Still, M & S*	1 Bottle/500ml	100	20	0.0	5.0	0.0	0.0
Mineral, Touch of Fruit, Still, Volvic*	1fl oz/30ml	7	23	0.0	5.5	0.0	0.0
Orange & Peach, Touch of Fruit, Volvic*	1 Bottle/400ml	93	23	0.0	5.5	0.0	0.0
Peach & Lemon, Still, M & S*	1 Bottle/500ml	100	20	0.0	5.0	0.0	0.0
Peach Flavoured, M & S*	1 Glass/250ml	13	5	0.0	1.0	0.0	0.0
Peach, Perfectly Clear, Silver Spring Mineral Water Co*	1 Bottle/500ml	4	1	0.0	0.0	0.0	0.0
Peach, Still, M & S*	1 Bottle/330ml	7	2	0.0	0.0	0.0	0.0
Spring, Apple & Raspberry Flavoured, Sainsbury's*	1fl oz/30ml	1	2	0.1	0.1	0.1	0.1

	Measure WEIGHT/INFO	per Measure KCAL	Nutrition Values per 100g / 100ml KCAL	PROT	CARB	FAT	FIBRE
WATER,							
Spring, Boysenberry, Shapers, Boots*	1 Bottle/700ml	7	1	0.0	0.1	0.0	0.0
Spring, Peach Flavour, Shapers, Boots*	1 Bottle/500ml	5	1	0.0	0.0	0.0	0.0
Spring, Peach Flavoured, No Added Sugar, Asda*	1 Glass/200ml	4	2	0.0	0.2	0.0	0.0
Spring, Peach Flavoured, Sainsbury's*	1 Glass/250ml	5	2	0.1	0.2	0.1	0.1
Spring, Raspberry & Mango, Shapers, Boots*	1 Bottle/500ml	7	1	0.0	0.1	0.0	0.0
Spring, Stawberry & Vanilla, Sainsbury's*	1 Glass/250ml	5	2	0.1	0.2	0.1	0.1
White Grape & Blackberry, Sparkling, Tesco*	1 Glass/200ml	4	2	0.0	0.5	0.0	0.0
WATERCRESS, Raw	1oz/28g	6	22	3.0	0.4	1.0	1.5
WATERMELON,							
Cantaloupe Style*	1 Segment/100g	19	19	0.6	4.2	0.1	1.0
Slices, M & S*	1 Pack/240g	72	30	0.4	7.0	0.3	0.5
WHEAT CRUNCHIES,							
Bacon, Crispy, Golden Wonder*	1 Bag/35g	172	491	11.1	55.9	24.9	2.8
Golden Wonder*	1 Pack/35g	172	491	11.1	55.9	24.8	0.0
Salt & Vinegar, Golden Wonder*	1 Bag/34g	165	484	10.5	54.5	24.9	2.8
Spicy Tomato, Golden Wonder*	1 Bag/35g	171	488	10.7	55.5	24.8	3.0
Worcester Sauce, Golden Wonder*	1 Bag/35g	170	487	10.7	54.9	24.9	3.0
WHEAT, Ebly*	1oz/28g	98	351	12.1	71.9	1.7	5.4
WHEATGERM	1oz/28g	100	357	26.7	44.7	9.2	15.6
WHELKS, Boiled	1oz/28g	25	89	19.5	0.0	1.2	0.0
WHISKEY,							
37.5% Volume	1 Shot/25ml	52	207	0.0	0.0	0.0	0.0
40% Volume	1 Shot/25ml	56	222	0.0	0.0	0.0	0.0
Jack Daniels*	1 Shot/25ml	56	222	0.0	0.0	0.0	0.0
Scotch, 37.5% Volume	1 Shot/25ml	52	207	0.0	0.0	0.0	0.0
Scotch, 40% Volume	1 Shot/25ml	56	222	0.0	0.0	0.0	0.0
Teacher's*	1 Shot/25ml	56	222	0.0	0.0	0.0	0.0
WHITE GRAPE JUICE,							
Sparkling, Sainsbury's*	1 Glass/200ml	120	60	0.1	14.5	0.1	0.1
Tesco*	1 Glass/200ml	130	65	0.1	15.6	0.0	0.0
WHITE PUDDING	1oz/28g	126	450	7.0	36.3	31.8	0.0
WHITEBAIT, In Flour, Fried	1oz/28g	147	525	19.5	5.3	47.5	0.2
WHITECURRANTS, Raw	1oz/28g	7	26	1.3	5.6	0.0	3.4
WHITING,							
In Crumbs, Fried In Blended Oil	1 Serving/180g	344	191	18.1	7.0	10.3	0.2
Raw	1oz/28g	23	81	18.7	0.0	0.7	0.0
Steamed	1 Serving/85g	78	92	20.9	0.0	0.9	0.0
WHOLEMEAL BRAN, Fox's*	1 Biscuit/14g	63	451	7.7	58.7	20.0	7.5
WIENER SCHNITZEL	1oz/28g	101	360	1.7	91.0	1.0	1.3
WINDERS, Real Fruit, Kellogg's*	1 Serving/18g	67	370	0.5	77.0	7.0	3.0
WINE GUMS,							
Co-Op*	1 Sweet/6g	20	337	3.5	80.8	0.0	0.0
Iceland*	1oz/28g	85	302	6.7	67.8	0.4	0.0
M & S*	1oz/28g	94	335	3.9	78.5	0.1	0.0
Maynards*	1 Sweet/5g	17	331	6.0	76.6	0.0	0.0
Mini, Co-Op*	1 Sweet/2g	7	330	6.0	76.0	0.1	0.0
WINE,							
Mulled, Homemade	1 Glass/120ml	227	196	0.1	25.2	0.0	0.0
Red	1 Glass/120ml	80	68	0.1	0.2	0.0	0.0
Rose, Medium	1 Glass/120ml	83	71	0.1	2.5	0.0	0.0
Strong Ale Barley	1 Can/440ml	290	66	0.7	6.1	0.0	0.0
White, Dry	1 Glass/120ml	77	66	0.1	0.6	0.0	0.0
White, Medium	1 Glass/120ml	87	74	0.1	3.0	0.0	0.0
White, Non Alcoholic, Ame*	1 Glass/120ml	46	38	0.0	9.5	0.0	0.0

	Measure WEIGHT/INFO	per Measure KCAL	Nutrition Values per 100g / 100ml KCAL	PROT	CARB	FAT	FIBRE
WINE,							
White, Sparkling	1 Glass/120ml	87	74	0.3	5.1	0.0	0.0
White, Sweet	1 Glass/120ml	110	94	0.2	5.9	0.0	0.0
WINKLES, Boiled	1oz/28g	20	72	15.4	0.0	1.2	0.0
WISPA,							
Bite, With Biscuit In Caramel, Cadbury's*	1 Bar/47g	240	510	6.4	56.9	28.6	0.0
Cadbury's*	1 Treatsize Bar/15g	83	550	7.1	53.9	34.2	0.0
Gold, Cadbury's*	1 Bar/52g	263	505	5.7	57.0	28.0	0.0
Mint, Cadbury's*	1 Bar/50g	275	550	7.0	54.7	33.6	0.0
WOK							
Chinese, Findus*	1 Serving/250g	113	45	1.5	9.5	0.2	0.0
Classic, Findus*	1 Serving/250g	113	45	2.0	7.5	0.5	0.0
Sambal Oelek, Findus*	1 Serving/200g	170	85	3.0	17.0	0.4	0.0
Thai, Findus*	½ Pack/250g	100	40	1.5	8.0	0.3	0.0
Vietnamese, Findus*	1 Serving/100g	25	25	1.5	4.5	0.5	0.0
WONTON,							
Chicken, Asda*	1 Wonton/15g	46	306	14.0	18.0	20.0	1.9
Chinese Prawn, Sainsbury's*	1 Wonton/16g	38	252	11.9	16.5	15.4	1.2
Prawn, Dim Sum Selection, Sainsbury's*	1 Wonton/10g	26	259	11.3	26.8	11.8	1.3
Prawn, M & S*	1 Wanton/10g	38	380	8.3	24.3	27.5	1.5
Vegetable, Malaysian Style, M & S*	1 Wonton/19g	46	240	5.9	31.9	9.8	1.3
WOTSITS,							
BBQ, Wotsits*	1 Bag/21g	109	521	7.2	55.8	29.9	1.2
Cheesy, Golden Wonder*	1 Bag/21g	114	541	8.8	50.8	33.6	1.2
Cheesy Wafflers, Golden Wonder*	1 Bag/31g	168	542	5.8	54.1	33.6	1.5
WRAP,							
All Day Breakfast, M & S*	1 Pack/196g	529	270	10.8	21.2	16.0	1.4
Aromatic Duck, Safeway*	1 Wrap/180g	376	209	9.1	21.3	9.7	1.6
Bean & Cheese, Tesco*	1 Wrap/105g	258	246	5.5	28.5	12.3	1.0
Beef In Black Bean, M & S*	1 Wrap/150g	338	225	10.2	20.5	11.4	1.6
Cajun Chicken Louisiana Style, Sainsbury's*	1 Pack/190g	395	209	11.1	23.9	7.6	0.0
Chicken & Bacon Caesar Salad, Asda*	1 Wrap/160g	565	353	18.0	20.8	22.0	0.9
Chicken & Cous Cous, BGTY, Sainsbury's*	1 Pack/230g	359	156	8.8	21.5	3.9	0.0
Chicken Caesar, M & S*	1 Pack/225g	675	300	11.9	20.5	19.1	1.4
Chicken Caesar, Tesco*	1 Wrap/110g	252	229	9.8	25.0	10.0	0.1
Chicken, Eat Smart, Safeway*	1 Pack/153g	230	150	12.5	19.7	1.9	2.0
Chicken Fajita, Asda*	1 Wrap/180g	369	205	9.4	20.6	9.4	0.4
Chicken Fajita Red, Yellow Peppers, Weight Watchers*	1 Pack/177g	297	168	9.0	24.7	3.7	1.7
Chicken Fajita, Tesco*	1 Wrap/110g	199	181	7.9	24.5	5.7	0.3
Chicken Jalfrezi, Boots*	1 Pack/215g	456	212	8.6	28.0	7.3	1.7
Chicken Salsa, HE, Tesco*	1 Wrap/240g	348	145	8.3	22.0	2.6	0.5
Chicken Salsa, HE, Tesco*	1 Pack/350g	529	151	8.0	23.8	2.6	0.5
Chicken Southern Style, Ginsters*	1 Wrap/150g	435	290	14.3	37.7	9.6	2.1
Chicken Sweet & Sour, Ginsters*	1 Wrap/150g	378	252	13.4	40.8	3.9	2.4
Chicken Thai Style, Boots*	1 Wrap/156g	290	186	11.0	21.0	6.4	2.2
Chicken Tikka, Ginsters*	1 Wrap/150g	278	185	8.9	25.5	5.3	1.6
Chicken Tikka Masala, Patak's*	1 Wrap/150g	252	168	7.8	19.3	6.6	0.0
Chicken With Stilton & Pear, Sainsbury's*	1 Serving/150g	264	176	25.4	2.1	7.3	0.1
Chilli Beef, COU, M & S*	1 Pack/179g	260	145	9.7	22.7	1.4	1.9
Chinese Chicken, M & S*	1 Wrap/155g	239	154	14.0	22.3	1.0	2.0
Chorizo Sausage, Black Olive & Bean, TTD, Sainsbury's*	1 Pack/237g	517	218	7.7	26.7	8.9	0.0
Duck, Food To Go, M & S*	1 Pack/257g	474	185	8.5	25.5	5.4	1.0
Fiery Mexican Cheese, Ginsters*	1 Wrap/150g	437	291	11.1	37.5	10.9	2.7
Goats Cheese & Tomato, TTD, Sainsbury's*	1 Serving/204g	420	206	7.0	25.6	8.4	0.0
Gressingham Duck & Hoi Sin Sauce, TTD, Sainsbury's*	1 Wrap/199g	354	178	9.3	24.8	4.6	0.0

W

WRAP,	Measure WEIGHT/INFO	per Measure KCAL	Nutrition Values per 100g / 100ml KCAL	PROT	CARB	FAT	FIBRE
Italian Chicken, Sainsbury's*	½ Pack/211g	395	187	15.7	6.2	11.0	0.9
Louisiana Style Chicken, GFY, Asda*	1 Pack/195g	355	182	11.0	31.0	1.5	2.0
Mexican Bean, GFY, Asda*	1 Pack/173g	303	175	5.0	31.0	3.4	2.3
Mexican Chicken, M & S*	1 Serving/218g	447	205	8.6	19.7	10.3	1.3
Mexican Style Chicken, Good Intentions, Somerfield*	1 Pack/220g	387	176	8.3	26.0	4.3	1.4
Mexican Sweet Potato & Three Bean, M & S*	1 Pack/222g	522	235	7.6	26.4	11.0	1.4
Mild Chicken Curry, Patak's*	1 Wrap/150g	239	159	8.1	21.3	6.0	2.8
Monterey Jack & Ham, Tesco*	1 Pack/200g	522	261	7.9	25.9	14.1	0.2
Moroccan Style Chicken & Cous Cous, GFY, Asda*	1 Pack/164g	307	187	12.0	32.0	1.2	1.8
Moroccan Style Cous Cous, Tesco*	1 Serving/240g	370	154	5.3	27.3	2.7	1.3
Morrocan Chicken, Shapers, Boots*	1 Serving/154g	271	176	9.6	26.0	3.7	1.7
Parma Ham Chicken, Perfectly Balanced, Waitrose*	½ Pack/198g	212	107	20.1	2.5	1.8	0.9
Peking Duck, Asda*	1 Wrap/172g	427	248	9.4	28.5	10.7	1.1
Peking Duck, Boots*	1 Wrap/229g	440	192	8.3	30.0	4.3	2.6
Peking Duck, Finest, Tesco*	1 Pack/200g	378	189	8.4	29.5	4.2	0.3
Peking Duck, Shell*	1 Wrap/173g	337	195	8.7	24.2	7.1	0.0
Peking Duck, Waitrose*	1 Pack/182g	319	175	10.0	25.9	3.5	1.6
Pepperoni, Tesco*	1 Wrap/153g	271	177	6.4	26.9	4.9	1.4
Pork Caribbean Spicy, Ginsters*	1 Wrap/150g	396	264	11.3	34.1	9.1	2.3
Red Thai Chicken, BGTY, Sainsbury's*	1 Pack/194g	384	198	11.3	29.3	3.9	1.0
Red Thai Prawns, Somerfield*	1oz/28g	81	288	10.0	20.0	19.0	0.0
Roasted Vegetable & Feta, BGTY, Sainsbury's*	1 Serving/200g	318	159	5.8	25.0	4.0	0.0
Sticky Chilli Chicken & Mango, Finest, Tesco*	1 Pack/192g	328	171	9.0	24.8	4.0	1.2
Tandoori Chicken, GFY, Asda*	1 Pack/167g	281	168	10.0	26.0	2.7	1.7
Thai Style Chicken, Tesco*	1oz/28g	50	178	7.1	26.9	4.7	0.3
Tortilla, Chicken, Asda*	1 Pack/125g	253	202	9.6	36.9	1.8	3.3
Tortilla, Chicken Fajita, Sutherland*	1 Pack/158g	379	240	13.0	27.0	9.0	0.0
Tortilla, Mediterranean Veg, Snack 'n' Go, Sainsbury's*	1 Wrap/202g	267	133	4.0	26.3	1.3	2.1
Tortilla, Vegetable, Asda*	1 Pack/125g	245	196	6.8	37.2	2.2	0.8
Tuna Nicoise, BGTY, Sainsbury's*	1 Pack/181g	273	151	11.0	18.0	3.9	0.0
Tuna Nicoise, HE, Tesco*	1 Wrap/117g	160	137	8.3	20.6	2.3	0.5
Tuna, Sweetcorn & Red Pepper, BGTY, Sainsbury's*	1 Pack/178g	306	172	11.5	21.2	4.6	2.1
Tuna, Tomato & Pepper Salad & Tomato, Weight Watchers*	1 Pack/182g	291	160	8.3	22.9	3.9	1.4

	Measure WEIGHT/INFO	per Measure KCAL	Nutrition Values per 100g / 100ml KCAL	PROT	CARB	FAT	FIBRE
YAM,							
Baked	1oz/28g	43	153	2.1	37.5	0.4	1.7
Boiled In Salted Water	1oz/28g	37	133	1.7	33.0	0.3	1.4
Boiled In Unsalted Water	1oz/28g	37	133	1.7	33.0	0.3	1.4
Raw	1oz/28g	32	114	1.5	28.2	0.3	1.3
YEAST,							
Bakers, Compressed	1oz/28g	15	53	11.4	1.1	0.4	0.0
Dried	1oz/28g	47	169	35.6	3.5	1.5	0.0
Extract	1 Tsp/9g	16	180	40.7	3.5	0.4	0.0
YOGHURT,							
Adore Vanilla With Choc Flakes, Ehrmann*	1 Pot/150g	215	143	3.1	17.0	7.0	0.0
Apple & Blackberry, Deep Fill Fruit, Ski*	1 Pot/160g	139	87	4.0	14.2	1.6	0.0
Apple & Blackberry, Organic, Yeo Valley*	1 Pot/125g	121	97	4.3	12.5	3.3	0.1
Apple & Blackberry, Perfectly Balanced, Waitrose*	1 Pot/125g	115	92	4.6	18.2	0.1	0.3
Apple & Pear, Low Fat, Sainsbury's*	1 Pot/125g	115	92	4.3	15.2	1.5	0.2
Apple & Prune, Fat Free, Yeo Valley*	1 Pot/125g	98	78	5.1	14.1	0.1	0.2
Apple & Spice Bio, Virtually Fat Free, Shape*	1 Pot/120g	67	56	5.6	7.3	0.1	0.2
Apple, 99% Fat Free, Mullerice, Muller*	1 Pot/150g	125	83	3.5	15.3	0.9	0.0
Apple Danish Fruit Pudding Style, HE, Tesco*	1 Pot/125g	99	79	4.1	14.1	0.7	0.2
Apple, Light, Muller*	1 Pot/200g	108	54	4.4	9.0	0.1	0.0
Apple, Mullerice, Muller*	1 Pot/200g	224	112	3.6	19.0	2.4	0.0
Apple Strudel Custard Style, Shape, St. Ivel*	1 Pot/100g	58	58	4.1	7.9	0.8	0.2
Apricot & Mango, 25% Extra Fruit, Low Fat, Asda*	1 Pot/125g	120	96	4.6	17.0	1.1	0.0
Apricot & Mango, Best There Is, Yoplait*	1 Pot/125g	130	104	4.7	17.4	1.6	0.0
Apricot & Mango, Low Fat, Tesco*	1 Pot/125g	126	101	4.9	16.3	1.8	0.0
Apricot & Mango Tropical Fruit, Ski*	1 Pot/125g	126	101	4.9	16.3	1.8	0.0
Apricot & Nectarine, Sunshine Selection, Sainsbury's*	1 Pot/125g	115	92	4.4	15.3	1.5	0.1
Apricot Bio, HE, Tesco*	1 Pot/125g	58	46	4.2	7.1	0.1	0.0
Apricot, Bio-Live, Fat Free, Rachel's Organic*	1 Pot/142g	81	57	3.5	10.5	0.1	0.0
Apricot Custard Style, Shapers, Boots*	1 Pot/146g	82	56	3.9	8.3	0.8	0.2
Apricot, French Style Smooth, Tesco*	1 Pot/125g	123	98	3.6	14.1	3.0	0.0
Apricot, Low Fat, Benecol*	1 Pot/150g	119	79	3.7	14.6	0.6	0.0
Apricot, Low Fat, Organic, Sainsbury's*	1 Pot/125g	103	82	5.3	13.0	1.0	0.1
Apricot, Low Fat, Organic, Somerfield*	1 Pot/150g	153	102	6.0	17.0	2.0	0.0
Apricot, Low Fat, Sainsbury's*	1 Pot/125g	115	92	4.3	15.2	1.5	0.1
Apricot, Low Fat, Tesco*	1 Pot/125g	111	89	4.9	13.4	1.7	0.2
Apricot, Organic, Low Fat, Tesco*	1 Pot/125g	111	89	5.3	14.6	1.0	0.2
Apricot, Organic, Yeo Valley*	1 Pot/150g	146	97	4.3	12.4	3.3	0.1
Apricot, Smooth Set French, Sainsbury's*	1 Pot/125g	100	80	3.5	13.6	1.2	0.0
Apricot, Vitality, Muller*	1 Pot/200g	196	98	4.7	15.8	1.8	0.0
Apricot Wholemilk, Organic, Sainsbury's*	1 Pot/150g	125	83	3.5	9.4	3.5	0.1
Bakewell Tart Compote Custard Style, HE, Tesco*	1 Pot/125g	100	80	4.2	13.8	0.9	0.3
Banana & Orange, Low Fat, 25% Extra Fruit, Asda*	1 Pot/125g	125	100	4.6	18.0	1.1	0.0
Banana, Childrens, Co-Op*	1 Pot/125g	124	99	3.7	15.1	2.6	0.2
Banana Choco Flakes Corner, Muller*	1 Pot/150g	218	145	4.1	22.5	4.3	0.0
Banana, Light, Muller*	1 Pot/200g	106	53	4.4	8.7	0.1	0.0
Banana, Low Fat, Asda*	1 Pot/150g	149	99	4.6	18.0	1.0	0.1
Banana, Low Fat, Sainsbury's*	1 Pot/125g	116	93	4.4	15.4	1.5	0.1
Banana, Low Fat, Tesco*	1 Pot/125g	128	102	4.9	16.8	1.7	0.1
Banana Smooth, M & S	1 Pot/150g	165	110	4.8	19.3	1.7	0.2
Banana Toffee, Low Fat, Somerfield*	1 Pot/125g	123	98	4.1	18.0	1.1	0.0
Banoffee, Low Fat, Asda*	1 Pot/125g	126	101	4.6	18.2	1.2	1.0
Berry Sunshine Grove, Shape*	1 Pot/100g	63	63	4.7	8.3	1.0	0.2
Bio Activia With Cereals, Danone*	1 Pot/125g	123	98	4.1	15.6	2.1	0.0
Bio Activia With Prunes, Danone*	1 Pot/125g	124	99	3.3	15.2	2.8	0.0

YOGHURT,	Measure WEIGHT/INFO	per Measure KCAL	Nutrition Values per 100g / 100ml KCAL	PROT	CARB	FAT	FIBRE
Bio Activia With Raspberry, Danone*	1 Pot/125g	113	90	3.6	13.0	2.8	0.0
Bio Fruits With Cherries, 0% Fat, Danone*	1 Pot/125g	65	52	3.6	9.1	0.1	0.0
Bio-Live Wholemilk With Maple Syrup, Rachel's Organic*	1 Pot/142g	139	98	3.5	13.0	3.5	0.0
Black Cherry, BGTY, Sainsbury's*	1 Pot/125g	64	51	4.7	7.6	0.2	0.1
Black Cherry, COU, M & S*	1 Pot/150g	68	45	4.2	5.9	0.1	0.1
Black Cherry, Economy, Tesco*	1 Pot/125g	85	68	3.0	11.9	1.0	0.1
Black Cherry, Extra Fruit, Low Fat, Ski*	1 Pot/125g	120	96	3.4	17.2	1.5	0.1
Black Cherry, Extremely Fruity, M & S*	1 Pot/200g	220	110	4.9	18.4	1.5	0.2
Black Cherry, Fat Free, Safeway*	1 Pot/125g	75	60	5.2	9.2	0.0	0.1
Black Cherry, Fat Free, Weight Watchers*	1 Pot/120g	55	46	4.2	7.0	0.1	0.1
Black Cherry, Fayrefield*	1 Pot/140g	185	132	4.0	17.4	5.1	0.0
Black Cherry, Frozen, M & S*	1 Pot/125g	164	131	3.1	27.1	1.1	0.5
Black Cherry Live Bio, Perfeclty Balanced, Waitrose*	1 Pot/125g	115	92	4.6	18.3	0.1	0.1
Black Cherry, Live, Turner's Dairies*	1 Pot/125g	86	69	4.9	11.9	0.3	0.0
Black Cherry, Low Fat, Asda*	1 Pot/150g	143	95	4.6	17.4	1.0	0.2
Black Cherry, Low Fat, Co-Op*	1 Pot/150g	128	85	3.2	16.0	0.9	0.4
Black Cherry, Low Fat, Sainsbury's*	1 Pot/125g	118	94	4.2	16.1	1.4	0.1
Black Cherry, Low Fat, Somerfield*	1 Pot/150g	116	77	3.0	14.0	1.0	0.0
Black Cherry, Low Fat, Tesco*	1 Pot/125g	124	99	4.9	16.0	1.7	0.1
Black Cherry, M & S*	1 Pot/150g	149	99	4.8	16.5	1.6	0.2
Black Cherry, So-Good*	1 Pot/120g	92	77	2.1	16.6	1.3	0.0
Black Cherry, Virtually Fat Free, Shapers, Boots*	1 Pot/125g	71	57	5.3	8.8	0.1	0.1
Blackberry & Apple, Best There Is, Yoplait	1 Pot/124g	133	107	4.7	18.0	1.6	0.0
Blackberry & Apple, BGTY, Sainsbury's*	1 Pot/122g	61	50	4.7	7.2	0.2	0.3
Blackberry & Apple, Low Fat, Sainsbury's*	1 Pot/125g	116	93	4.3	15.5	1.5	0.2
Blackberry & Raspberry Flip, Morrisons*	1 Pot/175g	207	118	3.4	15.8	4.6	0.5
Blackberry & Raspberry, Fruit Corner, Muller*	1 Pot/175g	193	110	3.7	15.0	3.9	0.0
Blackberry & Raspberry, Low Fat, Ski*	1 Pot/126g	67	53	5.7	7.2	0.0	2.0
Blackberry, BGTY, Sainsbury's*	1 Pot/150g	107	71	3.4	13.5	0.4	1.6
Blackberry, Weight Watchers*	1 Pot/120g	49	41	4.2	5.8	0.1	0.3
Blackcherry, Everyday, Low Fat, Co-Op*	1 Pot/125g	88	70	3.0	13.0	0.7	0.0
Blackcurrant & Vanilla, TTD, Sainsbury's*	1 Pot/143g	136	95	3.6	13.6	2.9	1.0
Blackcurrant, BGTY, Sainsbury's*	1 Pot/200g	100	50	4.8	7.3	0.2	0.1
Blackcurrant, Childrens, Co-Op*	1 Pot/125g	120	96	3.7	14.2	2.7	0.2
Blackcurrant, Low Fat, Sainsbury's*	1 Pot/125g	116	93	4.2	15.9	1.4	0.6
Blackcurrant, Low Fat, Tesco*	1 Pot/125g	110	88	4.9	13.2	1.7	0.4
Blackcurrant, M & S*	1 Pot/150g	147	98	4.8	16.1	1.6	0.8
Blackcurrant Smooth, Ski*	1 Pot/125g	129	103	5.0	16.4	1.9	0.0
Blackcurrant, Vitually Fat Free, Morrisons*	1 Pot/200g	114	57	5.4	8.4	0.2	0.2
Blackcurrant With Liquorice, Tesco*	1 Pot/150g	138	92	4.6	15.8	1.1	0.4
Blueberry Bio, Co-Op*	1 Pot/125g	141	113	4.5	16.5	2.8	0.4
Blueberry Flip, Morrisons*	1 Pot/175g	201	115	3.1	15.1	4.6	0.5
Blueberry, Fruit Corner, Muller*	1 Pot/175g	196	112	3.7	15.5	3.9	0.0
Blueberry, Light, Muller*	1 Pot/200g	98	49	4.4	7.7	0.1	0.0
Blueberry, Low Fat, Somerfield*	1 Pot/150g	131	87	4.0	16.0	1.0	0.0
Blueberry, M & S*	1 Pot/150g	141	94	4.7	15.8	1.6	0.4
Blueberry, Starbucks*	1 Pot/130g	116	89	4.4	17.8	0.0	0.0
Blueberry, Wholemilk, Organic, Sainsbury's*	1 Pot/150g	123	82	3.5	9.2	3.5	0.1
Caramel & Praline, Indulgent Greek Style, Somerfield*	1 Pot/125g	245	196	4.0	28.0	8.0	0.0
Champagne Rhubarb, Finest, Tesco*	1 Pot/150g	213	142	3.3	16.8	6.9	0.2
Cherry Bio, Co-Op*	1 Pot/125g	144	115	4.5	17.0	2.8	0.1
Cherry Flip, Morrisons*	1 Pot/175g	219	125	3.4	17.6	4.6	0.5
Cherry, Fruit Corner, Muller*	1 Pot/175g	193	110	3.7	15.0	3.9	0.0
Cherry, Light, Muller*	1 Pot/200g	100	50	4.4	7.9	0.1	0.0

Y

YOGHURT,	Measure WEIGHT/INFO	per Measure KCAL	KCAL	PROT	CARB	FAT	FIBRE
Cherry, Low Fat, Asda*	1 Pot/125g	120	96	4.6	17.0	1.1	0.0
Cherry, Low Fat, Benecol*	1 Pot/150g	122	81	3.8	15.2	0.6	0.0
Cherry Morello Bio, Tesco*	1 Pot/124g	51	41	4.4	5.4	0.2	0.9
Cherry, Muller*	1 Pot/150g	177	118	3.3	17.0	3.7	0.0
Cherry Pie Layered Custard Style, HE,Tesco*	1 Pot/125g	99	79	4.1	13.9	0.8	0.2
Cherry, Somerfield*	1 Pot/125g	61	49	5.0	7.0	0.0	0.0
Cherry, Virtually Fat Free Bio, Morrisons*	1 Pot/200g	120	60	5.4	9.2	0.2	0.0
Chocolate & Orange, COU, M & S*	1 Pot/200g	90	45	4.2	6.0	0.4	0.2
Chocolate & Toffee Selection, Shape*	1 Pot/100g	99	99	4.6	15.4	1.8	0.0
Chocolate, Light, Muller*	1 Pot/200g	108	54	4.8	8.1	0.3	0.0
Chocolate, Mullerice, Muller*	1 Pot/200g	246	123	3.4	21.5	2.6	0.0
Chocolate, Seriously Smooth, Waitrose*	1 Pot/125g	158	126	6.0	20.1	2.4	0.1
Chocolate, Shape*	1 Pot/100g	111	111	4.9	17.4	2.0	0.2
Chocolate, Vitaline*	1 Pot/125g	103	82	3.5	15.8	0.5	0.0
Citrus Fruit, Fat Free, Weight Watchers*	1 Pot/120g	52	43	4.1	6.3	0.1	0.2
Citrus Fruit, Tesco*	1 Serving/117g	53	45	4.2	6.5	0.1	0.1
Coconut, Muller*	1 Pot/150g	156	104	3.4	13.0	3.9	0.0
Country Berries, Virtually Fat Free, Light, Muller*	1 Pot/200g	104	52	4.4	8.3	0.1	0.0
Cranberry & Apple, Bio Live Fat Free, Organic, Yeo Valley*	1 Serving/100g	74	74	5.1	13.1	0.1	0.2
Cranberry & Blackcurrant, Fat Free, Bio, Shape*	1 Pot/120g	54	45	4.6	5.7	0.1	0.3
Cranberry & Blackcurrant, Low Fat Bio, Ocean Spray*	1 Pot/150g	147	98	4.6	17.4	1.1	0.0
Cranberry & Pink Grapefruit, Low Fat Bio, Ocean Spray*	1 Pot/125g	118	94	4.6	16.5	1.1	0.0
Cranberry & Raspberry, Low Fat Bio, Ocean Spray*	1 Pot/150g	144	96	4.6	17.0	1.1	0.0
Cranberry & Raspberry, Perfectly Balanced, Waitrose*	1 Pot/150g	135	90	4.5	17.8	0.1	0.6
Cranberry Classic, Low Fat Bio, Ocean Spray*	1 Pot/150g	144	96	4.6	17.0	1.1	0.0
Custard Style Apple & Blackberry, Co-Op*	1 Pot/150g	195	130	3.7	15.9	5.3	0.1
Custard Style Gooseberry, Co-Op*	1 Pot/150g	216	144	3.7	19.3	5.3	0.3
Custard Style, HE, Tesco*	1 Pot/125g	70	56	4.0	8.4	0.7	0.1
Custard Style, Low Fat, Sainsbury's*	1 Serving/100g	110	110	5.4	18.1	1.9	0.2
Custard Style Rhubarb, Co-Op*	1 Pot/150g	203	135	3.7	17.2	5.3	0.3
Dairy Toffee, Shape*	1 Pot/100g	99	99	4.6	15.4	1.8	0.0
Deep Fill Fruit, Ski*	1 Pot/160g	138	86	4.0	13.8	1.6	0.0
Devon Toffee, Low Fat, Sainsbury's*	1 Pot/126g	137	109	4.3	19.6	1.5	0.0
Double Caramel, Frozen, Dream*	1 Serving/50g	88	175	4.0	28.0	5.0	0.0
Exotic, COU, M & S*	1oz/28g	13	45	4.3	6.0	0.1	0.2
Exotic Fruits French Set Wholemilk, Asda*	1 Pot/125g	125	100	3.6	14.1	3.2	0.0
Farmhouse Blackberry, BGTY, Sainsbury's*	1 Pot/150g	107	71	3.4	13.5	0.4	1.6
Farmhouse Peaches, BGTY, Sainsbury's*	1 Pot/150g	134	89	3.2	17.8	0.4	0.3
Farmhouse Raspberry, BGTY, Sainsbury's*	1 Pot/150g	107	71	3.3	13.6	0.4	2.0
Farmhouse Strawberries & Clotted Cream, TTD, Sainsbury's*	1 Pot/150g	155	103	3.6	12.5	4.5	0.3
Farmhouse Strawberry & Redcurrant, Ann Forshaw's*	1 Pot/150g	194	129	3.8	17.4	4.9	0.2
Farmhouse Strawberry, BGTY, Sainsbury's*	1 Pot/150g	107	71	3.2	13.7	0.4	0.5
Florida Orange Summer, Onken*	1oz/28g	28	100	3.9	15.1	2.7	0.0
Forest Fantasy, Frozen, Thorntons*	1oz/28g	48	170	1.8	26.2	6.1	0.5
Forest Fruits, French Set Wholemilk, Asda*	1 Pot/125g	125	100	3.6	14.1	3.2	0.0
Forest Fruits, M & S*	1 Pot/150g	149	99	4.7	16.8	1.6	0.5
French Set, Low Fat, Iceland*	1 Pot/125g	100	80	3.6	13.6	1.2	0.0
French Style, Tesco*	1 Pot/125g	123	98	3.6	14.1	3.0	0.0
Fruit & Nut Layer, Indulgent Greek Style, Somerfield*	1 Pot/125g	214	171	3.0	24.0	7.0	0.0
Fruit Bio, Low Fat, Sainsbury's*	1 Pot/150g	156	104	4.6	18.9	1.1	0.3
Fruit, Low Fat	1 Pot/120g	108	90	4.1	17.9	0.7	0.0
Fruit Of The Forest, Smooth Set, Co-Op*	1 Pot/125g	95	76	3.7	12.5	0.9	0.0
Fruit Whole Milk	1 Pot/150g	158	105	5.1	15.7	2.8	0.0
Fudge Layer, Indulgent Greek Style, Somerfield*	1 Pot/125g	226	181	3.0	26.0	7.0	0.0

Nutrition Values per 100g / 100ml

Y

YOGHURT,	Measure WEIGHT/INFO	per Measure KCAL	Nutrition Values per 100g / 100ml KCAL	PROT	CARB	FAT	FIBRE
Fudge, Thick & Creamy, Co-Op*	1 Pot/150g	197	131	3.8	17.6	5.0	0.0
Fudge, Thick & Creamy, M & S*	1 Pot/150g	195	130	4.4	17.3	5.0	0.7
Goats Whole Milk	1 Carton/150g	95	63	3.5	3.9	3.8	0.0
Gooseberry Custard Style, Shapers, Boots*	1 Pot/151g	106	70	3.9	12.0	0.7	0.2
Gooseberry Custard Style, Somerfield*	1 Pot/125g	151	121	3.0	17.0	5.0	0.0
Gooseberry, Low Fat, Sainsbury's*	1 Pot/125g	113	90	4.4	14.6	1.5	0.2
Greek, 0% Fat, Total*	1 Pot/150g	84	56	10.0	4.0	0.0	0.0
Greek, Light, Total*	1 Pot/150g	120	80	6.0	3.0	5.0	0.0
Greek Natural, Half Fat, Safeway*	1 Serving/100g	101	101	5.7	8.1	5.1	0.0
Greek, Original, Total*	1oz/28g	36	130	6.0	4.0	10.0	0.0
Greek, Shape*	1 Serving/100g	108	108	7.1	12.7	2.7	0.0
Greek Style, BGTY, Sainsbury's*	1 Pot/500g	475	95	6.2	6.4	5.0	0.0
Greek Style Honey, Co-Op*	1 Pot/150g	228	152	4.0	13.8	8.5	0.0
Greek Style Lemon, Shape*	1 Pot/100g	115	115	7.6	10.7	3.6	0.0
Greek Style Natural, BGTY, Sainsburys*	1 Serving/50g	48	95	6.2	6.4	5.0	0.0
Greek Style Natural, Bio-Live, Rachel's Organic*	1 Pot/450g	513	114	3.7	4.6	9.0	0.0
Greek Style Natural, Organic, Tesco*	1oz/28g	37	133	4.5	6.2	10.0	0.0
Greek Style Natural, Somerfield*	1oz/28g	36	129	5.0	5.0	10.0	0.0
Greek Style Orange, Shape*	1 Pot/100g	105	105	7.7	9.4	3.6	0.1
Greek Style, Sainsbury's*	1 Serving/200g	258	129	4.6	4.8	10.2	0.0
Greek Style With Honey, Asda*	1 Pot/150g	225	150	4.0	13.9	8.7	0.0
Greek Style With Honey, Somerfield*	1oz/28g	43	152	4.0	15.0	9.0	0.0
Greek Style With Strawberries, Asda*	1 Pot/125g	159	127	3.2	13.6	6.6	0.2
Greek Style With Strawberry, Morrisons*	1 Pot/125g	163	130	3.3	14.4	6.6	0.0
Greek Style With Toffee & Hazelnuts, Asda*	1 Pot/125g	230	184	3.7	23.1	8.6	0.1
Greek Style With Tropical Fruits, Asda*	1 Pot/125g	164	131	3.3	14.5	6.6	0.3
Handmade Farmhouse Fig & Vanilla, TTD, Sainsbury's*	1 Pot/150g	150	100	3.6	15.5	2.9	0.2
Hazelnut, Low Fat, Asda*	1 Pot/125g	150	120	4.8	20.2	2.3	0.1
Hazelnut, Low Fat, Tesco*	1 Pot/125g	133	106	4.4	16.1	2.7	0.1
Hazelnut, Morrisons*	1 Pot/150g	159	106	3.9	16.9	2.6	0.0
Hazelnut, Seriously Nutty, Waitrose*	1 Pot/150g	179	119	5.3	17.7	3.0	0.2
Hazlenut Crunchy, Jordans*	1oz/28g	43	154	5.2	22.2	4.0	1.1
Hazlenut, Low Fat, Safeway*	1 Pot/150g	179	119	4.9	19.3	2.5	0.2
Hazlenut, Low Fat, Somerfield*	1 Pot/150g	126	84	4.0	15.0	1.0	0.0
Hint Of Coconut, Bio Activia, Danone*	1 Pot/125g	119	95	3.6	13.2	3.1	0.0
Honey & Ginger, Tesco*	1 Pot/150g	150	100	4.6	18.0	1.1	0.0
Honey & Greek, Total*	1 Pot/150g	245	163	4.8	19.2	8.0	0.0
Honey & Multigrain, Breakfast Selection, Sainsbury's*	1 Pot/125g	126	101	4.4	17.4	1.5	0.2
Honey, Low Fat, Asda*	1 Pot/125g	130	104	4.6	19.0	1.1	0.0
Jaffa Orange, Low Fat, Co-Op*	1 Pot/150g	126	84	3.9	15.0	0.9	0.4
Jaffa Orange, Morrisons*	1 Pot/150g	134	89	3.6	16.2	1.1	0.0
Kellogg's Frosties Crunch Corner, Muller*	1 Pot/150g	185	123	4.0	20.1	2.9	0.0
Layered, Eat Smart, Safeway*	1 Pot/125g	81	65	4.1	11.3	0.1	0.4
Lemon & Lime, Bio, Shape*	1 Pot/120g	54	45	5.7	5.7	0.1	0.1
Lemon & Lime, Fat Free, Shape*	1 Pot/120g	61	51	4.5	7.3	0.1	0.1
Lemon & Lime, Light, Muller*	1 Pot/200g	106	53	4.7	8.2	0.1	0.0
Lemon & Lime, Weight Watchers*	1 Pot/119ml	50	42	4.1	5.9	0.1	0.0
Lemon Cheescake Corner, Muller*	1 Pot/150g	224	149	3.7	23.9	4.3	0.0
Lemon, COU, M & S*	1 Pot/200g	80	40	4.2	5.4	0.1	0.0
Lemon Curd, Channel Island, M & S*	1 Pot/150g	225	150	5.4	20.2	5.1	0.1
Lemon Curd, Sainsbury's*	1 Pot/150g	182	121	4.1	17.7	3.7	0.2
Lemon, Fat Free, Weight Watchers*	1 Pot/120g	49	41	4.0	5.8	0.1	0.0
Lemon French Set Wholemilk, Asda*	1 Pot/125g	125	100	3.6	14.1	3.2	0.0
Lemon Lime Mousse, Shapers, Boots*	1 Pot/90g	89	99	4.2	11.0	4.2	0.1

Y

YOGHURT,	Measure WEIGHT/INFO	per Measure KCAL	Nutrition Values per 100g / 100ml KCAL	PROT	CARB	FAT	FIBRE
Lemon, Lite, Biopot, Onken*	1 Serving/100g	44	44	5.2	5.3	0.2	0.1
Lemon, Low Fat, Safeway*	1 Pot/150g	155	103	4.6	18.7	1.1	0.1
Lemon, Organic, Evernat*	1oz/28g	27	95	3.9	12.4	3.4	0.0
Lemon Smooth Set, Co-Op*	1 Pot/125g	95	76	3.7	12.5	0.9	0.0
Lemon, Smooth Set French, Low Fat, Sainsbury's*	1 Pot/125g	100	80	3.5	13.6	1.2	0.0
Lemon Sunshine Grove, Low Fat, Shape*	1 Pot/100g	64	64	4.6	8.5	1.0	0.0
Lemon, Thick & Creamy, Channel Island, M & S*	1 Pot/150g	195	130	4.2	17.6	5.1	1.0
Loganberry, Low Fat, Sainsbury's*	1 Pot/125g	111	89	4.2	14.5	1.5	0.2
Low Calorie	1 Pot/120g	49	41	4.3	6.0	0.2	0.0
Low Fat, Organic, Somerfield*	1 Pot/150g	120	80	6.0	8.0	3.0	0.0
Mandarin, Longley Farm*	1 Pot/150g	161	107	4.9	13.3	3.8	0.0
Mandarin, Low Fat, Safeway*	1 Pot/150g	141	94	4.6	16.4	1.1	0.2
Mango & Guava, Fat Free, Weight Watchers*	1 Pot/120g	55	46	4.1	6.8	0.1	0.3
Mango & Guava, Sunshine Selection, Sainsbury's*	1 Pot/125g	145	116	5.4	19.3	1.9	0.3
Mango & Pineapple, BGTY, Sainsbury's*	1 Pot/124g	63	51	4.6	7.6	0.2	0.2
Mango Bio, HE, Tesco*	1 Pot/125g	59	47	4.7	6.8	0.1	0.2
Mango Bio, Virtually Fat Free, Shape*	1 Pot/120g	60	50	4.7	6.8	0.1	0.2
Mango, Low Fat, Somerfield*	1 Pot/150g	135	90	4.0	17.0	1.0	0.0
Mango, Low Fat, Tesco*	1 Pot/125g	111	89	4.9	13.6	1.7	0.3
Mango Smooth, M & S*	1 Pot/150g	158	105	4.7	18.0	1.6	0.5
Maple Toffee, Low Fat, Somerfield*	1 Pot 150g	140	93	4.0	18.0	1.0	0.0
Mississippi Mud Pie Corner, Muller*	1 Pot/150g	254	169	4.1	26.3	5.3	0.0
Morello Cherry Duo, Co-Op*	1 Pot/175g	219	125	3.0	18.0	5.0	0.5
Morello Cherry, HE, Tesco*	1 Pot/125g	58	46	4.2	7.1	0.1	0.1
Muesli Nut, Low Fat	1 Pot/120g	134	112	5.0	19.2	2.2	0.0
Natural, Activia Low Fat, Danone*	1 Pot/125g	86	69	4.1	5.6	3.4	0.0
Natural Bio Activia, Low Fat, Danone*	1 Pot/125g	75	60	4.7	6.1	1.9	0.0
Natural Bio, Co-Op*	1 Pot/150g	117	78	4.8	5.5	3.6	0.0
Natural Bio, Fat Free, Waitrose*	1 Pot/150g	90	60	6.1	8.6	0.1	0.0
Natural Bio Garde Plus Live, Little Swallow*	1oz/28g	20	72	4.2	5.3	3.5	0.0
Natural Bio, GFY, Asda*	1oz/28g	17	62	6.0	9.0	0.2	0.0
Natural Bio, Low Fat, Sainsbury's*	1 Serving/100g	48	48	4.0	4.6	1.5	0.0
Natural Bio Set, Low Fat, Sainsbury's*	1 Pot/150g	78	52	3.9	5.7	1.5	0.0
Natural Bio, Virtually Fat Free, Tesco*	1 Serving/100g	47	47	5.5	5.8	0.2	0.0
Natural Biopot, Set, Onken*	1 Pot/150g	101	67	3.9	4.8	3.6	0.0
Natural, Danone*	1 Pot/125g	71	57	3.2	3.8	2.9	0.0
Natural, Fat Free, Organic, Rachel's Organic*	1 Pot/500g	180	36	3.9	4.8	0.1	0.0
Natural Greek Style, Asda*	1oz/28g	36	129	4.6	4.8	10.8	0.0
Natural Greek Style, HE, Tesco*	1oz/28g	22	79	6.5	4.0	4.1	0.0
Natural, Low Fat, Asda*	1oz/28g	17	62	6.1	7.1	1.0	0.0
Natural, Low Fat, Budgens*	1 Serving/112g	65	58	5.1	7.5	0.8	0.0
Natural, Low Fat, Co-Op*	1 Pot/150g	93	62	5.6	6.3	1.0	0.0
Natural, Low Fat, Live, Waitrose*	1 Pot/175g	114	65	5.8	8.2	1.0	0.0
Natural, Low Fat, Morrisons*	1 Pot/150g	84	56	5.2	6.2	1.2	0.0
Natural, Low Fat, Tesco*	1 Pot/150g	90	60	5.6	5.8	1.1	0.0
Natural, Low Fat, TTD, Sainsbury's*	1 Pot/125g	80	64	6.7	4.6	1.8	0.0
Natural, Netto*	1 Serving/50g	40	80	4.8	6.9	3.7	0.0
Natural, Organic, Evernat*	1oz/28g	29	104	3.9	12.9	4.1	0.0
Natural, Organic, Fat Free, Yeo Valley*	1 Serving/100g	58	58	5.9	8.4	0.1	0.0
Natural, Organic, Low Fat, Sainsbury's*	1oz/28g	20	71	6.2	8.8	1.2	0.0
Natural, Organic, Sainsbury's*	1oz/28g	20	71	6.3	9.0	1.1	0.0
Natural, Organic, Yeo Valley*	1 Pot/150g	120	80	4.7	6.9	3.7	0.0
Natural Set, Asda*	1oz/28g	16	57	5.1	6.8	1.0	0.0
Natural Set, Low Fat, Waitrose*	1 Pot/150g	99	66	5.7	8.1	1.2	0.0

Y

YOGHURT,	Measure WEIGHT/INFO	per Measure KCAL	Nutrition Values per 100g / 100ml KCAL	PROT	CARB	FAT	FIBRE
Natural, Very Low Fat Bio, Somerfield*	1 Pot/150g	98	65	7.0	9.0	0.0	0.0
Natural, Weight Watchers*	1 Serving/100g	44	44	4.8	5.3	0.1	1.6
Natural, Wholemilk, Organic, Sainsbury's*	1 Pot/125g	86	69	3.7	5.0	3.8	0.1
Natural With Prunes, Bio Activia, Danone*	1 Pot/125g	124	99	3.3	15.2	2.8	0.0
Nectarine & Apricot, BGTY, Sainsbury's*	1 Serving/123g	63	51	4.7	7.6	0.2	0.2
Nectarine & Apricot Bio, Virtually Fat Free, Shape*	1 Pot/120g	53	44	4.8	5.3	0.1	0.1
Nectarine & Orange, Best There Is, Yoplait	1 Pot/122g	131	107	4.7	18.0	1.6	0.0
Nectarine & Orange, Channel Island, M & S*	1 Pot/150g	158	105	4.5	14.7	3.3	0.3
Nectarine & Orange, Frozen, M & S*	1oz/28g	33	119	3.3	24.3	1.0	0.7
Nectarine & Orange, M & S*	1 Pot/150g	147	98	4.9	16.0	1.6	0.3
Nectarine & Orange, Virtually Fat Free, Shape*	1 Pot/120g	55	46	4.7	5.8	0.1	0.1
Nectarine & Orange, Virtually Fat Free, Tesco*	1 Pot/125g	58	46	4.1	7.2	0.1	0.0
Nectarine & Passion Fruit, BGTY, Sainsbury's*	1 Pot/151g	122	81	3.2	16.3	0.4	0.6
Nectarine & Passion Fruit, Fat Free, Weight Watchers	1 Pot/120g	54	45	4.2	6.6	0.1	0.1
Nectarine & Raspberry, Low Fat, Somerfield*	1 Pot/150g	134	89	4.0	17.0	1.0	0.0
Nectarine & Raspberry, Very Low Fat, Somerfield*	1 Pot/125g	60	48	5.0	7.0	0.0	0.0
Nectarines & Greek Style, Food To Go, M & S*	1 Pack/200g	100	50	2.9	6.3	2.1	1.0
Orange & Guava Tropical Fruit, Ski*	1 Pot/125g	128	102	4.9	16.3	1.9	0.0
Orange & Lemon, BGTY, Sainsbury's*	1 Pot/125g	63	50	4.7	7.3	0.2	0.2
Orange & Nectarine, Weight Watchers*	1 Pot/120g	54	45	4.2	6.5	0.1	0.1
Orange, Fat Free, Shape*	1 Pot/120g	61	51	4.5	8.7	0.2	0.1
Orange, Low Fat, Tesco*	1 Pot/125g	111	89	4.9	13.5	1.7	0.2
Orange, Truly Fruity, Bio, Shape*	1oz/28g	14	51	4.5	7.2	0.1	0.1
Orange With Chocolate Flakes, Shape*	1 Pot/150g	140	93	4.6	11.8	2.8	0.2
Original, 99% Fat Free, Mullerice, Muller*	1 Pot/150g	108	72	3.9	11.8	1.0	0.0
Original, Thick & Creamy, Muller*	1oz/28g	31	109	4.8	11.3	5.0	0.0
Papaya & Passion Fruit, Virtually Fat Free, Shape*	1 Pot/120g	59	49	4.7	6.5	0.1	0.1
Passion Fruit & Peach, Fruit Corner, Muller*	1 Pot/175g	186	106	3.7	14.1	3.9	0.0
Peach & Apricot, COU, M & S*	1 Pot/150g	68	45	4.2	5.7	0.1	0.2
Peach & Apricot Extremely Fruity, M & S*	1 Pot/200g	194	97	4.8	15.8	1.6	0.4
Peach & Apricot, Fruit Corner, Muller*	1oz/28g	31	110	3.7	15.0	3.9	0.0
Peach & Apricot, M & S*	1oz/28g	27	97	4.8	15.8	1.6	0.4
Peach & Apricot, Shape*	1 Pot/120g	54	45	4.6	5.8	0.1	0.1
Peach & Maracuya, Light, Muller*	1 Pot/200g	100	50	4.4	7.9	0.1	0.0
Peach & Passion Fruit, Balanced Lifestyle, Aldi*	1 Serving/100g	49	49	4.3	7.3	0.3	0.5
Peach & Passion Fruit, Eat Smart, Safeway*	1 Pot/125g	69	55	5.2	8.5	0.1	0.3
Peach & Passion Fruit Flip, Morrisons*	1 Pot/175g	89	51	3.9	8.2	0.3	0.6
Peach & Passion Fruit, Lite Biopot, Onken*	1 Serving/100g	45	45	4.6	6.0	0.2	0.2
Peach & Passion Fruit, Low Fat, Somerfield*	1 Pot/150g	132	88	4.0	16.0	1.0	0.0
Peach & Passion Fruit, Organic, Muller*	1 Pot/150g	147	98	3.9	16.6	1.8	0.0
Peach & Passion Fruit, Very Low Fat, Somerfield*	1 Pot/125g	61	49	5.0	7.0	0.0	0.0
Peach & Pear Smooth Set, Co-Op*	1 Pot/125g	95	76	3.7	12.5	0.9	0.0
Peach & Pineapple, Fat Free, Weight Watchers*	1 Pot/120g	53	44	4.1	6.5	0.1	0.1
Peach & Pineapple, Light, Ski*	1 Pot/125g	68	54	5.7	7.5	0.1	2.0
Peach & Raspberry Custard Style, Fat Free, Shape*	1 Pot/170g	77	45	4.1	6.3	0.1	0.2
Peach & Raspberry, M & S*	1 Pot/150g	144	96	4.8	15.7	1.6	0.4
Peach & Vanilla Flip, Morrisons*	1 Pot/175g	212	121	3.4	16.5	4.6	0.6
Peach & Vanilla, HE, Tesco*	1 Pot/125g	55	44	4.8	6.0	0.1	0.1
Peach & Vanilla, Thick & Creamy, Co-Op*	1 Pot/150g	180	120	3.6	16.0	4.6	0.1
Peach, BGTY, Sainsbury's*	1 Pot/125g	61	49	4.7	7.2	0.2	0.2
Peach Bio, Co-Op*	1 Pot/125g	133	106	4.5	14.6	2.8	0.1
Peach Bio, Virtually Fat Free, Shape*	1 Pot/120g	55	46	4.7	5.8	0.1	0.1
Peach Custard Style, Low Fat, Sainsbury's*	1 Pot/125g	110	88	4.4	14.2	1.5	0.1
Peach Duo, Co-Op*	1 Pot/175g	210	120	3.0	17.0	5.0	0.6

YOGHURT,	Measure WEIGHT/INFO	per Measure KCAL	KCAL	PROT	CARB	FAT	FIBRE
Peach, Economy, Sainsbury's*	1 Pot/125g	93	74	2.8	14.7	0.4	0.0
Peach, Extra Fruit, Low Fat, Ski*	1 Pot/125g	114	91	3.5	15.7	1.5	0.1
Peach, Fat Free, Weight Watchers*	1 Pot/118g	53	45	4.2	6.7	0.1	0.2
Peach, Low Fat, Asda*	1 Pot/125g	119	95	4.6	17.4	1.0	0.2
Peach, Low Fat, Co-Op*	1 Pot/150g	122	81	3.7	14.6	0.8	0.4
Peach, Low Fat, Muller*	1 Pot/150g	152	101	4.8	16.1	1.9	0.0
Peach, Low Fat, Ski*	1 Pot/125g	126	101	4.9	16.3	1.8	0.0
Peach, Low Fat, Yeo Valley*	1 Pot/125g	113	90	4.6	15.3	1.1	0.1
Peach Melba, Everyday Low Fat, Co-Op*	1 Pot/125g	88	70	3.0	13.0	0.7	0.0
Peach Melba, Low Fat, Tesco*	1 Pot/125g	80	64	2.7	11.7	0.7	0.1
Peach, Passion Fruit & Wholegrain, Tesco*	1 Pot/175g	175	100	4.7	17.9	1.1	0.2
Peach, Pineapple Passion Fruit, Very Low Fat, Loseley*	1 Pot/140g	99	71	3.3	14.3	0.0	0.0
Peach, Shape*	1 Pot/120g	55	46	4.7	5.8	0.1	0.1
Peach, Smooth, Ski*	1 Pot/125g	128	102	4.9	16.3	1.9	0.0
Peaches, Bio Activia 0%, Danone*	1 Pot/125g	64	51	3.7	8.9	0.0	0.0
Peanut Toffee, Low Fat, Somerfield*	1 Pot/150g	131	87	4.0	15.0	1.0	0.0
Pear & Butterscotch, Finest, Tesco*	1 Pot/150g	413	275	5.0	32.3	14.0	0.5
Pear & Ginger, COU, M & S*	1oz/28g	13	45	4.0	5.8	0.1	0.3
Pineapple & Papaya, Ski*	1 Pot/125g	126	101	4.9	16.3	1.8	0.0
Pineapple & Passion Fruit, Sunshine Selection, Sainsbury's*	1 Pot/125g	115	92	4.3	15.2	1.5	0.1
Pineapple & Peach, Virtually Fat Free, Light, Muller*	1 Pot/200g	106	53	4.4	8.7	0.1	0.0
Pineapple Bio, Virtually Fat Free, Shape*	1 Pot/120g	56	47	4.7	5.9	0.1	0.1
Pineapple, Channel Island, M & S*	1 Pot/150g	165	110	4.3	15.9	3.3	0.3
Pineapple, Extremely Fruity, M & S*	1 Pot/200g	200	100	4.3	17.6	1.4	0.2
Pineapple, Finest, Tesco*	1 Pot/200g	220	110	3.5	17.5	2.9	0.2
Pineapple, Low Fat, Somerfield*	1 Pot/150g	134	89	4.0	17.0	1.0	0.0
Pineapple, Low Fat, Tesco*	1 Pot/125g	111	89	4.6	13.4	1.7	0.0
Pineapple, Passion Fruit, Guava, Fat Free, Weight Watchers*	1 Pot/120g	54	45	4.1	6.6	0.1	0.1
Pineapple, Truly Fruity, Shape*	1 Pot/120g	61	51	4.5	7.3	0.1	0.1
Pineapple, Weight Watchers*	1 Pot/120g	52	43	4.1	6.3	0.1	0.1
Pink Grapefruit, Breakfast Selection, Sainsbury's*	1 Pot/117g	109	93	4.2	15.9	1.4	0.1
Pink Grapefruit Fruit Corner, Muller*	1 Pot/175g	189	108	4.1	13.9	4.0	0.0
Pink Grapefruit, Weight Watchers*	1 Pot/120g	52	43	4.1	6.3	0.1	0.2
Plain, Low Fat	1 Pot/120g	67	56	5.1	7.5	0.8	0.0
Plum, Low Fat, Orchard Grove, Shape*	1 Pot/100g	63	63	4.7	8.3	1.0	0.2
Prune, Breakfast Selection, Sainsbury's*	1 Pot/125g	119	95	4.2	16.3	1.4	0.2
Rapsberry & White Chocolate, Low Fat, Shape*	1 Pot/100g	101	101	4.7	15.6	1.8	0.1
Raspberry & Blackberry Bio, Fat Free, Shape*	1 Pot/120g	54	45	4.6	5.6	0.1	0.2
Raspberry & Blackberry, Thick & Creamy, Co-Op*	1 Pot/150g	188	125	3.6	17.3	4.6	0.1
Raspberry & Blackcurrant, Ski*	1 Pot/125g	129	103	4.4	14.6	3.0	0.0
Raspberry & Cranberry, Light, Muller*	1 Pot/200g	104	52	4.4	8.3	0.1	0.0
Raspberry & Elderberry, Organic, Onken*	1 Serving/50g	53	106	3.8	15.0	3.1	0.0
Raspberry & Orange, Organic, Fat Free, Yeo Valley*	1 Serving/100g	77	77	5.1	13.7	0.1	0.1
Raspberry & Redcurrant, Low Fat, Sainsbury's*	1 Pot/125g	109	87	4.2	14.5	1.4	0.5
Raspberry, BGTY, Sainsbury's*	1 Pot/125g	64	51	4.4	7.9	0.2	2.0
Raspberry Bio, HE, Tesco*	1 Pot/125g	65	52	4.7	7.9	0.2	0.4
Raspberry, Bio Pot, Onken*	1 Pot/150g	153	102	4.4	15.1	2.7	0.0
Raspberry Bio, Virtually Fat Free, Shape*	1 Pot/120g	56	47	4.7	6.1	0.1	0.2
Raspberry, COU, M & S*	1 Pot/150g	68	45	4.2	5.5	0.1	0.3
Raspberry, Economy, Sainsbury's*	1 Pot/125g	85	68	3.0	11.9	1.0	0.0
Raspberry, Everyday, Low Fat, Co-Op*	1 Pot/125g	88	70	3.0	13.0	0.7	0.0
Raspberry Extremely Fruity, M & S*	1 Pot/200g	190	95	5.0	15.6	1.5	0.5
Raspberry, Fat Free, Weight Watchers*	1 Pot/120g	49	41	4.2	5.7	0.1	0.3
Raspberry, French Set Wholemilk, Asda*	1 Pot/125g	125	100	3.6	14.1	3.2	0.0

(Nutrition Values per 100g / 100ml)

Y

YOGHURT,	Measure WEIGHT/INFO	per Measure KCAL	KCAL	PROT	CARB	FAT	FIBRE
			Nutrition Values per 100g / 100ml				
Raspberry, Frozen, Handmade Farmhouse, Sainsbury's*	1 Serving/100g	132	132	2.7	21.8	3.8	2.2
Raspberry, Frozen, Orchard Maid*	1 Serving/80ml	89	111	2.8	19.9	2.1	0.0
Raspberry, HE, Tesco*	1 Pot/125g	49	39	4.4	5.0	0.2	1.0
Raspberry, Low Fat, Asda*	1 Pot/125g	121	97	4.7	17.0	1.1	0.0
Raspberry, Low Fat, Benecol*	1 Pot/125ml	100	80	3.8	14.5	0.7	0.0
Raspberry, Low Fat, Budgens*	1 Pot/125g	121	97	4.7	17.0	1.1	0.2
Raspberry, Low Fat, Co-Op*	1 Pot/150g	120	80	4.0	13.6	1.0	0.4
Raspberry, Low Fat, Muller*	1 Pot/150g	152	101	4.8	16.1	1.9	0.0
Raspberry, Low Fat, Safeway*	1 Pot/150g	143	95	4.7	16.5	1.1	0.3
Raspberry, Low Fat, Sainsbury's*	1 Pot/125g	115	92	4.4	15.2	1.5	0.2
Raspberry, Low Fat, Ski*	1 Pot/125g	125	100	4.9	15.9	1.9	0.0
Raspberry, Low Fat, Somerfield*	1 Pot/150g	128	85	4.0	16.0	1.0	0.0
Raspberry, Low Fat, Tesco*	1 Pot/125g	123	98	4.9	15.5	1.8	0.3
Raspberry, M & S*	1 Pot/150g	144	96	4.9	15.4	1.6	0.6
Raspberry, Mullerice, Muller*	1 Pot/200g	228	114	3.4	20.0	2.3	0.0
Raspberry, Organic, Fat Free, Rachel's Organic*	1 Serving/142g	78	55	3.6	10.0	0.1	0.0
Raspberry, Organic, Low Fat, Tesco*	1 Pot/125g	109	87	5.3	14.1	1.0	0.1
Raspberry, Organic, Yeo Valley*	1 Pot/150g	144	96	4.4	12.3	3.3	0.1
Raspberry, Pavlova, Corner, Muller*	1 Pot/150g	230	153	3.4	24.4	4.7	0.0
Raspberry, Seriously Fruity, Low Fat, Waitrose*	1 Pot/150g	149	99	4.8	16.2	1.7	0.3
Raspberry, Ski*	1 Pot/125ml	125	100	4.9	15.9	1.9	0.0
Raspberry, Smooth, M & S*	1 Pot/150g	150	100	4.9	16.2	1.6	0.5
Raspberry, Smooth Set, Co-Op*	1 Pot/125g	95	76	3.7	12.5	0.9	0.0
Raspberry, Very Low Fat, Somerfield*	1 Pot/125g	60	48	5.0	6.0	0.0	0.0
Raspberry, Vitality, Muller*	1oz/28g	27	97	4.8	15.4	1.8	0.0
Raspberry, WTF, Sainsbury's*	1 Pot/151g	104	69	3.3	13.6	0.1	2.1
Red Cherries, Bio Activia 0%, Danone*	1 Pot/125g	65	52	3.6	9.1	0.0	0.0
Red Cherry, Bio, Shape*	1 Pot/120g	58	48	4.6	6.4	0.1	0.1
Red Cherry, Light, 99.9% Fat Free, Ski*	1 Pot/125g	73	58	4.9	9.2	0.1	1.2
Red Cherry, Virtually Fat Free, Shape*	1 Pot/120g	67	56	4.7	6.3	0.1	0.1
Red Cherry, Virtually Fat Free, Ski*	1 Pot/125g	64	51	4.5	7.7	0.2	2.0
Rhubarb, Crumble Corner, Muller*	1 Pot/150g	222	148	3.3	21.7	5.3	0.0
Rhubarb Crumble Duo, Co-Op*	1 Pot/140g	190	136	4.5	20.6	3.5	0.3
Rhubarb Crumble Layered Style, HE, Tesco*	1 Pot/125g	93	74	4.1	12.9	0.7	0.2
Rhubarb Custard Style, Somerfield*	1 Pot/125g	149	119	3.0	16.0	5.0	0.0
Rhubarb, Eat Smart, Safeway*	1 Pot/125g	69	55	5.1	7.8	0.1	0.2
Rhubarb, Extremely Fruity, M & S*	1 Pot/150g	158	105	4.5	18.2	1.4	0.4
Rhubarb, Farmhouse, Sainsbury's*	1 Pot/150g	149	99	4.3	13.4	3.1	0.3
Rhubarb, Live Bio, Perfectly Balanced, Waitrose*	1 Pot/151g	131	87	4.6	17.0	0.1	0.2
Rhubarb, Low Fat, Asda*	1 Pot/125g	110	88	4.6	15.0	1.1	0.0
Rhubarb, Low Fat, Safeway*	1 Pot/150g	137	91	4.6	15.7	1.1	0.1
Rhubarb, M & S*	1 Pot/150g	149	99	4.4	17.4	1.4	0.3
Rhubarb, Very Low Fat, Somerfield*	1 Pot/125g	58	46	5.0	6.0	0.0	0.0
Rum Raisin Crunch Corner, Muller*	1 Pot/150g	219	146	4.2	22.0	4.6	0.0
Sheep's Milk, Total*	1oz/28g	25	90	4.8	4.3	6.0	0.0
Smooth Strawberry, Ski*	1 Pot/125g	126	101	4.9	16.1	1.9	0.0
Smooth Toffee & Apple, Low Fat, Co-Op*	1 Pot/125g	150	120	6.0	22.0	1.0	0.1
Smooth Toffee & Orange, Co-Op*	1 Pot/125g	181	145	6.0	27.0	1.0	0.0
Smooth Toffee, Eat Smart, Safeway*	1 Pot/125g	69	55	5.1	8.7	0.1	0.0
Smooth Vanilla, Eat Smart, Safeway*	1 Pot/125g	69	55	5.0	8.3	0.1	0.0
Soya	1oz/28g	20	72	5.0	3.9	4.2	0.0
Spanish Lemon, Onken*	1 Serving/100g	100	100	3.9	15.1	2.7	0.0
Spiced Rhubarb, COU, M & S*	1oz/28g	13	45	4.3	5.5	0.1	0.2
Srawberry, Organic, Bio Live, Yeo Valley*	1 Serving/100g	100	100	4.2	12.1	3.9	0.1

YOGHURT,	Measure WEIGHT/INFO	per Measure KCAL	Nutrition Values per 100g / 100ml KCAL	PROT	CARB	FAT	FIBRE
Sticky Toffee Pudding Corner, Muller*	1 Pot/150g	239	159	3.6	24.7	5.1	0.0
Strawberry & Orange Crunch Corner, Muller*	1 Pot/150g	218	145	4.1	22.5	4.3	0.0
Strawberry & Raspberry, Bio Live Organic, Yeo Valley*	1 Pot/125g	125	100	4.2	12.0	3.9	0.1
Strawberry & Raspberry, HE, Tesco*	1 Pot/125g	58	46	4.2	7.0	0.1	0.0
Strawberry & Raspberry, Low Fat, Asda*	1 Pot/150g	143	95	4.6	17.4	1.0	0.2
Strawberry & Raspberry, Low Fat, Sainsbury's*	1 Pot/125g	109	87	4.2	14.3	1.4	0.2
Strawberry & Rhubarb, Low Fat, Somerfield*	1 Pot/125g	108	86	4.1	15.6	0.8	0.1
Strawberry & Vanilla, Low Fat, Somerfield*	1 Pot/125g	109	87	4.0	15.9	0.8	0.1
Strawberry & Vanilla, M & S*	1 Pot/150g	143	95	4.8	15.4	1.6	0.2
Strawberry & Vanilla, Weight Watchers*	1 Pot/120g	54	45	4.2	6.8	0.1	0.1
Strawberry & Wholegrain Bio Break, Tesco*	1 Pot/175g	175	100	4.7	17.8	1.1	0.2
Strawberry & Wild Strawberry, Weight Watchers*	1 Pot/120g	49	41	4.2	5.8	0.1	0.1
Strawberry, 99% Fat Free, Mullerice, Muller*	1 Pot/150g	107	71	3.5	12.2	0.9	0.0
Strawberry, Balanced Lifestyle, Aldi*	1 Pot/150g	72	48	4.1	7.1	0.3	0.5
Strawberry, Best There Is, Yoplait*	1 Pot/125g	135	108	4.8	15.8	1.6	0.0
Strawberry, BGTY, Sainsbury's*	1 Pot/123g	64	52	4.7	7.7	0.2	0.1
Strawberry Bio & Cereal Clusters, Rumblers*	1 Pot/168g	267	159	4.3	22.4	5.8	1.1
Strawberry, Bio Activia 0% Fat, Danone*	1 Pot/125g	63	50	3.8	8.4	0.0	0.0
Strawberry Bio, Co-Op*	1 Pot/125g	143	114	4.5	16.7	2.8	0.1
Strawberry Bio, HE, Tesco*	1 Pot/125g	61	49	4.7	7.0	0.2	0.2
Strawberry Bio, Virtually Fat Free, Shape*	1 Pot/120g	55	46	4.7	5.7	0.1	0.1
Strawberry, Bio Virtually Fat Free, Tesco*	1 Pot/125g	50	40	4.4	5.3	0.2	0.9
Strawberry, Bio-Live Fat Free, Rachel's Organic*	1 Pot/142g	81	57	3.5	10.5	0.1	0.0
Strawberry, Biopot Wholegrain, Onken*	1 Serving/100g	109	109	4.7	16.5	2.7	0.0
Strawberry, Childrens, Co-Op*	1 Pot/125g	121	97	3.5	14.9	2.7	0.2
Strawberry, COU, M & S*	1 Pot/125g	63	50	4.3	6.4	0.1	0.1
Strawberry, Crisp, Jordans*	1oz/28g	38	137	4.8	22.8	3.3	1.1
Strawberry Crumble, Brooklea, Aldi*	1 Pot/140g	181	129	3.4	19.5	4.2	0.8
Strawberry, Crumble Corner, Muller*	1 Pot/150g	222	148	3.3	21.7	5.3	0.0
Strawberry Crumble Duo, Co-Op*	1 Pot/140g	185	132	4.5	19.7	3.5	0.2
Strawberry, Custard Style, Somerfield*	1 Pot/125g	153	122	3.0	17.0	5.0	0.0
Strawberry Dessert, Frozen, Tesco*	1 Pot/60g	82	136	2.6	26.5	2.2	0.8
Strawberry Drinking, Live & Mild, Bio Green*	1 Bottle/250ml	240	96	3.0	14.1	2.9	0.0
Strawberry, Duo, Co-Op*	1 Pot/175g	219	125	3.0	17.0	5.0	0.7
Strawberry, Eat Smart, Safeway*	1 Pot/125g	69	55	5.1	8.3	0.1	0.3
Strawberry, Everyday Low Fat, Co-Op*	1 Pot/125g	88	70	3.0	13.0	0.7	0.0
Strawberry, Extremely Fruity, M & S*	1 Pot/200g	190	95	4.8	15.4	1.6	0.2
Strawberry, Fat Free, Waitrose*	1 Pot/150g	135	90	4.6	17.8	0.1	0.1
Strawberry, Fat Free, Weight Watchers*	1 Pot/120g	52	43	4.1	6.2	0.1	0.1
Strawberry Flip, Morrisons*	1 Pot/175g	215	123	3.4	17.1	4.6	0.7
Strawberry, Frozen, M & S*	1oz/28g	35	125	3.1	24.9	1.2	0.6
Strawberry, Fruit Corner, Muller*	1 Pot/175g	207	118	3.7	17.1	3.9	0.0
Strawberry, Granose*	1oz/28g	25	90	4.5	15.5	1.6	0.0
Strawberry, Light & Refreshing, Campina*	1 Pot/125g	110	88	2.5	16.9	1.1	0.0
Strawberry, Light, 99.9% Fat Free, Ski*	1 Pot/125g	60	48	4.7	7.7	0.1	1.0
Strawberry, Light, Muller*	1 Pot/200g	106	53	4.4	8.7	0.1	0.0
Strawberry, Lite, Onken*	1 Pot/235g	110	47	5.2	6.1	0.2	0.2
Strawberry, Live, Turner's Dairies*	1 Pot/125g	86	69	4.9	11.9	0.3	0.0
Strawberry, Low Fat, Asda*	1 Pot/125g	114	91	4.4	16.0	1.0	0.0
Strawberry, Low Fat, Benecol*	1 Pot/150g	119	79	3.7	14.8	0.6	0.0
Strawberry, Low Fat Bio, Shape*	1 Pot/100g	56	56	4.9	5.9	1.1	0.1
Strawberry, Low Fat, Budgens*	1 Pot/125g	113	90	4.6	15.5	1.1	0.1
Strawberry, Low Fat, Co-Op*	1 Pot/150g	129	86	3.9	15.5	0.9	0.3
Strawberry, Low Fat, Organic, Muller*	1 Pot/150g	147	98	3.9	16.6	1.8	0.0

YOGHURT,	Measure WEIGHT/INFO	per Measure KCAL	Nutrition Values per 100g / 100ml KCAL	PROT	CARB	FAT	FIBRE
Strawberry, Low Fat, Organic, Sainsbury's*	1 Pot/125g	100	80	5.3	12.6	1.0	0.1
Strawberry, Low Fat, Organic, Somerfield*	1 Pot/150g	153	102	6.0	17.0	2.0	0.0
Strawberry, Low Fat, Safeway*	1 Pot/150g	138	92	4.6	16.0	1.1	0.1
Strawberry, Low Fat, Sainsbury's*	1 Pot/125g	115	92	4.3	15.2	1.5	0.1
Strawberry, Low Fat, Ski*	1 Pot/125g	124	99	4.8	15.8	1.8	0.0
Strawberry, Low Fat, SmartPrice, Asda*	1 Pot/125g	85	68	2.2	13.0	0.8	0.0
Strawberry, Low Fat, Spelga*	1 Pot/125g	129	103	4.5	18.0	1.8	0.0
Strawberry, Low Fat, Tesco*	1 Pot/125g	110	88	4.8	13.6	1.6	0.1
Strawberry, Low Fat, Value, Tesco*	1 Pot/125g	81	65	2.7	11.8	0.7	0.1
Strawberry, M & S*	1 Pot/150g	143	95	4.8	15.4	1.6	0.2
Strawberry Mousse, Shapers, Boots*	1 Pot/90g	88	97	4.1	11.0	4.1	0.1
Strawberry, Mullerrice, Muller*	1 Pot/200g	230	115	3.4	20.0	2.4	0.0
Strawberry, Organic, Bio Live, Fat Free, Yeo Valley*	1 Pot/125g	98	78	5.1	14.3	0.1	0.1
Strawberry, Organic, Frozen, Yeo Valley*	1 Serving/100g	139	139	4.7	23.9	2.7	0.3
Strawberry, Organic, Low Fat, Tesco*	1 Pot/125g	104	83	5.3	13.2	1.0	0.1
Strawberry, Organic, Yeo Valley*	1 Pot/150g	144	96	4.3	12.4	3.3	0.1
Strawberry, Seriously Fruity, Low Fat, Waitrose*	1 Pot/150g	152	101	4.8	16.6	1.7	0.2
Strawberry, Ski*	1 Pot/125g	111	89	3.4	15.3	1.5	0.9
Strawberry, Smooth, M & S*	1 Pot/150g	150	100	4.8	16.1	1.6	0.2
Strawberry, Smooth Set, Co-Op*	1 Pot/125g	95	76	3.7	12.5	0.9	0.0
Strawberry, So-Good*	1oz/28g	25	90	2.0	16.4	1.4	0.0
Strawberry, Thick & Creamy, Channel Island, M & S*	1 Pot/150g	135	90	3.4	13.6	3.0	1.4
Strawberry, Thick & Creamy, Co-Op*	1 Pot/150g	182	121	3.6	16.4	4.6	0.1
Strawberry, Very Low Fat, Bio, Somerfield*	1 Pot/200g	100	50	5.0	7.0	0.0	0.0
Strawberry, Very Low Fat, Loseley*	1 Pot/140g	92	66	3.3	13.0	0.1	0.0
Strawberry, Very Low Fat, Somerfield	1 Pot/125g	60	48	5.0	6.0	0.0	0.0
Strawberry, Virtually Fat Free Bio, Morrisons*	1 Pot/200g	114	57	5.4	8.4	0.2	0.0
Strawberry, Virtually Fat Free, Organic, Yeo Valley*	1 Pot/125g	98	78	5.1	14.3	0.1	0.1
Strawberry, Virtually Fat Free, Shapers, Boots*	1 Pot/125g	67	54	5.2	8.1	0.1	0.1
Strawberry, Virtually Fat Free, Ski*	1 Pot/127g	61	48	4.5	7.1	0.2	2.0
Strawberry, Vitality Probiotic, Muller*	1 Pot/175g	170	97	4.7	15.6	1.8	0.0
Strawberry, Wholemilk, Organic, Sainsbury's*	1 Pot/150g	123	82	3.5	9.2	3.5	0.1
Summer Berries, Fat Free, Shape*	1 Pot/120g	55	46	4.6	6.0	0.1	0.2
Summerfruits Bio, Boots*	1 Pot/150g	140	93	4.1	13.0	2.7	0.4
Summerfruits, M & S*	1oz/28g	27	96	4.8	15.6	1.6	0.5
Toffee & Milk Choco Hoops, Crunch Corner, Muller*	1oz/28g	45	161	4.7	22.3	5.9	0.0
Toffee, 99% Fat Free, Mullerice, Muller*	1 Pot/150g	119	79	3.3	14.3	1.0	0.0
Toffee Apple, COU, M & S*	1 Pot/200g	90	45	4.2	6.3	0.2	0.2
Toffee Apple, Indulgent Greek Style, Somerfield*	1 Pot/125g	225	180	3.0	27.0	7.0	0.0
Toffee Bio, HE, Tesco*	1 Pot/125g	48	38	4.4	4.2	0.4	0.8
Toffee, Childrens, Co-Op*	1 Pot/125g	143	114	3.6	18.6	2.8	0.0
Toffee, Economy, Sainsbury's*	1 Pot/126g	91	72	3.0	12.8	1.0	0.0
Toffee Flavour, Virtually Fat Free Bio, Morrisons*	1 Pot/200g	110	55	5.3	8.1	0.2	0.0
Toffee, Light, Muller*	1 Pot/200g	106	53	4.4	8.5	0.1	0.0
Toffee, Light, Ski*	1 Pot/120g	60	50	4.6	7.7	0.2	0.6
Toffee, Low Fat, Asda*	1 Pot/150g	174	116	4.6	22.0	1.1	0.0
Toffee, Low Fat, Budgens*	1 Pot/125g	145	116	4.7	21.6	1.2	0.0
Toffee, Low Fat, Co-Op*	1 Pot/150g	125	83	3.8	15.0	0.9	0.2
Toffee, Low Fat, Safeway*	1 Pot/150g	174	116	4.7	21.6	1.2	0.0
Toffee, Low Fat, SmartPrice, Asda*	1 Pot/125g	96	77	2.2	15.0	0.9	0.0
Toffee, Low Fat, Somerfield*	1 Pot/150g	149	99	3.0	19.0	1.0	0.0
Toffee, Low Fat, Tesco*	1 Pot/125g	158	126	5.0	22.3	1.9	0.0
Toffee, M & S*	1 Pot/150g	180	120	4.9	21.6	1.7	0.0
Toffee, Seriously Smooth, Low Fat, Waitrose*	1 Pot/150g	156	104	4.7	16.5	2.1	0.1

	Measure WEIGHT/INFO	per Measure KCAL	KCAL	PROT	CARB	FAT	FIBRE
			Nutrition Values per 100g / 100ml				
YOGHURT,							
Toffee, Very Low Fat Bio, Somerfield*	1 Pot/200g	100	50	5.0	7.0	0.0	0.0
Toffee, Virtually Fat Free, Boots*	1 Pot/125g	69	55	5.1	8.3	0.1	0.0
Toffee, Weight Watchers*	1 Pot/120g	52	43	4.2	6.2	0.1	0.0
Tropical Fruit, Greek Style, Asda*	1 Pot/125g	170	136	3.3	15.0	7.0	0.0
Unsweetened Natural, Bio, M & S*	1 Pot/225g	135	60	5.6	5.5	1.8	0.0
Vanilla & Chocolate Flakes, Low Fat Bio, Shape*	1 Pot/150g	140	93	4.5	12.0	2.7	0.0
Vanilla & Pineapple, Nestle*	1 Pot/125g	120	96	4.2	16.7	1.5	0.0
Vanilla, Bio-Live, Low Fat, Rachel's Organic*	1 Pot/142g	104	73	3.7	10.5	1.8	0.0
Vanilla, Breakfast, Tesco*	1 Pot/150g	108	72	2.9	13.9	0.5	0.0
Vanilla, Channel Island, M & S*	1 Pot/150g	173	115	4.5	16.5	3.5	0.0
Vanilla Choco Balls, Crunch Corner, Muller*	1 Pot/150g	218	145	4.1	22.5	4.3	0.0
Vanilla, COU, M & S*	1 Pot/200g	90	45	4.1	6.1	0.1	0.0
Vanilla Custard, Mullerice, Muller*	1 Pot/200g	250	125	3.3	22.1	2.6	0.0
Vanilla Flavour, Organic, Low Fat, Tesco*	1 Pot/125g	114	91	5.3	15.3	1.0	0.0
Vanilla, French Set Wholemilk, Asda*	1 Pot/125g	125	100	3.6	14.1	3.2	0.0
Vanilla, Frozen, Less Than 5% Fat, Tesco*	1 Pot/120g	179	149	8.1	23.8	2.4	0.7
Vanilla, Light, Muller*	1 Pot/200g	106	53	4.6	8.2	0.1	0.0
Vanilla, Live, Bio, Green Dairy*	1 Bottle/250ml	263	105	2.5	17.7	2.9	0.0
Vanilla, Low Fat, Tesco*	1 Pot/125g	125	100	4.9	16.3	1.7	0.0
Vanilla, Organic, Low Fat, Sainsbury's*	1 Pot/125g	114	91	5.3	15.3	1.0	0.0
Vanilla, Seriously Smooth, Low Fat, Waitrose	1 Pot/150g	149	99	4.7	16.3	1.7	0.0
Vanilla, Smooth Set, Co-Op*	1 Pot/125g	95	76	3.7	12.5	0.9	0.0
Vanilla, Thick & Creamy, Waitrose*	1 Pot/150g	188	125	4.2	20.6	2.9	0.0
Vanilla, Thickie, Innocent*	1 Bottle/250ml	200	80	2.4	12.2	2.0	0.0
Vanilla, Very Low Fat Bio, Somerfield*	1 Pot/200g	98	49	5.0	7.0	0.0	0.0
Vanilla, Virtually Fat Free, Shapers, Boots*	1 Pot/125g	66	53	5.0	7.9	0.1	0.0
Vanilla, Virtually Fat Free, Ski*	1 Pot/120g	59	49	4.7	7.2	0.2	0.6
Vanilla, Virtually Fat Free, Yeo Valley*	1 Pot/150g	122	81	5.1	15.0	0.1	0.0
Vanilla, Weight Watchers*	1 Pot/120g	49	41	4.2	5.7	0.1	0.0
Vitality Probiotic, Low Fat, Muller*	1 Pot/175g	170	97	4.7	15.6	1.8	0.0
Whisp, M & S*	1 Pot/100g	115	115	4.5	13.9	4.1	0.1
White Peach, Seriously Fruity, Waitrose*	1 Pot/150g	152	101	4.8	16.5	1.7	0.2
Whole Milk, Plain	1oz/28g	22	79	5.7	7.8	3.0	0.0
Wholemilk, Organic, M & S*	1fl oz/30ml	27	90	6.1	7.4	3.6	0.0
Winter Medley, COU, M & S*	1 Pot/150g	68	45	4.2	6.2	0.1	0.1
With Vanilla, Bio-Live, Low Fat, Rachel's Organic*	¼ Pot/115g	84	73	3.7	10.5	1.8	0.0
YOGHURT COATED,							
Almonds, Holland & Barrett*	1 Pack/100g	536	536	10.9	45.3	37.0	2.8
Brazil Nuts, Nature's Harvest, Holland & Barrett*	1 Brazil Nut/25g	136	543	6.6	48.3	38.8	1.4
Hazelnuts, Holland & Barrett*	1 Pack/100g	546	546	7.7	45.0	39.8	2.5
Peanuts & Raisins, Nature's Harvest, Holland & Barrett*	1 Pack/100g	465	465	8.9	54.3	25.8	2.0
Pineapple Pieces, Holland & Barrett*	1 Pack/100g	344	344	2.1	46.8	19.3	0.6
YOGHURT DRINK,							
Yoghurt Drink	1floz/30ml	19	62	3.1	13.1	0.0	0.0
Blueberry & Blackcurrent, Orchard Maid*	1 Carton/250ml	148	59	1.6	13.6	0.0	0.0
Light, Yakult*	1 Pot/66ml	31	47	1.3	12.2	0.0	1.8
Raspberry & Passion Fruit, Everybody, Yoplait*	1 Bottle/90g	60	67	2.6	12.2	0.9	0.0
Yakult*	1 Pot/65ml	51	78	1.4	17.8	0.1	0.0
YORKIE,							
Honeycomb, Nestle*	1 Bar/65g	331	509	5.7	63.6	25.8	0.0
Nestle*	1 Bar/24g	121	504	6.8	60.4	26.1	1.2
Original, Nestle*	1 Bar/70g	368	525	6.5	58.6	29.4	0.0
Raisin & Biscuit, Nestle	1 Bar/63g	307	487	5.9	60.5	24.6	0.0
YORKSHIRE PUDDING							

Y

YORKSHIRE PUDDING,	Measure WEIGHT/INFO	per Measure KCAL	Nutrition Values per 100g / 100ml KCAL	PROT	CARB	FAT	FIBRE
Yorkshire Pudding	1oz/28g	58	208	6.6	24.7	9.9	0.9
3", Baked, Aunt Bessie's*	1 Pudding/36g	91	252	9.0	36.4	7.9	1.7
7", Baked, Aunt Bessie's*	1 Pudding/110g	290	264	8.5	37.4	9.0	2.0
Asda*	1 Pudding/30g	97	322	10.0	39.0	14.0	0.5
Baked, Morrisons*	1 Pudding/33g	106	322	10.0	39.0	14.0	0.5
Filled, Roast Chicken, COU, M & S*	1 Pudding/150g	210	140	12.6	15.7	2.7	0.9
Four Minute, Aunt Bessie's*	1 Pudding/18g	59	326	9.6	38.4	14.8	2.1
Giant, Aunt Bessie's*	1 Pudding/110g	290	264	8.5	37.4	9.0	2.0
Great Value, Asda*	1 Pudding/13g	34	260	10.0	37.0	8.0	2.8
Individual, Aunt Bessie's*	1 Pudding/18g	59	326	9.6	38.4	14.8	2.1
Large, Safeway*	1 Pudding/45g	123	273	8.5	41.1	8.3	2.5
Mini, Asda*	1 Pudding/13g	34	260	10.0	37.0	8.0	2.8
Mini, Farmfoods*	1 Pudding/3g	8	281	9.6	43.2	7.7	1.9
Ready Baked, SmartPrice, Asda*	1 Pudding/12g	36	297	10.0	44.0	9.0	2.8
Ready To Bake, Aunt Bessie's*	1 Pudding/17g	42	246	8.5	35.1	8.0	1.7
Ready To Bake, Sainsbury's*	1 Pudding/18g	48	263	9.9	35.9	8.9	1.3
Sausage & Onion Gravy Filled, Safeway*	1 Pudding/300g	540	180	6.2	18.0	9.2	1.2
Steak & Vegetable, COU, M & S*	1 Pudding/150g	188	125	9.6	14.9	2.7	0.9
Traditional Style, Asda*	1 Pudding/30g	97	322	10.0	39.0	14.0	0.5
Unbaked, Iceland*	1 Pudding/18g	47	263	9.9	35.9	8.9	1.3
YULE LOG, Chocolate, Sainsbury's*	1/8 Log/48g	186	382	5.1	46.5	19.6	0.7

About Weight Loss Resources

Set up in January 2001, the Weight Loss Resources web site is home to the biggest online calorie and nutrition database in the UK. www.weightlossresources.co.uk enables users to tap in their height, weight, age and basic activity level; then set an initial weight loss goal. The computer works out body mass index and healthy weight range, calculates how many calories are needed each day to lose weight at the chosen rate, and predicts the date an individual's weight loss goal will be achieved.

Users then keep an online food diary, drawing from a database with calorie, fat, fibre, protein, carbohydrate and alcohol values for over 18,000 UK foods and drinks. The food diary also keeps track of how many portions of fruit and veg are eaten in a day, and produces a nutrition profile pie chart so users can see the proportion of calories from fat, protein, carbohydrate and alcohol. Users also record any exercise taken and the programme keeps a running total of calories consumed, calories used in exercise, and calories left for the day. At the end of a week users get reports and graphs on their weight, nutrition and body fat.

The site offers a range of nutritious low fat recipes for those who need guidance and a bit of inspiration. There is also the facility for users to input their own recipes and get the calorie and nutrition info on them. This enables favourites to be modified if they prove to be too high in calories and fat. There is a research database which can be searched for information on things like vitamins and other important nutrients, plus soundly based articles on healthy diet, weight loss and fitness issues. A Members' Forum provides support, help and advice through message boards and chat rooms.

The Weight Loss Resources system is also available as a paper-based kit for people who do not have regular internet access.

Feedback

If you have any comments or suggestions about the Calorie, Carb & Fat Bible, or would like further information on Weight Loss Resources, please call, email or write to them:

Email	helpteam@weightlossresources.co.uk
Tel	01733 345592
Address	Weight Loss Resources, FREEPOST ANG30222, PE2 9BR